Lecture Notes in Computer Science   10406

Commenced Publication in 1973
Founding and Former Series Editors:
Gerhard Goos, Juris Hartmanis, and Jan van Leeuwen

More information about this series at http://www.springer.com/series/7407

Osvaldo Gervasi · Beniamino Murgante
Sanjay Misra · Giuseppe Borruso
Carmelo M. Torre · Ana Maria A.C. Rocha
David Taniar · Bernady O. Apduhan
Elena Stankova · Alfredo Cuzzocrea (Eds.)

Computational Science and Its Applications – ICCSA 2017

17th International Conference
Trieste, Italy, July 3–6, 2017
Proceedings, Part III

 Springer

Editors

Osvaldo Gervasi
University of Perugia
Perugia
Italy

Beniamino Murgante
University of Basilicata
Potenza
Italy

Sanjay Misra
Covenant University
Ota
Nigeria

Giuseppe Borruso
University of Trieste
Trieste
Italy

Carmelo M. Torre
Polytechnic University of Bari
Bari
Italy

Ana Maria A.C. Rocha
University of Minho
Braga
Portugal

David Taniar
Monash University
Clayton, VIC
Australia

Bernady O. Apduhan
Kyushu Sangyo University
Fukuoka
Japan

Elena Stankova
Saint Petersburg State University
Saint Petersburg
Russia

Alfredo Cuzzocrea
University of Trieste
Trieste
Italy

ISSN 0302-9743   ISSN 1611-3349 (electronic)
Lecture Notes in Computer Science
ISBN 978-3-319-62397-9   ISBN 978-3-319-62398-6 (eBook)
DOI 10.1007/978-3-319-62398-6

Library of Congress Control Number: 2017945283

LNCS Sublibrary: SL1 – Theoretical Computer Science and General Issues

Printed on acid-free paper

This Springer imprint is published by Springer Nature
The registered company is Springer International Publishing AG
The registered company address is: Gewerbestrasse 11, 6330 Cham, Switzerland

Preface

These multiple volumes (LNCS volumes 10404, 10405, 10406, 10407, 10408, and 10409) consist of the peer-reviewed papers from the 2017 International Conference on Computational Science and Its Applications (ICCSA 2017) held in Trieste, Italy, during July 3–6, 2017.

ICCSA 2017 was a successful event in the ICCSA conference series, previously held in Beijing, China (2016), Banff, Canada (2015), Guimarães, Portugal (2014), Ho Chi Minh City, Vietnam (2013), Salvador, Brazil (2012), Santander, Spain (2011), Fukuoka, Japan (2010), Suwon, South Korea (2009), Perugia, Italy (2008), Kuala Lumpur, Malaysia (2007), Glasgow, UK (2006), Singapore (2005), Assisi, Italy (2004), Montreal, Canada (2003), (as ICCS) Amsterdam, The Netherlands (2002), and San Francisco, USA (2001).

Computational science is a main pillar of most present research as well as industrial and commercial activities and plays a unique role in exploiting ICT innovative technologies. The ICCSA conference series have been providing a venue to researchers and industry practitioners to discuss new ideas, to share complex problems and their solutions, and to shape new trends in computational science.

Apart from the general tracks, ICCSA 2017 also include 43 international workshops, in various areas of computational sciences, ranging from computational science technologies to specific areas of computational sciences, such as computer graphics and virtual reality. Furthermore, this year ICCSA 2017 hosted the XIV International Workshop on Quantum Reactive Scattering. The program also features three keynote speeches and four tutorials.

The success of the ICCSA conference series in general, and ICCSA 2017 in particular, is due to the support of many people: authors, presenters, participants, keynote speakers, session chairs, Organizing Committee members, student volunteers, Program Committee members, international Advisory Committee members, international liaison chairs, and various people in other roles. We would like to thank them all.

We would also like to thank Springer for their continuous support in publishing the ICCSA conference proceedings.

July 2017

Giuseppe Borruso
Osvaldo Gervasi
Bernady O. Apduhan

Welcome to Trieste

We were honored and happy to have organized this extraordinary edition of the conference, with so many interesting contributions and participants coming from more than 46 countries around the world!

Trieste is a medium-size Italian city lying on the north-eastern border between Italy and Slovenia. It has a population of nearly 200,000 inhabitants and faces the Adriatic Sea, surrounded by the Karst plateau.

It is quite an atypical Italian city, with its history being very much influenced by belonging for several centuries to the Austro-Hungarian empire and having been through several foreign occupations in history: by French, Venetians, and the Allied Forces after the Second World War. Such events left several footprints on the structure of the city, on its buildings, as well as on culture and society!

During its history, Trieste hosted people coming from different countries and regions, making it a cosmopolitan and open city. This was also helped by the presence of a commercial port that made it an important trade center from the 18th century on. Trieste is known today as a 'City of Science' or, more proudly, presenting itself as the 'City of Knowledge', thanks to the presence of several universities and research centers, all of them working at an international level, as well as of cultural institutions and traditions. The city has a high presence of researchers, more than 35 per 1,000 employed people, much higher than the European average of 6 employed researchers per 1,000 people.

The University of Trieste, the origin of such a system of scientific institutions, dates back to 1924, although its roots go back to the end of the 19th century under the Austro-Hungarian Empire. The university today employs nearly 1,500 teaching, research, technical, and administrative staff with a population of more than 16,000 students.

The university currently has 10 departments: Economics, Business, Mathematical, and Statistical Sciences; Engineering and Architecture; Humanities; Legal, Language, Interpreting, and Translation Studies; Mathematics and Geosciences; Medicine, Surgery, and Health Sciences; Life Sciences; Pharmaceutical and Chemical Sciences; Physics; Political and Social Sciences.

We trust the participants enjoyed the cultural and scientific offerings of Trieste and will keep a special memory of the event.

Giuseppe Borruso

Organization

ICCSA 2017 was organized by the University of Trieste (Italy), University of Perugia (Italy), Monash University (Australia), Kyushu Sangyo University (Japan), University of Basilicata (Italy), and University of Minho, (Portugal).

Honorary General Chairs

Antonio Laganà   University of Perugia, Italy
Norio Shiratori   Tohoku University, Japan
Kenneth C.J. Tan   Sardina Systems, Estonia

General Chairs

Giuseppe Borruso   University of Trieste, Italy
Osvaldo Gervasi   University of Perugia, Italy
Bernady O. Apduhan   Kyushu Sangyo University, Japan

Program Committee Chairs

Alfredo Cuzzocrea   University of Trieste, Italy
Beniamino Murgante   University of Basilicata, Italy
Ana Maria A.C. Rocha   University of Minho, Portugal
David Taniar   Monash University, Australia

International Advisory Committee

Jemal Abawajy   Deakin University, Australia
Dharma P. Agrawal   University of Cincinnati, USA
Marina L. Gavrilova   University of Calgary, Canada
Claudia Bauzer Medeiros   University of Campinas, Brazil
Manfred M. Fisher   Vienna University of Economics and Business, Austria
Yee Leung   Chinese University of Hong Kong, SÀR China

International Liaison Chairs

Ana Carla P. Bitencourt   Universidade Federal do Reconcavo da Bahia, Brazil
Maria Irene Falcão   University of Minho, Portugal
Robert C.H. Hsu   Chung Hua University, Taiwan
Tai-Hoon Kim   Hannam University, Korea
Sanjay Misra   University of Minna, Nigeria
Takashi Naka   Kyushu Sangyo University, Japan

Rafael D.C. Santos   National Institute for Space Research, Brazil
Maribel Yasmina Santos   University of Minho, Portugal

Workshop and Session Organizing Chairs

Beniamino Murgante   University of Basilicata, Italy
Sanjay Misra   Covenant University, Nigeria
Jorge Gustavo Rocha   University of Minho, Portugal

Award Chair

Wenny Rahayu   La Trobe University, Australia

Publicity Committee Chair

Stefano Cozzini   Democritos Center, National Research Council, Italy
Elmer Dadios   De La Salle University, Philippines
Hong Quang Nguyen   International University (VNU-HCM), Vietnam
Daisuke Takahashi   Tsukuba University, Japan
Shangwang Wang   Beijing University of Posts and Telecommunications,
                             China

Workshop Organizers

Agricultural and Environmental Big Data Analytics (AEDBA 2017)

Sandro Bimonte   IRSTEA, France
André Miralles   IRSTEA, France

Advances in Data Mining for Applications (AMDMA 2017)

Carlo Cattani   University of Tuscia, Italy
Majaz Moonis   University of Massachusettes Medical School, USA
Yeliz Karaca   IEEE, Computer Society Association

Advances Smart Mobility and Transportation (ASMAT 2017)

Mauro Mazzei   CNR, Italian National Research Council, Italy

Advances in Information Systems and Technologies for Emergency Preparedness and Risk Assessment and Mitigation (ASTER 2017)

Maurizio Pollino   ENEA, Italy
Marco Vona   University of Basilicata, Italy
Beniamino Murgante   University of Basilicata, Italy

Advances in Web-Based Learning (AWBL 2017)

Mustafa Murat Inceoglu　　Ege University, Turkey
Birol Ciloglugil　　Ege University, Turkey

Big Data Warehousing and Analytics (BIGGS 2017)

Maribel Yasmina Santos　　University of Minho, Portugal
Monica Wachowicz　　University of New Brunswick, Canada
Joao Moura Pires　　NOVA de Lisboa University, Portugal
Rafael Santos　　National Institute for Space Research, Brazil

Bio-inspired Computing and Applications (BIONCA 2017)

Nadia Nedjah　　State University of Rio de Janeiro, Brazil
Luiza de Macedo Mourell　　State University of Rio de Janeiro, Brazil

Computational and Applied Mathematics (CAM 2017)

M. Irene Falcao　　University of Minho, Portugal
Fernando Miranda　　University of Minho, Portugal

Computer-Aided Modeling, Simulation, and Analysis (CAMSA 2017)

Jie Shen　　University of Michigan, USA and Jilin University, China
Hao Chenina　　Shanghai University of Engineering Science, China
Chaochun Yuan　　Jiangsu University, China

Computational and Applied Statistics (CAS 2017)

Ana Cristina Braga　　University of Minho, Portugal

Computational Geometry and Security Applications (CGSA 2017)

Marina L. Gavrilova　　University of Calgary, Canada

Central Italy 2016 Earthquake: Computational Tools and Data Analysis for Emergency Response, Community Support, and Reconstruction Planning (CIEQ 2017)

Alessandro Rasulo　　Università degli Studi di Cassino e del Lazio
　　　　　　　　　　　Meridionale, Italy
Davide Lavorato　　Università degli Studi di Roma Tre, Italy

Computational Methods for Business Analytics (CMBA 2017)

Telmo Pinto   University of Minho, Portugal
Claudio Alves   University of Minho, Portugal

Chemistry and Materials Sciences and Technologies (CMST 2017)

Antonio Laganà   University of Perugia, Italy
Noelia Faginas Lago   University of Perugia, Italy

Computational Optimization and Applications (COA 2017)

Ana Maria Rocha   University of Minho, Portugal
Humberto Rocha   University of Coimbra, Portugal

Cities, Technologies, and Planning (CTP 2017)

Giuseppe Borruso   University of Trieste, Italy
Beniamino Murgante   University of Basilicata, Italy

Data-Driven Modelling for Sustainability Assessment (DAMOST 2017)

Antonino Marvuglia   Luxembourg Institute of Science and Technology, LIST,
                          Luxembourg
Mikhail Kanevski   University of Lausanne, Switzerland
Beniamino Murgante   University of Basilicata, Italy
Janusz Starczewski   Częstochowa University of Technology, Poland

Databases and Computerized Information Retrieval Systems (DCIRS 2017)

Sultan Alamri   College of Computing and Informatics, SEU, Saudi
                          Arabia
Adil Fahad   Albaha University, Saudi Arabia
Abdullah Alamri   Jeddah University, Saudi Arabia

Data Science for Intelligent Decision Support (DS4IDS 2016)

Filipe Portela   University of Minho, Portugal
Manuel Filipe Santos   University of Minho, Portugal

Deep Cities: Intelligence and Interoperability (DEEP_CITY 2017)

Maurizio Pollino	ENEA, Italian National Agency for New Technologies, Energy and Sustainable Economic Development, Italy
Grazia Fattoruso	ENEA, Italian National Agency for New Technologies, Energy and Sustainable Economic Development, Italy

Emotion Recognition (EMORE 2017)

Valentina Franzoni	University of Rome La Sapienza, Italy
Alfredo Milani	University of Perugia, Italy

Future Computing Systems, Technologies, and Applications (FISTA 2017)

Bernady O. Apduhan	Kyushu Sangyo University, Japan
Rafael Santos	National Institute for Space Research, Brazil

Geographical Analysis, Urban Modeling, Spatial Statistics (Geo-and-Mod 2017)

Giuseppe Borruso	University of Trieste, Italy
Beniamino Murgante	University of Basilicata, Italy
Hartmut Asche	University of Potsdam, Germany

Geomatics and Remote Sensing Techniques for Resource Monitoring and Control (GRS-RMC 2017)

Eufemia Tarantino	Polytechnic of Bari, Italy
Rosa Lasaponara	Italian Research Council, IMAA-CNR, Italy
Antonio Novelli	Polytechnic of Bari, Italy

Interactively Presenting High-Quality Graphics in Cooperation with Various Computing Tools (IPHQG 2017)

Masataka Kaneko	Toho University, Japan
Setsuo Takato	Toho University, Japan
Satoshi Yamashita	Kisarazu National College of Technology, Italy

Web-Based Collective Evolutionary Systems: Models, Measures, Applications (IWCES 2017)

Alfredo Milani	University of Perugia, Italy
Rajdeep Nyogi	Institute of Technology, Roorkee, India
Valentina Franzoni	University of Rome La Sapienza, Italy

Computational Mathematics, and Statistics for Data Management and Software Engineering (IWCMSDMSE 2017)

M. Filomena Teodoro   Lisbon University and Portuguese Naval Academy,
                                         Portugal
Anacleto Correia   Portuguese Naval Academy, Portugal

Land Use Monitoring for Soil Consumption Reduction (LUMS 2017)

Carmelo M. Torre   Polytechnic of Bari, Italy
Beniamino Murgante   University of Basilicata, Italy
Alessandro Bonifazi   Polytechnic of Bari, Italy
Massimiliano Bencardino   University of Salerno, Italy

Mobile Communications (MC 2017)

Hyunseung Choo   Sungkyunkwan University, Korea

Mobile-Computing, Sensing, and Actuation - Fog Networking (MSA4FOG 2017)

Saad Qaisar   NUST School of Electrical Engineering and Computer
                                       Science, Pakistan
Moonseong Kim   Korean Intellectual Property Office, South Korea

Physiological and Affective Computing: Methods and Applications (PACMA 2017)

Robertas Damasevicius   Kaunas University of Technology, Lithuania
Christian Napoli   University of Catania, Italy
Marcin Wozniak   Silesian University of Technology, Poland

Quantum Mechanics: Computational Strategies and Applications (QMCSA 2017)

Mirco Ragni   Universidad Federal de Bahia, Brazil
Ana Carla Peixoto   Universidade Estadual de Feira de Santana, Brazil
  Bitencourt
Vincenzo Aquilanti   University of Perugia, Italy

Advances in Remote Sensing for Cultural Heritage (RS 2017)

Rosa Lasaponara   IRMMA, CNR, Italy
Nicola Masini   IBAM, CNR, Italy Zhengzhou Base, International
                        Center on Space Technologies for Natural and
                        Cultural Heritage, China

Scientific Computing Infrastructure (SCI 2017)

Elena Stankova   Saint Petersburg State University, Russia
Alexander Bodganov   Saint Petersburg State University, Russia
Vladimir Korkhov   Saint Petersburg State University, Russia

Software Engineering Processes and Applications (SEPA 2017)

Sanjay Misra   Covenant University, Nigeria

Sustainability Performance Assessment: Models, Approaches and Applications Toward Interdisciplinarity and Integrated Solutions (SPA 2017)

Francesco Scorza   University of Basilicata, Italy
Valentin Grecu   Lucia Blaga University on Sibiu, Romania
Jolanta Dvarioniene   Kaunas University, Lithuania
Sabrina Lai   Cagliari University, Italy

Software Quality (SQ 2017)

Sanjay Misra   Covenant University, Nigeria

Advances in Spatio-Temporal Analytics (ST-Analytics 2017)

Rafael Santos   Brazilian Space Research Agency, Brazil
Karine Reis Ferreira   Brazilian Space Research Agency, Brazil
Maribel Yasmina Santos University of Minho, Portugal
Joao Moura Pires   New University of Lisbon, Portugal

Tools and Techniques in Software Development Processes (TTSDP 2017)

Sanjay Misra   Covenant University, Nigeria

Challenges, Trends, and Innovations in VGI (VGI 2017)

Claudia Ceppi	University of Basilicata, Italy
Beniamino Murgante	University of Basilicata, Italy
Lucia Tilio	University of Basilicata, Italy
Francesco Mancini	University of Modena and Reggio Emilia, Italy
Rodrigo Tapia-McClung	Centro de Investigación en Geografía y Geomática "Ing Jorge L. Tamayo", Mexico
Jorge Gustavo Rocha	University of Minho, Portugal

Virtual Reality and Applications (VRA 2017)

Osvaldo Gervasi	University of Perugia, Italy

Industrial Computational Applications (WICA 2017)

Eric Medvet	University of Trieste, Italy
Gianfranco Fenu	University of Trieste, Italy
Riccardo Ferrari	Delft University of Technology, The Netherlands

XIV International Workshop on Quantum Reactive Scattering (QRS 2017)

Niyazi Bulut	Fırat University, Turkey
Noelia Faginas Lago	University of Perugia, Italy
Andrea Lombardi	University of Perugia, Italy
Federico Palazzetti	University of Perugia, Italy

Program Committee

Jemal Abawajy	Deakin University, Australia
Kenny Adamson	University of Ulster, UK
Filipe Alvelos	University of Minho, Portugal
Paula Amaral	Universidade Nova de Lisboa, Portugal
Hartmut Asche	University of Potsdam, Germany
Md. Abul Kalam Azad	University of Minho, Portugal
Michela Bertolotto	University College Dublin, Ireland
Sandro Bimonte	CEMAGREF, TSCF, France
Rod Blais	University of Calgary, Canada
Ivan Blečić	University of Sassari, Italy
Giuseppe Borruso	University of Trieste, Italy
Yves Caniou	Lyon University, France
José A. Cardoso e Cunha	Universidade Nova de Lisboa, Portugal
Rui Cardoso	University of Beira Interior, Portugal
Leocadio G. Casado	University of Almeria, Spain
Carlo Cattani	University of Salerno, Italy

Mete Celik	Erciyes University, Turkey
Alexander Chemeris	National Technical University of Ukraine KPI, Ukraine
Min Young Chung	Sungkyunkwan University, Korea
Gilberto Corso Pereira	Federal University of Bahia, Brazil
M. Fernanda Costa	University of Minho, Portugal
Gaspar Cunha	University of Minho, Portugal
Alfredo Cuzzocrea	ICAR-CNR and University of Calabria, Italy
Carla Dal Sasso Freitas	Universidade Federal do Rio Grande do Sul, Brazil
Pradesh Debba	The Council for Scientific and Industrial Research (CSIR), South Africa
Hendrik Decker	Instituto Tecnológico de Informática, Spain
Frank Devai	London South Bank University, UK
Rodolphe Devillers	Memorial University of Newfoundland, Canada
Prabu Dorairaj	NetApp, India/USA
M. Irene Falcao	University of Minho, Portugal
Cherry Liu Fang	U.S. DOE Ames Laboratory, USA
Edite M.G.P. Fernandes	University of Minho, Portugal
Jose-Jesús Fernandez	National Centre for Biotechnology, CSIS, Spain
María Antonia Forjaz	University of Minho, Portugal
María Celia Furtado Rocha	PRODEB-Pós Cultura/UFBA, Brazil
Akemi Galvez	University of Cantabria, Spain
Paulino Jose Garcia Nieto	University of Oviedo, Spain
Marina Gavrilova	University of Calgary, Canada
Jerome Gensel	LSR-IMAG, France
María Giaoutzi	National Technical University, Athens, Greece
Andrzej M. Goscinski	Deakin University, Australia
Alex Hagen-Zanker	University of Cambridge, UK
Malgorzata Hanzl	Technical University of Lodz, Poland
Shanmugasundaram Hariharan	B.S. Abdur Rahman University, India
Eligius M.T. Hendrix	University of Malaga/Wageningen University, Spain/The Netherlands
Tutut Herawan	Universitas Teknologi Yogyakarta, Indonesia
Hisamoto Hiyoshi	Gunma University, Japan
Fermin Huarte	University of Barcelona, Spain
Andrés Iglesias	University of Cantabria, Spain
Mustafa Inceoglu	EGE University, Turkey
Peter Jimack	University of Leeds, UK
Qun Jin	Waseda University, Japan
Farid Karimipour	Vienna University of Technology, Austria
Baris Kazar	Oracle Corp., USA
Maulana Adhinugraha Kiki	Telkom University, Indonesia
DongSeong Kim	University of Canterbury, New Zealand
Taihoon Kim	Hannam University, Korea
Ivana Kolingerova	University of West Bohemia, Czech Republic

Additional Reviewers

A. Alwan Al-Juboori Ali	School of Computer Science and Technology, China
Aceto Lidia	University of Pisa, Italy
Acharjee Shukla	Dibrugarh University, India
Afreixo Vera	University of Aveiro, Portugal
Agra Agostinho	University of Aveiro, Portugal
Aguilar Antonio	University of Barcelona, Spain
Aguilar José Alfonso	Universidad Autónoma de Sinaloa, Mexico
Aicardi Irene	Politecnico di Torino, Italy
Alberti Margarita	University of Barcelona, Spain
Alberto Rui	University of Lisbon, Portugal
Ali Salman	University of Magna Graecia, Italy
Alvanides Seraphim	University at Newcastle, UK
Alvelos Filipe	Universidade do Minho, Portugal
Amato Alba	Seconda Università degli Studi di Napoli, Italy
Amorim Paulo	Instituto de Matemática da UFRJ (IM-UFRJ), Brazil
Anderson Roger	University of California Santa Cruz, USA
Andrianov Serge	Saint Petersburg State University, Russia
Andrienko Gennady	Fraunhofer-Institut für Intelligente Analyse- und Informationssysteme, Germany
Apduhan Bernady	Kyushu Sangyo University, Japan
Aquilanti Vincenzo	University of Perugia, Italy
Asche Hartmut	Potsdam University, Germany
Azam Samiul	United International University, Bangladesh
Azevedo Ana	Athabasca University, USA
Bae Ihn-Han	Catholic University of Daegu, South Korea
Balacco Gabriella	Polytechnic of Bari, Italy
Balena Pasquale	Polytechnic of Bari, Italy
Barroca Filho Itamir	Universidade Federal do Rio Grande do Norte, Brazil
Behera Ranjan Kumar	Indian Institute of Technology Patna, India
Belpassi Leonardo	National Research Council, Italy
Bentayeb Fadila	Université Lyon, France
Bernardino Raquel	Universidade da Beira Interiore, Portugal
Bertolotto Michela	University Collegue Dublin, UK
Bhatta Bijaya	Utkal University, India
Bimonte Sandro	IRSTEA, France
Blecic Ivan	University of Cagliari, Italy
Bo Carles	ICIQ, Spain
Bogdanov Alexander	Saint Petersburg State University, Russia
Bollini Letizia	University of Milano-Bicocca, Italy
Bonifazi Alessandro	Polytechnic of Bari, Italy
Bonnet Claude-Laurent	Université de Bordeaux, France
Borgogno Mondino Enrico Corrado	University of Turin, Italy
Borruso Giuseppe	University of Trieste, Italy

Bostenaru Maria	Ion Mincu University of Architecture and Urbanism, Romania
Boussaid Omar	Université Lyon 2, France
Braga Ana Cristina	University of Minho, Portugal
Braga Nuno	University of Minho, Portugal
Brasil Luciana	Instituto Federal Sao Paolo, Brazil
Cabral Pedro	Universidade NOVA de Lisboa, Portugal
Cacao Isabel	University of Aveiro, Portugal
Caiaffa Emanuela	Enea, Italy
Campagna Michele	University of Cagliari, Italy
Caniato Renhe Marcelo	Universidade Federal de Juiz de Fora, Brazil
Canora Filomena	University of Basilicata, Italy
Caradonna Grazia	Polytechnic of Bari, Italy
Cardoso Rui	Beira Interior University, Portugal
Caroti Gabriella	University of Pisa, Italy
Carravilla Maria Antonia	Universidade do Porto, Portugal
Cattani Carlo	University of Salerno, Italy
Cefalo Raffaela	University of Trieste, Italy
Ceppi Claudia	Polytechnic of Bari, Italy
Cerreta Maria	University Federico II of Naples, Italy
Chanet Jean-Pierre	UR TSCF Irstea, France
Chaturvedi Krishna Kumar	University of Delhi, India
Chiancone Andrea	University of Perugia, Italy
Choo Hyunseung	Sungkyunkwan University, South Korea
Ciabo Serena	University of l'Aquila, Italy
Coletti Cecilia	University of Chieti, Italy
Correia Aldina	Porto Polytechnic, Portugal
Correia Anacleto	CINAV, Portugal
Correia Elisete	University of Trás-Os-Montes e Alto Douro, Portugal
Correia Florbela Maria da Cruz Domingues	Instituto Politécnico de Viana do Castelo, Portugal
Cosido Oscar	University of Cantabria, Spain
Costa e Silva Eliana	University of Minho, Portugal
Costa Graça	Instituto Politécnico de Setúbal, Portugal
Costantini Alessandro	INFN, Italy
Crispim José	University of Minho, Portugal
Cuzzocrea Alfredo	University of Trieste, Italy
Danese Maria	IBAM, CNR, Italy
Daneshpajouh Shervin	University of Western Ontario, USA
De Fazio Dario	IMIP-CNR, Italy
De Runz Cyril	University of Reims Champagne-Ardenne, France
Deffuant Guillaume	Institut national de recherche en sciences et technologies pour l'environnement et l'agriculture, France
Degtyarev Alexander	Saint Petersburg State University, Russia
Devai Frank	London South Bank University, UK
Di Leo Margherita	JRC, European Commission, Belgium

Dias Joana	University of Coimbra, Portugal
Dilo Arta	University of Twente, The Netherlands
Dvarioniene Jolanta	Kaunas University of Technology, Lithuania
El-Zawawy Mohamed A.	Cairo University, Egypt
Escalona Maria-Jose	University of Seville, Spain
Faginas-Lago, Noelia	University of Perugia, Italy
Falcinelli Stefano	University of Perugia, Italy
Falcão M. Irene	University of Minho, Portugal
Faria Susana	University of Minho, Portugal
Fattoruso Grazia	ENEA, Italy
Fenu Gianfranco	University of Trieste, Italy
Fernandes Edite	University of Minho, Portugal
Fernandes Florbela	Escola Superior de Tecnologia e Gest ão de Bragancca, Portugal
Fernandes Rosario	USP/ESALQ, Brazil
Ferrari Riccardo	Delft University of Technology, The Netherlands
Figueiredo Manuel Carlos	University of Minho, Portugal
Florence Le Ber	ENGEES, France
Flouvat Frederic	University of New Caledonia, France
Fontes Dalila	Universidade do Porto, Portugal
Franzoni Valentina	University of Perugia, Italy
Freitas Adelaide de Fátima Baptista Valente	University of Aveiro, Portugal
Fusco Giovanni	Università di Bari, Italy
Gabrani Goldie	Tecpro Syst. Ltd., India
Gaido Luciano	INFN, Italy
Gallo Crescenzio	University of Foggia, Italy
Garaba Shungu	University of Connecticut, USA
Garau Chiara	University of Cagliari, Italy
Garcia Ernesto	University of the Basque Country, Spain
Gargano Ricardo	Universidade Brasilia, Brazil
Gavrilova Marina	University of Calgary, Canada
Gensel Jerome	IMAG, France
Gervasi Osvaldo	University of Perugia, Italy
Gioia Andrea	Polytechnic University of Bari, Italy
Giovinazzi Sonia	University of Canterbury, New Zealand
Gizzi Fabrizio	National Research Council, Italy
Gomes dos Anjos Eudisley	Universidade Federal da Paraíba, Brazil
Gonzaga de Oliveira Sanderson Lincohn	Universidade Federal de Lavras, Brazil
Gonçalves Arminda Manuela	University of Minho, Braga, Portugal
Gorbachev Yuriy	Geolink Technologies, Russia
Grecu Valentin	University of Sibiu, Romania
Gupta Brij	Cancer Biology Research Center, USA
Hagen-Zanker Alex	University of Surrey, UK

Hamaguchi Naoki	Tokyo Kyoiku University, Japan
Hanazumi Simone	University of Sao Paulo, Brazil
Hanzl Malgorzata	University of Lodz, Poland
Hayashi Masaki	University of Calgary, Canada
Hendrix Eligius M.T.	Operations Research and Logistics Group, The Netherlands
Henriques Carla	Inst. Politécnico de Viseu, Portugal
Herawan Tutut	State Polytechnic of Malang, Indonesia
Hsu Hui-Huang	National Chiao Tung University, Taiwan
Ienco Dino	La Maison de la télédétection de Montpellier, France
Iglesias Andres	Universidad de Cantabria, Spain
Imran Rabeea	NUST Islamabad, Pakistan
Inoue Kentaro	National Technical University of Athens, Greece
Josselin Didier	Université d'Avignon et des Pays de Vaucluse, France
Kaneko Masataka	Kisarazu National College of Technology, Japan
Kang Myoung-Ah	Blaise Pascal University, France
Karampiperis Pythagoras	National Center of Scientific Research, Athens, Greece
Kavouras Marinos	University of Athens, Greece
Kolingerova` Ivana	University of West Bohemia, Czech Republic
Korkhov Vladimir	Saint Petersburg State University, Russia
Kotzinos Dimitrios	University of Cergy Pontoise, France
Kulabukhova Nataliia	Saint Petersburg State University, Russia
Kumar Dileep	SR Engineering College, India
Kumar Lov	National Institute of Technology, Rourkela, India
Kumar Pawan	Institute for Advanced Study, Princeton, USA
Laganà Antonio	University of Perugia, Italy
Lai Sabrina	Università di Cagliari, Italy
Lanza Viviana	Lombardy Regional Institute for Research, Italy
Lasala Piermichele	Università di Foggia, Italy
Laurent Anne	Laboratoire d'Informatique, de Robotique et de Microélectronique de Montpellier, France
Lavorato Davide	University of Rome, Italy
Le Duc Tai	Sungkyunkwan University, South Korea
Legatiuk Dmitrii	Bauhaus University, Germany
Li Ming	University of Waterloo, Canada
Lima Ana	University of São Paulo (UNIFESP), Brazil
Liu Xin	École polytechnique fédérale de Lausanne, Switzerland
Lombardi Andrea	University of Perugia, Italy
Lopes Cristina	Instituto Superior de Contabilidade e Administracao do Porto, Portugal
Lopes Maria João	Instituto Universitário de Lisboa, Portugal
Lourenço Vanda Marisa	Universidade NOVA de Lisboa, Portugal
Machado Jose	University of Minho, Portugal
Maeda Yoichi	Tokai University, Japan
Majcen Nineta	Euchems, Belgium
Malonek Helmuth	Universidade de Aveiro, Portugal

Mancini Francesco	University of Modena and Reggio Emilia, Italy
Mandanici Emanuele	Università di Bologna, Italy
Manganelli Benedetto	Università degli studi della Basilicata, Italy
Manso Callejo Miguel Angel	Universidad Politécnica de Madrid, Spain
Margalef Tomas	Autonomous University of Barcelona, Spain
Marques Jorge	University of Coimbra, Portugal
Martins Bruno	Universidade de Lisboa, Portugal
Marvuglia Antonino	Public Research Centre Henri Tudor, Luxembourg
Mateos Cristian	Universidad Nacional del Centro, Argentina
Mauro Giovanni	University of Trieste, Italy
McGuire Michael	Towson University, USA
Medvet Eric	University of Trieste, Italy
Milani Alfredo	University of Perugia, Italy
Millham Richard	Durban University of Technoloy, South Africa
Minghini Marco	Polytechnic University of Milan, Italy
Minhas Umar	University of Waterloo, Ontario, Canada
Miralles André	La Maison de la télédétection de Montpellier, France
Miranda Fernando	Universidade do Minho, Portugal
Misra Sanjay	Covenant University, Nigeria
Modica Giuseppe	Università Mediterranea di Reggio Calabria, Italy
Molaei Qelichi Mohamad	University of Tehran, Iran
Monteiro Ana Margarida	University of Coimbra, Portugal
Morano Pierluigi	Polytechnic University of Bari, Italy
Moura Ana	Universidade de Aveiro, Portugal
Moura Pires João	Universidade NOVA de Lisboa, Portugal
Mourão Maria	ESTG-IPVC, Portugal
Murgante Beniamino	University of Basilicata, Italy
Nagy Csaba	University of Szeged, Hungary
Nakamura Yasuyuki	Nagoya University, Japan
Natário Isabel Cristina Maciel	University Nova de Lisboa, Portugal
Nemmaoui Abderrahim	Universidad de Almeria (UAL), Spain
Nguyen Tien Dzung	Sungkyunkwan University, South Korea
Niyogi Rajdeep	Indian Institute of Technology Roorkee, India
Novelli Antonio	University of Bari, Italy
Oliveira Irene	University of Trás-Os-Montes e Alto Douro, Portugal
Oliveira José A.	Universidade do Minho, Portugal
Ottomanelli Michele	University of Bari, Italy
Ouchi Shunji	Shimonoseki City University, Japan
Ozturk Savas	Scientific and Technological Research Council of Turkey, Turkey
P. Costa M. Fernanda	Universidade do Minho, Portugal
Painho Marco	NOVA Information Management School, Portugal
Panetta J.B.	Tecnologia Geofísica Petróleo Brasileiro SA, PETROBRAS, Brazil

Pantazis Dimos	Otenet, Greece
Papa Enrica	University of Amsterdam, The Netherlands
Pardede Eric	La Trobe University, Australia
Parente Claudio	Università degli Studi di Napoli Parthenope, Italy
Pathan Al-Sakib Khan	Islamic University of Technology, Bangladesh
Paul Prantosh K.	EIILM University, Jorethang, Sikkim, India
Pengő Edit	University of Szeged, Hungary
Pereira Ana	IPB, Portugal
Pereira José Luís	Universidade do Minho, Portugal
Peschechera Giuseppe	Università di Bologna, Italy
Pham Quoc Trung	HCMC University of Technology, Vietnam
Piemonte Andreaa	University of Pisa, Italy
Pimentel Carina	Universidade de Aveiro, Portugal
Pinet Francois	IRSTEA, France
Pinto Livio	Polytechnic University of Milan, Italy
Pinto Telmo	Universidade do Minho, Portugal
Pinet Francois	IRSTEA, France
Poli Giuliano	Université Pierre et Marie Curie, France
Pollino Maurizio	ENEA, Italy
Portela Carlos Filipe	Universidade do Minho, Portugal
Prata Paula	Universidade Federal de Sergipe, Brazil
Previl Carlo	University of Quebec in Abitibi-Témiscamingue (UQAT), Canada
Prezioso Giuseppina	Università degli Studi di Napoli Parthenope, Italy
Pusatli Tolga	Cankaya University, Turkey
Quan Tho	Ho Chi Minh, University of Technology, Vietnam
Ragni Mirco	Universidade Estadual de Feira de Santana, Brazil
Rahman Nazreena	Biotechnology Research Centre, Malaysia
Rahman Wasiur	Technical University Darmstadt, Germany
Rashid Sidra	National University of Sciences and Technology (NUST) Islamabad, Pakistan
Rasulo Alessandro	Università degli studi di Cassino e del Lazio Meridionale, Italy
Raza Syed Muhammad	Sungkyunkwan University, South Korea
Reis Ferreira Gomes Karine	Instituto Nacional de Pesquisas Espaciais, Brazil
Requejo Cristina	Universidade de Aveiro, Portugal
Rocha Ana Maria	University of Minho, Portugal
Rocha Humberto	University of Coimbra, Portugal
Rocha Jorge	University of Minho, Portugal
Rodriguez Daniel	University of Berkeley, USA
Saeki Koichi	Graduate University for Advanced Studies, Japan
Samela Caterina	University of Basilicata, Italy
Sannicandro Valentina	Polytechnic of Bari, Italy
Santiago Júnior Valdivino	Instituto Nacional de Pesquisas Espaciais, Brazil
Sarafian Haiduke	Pennsylvania State University, USA

Santos Daniel	Universidade Federal de Minas Gerais, Portugal
Santos Dorabella	Instituto de Telecomunicações, Portugal
Santos Eulália	SAPO, Portugal
Santos Maribel Yasmina	Universidade de Minho, Portugal
Santos Rafael	University of Toronto, Canada
Santucci Valentinoi	University of Perugia, Italy
Sautot Lucil	MR TETIS, AgroParisTech, France
Scaioni Marco	Polytechnic University of Milan, Italy
Schernthanner Harald	University of Potsdam, Germany
Schneider Michel	ISIMA, France
Schoier Gabriella	University of Trieste, Italy
Scorza Francesco	University of Basilicata, Italy
Sebillo Monica	University of Salerno, Italy
Severino Ricardo Jose	Universidade de Minho, Portugal
Shakhov Vladimir	Russian Academy of Sciences (Siberian Branch), Russia
Sheeren David	Toulouse Institute of Technology, France
Shen Jie	University of Michigan, USA
Silva Elsa	INESC Tec, Porto, Portugal
Sipos Gergely	MTA SZTAKI Computer and Automation Research Institute, Hungary
Skarga-Bandurova Inna	Technological Institute of East Ukrainian National University, Ukraine
Skoković Dražen	University of Valencia, Spain
Skouteris Dimitrios	SNS, Italy
Soares Inês Soares Maria Joana	Universidade de Minho, Portugal
Soares Michel	Federal University of Sergipe, Brazil
Sokolovski Dmitri	Ikerbasque, Basque Foundation for Science, Spain
Sousa Lisete	Research, FCUL, CEAUL, Lisboa, Portugal
Stener Mauro	Università di Trieste, Italy
Sumida Yasuaki	Center for Digestive and Liver Diseases, Nara City Hospital, Japan
Suri Bharti	Guru Gobind Singh Indraprastha University, India
Sørensen Claus Aage Grøn	University of Aarhus, Denmark
Tajani Francesco	University of Rome, Italy
Takato Setsuo	Kisarazu National College of Technology, Japan
Tanaka Kazuaki	Hasanuddin University, Indonesia
Taniar David	Monash University, Australia
Tapia-McClung Rodrigo	The Center for Research in Geography and Geomatics, Mexico
Tarantino Eufemia	Polytechnic of Bari, Italy
Teixeira Ana Paula	Federal University of Ceará, Fortaleza, Brazil
Teixeira Senhorinha	Universidade do Minho, Portugal
Teodoro M. Filomena	Instituto Politécnico de Setúbal, Portugal
Thill Jean-Claude	University at Buffalo, USA
Thorat Pankaj	Sungkyunkwan University, South Korea

Tilio Lucia	University of Basilicata, Italy
Tomaz Graça	Instituto Politécnico da Guarda, Portugal
Torre Carmelo Maria	Polytechnic of Bari, Italy
Totaro Vincenzo	Polytechnic University of Bari, Italy
Tran Manh Hung	University of Danang, Vietnam
Tripathi Ashish	MNNIT Allahabad, India
Tripp Barba Carolina	Universidad Autónoma de Sinaloa, Mexico
Tut Zohra Fatema	University of Calgary, Canada
Upadhyay Ashish	Indian Institute of Public Health-Gandhinagar, India
Vallverdu Jordi	Autonomous University of Barcelona, Spain
Valuev Ilya	Russian Academy of Sciences, Russia
Varela Leonilde	University of Minho, Portugal
Varela Tania	Universidade de Lisboa, Portugal
Vasconcelos Paulo	Queensland University, Brisbane, Australia
Vasyunin Dmitry	University of Amsterdam, The Netherlands
Vella Flavio	University of Rome, Italy
Vijaykumar Nandamudi	INPE, Brazil
Vidacs Laszlo	University of Szeged, Hungary
Viqueira José R.R.	Agricultural University of Athens, Greece
Vizzari Marco	University of Perugia, Italy
Vohra Varun	Japan Advanced Institute of Science and Technology (JAIST), Japan
Voit Nikolay	Ulyanovsk State Technical University Ulyanovsk, Russia
Walkowiak Krzysztof	Wroclaw University of Technology, Poland
Wallace Richard J.	University College Cork, Ireland
Waluyo Agustinus Borgy	Monash University, Melbourne, Australia
Wanderley Fernando	FCT/UNL, Portugal
Wei Hoo Chong	Motorola, USA
Yamashita Satoshi	National Research Institute for Child Health and Development, Tokyo, Japan
Yamauchi Toshihiro	Okayama University, Japan
Yao Fenghui	Tennessee State University, USA
Yeoum Sanggil	Sungkyunkwan University, South Korea
Zaza Claudio	University of Foggia, Italy
Zeile Peter	Technische Universität Kaiserslautern, Germany
Zenha-Rela Mario	University of Coimbra, Portugal
Zoppi Corrado	Università di Cagliari, Italy
Zullo Francesco	University of l'Aquila, Italy
Zunino Alejandro	Universidad Nacional del Centro, Argentina
Žemlička Michal	Univerzita Karlova, Czech Republic
Živković Ljiljana	University of Belgrade, Serbia

Sponsoring Organizations

ICCSA 2017 would not have been possible without the tremendous support of many organizations and institutions, for which all organizers and participants of ICCSA 2017 express their sincere gratitude:

University of Trieste, Trieste, Italy
(http://www.units.it/)

University of Perugia, Italy
(http://www.unipg.it)

University of Basilicata, Italy
(http://www.unibas.it)

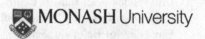

Monash University, Australia
(http://monash.edu)

Kyushu Sangyo University, Japan
(www.kyusan-u.ac.jp)

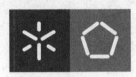

Universidade do Minho
Escola de Engenharia

Universidade do Minho, Portugal
(http://www.uminho.pt)

Contents – Part III

Workshop on Cities, Technologies and Planning (CTP 2017)

**Workshop on Deep Cities: Intelligence and Interoperability
(DEEP CITY 2017)**

Workshop on Econometrics and Multidimensional Evaluation in the Urban Environment (EMEUE 2017)

Workshop on Emotion Recognition (EMORE 2917)

Workshop on Chemistry and Materials Sciences and Technologies (CMST 2017)

Acetone-Water Mixtures: Molecular Dynamics Using a Semiempirical Intermolecular Potential

Noelia Faginas-Lago[1($\boxtimes$)], Margarita Albertí[2], Andrea Lombardi[1], and Federico Palazzetti[1]

[1] Dipartimento di Chimica, Biologia e Biotecnologie,
Università di Perugia, Perugia, Italy
noelia.faginaslago@unipg.it
[2] IQTCUB, Departament de Ciència de Materials i Química Física,
Universitat de Barcelona, Barcelona, Spain

Abstract. A theoretical study of some acetone -water solutions is performed considering a total number of molecules equal to 1000. A force field for the water-acetone interaction is presented. To this purpose we have considered four interaction centers on the acetone molecule and only one on the small water molecule. Then, the non electrostatic intermolecular interaction between pairs of interaction centers placed on different molecules has been modeled adopting Improved Lennard-Jones (ILJ) functions, which sum has been combined with the electrostatic interaction contribution (derived from the charge distributions on the molecules). The potential model has been used to perform some preliminary Molecular Dynamic simulations of the density at $298.15 \, K$ of temperature and 1 atm of pressure for two different values of the acetone molar fractions, $x_{acet} = 0.745$ and 0.986. The systems, formed by 1000 molecules, were previously thermalized at the selected temperature using the NVT ensemble. Production runs have been performed from the equilibrated systems using the NpT ensemble.

Keywords: Molecular Dynamics · Empirical potential energy surface · Acetone-water solution · DL_POLY

1   Introduction

Acetone (systematically named propanone) is the organic compound with the formula $CH_3\text{-}CO\text{-}CH_3$. It is a colorless, volatile, flammable liquid, and is the simplest ketone. Acetone is miscible with water and serves as an important solvent in its own right, typically for cleaning purposes in the laboratory. About 6.7 million tonnes were produced worldwide in 2010. It is a common building block in organic chemistry. Familiar household uses of acetone are as the active ingredient in nail polish remover and as paint thinner. Acetone is produced and disposed of in the human body through normal metabolic processes. It is normally present in blood and urine. People with diabetes produce it in larger amounts. Reproductive toxicity tests show that it has low potential to cause

© Springer International Publishing AG 2017
O. Gervasi et al. (Eds.): ICCSA 2017, Part III, LNCS 10406, pp. 3–13, 2017.
DOI: 10.1007/978-3-319-62398-6_1

reproductive problems. Pregnant women, nursing mothers and children have higher levels of acetone [1]. Ketogenic diets that increase acetone in the body are used to counter epileptic attacks in infants and children who suffer from recalcitrant refractory epilepsy.

There are two main ways of manufacturing propanone, both produced from propene. One of them is via cumene and the other one via isopropanol. By far the most important route is the cumene process [2–4]. Acetone is able to dissolve a wide range of chemical compounds, including polar, non-polar and polymeric materials [5,6] and is very soluble in water. Accordingly, most of the acetone production is used as a solvent, the properties as a solvent being known for a long time. [7] Due to the capability to dissolve different chemical compounds, acetone is often the primary component of cleaning agents, which present specific benefits because being effective and not expensive, they have a very low toxicity. Moreover, acetone is also important in the chemical industry, being widely used in the production of methyl methacrylate [8] and bisphenol A [9].

Owing to the central role of water in everyday life, water is the most investigated solvent. However, the understanding of the solvation mechanisms in solutions of organic solvents is crucial to improve the efficiency of processes of technological interest. [10–13] From an experimental point of view, to obtain detailed dynamical information on simple and complex liquids, spectroscopic methods based on a second rank molecular property, such as the polarizability anisotropy, can be suitably applied [12]. On another hand, Molecular Dynamics (MD) simulations is a theoretical powerful tool to analyze extensively the structural rearrangement of pure solvents, solution mixtures and the combustion processes. However, the accuracy of the results depends largely on the reliability of the interaction potential. In the last years some of us have formulated a potential energy function [14] to describe the non permanent charge interactions (V_{nel}), which combined with the electrostatic contributions (V_{el}), when present, is able to describe accurately ionic and neutral systems. In such model, the relevant parameters of V_{nel} are derived from the values of the molecular polarizability. On another hand, polarization effects are indirectly considered by increasing the value of the dipole moment of the molecules in respect with those corresponding to gas phase. Such formulation has been proved to be adequate not only to describe systems on gas phase (see for instance Refs. [15–17]) but also the liquid behavior of water [18–20], acetonitrile [13], ammonia [21] and acetone [22]. All the previous results encouraged us the use of the same methodology to construct the acetone-water force field.

The original potential model used here is based on a formulation of the non electrostatic approach to the intermolecular interaction that exploits the decomposition of the molecular polarizability [23] into effective components associated with atoms, bonds or groups of atoms of the involved molecules. This type of contribution to the intermolecular energy was already applied in the past to the investigation of several neutral [24–32] and ionic [33–35] systems, often involving weak interactions [24,36], difficult to calculate. The adequacy of such potential energy functions to describe several intermolecular systems was proved by comparing energy and geometry predictions at several configurations with ab initio calculations.

In the present paper, we present the preliminary theoretical results of the potential model, based in a modification of the Lennard Jones (LJ) function which is applied to investigate the mixture of acetone, (CH_3-CO-CH_3) and water (H_2O). The paper is organized as follows: in Sect. 2, we outline the construction of the potential energy function. We give in Sect. 3 the details of the Molecular Dynamics simulations. Preliminary results are presented in Sect. 4 and concluding remarks are given in Sect. 5.

2   Potential Energy Surface

In our model, the total potential energy of the acetone-water system for a given configuration, say V_{cfg}, is represented assuming the separability of electrostatic (V_{el}) including only permanent electric multipole contributions and nonelectrostatic interactions (V_{nel}), due to size (or Pauli) repulsion plus dispersion and induction attraction. V_{nel}, appearing from the balancing of dispersion and induction attraction forces, dominant at long range, and exchange (size) repulsion forces, dominant at short range, is, in general, the interaction component more difficult to formulate. In our model, it is constructed using Improved Lennard-Jones (ILJ) functions, [20, 37] which, in comparison with the Lennard-Jones ones (LJ), improve the description of the interaction at both short and long range [14, 38].

$$V_{ILJ}(r) = \varepsilon \left[\frac{m}{n(r) - m} \left(\frac{r_0}{r} \right)^{n(r)} - \frac{n(r)}{n(r) - m} \left(\frac{r_0}{r} \right)^{m} \right] \qquad (1)$$

V_{ILJ} represents the nonelectrostatic contributions between two pairs of interaction centers placed on different molecules. In fact, depending on the complexity and nature of the investigated systems, the interaction centers can be placed on atoms, bonds or groups of atoms (for details about the choice of interacting centers see ref. [36]). Following the guidelines developed in a previous work [22], we have considered four interaction centers on the acetone molecule. Two of them are placed on the C atoms of the methyl groups, represented by CM, and the other two placed on the C and O atoms of the $C = O$ group, described by C and O respectively. This means that the acetone molecule is given by a rigid set of four interaction sites, located on oxygen and carbon atoms. The representation of the acetone is given in Fig. 1.

Only one interaction center placed on the oxygen atom (represented by OW) has been considered for the water molecule, which also is treated as a rigid body [18, 39]. The potential model of water has been tested and validated in previous studies including both liquid water [20, 40] and alkali ion aqueous solutions [15, 41].

According with the interaction centers considered, the V_{nel} contributions due to the pair CH_3-CO-CH_3-CH_3-CO-CH_3, CH_3-CO-CH_3-H_2O and H_2O-H_2O interactions are constructed as a sum of of eight, four and one V_{ILJ} interaction terms, respectively.

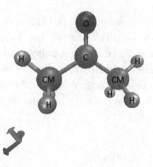

Fig. 1. Graphical representation of the labeled atoms in the acetone molecule.

In Eq. 1, ε, r_0 and m are pair specific parameters and r is the distance between the positions of the two interacting centers placed on different molecules. The first term of the bracketed sum in Eq. 1 (the positive one) represents the size-repulsion contribution arising from each pair, while the second term (negative) represents the effective dispersion attraction contribution for the given pair of centers. The exponent $n(r)$ of the first term modulates the falloff of the repulsion and controls the strength of the attraction as a function of r as follows:

$$n(r) = \beta + 4.0 \left(\frac{r}{r_0}\right)^2 \tag{2}$$

with β being an adjustable parameter able to modulate the hardness of the interaction [14]). The introduction of this modulating parameter (not present in the standard Lennard-Jones function (LJ)) provides ILJ with the possibility of indirectly taking into account some effects of the induction, charge transfer and atom clustering. The parameter β also corrects the dependence of the interaction on the internuclear distance, improving the LJ function in the asymptotic region. For a full account of the advantages of the ILJ function see Refs. [14, 15, 42, 43] and references therein.

In the interactions between neutral molecules m is set equal to 6. The relevant parameters describing (for each pair) the depth of the potential well (ε) and its location (r_0) are evaluated using effective values of the polarizability associated to each interaction center [44] and being compatible with the molecular polarizability. According with the interaction centers considered in the acetone and water molecules, the list of the ε and r_0 parameters used in the present work is given in Table 1.

Due to the relative role played by β and the dipole moment (μ), the specific values selected for β can depend on the selected value of μ [20]. In fact, small modifications of β can be compensated by varying μ. Due to this fact, in the present paper we have analized the modulation of the β parameter as a function of various charge distributions assigned to the water molecules. The modulation of β can also partially compensate the case of different representations of the charge distributions and indirectly include other less important interaction effects at intermediate and short distances [13, 18–21, 39].

Table 1. ε (well depth), r_0 (equilibrium distance) parameters used to define V_{nel} for the acetone-acetone, acetone-water and water-water intermolecular pair interactions using ILJ functions. The atoms are named as in Fig. 1.

Interaction partners	ε/meV	r_0/Å
CM-CM	11.362	4.053
C-C	6.520	3.628
O-O	5.160	3.398
CM-C	8.819	3.866
CM-O	6.688	3.789
C-O	5.640	3.521
CM-OW	9.881	3.908
OW-OW	9.060	3.730
C-OW	7.660	3.683
O-OW	9.100	3.754

3 The Simulation Protocol of the Molecular Dynamics

Classical molecular dynamics simulations were performed using the DL_POLY [45] molecular dynamics simulation package. We performed classical MD simulations of the mixture formed by $(CH_3\text{-}CO\text{-}CH_3)_n$ - $(H_2O)_m$ with $n + m = 1000$, being the corresponding molar fraction $n/1000$ represented by x_{acet}. Two different ensembles NVT and NpT were applied. In the first the number of particles, N, volume, V, and temperature, T, are conserved, while in the NpT ensemble the volume of the cell box can vary. For this reason, we have equilibrated the system at constant volume (NVT ensemble) (compatible qith the density value) to obtain the selected temperature using a Berendsen thermostat [46]. Then, with the equilibrated configuration of the system we have performed a NpT simulation, allowing fluctuations of the volume, to calculate the density predicted by own potential model. Cubic boundary conditions have been imposed in all simulations. Our simulations were carried out at the temperature of 298.15 K, to allow the comparison with the experimental results [47]. The NVT simulations have been performed along 1 ns, while the time for the NpT simulations was set equal to 3 ns. Obviously, only the NpT results have been considered to perform the final statistics.

4 The Acetone-Water Mixtures

In the present section we present preliminary results obtained using selected values of the charge distribution and of some β parameters. Such calculations have been suggested by the difficulties to reproduce accurate values of some properties of the acetone aqueous solutions in the whole range of molar fractions. [48] Such failure of the potential models has been attributed to the microscopic structure of the solution. In the ref. [48], the authors indicate the relation between the hydrogen-bond network and the concentration fluctuations. This originates visible clustering of the solution at all acetone mole fractions. This fact could suggest the use of different charge distributions for the different concentrations and in this preliminar study we test water dipole moment values in the 2.3 D-2.43 D range. The value of 2.3 D was suggested previously in our model for rigid water molecules. [18] In order to test if the same charge distribution can be used for the whole concentration range, at first different water charge distributions have been considered, together with different values of β in the ILJ function, for the molar fractions of $x_{acet} = 0.745$ and 0.986. The different charge distributions and β values considered are given in Table 2.

Table 2. Water molecule charge distributions and β of pair interactions involving water.

q_{OW}/q_{HW}	β_{OW-OW}	β_{CM-OW}	β_{C-OW}	β_{O-OW}
$-0.8828/0.4414$	7.00	8.00	8.00	8.00
$-0.8460/0.4230$	6.60	8.00	8.00	8.00
$-0.8460/0.4230$	6.60	7.00	7.00	7.00
$-0.8644/0.4332$	6.80	8.00	8.00	8.00
$-0.8460/0.4230$	6.60	6.60	6.60	6.60
$-0.8460/0.4230$	6.60	6.60	7.00	7.00

The solutions have been simulated at p = 1 atm and T = 298.15 K for the two different molar fractions indicated before. The density values of the solutions have been calculated and the results are presented in Fig. 2. In the figure, the fill circles linked by a straight line are the extrapolated experimental values [47]. Following the Table 2, the triangles up correspond to the density values obtained using the charge distribution and β values given in the first row of the Table. The results obtained using charges and β values given on the second row are represented by the diamonds, while the ones corresponding to the third, fourth, fifth and sixth rows are represented by squares circles, plus and stars, respectively.

In general it seems that higher dipole moments for water reproduce better the density values than the lower ones. As it can be seen in Fig. 2, the best value of the density obtained for the small molar fraction investigated ($x_{acet} = 0.745$) is obtained when the charge distribution and β values given on the first row of the Table are used. However, for $x_{acet} = 0.986$, the density value closer to the experimental one is obtained using the parameters given in the last row of the Table. Moreover, independently of the parameters used, the slope of the density values with the molar fraction is very different of the experimental one. The previous results seem to indicate that very different dipole moments of the molecules should be used to obtain reasonable results for acetone-water solutions at different concentrations. In fact, as it has been indicated by Perera and

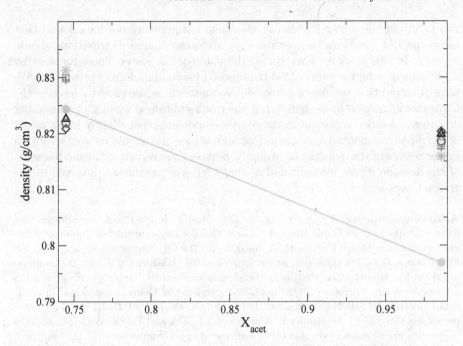

Fig. 2. Density values, ρ as a function of molar fraction of the acetone. The results linked by a straight line indicate the experimental values extrapolate from the literature [47]. Each set of values (different legends) indicate the values of the density obtained from the MD simulations using the different values of the β and charges distributions from water molecules indicated in the Table 2. (See explication in the text)

Sokolic [48] the deficiency of most potential models for acetone-water mixtures is due to the relation between the hydrogen-bond network and the concentration fluctuations, as well as the role played by acetone in their spatial organization (which is mainly due to the charge distribution). The high values obtained for the density when the molar fraction of acetone is increased to 0.986 indicates that the interaction potential is too attractive for the higher molar fractions of acetone. Due to the small number of water molecules, such behavior must be attributed mainly to the acetone interactions. In fact, in our previous paper on liquid acetone, we calculated density values slightly higher than the experimental ones [22, 49].

5   Conclusions

In this paper we have done the preliminary theoretical calculations to study the properties of acetone-water mixtures by classical MD simulations by using a semiempirical intermolecular potential energy surface based on the ILJ pair function to decribe the non electrostatic interaction contribution. By considering two values of the molar fraction at the same temperature, we have found that using the ILJ functions to describe V_{nel}, different charge distributions should be used. In this work we have varied the value of the water dipole moment by slightly increasing the value of 2.3 D proposed for rigid molecules previously. We have observed that the use of higher dipole moments is adequate to describe the lower molar fraction investigated, but the results obtained when a small number of water molecules is present in the solutions indicates that slightly lower values of the dipole moment of acetone and/or high values of β should be used to obtain better results of the density. Accordingly, perspectives regard to the modification of the acetone dipole moment and of the β_{CM-OW} parameter (involved in the H-bond network).

Acknowledgement. M. Noelia Faginas Lago and Federico Palazzetti acknowledge financial support from Fondo Ricerca di Base 2015 del Dipartimento di Chimica, Biologia e Biotecnologia dell'Università di Perugia and the OU Supercomputing Center for Education & Research (OSCER) at the University of Oklahoma (OU) for the computing time. M. Albertí acknowledges financial support from the Ministerio de Educación y Ciencia (Spain, Projects CTQ2013-41307-P) and to the Comissionat per a Universitats i Recerca del DIUE (Generalitat de Catalunya, Project 201456R25). The Centre de Serveis Científics i Acadèmics de Catalunya CESCA and Fundació Catalana per a la Recerca are also acknowledged for the allocated supercomputing time. A. Lombardi also acknowledges financial support to MIUR-PRIN 2010–2011 (contract 2010ERFKXL 002).

References

1. Council, A.C.: Acetone VCCEP submission (2013)
2. Andrigo, P., Caimi, A., d'Oro, P.C., Fait, A., Roberti, L., Tampieri, M., Tartari, V.: Phenol-acetone process: cumene oxidation kinetics and industrial plant simulation. Chem. Eng. Sci. **47**, 2511–2516 (1992)
3. Sifniades, S., Levy, A.: "Acetone" in Ullmann's Encyclopedia of Industrial Chemistry. Willey-VCH, Weinheim (2005)
4. Zakoshansky, V.: The cumene process for phenol-acetone product. Pet. Chem. **47**, 301–313 (2007)
5. Evchuk, Y., Musii, R., Makitra, R., Pristanskii, R.: Solubility of polymethyl methacrylate in organic solvents. Russ. J. Appl. Chem. **78**, 1576–1580 (2005)
6. Hadi Ghatee, M., Taslimian, S.: Investigation of temperature and pressure dependent equilibrium and transport properties of liquid acetone by molecular dynamics. Fluid Phase Equilib. **358**, 226–232 (2013)
7. Remler, R.: The solvent properties of acetone. Eng. Chem. **15**, 717–720 (1923)
8. Nagai, K.: New developments in the production of methyl methacrylate. Appl. Catal. A **221**, 367–377 (2001)
9. Uglea, C., Negulescu, I.: Synthesis and Characterization of Oligomers. CRC Press, New York (1991)
10. Asada, M., Fujimori, T., Fujii, K., Umebayashi, Y., Ishiguro, S.I.: Solvation structure of magnesium, zinc, and alkaline earth metal ions in N, N-dimethylformamide, N, N-dimethylacetamide, and their mixtures studied by means of raman spectroscopy and DFT calculations - ionic size and electronic effects on steric congestion. J. Raman Spectrosc. **38**, 417–426 (2007)

11. Mollner, A., Brooksby, J., Loring, I., Palinkas, G., Fawcett, W.R.: Ion-solvent inter-actions in acetonitrile solutions of lithium iodide and tetrabutylammonium iodide. J. Phys. Chem. A **108**, 3344–3349 (2004)

12. Palombo, F., Paolantoni, M., Sassi, P., Morresi, A., Giorgini, M.: Molecular dynam-ics of liquid acetone determined by depolarized rayleigh and low-frequency raman scattering spectroscopy. Phys. Chem. Chem. Phys. **13**, 16197–16207 (2011)

13. Albertí, M., Amat, A., De Angelis, F., Pirani, F.: A model potential for acetonitrile: from small clusters to liquid. J. Phys. Chem. B **117**, 7065–7076 (2013)

14. Pirani, F., Albertí, M., Castro, A., Moix, M., Cappelletti, D.: Atom-bond pairwise additive representation for intermolecular potential energy surfaces. Chem. Phys. Lett. **394**, 37–44 (2004)

15. Faginas-Lago, N., Lombardi, A., Albertí, M., Grossi, G.: Accurate analytic inter-molecular potential for the simulation of Na^+ and K^+ ion hydration in liquid water. J. Mol. Liq. **204**, 192–197 (2015)

16. Albertí, M., Lago, N.F., Laganà, A., Pirani, F.: A portable intermolecular potential for molecular dynamics studies of NMA-NMA and NMA-H_2O aggregates. Phys. Chem. Chem. Phys. **13**, 8422–8432 (2011)

17. Albertí, M.: Rare gas-benzene-rare gas interactions: Structural properties and dynamic behavior. J. Phys. Chem. A **114**, 2266–2274 (2010)

18. Albertí, M., Aguilar, A., Bartolomei, M., Cappelletti, D., Laganà, A., Lucas, J., Pirani, F.: A study to improve the Van der Waals component of the interaction in water clusters. Phys. Scr. **78**, 058108 (2008)

19. Albertí, M., Aguilar, A., Bartolomei, M., Cappelletti, D., Laganà, A., Lucas, J.M., Pirani, F.: Small water clusters: the cases of rare gas-water, alkali ion-water and water dimer. In: Gervasi, O., Murgante, B., Laganà, A., Taniar, D., Mun, Y., Gavrilova, M.L. (eds.) ICCSA 2008. LNCS, vol. 5072, pp. 1026–1035. Springer, Heidelberg (2008). doi:10.1007/978-3-540-69839-5_78

20. Faginas-Lago, N., Huarte Larrañaga, F., Albertí, M.: On the suitability of the ILJ function to match different formulations of the electrostatic potential for water-water interactions. Eur. Phys. J. D **55**(1), 75 (2009)

21. Albertí, M., Amat, A., Farrera, L., Pirani, F.: From the $(NH_3)_{2-5}$ clusters to liquid ammonia: molecular dynamics simulations using the NVE and NpT ensembles. J. Mol. Liq. **212**, 307–315 (2015)

22. Faginas-Lago, N., Albertí, M., Lombardi, A.: Acetone clusters molecular dynam-ics using a semiempirical intermolecular potential. In: Gervasi, O., et al. (eds.) ICCSA 2016. LNCS, vol. 9786, pp. 129–140. Springer, Cham (2016). doi:10.1007/978-3-319-42085-1_10

23. Pirani, F., Cappelletti, D., Liuti, G.: Range, strength and anisotropy of intermole-cular forces in atom-molecule systems: an atom-bond pairwise additivity approach. Chem. Phys. Lett. **350**(3–4), 286–296 (2001)

24. Albertí, M., Castro, A., Laganà, A., Pirani, F., Porrini, M., Cappelletti, D.: Prop-erties of an atom-bond additive representation of the interaction for benzene-argon clusters. Chem. Phys. Lett. **392**(4–6), 514–520 (2004)

25. Bartolomei, M., Pirani, F., Laganà, A., Lombardi, A.: A full dimensional grid empowered simulation of the $CO_2 + CO_2$ processes. J. Comput. Chem. **33**(22), 1806–1819 (2012)

26. Lombardi, A., Faginas-Lago, N., Pacifici, L., Costantini, A.: Modeling of energy transfer from vibrationally excited CO_2 molecules: Cross sections and probabilities for kinetic modeling of atmospheres, flows, and plasmas. J. Phys. Chem. A **117**(45), 11430–11440 (2013)

27. Lago, N.F., Albertí, M., Laganà, A., Lombardi, A., Pacifici, L., Costantini, A.: The molecular stirrer catalytic effect in methane ice formation. In: Murgante, B., et al. (eds.) ICCSA 2014. LNCS, vol. 8579, pp. 585–600. Springer, Cham (2014). doi:10.1007/978-3-319-09144-0_40

28. Lombardi, A., Laganà, A., Pirani, F., Palazzetti, F., Lago, N.F.: Carbon oxides in gas flows and earth and planetary atmospheres: state-to-state simulations of energy transfer and dissociation reactions. In: Murgante, B., et al. (eds.) ICCSA 2013. LNCS, vol. 7972, pp. 17–31. Springer, Heidelberg (2013). doi:10.1007/978-3-642-39643-4_2

29. Falcinelli, S., et al.: Modeling the intermolecular interactions and characterization of the dynamics of collisional autoionization processes. In: Murgante, B., et al. (eds.) ICCSA 2013. LNCS, vol. 7971, pp. 69–83. Springer, Heidelberg (2013). doi:10.1007/978-3-642-39637-3_6

30. Lombardi, A., Lago, N.F., Laganà, A., Pirani, F., Falcinelli, S.: A bond-bond portable approach to intermolecular interactions: simulations for N-methylacetamide and carbon dioxide dimers. In: Murgante, B., Gervasi, O., Misra, S., Nedjah, N., Rocha, A.M.A.C., Taniar, D., Apduhan, B.O. (eds.) ICCSA 2012. LNCS, vol. 7333, pp. 387–400. Springer, Heidelberg (2012). doi:10.1007/978-3-642-31125-3_30

31. Laganà, A., Lombardi, A., Pirani, F., Gamallo, P., Sayós, R., Armenise, I., Cacciatore, M., Esposito, F., Rutigliano, M.: Molecular physics of elementary processes relevant to hypersonics: atom-molecule, molecule-molecule and atom-surface processes. Open Plasma Phys. J. **7**, 48 (2014)

32. Faginas-Lago, N., Albertí, M., Costantini, A., Laganà, A., Lombardi, A., Pacifici, L.: An innovative synergistic grid approach to the computational study of protein aggregation mechanisms. J. Mol. Model. **20**(7), 2226 (2014)

33. Albertí, M., Castro, A., Laganá, A., Moix, M., Pirani, F., Cappelletti, D., Liuti, G.: A molecular dynamics investigation of rare-gas solvated cation-benzene clusters using a new model potential. J. Phys. Chem. A **109**(12), 2906–2911 (2005)

34. Albertí, M., Aguilar, A., Lucas, J., Pirani, F.: Static and dynamic properties of anionic intermolecular aggregates: the I-benzene-Ar_n case. Theoret. Chem. Acc. **123**(1–2), 21–27 (2009)

35. Lago, N.F., Albertí, M., Laganà, A., Lombardi, A.: Water $(H_2O)_m$ or Benzene $(C_6H_6)_n$ aggregates to solvate the K^+? In: Murgante, B., Misra, S., Carlini, M., Torre, C.M., Nguyen, H.-Q., Taniar, D., Apduhan, B.O., Gervasi, O. (eds.) ICCSA 2013. LNCS, vol. 7971, pp. 1–15. Springer, Heidelberg (2013). doi:10.1007/978-3-642-39637-3_1

36. Albertí, M.: Rare gas-benzene-rare gas interactions: structural properties and dynamic behavior. J. Phys. Chem. A **114**(6), 2266–2274 (2010)

37. Pirani, F., Brizzi, S., Roncaratti, L., Casavecchia, P., Cappelletti, D., Vecchiocattivi, F.: Beyond the lennard-jones model: a simple and accurate potential function probed by high resolution scattering data useful for molecular dynamics simulations. Phys. Chem. Chem. Phys. **10**, 5489–5503 (2008)

38. Albertí, M., Lago, N.F., Pirani, F.: Ar Solvation shells in K(+)-HFBz: from cluster rearrangement to solvation dynamics. J. Phys. Chem. A **115**(40), 10871–10879 (2011)

39. Albertí, M., Aguilar, A., Cappelletti, D., Laganà, A., Pirani, F.: On the development of an effective model potential to describe ater interaction in neutral and ionic clusters. Int. J. Mass Spectrom. **280**, 50–56 (2009)

40. Albertí, M., Faginas-Lago, N.: Competitive solvation of K^+ by C_6H_6 and H_2O in the $K^+(C_6H6)n-(H_2O)m$ (n = 1–4; m = 1–6) aggregates. The European Physical Journal D 67(4) (2013)

41. Faginas-Lago, N., Lombardi, A., Albertí, M.: Aqueous n-methylacetamide: New analytic potentials and a molecular dynamics study. J. Mol. Liq. **224**, 792–800 (2016)

42. Lombardi, A., Faginas-Lago, N., Gaia, G., Palazzetti, F., Aquilanti, V.: Collisional energy exchange in CO_2-N_2 gaseous mixtures. In: Gervasi, O., Murgante, B., Misra, S., Rocha, A.M.A.C., Torre, C.M., Taniar, D., Apduhan, B.O., Stankova, E., Wang, S. (eds.) ICCSA 2016, pp. 246–257. Springer International Publishing, Cham (2016)

43. Albertí, M., Lago, N.F.: Ion size influence on the Ar solvation shells of $M^+C_6F_6$ clusters (M = Na, K, Rb, Cs). J. Phys. Chem. A **116**(12), 3094–3102 (2012)

44. Cambi, R., Cappelletti, D., Liuti, G., Pirani, F.: Generalized correlations in terms of polarizability for Van der waals interaction potential parameter calculations. J. Chem. Phys. **95**(3), 1852–1861 (1991)

45. Smith, W., Yong, C., Rodger, P.: DL_POLY: Application to molecular simulation. Mol. Simul. **28**(5), 385–471 (2002)

46. Berendsen, H.J.C., Postma, J.P.M., van Gunsteren, W.F., DiNola, A., Haak, J.R.: Molecular dynamics with coupling to an external bath. J. Chem. Phys. **81**, 3684 (1984)

47. Beronius, P.: Ionic association and ion solvent interactions. The conductance of lithium bromide in acetone-water mixtures at 15–35 °C. Acta Chem. Scand. A **31**, 869–876 (1977)

48. Perera, A., Sokolic, F.: Modeling nonionic aqueous solutions: the acetone-water mixture. J. Chem. Phys. **121**, 11272–11282 (2004)

49. Faginas Lago, N., Albertí, M., Lombardi, A., Pirani, F.: A force field for acetone: the transition from small clusters to liquid phase investigated by molecular dynamics simulations. Theoret. Chem. Acc. **135**(7), 161 (2016)

Synchronized Content and Metadata Management in a Federation of Distributed Repositories of Chemical Learning Objects

Sergio Tasso[1], Simonetta Pallottelli[1], Osvaldo Gervasi[1(✉)],
Razvan Tanase[1], and Marina Rui[2]

[1] Department of Mathematics and Computer Science, University of Perugia,
via Vanvitelli, 1, 06123 Perugia, Italy
{sergio.tasso,simonetta.pallottelli,osvaldo.gervasi}@unipg.it,
tangent.jotey@gmail.com
[2] Department of Chemistry and Industrial Chemistry, University of Genoa,
via Dodecaneso, 31, 16146 Genoa, Italy
marina@chimica.unige.it

Abstract. The paper deals with the synchronization mechanism among the servers of a federation of distributed repositories for the constant updating of the didactic-scientific material, its properties and its locations. A shared metadata database is the synchronization point of reference and it allows to improve performance in terms of searching and downloading. The proposed federation is meant to deal with a large variety of different contents though the discussed prototype implementation is concerned with scientific and educational subjects in particular. Additional elements of evaluation are the capability of enhancing collaboration and fault tolerance.

Keywords: Repository · Synchronization · Learning objects · Content sharing

1 Introduction

Thanks to their advanced tools and interoperable environments, the new technologies, make available, any time and any place, learning object [1, 2] and repository facilities needful both for training and information.

The content, repository platforms and e-learning systems can share in these environments, are manifold. For our job, it is particularly interesting to note that repository platforms, because of their powerful and flexible structure, allow a full management of Learning Object Metadata (LOM).

In the current view, the e-learning content design implies the application of a development model featured by material serialization, which has the ultimate goal of obtaining self-consistent learning units (typically learning objects) in SCORM format.

In this context it suits the Glorep system [3], which, in order to facilitate the learning objects (LOs) phases production, proposes a shared and distributed solution for the education content, aimed at reuse, after a suitable classification and indexing [4, 5].

© Springer International Publishing AG 2017
O. Gervasi et al. (Eds.): ICCSA 2017, Part III, LNCS 10406, pp. 14–28, 2017.
DOI: 10.1007/978-3-319-62398-6_2

The project is part of other research carried out within the workgroup which has provided interesting ideas for the construction of the materials and for their treatment, also in view of an extension of the taxonomy so far considered [6–10].

2 The Glorep Project

The leaders of the Glorep project (Grid Learning Object Repository) [11–15] are the Mathematics and Computer Science Department and the Department of Chemistry, Biology and Biotechnology of the University of Perugia. This project involves other Chemistry Departments of Italian and foreign Universities, among which there are the ones of Genoa and Thessaloniki (Greece) and is focused at implementing a federation of repositories, supported by a cluster of SMEs (small and medium-sized enterprises) coordinated by ECTN, in which the information is processed by LOs.

The aim of this activity is to integrate different software tools in order to enhance the Glorep strength and efficiency for making it the reference product of the Virtual Research environment [16, 17] called for funding at the recent EINFRA-9-2015 Horizon 2020 call [18].

Then, Glorep, the federation of distributed and shared repository is especially builded for:

- Making available to a large community of teaching and learning the didactic *and* scientific content they produced.
- Offering an environment that ensures the dynamic improvement of materials available through the correct storage and cataloging of revised versions

The federation is composed by repositories with equal rank, responsibilities, duties and functions, which exchange among them the whole information about available LOs [19, 20].

Glorep assigns to the modular CMS Drupal [21–23], the role of collecting, managing and tracing the information on the distributed and collaborative networks.

Drupal is a free and open source content-management framework written in PHP and distributed under the GNU GPL. It is powerful, flexible and customizable according to the opinion of the Web community made of more than a million of users, with more than one hundred developers. As already said, it is modular and highly flexible, provided with more than 30 thousand modules to extend and customize its functionalities. Moreover, it is multiplatform.

It should note that the Drupal modularity is due to a bunch of modules that perform only primary functions, but complemented, by its own developers, by APIs (Application Programming Interface) which allow creating a lot of additional modules to extend its functionality according to needs.

2.1 The GLOREP Features

There are various modules of Glorep interacting in order to allow a simple and quick input and to find a LO. Whereas there are only two main features allowing the concerned modules to be effective and efficient: the use of the Dewey Decimal Classification (DDC) [24] cataloging system and the use of IEEE LOM [25, 26].

Starting from the Drupal configuration standard, we implemented four new modules in order to manage the wide federation and its contents:

- *LinkableObject* - To manage the LO: it enables the LO creation and upload it to the servers. It also allows managing LO permissions, defining who can create and who can view and download the learning material.
- *SearchLO* - To manage a distributed search of LO on wide federation: it is a searching system of LO easy and intuitive.
- *TaxAssistant* - To manage LO classification step: it analyses the related metadata entered by the user in order to help with the selection of the category better related to the LO.
- *CollabRep* - To manage the federation: it can be used to create, join and quit a federation, and it performs synchronization recovery measures in case of communication issues during updates.

Recently, fundamental changes have been made about synchronizing federated servers. In particular, the old *Collabrep* module has been replaced with the new *GlorepSyncIO* stand-alone daemon (as you can see in Fig. 1).

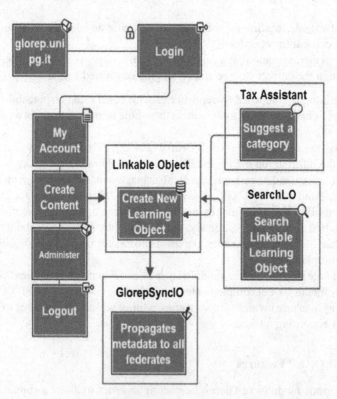

Fig. 1. The new schema of a Glorep server

3   The Synchronization Mechanism of GlorepSyncIO

3.1   Server.php

The main file of the entire daemon is called *server.php*, this is where everything comes together and where most of the defined methods are being put to use in order to achieve the main goal of the project: synchronization. This is the meat of the code [27, 28].

Before starting to talk about the mechanisms that are behind everything, we must first understand exactly what the exact problem is we are trying to solve at this point. We have a situation where a variable number of servers must provide data for a different number of applications (in this case a web application). Each server has their own database, containing data gathered from their users through forms, or any other kind of data input. At this point, each server has its storage of data. But, what if these servers would exchange data between them?

<u>Proposition</u>

One way of approaching this problem would be to directly transfer data from one server to another. Directly exchanging data sounds like a good idea, if the number of servers is not variable. We know, however, that our number of servers is variable, meaning that anyone can choose to leave or join the federation.

This implies other problems, such as allowing every server to detect and distinguish between the two events of leaving and joining the federation.

The resource cost of this method is also directly proportional to the number of servers of the federation, meaning that the more servers there are the more resources it will cost to keep everyone updated. This way of approaching is clearly a bad one.

Instead of using a direct point-to-point communication, a central database could serve as an easier way of communication between servers (see Fig. 2).

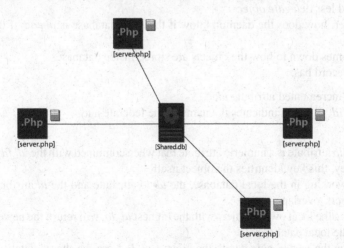

Fig. 2. The sharedBD based approach

The central piece is a database, nothing more. We will be calling that "shared database" from now on. In this mechanism, each server also has its own copy of the database stored locally.

3.2   Objects and Owners

The local database stores all kinds of objects gathered from around the federation, however we must distinguish between the ones created by the local federate and the ones created by other federates, to do so we define:

- *Owned Objects*:
  - The only objects the daemon will upload to the shared database are the ones belonging to the local federate.
- *Delegate Objects*:
  - The objects the local daemon must only download from the shared database.

3.3   Uploading

Let's say we are hosting one of these servers. Every N seconds, if the shared database is behind, the daemon would attempt to upload the local objects to the shared database. Understanding the meaning of *being ahead* or *being behind* is key.

We will say the local database *is ahead* of the shared database when the *owned objects* stored locally outnumber the *owned objects* stored on the shared database.

We will say the local database *is behind* the shared database when the *delegate objects* stored on the shared database outnumber the ones stored locally.

Note that this mechanism implies that the local database could be both *behind* and *ahead* of the shared database, in fact, the local database could contain more *owned objects*, and less d*elegate objects*.

However, how does the daemon know if the local database is *ahead* of the shared database?

It all comes down to how the objects are stored inside databases.

Every record has:

- ,an auto-incremented attribute *id*,
- a string *id_fd* which indicates the name of the federate and
- an *id_lo*.

The *id_lo* attribute is a numeric attribute that when combined with the *id_fd* produces a unique key, this key identifies the object itself.

When working in the local database, the *id_lo* attribute and the *id* attribute, of the *owned objects*, overlap.

Selecting the local owned object with the highest *id_lo*, will return the newest *owned object* on the local database.

Selecting the *owned object* with the highest *id_lo* from the shared database, on the other hand, will return the newest *owned object* stored on the shared database.

The last step in finding out whether the local database is *behind* or *ahead*, is to compare the two objects.

If they both have the same *id_lo*, it means the local database is *not ahead*.

If the shared object has a lower *id_lo*, it means the local database is *ahead*.

If the shared object has a higher *id_lo*, there will never be an instance when the shared database will be *ahead* of the local database regarding the *owned objects*.

When the local database is ahead, simply passing along as offset the *id_lo* of the last known proprietary object from the shared database to a devoted method (Sync::upload_after_offset($offset, $local_db, $shared_db, $federate_name)), it will upload every missing object to the shared database.

3.4 Downloading

Once established that the local database is behind, the download routine can start.

The download routine uses the method Sync::download_after_offset($offset, $local_db, $shared_db, $federate_name) to download the missing *delegate objects*.

This time the last *delegate objects* must be compared.

If they both have the same *id_lo*, it means the local database is *not behind*.

If the shared object has a higher *id_lo*, it means the local database is *behind*.

If the shared object has a lower *id_lo*, the local database will never be *ahead* of the shared database regarding the *delegate objects*, that's because the *delegate objects* are downloaded from the shared database to begin with.

When the local database is *behind*, the download routine will download each object to the local database.

Each time an object is *being* retrieved from the shared database, a delete query is executed. This query will delete every object in the local database that uses the same *id_fd* and the same *id_lo* of the object that is about to be pushed in the database.

This mechanism allows the federates to overwrite their *own objects* and propagate the changes across the federation network.

3.5 Updating

Every iteration, after executing the upload routine and the download routine, a third routine is executed. In order to keep the shared database updated with every change that passes locally, the daemon iterates through a table stored in the local database called *lo_update_log*, this table is populated by a MySql trigger, which executes every time an object is updated locally.

Through the iteration, GlorepSyncIO, will retrieve the *owned objects* referenced in *lo_update_log*, which are not *draft*, and it will propagate the changes to the shared database.

The changes are propagated by simply sending the whole object with the new metadata, this object will be then stored in the shared database, and every other server that executes the download routine, will notice that the object is a duplicate and will overwrite the existing one/s (Fig. 3).

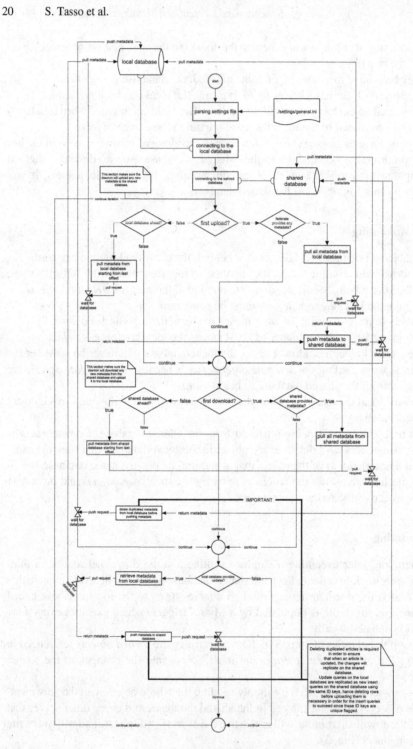

Fig. 3. The GlorepSyncIO schema

4 The GlorepSyncIO Components

The GlorepSyncIO daemon uses messages, readers and writers. Figure 4 shows the main features of each of these components used by GlorepSyncIO daemon.

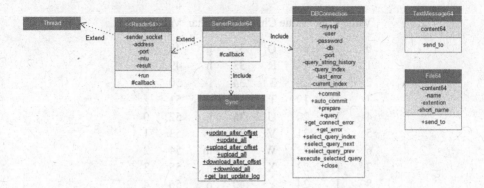

Fig. 4. The GlorepSyncIO class diagram

4.1 Messages

Once a machine is connected through a socket to our daemon, there are two types of messages that can be sent to us. The first one is a text message using the *TextMessage64* class, and the second type is a file using the *FileMessage64* class.

4.1.1 FileMessage64

The FileMessage64 class will create a FileMessage64 object, which will contain the data of the specified file. The data will not be stored as binary; instead, the binary string will be converted into a base64 string, and will be stored as such.

The reason behind storing a base64 string is quite simple: before sending our message, we want to wrap our file inside a JSON (JavaScript Object Notation) object [29], so we can send some side information about our file, such as the file's name, size, and type and we want to avoid JSON parsing errors in doing so.

JSON objects are very light and have a very simple syntax, thus are very easy to parse, however this is a double-edged sword.

Let's say I want to send a file as a binary string (which, again, we are not doing).

The actual string will not be stored as binary numbers in your variable; instead, it will be hashed using the Unicode standard.

Your file's contents will probably look something like this:

[…] &ÖS¥ýC´¤î#^#¤"#úP#Ü´{Ë[@#ÇŒh‰¾‹Tä☐#–Rù5w´Î-'±V>·#OwjÑO,,Õ […]

As you can see, the domain of the string contains some JSON wild characters such as "{", which could escape the JSON encoding algorithm.

One way to avoid this problem is to convert our binary string into a base64 string since the base64 alphabet table is much smaller and does not contain any wild characters that JSON might not like. Figure 5 shows the base64 characters table.

Value	Char	Value	Char	Value	Char	Value	Char
0	A	16	Q	32	g	48	w
1	B	17	R	33	h	49	x
2	C	18	S	34	i	50	y
3	D	19	T	35	j	51	z
4	E	20	U	36	k	52	0
5	F	21	V	37	l	53	1
6	G	22	W	38	m	54	2
7	H	23	X	39	n	55	3
8	I	24	Y	40	o	56	4
9	J	25	Z	41	p	57	5
10	K	26	a	42	q	58	6
11	L	27	b	43	r	59	7
12	M	28	c	44	s	60	8
13	N	29	d	45	t	61	9
14	O	30	e	46	u	62	+
15	P	31	F	47	V	63	/

Fig. 5. The table of base64 characters

4.1.2 TextMessage64

The TextMessage64 class acts almost identically to File64, they both send a stream of data to the other end of the channel, and they both convert the message in base64, to avoid the same parsing issue discussed above. The only difference here is the header of the package that is being sent. While File64 would send a JSON object containing the file's content, name, size and type, TextMessage64 would send an object containing the message and the type of its contents (which is set to "text-plain").

After the content of the message has been encoded (being either File64 or TextMessage64), it will then be wrapped inside a JSON Object, this object will then be also encoded into a base64 string. Finally, the string is then sent to the receiver.

4.2 Readers

Readers are a way for the server to read messages sent to their socket.

Reader64 is an abstract class which extends *Thread*, thus *Reader64* will define the method called *run*. Reader has a defined construct; it requires a socket (which will be used to read the incoming data) and a Maximum Transmission Unit (MTU) (which is used to read chunks of bytes from the stream of data).

Reader will start reading chunks of data from the socket buffer, each chunk will be appended to a temporary variable until there's nothing left inside the buffer.

Once the message has been read, it's contents encoded in base64 will be passed to an abstract callback method, along with the sender's IPv4 address and the port of the sending application.

The message that is being received at this point is nothing more that a base64 encoded string. Before passing the string to the callback method the string is decoded from Base64 into a JSON object, so there's no need to decode it afterwards.

Reader64 is an abstract class, thus, it cannot be instantiated and hence *ServerReader64* is needed.

ServerReader64 extends *Reader64* and it defines the body of the callback method, which is named *callback* which provides 3 parameters: the message, the IPv4 address, the port number of the sending application.

4.3   Writers

Writers are a simplified way to send JSON encoded messages through a socket.

Writer64 is an abstract class which extends *Thread*. It also have an abstract callback method, which will later be defined by the *TextWriter64* and *FileWriter64* classes, as they both extend *Writer64*.

4.3.1   TextWriter64 and FileWriter64

TextWriter64 and *FileWriter64* both extend *Writer64*, hence they both have to define a protected method called *callback*. This callback method takes one single attribute, and that is the socket to which the message is supposed to be written. Both these classes only exist to provide some "sugar syntax" [30] when sending data to the daemon. They are by no means required, in any situation, but they do help as they create a connection behind the scenes, and then they properly close it, all in one single line of code when creating an instance of the class itself.

4.4   DBConnection

DBConnection class does not extend *mysqli* (MySQL Improved Extension) [31], instead it uses a private *mysqli* object in order to connect to the database, and provides a limited number of methods to query the database in question.

When queries are sent to the database they are also saved to *DBConnection* inside an array, this allows *DBConnection* to quickly move backwards and forwards through the queries and execute them multiple times. Prepared statements are not saved when executed. *DBConnection* makes use of the *mysqli* construct and has the user to pass along the same parameters they would pass to *mysqli* (hostname, username, password, database, port), however, instead of providing these parameters hard-coding them, the invoker can also only provide the first two parameters, referencing the *./settings/ general.ini* file.

Using the second method might prove a bit more flexible, since the strings are fetched from a file which can be easily edited at runtime.

The first parameter passed to the *DBConnection* construct must indicate which of the two available databases it must connect to: the local database or the shared database.

The following keywords indicate the local database: *local, localhost, 127.0.0.1*.

These strings are not treated as IP addresses; they are just convenient, easy to remember predefined strings, nothing more.

The following keywords indicate the shared database: *shared, sharedhost*.

4.5   Sync

The *Sync* class provides the methods used in the synchronization mechanism in *server.php*, and *ServerReader* class.

4.5.1   Available Methods

```
Sync::upload_after_offset(
        int              $offset,
        DBConnection     $local_db,
        DBConnection     $shared_db,
        string           $my_fed
        )
```

Parameters description:

$offset
> Offset from which objects will start being selected from database $local_db.

$local_db
> Database from which the data will be selected.

$shared_db
> Database to which the data will be uploaded.

$my_fed
> Name of the local federate.

Selects objects from $local_db starting from $offset and uploads them to $shared_db.

> Sync::download_after_offset(
>> int $offset,
>> DBConnection $local_db,
>> DBConnection $shared_db,
>> string $my_fed
>>)

Parameters description:

$offset

> Offset from which objects will start being selected from database $local_db.

$local_db

> Database from which the data will be selected.

$shared_db

> Database to which the data will be uploaded.

$my_fed

> Name of the local federate.

Selects objects from $shared_db starting from $offset and uploads them to $local_db.

After the remote object has been obtained and saved in memory, this method executes one more step before writing the object in the local database.

Before writing the object in the local database, <u>every other object with the same *id_lo* and *id_fd* will be deleted regardless the circumstances</u>.

> Sync::get_last_update_log(
> DBConnection $local_db
>)

> Parameters description
> $local_db
>> Database from which the data will be selected.

Returns the last row from table *update_log* in database $local_db. Table *update_log* is used as a support table; no application should insert records in this table directly. The local database uses a trigger in order to insert records in *update_log*. The trigger will listen for an update event on the general table and insert a row in *update_log* afterwards, using the value of the *id_lo* attribute of the new object as the *local_id* attribute of the new record in the *update_log* table.

```
update_after_offset(
        int             $offset,
        DBConnection    $local_db,
        DBConnection    $shared_db,
        string          $my_fed
        )
```

Parameters description
$offset
      Offset from which updates will start being selected from database $local_db.
$local_db
      Database from which updates will be uploaded from.
$shared_db
      Database to which the updates will be uploaded.
$my_fed
      Name of the local federate.

Selects rows from *update_log* starting from $offset. For each fetched row the relative object from the general table is retrieved. If the object's status is *draft* or the object's *id_fd* is not the same as the local federate's name then do nothing.

Otherwise, the object will be uploaded to the shared database.

Finally, delete the currently selected record from update_log table and skip to the next record.

5   Conclusion and Future Work

The new stand-alone synchronization daemon GlorepSyncIO discussed in the present paper allows an efficient synchronization among the servers of the federation of distributed repositories of chemical learning objects Glorep.

The change from the previous configuration is due to the separation of the synchronization mechanism from the CMS hosting the local server.

The GlorepSyncIO daemon executes the synchronization routine once every N seconds. This way of proceeding might not be enough. In some cases we might want to directly query the daemon and force the synchronization routine using a RPC. Sockets allow the daemon to accept incoming (and request) connections from other machines and read the incoming message, which in this case would be a Remote Procedure Call (RPC).

Acknowledgements. The authors acknowledge ECTN (VEC standing committee) and the EC2E2 N 2 LLP project for stimulating debates and providing partial financial support. Thanks are due also to EGI and IGI and the related COMPCHEM VO for the use of Grid resources.

References

1. Raju, P., Ahmed, V.: Enabling technologies for developing next-generation learning object repository for construction. Autom. Constr. **22**, 247–257 (2012)
2. Sampson, D.G., Zervas, P.: Learning object repositories as knowledge management systems. Knowl. Manage. E-Learn. **5**(2), 117–136 (2013)
3. G-Lorep, March 2016. http://glorep.unipg.it
4. Xu, H.: Faculty use of a learning object repository in higher education. VINE J. Inf. Knowl. Manage. Syst. **46**(4), 469–479 (2016)
5. Nejdl, W., Tochtermann, K. (eds.): EC-TEL 2006. LNCS, vol. 4227. Springer, Heidelberg (2006). doi:10.1007/11876663
6. Franzoni, V., Mencacci, M., Mengoni, P., Milani, A.: Heuristics for semantic path search in wikipedia. In: Murgante, B., et al. (eds.) ICCSA 2014. LNCS, vol. 8584, pp. 327–340. Springer, Cham (2014). doi:10.1007/978-3-319-09153-2_25
7. Franzoni, V., Milani, A.: Semantic context extraction from collaborative networks. In: Proceedings of the 2015 IEEE 19th International Conference on Computer Supported Cooperative Work in Design, CSCWD 2015. IEEE Press (2015). doi:10.1109/CSCWD. 2015.7230946
8. Franzoni, V., Milani, A.: PMING distance: a collaborative semantic proximity measure. In: Proceedings of 2012 IEEE/WIC/ACM International Conference on Intelligent Agent Technology, IAT 2012, pp. 442–449. IEEE Press (2012). doi:10.1109/WI-IAT.2012.226
9. Franzoni, V., Milani, A.: Heuristic semantic walk for concept chaining in collaborative networks. Int. J. Web Inf. Syst. **10**(1), 85–103 (2014). doi:10.1108/IJWIS-11-2013-0031. Emerald
10. Franzoni, V., Chiancone, A., Milani, A.: A multistrain bacterial diffusion model for link prediction. Int. J. Pattern Recogn. Artif. Intell. **31**(9), 12–24 (2017). doi:10.1142/ S0218001417590248. World Scientific
11. Pallottelli, S., Tasso, S., Pannacci, N., Costantini, A., Lago, N.F.: Distributed and collaborative learning objects repositories on grid networks. In: Taniar, D., Gervasi, O., Murgante, B., Pardede, E., Apduhan, B.O. (eds.) ICCSA 2010. LNCS, vol. 6019, pp. 29–40. Springer, Heidelberg (2010). doi:10.1007/978-3-642-12189-0_3
12. Tasso, S., Pallottelli, S., Bastianini, R., Lagana, A.: Federation of distributed and collaborative repositories and its application on science learning objects. In: Murgante, B., Gervasi, O., Iglesias, A., Taniar, D., Apduhan, B.O. (eds.) ICCSA 2011. LNCS, vol. 6784, pp. 466–478. Springer, Heidelberg (2011). doi:10.1007/978-3-642-21931-3_36
13. Tasso, S., Pallottelli, S., Ferroni, M., Bastianini, R., Laganà, A.: Taxonomy management in a federation of distributed repositories: a chemistry use case. In: Murgante, B., Gervasi, O., Misra, S., Nedjah, N., Rocha, A.M.A.C., Taniar, D., Apduhan, B.O. (eds.) ICCSA 2012. LNCS, vol. 7333, pp. 358–370. Springer, Heidelberg (2012). doi: 10.1007/978-3-642-31125-3_28
14. Tasso, S., Pallottelli, S., Ciavi, G., Bastianini, R., Laganà, A.: An efficient taxonomy assistant for a federation of science distributed repositories: a chemistry use case. In: Murgante, B., Misra, S., Carlini, M., Torre, C.M., Nguyen, H.-Q., Taniar, D., Apduhan, B.O., Gervasi, O. (eds.) ICCSA 2013. LNCS, vol. 7971, pp. 96–109. Springer, Heidelberg (2013). doi: 10.1007/978-3-642-39637-3_8
15. Tasso, S., Pallottelli, S., Rui, M., Laganá, A.: Learning objects efficient handling in a federation of science distributed repositories. In: Murgante, B., et al. (eds.) ICCSA 2014. LNCS, vol. 8579, pp. 615–626. Springer, Cham (2014). doi:10.1007/978-3-319-09144-0_42

16. Mariotti, M., Gervasi, O., Vella, F., Cuzzocrea, A., Costantini, A.: Strategies and systems towards grids and clouds integration: a DBMS-based solution. Future Gener. Comput. Syst. (2017). doi:https://doi.org/10.1016/j.future.2017.02.047
17. Costantini, A., Gervasi, O., Zollo, F., Caprini, L.: User interaction and data management for large scale grid applications. J. Grid Comput. **12**(3), 485–497 (2014)
18. Laganà, A.: Horizon 2020 proposal for Research and Innovation actions Chemistry, Molecular & Materials Sciences and Technologies Virtual Research Environment (CMMST-VRE) Call EINFRA-9-2015 (2015)
19. Pallottelli, S., Tasso, S., Rui, M., Laganà, A., Kozaris, I.: Exchange of learning objects between a learning management system and a federation of science distributed repositories. In: Gervasi, O., Murgante, B., Misra, S., Gavrilova, M.L., Rocha, A.M.A.C., Torre, C., Taniar, D., Apduhan, B.O. (eds.) ICCSA 2015. LNCS, vol. 9156, pp. 371–383. Springer, Cham (2015). doi:10.1007/978-3-319-21407-8_27
20. Tasso, S., Pallottelli, S., Laganà, A.: Mobile device access to collaborative distributed repositories of chemistry learning objects. In: Gervasi, O., et al. (eds.) ICCSA 2016. LNCS, vol. 9786, pp. 443–454. Springer, Cham (2016). doi:10.1007/978-3-319-42085-1_34
21. Olteanu, C.: Learning Management System and Shareable Content Object Reference Model. Manag. J. **6**(1), 106–109 (2007). Faculty of Business and Administration - University of Bucharest
22. Drupal, January 2016. http://drupal.org
23. System requirements, January 2016. https://drupal.org/requirements
24. Ahn, J., Lin, X., Khoo, M.: Dewey decimal classification based concept visualization for information retrieval. In: CEUR Workshop Proceedings, vol. 1311, pp. 7–14 (2014)
25. 1484.12.1 IEEE Standard for Learning Object Metadata, March 2017. http://ieeexplore.ieee.org/document/1032843
26. McClelland, M.: Metadata standards for educational resources. Computer **36**(11), 107–109 (2003)
27. PHP Threads, March 2017. http://php.net/manual/en/book.pthreads.php
28. PHP Thread class, March 2017. http://php.net/manual/en/class.thread.php/
29. Introducing JSON, March 2017. http://www.json.org/
30. March 2017. http://www.quora.com/What-is-syntactic-sugar-in-programming-languages
31. PHP Manual-MySQL Extension, March 2017. http://php.net/manual/en/book.mysqli.php

Open Molecular Science
for the Open Science Cloud

Antonio Laganà[1]($\boxtimes$) (iD), Gabor Terstyanszky[2](iD), and Jens Krüger[3](iD)

[1] Master-UP S.r.l., Via Elce di Sotto, 806123 Perugia, Italy
lagana05@gmail.com
[2] Computer Science Department, University of Westminster,
115 New Cavendish Street, London W1W 6UW, UK
terstyg@gmail.com
[3] Compute Center (ZDV), University of Tübingen,
Wächterstrasse 76, 72074 Tübingen, Germany
jens.krueger@uni-tuebingen.de

Abstract. The Open Science Cloud project is getting off the ground within EINFRA 12 (a) under the joint action of EGI.eu, INDICO and EUDAT. To this end several pilots have been selected to provide its core services. In this paper, the characteristics of the (not selected for funding) Open Molecular Science pilot SUMO-Chem are described and further referring to two particularly innovative services: the distributed ab initio collaborative simulator of molecular processes GEMS and the prosumer based self evaluation handler of molecular knowledge e-tests.

Keywords: Open Molecular Science · Open Science Cloud · Molecular Simulator · e-tests

1 Introduction

"There is a revolution happening in the way science works. Every part of the scientific method is nowadays becoming an open, collaborative and participative process (Commissioner Moedas, Annual Joint Programming Conference of the DG Research & Innovation of the European Commission June 2015). Indeed, Open science is a potentially revolutionary approach to discovery and innovation through scientific research and data dissemination to all levels of the society. However, the term Open science is quite often referred to as Open access (see the European Commission initiative aimed to improve knowledge circulation by making research findings available free of charge for readers [1]) that is usually considered as a natural consequence of the prevalent public nature of research funding. Science openness, instead, implies much more than Open access. There are, in fact, different understandings about open science referring to (a) the technological research infrastructure, (b) the accessibility of knowledge creation for the general public, (c) the measurements of impact for scientific contributions, (d) the access to knowledge for both scientists and non-professionals, (e) the

O. Gervasi et al. (Eds.): ICCSA 2017, Part III, LNCS 10406, pp. 29–43, 2017.
DOI: 10.1007/978-3-319-62398-6_3

collaborative research. In other words Open science covers producing and/or collecting, analysing, publishing, critiquing, re-analysing, re-producing and reusing data for research, innovation and training within a collaborative and workflow-based process. Worldwide Open science players are large scientific bodies like the Open Knowledge Foundation (OKF) that is a worldwide non-profit network of people interested in openness and in using advocacy, technology and training to unlock information and enable the sharing of knowledge [2]. Among the other bodies is the Open Science Framework (OSF) [3] that provides free and open source project management support for researchers across the entire research lifecycle leveraging on a flexible repository for storing and archiving research data, protocols, and materials is another worldwide player as well. Using OSF tools researchers can work on projects privately with a limited number of collaborators and make parts of their projects public, or make the whole project publicly accessible for broader dissemination. As a workflow system, researchers can connect the many services they use to streamline their process and increase efficiency. SHIWA represents a successful project enabling workflow interoperability [4]. By focusing more on Molecular Science MoSGrid represents an example aiming and achieving the goals of an open science gateway [5]. An informal group of chemists who promote open data, open source and open standards in MS is Blue Obelisk that was initiated in 2005 [6–8] to associate multiple open source cheminformatics projects.

2 Chemistry and Open Science Initiatives

Specific European modern networking initiatives operating in the field of Open Science are INDICO (an open source data and computing platform software that is deployable on multiple hardware and provisioned over hybrid, private or public e-Infrastructure) [9], EUDAT (a collaborative data infrastructure offering heterogeneous research data management services and storage resources to ensure data is shared and preserved across borders and disciplines) [10], EGI (a publicly federated e-Infrastructure relying on over 300 data centres and cloud providers offering a range of compute, storage, data and support services spread across Europe and worldwide) [11], OpenAIRE (a service aimed at providing Metadata interoperability, common policy directions and agnostic approaches to choose among different solutions) [12]. Various community projects have been developed as a result of the activities of the above mentioned European open science infrastructures like the Virtual Organizations (VO)s and the Virtual Research Communities (VRC)s established for various disciplines. The community projects which have mostly exploited the use of the European Open science infrastructures are those belonging in decreasing order to physics, life sciences, earth sciences, applied engineering, etc. In the list Chemistry and Molecular Science (MS) do not appear at all (unless one considers them as a possible subset of other scientific communities). These days the EOSCpilot project [13] is getting off the ground to support the first phase in the development of European Commissions flagship initiative, the European Open Science Cloud (EOSC): a trusted and open environment for the European scientific community to share, store and re-use scientific data. The project brings together stakeholders from research infrastructures and e-Infrastructure providers and will engage with related funders and policy makers to create an open environment to use research data, knowledge and services. The European Open Science Cloud for Research pilot (EOSCpilot) project is supporting the first phase in the development of EOSC) and will address some of the key reasons why European research is not yet fully tapping into the potential of data. Specifically, it will reduce fragmentation between data infrastructures by working across scientific and economic domains, countries and governance models, and improve interoperability between data infrastructures by demonstrating how data and resources can be shared even when they are large and complex and in varied formats. These actions will build on and leverage already available resources and capabilities from research infrastructure and e-infrastructure organisations to maximise their use across the research community. The EOSC pilot project will improve the ability to reuse data resources and provide an important step towards building a dependable open-data research environment where data from publicly funded research is always open and there are clear incentives and rewards for the sharing of data and resources. Open Molecular Science (OMS) did not find its way among the approved EOSC pilots. This is due to a large extent to the insufficient attention paid by the chemistry community to Open Science in spite of the fact that, in the last 10 years within the activities of the COST actions D23 [14] and D37 [15], of the COMPCHEM VO [16] and of the CMMST VRC [17] an embryo presence of the OMS community among the Open Science ones has been developed. In particular, attempts in this direction have been made by the former Computational Chemistry (at present Computational and Theoretical Chemistry) Division of the European Chemical and Molecular Science (EuCheMS) [18] Association and by the European Chemistry Thematic Network (ECTN) Association [19].

3   The Collaborative Open Molecular Science Project

The EuCheMS Association consists of about 160,000 members who are either Computational or Experimental Chemists operating in a wide area of research, professional, production, research and educational activities while the ECTN Association consists of over than one hundred Higher Education Institutions (HEI)s whose central mission is the development of OMS within Higher education. Both EuCheMS and ECTN associations bear specific interests in building an OMS community at EU level by fostering the conversion of the present attitude of their members to act largely as isolated islands into a collaborative creation and delivery of community knowledge. In this paper we illustrate the strategy behind the project of gathering the isolated MS islands of competences and e-infrastructure resources of the two associations aimed to integrate them in an OMS community allowing researchers, developers and teachers to run their theoretical, computational, experimental and educational activities through an intuitive and seamless virtual access to the different levels of their expertise and skills and the sharing at all levels of the associated knowledge.

The first objective of this project consists in building a collaborative management of data covering the whole lifecycle of OMS knowledge using metadata, ontologies and provenance based on advanced data and computing services. To this end the community will build on the existing thematic VOs and VRCs (like the COMPCHEM VO and the CMMST VRC) to create a continent out of the existing islands. This will help the members of the community in exchanging best practices, relying on trans-national and virtual access to research facilities, compute and data resources for both academia and industry so as establish a worldwide EU-based virtual community. The project consortium will incorporate as stakeholders research facilities, technology providers, research teams and SMEs to target such goals and gain access to large European computing and data resources when running productive activities, laboratory experiments, high-performance simulations and exchange of produced data. To this end the project will:

1. gather together the researchers and companies running simulations in Computational and Experimental Chemistry within a network of European, regional and national research facilities and e-infrastructure resources and services;
2. ensure intuitive, seamless and virtual access to key European, regional and national research facilities and e-infrastructure resources and services considering different levels of expertise and skills of the members;
3. support efficient management of scientific data including creating, publishing, accessing, curating, preserving data using metadata, ontologies and provenance based on advanced data and computing services;
4. enable and support multi-disciplinary activities in cooperation with ESFRI and other major European initiatives to address societal challenges.

In doing this, particular emphasis will be given to the thematic areas of interest for the Chemistry community like environmental care, climate control, energy efficiency, renewable energy sources, waste management, etc. In particular the need for networking, trans-national and/or virtual access, standardisation and common access procedures will be developed and made available to the users. The project aims at supporting the whole data life cycle from creating, publishing, accessing, curating and, preserving the data using metadata, ontologies and provenance. Data resources to be used in experiments and simulations will be linked to ESFRI projects relevant to Molecular sciences (ECCSEL (Energy), IAGOS (Environmental Sciences), ELI (Physical Sciences and Engineering), etc.). The second objective of the project consists in building a collaborative educational system in which not only standards of teaching and learning are set at continental (Europe) level but also the creation of learning materials (Libraries of Questions and answers, eChemTest disciplinary areas and levels, Learning Objects (LO)s, online courses, etc.) and the assessment of chemical knowledge is cooperatively built and fully shared.

4 An OMS Research Infrastructure

Recent emblematic OMS participated by EuCheMS (through its former Computational Chemistry division) and ECTN (through its Virtual Education Community (VEC) committee) are reported in refs. [20,21]. Here we analyse in some detail SUMO-chem (the very recent OMS RIA proposal 731010-1 submitted to the call H2020-INFRAIA-2016–2017 (INFRAIA-02-2017) by Gabor Terstyanszky [22]).

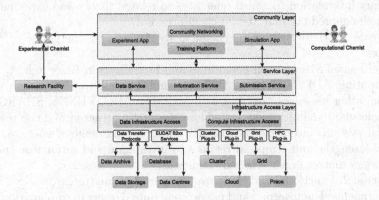

Fig. 1. The Architecture enabling convenient access for researchers to the data and compute infrastructure.

SUMO-chem relies on four layers of services as depicted in Fig. 1. Experimentalists and Computational chemist generate their application specific data. This is handled on an abstract level by the service layer which points onto the infrastructure access layer, bridging the connection to data and compute infrastructure. Consequently the whole life cycle ranging from experiment or simulation to data storage is covered.

In this framework the Grid Empowered Molecular Simulator (GEMS) is intended for collaborative handling of cloud based computational and experimental techniques [23] (https://www.egi.eu/use-cases/research-stories/). The distributed simulator GEMS is based on the highest level possible *ab initio* determination of intra and intermolecular interactions and on the accurate calculation of the experimental observables out of detailed dynamical quantities computed at the most accurate level for both gas and condensed phases. GEMS is structured to compose à la carte these computer applications and data made available for collaboration by different partners and further compose applications and data for simulating the evolution in time of multiple interleaved elementary processes in kinetics, as well as their combination with statistical, fluid dynamics and/or condensed phase treatments. This is aimed at allowing the grounding on *ab initio* approaches of the accurate modelling of important phenomena and the developing of innovative technological solutions to important societal challenges.

In fact, after repeated checks of the procedure comparing theoretical predictions versus experimental measurements, the gained confidence on the use of GEMS for the specific use-case enables its use as a service for situations in which no experiment is feasible. The combination of the appropriate software packages leads to the design of more advanced experiments and to the creation of more accurate simulations also of the industrial apparatuses.

In the SUMO-chem project the following use-cases are considered as examples at different levels of data complexity, of accuracy of the theoretical approaches used, of interplay between theory and experiment, of the statistical averaging of elementary information (detailed references to related theory and experiment is given in the quoted original SUMO-chem proposal):

Use-case 1: Highly accurate chemical dynamics and energetics of small molecules.

Experiments: Synchrotron beam-lines and Free Electron Laser light.

Computing: ADF, NWCHEM, DALTON and other electronic structure packages from other use-cases, together with MCDTH, ABC, VENUS, SHARC and other molecular dynamics codes suited for investigating reactive and non reactive molecular systems interacting with radiation in a wide range of energies, photon field strengths and temporal regimes to investigate and rationalize specific properties of matter under selected conditions.

Use case 2: Functional and structural properties of matter.

Experiments: Femtosecond and nanosecond pulsed lasers in combination with pump-probe and laser spectroscopy, time-of-flight mass spectrometry and ion and photoelectron imaging techniques.

Computing: MOLPRO, MOLCAS, GAUSSIAN and other electronic structure packages from other use-cases to study the dynamics, stereo-dynamics and quantum control of molecular processes including molecular photo-dissociation and photo-chemistry and bimolecular reactive and inelastic collisions and material science with lasers.

Use case 3: Plasmas in non-equilibrium conditions.

Experiments: Plasmas in non-equilibrium conditions.

Computing: DSMC (Direct Simulation Monte Carlo), PIC (Particle-in-Cell), EPDA (elementary processes data aggregator), PLASMA-FLU and Boltzmann transport equations (BTE) for beyond nano research.

Use case 4: Spectroscopy of metal complexes.

Experiments: Non-linear and time-resolved spectra of metal complexes using x-ray absorption, flash laser and linear and time-resolved spectroscopy.

Computing: ORCA, Jaguar, MOPAC, DFTB+, MNDO99 and packages from other use-cases to compare the results with simulated spectra and find the best matching molecular structures.

Use case 5: Renewable energy storage as chemicals.

Experiments: Methane and clathrate hydrates formation reactors, beam-beam and beam gas scattering.

Computing: ZACROS, APH3D (both time dependent and time independent), RWAVEPR and codes from other use-cases to design complex kinetic systems involving gas and solid state catalysed processes using efficiency parameters derived from ab initio studies checked against highly detailed measurements of the corresponding elementary gas phase processes obtained from experiments.

Use case 6: Cleaner combustion.

Experiments: Elementary reactors (sodium-cooled fast and plug flow reactor) and complex systems (engine and cyclonic burners) enhanced by analytical chemistry techniques (GC/MS, HPLC) and advanced optical diagnostics (spectroscopic and laser-induced fluorescence - LIF- measurements).

Computing: CRECK, Pope, ANOVA (variance analysis), Tukey/Dunnett modelling software, other codes from other use-cases to complement the experiments by validating the experimental results and optimizing the combustion process.

Use case 7: Secure, clean and efficient energy production.

Experiments: Functional tests, fabrication technologies and materials characterization apparatuses.

Computing: CPMD, Quantum espresso, GOMACS, LAMPS, CP2K codes and the virtual laboratory at ENEA to develop market affordable, cost-effective and resource efficient solutions for the energy system based on low-carbon technologies by designing new materials at the nano-scale level, combining experimental and numerical results and speeding up the production of specialized nano-materials for energy applications.

Use case 8: Optimization of Biodiesel Production.

Experiments: Experimental prototype rector.

Computing: QM/MM multi-scale, EVB Empirical Valence Bond MOLARIS, Q, other codes from other use-cases to investigate kinetic and thermodynamic parameters of high complexity associated with biodiesel synthesis.

In spite of the difficulty of the overall SUMO-chem in getting funded, some of its use cases have progressed to the point of deserving to be considered for future EOSC services and being illustrated at the School on Open Science Cloud organized by Master-up srl in collaboration with the University of Perugia and INFN within the activities of the ITN-EJD-642294_TCCM.

5 The General Frame of the SUMO-chem Research Infrastructure

The experimental platform of the proposed research infrastructure is made of the ELETTRA synchrotron facility and FERMI free electron laser facility of Trieste, the LENS non-linear spectroscopy facility of Firenze, the FLASH free electron laser and the PETRA III accelerator of Hamburg, the crossed beams and beam gas facility of Perugia, the Plasma facility of Bari, the Ultrafast laser spectroscopy facility of Madrid, the shock wave combustor, the Laboratory burners, the Jet-stirred and plug flow reactor and the Shock wave spectroscopy facilities of Nancy, the cyclonic and engine burner and the sodium-cooled fast and plug flow reactor of Napoli, the experimental kinetics laboratory of Ljubljana, the

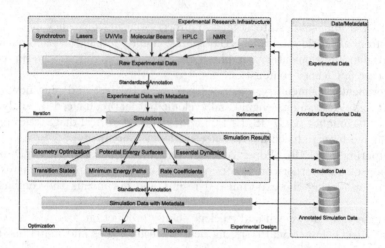

Fig. 2. Data flows within the community

UV/Vis and Raman facilities of Aachen. The experimental platform is paralleled by the EGI.eu grid federated cloud of Amsterdam, the supercomputing centres of CINECA in Casalecchio di Reno, of ENEA CMAST and CRESCO in Roma, of RECAS in Bari, of ZIH in Dresden, of MoSGrid in Germany, of UCM in Madrid, of the National Institute of Chemistry in Ljubljana, of the Conca Openstack Cloud and Linux Cluster in Perugia and of the Flavus cluster in Tubingen.

Members data resources (ranging from experimental measurements recorded either in their own laboratory or over large infrastructure facilities) specific to given analyses and simulation applications, are usually stored in a way (their

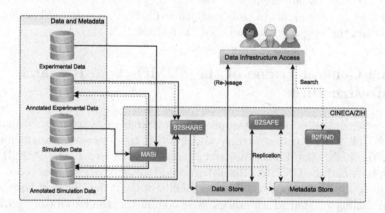

Fig. 3. Data management using EUDAT and MASi services for data ingestion, storage, replication and search (Remark: Data flows are indicated by bold lines, flow of metadata is shown as dashed line).

own data structures and formats) that needs to be ported to a uniform, open metadata format accompanied by robust ontologies. To this end the already mentioned virtual continent was going to be created out of the islands by connecting them via a 3rd generation science gateway (see Fig. 1). Researchers as the citizens of this continent will use data as a common currency for communication among the islands. There will be two-way communication between Computational and Experimental Chemistry in the continent. Researchers will run experiments and publish results. Analyzing this data Computational Chemists will design simulations that can complement experiments to produce new research achievements.

The same kind of cooperation will be supported from the other end, i.e. researchers will run simulations whose results can be further checked in experiments. The architecture, shown in Fig. 1, combines four key entities: research facilities, computing/data resources, science gateway and researchers at three different layers: community, service and infrastructure access layer. It will support training activities and community building. This layer will also provide a development environment for Computational Chemists enabling them to access the submission service to run simulations. The service layer will connect researchers to the research facilities and e-infrastructure resources using micro-services managed by a service orchestrator. The set of micro-services will contain a data, information, monitoring, resource broker, submission, visualization, etc. services. Figure 1 contains three of these services as an example. As shown in Fig. 1 here will be two-way communication between Computational and Experimental Chemistry in the continent. Researchers will run experiments and publish results. Analysing this data Computational Chemists will design simulations that can complement experiments to produce new research achievements. The same kind of cooperation will be supported from the other end, i.e. researchers will run simulations that results can be further checked in experiments. Access to European, national and regional data archives, databases, data centres and data storages using either basic data transfer protocols or advanced B2xx services will be provided to the other members of the community including companies and educational Institutions. The science gateway will enable researchers to access research facilities, computing and data resources. It will have three layers: community, service and infrastructure access. The community layer will offer social media type services allowing Experimental Chemists to run experiments on remotely available research facilities. This layer will provide access to the submission service to run simulations. It will also support training activities and community building. The service layer will connect researchers to the research facilities and e-infrastructure resources using micro-services managed by a service orchestrator. The set of micro-services will contain a data, information, monitoring, resource broker, submission, visualization, etc. service. The major innovation will be the data service that will connect Experimental and Computational Chemists through scientific data. Experimental Chemists will use the data service to manage experimental data while Computational Chemists will run simulations through the submission service using the data service. The submission service will support running jobs, pipelines and workflows. The infrastructure access layer will have two services: computing and data infrastructure access service. The first one will manage access to major computing resources such as cloud, cluster, grid and supercomputer. The second one will manage data using different types of data resources, such as data archives, databases, data collections, data storages using EUDAT B2xx and MASi services, and major data transfer protocols.

6 Molecular Science Data Interoperability

Data interoperability is a major technical challenge because data must enable cooperation inside and among sub-domains of Chemistry involving both Computational and Experimental Chemists. In Chemistry the data-life-cycle ranges from primary experimental data over simulation results to fully annotated scientific data. We will develop a data management approach that will facilitate reusability and consequently reproducibility using metadata. Experimental researchers produce a large volume of primary data in many different data formats. These differences make it difficult to share data among researchers and harness it. Storing and sharing primary experimental data might not be meaningful because it does not contain information about how it was obtained and processed. Adding metadata to primary data, particularly provenance information supports sharing scientific data.

Metadata can describe the method and the equipment used, measurement protocol applied, conditions and parameters specified, etc. These information enable researchers to evaluate the experiment itself and to decide further usage of data. The same approach must be followed with simulated data as illustrated in Fig. 2. Similarly to experimental data, significant efforts have been spent to describe computing resources needed, implementation methods used and scientific analysis applied in simulations.

There are a few approaches that support the transparent storage and sharing of scientific simulation data. Markup languages like CML or its derivate MSML offer ontologies for the hierarchical representation of simulation protocols as workflows including relevant input and output data, as well as the analysis [24]. QC-ML and consequently Q5Cost follow a similar tree representation overall focusing more on quantum chemical simulation data.

The proposal will build on the experience with MSML and Q5Cost to create a uniform standardized representation of the whole data life cycle ranging from initial experimental data to the analysis of simulation data. It is anticipated to feed the metadata to B2FIND making it available beyond the closer Computational Chemistry community. Special emphasis will be put into the storage of good protocols, accepted in the field, on a meta level. By representation through an XML based markup language individual tasks along such community workflows are decoupled from actual implementations e.g., specific software packages while maintaining the actual purpose of the respective task. For example the geometry optimization of a given molecule can be accomplished with numerous tools, while the final conformation should be sufficiently comparable among all implementations. A meta description of such tasks supports the reproducibility and sustainability of scientific protocols in the best possible way.

The data will be hosted by CINECA and ZIH data centres employing a federated storage solution compliant with EUDAT approaches as depicted in Fig. 3. Annotated primary data from experiments and simulations will be transferred via the MASi service uploading valuable content to the community data hub. The access to individual data sets will be handled via groups and access control lists allowing fine-grained control about what is shared with whom, which is especially important prior to scientific publication in compliance with existing scientific data policies of the facilities. The security of the data and metadata will be ensured through the usage of European AAI services utilizing federated identities (eduGAIN) wherever feasible. We will closely observe the results of the European AARC project and their goal to create an interdisciplinary AAI solution based on existing systems and evaluate its applicability within the proposed project.

To this end the Chemistry community will cooperate with a wide range of associations and organisations like COMPCHEM (EU Computational Chemistry VO), CMMST (EU Chemistry, Molecular and Materials Science and Technologies Virtual Research Community), CHEM.VO.IBERGRID (EGI-Inspire VO), MoSGrid. It will also collaborate with European and national research projects like DFG Priority Program 1740 (Reactive Bubbly Flows), EoCoE (Energy Oriented Centre of Excellence), Multi-scalSOLAR COST project (multiscale simulations of materials for PV technologies) and KIC Raw Materials (European Network for critical raw materials). The science gateway will be built on open source frameworks and services mainly developed within European research projects such as EDGI, ER-flow, SHIWA and SCI-BUS while B2xx services were developed by EUDAT.

7 GEMS

Among the OMS use cases considered in SUMO-chem there are some in which the use of the GEMS *ab initio* MS simulator as a service is fundamental. We consider here the Progeo applications devoted to the simulation of the production of methane from waste flue CO_2 gases. Experimental measurements of methane yields of ProGeo have been carried out using CO_2 bottles. The measurements show a complete compatibility with the catalyser used for the methanation process in ProGeo. A key element for a quantitative measure of the reaction yield is the regular monitoring of the temperature both along the central axis of each channel (maximum temperature) and along the peripheral axis (minimum temperature). The methanation reaction (the $H_2 + CO_2$ Sabatier [25] reaction) occurs mainly on the top segment of the reactor close to the inlet (90% in the first 200 mm). The threshold temperature is 240° C and the range of temperature of optimal yield is 300 – 350° C. The molar ratio has a significant impact on the percentage of produced methane with the optimum value of the CO_2/H_2 ratio being 1/5. Computational simulations of methane production based on the catalytic action of a commercial catalyst are carried out by composing the complex kinetics by means of all the (possibly significantly) contributing elementary processes. To this end we use the ZACROS [26] package, a Kinetic Monte Carlo (KMC) [27,28] set of codes written in Fortran 2003. ZACROS leverages on the Graph-Theoretical KMC methodology coupled with cluster expansion Hamiltonians for the ad-layer energetics and Brønsted-Evans-Polanyi relations for the activation energies of elementary events [27]. ZACROS enables researchers in the areas of Computational Catalysis and Surface Science to perform dynamic modelling of adsorption, desorption, surface diffusion, and reaction processes on heterogeneous catalysts. In ZACROS, rate coefficients r_i for all the elementary processes i potentially participating in the mechanism, need to be provided as a product of a pre-exponential factor A and an exponential term $\exp(-E_p/k_BT)$, where k_B is the usual Boltzmann constant and T the temperature. This formulation incorporates the information on the PES of the related elementary process p (for the direct or forward "f" and for the reverse or backward "b") for which E_p is the difference between the energy associated with the stationary point of the potential Minimum Energy Path at the transition state and that associated with the original asymptote of the process. In low level approximations to r_i, the pre-exponential factor A can be given the expression kT/h where h is the Plank constant, for pure gaseous species while for gaseous species adsorbed on the surface of a catalyser the mostly used expression for the reaction rate r_i is the well known Hertz-Knudsen equation $r_i^{ad} = S_{0,i}A_{site}p_i(2\pi m_i k_B T)^{-1/2}$ where $S_{0,i}$ is the sticking coefficient for which we took value 1 in our work, A_{site} is the area of the adsoprtion site, p_i is the partial pressure of the species i and m_i its mass. A more accurate formulation of the rate coefficients makes use of the partition functions of both the intermediate state (incorporating so far the information about the remaining degrees of freedom) and the reactants: $A = (k_BT/h)(Q^{\ddagger}/Q_r)$ where $Q^{\ddagger}$ is the partition function of the transition state and Q_r the partition function of the reactants r. For it use is made of the VASP code [29]. Each partition function is usually calculated considering that rotations and translations are hindered, due to the fact that they are adsorbed, and therefore can be assimilated to vibrational degrees of freedom.

8   ECHEMTEST$^+$

In order to provide another example of collaborative OSM projects we refer here to ECHEMTEST$^+$. ECHEMTEST$^+$ is a project of the ECTN Association coordinated by its VEC standing committee that manages a Europe wide network of National Test Centres (NTC)s and Accredited Test Sites (ATS). Within ECHEMTEST$^+$ ECTN takes care of EChemTest (the English e-test libraries of questions and answers on chemical knowledge produced in the past 20 years by the ECTN members for levels ranging from schools to Master degrees), administers related Self Evaluation Sessions (SES)s, provides translations into national languages, promotes the harmonization of the OMS knowledge over Europe, supports the development of a distributed repository of Learning Objects (LO)s, enhances the use of Massive Open Online Courses (MOOC), etc. ECHEMTEST$^+$ activities are technically operated by the SME Master-UP s.r.l [30] operating under the umbrella organization of ECTN. The running of EChemTest activities is the key OMS Cloud service provided within the ECHEMTEST$^+$ project to the members of the ECTN association. In particular, a large number of EChemTest SESs are run for academic use (credits assignment, curricula definition, dispersion mitigation, etc.) and for individual European Proficiency certificates. In order to deliver these service in a professional way over all Europe (and beyond it), the network of test centers has been extended to HEIs in Vienna (A), Thessaloniki (GR), Budapest (HU), Krakow (PL), Helsinki (FI), Madrid (ES), Perugia (IT), Milan (IT), Genoa (IT), Naples (IT), Kazan (RU), and Amsterdam (NL). Furthermore EOL (an Open Source software developed by Master UP to the end of running flexibly SESs for both academic and personal use (e.g. award proficiency certificates). This has led also to the development of a set of auxiliary e-learning tools aimed at supporting Virtual laboratory activities, professional career developments as well as an extension to other applications and scientific disciplines, related assessment, certification, training and job selection.

9 Conclusions

In spite of the fact that the project discussed in this paper was not selected as a pilot for the EOSC proposal to H2020, it offers an overview of the directions in which the Molecular Science community is moving to the end of implementing an Open Science Cloud. In particular, the project leverages on the on-going work of the COMPCHEM VO, MoSGrid and the CMMST VRC (with the support of the Computational and Theoretical Chemistry Division of EuCheMS and the Virtual Education Community of ECTN) to the end of providing Higher Education Institutions, research centres and companies with tools suited for handling Molecular science Computational and Experimental information, with intuitive, seamless and virtual access to e-infrastructure resources and services, with means for creating, publishing, accessing, curating, preserving data in order to enable multi-disciplinary innovation aimed to address societal challenges. In this spirit the implementation of two advanced use cases (respectively on clean energy and on line education) are described in detail in order to show how the OMS community can work to implement an Open Science Cloud.

Acknowledgments. The authors acknowledge the support of COMPCHEM VO, CMMST VRC, EuCheMS, ITN-EJD-642294_TCCM and ECTN.

References

1. New statements are constantly developed, such as the Amsterdam, Call for Action on Open Science to be presented to the Dutch Presidency of the Council of the European Union in late May (2016)
2. https://okfn.org/about/. Accessed 18 Feb 2017
3. https://cos.io/our-products/open-science-framework/. Accessed 18 Feb 2017
4. Kacsuk, P., Terstyanszky, G., Balasko, A., Karoczkai, K., Farkas, Z.: Executing multi-workflow simulations on a mixed grid/cloud infrastructure using the SHIWA and SCI-BUS technology. Advances in Parallel Computing, vol. 23, pp. 141–160 (2013)
5. Krueger, J., Grunzke, J.R., Gesing, S., Breuers, S., Brinkmann, A., de la Garza, L., Kohlbacher, O., Kruse, M., Nagel, W.E., Packschies, L., Mueller-Pfefferkorn, R., Schaefer, P., Schaerfe, C., Steinke, T., Schlemmer, T., Warzecha, K., Zink, A., Herres-Pawlis, S.: The MoSGrid science gateway a complete solution for molecular simulations. J. Chem. Theory Comput. **10**(6), 2232–2245 (2014). doi:10.1021/ct500159h
6. Murray-Rust, P.: The blue obelisk. CDK News **2**, 43–46 (2005)
7. Guha, R., Howard, M.T., Hutchison, G.R., Murray-Rust, P., Rzepa, H., Steinbeck, C., Wegner, J., Willighagen, E.L.: The blue obelisk-interoperability in chemical informatics. J. Chem. Inf. Model. **46**(3), 991–998 (2006). doi:10.1021/ci050400b. PMID 16711717
8. O'Boyle, N., Guha, R., Willighagen, E.L., Adams, S.E., Alvarsson, J., Bradley, J.C., Filippov, I.V., Hanson, R.M., Hanwell, M.D., Hutchinson, G.R., James, C.A., Jeliazkova, N., Lang, A., Langer, K.M., Lonie, D.C., Lowe, D.M., Pansanel, J., Pavlov, D., Spjuth, O., Steinbeck, C., Tenderholt, A.L., Theisen, T.J., Murray-Rust, P.: Open data, open source and open standards in chemistry: the blue obelisk five years on. J. Chem. Inf. 3 (2011)
9. https://indico.cern.ch/. Accessed 18 Feb 2017
10. https://www.eudat.eu/. Accessed 18 Feb 2017
11. https://www.egi.eu/. Accessed 18 Feb 2017
12. https://www.openaire.eu. Accessed 18 Feb 2017
13. https://www.egi.eu/about/newsletters/eoscpilot-getting-the-european-open-science-cloud-off-the-ground/. Accessed 18 Feb 2017
14. http://www.cost.eu/COST_Actions/cmst/D23. Accessed 18 Feb 2017
15. http://www.cost.eu/COST_Actions/cmst/D37. Accessed 18 Feb 2017
16. Laganà, A., Riganelli, A., Gervasi, O.: On the structuring of the computational chemistry virtual organization COMPCHEM. In: Gavrilova, M., Gervasi, O., Kumar, V., Tan, C.J.K., Taniar, D., Laganá, A., Mun, Y., Choo, H. (eds.) ICCSA 2006. LNCS, vol. 3980, pp. 665–674. Springer, Heidelberg (2006). doi:10.1007/11751540_70
17. Laganà, A.: Towards a CMMST VRC. VIRT&L-COMM.2.2012.2
18. http://www.euchems.eu/divisions/computationalchemistry.Html
19. http://ectn-assoc.cpe.fr/
20. A. Laganà, Research and innovation actions. chemistry, molecular & materials sciences and technologies virtual research environment (CMMST-VRE). VIRT&L-COMM.6.2014.1
21. Laganà, A.: The molecular science community for open science. VIRT&L-COMM.6.2016.6

22. Terstyanszky, G., Laganà, A., Cardini, G., Krueger, J., Stare, J., Bañares, L., Celino, M., de Joannon, M., Grunzke, R., Richter, R., Vianello, R., Herres-Pawlis, S.: The sumo-chem H2020 proposal, (VIRT&L-COMM. 6.2016 News September 16).http://www.hpc.unipg.it/ojs/index.php/virtlcomm/issue/view/17

23. Laganà, A., Costantini, A., Gervasi, O., Faginas-Lago, N., Manuali, C., Rampino, S.: COMPCHEM: progress towards GEMS a grid empowered molecular simulator and beyond. J Grid Comput. **8**, 71–86 (2010). doi:10.1007/s10723-010-9164-x

24. Grunzke, R., Krueger, J., Jakel, R., Nagel, W.E., Herres-Pawlis, S., Hoffmann, A.: Metadata management in the MoSGrid science gateway - evaluation and the expansion of quantum chemistry support. J. Grid Comput. 1–13 (2016)

25. Birbara, P.J., Sribnik, F.: Development of an improved Sabatier reactor. Am. Soc. Mech. Eng. **7936**, 1–10 (1979)

26. http://zacros.org/. Accessed 18 Feb 2017

27. Martì Alliod, C.: Networked computing for ab initio modeling the chemical storage of alternative energy: second term report (December 2015 - February 2016) VIRT&L-COMM. 15.2016 News March 16. http://www.hpc.unipg.it/ojs/index.php/virtlcomm/issue/view/15

28. Mueller-Krumbhaar, H., Binder, K.: Dynamic properties of the monte carlo method in statistical mechanics. J. Stat. Phys. **8**, 1–24 (1973). doi:10.1007/BF01008440

29. https://www.vasp.at/. Accessed 18 Feb 2017

30. http://www.master-up.it/. Accessed 18 Feb 2017

Determination of Volatile Aroma Composition Profiles of Coco de Mèr (Lodoicea Maldivica) Fruit: Analytical Study by HS-SPME and GC/MS Techniques

Bartolomeo Sebastiani[1], Donatella Malfatti[2,3], Martino Giorgini[2], and Stefano Falcinelli[4(✉)]

[1] Department of Chemistry Biology and Biotechnologies,
University of Perugia, Via Elce di Sotto, 8, 06123 Perugia, Italy
bartolomeo.sebastiani@unipg.it
[2] Vis Medicatrix Naturae s.r.l, 50034 Marradi, FI, Italy
[3] Studio Malfatti, Via R. Omicini 181, 06124 Perugia, Italy
[4] Department of Civil and Environmental Engineering,
University of Perugia, Via G. Duranti 93, 06125 Perugia, Italy
stefano.falcinelli@unipg.it

Abstract. This work reports the detection and identification of volatile chemical compounds in fruit kernel of "Lodoicea maldivica" coco nucifera palm by gas chromatographic method. The analysis was performed by HS-SPME and GC/MS techniques to determine volatile aroma composition profiles in internal and external pulp. No qualitative differences in flavor composition were observed between two pulp parts, but there were notable variations in the abundance levels of the prominent compounds. Computational method was used to extract individual component mass spectra from GC/MS data files by using the AMDIS version 2.65 software. With such a procedure we are able to construct our own mass spectra library determining retention indices for chemical compounds of our interest in the used specific experimental conditions.

Keywords: GC/MS analysis · Gas chromatography · Mass spectrometry · HS-SPME · Volatile aroma · "coco de mer" · Lodoicea maldivica

1 Introduction

The Lodoicea Maldivica is a particular plant, commonly named "Coco de mer" or "double coconut": it is a native palm of the Seychelles Islands in the Indian Ocean (see left panel of Fig. 1). It is considered as the last witness of the old continent Gondwana, (formed by Africa, Madagàscar and India assembled together), which 65 millions of years ago was split into a number of lands leaving Seychelles alone.

This kind of palms (see right-higher panel of Fig. 1) are enormous reaching about 40 m of height and more than 300 years of age [1]. They grow exclusively in the Mai Valley in the islands of Praslin and Curieuse.

© Springer International Publishing AG 2017
O. Gervasi et al. (Eds.): ICCSA 2017, Part III, LNCS 10406, pp. 44–59, 2017.
DOI: 10.1007/978-3-319-62398-6_4

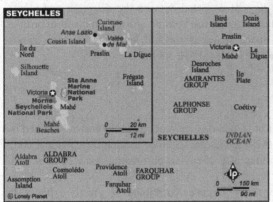

Fig. 1. Left side: The Seychelles islands; in the map are indicated the areas ("World Heritage Site" designed in 1983 by UNESCO) where the Lodoicea maldivica palms exclusively grow (the Vallée de Mai in the Praslin and Curieuse islands). Right side: in the upper panel is reported an image of the female palm, whereas in the lower panel a coconut from such a female palm, (commonly named "Coco de mer") can be seen, showing its impressive resemblance with the female pubes.

The about 4000 palms of the Coco de Mer are protected by UNESCO since 1983 [2], and the local government allows to pick up only 3000 coconuts every year which are sold at high price (about 12,500 Euros for each coconut). The peculiarity of the "Coco de mer" is the impressive resemblance with the female pubes, because it has generally two lobes suggesting a double coconut, as it is shown in the right-lower panel of Fig. 1. For this reason in the ancient times people attribute to Coco de Mer supernatural powers, since it was used as aphrodisiac in the Middle Ages. It is the largest known seed (about 50 cm long and up to 30 kg of weight), and it takes about 7 years to ripen [1].

From a commercial point of view the Middle East and China are the major importers of "Coco de mer", because in such countries it has been used for centuries both in traditional and ayurvedic medicine. Actually, the "Coco de mer" is the symbol of the Seychelles Islands. It has to be noted that, despite its peculiarity and world-famous image, the literature concerning the chemical characterization of the "Coco de mer" is still very limited, with the exception of a recent paper by Rist *et al.* concerning an investigation for a sustainable harvesting of "Coco de mer" [3]. Our analytical effort aims to fill this lack highlighting the main properties and possible uses from a nutritional and pharmacological point of view. In fact, this work intend to complete previous investigations performed in our laboratory in order to determine the chemical composition in fruit kernel of a sample of Lodoicea maldivica coconut. We have already published the concentration of phytosterols (24.6 µg/g for the external kernel portion, and 22.5 µg/g for the internal ones) and fatty acid composition by GC/MS technique [4, 5]. Here we present recorded data on the detection and identification of chemical compounds characterizing the volatile aroma composition profiles both on internal and external pulp of the analysed coconut, by using the same experimental analytical technique coupled with HS-SPME method.

2 Experimental

The volatile organic fraction flavour of "Coco de mer" coconut pulp was determined by the use of has mass spectrometry (MS) technique in order to identify chemical compounds responsible for the fruits aroma, after their gas chromatographic (GC) separation (GC/MS technique).

The wide use of the GC/MS for many purposes contributes to greatly expand MS applications and uses, because such a diagnostic technique is a powerful and universal analytical method able in principle to detect and recognize any chemical compound. For such a reason, MS is one of the most widely used technique in chemistry, being applied in research as well as in analytical studies passing from fundamental research [6–9], environmental [10–12], combustion [13–16] and atmospheric chemistry [17–21], to bio-medical and forensic applications [22], up to astrochemistry [23–26].

2.1 Characteristics of Used Reagents and Standards

For samples preparation, purification and analysis we used only reagents of analytical grade purity. In particular in the analytical extraction procedure solvent a mixture of hexane-acetone (1:1, v/v) was used. Such reagents were purchased from Sigma-Aldrich (Deisenhofen, Germany) having a purity grade ≥ 98% and ≥ 99%, respectively In order to determine a linear retention index, we have used a n-alkane calibration standard solution C6-C44, (ASTM method D2887), provided by Superchrom (Milano, Italy).

2.2 Experimental Devices and Apparatuses

An Ultra Turrax T25 device, being the high-performance dispersing instrument commonly used for the treatment and preparation of fruits kernel as well as for officinal herbs, was used to ensure perfect complete homogenization coconut samples. In the HS-SPME extraction procedure of the volatile flavour compounds collection a 65 µm mixed bipolar porous fiber coating PDMS/DVB (volume phase 357×10^{-9} cm^3) provided by Supelco Co (Bellafonte, PA, USA) was employed. In order to apply the normal-phase SPE extraction method, plastic syringe barrels (4 ml) were handmade packed with 1 g silica gel (Bondesil-SI 40 µm, Varian), previously conditioning overnight at 130 °C and capped with polymeric frits. Before to be used, the SPE cartridges were pre-conditionated with hexane-methyl tert-buthyl ether (99:1, v/v). The analysis of the extracted samples was performed using a Chrompack CP 3800 gas chromatograph equipped with 1079 split-splitless injector and coupled to an ion trap detector Saturn 2200 Varian Inc.

(Walnut Creek, CA, USA) operating in positive electron and liquid chemical ionization mode. The data acquisition and the quantitative analysis were achieved with Varian Saturn GC/MS Workstation system software, version 5.41 (Walnut Creek, CA, USA).

2.3 Plant Material

The coconut of Lodoicea Maldivica was obtained by a female palm from the Vallée de Mai National Park, in the Praslin island of Seychelles. It was a coconut about seven-eight years old harvested at an advanced maturation degree. The fruit was frozen and stored up at −10 °C from Seychelles islands to Italy and up to the analysis. It was a coco-nut of about 5.4 kg of weight. The coconut dimensions were the following: 32 cm in length with polar and equatorial diameters of about 7 and 24 cm, respectively. It was characterized by the presence of two different portions of the internal pulp so-called endosperm tissue: a more hard and external kernel of 25 mm thickness of grey-white colour (named in the text as sample A), covering one soft and whitish inner part of about 15 mm thickness (sample B). No watery endosperm was found into the coco-nut, indicating a probable advanced degree of maturation.

2.4 Sample Preparation

The analysed coconut, was first defrosted and then husked and split using a knife. In the sampling procedure we have used two distinct portions of the coconut kernel corresponding to different pulp consistency. Such samples were treated following standard procedures published by ISTISAN 97/23 report [27]. According to the procedure already used in our previous analytical study on "Coco de mer" [4, 5], both external and internal layers of the fruit pulp were scooped by a stainless steel spoon and care was taken to not scrape off the peel; after they were ground with "Ultra Turrax" T25. The fresh fruit pulp was finely grounded, thoroughly homogenized, stored in clean glass jar and frozen at −18 °C in the dark until being analysed the aroma flavor composition. Finally, a quantity of about 100 g of both samples has been taken, by using the "quartatura" technique following the ISTISAN 97/23 method [27], and then submitted to analysis. This work was carried out within a 90 day period after harvest.

2.5 HS-SPME Extraction

HS-SPME (static head space-solid phase micro extraction) technique has been used for double coco-nut volatile flavour analysis. The fruit pulp was treated according to the UNI 10899 analytical method. A sample share of 3.0 g, A and B, have been seals by teflon-lined septum aluminium caps in specific head space glass vials (20 ml). For volatile collection, headspace was manually sampled over solid fresh pulp heated at 40 °C for a 15 min sorption period on 65 μm mixed bipolar porous fiber coating PDMS/DVB (volume phase 357×10^{-9} cm^3) (Supelco Co, Bellafonte, PA, USA). The extraction range for this SPME coating phase is 50-300 molecular weight units. Before sampling the fiber was thermally conditioned in the GC injection port following the manufacturer specifications. After volatile fraction sampling, the fiber was desorbed at 250 °C for 0.8 min for GC/MS analysis.

2.6 Experimental Conditions for GC/MS Analysis

To characterize the volatile flavour, the GC/MS analysis was performed by thermal desorbing the fiber, used in SPME extraction (see Sect. 2.4), inside the injector (narrow-bore Supelco 0.75 mm I.D. GC-SPME inlet liner) at 250 °C operating in split mode with a ratio of 1:2 and using the following operative conditions: (i) a low-bleed/MS CP-Sil8 CB capillary column (30 m × 0.25 mm, 0.25 μm film thickness - Chrompack, Middelburg, The Netherlands); 0.8 ml/min He carrier gas constant flow; (ii) a 40 °÷270 °C thermal program of 25 min with a temperature rise of 15°C/min; (iii) transfer line temperature of 240 °C; manifold temperature of 90 °C; ITD temperature of 150 °C; electron impact ionization mode at 70 eV and EM voltage 2000 V, full scan acquisition in the 40÷250 uma range at 1 s/scan. For positive identification of complex flavour fraction, analyses were also performed using ion-trap system in positive chemical ionization mode with acetonitrile. Chemical compounds not qualitatively confirmed by a direct comparison with available mass spectra databases were considered not identified (NI) when MSMS diagnostics or internal standard procedure cannot be used for their proper identification. In such cases, we cannot use the recorded data to implement our mass spectra library with the relative retention indices, using the computational procedure described in Sect. 3. For such a purpose an additional effort respect to the present investigation appear to be necessary.

2.7 Reliability of the Analytical Procedure

The used analytical method and procedure were tested in order to determine their recovery and repeatability. We were able to minimize the variation in accurate and precise determination of identified volatile chemical compounds. For such a purpose distinct samples were taken in triplicate and for each different sample three injections were performed. With such a procedure we have obtained recoveries up to 90%. The reproducibility of replicate measurements was estimated as ±10%.

3 The Computational Procedure for GC/MS Chemical Compound Identification

In developing a computational approach to identify volatile and non volatile chemical compounds, we have leveraged our experience in simulation and computational procedures mainly applied to characterize intermolecular interactions [28–30], and to predict energetic and structure of ionic species [31–34]. In order to extract the individual component spectra from GC/MS data files a specific computational method, employing a commercial dedicated software to identify target compounds by matching mass spectra in a reference library, was used. The "Automated Mass Spectrometry Deconvolution and Identification System" (AMDIS) – version 2.65 software was used.

The description of the AMDIS software and of the main characteristics of our used computational procedure have already been given in a previous paper to which we refers for the related details and references [5]. Here we limit our description to the main steps of such a methodology. The AMDIS software extracts pure component spectra from complex GC/MS or LC/MS data files and searches against specialized libraries or the commonly used NIST library. This module was developed at the "National Institute of Standards and Technology" (NIST) USA. AMDIS can operate as a "black box" chemical identifier, displaying all identifications that meet a user-selectable degree of confidence. First of all, the chemical compounds identification procedure has been performed by internal standards and retention times. In our case we can compare the obtained mass spectra of the analysed chemical compounds with the Electron Ionization (EI) mass spectral library that is interfaced with our GC/MS-MS apparatus. It consists of NIST 11 MS/MS Library containing more than 250,000 spectra of about 230,000 unique compounds (see http://www.sisweb.com/software/ms/ nistsearch.htm). In this commercial library, besides spectra, typical data include name, formula, molecular structure, molecular weight, CAS number, list of peaks, synonyms, and estimated and/or measured retention index.

In our computational procedure, we are able to build our own mass spectra library, by using the AMDIS software as a processing tool for our collected GC/MS data files. In such a way we are able to collect and store mass spectra of any chemical compound and implement our library data determining retention indices for chemical compounds of our interest in any specific experimental condition used for the analysis. Our computational methodology is based on a specific algorithm built on the Van Den Dool and Kratz equation [5, 35–37], as discussed in a previous publication (for more details see ref. 4, and references therein). In the present work, the linear retention index (I^T) values for identified compounds were calculated using the retention time data obtained by analyzing the series of normal alkanes ranging from C5 to C44. The used chromatographic conditions for the analysis are those relative of volatile aroma compound fraction determination discussed in Sect. 2.6.

As previously discussed [5] the evaluation of the noise in the recorded GC/MS data is of crucial importance. For such a reason, in the performed experiment and computational procedure, it is essential to perform a proper and rigorous noise analysis. The required main step is to extract the "noise factor" from the GC/MS data file. For such a purpose the suggestion by Stein and Scott [38] has been fulfilled, considering the main characteristics of the ion detector mounted in our experimental apparatus. It is a channel electron multiplier, a specific detector able to reveal both excited and ionic species, and largely used in mass spectrometry [39–42]. This high performance detector generates output signals that fluctuate by an average amount proportional to the square root of the signal intensity [43]. The knowledge of the proportionality factor allows us to estimate the magnitude of the noise factor, N_f, for any signal strength, according to the simple following equation:

$$N_f = \frac{R_D}{\sqrt{I}} \qquad (1)$$

where R_D is the average random deviation and I is the recorded signal by the detector. In our applied procedure, the square root of a signal multiplied by N_f is the magnitude of this signal in "noise units", representing the typical scan-to-scan variation arising from ion-counting noise at a given abundance level. In their work, Stein and Scott shown that N_f was independent of both signal intensity level and m/z value and that run-to-run consistency for data files acquired on a single instrument was good (N_f variations of less than 10%) [38]. By analyzing the proper behavior of well-tuned commercial mass spectrometers, including quadrupole and ion trap instruments, being the case of our used GC/MS device, it has been found that the N_f fell in the range 0.5 to 10. However, some dependence on signal strength was noticed at low signal levels in the presence of large amounts of spurious signal. Proper signal threshold setting eliminated this problem, and no adverse effects attributable to the averaging of multiplier signals ("centroiding") were noted [38].

4 Results and Discussion

Analytical data concerning the chemical characterization of "Coco de mer" are scarce. The only exception are the data recently published by our research group related to the lipidic fraction characterization of this special kind of coconut. In our previous studies we reported a comprehensive overview of free sterol and fatty acid profiles, in order to highlight the nutritional and farmacological characteristics of such edible coconut [5, 36]. In particular, our first analytical attempt, has indicated that the total phytosterols concentration is too low in order to allow the "Coco de mer" being considered of interest from a pharmacological or dietary point of view. This conclusion comes from the fact that the estimated daily dietary intakes of plant sterols required to obtain a 10–15% lowering in blood low-density lipoprotein (LDL) cholesterol is of about 1.5-3.0 g/day, and consequently the "Coco de mer" does not seem to be indicated for such a purpose. In the present study we have extended the analytical characterization of the "Coco de mer" to the determination of the volatile aroma composition profile in the internal and external portion of fruit pulp.

4.1 The Flavour Fraction of "Coco de Mer"

Volatile and semi-volatile compounds are responsible for the fruits aroma and flavour. In general, a same fruit variety, but growing in different geographical places, could produce a dissimilar volatile composition fingerprint. For that reason, actually, the analytical determination of the volatile aroma compound fraction is a fast way to perform foodstuffs quality controls. The flavour profiles collected from the two different portions of the external kernel and internal pulp (sample A and B, respectively) shown the presence of 117 compounds. The chromatographic peaks related to such chemical species are visible in Fig. 2 where it is shown the reconstructed total ion current (TIC) comparative GC/MS profiles of the samples A and B as recorded by using the experimental conditions for GC/MS analysis reported in Sect. 2.6. Among the detected

117 volatile chemical compounds, 96 were positively identified, while 21 were only tentatively identified and reported in the synoptic Tables 1, 2, 3 and 4 as NI acronym.

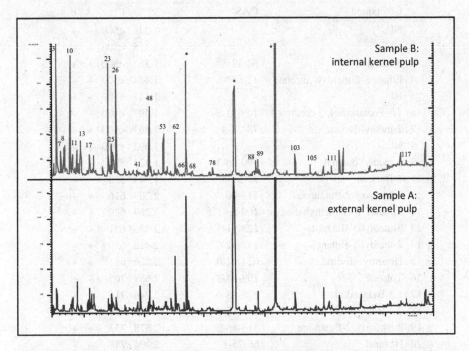

Fig. 2. Reconstructed total ion current comparative GC/MS profiles of the two kernel parts (A = external, B = internal) of *Coco de mer* fruit showing all analysed components. See Tables 1, 2, 3 and 4 for list peak numbers. * Blank PDMS fiber peaks.

The molecular weights of revealed compounds was ranged from 46 to 370 respectively for the ethanol and the di(2-hethylexyl)adipate. The GC/MS chromatogram comparison for each of the two analyses exhibited very similar qualitative aroma patterns, showing that the two portions of the kernel fruit produce identical qualitative flavours. In Tables 1, 2, 3 and 4 the identified analytes were reported in order of gas-chromatographic elution with their respective CAS numbers, absolute retention times and linear retention indices: they are belonging to the compound families of the unsaturated hydrocarbons (terpenic compounds), saturated alcohols, diols, aldehydes, ketons, esters, arenes and heterocyclic compounds. More than 20% of the volatile compounds are unsaturated hydrocarbons, monoterpenes (m/z 136 corresponding to $C_{10}H_{16}$), like α- and β-pinene, camphene, α-, β- and γ-terpinene, limonene, and other terpenoids (m/z 152 corresponding to $C_{10}H_{16}O$), like tujone, camphor, and pinocamphone, including one sesquiterpene like β-farnesene (m/z 204 corresponding to $C_{15}H_{24}$). Studies carried out on other fruits, like cucumis melos and prickly pears, would underline the presence of the sesquiterpenes correlated to fruit aging [44]. Terpenic compounds are a class of secondary phyto-constituent particularly wide.

Table 1. List of purgeable volatile components detected in external (A) and internal kernel (B) of "Coco de mer" fruit and their relative chemical abstract service (+ present; − absent) − first group (peaks number 1–35).

	Compound	CAS[a]	R_t^b	I^{Tc}	A	B
1	NI	−	1.248	<500	+	+
2	NI	−	1.315	<500	+	+
3	Ethanol	64-17-5	1.382	<500	+	+
4	Ethanol, 2-metoxy-, acetate	110-49-6	1.444	<500	+	+
5	NI	−	1.447	<500	+	+
6	1,3-Pentanediol, 2-methyl-	149-31-5	1.497	<500	+	+
7	2-methyl-Butane	78-78-4	1.563	<500	+	+
8	NI	−	1.692	<500	+	+
9	3-methyl butanal	590-86-3	1.922	520	+	−
10	1-Butanol	71-36-3	1.943	528	+	+
11	3-hydroxy-2-Butanone	513-86-0	2.209	616	+	+
12	Ethanol, 2-(1-methylethoxy)-	109-59-1	2.269	629	+	+
13	3-methyl-1-Butanol	123-51-3	2.376	651	+	+
14	2-methyl-1-Butanol	137-32-6	2.418	659	+	+
15	Dimethyl disulfide	624-92-0	2.526	681	+	+
16	Toluene	108-88-3	2.659	705	+	+
17	1,3-Butanediol	107-88-0	2.746	716	+	+
18	2,3-Butanediol	513-85-9	2.826	726	+	+
19	3-hydroxy-2-Butanone	513-86-0	2.878	733	+	+
20	Hexanal	66-25-1	2.994	748	+	+
21	Ethyl 2-methylbutyrate	7452-79-1	3.311	788	+	+
22	Ethylbenzene	100-41-4	3.494	809	+	+
23	1-Hexanol	111-27-3	3.510	810	+	+
24	m + p-Xylene	108-38-3 /106-42-3	3.592	819	+	+
25	2-Heptanone	110-43-0	3.724	832	+	+
26	2-Heptanol	543-49-7	3.823	842	+	+
27	o-Xilene	95-47-6	3.830	843	+	+
28	2-butoxy Ethanol	111-76-2	3.924	852	+	+
29	δ-3-Carene	13466-78-9	4.143	875	−	+
30	1R-α-Pinene	7785-70-8	4.246	885	+	+
31	NI	−	4.310	891	+	+
32	Camphene	79-92-5	4.391	900	+	+
33	Benzene, -1,2,4-trimethyl-	95-63-6	4.440	904	+	+
34	γ-Terpinene	99-85-4	4.458	906	+	+
35	2,4-dimethyl Decene	74421-03-7	4.473	907	+	+

[a] CAS = Chemical Abstract Service; [b] R_t absolute retention time; [c] I^T Retention indices of normal chain aliphatic on a CP-Sil8 CB column; NI = Not Identified.

Table 2. List of purgeable volatile components detected in external (A) and internal kernel (B) of "Coco de mer" fruit and their relative chemical abstract service (+ present; − absent) − second group (peaks number 36–70).

	Compound	CAS[a]	R_t^b	I^{Tc}	A	B
36	1,3,5-trimethyl benzene	108-67-8	4.522	912	+	+
37	Heptanol	53535-33-4	4.574	917	+	+
38	1,2,3-trimethyl Benzene	526-73-8	4.604	920	+	+
39	Sabinene	3387-41-5	4.654	924	+	+
40	Phenol	108-95-2	4.702	929	+	+
41	L-β-Pinene	18172-67-3	4.735	932	+	+
42	Furan, 2-pentyl-	3777-69-3	4.754	934	+	+
43	1-Ottanol, 2-methyl-	818-81-5	4.792	937	+	+
44	Benzene, -1,2,3-trimethyl-	526-73-8	4.858	943	+	+
45	3-Carene	13466-78-9	4.990	956	+	+
46	5-Undecene, 9-methyl-, (Z)-	74630-65-2	5.041	960	+	+
47	3-Caren-2-ol	none	5.173	973	+	+
48	Limonene	138-86-3	5.256	981	+	+
49	Eucalyptol	470-82-6	5.307	985	+	+
50	1-Octene	111-66-0	5.396	994	−	+
51	α-Terpinene	99-85-4	5.553	1008	+	+
52	1-Octanol	111-87-5	5.636	1016	+	+
53	1-Octyn-3-ol, 4-ethyl-	5877-42-9	5.817	1033	+	+
54	β-Terpinene	99-86-5	5.874	1039	+	+
55	Phenol, 2-methoxy- (guaiacol)	90-05-1	5.920	1043	+	+
56	Ethyl caprilate	106-32-1	5.946	1046	+	+
57	Fenchone	1195-79-5	5.969	1048	+	+
58	1,9,-Nonanediol	3937-56-2	6.003	1051	+	+
59	3-Undecyne	60212-30-8	6.018	1052	+	+
60	d-Isothuyone	471-15-8	6.095	1060	+	+
61	Thujone	546-80-5	6.213	1071	−	+
62	Benzenamine, N-etil-	103-69-5	6.317	1081	+	+
63	1,7-Nonadiene, 4,8-dimethyl-	62108-28-5	6.431	1091	+	+
64	Camphor	76-22-2	6.560	1104	+	+
65	p-Menthone	89-80-5	6.663	1114	+	+
66	Pinocamphone	547-60-4	6.714	1119	+	+
67	2H-Benzocyclohepten-2-one, decahydro-4α-methyl-, *trans*	55103-64-5	6.772	1124	+	+
68	exo-Isocamphanone	3649-86-3	6.844	1131	+	+
69	Ethyl laurate	106-33-2	6.878	1135	+	+
70	NI	−	6.919	1139	+	+

[a] CAS = Chemical Abstract Service; [b] R_t absolute retention time; [c] I^T Retention indices of normal chain aliphatic on a CP-Sil8 CB column; NI = Not Identified.

Table 3. List of purgeable volatile components detected in external (A) and internal kernel (B) of "Coco de mer" fruit and their relative chemical abstract service (+ present; − absent) − third group (peaks number 71–100).

	Compound	CAS[a]	R_t^b	I^{Tc}	A	B
71	β-Citronnellol	106-22-9	7.018	1148	+	+
72	NI	−	7.365	1182	+	+
73	Hydrocinammic alcohol	122-97-4	7.380	1184	+	+
74	Ocimene	2974-87-2	7.407	1186	−	+
75	Benzothiazole	95-16-9	7.424	1188	+	+
76	Bornyl acetate	76-49-3	7.836	1216	+	+
77	NI	−	7.872	1217	+	+
78	Anethol	104-46-1	7.906	1219	+	+
79	Benzene, ethyl-1,2-dimethoxy-	none	8.118	1261	+	+
80	Eugenol	97-53-0	8.495	1302	+	−
81	Tetradecanal	124-25-4	8.911	1347	+	+
82	2(4H)-Benzofuranone	17092-92-1	9.180	1376	+	+
83	5,9-Undecadien-2-one, 6,10-dimethyl	689-67-8	9.242	1382	+	−
84	NI	−	9.290	1388	+	+
85	NI	−	9.439	1404	−	+
86	Pentadecanol	629-76-5	9.561	1419	+	−
87	NI	−	9.617	1425	+	+
88	p-n-Amyloxyphenol	18979-53-8	9.643	1428	+	+
89	Butylated hydroxytoluene	128-37-0	9.760	1442	+	+
90	4-Carene	none	9.811	1449	−	+
91	NI	−	10.140	1488	+	+
92	NI	−	10.204	1496	+	+
93	1-Decanol, 2-hexyl-	2425-77-6	10.292	1506	+	+
94	NI	−	10.584	1542	+	+
95	2-Undecene, 2,5-dimethyl	49622-16-4	10.635	1548	+	+
96	NI	−	10.793	1567	−	+
97	NI	−	10.800	1568	+	+
98	Butyl fumarate	105-75-9	10.910	1581	+	+
99	N-Acetylmethionina	65-82-7	10.917	1582	+	+
100	2-Nonenal	2463-53-8	11.081	1601	+	+

[a] CAS = Chemical Abstract Service; [b] R_t absolute retention time; [c] I^T Retention indices of normal chain aliphatic on a CP-Sil8 CB column; NI = Not Identified.

They represent the most therapeutic interesting class of the biogenic volatile compounds, showing relevant anti-inflammatory and anti-microbic activity for man and animals. Furthermore terpenoids are made use as constituents to prepare essential oils, medicinal essences of the international pharmacopoeia, to treat disturbs at bronchial level, as well as of rheumatic and neuralgic disturbs [45, 46]. The therapeutic effect is mainly due to their antioxidant activity [46]. Besides in the recent years it had demonstrated that this class of chemical compounds is active in the prevention of

Table 4. List of purgeable volatile components detected in external (A) and internal kernel (B) of "Coco de mer" fruit and their relative chemical abstract service (+ present; − absent) – first group (peaks number 101–117).

	Compound	CAS[a]	R_t^b	I^{Tc}	A	B
101	Nonal	111-84-2	11.195	1617	+	+
102	NI	–	11.208	1619	+	+
103	Cyclohexane, 1-(cyclohexylmethyl)-4-(methylethyl)-	54965-61-6	11.257	1625	+	+
104	NI	–	11.365	1640	+	+
105	Methyl Tetradecanoate, 2-metil-	55551-09-1	11.888	1711	–	+
106	NI	–	11.938	1717	–	+
107	Isopropyl myristate	110-27-0	12.104	1739	+	+
108	2,6,10,14-Hexadecatetraenoic acid, 3,7,11,15-tetramethyl-, methyl ester	none	12.221	1754	+	+
109	Cyclohexane, 3,4-bis(1-methyletenyl)-1,1-dimethyl-	61142-74-3	12.238	1756	+	+
110	Ethyl tridecanoate	28267-29-0	12.247	1757	+	+
111	β-Farnesene	18794-84-8	12.735	1824	+	+
112	Ethyl palmitate	628-97-7	13.252	1903	+	+
113	NI	–	13.286	1908	–	+
114	Ethyl linoleate	544-35-4	14.309	2065	+	+
115	2-Mercaptobenzothiazole	149-30-4	14.531	2103	+	+
116	Di(2-ethylhexyl)adipate	103-23-1	15.638	2287	+	+
117	NI	–	15.690	2296	+	+

[a] CAS = Chemical Abstract Service; [b] R_t absolute retention time; [c] I^T Retention indices of normal chain aliphatic on a CP-Sil8 CB column; NI = Not Identified.

arteriosclerosis, stroke and heart attack, inhibiting the low density lipoprotein (LDL) oxidation which is cause of these pathologies [47].

Among non-terpenic compounds, the remaining part of investigated volatile aroma reveals the presence of several saturated alcohols like ethanol, 1-butanol, 2- and 3-methylbutan-1-ol, 1-hexanol, 1- and 2-heptanol, 1-octanol, 2-methyloctan-1-ol together with some diols, aldehydes and ketons. Nine compounds (see comparative synoptic Tables 1, 2, 3 and 4) were only detected from internal pulp (sample B) whereas only four, the 3-methyl butanal, eugenol, 6,10-dimethyl undecadien-2-one and pentadecanol are present in external kernel (sample A). This indicate that these volatile molecules could not be detected because their very low concentrations below the instrumental detection limits. The presence in the "Coco de mer" flavour of some aldehydes, such as 3-methyl butanal, hexanal, 2-nonenal and tetradecanal can probably result from the exposure of coconut pulp to the ultraviolet light. In fact the unsaturated fatty acids inside the fruit are easily oxidized by ultraviolet light exposition to form aldehydic compounds. For example the hexanal is considered the predominant autoxidation byproduct of linoleic acid [48]. This component produce a so called off-flavour. Another off-flavour compound from oxidation of fats is the dimethyldisulfide [44], that is revealed both in external and internal pulp portions. Generally sulfur compounds, even in very small concentration, can influence the sensorial properties of a fruit aroma [49]. The alcohols (C2, C4-C9 and C15) found in the head space of double coco-nut mainly occurs naturally as products of fermentation processes and therefore their presence is an indicator of the fruit state preservation. However these alcoholic components are present in most of the more widespread fruits aroma. The only identified carbonylic compounds, further 3-methyl butanal, hexanal, 2-nonenal and tetradecanal, were the 3-hydroxy-2-butanone, 2(4H)-benzofuranone and 2-hepatnone in both samples and 6,10-dimethyl-5,9-undecadien-2-one, found only in the sample A. Among them the 3-hydroxybutan-2-one has been revealed in some fruits as the predominant compound and was found in smaller amount in several other tropical fruits such as cupuacu, sapota, cashew-apple, annona, guava and feijoa [49]. The ester fraction was represented by methyl ester of 2-methyltetradecanoate (absent in sample A), ethyl ester of 2-methylbutyrate, caprilate, laurate, tridecanoate, palmitate, linoleate and dibutyl ester of fumarate and isopropyl myristate. The same alcohols, carbonyls and esters were also found as characteristic compounds in aroma flavour of cocumis melo [48]. Arenes and heterocyclic fraction, like toluene, alkyl-benzenes, buthylated hydroxytoluene and n-ethyl aniline, were characterized in the analysed samples. The alkyl arenes are also reported by Narain *et al.* in their study on caja-umbu (Spondias sp.) fruits [50]. Seeing that the biogenic origin of these compounds are not definite, it is supposed probably to come from ubiquitous anthropogenic pollution contamination. The only identified nitrogen and sulfur compound, benzothiazole (in both samples A and B), was also found in Parinari fruit flavour study by Joulain *et al.* [51] as well as the alkyl furans and alkenes in volatile fraction in caja-umbu fruits [50]. Four volatile flavour components are diols with 4, 5 and 9 carbon atom skeleton respectively 1,3- and 2,3-butanediol, 2-methyl-1,3-pentanediol and 1,9-nonanediol. Unfortunately, on our knowledge, there have been no reports concerning these specific analytes about their presence on fruit aroma. Only the octane-1,3-diol and its derivatives was identified by Beuerle *et al.* as a natural apple constituent [52]. The 2,3-butane diol isomers were also identified as volatile compounds in Baga wine by Rocha *et al.* [53], as well as phenolic compounds like phenol and methoxy phenol (guaiacol). Although the diols are generally considered to be intermediates of fatty acid metabolism, their biosynthesis is discussed controversially [52].

Semi quantitative analysis show generally a total amounts of volatile analytes, measured as total ion counts, smaller in the coco-nut external kernel (sample A) than in internal pulp (sample B) and their relative abundances change, as can be seen by comparing the of chromatographic profiles peak area (see Fig. 2). In the internal pulp the upper chromatogram of Fig. 2 put in evidence a remarkable and clear increase of the peaks related to alcoholic compounds (like ethanol, 1-butanol, 3-methyl-1-butanol, 1-hexanol, 2-heptanol and 4-ethyl-1-octin-3-ol), to ester fraction (like methyl ester of 2-methyltetradecanoate and ethyl ester of palmitate) and to alkane (like 2-methyl butane). Interestingly a clear increase in the same fruit pulp part of one monoterpenic and sesquiterpene species, (limonene and β-farnesene), becomes present besides p-n-amyloxyphenol. Significant decrease of pinocamphone, 2,3-butandiol, 2-methyl octanol and benzothiazole has been observed, accompanied by a constant concentration of n-ethyl aniline, anethol and 3-hydroxy-2-butanone.

5 Conclusions

The main goal of the present study is to complete a previous chemical characterization by a GC/MS analytical investigation of the "Coco de mer" fruits. In fact, despite "Coco de mer" is the symbol of the Seychelles Islands, the literature concerning the chemical characterization of such a kind of coconut is still very limited. In our knowledge, our data (collected by HS-SPME and GC/MS techniques) are the first experimental attempt in order to determine the volatile organic fraction flavour of "Coco de mer" coconut pulp. The flavour profiles collected from the two different portions of the external kernel and internal pulp shown the presence of 117 volatile chemical compounds, 96 were positively identified, while 21 were only tentatively identified and reported in the synoptic Tables 1, 2, 3 and 4 as NI acronym. The semi-quantitative approach adopted in this preliminary study allows to establish the relative concentration of different biological volatile organic compounds for each fruit parts under investigation. The presence of cyclic monoterpene hydrocarbons with two double chains (α-, β- and γ-terpinenes, sabinene, and other) is important because these compounds are shown to have very high antioxidant activity (80–98%) [54]. Finally, computational method was used to extract individual component mass spectra from GC/MS data files by using the AMDIS version 2.65 software. With such a procedure we are able to construct our own mass spectra library determining retention indices for chemical compounds of our interest in the used specific experimental conditions. Our mass spectra database building up is still in progress and recently has been uploaded in order to consider a wider range of possible application not only in analytical chemistry but also in physical chemistry and astrochemistry [55–58].

Acknowledgments. Prof. Gian Gualberto Volpi died during the preparation of the manuscript. This work and our future endeavours are dedicated to him, whose example, intellectual honesty and genuine love of chemistry continue to inform our scientific life. Financial support by the "VIS MEDICATRIX NATURAE s.r.l." – Marradi (FI – Italy) is gratefully acknowledged by the authors.

References

1. Savage, A.J.P., Ashton, P.S.: Biotropica **15**, 15–25 (1983)
2. Fleischmann, K., Edward, P.J., Ramseier, D., Kollmann, J.: Afr. J. Ecol. **43**, 291–301 (2005)
3. Rist, L., Kaiser-Bunbury, C.N., Fleischer-Dogley, F., Edwards, P., Bunbury, N., Ghazoul, J.: Forest Ecol. Manage. **260**, 2224–2231 (2010)
4. Falcinelli, S., Giorgini, M., Sebastiani, B.: Applied Engineering Sciences. In: Deng, W. (ed.) Taylor & Francis Group, London, Chap. 19, pp. 99–104 (2015). ISBN: 978-1-138-02649-0
5. Falcinelli, S., Bettoni, M., Giorgini, F., Giorgini, M., Sebastiani, B.: Chemical character-ization of "Coco de Mer" (Lodoicea Maldivica) fruit: phytosterols and fatty acids composition. In: Gervasi, O., Murgante, B., Misra, S., Gavrilova, Marina L., Rocha, A.M.A.C., Torre, C., Taniar, D., Apduhan, Bernady O. (eds.) ICCSA 2015. LNCS, vol. 9156, pp. 308–323. Springer, Cham (2015). doi:10.1007/978-3-319-21407-8_23
6. Cappelletti, D., Bartocci, A., Grandinetti, F., et al.: Chem. Eur. J. **21**, 6234–6240 (2015)

7. Cappelletti, D., Candori, P., Falcinelli, S., Albertì, M., Pirani, F.: Chem. Phys. Lett. **545**, 14–20 (2012)
8. Brunetti, B., Candori, P., Cappelletti, D., et al.: Chem. Phys. Lett. **539–540**, 19–23 (2012)
9. Balucani, N., Bartocci, A., Brunetti, B., Candori, P., et al.: Chem. Phys. Lett. **546**, 34–39 (2012)
10. Falcinelli, S., Fernandez-Alonso, F., Kalogerakis, K., Zare, R.N.: Mol. Phys. **88**, 663–672 (1996)
11. Tosi, P., Correale, R., Lu, W., et al.: Phys. Rev. Lett. **82**, 450–452 (1999)
12. Falcinelli, S., Bartocci, A., Cavalli, S., Pirani, F., Vecchiocattivi, F.: Chem. Eur. J. **22**, 764–771 (2016)
13. Balucani, N., Leonori, F., Nevrly, V., et al.: Chem. Phys. Lett. **602**, 58–62 (2014)
14. Cavallotti, C., Leonori, F., Balucani, N., Nevrly, V., et al.: J. Phys. Chem. Lett. **5**, 4213–4218 (2014)
15. Leonori, F., Balucani, N., Nevrly, V., Bergeat, A., et al.: J. Phys. Chem. C Nanomater. Interfaces **119**, 14632–14652 (2015)
16. Vanuzzo, G., Balucani, N., Leonori, F., Stranges, D., et al.: J. Phys. Chem. Lett. **7**, 1010–1015 (2016)
17. Falcinelli, S., Pirani, F., Vecchiocattivi, F.: Atmosphere **6**, 299–317 (2015)
18. Falcinelli, S., Rosi, M., Candori, P., Farrar, J.M., et al.: ICCSA 2014, Part I. LNCS 8579, pp. 554–570 (2014). doi:10.1007/978-3-319-09144-0_38
19. Falcinelli, S., Bartocci, A., Candori, P., Pirani, F., Vecchiocattivi, F.: Chem. Phys. Lett. **614**, 171–175 (2014)
20. Falcinelli, S., Candori, P., Bettoni, M., Pirani, F., Vecchiocattivi, F.: J. Phys. Chem. A **118**, 6501–6506 (2014)
21. Brunetti, B.G., Candori, P., Falcinelli, S., Pirani, F., Vecchiocattivi, F.: J. Chem. Phys. **139**, 164305 (2013)
22. Eberlin, L.S., Tibshirani, R.J., Zhang, J., Longacre, T.A., Berry, G.J., Bingham, D.B., Norton, J.A., Zare, R.N., Poultsides, G.A.: Proc. Natl. Acad. Sci. U.S.A. **111**, 2436–2441 (2014)
23. Alagia, M., Bodo, E., Decleva, P., et al.: Phys. Chem. Chem. Phys. **15**, 1310–1318 (2013)
24. Falcinelli, S., Rosi, M., Candori, P., Farrar, J.M., et al.: Planet. Space Sci. **99**, 149–157 (2014)
25. Schio, L., Li, C., Monti, S., Salén, P., Yatsyna, V., Feifel, R., et al.: Phys. Chem. Chem. Phys. **17**, 9040–9048 (2015)
26. Pei, L., Carrascosa, E., Yang, N., et al.: J. Phys. Chem. Lett. **6**, 1684–1689 (2015)
27. Rapporti ISTISAN 97/23: Multiresidue analytical procedures for pesticides residues in vegetable products. Italian National Institute for Health, Rome (1997). (ISSN 1123-2117)
28. Alagia, M., Candori, P., Falcinelli, S., Lavollée, M., Pirani, F., Richter, R., Stranges, S., Vecchiocattivi, F.: J. Chem. Phys. **126**, 201101 (2007)
29. Lombardi, A., Faginas Lago, N., Laganà, A., et al.: ICCSA 2012, Part I. LNCS 7333, pp. 387–400 (2012). doi:10.1007/978-3-642-31125-3_30
30. Falcinelli, S., Rosi, M., Candori, P., Vecchiocattivi, F., et al.: ICCSA 2013. Part I, Lecture Notes in Computer Science LNCS **7971**, 69–83 (2013). doi:10.1007/978-3-642-39637-3_6
31. Teixidor, M.M., Pirani, F., Candori, P., et al.: Chem. Phys. Lett. **379**, 139–146 (2003)
32. Alagia, M., Biondini, F., Brunetti, B.G., Candori, P., et al.: J. Chem. Phys. **121**, 10508–10512 (2004)
33. Alagia, M., Candori, P., Falcinelli, S., Lavollée, M., et al.: Phys. Chem. Chem. Phys. **12**, 5389–5395 (2010)
34. Alagia, M., Brunetti, B.G., Candori, P., et al.: J. Chem. Phys. **120**, 6980–6984 (2004)
35. Abidi, S.L.: J. Chromatogr. A **935**, 173–201 (2001)

36. Falcinelli, S., Giorgini, M., Sebastiani, B.: Abstract of Papers of The American Chemical Society, vol. 248, Meeting Abstract: 244-AGFD - 248th National Meeting of the American-Chemical-Society (ACS), San Francisco, CA (USA), August 13, 2014. ISSN: 0065-7727

37. Van Den Dool, H., Kratz, P.D.: J. Chromatogr. A **11**, 463–471 (1963)

38. Stein, S.E., Scott, D.R.: J. Am. Soc. Mass Spectrom. **5**, 859–866 (1994)

39. Brunetti, B., Candori, P., Falcinelli, S., Lescop, B., et al.: Eur. Phys. J. D **38**, 21–27 (2006)

40. Alagia, M., Candori, P., Falcinelli, S., Pirani, F., et al.: Phys. Chem. Chem. Phys. **13**, 8245–8250 (2011)

41. Alagia, M., Callegari, C., Candori, P., et al.: J. Chem. Phys. **136**, 204302 (2012)

42. Falcinelli, S., Rosi, M., Cavalli, S., Pirani, F., Vecchiocattivi, F.: Chem. Eur. J. **22**, 12518–12526 (2016)

43. Pool, W.G., Leeuw, J.W., van de Graaf, B.J.: Mass Spectrom. **32**, 438–443 (1997)

44. Di Cesare, L.F., d'Angelo, V., Testoni, A.: Industrie Alimentari XXXIV, pp. 1152–1157 (1995)

45. Kohlert, C., van Rensen, I., Marz, R., Schindler, G., Graefe, E.U., Veit, M.: Planta Med. **66**, 495–505 (2000)

46. Graßmann, J., Hippeli, S., Vollmann, R., Elstner, E.F.: J. Agric. Food Chem. **51**, 7576–7582 (2003)

47. Graßmann, J., Hippeli, S., Spitzenberger, R., Elstner, E.F.: Phytomedicine **12**, 416–423 (2005)

48. Larsen, T.O.: Int. Dairy J. **8**, 883–887 (1998)

49. Alves, G.L., Franco, M.R.B.: J. Chromatogr. A **985**, 297–301 (2003)

50. Narain, N., de Sousa Galvão, M., Madruga, M.S.: Food Chem. **102**, 726–731 (2007)

51. Joulain, D., Casazza, A., Laurent, R., Portier, D., Guillamon, N., Pandya, R., et al.: J. Agr. Food Chem. **52**, 2322–2325 (2004)

52. Beuerle, T., Schreier, P., Brunerie, P., Bicchi, C., Schwab, W.: Phytochemistry **43**, 145–149 (1996)

53. Rocha, S.M., Rodrigues, F., Coutinho, P., Delgadillo, I., Coimbra, M.A.: Anal. Chim. Acta **513**, 257–262 (2004)

54. Misharina, T.A., Polshkov, A.N.: Appl. Biochem. Microb. **41**, 610–618 (2005)

55. Biondini, F., Brunetti, B.G., Candori, P., et al.: J. Chem. Phys. **122**, 164307 (2005)

56. Falcinelli, S.: Acta Phys. Pol., A **131**(1), 112–116 (2017). doi:10.12693/APhysPolA.131.112

57. Falcinelli, S., Candori, P., Pirani, F., Vecchiocattivi, F.: Phys. Chem. Chem. Phys. **19**(10), 6933–6944 (2017). doi:10.1039/C7CP00614D

58. Sebastiani, B., Giorgini, M., Falcinelli, S.: Chemistry & Biodiversity (2017, in press). doi:10.1002/cbdv.201700109

Automated Simulation of Gas-Phase Reactions on Distributed and Cloud Computing Infrastructures

Sergio Rampino[1]([✉]), Loriano Storchi[2], and Antonio Laganà[3]

[1] Scuola Normale Superiore, Piazza dei Cavalieri 7, 05126 Pisa, Italy
sergio.rampino@sns.it
[2] Dipartimento di Farmacia, Università degli Studi 'G. D'Annunzio',
Via dei Vestini 31, 66100 Chieti, Italy
loriano@storchi.org
[3] Dipartimento di Chimica, Biologia e Biotecnologie,
Università degli Studi di Perugia, Via Elce di Sotto 8, 06123 Perugia, Italy
lag@dyn.unipg.it

Abstract. The Grid Empowered Molecular Simulator GEMS enabling fully ab initio virtual experiments through rigorous theoretical and computational procedures has been upgraded with a novel scheme for automated generation of three-atom potential energy surfaces. The scheme is based on a space-reduced formulation of the so-called bond-order variables allowing for a balanced representation of the attractive and repulsive regions of a diatom configuration space. The deployment and use of the resulting upgraded machinery on distributed and cloud computing infrastructures is also discussed.

Keywords: Molecular simulator · Reaction dynamics · Potential energy surface · Bond order · Distributed and cloud computing

1 Introduction

The recent evolution of Grid technologies has fostered the formation of Virtual Organizations (VO, http://www.egi.eu/community/vos/) and Virtual Research Communities (VRC, http://www.egi.eu/community/vos/vrcs/) within EGI (the European Grid Infrastructure, http://www.egi.eu/). In the molecular science environment this process has led to the formation of the COMPCHEM VO (https://www3.compchem.unipg.it/compchem/) [1] and of the Chemistry, Molecular & Materials Science and Technology (CMMST) VRC [2].

The specific goals of the CMMST VRC are those of meeting the user requirements for an efficient access and use of high throughput (HTC) and high performance (HPC) computing resources, enabling the composition of higher level of complexity applications through the sharing of hardware and software [3], developing a new collaborative model of carrying out research grounded on a quality evaluation of the work done for the community [4]. This is achieved

© Springer International Publishing AG 2017
O. Gervasi et al. (Eds.): ICCSA 2017, Part III, LNCS 10406, pp. 60–73, 2017.
DOI: 10.1007/978-3-319-62398-6_5

by assembling a set of inter-linkable applications useful to build higher level of complexity multi-scale computational procedures, exploit the tools offered by EGI to support the activities of a distributed computing community and further develop applications and tools specific of its partners. Such articulation is meant to enable the selection of the provided resources (from personal systems to supercomputers) and services (from number crunching to massive data handling on heterogeneous platforms) [5,6]. The quality of service (QoS) parameters of the products provided and of the resources used are utilized also to build a metrics on which grounding the rewarding of the work done for the community through a credit acquisition/redemption system.

The most advanced community service offered by CMMST to its members leveraging on the computing platforms accessible through COMPCHEM is the so called Grid Empowered Molecular Simulator (GEMS) [7]. GEMS is a distributed workflow that gathers together the codes implemented by the members of the community bearing the complementary competences necessary to assemble the most accurate treatment of the tackled molecular problem. As recently quoted in the EGI.eu website under the headings "What happens when molecules collide" (https://www.egi.eu/use-cases/research-stories/) GEMS is the simulator of election when one needs to compute accurately and effectively the efficiency of processes in which molecules collide to react, dissociate, exchange energy and deform. Using GEMS, as will be listed in some detail later, applications to interstellar clouds, atmospheric entry, energy transfer processes, materials' properties, renewable energies utilization, combustions, etc. have been assembled for distributed execution [8–10].

In the present paper we discuss recent upgrades of GEMS for its use on distributed and cloud computing infrastructures. In Sect. 2 the structure and workflow of GEMS is briefly reviewed. In Sect. 3 we discuss some issues related to a Cloud OpenStack implementation of GEMS. In Sect. 4 we detail a novel procedure for automated generation of the PES withing this workflow. In Sect. 5 we illustrate calculations on a prototypical ($H + H_2$) study case. In Sect. 6 we draw some conclusions and outline perspectives for future work.

2   Structure and Workflow of GEMS

The molecular simulator GEMS has been described in detail elsewhere [5,7,11,12], especially with a focus on its use for the a priori modeling of elementary reactive processes [13–16]. We thus limit here to briefly review its foundations.

GEMS leverages on the Grid infrastructure of EGI in which a synergistic use of CMMST information is made. In particular, GEMS manages a workflow that is articulated into four modules (Interaction, Fitting, Dynamics, and Statistics) featuring a high degree of interoperability thanks to the definition of the common data formats Q5Cost/D5Cost [17,18] (see a scheme in Fig. 1). The four blocks are part of a workflow designed to enable the coordinated execution of in-house developed and commercial codes on the distributed platform of the European Grid Infrastructure (EGI) [19] by properly selecting compute resources among the high-performance computing (HPC) and high-throughput computing (HTC) available ones. In particular, the first module (Interaction) deals with the sampling, through high-level electronic-structure calculations, of the potential energy surface (PES) on which a chemical reaction takes place. In the second module (Fitting) an analytic representation of the PES is obtained through fitting or interpolation procedures using the data produced in Interaction. In the third module (Dynamics) dynamical calculations are performed on the PES generated by Fitting. In the fourth module (Statistics), the required statistical averaging is performed on the outcome of Dynamics to get estimates of experimental observables such as cross sections and reaction rate coefficients.

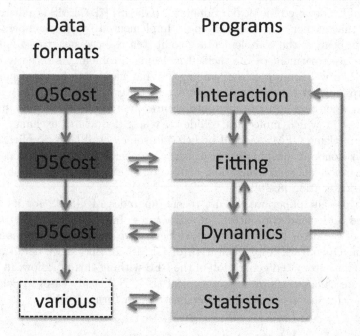

Fig. 1. Scheme of the workflow of the molecular simulator GEMS. Data formats fostering interoperability among the codes used in the various modules are also reported.

GEMS has been successfully used to study the dynamics and compute the reactive probabilities/cross sections and rate coefficients (through the J-shifting approximation [20]) of atom-diatom systems such as $H + H_2$ [18], $Li + FH$ [16], $N + N_2$ [21,22], $O + O_2$ [23,24] and $OH + CO$ [25–27], where PESs were already available. However, while electronic-structure and fitting programs are already incorporated into GEMS, only quite recently an automated procedure for a full generation of the PES including an optimal choice of geometries at which ab initio calculations should be carried out has been devised [28] and applied to the study of the astrochemical process $C + CH^+$ [29,30].

3   A Cloud OpenStack Implementation of GEMS

GEMS and its blocks are a typical distributed computing procedures that can exploit the typical utilities of a cloud environment [31] like producing, transmitting, archiving, reusing on pre-existing and configurable resources made available on Internet by other users, centers and facilities. A characteristic of the cloud is the fact that the resources are not ad hoc configured by the providers for a specific user. However, they are quickly and conveniently made available to the user out of a pool of shared resources through automated procedures following its specific requests. At the end of its application the user releases the resources which become available for further use. There are three main service typologies in cloud computing [32]:

- SaaS (Software as a Service) - provision of computer programs installed on a remote server most often through a web server;
- DaaS (Data as a Service) - provision of data with modalities typical of local disks;
- HaaS (Hardware as a Service) - provision of compute service for elaboration of data supplied by and returned to the user;

that the new (cloud) version of GEMS targets. This is that the various blocks of GEMS (and within each block its different components) are articulated in a way that codes developed by different users can be inserted as SaaS and the data they produce can be offered as DaaS. Moreover, when the GEMS procedure includes an interaction with the experiment (say for input/checks to/of computer simulations) also HaaS is activated. This differentiates the cloud approach of GEMS, being implemented at present, from its previous grid computing oriented one targeted to distributed computing of the different components of the simulator. The new cloud implementation of GEMS will address also two other important services:

- PaaS (Platform as a Service) - the execution is given in charge, as remote, to a software platform made of various services;
- IaaS (Infrastructure as a Service) - both virtual and hardware (servers, networking, memory, storage, backup, etc.) resources are made available upon request when needed.

The cloud IaaS provides the user with resources as they were implemented on "standard" systems (personal servers and peripherals). Within this perspective using OpenStack a IaaS for GEMS is being implemented for use by the local Chemistry and Physics community that will be shared between INFN, the University of Perugia and the University of Chieti and will be used within the School on Open Science Cloud for training the students of ITN-EJD-642294_TCCM (4–10 June 2017).

The resulting Cloud enabled GEMS application is able to automatically select and instantiate a given set of resources (i.e. number of Virtual Machines) as a function of the molecular system dimension via the OpenStack REST API [33].

Almost all the components of the workflow can easily distributed in an embarrassingly parallel approach [34], without the explicit need for high throughput and very low latency network infrastructures such as for instance InfiniBand, or different kind of specialized hardware such as GPGPUs. However, in future releases one may try to explore also the support for Docker containers, that provide an easy and efficient way to exploit specialized hardware (see for instance [35]).

The infrastructure where a first cloud enabled version of GEMS has been deployed is made of three main hardware resources geographically distributed in three research centers, namely: Perugia Physics Department (PPD), Perugia Chemistry Department (PCD) and Chieti Pharmacy Department (CPD). The infrastructure is based on OpenStack Mitaka release. The central controller (the so called Cloud Master) is installed at the PPD (where all the main components of OpenStack have been deployed and configured) while all the Nova Compute Nodes are distributed among the three centers.

4 Automated Generation of the PES

One of the most common approaches in generating a single-valued potential energy surface (PES) for use in dynamics calculations of atom-diatom exchange reactions of the type $A + BC \rightarrow AB + C$, is to sample the potential energy (the energy of a selected electronic state) computed with high level ab initio methods for a finite number of nuclear configurations (geometries) and to fit or interpolate the obtained set of energies with an appropriate analytic formulation. Ideally, ab initio energies should be computed for a large number of geometries on a dense grid sampling the available configuration space and allowing to reproduce all of the topological features of the PES such as asymptotic atom-diatom channels, saddles and wells. However, ab initio calculations are often computationally highly demanding, and some of them might require additional care as might have not converged to the desired electronic state. Therefore, a wise choice of an as small as possible set of geometries optimally sampling configuration space turns out often to be crucial.

In the following, we shall focus on the two topics of configuration-space sampling (i.e., choosing the set of geometries) and that of fitting/interpolating the obtained values.

A. Configuration-space sampling. A common way of sampling the three-atom configuration space for $A + BC \rightarrow AB + C$ reactions is to use the following internal coordinates:

- the interatomic distance of the reactant diatomic (r_1)
- the interatomic distance of the product diatomic (r_2)
- the angle formed by these two distances (ϕ)

and to adopt regular grids defined on these coordinates.

One of us has recently published a more efficient scheme, namely the space-reduced bond-order (SRBO) scheme [28], which introduces a diatom-tailored force-based metric to better sample the configuration space of the diatoms. In the SRBO scheme, use is made of properly defined diatomic bond-order (BO) variables $n = \exp[-\beta(r - r_e)]$ (with r being the diatom internuclear distance and r_e its equilibrium value) where β is relaxed so as to reach a desired ratio f between the sampled attractive $(0 < n < 1)$ and repulsive $(1 < n < \exp[\beta r_e])$ regions of the diatom configuration space. A proper tuning of f and the adoption of regular grids in SRBO variables allows for a wise, process-oriented selection of geometries providing a small, most informative set of electronic energies [28].

Whereas in principle one may define the SRBO grid on the whole diatom configuration space ranging from $n = 0$ (infinite distance) to $n = \exp[\beta r_e]$ (collapsed atoms), it turns useful to introduce two boundary values n_{min} and n_{max} to avoid including points in the highly repulsive regions (not accessible to the dynamics) or the long-range weakly attractive potential regions. Diatom tailored values of n_{min} and n_{max} can be obtained by the equilibrium property (equilibrium distance r_e, dissociation energy D_e and force constant k_e) of the considered diatom through a Morse modeling of the potential by setting the parameters V_{fact} and V_{thrs}. V_{fact} sets a boundary where the Morse potential is exactly V_{fact} times the dissociation energy. V_{thrs} sets a boundary where the Morse potential has reached the dissociation energy within a certain threshold. The reader is referred to Ref. [28] for further details on these aspects.

Accordingly, the workflow for setting up a one-dimensional SRBO grid for a given diatom is as follows:

- compute r_e, D_e and k_e (this is done trough a geometry-optimization calculation) for the diatom in the proper electronic state
- choose suitable values for f, V_{fact}, and V_{thrs} (space-ratio and bounding parameters)
- get a regular grid in the considered segments of $n = \exp[-\beta(r - r_e)]$

The full three-dimensional SRBO grid (on which ab initio calculations should be carried out for studying reaction A + BC $\rightarrow$ AB + C) can then be constructed by the two one-dimensional SRBO grids for the reactant and product diatoms and a regular grid in the angular coordinate ϕ.

B. Fitting or interpolation. Once the three-dimensional SRBO grid has been set up, ab initio calculations have to be carried out yielding the energy of the selected electronic state at each point of the SRBO grid. The obtained set of energies is ready to be either fit or interpolated with a suitable analytic functional form. Aguado and Paniagua have made available a code (GFIT3C) [36] for fitting a set of two-body and three-body ab initio energies with the Aguado-Paniagua functional form [37]. Another successful approach is that based on the so-called modified Shepard (local) interpolation [38,39], whereby the potential energy is written as a weighed sum of second-order Taylor expansions around a set of ab initio energies (note that for this the second order derivatives of the electronic energies are required and a suitable ab initio method should be chosen).

Summary. The workflow for the above devised procedure can be summarized as follows. Once the desired electronic states have been chosen for the possible atoms, diatoms and the triatom of the A + BC reactive system, the following steps are performed:

1. Compute two-body equilibrium properties (r_e, D_e, k_e) of the reactant and product diatoms
2. Set f, V_{fact}, V_{thrs} and set up two one-dimensional SRBO grids for these diatoms
3. Set up a regular grid on the angular coordinate ϕ and assemble the full three-dimensional SRBO grid
4. Compute two-body and three-body electronic energies at the points of the three-dimensional SRBO grid
5. Fit or interpolate the computed energies to get an analytic representation of the PES

5   Calculations on the H + H_2 Prototype

To illustrate how the above scheme works on a real case, we report in this section calculations on the H + H_2 prototypical system.

Computational details. Configuration-space sampling was performed according to the SRBO scheme [28] (see later on for details). A computer program for generating one-dimensional SRBO grids starting from input parameters r_e, D_e, k_e, V_{fact}, V_{thrs}, and f is made available.[1]

Ab initio calculations were carried out at full configuration-interaction (FCI) level of theory with the MOLPRO package [40] version 2010.1 using Dunning's correlation-consistent basis sets cc-pVTZ (hereafter VTZ) [41].

The AP fit was carried out using the GFIT3C program [36], employing a 6th-degree polynomial fit for the two-body term and a 9th-degree polynomial fit for the three-body term. The correct permutational symmetry was ensured by setting input parameter INDICE = 1 (specifying an A_3 system as opposed to AB_2 or ABC, with A, B and C labelling the three atoms).

Reactive scattering calculations on the H + H_2 → H_2 + H atom-exchange reaction for total angular momentum $J = 0$ and total-energy range 0.4–1.4 eV were carried out within a time-independent (TI) hyperspherical-coordinate formalism as implemented in the ABC program [42] by setting input parameters emax = 2.4 eV (maximum internal energy in any channel), jmax = 50 (maximum rotational quantum number in any channel), rmax = 12.0 a_0 (maximum hyperradius) and mtr = 150 (number of log-derivative propagation sectors).

---

[1] A Fortran computer program for constructing SRBO grids is available at http://www.srampino.com/code.html#Pestk or upon request to info@srampino.com.

A typical set of input data adopted for the ABC code is given in Table 1.

Table 1. Typical input parameters adopted for the present TI calculations.

Total angular momentum quantum number	0
Triatomic parity eigenvalue	1
Diatomic parity eigenvalue	1
Maximum internal energy in any channel (eV)	2.4
Maximum rotational quantum number of any channel	50
Helicity truncation parameter	0
Maximum hyperradius (bohr)	12.0
Number of log derivative propagation sectors	150
Initial scattering energy (eV)	0.4
Scattering energy increment (eV)	0.01
Total number of scattering energies	101
Maximum value of v for which output is required	0
Maximum value of j for which output is required	0

Results. For the three-body configuration-space sampling of H_3, an SRBO three-dimensional grid defined on internal coordinates r_1 and r_2 (two bond distances) and ϕ (the angle formed by the related bonds) was adopted. To the purpose of constructing the one-dimensional SRBO grids on r_1 and r_2, the FCI/VTZ values of $r_e = 1.7576$ a_0, $D_e = 0.1727$ E_H, $k_e = 0.3707$ $E_H a_0^{-2}$ were used. SRBO parameters were set to $V_{fact} = 2.0$, $V_{thrs} = 0.001$ and $f = N_a/N_r$, with N_a set to 6 and N_r set to 3 (this means 6 points in the attractive region and 3 in the repulsive region for a total number of 10 points, including the equilibrium geometry which is neither attractive nor repulsive). A regular grid of five values ranging from 180° (collinear configuration) to 60° in steps of 30° was set up for the angular coordinate ϕ.

Due to the symmetry of the system, for each angle only $\frac{(N_r+N_a+1)\times[(N_r+N_a+1)+1]}{2}$ rather than $(N_r + N_a + 1)^2$ grid points were computed (only the points for which $r_2 \leq r_1$). The FCI/VTZ saddle point ($r_1 = r_2 = 1.7576$ a_0, $\phi = 180°$) was also added to the ensemble of points. The corresponding final three-dimensional grid is made of $N = \frac{(N_r+N_a+1)\times[(N_r+N_a+1)+1]}{2} \times 5 + 1 = 276$ points (where the plus one accounts for the just mentioned H_3 transition-state geometry). For illustrative purposes, the points of the fixed angle ($\phi = 180°$) two-dimensional SRBO grid in r_1 and r_2 are depicted in Fig. 2. As apparent from the figure, the distribution of the computed ab initio points indicates a fair coverage of the molecular geometry space by the SRBO grid used for the calculations, with a denser concentration in the high-gradient regions of the potential. The figure also shows the smoothness of the fitted PES and the occurrence of a barrier the strong the interaction region.

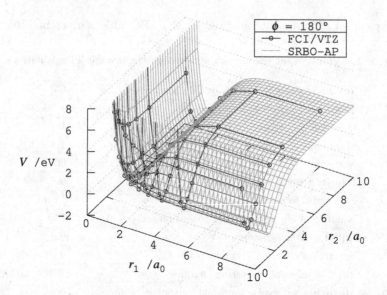

Fig. 2. Scheme of a fixed angle ($\phi = 180°$) two-dimensional SRBO grid in r_1 and r_2 used for the three-dimensional H_3 testcase. Computed FCI/VTZ points together with the SRBO-AP fitted surface are also shown. The energy zero is set to the bottom of the reactant valley.

To carry out the dynamical calculations we went through the next module of GEMS Dynamics. The $J = 0$ state-specific ($v = 0, j = 0$) quantum reactive probabilities for the H + H_2 exchange reaction on the generated PES were calculated for a grid of total energy values ranging from 0.4 eV to 1.4 eV in steps of 0.01 eV and are compared in Fig. 3 with results obtained using the

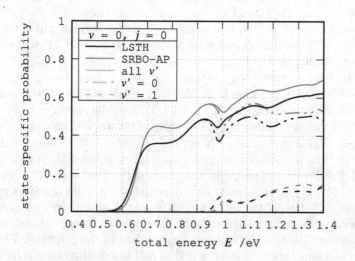

Fig. 3. $J = 0$ state-specific ($v = 0$, $j = 0$) reactive probabilities plotted as a function of the total energy E.

popular LSTH PES [43–46]. A resolution of these state-specific quantities in the product vibrational state (for the vibrational channels $v' = 0$ and $v' = 1$ open in the considered energy range) is also shown in the Figure. As apparent from the Figure, the PESs provide qualitatively similar reactive probabilities, with the SRBO-AP PES slightly reducing the threshold and enhancing reactivity at the near-threshold region, though being less reactive in the higher energies region.

6   Conclusions and Future Work

In this paper the innovative synergistic distributed computing model developed by the COMPCHEM VO and constituting the angular stone of the CMMST VRC is adopted for a full dimensional quantum study of the $H + H_2$ reaction. For this purpose the exploitation of a quality based combined access to HTC and HPC computing resources and of a workflow approach enabling the composition of complementary/competitive codes has allowed the implementation of an efficient computational machinery able to tackle higher level of complexity applications like the fully ab initio simulation of data produced in CMB experiments.

The calculations presented here focus on the benchmark $H + H_2$ system in order to illustrate as a single workflow implementation of GEMS can work on a combined HTC-HPC platform. More complex applications can be assembled using the machinery illustrated in the paper when the single modules of GEMS are used to describe more complex molecular processes, to evaluate more statistically averaged properties, to compose multiscale simulations of different atomistic granularity. In that case use of metaworkflows will be made to combine simpler (atomistic) workflows à la carte. In doing this particular care has to be put in handling members' data resources (ranging from experimental measurements recorded either in an individual laboratory or over large infrastructure facilities) specific to given analyses and simulation applications. These are usually stored in data structures and formats specific of the particular laboratory and will need to be ported to a uniform, open metadata format accompanied by robust ontologies.

For this reason next evolution of GEMS towards two-way communications between Computational and Experimental Chemists in the cloud will have to be implemented to facilitate the cooperative use of molecular simulations whose results can be further checked in experiments whose outcomes will fuel the design and running of simulations that can complement experiments to produce new research achievements. To this end a data management support that will facilitate re-usability and consequently reproducibility of the handled information using metadata will have to be developed. Experimental researchers produce a large volume of primary data in many different data formats that make it difficult to share data among researchers. Furthermore, storing and sharing primary experimental data might not be meaningful because it does not contain information about how it was obtained and processed. Accordingly, a system of metadata to primary data (particularly provenance information) will have to be designed and implemented in GEMS in the future.

Acknowledgments. The authors acknowledge financial support from EGI Inspire contract 261323, MIUR PRIN grant 2008 KJX4 SN_003, ESA ESTEC 21790/08/NL/HE and ITN-EJD-642294_TCCM. Thanks are also due to CINECA and COMPCHEM for computer time allocation, and to Mirko Mariotti, Giuseppe Vitillaro, Manuel Ciangottini and Daniele Spiga for technical support and helpful discussions.

References

1. Laganà, A., Riganelli, A., Gervasi, O.: On the structuring of the computational chemistry virtual organization COMPCHEM. In: Gavrilova, M., Gervasi, O., Kumar, V., Tan, C.J.K., Taniar, D., Laganá, A., Mun, Y., Choo, H. (eds.) ICCSA 2006. LNCS, vol. 3980, pp. 665–674. Springer, Heidelberg (2006). doi:10.1007/11751540_70

2. Costantini, A.: Laganà: towards a CMMST VRC virtual team project report. https://documents.egi.eu/public/RetrieveFile?docid=2221&version=1&filename=CMMSTVT-Report_Final_6.0.pdf. Accessed 28 Apr 2017

3. Costantini, A., Gervasi, O., Laganà, A.: A fault tolerant workflow for CPU demanding calculations. In: Murgante, B., Gervasi, O., Iglesias, A., Taniar, D., Apduhan, B.O. (eds.) ICCSA 2011. LNCS, vol. 6784, pp. 387–396. Springer, Heidelberg (2011). doi:10.1007/978-3-642-21931-3_30

4. Manuali, C., Laganà, A.: A grid credit system empowering virtual research communities sustainability. In: Murgante, B., Gervasi, O., Iglesias, A., Taniar, D., Apduhan, B.O. (eds.) ICCSA 2011. LNCS, vol. 6784, pp. 397–411. Springer, Heidelberg (2011). doi:10.1007/978-3-642-21931-3_31

5. Manuali, C., Laganà, A., Rampino, S.: GriF: a grid framework for a web service approach to reactive scattering. Comput. Phys. Commun. **181**(7), 1179–1185 (2010)

6. Manuali, C., Laganà, A.: GriF: a new collaborative framework for a web service approach to grid empowered calculations. Future Generation Comput. Syst. **27**(3), 315–318 (2011)

7. Laganà, A., Costantini, A., Gervasi, O., Faginas Lago, N., Manuali, C., Rampino, S.: COMPCHEM: progress towards GEMS a grid empowered molecular simulator and beyond. J. Grid Comput. **8**(4), 571–586 (2010)

8. Esposito, F., Garcia, E., Laganà, A.: Comparisons and scaling rules between N + N_2 and N_2 + N_2 collision induced dissociation cross sections from atomistic studies. Plasma Sources Sci. Technol. **26**(4), 045005 (2017)

9. Faginas Lago, N., Albertí, M., Laganà, A., Lombardi, A., Pacifici, L., Costantini, A.: The molecular stirrer catalytic effect in methane ice formation. In: Murgante, B., et al. (eds.) ICCSA 2014. LNCS, vol. 8579, pp. 585–600. Springer, Cham (2014). doi:10.1007/978-3-319-09144-0_40

10. Lombardi, A., Faginas-Lago, N., Pacifici, L., Grossi, G.: Energy transfer upon collision of selectively excited CO_2 molecules: state-to-state cross sections and probabilities for modeling of atmospheres and gaseous flows. J. Chem. Phys. **143**(3), 034307 (2015)

11. Rampino, S.: Workows and data models for atom diatom quantum reactive scattering calculations on the Grid. Ph.D. thesis, Università degli Studi di Perugia (2011)

12. Rampino, S., Faginas Lago, N., Laganà, A., Huarte-Larrañaga, F.: An extension of the grid empowered molecular simulator to quantum reactive scattering. J. Comput. Chem. **33**(6), 708–714 (2012)

13. Rampino, S., Skouteris, D., Laganà, A., Garcia, E.: A comparison of the isotope effect for the N + N$_2$ reaction calculated on two potential energy surfaces. In: Gervasi, O., Murgante, B., Laganà, A., Taniar, D., Mun, Y., Gavrilova, M.L. (eds.) ICCSA 2008. LNCS, vol. 5072, pp. 1081–1093. Springer, Heidelberg (2008). doi:10. 1007/978-3-540-69839-5_82

14. Laganà, A., Faginas Lago, N., Rampino, S., Huarte Larrañaga, F., García, E.: Thermal rate coefficients in collinear versus bent transition state reactions: the N + N$_2$ case study. Phys. Scr. **78**(5), 058116 (2008)

15. Rampino, S., Pirani, F., Garcia, E., Laganà, A.: A study of the impact of long range interactions on the reactivity of N + N$_2$ using the Grid Empowered Molecular Simulator GEMS. Int. J. Web Grid Serv. **6**(2), 196–212 (2010)

16. Laganà, A., Rampino, S.: A grid empowered virtual versus real experiment for the barrierless Li + FH → LiF + H reaction. In: Murgante, B., et al. (eds.) ICCSA 2014. LNCS, vol. 8579, pp. 571–584. Springer, Cham (2014). doi:10.1007/ 978-3-319-09144-0_39

17. Rossi, E., Evangelisti, S., Laganà, A., Monari, A., Rampino, S., Verdicchio, M., Baldridge, K.K., Bendazzoli, G.L., Borini, S., Cimiraglia, R., Angeli, C., Kallay, P., Lüthi, H.P., Ruud, K., Sanchez-Marin, J., Scemama, A., Szalay, P.G., Tajti, A.: Code interoperability and standard data formats in quantum chemistry and quantum dynamics: the Q5/D5Cost data model. J. Comput. Chem. **35**(8), 611–621 (2014)

18. Rampino, S., Monari, A., Rossi, E., Evangelisti, S., Laganà, A.: A priori modeling of chemical reactions on computational grid platforms: workflows and data models. Chem. Phys. **398**, 192–198 (2012)

19. EGI.eu: The European Grid Infrastructure. http://www.egi.eu/. Accessed 15 Mar 2017

20. Bowman, J.M.: Reduced dimensionality theory of quantum reactive scattering. J. Phys. Chem. **95**(13), 4960–4968 (1991)

21. Rampino, S., Skouteris, D., Laganà, A., García, E., Saracibar, A.: A comparison of the quantum state-specific efficiency of N + N$_2$ reaction computed on different potential energy surfaces. Phys. Chem. Chem. Phys. **11**, 1752–1757 (2009)

22. Rampino, S., Garcia, E., Pirani, F., Laganà, A.: Accurate quantum dynamics on grid platforms: some effects of long range interactions on the reactivity of N + N$_2$. In: Taniar, D., Gervasi, O., Murgante, B., Pardede, E., Apduhan, B.O. (eds.) ICCSA 2010. LNCS, vol. 6019, pp. 1–12. Springer, Heidelberg (2010). doi:10.1007/ 978-3-642-12189-0_1

23. Rampino, S., Skouteris, D., Laganà, A.: The O + O$_2$ reaction: quantum detailed probabilities and thermal rate coefficients. Theor. Chem. Acc. Theory Comput. Model. **123**(3/4), 249–256 (2009)

24. Rampino, S., Skouteris, D., Laganà, A.: Microscopic branching processes: the O + O$_2$ reaction and its relaxed potential representations. Int. J. Quantum Chem. **110**(2), 358–367 (2010)

25. Laganà, A., Garcia, E., Paladini, A., Casavecchia, P., Balucani, N.: The last mile of molecular reaction dynamics virtual experiments: the case of the OH(n = 1–10) + CO(j = 0–3) reaction. Faraday Discuss. **157**, 415–436 (2012)

26. Laganá, A., Balucani, N., Crocchianti, S., Casavecchia, P., Garcia, E., Saracibar, A.: An extension of the molecular simulator GEMS to calculate the signal of crossed beam experiments. In: Murgante, B., Gervasi, O., Iglesias, A., Taniar, D., Apduhan, B.O. (eds.) ICCSA 2011. LNCS, vol. 6784, pp. 453–465. Springer, Heidelberg (2011). doi:10.1007/978-3-642-21931-3_35

27. Garcia, E., Saracibar, A., Laganà, A.: On the anomaly of the quasiclassical product distributions of the OH + CO → H + CO_2 reaction. Theoret. Chem. Acc. **128**(4), 727–734 (2011)

28. Rampino, S.: Configuration-space sampling in potential energy surface fitting: a space-reduced bond-order grid approach. J. Phys. Chem. A **120**(27), 4683–4692 (2016)

29. Rampino, S., Pastore, M., Garcia, E., Pacifici, L., Laganà, A.: On the temperature dependence of the rate coefficient of formation of C_2^+ from C + CH^+. Mon. Not. R. Astron. Soc. **460**(3), 2368–2375 (2016)

30. Pacifici, L., Pastore, M., Garcia, E., Laganà, A., Rampino, S.: A dynamics investigation of the C + CH^+ → C_2^+ + H reaction on an ab initio bond-order like potential. J. Phys. Chem. A **120**(27), 5125–5135 (2016)

31. Mell, P., Grance, T.: The NIST definition of cloud computing. http://nvlpubs.nist.gov/nistpubs/Legacy/SP/nistspecialpublication800-145.pdf. Accessed 15 Mar 2017

32. Magoulés, F., Roux, F.X., Houzeaux, G.: Parallel Scientific Computing. Wiley-ISTE, London (2015)

33. OpenStack: Open source software for creating private and public clouds. https://www.openstack.org/. Accessed 15 Mar 2017

34. Storchi, L., Tarantelli, F., Laganà, A.: Computing molecular energy surfaces on a grid. In: Gavrilova, M., Gervasi, O., Kumar, V., Tan, C.J.K., Taniar, D., Laganá, A., Mun, Y., Choo, H. (eds.) ICCSA 2006. LNCS, vol. 3980, pp. 675–683. Springer, Heidelberg (2006). doi:10.1007/11751540_71

35. INDIGO-Datacloud: Towards a sustainable european PaaS-based cloud solution for e-Science. https://www.indigo-datacloud.eu/. Accessed 15 Mar 2017

36. Aguado, A., Tablero, C., Paniagua, M.: Global fit of ab initio potential energy surfaces I. Triatomic systems. Comput. Phys. Commun. **108**(23), 259–266 (1998)

37. Aguado, A., Paniagua, M.: A new functional form to obtain analytical potentials of triatomic molecules. J. Chem. Phys. **96**(2), 1265–1275 (1992)

38. Shepard, D.: A two-dimensional interpolation function for irregularly-spaced data. In: Proceedings of the 1968 23rd ACM National Conference, ACM 1968, pp. 517–524. ACM, New York (1968)

39. Collins, M.A.: Molecular potential-energy surfaces for chemical reaction dynamics. Theoret. Chem. Acc. **108**(6), 313–324 (2002)

40. Werner, H.J., Knowles, P.J., Knizia, G., Manby, F.R., Schütz, M., Celani, P., Korona, T., Lindh, R., Mitrushenkov, A., Rauhut, G., Shamasundar, K.R., Adler, T.B., Amos, R.D., Bernhardsson, A., Berning, A., Cooper, D.L., Deegan, M.J.O., Dobbyn, A.J., Eckert, F., Goll, E., Hampel, C., Hesselmann, A., Hetzer, G., Hrenar, T., Jansen, G., Köppl, C., Liu, Y., Lloyd, A.W., Mata, R.A., May, A.J., McNicholas, S.J., Meyer, W., Mura, M.E., Nicklass, A., O'Neill, D.P., Palmieri, P., Pflüger, K., Pitzer, R., Reiher, M., Shiozaki, T., Stoll, H., Stone, A.J., Tarroni, R., Thorsteinsson, T., Wang, M., Wolf, A.: Molpro, version 2010.1, a package of ab initio programs (2010). http://www.molpro.net. Accessed 15 Mar 2017

41. Dunning, T.H.: Gaussian basis sets for use in correlated molecular calculations. I. The atoms boron through neon and hydrogen. J. Chem. Phys. **90**(2), 1007–1023 (1989)

42. Skouteris, D., Castillo, J.F., Manolopoulos, D.E.: ABC: a quantum reactive scattering program. Comput. Phys. Commun. **133**(1), 128–135 (2000)

43. Liu, B.: Ab initio potential energy surface for linear h_3. J. Chem. Phys. **58**(5), 1925–1937 (1973)

44. Siegbahn, P., Liu, B.: An accurate three-dimensional potential energy surface for H_3. J. Chem. Phys. **68**(5), 2457–2465 (1978)

45. Truhlar, D.G., Horowitz, C.J.: Functional representation of Liu and Siegbahn's accurate ab initio potential energy calculations for $H + H_2$. J. Chem. Phys. **68**(5), 2466–2476 (1978)

46. Truhlar, D.G., Horowitz, C.J.: Erratum: functional representation of Liu and Siegbahn's accurate abinitio potential energy calculations for $H + H_2$. J. Chem. Phys. **71**(3), 1514–1514 (1979)

Workshop on Computational Optimization and Applications (COA 2017)

A Global Score-Driven Beam Angle Optimization in IMRT

Humberto Rocha[1,2(✉)], Joana M. Dias[1,2], Tiago Ventura[2,3,4],
Brígida C. Ferreira[2,5], and Maria do Carmo Lopes[2,3,4]

[1] CeBER and Faculdade de Economia, Universidade de Coimbra,
3004-512 Coimbra, Portugal
hrocha@mat.uc.pt, joana@fe.uc.pt
[2] INESC-Coimbra, 3030-290 Coimbra, Portugal
bcf@estsp.ipp.pt
[3] Serviço de Física Médica, IPOC-FG, EPE, 3000-075 Coimbra, Portugal
{tiagoventura,mclopes}@ipocoimbra.min-saude.pt
[4] Departamento de Física, Universidade de Aveiro, 3810-193 Aveiro, Portugal
[5] School for Allied Health Technologies, 4400-330 Porto, Portugal

Abstract. Radiation therapy is one of the main treatment modalities
for cancer. The objective of radiation therapy is to eliminate all cancer cells by delivering a prescribed dose of radiation to the tumor volume while sparing at the same time the surrounding tissues. Intensity-
modulated radiation therapy (IMRT) is a sophisticated technologically-
driven type of radiation therapy where non-uniform radiation fields are
used to irradiate the patient from different beam angle directions. Appropriate selection of beam irradiation directions – beam angle optimization
(BAO) problem – enhance the quality of the treatment plan. The BAO
problem is a very difficult global non-convex optimization problem for
which there are few or none commercial solutions. Typically, the BAO
procedure is driven by the outcome of the fluence map optimization
(FMO) problem – the problem of calculating the most adequate radiation intensities. However, functions used for modeling the FMO problem
have little clinical meaning. Typically, selection/validation of treatment
plans is done considering a set of dosimetric measures. In this study, we
propose a treatment plan global score, based on dosimetric criteria and
its relative importance, as alternative plan's quality measure to drive
the BAO procedure. For the clinical case of nasopharyngeal tumor, the
use of a global score to drive the BAO procedure lead to higher quality
treatment plans. For similar target coverage, an improved organ sparing
was obtained.

Keywords: IMRT · Beam angle optimization · Global score

1 Introduction

The number of cancer patients and deaths due to cancer is expected to increase
in the coming years. More than half of the cancer patients will be treated with

O. Gervasi et al. (Eds.): ICCSA 2017, Part III, LNCS 10406, pp. 77–90, 2017.
DOI: 10.1007/978-3-319-62398-6_6

radiation therapy, either with curative intent or simply to palliate the symptoms. Radiation therapy aims to eliminate all cancer cells by delivering a prescribed dose of radiation to the cancerous tissues while sparing the surrounding healthy organs. Intensity-modulated radiation therapy (IMRT) is a sophisticated technologically-driven type of radiation therapy where the radiation beam is discretized into a set of small beamlets with different intensities by means of a multileaf collimator. Calculating the most adequate radiation intensities – fluence map optimization (FMO) problem – using this discretization of the radiation beam enhances an accurate control of the radiation doses received by different structures.

In IMRT, radiation is typically generated by a linear accelerator (linac) mounted on a C-arm gantry that can rotate along a central axis. Radiation beams from selected directions intersect the tumor, depositing in an additive way the total radiation dose in the tumor while trying to spare the surrounding organs that only receive radiation from a small subset of radiation beams. Typically, equispaced coplanar irradiation directions, i.e. evenly spaced directions laying on the rotation plane of the linac's gantry, are used in clinical practice. However, evidence shows that appropriate selection of beam irradiation directions – beam angle optimization (BAO) problem – can enhance the quality of the treatment plan [11]. Furthermore, for some types of cancer cases, e.g. intra-cranial tumors, the use of noncoplanar incidence directions improves substantially the treatment plan quality [5].

BAO and FMO problems can be solved separately, considering dosimetric surrogates or geometric features as quality measures of the beam ensembles [3,17]. Alternatively, BAO and FMO problems can be solved simultaneously and the optimal value of the FMO problem is used as quality measure of the beam ensembles [2,10,18]. Optimality and reliability is only granted by the second approach since beam angle directions for IMRT are often non-intuitive [23]. However, the objective functions usually used to drive the FMO problem are simple mathematical formulations with little or none clinical relevance. Thus, although the optimal FMO value is a beam ensemble score that is better correlated with treatment plan's quality than alternative dosimetric surrogates, it is far from being the ideal score. In this study, we propose BAO driven by a treatment plan global score as presented by Ventura et al. [24]. A clinical case of nasopharyngeal tumor, already treated at the Portuguese Institute of Oncology of Coimbra (IPOC), is used to acknowledge the performance of this novel approach. The remainder of the paper is organized as follows. Formulation of the BAO problem is presented in the Section 2. In Sect. 3 we briefly describe the derivative-free optimization methods used to tackle the BAO problem. Computational tests are presented in Sect. 4 followed by the conclusion's Section.

2   Noncoplanar BAO in IMRT Treatment Planning

The BAO problem can generically belong to two distinct classes of optimization problems. In a first class, BAO is formulated as a combinatorial optimization problem, considering a discrete sample of all continuous beam angle directions. Since exhaustive searches are not recommended due to computational time, many different algorithms have been proposed, including gradient search [10], neighborhood search [2], simulated annealing [14], genetic algorithms [13], branch-and-prune [16], hybrid approaches [6] or iterative BAO [9]. Regardless of the algorithm used, it is not possible to calculate, in a polynomial run time, the optimal solution of the combinatorial BAO problem (NP hard problem) [4]. In a second class, a completely different methodological approach is considered. BAO is formulated as a continuous global optimization problem considering all possible beam angle directions around the tumor [19–22]. Here, a continuous formulation of the noncoplanar BAO problem is considered as described next.

2.1 Noncoplanar BAO Model

Let n be the number of noncoplanar beam angle directions defined *a priori* by the treatment planner. Let ϕ denote the couch angle and θ denote the gantry angle. An unbounded formulation can be considered as angles $-5°$ and $355°$ or angles $365°$ and $5°$ are equivalent. While collisions between the patient/couch and the gantry never occur for coplanar optimization (for a fixed couch position at $\phi = 0$), for some noncoplanar beam directions candidates collisions would occur. Thus, the choice of noncoplanar beam directions has collision restrictions. In order to maintain an unbounded formulation, collision restrictions are embedded in the objective function in the form of a penalty. A mathematical formulation for the noncoplanar BAO problem can then be obtained by considering a measure/score (objective function) such that the best beam ensemble corresponds to the function's minimum:

$$\min f\Big((\theta_1, \phi_1), \ldots, (\theta_n, \phi_n)\Big)$$
$$\text{s.t. } \Big(\theta_1, \ldots, \theta_n, \phi_1, \ldots, \phi_n\Big) \in \mathbb{R}^{2n}. \tag{1}$$

In this study, two different objective functions $f\Big((\theta_1, \phi_1), \ldots, (\theta_n, \phi_n)\Big)$ that measure the quality of a beam ensemble $(\theta_1, \phi_1), \ldots, (\theta_n, \phi_n)$ will be compared. The first, widely used, corresponds to the optimal value of the FMO problem for each fixed beam ensemble and incorporates a penalization for beam direction candidates where collision between the patient/couch and the gantry occur:

$$f\Big((\theta_1, \phi_1), \ldots, (\theta_n, \phi_n)\Big) = \begin{cases} +\infty & \text{if collisions occur} \\ \text{optimal value of the FMO} & \text{otherwise.} \end{cases}$$

The second, corresponds to a treatment plan's quality global score for each beam ensemble and it also incorporates a penalization for beam direction candidates where collision between the patient/couch and the gantry occur:

$$f\Big((\theta_1, \phi_1), \ldots, (\theta_n, \phi_n)\Big) = \begin{cases} +\infty & \text{if collisions occur} \\ \text{plan's quality global score} & \text{otherwise.} \end{cases}$$

FMO formulation/resolution and treatment plan's quality global score used to drive BAO are presented next.

2.2 FMO Formulation and Resolution

The FMO problem is usually formulated as a weighted sum function with conflicting objectives. Furthermore, constraints are often implemented as objectives, which difficult the trade-off between objectives without violating constraints [15]. Thus, a multicriteria approach is the most suitable formulation for the FMO problem. Here, the FMO problem formulation considers an *a priori* multicriteria optimization approach based on a prescription called wish-list [7–9].

Table 1 displays the wish-list constructed for the clinical case of nasopharyngeal tumor tested. Nasopharyngeal tumor cases are usually complex tumors to treat with radiotherapy, given the close proximity of multiple healthy structures. For simplicity, the organs at risk (OARs) in the wish-list are limited to the spinal cord, brainstem, parotids and oral cavity. For the nasopharyngeal case in study, two dose levels were defined for the planning target volume (PTV), tumor to be treated plus some safety margins: a higher dose level (70 Gy) was defined for the tumor (PTV_{70}) and a lower dose level (59.4 Gy) was defined for the lymph nodes ($PTV_{59.4}$). Several auxiliary structures were defined by computerized volume expansions to support the dose optimization. To prevent possible overirradiation in the lymph nodes, $PTV_{59.4}$ shell was created by removing a 10 mm margin of PTV_{70} to $PTV_{59.4}$. To improve target coverage and conformity, two auxiliary ring shape structures, Ring PTV_{70} and Ring $PTV_{59.4}$, were created with 10 mm of thickness at 10 mm distance from PTV_{70} and $PTV_{59.4}$, respectively. External Ring, a ring of 10 mm thickness, was created next to the patient outer contour to prevent possible high values of dose entrance.

The wish-list contains 9 hard constraints and 10 prioritized objectives based on the prescribed/tolerance doses for the different structures included in the treatment planning optimization. All constraints are maximum-dose constraints and have to be strictly fulfilled. Objectives are optimized following a priority order defined *a priori* in the wish-list. Objectives with higher priorities are addressed first and thus are more likely to be fulfilled. For spinal cord and brainstem, organs whose functionality is jeopardized even if only a small subunit is damaged (serial organs), maximum-dose constraints are considered. For parotids, the larger salivary glands, and oral cavity, that contains the remaining salivary glands, mean-dose constraints are considered because the salivary glands are parallel type organs, i.e., organs whose function is not jeopardized if only a small portion is injured.

The logarithmic tumor control probability ($LTCP$) was considered for the target dose optimization [9],

$$LTCP = \frac{1}{N_T} \sum_{l=1}^{N_T} e^{-\alpha(D_i - T_i)},$$

where N_T is the number of voxels in the PTV, D_i is the dose in voxel i, T_i is the prescribed dose, and α is the cell sensitivity parameter. $LTCP$ penalizes

Table 1. Wish-list for the nasopharyngeal tumor case.

	Structure	Type	Limit			
Constraints	$PTV_{59.4}$	maximum	63.6 Gy (=107% of prescribed dose)			
	PTV_{70}	maximum	74.9 Gy (=107% of prescribed dose)			
	$PTV_{59.4}$ shell	maximum	63.6 Gy (=107% of prescribed dose)			
	Spinal cord	maximum	45 Gy			
	Brainstem	maximum	54 Gy			
	Ring $PTV_{59.4}$	maximum	50.5 Gy (=85% of prescribed dose)			
	Ring PTV_{70}	maximum	59.5 Gy (=85% of prescribed dose)			
	External Ring	maximum	45 Gy			
	Body	maximum	70 Gy			
	Structure	Type	Priority	Goal	Parameters	Sufficient
Objectives	$PTV_{59.4}$	LTCP	1	1	$T_i = 59.4$ Gy; $\alpha= 0.75$	0.5
	PTV_{70}	LTCP	2	1	$T_i = 70$ Gy; $\alpha= 0.75$	0.5
	$PTV_{59.4}$ shell	LTCP	3	1	$T_i = 59.4$ Gy; $\alpha= 0.75$	0.5
	External ring	maximum	4	42.75 Gy	–	–
	Spinal cord	maximum	5	42.75 Gy	–	–
	Brainstem	maximum	6	51.3 Gy	–	–
	Parotids	mean	7	50 Gy	–	–
	Oral cavity	mean	8	45 Gy	–	–
	Parotids	mean	9	26 Gy	–	–
	Oral cavity	mean	10	35 Gy	–	–

doses lower than prescribed while the value slowly tends to zero for doses D_i higher than the prescribed dose T_i. The ultimate goal is to obtain $LTCP = 1$ corresponding to an homogeneous dose equal to T_i. An increase in the α value can improve the tumor coverage, i.e. the volume of the PTV that receives at least 95% of the prescribed dose.

The FMO problem formulated using the described wish-list was solved by a primal-dual interior-point algorithm, $2pec$ [7], tailored for multicriteria IMRT treatment planning. This algorithm generates a single Pareto optimal IMRT plan, in an automated way, for a fixed number of beam directions [7]. The $2pec$ algorithm performs in two stages. In the first stage, all objectives are sequentially optimized, following the wish-list priorities, respecting the hard constraints. To assure flexibility for lower level objectives improvement, the optimization of tumor objectives ($LTCP$) halts at a predefined sufficient value. After the optimization of each objective, a constraint is added to assure that the outcome of higher-order priorities are kept during the optimization of lower level priority objectives. At the end of the first stage, the treatment plan obtained fulfills all hard constraints of the wish-list as well as the goal for each objective or a higher value if the constraints prevent a better outcome. In the second stage, all objectives, except tumor ($LTCP$) objectives, are fully optimized following the priority sequence of the wish-list. For more details on $2pec$ interior-point algorithm see Breedveld et al. [7].

The optimal value of the FMO problem is used to drive the BAO problem as a black-box function. Thus, the conclusions drawn considering the BAO problem coupled with this particular formulation/resolution of the FMO problem, are also valid if different formulations/resolutions are considered.

2.3   Global Score for Treatment Plan Quality

A Global Score (GS) aiming to represent more accurately the overall quality of a treatment plan is proposed as alternative measure to guide the BAO procedure. Similarly to the treatment plan global score presented by Ventura et al. [24], GS is a weighted sum of individual scores assigned to each structure involved in the treatment planning optimization process:

$$GS = \sum_i w_i \times Score_i, \qquad (2)$$

where w_i is the relative weight assigned to structure i and $Score_i$ is the score assigned to structure i. Thus, a relative weight must be assigned to each structure, based on its clinical relevance, and each structure's score, computed considering dosimetric goals typically inspected during treatment plan selection/validation, should express the fulfillment of the treatment prescription for that structure. Relative weights should be customized for each type of tumor in order to reflect the relative importance given by the radiation oncologist to the different planning objectives [24].

Clinical dose metrics typically used to verify organ sparing correspond to the maximum or mean tolerance doses, depending on the type of organ (serial or parallel, respectively). For tumor coverage, a clinical dose metric commonly used is the dose that 95% of the tumor volume receive (D_{95}). Typically more than 95% of the prescribed dose is required. Table 2 depicts the prescribed and tolerance doses as well as the clinical dose metrics and corresponding weights considered for the nasopharyngeal tumor case tested. The weights selected consider PTV dose metrics as the most important, followed by the serial organs (spinal cord and brainstem) dose metrics, with half of the importance of PTVs, and the remaining structures with half of the importance of serial organs. The score for each structure corresponds to the ratio between clinical dose metrics and the corresponding planned doses. For the OARs, the score is given by

$$Score_{OAR} = \frac{D_P}{D_C}, \qquad (3)$$

where D_C is the OAR clinical dose metric and D_P the corresponding planned dose. For the PTVs, the score is given by

$$Score_{PTV} = \frac{D_C}{D_P}, \qquad (4)$$

where D_C is the PTV clinical dose metric and D_P the corresponding planned dose. Thus, a value of one is expected if the dose for that structure is equal to

Table 2. Prescribed and tolerance doses for tumor volumes and OARs. Clinical dose metrics considered for plan's quality evaluation and respective weights.

Structure	Tolerance Dose		Prescribed dose	Clinical dose metrics	w_i
	Mean	Max			
PTV$_{70}$	–	–	70.0 Gy	$D_{95} \geq 66.5$ Gy	0.25
PTV$_{59.4}$	–	–	59.4 Gy	$D_{95} \geq 56.4$ Gy	0.25
Brainstem	–	54 Gy	–	$D_{max} \leq 54$ Gy	0.125
Spinal cord	–	45 Gy	–	$D_{max} \leq 45$ Gy	0.125
Left parotid	26 Gy	–	–	$D_{mean} \leq 26$ Gy	0.0625
Right parotid	26 Gy	–	–	$D_{mean} \leq 26$ Gy	0.0625
Oral cavity	45 Gy	–	–	$D_{mean} \leq 45$ Gy	0.0625
Body	–	70 Gy	–	$D_{max} \leq 70$ Gy	0.0625

the respective clinical dose metric value. A score inferior to one is obtained for an improved target coverage or organ sparing. Overall, lower values of GS imply treatment plans with better quality considering the metrics typically used to evaluate/compare treatment plans.

3   Pattern Search Methods

The highly non-convex nature of the noncoplanar BAO problem advises the selection of a derivative-free method. In previous works, we showed that a beam angle ensemble can be improved in a continuous manner using derivative-free algorithms. Pattern search methods (PSM) were selected for the resolution of the continuous BAO problem as they have the ability to avoid local entrapment and need a reduced number of function (FMO) evaluations to converge [1,19–22]. Each iteration of PSM have two steps with different purposes. In the first step, named search step, a global search is performed attempting to improve the outcome of the current best iterate. This global search is free of rules, except being finite, and can use any heuristic, strategy or method. If the first step fails, i.e. if the search step is empty or the procedure used was not able to improve the outcome of the current best iterate, the second step, named poll step, use the directions of positive bases to explore the neighborhood of the current best iterate. A positive basis is defined by a set of nonzero vectors (directions) that positively span the entire search space while no subset does. The main reason for using positive bases for optimization purposes is that at least one of its vectors (directions) can provide an improvement on the objective function value unless the current iterate is a stationary point [12]. An example of a positive basis is the set of $2n$ vectors $[I \quad - I]$ where $I = [e_1 \ldots e_n]$ is the identity matrix. In terms of BAO, following each direction of this positive basis corresponds to the rotation of each beam direction clockwise and counter-clockwise for a certain amount (step-size) at each iteration.

For a matter of computational time efficiency, the pattern search method implemented considers no trial points in the search step. The positive basis considered in the poll step is $[I - I]$. Algorithm 1 displays the parallel PSM algorithm used.

Algorithm 1. Parallel PSM algorithm
___

Initialization:

- Set $k \leftarrow 0$;
- Choose $\mathbf{x}^0 \in \mathbb{R}^{2n}$, $\alpha_0 > 0$ and α_{min};

Iteration:

1. Compute in parallel $f(\mathbf{x}), \forall \mathbf{x} \in \mathcal{N}(\mathbf{x}^k) = \{\mathbf{x}^k \pm \alpha_k e_i, i = 1, \ldots, n\}$.
2. If search is successful, i.e. $\min_{\mathcal{N}(\mathbf{x}^k)} f(\mathbf{x}) < f(\mathbf{x}^k)$ then
   $\mathbf{x}^{k+1} \leftarrow \operatorname{argmin}_{\mathcal{N}(\mathbf{x}^k)} f(\mathbf{x})$;
   $\alpha_{k+1} \leftarrow \alpha_k$;
   Else
   $\mathbf{x}^{k+1} \leftarrow \mathbf{x}^k$;
   $\alpha_{k+1} \leftarrow \frac{\alpha_k}{2}$;
3. If $\alpha_{k+1} \geq \alpha_{min}$ return to step 1 for a new iteration and set $k \leftarrow k + 1$.

---

4 Computational Results

Computational tests were performed on a Dell Precision T5600 with Intel Xeon processador 64 GB 1600 MHz. YARTOS, an in-house optimization suite developed in MATLAB at Erasmus MC Cancer Institute in Rotterdam, was used to import DICOM images, optimize dose distributions and compute and visualize dose. YARTOS optimizer, $2p\epsilon c$, was used to compute the optimal value of the FMO problem and thus to obtain the optimal fluences for a given beam direction ensemble.

The initial step-size considered by the implemented PSM algorithm was $\alpha_0 = 2^5 = 32$ and the minimal value allowed was one, defining the stopping criteria. By choosing the initial step-size as a power of two, since step-size is halved at unsuccessful iterations, all beam directions considered are integer until the step-size becomes inferior to one which is the termination criteria.

Both the optimal value of the FMO problem and GS were used to guide the PSM during the optimization of the noncoplanar BAO problem for a clinical case of nasopharyngeal tumor already treated at IPOC.

Treatment plans with seven equispaced coplanar beam directions are commonly used to treat intra-cranial tumor cases. Therefore, treatment plans of seven noncoplanar beam directions were obtained using the optimal value of the FMO problem (f) and GS to guide the PSM and were denoted BAO_f and BAO_{GS}, respectively. These plans were compared with the typical seven-beam equispaced coplanar treatment plan denoted *Equi*. The objective of these comparisons is twofold. First, to compare the two measures of quality of a given beam ensemble. Second, to benchmark the noncoplanar results obtained with a coplanar plan typically used in clinical practice.

Table 3. Results of the beam angle optimization processes.

	Optimal FMO		Global score	
	value	% decrease	value	% decrease
Equi	542.47	–	0.924	–
BAO_f	501.72	7.5 %	0.899	2.5%
BAO_{GS}	502.25	7.4 %	0.856	6.8%

Table 3 depicts the results of the BAO processes both in terms of optimal FMO value and GS. BAO_f treatment plans, obtained considering the optimal value of the FMO to guide the BAO procedure, achieve a 7.5% reduction of the optimal FMO value compared to *Equi* treatment plans. However, the improvement obtained in terms of GS was only 2.5%. On the other hand, BAO_{GS} treatment plans, obtained considering GS to guide the BAO procedure, achieved a 6.8 % reduction of GS value compared to *Equi* treatment plans which corresponded to a 7.4% reduction on the optimal FMO value. The history of the BAO processes considering the optimal FMO value and GS value as objective functions are displayed in Fig. 1. Since PSM are non-increasing iterative methods, i.e. the next iterate only replaces the current one if its objective function value improves the best known so far, we can verify that the curves of the measures used to drive the BAO process are non-increasing. However, the behavior of the other measure is different meaning that an improvement in one measure do not necessarily imply an improvement in the other. In particular, improvements in the optimal FMO value have poor correspondence with similar improvements in the GS value.

Regardless of objective function improvement, either optimal FMO value or GS value, the quality of the results is typically acknowledged by different dose metrics. These dose metrics, considered for construction of GS, are displayed in Table 4. By simple inspection it is possible to realize that BAO_{GS} clearly outperforms both BAO_f and *Equi* treatment plans. For similar target coverage, an enhanced organ sparing is clearly obtained by BAO_{GS} treatment plans. Comparison of the three treatment plans is straightforward using the graphical analysis proposed in SPIDERplan [24]. Figure 2 displays customized radar plots that include the different structures considered for treatment planning optimization. The circular plotting area is divided into sections with an angular amplitude corresponding to the relative weight of the respective structure. Each structure's score is represented by a point on the bisector of the corresponding section that is exactly the score value away from the radar's center. The radar inner circle has unitary radius which corresponds to the situation where the dosimetric goal defined for each structure is met as an equality. Optimal scores will converge

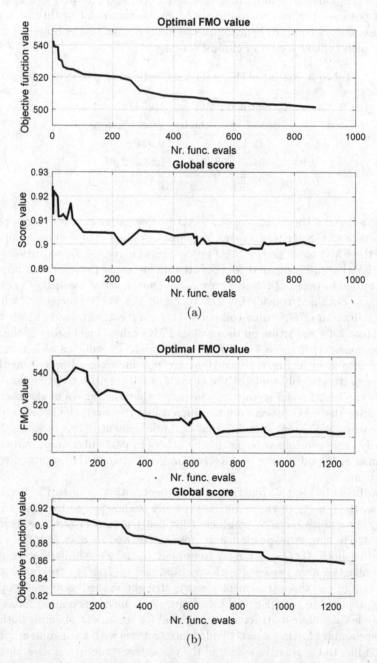

Fig. 1. History of the BAO procedure considering the optimal FMO value as objective function – 1(a) and considering GS value as objective function – 1(b), respectively.

Table 4. Target coverage and organ sparing obtained by treatment plans.

Structure (Dose goal)	*Equi*	*BAO$_f$*	*BAO$_{GS}$*
PTV$_{70}$ (at 95 % volume)	65.4 Gy	65.3 Gy	65.4 Gy
PTV$_{59.4}$ (at 95 % volume)	56.2 Gy	56.0 Gy	56.0 Gy
Brainstem (Max dose)	42.6 Gy	40.9 Gy	35.3 Gy
Spinal cord (Max dose)	32.0 Gy	34.7 Gy	25.7 Gy
Right parotid (Mean dose)	21.3 Gy	19.1 Gy	18.4 Gy
Left parotid (Mean dose)	28.2 Gy	22.3 Gy	23.2 Gy
Oral Cavity (Mean dose)	32.2 Gy	23.8 Gy	21.4 Gy
Body (Max dose)	76.0 Gy	77.2 Gy	76.0 Gy

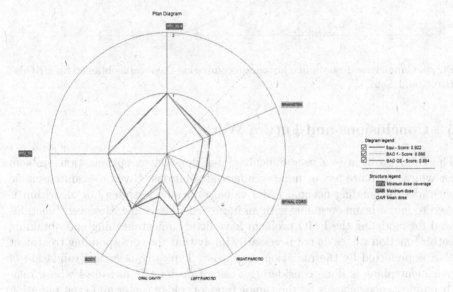

Fig. 2. Radar plots obtained by BAO_{GS}, BAO_f and *Equi*.

to the radar plot center while increasing deviations from prescribed/tolerance doses will converge to the outer circle with radius equal to two. The polygon that connects all scores represents the quality of the treatment plan. The inner treatment plan, corresponding to BAO_{GS} treatment plan, is easily identified as the best treatment plan.

In clinical practice, treatment plans are also typically compared using their cumulative dose-volume histograms (DVHs). Figure 3 display the DVH results for the three treatment plan. The DVH curves also show that for similar target coverage, an improved organ sparing is obtained by BAO_{GS} treatment plans. In particular, salivary glands are better spared which prevents xerostomia. This is a common complication of radiation therapy for head-and-neck cancer cases causing difficulties to swallow and decreasing the patient's quality of life. Thus, the enhanced salivary glands sparing is of the utmost interest.

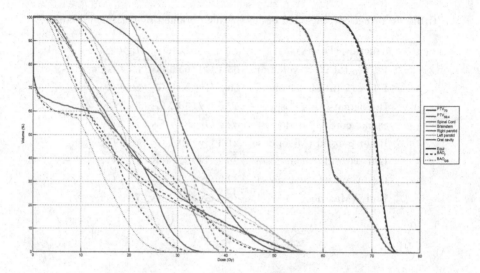

Fig. 3. Cumulative dose volume histogram comparing the results obtained by BAO_{GS}, BAO_f and $Equi$.

5   Conclusions and Future Work

The BAO problem is a very difficult global non-convex optimization problem for which there are few or none commercial solutions. Given a beam ensemble with a corresponding optimal FMO value, typically a strategy or algorithm is used to find a beam ensemble with an improved FMO value. However, functions used for modeling the FMO problem have little clinical meaning and obtaining better function values do not necessarily imply that the corresponding treatment plan is preferred by the radiation oncologist. Typically, selection/validation of treatment plans is done considering a set of dosimetric measures whose relative importance depends on the tumor type, oncology center and even radiation oncologist. Nevertheless, assuming that the decision maker's preferences (relative importance of the different, possibly conflicting, dosimetric criteria) can be established *a priori*, it is possible to define a measure based on dosimetric criteria and its relative importance that correlates better with the quality of the treatment plan. In this study, we propose a treatment plan global score, as presented by Ventura et al. [24], as alternative plan's quality measure to guide the BAO procedure.

For the clinical case of nasopharyngeal tumor tested, the use of GS to drive the BAO procedure leads to higher quality treatment plans. For similar target coverage, an improved organ sparing is obtained by BAO_{GS} treatment plans. It is important to highlight that BAO driven by GS value obtained, as expected, a much better final GS value than $Equi$ treatment plan, but also leads to a final optimal FMO value similar to the one obtained by BAO driven by the optimal FMO value. On the other hand, BAO driven by the optimal FMO value obtained, as expected, a much better final optimal FMO value than *Equi* treatment plan, but only a small improvement on GS value compared to the one obtained by BAO driven by GS. This result implies that improving the optimal FMO value does not necessarily improve GS, i.e. dose gains reflected in the optimal FMO value do not translate directly into dosimetric goals gains, while improving GS corresponds more often to a better optimal FMO value.

In future work, a GS incorporating more structure's dosimetric measures, with weights clinically validated, should be further tested to acknowledge its advantage on driving a BAO procedure. Furthermore, one of the disadvantages of using the optimal FMO value to drive the BAO procedure is that the optimal beam ensemble found is jeopardized if a different fluence optimizer is used. It is worth to test if BAO driven by GS decreases the dependence on the fluence optimizer, i.e. if the optimal beam ensemble found using a given treatment planning system shows the same benefits when used in a different treatment planning system.

Acknowledgements. This work has been supported by the Fundação para a Ciência e a Tecnologia (FCT) under project grant UID/MULTI/00308/2013.

References

1. Alberto, P., Nogueira, F., Rocha, H., Vicente, L.N.: Pattern search methods for user-provided points: Application to molecular geometry problems. SIAM J. Optim. **14**, 1216–1236 (2004)
2. Aleman, D.M., Kumar, A., Ahuja, R.K., Romeijn, H.E., Dempsey, J.F.: Neighborhood search approaches to beam orientation optimization in intensity modulated radiation therapy treatment planning. J. Global Optim. **42**, 587–607 (2008)
3. Bangert, M., Oelfke, U.: Spherical cluster analysis for beam angle optimization in intensity-modulated radiation therapy treatment planning. Phys. Med. Biol. **55**, 6023–6037 (2010)
4. Bangert, M., Ziegenhein, P., Oelfke, U.: Characterizing the combinatorial beam angle selection problem. Phys. Med. Biol. **57**, 6707–6723 (2012)
5. Bangert, M., Ziegenhein, P., Oelfke, U.: Comparison of beam angle selection strategies for intracranial imrt. Med. Phys. **40**, 011716 (2013)
6. Bertsimas, D., Cacchiani, V., Craft, D., Nohadani, O.: A hybrid approach to beam angle optimization in intensity-modulated radiation therapy. Comput. Oper. Res. **40**, 2187–2197 (2013)
7. Breedveld, S., Storchi, P., Keijzer, M., Heemink, A.W., Heijmen, B.: A novel approach to multi-criteria inverse planning for IMRT. Phys. Med. Biol. **52**, 6339–6353 (2007)
8. Breedveld, S., Storchi, P., Heijmen, B.: The equivalence of multicriteria methods for radiotherapy plan optimization. Phys. Med. Biol. **54**, 7199–7209 (2009)
9. Breedveld, S., Storchi, P., Voet, P., Heijmen, B.: iCycle: integrated, multicriterial beam angle, and profile optimization for generation of coplanar and noncoplanar IMRT plans. Med. Phys. **39**, 951–963 (2012)
10. Craft, D.: Local beam angle optimization with linear programming and gradient search. Phys. Med. Biol. **52**, 127–135 (2007)

11. Das, S.K., Marks, L.B.: Selection of coplanar or non coplanar beams using three-dimensional optimization based on maximum beam separation and minimized non-target irradiation. Int. J. Radiat. Oncol. Biol. Phys. **38**, 643–655 (1997)
12. Davis, C.: Theory of positive linear dependence. Am. J. Math. **76**, 733–746 (1954)
13. Dias, J., Rocha, H., Ferreira, B.C., Lopes, M.C.: A genetic algorithm with neural network fitness function evaluation for IMRT beam angle optimization. Cent. Eur. J. Oper. Res. **22**, 431–455 (2014)
14. Dias, J., Rocha, H., Ferreira, B.C., Lopes, M.C.: Simulated annealing applied to IMRT beam angle optimization: A computational study. Physica Med. **31**, 747–756 (2015)
15. Dias, J., Rocha, H., Ventura, T., Ferreira, B.C., Lopes, M.C.: Automated fluence map optimization based on fuzzy inference systems. Med. Phys. **43**, 1083–1095 (2016)
16. Lim, G.J., Cao, W.: A two-phase method for selecting IMRT treatment beam angles: Branch-and-Prune and local neighborhood search. Eur. J. Oper. Res. **217**, 609–618 (2012)
17. Llacer, J., Li, S., Agazaryan, N., Promberger, C., Solberg, T.D.: Noncoplanar automatic beam orientation selection in cranial IMRT: a practical methodology. Phys. Med. Biol. **54**, 1337–1368 (2009)
18. Mišić, V.V., Aleman, D.M., Sharpe, M.B.: Neighborhood search approaches to non-coplanar beam orientation optimization for total marrow irradiation using IMRT. Eur. J. Oper. Res. **205**, 522–527 (2010)
19. Rocha, H., Dias, J., Ferreira, B.C., Lopes, M.C.: Selection of intensity modulated radiation therapy treatment beam directions using radial basis functions within a pattern search methods framework. J. Glob. Optim. **57**, 1065–1089 (2013)
20. Rocha, H., Dias, J., Ferreira, B.C., Lopes, M.C.: Beam angle optimization for intensity-modulated radiation therapy using a guided pattern search method. Phys. Med. Biol. **58**, 2939–2953 (2013)
21. Rocha, H., Dias, J., Ferreira, B.C., Lopes, M.C.: Pattern search methods framework for beam angle optimization in radiotherapy design. Appl. Math. Comput. **219**, 10853–10865 (2013)
22. Rocha, H., Dias, J., Ventura, T., Ferreira, B.C., Lopes, M.C.: A derivative-free multistart framework for an automated noncoplanar beam angle optimization in IMRT. Med. Phys. **43**, 5514–5526 (2016)
23. Stein, J., Mohan, R., Wang, X.H., Bortfeld, T., Wu, Q., Preiser, K., Ling, C.C., Schlegel, W.: Number and orientation of beams in intensity-modulated radiation treatments. Med. Phys. **24**, 149–160 (1997)
24. Ventura, T., Lopes, M.C., Ferreira, B., Khouri, L.: SPIDERplan: A tool to support decision-making in radiation therapy treatment plan assessment. Rep. Pract. Oncol. Radiother. **21**, 508–516 (2016)

Automated Radiotherapy Treatment Planning Using Fuzzy Inference Systems

Joana Dias[1,2], Humberto Rocha[1,2(✉)], Tiago Ventura[3],
Brígida Ferreira[4], and Maria do Carmo Lopes[3,5]

[1] CeBER and Faculdade de Economia, Universidade de Coimbra,
3004-512 Coimbra, Portugal
joana@fe.uc.pt, hrocha@mat.uc.pt
[2] Inesc-Coimbra, Rua Sílvio Lima, Pólo II, 3030-290 Coimbra, Portugal
[3] Serviço de Física Médica, IPOC-FG, EPE, 3000-075 Coimbra, Portugal
{tiagoventura,mclopes}@ipocoimbra.min-saude.pt
[4] School for Allied Health Technologies, Porto, Portugal
brigida@ua.pt
[5] I3N, Departamento de Física, Universidade de Aveiro,
3810-193 Aveiro, Portugal

Abstract. Radiotherapy is one of the treatments available for cancer patients, aiming to irradiate the tumor while preserving healthy structures. The planning of a treatment is a lengthy trial and error procedure, where treatment parameters are iteratively changed and the delivered dose is calculated to see whether it complies with the desired medical prescription. In this paper, a procedure based on fuzzy inference systems (FIS) for automated treatment planning is developed, allowing the calculation of high quality treatment plans without requiring human intervention. The procedure is structured in two different phases, incorporating the automatic selection of the best set of equidistant beam irradiation directions by an enumeration procedure. The developed method is extensively tested using ten head-and-neck cancer cases.

Keywords: Fuzzy inference systems · Radiotherapy planning · IMRT · Optimization · Decision problem

1 Introduction

Radiation therapy is, along with surgery and chemotherapy, one of the main treatments for cancer patients. Radiation has the capability of damaging and killing cells. The main objective is to be able to kill all cancer cells (that have more difficulties recovering from radiation), and at the same time spare as most as possible healthy cells. The treatment is usually performed applying a linear accelerator, mounted on a gantry that can rotate along a central axis parallel to the couch where the patient lays immobilized. The rotation of the couch along with the rotation of the gantry allows radiation to be delivered from almost any direction (angle) around the tumor. Nevertheless, most of the times, it is the equidistant coplanar angle configuration that is considered (only angles that lay in the plane of rotation of the gantry are considered). There are different

© Springer International Publishing AG 2017
O. Gervasi et al. (Eds.): ICCSA 2017, Part III, LNCS 10406, pp. 91–106, 2017.
DOI: 10.1007/978-3-319-62398-6_7

radiotherapy treatment modalities: 3D-conformal, Intensity Modulated Radiation Therapy (IMRT), Arc-Therapy, for instance. In this work, our focus is on IMRT treatments, although the developed methodology can also be extended to other radiotherapy modalities. In IMRT it is possible to modulate the radiation intensity due to the use of a multileaf collimator, that is composed of pairs of individual leaves, moving independently and blocking the radiation beam. This allows not only the conformal shaping of the treatment beams to the tumor shape, but also the possibility of achieving radiation intensity maps: each radiation beam can be interpreted as a set of individual beamlets. Before a radiotherapy treatment can be delivered, CT-scans are taken allowing a 3D discretization of the patient into voxels, and a delineation of all important structures (Planning Target Volumes – PTV – and healthy organs that are meant to be spared known as Organs at Risk – OAR). A radiation dose prescription defines minimum dose coverage constraints for the PTVs and maximum allowed radiation doses to OARS. Having as input the 3D discretization of the patient and the desired prescription, the treatment planner will try to generate a treatment plan. The treatment planning procedure uses software that simulates the treatment and calculates the radiation dose that is being deposited in each voxel (Treatment Planning System – TPS). The planner needs to define *a priori* the radiation beam angles and a set of parameters that are TPS dependent, but are usually weights and lower and/or upper bounds. With these parameters fixed, the TPS will run an optimization procedure (IMRT Fluence Map Optimization – FMO) that will generate the optimal radiation intensity associated with each beamlet from each of the angles to be used in the treatment (fluence maps), so that the dose that is being deposited in each voxel (measured in Gy) is calculated. The commonly used trial-and-error treatment planning procedure is a lengthy and cumbersome process, taking from several hours to several days for each patient. The quality of the treatment plan is highly dependent on the planner, and it is not possible to know whether more time and effort will be rewarded with a better quality treatment plan. Automating the treatment planning procedure will constitute an important breakthrough in this area. Probably the best known and general developed approach so far is *iCycle* [1] and other related works [2, 3]. In this paper, we present an approach where the trial-and-error procedure is replaced by an automated procedure that optimizes fluence maps by using FIS. The way in which the planner drives the TPS aiming at calculating better plans is based on his own reasoning and it is not possible to describe this process in a rigorous mathematical form. Moreover, two different planners will most probably have different reasoning. Nevertheless, it is possible to think of some simple rules that will certainly be followed. If, for instance, structure *A* is an OAR and it is receiving a higher dose than what is desired, then the importance of this structure in the FMO should be increased. This kind of simple rules can be defined for each structure and can be the basis of an automated procedure that guides the search process towards an acceptable treatment plan.

Fuzzy logic has been applied before to radiotherapy planning. Li and Yin [4] apply fuzzy logic to determine the best prescription for the normal tissue. Yan et al. [5, 6] apply a fuzzy inference system (FIS) composed of eight rules that changes the *a priori* defined weights assigned to each structure. This work is further extended in [7] by a neuro-fuzzy inference system that uses a trained neural network to determine the parameters of the fuzzy inference system. Our approach is different from the cited works since it mimics the planner's trial-and-error procedure, and the implicit rules that the planner uses, in an automated way and automatically changing all the parameters available and not only weights. Furthermore, if a feasible treatment plan is found, the algorithm will try to automatically improve this plan by increasing PTV coverage and/or achieving better organ sparing. If a feasible plan is not found, then it will calculate a plan that complies as much as possible with the medical prescription. The present approach builds on the work of Dias et al. [8], adapting it so that it accommodates the choice of the best equidistant beam angle geometry, without increasing the planner's workload. Furthermore, extensive computational tests were performed to assess the effect of using different parameters in the fuzzy inference system. The proposed methodology is applied to ten retrospectively treated head-and-neck cancer cases at the Portuguese Oncology Institute of Coimbra (IPOCFG). In Sect. 2, the IMRT treatment planning procedure is explained. In Sect. 3, the FMO is detailed. The algorithm is described in Sect. 4. In Sect. 5, computational results are shown, and discussed in Sect. 6.

2 IMRT Treatment Planning

The aim of IMRT treatment planning is to achieve a treatment plan that satisfies all dosimetry treatment constraints. The dosimetry constraints can take a variety of forms, depending on whether they relate to OAR or PTV. Considering OAR, for instance, there are generally constraints that limit the maximum or mean dose that the OAR can receive. The constraints to consider will depend on the organs' functionality. OARs can be classified as being serial or parallel organs. For serial organs even if only a small percentage of the organ is over-irradiated then the whole organ's functionality is jeopardized (spinal cord, for instance). It is thus necessary to guarantee that the maximum dose received anywhere within the organ is upper bounded. Other organs can still perform their function even if a small percentage of the organ is damaged (lung, for instance). In this case, a dose volume condition has to be preserved and can be expressed, for instance, by guaranteeing that the mean dose received is not above a given threshold. Regarding PTV, the medical prescription defines a desired dose and also dose-volume constraints. As an example, consider a patient that has different PTV structures that can be clustered in two groups: PTVs where the desired dose is 70 Gy (PTV70) and PTVs where the desired dose is 59.4 Gy (PTV59). Consider also that structures belonging to PTV70 are inside structures belonging to PTV59. For each of the PTV structures, a constraint could state that at least 95% of the PTV volume ($D_{95\%}$) receives at least 95% of the prescribed dose. For PTVs, maximum doses should not be exceeded. No PTV voxel should receive, for instance, more than 107% of the prescribed dose ($V_{107\%}$). If PTV70 is inside PTV59, then it is not possible to consider that no voxel in PTV59 will receive more than 63.6 Gy since we aim at achieving 70 Gy for PTV70. In this case, the percentage of voxels in PTV59 that are allowed to receive more than the maximum desired dose is limited. Table 1 presents an example of such dosimetry constraints. According to Table 1, a treatment plan will be considered in accordance with the medical prescription if and only if:

Table 1. Prescribed doses for the structures considered for FMO

Structure	Type of constraint		Limit
Spinal cord	Maximum dose	Lower than	45 Gy
Brainstem	Maximum dose	Lower than	54 Gy
Left parotid	Mean dose	Lower than	26 Gy
Right parotid	Mean dose	Lower than	26 Gy
PTV_{70}	$D_{95\%}$	Greater than	66.5 Gy
PTV_{70}	Maximum dose	Lower than	74.9 Gy
PTV_{59}	$D_{95\%}$	Greater than	56.4 Gy
PTV_{59}	$V_{107\%}$	Lower than	Percentage of PTV_{70} volume inside PTV_{59} plus a 10% margin
Body	Maximum dose	Lower than	80 Gy

- There is no voxel belonging to the spinal cord receiving more than 45 Gy;
- There is no voxel belonging to the brainstem receiving more than 54 Gy;
- The mean dose in the parotids does not exceed 26 Gy;
- 95% of the voxels in PTV_{70} are receiving at least 66.5 Gy;
- No voxel belonging to PTV_{70} receives more than 74.9 Gy;
- 95% of the voxels in PTV_{59} are receiving at least 56.4 Gy;
- The percentage of voxels in PTV_{59} that are allowed to receive more than 107% of the prescribed dose are limited to the percentage of PTV_{70} volume inside PTV_{59} plus a 10% margin.

In the planning of every single treatment, the questions that need to be answered are: *Is this medical prescription attainable? If it is, what is the treatment plan that complies with all the constraints? If it is not, how can we comply as much as possible with the medical prescription?*

The objective of a treatment planning procedure is thus to reach a solution that satisfies all the inequalities defined by the dose-volume constraints. It is not an optimization problem that needs to be solved, in the sense that no objective function needs to be defined. It is rather a feasibility problem, in the sense that what the planner really needs is to find a feasible solution. One of the difficulties encountered with this feasibility problem is the fact that the dose-volume constraints that have to be considered are not simple to represent in tractable mathematical programming models. To tackle this problem we will consider a procedure that iteratively solves an unconstrained optimization problem with parameters being changed automatically.

3 Fluence Map Optimization

The therapeutic radiation dose is delivered through a set of radiation beams usually determined *a priori*. Each beam can be interpreted as being discretized in a set of beamlets. It is then necessary to determine the intensity of each of these beamlets, defining the fluence map (FMO problem). FMO has been mainly tackled by constrained optimization models such that an objective function is optimized subject to a set of dose requirements [9–14]. The objective function usually considers a weighted sum of deviations from prescribed doses (underdose for PTVs and overdose for OARs). It is possible to find examples of linear models [15], mixed integer linear models [16], nonlinear models [17, 18], multiobjective models [19] and parallel programming approaches [20, 21]. In this paper, a voxel-based convex penalty non-linear model for FMO is used. The objective function considers the minimization of the sum of the penalties associated with each voxel, calculated as the square difference between the amount of dose received by the voxel and a given upper and/or lower bound. There are only linear nonnegativity constraints on the intensity (fluence) values. Considering that beam angles have already been fixed, let V represent the number of voxels, N the number of beamlets and D the dose matrix, such that D_{ij} represents the contribution of beamlet j to the total dose deposited in voxel i. The total dose received by voxel i can be calculated as $\sum_{j=1}^{N} D_{ij}w_j$ with w_j representing the intensity of beamlet j. Let U_i be the upper bound associated with voxel i, L_i the lower bound associated with voxel i, $\underline{\lambda}_i$ and $\overline{\lambda}_i$ the penalty weights of underdose and overdose of voxel i, respectively. The FMO model can be defined as follows, where $(\bullet)_+ = \max\{0, \bullet\}$:

$$f(w) = Min_w \sum_{i=1}^{V} \left[\underline{\lambda}_i \left(L_i - \sum_{j=1}^{N} D_{ij}w_j \right)_+^2 + \overline{\lambda}_i \left(\sum_{j=1}^{N} D_{ij}w_j - U_i \right)_+^2 \right] \quad (1)$$

$$\text{s.t. } w_j \geq 0, \quad j = 1, \ldots, N \quad (2)$$

Although this formulation allows unique weights and unique upper/lower bounds for each voxel, in the current approach weights are assigned by structure only. Considering a given structure S we can thus define $\overline{\lambda}_S$, $\underline{\lambda}_S$, U_S and L_S such that $\overline{\lambda}_i = \overline{\lambda}_S, \forall i \in S$, $\underline{\lambda}_i = \underline{\lambda}_S, \forall i \in S$, $U_i = U_S, \forall i \in S$ and $L_i = L_S, \forall i \in S$. This nonlinear formulation implies that a very small amount of deviation from the established bounds may be accepted, but larger deviations are decreasingly tolerated. We have chosen to work with this model for two main reasons: (1) the fact that it is an unconstrained problem guarantees that it will always be possible to find an admissible solution for the optimization problem (although it may not be feasible for the original treatment planning problem); (2) it is a convex problem that can be solved by known optimization algorithms. The main disadvantage of this model consists in the difficulty of predicting the impact that changes in the model parameters (namely weights and bounds) will have in the optimal solution calculated. Although this FMO model was chosen, the developed methodology could be extended to deal with different FMO models. It should be stressed that the value of the objective function has absolutely no clinical meaning whatsoever. The quality of the solution is not assessed by looking at the FMO objective function value but rather by looking at the dosimetry values. This means that the FMO objective function should be interpreted as nothing more than a technical tool that guides the optimization algorithm to interesting regions of the solution space, where feasible solution of the treatment planning problem can be found. If a planner were to work with such a FMO through a TPS, he would be asked to define *a priori* all the model's parameters: weights and upper and lower bounds. Looking at the objective function (1), and considering a given current solution w, how would the planner change the model's parameters to obtain a better solution? Let's imagine that for a given OAR S the maximum allowed dose in the current solution is not being respected. Then, in order for the optimization algorithm to produce a solution that spares S more than it is being spared, two things can be done: either one increases the upper weight associated with S $(\overline{\lambda}_S)$ or one changes (decreases) the corresponding upper bound (U_S). Both

options will increase $\overline{\lambda}_i \left(\sum_{j=1}^{N} D_{ij}w_j - U_i \right)_+^2$ for all voxels $i \in S$ that fail to respect the

prescribed dose. Although it is easy enough to see the direction into which the model's parameters should be changed in order to reach solutions that are more in accordance with the desired medical prescription, there is not a straightforward way of automatically determining the best change in the parameters. It is expected that larger deviations between the dosimetry results and the desired doses should correspond to more pronounced changes in the parameters. The main idea in the developed methodology is to drive this iterative procedure by resorting to FIS, that will mimic the reasoning of the human planner.

4   Automated FMO by Fuzzy Inference Systems

The proposed methodology will automatically change the FMO model's parameters in each iteration, by considering the deviations between the current and the desired dosimetry results. These changes will drive the FMO algorithm to search more promising regions of the searchable surface, until a plan complying as much as possible with the desired prescription is attained.

4.1   Initialization

The initial FMO model's parameters are defined by the dosimetry constraints. OARs, for instance, will only have upper bounds and will not have any lower bounds. Upper bounds are equal to the maximum dose or to the mean dose allowed, depending on the type of OAR. Regarding PTVs, both upper and lower bounds are defined. Upper bounds are usually considered as being equal to the maximum allowed dose (107% of the prescribed dose, for instance). Lower bounds are equal to the minimum required dose. Regarding the weights to assign to each structure, every structure begins by having a weight equal to 1. The only exception to this rule is when PTVs are inside other PTVs. Actually, the inner PTVs are subject to contradicting constraints, since each voxel will belong to more than one structure. In this case, and if the inner PTV is much smaller than the outer PTV, it is better to give an increased weight to the inner PTV. It should be pointed out that these weights will be automatically updated by the algorithm, so the initial weights will not have an impact in the quality of the final outcome (they can, however, have an impact in the total computational time, and this initialization will simply give the algorithm a better starting point). Weight initialization different than 1 could also be thought for special cases of very tiny OARs that are in close proximity to other OARs or PTVs (the case of crystalline lens, for instance), or for OARs that the planner knows that will be especially difficult to spare. It should be stressed that all weights could be initialized to 1: the algorithm will update these weights if necessary, at the cost of increased computational time.

4.2 Fuzzy Inference Systems

At each iteration, the FMO is optimized and dosimetry results are calculated. For each structure, the algorithm will check whether the defined constraints are being satisfied or not, and changes the model parameters in accordance. Upper/lower bounds are updated first, and weights are only changed if updating bounds proves not to be sufficient to attain the desired goals. Actually, changing bounds will potentially affect a greater number of voxels, therefore the penalty associated with the structure will be greater than changing only weights. When only weights are changed there will be a smaller number of voxels contributing to the objective function value. For a given structure S, if there is a deviation equal to d between the desired dosimetry metric and the current one, the corresponding bounds U_S and L_S are changed according to very simple common sense rules: if d is *large* then increase (decrease) $L_S(U_S)$ by a *large* amount; if d is *medium* then increase (decrease) $L_S(U_S)$ by a *medium* amount; if d is *small* then increase (decrease) $L_S(U_S)$ by a *small* amount. As it is not possible to define in a crisp way the notion of *large*, *medium* or *small*, these linguistic concepts are represented through the use of fuzzy sets and FIS is used to determine how much U_S and L_S should be changed. These concepts are represented resorting to triangular and trapezoidal membership functions, where d is measured as a percentage in relation to the desired value and the change in the bound is also measured in percentage. Linguistic concepts related to the current deviation are defined in Eqs. (3) to (5), and are also depicted in Fig. 1 (considering $a = 5$). Equations (6) to (8) define the membership functions representing the linguistic concepts associated with the change in the bounds (depicted in Fig. 2, for $b = 10$). A Mamdani type implication rule was considered [22]. This means that the Mamdani implication operator (min operator) is applied between the resulting antecedent membership function and the consequent membership function for all three fuzzy rules. The defuzzification technique is the Centroid Defuzzification

Technique (center of gravity), calculated as $\dfrac{\int \mu(z) \cdot z \partial z}{\int \mu(z) \partial z}$, where $\mu(z)$ represents the function that results from the fuzzy inference system.

$$\mu_{d\_small}(x) = \begin{cases} \frac{a-x}{a}, x < a\% \\ 0, x \geq a\% \end{cases} \tag{3}$$

$$\mu_{d\_medium}(x) = \begin{cases} 0, x \leq 2\% \\ \frac{x-(a-3)}{4}, (a-3)\% < x \leq (a+1)\% \\ \frac{(a+5)-x}{4}, (a+1)\% < x < (a+5)\% \\ 0, x \geq (a+5)\% \end{cases} \tag{4}$$

$$\mu_{d\_l\,arg\,e}(x) = \begin{cases} 0, x \leq (a+2)\% \\ \frac{x-(a+2)}{5}, (a+2)\% < x \leq (a+7)\% \\ 1, x > (a+7)\% \end{cases} \tag{5}$$

$$\mu_{c\_small}(x) = \begin{cases} \frac{b-x}{b}, x < b\% \\ 0, x \geq b\% \end{cases} \tag{6}$$

$$\mu_{c\_medium}(x) = \begin{cases} 0, x \leq (b-5)\% \\ \frac{x-(b-5)}{5}, (b-5)\% < x \leq b\% \\ \frac{(b+5)-x}{5}, b\% < x < (b+5)\% \\ 0, x \geq (b+5)\% \end{cases} \tag{7}$$

$$\mu_{c\_l\,arg\,e}(x) = \begin{cases} 0, x \leq b\% \\ \frac{x-b}{10}, b\% < x \leq (b+10)\% \\ 1, x > (b+10)\% \end{cases} \tag{8}$$

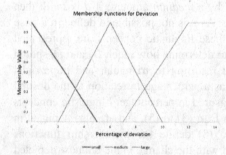

Fig. 1. Percentage of Deviation Membership Functions

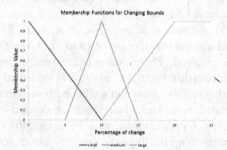

Fig. 2. Percentage of Change in the Bound Membership functions

The chosen membership functions result in an algorithm behaviour that will change the bounds in a continuous and smooth way. If different thresholds are considered (different values for a and b), more or less accentuated changes in bounds will be achieved that could lead to either similar results in less computational time or difficulties in achieving convergence towards a feasible solution. In many situations, it is possible to achieve admissible treatment plans by changing upper and lower bounds only. However, in more complicated cases, it will also be necessary to change structures' weights, namely when an upper bound is reaching very low values, or when a lower bound is increasing towards very large values. In this case, the algorithm will change the corresponding structure's weights, also resorting to a set of fuzzy rules, and following the same reasoning as before. Weights $\overline{\lambda}_S$ are changed whenever U_S reaches less than $l\%$ of its initial value. Weights $\underline{\lambda}_S$ are changed whenever L_S reaches more than u times its original value. Whenever the weights are updated, the upper and lower bounds take their initial values. If we increase (decrease) the l value (u value) for updating $\overline{\lambda}_S(\underline{\lambda}_S)$, then the weights will be updated more often. The weights are changed by using fuzzy rules similar to the ones already described: the current deviation is characterized as being *small*, *medium* or *large* according to (3)–(5). The change in the weights is given as a nominal change determined by the membership functions depicted in Eqs. (9)–(11). Parameter c can be used to change the behaviour of the FIS regarding the magnitude of changes in the weights.

$$\mu_{w\_small}(x) = \begin{cases} 1, x \leq c \\ \frac{c-x}{2}, c < x \leq (c+2) \\ 0, x \geq (c+2) \end{cases} \tag{9}$$

$$\mu_{w\_medium}(x) = \begin{cases} 0, x \leq (c-2) \\ \frac{x-(c-2)}{3}, (c-2) < x \leq (c+2) \\ \frac{(c+5)-x}{3}, (c+2)\% < x < (c+5) \\ 0, x \geq (c+5) \end{cases} \tag{10}$$

$$\mu_{w\_l\,arg\,e}(x) = \begin{cases} 0, x \leq (c+2) \\ \frac{x-(c+2)}{2}, (c+2) < x \leq (c+4) \\ 1, x > (c+4) \end{cases} \tag{11}$$

4.3 The Whole Procedure

After initialization, the algorithm will run for a predetermined number of iterations (*Nmax*) or until a plan complying with all the desired dosimetry results is reached. At each iteration, the bounds and weights are changed, in accordance with the deviations between the current and the desired solution, and the FMO is solved again. If *Nmax* is reached without an admissible treatment plan being found, then the algorithm will choose to relax some of the dosimetry constraints, trying to look for a plan that will not comply completely with the desired specifications, but that will comply as much as possible. The way the algorithm relaxes the dosimetry constraints is guided by the planner's preferences. The planner can choose, from the existing constraints, which of them he is more willing to relax. He can also assign a priority to each of these constraints, so that the highest the priority, the less relaxed the constraint will be. The relaxation of a given constraint is considered by calculating an admissibility slack for that constraint, such that if the deviation between the desired and the current dosimetry value is within that slack the constraint is considered as being satisfied. The value of this slack is calculated as a percentage value by using a FIS that takes as input the priority of the corresponding structure (the higher the priority the lowest the slack). The set of rules that are considered are as follows: if the priority is *high* then the slack is *small*; if the priority is *low* then the slack is *large*; if the priority is *medium* then the slack is *medium*. Linguistic concepts *high, low, medium, small, large* are defined in a similar manner as similar concepts already described. If the algorithm was able to comply with all the defined constraints before reaching the maximum number of iterations, then it will try to improve even further the treatment plan. This means that a new feasibility problem is considered, with constraints that are harder to satisfy. This can be done in two phases, also considering the planner's preferences. If the planner thinks it is important to try to obtain a better PTV coverage, then he can signalize the PTVs as being structures to improve. The algorithm will be more demanding regarding PTV coverage than initially defined. The path that the algorithm takes in attempting to increase PTV coverage can be configured by the planner. As an example: the PTV constraint of having 95% of the volume receiving at least 95% of the prescribed dose is changed to 96% of the volume receiving 95% of the prescribed dose, and so on, as long as it is possible to improve PTV coverage. When the algorithm is no longer capable of improving PTV coverage, it considers the best admissible plan found so far, fixes the desired PTV coverage as being equal to what was achieved, and tries to improve OARs in the second phase of the algorithm. In this second phase, the OARs' constraints are more demanding regarding their allowed maximum or mean doses (the desired values will be decreased). The decrease that is considered is given, once again, by a FIS that looks at how far the current dose received by an OAR is from the admissibility tolerance dose. If the dose received by the OAR is very close to its upper admissible limit, then the algorithm will not be very demanding. If the OAR is satisfying its constraint by a large amount, then the algorithm will be more demanding. Whenever the desired value is changed, a slack is considered so that the algorithm has some flexibility in the search for better solutions (nevertheless guaranteeing that the initial desired values are always attained). Slacks are calculated through a FIS system, similar to the one described above. The procedure is repeated until it is not possible to find an admissible solution or a maximum number of iterations is reached.

The algorithm will test different sets of equidistant beam angles, trying to find out the best set of angles. At the present moment, different beam angle sets are considered one at a time, in sequential executions of the algorithm. However, only the first phase of the algorithm is run for every set of angles to be considered. OAR improvement is run for the set of angles that achieved better PTV coverage only. Actually, when the OAR constraints are being satisfied, the preferred treatment plan is usually the one that better irradiates the PTVs. The whole procedure is described next.

1. Choose a set of radiation beam angles. *improve*←0; *IT*←0.
2. Initialize all the model's parameters; *it*←0.
3. Solve the FMO with the current parameters; *it*←*it* +1; *IT*←*IT* +1.
4. Do the dosimetry calculations. *Admissible*←*true*.
5. For each structure *S*
   (a) If there is a deviation between the current dosimetry metrics and the desired ones, change the upper/lower bounds associated with *S* according to the FIS. *Admissible*←*false*.
   (b) If the upper/lower bound has reached a predetermined threshold, then change the corresponding weight according to the FIS. Reset all upper and lower bounds to their initial values.
6. If *Not Admissible* go to 7, else
   (a) If *improve* then change the desired dosimetry constraints for selected OARs, trying to spare these OARs more. Go to 3.
   (b) Else go to 10.
7. If *it* ≤ *Nmax* then go to 3, else go to 8.
8. If *improve* then stop. If *IT* = *MaxIter* then go to 11, else go to 9.
9. Relax some of the defined constraints according to the planner's preferences. *it*←0. Go to 3.
10. Improve the current PTV coverage, by being more demanding regarding the dosimetry constraints. Go to 2.
11. If every set of angles was already considered, then go to 12. Else, select a different set of angles and go to 2.
12. If *improve* then stop, else *improve* ←1 and go to 13.
13. Consider the beam angle solution that resulted in better PTV coverage. Starting from the best solution found so far, improve the OARs sparing by being more demanding with the defined dosimetry constraints for selected structures. *it*←0. Go to 2.

5 Computational Results

This algorithm was applied to ten head-and-neck cancer cases identified as cases where proper PTV coverage and OAR sparing was difficult to obtain in clinical practice. The OARs considered were the spinal cord, the brainstem and the parotid glands. There are two or more PTVs with different prescribed doses. The desired dosimetry constraints are the ones depicted in Table 1. In clinical practice, most of the times, these cases are treated with 5 up to 11 beam angles. In this paper 9 beam angles plans are considered. It is also common to choose the equidistant solution starting at angle 0°. In these computational experiments, every equidistant beam angle solution was tried, considering a 5° discretization. Tests were performed on an Intel Core i7 CPU 2.8 GHz computer with 4 GB RAM and Windows 7. CERR 3.2.2 version [23] and MATLAB 7.4.0 (R2007a) were used. The dose was computed using CERR's pencil beam algorithm (QIB), with corrections for heterogeneities. For each of the ten head-and-neck cases, the sample rate used for Body was 32 and for the remaining structures was 4 (meaning that each set of 32 Body voxels was considered as one voxel in the optimization procedure and, for all other structures, one out of 4 voxels was used in the optimization procedure). To address the convex non-linear formulation of the FMO problem we used a trust-region-reflective algorithm (fmincon) of MATLAB 7.4.0 (R2007a) Optimization Toolbox. FIS were implemented resorting to the Fuzzy Sets Toolbox. The termination criteria for the algorithm are as follows: for each of the beam angles' set, the algorithm will stop after 20 iterations without being able to find an admissible solution ($Nmax = 20$), or if 200 iterations in total are reached ($MaxIter = 200$). The weights are being initialized as follows: if the inner PTV volume is less than 5% of the outer PTV volume, then the weight of the inner PTV will be equal to 50; if the volume is greater than 5% but less than or equal to 10%, then the weight will be equal to 10; in all other cases, it will be equal to 5. The choice of these weights can be seen as arbitrary, and it is indeed. These weights are as good as any others that represent the same idea: the smaller the inner PTV in relation with the outer PTV, the greater the weight we should assign to it. The algorithm was run considering different values for the parameters a, b, c, l and u to assess whether the algorithm is or is not very sensible to these parameters. Simultaneously decreasing a and increasing b will make the update of lower and upper bounds more accentuated. Increasing l and decreasing u will make the weights be updated more often, and increasing c will make the updates steeper. Eight different configurations were tested. Table 2 shows the number of iterations needed to reach a first feasible treatment plan. The minimum number of iterations for each case is shown in squares. It can be seen that it is possible to achieve a feasible treatment for all combinations tested except for one case and one configuration. The algorithm presents the expected behavior: for higher values of a and lower values of b it takes longer to reach feasibility. However, it may present problems converging if it tries to adjust too quickly. The update of weights has little influence in the algorithm's behavior. To analyze computational time and treatment plan quality, we fixed the parameters to $a = 5$, $b = 10$, $l = 30\%$, $u = 1.5$ and $c = 5$. Table 3 shows the computational time in minutes that the algorithm took to find the first treatment plan complying with all the dosimetry constraints, and also the total computational time (comprising the OAR improvement phase for the best equidistant beam angle set chosen). It is possible to see that the algorithm reaches a first admissible treatment plan in a very short period of time. The total computational time is compatible with clinical practice. The equidistant solution starting from $0°$ was the best equidistant angle solution for only 3 out of the 10 cases. This reinforces the idea that beam angle optimization is of the utmost importance.

Table 2. Number of iterations until the first feasible solution is found

Cases	$l = 15\%$, $u = 2$, $c = 3$										$l = 30\%$, $u = 1.5$, $c = 5$									
	1	2	3	4	5	6	7	8	9	10	1	2	3	4	5	6	7	8	9	10
$a = 10$, $b = 5$	16	23	11	14	36	23	12	20	12	30	16	23	11	14	36	23	12	20	12	30
$a = 5$, $b = 10$	7	10	4	4	16	10	4	7	7	69	7	10	4	4	15	10	4	7	7	26
$a = 3$, $b = 12$	68	6	4	5	14	44	5	5	14	35	23	6	4	5	13	19	5	5	15	39
$a = 3$, $b = 15$	18	6	4	5	15	40	15	5	17	—	18	6	4	5	27	37	5	5	26	45

Table 3. Computational time in minutes

Time (minutes)	1	2	3	4	5	6	7	8	9	10
First admissible solution	12	25	8	7	15	21	8	9	4	25
Total computational time	539	717	618	155	95	236	363	405	358	407

For all cases, it was possible to find treatment plans complying with the desired PTV coverage. Figures 3 and 4 depict the dose received for at least 95% of the PTV volume, for each one of the cases. An admissible plan should attain at least 95% of the desired dose, meaning that all points in the charts should be above the horizontal line which is indeed guaranteed. For all patients that have several different PTV70 and/or PTV59 structures, a weighted average considering the number of voxels in each structure was calculated, so that a single number could be shown in the chart, for ease in the presentation of results. It is, however, important to stress that the dosimetry constraints are fulfilled for all individual PTV structures. For OARs, it is important to guarantee that maximum admissible doses are not exceeded. The algorithm produced plans that guarantee all the dosimetry constraints for all OARs (Figs. 5, 6, 7 and 8). The depicted lines represent the maximum admissible value, so all values should be under these lines. This is exactly what is happening in all cases.

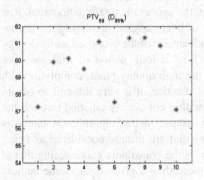

Fig. 3. Target irradiation metrics for PTVs

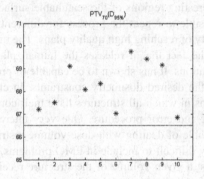

Fig. 4. Target irradiation metrics for PTVs

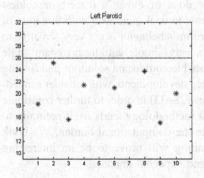

Fig. 5. Left parotid mean dose

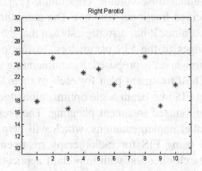

Fig. 6. Right parotid mean dose

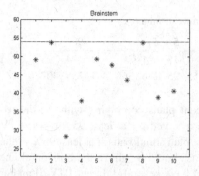
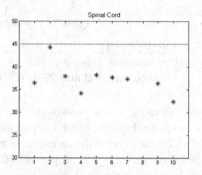

Fig. 7. Brainstem maximum dose   **Fig. 8.** Spinal cord maximum dose

6 Discussion and Conclusions

A methodology based on FIS that is able to attain admissible IMRT treatment plans in an automated way is described. The inputs to the algorithm are the patient's CT-scans with information regarding all the structures of interest and the desired dosimetry constraints. The algorithm will iteratively solve FMO problems, changing in an automated way the model's parameters, and driving the optimization process into interesting regions of the searchable surface. As the process is totally automated, it is possible to repeat the process for different sets of beam angles, increasing the probability of reaching high quality plans. The main advantage of the proposed methodology is the fact that it releases the human planner from a long period of trial-and-error iterations. It has shown to be capable of producing high quality plans, complying with all the desired dosimetry constraints. In clinical practice, it is very difficult to obtain plans in which all structures have their corresponding constraints satisfied through the trial and error procedure. One very interesting feature of this algorithm is that it is capable of dealing with dose-volume restrictions that are usually considered as being very difficult to include in FMO problems, namely the constraints guaranteeing that at most a given volume of the structure receives more than a given dose. Some authors have developed models using dose-volume histogram constraints [24–26], but these constraints have the drawback of creating a non-convex feasibility space, with many local minima. It can also be useful to consider the mean-tail-dose rather than conventional dose-volume constraints [27] (mean dose of either a hottest or coldest specified fractional volume). The algorithm is able to deal quite well with this kind of constraints. It has also been shown that the algorithm's behavior is not very sensitive to changes in the FIS parameters. In this paper a very simple equidistant beam angle optimization is proposed, by enumerating the possible equidistant solutions and finding the best treatment plan for each of them. Further developments will consider embedding FIS into beam angle optimization algorithms [28–33] in order to further contribute to automated treatment planning. The presented methodology lends itself naturally to parallel implementations, which will help tackle the computational burden. We think that using FIS for radiotherapy treatment planning will prove to be an interesting research direction with important applications and expected impacts.

Acknowledgments. This work has been supported by the Fundação para a Ciência e a Tecnologia (FCT) under project grant UID/MULTI/00308/2013.

References

1. Breedveld, S., Storchi, P.R.M., Voet, P.W.J., Heijmen, B.J.M.: iCycle: Integrated, multicriterial beam angle, and profile optimization for generation of coplanar and noncoplanar IMRT plans. Med. Phys. **39**, 951–963 (2012)
2. Breedveld, S., Storchi, P.R.M., Keijzer, M., Heemink, A.W., Heijmen, B.J.M.: A novel approach to multi-criteria inverse planning for IMRT. Phys. Med. Biol. **52**, 6339 (2007)
3. Voet, P.W.J., Dirkx, M.L.P., Breedveld, S., Fransen, D., Levendag, P.C., Heijmen, B.J.M.: Toward fully automated multicriterial plan generation: a prospective clinical study. Int. J. Radiat. Oncol. Biol. Phys. **85**, 866–872 (2013)
4. Li, R.-P., Yin, F.-F.: Optimization of inverse treatment planning using a fuzzy weight function. Med. Phys. **27**, 691–700 (2000)
5. Yan, H., Yin, F.F., Guan, H., Kim, J.H.: Fuzzy logic guided inverse treatment planning. Med. Phys. **30**, 2675–2685 (2003)
6. Yan, H., Yin, F.-F., Willett, C.: Evaluation of an artificial intelligence guided inverse planning system: clinical case study. Radiother. Oncol. **83**, 76–85 (2007)
7. Stieler, F., Yan, H., Lohr, F., Wenz, F., Yin, F.-F.: Development of a neuro-fuzzy technique for automated parameter optimization of inverse treatment planning. Radiat. Oncol. **4**, 39 (2009)
8. Dias, J., Rocha, H., Ventura, T., Ferreira, B., Lopes, M.D.C.: Automated fluence map optimization based on fuzzy inference systems. Med. Phys. **43**, 1083–1095 (2016)
9. Lim, G.J., Choi, J., Mohan, R.: Iterative solution methods for beam angle and fluence map optimization in intensity modulated radiation therapy planning. OR Spektrum **30**, 289–309 (2008)
10. Lodwick, W.A., McCourt, S., Newman, F., Humphries, S.: Optimization methods for radiation therapy plans. In: Börgers, C., Natterer, F. (eds.) Computational Radiology and Imaging: Therapy and Diagnostics (1999)
11. Shepard, D.M., Ferris, M.C., Olivera, G.H., Mackie, T.R.: Optimizing the delivery of radiation therapy to cancer patients. SIAM Rev. **41**, 721–744 (1999)
12. Holder, A.: Designing radiotherapy plans with elastic constraints and interior point methods. Health Care Manag. Sci. **6**, 5–16 (2003)
13. Ólafsson, A., Wright, S.J.: Linear Programming Formulations and Algorithms for Radiotherapy Treatment Planning. Optim. Methods Softw. **21**, 201–231 (2006)
14. Preciado-Walters, F., Langer, M.P., Rardin, R.L., Thai, V.: Column generation for IMRT cancer therapy optimization with implementable segments. Ann. Oper. Res. **148**, 65–79 (2006)
15. Romeijn, H.E., Ahuja, R.K., Dempsey, J.F., Kumar, A., Li, J.G.: A novel linear programming approach to fluence map optimization for intensity modulated radiation therapy treatment planning. Phys. Med. Biol. **48**, 3521–3542 (2003)
16. Lee, E.K., Fox, T., Crocker, I.: Integer programming applied to intensity-modulated radiation therapy treatment planning. Ann. Oper. Res. **119**, 165–181 (2003)
17. Cheong, K., Suh, T., Romeijn, H., Li, J., Dempsey, J.: Fast nonlinear optimization with simple bounds for IMRT planning. Med. Phys. **32**, 1975 (2005)

18. Aleman, D.M., Kumar, A., Ahuja, R.K., Romeijn, H.E., Dempsey, J.F.: Neighborhood search approaches to beam orientation optimization in intensity modulated radiation therapy treatment planning. J. Global Optim. **42**, 587–607 (2008)
19. Craft, D.L., Halabi, T.F., Shih, H.A., Bortfeld, T.R.: Approximating convex Pareto surfaces in multiobjective radiotherapy planning. Med. Phys. **33**, 3399–3407 (2006)
20. Men, C., Gu, X., Choi, D., Majumdar, A., Zheng, Z., Mueller, K., Jiang, S.B.: GPU-based ultrafast IMRT plan optimization. Phys. Med. Biol. **54**, 6565 (2009)
21. Ziegenhein, P., Kamerling, C.P., Bangert, M., Kunkel, J., Oelfke, U.: Performance-optimized clinical IMRT planning on modern CPUs. Phys. Med. Biol. **58**, 3705–3715 (2013)
22. Mamdani, E.H., Assilian, S.: An experiment in linguistic synthesis with a fuzzy logic controller. Int. J. Hum Comput Stud. **51**, 135–147 (1999)
23. Deasy, J.O., Blanco, A.I., Clark, V.H.: CERR: A computational environment for radiotherapy research. Med. Phys. **30**, 979–985 (2003)
24. Deasy, J.O.: Multiple local minima in radiotherapy optimization problems with dose–volume constraints. Med. Phys. **24**, 1157 (1997)
25. Zarepisheh, M., Shakourifar, M., Trigila, G., Ghomi, P.S., Couzens, S., Abebe, A., Noreña, L., Shang, W., Jiang, S.B., Zinchenko, Y.: A moment-based approach for DVH-guided radiotherapy treatment plan optimization. Phys. Med. Biol. **58**, 1869–1887 (2013)
26. Scherrer, A., Yaneva, F., Grebe, T.,Küfer, K.H.: A new mathematical approach for handling DVH criteria in IMRT planning. J. Glob. Optim. **61**, 407–428 (2015)
27. Romeijn, H.E., Ahuja, R.K., Dempsey, J.F., Kumar, A.: A new linear programming approach to radiation therapy treatment planning problems. Oper. Res. **54**, 201–216 (2006)
28. Rocha, H., Dias, J., Ferreira, B.C., Lopes, M.C.: Selection of intensity modulated radiation therapy treatment beam directions using radial basis functions within a pattern search methods framework. J. Glob. Optim. **57**, 1065–1089 (2013)
29. Rocha, H., Dias, J., Ferreira, B.C., Lopes, M.C.: Beam angle optimization for intensity-modulated radiation therapy using a guided pattern search method. Phys. Med. Biol. **58**, 2939–2953 (2013)
30. Rocha, H., Dias, J., Ferreira, B.C., Lopes, M.C.: Pattern search methods framework for beam angle optimization in radiotherapy design. Appl. Math. Comput. **219**, 10853–10865 (2013)
31. Dias, J., Rocha, H., Ferreira, B.C., Lopes, M.C.: A genetic algorithm with neural network fitness function evaluation for IMRT beam angle optimization. Cent. Eur. J. Oper. Res. **22**, 431–455 (2014)
32. Dias, J.M., Rocha, H., Ferreira, B., Carmo Lopes, M.: IMRT beam angle optimization using DDS with a cross-validation approach for configuration selection. In: Murgante, B., et al. (eds.) ICCSA 2014. LNCS, vol. 8580, pp. 1–16. Springer, Cham (2014). doi:10.1007/978-3-319-09129-7_1
33. Dias, J., Rocha, H., Ferreira, B., Lopes, M.C.: Simulated annealing applied to IMRT beam angle optimization: a computational study. Phys. Medica Eur. J. Med. Phys. **30**, 747–756 (2014)

Continuous Relaxation of MINLP Problems by Penalty Functions: A Practical Comparison

M. Fernanda P. Costa[1]([⊠]), Ana Maria A.C. Rocha[2],
and Edite M.G.P. Fernandes[2]

[1] Centre of Mathematics, University of Minho, 4800-058 Guimarães, Portugal
mfc@math.uminho.pt
[2] Algoritmi Research Centre, University of Minho, 4710-057 Braga, Portugal
{arocha,emgpf}@dps.uminho.pt

Abstract. A practical comparison of penalty functions for globally solving mixed-integer nonlinear programming (MINLP) problems is presented. The penalty approach relies on the continuous relaxation of the MINLP problem by adding a specific penalty term to the objective function. A new penalty algorithm that addresses simultaneously the reduction of the error tolerances for optimality and feasibility, as well as the reduction of the penalty parameter, is designed. Several penalty terms are tested and different penalty parameter update schemes are analyzed. The continuous nonlinear optimization problem is solved by the deterministic DIRECT optimizer. The numerical experiments show that the quality of the produced solutions are satisfactory and that the selected penalties have different performances in terms of efficiency and robustness.

Keywords: MINLP · Continuous relaxation · Penalty function · DIRECT

1 Introduction

In a continuous relaxation context, the mixed-integer nonlinear programming (MINLP) problem is formulated as a continuous bound constrained nonlinear programming (BCNLP) problem, by adding a special penalty function to the objective function in order to penalize integrality violation. In this study, we extend the work presented in [1,2] by using an exact method with guaranteed convergence to solve the BCNLP problem. The deterministic DIRECT optimizer [3] is selected. Further, a new penalty-type algorithm is designed. At each iteration k, the algorithm computes a δ^k-global minimizer of the BCNLP problem and reduces the error tolerances – for the optimality, δ^k, and for feasibility, η^k – when the integrality violation is at a satisfactory level. The performance of the algorithm is analyzed by using a practical comparison that involves six special penalty functions. Three well-known penalty functions taken from [4] and three

© Springer International Publishing AG 2017
O. Gervasi et al. (Eds.): ICCSA 2017, Part III, LNCS 10406, pp. 107–118, 2017.
DOI: 10.1007/978-3-319-62398-6_8

other recently proposed in [1,2] are investigated. The problem to be addressed
has the form:

$$\min f(x)$$
$$\text{subject to } x \in C \subset \mathbb{R}^n$$
$$x_i \in \mathbb{R} \text{ for } i \in I_c \subseteq I \equiv \{1,\ldots,n\} \tag{1}$$
$$x_j \in \mathbb{Z} \text{ for } j \in I_d \subseteq I \text{ (in particular } x_j \in \{0,1\})$$
$$I_c \cap I_d = \emptyset \text{ and } I_c \cup I_d = I$$

where f is a nonlinear continuous function, $|I_c|$ and $|I_d|$ give the number of con-
tinuous and integer variables respectively and the set C, assumed to be compact,
is $C = \{x \in \mathbb{R}^n : l_i \leq x_i \leq u_i, i \in I\}$ (l and u are the vectors of the lower and
upper bounds on the variables respectively). Since $x_j \in \mathbb{Z}$ for $j \in I_d$, we define
the feasible region of problem (1) as follows:

$$W = \{x \in C \subset \mathbb{R}^n : x_j \in \mathbb{Z} \text{ for } j \in I_d\}. \tag{2}$$

The continuous relaxation of a MINLP is obtained by relaxing the integrality
conditions from $x_j \in \mathbb{Z}$, $j \in I_d$ to $x_j \in \mathbb{R}$, $j \in I_d$ (assuming that the f values
can be computed for $x_j \in \mathbb{R}$, $j \in I_d$). We note that the presence of integer
variables implies that the feasible region W is not convex. There are two classes
of MINLP problems. In the context of problem (1), if the function f is convex,
the MINLP problem is called convex; otherwise it is called nonconvex. A convex
MINLP problem is easier to solve than a nonconvex one, since its continuous
relaxation is itself a convex problem, and therefore likely to be tractable, at
least in theory. By contrast, the continuous relaxation of a nonconvex MINLP is
itself a global optimization problem, and therefore likely to be NP-hard. Reviews
on MINLP techniques and applications are available in [5,6].

An exact continuous reformulation of MINLP problems using a specific class
of penalty terms is studied in [4,7]. The equivalence between the MINLP problem and the continuous reformulated penalty problem is therein established. This
issue concerned with penalty functions for problems with binary variables has
been addressed in [8,9]. Although any bounded MINLP problem can be reformulated as a mixed-binary programming problem, this strategy can be troublesome
and is not recommended in practice. The use of particular penalty terms to penalize integer constraints violation directly is preferred. In this context, a penalty
term based on the 'erf' function is proposed and compared with other penalty
alternatives available in the literature (see [1]). In [2], two different penalty functions are proposed. The hyperbolic tangent function and the inverse hyperbolic
sine function are designed and their properties are established. The equivalence
property between problem (1) and its continuous relaxation is studied. Another
proposal, that can be seen in [10], transforms the MINLP problem into an equivalent nonlinear programming (NLP) problem by adding to the original constraints
some linear and quadratic constraints. Then, a penalty function is used to transform the NLP problem into an unconstrained one. In [11], a new exact and
smooth penalty function for the MINLP problem is presented by augmenting
only one variable whatever the number of constraints.

In the sequence of the specific penalty approach, a continuous reformulation of the problem (1) comes out, by relaxing the integer constraints on the variables and adding a particular penalty term to the objective function f,

$$\min \psi(x; \varepsilon) \equiv f(x) + P(x; \varepsilon)$$
$$\text{subject to } x \in C \qquad\qquad (3)$$
$$x_i \in \mathbb{R} \text{ for } i = 1, \ldots, n,$$

where $\varepsilon \in \mathbb{R}^+$ is the penalty parameter and $P(x; \varepsilon)$ is the penalty term. Under suitable assumptions on the function f and the penalty $P(\cdot; \varepsilon)$, the function $\psi(\cdot; \varepsilon)$ in (3) is 'exact' in the sense that there exists a positive $\bar{\varepsilon}$ such that for $\varepsilon \in (0, \bar{\varepsilon}]$, problems (1) and (3) are equivalent, i.e., problems (1) and (3) have the same global minimizers [4,7].

In this study, we aim to address two important issues related to a penalty-type algorithm for solving MINLP problems. First, a new algorithm that is able to compute a sequence of approximations with error tolerances increasingly smaller on the optimality and on the integer infeasibility, is proposed. Second, using a set of penalty terms already available in the literature, we analyze their practical behavior when solving a benchmark set of bound constrained MINLP problems. We have also used an exact global optimizer for solving the continuous BCNLP problem, the DIRECT optimizer. Furthermore, this study also aims to analyze the relative performance of the penalty functions, within the exact penalty algorithm context, when different ε initialization and update schemes are tested.

This paper is organized as follows. In Sect. 2, we present the new penalty-based algorithm, by explaining the main ideas behind the penalty parameter and error tolerance updates, and illustrate the penalty functions used in the comparative experiments. In Sect. 3, the DIRECT optimizer is briefly described. Section 4 presents the results of the numerical experiments and some comparisons and Sect. 5 contains the conclusions of the present study.

2 Penalty Algorithm

In this section, we propose a penalty algorithm to solve MINLP problems. Based on the equivalence statement between the problems (1) and (3), when some suitable penalty terms are used to penalize integrality violation, a finite sequence of BCNLP problems (3) is solved. It has been proven that there exists a positive $\bar{\varepsilon}$ such that for $\varepsilon \in (0, \bar{\varepsilon}]$, both problems have the same global minimizers [4]. For the design of the penalty algorithm, we need the following definitions:

Definition 1. *Let ε^k be fixed at iteration k and let $\psi(x; \varepsilon^k)$ be a continuous objective function defined over a bounded space $C \subset \mathbb{R}^n$. The approximation $x^k \in C$ (to the global optimal of problem (3)) is a δ^k-global minimizer of the problem (3) if $\psi(x^k; \varepsilon^k) \leq \min_{x \in C} \psi(x; \varepsilon^k) + \delta^k$, where $\delta^k > 0$ is the error bound which reflects the accuracy required for the approximation.*

Definition 2. *Let η^k be fixed at iteration k and let $z^k = [x^k]_r$ be a feasible approximation, where $z_i^k \in \mathbb{Z}, i \in I_d$ results from rounding x_i^k to the nearest integer and $z_j^k = x_j^k$ for $j \in I_c$. The point $x^k \in C$ is an η^k-feasible approximation to the problem (1) if $\|x^k - z^k\|_\infty \leq \eta^k$ where $\eta^k > 0$ is the error bound which reflects the accuracy required for the approximation.*

Thus, it is shown in Algorithm 1 the main steps for finding a global solution to problem (1). At iteration k and for a fixed value of ε^k, the algorithm computes x^k, a δ^k-global minimizer of problem (3), which is an approximation to the global minimizer of (1). It is assumed that the sequence $\{x^k\}$ converges to the optimal solution x^* of (1), as long as $\eta^k \to 0$ and $\delta^k \to 0$, and a finite set of decreasing ε^k values are tested. The algorithm imposes the lower bound $\underline{\varepsilon}$ to prevent the BCNLP problem of becoming very hard to be solved. On the other hand, in practical terms, the sufficiently small positive error bounds $\underline{\eta}$ and $\underline{\delta}$, for η^k and δ^k respectively, are used to reflect the accuracy required for the solution.

Data: f^*, $k_{\max}$, $0 < \underline{\varepsilon} \ll 1$, $0 < \underline{\delta} \ll 1$, $0 < \underline{\eta} \ll 1$, $\varepsilon^1 > \underline{\varepsilon}$, $\delta^1 > \underline{\delta}$, $\eta^1 > \underline{\eta}$,
$\quad\sigma_\varepsilon \in (0,1), \sigma_\delta \in (0,1), \sigma_\eta \in (0,1)$;
Set $k = 1$;
repeat
$\quad$ Compute a δ^k-global minimizer x^k of problem (3) such that

$$\psi(x^k; \varepsilon^k) \leq \psi(x; \varepsilon^k) + \delta^k, \quad \text{for all } x \in C; \tag{4}$$

$\quad$ **if** $\|x^k - z^k\|_\infty > \eta^k$ **then**
$\quad\quad|\quad$ Set $\varepsilon^{k+1} = \max\{\sigma_\varepsilon \varepsilon^k, \underline{\varepsilon}\}$, $\delta^{k+1} = \delta^k$, $\eta^{k+1} = \eta^k$;
$\quad$ **else**
$\quad\quad|\quad$ Set $\varepsilon^{k+1} = \varepsilon^k$, $\delta^{k+1} = \max\{\sigma_\delta \delta^k, \underline{\delta}\}$, $\eta^{k+1} = \max\{\sigma_\eta \eta^k, \underline{\eta}\}$;
$\quad$ **end**
$\quad$ Set $k = k + 1$;
until $(\|x^k - z^k\|_\infty \leq \underline{\eta}$ and $|f(x^k) - f^*| \leq \underline{\delta})$ or $k > k_{\max}$;

Algorithm 1. Penalty algorithm for MINLP problems

To check when the update of the penalty parameter is timely, the algorithm resorts to Definition 2. Thus, the penalty parameter is reduced whenever the computed approximation x^k is not an η^k-feasible approximation; otherwise the value is maintained. Further, when x^k satisfies the definition of an η^k-feasible approximation, the error tolerance parameters δ^k and η^k are reduced so that a better approximation to the global solution of the problem (3) can be found. The algorithm stops when the computed iterate x^k is in a $\underline{\eta}$ vicinity of a feasible point and is within an error of $\underline{\delta}$ of the global minimum $\overline{f}^*$. We note that the use of the known global solution to stop the algorithm has the goal of analyzing its real effectiveness.

We note that any global optimizer for BCNLP problems can be used to compute the δ^k-global minimizer x^k. Since finding a global minimizer is much more difficult than finding a local one, the algorithms specially tailored for local optimization may converge to a local minimizer and the convergence entirely depends on the starting approximation. Thus, the global optimizer DIRECT is used to find a solution that satisfies (4) (see the details in the next section).

We now illustrate the set of penalty terms that will be used to solve MINLP problems, in this penalty algorithm context. Three popular penalty terms [4, 7, 8] are:

$$P(x; \varepsilon) = \sum_{\substack{j \in I_d}} \min_{\substack{l_j \leq d_i \leq u_j \\ d_i \in \mathbb{Z}}} \log\left(|x_j - d_i| + \varepsilon\right), \tag{5}$$

$$P(x; \varepsilon) = \frac{1}{\varepsilon} \sum_{\substack{j \in I_d}} \min_{\substack{l_j \leq d_i \leq u_j \\ d_i \in \mathbb{Z}}} \left\{[|x_j - d_i| + \varepsilon]^p\right\}, \ 0 < p < 1, \tag{6}$$

and

$$P(x; \varepsilon) = \frac{1}{\varepsilon} \sum_{\substack{j \in I_d}} \min_{\substack{l_j \leq d_i \leq u_j \\ d_i \in \mathbb{Z}}} \left\{[1 + \exp\left(-\rho|x_j - d_i|\right)]^{-1}\right\}, \ \rho > 0. \tag{7}$$

The two most recently proposed penalty terms for solving MINLP problems are based on the hyperbolic tangent function, tanh(·),

$$P(x; \varepsilon) = \frac{1}{\varepsilon} \sum_{\substack{j \in I_d}} \min_{\substack{l_j \leq d_i \leq u_j \\ d_i \in \mathbb{Z}}} \tanh\left(|x_j - d_i| + \varepsilon\right) \tag{8}$$

and on the inverse hyperbolic sine, asinh(·), both differentiable and strictly increasing functions on $[0, +\infty)$ [2],

$$P(x; \varepsilon) = \sum_{\substack{j \in I_d}} \min_{\substack{l_j \leq d_i \leq u_j \\ d_i \in \mathbb{Z}}} \mathrm{asinh}\left(\frac{1}{\varepsilon}|x_j - d_i| + \varepsilon\right). \tag{9}$$

Finally, the penalty term proposed in [1] uses the 'erf' function,

$$P(x; \varepsilon) = \frac{1}{\varepsilon} \sum_{\substack{j \in I_d}} \min_{\substack{l_j \leq d_i \leq u_j \\ d_i \in \mathbb{Z}}} \left\{\mathrm{erf}\left(|x_j - d_i| + \varepsilon\right)\right\} \tag{10}$$

and has been also selected for this study.

The six plots in Fig. 1 show the behavior of the above illustrated penalty terms when four different values of ε are used (10, 1, 0.1 and 0.01). Figure 1(a) displays the penalty term based on the 'log' function (see (5)), while Fig. 1(b) and (c) illustrate the behavior of the penalty terms presented in (6) and (7) respectively. In Fig. 1(d), we show the behavior of the hyperbolic tangent function, and in Fig. 1(e) the inverse hyperbolic sine is plotted. Finally, the 'erf' function is plotted in Fig. 1(f). As it can be seen, the functions (6), (7), (8), (9) and (10) are positive for $\varepsilon > 0$ while the function (5) may reach negative values. The hyperbolic tangent function and the 'erf' function have similar behaviors as a function of ε and the penalty functions that provide a faster penalty increase, as the integrality violation increases, are the functions (6), (7), (8) and (10).

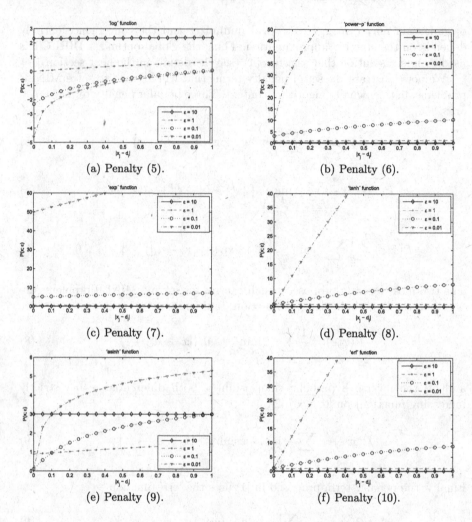

(a) Penalty (5).   (b) Penalty (6).

(c) Penalty (7).   (d) Penalty (8).

(e) Penalty (9).   (f) Penalty (10).

Fig. 1. Behavior of the penalty terms, for four different values of ε.

3 DIRECT Optimizer

When solving a nonconvex optimization problem, a global optimizer is recommended so that there exists some guarantee of convergence to a global solution and to avoid convergence to a local one.

This section aims to briefly describe the main ideas behind a partition-based algorithm, called DIRECT [3], that is capable of searching for a global optimal solution to the BCNLP problem by defining a sequence of partitions of the search region C. The DIRECT (DIviding RECTangles) algorithm has been originally proposed to obtain global solutions to continuous BCNLP problems [3], where the objective penalty function ψ must satisfy a Lipschitz condition

$$|\psi(x_1; \cdot) - \psi(x_2; \cdot)| \leq K\|x_1 - x_2\| \text{ for all } x_1, x_2 \in C,$$

for $K > 0$, by producing finer and finer partitions of the hyperrectangles generated from C. The algorithm is a modification of the standard Lipschitzian approach that does not require any derivative information or the value of the Lipschitz constant K. DIRECT has the ability to explore potentially optimal regions aiming to converge to the global optimum, while avoiding being trapped in local optima. This search is carried out by dividing all hyperrectangles that are potentially optimal. Notice the following definition:

Definition 3. *Given the partition $\{C^i : i \in J\}$ of C, let ν be a positive constant and let $\psi_{\min}$ be the current best objective function value. A hyperrectangle j is said to be potentially optimal if there exists some rate-of-change constant $\hat{K} > 0$ such that*

$$\psi(c_j; \cdot) - \hat{K}d_j \leq \psi(c_i; \cdot) - \hat{K}d_i, \text{ for all } i \in J$$
$$\psi(c_j; \cdot) - \hat{K}d_j \leq \psi_{\min} - \nu|\psi_{\min}| \tag{11}$$

where c_j is the center and d_j is a measure of the size of the hyperrectangle j.

We note that the use of $\hat{K}$ intends to show that it is not the Lipschitz constant. The division of the potentially optimal hyperrectangles is carried out only along the dimensions of maximal size, the division is into thirds and follows a specific order. The reader is referred to [3, 12, 13] for details. A subsequential convergence result for the DIRECT algorithm is established in [14]. In [3], the DIRECT algorithm for solving the BCNLP problem is described by its six main steps:

1. In the initialization step, the search space C is normalized to an n-dimensional unit hypercube, the center point c_1 and $\psi(c_1; \cdot)$ are determined, $\psi_{\min}$, the iteration counter and the set of indices of partition-based hyperrectangles are initialized.
2. In the selection step, for each partition of C, the set of potentially optimal hyperrectangles are identified.
3. In the sampling step, for each potentially optimal hyperrectangle, the set of dimensions with the maximum size is identified, and the objective function ψ is sampled at center points along those identified dimensions.
4. In the division step, using a specific order, hyperrectangles are divided into thirds along those identified dimensions.
5. The iteration step aims to update $\psi_{\min}$, the set of indices of partition-based hyperrectangles, and the set of potentially optimal hyperrectangles not yet explored.
6. In the termination step, the stopping conditions are checked so that steps 2–5 are repeated or the algorithm is terminated.

In the Algorithm 1 context, the δ^k-global minimizer of problem (3) is found when the condition (4) illustrated in the algorithm is satisfied. However, during this algorithm's practical evaluation (assuming that f^* is provided) the DIRECT optimizer terminates when the condition

$$\psi(x^k; \varepsilon^k) \leq f^* + \mathcal{C}(\varepsilon^k) + \delta^k$$

holds for the iterate x^k. For fixed ε^k, the term $\mathcal{C}(\varepsilon^k) \equiv P(x^*; \varepsilon^k) = P(\bar{x}; \varepsilon^k)$ is constant for any $\bar{x} \in W$, and equals $|I_d| \log(\varepsilon^k)$ for the penalty (5), $|I_d|(\varepsilon^k)^{p-1}$ for the penalty (6), $|I_d|(2\varepsilon^k)^{-1}$ for the penalty (7) (with $\rho = 1$), $|I_d|(\varepsilon^k)^{-1} \tanh(\varepsilon^k)$ for the penalty (8), $|I_d| \operatorname{asinh}(\varepsilon^k)$ for the penalty (9) and $|I_d|(\varepsilon^k)^{-1} \operatorname{erf}(\varepsilon^k)$ for the penalty (10).

Alternatively, DIRECT is stopped when the first, a maximum number of iterations, or a maximum number of function evaluations, is reached.

4   Numerical Experiments

In this section, a practical comparison of the penalty terms illustrated in Sect. 2, for solving MINLP problems, in the context of the proposed Algorithm 1 and using the DIRECT optimizer for solving the continuous BCNLP problem (3), is presented. The numerical experiments were carried out on a PC Intel Core 2 Duo Processor E7500 with 2.9 GHz and 4Gb of memory RAM. The algorithm was coded in Matlab Version 8.1 (R2013a).

The comparisons rely on 18 instances of 14 well-known MINLP problems. Eight problems have $n = 2$ variables, three have $n = 4$ variables, problem Dixon-Price is tested with $n = 2$ and $n = 4$, problem Sum Squares is tested with $n = 5$, and problems Ackley, Levy and Rastrigin are tested with $n = 5$ and 10. See [2] for the full description of the problems.

The parameters in the Algorithm 1 are set as follows: $\delta^1 = 1$, $\eta^1 = 1$, $\underline{\delta}$=1E-04, $\underline{\eta}$=1E-08, $\sigma_\delta = 0.1$, $\sigma_\eta = 0.1$ and $k_{\max} = 20$. The threshold number of iterations and function evaluations in the DIRECT solver are set to 100 and 50000 respectively. Other parameters for the penalty functions are $p = 0.5$ and $\rho = 1$.

The two parameters ε^1 (initialization of the penalty parameter) and σ_ε (the reduction factor) are analyzed in terms of penalty sensitivity, i.e., we aim to conclude if any of the penalty terms performs consistently better than the others for some pair of values of the parameters. During these experiments $\underline{\varepsilon}$ is set to 1E-12. The comparisons are made by using a graphical procedure to visualize the differences in the performance of the six penalty terms, in relative terms on the 18 instances, known as performance profiles [15]. The performance is analyzed in terms of the efficiency of the penalty. Thus, for the performance metric, P_m, the number of function evaluations is used. The performance function of case j in comparison is the (cumulative) distribution function $F_j(\tau)$ (for P_m), i.e., is the 'probability' that the case j is within a factor τ of the best possible case. For each j, the $F_j(\tau)$ is a (weakly) monotonically increasing function in τ. A performance profile is the plot of all functions $F_j(\cdot)$. The higher the 'probability' the better. A higher value for $\tau = 1$ means that the corresponding case achieves the smallest metric value, i.e., the fewer number of function evaluations, mostly.

The performance profile for the configuration $\varepsilon^1 = 10$ and $\sigma_\varepsilon = 0.1$ is shown in Fig. 2. We also show in Table 1 the percentage of success (in %) for each penalty. Here, the run with a certain penalty is considered a success if the algorithm terminates with the solution x^k that satisfies the conditions $\|x^k - z^k\|_\infty \leq \underline{\eta}$ and $|f(x^k) - f^*| \leq \underline{\delta}$, for the given values of $\underline{\eta}$ and $\underline{\delta}$.

From the Fig. 2 (and for $\tau = 1$) we may conclude that the probability that the 'log' function, as well as the 'asinh' function, are the winners on a given problem is about 0.39 since each one of them requires fewer function evaluations than the other penalty functions in seven of the 18 instances. The 'power-p' function has a probability of winning of 0.22 (requiring fewer function evaluations in four of the 18 instances). The other penalties in comparison did not reach the smallest number of function evaluations in any of the tested instances. Although being one of the most efficient (with the configuration $\varepsilon^1 = 10$, $\sigma_\varepsilon = 0.1$), the 'log' function is the least robust with a percentage of success of 78%, against 83% of the other penalties (see the percentages along the first row of the Table 1).

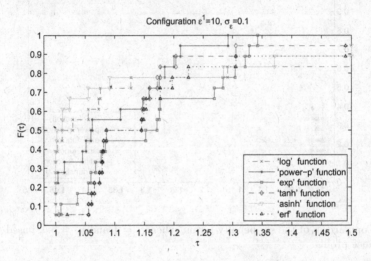

Fig. 2. Comparison of the six penalty terms, when $\varepsilon^1 = 10$ and $\sigma_\varepsilon = 0.1$, based on the performance profile.

Table 1. Percentage of success (%) for each penalty and each configuration

Configuration	'log'	'power-p'	'exp'	'tanh'	'asinh'	'erf'
$\varepsilon^1 = 10$, $\sigma_\varepsilon = 0.1$	78	83	83	83	83	83
$\varepsilon^1 = 1$, $\sigma_\varepsilon = 0.5$	61	78	83	83	72	83
$\varepsilon^1 = 0.1$, $\sigma_\varepsilon = 0.5$	56	67	67	67	56	67

Figure 3 shows the performance profile when $\varepsilon^1 = 1$ and $\sigma_\varepsilon = 0.5$ are considered. We may conclude that the penalty with the highest probability of winning, requiring fewer function evaluations to reach the global solution, is the 'power-p', 0.44, followed by the 'asinh' function with a probability of 0.22, by the 'erf' with a probability of 0.17 and by 'log' and 'tanh', both with probability of 0.11. The percentages of success of this configuration are shown along the second row of the Table 1. The penalties 'exp', 'tanh' and 'erf' are the most robust.

On the other hand, by analyzing the performance functions in Fig. 4, where the configuration $\varepsilon^1 = 0.1$ and $\sigma_\varepsilon = 0.5$ is tested, it is possible to conclude that the most efficient penalty is the 'power-p' with a probability of winning of 0.61, followed by the 'erf' penalty with a probability of 0.22, by the 'log' with probability of 0.11 and by the 'exp' with probability of 0.06. Further, from the percentages shown in the third row of the Table 1, we conclude that this is the configuration that produces the worst results, in the sense that the required final

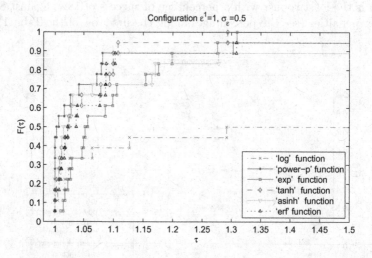

Fig. 3. Comparison of the six penalty terms, when $\varepsilon^1 = 1$ and $\sigma_\varepsilon = 0.5$, based on the performance profile.

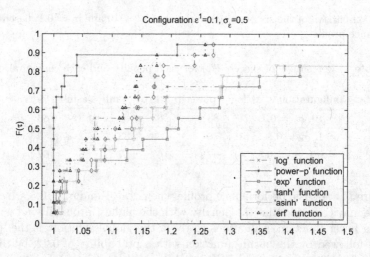

Fig. 4. Comparison of the six penalty terms, when $\varepsilon^1 = 0.1$ and $\sigma_\varepsilon = 0.5$, based on the performance profile.

error tolerances for the optimality, $\underline{\delta}$, and for the feasibility, $\underline{\eta}$, are attained for a much smaller number of instances, being even so the penalties 'power-p', 'exp', 'tanh' and 'erf' the most robust.

5 Conclusions

In this paper, we have developed a new penalty algorithm for solving nonconvex MINLP problems. The algorithm is based on a continuous relaxation of the MINLP problem by adding to the objective function a specific penalty term that aims to penalize integrality violation. The algorithm computes (a sequence of) δ^k-global minimizers of a BCNLP problem, for a decreasing sequence of δ^k values, using the DIRECT optimizer. A sequence of decreasing error tolerances, incorporated in the algorithm to measure integer infeasibility, is used to check when the update of the penalty parameter is timely. Six penalty terms are tested in the proposed algorithm context.

Numerical experiments have been carried out to analyze the penalty term sensitivity to the initialization and update scheme of the penalty parameter. The comparisons are based on the performance profile relative to an efficiency metric. With this comparative study, we are able to conclude that the selected penalties behave differently as far as the efficiency metric is concerned. Two penalties, one based on a power function and the other based on the 'asinh' function, are consistently the most efficient, and the penalties with the power term and with the 'log' function are less sensitive to changes in ε. On the other hand, penalties 'asinh' and 'erf' are the ones whose performances vary the most with the penalty parameter values. It has been shown that the configuration that uses 10 as the initial value and 0.1 as the reduction factor produces the best results in terms of number of instances that converged to the global solution with the required accuracy. Overall, in comparative terms, we may say that the penalties 'exp', 'tanh' and 'erf' are consistently more robust and the penalties 'power-p' and 'asinh' require in general fewer function evaluations.

Acknowledgments. The authors wish to thank two anonymous referees for their comments and suggestions.

This work has been supported by COMPETE: POCI-01-0145-FEDER-007043 and FCT - Fundação para a Ciência e Tecnologia, within the projects UID/CEC/00319/2013 and UID/MAT/00013/2013.

References

1. Francisco, R.B., Costa, M.F.P., Rocha, A.M.A.C., Fernandes, E.M.G.P.: Comparison of penalty functions on a penalty approach to mixed-integer optimization. In: AIP Conference Proceedings, vol. 1738 (ICNAAM 2015), pp. 300008-1–300008-4 (2016)
2. Costa, M.F.P., Rocha, A.M.A.C., Francisco, R.B., Fernandes, E.M.G.P.: Firefly penalty-based algorithm for bound constrained mixed-integer nonlinear programming. Optimization **65**(5), 1085–1104 (2016)

3. Jones, D.R., Perttunen, C.D., Stuckman, B.E.: Lipschitzian optimization without the Lipschitz constant. J. Optim. Theory Appl. **79**(1), 157–181 (1993)
4. Lucidi, S., Rinaldi, F.: Exact penalty functions for nonlinear integer programming problems. J. Optim. Theory Appl. **145**(3), 479–488 (2010)
5. Burer, S., Letchford, A.N.: Non-convex mixed-integer nonlinear programming: a survey. Surv. Oper. Res. Manage. Sci. **17**(2), 97–106 (2012)
6. Boukouvala, F., Misener, R., Floudas, C.A.: Global optimization advances in mixed-integer nonlinear programming, MINLP, and constrained derivative-free optimization, CDFO. Eur. J. Oper. Res. **252**(3), 701–727 (2016)
7. Lucidi, S., Rinaldi, F.: An exact penalty global optimization approach for mixed-integer programming problems. Optim. Lett. **7**(2), 297–307 (2013)
8. Murray, W., Ng, K.-M.: An algorithm for nonlinear optimization problems with binary variables. Comput. Optim. Appl. **47**(2), 257–288 (2010)
9. Shandiz, R.A., Mahdavi-Amiri, N.: An exact penalty approach for mixed integer nonlinear programming problems. Am. J. Oper. Res. **1**(3), 185–189 (2011)
10. Yu, C., Teo, K.L., Bai, Y.: An exact penalty function method for nonlinear mixed discrete programming problems. Optim. Lett. **7**(1), 23–38 (2013)
11. Ma, C., Zhang, L.: On an exact penalty function method for nonlinear mixed discrete programming problems and its applications in search engine advertising problems. Appl. Math. Comput. **271**, 642–656 (2015)
12. Gablonsky, J.M., Kelley, C.T.: A locally-biased form of the DIRECT algorithm. J. Global Optim. **21**(1), 27–37 (2001)
13. Finkel, D.E.: DIRECT Optimization Algorithm User Guide. North Carolina State University, Center for Research in Scientific Computation (2003)
14. Finkel, D.E., Kelley, C.T.: Convergence analysis of the DIRECT algorithm. Technical Report CRSC-TR04-28, Center for Research in Scientific Computation, North Carolina State University (2004)
15. Dolan, E.D., Moré, J.J.: Benchmarking optimization software with performance profiles. Math. Program. Ser. A **91**(2), 201–213 (2002)

Combining Filter Method and Dynamically Dimensioned Search for Constrained Global Optimization

M. Joseane F.G. Macêdo[1], M. Fernanda P. Costa[2], Ana Maria A.C. Rocha[3]([✉]), and Elizabeth W. Karas[4]

[1] Department of Exact and Natural Sciences,
Federal Rural University of Semi-Árido, Mossoró 59625-900, Brazil
joseane@ufersa.edu.br
[2] Department of Mathematics and Applications, Centre of Mathematics,
University of Minho, Campus de Gualtar, 4710-057 Braga, Portugal
mfc@math.uminho.pt
[3] Department of Production and Systems, Algoritmi Reasearch Centre,
University of Minho, Campus de Gualtar, 4710-057 Braga, Portugal
arocha@dps.uminho.pt
[4] Department of Mathematics, Federal University of Paraná,
Curitiba 81531-980, Brazil
ewkaras@ufpr.br

Abstract. In this work we present an algorithm that combines the filter technique and the dynamically dimensioned search (DDS) for solving nonlinear and nonconvex constrained global optimization problems. The DDS is a stochastic global algorithm for solving bound constrained problems that in each iteration generates a randomly trial point perturbing some coordinates of the current best point. The filter technique controls the progress related to optimality and feasibility defining a forbidden region of points refused by the algorithm. This region can be given by the flat or slanting filter rule. The proposed algorithm does not compute or approximate any derivatives of the objective and constraint functions. Preliminary experiments show that the proposed algorithm gives competitive results when compared with other methods.

Keywords: Global optimization · Dynamically dimensioned search algorithm · Filter methods

1 Introduction

Many engineering optimization problems are complex, nonconvex and non-smooth. Additionally some of them are defined as black-box problems that involve computational expensive computer simulations for which one cannot accurately approximate derivatives. To solve this type of problems, traditional gradient-based methods might not be suitable. In this context, stochastic methods are attractive because they are computationally simple and derivative-free.

© Springer International Publishing AG 2017
O. Gervasi et al. (Eds.): ICCSA 2017, Part III, LNCS 10406, pp. 119–134, 2017.
DOI: 10.1007/978-3-319-62398-6_9

Most stochastic methods were primary developed for unconstrained problems and then extended to constrained ones. An important class of methods for constrained optimization are the penalty methods, which seek the solution by replacing the original constrained problem by a sequence of unconstrained subproblems, where the constraint functions are combined with the objective function to define a penalty function.

An alternative to penalty methods to handle constrained optimization problems is the filter method introduced by Fletcher and Leyffer in [1]. This method is based on the concept of dominance, borrowed from multicriteria optimization, to build a filter that accepts iterates if they improve the objective function or improve a constrained violation function, based on *Pareto domination rule*. One of the advantages of this method when compared to the penalty method is that it avoids the initialization and updating of the penalty parameters that are associated with the penalization of the constraints. Filter methods have been combined with trust-region approaches [2,3], SQP techniques [4,5], inexact restoration algorithms [6,7], interior point strategies [8] and line-search algorithms [9–11]. They also have been extended to other areas of optimization such as nonlinear equations and inequalities [12–15], nonsmooth optimization [16,17], unconstrained optimization [18,19], complementarity problems [20,21] and derivative-free optimization [22–25].

The Dynamically Dimensioned Search (DDS) algorithm was introduced in [26] for automatic calibration of watershed simulation models (WDS). Since the calibration problems have many parameters/variables, DDS proved to be a simple and robust tool for computationally expensive models. In [27], a new global optimization algorithm for WDS optimization, called hybrid discrete dynamically dimensioned search, combines two local search heuristics with a discrete DDS search strategy adapted from the continuous DDS algorithm. Another derivative-free heuristic based on DDS algorithm for optimization of expensive black-box objective functions subject to inequality constraints using surrogate model-based methods was developed in [28,29].

Our contribution is to extend the DDS Algorithm for nonlinear nonconvex and nonsmooth constrained global optimization problems by incorporating a filter technique to handle the constraints.

The problem to be addressed is of the following form:

$$\begin{aligned}
\text{minimize} \quad & f(x) \\
\text{subject to} \quad & g(x) \leq 0 \\
& x \in \Omega,
\end{aligned} \tag{1}$$

where $f : \mathbb{R}^n \to \mathbb{R}$, $g : \mathbb{R}^n \to \mathbb{R}^m$ are nonlinear functions and $\Omega = \{x \in \mathbb{R}^n : -\infty < \ell \leq x \leq u < \infty\}$. Since we do not assume that the functions f and g are differentiable and convex, many local minima may exist in the feasible region $\Omega_F = \{x \in \Omega : g(x) \leq 0\}$.

The paper is organized as follows. Section 2 briefly describes the DDS algorithm and Sect. 3 presents the filter technique to handle the constrained optimization problem. Section 4 presents the proposed algorithm that combines the

DDS algorithm with the filter technique. In Sect. 5, numerical experiments for two sets of test problems are reported. The paper is concluded in Sect. 6.

2 Dynamically Dimensioned Search Algorithm

In this section, we briefly describe the DDS algorithm developed by Tolson and Shoemaker [26] for calibration problems that arise in the context of watershed simulation models. These type of problems involve many parameters to estimate (that correspond to decision variables), and are modeled as bound constrained optimization problems. Thus, the DDS Algorithm aims to solve a bound constrained global optimization problem in the following form

$$\underset{x \in \Omega}{\text{minimize}} \quad f(x),$$

where $f : \mathbb{R}^n \to \mathbb{R}$ is a nonlinear function in the compact set Ω.

The DDS algorithm is a point-to-point stochastic based heuristic global search algorithm. The main features of the DDS are no parameter tuning and the search strategy of finding good global solutions is scaled within a user-specified maximum number of function evaluations (k_{max}). At the beginning, the algorithm searches globally, and becomes a more local search as the number of iterations approaches the maximum allowable number of function evaluations. The transition from global to local search is achieved by dynamically and probabilistically reducing the number of dimensions to be perturbed in the neighborhood of the current best solution. Thus, at each iteration k, a trial candidate solution/point x_{trial}^k is obtained by perturbing the current best x_{best}^k only in the randomly selected dimensions. These perturbation magnitudes are randomly sampled from a normal distribution with a mean of zero and a standard deviation σ. Therefore, having selected a subset $I_{perturb}$ of dimensions to be perturbed, the trial x_{trial}^k is componentwised computed by:

$$x_{trial,i}^k = \begin{cases} x_{best,i}^k + N(0, \sigma_i^2) & \text{if } i \in I_{perturb} \\ \\ x_{best,i}^k & \text{otherwise} \end{cases} \tag{2}$$

with a standard deviation $\sigma_i = r(u_i - \ell_i)$ being r a scalar neighborhood size perturbation parameter. Here $x_{trial,i}^k$, $x_{best,i}^k$ and σ_i denote the ith coordinate of the respective vector. If $x_{trial}^k \notin \Omega$ then the trial point is projected onto Ω.

To choose the new best point for the next iteration a greedy procedure between the current best x_{best}^k and the trial candidate x_{trial}^k is performed. The current best x_{best}^k and the trial x_{trial}^k are compared with each other and if the trial decreases the objective function value ($f(x_{trial}^k) < f(x_{best}^k)$), then the trial candidate is moved to the next iteration as the current best point; otherwise, the current best is preserved to the next iteration. A formal description of the DDS algorithm is presented in Algorithm 1.

Algorithm 1. DDS Algorithm

Require: $r = 0.2$, k_{max}
1: Initialization
      Generate $x^1 \in \Omega$
      Set $k = 1$, $x_{best}^k = x^k$, $f_{best}^k = f(x^k)$, $I_{perturb} = \emptyset$
2: **while** $k \leq k_{max}$ **do**
3:    Compute the probability of perturbing the decision variables:
      $$P_k = 1 - \frac{\ln(k)}{\ln(k_{max})}$$
4:    Select coordinates to perturb:
      Generate uniform random numbers $\omega_i \in [0,1]$, for $i = 1, \ldots, n$
      Set $I_{perturb} = \{i : \omega_i < P_k\}$
      if $I_{perturb} = \emptyset$ **then**
          Select a random number $i \in \{1, \cdots, n\}$
          Set $I_{perturb} = \{i\}$
      endif
5:    Generate x_{trial}^k using (2)
6:    Project x_{trial}^k onto Ω, if necessary
7:    Evaluate $f(x_{trial}^k)$
8:    Select the best point:
      if $f(x_{trial}^k) < f_{best}^k$ **then**
          Set $x_{best}^{k+1} = x_{trial}^k$, $f_{best}^{k+1} = f(x_{trial}^k)$
      endif
9:    Set $k = k + 1$
10: **end while**

---

3   Filter Methods

In this section we give a brief description of filter methods originally introduced by Fletcher and Leyffer in [1] as an alternative way for globalizing nonlinear programming methods without using any penalty or merit function. The filter methods avoid the problematic issues related to the initial value of the penalty parameter and the tuning of their values throughout the iterative process, which greatly affects the performance of the algorithms.

Filter methods regard (1) as a bi-objective optimization problem that minimizes both the objective function f and a non-negative constraint violation function $h : \mathbb{R}^n \to \mathbb{R}^+$ defined by

$$h(x) = \|g^+(x)\| \tag{3}$$

where $\|g^+(x)\| = \|\max\{0, g(x)\}\|$ for some norm. The filter methods use the concept of dominance from multiobjective optimization, attempting to minimize both functions, but a certain emphasis is put on h, since convergence to a feasible point must be ensured. According to [1], a point x^j (or the corresponding pair $(f(x^j), h(x^j))$) dominates a point x^ℓ (or the corresponding pair $(f(x^\ell), h(x^\ell))$ if

$$f(x^\ell) \leq f(x^j) \text{ and } h(x^\ell) \leq h(x^j).$$

A filter $\mathcal{F}$ is a set of pairs $\{(f^j, h^j)\}$ such that no pair is dominated by any of the others, where $(f^j, h^j) = (f(x^j), h(x^j))$. As proposed in [1], to avoid the acceptance of filter entries close to the boundary formed by the set of all pairs dominated by the filter, the acceptability of the pair $(f(x), h(x))$ to the filter must satisfy a sufficient reduction condition in the form of an *envelope* over all $(f^j, h^j) \in \mathcal{F}$:

$$f(x) < f^j - \alpha h^j \quad \text{or} \quad h(x) < (1 - \alpha)h^j, \quad \forall (f^j, h^j) \in \mathcal{F} \tag{4}$$

where $\alpha \in (0, 1)$ is a given constant. A filter based on this acceptance rule is designated by *flat filter*. In [30] a slightly different acceptance condition for defining this filter envelope is proposed:

$$f(x) < f^j - \alpha h(x) \quad \text{or} \quad h(x) < (1 - \alpha)h^j, \quad \forall (f^j, h^j) \in \mathcal{F}. \tag{5}$$

A filter based on this acceptance rule is called by *slanting filter*. A typical filter entry is illustrated in Fig. 1, where the shaded area shows the region dominated by the entry (f^j, h^j) and the *envelope*, in a flat filter (on the left) and in a slanting filter (on the right).

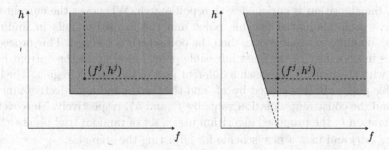

Fig. 1. A typical flat and slanting filter on one entry

Usually, the filter is initialized to be empty $\mathcal{F}_1 = \emptyset$ or with one filter entry that imposes an upper bound for acceptable values on h, $\mathcal{F}_1 = \{(-\infty, h_{\max})\}$ for some $h_{\max} \geq h^1$. In each iteration k, a point x^{k+1} is computed in a such way that the pair (f^{k+1}, h^{k+1}) satisfies the condition (4) (or (5)) for $\mathcal{F} = \mathcal{F}_k \cup \{(f^k, h^k)\}$. If the constraint violation is small and a predicted reduction on f holds, then instead of the filter acceptance criterion, a sufficient reduction on f is required. In case of success, this type of iteration is called a f-type iteration and all the others as h-type iteration (see [1] for more details). On the other hand, in [2,6], an iteration is considered an h-type whenever the function f increases along of the iteration, and all the others as f-type iteration. Such classification of the iterations is used for updating the filter. Throughout the optimization, the filter is updated only at h-type iterations, i.e., in such iterations the pair (f^k, h^k) is added to filter $\mathcal{F}_k$. If the filter is not updated, it remains unchanged, i.e.,

$\mathcal{F}_{k+1} = \mathcal{F}_k$ and the entry $\{(f^k, h^k)\}$ is discarded. Thus, the filter is updated as follows:

$$\mathcal{F}_{k+1} = \begin{cases} \mathcal{F}_k \cup \{(f^k, h^k)\} & \text{if } k \text{ is an } h\text{-type iteration} \\ \mathcal{F}_k & \text{otherwise.} \end{cases} \quad (6)$$

Whenever a new entry (f^k, h^k) is added to the filter, all entries that are dominated by (f^k, h^k) are removed from the filter. Furthermore, the updating (6) prevents the addition of feasible iterates to the filter. In fact, whenever x^k is a feasible point then x^{k+1} must decrease f to be accepted by the filter $\mathcal{F}_k \cup \{(f^k, 0)\}$. So, the iteration is a f-type, and consequently the entry $(f^k, 0)$ is discarded.

4 The Proposed Algorithm

In the previous sections we presented the DDS algorithm for bound constrained optimization, and the filter technique for handling constraints. We now present a global algorithm that combines the filter methodology and the DDS, for solving nonlinear constrained problems. The proposed algorithm uses the filter methodology that is able to guarantee sufficient progress towards feasible and optimal solutions of (1), by exploring both feasible and infeasible regions. Furthermore, the filter method allows to select the best non-dominated points, being the least infeasible ones. To promote the exploration of other promising areas of the search region, the algorithm is enriched with a poll-search. Whenever the current best point is a non-dominated feasible point and the algorithm fails in finding a new non-dominated feasible one, then the poll-search is invoked. This procedure searches in a vicinity of the least infeasible point found up to the current iteration k, with the hope to approach a different part of the feasible region. The least infeasible point will be denoted by x_I^k, and the corresponding objective function value and the constraint violation value by f_I^k and h_I^k, respectively. Moreover, at each iteration k, the proposed algorithm uses a set of random trial points $x_{trial_j}^k$ $(j = 1, ..., n_t)$ and uses a new scheme for adjusting the step size.

4.1 Initialization

At iteration $k = 1$, an initial point is randomly generated in the search space Ω as follows

$$x^1 = \ell + \xi(u - \ell), \quad (7)$$

where each component of the vector ξ is a uniformly distributed random number in $[0, 1]$. The initial filter is an empty set, $\mathcal{F}_1 = \emptyset$, the current best point is $x_{best}^1 = x^1$, $(f_{best}^1, h_{best}^1) = (f(x^1), h(x^1))$ and $(f_I^1, h_I^1) = (-\infty, +\infty)$.

4.2 Probability Computation

As in [26], at iteration k, the algorithm computes the probability of perturbing the coordinates of the current best point as follows:

$$P_k = 1 - \frac{\ln(k)}{\ln(k_{max})} \quad (8)$$

where k_{max} is the maximum number of iterations.

4.3   Set of Trial Points

At iteration k, the algorithm computes a set of n_t trial points. First, for each $j \in \{1, \cdots, n_t\}$ are generated n uniform random numbers $\omega_{j,1}, \cdots, \omega_{j,n}$ in $[0, 1]$. These random numbers are used to define the coordinate index set of the current best point x_{best}^k to be perturbed in the following way:

$$I_{perturb_j} = \{i : \omega_{j,i} < P_k\},$$

where the probability P_k is given in (8). If $I_{perturb_j}$ is an empty set, then a coordinate index i is randomly selected from $\{1, ..., n\}$, and $I_{perturb_j} = \{i\}$. Then, the trial point $x_{trial_j}^k$, for $j \in \{1, ..., n_t\}$, is obtained by:

$$x_{trial_j,i}^k = \begin{cases} x_{best,i}^k + \gamma_k N(0, \sigma_i^2) & \text{if } i \in I_{perturb_j} \\ \\ x_{best,i}^k & \text{otherwise,} \end{cases} \tag{9}$$

where $\gamma_k \in (0, 1]$ is a randomization parameter. Note that (9) differs from (2) by this parameter that adjusts the step-size. If $x_{trial_j}^k \notin \Omega$, then the trial point is projected onto Ω. Let $T^k = \{x_{trial_1}^k, ..., x_{trial_{n_t}}^k\}$ be the set of the trial points generated.

4.4   Selection of the Non-Dominated Trial Best Points

Given the set of trial points $T^k = \{x_{trial_1}^k, ..., x_{trial_{n_t}}^k\}$, identify the set of non-dominated trial points $T_{ND}^k \subseteq T^k$, i.e., the points $x_{trial_j}^k \in T^k$ that verify the condition (4) (or (5)) for $\mathcal{F} = \mathcal{F}_k \cup \{(f_{best}^k, h_{best}^k)\}$.

If $T_{ND}^k \neq \emptyset$, then two trial best points, denoted by x_{bt}^k, and x_{It}^k, are selected using the following definition:

Definition 1. *(trial best points)*

1. *If there exist feasible points in T_{ND}^k, then x_{bt}^k is the feasible trial point with the smallest objective function value.*
2. *If there exist no feasible points in T_{ND}^k, then x_{bt}^k is the trial point with the least constraint violation value.*
3. *If $T_{ND}^k \backslash \{x_{bt}^k\} \neq \emptyset$, then x_{It}^k is the trial point with the least constraint violation value in this set.*

If $T_{ND}^k = \emptyset$, then the poll-search will be invoked.

4.5   Updating the Best Point

Given x_{bt}^k, the new best point is updated when $h(x_{bt}^k) \leq h(x_{best}^k)$, which means that $x_{best}^{k+1} = x_{bt}^k$. If a new best point is obtained, then the iteration k is declared successful. Otherwise, the poll-search will be invoked with x_I^k, the least infeasible point found up to the iteration k. This point is updated as $x_I^k = x_{It}^k$ when $0 < h(x_{It}^k) < h(x_I^k)$.

4.6 Poll-Search

In the poll-search we set $T^k = T_{ND}^k = \emptyset$ and the vicinity of x_I^k is explored. Here, new n_t trial points are randomly generated using (9) but considering x_I^k instead of x_{best}^k. Then, a new set of non-dominated trial points T_{ND}^k is identified. If $T_{ND}^k \neq \emptyset$, new points x_{bt}^k and x_I^k are selected using Definition 1. If the poll-search also fails in finding a new non-dominated point, the iteration k is declared unsuccessful and the step size γ_k will be reduced.

4.7 Updating the Step Size

The parameter γ_k is updated using the following formula:

$$\gamma_{k+1} = \begin{cases} \mu\gamma_k & \text{if } k \text{ is an unsuccessful iteration} \\ \gamma_k & \text{otherwise,} \end{cases} \tag{10}$$

where $0 < \mu < 1$. This parameter controls the randomness, or equivalently, the diversity of the generated points. At the beginning of the iterative process, the parameter must take large values to increase the diversity of the points. Throughout the optimization process its value must decrease in order to fine tuning the points since the effort is focused on exploitation.

4.8 Updating the Filter

Whenever the iteration k is successful, the filter $\mathcal{F}_k$ is updated using formula (6). More precisely, x_{best}^{k+1} verifies the condition (4) (or (5)) for $\mathcal{F}_k \cup \{(f_{best}^k, h_{best}^k)\}$ and the filter is updated as follows:

$$\mathcal{F}_{k+1} = \mathcal{F}_k \cup \{(f_{best}^k, h_{best}^k)\} \quad \text{if} \quad f_{best}^{k+1} \geq f_{best}^k \quad (h\text{-type iteration}). \tag{11}$$

Otherwise, the filter remains unchanged $\mathcal{F}_{k+1} = \mathcal{F}_k$ and (f_{best}^k, h_{best}^k) is discarded. Whenever a new entry (f_{best}^k, h_{best}^k) is added to the filter, all entries dominated by (f_{best}^k, h_{best}^k) are removed from the filter.

4.9 Stopping Criteria

The stopping criterion of the algorithm is based on the constraint violation and objective function values. Thus, the algorithm stops when the best point x_{best}^k, at iteration k, satisfies

$$f(x_{best}^k) \leq f^* + \varepsilon_f \quad \text{and} \quad h(x_{best}^k) \leq \varepsilon_h \tag{12}$$

where $\varepsilon_f > 0$ is the accuracy error bound on the function value, $\varepsilon_h > 0$ is a small tolerance on the constraint violation and f^* is the best-known solution. For other problems where f^* is not known, the absolute difference between the objective function values of consecutive iterations can be compared with ε_f to decide termination. Besides, if (12) does not hold, the algorithm has an alternative stopping rule based on the maximum number of iterations (k_{max}).

4.10   The Algorithm

A formal description of the proposed algorithm is presented in Algorithm 2.

5   Numerical Experiments

In this section we report the numerical experiments to illustrate the practical performance of Algorithm 2 with the flat or the slanting filter. First, a set of 20

Algorithm 2

Require: $r = 0.2$, $\sigma_{min} > 0$, $\mu \in (0,1)$, $\gamma_1 \in (0,1)$, $\varepsilon_f > 0$, $\varepsilon_h > 0$, n_t, k_{max}

1: Set $k = 1$, $\mathcal{F}_1 = \emptyset$, $exist = 0$
2: Initial point:
        Compute a random initial point x^k by (7). Evaluate $(f^k, h^k) = (f(x^k), h(x^k))$
        Set $x^k_{best} = x^k$, $(f^k_{best}, h^k_{best}) = (f^k, h^k)$, $(f^k_I, h^k_I) = (-\infty, \infty)$
3: **while** the stopping criterion is not satisfied **do**
4:    Set $success = 0$
5:    Compute the probability P_k by (8)
6:    Generate n_t trial points using (9): $T^k = \{x^k_{trial_j} \mid j = 1, \ldots, n_t\}$
7:    Evaluate f and h at the trial points: $(f(x^k_{trial_j}), h(x^k_{trial_j}))$ for $j = 1, \ldots, n_t$
8:    Select the non-dominated trial points:
        $T^k_{ND} = \{x^k_{trial_j} \in T^k \mid (f(x^k_{trial_j}), h(x^k_{trial_j}))$ satisfies (4) (or (5)) for $\mathcal{F}_k \cup$
        $\{(f^k_{best}, h^k_{best})\}\}$
9:    **if** $T^k_{ND} \neq \emptyset$ **then**
10:      Select x^k_{bt} and x^k_{It} in T^k_{ND} by Definition 1
11:      **if** $h(x^k_{bt}) \leq h^k_{best}$ **then**
12:        Set $x^{k+1}_{best} = x^k_{bt}$, $(f^{k+1}_{best}, h^{k+1}_{best}) = (f(x^k_{bt}), h(x^k_{bt}))$, $success = 1$
13:      **end if**
14:      **if** $h(x^k_{It}) < h^k_I$ **then**
15:        Set $x^k_I = x^k_{It}$, $exist = 1$
16:      **end if**
17:    **end if**
18:    **if** $(success = 0)$ and $(exist = 1)$ and $(h^k_{best} = 0)$ **then**
19:      Repeat steps 6-8 with x^k_I instead of x^k_{best}. Repeat steps 9-17
20:    **end if**
21:    **if** $(success = 1)$ **then**
22:      Set $\gamma_{k+1} = \gamma_k$
23:      **if** $f^{k+1}_{best} > f^k_{best}$ **then**
24:        $\mathcal{F}_{k+1} = \mathcal{F}_k \cup \{(f^k_{best}, h^k_{best})\}$
25:      **else**
26:        $\mathcal{F}_{k+1} = \mathcal{F}_k$
27:      **end if**
28:    **else**
29:      Set $x^{k+1}_{best} = x^k_{best}$, $(f^{k+1}_{best}, h^{k+1}_{best}) = (f^k_{best}, h^k_{best})$, $\gamma_{k+1} = \mu\gamma_k$, $\mathcal{F}_{k+1} = \mathcal{F}_k$
30:    **end if**
31:    Set $(f^{k+1}_I, h^{k+1}_I) = (f^k_I, h^k_I)$
32:    Set $k = k + 1$
33: **end while**

---

small constrained global optimization problems are tested, where the number
of variables ranges from 2 to 10 and the number of constraints ranges from 1
to 12, described in [31]. Second, nine well-known engineering design problems
presented in [32] are used, where the number of design variables ranges from 2
to 8 and the number of inequality constraints ranges from 1 to 11. The tests
were performed in a notebook ASUSTek Intel Core i7-6700HQ, CPU 2.60 GHz,
with 16GB RAM, 64-bit, using `Matlab` R2015a.

We considered the Algorithm 2 with the two different filters discussed in
Sect. 3: the flat filter based on the rule (4), denoted as `A2-FF`, and the slanting
filter based on the rule (5), denoted as `A2-SF`. The following parameters were
fixed: $k_{max} = 300$, the maximum number of iterations; $n_t = 5n$, number of trial
points (where n is the dimension of the problem); $\gamma_1 = 1$, the initial randomization parameter related to the step size; and $\mu = 0.8$, the constant used in (10).
We adopted the stopping criterion (12) with $\varepsilon_f = 10^{-4}$ and $\varepsilon_h = 10^{-8}$, as considered in [25]. Problems with equality constraints $\psi(x) = 0$ were reformulated
into inequalities using $\psi(x) - \delta \leq 0$ and $-\psi(x) - \delta \leq 0$, where $\delta = 10^{-4}$.

To put our approach in perspective, the first set of problems were addressed
by two distinct solvers: the Filter-based Artificial Fish Swarm algorithm (`P-BF
AFS`) proposed in [25] and the Exact Penalty Global Optimization algorithm
(`EPGO`) proposed in [33].

Table 1 lists the results for solving the problems from [31] obtained after
30 independent runs. The first columns display the data of the problem: the
identification (**P**); the dimension (n); the known global optimum (f^*). The next
columns display for each solver the obtained results among the 30 runs: the best
solution obtained (f_{best}), the median (f_{med}), the infeasibility measure at the
best point (h_{best}), the median of infeasibility measure (h_{med}) and the average of
number of function evaluations ($n_{f_{avg}}$) to reach the value f_{best}.

From the results, we may conclude that the proposed algorithm performs reasonably well. It is able to reach the target solution with good accuracy, except
for Problems 1, 2b and 13. Therefore, the Algorithm 2 reached the f^* solution
in 17 out of the 20 problems, while the `P-BF AFS` and the `EPGO` reached the
best known solution in 16 and 13 problems, respectively. When we compare our
results with those in `P-BF AFS`, we conclude that the quality of the obtained solutions is comparable although our algorithm required a larger number of function
evaluations. On the other hand, `EPGO` is the most computationally expensive.
When comparing the two solvers based on the Algorithm 2, for six problems the
solvers obtained the same f_{best}, whereas the `A2-FF` finds the best solutions for
eight problems while `A2-SF` for six problems. In terms of $n_{f_{avg}}$, there are no
significant differences between the solvers.

Finally, the next experiment aims to show the effectiveness of the proposed
algorithm when solving more complex and real application problems. Thus, the
second set of test problems comprises nine problems that arise from well-known
engineering design problems described in [32]. Table 2 lists the results obtained
after 30 independent runs for the developed solvers `A2-FF` and `A2-SF`. All the
parameter settings are the same as for the previous experiment.

Table 1. Numerical results for the problems described in [31]

P	n	f^*	Solver	f_{best}	f_{med}	h_{best}	h_{med}	$n_{f_{avg}}$
1	5	2.9313e-02	A2-FF	0.3051	115.1234	8.25e-04	2.22e-04	8355
			A2-SF	0.1978	237.3387	1.43e-04	6.49e-05	9479
			P-BF AFS	0.0956	1.4665	7.84e-07	*	6945
			EPGO	0.0625		2.35e-07		39575
2a	9	−4.0000e02	A2-FF	−398.300	−84.0701	0.00e00	0.00e00	15476
			A2-SF	−395.875	−312.4870	0.00e00	0.00e00	14994
			P-BF AFS	−358.650	−308.664	0.00e00	*	7068
			EPGO	−134.113		8.43e-04		115107
2b	9	−6.0000e02	A2-FF	−386.276	−298.406	0.00e00	0.00e00	14127
			A2-SF	−384.423	−301.721	0.00e00	0.00e00	14743
			P-BF AFS	−378.317	−274.472	0.00e00	*	6963
			EPGO	−768.457		5.30e-04		120057
2c	9	−7.5000e02	A2-FF	−738.748	−703.827	0.00e00	0.00e00	14532
			A2-SF	−747.021	−702.915	0.00e00	0.00e00	14630
			P-BF AFS	−697.452	−657.349	0.00e00	*	7189
			EPGO	−82.977		8.43e-04		102015
2d	10	−4.0000e02	A2-FF	−399.234	−381.142	0.00e00	0.00e00	13682
			A2-SF	−399.900	−347.957	0.00e00	0.00e00	14286
			P-BF AFS	−399.118	−394.563	0.00e00	*	6526
			EPGO	−385.170		0.00e00		229773
3a	6	−3.8880e-01	A2-FF	−0.3886	−0.3746	0.00e00	0.00e00	16545
			A2-SF	−0.3878	−0.3747	0.00e00	0.00e00	15858
			P-BF AFS	−0.3888	−0.3842	5.22e-04	*	7495
			EPGO	−0.3861		1.02e-06		48647
3b	2	−3.8881e-01	A2-FF	−0.3888	−0.3881	0.00e00	0.00e00	6499
			A2-SF	−0.3888	−0.3883	0.00e00	0.00e00	6512
			P-BF AFS	−0.3888	−0.3888	0.00e00	*	1041
			EPGO	−0.3888		0.00e00		3449
4	2	−6.6666e00	A2-FF	−6.6666	−5.8325	0.00e00	0.00e00	5726
			A2-SF	−6.6666	−6.6662	0.00e00	0.00e00	5483
			P-BF AFS	−6.6667	−6.6665	0.00e00	*	493
			EPGO	−6.6666		0.00e00		3547
5	3	2.0116e02	A2-FF	201.159	201.159	1.26e-06	4.43e-02	3074
			A2-SF	201.159	201.157	0.00e00	3.57e-02	2930
			P-BF AFS	201.159	201.159	8.11e-07	*	2999
			EPGO	201.159		1.66e-04		14087

Table 1. *(Continued)*

P	n	f^*	Solver	f_{best}	f_{med}	h_{best}	h_{med}	$n_{f_{avg}}$
6	2	3.7629e02	A2-FF	376.302	376.905	0.00e00	0.00e00	5872
			A2-SF	376.305	376.986	0.00e00	0.00e00	6079
			P-BF AFS	376.293	376.304	0.00e00	*	1335
			EPGO	0.4701		2.05e-05		1523
7	2	-2.8284e00	A2-FF	−2.8283	−2.8219	0.00e00	0.00e00	5114
			A2-SF	−2.8284	−2.8230	0.00e00	0.00e00	4829
			P-BF AFS	−2.8284	−2.8283	0.00e00	*	920
			EPGO	−2.8058		0.00e00		13187
8	2	−1.1870e02	A2-FF	−118.704	−86.402	0.00e00	0.00e00	5854
			A2-SF	−118.703	−115.138	0.00e00	0.00e00	5904
			P-BF AFS	−118.704	−118.698	0.00e00	*	1521
			EPGO	−118.704		0.00e00		7621
9	6	−1.3402e01	A2-FF	−13.4018	−13.3906	0.00e00	0.00e00	8466
			A2-SF	−13.4019	−13.3916	0.00e00	0.00e00	8187
			P-BF AFS	−13.4018	−13.4007	0.00e00	*	1839
			EPGO	−13.4026		1.35e-04		68177
10	2	7.4178e-01	A2-FF	0.7418	0.7431	0.00e00	0.00e00	5708
			A2-SF	0.7419	0.7436	0.00e00	0.00e00	5733
			P-BF AFS	0.7418	0.7418	0.00e00	*	2126
			EPGO	0.7420		0.00e00		6739
11	2	−5.0000e-01	A2-FF	−0.5000	−0.4995	0.00e00	0.00e00	5533
			A2-SF	−0.5000	−0.4982	0.00e00	0.00e00	6135
			P-BF AFS	−0.5000	−0.5000	0.00e00	*	782
			EPGO	−0.5000		0.00e00		3579
12	2	−1.6739e01	A2-FF	−16.7255	−15.3324	0.00e00	8.83e-06	4231
			A2-FF	−16.6486	−15.5805	0.00e00	3.02e-05	4159
			P-BF AFS	−16.7389	−16.7389	0.00e00	*	35
			EPGO	−16.7389		5.36e-06		3499
13	3	1.8935e02	A2-FF	267.923	282.729	0.00e00	4.38e-01	4717
			A2-SF	278.942	280.580	1.45e-05	3.30e-01	4601
			P-BF AFS	189.345	253.937	0.00e00	*	4031
			EPGO	195.955		9.21e-04		8085
14	4	−4.5142e00	A2-FF	−4.5133	−4.4766	0.00e00	0.00e00	8717
			A2-SF	−4.5142	−4.4808	0.00e00	0.00e00	8520
			P-BF AFS	−4.5142	−4.5139	0.00e00	*	2028
			EPGO	−4.3460		9.22e-05		19685

Table 1. *(Continued)*

P	n	f^*	Solver	f_{best}	f_{med}	h_{best}	h_{med}	$n_{f_{avg}}$
15	3	0.0000e00	A2-FF	0.0000	0.0000	6.90e-05	1.21e-02	4501
			A2-SF	0.0000	0.0000	2.03e-05	1.91e-02	4729
			P-BF AFS	0.0000	0.0000	9.11e-07	*	3593
			EPGO	0.0000		4.94e-05		1645
16	5	7.0492e-01	A2-FF	0.7049	0.7050	0.00e00	0.00e00	138
			A2-SF	0.7049	0.7050	0.00e00	0.00e00	121
			P-BF AFS	0.7049	0.7049	0,00e00	*	447
			EPGO	0.7181		2.00e-04		22593

*not available

Table 2. Numerical results for the problems described in [32]

P	n	f^*	Solver	f_{best}	f_{med}	h_{best}	h_{med}	$n_{f_{avg}}$
Cylindrical Vessel	5	5868.7650	A2-FF	5978.6504	6384.3347	0.00e00	0.00e00	11151
			A2-SF	5898.3626	6327.0383	0.00e00	0.00e00	10966
Disc Brake	4	0.1274	A2-FF	0.1274	0.1355	0.00e00	0.00e00	8916
			A2-SF	0.1274	0.1283	0.00e00	0.00e00	6770
Four Bar Truss	4	1400.0000	A2-FF	1400.0000	1400.0000	0.00e00	0.00e00	276
			A2-SF	1400.0000	1400.0000	0.00e00	0.00e00	336
Heat Exchanger	8	7049.2480	A2-FF	7144.4819	9383.1025	0.00e00	0.00e00	16781
			A2-SF	7075.0293	8340.3915	0.00e00	0.00e00	17826
Speed Reducer	7	2994.4991	A2-FF	2994.4840	2994.4971	0.00e00	0.00e00	14771
			A2-SF	2994.4840	2994.5185	0.00e00	0.00e00	15146
Tubular Column	2	26.5313	A2-FF	26.5386	26.6533	0.00e00	0.00e00	5883
			A2-SF	26.5342	26.6429	0.00e00	0.00e00	5884
Tension Spring	3	0.0127	A2-FF	0.0127	0.0144	0.00e00	0.00e00	6976
			A2-SF	0.0127	0.0140	0.00e00	0.00e00	7598
Three Bar Truss	2	263.8958	A2-FF	263.9017	263.9764	0.00e00	0.00e00	6514
			A2-SF	263.9086	264.0120	0.00e00	0.00e00	6649
Welded Beam	4	2.3809	A2-FF	2.5380	4.2294	0.00e00	0.00e00	10966
			A2-SF	2.5942	5.2176	0.00e00	0.00e00	11016

From the results for this set of problems, we may conclude that our algorithm is able to reach the target solution with good accuracy, except for Cylindrical Vessel, Heat Exchanger and Welded Beam problems. Furthermore, the performance of the solvers A2-FF and A2-SF is similar.

6   Conclusions

This paper presents the DDS algorithm combined with the filter method to solve nonlinear and nonconvex constrained global optimization problems. The

DDS algorithm was developed for calibration problems that arise in the context of WSM, modeled as bound constrained optimization problems. The proposed algorithm is an extension of the DDS algorithm incorporating a filter method that reformulates the optimization problem as a bi-objective optimization one, aiming to minimize the objective and the constraint violation functions. The reported numerical results show the effectiveness of the proposed algorithm and its competitive practical performance when compared with a penalty framework and with a filter-based stochastic global AFS algorithm from the literature.

Future developments will focus on the decrease of the computational cost and the solution of larger dimensional problems. A study of the convergence of the algorithm will be carried out in the future.

Acknowledgments. The first author thanks a scholarship supported by the International Cooperation Program CAPES/ COFECUB at the University of Minho. The second and third authors thanks the support given by FCT (Fundação para Ciência e Tecnologia, Portugal) in the scope of the projects: UID/MAT/00013/2013 and UID/CEC/00319/2013. The fourth author was partially supported by CNPq-Brazil grants 308957/2014-8 and 401288/2014-5.

References

1. Fletcher, R., Leyffer, S.: Nonlinear programming without a penalty function. Math. Program. **91**, 239–269 (2002)
2. Periçaro, G.A., Ribeiro, A.A., Karas, E.W.: Global convergence of a general filter algorithm based on an efficiency condition of the step. Appl. Math. Comput. **219**, 9581–9597 (2013)
3. Ribeiro, A.A., Karas, E.W., Gonzaga, C.C.: Global convergence of filter methods for nonlinear programming. SIAM J. Optim. **19**(3), 1231–1249 (2008)
4. Fletcher, R., Gould, N.I.M., Leyffer, S., Toint, P.L., Wachter, A.: Global convergence of trust-region SQP-filter algorithm for general nonlinear programming. SIAM J. Optim. **13**, 635–659 (2002)
5. Wang, X., Zhu, Z., Zuo, S., Huang, Q.: An SQP-filter method for inequality constrained optimization and its global convergence. Appl. Math. Comput. **217**(24), 10224–10230 (2011)
6. Gonzaga, C.C., Karas, E.W., Vanti, M.: A globally convergent filter method for nonlinear programming. SIAM J. Optimiz. **14**(3), 646–669 (2003)
7. Karas, E.W., Oening, A.P., Ribeiro, A.A.: Global convergence of slanting filter methods for nonlinear programming. Appl. Math. Comput. **200**, 486–500 (2008)
8. Ulbrich, M., Ulbrich, S., Vicente, L.N.: A globally convergent primal-dual interior-point filter method for nonlinear programming. Math. Program. **100**(2), 379–410 (2004)
9. Gu, C., Zhu, D.: A secant algorithm with line search filter method for nonlinear optimization. Appl. Math. Model. **35**(2), 879–894 (2011)
10. Pei, Y., Zhu, D.: A trust-region algorithm combining line search filter technique for nonlinear constrained optimization. Int. J. Comput. Math. **91**(8), 1817–1839 (2014)
11. Wächter, A., Biegler, L.T.: Line search filter methods for nonlinear programming: motivation and global convergence. SIAM J. Optimiz. **16**(1), 1–31 (2005)

12. Echebest, N., Shuverdt, M.L., Vignau, R.P.: A derivative-free method for solving box-constrained underdetermined nonlinear systems of equations. Appl. Math. Comput. **219**, 3198–3208 (2012)
13. Fletcher, R., Leyffer, S.: Filter-type algorithms for solving systems of algebraic equations and inequalities. In: di Pillo, G., Murli, A. (eds.) Advances in Optimization and Numerical Analysis. High Performance Algorithms and Software for Nonlinear Optimization, pp. 259–278. Kluwer (2003)
14. Gould, N.I.M., Leyffer, S., Toint, P.L.: A multidimensional filter algorithm for nonlinear equations and nonlinear least-squares. SIAM J. Optimiz. **15**(1), 17–38 (2004)
15. Gould, N.I.M., Toint, P.L.: FILTRANE, a Fortran 95 filter-trust-region package for solving least-squares and nonlinear feasibility problems. ACM T. Math. Software **33**(1), 3–25 (2007)
16. Karas, E.W., Ribeiro, A.A., Sagastizábal, C., Solodov, M.: A bundle-filter method for nonsmooth convex constrained optimization. Math. Program. **116**, 297–320 (2009)
17. Peng, Y., Feng, H., Li, Q.: A filter-variable-metric method for nonsmooth convex constrained optimization. Appl. Math. Comput. **208**(1), 119–128 (2009)
18. Gould, N.I.M., Sainvitu, C., Toint, P.L.: A filter-trust-region method for unconstrained optimization. SIAM J. Optimiz. **16**(2), 341–357 (2006)
19. Yang, Z., Sun, W.: A filter-trust-region method for LC^1 unconstrained optimization and its global convergence. Anal. Theor. Appl. **24**(1), 55–66 (2008)
20. Long, J., Ma, C., Nie, P.: A new filter method for solving nonlinear complementarity problems. Appl. Math. Comput. **185**(1), 705–718 (2007)
21. Long, J., Zeng, S.: A new Filter-Levenberg-Marquart method with disturbance for solving nonlinear complementarity problems. Appl. Math. Comput. **216**(2), 677–688 (2010)
22. Audet, C., Dennis Jr., J.E.: A pattern search filter method for nonlinear programming without derivatives. SIAM J. Optim. **14**(4), 980–1010 (2004)
23. Echebest, N., Shuverdt, M.L., Vignau, R.P.: An inexact restoration derivative-free filter method for nonlinear programming. Comput. Appl. Math. **36**(1), 693–718 (2017)
24. Ferreira, P.S., Karas, E.W., Sachine, M., Sobral, F.N.C.: Global convergence of a derivative-free inexact restoration filter algorithm for nonlinear programming. Optimization **66**, 271–292 (2017)
25. Rocha, A.M.A.C., Costa, M.F.P., Fernandes, E.M.G.P.: A filter-based artificial fish swarm algorithm for constrained global optimization: theoretical and practical issues. J. Global Optim. **60**, 239–263 (2014)
26. Tolson, B.A., Shoemaker, C.A.: Dynamically dimensioned search algorithm for computationally efficient watershed model calibration. Water Resour. Res. 43 (2007)
27. Tolson, B.A., Asadzadeh, M., Zecchin, A.: Hybrid discrete dynamically dimensioned search (hd-dds) algorithm for water distribution system design optimization. Water Resour. Res. 45 (2009)
28. Regis, R.G.: Stochastic radial basis function algorithms for large-scale optimization involving expensive black-box objective and constraint functions. Comput. Oper. Res. **38**, 837–853 (2011)
29. Regis, R.G.: Constrained optimization by radial basis function interpolation for high-dimensional expensive black-box problems with infeasible initial points. Eng. Optimiz. **46**, 218–243 (2014)

30. Chin, C.M., Fletcher, R.: On the global convergence of an SLP-filter algorithm that takes EQP steps. Math. Program. **96**(1), 161–177 (2003)
31. Birgin, E.G., Floudas, C.A., Martínez, J.M.: Global minimization using an augmented Lagrangian method with variable lower-level constraints. Math. Program. **125**(1), 139–162 (2010)
32. Rocha, A.M.A.C., Fernandes, E.M.G.P.: Hybridizing the electromagnetism-like algorithm with descent search for solving engineering design problems. Int. J. Comput. Math. **86**, 1932–1946 (2009)
33. Pillo, G.D., Lucidi, S., Rinaldi, F.: An approach to constrained global optimization based on exact penalty functions. J. Glob. Optim. **54**, 251–260 (2012)

Optimal Schedule of Home Care Visits
for a Health Care Center

Filipe Alves[1], Ana I. Pereira[1,2(✉)], Florbela P. Fernandes[1], Adília Fernandes[1],
Paulo Leitão[1,3], and Anabela Martins[4]

[1] Polytechnic Institute of Bragança, 5301-857 Bragança, Portugal
{filipealves,apereira,fflor,adilia,pleitao}@ipb.pt
[2] Algoritmi R&D Centre, University of Minho, Campus de Gualtar,
4710-057 Braga, Portugal
[3] LIACC, University of Porto, R. Campo Alegre 1021,
4169-007 Porto, Portugal
[4] ULSNE, Unidade Local de Saúde do Nordeste,
Av. Abade de Baçal, 5301-852 Bragança, Portugal
apaula.martins@ulsne.min-saude.pt

Abstract. The provision of home health care services is becoming an
important research area, mainly because in Portugal the population is
ageing. Home care visits are organized taking into account the medical
treatments and general support that elder/sick people need at home. This
health service can be provided by nurse teams from Health Care Centers.
Usually, the visits are manually planned and without computer support.
The main goal of this work is to carry out the automatic schedule of home
care visits, of one Portuguese Health Care Center, in order to minimize
the time spent in all home care visits and, consequently, reduce the costs
involved. The developed algorithms were coded in MatLab Software and
the problem was efficiently solved, obtaining several schedule solutions of
home care visits for the presented data. Solutions found by genetic and
particle swarm algorithms lead to significant time reductions for both
nurse teams and patients.

Keywords: Genetic Algorithm · Particle Swarm Optimization · Health
care services · Optimization · Scheduling

1 Introduction

Advances in health care, declining fertility rates and longer life expectancy have
led to an increasing number of elderly people in European society, namely, in
Portuguese society. Consequently, the number of people who needs home care
services is growing over the years. This scenario — to provide home care services — is not only advantageous to elder/sick people but also to the National
Health System since it is economically advantageous to keep people at home
instead of providing them with a hospital bed [11,15].

© Springer International Publishing AG 2017
O. Gervasi et al. (Eds.): ICCSA 2017, Part III, LNCS 10406, pp. 135–147, 2017.
DOI: 10.1007/978-3-319-62398-6_10

The home-based care provided by public or private entities has been the subject of recent research mainly in the operations research area with particular attention on route's optimization and on the staff teams composition that provide this kind of services [2,3,11,14].

The Portuguese public health system consists in two types of units: Hospitals and Health Care Centers. The Health Care Centers are closer to the population since they follow up their patients continuously and the home care services are performed by nurse teams of these Units. In this context, Health Care Centers have to perform the schedule of the nurse teams inside and outside of the Health Care Centers.

The schedule of the home care visits provided by the Health Care Centers teams depends on the patients and nurses profiles. This represents a complex problem being its main goal to minimize the time needed, by the nurses team, to perform all the home care visits and return to the Health Care Center. The schedule of the home care visits provided by the Health Care Centers can be seen as a vehicle routing problem with specific conditions [10].

The paper is organized as follows: first, it is given a description of the real problem and its mathematical formulation; then it is presented a summary of the genetic algorithm method (GA) and the particle swarm optimization method (PSO) since they were the selected methods to solve the problem. After, numerical results are presented and a comparison is made between the different algorithms used. Finally, some conclusions and future work ideas are given.

2   Problem Description

For a given day, a Health Care Center need to provide the schedule of all nurses team to perform the tasks inside and outside of the Health Care Center. In this paper, it is studied the problem to schedule the tasks outside the Health Care Center, particularly, to find the home care visits schedule for a given day, in order to minimize the travel time to perform all visits. Then, the main objective of this study is to perform automatic planning of home care visits by a nurses team of a Health Care Center of Bragança (HUB), Bragança, Portugal, aiming to minimize all the time spent by the nurses to perform all home care visits.

This optimization problem, related with the HUB, is formulated and solved as follows.

2.1   Assumptions

In the developed model it was assumed, without loss of generality, that:

A.1 Patients who live in the area of HUB can have different profiles.

A.2 A patient profile is assumed to be known *a priori* and does not change during the home care visit.

A.3 The number and average duration of the treatments that characterize a patient profile are known and are the same among the patients who have the same profile.

A.4 The number of patients who need home care services and assigned to a working day is known in advance and does not change during that day.

A.5 Human resources (nurses) that perform home care visits have different profiles, this means that not all the nurses perform all the treatments.

A.6 All the patients assigned to a working day are covered which means that all the patients admitted to the home care visits have to be assigned to a set of nurses.

A.7 The number of nurses assigned to a working day is known in advance.

A.8 The time of travel between all the localities is also known in advance.

A.9 All the travels begin and end up in the HUB.

2.2   Mathematical Formulation

Taking into account all the above assumptions for a working day, consider the following general and fixed variables:

- N is the total number of nurses assigned for home care visits.
- P is the total number of patients that need some treatments at their homes.
- L is the total number of different patients' locations.

Another mathematical entities are needed to obtain the final formulation, such as:

- The list of all different treatments and the time needed to perform each treatment.
- The list of the treatments that each nurse can perform.
- The time matrix that presents the time needed to travel between all the different locations.
- The list representing the patient treatment needs.
- The locations of all patients.

Consider the variable $(p; n) = (p_1, ..., p_P; n_1, ..., n_P)$, where the patient p_i will be visited by the nurse n_i, for $i = 1, ..., P$, and $p \in \{1, \cdots, P\}^P$ and $n \in \{1, \cdots, N\}^P$.

Then, for a given $(p; n)$ it is possible to define the nurse schedule and also the total time needed by each nurse to finish her work. So, consider the objective function $tt(p; n)$, $n = 1, .., N$ defined as

$$f(p; n) = \max_{n=1,...,N} tt(p; n) \qquad (1)$$

which represents the time spent by the nurses to perform all treatments, including the returning journey to the HUB.

Then the constrained integer optimization problem will be defined as

$$\min f(p; n)$$
$$\text{s.t. } 1 \leq p_i \leq P, \ i \in \{1, ..., P\}, p_i \text{ integer} \qquad (2)$$
$$1 \leq n_j \leq N, \ j \in \{1, ..., P\}, n_j \text{ integer}$$

where all the patients need to be treated $\cup_{i=1}^{P} p_i = \{1, ..., P\}$ and the nurse n_i needs to perform all the treatments of the patient p_i, for $i = 1, ..., P$.

2.3   Real Data

It is intended to apply the developed mathematical model to a real problem of the HUB. The data provided by the HUB concern the day April 18, 2016, [1]. The home care services provided by the assigned nurses to this job can be classified into five different treatments (or home care visits) presented in Table 1.

The HUB has twelve nurses designated to perform home care visits during the day in study. Table 2 shows the allocation of the five treatments by each nurse as well as the average time treatment required.

Table 1. Characterization of the different treatments provided by the nurses.

Treatment	Description	Characterization
T.1	Curative	Treatments, for example, pressure ulcer, venous ulcer, surgical wounds, traumatic wounds, ligaments, remove suture material, burns, evaluation and dressing of wound dressings
T.2	Surveillance and Rehabilitation	Evaluation, implementation and patient monitoring
T.3	Curative and Surveillance	Wound treatment, watch over bandage, frequency and tension monitoring, teach and instruct the patient of the complications and pathologies
T.4	Surveillance	Assess risk of falls, self-care, patient behaviors and still the providers knowledge. Monitor, height, tension and heart rate. Patients dietary and medical regimen
T.5	General	Evaluate, support and teach about mourning

Table 2. Treatments performed by the nurses.

	T.1 (30 min)	T.2 (60 min)	T.3 (75 min)	T.4 (60 min)	T.5 (60 min)
Nurse 1	X			X	
Nurse 2	X	X		X	
Nurse 3	X			X	
Nurse 4	X		X	X	
Nurse 5	X			X	
Nurse 6	X			X	X
Nurse 7	X		X	X	
Nurse 8	X			X	
Nurse 9	X			X	
Nurse 10	X			X	
Nurse 11	X			X	
Nurse 12	X			X	

On April 18, there were thirty one patients who needed home care visits by HUB.

Each patient, represented in the first column of Table 3 by P($\cdot$), required specific medical assistance — one or more different treatments, from the 5 treatments that the nurses can perform.

Table 3. Summary of which kind of treatments each patient needs.

	T.1	T.2	T.3	T.4	T.5
P(1)	X				
P(2)	X				
P(3)	X				
P(4)	X				
P(5)		X			
P(6)		X			
P(7)		X			
P(8)	X				
P(9)	X				
P(10)	X				
P(11)	X				
P(12)	X				
P(13)	X				
P(14)	X				
P(15)			X		
P(16)				X	
P(17)	X				
P(18)					X
P(19)	X				
P(20)			X		
P(21)				X	
P(22)	X				
P(23)	X				
P(24)	X				
P(25)				X	
P(26)				X	
P(27)				X	
P(28)				X	
P(29)				X	
P(30)				X	
P(31)				X	

The thirty-one patients are from twelve different locations of the Bragança region, that belong to the action area of the HUB.

In Table 4, the locations are represented by the corresponding abbreviation. From hereafter it will be used only these abbreviations. In third column it is shown the related number of patients who need health care. The major part of the patients (18) are from Bragança city while 13 patients are from rural localities around Bragança.

The time required to travel between two locations is shown in Table 5. It was assigned 15 min to travel between two different places, in the same location.

Table 4. Short name of the locations and total number of patients in each locality.

Localities	Abbreviations	Number of patients
Bragança	Bg	18
Parada	Pa	2
Rebordainhos	Re	1
Carrazedo	Car	1
Espinhosela	Esp	1
Rebordãos	R	1
Salsas	Sal	1
Serapicos	Se	1
Outeiro	Ou	1
Meixedo	M	1
Bragada	Bda	1
Milhão	Mil	2

Table 5. Data about travel times between different locations (in minutes).

	Bg	Pa	Re	Car	Esp	R	Sal	Se	Ou	M	Bda	Mil
Bg	15	28	25	26	20	14	23	31	23	20	22	24
Pa	28	15	27	39	37	25	25	23	27	40	26	36
Re	25	27	15	33	34	22	12	20	32	37	14	33
Car	26	39	33	15	24	23	34	42	38	39	33	39
Esp	20	37	34	24	15	24	32	40	33	18	31	34
R	14	25	22	23	24	15	20	28	26	27	19	27
Sal	23	25	12	34	32	20	15	8	30	34	9	31
Se	31	23	20	42	40	28	8	15	38	42	17	39
Ou	23	27	32	38	33	26	30	38	15	29	30	14
M	20	40	37	39	18	27	34	42	29	15	34	31
Bda	22	26	14	33	31	19	9	17	30	34	15	31
Mil	24	36	33	39	34	27	31	39	14	31	31	15

Based on all the presented data, the objective is to obtain the nurses schedule, in order to minimize the total time needed by each nurse to provide all the treatments to all the patients and return to the Health Center.

To solve the minimization problem presented in (2), two different optimization methods were used: Genetic Algorithm and Particle Swarm Optimization method.

3   Optimization Methods

Two global optimization methods were used to solve the nonlinear optimization problem defined in (2): Genetic Algorithm and Particle Swarm Optimization method. Both methods are population-based methods and a brief summary of them follows.

3.1   Genetic Algorithm - GA

The Genetic Algorithm (GA) was proposed by Holland [6] and it is based on the theory of the species evolution.

GA is a stochastic method, whose mechanism is based on simplifications of evolutionary processes observed in nature, namely selection, mutation and crossover [5,7,9,13]. As opposed to many other optimization methods, genetic algorithm works with a population of solutions instead of one single solution. In GA, the solutions are combined to generate new ones until a satisfactory solution is obtained, i.e. until the stop criteria is met.

The genetic algorithm applied in this work is summarized by the following algorithm.

Algorithm 1. Genetic Algorithm

1: Generates a randomly population of individuals, $\mathcal{P}^0$, with dimension N_{pop}. Set $k = 0$.
2: **while** stopping criterion is not met **do**
3:     Set $k = k + 1$.
4:     $\mathcal{P}' = $ Apply crossover procedure in population $\mathcal{P}^k$.
5:     $\mathcal{P}'' = $ Apply mutation procedure in population $\mathcal{P}^k$.
6:     $\mathcal{P}^{k+1} = NP$ best individuals of $\{\mathcal{P}^k \cup \mathcal{P}' \cup \mathcal{P}''\}$.

The initial population, $\mathcal{P}^0$ consists of N_{pop} individuals, where each one represents a feasible schedule (all constraints are satisfied).

The iterative procedure terminates after a maximum number of iterations (number of generations) or after a maximum number of function evaluations.

3.2 Particle Swarm Optimization - PSO

The Particle Swarm Optimization (PSO) was developed by Kennedy and Eberhart [8] and it is based on natural social intelligent behaviors.

PSO is a computational method that optimizes a given problem by iteratively measuring the quality of the various solutions. This method consists in optimizing an objective function through the exchange of information between individuals (particles) of a population (swarm). The PSO idea is to perform a set of operations and move each particle to promising regions in the search space. The Particle Swarm Optimization method also works with a population of solutions and stops when the stop criteria is met [12,16].

At each iteration the velocity of each individual is adjusted. The velocity calculation is based on the best position found by the neighborhood of the individual, the best position found by the particle itself - *xbest* and the best position found by the whole population, taking into account all individual - *gbest* or the best position overall [4].

The particle swarm optimization method applied in this work is summarized by the following algorithm.

Algorithm 2. Particle Swarm Optimization Algorithm

1: Generates a randomly population of individuals, $\mathcal{P}^0$, with dimension N_{pop}.
2: Set the values of w, c_1, r_1. Define c_2, r_2 random numbers in $[0, 1]$. Set $v_i = 1$, for $i = 1, ..., N_{pop}$, and $k = 0$.
3: **while** stopping criterion is not met **do**
4:     Set $k = k + 1$.
5:     Update the value of $xbest_i$ for the individual with index i, for $i = 1, ..., N_{pop}$.
6:     Update the value of $gbest$ for all population $\mathcal{P}^j$, for $j = 1, ..., k$.
7:     Update the individual velocity according to:

$$v_i^{k+1} = wv_i^k + c_1 r_1 (xbest_i - x_i^k) + \lfloor c_2 r_2 \rceil (gbest - x_i^k).$$

8:     Update the individual position according to: $x_i^{k+1} = x_i^k + v_i^{k+1}$.
9:     If necessary, adapt x_i^{k+1} to a feasible schedule.

During the iterative process if x_i^{k+1} is not a feasible solution, the coordinate that is not feasible will be projected to the feasible region.

The iterative procedure terminates after a maximum number of iterations or after a maximum number of function evaluations.

4 Results and Discussion

The main objective is to produce the nurses' schedules for the home care visits of the Health Care Center of Bragança for April 18, 2016.

The daily route carried out on April 18 by the Health Care Center of Bragança was made manually, that is, without any mathematical model or subject to computational mechanisms.

The nurses' schedules were collected [1]. Figure 1 presents the schedule made available by the Health Care Center on April 18 for the twelve nurses that performed the home care visits in that day.

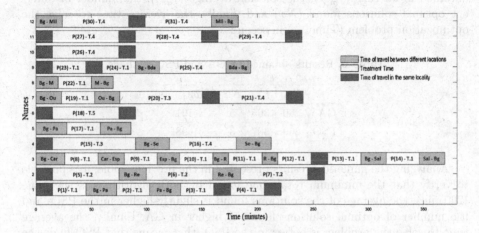

Fig. 1. Schedule carried out by the Health Care Center (manually)

The time needed to each nurse to perform the health treatment is represented by no color. The light gray color show the time of travel between different locations. The assigned 15 min ride between to different houses in the same city is represented by the dark gray color.

Regarding the identification of patients and treatments, P(1) - T.1 represents Patient 1 who needs Treatment 1. For example, the schedule of the Nurse 8 will be: moves from the HUB to the village of Meixedo (Bg - M) to execute the home care visit of Patient 22, that requires the Treatment 1 (P(22) - T.1). After this, the nurse returns to the point of origin, the Health Care Center (M - Bg). For this nurse, the time spent in this home care visit was 70 min.

Analyzing the scheduling carried out by the Health Care Center, it is possible to conclude that all nurses have different work schedules. The number of patients that each nurse visits change from 1 (Nurse 8) to 7 (Nurse 3) and it is Nurse 3 who has the highest time to provide the home care visits.

On this working day, the total time needed on home visits ended after 369 min.

In an attempt to plan the nurses' schedule automatically two computational algorithms were used — GA and PSO. The numerical results were obtained using an Intel(R) Core(TM) i7 CPU 2.2GHz with 6.0 GB of RAM and using the MatLab software. The fix variable for both methods were $N_{pop} = 30$, $w = 1$ and $c_1 = r_1 = 2$.

Since the methods used are stochastic methods, each implementation was tested with 100 executions in order to evaluate the results obtained and compare them with the ones obtained from the Health Care Center. Both methods used the same stop criteria, limit the number of function evaluation to 5000 or after 1000 iterations.

Both methods had 100% of successful rate since they found a feasible solution in all runs.

Table 6 presents the summary of both methods, such as: the best solution obtained in all runs (f^*_{min}), the solution average (f^*_{avg}), the number of different optimal solutions found (Nx) and, finally, the average time to solve the optimization problem (Time$_{avg}$) in seconds.

Table 6. Results obtained by GA and PSO methods.

	f^*_{min}	f^*_{avg}	Nx	Time$_{avg}$ (s)
GA	260	305	5	191
PSO	260	307	3	98

Analyzing the numerical results presented in the previous table, it is possible to verify that the minimum total time found by both algorithms is the same (260 min), the average of the solutions found is slightly higher in the PSO, and the number of optimal solutions found is higher in GA. Finally, the average time to solve the problem is better in the PSO, that means that PSO finds the problem solution faster than GA.

In both methods, it was obtained more than one optimal solution (three by the PSO and five by the GA), so the methods find different nurses schedules with the same minimum (260 min). This allows that the Health Care Center can choose one of those nurses' schedules.

Figure 2 depicts one obtained solution using GA.

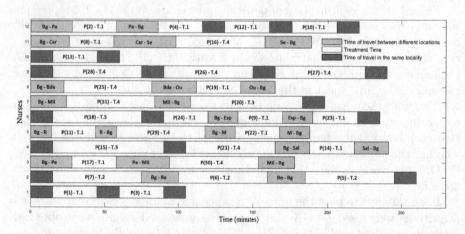

Fig. 2. Optimal nurses' schedules using GA

Analyzing Fig. 2 it is possible to see that the minimum time needed to the last nurse perform all the visits and return to the Health Care Center is 260 min. This value is less than the related value in the manual schedule (369 min). Only two nurses have more than 3 patients — Nurse 6 and Nurse 12. This means that the nurses' schedule produced by the algorithm are more balanced in comparison with the Health Care Center schedule (Fig. 1).

Analyzing Fig. 2, is possible to conclude that all real restrictions are met, accordingly to the data from the Health Care Center.

The next figure, Fig. 3, depicts one obtained solution using PSO algorithm.

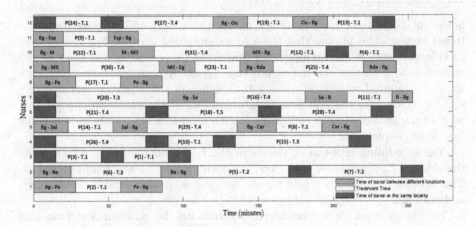

Fig. 3. Optimal nurses' schedules using PSO

From Fig. 3 it is possible to see that the minimum time needed to the last nurse perform all the visits and return to the Health Care Center was 260 min (the same value as the one obtained with GA). Both solutions obtained by both methods have a significant time reduction (109 min) when compared to the HUB manual planning, which was 369 min. However, the GA schedule is more homogeneous than the PSO schedule.

To show (in an easy and fast way) the time spent by each nurse, using both methods, and compare it with the related time obtained manually by the HUB, Table 7 list for each nurse (first row), the time needed to finish the home care visits done manually (second row), the time spent obtained using GA (third row) and the time spent obtained with PSO (fourth row).

Table 7. Total time spent by each nurse in home care visits.

	\multicolumn{12}{c}{Nurses}											
	1	2	3	4	5	6	7	8	9	10	11	12
HUB	221	260	369	212	86	90	241	70	194	90	240	183
GA	105	260	178	241	188	235	198	165	240	60	189	221
PSO	86	260	105	225	218	240	253	86	242	255	70	241

From the above table it is possible to state that with both algorithms, the maximum time spent by the nurses never exceeded 260 min. In turn, the maximum time spent by the nurses in HUB scheduling is 369 min (greater than both computational solutions).

4.1 Conclusions and Future Work

Since, in HUB, home care visits are planned manually and without computational support, this implies that the solution obtained may not be the best one. In this way, and in an attempt to optimize the process, it is necessary to use strategies to minimize the maximum time spent by each nurse on home care routes, without, however, worsening the quality of the provided services and, always, looking for the best schedules organization. Optimization can be used very advantageously in the context of Health Care Centers scheduling for home care aged people visits.

The scheduling problem of nurses in the HUB was efficiently solved using the GA and PSO methods. Moreover, the optimal solution was found quite fast. This approach represents a gain for all the involved people, health professionals and patients.

For future work, it is possible to reformulate the problem and take into account the number of vehicles available in the Health Care Center and use multi-objective approach to minimize not only the maximum time for each nurse, but also the total time spent by all nurses.

Acknowledgments. This work has been supported by COMPETE: POCI-01-0145-FEDER-007043 and FCT – Fundação para a Ciência e Tecnologia within the Project Scope: UID/CEC/00319/2013.

References

1. Alves, F.: Estudo sobre os procedimentos ótimos de visitas domiciliárias em unidades de saúde, Instituto Politécnico de Bragança (Master thesis), pp. 61–84 (2016)
2. Benzarti, E., Sahin, E., Dallery, Y.: Operations management applied to home care services: analysis of the districting problem. Decis. Support Syst. **55**, 587–598 (2013)
3. Bertels, S., Fahle, T.: A hybrid setup for a hybrid scenario: combining heuristics for the home health care problem. Comput. Oper. Res. **33**, 2866–2890 (2006)
4. Bratton, D., Kennedy, J.: Defining a standard for particle swarm optimization. In: IEEE Swarm Intelligence Symposium (2007)
5. Curralo, A., Pereira, A.I., Barbosa, J., Leitão, P.: Sensibility study in a flexible job shop scheduling problem. In: AIP Conference Proceedings, pp. 634–637 (2013)
6. Holland, J.H.: Adaptation in Natural and Artificial Systems. An Introductory Analysis with Application to Biology, Control, and Artificial Intelligence. University of Michigan Press, Ann Arbor (1975)
7. Holland, J.H., Goldberg, D.: Genetic Algorithms in Search, Optimization and Machine Learning. Addison-Wesley, Reading (1989)

8. Kennedy, J.: Particle swarm optimization. In: Sammut, C., Webb, G.I. (eds.) Encyclopedia of Machine Learning, pp. 760–766. Springer, New York (2011)
9. Kumar, M., Husian, M., Upreti, N., Gupta, D.: Genetic algorithm: review and application. Int. J. Inf. Technol. Knowl. Manage. **2**, 451–454 (2010)
10. Kumar, S.N., Panneerselvam, R.: A survey on the vehicle routing problem and its variants. Intell. Inf. Manage. **4**, 66–74 (2012)
11. Nickel, S., Schröder, M., Steeg, J.: Mid-term and short-term planning support for home health care services. Eur. J. Oper. Res. **219**, 574–587 (2012)
12. Poli, R., Kennedy, J., Blackwell, T.: Particle swarm optimization. Swarm Intell. **1**, 33–57 (2007)
13. Rao, S.S., Rao, S.S.: Engineering Optimization: Theory and Practice. Wiley, Hoboken (2009)
14. Rasmussen, M.S., Justesen, T., Dohn, A., Larsen, J.: The home care crew scheduling problem: preference-based visit clustering and temporal dependencies. Eur. J. Oper. Res. **219**, 598–610 (2012)
15. Rest, K.D.: Supporting urban home health care in daily business and times of disasters. IFAC Proc. Vol. (IFAC-PapersOnline) **48**, 686–691 (2015)
16. Simões, G.J., Ebecken, N.F.F.: Algoritmo genético e enxame de partículas para a otimização de suportes laterais de fornos. Revista Internacional de Métodos Numéricos para Cálculo y Diseño en Ingeniería **32**, 7–12 (2016)

Neighborhood Analysis on the University Timetabling Problem

Edmar Hell Kampke[(✉)], Erika Almeida Segatto[(✉)],
Maria Claudia Silva Boeres[(✉)], Maria Cristina Rangel[(✉)],
and Geraldo Regis Mauri[(✉)]

Optimization Lab, Federal University of Espírito Santo, Vitória, ES, Brazil
{edmar.kampke,geraldo.mauri}@ufes.br,
{easegatto,boeres,crangel}@inf.ufes.br

Abstract. Metaheuristics define and explore a set of different neighborhoods, in general, adapted to specific characteristics of a problem. The quality of the solution found relies on the efficiency of the neighborhood used on the local search phase, therefore it is very important to research about the movements or combination of them which compose the neighborhood structure. This paper is based on a recent work reported on literature that deals with four standard movements for the university timetabling problem. This work complements the analysis already done so far, adding five new movements widely known in the literature. Two of then are specific for the restrictions adopted by the curriculum-based formulation proposed on the Second International Timetabling Competition (ITC-2007). The Steepest Descent (SD) algorithm was implemented to study each movement separately and combined. This analysis shows that the quality of the solutions is highly affected by the movements chosen, since the ratio between the worst and best solution (in terms of objective function value), can be up to 13.5.

Keywords: University timetabling problem · Neighborhood analysis · Steepest Descent

1 Introduction

The allocation of resources into slots respecting a set of constraints is the deal of scheduling problems [7]. Timetabling is a specific type of scheduling with a wide variety of applications, such as employees scale [3] and sports championships matches scheduling [15]. More specifically, educational timetabling is concerned with to the allocation of a set of lectures in a predetermined number of timeslots, satisfying various constraints involving teachers, students and physical space [17].

Real world timetabling problems are usually hard to solve manually, because they often require a great amount of time and resources. The timetabling problem is classified as NP-complete for most of the formulations [18]. Therefore, the timetabling research community organizes competitions on this issue, known as the International Timetabling Competition (ITC), in order to promote the

© Springer International Publishing AG 2017
O. Gervasi et al. (Eds.): ICCSA 2017, Part III, LNCS 10406, pp. 148–164, 2017.
DOI: 10.1007/978-3-319-62398-6_11

discussion of several formulations, resolution techniques and provide real world instances for benchmarks. Three ITC editions have already held: ITC-2002, ITC-2007 and ITC-2011. The first two are dedicated to the university timetabling problem and the last to the high school timetabling problem.

The literature for timetabling solution techniques can be broadly inserted into three important research areas: mathematical programming, logic programming and metaheuristics. We observe that the majority of the recent works for the University Timetabling Problem use metaheuristic procedures, such as Genetic Algorithms [6], Tabu Search [11], Simulated Annealing [2] and Greedy Randomized Adaptive Search Procedures (GRASP) [7]. Metaheuristics are widely used due to simplicity of methods and quality of solutions found, according to Lewis [9]. Metaheuristics are intelligent local search procedures with the ability to explore the space of solutions and thus escape from local optimums. The main idea of these procedures is to apply a small modification (movement) to a solution s to get a new solution s' (neighbor) [14]. The neighborhood of s is defined by a set of solutions s' obtained by applying movements on s. Building a good neighborhood increases search capacity and, consequently, leads to satisfactory results [14].

Müller [13] proposes an algorithm with four steps that has been applied successfully to the Curriculum-Based Course Timetabling (CB-CTT) problem for the third track of ITC-2007. The first step is the generation of an initial solution with a graph coloring algorithm. The other steps are three successive local search procedures using, respectively, hill climbing [16], great deluge [5] and simulated annealing [8], with specific movements for the CB-CTT problem. Müller was the ITC-2007 winner.

Lü et al. [12] analyze four standard local search movements for the University Timetabling problem, adapted for the CB-CTT problem formulation. The authors studied these movements separately and combined, according to three criteria: (i) the percentage of improving neighbors; (ii) the improvement strength, that is, the biggest variation among all differences between the current solution and a best improving neighbor; (iii) the number of search steps. They observed that successive combination of the two best movements when applied alone, produced the best results, considering the defined criteria. The local search technique Steepest Descent algorithm (SD) was chosen to be used in the analysis, as in [12]. The SD is a local search procedure that analyzes all neighbors of solution s. If the best neighbor s' is better than s, then the search restarts with s' and ends when it does not find better neighbor than the current solution. Bolaji et al. [1] also present a study related to movements in the local search procedures for the university examination timetabling problem. They use an artificial bee colony algorithm with local search neighborhood composed of three movements which were also analyzed in [12].

In this work we intend to extend the study carried out in [12], analyzing additional movements which are specific for the CB-CTT problem. Some of them were proposed by Müller [13].

For comparison purposes, we decided to reimplement the movements described in [12], once their code was not available to us, performing all the tests in the same computational environment.

This paper is organized as follows. In Sect. 2, we describe the CB-CTT problem formulation for the university timetabling problem, adopted in the third track of ITC-2007. Section 3 outlines the movements and algorithms we intend to analyze. Computational experiments results are reported in Sect. 4 and conclusions are drawn in Sect. 5.

2   Problem Description

The CB-CTT problem deals with the weekly assignment of a set of lectures for several university courses to specific periods and rooms, where conflicts between courses are set according to curricula published by the university. The wide acceptance of this formulation is due to its good representation of the real problems that often arise in higher educational institutions. We describe briefly some elements of the CB-CTT problem below. Its whole formulation description can be found in [4].

Let d be the number of weekly school days, usually five or six, of a timetable T. Each day of T is split into a fixed number of slots q, which is equal for all days. In this work, differently from the formal definition [4], a period is a slot of T, ranged from 1 to $d \times q$. For example, if $d = 5$ and $q = 4$ for a given university timetabling, than the number of periods in this university is 20. Considering nr the total number of rooms, a timeslot t is defined as a pair (p, r), where p is a period and r a room in the range of 1 to nr.

A solution (or timetable) of the CB-CTT problem represents the assignment of a timeslot to all lectures of each course of a curriculum. Hard and soft constraints can be established. The hard constraints must always be respected and any violation of these restrictions generates an unfeasible timetable. On the other hand, the soft constraints must be satisfied as much as possible, and few violations indicate better timetabling solutions. The hard (denoted by **H1.** to **H4.**) and soft (denoted by **S1.** to **S4.**) constraints are:

- **H1.** *Lectures:* All lectures of a course must be assigned to distinct period and room.
- **H2.** *Room Occupancy:* Any two lectures cannot be assigned in the same period and in the same room.
- **H3.** *Conflicts:* Lectures of courses of the same curriculum or taught by the same teacher cannot be assigned in the same period, i.e., any period cannot have an overlapping of students or teachers.
- **H4.** *Availability:* If the teacher of a course is not available at a given period, then no lectures of the course can be assigned to that period.

- **S1.** *Room Capacity:* For each lecture, the number of students attending the course should not be greater than the capacity of the room hosting the lecture.

- **S2.** *Room Stability:* All lectures of a course should be scheduled at the same room. If this is impossible, the number of occupied rooms for these lectures should be as few as possible.
- **S3.** *Minimum Working Days:* The lectures of a course should be spread over a minimum number of days.
- **S4.** *Curriculum Compactness:* For a given curriculum, a violation is counted if there is one lecture not adjacent to any other lecture belonging to the same curriculum within the same day, which means that the weekly schedule of students should be as compact as possible.

The CB-CTT objective function f considers the number of conflicts of hard constraints for a feasible solution s as zero and counts the number of conflicts of each soft constraint with different penalties. So, $f_{Hard}(s) = 0$ and $f_{Soft}(s) = \sum_{i=1}^{4} \alpha_i \cdot \omega_i$, where α_i and ω_i are respectively the penalty and total number of conflicts of each soft constraint i. The CB-CTT problem formulation defines the values of α_i. These values are fixed and set to $\alpha_1 = 1$, $\alpha_2 = 1$, $\alpha_3 = 5$ and $\alpha_4 = 2$.

Thus, an optimum solution for the CB-CTT problem must be feasible (i.e., the hard constraints are satisfied) and must minimize the function f given by $f(s) = f_{Hard}(s) + f_{Soft}(s)$.

3   Neighborhoods and Algorithms

In this work, we intend to study several types of movements known in the literature to solve the University Timetabling problem. For this purpose, we implement the heuristic proposed by Lü and Hao [11], that constructs a solution s in a greedy way. This solution is submitted to the Steepest Descent local search method (SD) [14]. This method uses a neighborhood structure to explore the search space in order to find some solution s' with $f(s') < f(s)$, until there is no further improvement. In this section, we describe how we generate an initial solution s as input to SD, using Lü and Hao method (Sect. 3.1). Furthermore, we also briefly describe all movements we analyze in order to identify which of them leads the local search procedures to good solutions, in the same way as [1] and [12] (Sect. 3.2). These movements compose individually or in combination the neighborhood structures used for the SD algorithm described in Sect. 3.3.

3.1   Initial Solution

A sequential greedy heuristic starts to allocate lectures, one by one, in an empty timetable s, until all courses lectures are in s. Each heuristic iteration performs two distinct choices: first, a lecture l is selected among those not yet assigned to s, and then a timeslot t, still available, is chosen to allocate the lecture l. A timeslot t is available for a lecture l, if, when allocating l in t, an unfeasible timetable is not generated.

We apply the priority criteria for the lecture and timeslot choices proposed by Lü and Hao [11]. First, we compute the ratio between the number of available periods and the number of unassigned lectures for each course. Lectures of the courses with the smallest ratios have priority. Given a selected lecture l of course c, the next step is to choose an available timeslot t. Thus, for all available timeslots, we consider the total number of unassigned lectures that become unavailable after assigning the lecture l in timeslot t. In addition, this selection takes into account the soft constraints penalties incurred when allocating l in t. The timeslot with smallest sum of calculated values is chosen. For all the instances tested in this work, feasible solutions were generated with these priority criteria.

3.2   Movements

In this section we describe a set of nine movements, widely known in the literature, that we consider to compose the neighborhood structures of the local search procedures of the SD algorithm. We denote each movement by m and the application of m to a solution s generates a neighbor solution s', given by $s \oplus m$. The symbol $\oplus$ represents the transformation imposed over s by the movement m, generating a new solution s'.

- **Move (M).** *Move* is a standard movement used in local search procedures for timetabling problems. This movement consists simply in moving one lecture l at timeslot t_1 to an empty timeslot t_2 [12]. Move the lecture l from timeslot t_1 to timeslot t_2, leaving t_1 empty. Both the lecture l and the empty timeslot t_2 are randomly selected. This movement is similar to *SimpleMove*, described in [12].
- **Swap (S).** *Swap* is another standard movement. In this case, lectures l_1 and l_2 assigned to timeslots t_1 and t_2, respectively, are randomly selected. The *Swap* movement consists of exchanging the lecture l_1 from timeslot t_1 to timeslot t_2, and the lecture l_2 from timeslot t_2 to timeslot t_1 [12]. This movement is similar to *SimpleSwap*, described in [12].
- **Simple Kempe Chain Move (KS).** The KS movement select randomly two different periods p_1 and p_2 (in the same day of the timetable or not). Then, given subsets of lectures L_1 and L_2, respectively allocated to the periods p_1 and p_2, KS tries to assign lectures from L_1 to p_2 and lectures from L_2 to p_1, ensuring the feasibility of the neighbor solution [20].
  To apply KS to a candidate solution s, we consider a bipartite graph G where the vertices represent timeslots of s. One of G partitions represent the timeslots associated to the period p_1 and the other, the timeslots associated to p_2. The edges between G partitions link timeslots with lectures that must remain in different periods. In other words, there will be an edge between each two timeslots with lectures that are carried out by the same teacher or belonging to the same curriculum.
  Given the graph G, a KS movement is represented by a connected component in G. Note that more than one Kempe chain can be found in a graph. In this case, one of them is chosen randomly and all the lectures of the selected chain will belong to L_1 or L_2. If the number of lectures assigned to the periods p_1 and p_2 in the selected Kempe chain is not higher than the number of available rooms, the KS movement is effectively applied, otherwise, it is discarded.

This violation is called room allocation violation and is related to the hard constraint **H2**. The movement KS is similar to *KempeMove*, described in [12].

- **Extended Kempe Chain Move (KE).** The extended Kempe chain move is very similar to the simple Kempe chain move [12]. One of the differences is the associated graph G. In addition to the edges generated in the simple Kempe chain version, there exists edges between each two timeslots for the same room (one of them in period p_1 and the other in period p_2), added with the intention of escaping from the room allocation violation. Another difference we point out is related to the application of the KE move in G, that can be understood as several simple Kempe chain moves. The KE move can choose lectures from more than one connected component, in an attempt to expand the exploration of the search space. This movement is similar to *KempeSwap*, described in [12].

The next five movements are proposed by Müller in [13].

- **Time Move (TM).** In this movement, a lecture l allocated in period p_i and room r (timeslot t_i) is randomly selected. The first non-conflicting period p_j with $j > i$ at the same room r (timeslot t_j) is also selected and then, **M** is applied moving l to t_j, if t_j is an empty timeslot or **S** is applied, otherwise. If the TM movement incurs in a hard constraint violation, the next periods after p_j at the same room r are verified.

- **Room Move (RM).** This movement is similar to the previous one. Initially, a lecture l allocated in period p and room r_i (timeslot t_i) is randomly selected. Then, the first non-conflicting room r_j with $j > i$ at the same period p (timeslot t_j) is also selected and then, M is applied moving l to t_j, if t_j is an empty timeslot or S is applied, otherwise. If the RM movement incurs in a hard constraint violation, the next rooms after r_j at the same period p are verified.

- **Lecture Move (LM).** For this movement, a lecture l_1 allocated in timeslot t_1 is randomly selected. Then a timeslot t_2 is also randomly selected. If t_2 is an empty timeslot, M is applied, moving l to t_2. Otherwise, S is applied. We highlight that the difference of LM to M and S is that, when the movement LM selects a timeslot t_2, it does not distinguish an empty from a non-empty timeslot, as is the case of the M and S movements.

- **Room Stability Move (RS).** Room Stability Move attempts a set of switches in order to minimize the Room Stability soft constraint (**S2**) [13]. A course c that violates this constraint is selected randomly and a room r with one or more lectures of c is also selected. Then all lectures of c which are not allocated in r are moved to r, keeping the same periods as before. If there is another lecture already allocated on r, a S move switches them.

- **Minimum Working Days Move (MWD).** The purpose of this movement is to minimize the penalty of the Minimum Working Days soft constraint (**S3**) [13]. A course c that violates this constraint is selected randomly and a day d_1 with two or more lectures of c is also selected. Then a day d_2 without c lectures allocated is also chosen. Thereafter, a timeslot t of d_2 is selected. If t has no lecture assigned, M is applied, moving a lecture of c (allocated in d_1) to t. Otherwise, S is applied.

3.3   Local Search

The whole set of movements described in Sect. 3.2 are tested as neighborhood components of the Steepest Descent (SD) algorithm [14] we implemented in this work, following the same methodology and definitions of Lü et al. [12].

Let $M(s)$ be the set of all feasible moves which can be applied to a solution s. Thus, the neighborhood $N(s)$ of s is defined by: $N(s) = \{s' = s \oplus m : \forall m \in M(s)\}$ [10].

The SD implemented is a simple best improvement local search (Algorithm 1). Starting from an initial solution s, the algorithm set both the best solution (s^*) and the current solution ($s_{current}$) to s (lines 1 and 2). Then, it iteratively (lines 3 to 9) checks the application of a movement m' from $M(s^*)$ over s^*, choosing the best neighbor $s^* \oplus m'$ of $N(s^*)$ in terms of the objective function f (line 4). The current solution $s_{current}$ is then replaced by $s^* \oplus m'$ of $N(s^*)$ (line 5). If this solution is better than s^*, the latter is updated (lines 6 to 8). The algorithm SD stops when there is no more feasible movement in $N(s^*)$ which improves the solution s^*.

Algorithm 1. Steepest Descent

Input: Initial solution s
Output: Best solution found s^*

1 $s^* \leftarrow s$;

2 $s_{current} \leftarrow s$;

3 **while** $s_{current} = s^*$ **do**

4 $\quad$ choose $m' \in M(s^*)$, such that $f(s^* \oplus m') = min_{m \in M(s)} f(s^* \oplus m)$;

5 $\quad$ $s_{current} \leftarrow s^* \oplus m'$;

6 $\quad$ **if** $f(s_{current}) < f(s^*)$ **then**

7 $\quad\quad$ $s^* \leftarrow s_{current}$;

8 $\quad$ **end**

9 **end**

---

4   Computational Experiments

The proposed algorithm was tested on a set of 21 instances (named comp01 $\sim$ comp21), the same used in the ITC-2007 and available at the website http://satt. diegm.uniud.it/ctt. Therefore, in this section, we present the implementation details of the proposed algorithm (Sect. 4.1), how the neighborhood structures have been defined and the methodology adopted for the experiments (Sect. 4.2). In Sect. 4.3, the results are discussed and analyzed.

4.1   Implementation Details

The SD algorithm was implemented in C++, using the object oriented paradigm. We highlight as its main classes *the problem*, which contains all the information of the CB-CTT formulation, including the hard and soft constraints and *the solution*, which contains three vectors. One of them represents effectively the timetable composed with all possible $d \times q \times nr$ timeslots and the other two represent, respectively, the set of timeslots that contains a lecture assigned and the set of those that are empty. Both contain maximum dimension $d \times q \times nr$. With these three vectors, we aim to facilitate the choice of the lectures to be modified by the local search.

Furthermore, each timetable (solution) contains four associated matrices. Three of them are two-dimensional and binary (0 or 1). They report:

- If a room i is used by a course j, then the ij position in the first matrix is 1, otherwise is 0.
- The ij position of the second matrix is 1, if one or more lectures of course j are assigned on day i, otherwise is 0.
- For the third matrix, if some course of curricula i has one lecture assigned in period j, then the ij position is 1, otherwise is 0.

The fourth matrix is three-dimensional, where each ijk position has a struct with all data from lecture l of course c, only if c belongs to curriculum i and is assigned to slot k of day j, otherwise is empty. The purpose of these associated matrices is to allow the fast access of the information in the recalculation of the objective function when performing a movement. This representation strategy is very similar to [19].

The code was compiled using $g++$, version 4.8.4 with -O3 optimization flag. The results were generated on a computer with a hardware Intel Core i5-3570 CPU 3.40 GHz 4, 8 GB memory and ubuntu 14.04 64 bit.

4.2   Neighborhood Analysis Procedure

The methodology we adopt for the experiments consider sixteen tests representing different neighborhood structures. Each test is performed 50 times for each instance. The average of all results obtained is computed.

The tests set is split considering simple and combined neighborhoods structures. The former is composed of a single type of movement of the whole list described in Sect. 3.2. The latter consider the combination of two or three types of movements, chosen among those of the list aforementioned. Our expectation is to increase the search capability of the neighborhood in order to find better results.

In this work, we investigate two distinct local search strategies, proposed in [12], for exploring the combined neighborhoods, denoted by union ($\cup$) and sequence ($\rightarrow$). In the union strategy, for a given solution s and k different movements $m_1 \sim m_k$, we generate all s neighbors using each of the k movements. Thus, all these solutions will compose s neighborhood. The best neighbor of s is chosen and this process is repeated until there is no further improvement.

In the sequence strategy, for a given solution s and k different movements $m_1 \sim m_k$, we apply the local search procedure over s using m_1. The best neighbor s' is submitted as initial solution, to the same local search procedure, using m_2

and so on, following the sequence of movements until m_k. This process is repeated until no further improvement is possible.

Based on the neighborhoods comparison criteria adopted in [12], we record details of the performed runs as best result found with each neighborhood, the number of SD iterations, the size of the neighborhood measured as the average $M(s)$ cardinality over SD iterations and the percentage of improving neighbors.

4.3 Computational Experiments Results

In this section we present the results and analysis for the computational tests performed with the SD algorithm using simple and combined neighborhoods.

Simple Neighborhoods. Table 1 presents the results obtained for SD with simple neighborhoods. The first column of this table indicates the instance names and the following depict the results obtained using singly each movement described in Sect. 3.2, which are: Lecture Move (LM), Move (M), Swap (S), Room Move (RM), Room Stability Move (RS), Extended Kempe Chain Move (KE), Time Move (TM), Simple Kempe Chain Move (KS) and Minimum Working Days (MWD). The numbers in this table, which are rounded down, represent the average cost over 50 SD runs, relative to the soft constraint violations

Table 1. Average cost of solutions found using simple neighborhoods

Instance	LM	M	S	RM	RS	KE	TM	KS	MWD
comp01	25	251	29	288	228	294	313	320	330
comp02	190	209	304	408	499	476	485	467	507
comp03	210	235	336	385	448	416	427	442	461
comp04	182	195	349	396	581	626	669	676	666
comp05	638	730	785	816	895	877	914	910	939
comp06	233	287	388	573	884	1180	1243	1333	1362
comp07	238	361	335	664	979	1238	1302	1426	1468
comp08	149	171	338	455	668	692	783	843	826
comp09	220	249	394	515	570	540	562	572	588
comp10	204	243	369	611	714	644	726	825	815
comp11	24	58	148	91	210	154	343	320	350
comp12	673	1140	913	1109	1243	1742	1707	1694	1752
comp13	215	226	407	436	772	1024	1013	1066	1088
comp14	221	247	547	479	865	934	931	952	935
comp15	210	235	336	385	448	416	427	442	461
comp16	233	273	491	677	936	748	879	1007	1013
comp17	253	312	377	639	708	810	925	947	993
comp18	204	217	305	296	369	481	558	540	503
comp19	236	262	340	380	423	463	485	472	487
comp20	286	421	609	633	1316	1640	1716	1726	1805
comp21	258	313	435	610	656	761	953	1001	1013

penalty, since all solutions found are feasible. The cells are colored following a criterion: each row have nine cells with different shades of gray. The darkest cell contains the best result found for the instance, the second darker, the second best, and so on respectively, up to the lightest, which contains the worst solution found. Note that this criterion is also applied to the columns: the darker the column, the better is the quality of the related movement results, inducing the display order of the movements in the table.

We can observe that the **LM** results outperform those of all other movements. Comparing the best move (**LM**) with the second best (**M**), we observe that the improvement range is 4.98% (comp13) to 90.16% (comp01). From the best (**LM**) to the worst move (**MWD**), the improvement range is 32.02% (comp05) to 93.13% (comp11).

The graphics of Fig. 1a to c show respectively the number of SD iterations, the average $M(s)$ cardinality over SD iterations and the percentage of improving neighbors, considering all the neighborhoods composed by each of the nine movements (**LM** to **MWD**) evaluated.

We can see from Fig. 1a that the neighborhoods with better results in Table 1 are associated to those with the larger number of iterations. The lines in the graph are plotted over normalized values (that varies from 0 to 1) and computed as $h = (g - g_{min})/(g_{max} - g_{min})$, where g is the value measured for each graphic and g_{min} (g_{max}) is the minimum (maximum) value obtained over all movements. Those plotted near to one represent the movements with the largest number of iterations, while the other perform the smallest number of iterations. In theory, a neighborhood is better explored as more iterations are executed. We observe the display order of the movements, from the best to the worst, in Table 1 match with the order of the lines representing each movement in Fig. 1a.

Figure 1b shows the neighborhood size for each movement and instance. The best results are those generated by the **KS** move. The worst values are for the instances comp5, comp12 and comp18, which are known as containing a large amount of unavailability. With respect to the Kempe movements, **KS** and **KE**, when compared to each other we observe that, although **KS** generated more neighbors than **KE** (Fig. 1b), it is less effective in terms of number of SD iterations performed. As they are similar neighborhoods, we suggest **KE** is more suitable than **KS** for CB-CTT problem.

The **LM** move, with the best results in Table 1, however, produces a neighborhood size not so high, but even so, higher than **M** and **S**. Note that this movement is composed of these other two. We observe from Fig. 1b, that the **LM** neighborhood size is similar to the sum of **M** and **S** neighborhood sizes. For this reason we expected that **LM** performs similar to **M** ∪ **S**, since preliminary tests confirmed this statement.

TM and **MWD** generated the smallest neighborhood sizes. We attribute this behavior to the fact that these movements are dedicated to specific soft constraints of the CB-CTT problem. Consequently, these movements generate a smaller number of possible neighbors.

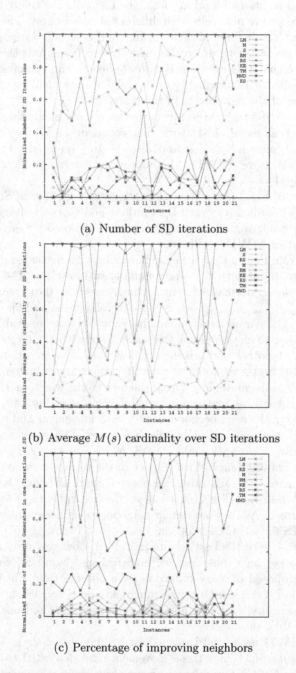

(a) Number of SD iterations

(b) Average $M(s)$ cardinality over SD iterations

(c) Percentage of improving neighbors

Fig. 1. Comparisons measures for the SD algorithm for simple neighborhoods

Opposite to Fig. 1b, in the Fig. 1c, the specific movements **TM** and **MWD** generate a significant higher percentage of improving neighbors. This means that these movements are effective as, despite generating few neighbors, most of them decrease the value of the objective function f. The best movement **LM**, in terms of the objective function values, generates few improving neighbors, when comparing to the neighborhood size. We believe that this behavior is due to the fact that this movement produces a greater amount of neighbors (Fig. 1b), improving the search space exploration.

We underline that **RM** and **RS** change, in a similar way, the lecture rooms of a candidate neighbor. We observe from Table 1 that **RM** performs better than **RS**, as it probably generates good neighbours that were not produced by **RS**.

With respect to the simple movements described in [12], that we similarly implemented in this work, we observed the best results were obtained by *KempeSwap*, followed by *SimpleMove*, *SimpleSwap* and *KempeMove*. In this work, **M** is the best, followed by **S**, **KE** and **KS**. Although the sequence is not the same, we highlight that, in both cases, **M** (*SimpleMove*) outperforms **S** (*SimpleSwap*) as well as **KE** (*KempeSwap*) outperforms **KS** (*KempeMove*).

Combined Neighborhoods. Seven combined neighborhoods (i) **LM** ∪ **RM**; (ii) **LM** ∪ **TM**; (iii) **RM** ∪ **TM**; (iv) **LM** ∪ **RM** ∪ **TM**; (v) **LM** → **KE**; (vi) **LM** → **RS** and (vii) **LM** → **MWD** were generated from the single movements **LM**, **RM**, **TM**, **KE**, **RS** and **MWD**.

This strategy was adopted because **LM** was the movement with the best behavior among all simple neighborhoods tested. For that reason the **LM** movement was used in most of combined neighborhoods. The four first (union) combined neighborhoods of the list above are all possible combinations between **LM**, **RM** and **TM** movements. They were chosen because they are the most similar to a simple **M** or **S**. The last three (sequence) combined neighborhoods represent the sequence between a **LM** and other movement with a very different structure from **M** and **S**. We highlight that the tests of the sequence combinations were performed without limitation of SD iterations per movement, according to the definition of the Sect. 4.2.

Considering the sequence **LM** → **KE**, the best improvement obtained in relation to **LM** was for instance comp11 with reduction of 2.99% whereas for the instances comp01, comp05, comp13 and comp19, we observed no improvement. Analyzing the other sequence neighborhoods, **LM** → **MWD** and **LM** → **RS**, the results achieved were similar to **LM**, showing that the diversification was not able to generate neighbors that escaped the local minimum. It is important to note the sequence combination worst case provides the same result obtained by the simple neighborhood **LM**.

In order to make the sequence combination more efficient, we limited the number of SD iterations for each neighborhood, based on exhaustive preliminary tests. The best limit value found was 20 SD iterations. The average objective function f found with this limit, for each instance, are presented in Table 2 along with the respective f values for the union combinations aforementioned.

Table 2. Average soft cost of solution found using combined neighborhoods

Instance	LM → KE	LM → MWD	LM → RS	LM ∪ TM	LM ∪ RM	LM ∪ RM ∪ TM	RM ∪ TM
comp01	24	25	25	25	25	25	310
comp02	188	188	188	188	190	189	483
comp03	211	211	211	209	210	210	417
comp04	176	182	188	185	182	184	568
comp05	636	638	641	638	638	638	912
comp06	230	231	231	234	233	235	997
comp07	232	236	231	238	240	241	971
comp08	149	152	149	150	149	150	582
comp09	224	221	221	222	222	221	559
comp10	207	203	203	205	207	206	629
comp11	26	24	21	24	24	24	327
comp12	629	673	679	677	680	678	1707
comp13	216	212	216	215	215	215	891
comp14	221	213	227	221	224	226	902
comp15	211	211	211	209	210	210	417
comp16	222	229	230	230	234	233	721
comp17	250	258	254	258	255	254	873
comp18	199	201	204	204	204	204	558
comp19	235	236	235	236	234	235	468
comp20	280	280	274	287	286	286	1337
comp21	259	264	258	262	257	261	753

It is worth noting that for the union combination tests there is no limit of SD iterations. The display structure of Table 2 is analogous to Table 1.

From Table 2 we can see that the combination **LM → KE** (with limited iterations) presents the best result for 10 instances, among all combined movements tested. Comparing the results of **LM** and **LM → KE**, the latter improved the f value for 12 of the 21 instances tested. For these 12 instances, the improvement range is from 0.31% (comp5) to 6.54% (comp12). For the remaining instances, two ties are achieved (comp8 and comp14) and for the others seven, unfortunately, we got worse results with this combined movement. In this case, the worsening range is from −8.33% (comp11) to −0.39% (comp21). Given f_{LM} and $f_{LM \to KE}$ respectively the objective function f values for **LM** and **LM → KE**, we point out that the percentages of gain and loss from $f_{LM \to KE}$ to f_{LM} were computed as $100 \cdot (1 - f_{LM \to KE}/f_{LM})$. Nevertheless, when considering the average f cost variation for all instances, an improvement of 1.51% is obtained. None of the union combinations achieved improvement in comparison to **LM**.

Comparing the best sequence move (**LM → KE**) with the second best (**LM → MWD**) (similar to the comparison performed in Sect. 4.3), we observe there exists f cost improvement for 12 instances, with improvement ranging from 0.31% (comp5) to 6.54% (comp12). From the best sequence move (**LM → KE**) to the worst sequence move (**LM → RS**), 9 instances improved with the range between 0.43% (comp6) and 7.36% (comp12). With respect to the union

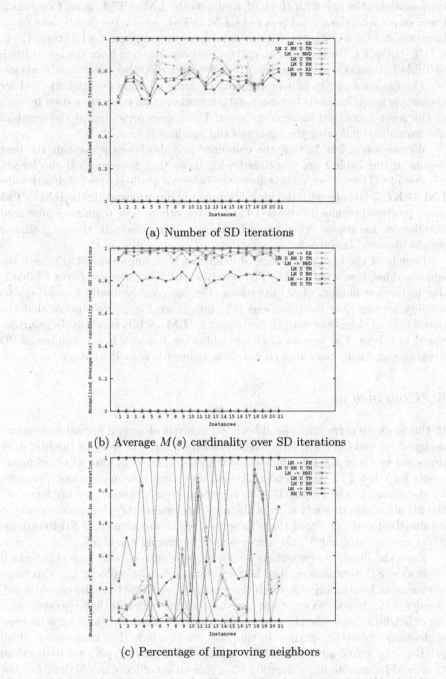

(a) Number of SD iterations

(b) Average $M(s)$ cardinality over SD iterations

(c) Percentage of improving neighbors

Fig. 2. Comparisons measures for the SD algorithm for combined neighborhoods

combinations, the one with the best results is the **LM ∪ TM** move. Comparing these values with the second best move **LM ∪ TM**, we observe there exists f cost improvement for 8 instances, with improvement ranging from 0.44% (comp12) to 1.71% (comp16). We highlight that the union combination from the last column of Table 2 presents results significantly worse than the other union combinations.

The graphics of Fig. 2a to c present the same measure evaluations used for the simple neighborhoods (see Sect. 4.3), considering all those composed by each of the seven combined movements used. The values presented in the graphics are normalized following the design of the previous figures.

We can see in Fig. 2a that the combined neighborhoods presenting the best results in the Table 2 are associated with those that have reached the largest number of SD iterations, analogous to the behavior of the simple neighborhoods. **LM → KE** is the one with the largest number of iterations while the **RM ∪ TM** move produced results much lower than all the others. The remaining presented numbers of iterations closer to each other, which reflects in the very similar results observed in Table 2.

Despite of the high percentage of neighbors with improvement (Fig. 2c), the combined neighborhood **RM ∪ TM** obtained the worst average f cost (Table 2) due to the low number of SD iterations (Fig. 2a) combined with low $M(s)$ cardinality average over the iterations (Fig. 2b). From Fig. 2c we observe that the percentage of neighbors with improvement of **LM → KE** is relatively low compared to others. The success of this neighborhood resides in the number of SD iterations and neighbors at each iteration, achieving a good solution.

5　Conclusions

In this work we carry out a neighborhood analysis of several known movements designed for the CB-CTT formulation, based on a recent work of the literature proposed by Lü et al. [12], which deals with the analysis of four standard movements for CB-CTT. We extend this analysis to five new movements, proposed by the winner of the ITC-2007 [13]. For comparison purposes, we implemented the SD algorithm to study each of the nine movements chosen separately and in combination and calculated three measures, which are number of SD iterations, $M(s)$ average cardinality and percentage of improving neighbors.

From the simple movements neighborhoods results, we conclude those which allow more SD iterations reached better solutions for the problem, i.e., this number seems to be strongly related to the quality (f value) of the solution obtained. Besides that, the second and third measures results indicates that a greater number of neighbors generated by a movement does not necessarily imply the increase of neighbors of better quality. In this way, we conclude that movements which privilege the search intensification (i.e., more SD iterations) perform better than those which promote diversification (i.e., generation of more neighbors), but not always with high f improvement. From this set of movements, **LM** outperforms all the others. It can achieve, in average over all instances, a gain of up to 72.21%, relative to the movement with the worst results (**MWD**).

From the combined movements neighborhoods results, we conclude those which are combined with **LM** always achieve better values for all measures computed. The best results are obtained by **LM** → **KE**, combining **LM** (more intensification) with **KE** (more diversification). In addition, we observe that the sequence combination neighborhoods performed slightly better than those generated by the union combination movements. The first improved by up to 1.51%, in averàge over all instances, the results of **LM**, while the latter did not achieve the same improvement success.

The input data, the source codes implemented in this work and a readme file are available in https://bitbucket.org/timetablingufes/iccsa-2017/.

Acknowledgments. We want to express our thanks to Conselho Nacional de Desenvolvimento Científico e Tecnológico - CNPq (processes 454569/2014-9 and 301725/2016-0) and Fundação de Amparo à Pesquisa e Inovação do Espírito Santo - FAPES (processes 67656021/2014, 67627153/2014, 70232628/2015 and 73290475/2015) for financial support.

References

1. Bolaji, A.L., Khader, A.T., Al-Betar, M.A., Thomas, J.J.: The effect of neighborhood structures on examination timetabling with artificial bee colony. In: Proceedings of the 9th International Conference on the Practice and Theory of Automated Timetabling, pp. 29–31 (2012)
2. Ceschia, S., Di Gaspero, L., Schaerf, A.: Design, engineering, and experimental analysis of a simulated annealing approach to the post-enrolment course timetabling problem. Comput. Oper. Res. **39**(7), 1615–1624 (2012)
3. Della Croce, F., Salassa, F.: A variable neighborhood search based matheuristic for nurse rostering problems. Ann. Oper. Res. **218**(1), 185–199 (2014)
4. Di Gaspero, L., Schaerf, A., McCollum, B.: The second international timetabling competition (ITC-2007): curriculum-based course timetabling (track 3). Technical report (2007)
5. Dueck, G.: New optimization heuristics: the great deluge algorithm and the record-to-record travel. J. Comput. Phys. **104**(1), 86–92 (1993)
6. Erben, W., Keppler, J.: A genetic algorithm solving a weekly course-timetabling problem. In: Burke, E., Ross, P. (eds.) PATAT 1995. LNCS, vol. 1153, pp. 198–211. Springer, Heidelberg (1996). doi:10.1007/3-540-61794-9_60
7. Kampke, E.H., de Souza Rocha, W., Boeres, M.C.S., Rangel, M.C.: A grasp algorithm with path relinking for the university courses timetabling problem. In: Proceeding Series of the Brazilian Society of Computational and Applied Mathematics, vol. 3(2), pp. 1081–1087 (2015)
8. Kirkpatrick, S.: Optimization by simulated annealing: quantitative studies. J. Stat. Phys. **34**(5), 975–986 (1984)
9. Lewis, R.: A survey of metaheuristic-based techniques for university timetabling problems. OR Spectr. **30**(1), 167–190 (2008)
10. Lü, Z., Hao, J.-K.: Solving the course timetabling problem with a hybrid heuristic algorithm. In: Dochev, D., Pistore, M., Traverso, P. (eds.) AIMSA 2008. LNCS, vol. 5253, pp. 262–273. Springer, Heidelberg (2008). doi:10.1007/978-3-540-85776-1_22
11. Lü, Z., Hao, J.K.: Adaptive tabu search for course timetabling. Eur. J. Oper. Res. **200**(1), 235–244 (2010)

12. Lü, Z., Hao, J.K., Glover, F.: Neighborhood analysis: a case study on curriculum-based course timetabling. J. Heuristics **17**(2), 97–118 (2011)
13. Müller, T.: ITC 2007 solver description: a hybrid approach. Ann. Oper. Res. **172**(1), 429–446 (2009)
14. Papadimitriou, C.H., Steiglitz, K.: Combinatorial Optimization: Algorithms and Complexity. Courier Corporation, Mineola (1982)
15. Ribeiro, C.C., Urrutia, S.: Scheduling the Brazilian soccer tournament: solution approach and practice. Interfaces **42**(3), 260–272 (2012)
16. Russell, S., Norvig, P.: Artificial intelligence: a modern approach, pp. 111–113. Prentice-Hall, Englewood Cliffs, New Jersey (1995)
17. Santos, H.G., Uchoa, E., Ochi, L.S., Maculan, N.: Strong bounds with cut and column generation for class-teacher timetabling. Ann. Oper. Res. **194**(1), 399–412 (2012)
18. Schaerf, A.: A survey of automated timetabling. Artif. Intell. Rev. **13**(2), 87–127 (1999)
19. Teoh, C.K., Abdullah, M.Y.C., Haron, H.: Effect of pre-processors on solution quality of university course timetabling problem. In: Proceedings of the 2015 IEEE Student Conference on Research and Development, pp. 472–477 (2015)
20. Tuga, M., Berretta, R., Mendes, A.: A hybrid simulated annealing with kempe chain neighborhood for the university timetabling problem. In: Proceedings of the 6th IEEE/ACIS International Conference on Computer and Information Science (ICIS 2007), pp. 400–405 (2007)

On Grid Aware Refinement
of the Unit Hypercube and Simplex:
Focus on the Complete Tree Size

L.G. Casado[1], E.M.T. Hendrix[2(✉)], J.M.G. Salmerón[1], B. G.-Tóth[3],
and I. García[2]

[1] University of Almería (ceiA3), Almería, Spain
{josemanuel,leo}@ual.es
[2] Universidad de Málaga, Málaga, Spain
{eligius,igarciaf}@uma.es
[3] Szeged University, Szeged, Hungary
tothbog@gmail.com

Abstract. Branch and bound (BnB) Global Optimization algorithms
can be used to find the global optimum (minimum) of a multiextremal
function over the unit hypercube and unit simplex with a guaranteed
accuracy. Subdivision strategies can take the information of the evaluated points into account leading to irregular shaped subsets. This study
focuses on the passive generation of spatial subdivisions aiming at evaluating points on a predefined grid. The efficiency measure is in terms of
the complete tree size, or worst case BnB scenario, with a termination
criterion on the subset size. Longest edge bisection is used as a benchmark. It is shown that taking the grid for a given termination tolerance
into account, other general partitions exist that improve the BnB upper
bound on the number of evaluated points and subsets.

Keywords: Branch and bound · Division · Covering · Unit hypercube ·
Unit simplex

1 Introduction

Global Optimization (GO) branch and bound (BnB) algorithms attempt to find
the global optimum of an optimization problem with a guaranteed accuracy
performing an exhaustive search [8,11,13]. Using grid search as a benchmark,
BnB reduces its computational burden avoiding evaluation of subregions where
the global solution is proven not to exist based on calculating objective function
or constraint bounds. Grid search is a passive method (like pure random search)
where the next point to be evaluated does not depend on the objective function
values of the evaluated points. Our focus is on subdivision methods in BnB,
where the chosen subdivision does not depend on the evaluated values, leading
to a predictable size of the complete search tree. Given this context, the research
question is how the subdivision can be designed in such a way that by taking

© Springer International Publishing AG 2017
O. Gervasi et al. (Eds.): ICCSA 2017, Part III, LNCS 10406, pp. 165–180, 2017.
DOI: 10.1007/978-3-319-62398-6_12

the grid points into account. Additionally, we are interested in spatial divisions with a small branching factor, i.e. a small number of sub-spaces generated by a division, to obtain a complete search tree that is as small as possible. We consider the unit hypercube $S_1 = [0,1]^d$ as search space and focus further on the unit simplex defined as

$$S_1 = \{x \in \mathbb{R}^d \mid \sum_{j=1}^{d} x_j = 1; \; x_j \geq 0, \forall j\}, \tag{1}$$

which is the search region for several challenging GO problems [4,7,9].

Grid search is one of the simplest algorithms that can be applied trying to find a minimum point x^* such that $f^* = f(x^*) = \min_{x \in S_1} f(x)$, where the search space $S_1 \subset \mathbb{R}^d$ is the unit hypercube or the unit simplex. However, evaluating all grid points with a given tolerance (mesh size) α is not appealing, because the number of points increases strongly with the dimension d and as α decreases. Moreover, the best evaluated point $\hat{x}$, in term of its objective function value $\hat{f} = f(\hat{x})$, can be at further distance than α from a global minimum point x^*.

GO BnB methods provide a guarantee exploiting structure of the problem to be solved, [8]. A basic test in BnB discards a sub-problem when the upper bound $\hat{f}$ (objective function value of the best point found) is smaller than the lower bound of a given sub-problem. Due to the possibility of a rejection of a sub-problem, the branching factor (number of sub-problems generated in a partition) is usually low, even when multi-section is applied [3,12,14]. Longest edge bisection (LEB) has the lowest branching factor; two sub-problems with the same volume are generated. LEB has been used in literature as a comparison benchmark in different GO BnB methods due to its simplicity and its convergence properties. Division methods may make use of the information about the objective function obtained during the search [5,10,12,17]. On one hand, doing so aims at finding better bounds. On the other hand, they hinder the estimation of the left-over work, related to the unpredictable shape of the sub-problems and the difficulty of determining an upper bound on the final tree size.

This paper studies passive spatial division methods with a small branching factor, with two aims: (i) to improve the efficiency of LEB in generating the complete tree, and (ii) to facilitate the estimation of the left-over work. Let $w(S)$ be the width of a sub-problem S, i.e. the euclidean norm length of its longest edge. In our study, the complete tree is built and a tolerance ϵ determines when a sub-problem S is not further divided, $w(S) \leq \epsilon w(S_1)$.

One question is how to design a division method helping the estimation of the left-over work. Knowing the size of a complete sub-tree from a given tree node, provides an upper bound of its left-over work. An approximation can be derived in GO BnB algorithms by heuristically applying exponential smoothing of previous pruning to the remaining complete sub-tree size [2].

This paper is organized as follows. Section 2 defines the α-grid and presents an algorithm to generate it on the unit simplex. Section 3 describes a longest edge bisection refinement algorithm and shows how to improve it by considering the α-grid for the unit hypercube, giving the basis for the unit simplex refinement, which is studied in Sect. 4. Numerical results are shown in Sect. 5. The main conclusions and future research are described in Sect. 6.

2 The α-grid

We focus the study on new refinements for a BnB algorithm with accuracy ϵ that evaluates points being vertices of the subsets such that these points coincide with grid points on S_1. This does not occur for each choice of the accuracy ϵ. In principle, the largest value for the grid size α given accuracy ϵ is

$$\alpha = \frac{1}{\lceil \frac{1}{\epsilon} \rceil}, \tag{2}$$

which coincides with $G = \lceil \frac{1}{\epsilon} \rceil$ parts on each axis and $G + 1$ grid point per axis, whereas two of them represent vertices of S_1. Consider the unit hypercube $S_1 = [0, 1]^d$.

Definition 1. *The α-grid in the unit hypercube is a mesh of points where points $x, y \in \alpha$-grid are neighbours if $\exists i$, such that, $y_i = x_i \pm \alpha$ and $y_k = x_k$, for $k \neq i$.*

The number of α-grid points $(G + 1)^d$ grows exponentially in dimension d.

Definition 2. *The α-grid in the unit simplex is a mesh of points where two points $x, y \in \alpha$-grid are neighbours if $\exists i, j, \ i \neq j$ such that, $y_i = x_i + \alpha$, $y_j = x_j - \alpha$ and $y_k = x_k$, for $k \neq i, j$.*

For the unit simplex, the number of the α-grid points [4] is not as bad as for the unit hypercube:

$$\sum_{k=1}^{d-1} \binom{G+1}{k} \binom{d-2}{k-1}. \tag{3}$$

For instance, having $d = 5$ and $G = 9$, the number of the α-grid points for the unit hypercube is 10^5 and just 715 for the unit simplex. This difference becomes more clear when considering the unit simplex as a $d - 1$ dimensional polytope. For instance, the unit simplex is a triangle for $d = 3$ and a tetrahedron for $d = 4$. Moreover, the volume of the unit simplex in d dimensions is smaller than the volume of unit hypercube in dimension $d - 1$.

Algorithm 1. GenUSimplexGrid (ϵ, d)

Require:
    ϵ: User accuracy,
    d: Dimension
1: $G := \lceil \frac{1}{\epsilon} \rceil$ *Number of grid segments per axis*
2: $\Lambda := \emptyset$ *Set of grid points*
3: $P = (P_1, \ldots, P_d) := (0, \ldots, 0)$
4: GenUSimplexGridRec$(P, G + 1, d)$ *See Algorithm 2*
5: **return** Λ

To check whether a general partition method visits the α-grid points, they can be generated by Algorithm 1. In fact, it initiates the parameters for the recursive Algorithm 2. The argument $PpLRec$ determines the number of points per line (see line 1) and $dTofix$ is used to fix the number of slots of the coordinate $dTofix$ in the vector P (see line 2). The recursion calls are performed with proper $PpLRec$ and $dTofix$ values (see line 4) until the coordinate to be fixed is 2 (see line 3). In such case, the $PpLRec$ points in terms of the number of slots stored in P are calculated by varying P_2 (see line 2) and P_1 (see line 6). The new grid point is calculated by dividing P by the number of slots per initial edge G and it is stored in Λ. After Algorithm 2 completion, Algorithm 1 returns the set of α-grid points stored in Λ.

Algorithm 2. GenUSimplexGridRec(P, $PpLRec$, $dToFix$)

Require:
  Global variables G, d and Λ of Algorithm 1,
  P: A d vector indexing the grid points per axis,
  $PpLRec$: Number of points per line in recursive call,
  $dToFix$: Dimension to be fixed.
1: **for** $k := 0$ to $PpLRec - 1$ **do**
2:    $P_{dToFix} := k$
3:    **if** $dToFix > 2$ **then**
4:       GenUSimplexGridRec (P, $PpLRec - k$, $dToFix - 1$)
5:    **else**
6:       $P_1 := G - \sum_{j=2}^{d} P_j$
7:       Store $\frac{1}{G} P$ in Λ
8:    **end if**
9: **end for**

---

3   Search Refinement Algorithm

Algorithm 3 represents an iterative refinement procedure with Longest Edge Bisection generating two new sub-problems at each division. We first focus on instances where LEB is not necessarily the best passive spatial division option to generate the complete search tree for a given accuracy ϵ.

3.1   Unit Hypercube Partition

As studied in [2], applying LEB on an hypercube will generate a binary tree where the number of levels L can be determined from the number of times m to halve the width. The final solutions have a width $w(S) \le \epsilon w(S_1)$, and the number m is determined by $\frac{1}{2^m} \le \epsilon$ such that $m = \lceil \log_2(\frac{1}{\epsilon}) \rceil = \lceil -\log_2 \epsilon \rceil$. The depth of the complete BnB binary tree is $L = m \cdot d$ and the total number of nodes is $2^{L+1} - 1$. Notice that the last level of the tree has 2^L nodes. That number is the same as the total number of nodes at all higher levels plus one.

Given the choice for G in the range $2^{m-1} < G \le 2^m$, LEB only visits the grid if $G = 2^m$. If the mesh size does not correspond to $G = 2^m$, the corresponding grid may not be visited by iterative LEB. Therefore, we focus on other division rules that may generate points on the α-grid.

Algorithm 3. SR (S_1, ϵ).

Require:
  S_1: the initial search space,
  ϵ: accuracy
1: $\Lambda := \{1\}$ *Set of leaf indices; sub-problems not yet split*
2: $ns := 1$ *Number of sub-problems*
3: **while** $\Lambda \neq \emptyset$ **do**
4:    Extract a sub-problem i from Λ
5:    **if** $w(S_i) > \epsilon w(S_1)$ **then**   *Final accuracy not reached*
6:       $LE := \text{SelectLE}(S_i)$ *Select the LE to divide*
7:       $\{S_{2i}, S_{2i+1}\} := \text{LEB}(S_i, LE)$ *Division rule*
8:       Store simplices $2i$ and $2i + 1$ in Λ.
9:       $ns := ns + 2$.
10:   **end if**
11: **end while**
12: **return** ns

Definition 3. *An α-aware two part division of the unit hypercube selects as division point an α-grid point on a longest edge nearest to its middle point.*

The α-aware division assures that only α-grid points are evaluated in the worst case. The division point for a real BnB algorithm with pruning should be selected using the structure of the problem to solve in order to increase the pruning of the tree. Figure 1 shows an example of two binary trees for the unit hypercube in $\mathbb{R}^2$ with $\frac{1}{3} \leq \epsilon < \frac{1}{2}$. Iterative LEB visits a grid with $G = 4$ parts per axis, resulting in 31 sub-problems and 16 vertex evaluations. The α-aware division uses $G=3$, evaluating 17 sub-problems and 9 vertices. This reduces the evaluation to 45% of sub-problems and 44% of vertices to reach the same accuracy. However, it is more difficult to determine the sub-tree size compared to LEB. The following can be observed in the division of the unit hypercube to generate a binary tree:

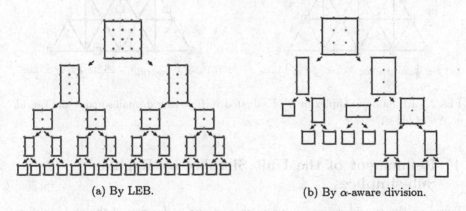

        (a) By LEB.   (b) By α-aware division.

Fig. 1. Iterative division of the unit hypercube in $\mathbb{R}^2$ for $\frac{1}{3} \leq \epsilon < \frac{1}{2}$

1. α-aware division allows reduction of the grid size generated by LEB when there exists a $G \neq 2^m$ satisfying (2).
2. The worst case (not shared with other boxes or sub-problems) number of new vertices in a division is 2^{d-1}.
3. Division always generates hyperplanes parallel to the initial edges.
4. New edges have a length that is a multiple of the mesh size α.

3.2 Unit Simplex Partition

Simplicial partition sets and corresponding bisection has an advantage that the maximum number of newly generated vertices in a division for the worst case is just one [16]. As shown in [1], the existence of branches with different number of tree levels complicates determination of a sub-tree size beforehand. Moreover, for $d > 3$ there is usually more than one longest edge in irregular sub-simplices; different longest edge selections for bisection usually generate different sub-tree sizes [1]. Actually, finding the smallest tree size is a challenging problem [15].

Moreover, in contrast to unit hypercube partition, LEB or the α-aware division generates also planes that are not parallel to the initial edges, generating edges that are in size not a multiple of the mesh size. For this reason, there exist points to be evaluated that are not on the α-grid as illustrated for $\mathbb{R}^3$ in Fig. 2. For $\epsilon = \frac{1}{4}$, LEB generates 47 simplices and 19 vertices, whereas the α-grid with $G=4$ has only 15 points. For $\epsilon = \frac{1}{3}$ the number of generated simplices and vertices by LEB is equal to those for $\epsilon = \frac{1}{4}$, but the number of α-grid points with $G=3$ is only 10. This motivates the study of general partition methods that just visit the α-grid points.

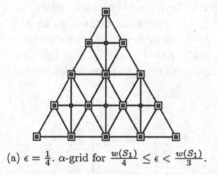
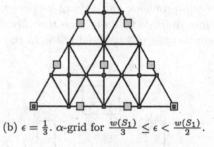

(a) $\epsilon = \frac{1}{4}$. α-grid for $\frac{w(S_1)}{4} \leq \epsilon < \frac{w(S_1)}{3}$.   (b) $\epsilon = \frac{1}{3}$. α-grid for $\frac{w(S_1)}{3} \leq \epsilon < \frac{w(S_1)}{2}$.

Fig. 2. LEB on unit simplex in $\mathbb{R}^3$. Evaluated vertices as red small squares and α-grid as yellow big squares

4   Refinement of the Unit Simplex by Regular Sub-simplices

Based on the considerations in previous sections, a division of the unit simplex should use hyperplanes parallel to the initial edges and generate sub-problems having edges of size that is a multiple of α, see Eq. (2).

4.1 Two Uniform Simplex Cover on the α-grid

The Two Uniform Simplex Cover (2USC) introduced in [6], divides a regular simplex in d overlapping regular sub-simplices with a reduction factor $\beta \geq \frac{d-1}{d}$ and has two sub-simplices per edge. One of the advantages of the 2USC refinement method is storage saving, because the identification of a regular sub-simplex only requires storing its centre and radius. The disadvantage is that for $d > 3$ the resulting subsimplices overlap. Fortunately, in [6] it is shown how a simplex evaluation can be saved in the refinement, when its area is already covered by another simplex not yet split. Moreover, the 2USC-Grid division studied in [6] reduces the number of simplex and vertex evaluations of the 2USC by forcing the vertices to lay on a grid. In that analysis, the considered stopping criterion was $w(S) \leq \epsilon w(S_1)$. The question here is how to adapt the termination criterion taking into account the overlap of the sub-simplices. The final goal is to reduce the number of simplex and vertex evaluations with the guarantee of visiting all α-grid points during the refinement.

To investigate this question, we can consider just one edge of the simplex due to the regularity of the division. Let S^ℓ denote a sub-simplex leaf of the d-ary tree, and $S^{\ell-1}$ a simplex at the last but one level of the tree, which generates S^ℓ after its regular refinement. We would like the last refinement to have exactly the reduction factor $\frac{d-1}{d}$. So,

$$w(S^\ell) = \frac{d-1}{d} w(S^{\ell-1}). \qquad (4)$$

Figure 3 shows two examples for $d{=}3$ and $d{=}4$. It illustrates

$$w(S^\ell) = \alpha(d-1)w(S_1), \qquad (5)$$

to be used as new termination criterion. For $G \geq d$ (see Eq. (2)) and $d > 3$, performing one division implies the existence of additional α-grid points on the edge segment of S^ℓ. Additional adjacent leaf simplices are needed, having their vertices at those points. Three of the α-grid points on the edge segment of S^ℓ are always visited, two from S^ℓ itself and one from an adjacent leaf sub-simplex in the 2USC division. This means that the number of grid points $G+1$ should fulfil

$$G \geq 2d - 3. \qquad (6)$$

How to obtain the sequence of reduction factors in the refinement from the root to a leaf of the complete tree? The sequence of sub-simplex size αk_i on each level i of the tree can be determined in forward mode, taking into account that the size of every sub-simplex should be a multiple of α:

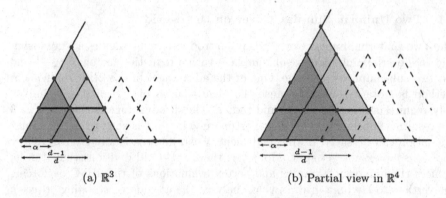

(a) $\mathbb{R}^3$.   (b) Partial view in $\mathbb{R}^4$.

Fig. 3. Leaf simplex by 2USC on the α-grid

$$
\begin{aligned}
w(S_1 = S^0) = \alpha k_0 \qquad\qquad & k_0 = G \\
w(S^1) = \alpha k_1, \qquad\qquad & k_1 = \left\lceil k_0 \frac{d-1}{d} \right\rceil \\
w(S^2) = \alpha k_2, \qquad\qquad & k_2 = \left\lceil k_1 \frac{d-1}{d} \right\rceil \\
\cdots \qquad\qquad\qquad& \\
w(S^{\ell-2}) = \alpha k_{\ell-2}, \qquad & k_{\ell-2} = \left\lceil k_{\ell-3} \frac{d-1}{d} \right\rceil \\
w(S^{\ell-1}) = \alpha k_{\ell-1}, \quad k_{\ell-1} = d = & \left\lceil k_{\ell-2} \frac{d-1}{d} \right\rceil \\
w(S^{\ell}) = \alpha k_{\ell}, \quad k_{\ell} = d - 1 = & \left\lceil k_{\ell-1} \frac{d-1}{d} \right\rceil .
\end{aligned}
\tag{7}
$$

This sequence determines the reduction factors to be used on each level of the search tree.

Termination criterion (5), initial condition (6) and reduction factors (7) as such are not sufficient conditions to visit the α-grid points. Condition (6) determines G in order to visit all grid points on every edge (2-face), but does not guarantee all grid points on the larger n-faces, $n = 3$, $\ldots$, d are generated, as illustrated in Fig. 4. Therefore, the number of grid points G must be increased accordingly. However, if there exists a dimension $\hat{n}$ for which all grid points on an $\hat{n}$-face are vertices for some simplices, then it is true for all other $\hat{n}$-faces. The number of hyperplanes (new grid points on an edge) needed to visit the 3-face is $d - 2$. The number of n-faces where non-vertex grid points still exist is also $d-2$, e.g. for $d = 5$, the 3-, 4-, and 5-face has unvisited grid points in its interior. Therefore, the number of grid segments has to be at least

$$
G \geq 2d - 3 + (d-2)^2 = d^2 - 2d + 1 = (d-1)^2,
\tag{8}
$$

to visit all α-grid points. For instance, for $d = 10$, one can take $G \geq 81$ or $\epsilon \leq 0.012345679$.

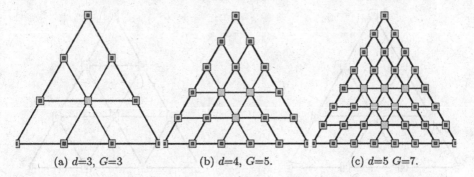

(a) d=3, G=3   (b) d=4, G=5.   (c) d=5 G=7.

Fig. 4. 2USC evaluated points in red following conditions (5), (6) and (7), grid points in yellow on 3 faces of the unit simplex

4.2 Refinement Using 2∇USC

The 2∇-uniform-simplex-cover (2∇USC) introduced in [6] refines a regular simplex in $d+1$ regular sub-simplices. In contrast to 2USC, d of them have the same orientation using a reduction factor $\frac{d-2}{d-1} \leq \rho < \frac{d-1}{d}$ and one non-overlapped inverted sub-simplex has a reduction factor $\varrho = d(1 - \rho) - 1$. In 2∇USC, the sub-simplices overlap less than in 2USC, but the sub-simplices are not equally oriented and sized. 2∇USC requires a delicate choice of the reduction factor ρ. In order to have a value for ρ being a multiple of α, ρ may be greater or equal to $(d - 1)/d$. In that case, the reduction factor of the inverted simplex $\varrho \leq 0$. This means that the inverted sub-simplex does not exist and 2∇USC reduces to 2USC. Consequently, the maximum overlap for 2∇USC of the sub-simplices is equal to that of 2USC.

4.3 Refinement Using 2MUSC

We now introduce 2-mixed-uniform-simplex-cover refinement (2MUSC) combining 2USC and 2∇USC in the refinement of the unit simplex. Depending on the current simplex, either a reduction factor ρ or β is applied to force vertices of the generated sub-simplices to be on the α-grid. Figure 5 shows an example for $d = 3$ and $G = 3$, where first 2USC is applied, followed by a 2∇USC refinement of the sub-simplices generated by 2USC.

The question is how to choose the reduction factors and when to select 2USC or 2∇USC such that we obtain the desired cover of the grid in an efficient way. Our analysis starts again at the leafs of the tree. Assume we would like to use the less overlapping 2∇USC as last refinement in 2MUSC, where the size of a leaf sub-simplex S^ℓ is a multiple of α. Similar as seen before, it can be derived that the termination criterion can be relaxed to

$$w(S^\ell) = \alpha(d - 2)w(S_1). \tag{9}$$

We now focus on the possible reduction factors. Because we want the size of all generated sub-simplices to be a multiple of α, there exist cases where the

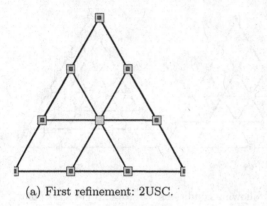
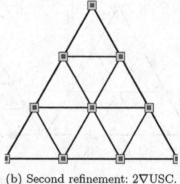

(a) First refinement: 2USC.   (b) Second refinement: 2∇USC.

Fig. 5. 2MUSC for $d = 3$ and $G = 3$

reduction factor cannot equals $\frac{d-2}{d-1}$, but should be chosen larger. For the selection of the refinement method, we can choose 2∇USC, if the new reduction factor ρ is smaller than $\frac{d-1}{d}$. Otherwise, a 2USC refinement is applied. The sequence (10) shows the derivation of the sequence of size αk_i of sub-simplices at each level i.

$$w(S^0) = \alpha k_0 \qquad k_0 = G$$

$$w(S^1) = \alpha k_1, \qquad k_1 = \left\lceil k_0 \frac{d-2}{d-1} \right\rceil \begin{cases} 2\nabla\text{USC, if } \left\lceil k_0 \frac{d-2}{d-1} \right\rceil < k_0 \frac{d-1}{d} \\ 2\text{USC, otherwise.} \end{cases}$$

$$w(S^2) = \alpha k_2, \qquad k_2 = \left\lceil k_1 \frac{d-2}{d-1} \right\rceil \begin{cases} 2\nabla\text{USC, if } \left\lceil k_1 \frac{d-2}{d-1} \right\rceil < k_1 \frac{d-1}{d} \\ 2\text{USC, otherwise.} \end{cases}$$

$$\dots$$

$$w(S^{l-1}) = \alpha k_{l-1}, \; k_{l-1} = \left\lceil k_{l-2} \frac{d-2}{d-1} \right\rceil \begin{cases} 2\nabla\text{USC, if } \left\lceil k_{l-2} \frac{d-2}{d-1} \right\rceil < k_{l-2} \frac{d-1}{d} \\ 2\text{USC, otherwise.} \end{cases}$$

$$w(S^l) = \alpha k_l, \qquad k_l = \left\lceil k_{l-1} \frac{d-2}{d-1} \right\rceil (2\nabla\text{USC}),$$

$$(10)$$

where $k_{l-1} = d - 1$ and $k_l = d - 2$.

Table 1 illustrates the selection in 2MUSC combining 2USC and 2∇USC in the refinement process. Depending on the dimension d and the number of segments per axis G, a sequence appears that chooses between the two covering methods. Notice that when the number of segments G is a power of two and $\rho = 1/2^j$, $j \in \mathbb{N}^+$, only 2∇USC is applied. This happens for $d = 3$ and $G = 16$, but it is not the case for $d = 4$ and $G = 16$. This illustrates that it is not straightforward to come up with a sequence of reduction factors for a given dimension d and number of segments G. However, it can be calculated beforehand.

Table 1. Combining 2USC (2) and 2∇USC (2∇) in 2MUSC for varying dimension d and number of segments G.

G	$d = 3,\ \rho = 1/2$			$d = 4,\ \rho = 2/3$		
	4	6	16	4	8	16
	2∇	2∇	2∇	2	2	2∇
	2∇	2	2∇	2∇	2∇	2∇
		2∇	2∇	2	2	
			2∇	2∇	2∇	
				2		
				2∇		

Because the sequence of reduction factors depends on d and G and is not known beforehand, we should determine the maximum value for the number of segments G to guarantee covering an α-grid by 2MUSC in a computational way.

5   Experiments

The α-aware division of a unit hypercube as outlined in Sect. 3.1, is straightforward and its advantage over longest edge bisection for the worst case is well defined. As discussed, to have a well balanced alternative for the unit simplex, requires computing reduction factors. To see the effect of the described refinement of a unit simplex, we report on several numerical experiments.

Due to the high computational cost of generating the complete tree when dimension d and the number of segments G increases, the design of experiments is limited to $d = 3$, 4 and 5, and $G \in \{2, 3, \ldots, 17\}$. To obtain results in a reasonable amount of time for larger values, parallel computing is a must.

5.1   Computational Considerations

Due to rounding of computer real arithmetic, special care has to be taken when two real values are compared. For instance, to see if a vertex of a sub-simplex is a grid point. In the experiments we use the function $EQ(a, b)\{| a - b | < Th\}$ with a threshold value $Th = 10^{-15}$, to evaluate $a = b$. For the same reason, the computation of k_i in (7) using the math library of the gcc C compiler is performed in the following way:

```
if ( EQ( d−1/d kᵢ, round(d−1/d kᵢ) ) ) then
    kᵢ₊₁:=round(d−1/d kᵢ)
else
    kᵢ₊₁:=ceil(d−1/d kᵢ)
end if
```

A similar approach is used in (10). Notice that, interestingly enough, in principle no rounding errors occur iteratively bisecting the unit simplex, as the generated fractional numbers are represented exactly in a digital computer.

5.2   Numerical Results

The design of experiments is given in Table 2. The instances are defined by the number of grid segments G and the dimension d. For each experiment we measure the number of evaluated simplices (N.S.), the number of evaluated vertices (N.V.) and the number of visited α-grid points (N.G.).

Table 2. Number of grid points.

G	ϵ	$d=3$	$d=4$	$d=5$
2	0.5	6	10	15
3	0.$\dot{3}$	10	20	35
4	0.25	15	35	70
5	0.2	21	56	126
6	0.1$\dot{6}$	28	84	210
7	0.1429	36	120	330
8	0.125	45	165	495
9	0.$\dot{1}$	55	220	715
10	0.1	66	286	1,001
11	0.0909	78	364	1,365
12	0.08$\dot{3}$	91	455	1,820
13	0,0769	105	560	2,380
14	0.0714	120	680	3,060
15	0.0$\dot{6}$	136	816	3,876
16	0.625	153	969	4,845
17	0.0588	171	1,140	5,985

Longest edge bisection as described in Algorithm 3 and the 2USC and 2MUSC refinements are run, where the reduction factors of the two last methods are taken as described in Sects. 4.1 and 4.3, respectively.

Table 3 shows the result for the first longest edge bisection. For $d=3$ there exists just one longest edge for irregular simplices generated in the unit simplex refinement by LEB. But for $d > 3$ the number of longest edges for an irregular simplex can be larger than 1. The chosen first longest edge depends on the coding and storing of the vertices and edges, i.e. the index number assigned to each vertex of the simplex. The new vertex usually has the same index as the one it substitutes. Grey background in the cells of Tables 3, 4 and 5 indicates the instances where all the α-grid points are covered. For $d = 3$ in Table 3, the α-grid is visited when $G = 2^j$ but the number of vertices is larger than the number of the α-grid points. For a higher dimension d, α-grid points are missed for $G = 2^j$ and $j > 2$, because a final non regular pattern mesh is generated. The study reveals that LEB is not appealing for the complete tree, when it is compared with the direct evaluation of the α-grid and the difficulty of the instance increases. For the hardest instance in the test bed ($d=5$, $G=17$), the number of evaluated points and simplices by LEB is x19 and x528 the corresponding number of α-grid points. In other words, the pruning of the corresponding BnB should be really effective to avoid so many evaluations.

Table 3. Iterative longest edge bisection selecting the first longest edge. N.S., N.V., and N.G. are the number of simplices, vertices and covered α-grid points, respectively.

	$d=3$			$d=4$			$d=5$		
G	N.S.	N.V.	N.G.	N.S.	N.V.	N.G.	N.S.	N.V.	N.G.
2	11	7	6	63	18	10	379	46	15
3	47	19	3	375	72	4	3,157	251	5
4	47	19	15	507	92	35	6,319	438	70
5	191	61	3	2,013	324	4	25,095	1,572	5
6	191	61	6	2,951	427	10	48,609	2,711	15
7	191	61	36	2,987	431	4	57,087	3,035	5
8	191	61	45	4,027	571	163	99,563	5,081	485
9	511	153	3	9,403	1,160	4	232,953	10,145	5
10	767	217	6	15,327	2,035	10	382,245	18,071	15
11	767	217	3	18,447	2,400	4	464,759	22,114	5
12	767	217	15	22,951	2,842	35	764,163	33,663	70
13	767	217	3	23,711	2,924	4	888,721	38,858	5
14	767	217	6	23,711	2,924	10	910,205	39,911	15
15	767	217	3	30,463	3,754	4	1,360,527	57,666	5
16	767	217	153	32,167	3,959	928	1,577,047	67,162	4,540
17	2,047	561	3	71,111	7,544	4	3,160,751	111,515	5

Table 4 shows results for the experimental design running iterative 2USC refinement considering (5) and (7). Typically, it is not necessary to report the number of covered grid points N.G., because all vertices are α-grid points. Simplices that are completely covered by other pending simplices are not evaluated and therefore not included in the count of the number of evaluated simplices N.S.

Notice that to perform at least one refinement, the number of segments G should exceed the dimension d, i.e. $G \geq d$. Moreover, the number of segments G needed to visit the α-grid should fulfil (8). Table 3 shows that the number of simplex and vertex evaluations is in general smaller for G segments satisfying (8) than having a smaller or equal number of segments G using LEB. The saving increases significantly when the number of segments G satisfies (8), because only the α-grid points are evaluated.

Table 5 shows the results when refinement is carried out according to the 2MUSC method. Comparing the data in Tables 4 and 5 shows that the minimum number of segments G that guarantees covering all the α-grid points is smaller for 2MUSC than for 2USC. Actually for $d = 3, 4, 5$, 2MUSC only requires

Table 4. 2USC on α-grid partition. All vertices are α-grid points.

G	d=3 N.S.	d=3 N.V.	d=4 N.S.	d=4 N.V.	d=5 N.S.	d=5 N.V.
2						
3	4	9				
4	10	15	5	16		
5	20	21	15	40	6	25
6	28	28	35	74	21	75
7	49	36	70	116	56	175
8	56	45	111	164	126	340
9	73	55	195	220	252	580
10	118	66	255	286	431	900
11	122	78	420	364	761	1,300
12	139	91	575	455	1,101	1,785
13	172	105	669	560	1,816	2,365
14	263	120	1,033	680	2,352	3,055
15	295	136	1,270	816	3,356	3,875
16	283	153	1,613	969	5,176	4,845
17	308	171	1,743	1,140	6,101	5,985

$G \geq 2, 3, 7$ and 2USC needs at least $G \geq 4, 9, 16$, respectively. On the other hand, the number of simplex evaluations is larger when 2MUSC refinement is used. However, 2USC has more overlap among simplices than 2MUSC.

The sequence of reduction factors for 2USC and 2MUSC can be calculated beforehand. In this way, also the size of the complete tree, with all branches

Table 5. 2MUSC on α-grid partition. All vertices are α-grid points.

G	d=3 N.S.	d=3 N.V.	d=4 N.S.	d=4 N.V.	d=5 N.S.	d=5 N.V.
2	5	6				
3	13	10	6	20		
4	21	15	19	35	7	30
5	38	21	45	56	26	96
6	53	28	72	84	71	200
7	66	36	146	120	161	330
8	85	45	179	165	287	495
9	125	55	259	220	557	715
10	153	66	472	286	796	1,001
11	178	78	518	364	1,431	1,365
12	213	91	622	455	2,087	1,820
13	234	105	839	560	2,642	2,380
14	265	120	1,408	680	4,367	3,060
15	306	136	1,664	816	5,571	3,876
16	341	153	1,660	969	7,463	4,845
17	439	171	1,887	1,140	8,792	5,985

having the same tree levels can be determined. It is interesting to highlight that the minimum reduction factors, β for 2USC and ρ for 2MUSC, are usually smaller than 1/2 which is the volume reduction used by LEB. Therefore, the convergence of LEB should be quicker than the studied USC partitions. However, the results in the tables show the contrary. This is caused by not evaluating a generated subsimplex covered by other pending simplices (otherwise its search region would be evaluated more than one time). Therefore, the complete trees generated by 2USC and 2MUSC have branches with different tree levels. Studying their convergence properties is a challenge for future research.

6   Conclusions and Future Research

This paper studies passive spatial refinement methods on the unit hypercube and unit simplex. The question is how the complete tree size and the number of evaluated points of new grid aware methods behave compared to the well known Longest Edge Bisection (LEB). The complete tree size provides an upper bound on the pending work for branch and bound (BnB) methods. Numerical results show that the studied grid aware methods (2USC and 2MUSC) outperform LEB by resulting in much better bounds for the pending work and that they can be tuned to visit just the grid points. 2USC generates a smaller tree than 2MUSC, but 2MUSC shows less overlap. Moreover, grid aware methods facilitate the estimation of the left-over work, because the hight of the complete tree (worst BnB case) can be calculated beforehand. This is not the case for LEB on a simplex. The studies provide the foundation for further research on BnB methods for instances where the pruning in the BnB tree is low. These studies will be tackled in future work.

Acknowledgments. This work has been funded by grants from the Spanish Ministry (TIN2015-66680), in part financed by the European Regional Development Fund (ERDF). J.M.G. Salmerón is a fellow of the Spanish FPU program.

References

1. Aparicio, G., Casado, L.G., G-Tóth, B., Hendrix, E.M.T., García, I.: Heuristics to reduce the number of simplices in longest edge bisection refinement of a regular n-simplex. In: Murgante, B., Misra, S., Rocha, A.M.A.C., Torre, C., Rocha, J.G., Falcão, M.I., Taniar, D., Apduhan, B.O., Gervasi, O. (eds.) ICCSA 2014. LNCS, vol. 8580, pp. 115–125. Springer, Cham (2014). doi:10.1007/978-3-319-09129-7_9
2. Berenguel, J.L., Casado, L.G., García, I., Hendrix, E.M.T.: On estimating workload in interval branch-and-bound global optimization algorithms. J. Global Optim. **56**(3), 821–844 (2013)
3. Casado, G.L., García, I., Csendes, T.: A new multisection technique in interval methods for global optimization. Computing **65**(3), 263–269 (2000)
4. Casado, L.G., Hendrix, E.M.T., García, I.: Infeasibility spheres for finding robust solutions of blending problems with quadratic constraints. J. Global Optim. **39**(2), 215–236 (2007)

5. Csendes, T., Ratz, D.: Subdivision direction selection in interval methods for global optimization. SIAM J. Numer. Anal **34**, 922–938 (1997)
6. G.-Tóth, B., Hendrix, E.M.T., Casado, L.G., García, I.: On refinement of the unit simplex using regular simplices. J. Global Optim. **64**(2), 305–323 (2016)
7. Hendrix, E.M.T., Pínter, J.: An application of Lipschitzian global optimization to product design. J. Global Optim. **1**, 389–401 (1991)
8. Hendrix, E.M.T., Tóth, B.G.: Introduction to Nonlinear and Global Optimization. Springer, New York (2010)
9. Hendrix, E.M.T., Casado, L.G., García, I.: The semi-continuous quadratic mixture design problem: Description and branch-and-bound approach. Eur. J. Oper. Res. **191**(3), 803–815 (2008)
10. Horst, R.: On generalized bisection of n-simplices. Math. Comput. **66**(218), 691–698 (1997)
11. Horst, R., Tuy, H.: Global Optimization (Deterministic Approaches). Springer, Berlin (1990)
12. Kuno, T., Ishihama, T.: A generalization of ω-subdivision ensuring convergence of the simplicial algorithm. Comput. Optim. Appl. **64**(2), 535–555 (2016)
13. Locatelli, M., Schoen, F.: Global Optimization: Theory, Algorithms, and Applications. SIAM, Philadelphia (2013)
14. Markót, M., Fernández, J., Casado, L., Csendes, T.: New interval methods for constrained global optimization. Math. Program. **106**(2), 287–318 (2006)
15. Salmerón, J.M.G., Aparicio, G., Casado, L.G., García, I., Hendrix, E.M.T., G.-Tóth, B.: Generating a smallest binary tree by proper selection of the longest edges to bisect in a unit simplex refinement. J. Comb. Optim. **3**, 389–402 (2017)
16. Todd, M.J.: The Computation of Fixed Points and Applications. Lecture Notes in Economics and Mathematical Systems, vol. 124. Springer, Heidelberg (1976)
17. Tuy, H.: Effect of the subdivision strategy on convergence and efficiency of some global optimization algorithms. J. Global Optim. **1**(1), 23–36 (1991)

Workshop on Cities, Technologies and Planning (CTP 2017)

Identifying and Using Key Indicators to Determine Neighborhood Types in Different Regions

Harutyun Shahumyan[1]($\boxtimes$), Chao Liu[2], Brendan Williams[1],
Gerrit Knaap[2], and Daniel Engelberg[2]

[1] School of Architecture, Planning and Environmental Policy,
University College Dublin, Dublin, Ireland
{harutyun.shahumyan, brendan.williams}@ucd.ie
[2] National Center for Smart Growth, University of Maryland,
College Park, MD, USA
{cliu8, gknaap}@umd.edu, dengelberg2@gmail.com

Abstract. Identification of a key indicators capturing essential patterns in a region can be a cost-effective solution for neighborhood classification and targeted policy making. Yet, such a "core" set of indicators can vary from region to region. Here, we define set of indicators measuring education, housing, accessibility, and employment which can be used to classify neighborhoods. We test these indicators in two study regions: the Baltimore Metropolitan Area and the Greater Dublin Region. We apply factor analysis to distill indicators to smaller sets that capture differences in neighborhood types in terms of social, economic, and environmental dimensions. We use factors loadings in cluster analyzes to identify unique neighborhood types spatially. Comparison of the core set of indicators and clustering patterns for case study regions sheds new lights on the important factors for both regions. The proposed approach will help compare variations in neighborhood types between and within different regions internationally.

Keywords: Indicators · Factor analysis · Cluster analysis · Baltimore · Dublin

1 Introduction

Well-structured indicators can improve the understanding of urban neighborhoods, address the issues and barriers to improved neighborhood development policies, and further steer the policy for a better guidance and identification of potential targeted area [1–3]. A large set of indicators and neighborhood classification methods have been developed for different purposes by urban planners, scholars and local government agencies. Using one indicator or multiple indicators separately is unlikely to reflect real-world situations where decisions are often made based on several competing factors. A clear focus is often placed on a number of key indicators or composite indices in urban planning literature and policy. However, such indices are usually data-hungry, demanding lots of effort and time to compose. Therefore, identification of a key or "core" set of indicators capturing essential patterns in a region can be a

© Springer International Publishing AG 2017
O. Gervasi et al. (Eds.): ICCSA 2017, Part III, LNCS 10406, pp. 183–199, 2017.
DOI: 10.1007/978-3-319-62398-6_13

cost-effective and desirable solution. Yet, such "core" sets can vary significantly from region to region and even more from country to country. This research suggests an approach to identify a set of indicators that can be effectively applied for different regions. We test this approach on two contrasting urban spatial contexts of similar population size, one in Europe and one in USA. We apply an existing analysis framework of neighborhood classification in Ireland [4] and Maryland [5] using the same set of indicators, covering education, housing, accessibility, health and employment sectors at the electoral division level for the Greater Dublin Region (GDR) and at the census tract level for the Baltimore Metropolitan Area (BMA).

2 Methodology

2.1 Data Sources and Neighborhood Definition

The data for this study are mostly obtained from US 2010 and Ireland 2011 census datasets as well as from GeoDirectory[1], CORINE[2], US Longitudinal Employer-Household Dynamics, and Maryland Department of Health and Mental Hygiene. The electoral divisions in Ireland and census tracts in Maryland are relatively comparable in size and were used as geographic units for further quantitative analyses. For simplicity, hereafter, we will call those census units just "neighborhood". For each indicator described below, data was gathered or aggregated at the neighborhood level.

2.2 Indicator Selection Process

The initial list of 25 variables was selected based on the previous relevant research on opportunity mapping and neighborhood classification [4–7]; and in consultation with experts, researchers and policy makers both from Ireland and USA. Those variables can be categorized under three main areas:

- Socio-economic indicators: population change and density, age dependency ratio, (un)employment rates, number of jobs, number of people by their education degree, and household ownership rates.
- Health indicators: infant mortality, teen birth rates and low birthweight rates
- Accessibility indicators: travel time; bus service coverage; distances to roads, rails stations, coastline, hospitals, schools, universities, companies and recreational facilities (green urban areas, beaches, forest, sport and leisure facilities).

However, this list is neither exhaustive nor binding. We use them only to demonstrate the capabilities of the suggested approach and its potential applicability for decision makers worldwide. The main goal of this research was to identify a "core" set from a list of frequently used indicators which could be used to characterize the neighborhoods by their socio-economic and accessibility opportunities in various regions. The emphasis

---

[1] Irish postal address and geographic coordinates database.

[2] A map of the European environmental landscape which includes 44 land cover classes.

was on locating clusters of neighborhoods using those variables for targeted planning policy. In this article, the approach was tested on two case study regions presented below.

2.3 Study Regions

The Greater Dublin Region (GDR) is Ireland's most densely populated region with 1.9 million people stretched over 7,800 km^2 (Fig. 1). The GDR was the principal beneficiary of the 'Celtic Tiger' [8] and experienced strong economic and population growth from the late 1990s to 2007; followed by a financial crisis and economic recession from 2007 to 2014; and a strong recovery from 2014 to 2016. Meanwhile, the realities of recent development patterns differ substantially from stated policy in the National Spatial Strategy [9] and from international best practice in many cases. A lack in provision of housing close to the economic core areas created a continuing push of employment related housing demand at increasing distances from Dublin. The dispersal of housing, retail and employment activities in a fragmented manner across GDR has major implications for the environment, infrastructure and service provision. Moreover, population in the GDR is projected to grow over 400 thousand and will account for 42.4 per cent of the total population in Ireland by 2031 [10] adding more challenges for local policy making.

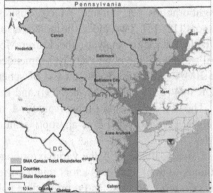

Fig. 1. Greater Dublin region   **Fig. 2.** Baltimore metropolitan area

The Baltimore Metropolitan Area (BMA), with a population over 2.3 million and stretching over 5,700 km^2, is one of the twenty largest metropolitan regions in the US (Fig. 2). According to the most recent projections from Baltimore Metropolitan Council, population in the region is expected to grow nearly 300,000 by 2030, while job growth will be over 50%, reaching an estimated 1.96 million jobs by 2030. Though the Baltimore-Washington region is diverse as a whole, a high level of racial and economic segregation remains in older parts of the region as a result of historic inequities. In particular, poverty and racial segregation remains high within Baltimore

City, though the majority of the regions poor now live in suburban communities. Among the US 100 most populous cities, Baltimore rank as the 9th least diverse city at the neighborhood level and the 7th most segregated city. Associated with the increased poverty rate within Baltimore city has been the depopulation of the City itself. Driven by deindustrialization, Baltimore's population dropped from nearly 1,000,000 during World War II to around 620,000, where it has currently stabilized. The population loss in the core, however, never prevented the region from growing as a whole.

2.4 Data Analysis

Exploratory Factor Analysis (EFA) was applied to summarize data so that relationships and patterns of selected indicators can be interpreted, understood and compared for the case study regions. EFA was used to reduce the initial set of 25 indicators into a set of 12 indicators covered by 4 factors. The factor scores then have been applied in cluster analysis to identify clusters of similar neighborhoods in the GDR and the BMA. The R statistical package was used for statistical analysis and ArcGIS was used for spatial analysis and mapping.

Explanatory Factor Analysis (EFA). Based on the EFA requirements [11], the data was first screened for outliers, missing values and extreme correlation. As a result, the total number of variables was reduced to 22. The number of neighborhoods in GDR and BMA are 628 and 660, respectively, yielding approximately a ratio of over 27 neighborhoods per variable, which satisfies a validity measure suggested by several authors [12–15]. Two model fit indices also suggest that our variables and samples are suitable for factor analysis: the Kaiser-Meyer-Olkin measure of sampling adequacy [16] was above the commonly recommended value of 0.5 both for the GDR (0.83) and the BMA (0.88); the Bartlett's test of sphericity [12, 13] was significant both for the GDR ($\chi2$ (231) = 12325.5, p < .00) and the BMA ($\chi2$ (231) = 9654.6, p < .00).

The Kaiser's criteria (eigenvalue > 1 rule) [17], the Scree test [18] and parallel analysis [19] indicated 5 as appropriate number of factors for the GDR and 4 for the BMA.

Usually, in the EFA the varimax orthogonal rotation is appropriate, if there are no grounds to think that the factors might correlate [11]. Otherwise, oblique rotation may render a more accurate and reproducible solution. But, as highlighted by Costello and Osborne [20], if the factors are truly uncorrelated, orthogonal and oblique rotation produce nearly identical results. Both varimax and oblique rotation have been applied in this research and as the outputs were quite similar, the results of the oblique rotation have been used for further analysis.

In general, maximum likelihood and principal axis (PA) approaches are the most commonly used factor analysis extraction methods for the EFA. However, the PA approach is considered more suitable for data with non-normal distributions [20]. In this research, Quantile-Comparison Plots and Shapiro-Wilks test, showed that almost all our variables have non-normal distribution for both regions. Therefore, the factor analysis have been applied with PA method.

The factor analyses extracted five factors for the GDR (labeling by D1-D5 in red in Fig. 3) and four factors for the BMA (labelling by B1-B4 in green). The results revealed that few variables contribute to two factors. However, in such cases the loading is higher for one factor than for the other, so the variable was considered as part of the factor with the higher loading value.

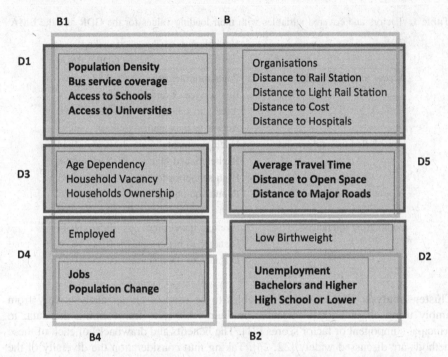

Fig. 3. Variable grouping within factors for GDR (D) and BMA (B). (Color figure online)

Interestingly, the indicators grouping patterns within factors have some similarity for two regions. The overlapping indicators in Fig. 3 corresponding to certain factors in two study areas are highlighted in bold. Aiming to find the similar factors influencing on both regions we have re-run factor analyses by using only selected overlapping 12 variables. All relevant tests described above were repeated and supported the factorability of this set of variables too. In the case of GDR, Kaiser's criteria has indicated four as the appropriate number for factor extraction while the parallel analysis has suggested three as the optimal number of factors. In the case of BMA, both tests indicated four as the appropriate number for factor extraction. In order to maintain consistency between two regions, we have applied a four factor solution for both regions.

Table 1 summarizes the results of the 4-factor solution for 12 short listed variables. The analysis revealed that the variables contribute to four factors: (1) Access to transport and education, (2) Low skilled unemployment, (3) Population change and (4) Commuting tolerance. Population density, bus service, access to schools, and access to universities, education attainment, population change, jobs and open space indicators behave in a relatively similar ways in both regions. Two variables (Average Travel Time and Distance to Major Roads) contribute differently, which suggests that people have different commuting tolerance in two regions. When comparing commuters in both GDR and BMA, it seems that people in GDR have less commuting tolerance than the people in BMA, given that the average commuting time in BMA is about 6 min longer.

Table 1. Factors and covered variables with their loading values for the GDR and the BMA

Factors	Variables	Loading	
		GDR	BMA
Access to transport and education	Population density	+0.88	+0.67
	Bus service coverage	+0.72	+0.74
	Access to schools	+0.96	+0.90
	Access to universities	+0.92	+0.92
Low skilled unemployment	Unemployment	+0.75	+0.44
	Bachelors and higher	−0.93	−0.96
	High school or lower	+0.86	+0.85
Population change	Population change	+0.80	+0.35
	Jobs	+0.47	+0.98
Commuting tolerance	Average travel time	−0.50	+0.44
	Distance to major roads	−0.34	+0.65
	Distance to open space	+0.36	+0.64

Cluster Analysis. The choice of variables to be used in cluster analysis vary from simply using all individual variables or their subsets, to transforming the data, to principal component or factor scores [21]. The benefits and drawbacks of each of these methods are discussed widely [22, 23]. Taking into consideration the diversity of the study regions as well as dissimilar scales and correlation patterns of included variables, we have used EFA factor scores described above to identify and compare the clustering pattern of the neighborhoods in the GDR and the BMA.

Firstly, a hierarchical clustering method was applied and indicated that the neighborhoods in both regions can be classified into three or four clusters. Both options have been then implemented through the k-means clustering analysis. Further analysis however showed that the most relevant and comparable for two regions is three cluster option, which is presented below in more details.

3   Results

The neighborhood statistics reflected in the Tables 2 and 3 indicate that the GDR and the BMA are comparable for most of the indicators we explored. However, on average the GDR neighborhoods have a four-time larger increase in population in ten years compared with the BMA neighborhoods. Baltimore city center lost population while

Table 2. Area and population characteristics of the neighborhoods of the GDR and the BMA.

	GDR electoral division	BMA census track
Number of units	628	660
Counties covered	5	6
Area (km^2)		
Mean	12.45	8.64
Minimum	0.14	0.15
Maximum	76.38	152.74
Sum	7,816.77	5,774.56
Population		
Mean	3,009	4,063
Minimum	87	0
Maximum	35,970	11,137
Sum	1,889,949	2,384,938

Table 3. Descriptive statistics of the indicators for GDR and BMA

	GDR	BMA	Difference
Population Change	**19.84**	**4.80**	**76%**
Population Density	**2372.80**	**2227.33**	**6%**
Age Dependency	0.49	0.33	33%
Employed	1242.99	1874.09	−51%
Unemployment	**0.08**	**0.08**	**0%**
Organizations	19808.01	18296.12	8%
Jobs	**1049.27**	**1863.81**	**−78%**
Bachelors and Higher	**0.18**	**0.22**	**−22%**
High School or Lower	**0.33**	**0.27**	**18%**
Household Vacancy	0.12	0.09	25%
Households Ownership	0.72	0.66	8%
Low Birthweight	1.86	0.10	95%
Average Travel Time	**23.74**	**29.65**	**−25%**
Bus Service Coverage	**19.33**	**36.65**	**−90%**
Distance to Major Roads	**0.83**	**0.62**	**25%**
Distance to Rail Station	7.56	10.25	−36%
Distance to Light Rail Station	22.14	10.66	52%
Distance to Cost	15.69	10.04	36%
Distance to Hospitals	6.15	4.77	22%
Distance to Open Space	**1.72**	**0.71**	**59%**
Access to Schools	**60.74**	**26.62**	**56%**
Access to Universities	**44.78**	**4.94**	**89%**

The variables highlighted in bold are shortlisted indicators used in further analysis.

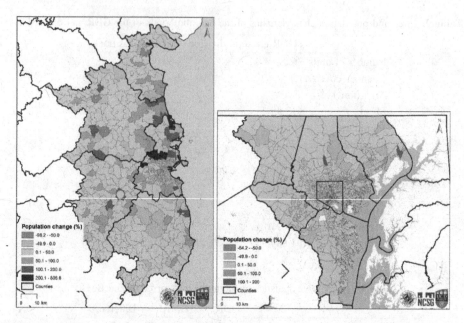

Fig. 4. Population change over 10 years (These and below maps have similar scale and value ranges for both regions to allow direct comparison.)

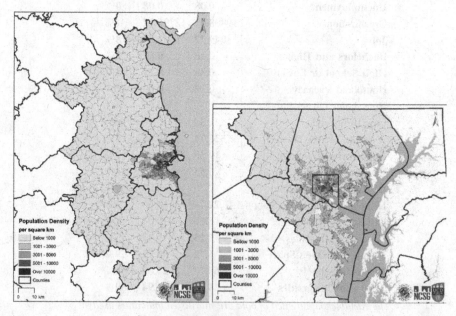

Fig. 5. Population density per square km

Dublin city experienced population growth in inner city regeneration areas and decreases in population in some suburban areas (Fig. 4). The higher levels of population growth in both regions were in the peri urban or commuter areas. Other indicators with over 50% different values between GDA and BMA are Unemployment, Jobs, Low Birthweight, Bus Service Coverage, Distances to Light Rail Station and to Open Space, as well as Access to Schools and to Universities (Table 3).

The population density map varies: while Dublin has a historic compact core area, Baltimore is more multi-centric, with the City of Baltimore being the major population core of the region (Fig. 5). The extensive suburbs are of a generally low density.

The GDR has relatively homogenous unemployment rate all over the region. In the BMA the very high unemployment rate is registered in the city center, while the surrounding counties mostly have low unemployment rate. The unemployment rate within parts of central Baltimore are far greater than anywhere in Dublin, while suburban areas have generally lower unemployment than Dublin (Fig. 6).

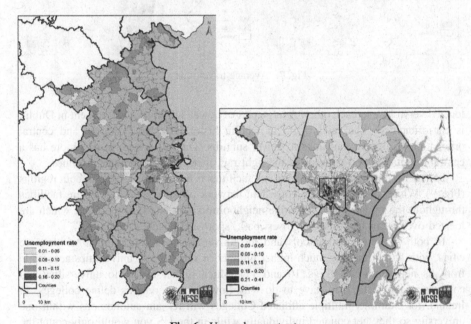

Fig. 6. Unemployment rate

The GDR has relatively low average travel time (Fig. 7). Long commute times in Baltimore are concentrated in exurban areas far from job centers and in the central city, where many families rely on public transit.

Dublin has a wide network of bus dominated public transport but frequencies are poor due to dispersed population in suburbs (Fig. 8). Baltimore has a similar pattern with the City of Baltimore heavily reliant on bus and other counties rely on the local bus system to get public transit accessibility. Though access to bus stops seems quite high in Baltimore city, not all those bus routes have high frequency and some stops are

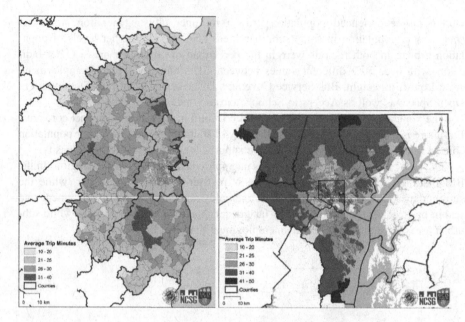

Fig. 7. Average travel time

located very close to each other. A large part of newer suburban development in Dublin is car orientated. The rail system in Dublin historically has a coastal and central orientation with weak rail links to newer suburbs. The rail system in Baltimore has a central orientation and consists of the light rail, metro, and commuter rail lines.

In general the distance to recreational facilities is mostly up to 4 km in both regions (Fig. 9). While, the BMA has a consistent network of park, sport and leisure facilities throughout the region, there are some neighborhoods in North of the GDR which are located over 8 km far from the closest park, sport and leisure facilities.

In both regions most schools and the universities are concentrated within core cities, with Dublin having much higher number of schools and universities accessible from its neighborhoods (Figs. 10 and 11). Much higher access to universities and colleges in the GDR may have to do with how the two regions define colleges. In Ireland, for example, multiple affiliated Colleges will remain autonomous within one university so they get counted individually while in the US you would only count the one University. Therefore, in future, comparing student numbers instead might be more useful as the differences in institutional governance may skew the results.

Spatial clusters of the neighborhoods are mapped using the results of both hierarchical and k-mean clustering analysis. Multiple iterations have been conducted by using three and four cluster options, mostly achieving similar neighborhood classification patterns. However, explanation and comparison purposes the results of hierarchical clustering with three cluster option seemed to be more relevant for the study regions and described below.

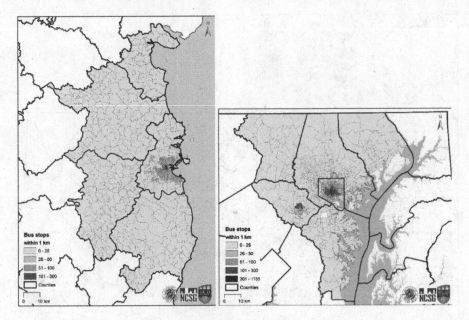

Fig. 8. Number of bus stops within 1 km

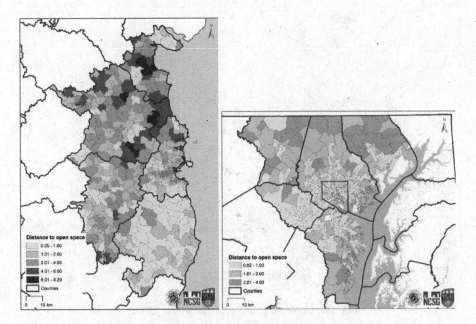

Fig. 9. Distance to recreational facilities (open space)

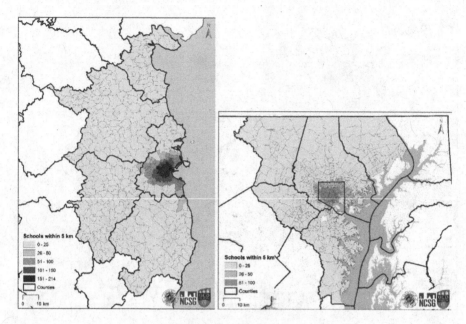

Fig. 10. Schools within 5 km

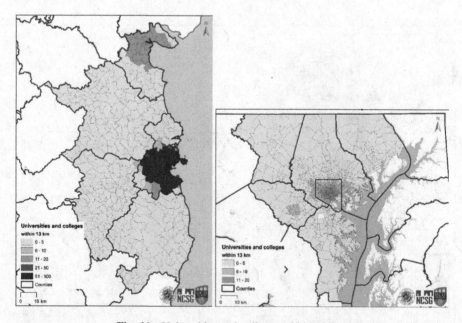

Fig. 11. Universities and colleges within 13 km

For the GDR, cluster 1 represents low and middle income population areas, which are mostly located in the North and South-East parts of Dublin city (Fig. 12). Those neighborhoods account for 25% of all neighborhoods in the GDR (Fig. 13). Cluster 2 represents high income population centers covering South Dublin and part of its North-East coastal areas. Cluster 2 covers 16% of all neighborhoods in the GDR. Cluster 3 covers mostly low income, low density suburban and rural areas in the surrounding counties of Dublin city. However, those areas include also some high income population. Cluster 3 accounts over 59% of all neighborhoods in the GDR.

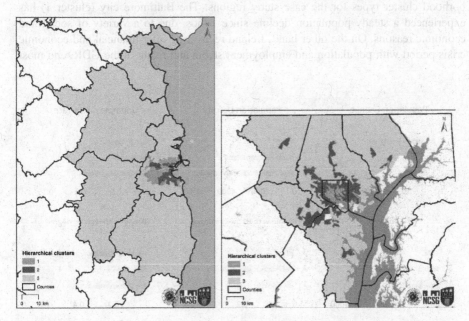

Fig. 12. Hierarchical clustering of the neighborhoods in the GDR (left) and the BMA (right).

Fig. 13. The distribution of the neighborhoods according to Hierarchical clustering

For the BMA, cluster 1 represents low income, mostly black communities, with low education levels and decreasing population. The Baltimore city center includes mainly neighborhoods with cluster type 1 (Fig. 12), accounting 40% of the total (Fig. 13). Cluster 2 represents high and middle density job/populations centers, including middle and upper income population areas with higher diversity but still with some segregation among them. These neighborhoods account for 44% and relocated mostly in the suburbs of Baltimore region. Cluster 3 covers both rural and low density suburban residential areas with generally moderate to high income population. The surrounding counties of Baltimore city include mostly neighborhoods with cluster type 3, which although cover vast area, accounts only 16% of all neighborhoods in the BMA.

The comparison of the mean values of the indicators by neighborhood cluster types shows that despite of some similarity in spatial patterns a few of those indicators are quite different for the GDR and the BMA. Figure 14 presents indicators by neighborhood cluster types for the case study regions. The Baltimore city (cluster 1) has experienced a steady population decline since 1950s, due to a variety of social and economic reasons. On the other hand, Ireland recovering after financial and economic crisis period with population and employment stable and rising in the GDR, and most

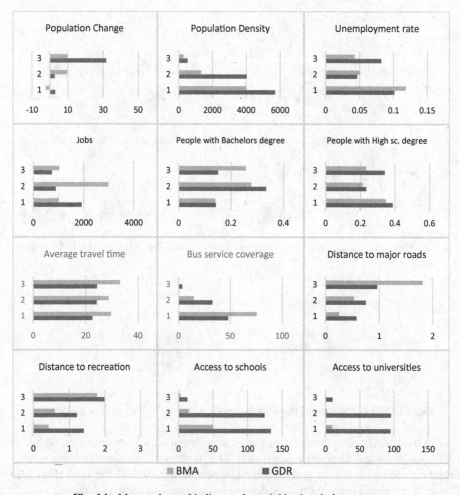

Fig. 14. Mean values of indicators by neighborhood cluster types.

significantly in the surrounding counties of Dublin city (cluster 3). The contrasting population change can be the driving force that leads to relatively stronger job concertation and population density in Dublin city (clusters 1 and 2). The BMA in general has much lower population densities within all three clusters. The unemployment rate is highest in North and North-East Dublin (cluster 1) and in Baltimore city center (cluster 1). Interestingly, for the GDR, jobs are mostly located in the same area (cluster 1), while in case of the BMA, jobs are more concentrated in the suburbs of Baltimore city (cluster 2), being much higher not only in the region, but also compared with the GDR. Education attainment can also play a critical role in affecting the neighborhood typology. Thus, the residents with Bachelor or higher degree live mostly in South Dublin (cluster 2), while people with high school degree only are located mostly in North Dublin and in surrounding counties. In case of the BMA, the people with Bachelor or higher degree live mostly in Baltimore suburbs and suburban areas (clusters 2 and 3), while people with high school degree only are located more in Baltimore City (cluster 1).

The average travel time is less in all clusters types of the GDR compared with the BMA relevant clusters - with the longest travel time in the suburban neighborhoods of both regions (cluster 3). Dublin has a wide network of public transport but frequencies are poor due to dispersed population in suburbs. Baltimore has a similar pattern. Though access to bus stops is higher in Baltimore, not all those bus routes have high frequency and some stops are located very close to each other. In the GDR suburban neighborhoods (cluster 3) are the furthest from the major roads but essentially closer compared with the BMA suburban neighborhoods (cluster 3). In contrast, for Dublin city (clusters 1 and 2) distance to major roads is relatively longer compared with the neighborhoods in Baltimore city (cluster 1) and suburbs (cluster 2). In all neighborhood cluster types, distance to recreation facilities is longer for the GDR compared with the BMA, with South Dublin being closest and the surrounding counties being farthest. The Baltimore city suburbs (cluster 2) are closest to the open areas while the suburban areas are furthest (cluster 3). The GDR has essentially higher level of access to schools and universities compared with the BMA. Within regions the most access is available from Dublin city (cluster 1 and 2) and Baltimore city (cluster 1).

4 Conclusion

In this research, we distill indicators to a core set that can capture essential differences in neighborhood types in terms of social, economic, and environmental dimensions. It is interesting to see the similarity of the two regions that the key component indicators are consistent among major factors between two cases. We use these factors' loadings in cluster analyzes to identify unique neighborhood types spatially in the GDR and the BMA. We found that the same set of the core factors actually behave differently due to their own local history, development trajectory, and socio-economic characteristics. Comparison of the core set of indicators and spatial clustering patterns sheds new lights on the important factors for both regions.

The proposed approach will help compare variations in neighborhood types in different regions. In examining indicators related to the recent evolutions in the cities tested it is clear that traditional central location preferences can be seen as stronger in the Dublin example. While analysis of both region's key indicators illustrate periods of economic restructuring, in recovery the Dublin central area neighborhoods show indicators of regeneration and recovery to a greater extent than Baltimore. In addition, this analysis supports a view that while there may be no perfect set of indicators for a sustainable neighborhood, accessibility indicators as a general principle should play a substantial role in such policy discussions.

The approach is based on an understanding that the process of identifying and examining core indicators of neighborhood types and clusters is improved by working with more than one case study as this assists in overcoming local bias or interpretation which can be inherent in single case study analysis. A single case analysis can be very specific in terms of scale, policy and institutional context and actors involved. This research is attempting to achieve a more generalized insight which is valid across locations and contexts.

Acknowledgments. This research was supported by a Marie Curie International Outgoing Fellowship (GeoSInPo) within the 7th European Community Framework Program.

References

1. Sawicki, D.S., Flynn, P.: Neighborhood indicators - a review of the literature and an assessment of conceptual and methodological issues. J. Am. Plan. Assoc. **62**(2), 165–183 (1996)
2. Dluhy, M., Swartz, N.: Connecting knowledge and policy: the promise of community indicators in the United States. Soc. Indic. Res. **79**(1), 1–23 (2006)
3. Song, Y., Knaap, G.: Quantitative classification of neighborhoods: the neighborhoods of new single-family homes in the Portland metropolitan area. J. Urban Des. **12**(1), 1–24 (2007)
4. Shahumyan, H., et al.: Regional development scenario evaluation through land use modelling and opportunity mapping. Land **3**(3), 1180–1213 (2014)
5. Liu, C., Knaap, E., Knaap, G.: Reclassification of sustainable neighborhoods: an opportunity indicator analysis in baltimore metropolitan area. In: AESOP-ACSP Joint Congress, Dublin, Ireland (2013)
6. Reece, J., et al.: The geography of opportunity: mapping to promote equitable community development and fair housing in King county, WA. Kirwan Institute for the Study of Race and Ethnicity, Ohio State University, US (2010)
7. Reece, J., et al.: People, Place and Opportunity: Mapping Communities of Opportunity in Connecticut. Kirwan Institute for the Study of Race And Ethnicity, Ohio State University, US (2009)
8. Couch, C., Leontidou, L., Petschel-Held, G.: Urban sprawl in Europe: landscapes, land-use change & policy. Real Estate Issues, xix, 273 p. Blackwell, Oxford, Malden (2007)
9. NSS: National spatial strategy for Ireland 2002–2020: People, Places and Potential, D.o.t.E. a.L. Government, Editor, 160 p. Stationery Office, Dublin (2002)
10. CSO Regional Population Projections 2016–2031. CSO statistical release (2013)
11. Field, A.: Discovering Statistics Using IBM SPSS Statistics, 4th edn. Sage Publications Ltd., UK (2013)

12. Tabachnick, B.G., Fidell, L.S.: Using Multivariate Statistics. Pearson Education Inc., Boston (2007)
13. Hair, J., et al.: Multivariate Data Analysis, 4th edn. Prentice-Hall Inc., Upper Saddle River (1995)
14. Gorsuch, R.L.: Factor Analysis. Hillsdale Erlbaum, Newark (1983)
15. Comrey, A.L.: A First Course in Factor Analysis. Academic Press, New York (1973)
16. Kaiser, H.F.: An index of factorial simplicity. Psychometrika 39(1), 31–36 (1974)
17. Kaiser, H.F.: The application of electronic-computers to factor-analysis. Educ. Psychol. Measur. 20(1), 141–151 (1960)
18. Cattell, R.B.: The scree test for the number of factors. Multivar. Behav. Res. 1(2), 245–276 (1966)
19. Horn, J.L.: A rationale and test for the number of factors in factor-analysis. Psychometrika 30(2), 179–185 (1965)
20. Costello, A.B., Osborne, J.W.: Best practices in exploratory factor analysis: four recommendations for getting the most from your analysis. Pract. Assess. Res. Eval. 10(7), 1–9 (2005)
21. Fiedler, J.A., Mcdonald, J.J.: Market figmentation clustering on factor scores versus individual variables. In: Second Annual Advanced Research Techniques Forum, pp. 118–129 (1992)
22. Mooi, E., Sarstedt, M.: A Concise Guide to Market Research: The process. Data and Methods Using IBM SPSS Statistics. Springer, Heidelberg (2011)
23. Dolnicar, S., Grun, B.: Challenging factor-cluster segmentation. J. Travel Res. 47(1), 63–71 (2008)

Automated Valuation Methods in Atypical Real Estate Markets Using the Mono-parametric Approach

Marina Ciuna[1], Manuela De Ruggiero[2], Benedetto Manganelli[3],
Francesca Salvo[2(✉)], and Marco Simonotti[1]

[1] Department of Civil, Environmental, Aerospace and Materials Engineering,
University of Palermo, Viale delle Scienze, Ed. 8, 90128 Palermo, Italy
{marina.ciuna,marco.simonotti}@unipa.it
[2] Department of Environmental and Chemical Engineering,
University of Calabria, Via Pietro Bucci Cubo 46b, 87036 Rende, Italy
manueladeruggiero@gmail.com,
francesca.salvo@unical.it
[3] School of Engineering, University of Basilicata, Viale dell'Ateneo Lucano,
85100 Potenza, Italy
benedetto.manganelli@unibas.it

Abstract. The appraisal objectivity depends on the possibility to quickly and easily access to reliable real estate data in order to apply appropriate appraisal approaches. In order to ensure the objectivity of the real estate appraisals, in recent years Automated Valuation Methods (AVM) have been developed, integrating computerized real estate databases and programming languages. The Automated Valuation Methods proposed at international level usually recur to regression models, aimed to return appraisal equations based on reliable real estate databases. This approach is not applicable in some markets where lack of data does not allow the implementation of regression models. This paper proposes to implement a valuation automatic method in order to appraise properties located in atypical markets, structuring a procedural algorithm based on the mono-parametric approach and able to return punctual values related to the subject's specifics and to the market peculiarities in a very limited area. The paper proposes also the application of similarity degree coefficients in order to take into account the differences between the amounts of the real estate features, leading to the possibility to use the mono-parametric approach also when lack of data would not recommend it.

Keywords: Real estate market · Mono-parametric approach · Similarity degree · Automated Valuation Methods

1 Introduction

An Automated Valuation Method (AVM) is a calculation software with mathematical basis, able to produce market value appraisals based on the local real estate market, its parameters and the property characteristics, using information previously and separately

O. Gervasi et al. (Eds.): ICCSA 2017, Part III, LNCS 10406, pp. 200–209, 2017.
DOI: 10.1007/978-3-319-62398-6_14

collected and available in a computerized database. The distinguishing feature of an AVM is the use of mathematical models, so that AVM deeply differs from traditional valuation methods in which the appraiser physically inspects the property and relies mostly on experience and judgment to analyse real data and develop a market value appraisal.

The possibility offered by AVM compared to traditional valuation methods is to provide reliable values, in a fast, automatic, efficient, way, reducing costs, on condition that the database contains accurate and reliable data, that analysis is consistent with the appraisal theory accepted by international standards, that modelling is properly tested prior to application.

The application of such procedures is made possible by the presence of real estate comparison data previously collected in a computer database.

The reliability of the results produced by an AVM is obviously linked to the reliability of real estate data available in the support database, which must be continuously monitored and updated in order to verify its integrity.

If the application of automatic valuation methods is relatively simple in dynamics and transparent real estate markets, the specifications in static and viscous real estate markets, for which the simple data collection may be difficult if not impossible, is complex.

Internationally, AVM are generally set on multiple regression models, in order to prediction functions, valid throughout the study area. The lack of data obviously makes unenforceable deploying multiple regression models in atypical realities. In these contexts, it is considered more appropriate to provide procedural algorithms, that do not give back generally valid equations, but that are aimed to return punctual appraisals. In these situations, the AVM has to set in the computerized database tools able to select in the comparative mechanism few limited comparative properties, falling in a limited geographic area, resulting a very high level of detail that does not require extrapolation.

In this perspective, an interesting possibility is to use potentialities in the block programming tools, to implement flexible valuation procedures, in accordance with the guidelines provided by the international standards for automated valuations.

2 Literature Review

The idea of automating the sales comparison approach has appeared sporadically in the real estate literature over time and it has been used in some CAMA (Computer-Assisted Mass Appraisal) methods [1, 2]. Graaskamp and Robbins [3] developed an automated sales comparison system that they referred to as Market-Comp based on choosing small samples with very similar properties: an approach similar to 'sales comparison adjustment grids' used in conventional individual property appraisals. Detweiler and Radigan [4, 5] published an article describing their Computer-Assisted Real Estate Appraisal Sys-tem (CAREAS). Their work described a statistically derived dissimilarity index used to select comparables and a regression model to create adjustment factors. The use of sophisticated fitting techniques can account for different functional forms or, in some cases, the complete lack of functional relationships. Spline regressions, nonparametric regressions, autoregressive techniques and spatial heterogeneity modelling are some examples [6–10]. Incorporating spatial information in pricing models through the use of direct spatial modelling with Cartesian coordinates [11], geostatistical models [12, 13], or response surfaces [14] has improved the precision of price estimates. Other studies [15–19] have focused on improving sample selection by delineating submarkets of homes in which the marginal price contributions of independent variables are more likely to be similar. Predicted residuals from nearby sales (spatial errors) have been used in two separate but related ways in the literature. Case et al. [20], in particular, developed a two-stage method in which errors from a single-stage ordinary least squares (OLS) model are used as predictors in the two stage model; conversely, Pace and Gilley [21, 22], among others, used a simultaneous auto-regressive (SAR) model to account for nearby residuals in a single stage model.

Bourassa, Hoesli, and Cantoni [23, 24] recently have dealt with uses of autoregressive models.

The application of the International Valuation Standards [25] have prompted research to investigate the possibility of applying the AVM even in really complex real estate markets [26], for different issues at stake, including best practices, real-life constrains, administrative procedures, software capabilities, expert competences, modelling frame-works, background theories and more [27–30], taking account that real estate analysis needs portals and databases in order to manage deficits of the non-spatial methods [31].

As far as we know, the mono-parametric approach has never been applied in AVM, moreover because the hypothesis of application in order to obtain certifiable values are very difficult to find, especially in atypical markets. That is why the mono-parametric-approach is mainly used in order to obtain indicative values on real estate prices or as a verification of the results obtained by other processes. The question is still under investigation, assuming that the operative real estate practice in atypical markets is quite far from the best one [32].

3   Methods

International Valuation Standards group the appraisal procedures in three categories (market approach, cost approach, income approach), which have different procedural articulation and baseline data, but all use a comparative method.

There is not a method better than the others, but it is possible to choose from time to time the one that best meets the case study's specific requirements, based on the property's characteristics and on the availability of comparative data. If the necessary real estate data are available, it is possible to build up an automatic procedure for each methodology, characterizing and differentiating just for the model's specification and variable coefficients calibration.

Calibration is the determination of the adjustments or of the coefficients used in the AVM through market analysis. If most of the existing AVM today uses statistical tools such as multiple linear regression and nonlinear regression to calibrate the model coefficients, it is also possible to use various calibration methods based on comparison functions and appraisal criteria.

With reference to this alternative and since the aim of the proposed project is the implementation of punctual appraisal procedures, rather than the identification of valuation equations generally valid in the context of the case study market, the calibration can be carried out through the use of economic postulates and the construction of the comparison functions, respecting the specificities of each implemented method.

3.1 Mono-parametric Approach

In wider terms, the mono-parametric approach can be summarized through the following five basic steps:

1. identification of comparable properties as much as possible similar to the subject, and surveying of their prices and amounts of the selected parameters;
2. construction of a known price scale based on the size of the parameter;
3. integration of subject in the corresponding scale step proportionate to the amount of the owned parameter;
4. determination of the subject's market value based on the position occupied in the scale;
5. any adjustment to the appraised value.

The determination of the most probable market value is based on the following

$$V_x : \pi_x = P_y : \pi_y, \tag{1}$$

where

- V_x è is the subject's market value (unknown);
- π_x and π_y are the amounts of the comparison parameter, respectively for the subject and the comparable (both known);
- P_y is the comparable's price (known).

From the abovementioned proportion, the elementary linear relationship used for determining the appraised value is deduced, if you have n comparables:

$$V_x = \frac{\sum_{i=1}^{n} P_i}{\sum_{i=1}^{n} \pi_i} \cdot \pi_x, \tag{2}$$

where $P_i = p_i \cdot \pi_i$ and pi represent the unitary average price.

In practice, the appraised value is determined by defining the average unit price obtained as an average of prices compared with the parameter amounts for several comparison properties.

The mono-parametric approach requires both analysis and synthesis abilities: analysis of the multiple characteristics and peculiarities of subject and comparables, looking for similarities; synthesis of the complexity and pluralities that contribute to the formation of the market value in a unique, represented by the comparison parameter. These operations require, of course, a remarkable ability to investigate, an adequate knowledge of the appraisal condition and objectives, as well as a significant experience of the specific market.

It is necessary to underline that the mono-parametric approach can be used in a scientific way and with reliable results only if comparables' features are identical to those of the subject, except for the comparison parameter. Otherwise, the appraisal would ignore the incidence of the properties' characteristics, leading to approximate appraisal results.

In atypical markets, the ideal conditions for the application of the mono-parametric approach conflict with the lack of the comparison data that, even when available, usually do not meet the application requirements (being equal to less than comparison parameter).

In the comparables selection, it would be possible to define some limits of acceptability in the divergence of the amounts of real estate features, designed to drive the exclusion/inclusion of comparables in the sample. But, even when it was possible to define a limit numerical index, with a scientifical and credible approach, the exclusion of comparables in atypical markets would substantially lead to the absence of the comparison data and, therefore, to the inapplicability of the procedure itself.

However, the possibility to apply the mono-parametric approach can be done using rationality measures [33] able to synthesize the differences in the amount of the real estate characteristics into similarity coefficients aimed to differently "weight" the comparables in relation to the different similarity degree.

3.2 Measure of the Similarity Degree

A similarity coefficient provides a measure of the degree of similarity between the comparables, giving values between 0 and 1, the first corresponding to observations with no common elements, the second relating to the surveys that perfectly meet the criterion used to measure the similarity.

A measure able to detect the similarity of individual properties in the real estate sample has its foundation in the "closeness" between the amounts of property characteristics: greater comparability means greater proximity of the amounts of the real estate characteristics; less comparability means amounts that are more distant. The measure of the "degree of similarity" of comparable properties may be expressed, therefore, as a function of the difference between the amounts of the i-th feature of the comparable and those of the subject.

This difference can be expressed in terms of absolute value in the following way:

$$gs_a^{j^*} = \frac{\sum_{j=1}^{m} \sum_{i=1}^{n} \left| \frac{x_{ij}-x_{i0}}{\bar{x}_i} \right| - \sum_{i=1}^{n} \left| \frac{x_{ij}-x_{i0}}{\bar{x}_i} \right|}{(m-1) \cdot \sum_{j=1}^{m} \sum_{i=1}^{n} \left| \frac{x_{ij}-x_{i0}}{\bar{x}_i} \right|} \tag{3}$$

where $gs_a^{j^*}$ is the indicator of the degree of similarity of a j^* generic property of comparison and $\bar{x}_i$ is the average of the considered characteristic.

The difference between the amount of the i-th feature of the comparable and that corresponding to the subject can also be expressed in terms of square standardized distances, as follows:

$$gs_q^{j^*} = \frac{\sum_{j=1}^{m} \sum_{i=1}^{n} \left| \frac{x_{ij} - x_{i0}}{\bar{x}_i} \right|^2 - \sum_{i=1}^{n} \left| \frac{x_{ij} - x_{i0}}{\bar{x}_i} \right|^2}{(m-1) \cdot \sum_{j=1}^{m} \sum_{i=1}^{n} \left| \frac{x_{ij} - x_{i0}}{\bar{x}_i} \right|^2} \quad (4)$$

where $gs_q^{j^*}$ is the degree of similarity of a generic property of comparison j^*.

3.3   Weighted Single Parameter Reconciliation

Resorting to the similarity coefficients, the reconciliation of the average prices related to the parameter can therefore be weighted using the (3) and (4) coefficients, as:

$$V_x = \frac{\sum_{i=1}^{n} P_j \cdot gs_a^{j^*}}{\sum_{i=1}^{n} \pi_i} \cdot \pi_x \quad (5)$$

$$V_x = \frac{\sum_{i=1}^{n} P_j \cdot gs_q^{j^*}}{\sum_{i=1}^{n} \pi_i} \cdot \pi_x \quad (6)$$

By removing the hypothesis of equal probability, the reconciliation made using the similarity coefficients can also be applied to comparable samples that do not meet the ideal conditions for the application of the mono-parametric approach. In this way, the mono-parametric approach can be applied in a scientific and rigorous manner even in atypical markets with limited data.

3.4   AVM Method's Specification

The implementation of the mono-parametric approach in an AVM can be done according to international valuation standards in operational terms [34], making automatic the selection of the comparable properties, the data processing, the coefficients determination and the market value appraisal:

1. definition of the subject and its detection on the map;
2. definition of the subject buffer within which to search for comparables;
3. identification of the comparative properties;
4. parameter measurements both for the subject and for the comparables;
5. similarity degree coefficients and average updated prices measurements (coefficient calibration);
6. review of the appraised value.

The approach could choose the surface characteristic as the comparison parameter. This choice would be the best one because the surface variables are proxies ones, and they are able to represent the incidence, albeit approximately, of the other characteristics in their unitary average price.

The subject property (spatially represented by an element of punctual geometry) would be placed on the map with a geocoding operation. A buffer (parametric entities) could be applied in order to investigate surroundings, in which to search the comparative properties, which would be detected by intersection of the buffer area and the layer relative to sales data.

Once the comparables have been selected, the procedure would switch to coefficients calibration, represented by the measurements of the surface's unitary average price and of the similarity degree coefficients, calculated in additional fields as a ratio of the weighted sum of the sales updated prices (to current date) and the sum of the corresponding surfaces:

$$p_x = \frac{\sum_{i=1}^{n} P_j \cdot gs_a^{j*}}{\sum_{i=1}^{n} S_i} \cdot S_x \tag{7}$$

$$p_x = \frac{\sum_{i=1}^{n} P_j \cdot gs_q^{j*}}{\sum_{i=1}^{n} S_i} \cdot S_x \tag{8}$$

The value would be then calculated by multiplying the surface average price for the subject's surface as:

$$V_x = p_x \cdot S_x \tag{9}$$

The procedure's reliability would be verified by applying to every real estate data in the database, considered as subject with unknown value, in order to calculate the ratio test, valuating the discrepancy between the appraised values and real sales price, and verifying that the obtained differences are contained within the limits reported in literature [33, 35].

The automatic procedure may be implemented using the programming tools available in the GIS software, such as the ArcGis Model Builder.

The advantage of this choice lies in the extreme flexibility of use of the implemented tool that, while working on a specific real estate database, is independent from it. The proposed procedure, not providing the generalization inherent in the analysis of the regressive models, can be used in real contexts different from the pilot one, provided that the real estate database has the same structure as the original one.

In Model Builder, the procedure would appear as a flow diagram that represents the algorithm and documents the process adopted in a transparent way.

4 Conclusion

This study aimed to assess the possibility of applying the automatic valuation methods in atypical real estate markets for which, given the lack of data, it is not possible to implement statistical models. In particular, it was thought the opportunity to set procedural algorithms in place of analysis models with the aim of returning punctual appraisals of the market value of individual properties, controlling the subjective component which characterizes the traditional valuation in viscous real estate markets, through the use of computer software.

The proposed approach has been set on the application of the mono-parametric approach, appropriately weighting similarities and dissimilarities in the comparables using scientific coefficients in the reconciliation of the average updated prices.

This is a very interesting investigative option, because it allows an automated approach even in static and complex real estate markets.

The next step will be the test of the proposed approach in a real estate case study, for which the real estate database is already available, emphasizing that the proposed approach involves the implementation of an automatic procedure and not of an automatic model, so that the approach is independent from the used database and it can be applied in any case study.

References

1. Shenkel, W., Eidson, A.: Comparable sales retrieval systems. Apprais. J. **4**, 540–544 (1971)
2. Dilmore, G.: Appraising houses. Real Estate Apprais., 21–32, July–August 1974
3. Graaskamp, J., Robbins, M.: Business 868 lecture notes. University of Wisconsin, Madison (1987)
4. Detweiler, J., Radigan, R.: Computer-assisted real estate appraisal. Apprais. J. **64**, 91–101 (1996)
5. Detweiler, J., Radigan, R.: Computer-assisted real estate appraisal: a tool for the practicing appraiser. Apprais. J. **67**, 280–286 (1999)
6. Giudice, V., Manganelli, B., Paola, P.: Spline smoothing for estimating hedonic housing price models. In: Gervasi, O., Murgante, B., Misra, S., Gavrilova, M.L., Rocha, A.M.A.C., Torre, C., Taniar, D., Apduhan, B.O. (eds.) ICCSA 2015. LNCS, vol. 9157, pp. 210–219. Springer, Cham (2015). doi:10.1007/978-3-319-21470-2_15
7. Manganelli, B., Mare, G., Nesticò, A.: Using genetic algorithms in the housing market analysis. In: Gervasi, O., Murgante, B., Misra, S., Gavrilova, M.L., Rocha, A.M.A.C., Torre, C., Taniar, D., Apduhan, B.O. (eds.) ICCSA 2015. LNCS, vol. 9157, pp. 36–45. Springer, Cham (2015). doi:10.1007/978-3-319-21470-2_3
8. Manganelli, B., De Paola, P., Del Giudice, V.: Linear programming in a multi-criteria model for real estate appraisal. In: Gervasi, O., et al. (eds.) ICCSA 2016. LNCS, vol. 9786, pp. 182–192. Springer, Cham (2016). doi:10.1007/978-3-319-42085-1_14
9. Tajani, F., Morano, P., Locurcio, M., D'Addabbo, N.: Property valuations in times of crisis: artificial neural networks and evolutionary algorithms in comparison. In: Gervasi, O., Murgante, B., Misra, S., Gavrilova, M.L., Rocha, A.M.A.C., Torre, C., Taniar, D., Apduhan, B.O. (eds.) ICCSA 2015. LNCS, vol. 9157, pp. 194–209. Springer, Cham (2015). doi:10. 1007/978-3-319-21470-2_14
10. Helbich, M., Brunauer, W., Vaz, E., Nijkamp, P.: Spatial heterogeneity in hedonic house price models: the case of Austria. Urban Stud. **51**(2), 390–411 (2014)
11. Fik, T., Ling, D., Mulligan, G.: Modeling spatial variation in housing prices: a variable interaction approach. Real Estate Econ. **31**(4), 623–646 (2003)
12. Dubin, R.: Estimation of regression coefficients in the presence of spatially autocorrelated error terms. Rev. Econ. Stat. **70**(3), 466–474 (1998)

13. Manganelli, B., Pontrandolfi, P., Azzato, A., Murgante, B.: Using geographically weighted regression for housing market segmentation. Int. J. Bus. Intell. Data Min. 9(2), 161–177 (2014)
14. O'Connor, P.: Automated valuation models by model-building practitioners: Testing hybrid model structure and GIS location adjustments. J. Prop. Tax Assess. Adm. 5(2), 5–24 (2008)
15. Goodman, A., Thibodeau, T.: Housing market segmentation. J. Hous. Econ. 7, 121–143 (1998)
16. Goodman, A., Thibodeau, T.: Housing market segmentation and hedonic prediction accuracy. J. Hous. Econ. 12(3), 181–201 (2003)
17. Goodman, A., Thibodeau, T.: The spatial proximity of metropolitan area housing submarkets. Real Estate Econ. 35, 209–232 (2007)
18. Bourassa, S., Cantoni, E., Hoesli, M.: Spatial dependence, housing submarkets, and house price predictions. J. Real Estate Finan. Econ. 35, 143–160 (2007)
19. Borst, R., McCluskey, W.: The modified comparable sales method as the basis for a property tax valuations system and its relationship and comparison to spatially autoregressive valuation models. In: Kauko, T., d'Amato, M. (eds.) Mass Appraisal Methods: An International Perspective for Property Valuers, pp. 49–69. Wiley Blackwell, Chicester (2008)
20. Case, B., Clapp, J., Dubin, R., Rodriguez, M.: Modeling spatial and temporal house price patterns: A comparison of four models. J. Real Estate Finan. Econ. 29, 167–191 (2004)
21. Pace, R., Gilley, O.: Using the spatial configuration of data to improve estimation. J. Real Estate Finan. Econ. 14, 333–340 (1997)
22. Pace, R., Gilley, O.: Generalizing the OLS and grid estimators. Real Estate Econ. 1, 331–346 (1998)
23. Bourassa, S., Cantoni, E., Hoesli, M.: Predicting house prices with spatial dependence: a comparison of alternative methods. J. Real Estate Res. 32, 139–159 (2010)
24. Bourassa, S., Cantoni, E., Hoesli, M.: Robust repeat sales indexes. Real Estate Econ. 41(3), 517–541 (2013)
25. IVSC: International Valuation Standards. IVSC, London (2011)
26. d'Amato, M., Kauko, T.: Advances in Automated Valuation Modeling: AVM After the Non-Agency Mortgage Crisis. Springer, Heidelberg (2017)
27. Ciuna, M., Salvo, F., Simonotti, M.: An estimative model of automated valuation method in Italy. In: d'Amato, M., Kauko, T. (eds.) Advances in Automated Valuation Modeling: AVM After the Non-Agency Mortgage Crisis. SSDC, vol. 86, pp. 85–112. Springer, Cham (2017). doi:10.1007/978-3-319-49746-4_5
28. Ciuna, M., Salvo, F., Simonotti, M.: The multilevel model in the computer-generated appraisal: a case in Palermo. In: d'Amato, M., Kauko, T. (eds.) Advances in Automated Valuation Modeling: AVM After the Non-Agency Mortgage Crisis. SSDC, vol. 86, pp. 225–261. Springer, Cham (2017). doi:10.1007/978-3-319-49746-4_14
29. Ciuna, M., Ruggiero, M., Salvo, F., Simonotti, M.: Automatic research of the capitalization rate for the residential automated valuation: an experimental study in Cosenza (Italy). In: d'Amato, M., Kauko, T. (eds.) Advances in Automated Valuation Modeling: AVM After the Non-Agency Mortgage Crisis. SSDC, vol. 86, pp. 361–380. Springer, Cham (2017). doi:10.1007/978-3-319-49746-4_20
30. Ciuna, M., Ruggiero, M., Salvo, F., Simonotti, M.: Automated procedures based on market comparison approach in Italy. In: d'Amato, M., Kauko, T. (eds.) Advances in Automated Valuation Modeling: AVM After the Non-Agency Mortgage Crisis. SSDC, vol. 86, pp. 381–400. Springer, Cham (2017). doi:10.1007/978-3-319-49746-4_21

31. Schernthanner, H., Asche, H., Gonschorek, J., Scheele, L.: Spatial modeling and geovisualization of rental prices for real estate portals. In: Gervasi, O., et al. (eds.) ICCSA 2016. LNCS, vol. 9788, pp. 120–133. Springer, Cham (2016). doi:10.1007/978-3-319-42111-7_11

32. Simonotti, M., Salvo, F., Ciuna, M.: Appraisal value and assessed value in Italy. Int. J. Econ. Stat. **3**, 24–31 (2015)

33. Salvo, F., Simonotti, M., Ciuna, M., De Ruggiero, M.: Measurements of rationality for a scientific approach to the market oriented methods. J. Real Estate Lit. **2**, 403–427 (2016)

34. VV.AA.: *Standard on automated valuation models* (AVMs), International Association of Assessing Officers, Chicago (2003)

35. Salvo, F., Ciuna, M., De Ruggiero, M.: Property prices index numbers and derived indices. Prop. Manage. **32**(2), 139–153 (2014)

Urban Planning and Technological Innovation

Teresa Cilona[✉]

Department of Architecture, University of Palermo, Palermo, Italy
teresa.cilona@unipa.it

Abstract. Over the years, city and territory have been transformed disproportionately and the planning appears to have lost control over the dynamics of the events that, unfortunately, have caused indelible changes on urban and environmental systems. The reworking of alphanumeric and geographic data through the territorial information system can be useful as technical support and methodological knowledge capable of intervening and redeveloping the residential centers. In fact, cities and their dynamics can be visualized with tools and machinery capable of representing them in a graphic or schematic way. This study presents some Italian experiences of urban renewal made possible by territorial information systems. The achieved results attest that technological innovation represents a great opportunity for planning increasingly smart cities, in addition to having a greater influence on redevelopment processes in the government of the territory and improving services distribution and the decision making process.

Keywords: Technological innovation · Participation · Planning

1 Introduction

In urban planning the use of IT technologies is always becoming more valuable, both at the national and international level, due to the ability to obtain, in a short amount of time, information from different disciplines.

Territorial information systems represent urban centers and territories by crossing and sharing different data that is often complex, contradictory, and difficult to interpret. They are dynamic knowledge tools - essential for planning and for a large number of subjects - as their use allows the use of alphanumeric and geographic data, which represent the traditional heritage of the discipline.

Moreover, if we consider that in Italy the planning instruments are drawn up according to the requirements of the national planning law n. 1150 of 1942, the use of computer systems – that are more modern and flexible, quick and inexpensive, capable of being continually updated at the service of those who administer them as well as citizens themselves – represent, both for the government and the territory, a great achievement. In this paper we seek to analyze how territorial information systems affect and influence the processes of government of the land and cities. The objective, in fact, is to understand how technological innovation might affect the future planning of urban centers. In this scenario it is natural to ask:

© Springer International Publishing AG 2017
O. Gervasi et al. (Eds.): ICCSA 2017, Part III, LNCS 10406, pp. 210–223, 2017.
DOI: 10.1007/978-3-319-62398-6_15

1. What is the relationship between technological innovation and the drafting of planning instruments?
2. How much and for what purposes may territorial information systems affect the definition and management of analyzes, plans, and intervention strategies in the cities?
3. Can the use of territorial information systems be a factor of progress in city government and have a positive effect on recovery and regeneration policies?

Unfortunately, in some of the inquiries, as stated in Fig. 1, the data is not always comforting. It's possible to detect a clear separation between the institutional and the experimental levels, between the promotion of computerization and the poor implementation of innovative research results for planning methods and tools [1–5].

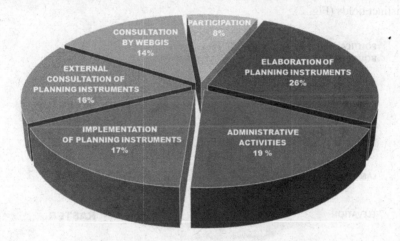

Fig. 1. Urban planning and technological activities

2   Territorial Government and Management

2.1   Information Tools for the Valorization of Land Resources

Among the information systems for the government of the territory we can distinguish between GIS and SIT, though often we tend to confuse the two terms as if they were the same thing. Below, we will try to clarify the difference between the two, eliminating any doubts. There are different definitions of GIS, an English acronym for *Geographical Information System,* and SIT, the Italian acronym for Territorial Information Systems[1]. In fact, the two systems differ in meaning of the words "geographical" and "territorial" [6].

According to the famous definition of Burrough (1986), *"The GIS is composed of a series of software instruments for collecting, storing, retrieving, transforming and*

---

[1] Murgante B.: Smart Cities and City Sensing, preface in G. Borga (2013), City Sensing. Approcci, metodi e tecnologie innovative per la Città intelligente.

displaying spatial data from the real world." According to *Mogorovich* (1988) it is *"The set of men, instruments and procedures (often informal) that allow the acquisition and distribution of data within the organization, that make them available upon request to those in need of carrying out any activities."*

GIS, aim to create a virtual model of the real world through simulations and mathematical models, in order to implement strategies for protection, enhancement and use of resources present in the area, sustainable as much as possible for the environment and for populations [7].

The SIT, clearly comprehend the concept of territory, understood as place in which policy, control, administrative power, social conflict, and higher-level spatial planning are exercised[2] [8]. In addition, among industry experts we can distinguish between proponents who use the two terms in the same way and those who believe the terms are two distinct fields (Fig. 2).

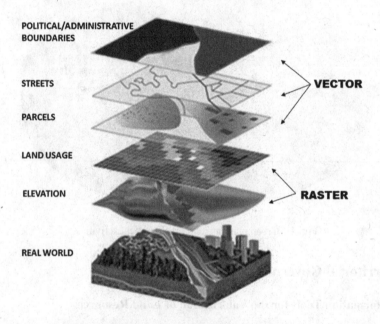

Fig. 2. Schematic – overlapping information and maps

The GIS, are geographic database management software, that permit us to examine graphic data and text simultaneously, to operate queries and overlay maps [9]. The SIT, include techniques, tools, procedures, human resources, and cartography[3] [10].

Ultimately, we can say as Fischer and Nijkamp (1992) do, that a territorial information system (SIT or GIS) can be defined as *"… an information system based on a*

---

[2] The debate in Italian urban planning on GIS between new perspectives and old misunderstandings, archive of urban and regional studies.

[3] The information concerns: place names, house numbering, Technical Regional Papers, Province Mapping, Orthophotos, Cadastral Cartography, etc.

computer that tries to capture, store, manipulate, analyze and display spatial data with associated attributes, in order to solve complex research, plan and manage problems".

The computer-territory couple was used for the first time by American planners, in the early 50s, when they experimented with the representation of the territory through mathematical models and processed geographic information through the computer.

The first significant experience of Geographical Information System was developed in Canada. The aim was to set up a *land inventory* for store and manage cartographic data through the computer.

The creation of the CGIS (Canada Geographical Information System) was a turning point. Operations important such as associating attributes to geographic elements, creating the topological data structure, elaborations (area measurements, scale change, adjoining sheets, and thematic crossings) were made. Moreover, in the same years at Universities, was developed software based on a grid system with data related to elementary cells, such as Symap and Grid (University of Harvard), Miads (US Forest Service), Geomap (University of Waterloo) [11].

In this way, with the introduction of computer graphics programs, computer science was applied to the territory, to know it better [12], to create and edit maps[4] [13].

The databases became Geographic Information Systems able to connect a series of information to a precise location of the territory.

In Europe, between 1998 and 2000, the exchange of knowledge was promoted[5] for the construction of digital archives containing territorial data on settlements [14, 15].

Very useful information was created to determine interventions of guardianship, enhancement, and preservation of the territory and of settlement heritage, redevelopment in recovery projects and sustainable development. In this regard, we recall the INSPIRE[6] [16], Directive 2007/2/CE, that established an infrastructure for territorial information in the European Community. The objective was to define environmental policies through the adoption of appropriate measures in the field of exchange, sharing, access and use of territorial data and interoperable services between the various levels of public administration. In this Directive the term *land use* [17–21] assumed particular relevance, which was devoted to forecasts of urban planning and transformations. In Italy, territorial information systems were first used in the 1980 s, with the drafting of some general planning instruments. The first experiments were carried out in Friuli Venezia Giulia, Tuscany, Emilia Romagna, Lombardy, and Piedmont: forward-looking regions, that established clear territorial policy objectives, with which they began the

---

[4] For example, a group led by Len Gaydos, USGS, at NASA Ames in Silicon Valley, have put together a simulation of urban growth in the San Francisco Bay Area as part of a wider project dealing with the human consequences of land use change. Urban development in the Bay Area from 1820 has been morphed together from old maps and since 1972 from satellite imagery.

[5] The network HISTOCITY was sponsored within the TMR (Training and Mobility of Researchers) Euro-Conferences Program IV EC R&D Framework Program, and coordinated by Maria Antonietta Esposito at the University of Florence in the period between 1998–2000.

[6] INfrastructure for SPatial InfoRmation in Europe. INSPIRE refers to 34 data layers that include geographic names, administrative units, land parcels, buildings and land use. The data model is defined by specific technical specifications, developed at the European level through a participatory process.

process of computerization of the regional technical cartography, using appropriate instruments for processing cartographic data. We recall, in this regard, the territorial and environmental geographic databases - used to generate the landscape plans - cartographic portals and the webGIS. Over the years, the territorial information systems changed from a tool of *inspection* to a tool of *management* for environmental issues or administrative and management activities of the Institutions. The spread of the technology, of internet and the versatility of the software [22–29] has made possible the development of application solutions that can be used in any place and by users that are not necessarily experts. See for example one of the first Italian experiences, the WebSIT of the Province of Padua (Fig. 3).

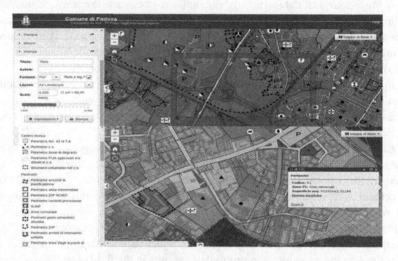

Fig. 3. Padua - example maps of webSIT consultation

For these reasons, in fact, interest has grown exponentially and has increased the number of users and applications in various fields such as: environment, civil protection, defense, agriculture, navigation telecommunications, etc.

2.2 Urban Planning Designs: Knowledge Systems

To draw up a planning instrument, a thorough awareness of the territory is necessary; of the origins and evolutionary processes of the city from surveys, verification, detection of building structures, from exploration and from historical sources.

For example, cadastral plans of the late nineteenth century superimposed over contemporary plans [30] allow us to reconstruct the territorial transformations that have occurred over time[7]. For Local Institutions, information technologies assume a great importance not only to describe, interpret reality, assess the impact of possible

---

[7] See the CASTORE project promoted by the Region of Tuscany that compares, on the internet, 12,000 historical cadastral maps with modern maps.

alternative choices, and monitor the implementation of the planbut, above all, because they make the planning and administrative activities of City Hall more transparent.

In particular, an IT environment in which alphanumeric information is closely connected with graphical information allow an operator to return to those areas of territory that meet certain conditions: infrastructure, services and equipment connected with the population, physical, material and social conditions of degradation. Typologically different information requires specific expertise, and the involvement of public and private entities, as well as the registration of modifications, to avoid becoming obsolete. Thanks to territorial information systems, an administrator, a technician or an ordinary citizen can visualize, in an urban center, buildings that have certain characteristics with the possibility of updating the information at any time. In this way, parallel handling of all information, making it traceable and sharing the data pushes towards the simplification of monitoring the territory and the definition of correct redevelopment strategies (Fig. 4).

Fig. 4. Territorial information systems

«…In the era of digital and relational democracy it is no longer possible to draw up development plans without a concrete system of specifics, that should be the tools of every administration, the result of coordination channels with other authorities, of the participation of actors and data users, and the definition of adequate rules [31] ».

3   Case Studies

The experience of urban regeneration that we propose concerns three Italian cities: Genoa, Naples and Palermo (Fig. 5).

All three of which are heterogeneous urban areas with different stories, morphologies, and linked traditions but that have the same experience of applying information systems towards urban redevelopment.

The investigations have been performed in two different ways.

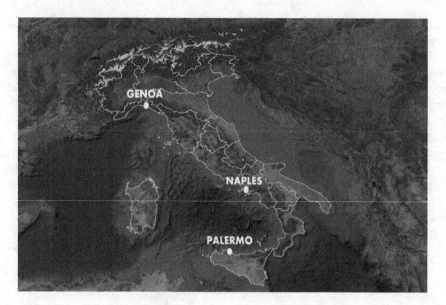

Fig. 5. The locations of Genoa, Naples, and Palermo in Italy

The first is that of direct detection, information was gathered through interviews with citizens, with the technicians responsible for the planning instrument, with experts in the information system, with freelancers and with simple users [32–36].

The second, instead, was through indirect detection.

The information is the result of the study of planning instruments, publications and articles in specialized journals and documents provided by municipalities.

The objective, as already mentioned in the introduction, is to understand how the information system affects and influences the urban recovery process. But let's proceed in order.

The first case analyzed is that of Genoa. The history of this city is similar to that of many other Italian cities: a past characterized by depopulation of the historic center, episodes of widespread crime, and economic crisis; factors that have caused degradation and neglect of the city center over the years.

But Genoa was a city that knew how to react.

The municipal government adopted an urban planning tool that was able to join urban, building, cultural, social and economic actions together by choosing to use information technology to develop an in-depth and updateable knowledge.

So to overcome the economic crisis it aimed to redevelop the port, industrial and urban areas by using its territorial information systems.

The restoration work was carried out with public and private funds by activating a real process of change, transformation and social substitution.

The city of Genoa began its experience using territorial information systems as a result of an agreement signed in 1997 with organizations, municipal companies and associations like the *Osservatorio Civis*[8] [37–40].

The system contains project specific data, has an interface accessible to all from which it is possible to visualize different zoom levels and information sheets.

All of this drives the design choices and reduces any errors that might cause a deterioration in the quality of life.

The interventions include: the recovery project of the ancient port, the arrangement of the waterfront, the construction of roads and parking lots, and feasibility studies related to waste disposal (Fig. 6).

(a)   (b)

(c)   (d)

Fig. 6. Genoa – (a) panoramic view of the harbor; (b, c and d) examples of urban development

The second case is that of Naples, which, unlike the Ligurian capital, has a past linked to the negative influences of the political class.

The city developed following the orthography of the land, where the outer walls, the main roads, the demolition of the fascist period, and speculative construction are all recognizable.

However, in the nineties, the planning activities of a new city administration managed to recover parts of the city center thanks to a variant of the PRG (General

---

[8] The observatory is very important in the preparation of planning instruments and in promoting and ensuring environmental sustainability, economic and social impact of projects on the territory.

Development Plan) [41–43] realized with the help of territorial information systems. The interventions made in preparation to the G7 were particularly significant - new roads, restoration of monumental buildings, palaces, rehabilitation of gardens and public squares such as Piazza Plebiscito.

The information system of the city of Naples was created in 1994 and reconstructs the historical urban transformation the city has undergone over the years, identifies the classification and the categories of intervention applied to heritage buildings, permits the visualization of maps, photos, surveys, identifies the equipment of the district, land use, constraints and realized recovery projects [44, 45].

In this regard, we point to the new sports facilities, the recreational play areas for children, the places of cultural aggregation, the reuse of reclaimed brownfield sites, the new port.

The objective is the communicability of the plan, the inspection of the transformation, the streamlining of implementation procedures of the planning instrument and knowledge management (Fig. 7).

(a)   (b)

(c)   (d)

Fig. 7. Naples – (a) panoramic View; (b and c) examples of urban development; (d) plebiscito square

The third case involves the city of Palermo. The Sicilian reality differs from Genoa and Naples because of the slowness of the technological innovation process within the public administration, in addition to a substantial shortage of urban planning and territorial tools [46].

Despite different changes undergone over time, the system of the city is now clearly visible. We identify two orthogonal roads that divide the city center into four districts, the development of the nineteenth-century city, the Haussmanian demolition, the changes of the fascist period, the havoc created after World War II, the expansion of real estate speculation [47–49].

Palermo is a city that, with great difficulty, tried to begin some useful experiments for the development of online services for citizens along with a risk map of the historic center for buildings and two particularly degraded areas.

The risk map, created thanks to the territorial information systems, contains: a collection of data, a register-city interchange model, the project of garden restoration, the construction of parking lots, the remediation of the underground, the arrangement of green areas, the implementation of infrastructure works, as well as the planning, management and transformation of the territory.

Finally, in the 2000s, the municipality activated a website with thematic maps, property use, consistency, constraints, and existing planning tools.

Even in this latter case, the use of information systems allows us to switch from the simple representation of territory acquisition, to updating and dissemination of information (Fig. 8).

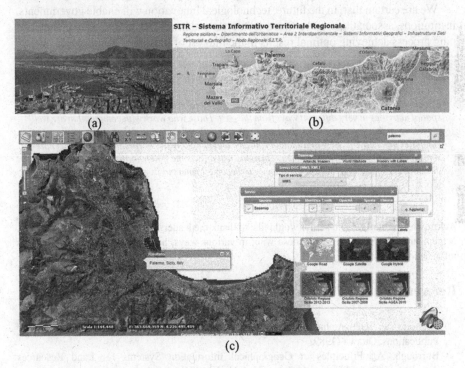

(a)   (b)

(c)

Fig. 8. Palermo - (a) panoramic view; (b and c) example of webSIT consultation.

4 Conclusions

From the analyzes carried out thus far we can affirm that information systems are useful for the collection and organization of data, the review and simulation of possible evolutions of the territory, the visualization and creation of maps, the communication of planning strategies to policy makers and the public [50].

Thanks to the diffusion of the web they allow, through participatory processes, an activity of information and involvement of the private.

The citizen, by signing into websites, can freely operate on planning instruments and address the development choices of the city and territory.

They represent, therefore, a trait d' union able to support the different phases of the plan. Unfortunately, in our country, territorial information systems are considered only as useful tools for creating databases, and their support to planning is still evolving [51–54].

We are at an early stage, often the local authorities use the territorial information systems to computerize their work, speed up administrative practices, to make visible the paper files that, if not digitized, could go missing [55].

We are certain that, in the future, technological innovation will enable governments, institutions, associations, and citizens to interact and intervene immediately in the planning process achieving optimal results in the interest of the entire community.

"The future of the city will be largely concerned with the use of new methods of analysis, modeling and design which are informed by computers. There is an urgent need to increase in our debate in the light of the way cities themselves are changing, the way activities are decentralizing in both time and space and the way new network forms are dispersing and concentrating spatial activities in very different ways from the past. Those who work with computation are well placed to make important contributions to this broader debate for the use of new forms of computer and network, new digital data sources, and new software across the net in itself represents the way the city is changing. New insights will only come if new forms of computation are developed, requiring all who study the city to become immersed in its intrinsic computability" [56, 57].

Acknowledgements. The author would like to thank the leaders of the municipalities of Genoa, Naples, and Palermo along with those who, in various ways, have collaborated to finding this information.

References

1. Aronoff, S.: Geographic Information Systems: a Management Perspective. WDL Publications, Ottawa (1989)
2. Burrough, A.: Principles of Geographical Information Systems for Land Resources Assessment. Oxford University Press, New York (1986)
3. Cortellessa, C.M.: Breve introduzione al GIS. Supplemento a Mondo Autocad 5 (1995)
4. Cowen, D.J.: Gis versus CAD versus DBMS: What are the Difference? PERS **54**, 1551–1554 (1988)
5. Camerata, F., De Marco, G., Magaudda, S., Ombuen, S., Pellegrino, G.: La pianificazione territoriale in Europa: una proposta di modello dati per il tema land use di INSPIRE. In: ASITA, 14° Conferenza nazionale ASITA, Brescia, 9–12 Novembre (2010)

6. Murgante, B.: Smart Cities and City Sensing, prefazione in City Sensing. Approcci, metodi e tecnologie innovative per la Città Intelligente, di G. Borga, FrancoAngeli (2013)
7. Laurini, R., Thompson, D.: Fundamentals of Spatial Information Systems. A.P.I.C. Series, No 37. Academic Press (1992)
8. Jogan, I., Patassini, D.: Il dibattito nell'urbanistica italiana sui GIS tra nuove prospettive e vecchi malintesi. archivio di studi urbani e regionali 67, p. 142 (2000)
9. Camerata, F., Mildorf, T., Ombuen, S., Vico, F.: Data interoperability for spatial planning: a tentative common description of European datasets concerning land use, in UDMS. In: Zlatanova, S., Ledoux, H., Fendel, E., Rumor, M. (eds.) Proceedings of the 28th Urban Data Management Symposium, Delft, 28–30 settembre 2011. CRC Press, Taylor & Francis Group, London (2012)
10. Eremitaggio, A.M., Procaccini, P., Ombuen, S., Vico, F., Zanetti, N.: Plan4all: l'armonizzazione dei dati per la pianificazione territoriale in accordo con INSPIRE. In: ASITA, 14° Conferenza Nazionale ASITA, Brescia, 9–12 Novembre (2010)
11. Catronuovo, D.: Introduzione ai sistemi informativi territoriali 129, Settembre 2011. www.agraria.org
12. Batty, M.: The computable city. In: Fourth International Conference on Computers in Urban Planning and Urban Management, Melbourne, Australia, 11–14 July 1995
13. Mildorf, T., Ombuen, S., Vico, F.: Plan4all: data interoperability for spatial planning. In: AESOP, 24th Annual Conference, Finland, 7–10 July 2010
14. Camuffo, A.: Il computer per il centro storico di Cittadella. In: Jatta, A., et al. (ed.) Sistemi informativi e pianificazione urbanistica Casa del Libro, Reggio Calabria (1980)
15. Craglia, M., Campagna, M.: Report on Advanced Regional Spatial Data Infrastructures in Europe (2009)
16. European Commission Joint Research Centre IES, vol. EUR 23716 EN, pp. 1–132 (2009)
17. Deplano, G.: Piano Quadro per il centro storico di Cagliari, Comune di Cagliari (1997)
18. Esposito, M.A.: HISTOCITY book. Alinea Editrice, Firenze (2000)
19. Camerata, F., De Marco, G., Magaudda, S., Ombuen, S., Pellegrino, G.: La pianificazione territoriale in Europa: una proposta di modello dati per il tema land use di INSPIRE. In: ASITA, 14° Conferenza nazionale ASITA, Brescia, 9–12 Novembre 2010
20. Camerata, F., Mildorf, T., Ombuen, S., Vico, F.: Data interoperability for spatial planning: a tentative common description of European datasets concerning land use. In: Zlatanova, S., Ledoux, H., Fendel, E., Rumor, M. (eds.) UDMS, Proceedings of the 28th Urban Data Management Symposium, Delft, 28–30 settembre 2011. CRC Press, Taylor & Francis Group, London (2012)
21. Eremitaggio, A.M., Procaccini, P., Ombuen, S., Vico, F., Zanetti, N.: Plan4all: l'armonizzazione dei dati per la pianificazione territoriale in accordo con INSPIRE. In: ASITA, 14° Conferenza Nazionale ASITA, Brescia, 9–12 Novembre 2010
22. Mildorf, T., Ombuen, S., Vico, F.: Plan4all: data interoperability for spatial planning, in AESOP. In: 24th Annual Conference, Finland, 7–10 July 2010
23. Iannuzzi, Y., Campagna, M.: SDI development and spatial planning in Sardinia. In: Informatica e Pianificazione Urbana e Territoriale, Casa Editrice Libria, Melfi (2010)
24. Iannuzzi, Y.: Spatial Data Infrastructure e geographic information a supporto dei processi di decisione nella pianificazione territoriale. In: La Pianificazione Urbanistica partecipativa nella società dell'informazione Deplano G., Edicom Edizioni, Montefalcone, Gorizia (2009)
25. Goodchild, M.F.: Citizens as Voluntary Sensors: Spatial Data Infrastructure in the World of Web 2.0 (2007)
26. Assini, N.: Pianificazione urbanistica e governo del territorio, cedam, Padova (2000)

222   T. Cilona

27. Giangrande, A., Mortola, E.: Progettazione e uso di una base di dati per il centro storico di Pietrasanta (1980)
28. Jatta, A., et Al.: In Sistemi informativi e pianificazione urbanistica (a cura di) Casa del Libro, Reggio Calabria (2012)
29. Lago, R., Vicario, A., Massari, R.: WebSIT: a netwrok for the distribution of territorial data on the province of Padua. In: Esposito M.A. (a cura di) HISTOCITY book, Aliena Editrice, Firenze (2000)
30. Peng, Z.R., Ming-Hsiang, T.: Internet GIS: Distributed Geographic Information Services for the Internet and wireless network. Wiley, Hoboken (2003)
31. Iannuzzi, Y., Campagna, M.: Built environment and geospatial technologies: experiences in Sardinia, Università degli Studi di Cagliari, DICAAR, Disegnare con numero speciale DoCo 2012 – Documentazione e Conservazione del Patrimonio Architettonico ed Urbano
32. GIS Development Guide. Local Government Technology Services State Archives And Records Administration Albany, New York (1999)
33. Marescotti, L.: I geographical information System, l'informatica e la pubblica amministrazione. Urbanistica Informazioni n **127**, 54–64 (1993)
34. Ombuen, S.: Informazione geografica digitale e risorse per il governo del territorio (2011). http://www.agenziaentrate.gov.it/wps/content/Nsilib/Nsi/Documentazione/Archivio/Agenzia+comunica/Prodotti+editoriali/Territorio+Italia/Archivio+Territorio+Italia+English+version/Territorio_Italia_n_1_2011_en/
35. Albano, A., Ghelli, G., Orsini, R.: Basi di dati relazionali e a oggetti. Zanichelli (1997)
36. Spaccapietra, S.: Modeling Spatial Data in the MADS Conceptual Model (1998)
37. Zimanyi, et al.: Proceedings of the International Symposium on Spatial Data Handling, SDH 98, Vancouver, Canada (1998)
38. Zeiler, M.: Modeling Our World. In: The ESRI Guide to Geodatabase Design. ESRI Press (1999)
39. Biallo, G.: I sistemi informativi geografici per la pianificazione e il governo del territorio, Urbanistica, 115, pp. 178–181 (2000)
40. Bobbio, R.: Nuovi piani e città antica, il PRG di Genova per il centro urbano. Urbanistica Informazioni **160**, 30 (1998)
41. Bobbio, R.: Rifare il pianod i Genova. Urbanistica Informazioni **192**, 90–92 (2003)
42. Bonora, F.: Genova aspettative e realtà ul litorale della città vecchia. Urbanistica Informazioni **178**, 55–56 (2001)
43. http://civis.comune.genova.it/startpage.htm
44. Campos Venuti, G.: Napoli e l'urbanistica riformista. Urbanistica **109**, 120–122 (1997)
45. Cocchia, C.: Relazione al PRG di Napoli. Urbanistica **15**, 100–109 (1995)
46. Comune di Napoli. Variante di salvaguardia al PRG, Dipartimento di pianificazione urbanistica di Napoli (2004)
47. Carrino, A., Donatini, F., Avolio, G., Fusco, G., Speranza, D.: Progetto DREAM, Rapporto finale della Convenzione di Ricerca DPGI Napoli – ENEL Produzione & Ricerca Pisa Maggio (2002)
48. Brancaccio, G.: Geografia, Cartografia e storia del Mezzogiorno, Guida, Napoli (1991)
49. Alessandro, S.: Linee Guida del Piano Territoriale Paesistico Regionale e il supporto del sistema informativo nella pianificazione territoriale in Sicilia. MondoGis **10**, 23–27 (1998)
50. Regione Siciliana Assessorato Territorio ed Ambiente. Servizio cartografico e informativo. www.artasicilia.net, www.cartosicilia.it
51. Bonnes, M.: Ambiente urbano, qualità e innovazione tecnologica, UNESCO, MAB 11, Italia, rapporto di ricerca (1993)

52. Cilona, T.: Future cities urban transformation and sustainable development. In: Gervasi, O., Murgante, B., Misra, S., Rocha, A.M.A.C., Torre, C., Taniar, D., Apduhan, Bernady O., Stankova, E., Wang, S. (eds.) ICCSA 2016. LNCS, vol. 9788, pp. 183–197. Springer, Cham (2016). doi:10.1007/978-3-319-42111-7_15

53. Biallo, G.: Il Gis e la pubblica amministrazione. MondoGis **10**, 9–10 (1998)

54. Biallo, G., Onorati, G., Massari, M.: Il Gis nei comuni italiani, risultati del sondaggio di Mondo Gis, prima parte. MondoGis **24**, 14–17 (2001)

55. Cilona, T.: Sustainability, territorial resources and social capital. Int. J. Sustainable Development Plann. **12**(4), 819–828 (2017). Encouraging a unified approach to achieve sustainability. SPECIAL ISSUE - The Sustainable City. WIT PRESS, Ashurst Lodge, Southampton, UK

56. Batty, M., Longley, P.: Fractal Cities: A Geometry of Form and Function. Academic Press, London and San Diego (1994)

57. Batty, M., Xie, Y.: Urban growth paths, unpublished paper, National Center for Geographic Information and Analysis, State University of New York at Buffalo, Buffalo, NY (1994)

Jewish Communities in Pre-war Central Poland as an Example of a Self-organising Society

Małgorzata Hanzl[✉]

Institute of Architecture and Town Planning, Lodz University of Technology,
Al. Politechniki 6A, 90-240 Lodz, Poland
mhanzl@p.lodz.pl

Abstract. The current paper presents the experience of mapping pre-war Jewish communities in pre-war central Poland. While going through a period of intensive social and cultural transformations these communities may be considered a proto-type of contemporary complex societies. The initial analytical framework, provided thanks to the GIS database and concatenation of attributes coming from various sources, makes some initial observations and conclusions possible. It confirms the thesis that Jewish communities in pre-war Poland may be considered an example of a self-organising society, one which could be considered a proto-type of contemporary postmodern cultural complexity. The current study provides the initial framework to map the morphology and spatial distribution of the complexity of everyday culture of use of space proper to this extremely diverse group.

Keywords: GIS · Self-organisation · Complexity

1 Introduction

A need for a more precise definition of the basic rules underpinning the form of urban settings may become satisfied when looking at past societies. This task calls for collab-orative approach extending beyond the scope of one single discipline, such as urban design. While the fragmentation and specialisation of science as well as historically established divisions result in huge discrepancies in the terminology and language used by researchers from various backgrounds, Lefebvre's call for a single discipline of urban science [1] requires a more heuristic approach and a more efficient use of the knowledge from the various disciplines. Some of these problems, which exist especially on the margins of social and technical fields, have already been addressed in the field of complexity science [2]. To begin with, the understanding of real life processes requires visualisation of distribution of actual groups of people. This first step provides frame-work for further systemic approach towards picturing the living conditions, describing of urban settings, and looking for understanding of meanings and actual cultures reflected in the forms of urban realm.

The current paper, structured around the case study of pre-war Jewish communities in central Poland, presents a method to elaborate the morphological typology of Jewish settlements. An attempt at typology shall enable an understanding of the processes which

© Springer International Publishing AG 2017
O. Gervasi et al. (Eds.): ICCSA 2017, Part III, LNCS 10406, pp. 224–238, 2017.
DOI: 10.1007/978-3-319-62398-6_16

influenced the forms of urban settings inhabited by this group. After this introduction, a theory of complex systems is briefly explained, with emphasis on context as an element affecting individual choices, and thus self-organisation processes. The case study follows, featuring a concise presentation of social diversity in the studied group. The method of analysis, key from the point of view of the conference topic, explained along with a brief summary of results, has made it possible to elaborate on the future development of the method.

2   The Theories of Complex Systems

The term complex systems defines systems which are both complex, which equals the inability to describe the causal relations between parts of a system on the one hand, and the emerging nature of phenomena associated with their functioning on the other, and open, so related to the surrounding environment [2]. Self-organisation, understood as the ability of a system to self-organise its internal structure [3, p. 49], is one of the basic features of complex systems. Self-organisation is explained by means of such theories as synergetics [4, 5], which deals with mutual relations of parts of a system and its functioning as a whole, and dissipative structures theory [6], which, applied to socioeconomic and particularly urban themes, focuses on fluctuations of people, values and information in cities [2].

While the theories of self-organisation of cities were elaborated in the second half of the twentieth century, the phenomena which they describe started even earlier. Complexity, as Portugali [3, p. 315] asserts, defines the phenomena which emerged along with the dissolution of high context, traditional cultures. Long established sets of norms, practices and meanings for a given community transformed and new ones emerged.

The relations between physical settings and the communities living there dispersed. The order of space, which according to Alexander [7] and Hanzl [8, 9] means the cultural framework which structures both human behaviour and the physical settings, has been changing in tandem. Although during this process of transformation from traditional, high context societies to low context ones it loses some of its former meaning, still the architectural and urban environment enables the screening and filtering of sensory data, which is the way information is conveyed [10, p. 2]. A proper understanding of the concept of the meaning of urban settings [11] is essential here because, as Haken [12], after [2] states, the key feature in how complex systems 'self-organize', is that they 'interpret', the information that comes from the environment. It also needs highlighting that an important part of the internal structure of human settlements results from the layout of pathways, as has been described in the widely recognised theory of Space Syntax by Hillier and Hanson [13].

Some light may be cast on the above issues thanks to the analysis of environments where contemporary complex societies started. The structures left behind when juxtaposed with their cultural background lets us read the past activities and social relations. The forms of urban environments, approached through culture related lenses, may lead to an understanding of the processes which led to the emergence of contemporary multicultural societies. The comprehension of the way multicultural communities developed and lived together through longer spans of time may help while creating new, more open environments which cater to the actual needs of citizens, with regard to their culture related requirements.

3 Case Study

The current paper presents the experience of mapping pre-war Jewish communities in towns and villages of Mazovian and Lodz voivodeships in central Poland, which went through a period of intensive transformations in the pre-war period. The focus on a group who lived surrounded by other cultures, gives the opportunity to follow their spatial foot-prints left in physical settings. The analysis is preceded by an in-depth study of the cultural habits in a diachronic approach [9]. Jewish communities in central Poland in the period directly preceding the Second World War consisted of several groups of varied levels of acculturation, system of values, adjustment to religious beliefs and political views. The overall picture characterised with complexity and represented what we understand as a contemporary heterogeneous society.

3.1 Social Structure Versus Urbanisation Processes

Jews, who made up a large share of the population, on the one hand preserved their own culture, on the other mixed with Polish and German citizens. Along with the acculturation processes, which progressed with time, Jewish daily lives also changed, together with the urban settings in which they lived. People, enticed by the emerging opportunities, tried to improve their living conditions or simply began looking for any kind of income. The period of the noble economy before the partitions of Poland in the end of the 18th century found many Jews still inhabiting small villages and manor houses, many still working as leaseholders, even if no longer dealing with propination. This situation continued due to the conservative nature of orthodox groups, and in some places lasted with only little changes until pre-war times. While in small villages the picture was quite clear and showed a traditional community with a few more educated representatives of intelligentsia, the growth of the population and the range of available occupations, lifestyles and political preferences, religious and social groups, resulted in a much more complex mosaic.

The larger cities, including Warsaw and Lodz, were surrounded with satellite cities and towns, while small - shtetls - villages continued their pace of life and, when it comes to the Jews living there, their traditional, religion-based culture. Many towns, starting from the period of the Kingdom of Poland, went through intensive development as newly established administrative centres. Many others developed as industrial centres, mainly, but not exclusively, for the textile industry. In many towns, new districts were developed, both by public authorities and by private owners and other, mostly private, towns were started from scratch.

The situation of development during the industrial era, overlapped with that of merchant urbanisation (terminology after [1, 2, p. 312]). Most of these urban centres, especially those hosting markets, accommodated large groups of Jews, their core population dealing with such crafts as tailoring, dressmaking, shoe-making, etc. Some towns had a longer or shorter tradition of Jewish settling, with various conditions for the accommodation of Jews. For instance, many towns formerly had the privilege, *non tolerandis judeorum*, which forced Jews to settle in the private domains of rich nobles. In other settlements, the Jewish presence was, until 1862, limited to specially established zones. Next to the commerce which developed in all urban conditions, the Jewish religious centres drew many, with the important Chasidic courts serving as major attractors. The Jewish faith and its requirements also encouraged specialised services, for instance the making of prayer shawls in Maków Mazowiecki. The acculturation processes of the interwar period further added to this mosaic, for instance the popularity of medicine as a profession was picked up by Jewish intelligentsia, leading to the development of towns which served as health resorts offering sophisticated and specialised health services. New forms of urban structures developed, along with the culture of spending holidays in the countryside.

4   Thesis

As a result of its historic development, each single town and each single Jewish community can be characterised with its own specific set of features [14, p. 195], which played a defined role in the urbanisation system. Each had its idiosyncrasy, which, in order to be understood, must be mapped spatially and with regard to time axis. While there is no one single approach to present all cases, still morphological typology needs to be developed to enhance understanding.

In spatial, social and cultural pluralism, the questions of human intentionality and socio-spatial emergence remain central to social theory [3, p. 142]. The correlation between individual preferences, values and intentions, and actual behaviour and actions, is subject to Portugali's theory of self-organisation [3]. Compared to Gidden's structuralism, which focuses on society and groups, the point of departure for Portugali [3] are individuals and their personal choices. The above considerations are in line with the empirical studies of the relations between Jews and Poles, especially in large cities, where more complex socio-cultural processes could occur. This is one of the possible paths for the further development of this research.

The current paper proposes a thesis that Jewish communities in pre-war Poland represented an example of a self-organising society, one which could be considered a prototype of contemporary postmodern cultural complexity. The mapping of this complexity is a challenge, a method for which is addressed in the current study. While challenging, an attempt at creating an image of actual distribution of Jewish citizens and examination of their social profile, gives a chance to establish a framework for further research on culture based analyses of morphological features of urban settings, in a way using the method defined by the famous study of London by Booth [15].

5 Method

The understanding of the relations between the patterns of everyday life and the social habits of the communities needs contemporary analytical tools. The complexity of patterns has been approached with the usage of a hierarchy of typologies. Three basic levels were used as a starting point for modelling - that of region (Fig. 1), that of town, and that of neighbourhood. The analysis led to the pinpointing of certain cases which although considered Jewish because of the high population share, at the same time represented different classes and varied significantly, including the way the structure could be mapped. The basic level was a single neighbourhood, with such features analysed as culture related notions of rhythms and sociometric layouts. The heuristic method of highlighting those elements of urban environments which were key for a given case have been applied. The theory, based on the anthropological concept of

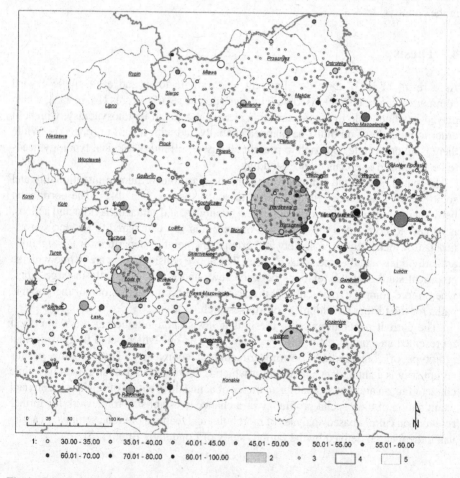

Fig. 1. Distribution of settlements with over 50 Jews where they provided for 30 and more percent of the total population

meaning and the quest for its reflection in spatial order as a feature attributed to physical forms of urban structures, supported the classification and understanding.

5.1 Database

While the making of the complete dataset needs a bottom-up approach with individual case studies, the general framework may already be defined, with an assumption however that the classification may be further extended. In order to achieve comprehensive results which could fully render the reality, the database needs to be scalable. The combination of values from several fields would give a matrix, determining the type of individual record. Concatenation of attributes should be done separately for various time periods.

The current study, departing from a more heuristic approach, starts by establishing a clear method of classification of lifestyles and values versus choice of living places. The requirement to render the actual complexity of the typology means avoiding any sort of predefined, closed and hierarchical structure. Instead, what we need is a scalable system of description which may accommodate both new categories - fields - and new record values, as necessary. Some historical documents have a predefined structure, which should be followed unaltered to convey its historical testimony, e.g., classification of settlements based on results of the 1921 census [16]. While the number of such comprehensive and closed documents is limited, they may be used as initial characteristics, giving the general picture and introducing background organisation. Another basic source of knowledge is statistics, which contains mainly quantitative data. For the sake of the final assessment, typology thresholds need to be introduced, referring to the quantities of Jewish populations, their percentage and the size of towns or villages.

The initial study covering the available statistical data may not only serve as a framework for further development but also reveals an image which may be used as a source of valuable insights into the dynamics of Jewish life in central Poland. The ArcGIS 10.1 has been used as a platform for mapping, with shapefiles created describing the situation at a few historical moments based on the data available. The shapefiles were afterwards combined in order to follow the processes of the emergence/collapse of Jewish communities. While the data coming from the origins of Jewish presence in Poland is fragmentary and refers to the established kahals only, the most recent available statistics, coming from 1921, contain exact numbers of Jewish inhabitants, down to a single person. This gives a very detailed picture of urban dynamics at this moment. Later census data of 1931 has not been published in a form enabling the analysis of population dynamics.

5.2 Data Sources

The statistical data and typology of urban centres were juxtaposed with the available knowledge on new industrial and administrative towns and districts started in the region in the 19th and 20th century, including the Jewish population. Here many sources were used, including databases held by: Polin Museum in Warsaw: www.shtetl.org.pl, YIVO Institute in New York, Jewish Gen and others, as well as available research on the development of industry and urbanisation, both during the period of the Kingdom of Poland and the interwar period.

Studies on individual towns and villages were also consulted, as well as numerous historical elaborations referring to the Jewish past in Poland. The full bibliography goes beyond the volume of the current paper and is presented in a book containing the final results of the current research (in press).

Chosen features included in the current set of attributes are listed in Table 1, along with a preliminary set of values. The final list is yet to be elaborated or, more likely, will be left open for possible extension. As a result, an initial framework typology of urban centres of various scales has been obtained, which shall allow for a more profound understanding and description of Jewish urban life in Poland in the period before World War II.

Table 1. Features included in the database set of attributes

Field	1765	1827	1921
Name	Name	Name	Name
Current name	Name	Name	Name
Population	–	Quantity	Quantity
Jewish pop.	Value: < 2000, > 2000	Quantity	Quantity
Share	–	%	%
Fairs/year	–	Quantity	–
Markets/week	–	Quantity	–
Masonry buildings	–	Quantity	Quantity
Wooden buildings	–	Quantity	Quantity
Buildings	–	Quantity	Quantity
Voivodeship	Name	Name	Name
Property	Value: n, k, ch	Value: p, r, ch	–
Type	–	–	Value – Table 2
Community board/ kehilla	All	All	yes/not
Bund	–	–	yes/not
Hasidic community	–	yes/not	yes/not
Number of dependent shtibles	–	–	Quantity
Administrative centre	–	yes/not	Value: capital, curcuit, voivod.
Industry	–	Type: t, m, …	Type: t, m, …
Notes	Text	Text	Text

6 Results

While the traditional society offered a livelihood in a highly defined and hierarchical structure, starting with the abolishment of the noble economy and along with the increasing industrialisation, the former stability was lost. Deprived of this economic base, with the changing conditions of local communities no longer providing sufficient support for their poor, Jewish masses were forced to look after themselves. Population growth and the shrinking market for their services in locations they had lived so far, together with the opportunities which opened up thanks to the development of industry and the growth of new administrative centres, forced crucial changes in Jewish society. This was the situation when, with the progressing development of secular education, and, as a consequence, individualism, more and more actors started planning and re-planning their individual activities, looking for new routines. For the Jewish population, accustomed to adjusting to the decisions of governing bodies, in the period of transition from a high context culture to a low context one again easily adjusted, however this time based more on individual and family decisions than that of community.

The model defined by Portugali [3, p. 243] as a new order-parameter plan applies to the current case study. With the constant migrations and adaptations to the situation of the already established or newly-formed urban centres being a typical reality for Jewish citizens in pre-war Poland. Both scenarios which Portugali distinguishes apply here: Jews became enslaved in the system of norms which ruled in the place before their arrival, and they affected the new reality, adjusting it to their needs and system of rules and values appropriate to their own culture. We may also establish a time-scale, as some larger and shorter processes coexisted in the system. Cities, for instance, which had served as primary or secondary administrative centres for years, were permanent magnets for Jewish communities, who had lived there since the Middle Ages. These processes provided the background for the much speedier development of industrial towns, some booming then declining very rapidly, others observing a more stable devel-opment, or, like Lodz, growing into a metropolis. Against the backdrop of economic activities, individual decisions were made, following individual preferences and systems of values, as well as the outset preconditions, such as economic capacities. We may presume that there was opposition between the highly centralised hierarchical and, to a large extent, oppressive nationalist practices of planning, and *"the highly distributed, diffused and decentralised urban tradition"* [3, p. 247].

The idea of self-organisation is crucial as it shifts the understanding of agency. In a historical sense, it has been up to now recognised that a society, especially the Jewish society in pre-war Poland, had very little influence on the actual appearance of cities, or at least it was hard to define. Looking at the same historical facts from the perspective of self-organisation, we start to recognise their role in the urbanisation process. As particularly mobile citizens, they significantly altered the dynamics of urban growth. Performing various professional activities, they undeniably influenced local economies. They also influenced the form of dwellings and tenements, which, originally universal and adaptable, had to now accommodate Jewish families, with their specific habits. Among the neighbourhoods they picked to live in, there were linear structures, more concentrated ones, and even those which adopted much more contemporary models of dispersed urbanisation. In certain settlements, differing models developed one next to another, representing different cultures of the usage of space.

6.1 The Regional Level

The demographic dynamics are comparatively high for the Jewish population, yet quantitative thresholds need to be defined in order to assess their representation in the settlement network of central Poland and provide an image at a given moment. In 1921, of the total number of 345 settlements in central Poland with a Jewish population larger than 50, 70 had a Jewish population of 50 percent or more. Among the multiplicity of towns and villages in central Poland, some of them very small, others reaching up to several hundred thousand, Jews were usually present in great numbers in the more urbanised ones - in 1921, in the 70 mentioned above, 25 possessed the status of a town, 27 were urban settlements and 10 still villages, most quickly urbanising to become towns in future or suburban colonies outside larger settlements (Table 2). The quantity of settlements with over 50 Jews where they provided for 30 and more percent of the total population, reached up to 182 (Fig. 1). In the case of smaller settlements, depending on the overall Jewish population in a given region, Jews were generally equally spread, with individual groups often counting no more than 5 individuals, which may point to a single family.

Table 2. Jewish settlements larger than 50 people and providing for more than 50% of the total population [16].

Profile	Quantity	Jewish population	
	Number	People	%
Towns	25	1429–6812	50–82
Urban settlements	27	218–3809	50–97
Villages	9	57–1085	53–100
Settlement	1	139	60
Summer resort	1	1108	63
Manors	2	65–148	52–54
Colonies	5	73–270	57–100

The classification of a town's profile refers mostly to those settlements with a population larger than 50, usually hosting a Jewish kehilla - a religious community. In the case of smaller settlements, the profile was chiefly rural, with Jewish families catering to the basic needs of the surrounding communities in terms of commerce and tavern-keeping. In larger communities, there were also other basic crafts offered, traditionally tailoring and shoemaking. Additionally, in many manors, small groups of Jews resided, perhaps being current or past leaseholders (Fig. 2). The scale of this phenomena varied between counties, depending on the importance of the manor economy in general, and the role of agriculture. Nonetheless, in some counties, such as Łowicz, apart from major towns, Jews were hardly present.

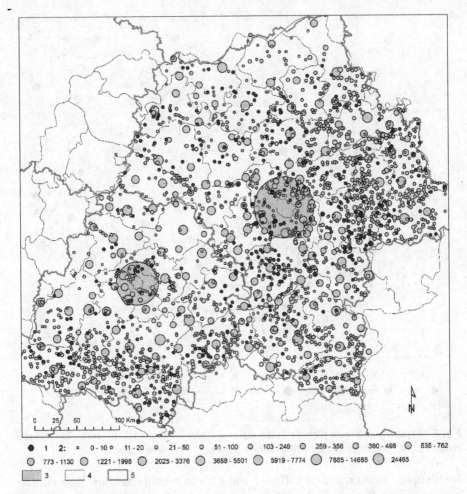

Fig. 2. Distribution of manors with Jewish dwellers. 1 – manors, 2 – regional centres: Łódź and Warsaw, 3 – contemporary voivodships borders, 4 – pre-war counties

When analysing the distribution of the Jewish population in the scale of a region (Fig. 3), two main patterns are noticeable, corresponding to the two main types of prevailing economies: agrarian and industrial. The main difference between the two patterns refers to the regularity of distribution and its internal dynamics.

6.2   The Town Level

The variety of Jewish culture in pre-war central Poland found its reflection in the variety of neighbourhoods inhabited by Jews. Each town had its own history, its own specific reasons for development and growth. The Jewish population might change over time, first growing then declining when the gentile citizens of many towns obtained the privilege non tolerandis judeorum or pogroms purged Jews out of towns. In some towns,

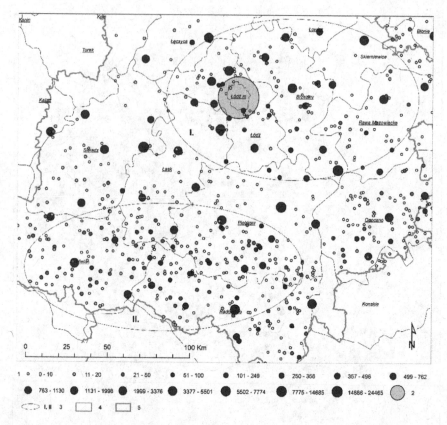

Fig. 3. Types of settlement patterns in the regional scale: I – industrial, II - rural, 2 – regional centres: Łódź, 3 – contemporary voivoideships borders, 4 – pre-war counties

Jewish zones were created or collapsed and even in certain cases lost their charters because of fires. Reasons for growth were multiple, in the era of industrial production, the most common were related to the development of specific industries, with textile or leather garment production predominating. Despite this, many towns and villages continued as before, servicing the neighbouring country with minor crafts and commerce.

There were also numerous religious centres, in most cases growing around the court of a Hasidic or Orthodox rabbi. Among centres of religious cults, the most spectacular examples of rapid growth were Ger (Góra Kalvaria), Przysucha and Aleksander (Aleksandrów Łódzki), all of them seats of famous Hasidic rabbis. Wodziński [17] analyses the impact of individual courts, measuring it with the numbers and an extent of the network of shtiblekhs – Fig. 4. Hasidism did not have a centralised structure, it consisted of several self-organised bottom-up movements which concentrated around leaders. With time, as Assaf [18] asserts since the 19th century Hasid groups used to be identified with dynasties and named after the towns and villages where they emerged. The influence of individual courts depended on the leaders' charisma and as Wodziński

[17] proves, the type of leadership. Wodziński [17] observes that the popularity of specific groups may be presented with a pareto curve, which confirms the thesis on the self-organisation character of the movement.

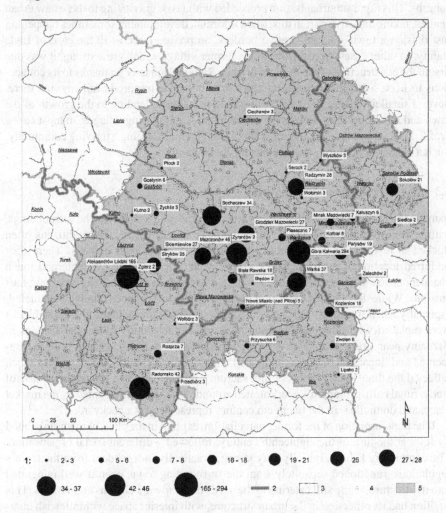

Fig. 4. The impact of individual courts, measured with the numbers of the network of shtiblekhs, after Wodziński [17]

The presence of a specialisation did not however exclude other activities, with commerce and crafts represented in all Jewish settlements. Smaller settlements maintained their unique profile and specialisation, their development leading to complexity, and the overlapping of several characteristics. These processes, accompanied by progressing acculturation and assimilation, meant districts inhabited by Jewish groups had specific features when it comes to social status, education, professional profile, religious observation, etc. This phenomenon though most explicit in the case of large metropolis, such as Warsaw and Lodz, is also observable in cities with long traditions of Jewish presence, such as Radom, Płock or Siedlce.

Rapidly developing towns and villages gained new extensions, such as colonies or suburbs. This rapid suburbanisation proceeded with Jews, gravitating to these new urban centres, taking an active part in this, often informal, development, sometimes happening just outside a town's administrative borders, on private land, as in the case of Lodz Bałuty. In other cases, like in Koluszki, a former village which grew strong, it was due first to the construction of the Warsaw Vienna Railway and later on thanks to its connections to Lodz and further to Kalisz and Poznań and the important railway hub there. Several smaller villages in its direct proximity urbanised, leading to the growth of the town and attracting Jews. Jews who settled in the neighbouring villages, in most cases, profited from the existing community facilities, together forming a thriving community. Such a cluster may or may not become an actual town.

6.3 The Neighbourhood Structure

In many towns, the districts inhabited by Jews became more urban than the surroundings, with urbanisation pressure and densities higher than elsewhere. Jewish citizens often flocked to historic medieval cores, which usually hosted local markets. There they preferred locations next to the river valley, which, firstly, were available and much cheaper due to the flood danger and, secondly, catered to their needs in terms of religious customs. While the plan of a town after the arrival of Jews remained relatively unaltered, especially when speaking of the network of public streets and squares, the urban blocks were replaced with new, masonry structures of a much more urban character, as in Brzeziny near Lodz. Moreover, the way space was used changed, from a more fragmented and linear one, into one integrated around typically Jewish focal points, which reflected the three main spheres of life: sacrum – represented by a synagogue, house of study, ritual bath, profanum – concentrated around work – and represented by the market place, and domicile – in the twentieth century represented by a backyard.

The transformation of the former parcellation, explicit in the plans of towns inhabited by Jews at the turn of the eighteenth century, followed a different social organisation. The community kehilla, initially very strong, practically independent from the town's regulations, functioned separately from the surrounding town, even if well integrated into its structure, while still catering to the needs of the town's citizens and visitors. This position had its reflection in the urban structure, with interior space within Jewish quarters seemingly unordered and uninviting to visitors, while for Jews serving as extensions of their dwellings and a space of interior circulation. The last observation confirmed by the tradition of eruvim - temporary cords distinguishing private space during Sabbath. With time this former hierarchical structure released, giving way to multiplicity of lifestyles, which were also reflected in the actual form of neighbourhoods. The features which are listed in the current paper are explained in more depth in other articles stemming from the current study [8, 9, 11, 19].

7   Conclusions and Future Research Paths

This paper provides a summary of the larger research on the most typical neighbourhoods inhabited by Jews in central Poland in the pre-war period. The initial analytical framework, provided thanks to the GIS database and concatenation of attributes coming from various sources, makes some initial observations and conclusions possible. Firstly, it confirms the thesis that Jewish communities in pre-war Poland may be considered an example of a self-organising society, one which could be considered a prototype of contemporary postmodern cultural complexity.

While the complexity of everyday culture of use of space is challenging, the current study provides the initial framework to map its morphology and spatial distribution. The data collected reveals the following features which differed between settlements and neighbourhoods:

- acculturation level and attitude towards religion,
- main professional profile of a settlement or of a neighbourhood,
- size of a community.

Additionally, characteristics changed over time, with new layers resulting from industrialisation and the development of modern administration, overlapping with the former urban centres coming from the period of merchant urbanisation [1, 3, p. 312]. The model of a new order-parameter plan [3, p. 243] entirely applies, Jewish citizens in pre-war Poland used to migrate and adjust to external conditions, either enslaved in the system of norms which ruled in the place before their arrival, or adapting it to their own needs.

An attempt at the classification of larger urban centres is given, distinguishing such types as industrial, administrative, commercial and religious ones. In the settlement network of smaller Jewish concentrations, two patterns have been noticed: a dynamic and a static one, linked to industrial and rural economies. The detailed analyses of census data in the scale of the urban region made it possible to follow the urban growth processes.

Further research aims at more in-depth illustration of the above characteristics, with the analyses of individual case studies. The data base framework may be further completed and extended in a bottom-up way, thanks to its open structure. Another challenge may be the examination of the spatial, social and cultural pluralism through the questions of human intentionality and socio-spatial emergence with relation to the meaning conveyed by the form of the urban settings.

Acknowledgements. The current study is a part of the research project financed by The National Science Centre of Poland UMO-2011/03/D/HS3/01630, entitled: "Morphological analysis of urban structures – the cultural approach. Case studies of Jewish communities in the chosen settlements of Lodz and Masovian voivodeships". Part of the methodological research was performed in SENSEable City Laboratory, Massachusetts Institute of Technology within the framework of a Fulbright Senior Research Award.

References

1. Lefebvre, H.: The Urban Revolution. University of Minnesota Press, Minneapolis (2003)
2. Portugali, J.: Complexity theory as a link between space and place. Environ. Plan. A **38**, 647–664 (2006)
3. Portugali, J.: Self-Organization and the City. Springer, Heidelberg (2000)
4. Haken, H., Portugali, J.: A synergetic approach to the self-organisation of cities. Environ. Plan. B Plan. Des. **22**, 35–46 (1995)
5. Haken, H.: Synergetics. An Introduction. Springer, Berlin (1983)
6. Prigogine, I., Stengers, I.: Order Out of Chaos. Bantam Books, New York (1984)
7. Alexander, C., Ishikawa, S., Silverstein, M.: Pattern Language. Oxford University Press, New York (1977)
8. Hanzl, M.: Towards understanding the complexity of urban culture - a case study of jewish communities in pre-war central Poland. In: Herneoja, A., Österlund, T., Markkanen, P. (eds.) Complexity & Simplicity - Proceedings of the 34th eCAADe Conference – Volume 2, pp. 49–58. University of Oulu, Oulu (2016)
9. Hanzl, M.: Morphological analysis of urban structures - the cultural approach. Case studies of Jewish communities in Lodz and Mazovian voivodeships. Wydawnictwo Politechniki Łódzkiej, Lodz (in press)
10. Hall, E.T.: Hidden Dimension. Doubleday, Garden City (1966)
11. Hanzl, M.: The meaning of public spaces. In: Bartolo, H., Bartolo, P.J.D.S., Alves, N.M.F., Mateus, A.J., Almeida, H.A. (eds.) Green Design, Materials and Manufacturing Processes, pp. 39–44. Taylor & Francis, London (2013)
12. Haken, H.: Information and Self-Organization. A Macroscopic Approach to Complex Systems. Springer, Heidelberg (2000)
13. Hillier, B., Hanson, J.: The Social Logic of Space. Cambridge University Press, Cambridge (2003)
14. Wodziński, M.: Żydzi w okresie zaborów. In: Sienkiewicz, W. (ed.) Atlas Historii Żydów Polskich, pp. 155–246. Demart SA, Warsaw (2010)
15. Booth, Ch.: On the City: Physical Pattern and Social Structure. Selected Writings. The University of Chicago Press, Chicago, London (1967)
16. Główny Urząd Statystyczny Rzeczypospolitej Polskiej, Skorowidz miejscowości Rzeczypospolitej Polskiej opracowany na podstawie wyników Pierwszego Powszechnego Spisu Ludności z dn. 30 września 1921 r. i innych źródeł urzędowych (1925)
17. Wodziński, M.: Space and spirit: on boundaries, hierarchies and leadership in Hasidism. J. Hist. Geogr. **53**, 63–74 (2016)
18. Assaf, D.: Chasydyzm: zarys historii. In: Galas, M. (ed.) Światło i słońce. Studia z dziejów chasydyzmu, pp. 11–38. Austeria, Kraków (2006)
19. Hanzl, M.: Culture as a determinant of city form - the case of the former jewish district in Lodz. In: Bovati, M., Caja, M., Floridi, G., Landsberger, M. (eds.) Cities in Transformation Research & Design: Ideas, Methods, Techniques, Tools, Case Studies, pp. 625–634. Politecnico di Milano/eAAe/ARCC, Milano (2014)

The *Time Machine*. Cultural Heritage and the Geo-Referenced Storytelling of Urban Historical Metamorphose

Letizia Bollini[(✉)] and Daniele Begotti

Department of Psychology, University of Milano-Bicocca,
Piazza dell'Ateneo Nuovo 1, 20126 Milan, Italy
letizia.bollini@unimib.it

Abstract. The digital revolution is changing the space and the concept of cultural heritage. Furthermore, mobile devices – thanks to geolocalization, augmented/ virtual reality, ubiquitous and multimodal interactions – transform the cultural storytelling in a pervasive and ongoing experience crossing seamlessly the boundaries between places of preservation and the historical remains spread in a territory. The paper proposes a design experience which explores the historical layering and evolution of the city of Milano through an interactive time machine. The cultural key chosen to read the historical development is the Manzoni's novel The Betrothed. According to the literary interpretation, three key periods have been explored along with the evolution of the urban representation. The historical period of the novel (XVII century) corresponding to the map drawn by Cartaro in 1581. Milan at the time of the author (1785–1873) before the Beruto's master plan that brought down the Spanish walls. And the contemporary city, where the novel itineraries are still recognizable. The time machine – the core features of the app PS 3.0 – is a dynamic way to visualize and experience the geo-referenced point of interests of the cultural paths that allow people to discover past in the present in a spatially-situated interaction.

1 Cultural Storytelling: A Way to the Historical Genius-Loci

Digitization, interactive museums, multimodal exhibitions, and virtual archives are one of the most valuable tools to preserve and spread the knowledge of the past. Furthermore, the mobile revolution is fostering the boundaries between the places pointed at maintaining cultural heritage and the environment daily lived by people, where vestiges of the past are still deeply embedded.

According to the ongoing evolution of the culture and practices of the preservation of cultural heritage, the new awareness in the historical and artistic field looks at two different phenomena. On one hand, people are more involved and engaged as active participants in the dissemination of culture. Not only in the technical field, where – since the revolution introduced by the Exploratorium in San Francisco (1969–2013) the concept of learning-by-doing has been shortly embraced as a way to spread the scientific culture by making it accessible, but also in the humanities. As proposed in the book the

© Springer International Publishing AG 2017
O. Gervasi et al. (Eds.): ICCSA 2017, Part III, LNCS 10406, pp. 239–251, 2017.
DOI: 10.1007/978-3-319-62398-6_17

Participatory Museum [1] and the blog Museum 2.0 [2] by Nina Simon, visitors' participation is one of the emerging issues in museum curation. The era of 2.0 culture can involve the community members and visitors to make cultural institutions more dynamic, relevant, essential places. One the other hand, digital communication technologies are breaking the boundaries of museums, archives, and Wunderkammers. The phenomenon has two sides. In a first place Internet, the web and mobile applications make information accessible everywhere, in every time, or – better to say: "right thing at the right place at the right time" as underlined by Levin [3] in a digital cross-device, always-connected ecosystem. People can retrieve information both if they are planning a visit (in a previous time), and after an exhibition already finished, even during the experience just using a smartphone, a tablet or other connected devices.

But technologies are also used to improve the exhibitions themselves, giving deeper, contextual information, as hands-on to facilitate the tour or be what has to be seen. In this last case, the virtual presence of historical or artistic heritage brings the ephemeral, lost, or immaterial *document* alive to the visitors' senses and cognitive experience: "The communicative act which is therefore performed expects to be a substitute for, or equivalent to, the fruition of art, of science, of the memory of the ephemeral aspect of the exhibition of the personal experience, whilst mediated by the spectator/user and his/her ability to relate to the material and emotional aspects of memory, aesthetics and knowledge. The great revolution introduced by digital technology is instead the ability to open up places and archives to collective, massive dimensions, and to the sharing of knowledge itself. Making knowledge coplanar, diachronic and distributed, beyond the four dimensions in a sort of new space-time relativity." [4].

1.1 En Plain Air Museums

Cultural heritage, however, is not limited to places deputized to their preservation, but also a diffuse presence in our everyday environment. Areas, where historical events took places, building where history is layered in their functional and architectural evolution, are heritage in themselves, worth to be known and explored. From this consideration, a cultural movement has started in the late 1980' aimed to make the environment itself a museum. Is the *open air museum* discussed by Rentzhog [5] as a "visionary idea".

A territory as Italy, where historical vestiges are long and deeply grounded in the space and national evolution from Romans to contemporary, is an open air museum in itself that needs to be told. In fact, the Unesco has estimated that Italy has the higher concentration of all the cultural and natural sites of the whole world: "As of 2016, Italy has a total of 51 inscribed properties, making it the state party with the most World Heritage Sites, followed by China with 50" [6]. The challenge is rather to make all this cultural information available to people, tourists, and citizens that live and experience this space to improve their knowledge and awareness.

For this pour pose digital technologies such as mobile, smartphones, Internet of Things, Augmented and Virtual reality could provide excellent support to spread and promote the cultural dissemination as proposed already in 2010 by Proctor in *The museum is mobile: cross-platform content design for audiences on the go* [7] at the annual conference *Museums and the Web*.

1.2 Situated Interactions

The mobile and proximity technologies enable a *context-aware interactions*: as described by Dey: "Context is any information that can be used to characterize the situation of an entity. An entity is a person, place, or object that is considered relevant to the interaction between a user and an application, including the user and applications themselves" [8]. A further definition of the relationship between the space ant the interaction with users mediated by technologies and mediated by the spatial experience and the difference between context and – simply – location, is presented by Schmidt et al. [9] suggesting that context is made from human factors and physical landscape intended as the system of places, environmental conditions and infrastructures (for a wider discussion of the concept of context-aware interactions see the work presented by the author at the ICCSA Conference in 2016 [10] and the survey conducted in 2000 by Chen and Kotz [11]). The context-aware approach, however, seems to be unbalanced in favor of a position more focused on the *hard* part – technology and its potentiality – rather on the *soft* one – the human beings and their needs, interests and motivation.

Situated interactions is a further concept that proposes and focuses in the user's perspective. In a paper proposed by Marti, Petrelli and Pucci the idea has been applied and tested in a project in the field of art in which the researches "describes metaphors and design strategies used to conceive and develop a hand-held, location-aware tourist guide that delivers information related to the surrounding space mainly by reacting to the physical movements of the visitors. The guide is designed to minimise the boundary between the physical space and the related information through a number of situated and contextual-aware interaction mechanisms" [12].

1.3 Human and Social Centered Design

Finally, moving from the places deputized to preserve cultural heritage to a living environment implies to face the people's experience not only to an individual but also to a social scale.

The everyday experience of residents, city users, tourist, students, and commuters is a way to culturally create, superimpose, and interpret the shared symbols, the common values or the historical totem. According to Lynch's work [13] about the construction of the social image of the city, some researchers have investigated the construction processes of the space identities in a changing and dynamic evolution caused by the presence, migrations, re-working of people under individual, social and historical circumstances [14]. In particular, the anthropologist Barbara Bender has explored the relationship between time and space in the identity construction of a landscape The temporal variable becomes the primary driver of the work-in-progress process: "Landscapes are created out of people's understanding and engagement with the world around them. They are always in process of being shaped and reshaped. Being of the moment and in process, they are always temporal. They are not a record but a recording, and this recording is much more than a reflection of human agency and action; it is *creative* of them. Landscapes provoke memory, facilitate (or impede) action. Nor are they *a* recording, for they are always polyvalent and multivocal. There is a historicity and spatiality to people's engagement with the world around them." [15].

2   The Betrothed 2.0: Telling History Through Cartography

According to the below mentioned on-going phenomena in the field of cultural heritage, ICT applied to spatial, situated and time interactions, and the social construction of the space identity, both physical and symbolic, the paper proposes a research experience in which this aspects have been investigated, projected and tested to define a conceptual and design framework in the field.

The Betrothed 2.0 mobile app was firstly presented at ICCSA 2013 [16]. It's a pilot of a smartphone geo-based application aimed to tell the story of the city of Milan in its historical evolution. The concept on which the PS2 is based uses a narrative escamotage to introduce people – both that already know the city or who've never been there – to a different perception of the urban space and its evolution.

The app tells the story through the eyes of one of the most famous Italian writers Alessandro Manzoni, who lived in the XIX century. He wrote *The Promessi Sposi* (*The Betrothed*) and set it in XVII century. In the book, one of the main character – Renzo Tramaglino – comes several times from Como Lake to Milan, where some of the most important and tragic events of the plot took place.

The app follows the paths made by the protagonist to present to the users the urban landscape emphasizing some important areas – the point of interest – already recognizable in the modern city or forever lost in its evolution.

Multimodal contents such as video and podcast present the storytelling of the city and the novel. Picture galleries, 3D representations, virtual models, and imagery proposes a comparison of the different historical thresholds: engraves, drawings or illustration in the first case, paints, sketches and the first black and white photographs in the second, photos mainly in the third. Augmented reality allows users to frame a mentioned point of interest – through push notification if the user enables them – to explore context-aware information and to experience situated interactions with the space of the city and its history.

The beta version of the application has even been validated with users according to environmental psychology [17] and user personas task-based test – already developed and used in spatial and visual interactive projects based on Esri and Open GIS technologies [18] – results have been discussed and improved in a second released: The Betrothed 3.0 in 2014 [19].

2.1   The Novel: The Cartaro's Map

As before mentioned, the first version of the app and its next evolution PS3 relies on three different historical thresholds: the XVII century, the XIX century and the contemporaneity.

The first map considered in the ones drawn by Mario Cartaro in 1581. Cartaro (Viterbo 1540 – Napoli 1620) was a well-known engraver and cartographer mainly active in Rome famous for archeological, religious and geographical subjects. In particular, it worths remembering the two big charts of Roma the modern one realized in 1576 and the archeological one in 1579 a work that already seems an analogical time machine aimed to visualize the temporal evolution of the Eternal City.

The Cartaro's map is – obviously – a pre geodetical representation of the city of Milan, and it's limited to the Spanish Walls (see Fig. 1). Although the chart dates back 41 years before the pestilence that spreads in North of Italy from 1629 to 1633, it is a good image of the city in XVII century where Manzoni set the novel. That is Milan as it was seen and experienced by Renzo Tramaglino in his trips.

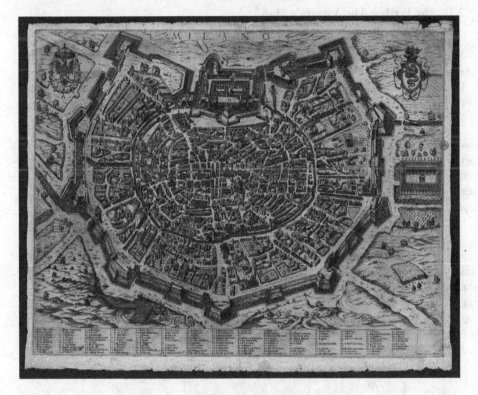

Fig. 1. The map of Milano drawn by Mario Cartaro in 1581. The document is kept at the *Biblioteca Nacional de Portugal* in Lisbon.

The map is a hybrid visualization of the space that uses a 3D language to shows and empathizes the urban structure and the most important political, religious and social symbols. In fact, the Sforza's Castle, the emblem of the secular power, is bigger than its real proportion compared to the rest of the buildings. Besides, it's positioned at north, in the center of the paper to underly its symbolic centrality even if it's placed in the North-West area of the city plan and its facade is South-East oriented. As noticed by Rumsey and Williams [20], people in the past were used to read maps both with a critical perspective and grounded in a previous knowledge.

Moreover in the former cartographer often draw maps gathering information from already existing historical maps rather than from direct field studies and topographical or direct surveys. Their works – say the authors – were *marvelous interpretation acts*.

Another open question is the nature itself of a map. A cartography could be produced and used to plan and control the future evolution of a territory. It means that it's the representation of the hoped city, not the real one especially when it's a sort of review work – as happened in the Berruto's master plan of Milano and the Napoleon period – or when the intervention has already been realized.

2.2   The Writer: The Artaria's Map

A second period considered in the research work is the XIX century. Alessandro Manzoni (Milano, 1785–1873) lived in Milan almost his entire life except for the years spent in Paris from 1805 to 1810. His home in the city center is now a house-museum where his memorabilia, books and other historical objects that belonged to him and his family are preserved and visited. In this period the city was changed by large urban

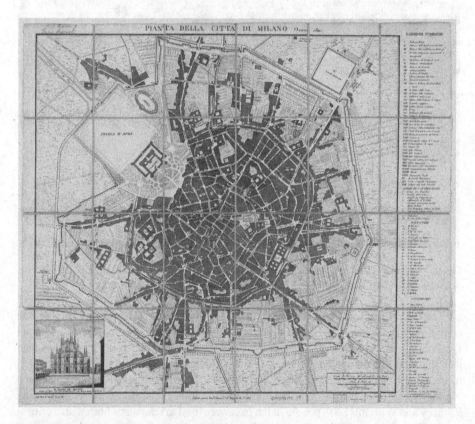

Fig. 2. The map of Milano drawn by Ferdinando Artaria and Gaspare Cagnogni in 1820. The document is kept at the *Harvard Library* in Cambridge, Boston.

interventions. The impact is impressive if we compare to maps of the Artaria Company stored in the Harvard Library.

The first is the master plan drawn by Ferdinando Artaria and Gaspare Cagnoni in 1820 (see Fig. 2). In that version, we see that the perimeter of the city is almost the same of the Cartaro's one. Milano still has an octagonal shape, the Lazzaretto – one of the key place of the novel – is outside the city boundaries and the center is surrounded by the Naviglio, the waterway channel ring, built in XII century and redesigned by Leonardo da Vinci in 1482 on behalf of the Duke Ludovico il Moro.

In less than 100 years the city had completely changed. The differences are well visible in the Artaria Company's map which dates back to 1910 (see Fig. 3). The Cesare Beruto's master plan – developed from 1884 to 1889 as a result of the historical changes brought by the unification of Italy as a whole state in 1861 – had destroyed the circle of

Fig. 3. The map of Milano of the Artaria's Company Ferdinando Sacchi and Sons published in 1910. The document is kept at the *Harvard Library* in Cambridge, Boston.

medieval walls – the Bastion – to give free space to the urban growth. The Lazzaretto has been dismissed, and the renovation of Duomo's Square and Piazza dei Mercanti (Merchants' Square) transforms the Dom in the physical and symbolic spatial center of the municipality. The Castle influence and importance has been partially declined, if not like a cultural heritage. The Navigli are still navigable, but the master plan provides for their closure, and they will be definitively undergrounded in 1928–30 under fascism that will give a new structure to the whole city and its rail network.

2.3   The Contemporaneity: The Google Map View

The contemporary city as almost canceled the main key point of the history as told by the novel and experienced by its author; nevertheless, some of the buildings have not been destroyed by the war or knocked down to make room to new edifications.

The center is almost unrecognizable due to post-war reconstruction and the renovation planned by the architect Gio Ponti in 1936–37 of Piazza San Babila and neighboring

Fig. 4. A detail of the Porta Venezia, Lazzaretto, and Via San Gregorio area as viewed in satellite version of Google Map.

areas. The places and events mentioned in *The Betrothed* are, at least, remembered by some commemorative plaques which allow you to locate the most non-existent places.

The Lazzaretto's surface is still recognizable in the satellite view of Google Map. Moving around, only the toponomastic – Via Lazzaretto, Via San Gregorio (see Fig. 4) – remind of the original destination of the area and allows you to define the extension. The only surviving buildings are the central chapel – now surrounded by condo and parking lots – and part of the perimeter wall of the San Gregorio's Parish.

3   The Betrothed 3.0: Time Machine

One of the key features of the PS3 application form mobile is the possibility to explore the historical maps of the city, layering the previous views to the contemporary digital map. Time become the river to explore the urban space in its historical presence and its intimate and hidden footsteps in a digital space-based and memory-related experience [21].

The time machine is a function already implemented in some experimental cultural projects. The Time machine of the *Faragola site* is one of the examples we've looked at to verify the already existing opportunities. The digital instrument is part of a wider project carried by the *Itinera Project* of the Foggia University and the iPad app *Chichen Itza*.

In the first case, the time machine compares information about the actual condition of the villa to the archeological evidence and reconstructions.

The time is subdivided into four different dates: the first period until 400 AC; the second one finishes in 450 AC, the third lasts until 700 AC, and then the Middle age. The transition along the time line are punctual and discontinuous; nevertheless, the project has a very powerful impact in describing historical phases and condition of the heritage. The second application, instead, implemented a virtual time-tour based on a three-dimensional virtual reconstruction of the archaeological site of Chichen Itza in Yucatan Peninsula. These cases have been analyzed to verify the possibilities given by technologies and real solutions implementing them in a real situation.

According to this first exploration and further mapping activities of already developed and tested experiences, PS3 itself has explored the timeline approach based on historical maps.

3.1   From Cartography to GIS

The georeferencing of old maps in modern reference systems is the same challenge faced by Bitelli et al. [22] and Guzzetti et al. [23]. Bitelli et al. georeferenced maps of Emilia-Romagna region, edited by Giovanni Antonio Magini in 1599 with four maps edited in XIX century. Guzzetti referenced five maps: one edited during 16th century, two during 17th and two during 19th century. Both the works aimed to georeference these historical material in webGIS. In order to georeference a map correctly, a system of point with known position and elevations is needed. This system of points, known as *Ground Control Points*, is essential to match objects and features with the geodetic map.

The most issue we must face in georeferencing pre-geodetic maps is related to the way cartographers changed their techniques through centuries and years. The science of measuring and representing the shape and size of the earth – geodesy – was born when, after the birth of regional stated in XVII, occidental governments started to plan and control the territory for civil and military aims. This trend spread in 1600 and 1700, thanks to the technological progresses in the topographic surveying tools (i.e. sextant, theodolite, telescope).

As highlighted in Bitelli work, pre-geodesic maps suffer of "not-always directly observable intrinsic deformations related both to the creation phase of the cartographic product (for example the type of cartographic representation adopted by the cartographer or the surveying and drawing methods) and to the conservation status. Moreover, scale is constant and unique on the whole map in modern cartography, but not on the pre-geodesic maps" [23]. This internal heterogeneity of the map was due to the lack of technical and scientific knowledge, but also to different methods and approaches adopted in different ways by the operators of the time, each one with their level of accuracy and precision.

For these reasons, as shown in works of Bitelli and Guzzetti works, the GCP method must be applied using the highest number of points in order to maximize precision. A former deformation analysis is required. These analysis consists in recognizing the homologous points of the old map and then in matching them on a control map, which is a more recent one we know is correct, according to the geodetic reference system.

To guarantee the possibility to have geo-referred contents both in the today map and in the historical cartography the project has adopted the Rumsey web-based GIS [20]. The mash-up of Google Heart and his digital maps collection, composed by 51,000 digitized elements and more than 150,000 geographical maps, can be seen at the URL: http://goo.gl/t1o3Tg.

The principles are easy to implement and efficacy: some control points – homologue points – are selected and fixed on the digital version of the analog map. Then, they are aligned with geographical points giving the coordinates. In the case of Milan's cartography, the points identified for the aligning process could be: the corners of the internal ring road correspondent to the old gate of the medieval/Spanish wall to access the city: The East Door – nowadays Porta Venezia – Porta Ticinese, Porta Romana, Porta Vercellina, Porta Comasina and Porta Nuova.

Then an algorithm *deform* and *bend* to adapt the historical source to the in the current map according to a process called *rubber sheeting*. Further correction can be "manually" imposed to improve precise alignment.

Albeit the proposed process, georeferencing an old map is pretty impossible due to a variety of problems: the mapping methods used before the introduction of aerial photography and photogrammetry have very imprecise scale proportions, orientations and distance measurement. The problem has been discussed at the XVII ASITA Conference (Scientific Association for Territorial and Environmental Information: http://www.asita.it/) where the issue has been raised by two different projects. The first one focused on the Bologna Territory and the second one on a Milan's Web-GIS of the Napoleon period [22, 23].

The PS3 adopted this approach and tried to improve a dynamic visual version of the transition among the three different maps and temporal levels (as presented in Fig. 5).

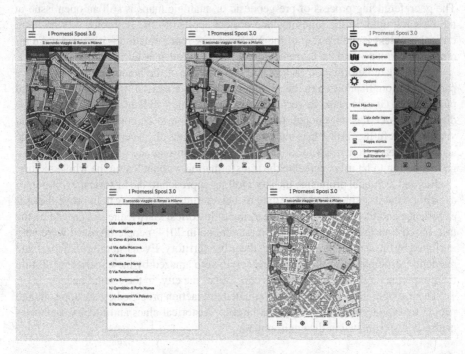

Fig. 5. The time machine: the transition between the different temporal levels according to the periodization of the app's storytelling approach based on the Manzoni's novel. The figures presents the second trip in Milan of Renzo Tramaglino.

The multimodal contents and figurative heritage associated with the point of interests geo-located in the app give a good understanding of the changes that the city has gone through. In Fig. 6 the three images allow to compare the before and after evolution of one of the more characteristic corner of Milan: Via San Marco.

Fig. 6. Milano in the '30 is no more a "water city": on the left the Conca delle Gabelle di San Marco has been completely emptied of water, in the middle the Naviglio during the covering work i 1929, on the left the place today.

4 Conclusions

The georeferencing process of pre-geodesic or analogic maps is still an open issue in the research field. In the time machine project applied to the Bethroted 3.0 the more critical problem is the overlap of the XVII century representation – it's even not a bi-dimensional map – and the current geobased systems such as GIS or Google map.

To calculate deformation factors and the increase of the homolog points is only a partial solution. In addition to that, analogical images are raster, when digital tools and platforms as Google map are vectorial instead. Zooming and enlarging the picture the digitized source has not enough quality and resolution to be correctly displayed and visualized. A further problem is represented by the streets displacement and their change across the years from 1928 to today. Varying the transparency of the map could be a good solution to let users perceive the transformation without losing the whole picture.

Beyond technical problems, the story telling approach to the historical evolution of a territory and its exploration according to a given timeline is a way to improve the user experience and the overall informal learning of historical knowledge. As proved by the task-based user test conducted in the pilot version in 2014, people involved were very intrigued by the serendipity discover of the urban territory. Even Literature teachers and residents participating in the in field research were amazed by the experience, despite their expertise of the novel, the first group, and of the city, in the second one.

The use of mobile devices and the situated interaction proposed by the app solicited people to explore in a sort of treasure hunt for historical clues and literary memories naturally disseminated in the environment.

Acknowledgments. Although the paper is a result of the joint work of all the authors, Letizia Bollini is in particular the author of Sects. 1, 2 and 4; and Daniele Begotti is the author of Sect. 3.

References

1. Simon, N.: The Participatory Museum. Lightning Source Inc., La Vergne (2010)
2. Simon, N.: Museum 2.0. http://museumtwo.blogspot.it/. Accessed 21 Mar 2017
3. Levin, M.: Designing Multi-Device Experiences. An Ecosystem Approach to User Experiences Across Devices. O'Reilly Media, Sebastopol (2014)
4. Bollini, L.: The digital space of knowledge: from archival forms to cultural knowledge-bases. Aggregations, narrations and migrations. In: Trocchianesi, R., Lupo, E. (eds.) Design & Cultural Heritage, pp. 53–66. Skirà, Milano (2013)
5. Rentzhog, S.: Open Air Museums: The History and Future of a Visionary Idea. Carlssons, Stockholm (2007)
6. UNESCO: World Heritage List. http://whc.unesco.org/en/list. Accessed 21 Mar 2017
7. Proctor, N.: The museum is mobile: cross-platform content design for audiences on the go. In: Museums and the Web 2010. Archives & Museum Informatics, Toronto, Canada (2010)
8. Dey, A.K.: Understanding and using context. Pers. Ubiquit. Comput. 5, 4–7 (2001)
9. Schmidt, A., Gellersen, H.W., Beigl, M.: There is more to context than location. Comput. Graph. 23(6), 893–901 (1999)

10. Bollini, L.: Digital Tom Thumb: A digital mobile and geobased signage system in public spaces orientation. In: Gervasi, O., et al. (eds.) ICCSA 2016. LNCS, vol. 9788, pp. 383–398. Springer, Cham (2016). doi:10.1007/978-3-319-42111-7_30

11. Chen, G., Kotz, D.: A survey of context-aware mobile computing research. Dartmouth Computer Science Technical report TR2000-381, Dartmouth College (2000)

12. Marti, P., Gabrielli, F., Pucci, F.: Situated interaction in art. J. Pers. Ubiquitous Comput. Archive **5**(1), 71–74 (2001)

13. Lynch, K.A.: The Image of the City. The MIT Press, Cambridge (1960)

14. Tilley, C.: Introduction: identity, place, landscape and heritage. J. Mater. Culture **11**(1–2), 7–32 (2006)

15. Bender, B.: Time and landscape. Curr. Anthropol. **43**(S4), 103–112 (2002). Special Issue Repertories of Timekeeping in Anthropology

16. Bollini, L., De Palma, R., Nota, R.: Walking into the past: design mobile app for the geo-referred and the multimodal user experience in the context of cultural heritage. In: Murgante, B., et al. (eds.) ICCSA 2013. LNCS, vol. 7973, pp. 481–492. Springer, Heidelberg (2013). doi:10.1007/978-3-642-39646-5_35

17. Francescato, D., Mebane, W.: How citizens view two great cities: Milano and Rome. In: Downs, R.M., Stea, D. (eds.) Image & Environment. Cognitive Mapping and Spatial Behaviors, pp. 131–147. Aldine Pub. Co, Chicago (1973)

18. Bollini, L., Cerletti, V.: Knowledge-sharing and management for local community: logical and visual georeferenced information access. In: Proceedings of the EISW (2009)

19. Bollini, L., De Palma, R., Nota, R., Pietra, R.: User experience & usability for mobile geo-referenced apps. A case study applied to cultural heritage field. In: Murgante, B., et al. (eds.) ICCSA 2014. LNCS, vol. 8580, pp. 652–662. Springer, Cham (2014). doi:10.1007/978-3-319-09129-7_47

20. Rumsey, D., Williams, M.: Historical maps in GIS. In: Past Time, Past Place: GIS for History, pp. 1–18 (2002). http://esriaustralia.com.au/u/lib/cms/past_time_past_place_c1sample.pdf. Accessed 21 Mar 2017

21. Bollini, L., Busdon, G., Mazzola, A.: GeoLapse. A digital space-based and memory-related time-capsule app. In: Gervasi, O., Murgante, B., Misra, S., Gavrilova, M.L., Rocha, A.M.A.C., Torre, C., Taniar, D., Apduhan, B.O. (eds.) ICCSA 2015. LNCS, vol. 9156, pp. 675–685. Springer, Cham (2015). doi:10.1007/978-3-319-21407-8_48

22. Bitelli, G., Gatta G., Di Cocco, I., Garberi, M.L.: La georeferenziazione dell'Atlante geografico d'Italia di Giovanni Antonio Magini in Emilia Romagna: i fogli del bolognese. In: 17ª Conferenza Nazionale ASITA. Riva del Garda, Trento, 7 Novembre 2013

23. Guzzetti, F., Iarossi, M.P., Meregalli, O., Privitera, A.: WebGis temporale delle carte storiche di Milano. In: 17ª Conferenza Nazionale ASITA. Riva del Garda, Trento, 7 Novembre 2013

Risk Prevention and Management. A Multi-actor and Knowledge-Based Approach in Low Density Territories

Alessandro Plaisant[(✉)], Miriam Mastinu, and Daniela Sini

Department of Architecture, Design and Urban Planning, University of Sassari, Sassari, Italy
{plaisant,mmastinu}@uniss.it, dansi91@live.it

Abstract. In the age of Big Data, the lack of relevant data, information and knowledge and the limits of the instruments and legislation for Risk Prevention and Management (RPM) do not allow decision makers to act efficiently and in a participatory way in territorial management. The task of this paper is to find a way to foster a proactive coordination between RPM instruments, practices and stakeholders, in order to identify consistent policy choices. A territorial organization model is defined, the Observatory for Territorial Participation (OTP), based on the following tasks: involvement of local actors; use of interactive computerized techniques and tools for decision support; access and sharing of big data and information in real time. The use of a "strategic planning" software, tested within a real setting, not only helps to focus the discussion and the process of definition of RPM policies, but it also leads at possible strategic organizational paths in the short, medium and long run.

Keywords: Participatory decision-making · Observatory for Territorial Participation · Risk management planning

1 Introduction: Few Remarks on Risk Management Planning

The reference framework of the logical and conceptual construction of RPM planning is the idea that it is possible and necessary to govern urban and territorial transformations (and risks consequently) in the current context of rapid changes, many of which having "external" causes and protagonists hard to tame to the obedience of traditional instruments of government. Therefore, faced with the creation of new supra-local government configurations we need new shapes of governance untied from formal institutions [7]. There are several problems related to the organization of environmental risk prevention measures. First of all, in most EU Member States, the risk issues are faced with a sectorial approach and disaster driven one, and specialist knowledge is still poorly integrated in governance processes [4]; second, there is a lack of a 'mutual' language between planning legislation and the several disciplines that deal with risk management [9]; third, public participation in RPM programs is taken into account in a later stage of the process, through the simple communication of measures, when they have been previously established [8].

© Springer International Publishing AG 2017
O. Gervasi et al. (Eds.): ICCSA 2017, Part III, LNCS 10406, pp. 252–265, 2017.
DOI: 10.1007/978-3-319-62398-6_18

In the age of Big Data, too many areas of expertise, who deal with environmental management, lack in data, information and knowledge, and this sets to limit decision-making processes. Despite the impossibility to create safety measures in the entire area of interest, it is necessary to know how to cope with risk and handle emergencies: in other words, how to realize a targeted management of hazard. It is crucial to increase the collective sensitivity and mutual learning regarding these phenomena, which are not just limited to the areas at very high risk.

A systemic analysis of legislation at European, national and local levels is carry out with the aim of highlighting a number of mandatory requirements for the risk management cycle. It is relevant to note that in the current framework of policies, directives and conventions, the European and national legislations contextualize the risk management at different levels of government. The Commission Directive 98/22/EC establishes the first Community action program aimed at promoting Civil Protection. Yet, the EU Water Framework Directive 2000/60/EC aims at establishing a framework in the field of water policy for the protection of inland surface waters, transitional waters, coastal waters and groundwater. Last but not least, art. 10 of the Flood Directive 2007/60/EC, which institutes a framework for flood risk management, aims to promote interaction processes at all levels of urban planning and 'active' involvement of citizens in the flood management cycle [11]. Moreover, by analyzing the framework of current policies and practices at national and regional levels, we consider the Italian Hydro-geological Watershed Plan (*Piano Stralcio per l'Assetto Idrogeologico*) as the reference system to pursue prevention objectives and hydro-geological risk reduction.

In February 1992, after the catastrophic events that affected the Country, the Italian Law n. 225/92 - constitution of the National Civil Protection Service (*Istituzione del Servizio Nazionale della Protezione Civile*), recognizes "organized and non-occasional voluntary work and assigns it the role of component" (art. 6) and of "operating unit" of the National Service (art. 11) ensuring "its involvement in any Civil Protection activity, with approval of dedicated regulations" (art. 18). The Civil Protection activities are aimed at the protection and preservation of life, settlements and environment, against damage caused by natural disasters or by humans in order to mitigate, manage and anticipate the possibility of any possible risk scenarios. The development of small groups and associations as part of local administration led to improve skills and to combine civil protection voluntary work with the public services. According to the Decree n. 49/2010, art. 11, which implemented the Flood Directive into national legislation, Civil Protection and Regions are also in charge to foster stakeholder participation in the defining of the basin plans. The diagram (Fig. 1) shows that the mayor is the fundamental actor at a local level, and plays a crucial role for emergency management: despite having no direct contact with the intermediate bodies, he/she acts in accordance with the general guidelines of the civil protection plan in relation to the alert that is communicated, following possible risk scenarios for the municipality. It emerges that the top-down transmission of data from the national level to the regional and the local one, reaches the mayor, who can only act through ordinances according to the Civil Protection recommendations. In the first place, the problem of a municipal management level, based only on ordinances, highlights the lack of coordination and interaction between policy-makers of the neighboring municipalities, who share mutual risk factors (e.g. a river flood). In fact, several types of hazards goes beyond administrative boundaries.

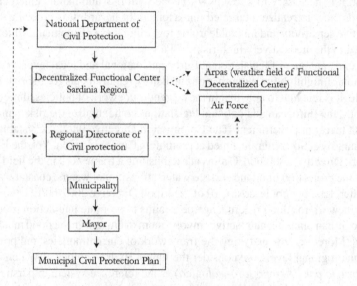

Fig. 1. Civil protection management diagram

Then it underlies the lack of an operational structure capable of managing real-time information on the gravity of the expected event. Therefore, all the limits affecting the environmental risk concern: the lack of coordination between the various authorities and institutions in charge for risk management, which – with fragmentary and sometimes conflicting competencies – lead to undesirable consequences for prevention; the deficiency of cooperative and strategic planning among public authorities; the different types of risks management which take place at the supra-local government level. The risk management plans are often inflexible because they cope with emergencies through technical parameters and criteria, established at a upper level, coming from general requirements, which exclude local knowledge and the context in which they act. That limits the role of public participation in programs management and risk prevention, which is often previously established at the highest levels of government. It comes out the lack of a bottom up participatory process in the initial stages to foster the necessary exchange of information between local communities, public authorities and techno-structures.

Therefore, in order to ensure an effective risk management, and local development consequently, it is necessary to carry out a systemic overview of the risk-oriented legislations, practices and instruments at different levels of government (with specific goals, actions, areas of competence). It is relevant to note that most of the aims refer to three main categories of options: a. prevention and preparedness; b. information; c. response. Hence, the risk management and assessment tools can be organized following these three stages aimed at defining a territorial organization model.

In other words, our efforts to review European, national and regional instruments for risk management and prevention aim at organizing three sets of policy options that lead the policymaking process: a. to ensure territorial safety standards, through the definition of structural and non-structural interventions, to mitigate the damage caused by a calamitous event and to implement preventive measures; b. to foster accessibility to information, allowing the 'proactive' participation of all the involved actors, including citizens and the local associations, and ensuring the proper management and emergency coordination; c. to encourage the landscape protection highlighting how proper risk mitigation may lead to positive effects for local development in a specific area.

2   A Territorial Organization Model for Risk Management: The Observatory for the Territorial Participation (OPT)

In Italy, the current policies and practices for risk prevention and management (RPM) are affected by the lack of coordination among different levels of government, by the sectorial management of the interventions and by the difficulty to integrate planning directions and prevention measures, especially in low-density residential areas.

On this basis, a risk management process, on the one hand, aims at the definition of the RPM policy options and, on the other hand, at activating a multi-actor decision-making process in order to support their evaluation in a participatory way. As such, the participatory process fosters a proactive coordination between RPM instruments and practices with public actors. Hence, the definition of a territorial organization model for risk management – the Observatory for the Territorial Participation (OTP) may be the opportunity to foster participation in the risk-oriented debate [3, 10], based on the involvement of local actors and citizens, on the use of interactive computerized techniques and tools for decision support and on the access and sharing of big data and information in real time. It involves local public services and dynamics of cooperation and self-organization linked to social and production processes.

An OTP, a multi-stakeholder governance model, which is flexible and adaptable, is developed as a network of operational spaces of interaction to prevent and coordinate emergency situations and to ensure a dialogue among a number of actors, by crossing administrative and sectoral boundaries and by integrating technical knowledge (the experts and the techno-structures) and context information (the citizens and all subjects involved). In particular, it acts as an interface between decision-makers citizens, local authorities, third sector and privates, operating in the contexts and collecting local data, knowledge and observations in real time and it represents an innovative and operational approach in the public and private dimension of RPM (Fig. 2).

The OTP has the potential to act as an organized space of interaction, supported by specific conventional and advanced ICTs instruments (e.g. sensor technologies, telematics access and open mapping, but also instruments aiding decisions on and evaluation of policies). It should guarantee that all subjective rationalities – those representing institutional ownership, technical knowledge and the context, are represented and organized according to a system of common rules. It can help exercise urban functions in a

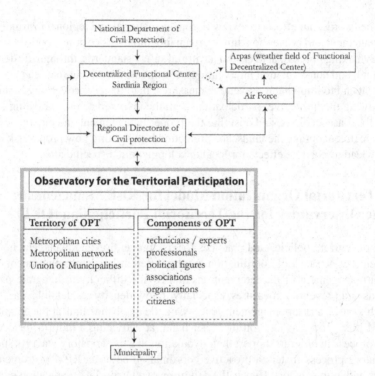

Fig. 2. The model of the observatory for the territorial participation (OTP).

shared way, by the development of a common vision about RPM in a wider framework, e.g. quality of life, use of public spaces and services.

Its adaptability to the current policies of specific contexts and needs is associates with the easy usability through simple operating procedures supported by ICT' services/ e-participation tools (e.g. a crowdsourcing platform provides OTP with the gathering of environmental data and knowledge about perceived needs and spatial and social relationships along with workshops, public discussions, meetings, reports). For this reason, through a coordinated operation of the network, the OTP allows an active participation among the different actors who are in charge for RPM, and allows them to interact with experts, professionals and political figures (third sector, voluntary and other organizations), so as to give a mutual contribution to the definition of the management action plans and interventions. This means adjusting tasks and competencies of the techno-structures of public authorities to a new generations of tools and strategies, in order to deal with complex situations.

The four step for identification of an OTP organizational perimeter can be summarized as follows: 1. a desk analysis on current EU/national/regional framework in order to identify policies, objectives and actions related to risk management cycle: prevention and preparedness; information; response; 2. identification of local key actors and stakeholders in order to clearly outline available financial, human and social resources and the vitality of local communities expressed by self-organized, volunteer or cooperative forms of production and service supply; 3. definition of the operating area to be involved through the analysis of the present risk patterns and local socio-spatial relationships in terms of distribution and accessibility of dwellings, services, facilities; 4. construction of alternative scenarios for risk management.

3   A Decision Support and Evaluation Model for RPM Policymaking: The ASA Computer Software (Actors – Strategies – Actions)

The authors conducted a multi-actor policy-making experience to improve the Municipal Civil Protection Plan of a small town in Sardinia, Italy, recently approved by the municipal Council, and the construction of a possible OTP operating area (Fig. 3).

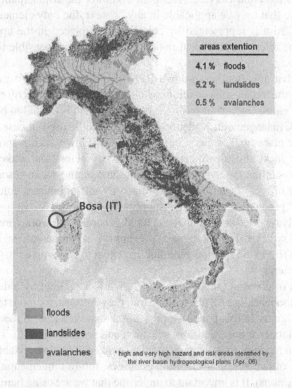

areas extention

4.1 %	floods
5.2 %	landslides
0.5 %	avalanches

Bosa (IT)

floods
landslides
avalanches   * high and very high hazard and risk areas identified by the river basin hydrogeological plans (Apr. 06)

Fig. 3. Location of the case study in the map of areas at high hydrogeological critical state (www.minambiente.it).

For this purpose, we tested a computer software package[1] for better organizational planning within an actual setting of Bosa Municipality, a town in middle-western Sardinia (about 8000 inhabitants; area: 128 km^2; population density: 62 pop/km^2).

The issue concerns the floods caused by the overflowing of the Temo River, that crosses the town and the territory of the Bosa Municipality. The Bosa municipality adopted the Unitary Development city Plan and the Hydro-geological Watershed Plan (HWP, see p. 2) identifies a huge high flood risk area (R4 – very high risk) in the urban area, while the coastal Bosa Marina area (R2 - medium risk), presents a return time of the alluvial phenomenon of 50 years. Given the involvement of the territory of Bosa with the risk-related problems (hydraulic, geomorphological and fire hazards), this municipality has drawn up its own Plan of Municipal Civil Protection, on the basis of operational guidelines established by the Italian Law n. 225/92 – constitution of the National Civil Protection Service. The plan commits the Municipality to prepare a general brochure that may be applicable in any context: the only element that refers to the territory of Bosa is represented by colored bands placed in the upper part of the brochure and the reference to a local radio station, that is responsible to inform about possible hazards.

The limits that affects this top-down RPM plan can be briefly summarized as: it considers only the urban area, excluding all the neighboring territory and without considering the entire catchment basin of the river, which is crucial to be evaluated for an effective risk management; it identifies the areas to be used in case of emergency, including public places and services, but without specifying who is responsible for their organization; it lacks the identification of local key actors and stakeholders which doesn't allow to outline the available financial, human and social resources (together with the vitality of local communities expressed by self-organised, volunteer or cooperative forms of production and service supply).

As previously reported according to the RPM general framework, three sets of policy options lead the policymaking process: a. prevention and preparedness; b. information; c. response, and reveal the specific geographic context to be involved in the OPT organizational perimeter.

The process of construction of a possible OPT is supported by a decision support and evaluation model called ASA (Actors-Strategies-Actions, for more technical details see [1]). In particular, in this paper we present the experience with the use of a multi-actor evaluation tool for policy options selection and prioritization [6]. The general aim of the evaluation model is to assist public policy-makers in defining viable and effective implementation of policy options (setting priorities, future implementation phases and sequencing of options). It is important to underline that we are using here a very abstract representation of time, whose discretization is not related to specifically defined time intervals. In order to compare sequences of policy options, they are evaluated with respect to three criteria:

– the *actors' interest* represents the interest of each actor for a single policy option. In this model, the interest criterion takes into account both the willingness of actors to

[1] ASA Software (2007), Laboratory of Analysis and Models for planning (LAMP), University of Sassari (web site: <http://www.lampnet.org>).

invest in an option, as well as actors' importance for its implementation. The rationale behind this concept is the idea that having for example two actors equally willing to invest in an option, the one considered more important for the implementation of the option should be of a greater importance (weight) for the overall evaluation of the option's interest.

- The *option relevance* criterion is modeling the effect of option on general RPM planning. Differently from the previous one, this criterion measures the option performance (the synergistic effects) in terms of benefits that different sequences of policy options have in reaching the overall goal defined by the RPM plan.
- The *resources criterion* refers to necessary resources for the implementation of the options (in terms of funds, work force, facilities, equipment, organizational capacity, *etc.*).

Taking into account some recent reviews on evaluation and urban and regional planning, we hold that these three criteria are essential for our purpose, as they represent the three fundamental dimensions of public policy decision-making, namely the effectiveness and efficacy of actions (the relevance criterion), the complexity of and the effects on the political arena (the interest criterion), and finally the efficiency and resource constraints (the resources criterion). The process has come to define 12 relevant policy options, better specified through interview with relevant local actors (authorities, service officers, policymakers) involved in risk-oriented specific practices and tasks at all level of government, consisting of more than 39 actions related to the objectives of the RPM plan. The set of evaluated options is reported in Table 1.

Table 1. The list of policy options emerged from the process.

A.1	Coordination for risk management (actions to ensure coordination between the various bodies in charge for risk management and the related tools)
A.2	No-structural measures (no-structural measures that prevent or reduce damage caused by a flood event)
A.3	Structural interventions on hydrographic network (structural interventions on water network to reduce the hazard event)
A.4	Safety of people (actions concerning safety of the people and infrastructures)
A.5	Mitigation damage (actions to mitigate hazards to the economy, productive and real property)
A.6	Territory maintenance (actions to ensure the maintenance of territory)
B.1	Prediction and prevention system (actions involving the use of tools for advanced prediction and propagation of flood events)
B.2	Improving communication (action to involve territorial networks)
B.3	Increasing knowledge and participation of local community
C.1	Coherence between land use and risks (actions for agricultural land uses appropriate to the existing risks)
C.2	Reduce the coastal vulnerability
C.3	Promote tourism development (to increase the value of local assets)

First of all, each option has been included in the software, specifying a title[2] and the supposed financial costs for technical implementation[3]. Each option holds elements favoring the emergence of relations involving places, subjects, economies of the territory for the construction of alternative RPM scenarios. The option relevance is a criterion representing the relevance of the policy option to pursuit each strategic goal, but this assessment cannot be divorced from the synergistic effects that different combinations of options could produce on the overall goals of the RPM plan. Thus, positive or negative or null synergistic effect between options will arise depending on the order of their implementation.

Each option is given a 'direct' relevance (RD), that is a score of relative importance[4]. It is calculated by taking into account the actions the option requires for helping to achieve each strategic option. Therefore, by matching two options we insert in the cell the corresponding average of the two relative importance scores. Finally, it can be added (or cut for negative synergy) a value[5] indicating the synergistic effects of each ordered pair of options for helping to achieve each strategic goal, when the sequence of implementation has been followed (Fig. 4).

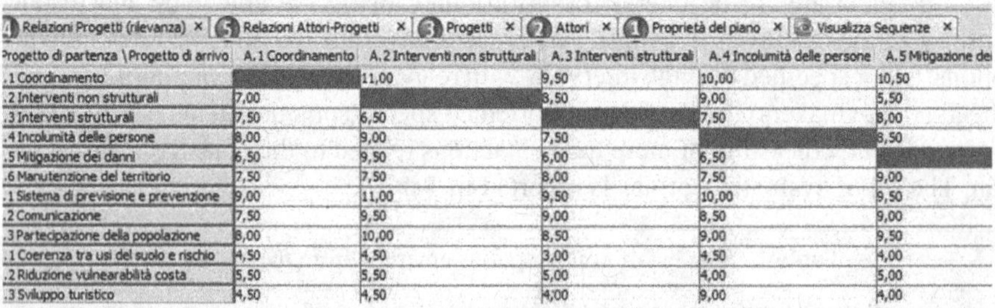

Relazioni Progetti (rilevanza) ×	Relazioni Attori-Progetti ×	Progetti ×	Attori ×	Proprietà del piano ×	Visualizza Sequenze ×		
Progetto di partenza \ Progetto di arrivo	A.1 Coordinamento	A.2 Interventi non strutturali	A.3 Interventi strutturali	A.4 Incolumità delle persone	A.5 Mitigazione dei
.1 Coordinamento		11,00	9,50	10,00	10,50
.2 Interventi non strutturali	7,00		8,50	9,00	5,50
.3 Interventi strutturali	7,50	6,50		7,50	8,00
.4 Incolumità delle persone	8,00	9,00	7,50		8,50
.5 Mitigazione dei danni	6,50	9,50	6,00	6,50	
.6 Manutenzione del territorio	7,50	7,50	8,00	7,50	9,00
.1 Sistema di previsione e prevenzione	9,00	11,00	9,50	10,00	9,50
.2 Comunicazione	7,50	9,50	9,00	8,50	9,00
.3 Partecipazione della popolazione	8,00	10,00	8,50	9,00	9,50
.1 Coerenza tra usi del suolo e rischio	4,50	4,50	3,00	4,50	4,00
.2 Riduzione vulnerabilità costa	5,50	5,50	5,00	4,00	5,00
.3 Sviluppo turistico	4,50	4,50	4,00	9,00	4,00

Fig. 4. ASA user interface: the matrix of option-to-option interdependencies.

The subsequent step was to define the space of interaction. It should have assured to represent all the involved actors which mutually concur to the construction of the OPT, be they deriving from expert knowledge or from the local community[6]. It should also be organized according to a system of common rules with the possibility of adequately

---

[2] The options have been nominated with the same identification number of the goals which they relates to. First capital letter refer to the three sets of policy options, numbers refer to policy options.

[3] Financial costs of technical implementation of options are ordinal variables expressing a measure, in this case using a scale ranging from 0 to 100.

[4] Direct Relevance (RD) is an ordinal variable expressing a measure, in this case using a scale ranging from 0 to 10.

[5] The value indicating the synergistic effects of each ordered pair of options is: low synergy (average value 0%); medium synergy (average value 25%); strong synergy (average value 50%); negative synergy.

[6] The results of the desk analysis on current RPM EU/national/regional framework (1) were better specified through interviews with relevant local authorities, emergency services as well as local policy makers.

representing the field of interest of each actor. The following categories of actors were defined and asked their local representative bodies for an interview about the RPM policy options and relative actions: 1. the Region of Sardinia, 2. the Municipality of Bosa, 4. the neighbouring municipalities, 5. The administrational techno-structures, 6. The educational institutions, 7. The civil protection and associations, 8. The forest Rangers, 9. The Police and port authority 10. The business operators (e.g. traders, hoteliers).

The actors' interest for options (Fig. 5) expresses the interest of the actors for single options and it is measured on two sub-criteria: 1. the influence level of each actor for single options; 2. the effort that actors are willing to invest in options

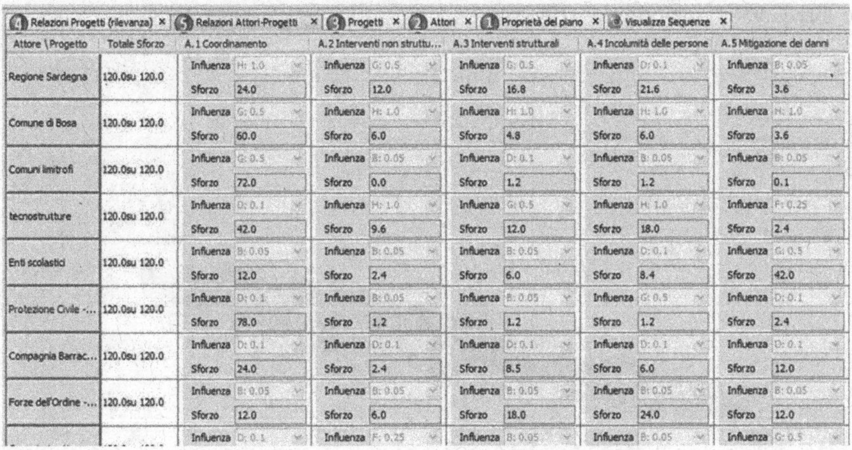

Relazioni Progetti (rilevanza) ×	Relazioni Attori-Progetti ×	Progetti ×	Attori ×	Proprietà del piano ×	Visualizza Sequenze ×		
Attore \ Progetto	Totale Sforzo		A.1 Coordinamento	A.2 Interventi non struttu...	A.3 Interventi strutturali	A.4 Incolumità delle persone	A.5 Mitigazione dei danni
Regione Sardegna	120.0su 120.0	Influenza	H: 1.0	G: 0.5	G: 0.5	D: 0.1	B: 0.05
		Sforzo	24.0	12.0	16.8	21.6	3.6
Comune di Bosa	120.0su 120.0	Influenza	G: 0.5	H: 1.0	H: 1.0	H: 1.0	H: 1.0
		Sforzo	60.0	6.0	4.8	6.0	3.6
Comuni limitrofi	120.0su 120.0	Influenza	G: 0.5	B: 0.05	G: 0.5	B: 0.05	B: 0.05
		Sforzo	72.0	0.0	1.2	1.2	0.1
tecnostrutture	120.0su 120.0	Influenza	D: 0.1	H: 1.0	G: 0.5	H: 1.0	F: 0.25
		Sforzo	42.0	9.6	12.0	18.0	2.4
Enti scolastici	120.0su 120.0	Influenza	B: 0.05	B: 0.05	B: 0.05	D: 0.1	G: 0.5
		Sforzo	12.0	2.4	6.0	8.4	42.0
Protezione Civile -...	120.0su 120.0	Influenza	D: 0.1	D: 0.1	B: 0.05	G: 0.5	D: 0.1
		Sforzo	78.0	1.2	1.2	1.2	2.4
Compagnia Barrac...	120.0su 120.0	Influenza	D: 0.1	D: 0.1	D: 0.1	D: 0.1	D: 0.1
		Sforzo	24.0	2.4	8.5	6.0	12.0
Forze dell'Ordine -...	120.0su 120.0	Influenza	B: 0.05	B: 0.05	B: 0.05	B: 0.05	B: 0.05
		Sforzo	12.0	6.0	18.0	24.0	12.0
		Influenza	D: 0.1	F: 0.25	B: 0.05	B: 0.05	G: 0.5

Fig. 5. ASA user interface: actors' importance and effort for each option user interface: the matrix of option-to-option interdependencies.

Hence, the influence level of actors in an option is modeled as an ordinal measure, the estimation of which is treated as an input data of the evaluation model. We have five "levels" of meaning for actors: a. 'key actor': the option cannot be activated without this actor (ratio value: 1); b. 'Compulsory actor': the option cannot be implemented without this actor (ratio value: 0,5); c. 'Conditioning actor': the actor has the possibility to influence the implementation of the option, but is not compulsory for its accomplishment (ratio value: 0,25); d. 'Marginal actor': the actor exercises only marginal and generic influence on the option (ratio value: 0,10); e. 'Non influential actor': the actor has no influence on the option[7] (ratio value: 0,05). The second sub-criteria to be included is the willingness of actors to invest in terms of time, money, human and financial resources, *etc.*, as well as actors' importance for the implementation of options in terms of comfort, liveability, sustainability, development, political consensus, *etc.* For an operational point

---

[7] For example, the actor with influence level 'b' is less important for the development of an option than the actor with influence level 'a', but in the same way, a couple of actors with influence level 'b', putting equal efforts, have the same importance for the general development of the option than an actor with influence level 'a'.

of view, the model allows each actor to assign a constant amount of effort points (having 12 options to compare, the total amount of effort points per each actor is 120). Note that multiplying the two values for each option-actor couple, the software allows the player to assess the interest of actors for each individual option.

After defined this information, it was possible to explore, within the domain of all the possible sequences of options, those sequences which form a Pareto-optimal frontier in terms of the three criteria of evaluation (interest, relevance and costs) [1].

In our case, the analysis of the outputs at the end of the execution of the model allowed us to come to few important observations, such as the identification of the options which are always present in highly valued sequences in terms of at least one of the three evaluation criteria[8] (Fig. 6).

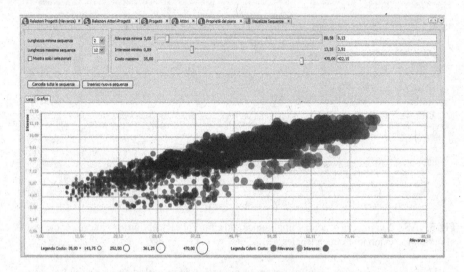

Fig. 6. ASA user interface: visual exploration of sequences of options.

Following this procedure for many Pareto-optimal sequences of different sizes, the options have been subdivided on the basis of their frequency in short (up to 5 options), medium (up to 10) and long (up to 15) sequences. In that way, we have identified options which we labeled "fundamental" options (present in more than 65% of all sequences), "relevant" options (present in 35–65% of sequences) and "correlated" options (present in less than 35% of sequences). The latter should not necessarily be irrelevant or inferior, as they could possibly acquire their importance if implemented together or subsequently to other fundamental and relevant options. Within this classification, it is possible to perform another distinction between "start-up" options (which appear at the beginning of sequences) and "concatenated" options (which may be relevant only if implemented in concatenation with some other options). Combining the two sets of information (frequency and positioning) of the options, we have selected three families of options,

---

[8] ASA user graphical interface represents each sequence of options as a "bubble". Optimal sequences are in the second quadrant (upper right).

with their respective objectives and actionIn particular, we shown that administrational structures do not have to activate or implement the strategic options all together, but they can implement them in different steps to better manage and to strength the RPM process. The three families are:

- *activating options* (with their respective actions), able to support and sustain the "take off" of the entire process of implementation of the RPM plan, composed of fundamental or relevant start-up options present in short, medium and long sequences;
- *supporting options* (and actions), capable to improve the efficacy and to guide the development of the implementation process after the initial activation, composed of fundamental or relevant options in medium and long sequences, but correlated in the short ones. Some options were considered supportive of the plan, if they appeared as start-up in some sequences, but did not appear in short sequences.
- *auxiliary options* (and actions), able to determine a consolidation of those already activated in the medium and long run, composed of correlated options in the short and medium sequences.

In the Table 2. we report the policy options following these typologies.

Table 2. The list of policy options emerged from the process.

Activating options	A.1, B.1
Supporting options	A.3, A.4, A.5, B.2, B.3, C.2, A.2, A.6
Auxiliary options	C.3, C.1

The evaluation process of options and, therefore, the related objectives and actions, allows us to understand the most effective sequences of options from the point of view of the RPM, given that all the actions are useful because they express different knowledge and technical expertise. The contexts are not to passively suffer the general indications that come from legislations, so it is necessary that the general requirements of risk management cycle, coming from the current framework of RPM policies, directives and conventions (prevention and preparedness, information, response), are tailored to specific contexts as well as the policy options.

In the territory of Bosa there are self-organized and collaborative associations that can be 'mobilized' and organized to cope with the emergency. Thus, we proceed to highlight local requirements and services that support RPM planning in terms of ensuring territorial safety standards, fostering accessibility to information and participation, encouraging the landscape protection. In this sense, the OTP, formed by a number of stakeholders, provides essential information, emergency procedures and organizes public services consequently in a collaborative way:

- *prevention and preparedness*: municipal operations centers (Centro Operativo Comunale – C.O.C.), social centers, educational structures, associations;
- *information*: C.O.C., educational structures, cultural services, municipal information points, associations;
- *response*: health services, sports services, voluntary associations, parks.

It is relevant to note that one of the limits concerns the risk management that is limited to the municipal level. In this regard, the OTP organizational perimeter corresponds to the network of the neighboring territories (the Union of Municipalities of Planargia and western Montiferru).

The proposal, on the one hand, supports current RPM tools and practices fostering dialogue and cooperation between stakeholders in the different steps of risk cycle and, on the other hand, establishes a network of municipalities that cope with common problems and hazards in a collaborative way. This network oversteps the boundaries of the Unitary Development City Plans and it can be helpful to define the system of linked pathways, urban functions and strategic spaces during and after the emergencies. That is also the goal of *Struttura Urbana Minima* (SUM – Minimal Urban Structure) of the national directions in terms of Civil Protection.

4   Conclusion

We conclude that this bottom-up approach to innovative RPM practices is extremely useful for three reasons.

First, it provides local authorities with a set of strategic options following an understandable, transparent and replicable itinerary. Second, it can help administrational structures to assign resources so as to prevent and to compensate for the damages adequately, fostering effective complementary countermeasure for unexpected losses from natural hazards (e.g. insurance coverage [5]).

Third, it encourages and enables citizens and visitors, planning communities and decision making practitioners to successfully organizing a number of basic services, pathways, urban functions and strategic spaces for coping with emergencies through simple operating procedures supported by ICT' services/e-participation tools.

Future research perspectives suggest to test the model in different territorial/hazard(s) contexts. Through this framework we can observe the interaction between risk analysis and strategy and between processes of social interaction and technology as well as the integration between technical, administrative and political skills of institutions and techno-structures with knowledge, practices, experiences and needs of local context [2].

References

1. Blecic, I., Cecchini, A., Plaisant, A.: Constructing strategies in strategic urban planning: A case study of a decision support and evaluation model. In: Murgante, B., Gervasi, O., Iglesias, A., Taniar, D., Apduhan, Bernady O. (eds.) ICCSA 2011. LNCS, vol. 6783, pp. 277–292. Springer, Heidelberg (2011). doi:10.1007/978-3-642-21887-3_22
2. Cecchini, A., Plaisant, A.: Better decisions for a better quality of life: the potential of rural districts supported by e-governance tools. In: Gervasi, O., Murgante, B., Misra, S., Gavrilova, Marina L., Rocha, A.M.A.C., Torre, C., Taniar, D., Apduhan, Bernady O. (eds.) ICCSA 2015. LNCS, vol. 9156, pp. 577–592. Springer, Cham (2015). doi:10.1007/978-3-319-21407-8_41
3. Fung, A.: Varieties of participation in complex governance. Public Adm. Rev. **66**, 66–75 (2006)

4. Galderisi, A., Menoni, S.: Rischi naturali, prevenzione, piano. Urbanistica **134**, 20–23 (2007)
5. Gizzi, F.T., Potenza, M.R., Zotta, C.: The insurance market of natural hazards for residential properties in Italy. Open J. Earthq. Res. 5, 35-61 (2016). http://dx.doi.org/10.4236/ojer. 2016.51004
6. Lycett, M., Rassau, A., Danson, J.: Programme management: A critical review. Int. J. Project Manage. **22**(4), 289–299 (2004)
7. Plaisant, A.: La partecipazione nel governo delle trasformazioni del territorio. Strumenti innovativi per costruire la città dei diritti. FrancoAngeli, Milano (2009)
8. Sanoff, H.: Community Participation Methods in Design and Planning. Wiley, New York (2000)
9. Segnalini, O.: Rischio e pianificazione urbanistica. In: Urbanistica, vol. 117, pp. 25–28 (2001)
10. Wehn, U., Evers, J.: Citizen Observatories of Water: Social Innovation via eParticipation? Presentation at ICT4S (ICT for Sustainability), pp. 24–27. Stockholm, Sweden (2014)
11. Wehn, U., Rusca, M., Evers, J., Lanfranchi, V.: Participation in flood risk management and the potential of citizen observatories: A governance analysis. Environ. Sci. Policy **48**, 225–236 (2015). Elsevier

Flickr as a Tool for the Analysis of Photographic Tourism: The Estimation of Geotagging Rate and Its Use for Mapping the World

Gian Pietro Zaccomer[1](✉) and Luca Grassetti[2]

[1] Dipartimento di Lingue e Letterature, Comunicazione, Formazione e Società (DILL),
University of Udine, Via Petracco 8, 33100 Udine, Italy
gianpietro.zaccomer@uniud.it
[2] Dipartimento di Scienze Economiche e Statistiche (DIES), University of Udine,
Via Tomadini 30, 33100 Udine, Italy
luca.grassetti@uniud.it

Abstract. The current digital revolution has a strong impact on the people life and on the research process in most of the scientific areas. Geography and cartography have been invested by the innovation connected with GIS. Moreover, they reacted to the new opportunities given by the new web applications founded on the dynamic paradigm of Web 2.0. In the geographic framework the possibility to self-supply the online contents brought to the Volunteered Geographic Information phenomenon. This study presents a number of preliminary results of a project aimed at reformulating the theoretical framework of Photographic Tourism. The research focuses on the integration of social media and web mapping as an application of neogeography. The estimation (based on a sample) of the proportion of geotagged photos loaded on Flickr during 2016 and the analysis of the spatial distribution of the considered sample are the main objectives of the paper.

Keywords: Social media · Volunteered Geographic Information · Neogeography · Application Programming Interface

1 Introduction

The digital revolution, also called the fourth industrial revolution, is influencing the production of goods and services. At the same time, it is conditioning the behaviour of the society and the people everyday life. The impact of this phenomenon regards both the economic framework (considering producers and consumers) and the general social framework (considering organisations and citizens).

Geography and Cartography are parts of this revolution. In fact, two main digital innovations caused relevant changes in these disciplines (Borruso 2013). The first one, observed during the 90s, is connected with the diffusion of Geographical Information Systems (GIS). These tools were developed as simple operational tools but, nowadays, they assume an independent scientific role for the spatial analysis. More recently, the transition from static to dynamic programming practice produced the change in the

© Springer International Publishing AG 2017
O. Gervasi et al. (Eds.): ICCSA 2017, Part III, LNCS 10406, pp. 266–281, 2017.
DOI: 10.1007/978-3-319-62398-6_19

paradigm of web applications (generally called "Web 2.0"). In particular, users are now directly involved in the data collection and modification. This means that the users of these innovative applications are consumers but also producers (the so-called "produsers" in Bruns 2006) of geotagged contents (photos, videos, texts, and so on).

The literature classifies this latter innovation by "recycling" the term new geography (or neogeography). This term has been previously used to denote a particular moment of the evolution of geographical thinking as, for instance, the introduction of quantitative approach during the 60s. The classical approaches to geography and cartography are based on precise and consolidated rules and protocols. On the contrary, the lack of precise basis and rules is the main characteristics of the "new geography 2.0" and the "cartography 2.0" (Mauro 2013). These new "virtual cartographic spaces" (Krasna 2014) are user-friendly. The way in which the users can interact with them gives the feeling to "know and master the world thanks to a simple click" (Scanu 2008, p. 13). A typical example of new geography is the so-called Map Mashup. This "technology" allows to integrate and jointly represent the spatial information coming from different applications (Butler 2006) by means of the Application Programming Interface (API).

The statistical methods applied to the neogeography and the technology involved in this field of study are surely naïve but the evolution also offers some opportunities. These are mainly connected with the "voluntary participation" of users in value co-creation. People involved in the process of data collection and analysis are geography and cartography enthusiasts. In Eisnor (2006) and Turner (2006) the authors introduce the new directions and the technological aspects of neogeography.

Goodchild (2007) discusses the role of "citizens as sensors" in the data collection process. The concept of Volunteered Geographic Information (VGI) is useful for describing the use of digital devices in the production, management, and diffusion of the geographical information. This concept can be considered as an advantage but it also implicitly requires the availability of a remote connection to the web as a "condicio sine qua non" for the production and diffusion of geographical voluntary information.

The digital revolution caused an epochal change in the approach to photography and in the use of photographic tools in the photographic tourism. For instance, every modern smartphone embodies a camera and consequently, everyone holds a camera in his pocket. This paper focuses on Flickr (a specific photographic social media) but it is also a pretext to deal with web mapping process. Flickr has been founded in 2002 in Vancouver. After a short time, it has been assimilated by Yahoo!. The service aims to promote the sharing of photos and related comments between the users. From 2006, after the beta testing stage, the automatic and manual geotagging of the photos has been introduced. This possibility allows to consider Flickr, along with Panoramio, as a case study in the analysis of the VGI.

The choice of Flickr as the main source of information has been guided by several reasons. First, Flickr is a well-known photographic social media that collects 13 billion objects (photos, images, screenshots and videos as private or public objects). Secondly, Panoramio service will be definitively abandoned in November 2017, and 500px represents a valid alternative for amateurs with superior photographic abilities only. Finally, Flickr also collects meta-data (useful for the classification of users) that are not included in Instagram. For all these reasons, the literature suggests that Flickr can be considered as a valid tool for the market analysis of tourism consumption (Iñiguez-Berrozpe et al. 2013). Moreover, Zielstra and Hochmair (2013) suggest that the accuracy of the geotagging process in Flickr is adequate for spatial analysis even if it is lower than in Panoramio. Last but not least, Flickr uses a specific API which resulted fundamental for the data collection.

Photographic Tourism is a specific form of Special Interest Tourism (see Palmer and Lester 2004 for further details). The final aim of the whole research project is to redefine the theoretical framework in which the Photographic Tourism is studied by including the components related to place marketing, social media, and VGI. The Photographic Tourist is, also, defined focusing on the "sensibility to place" in order to distinguish this figure from the simple tourist with a camera (Gogoi 2014).

The secondary aim of the project is to analyse the potential market for photographic tours. In particular, the study aims at understanding if this service can be shaped around the passionate photographers. The existence of a market niche for photographic tourism can be a key element for the adjustment of the seasonal behaviour of the tourism sector.

The present work starts from the explorative analysis about the photographic use of the social media introduced in Zaccomer et al. (2016). This study is based on a sample of 100 users of Flickr selected on the basis of their activity on the social media. The hypothesis is that the potential photographic tourists are most common in the group of users identified by a "real photographic use" of the social media. Sun (2010) suggests that these tourists can also be identified by considering their photographic equipment. The kind of equipment used by a photographer is one of the drivers of the quality of the photos but it also represents a proxy of the budget and of the willingness to pay for specific travel packages.

In the cited analysis the users are observed considering the characteristics of the last 100 photos uploaded on Flickr. The collected dataset includes: the users' characteristic (id and user's registry data), the behaviour of the users (use of groups, albums, tags, etc. for the photo classification), the geotagging data, the kind of photographic equipment, the kind of photos and the measure of the reputation of the users based on Flickr's Interestingness Algorithm (Michel 2013).

In the same work, the Authors also carry out a cluster analysis. The quantitative measures used at this step are: the number of followers for each following (IFOL, a measure of social media activity), the percentage of geotagged photos (IGEO, a measures of the "sensibility to place") and the percentage of "interesting" photos according to the algorithm used by Flickr (IBHL, a measure of the quality of the photos). The variable IGEO is the one presenting the largest discriminant capability. Notwithstanding, this information is missing in Flickr and for this reason it is necessary to estimate this parameter at the population level.

The present work aims at estimating the percentage of geotagged photos. In order to obtain a better representation of the phenomenon, the time series of Flickr uploads is analysed in order to identify specific seasonality. As stated in Borruso (2010) the current level of "spatial awareness" is facilitated by the increasing diffusion of spatial tools. The availability of geotagging technologies promote the users' capability in this field. For this reason, the descriptive analysis of the uploads trend is developed on the 2004–2016 data. The estimation of the proportion of geotagged photos is based on the 2016 data only.

The dataset is collected using the Flickr specific API (their main characteristics are fully described at the URL www.flickr.com/services/api/). Two ad-hoc scripts are used to select the data for the time series and for the 2016 sample respectively (see the acknowledgments at the end of this paper).

2   The Analysis of the Monthly Time Series of Uploads

The time series of the Flickr uploads from the 2004 (first year of activity) is studied here. In particular, only public photos (no videos, screenshots or private pictures) are considered in this work. The phenomenon is observed with a monthly period and consequently the seasonality must be treated in order to account for the classical infra-annual cyclical behaviours.

The dataset is characterized by a very long observational period: 13 years (156 monthly data) are considered summarizing almost 6 billion uploads. This sample size is sufficient to study the data by means of classical decomposition approach notwithstanding more complex models specifications as for instance considering a variable seasonality cannot be adopted.

The following analyses are developed considering the row data. The typical calendar based adjustments are not considered here because their effect is negligible if compared with the effect of the maintenance of the service. Moreover, these two effects cannot be separated as it is not possible to determine the full log of service's maintenance. A simple example can help understanding why the classical calendar adjustments cannot be used. In December 2016 the service has been down for five days. As a result, the activity time in this month is lower than the one in February 2016.

The graphical analysis of the time series, shown in Fig. 1, provides some broad indications. First, the series of uploads follows, at least until 2010, a sigmoid pattern typical of the introduction of new products or innovative services (as Flickr in 2004). In fact, it presents a first phase of slow growth due to the introduction of the network service, followed by a phase of rapid development. After the inflection point the curve tends to a saturation level.

The plot shows that the period from 2011 to 2013 is characterized by a slight increase in both the average level of the phenomenon and in its variability. From 2014 to 2016 this behaviour is exacerbated. The increase in the uploads after 2013 is probably linked with the market repositioning strategy adopted by Flickr in order to face the competition by Instagram and Facebook. In particular, Flickr adopted the concept of "photocracy", suppressing the Pro users (i.e. professional). This decision is based on the questionable opinion suggesting that the current technological level enables everyone to make "beautiful" photos.

Many good photographers transmigrated on other providers like 500px or Ipernity (automated scripts were also created for the automatic transfer from one service to the other). In order to recover these users, Flickr had to rethink its market strategy and restore

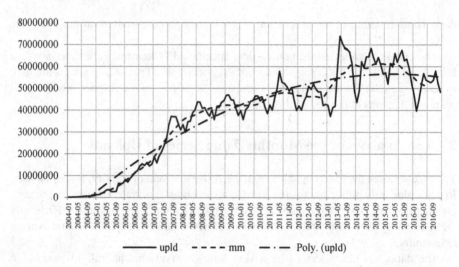

Fig. 1. Original time series of uploads (upld), moving averages (mm) and quadratic trend (Poli)

Pro users' service. These users pay to receive additional services as, for example, the possibility to control their own production through a statistical dashboard.

The graphical analysis shows that a relevant seasonal effect is present in the time series. In a first moment, the "classical approach" to time series analysis is considered in order to study the seasonality. The decomposition of the time series is based on the specification of classical Trend and Seasonality components (Di Fonzo and Lisi 2005). As just introduced the observed phenomenon presents an increasing variability. For this reason, the analysis is based on the multiplicative model. Consequently, the seasonality is expressed in terms of pure indices.

In order to define the seasonality, the original time series is de-trended considering the ratio between the observed measure and the estimated trend component. As a first result, the trend is identified using the functional approach. Given the peculiar behaviour of the phenomenon, the estimated models for the trend are not able to adapt to the entire time series. Moreover, the model estimates are cursed by the presence of autocorrelation in the residuals. For instance, the polynomial trend solutions (the quadratic form shown in Fig. 1 as Poli. (upld)) presents a very high goodness of fit (the 89.7% of the variability is explained by the quadratic trend). The parameters in the polynomial function are significant and the full model specification test suggests that the model is significant. Notwithstanding, the model residuals present positive and significant autocorrelations.

The non-linear growth curves (such as modified exponential, logistic, and Gompertz curves) are also adopted here. The estimation of the parameters of these functions presents some computational issues. In particular, the saturation level of the growth curves is difficult to obtain due to the high variability observed on the final stretch of the time series.

Finally, the non-functional analysis has been adopted to identify the underlying trend of the time series. In particular, the moving average approach is used in the following analysis. On one, hand this method is not based on underlying theoretical assumptions and for this reason it could be considered more reliable than the estimation of functional trends in this specific framework. On the other hand, this approach leads to data loss for the first half of 2004 and the second half of 2016.

This approach involves some specific sequential steps. First, the simple moving averages of order 12 are computed and centred (the obtained composition correspond to a weighted moving average of order 13). The ratios between the observed time series and the moving averages are computed (obtaining the so-called "row seasonality indexes"). Assuming a constant seasonality, these measures are used to compute the period specific seasonality indexes SI (the period specific arithmetic means). Finally, these indexes are adjusted to be suitable for the analysis of flow variables such as the one analysed here.

The outcome of such a procedure is summarized in Table 1. The seasonality indexes allow to identify the periods presenting a number of uploads larger (SI larger than one) and lower (SI lower than one) than the averaged trend value. The proposed approach represents an ad-hoc solution.

Table 1. Seasonality indexes

Month	Adjusted SI	Census SI	Month	Adjusted SI	Census SI
January	0.93	0.92	July	1.09	1.10
February	0.83	0.82	August	1.08	1.10
March	0.95	0.95	September	1.02	1.04
April	0.98	0.98	October	1.08	1.08
May	1.10	1.09	November	0.96	0.97
June	1.09	1.07	December	0.89	0.89

The "automatic" Census procedure (Shiskin et al. 1967) is applied in order to obtain a more robust result. Also this method is based on the computation of moving averages. The results of the Census method are compared to the ones of the ad-hoc solution in Table 1.

The first important result is that presence of seasonality is confirmed by both methods. The two methods bring to comparable results. The computed indexes are slightly different for some periods but the two methods are coherent in the identification of the positive or negative seasonal effects. In particular, a negative seasonality can be observed in the period between November and April. On the contrary, the number of uploads is larger than the trend value in the period between May and October.

Observing the values of the Census based seasonality indices the largest seasonal effects are observed in July and August with a number of uploads that is 10% larger than the averaged trend. On the other hand, a reduction of 18% is observed in February. This result is only partly related to the so-called calendar effect.

The obtained results have been validated considering the modern approach to the time series analysis based on the Box and Jenkins methodology (Box and Jenkins 1970).

The time series is modelled considering a seasonal stochastic process. The best specification among the so-called Seasonal ARIMA models is selected adopting the BIC criterion. In order to account for heteroscedasticity, the model is applied to the logarithmic transformation of the time series.

The final model specification follows an ARIMA $(1, 2, 1) \times (2, 0, 0)$. The estimated model is as:

$$y_t^* = \Delta^2 \ln\left(upld_t\right) = 0.15y_{t-1}^* - 0.96\varepsilon_{t-1} + 0.27y_{t-12}^* + 0.36y_{t-24}^* + \varepsilon_t. \qquad (1)$$

The estimation results suggest that: (a) the logarithmic time series must be differentiated twice in order to be considered stationary behaviour (coherently with the quadratic trend shown in Fig. 1); (b) non-seasonal component of the model shows both autoregressive and moving average terms of order 1; (c) the seasonal component includes only the autoregressive term of order 2. The values of the times series observed on the single periods (months) "remember" their behaviour of the past two years.

The results of the time series analysis can be summarised as follows. The upload behaviour of the users of Flickr is different in the two periods of the year identified by means of the classical decomposition approach. The stochastic model estimation confirms the significance of the seasonal component. The future analysis must account for this specific characteristic of the phenomenon starting from the sampling design process.

3   The Analysis of Users' Uploads in 2016

The next step in the analysis of upload behaviour regards the study of the geotagging habits of the Flickr users. Using the WebGIS tool of Flickr (World Map) it is possible to search for the geotagged photos. In particular, the results of a generic "everyone's uploads" search show that the total number of geotagged photos until 2016 is about 5 million (from www.flickr.com/map website).

The geotagging service was launched at the end of August 2006. The total number of photos uploaded from September 2006 is also available from the Flickr archives. The general rate of geotagging can be finally estimated. Its value is very low, i.e. about 0.1%. This result is obtained considering the information aggregated over a very long period. The quality of this measure cannot be evaluated by the users because metadata about the entire phenomenon is not available. For these reasons, a more accurate analysis is developed on a sample of Flickr users.

The specific sample design is based on two basic ideas. First of all, the geotagging service was an innovative service in 2006 but now it reached its saturation level. Secondly, the phenomenon is strongly affected by the evolution of photographers' equipment and the diffusion of smartphones. The growing availability of photographic tools, including a built-in GPS module, encourages the geotagging behaviour.

The hypothesis is that the geotagging of photographic contents is a growing phenomenon and that it is still evolving. In order to avoid unnecessary complications, the sample used for the estimation of the proportion of geotagged photos is selected considering the uploads observed during 2016. The sample has been selected considering two fundamental needs. In order to evaluate the inferential properties of the estimation results, the sample units must be randomly selected. In particular, the selection bias issue can be completely avoided considering a random sample selection process. Moreover, the results of the previous section highlight the seasonality of the upload phenomenon. For this reason, a better representation of the geotagging process can be obtained stratifying the sample over the observational sub-period (months). This solution allows studying the seasonality of the geotagging process.

The sampling process presents some criticisms. First of all, the list of the population units is not available because it is formed gradually during the observational period. The solution adopted in the present research is to sample the uploaded photos at regular intervals fixing the number of photos sampled in each occasion.

The size of sample units is predetermined in order to guarantee the monthly representativeness of the sample and it consider the possible presence of errors in the Flickr records. The sampling method considers the following steps.

1. Every day an automatic script is used to download the data forming a very large sample of pictures uploaded by the users of Flickr service. Consequently, the reference statistical unit is the photo, not the individual Flickr user.
2. Every hour during the day the script identify the latest 150 uploaded photos. For each picture, the upload time, the user's code, the rank, the number of views, comments, tags, notes and groups in which the photo is included are measured. Two other measures regarding the users are collected: the total number of loaded images and the number of followers. For the geotagged photos the WGS84 coordinates are observed. Flickr WebGIS software attributed these pictures to the reference country where they are uploaded.
3. The single day reports are generated by the script for every day of observation.

The information collected in the various reports has been processed in order to obtain a usable database. In particular, given the results of the data cleansing process, the final database presents the following features.

- The total amount of pictures observed every day is theoretically equal to 3600. This nominal sample size cannot be reached because a number of the uploaded pictures are deleted before the data collection. Moreover, some observations are lost because of errors in the downloaded records. Finally, the service has been suspended for maintenance several times during the observational period. For instance, the maintenance lasted almost 5 full days in December. For these reasons, the number of daily observations (excluding the days in which the service is down for 24 h) ranges from 3000 to 3500. The daily mean number of observed pictures over the year is 3241.
- The total number of monthly observations ranges from a maximum of 100 thousand pictures in July to a minimum of 86 thousand in December.
- Due to the issues listed in the previous paragraph, the final annual sample size is equal to 1.17 million corresponding to the 90% of the theoretical maximum size (1.3 million).
- The missing values can be considered as missing completely at random because the missing patterns are not related with the interest phenomenon (the geotagging process). For this reason, the hypothesis of self-selection can be rejected. Moreover, the sample size is not severely affected by missing values.

- During the year 2016 the total number of uploaded pictures is close to 612 million. The sampling proportion results to be 0.2%. This value seems to be very low but the sampling proportion is not a direct indicator of the sample quality. For instance, a sample size of 400 units is sufficient in order to obtain a 5% maximum error in the estimation of a proportion if the population is infinite (612 million represents a huge population size). The sample size rose to about 10000 units if the error must be at most equal to 1% (see Marbach 1992, p. 132 for further details). The considered sample size is therefore huge if compared to these benchmarks.

3.1 Estimating the Geotagging Rate

The analysis of geotagging rate can be based on the described sample. First of all, for each month, all the photos that were provided with geographic coordinates have been identified. The share of geotagging is then computed both on a monthly and yearly basis. The results are reported in Table 2. The rates are computed considering the date of upload and the date of collection.

Table 2. Monthly geotagging rates

Month	Date of collection			Date of loading		
	Photos	Geotagged photos	Geotagging rate %	Photos	Geotagged photos	Geotagging rate %
January	98278	9510	9.68	97004	9396	9.69
February	93449	9524	10.19	93422	9499	10.17
March	100077	10376	10.37	100079	10371	10.36
April	96412	9865	10.23	96346	9885	10.26
May	99095	9688	9.78	99068	9648	9.74
June	97137	9796	10.08	97068	9781	10.08
July	101100	10694	10.58	101080	10692	10.58
August	97792	10100	10.33	97732	10064	10.30
September	97843	9641	9.85	97797	9640	9.86
October	102755	10671	10.38	102691	10649	10.37
November	100132	9819	9.81	100142	9825	9.81
December	85976	6558	7.63	85907	6554	7.63
2016	1170046	116242	9.93	1168336	116004	9.93

The first analysis is developed considering the date of collection. The general rate of geotagging of photos uploaded to Flickr in 2016 is 9.93%. This rate is not constant over the observational period. The monthly report shows this behaviour with a rate ranging from 7.63% in December to 10.58% in July.

As mentioned before, both the yearly and the monthly estimates reported in Table 2 are obtained considering a maximum error lower than 1%. Every daily report also collects the effective date of the (first) loading.

The analysis of this information allows identifying some specific issues. First of all, the photos can be collected on a day different from the one of the upload. This can cause some time shifts also between months and years. Moreover, the software allows to revive the old photos. These photos are collected by the script but their reference is wrong. To refine the estimation of the geotagging rates, the sample has been cleaned by selecting only the pictures loaded for the first time in 2016. As the results in Table 2 reveal the issue is not very affecting (monthly and annual rates are substantially identical) but the correction can be easily obtained.

An ulterior analysis can be developed to study the seasonality of the geotagging rates. A first empirical evidence has already emerged looking to July and December data. The mean rate of geotagged photos for the period from May to October 2016 is equal to 10.16% while for the November-April period the same value is lower, i.e. 9.69%. A Chi-squared test can be adopted to evaluate the significance of the observed difference (0.47%). The value of the test statistic is 70.13 (the significance level is close to zero). The geotagging process is therefore associated with the period of the year.

Finally, both the upload and geotagging behaviours present a relevant seasonality. In the period between May and October, the analyses identified a higher number of uploads and a slightly larger proportion of geotagged photos too.

3.2 The Analysis of the Spatial Distribution of the Sample

A spatial analysis of the distribution of the phenomenon can be obtained restricting the study to the sub-sample of the geotagged photos only. These photos are associated with the geographical coordinates of the shot and where possible with the country. The overall mapping of the phenomenon is given in Fig. 2. Spatial analysis is then performed on the basis of the classification automatically obtained from the WebGIS.

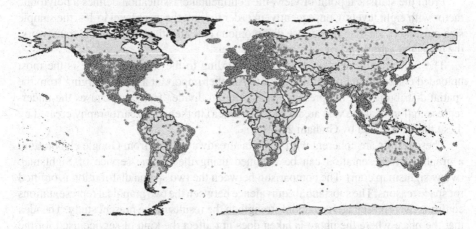

Fig. 2. The World spatial distribution of the geotagged photos

A preliminary data cleansing process is adopted to select the photos uploaded in 2016 and which have been attributed to a single country. The final sample size is about 115 thousand. Nearly one thousand photos are excluded because they are taken during navigation (as is easy to see from Fig. 2) or, in small part, because their records present corrupted geographical coordinates.

The countries that exceed the threshold of 5000 shots are only four: United States of America (almost 30 thousand photos), the United Kingdom (almost 12.5 thousand photos), Australia (about 7200 shots) and Italy (almost 5800 shots). These four countries represent the 48% of the full sample. The remaining sample units are spread all around the world.

The global spatial distribution is difficult to read and for this reason, the following analyses are based on the continental classification. A detailed view will be given for the 28 countries of the European Union.

Some countries, such as Russia and Turkey, are not uniquely included in one single continent. In order to aggregate the data at the continental level, these countries entered a generic transcontinental group (which also includes some other countries). This group collects the 2.1% of the sampled photos.

The Europe is the most "photographed continent": 37.3% of the photos comes from Europe (35.2% regards the 28 European Union countries). The 31% of the photos represent the north-central America countries. USA and Canada are the most represented nations (92.8% of the photos in this sub-sample).

The proportion of observations in Asia, Oceania, and South America are 15.6%, 7% and 6.1% respectively. The photos geotagged in Australia are the 91% of the total photos of Oceania.

The African continent presents a very low proportion of observations. This is due to the fact that Egypt was included in the transcontinental group. Moreover, in Africa, the access to Internet is less diffused.

From the statistical point of view, the continental classification defines a polytomic factor with eight levels. Consequently, in order to limit the error level to 1%, the sample size must be twice than in the case dichotomous classification. Also in this framework, the collected sample is large enough.

The fundamental result is then that, according to the sample, Europe is the most uploaded continent in Flickr during 2016. Another important aspect emerging from the spatial distributions is the presence of the digital divide. This issue causes the under-representation of some vast areas (such as Africa) in the virtual cartography created by these tools (as stated by Graham 2012).

These results are coherent with the data already available from Google elaboration: a graphical representation can be obtained using the on-line service of Sightsmap (www.sightsmap.com). The comparison between the two spatial distribution is omitted for space reasons. The substantial equivalence between the two graphical representations confirms the representativeness and strengthen the results of the present study. The idea that the place where the photo is taken does not affect the kind of service used for the photos upload is also supported.

The distribution of the photos within the 28 countries in EU (identified according to the three-letter ISO 3166 code) is given in Table 3 (and relative Fig. 3). More than one-third of the geotagged photos belongs to this geographical area. The other EU members present much smaller proportions of observations.

Table 3. Percentage distribution of sample in European Union (UE28)

Country	Weight %	Country	Weight %
GBR	30.9	DNK	1.0
ITA	14.4	FIN	0.9
ESP	10.7	ROU	0.6
FRA	10.3	HUN	0.6
DEU	9.3	HRV	0.5
POL	3.9	BGR	0.2
NLD	3.6	EST	0.2
SWE	2.5	MLT	0.2
PRT	1.9	LVA	0.2
BEL	1.7	SVN	0.2
GRC	1.6	LTU	0.1
IRL	1.5	SVK	0.1
AUT	1.5	LUX	0.1
CZE	1.2	CYP	0.1

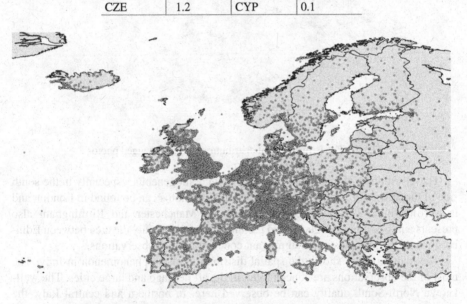

Fig. 3. The European spatial distribution of the geotagged photos

The information summarised in Table 3 show that the first five countries present proportions of observations significantly larger than the others. In particular, the top five EU nations represent nearly the 76% of the EU sample.

In a nutshell, it can be said that, for 2016, a third of the global is related with pictures taken in EU28. In this area, three out of four pictures are taken in UK, Italy, Spain, France or Germany. With the Brexit, Italy has a good chance of becoming the most "photographed" country in the area. In order to analyse the spatial distribution, a poly-tomic factor defining the 28 countries must be considered. The sample size necessary to ensure the maximum error of 1% is then much higher than in the previous cases. Notwithstanding the sample size is in this case about 40 thousand and consequently, it is sufficient to guarantee the same precision.

Table 3 shows that the UK (which includes also some pictures taken in Gibraltar) is the most "photographed" country in the EU (as in 2016 the Brexit was still not effective), with 30.9% of the sub-sample. Figure 4 represents the distribution of the geotagged photos on the UK.

Fig. 4. The British spatial distribution of the geotagged photos

The distribution of individual photos is quite homogeneous, especially in the south side of Great Britain. The highest concentration of photos can be found in London and its surroundings. The area between Liverpool, Manchester and Birmingham also presents a large number of geotagged pictures. In Scotland only the area between Edinburgh and Glasgow presents a significant concentration of observations.

The map in Fig. 5 shows the spatial distribution of the phenomenon in Italy. The most of the observations are concentrated in the art heritage and large cities. The well-known North-South duality can be observed here. In northern and central Italy, the distribution seems to be very close to the one of Switzerland and Western Austria, with peaks in the large urban areas.

The phenomenon in the South of Italy presents a lower density. The geotagged photos are mainly observed in the bay of Naples and the main cities of Puglia and Sicily. The South of Italy is, therefore, under-represented in the Flickr data sample. A possible explanation for this dualism can be found in the heterogeneous number of tourists and in the digital divide phenomenon. This is certainly an aspect that needs to be addressed in the further studies.

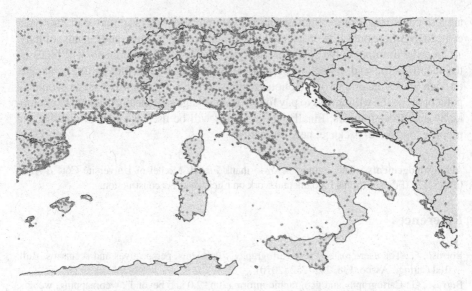

Fig. 5. The Italian spatial distribution of the geotagged photos

4 Conclusions and Discussion

The first important result of the present work is the estimation of the proportion of geotagged photos. This result is based on the sample of photos uploaded during 2016. On the basis of the sample estimates, we can state that the geotagging rate is about 10%. The seasonality estimated on the full sample shows that the period May-October presents a proportion significantly higher than rest of the year.

The analysis of the spatial distribution of the geotagged photos that have been uploaded on Flickr is very similar to the image given by the analysis of Panoramio data. Going into details, the spatial distributions of photos in the United Kingdom and Italy has been considered. In both sub-samples, the distribution is quite uneven. In particular, in Italy, the geotagged photos are concentrated in the big metropolitan areas and in the art heritage cities. Moreover, the density of the spatial distribution is lower in the southern regions.

On one hand, this peculiar behaviour can be due to the different number of users observed in the different regions. On the other hand, this can be considered as a proxy of the availability of web connections in the various areas. As stated in Graham (2012) the digital divide can cause severe biases in the web mapping process. The areas presenting a better Internet coverage are commonly more represented in the web mapping process.

The differences between South and North of Italy have been investigated in a study conducted using the OpenStreetMap (OSM) tool for participatory cartography. In Mauro (2013), the Author states that the effect of the digital divide on the quality of OSM cartography is higher than the one of the specific characteristics of the territories. The results for Italian sub-sample are coherent with those reported in Mauro (2013). They are also consistent with the findings of the exploratory survey (as reported in Zaccomer et al. 2016) where only 12% of selected Italian users lived in South (and Islands) of Italy.

In order to improve the statistical analyses, the future developments will focus on the identification and collection of a larger user dataset. The idea is to investigate, through Flickr, the propensity to photographic tourism and measure (from an economic point of view) the willingness to pay for a travel package specifically oriented to photography and photographers. Finally, these results will be used in order to identify and propose, in a travel package, new itineraries.

Acknowledgements. The Authors wish to thank Franck Michel of Université Côte d'Azur, CNRS, I3S (France) for his fundamental work on Flickr datasets construction.

References

Borruso, G.: The user-created "new-cartography". Problems, perspectives and scenarios. Bull. Ital Cartogr. Assoc. **138**, 241–252 (2010)

Borruso, G.: Cartography and geographic information "2.0 and beyond", webmapping, webgis. An introduction. Bull. Ital. Cartogr. Assoc. **147**, 7–15 (2013)

Box, G.E.P., Jenkins, G.M.: Time Series Analysis, Forecasting and Control. Holden-Day, San Francisco (1970)

Bruns, A.: Towards produsage: futures for user-led content production. In: Sudweeks, F., Hrachovec, H., Ess, C. (eds.) Proceedings of Cultural Attitude Towards Communication and Technology, pp. 275–284. Murdoch University, Perth (2006)

Butler, D.: Mashups mix data into global service. Nature **439**, 6–7 (2006)

Di Fonzo, T., Lisi, F.: Serie storiche economiche. Analisi statistiche e applicazioni. Carrocci, Roma (2005)

Eisnor, D.A.: What is neogeography anyway? Platial news and Neogeography (2006). http://platial.typepad.com/news/2006/05/what_is_neogeog.html

Gogoi, D.: A conceptual framework of photographic tourism. Int. J. Res. Appl. Nat. Soc. Sci. **8**, 109–114 (2014)

Goodchild, M.F.: Citizen as sensors: the world of volunteered geography. GeoJournal **69**, 211–221 (2007)

Graham, M.: Featured graphic: digital divide: the geography of Internet access. Environ. Plan. **44**, 1009–1010 (2012)

Iñiguez-Berrozpe, T., Plumed-Lasarte, M., Latorre-Martinez, M.P.: Flickr: tool for a market analysis of tourism consumption. In: Sáez-Martínez, F.J., Sánchez-Ollero, J.L., García-Pozo, A., Pérez-Calderón, E. (eds.) Managing the environment: sustainability and economic development of tourism, pp. 20–34. Chartridge Books, Oxford (2013)

Krasna, F.: Cartography 2.0 for an innovative tourism: along the Slovenian routes among nature, art and history: Kojnik's ring. Bull. Ital. Cartogr. Assoc. **151**, 91–104 (2014)

Marbach, G.: Le ricerche di mercato. UTET, Torino (1992)

Mauro, G.: Digital divide and collaborative mapping: the street network's growth in OpenStreetMap. A comparison between two Italian provinces, Benevento and Trento. Bull. Ital. Cartogr. Assoc. **147**, 93–108 (2013)

Michel, F.: Flickr explorer: what makes explored photos so special? (2013). Provided under license Creative Commons 3.0. http://www.flickr.com/photos/franckmichel

Palmer, C., Lester, J.O.: Photographic tourism. Shooting the innocuous, making meaning of tourist photographic behavior. In: Novelli, M. (ed.) Niche Tourism. Contemporary Issues, Trends and Cases, pp. 15–25. Butterworth-Heinemann Ltd., Oxford (2004)

Scanu, G.: Comments on the prospects of cartography. Bull. Ital. Cartogr. Assoc. **132–134**, 11–21 (2008)

Shiskin, J., Young, A.H., Musgrave, J.C.: The X-11 variant of the Census Method II seasonal adjustment program. Technical paper 15, Bureau of Census, US Department of Commerce, Washington DC (1967)

Sun, J.: Tourist tales: a case study on photography tourism in Yuanyang, China. In: Han, M., Graburn, N. (eds.) Tourism and Glocalization: Perspectives on East Asian Societies. Senri Ethnological Studies, vol. 76, pp. 111–130 (2010)

Turner, A.J.: Introduction to Neogeography. O'Reilly Media Inc., Sebastopol (2006)

Zaccomer, G.P., Marangon, F., Troiano, S.: Measurements of photographic tourism experiences: findings of an exploratory survey on Flickr users as new directions in tourism research. In: Volo, S., Maurer, O. (eds.) Book of Abstracts Consumer Behavior in Tourism Symposium 2016 Experiences, Emotions and Memories: New Directions in Tourism Re-search. Free University of Bozen, Bruneck (2016)

Zielstra, D., Hochmair, H.H.: Positional accuracy analysis of Flickr and Panoramio images for selected world regions. Journal of Spatial Science **58**, 251–273 (2013)

From *SMART Cities* to SMART City-Regions: Reflections and Proposals

Ilaria Greco[✉] and Angela Cresta

Department of Low, Economic, Management and Quantitative Methods,
University of Sannio, Via delle Puglie 1, 82100 Benevento, Italy
{ilagreco,cresta}@unisannio.it

Abstract. The paper introduce the rapid development of the "smart city" concept and its different meanings through a critical review of main bibliographical references: from the original concept of intelligent, digital and creative city, to the recent one of human smart city and SENSEable city, until to the integrated approach, who reads the "smartness" as condition for a continuous and ongoing process of growth and innovation [35].

In Europe, and also in Italy, the application of this concept has been mainly restricted to the urban scale, lacking a broader strategic and territorial vision. Starting with some reflections already developed by the authors on the subject [36], the article proposes a change of scale in the approach to the topic of the "smart city" (from urban scale to wide scale), which implies not only a conceptual transition (*Smart city* to *Smart city-region*), but the definition of completely different models and strategies.

The analysis considers the key role that the Europe's Growth Agenda recognizes to Regions in the development of new growth dynamic for Europe based on the definition of smart specialization strategies, and focuses on importance of identifying an Italian approach - *an Italian road map* - to smart cities, based on local potentialities. Finally, in the perspective of a new mutual balance between City and Region is presented the experience (to be defined) of the Northern global city-region Milano-Torino.

Keywords: Smart city · Smart region · Smart specialization · Planning

1 Introduction: A Geographical Vision of the SMART Concept[1]

Despite numerous studies, the wide literature, the various contributions on this topic and the many applications in models, actions and policies, we still do not have a shared definition of the term, or rather the concept of Smart City [18, 33]. For several years,

---

[1] The paper is the result of a common reflection of the authors; however, the single sections can thus be attributed to: Ilaria Greco paragraphs 1 and 2 and Angela Cresta paragraphs 3 e 4. The reflections presented are the result of participation at the *first International Smart Cities in Smart Regions 2016 Conference*, organized by Lahti University of Applied Sciences took place in May 10–12, 2016, Lahti, Finland.

© Springer International Publishing AG 2017
O. Gervasi et al. (Eds.): ICCSA 2017, Part III, LNCS 10406, pp. 282–295, 2017.
DOI: 10.1007/978-3-319-62398-6_20

the concept of Smart City was used as a "label Urban" [39], a fuzzy concept, often used improperly [48], declined with many different meanings.

At the beginning of the Nineties, David V. Gibson, George Kometsky and Raymond W. Smilor published the "Technopolis Phenomenon" (1992), a work in which the term Smart City was used for the first time connected to an urban development more and more dependent on technology and on innovation and globalization phenomena, mainly by an economic vision: the "smart city" as "intelligent city" [37].

In a few years, even in response to changes in the models and urban development policies, there was a rapid evolution of the idea of smart cities from "digital city", linked to the development of technological infrastructure (so-called *techno-centered approach,* developed by Cairney and Speaks, 2000; Washburn and Sindhu 2010), to "socially inclusive city" linked to the enhancement of social and human capital and participation practices (so-called *human-centered approach,* developed by Partridge, 2004; Berry and Glaeser, 2005) - what in our previous study we have defined as *SENSEable Cities* according to the concept of equity[2] [35], until the idea of smart city as "city with increased quality of life" (according to an *integrated approach,* supported by Kanter and Litow, 2009; Campbell, 2012; The European House-Ambrosetti 2012), according to an integration between technology and human and social capital to create the suitable condition for a continuous and ongoing process of growth and innovation.

The concept of "smart city" has thus been widely extended, taking on the meanings of interconnected, attractive, sustainable, comfortable and inclusive city [55].

Recently, the same EU and national policies have supported programs and projects for development of smart city as an opportunity to coordinate different sectoral strategies, emphasizing the role of cities as centers of innovation and territorial cohesion: see the *Integrated Strategic Energy Technology (SET) Plan* (2007–2013), the *European Program 2020,* the *EU Research and Innovation program Horizon 2020* (2014–2020), the *European Digital Agenda; PON Research and Competitiveness* 2007–2013, the *Italian Digital Agenda.*

In the Report of the European Smart Cities, in line with the new European vision for the future development of global cities (Horizon 2020 Urban Forum, Digital Agenda - Strategy 20.20.20, Decree Digitalia, etc.) is defined "A Smart City is a city well performing in six characteristics, built on the smart combination of endowments and activities of self-decisive, independent and aware citizens: mobility, environment, people, living, governance, economy". This is one of the most complete definition.

Despite the breadth of the concept, still few, however, are the studies and research that consider the concept of smartness as an opportunity to re-think the planning models of the contemporary city in a strategic and wider territorial vision that goes beyond the political and administrative boundaries of a city: the projects and the proposed models are aimed at punctual investments, unrelated to an organic vision of innovation and urban and regional development. The territorial logic is completely absent!

---

[2] According to concept of *SENSEable Citie,* a city should not just be smart, but its smartness must cover all the inhabitants. In the article cited, considering together the size of *smartness and equity* have been presented four different models of *Smart-Equity Cities: (i) Potential Smart/Equity City, (ii) Smart City; (iii) Senseable City, (iv) Equitable City.*

Most of the projects promoted to date at worldwide level, in fact, support sustainable mobility, energy saving, intelligent buildings, or a decrease in the environmental footprints of urban settlements. The same International and European rankings as the *Top Ten Global Smart Cities* and the *Top Ten Smartest European Cities* by Boyd Cohen [25], or the *European smart cities* in ESPON 2013 (ESPON Project 1.1.1), give an limited interpretation, measuring the smartness with mostly quantitative indicators related to urban scale in terms of: (i) investments in human and social capital; (ii) traditional (transport) and modern (ICT) communication infrastructure; (iii) sustainable economic development; (iv) quality of life.

Missing, therefore, a *geographical vision of the SMART concept* and this article is proposed as a first reflection for the construction of this vision in terms of innovation widespread in the territory.

2   Towards a Definition of *Smart City-Region*

Until now, in the approach to the topic of the smart city it lacked a change of scale. From the international literature and from the case studies it is evident that the application of this concept has been mainly restricted to the urban scale, through the definition of strategies of growth smart, sectorally declined, with punctual interventions or, even though integrated, of urban area.

Limiting the research to the European and Italian context, there are few cases in which the principles of smart cities have been applied to medium-sized cities, and even more, the experiences are limited to individual projects if we consider the smaller towns, however, they represent a specific and prevalent characteristic of the urban structure, both Italian and European. The smaller urban centers, in fact, are remained at the margins of global process of innovation and renewal of the urban areas, where the "smartness approach" is central, even in a European strategic vision for urban development [16].

The structure of the European and Italian urban model imposes, therefore, a revision of the concept and policies of smart cities, requiring the extension and application of the smart city model on large-scale, moving from the idea of "smart city" to that of "smart region/land", understood as intelligent city widespread to territorial level, consisting of clusters of common joined by a long-term prospect of development and innovation, passing from the intelligent planning of the city at the intelligent planning of the territories [36].

This means adopting a new approach to urban planning processes that sees the possibility of extending the benefits and new opportunities for development related to the use of a planning model smart (smart mobility, smart people, smart environment, smart economy, smart living, smart governance) to the peri-urban and infra-urban territories that are physically and functionally in the area of gravitation of the main urban pole - engine of innovation and the change - transforming the condition of the territories from marginal to complementary, according to an integrated and polycentric development model between strong nodes and weak nodes.

A perspective of growth and development that weaves, therefore, the potential and risks of most urban areas, of different rank, declinable in the definition of a strategy of smart city extended to large-scale, understood as "smart city-region" or, more simply, "smart region". The smart region is a geographical area in which through common and shared policies it will increase the competitiveness and attractiveness of the territory, with particular attention to social cohesion, spread of knowledge, creative growth, accessibility and freedom of movement, the usability of the environment (natural, historical architectural, urban spread) and quality of the landscape and the lives of citizens [15, 47].

A vision that in the geographical studies recalls the recent reflections on the definition of two other concepts:

(i) *"Global city-region"* [58], from the point of view of economic and political geography. It is the result of economic and social concentration processes that develop in territorial systems densely urbanized or characterized by a tendency toward spatial polarization. These centers put in relation the national system with the global economic system;

(ii) *"Mega-city region"* [38], which expresses the urban and regional geography perspective. It is a wide polycentric urbanized area, formed by multiple cities, physically separate, but functionally interconnected, which are concentrated around one or more major cities, forming economically very strong urban regions, connected by infrastructure networks traversed by flows of people, goods and information.

Compared to the possible forms of physical interconnection, social and economic of the centers in territorial systems of wide area, the definition of a smart region represents a great opportunity to enhance the specificity of the European and Italian urban system, allowing marginal areas (such as peri-urban and inter-urban areas, as well as small cities in peripheral regions, often penalized by high levels of digital divide) to participate in socio-economic processes and innovation in spatial and environmental regeneration plans, based on the improvement of ICT nodes and networks.

Certainly, the conceptual transition from smart city to smart region implies the definition of wider-scale smart very complex programs and projects. Their management requires, in fact, the involvement of all territorial institutions (local, regional, national and Community), functional institutions, businesses and citizens, as well as the development of a form of multi-level participate governance that integrates the top-down with a bottom-up approach to development [7].

In this perspective, increases awareness of the need to proceed through a systemic view and planning of wide-scale, which aims to focus resources (public and private), that continue to diminish, overcoming punctual size of the rider experiences implemented so far in the field of smart programmes and projects in urban areas, with the objective of stimulating an increased territorial (re)balance in the development processes [32].

This means creating a system of studies, skills and interests necessarily public-private and multidisciplinary at different scales (local, urban and regional) for the understanding of the phenomena and the development of innovative projects in terms of enhancement of physical space and strengthening of practices social and economic relationships. Only in this way will be possible to build an intelligent infrastructure at the regional scale for constant sharing of visions, goals, ideas and resources between urban polarities groups that are part of the same smart region (land).

The wide area approach integrates, in fact all levels of planning, from the timely to the metropolitan and regional, as well as lay the strategic foundation of the intelligent and shared development of the territory. The territories have to find the right combination of local resources and policies aimed at implementing strategies to re-think about innovative planning methods and practices of wide area.

This means rethinking the model of urban development, overcoming the dualistic vision to approach the Jacobs's thought and that is to consider the city in terms of complex system, as a set of different processes that generate changes and consolidations, as a system where you need to shift the focus from hard infrastructure to soft infrastructure, able to close the gap, improve the quality of life of citizens, think of new ways of seeing and designing the city and its metropolitan area into an integrated strategic vision.

The concept of Smart region has a double interpretive key, being able to be defined as "opportunistic" and "mobility" a concept: opportunistic because it could serve to transform cities in terms of spatial and functional view, define a new model of development and resource management, as well as expansion and relationship with a scope of wide reference area; mobility as potentially able to mobilize resources, both economic and financial, creative and human capital and transform them into opportunities, based on shared specialization strategies.

The change of scale involves, in fact, not only a conceptual transition (smart city to smart region), but the definition of models and strategies of smartness region completely different. If large cities can compete and, therefore, implement projects in all areas of a smart city (smart mobility, smart people, smart environment, smart economy, smart living, smart governance …), in the context of a smart region, smaller urban centers must focus attention on specific aspects, according to their vocation and territorial characterization.

The planning, the activities and the management of a smart region should leverage on what the land in which you are operating makes available, to evaluate different scenarios and sectors on which to focus. It is necessary, therefore, to develop a "*strategy of specialization*" based on two basic steps:

– identification of the potential offered by the area in order to identify specific areas that represent the identitary vocation of the smart region;
– capitalization of these specific resources in order to establish a competitive advantage on a global scale.

Only by establishing a clear and shared "specialization strategy" will be able to start a technology programming and planning process that is oriented to strengthening and enhancement of the existing. In this way, any intervention will be characterized by a systemic approach to the problems that characterize the territory, whose specific nature must become the starting point of all reasoning [13].

3   Smart Specialisation and Europe's Growth Agenda: An Italian Roadmap

"Smart Specialisation is one of the key innovations of the new programming period 2014–20 for the European Structural and Investment Funds. It's about creating a new growth dynamics and a transformation of the EU economies.(…) Linking up the Smart Specialisation Strategies between regions in related areas can create additional growth potential beyond the silo approach". Walter Deffaa, Director-General for Regional and Urban Policy[3].

Smart Specialisation is one of the key innovations of the new programming period 2014–20 for the European Structural and Investment Funds. It's about creating a new growth dynamics and a transformation of the EU economies towards innovation driven smart, sustainable and inclusive growth[4].

The national and regional research and innovation strategies for smart specialization (RIS3) are, in fact, territorial programs of integrated economic transformation launched by national and regional authorities in Europe to encourage more efficient use of European Structural and Investment Funds (ESI Funds) and achieve greater synergies between different EU policies, national and regional, as well as between public and private investments [29].

The theme of smart specialization is not new. It is, rather, the improvement and upgrading of an existing methodology for the programming of the Structural Funds in supporting innovation strategies at regional level has already been adopted by several international institutions, like the World Bank, the OECD and the International Monetary Fund (IMF). The most advanced regions are already engaging in similar strategic initiatives such as *Regions for Economic Change*[5] or the *Regional Observatory for Innovation*[6].

Compared to the new planning, the novelty lies in the fact that the Commission requires such strategies as a precondition for accessing FESR funding. The regions and the EU Member States should therefore implement strategies RIS3 before the operational programs in support of these investments are approved[7].

Among the inspiring principles of RIS3 policy we have to make innovation a priority for all regions, calling for policy makers to consider the interdependence of the different aspects of smart growth, sustainable and inclusive, responding to complex challenges and adapting the policy to the regional and local context.

---

[3] *"Smart Regions Conference: Driving Smart Specialisation Investments In Priority Areas For European Growth"*, 1st of June, 2016. http://ec.europa.eu/regional_policy/en/conferences/smart-regions/agenda/.

[4] Regulation (UE) n. 1301/2013, the European Parliament and of the Council of 17 Dec. 2013.

[5] http://europa.eu/legislation_summaries/regional_policy/review_and_future/g24240_it.htm.

[6] http://www.rim-europa.eu.

[7] http://ec.europa.eu/regional_policy/sources/docgener/presenta/smart_specialisation/smart_ris3_2012.pdf.

Smart specialization combines, in fact, two logics of political action:

- the definition of vertical priorities related fields, technologies and activities rather than generic priorities, pushing for greater cooperation between research, development and human capital;
- the inclusion of dynamism, competitive factors and entrepreneurial knowledge that combines science, technology and engineering with knowledge of market developments, the needs of businesses and emerging opportunities.

This is designed to achieve important goals of the smart growth processes of the territories:

- focus policy support and investments on key priorities, challenges and development needs based on knowledge of the national and regional capabilities;
- enhance the strengths, competitive advantages and excellence of each country or region;
- support technological innovation based on practice and promote investment in the private sector;
- ensure the full participation of actors involved and encourage innovation and experimentation.

The definition of a smart specialization strategy goes, in fact, through a process of transformation that engages the territories in a series of actions:

- the development of a vision for growth;
- the identification of its competitive advantage;
- the definition of strategic priorities;
- the use of smart policies and actions.

Currently are activated over 120 smart specialization strategies at national or regional levels, allocated funds for over 40 billion eur. Adding to this, the leverage effects for private investment and contributions from other EU instruments, we estimate That about 250 billion eur will be mobilized via the strategies. This is a massive contribution to the Investment Plan for Europe.

The objective is, in fact, promote the growing through synergies among the different EU funding tools - ESI Funds, INTERREG including and macro-regional strategies, Horizon2020, COSME and hopefully Also the European Fund for Strategic Investments (EFSI) to provide support to regions and countries that wish to align their Smart Specialization implementation around related priorities and to complement each other. A way to create and strengthen European value chains.

First projects are being launched, like fab-labs, testing facilities, incubators, research infrastructures, pilot plants, crowd-sourcing platforms, collaborative spaces and platforms to bring business and researchers together to translate their entrepreneurial discovery process in R & D, etc.

Although with some delay, also in Italy this challenge is now being rapidly taken up.

The first indications of the Italian Government were expressed by the Monti government (2011–2012). Has been stressed the importance of identifying an Italian approach - *an Italian road map* - to smart cities, based on local potentialities to be exploited and on local criticalities to be solved.

Even Francesco Profumo, Minister for Education, University and Research (2011–2013), in the program guidelines of his ministry, has stressed the importance of a smart urban development, emphasizing the need to organize actions at the regional level, in terms of smart region, especially in reference to the subsurface planning and upgrading the energy efficiency and anti-seismic [52].

The priority of extending the concept of smart city towards that smart region was also called by Marie Donnelly, Director of new energy and renewable sources, energy efficiency and innovation in the European Community. According to Donnelly smart technologies can be really effective only if they are developed and implemented in a coordinated manner, within a large-scale vision [13].

The Italian territory is characterized, in fact, the presence of more than 8,000 municipalities, of which 70% are small municipalities with a population of less than 5,000 inhabitants. In addition, from 1861 to date, the total concentration of the Italian population in these municipalities is lowered drastically, from 50% to 17%. These polarities of reduced dimensions are characterized by a strong local identity and relevant cultural values both material and immaterial to value, but they are also limited by a shortage of resources to invest in innovation processes. Small towns must therefore cooperate and "networking", joining the few available economic resources and leveraging the many cultural resources spread within their territories, which make it unique, as also emphasized by the IBM's *Smarter Town Initiative* devoted primarily the Italian case [30].

The same recent Decree Growth 2.0 approved by the Italian Government interpreted urban smartness as an opportunity for innovation of the production system and, therefore, for economy recovery in the current crisis.

We should follow the approach of smart specialization strategies promoted by the European Union and invest in land resources: villages, historic centers, cultural heritage spread, on Italian culture and its territory [34].

Several projects have recently been implemented or activated in the Italian cities, although most of the projects within the cities monitored by the National Observatory Smart City, the National Association of Italian Municipalities (ANCI).

This mainly refers to green, mobility, urban and environmental regeneration, renewable energy, and Smart Building (seismic and energy viewpoints). Moreover, the economic resources to date allocated to smart city projects are based on a large percentage of public resources which, however, are unlikely to be available in the coming years [22, 28, 31, 44]. They divide among: municipal funds (53%); regional funds (16%); public-private partnerships (10%); European funds (8%); national funds (6%); private sponsors and endowments (5%); other funds (2%).

A first experience, instead, of large-scale schemes is represented by inter-municipal projects related to smart economy, environment, governance and living within the Union of Municipalities of Romagna, or to the smart economy, environment, living and mobility within the Mountain Community Vallo di Diano (National Association of Italian Municipalities, Smart City National Observatory 2014). On the other hand, there is the experimental proposal for technological and governance innovation of the entire province of Mantova within the so-called *Mantova Smart Region project* [14].

4   A Possible Italian "Smart City/Region": The Northern Global City-Region Milano-Torino

The area between Turin and Milan is part of a wider macro-regional system that extends beyond the traditional administrative boundaries (metropolitan and regional) and is included in a wider context by now identified as Northern Italy global city-region [51, 58], from an economic perspective, or mega-city region [6, 7, 38], from a spatial perspective. A polycentric metropolitan system, by hardly recognizable boundaries, which entirely covers the area of the Po Valley and which is formed by a network of cities of varying size and importance, connected together by an articulated infrastructure system, placing itself in direct relation with the main global city-regions [47, 56].

Within this area, it develops a system of nodes and networks, observable into its components according to a multiscale approach, which overlap to traditional administrative boundaries, configured as "bonding agents" of a metropolitan region with a high landscape value, where emerge:

– major and minor urban centers, strongly integrated to the historic structure of the communication routes and the agricultural landscape;
– large commercial polarity and equipment for leisure;
– equipped sites for logistics activities;
– ecological networks and natural connections (rivers, mountains);
– infrastructures (from the historic road and river networks to the long and fast networks of European corridors V and XXIV, in part already made;
– new territorial configurations linked to the networks of knowledge and information flows.

The existence of a great city-region, which stretches from Milan to the entire Po Valley, requires enlargement of the conceptual space from "Smart city" to a "Smart city-region", or simply "Smart Region" [53], surpassing the localistic logic that is usually adopted by single municipalities in view of technological and socio-economic development [15]. This means to pay particular attention not only to the main urban centers but also, and especially, to the peri-urban and intra-urban areas and, consequently, remedying to their marginality with respect to the stronger nodes [46].

In this perspective, it was started the research *"The smart region between Turin and Milan. Mobile services such as territorial innovation driver in view of Expo 2015"*[8], aimed at testing the use of Information and Communication Technologies (ICT) for development, management and communication of an integrated system of services to the metropolitan region scale between Turin and Milan, also in view of the opportunities arising from the Milan Universal Exhibition 2015.

---

[8] It is part of a more comprehensive research that concerns the territorial configuration of the metropolitan region between Turin and Milan. .

The project, organized in application stages related to different themes and territorial components, has as main objective the development of a mobile service system to encourage new ways of using space and new collective behavior. At the same time, tries to overcome some of the main critical (in terms of cost, effectiveness and efficiency) inherent in the excessive fragmentation of the technologies and the continuous over-lapping of infrastructure, proposing to solicit, in the next stages, the coordination and integration of multiple platforms service, from the exploitation of the opportunities offered by the Expo 2015.

The use of new information and communications technologies is therefore assumed in research perspective as a factor capable of overcoming the idea of "smart city" towards a broader concept of "smart region". The intent is to promote new services, exploiting the opportunities offered by ICT, to produce positive effects not only on the major urban centers but, above all, on the peri-urban areas and infra-urban, making them more complementary and integrated to the strong nodes. ICT as a tool of governance of the post-event phase.

The first application part of the research was developed in the second semester of 2012 and, according to a strategy that could be considered smart specialization, had as its focus the area of the *University district of City Study* in Milan. This area was seen as experimental territorial laboratory for the project in which you can make a pool of knowledge, existing studies and projects. Specifically, research has used the Sustainable Campus Project promoted by the Polytechnic and the University of Milan. The project made use of the active participation of students, researchers, administrative staff and the community for the definition of targeted actions on the issue of quality of life and envi-ronmental sustainability, declining the concept of "smart" in the development of tech-nological systems in the field of mobile services.

The goal was to promote a conscious and virtuous behavior on the part of users aimed at optimizing the use of space and services available. Have been activated, in fact, five working smart tables regarding: *City, Accessibility, Environment, Energy and People*[9].

Later, research, also in view of participation in the Joint Open Lab sponsored by Telecom Italy and Politecnico di Milano on "smart spaces", has been oriented:

- completion of the Sustainable Campus project with the realization of the planned tech applications;
- extension of the study to the Local Identity Nuclei (NIL) defined by the Territorial Plan of the Municipality of Milan, with the aim of identifying suitable sites to accom-modate new "capacitor" of physical and virtual functions;
- extension of the experimentation made in the Campus of Città Study to other univer-sity campuses between Turin and Milan (Campus Novara- University of Eastern Piemonte and, thereafter, the Mirafiori Campus of Politecnico di Torino);
- connection the research with Expo 2015, promoting the activation of a comparison of the projects developed by Politecnico di Milano, Telecom Italy, Expo 2015 SpA and the Municipality of Milan.

---

[9] The first phase of the research results were presented to the seminar "Mobile Communications: sites and services. An experiment on Sustainable Campus (Politecnico di Milano, Department of Architecture and Urban Studies, January 21, 2013).

This project, although still experimental and under implementation, is surely a first example, very interested, of smart planning of large area, aimed both to technological innovation to social integration. It has encouraged, in fact, the participation of all local institutions (local, regional, national and Community) to the definition of policies, plans and projects of large area, in a synthesis of top down and bottom up approaches that can overcome localism and increase the effectiveness of individual proposals.

A strategic vision and a methodology that starts with the search then to become concrete projects, and could later be transferred to other areas and other territories and act as, therefore, as a stimulus to the smart planning of wide area.

References

1. AA.VV.: Smart Cities nel mondo, CITTALIA-fondazione ANCI Ricerche (2012)
2. AA.VV.: Smart Cities in Italia: un'opportunità nello spirito del Rinascimento per una nuova qualità della vita, ABB e The European House-Ambrosetti (2012). http://www.abb.it/
3. Alto, A., Mon Tonen, L.: Smart Cities in Smart Regions 2016, Conference Proceedings, The first International Smart Cities in Smart Regions 2016 Conference, Lahti University of Applied Sciences took place in May 10–12, 2016, Lahti, Finland (2016)
4. Associazione Nazionale Comuni Italiani, Osservatorio Nazionale Smart City. Vademecum per la città intelligente (2014). http://osservatoriosmartcity.it/il-vademecum
5. Annunziato, M.: La roadmap delle Smart Cities. Energia Ambiente Innov. **4–5**(1), 33–42 (2012)
6. Balducci, A.: Dall'area metropolitana alla regione urbana: forme efficaci di pianificazione. Impresa e Stato, 71 (2005)
7. Bassetti, P.: Milano glocal city. In: Camera di Commercio di Milano (ed.) Milano Produttiva. 22° Rapporto. Mondadori, Milano (2012)
8. Battisti, E., Battisti, F., Di Vita, S., Guerritore, C.: Expo Diffusa e Sostenibile. Unicopli, Milano (2011)
9. Bencardino, M.: Demographic changes and urban sprawl in two middle-sized cities of campania region (Italy). In: Gervasi, O., Murgante, B., Misra, S., Gavrilova, Marina L., Rocha, A.M.A.C., Torre, C., Taniar, D., Apduhan, Bernady O. (eds.) ICCSA 2015. LNCS, vol. 9158, pp. 3–18. Springer, Cham (2015). doi:10.1007/978-3-319-21410-8_1
10. Bencardino, M., Greco, I.: Smart Communities. Social Innovation at the Service of the Smart Cities. In: Papa, R. (ed.) Smart City Planning for Energy, Transportation and Sustainability of the Urban System, Special Issue, giugno 2014, pp. 39–51 (2014) (TEMA Journal of Land Use, Mobilità e Ambiente)
11. Bencardino, M., Granata, M.F., Nesticò, A., Salvati, L.: Urban growth and real estate income. a comparison of analytical models. In: Gervasi, O., Murgante, B., Misra, S., Rocha, A.M.A.C., Torre, C., Taniar, D., Apduhan, Bernady O., Stankova, E., Wang, S. (eds.) ICCSA 2016. LNCS, vol. 9788, pp. 151–166. Springer, Cham (2016). doi:10.1007/978-3-319-42111-7_13
12. Berry, C.R., Glaeser, E.L.: The divergence of human capital levels across cities. Pap. Reg. Sci. **84**, 407–444 (2005)
13. Berthon, B., Guittat, P.: Ascesa delle città intelligenti in "*Outlook*", 2–2011. Accenture (2011). http://www.accenture.com
14. Bolici, R., Mora, L.: Dalla smart city alla smart region. In: Bertello, A., Blanchetti, E. (eds.) City 2.0. Il futuro delle città. La sfida delle smart cities tra opportunità e necessità. Allea, Milano (2012)
15. Bonomi, A., Masiero, R.: Dalla Smart City alla Smart Land. Marsilio, Venezia (2014)

16. Boscacci, F., et al.: Smartness and Italian cities. A cluster analysis. In: Tema: Journal of Land Use, Mobility and Environment. Special issue Input 2014. Smart city planning for energy, transportation and sustainability of the urban systems (2014)
17. Campbell, T.: Beyond smart cities. How cities network, learn and innovate. Earthscan, Londra-New York (2012)
18. Caragliu, A., Del Bo, C., Njkamp, P.: Smart cities in Europe. Paper presented at the conference III Central European Conference in Regional Science, CERS (2009)
19. Cardone, M.: La rivoluzione delle smart city è in corso, QualEnergia.it (2012). http://www.qualenergia.it/articoli/20120802-la-rivoluzione-delle-smart-city-in-europa-e-negli-usa
20. Carta, M.: Città Creativa 3.0. Rigenerazione urbana e politiche di valorizzazione delle armature culturali. In: Cammelli, M., Valentino, P.A. (eds.) Citymorphosis. Politiche culturali per città che cambiano, pp. 213–221. Giunti, Firenze (2011)
21. Cairney, T., Speak, G.: Developing a "smart City": Understanding Information Technology Capacity and Establishing an Agenda for Change (2000). http://trevorcairney.com/wp-content/uploads/2012/11/IT_Audit.pdf
22. Cassa Depositi e Prestiti and Politecnico di Torino. Smart City. Progetti di sviluppo e strumenti di finanziamento. Cassa Depositi e Prestiti 2013. http://www.cdp.it/static/upload/rep/report-monografico-smart-city.pdf
23. Cittalia: Smart cities nel mondo, Roma: Cittalia e Fondazione Anci Ricerche (2011)
24. Cohen, B.: The Top 10 Smart Cities on the Planet (2012). www.fastcoexist.com /1679127/the-top-10-smart-cities-on-the-planet
25. Cohen, B.: The Top 10 Smartest European Cities (2013). Fonte: http://www.fastcoexist.coms
26. Comunicazione COM: 808 della Commissione al Consiglio, al Parlamento Europeo. Programma quadro di ricerca e innovazione "Orizzonte 2020" (2011)
27. De Luca, A.: Come (ri)pensare la smart city. EyesReg G. Sci. Reg. **2**(6), 143–146 (2012)
28. De Pascali, P.: Governance e tecnologie per il piano della smart city. In: Zoppi, C. (ed.) Valutazione e pianificazione delle trasformazioni territoriali nei processi di governance ed e-governance. Sostenibilità ed e-governance nella pianificazione del territorio. Franco Angeli, Milano (2012)
29. European Commission: Smart Specialisation and Europe's Growth Agenda, Regional and Urban Policy. Publications Office of the European Union, 2014. Luxembourg (2014)
30. Farioli, M.C.: Costruire le città digitali: casi ed esperienze italiani ed internazionali e modelli di business. La città a costo zero, Le Città Digitali, Milan, 30 June 2011 (2011)
31. Fiordalisi, M., Tripodi, A.: Smart city, progetti boom ma senza una strategia. Il Sole 24 Ore (2014)
32. Franz, G.: Smart City vs Città Creativa. Una via italiana all'innovazione delle città. Lulu Press, Milano (2012)
33. Giffinger, R., Kraman, H., Fertner, C., Kalasek, R., Pichler-Milanovic, N., Meijers, E.: Smart Cities - Ranking of European medium-sized cities. Centre of Regional Science, Vienna (2007). http://www.smart-cities.eu
34. Granelli, A.: Città intelligenti? Per una via italiana alle Smart Cities. Sassella Editore, Bologna (2012)
35. Greco, I., Bencardino, M.: The paradigm of the modern city: *SMART and SENSEable Cities* for smart, inclusive and sustainable growth. In: Murgante, B., Misra, S., Rocha, Ana Maria A.C., Torre, C., Rocha, J.G., Falcão, M.I., Taniar, D., Apduhan, Bernady O., Gervasi, O. (eds.) ICCSA 2014. LNCS, vol. 8580, pp. 579–597. Springer, Cham (2014). doi: 10.1007/978-3-319-09129-7_42

36. Greco, I., Cresta, A.: A smart planning for smart city: the concept of smart city as an opportunity to re-think the planning models of the contemporary city. In: Gervasi, O., Murgante, B., Misra, S., Gavrilova, Marina L., Rocha, A.M.A.C., Torre, C., Taniar, D., Apduhan, Bernady O. (eds.) ICCSA 2015. LNCS, vol. 9156, pp. 563–576. Springer, Cham (2015). doi:10.1007/978-3-319-21407-8_40

37. Gibson, D.V., Kozmetsky, G., Smilor, R.W. (eds.): The Technopolis Phenomenon: Smart Cities, Fast Systems, Global Networks. Rowman & Littlefield, New York (1992)

38. Hall, P., Kathy, P.: The Polycentric Metropolis: Learning from Mega-City Regions in Europe. Earthscan, London (2006)

39. Hollands, R.G.: Will the real smart city please stand up? Intelligent, progressive or entrepreneurial? City 12(3), 303–320 (2008)

40. Kanter, R.M., Litow, S.S.: Informed and Interconnected: A Manifesto for Smarter Cities, Working Paper 09-141, Harvard Business School (2009). http://www.hbs.edu/faculty/Publication%20Files/09-141.pdf

41. Komninos, N.: Intelligent Cities: Innovation, Knowledge Systems and Digital Spaces. Spon Press, London (2002)

42. Komninos, N.: Smart Cities are more competitive, sustainable and inclusive, Cities. Brief, n. 2 (2011)

43. Kotkin, J.: The World's Smartest Cities (2009). Fonte: http://www.forbes.com

44. Manfredini, F., et al.: Mobile phone network data: new sources for urban studies? In: Borruso, G. (ed.) Geographic Information Analysis for Sustainable Development and Economic Planning: New Technologies. IGI Global, Hershey (2012)

45. Milano Smart City: Progetti MIUR e POR-Regione Lombardia (2014). http://www.milanosmartcity.org/joomla/milanosmart/progetti-miur-e-por-regione-lombardia

46. Morandi, C., et al.: ICT: interfacce tra persone e luoghi. Sperimentazioni in corso per una smart (city-)region del Nord Italia: il territorio tra Torino e Milano verso l'Expo 2015 e oltre. Tema: Journal of Land Use, Mobility and Environment 1 (2013b)

47. Morandi, C., Rolando, A., Di Vita, S.: From Smart City to Smart Region. SAST. Springer, Cham (2016). doi:10.1007/978-3-319-17338-2

48. Nam, T., Pardo, T.A.: Conceptualizing smart city with dimensions of technology, people, and institutions. In: Proceedings of the 12th Annual International Conference on Digital Government Research (2009)

49. Papa, R.: Smart cities: researches, projects and good practices for the city. TeMA J. Land Use Mob. Environ. 6(1), 113–140 (2013)

50. Partridge, H.: Developing a human perspective to the digital divide in the Smart City (2004). http://eprints.qut.edu.au/1299/1/partridge.h.2.paper.pdf

51. Perulli, P., Pichierri, A.: La crisi italiana nel mondo globale. Economia e società del Nord. Einaudi, Torino (2010)

52. Profumo, F.: 10 January 2012, 2012-last update, Audizione Ministro Profumo

53. Rete Consultiva per Milano Glocal City: Milano smart-city region. Globus et Locus (Report), Milano (2013)

54. Rifkin, J.: Smart Regions, Smart Cities: a Digitally Interconnected and Ecologically Sustainable. Third Industrial Revolution Across the European Union, 7th European Summit of Regions and Cities, Bratislava, 2016 (2016)

55. Rosina, A.: "Città protagoniste", Le Scienze, numero speciale "Il futuro delle città" (2011)

56. Rolando, A.: Torino e Milano: territori intermedi e spazi aperti come opportunità di sviluppo di una smart region. In: De Magistris, A., Rolando, R. (eds.) Torino Milano: prospettive territoriali per una cooperazione competitiva, pp. 3–4. Atti e Rassegna Tecnica (2011)

57. Sassen, S.: Who needs to become 'smart' in tomorrow's cities', keynote speech at the LIFT Conference "The Future of Smart Cities" (2011)
58. Scott, A.J.: Global City-Regions. Trends, Theory, Policy. Oxford University Press, Oxford (2001)
59. Washburn, D., Sindhu, U.: Helping CIOs Understand "Smart City" Initiatives, Forrester Research Inc. (2010). http://www.uwforum.org/upload/board/forrester_help_cios_smart_city.pdf

An Approach for Semantically Enriching Volunteered Geographic Data with Linked Data

Liliane Soares da Costa[1], Italo Lopes Oliveira[2], Alexandra Moreira[1], and Jugurta Lisboa-Filho[1(✉)]

[1] Departamento de Informática, Universidade Federal de Viçosa (UFV), Viçosa, MG, Brazil
lilianesoaresnc@gmail.com, xandramoreira@yahoo.com.br,
jugurta@ufv.br
[2] Departamento de Informática e Estatística, Universidade Federal de Santa Catarina (UFSC), Florianópolis, SC, Brazil
italo.oliveira@posgrad.ufsc.br

Abstract. Volunteered geographic information (VGI), which pertains to geographic information voluntarily collected and shared, represents a paradigm shift in the way geographic information is created and shared. However, there are still hurdles in properly using such information. One alternative to improve the use of VGI is to use semantic enrichment. Semantic enrichment is a potential way of mitigating several issues that plague VGI such as low data quality, unreliability, and difficulty in use and recovery, among others. The present study discusses the possibility of semantically enriching volunteered geographic data using Linked Data and presents a simplified algorithm to automate this process.

Keywords: Volunteered geographic information · Semantic enrichment · Linked Data

1 Introduction

A huge amount of data and information is made available and consumed daily on the Internet. The evolution of web search engines has been revolutionizing the way these data are discovered, accessed, integrated, and used [1].

The convergence of interactive technologies via web with the growing amount of user-generated content on the internet has spawned a new way of producing geographic information. Citizens are using mobile devices to collect geographic information using web-based mapping interfaces to tag and annotate geographic characteristics or, for example, add geotag photographs. Such actions originated the term Volunteered Geographic Information (VGI), representing a paradigm shift in the way geographic information is created and shared [2]. However, just like conventionally generated geographic data (e.g., by companies or governmental agencies), properly discovering and using VGI still poses some challenges such as, for example, ambiguity in terminology. One of the ways to mitigate these issues is by adding semantics to VGI using Linked Data.

© Springer International Publishing AG 2017
O. Gervasi et al. (Eds.): ICCSA 2017, Part III, LNCS 10406, pp. 296–306, 2017.
DOI: 10.1007/978-3-319-62398-6_21

Semantic enrichment can be seen as the process of attributing greater meaning to metadata and data through the application of ancillary resources, in order to facilitate the understanding, integration and processing of data by people and machines. In other words, the semantic enrichment makes the data and metadata more qualified through the use of semantic attributed by pre-existing vocabularies, synonyms and provenance information [3].

The Linked Data concept arose to aid in the discovery, access, and use of online data. Linked Data are semi-structured data that allow specifying semantic relationships among themselves. Using such concept, data on the internet become semi-structured nodes of a semantic network, thus facilitating their use by systems and helping them be discovered and accessed [1].

The semantic relationships expressed by Linked Data allow data to be related to each other, which makes it easier for them to be discovered across different data repositories, besides allowing semantic searches to the performed from these data [4].

Given the use of semantic relationships to relate data and, therefore, improve sharing, the Linked Data concept has been suggested as an approach in semantic enrichment of VGI [5–7].

Nonetheless, manually adding semantics to VGI is a costly and tedious task. Automated semantic enrichment approaches allow VGI to be semantically enriched as needed by the application domain, besides allowing for a more thorough description of user-generated data. Requiring users to describe the semantics and semantic relationships of previously produced volunteered geographic data is impractical either due to the lack of user knowledge on how to properly specify data semantics or due to the burden of this task, which would prevent users from producing new geographic data.

This paper presents an approach that uses spatial operations to automate VGI semantic enrichment, which enables semantic analyses and, consequently, improves data discovery. Moreover, adding semantics to VGI allows finding or solving inconsistencies and ambiguities, thus improving the quality of user-generated data.

The remaining of the paper is structured as follows. Section 2 describes the basic concepts involved in the research. Section 3 presents some related works. Section 4 presents the work proposal, while Sect. 5 makes some final considerations.

2 Theoretical Framework

2.1 Volunteered Geographic Information

With the use of different types of technologies and tools, people are able to widely collect, publish, and make available data on different subjects and in different ways. This way, the amount of geospatial data generated is on the rise.

The advances associated with Web 2.0, particularly in the context of web mapping technologies, have driven innovation in online geographic information collection, sharing, and interaction. That makes way for VGI, which concerns geographic information voluntarily collected and shared by the general public [8].

The marked increase in VGI contributions leads to several new platforms and projects that use data and technologies in spatial decision-making, participatory planning, and citizen science. The potential use of VGI has been proven for urban management, damage from floods, fires, and earthquakes, and other important cases of risk, crisis, and natural disaster management [9].

Volunteered information may also be provided anonymously. This way, not all VGI contributions are altruistic or unbiased. Thus, according to Cooper et al. [10], the risks of using low-quality VGI are the same when the data come from an official provider since the source of the data does not impact the results of their use. The main difference may be that an official agency or commercial vendor could be considered legally liable for the data, although, in practice, that hardly ever happens because of exemption of liability.

To be able to contribute to any VGI platforms, the information has to correspond to a geographical position, being often necessary connection with Internet, smartphone or personal computer. VGI is sometimes the cheapest and often the only source of geographic data, particularly in areas where access to geographic information is considered a national security issue [9].

VGI may be found in simple ways, such as information on Wikipedia, which also provides spatial information in some cases. Other examples of projects involving volunteered geographic contributions are OpenStreetMap[1] (OSM) and Wikimapia[2].

OSM is known as one of the most complex and promising VGI projects. It allows users to download geospatial data free of cost and use them in personal projects [11]. Wikimapia allows users to use polygons to indicate points of interest (POI) in maps. It focuses mainly on describing places [12]. Projects such as OSM feature tools able to capture, display, produce, and spread information on a larger scale, besides enabling experiences for several purposes.

2.2 Linked Data

Linked Data refers to a style of publishing and interlinking semantic data on the web. The data are made available online in a way that they are easily processed by machines and their meaning/semantics are defined explicitly. Moreover, these data are linked bidirectionally to other external datasets [13].

The goal is to allow people to share data with well-defined semantic on the web as easily as documents are currently shared. Therefore, it targets massively sharing and reusing information in a global data space, besides allowing new data to be discovered [16]. The more a piece of data is interlinked to other data, the greater its value and usefulness.

One of the most commonly employed formats for linked data structuring is Resource Description Framework (RDF[3]). RDF is a generic data model based on graph structure that describes things in the world. The RDF model codes data as triplets: **subject, predicate, object.** The **subject** and **object** of a triplet are both Uniform Resource Identifiers (URI) that identify each resource, while the **object** may take on the value of a string.

---

[1] http://www.openstreetmap.org.
[2] http://www.wikimapia.org.
[3] https://www.w3.org/RDF/.

The **predicate** specifies how the **subject** and **object** are related and is also represented by a URI of a resource that describes such relationship [13].

Some Linked Data principles were introduced by [14], namely: Using URIs as resource names, use URIs for people, fruits, cars, but also for abstract concepts as love, war, statistics; using HTTP URIs so that people are able to find those names, whenever there is an HTTP GET request, something must be returned, in this case RDF; when someone searches for an URI, ensure that useful information can be obtained through those URIs, which must be represented in RDF format; and including links to other URIs so that other resources can be discovered, these links are RDF properties.

According to Berners-Lee et al. [13], similarly to geographic data, Linked Data must be published with several metadata in order to aid in their discovery and use. It is suggested by Hartig [15] that metadata related to Linked Data must contain, at least, the date of creation and method of creation.

The most well-known Linked Data example is project DBpedia[4], which is a semantic wiki. Wikipedia provides its information in a searchable format, usually RDF. Such queries may be performed using the SPARQL[5] language.

3   Related Works

According to Ronzhin [7], integrating a VGI set to the Linked Open Data (LOD) cloud provides advantages beyond only resources that are directly interlinked with the VGI set. That is because of the great interconnectivity between the set of data published as linked data.

The study [7] seeks to investigate to what extent the LOD cloud could help semantically enrich VGI in order to obtain better search results in the context of operations and crisis. Based on that, it is said that the use of URIs of an open knowledge database such as LinkedGeoData[6] (LGD) eliminates the possibility of ambiguity when indicating a place. The additional semantics obtained from structured information presented in LGD enables, for example, quick access to basic and useful knowledge on infrastructure objects and public buildings, which could be used to speed up and improve the decision-making process. Therefore, integrating VGI with relevant entities on the LOD cloud makes it possible to semantically enrich unstructured user-generated content with structured information presented in LOD.

Using the Linked Data concept, Azevedo [16] proposes a solution able to obtain heterogeneous data related to floods in the Rio Doce Basin (water basin located in southeast Brazil) from several public organizations by integrating and providing such data for visualization in a Geographic Information System (GIS). To that end, that author proposes converting data to RDF format, interlinking them, and visualizing them using SPARQL queries. The study employed experimental, proof-of-concept methodology and the Rio Doce Basin was the analysis unit.

---

[4] http://wiki.dbpedia.org/.

[5] http://www.sparql.org/.

[6] http://linkedgeodata.org/.

In the context of floods, visualizing, interacting with, and publicizing these data are the key for effective disaster management. In that realm, the Linked Data principles are a way of providing information shared on the web by offering a dataset on different subjects and sources and by making connections.

VGI has been successfully utilized in scenarios such as emergency response and is also increasingly integrated into commercial products. Based on an analysis of existing projects and research, [17] propose to extend the idea of VGI by introducing Volunteered Geographic Services (VGS). Instead of contributing information, volunteers can request or offer microservices to their local community. Therefore, it provides a flexible server framework that handles service requests and offers, and also implements a smartphone application developed using Google's Android platform. The server and mobile client are realized following the Linked Data paradigm and using Semantic Web technologies. In this paper, it discusses the idea behind VGS, motivate it using two scenarios, and explain the technical realization. It can be concluded, the data produced by VGS users may provide a rich source for spatial and temporal data analysis as well as pattern mining.

Semantic enrichment derived from knowledge on the relationships among geospatial data is a potential source of solutions to traditional issues when recovering geographic information [18]. This way, the study [18] discusses the applicability of Linked Data concepts to several issues, such as resolving ambiguity and recognizing the spatial context of documents. In addition, the study presents a list of challenges and opportunities for research on the recovery of geographic information and correlated topics.

4   A Method for VGI Enrichment with Linked Data

The present study is based on the hypothesis that semantic enrichment of VGI enables automatically adding information with no need for user input. The analyses on semantically enriched VGI may improve the decision-making process. Furthermore, the use of semantic relationships generated in such enrichment may help verify the reliability of VGI.

As a study case, the automated VGI semantic enrichment methods, the semantic analyses, and the reliability verification are implemented and tested in a VGI collection system called *Gota D'Água*[7] (Water Drop). This system was developed aiming to collect data through volunteered citizen contributions regarding water waste and shortages, a recurring issue in several regions of Brazil during the dry season.

The main goal of this research is to automate semantic enrichment of volunteered geographic data using Linked Data. The other goals are: Link issues identified by volunteers to the places affected or to user profiles, already converted into Linked Data; propose semantic analyses so as to demonstrate the usefulness of semantic enrichment of VGI; perform the semantic analyses proposed using the SPARQL query language; propose metrics to verify the reliability of semantically enriched VGI; verify whether semantic relationships via Linked Data allow attesting VGI reliability; and applying the approaches proposed in a VGI application.

---

[7] http://www.gotadaguaufv.com.br/.

The VGI dataset obtained by the *Gota D'Água* system was transformed into Linked Data using tools such as Triplify[8] and -ontop-[9]. Those tools transform existing data in a relational database into RDF data.

The POI to be used for the analyses (for example, verifying which places will be impacted by a leak in the water distribution network) are obtained from the LinkedGeoData (LGD) repository. That repository uses information collected by the OpenStreetMap project and makes it available as an RDF knowledge base according to the Linked Data principles. LGD interconnects those data with other knowledge bases of the Linking Open Data (LOD) initiative, such as DBpedia.

Two database management systems (DBMS) are used to store the data: PostGreSQL with the PostGIS extension and the open-source version of Virtuoso[10]. All data (Linked Data), i.e., data in the RDF format, are stored in the Virtuoso database, which allows them to be queried using the semantic query language SPARQL. PostGreSQL, with the PostGIS extension, is used to perform geospatial operations. Although there are DBMS that support spatial queries on RDF data (Strabon and Oracle, for example), geographic operations on RDF data are still less efficient than geographic queries performed in relational databases, which justifies the use of PostGreSQL+PostGIS.

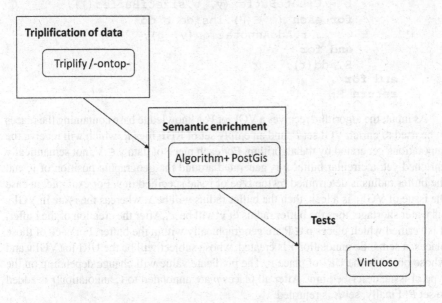

Fig. 1. Steps of the method for VGI enrichment with Linked Data.

With the data collected by the *Gota D'Água* system and the POI obtained using LinkedGeoData, analyses are proposed to take advantage of the semantic network provided by Linked Data, showing, for instance, how a given type of issue in water

---

[8] http://semanticweb.org/wiki/Triplify.html.

[9] http://ontop.inf.unibz.it/.

[10] http://virtuoso.openlinksw.com/.

distribution may impact places of a certain type (e.g., stores, hospitals). Moreover, the semantic analysis of data is used to verify the levels of reliability of data added to the *Gota D'Água* system. Reliability is measured based on the number of semantic relations an issue or user profile has. The larger the number of semantic relationships (e.g., the same issue has been reported by different users), the higher the likelihood of the data being reliable.

Figure 1 presents the flow of steps (outer boxes) in which the method is applied. As previously described, each step uses the tools needed (inner boxes) for its execution.

Algorithm 1 presents the method proposed for semantically enriching VGI.

```
ALGORITHM 1. Automatic Enrichment of VGI
    Require:
        V // VGI set
        P // Knowledge base with semantically well-
        described places with geographic coordinates
        R = empty set of rdf files;
    for each v ∈ V do
        // Creates buffer around v in meters
        b = CreateBuffer(v, v.sizeOfBuffer());
        for each (p ∈ P) inside b do
            r.AddAnnotation(v, p);
        end for
        R.add(r);
    end for
    return R;
```

As input, the algorithm receives a VGI set *V*, a knowledge base containing the places to be used to enrich VGI set *P*, and an empty set of RDF files *R*, which will receive the annotations generated by the algorithm. For each piece of data v ∈ V, not semantically enriched yet, a circular buffer *b* is generated around the geographic position of *v*, and the buffer radius is determined by the type of issue specified in *v*. For example, in case the issue of VGI *v* is a leak, then the buffer radius will be *x*, whereas the issue in VGI *v* ' is water shortage, thus the buffer radius of *v'* will be *x'*. After the creation of the buffer, it is verified which places p ∈ P are geographically within the buffer. For each of those places, a semantic annotation *r* is created, whose subject will be the URI for VGI *v* and whose object is the URI of place *p*. The predicate value will change depending on the type of issue described in *v*. After all places *p* are annotated to *v*, annotation *r* is added to set *R*. Finally, set *R* is returned.

The algorithm described considers the generation of a buffer around the issue submitted to the system. The buffer may have different shapes and sizes and may be adapted according to the issue. Figure 2 illustrates different buffer shapes.

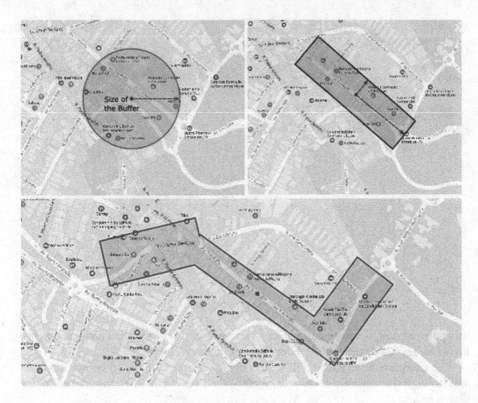

Fig. 2. Examples of buffer shapes.

5   Discussion

The *Gota D'Água* system, used in this work to obtain VGI, enables users from different parts of Brazil contribute by providing information on different types of problems related to lack and/or waste of water. When making the contribution, the place indicated by the user is identified by its geographical coordinates, and it is highlighted in the map for visualization, as seen in Fig. 3. In addition, users can choose the type of problem (e.g., leak, waste) and provide more detailed information, in form of text, image or video.

In the context of this work, a VGI has similarities to microblogging data, such as Twitter. Usually, both have low context attached to them. This happens due to the fact that users use small messages, either by limiting the system (e.g., Twitter limits posts to 140 characters), or because the user is very succinct in describing a problem, as occurs in the contributions of the *Gota D'Água* system.

However, although the descriptions of the user contributions in the *Gota D'Água* system are not detailed, in the use of this approach it is expected to demonstrate the semantic enrichment in the VGI starting from the triple coding in RDF.

The generation of RDF files from *Gota D'Água* VGI makes possible to ask questions to be answered by the system through the SPARQL language. Queries in SPARQL become easier than expressing the same query in SQL. In addition to the advantage of

Fig. 3. Identification of contribution location

using the SPARQL language, a query can be used to formulate complex queries involving several distributed RDF repositories on the Web [18].

The queries to be executed will answer the questions previously proposed after the validation of the semantic enrichment method, and the data will be transcribed in the search results.

A small number of contributions examined will be annotated manually, generating a set of ground truth. The proposed method should generate annotations similar to the set of ground truths, and a certain level of imprecision is expected.

The annotations associated with the described event are the basis for determining the radius of the buffer associated with the VGI. Its limits are delimited at the moment and arbitrarily, but will be used to demonstrate the application of the technique. Its size should be better adjusted to get closer to reality in the final implementation of the system.

The greatest difficulty of the research is to deal with brief description that the VGI contributions have. For example, in the *Gota D'água* system many contributions do not have any type of comments linked to them, based only on the type, geographical location and timestamp of the contribution. This lack of detail makes it impossible to use tools like Named Entity Recognition (NER)/Named Entity Disambiguation (NED) [19, 20] or other semantic enrichment methods that could generate new semantic annotations and, consequently, contribute to the results of the queries to be executed.

6   Final Considerations

Linked Data is a concept used to integrate data by simplifying the relationship schemas and enriching semantics. Although its use seems advantageous, the technology is new and several challenges must be overcome and areas of application have to be discovered

[21]. This paper describes the initial results of a research project whose final goal is to verify the applicability of Linked Data to semantic enrichment of VGI.

The importance of volunteered data is on the rise; however, such data often lack descriptive information. This research aims to add more information – namely, Linked Open Data (LOD) – to VGI in an automated fashion. The research results in a VGI set with annotations that point to LOD, which enables semantic and/or more complex queries to be performed on volunteered data. An example of such query is verifying which types of services will be affected by an issue/disaster.

Although the work proposal is a very simple algorithm, this simplicity can be considerate as an advantage. Such simplicity indicates that the algorithm proposed can be easily implemented by any organization or people that want to enrich semantically VGI. Moreover, the functions used in the algorithm (like the buffer creation) are already implemented in several databases, like PostgreSQL (with the extension PostGIS) and OracleDB.

As future works, a more complex algorithm can be proposed to generate more semantic annotation for VGI than the algorithm proposed in this work. To produce more annotations, semantic annotations tasks, like Named Entity Recognition (NER), Named Entity Disambiguation (NED), also called Entity Linking (EL), and Word Sense Disambiguation (WSD) will be integrated in the algorithm. In addition, social media posts can be considered as VGI, like the use of Twitter posts (tweets) in emergency management/communication [22, 23]. Although there are several works that enrich semantically social media posts using EL/NED [24, 25], the use of semantically enriched tweets in VGI systems has not properly studied yet.

Acknowledgements. This project was partially funded with resources from the agencies FAPEMIG and CAPES, with the support of the *Companhia Energética de Minas Gerais* (CEMIG).

References

1. Heath, T., Bizer, C.: Linked Data: Evolving the Web into a Global Data Space. Synthesis Lectures on the Semantic Web: Theory and Technology, 1st edn. Morgan & Claypool (2011)
2. Elwood, S., Goodchild, M.F., Sui, D.Z.: Researching volunteered geographic information: spatial data, geographic research, and new social practice. Ann. Assoc. Am. Geogr. **102**(3), 571–590 (2012)
3. Clarke, C.: A resource list management tool for undergraduate students based on linked open data principles. In: Aroyo, L., Traverso, P., Ciravegna, F., Cimiano, P., Heath, T., Hyvönen, E., Mizoguchi, R., Oren, E., Sabou, M., Simperl, E. (eds.) ESWC 2009. LNCS, vol. 5554, pp. 697–707. Springer, Heidelberg (2009). doi:10.1007/978-3-642-02121-3_51
4. Schade, S., Granell, C., Díaz, L.: Augmenting SDI with linked data. In: Workshop on Linked Spatiotemporal Data, in Conjunction with the 6th International Conference on Geographic Information Science (GIScience), Zurich (2010)
5. Ballatore, A., Bertolotto, M.: Semantically Enriching VGI in Support of Implicit Feedback Analysis. In: Tanaka, K., Fröhlich, P., Kim, K.-S. (eds.) W2GIS 2011. LNCS, vol. 6574, pp. 78–93. Springer, Heidelberg (2011). doi:10.1007/978-3-642-19173-2_8

6. Stadler, C., Lehmann, J., Höffner, K., Auer, S.: Linkedgeodata: a core for a web of spatial open data. Semant. Web **3**(4), 333–354 (2012)
7. Ronzhin, S.: Semantic enrichment of volunteered geographic information using linked data: a use case scenario for disaster management. Ph.D thesis, University of Twente (2015)
8. Goodchild, M.F.: Citizens as voluntary sensors: spatial data infrastructure in the world of web 2.0. Int. J. Spat. Data Infrastruct. Res. **2**, 4–32 (2007)
9. Neis, P., Zielstra, D.: Recent developments and future trends in volunteered geographic information research: the case of OpenStreetMap. Future Internet **6**(1), 76–106 (2014)
10. Cooper, A.K., Coetzee, S., Kaczmarek, I., Kourie, D.G., Iwaniak, A., Kubik, T.: Challenges for quality in volunteered geographical information. In: Proceedings of the AfricaGEO 2011 Conference, Cape Town, South Africa (2011)
11. Zielstra, D., Zipf, A.: A comparative study of proprietary geodata and volunteered geographic information for Germany. In: 13th AGILE International Conference on Geographic Information Science (2010)
12. Mummidi, L.N., Krumm, J.: Discovering points of interest from users' map annotations. GeoJournal **72**(3–4), 215–227 (2008)
13. Berners-Lee, T., Bizer, C., Heath, T.: Linked data-the story so far. Int. J. Semant. Web Inf. Syst. **5**(3), 1–22 (2009)
14. Berners-Lee, T., Chen, Y., Chilton, L., Connolly, D., Dhanaraj, R., Hollenbach, J., Sheets, D.: Tabulator: exploring and analyzing linked data on the semantic web. In: CITESEER. Proceedings of the 3rd International Semantic Web User Interaction Workshop, vol. 2006, p. 159 (2006)
15. Hartig, O.: Provenance information in the web of data. In: LDOW, vol. 538 (2009)
16. Azevedo, P.C.N.D.: Uma proposta para visualização de linked data sobre enchentes na bacia do rio doce. Projetos e Dissertações em Sistemas de Informação e Gestão do Conhecimento, vol. 2(1) (2013)
17. Savelyev, A., Xu, S., Janowicz, K., Mülligann, C., Thatcher, J., Luo, W.: Volunteered geographic services: developing a linked data driven location-based service. In: Proceedings of the 1st ACM SIGSPATIAL International Workshop on Spatial Semantics and Ontologies, pp. 25–31 (2011)
18. SPARQL Sparql 1.1 Overview. W3C, 2013. Disponível em Acesso em: 11 May 2017
19. Derczynski, L., Maynard, D., Rizzo, G., van Erp, M., Gorrell, G., Troncy, R., Bontcheva, K.: Analysis of named entity recognition and linking for tweets. Inf. Process. Manage. **51**(2), 32–49 (2015)
20. Han, X., Zhao, J.: Named entity disambiguation by leveraging wikipedia semantic knowledge. In: Proceedings of the 18th ACM Conference on Information and Knowledge Management, pp. 215–224. ACM (2009)
21. Moura, T.H.V.M, Davis Jr., C.: Linked Geospatial Data: desafios e oportunidades de pesquisa, p. 13. Santanche, A., Andrade, P.R. (eds.) (2013)
22. White, C.M.: Social media, crisis communication, and emergency management: leveraging web 2.0 technologies. CRC press (2011)
23. Gao, H., Barbier, G., Goolsby, R.: Harnessing the crowdsourcing power of social media for disaster relief. IEEE Intell. Syst. **26**(3), 10–14 (2011)
24. Yamada, I., Takeda, H., Takefuji, Y.: An end-to-end entity linking approach for tweets. In: 5th Workshop on Making Sense of Microposts: Big Things Come in Small Packages, # Microposts 2015, at the 24th International Conference on the World Wide Web, CEUR-WS (2015)
25. Guo, S., Chang, M.W., Kiciman, E.: To link or not to link? a study on end-to-end tweet entity linking. In: HLT-NAACL, pp. 1020–1030 (2013)

Demographic Data and Remote Sensing to Monitor Urban Growth: The Ho Chi Minh City (Vietnam) Case Study

Giovanni Mauro[1]([✉]), Andrea Favretto[1], and Duy Võ Hoàng[2]

[1] Department of Humanities, University of Trieste, Trieste, Italy
{gmauro,afavretto}@units.it
[2] Ton Duc Thang University, Ho Chi Minh, Vietnam
vohoangduy@tdt.edu.vn

Abstract. In the last decades Ho Chi Minh City (HCMC), Vietnam, has experienced a rapid urbanization. This town grows from 2.3 millions of inhabitants in the 1975 until 8 millions in the 2014. Therefore, understanding the land-cover changes is one of the main topics in order to monitor the process of urban development. In this paper we study the urban dynamics of HCMC using two Landsat scenes acquired on June of 1988 (sensor TM) and on February 2017 (sensor OLI/TIRS). We relate our main results with other sources, like demographic data and the participative maps of OpenStreetMap. So, we identify main land cover changes in this period, such as the most important demographic variations within the urban districts of HCMC.

Keywords: Ho chi minh city · Landsat TM · Landsat OLI/TIRS · Demographic data · Urban growth models

1 Introduction

Recent global demographic analysis highlights the constant population growth in the urban areas especially during the last decades. Globally, from the early years of this century more and more people live in these areas (about 54% in 2014). Currently, although Asia and Africa remain mostly rural (respectively 60% and 52% of their population live in the countryside), these two continents are urbanizing faster than other regions of the world. Considering the rank of the first fifty cities over 5 million inhabitants, in 1990 about 45% were Asiatic, while in the 2014 Asiatic cities are more than 60% (UN 2014).

Similar to other emerging megacities in South-East Asia, Ho Chi Minh City (HCMC) experienced in the last thirty years a remarkable demographic growth, becoming the largest metropolis in Vietnam. According to the official statistics, the urban region of HCMC metropolitan area has recently achieved almost 8 million of inhabitants (GSO 2015). For this reason HCMC is now facing several challenges regarding, for example, flooding (i.e., Storch and Downes 2011), water management (i.e., Phun Le Vo 2007), urban cooling (i.e., Son et al. 2017) and urban sprawl (Saksena et al. 2014). On the other side, HCMC is the most important financial city in Vietnam, with more than 53 industrial

© Springer International Publishing AG 2017
O. Gervasi et al. (Eds.): ICCSA 2017, Part III, LNCS 10406, pp. 307–326, 2017.
DOI: 10.1007/978-3-319-62398-6_22

zones designed to attract foreign investment and people from all across Vietnam (Kontgis et al. 2014).

Many Authors investigated the fast urban development of HCMC. Back in (Bolay et al. 1997) highlighted how HCMC occupies a "strategic position in the opening up process" of the whole country. Therefore, in spite of many critical issues, the urbanization of this area could represent a good opportunity for the entire Vietnam. However, also in (Drakakis-Smith and Dixon 1997) pointed out many environmental and social problems connected to the fast urban growth of HCMC. For this reason they hope for an "urgent need to reappraise the urbanization process in Vietnam in the context of its sustainability". Currently, sustainability is a key issue mainly because HCMC, for its location, is very vulnerable to the effects of climate change. Flooding, for example, has become one of the most pressing issues. Downes et al. (2016) describe the urban structure types of HCMC; they create a database filled with reliable information, very useful to plan economic activities or to build residential areas. This kind of database could be very important for a "future megacity", as Gubry and Huong defined HCMC (2004). The recent economic growth of HCMC, mainly as result of *Doi Moi* (or *Renovation*) state reforms (see Sect. 2), made the town more attractive and it cause a very large rural-urban migration. The decline of the residential control (very strict in the early '80) and a very low rate of unemployment in the urban areas of HCMC (about 2%) are the two most important pull factors driving this internal migration (Gabry and Huong 2005).

Remote sensing methodologies were also widely applied to study the urban growth of HCMC. However, although all these studies highlighted the massive growth of HCMC in a short time, their results appear to be quite different. Applying supervised classification and band ratios methodology on the Landsat TM and Spot images, Van et al. (2015), for instance, estimated a seven time growth of urban areas (from 60.1 Km^2 to 430.3 km^2) in the HCMC municipality during the 1989–2011 period. Son et al. (2012), instead, classified the albedo of three Landsat images (1990, 2002 and 2010) using the spectral linear mixture model (Adams et al. 1986). Their results put in evidence the big increase of built areas (from 168.2 km^2 in 1990 to 423.8 km^2 in 2010), but also how the growth was mainly along available infrastructures, in this way creating new satellites centers around the city. On the other hand, Thin and Kopec (2013) classify NDVI vegetation index on four Landsat scenes (1989, 2000, 2002 and 2005), estimating a very relevant increase of urban area in less of twenty years (from 102.9 Km^2 in 1989 to 522.1 km^2 in 2005). At last, Son et al. (2017) extracted the 'impervious surface' of HCMC, evaluating the mean surface reflectance of each band of Landsat TM and OLI images. In this way they observed almost triple values of this kind of land cover in only twenty years (from 104.9 Km^2 in the 1996 until 271.4 km^2 in 2016).

Overall, these researches put in evidence some problems to clearly identify land cover classes. These difficulties are mainly due to the great complexity of this area, characterized by a big variety of land cover types sometimes highly fragmented. Kontgis et al. (2014) underlined the difficulty to distinguish between bare ground and urban areas during the course of one year. At this regard they used 'dense stacks Landsat images'[1] for the 1990–2012 period. Thanks to this method they estimated a almost quintupling of urban land within a radius of 50 km from the city center.

Similarly to these studies, also this paper aims to analyze the recent urbanization of HCMC using remote sensing images and the official demographic data. Otherwise, we would like to test a standard and 'traditional' procedure, like the unsupervised classification, in order to verify its limits and potential in these complex territorial contexts. For these reasons, we classified two Landsat images: the first acquired on June of 1987 (Landsat 5, sensor TM), the second on February of 2017 (Landsat 8, sensor OLI). Then, we applied some change detection procedures in order to detect the main land cover changes in the studied period. Besides, as many Authors put in evidence (i.e., Simon 2008), the fast growth of the metropolis in Southeast Asia led in a first step to the creation of a peri-urban area and, then, of the so called *desakota* zone (a specific category of peri-urbanization, stretching along strips which connect build-up areas - see Sect. 2). In order to assess the main land cover changes along someone of these strips, we used the participative cartography of the OpenStreetMap (OSM) project. From the OSM vector layers we identified the main roads of HCMC. Then, we defined a buffer zone along this road network and we evaluated the main changes inside these specific areas in the considered period.

The paper is structured as follow. In Sect. 2 we shortly describe the general background of the Mega-Urban Regions (MURs) of the Southeast Asian country and, briefly, the recent history of HCMC. Section 3 is dedicated to the HCMC (and its districts) demographic trend. Section 4 presents the remote sensed used database. Section 5 describes the remote sensed image processing applied methodology. In the Sect. 6 the main results are presented and discussed. At last, in Sect. 7 we shortly present our final remarks.

2   General Background of the MURs in Southeast Asia: The HCMC Case Study

In the rapidly developing Southeast Asian Countries - like Vietnam - the fast rise of urbanization in the last decades created the so called Mega-Urban Regions (MURs) as, for instance, Manila, Jakarta, Bangkok, etc. (Jones and Douglas 2008). Usually, from the inner of the city to the rural areas we can identify three zones in the MURs (Fig. 1): the first is the 'core city', the second the 'peri-urban zone' and, finally, the third is the 'desakota zone' (Mc Gee 1991).

---

[1] The 'dense stacks Landsat images' are images composed by several bands of previously selected Landsat data. The different years stacked images are created and input to a multi-date composite change detection technique (Schneider 2012), in order to obtain the land cover changes of a studied area.

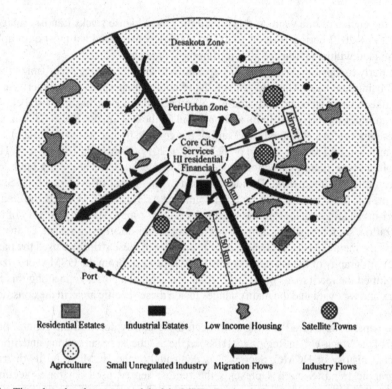

Fig. 1. The urban development model of the MURs Region in Southeast Asian countries (source: Mc Gee 1991).

As the capitalist cities of the developed Countries, the 'core city' is a sort of Central Business District (CBD). As is well known (i.e., Dematteis and Lanza 2011), CBD is the headquarter of the political, social, economic and cultural control activities. However, unlike North American metropolis, those of Southeast Asian Countries are centuries-old. For this reason often the inner city also keeps a residential function. Even if is difficult to precisely identify it, the peri-urban zone area is usually included between the inner core city and the outer zone of the urban area. Encompassing the urban fringes, it grew very quickly beyond the limits of the city, mainly at the expense of nearby rural areas. In this way the peri-urban zone generally becomes a new functional space of the MURs (mainly residential and industrial functions). Of course, one of the main driving forces to the spreading out of these areas is the transport system (Mc Gee and Shaharudin 2016). Besides, in the megacities of Southeast Asian countries (i.e., Jakarta, Calcutta, Bangkok, Shanghai, etc.), Mc Gee (1991) identified a different kind of land use area which borders these peri-urban zones, the desakota[2]. This area is often very fragmented, it is locally characterized by an high population density, a small-holder agriculture (mainly rice crop) and a well developed infrastructure of roads and canals. It is very attractive for the urban activities: lower labor costs have encouraged industrial relocation

---

[2] This word results from Indonesian words for village – desa – and town – kota (Mc Gee 1991).

in well-connected rural areas, located nearby (but outside) the city. However, environmental pressures (water and atmosphere pollution) and social issues (i.e., poverty and housing) are the main future challenges in these changing areas.

Formerly founded in the 1698 by the Nguyen Dynasty, the city of HCMC is located close of the mouth of the Saigon river, in an alluvial plain, mainly rice cropped (Nguyen et al. 2016). In the following three centuries, HCMC history has been quite turbulent. As it was built along the Saigon River, in the beginning HCMC was an important port. In the 1859 the town was completely destroyed by French. During the French occupation (1859–1954), a new name was adopted: Saigon. Several master plans deeply change the city, setting its grid-like planned streets and creating the lined avenues and several urban parks. It became famous for its beauty but also for its cosmopolitan atmosphere, so that it was considered as the "Pearl of the Far East". Between 1954 and 1975 it was the capital of the *Republic of Vietnam* in a divided Country and it hosted military headquarters of the US forces during the civil war. When the war ended, Saigon was renamed Ho Chi Minh City in honor of the revolutionary leader of Vietnam. In the following years a strong out-migration from HCMC occurred, mainly until 1979 (Gubry and Huong 2004). The economic stagnation and the lack of agricultural production in the early '80 s were the conditions to introduce in the 1986 the Doi Moi policy reforms. Following the example of China, also Vietnam aimed to create a "market-oriented socialist economy under state-guidance" (Beresford 2008). In the following thirty years several laws[3] deeply changed the land use rights and the house ownership, leading a lot of foreign investments and thus realizing the conditions for the strong growth of HCMC in a very short time (Nguyen et al. 2016). Nowadays HCMC is the economic and financial capital of Vietnam: according to the 2011 data (GSO 2011) HCMC generated the 21.1% of the Country GDP, while its rate of unemployment is about 3% (GSO 2015).

3   The Demographic Growth of Ho Chi Minh City

Ho Chi Minh City covers about 2,095 Km^2 and it is divided in 24 administrative areas (Fig. 2)[4]. Officially they are 5 rural districts, 6 semi-urban districts and 13 urban districts. The people living in the rural districts (1,600 km^2) are about 1,336,000; in the semi-urban districts (352 Km^2), about 2,157,000; finally in the urban districts (143 km^2), about 5,240,000 (GSO 2011).

---

[3] After the *Doi Moi* policy reforms (1986), the government of Vietnam introduced several land laws ('New Beginning' in the 1988, 'Joining The World' in the 1993, 'New Future' in the 2003 and 'Future and Beyond' in the 2013) enabling this Country to achieve remarkable economic targets in the last thirty years (Nguyen et al. 2016).

[4] The polygon vectors used in the figures of this paper are available in the following sources: (1) for the urban district polygons in Figs. 2, 4, 5 and 13, PUMA (Platform for Urban Management and Analysis), The World Bank, https://puma.worldbank.org/intro/index.php/downloads/25; (2) for the province administrative level in Fig. 2, Global Administrative level, http://www.gadm.org/country.

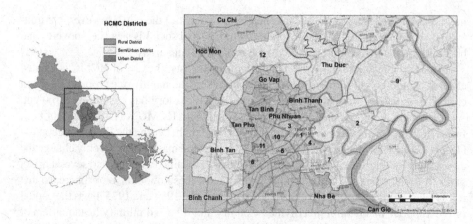

Fig. 2. The HCMC Districts. Basemap by OpenStreetMap (licensed by CC-BY-SA).

The population of HCMC has more than tripled over the last forty years (Fig. 3), mainly between 1989–2016. During the first period, after the civil war (1975–1979), there was a emigration from HCMC due to return of the "war refugees" to their village, to the measures of "relocation" towards countryside (New Economic Zone), but also to the illegal emigration abroad. However the Government officers coming from the north overcompensated this emigration. Between 1979 and 1989 the demographic growth was very slow: limited work opportunities and a very strict administrative residential control strongly limited the rise of this town. Otherwise, after the introduction of the Renovation policies (see note 3), HCMC experienced an impressive urban growth from 2.9 million (1989) to almost 8.5 million (2016). HCMC job opportunities and less intensive residential controls are pull factor for the neighboring rural people (Gubry and Thi Le 2004).

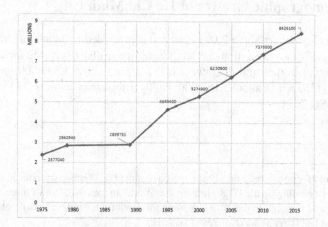

Fig. 3. Recent demographic evolution of HCMC population (sources of data: Department of Statistical Office of HCMC 1977–2001; GSO 2015).

As regard to the spatial distribution of this growth, the maps of density for the 1979–2010 highlight the 'demographic sprawl' between HCMC districts (Fig. 4). At the beginning (1979–1989) people is mainly concentrated in its historical districts (1, 3, 5 and 6) and in the just outside area (8, 10, 11, Phu Nhuan, Tan Phu, Tan Binh, Go Vap and Bin Thanh districts). Twenty years later the density of people grew in the semi-urban and rural districts in the northeast direction (12, Thu Duc, Binh Tan and Hoc Mon districts) but also in the southeast direction (7 and 2 districts).

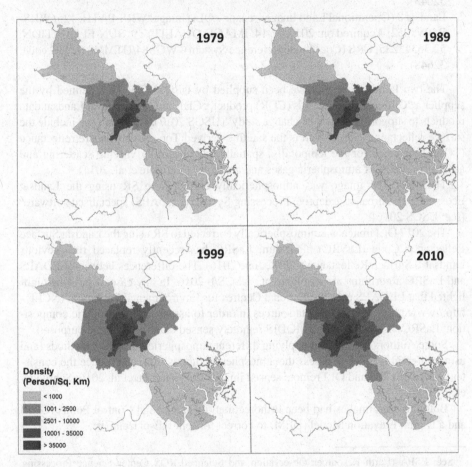

Fig. 4. Density (Person/Sq. Km) of the HCMC Districts during the 1979–2010 period (algorithm: manual classification) (sources: Department of Statistical Office of HCMC 1977–2001; Statistical office of HCMC 2010).

4 Database

We used the following remotely sensed images:

1. Landsat 5 (Thematic Mapper sensor – TM) image. WRS-PATH: 125; WRS-ROW: 052. Acquired on: 1988-06-22. IMAGE-QUALITY: 9. SUN-ELEVATION: 56.38103971. CRS (Coordinate Reference System): WGS84/UTM/48 (EPSG code: 32648);
2. Landsat 8 (Operational Land Imager sensor – OLI) image. WRS-PATH: 125; WRS-ROW: 052. Acquired on: 2017-02-14. IMAGE-QUALITY: 9. SUN-ELEVATION: 52.35343235. CRS (Coordinate Reference System): WGS84/UTM/48 (EPSG code: 32648).

The two Landsat scenes have been supplied by USGS[5]. They are defined by the supplier a "Climate Data Records (CDR) product". CDR are 'higher-level Landsat data products to support land surface change study' (USGS 2017). CDR also can include the surface reflectance (SR), which is the satellite derived Top of Atmosphere reflectance (TOA) "corrected for the temporally, spatially and spectrally varying scattering and absorbing effects of atmospheric gases and aerosols" (Vermote et al. 2016).

The 1988 TM image was atmospherically corrected to SR using the Landsat Ecosystem Disturbance Adaptive Processing System (LEDAPS) specialised software[6] (see: USGS 2016).

The 2017 OLI image was atmospherically corrected to SR using the Landsat Surface Reflectance Code (LaSRC) algorithm. LaSRC has recently replaced the previous Landsat 8 Surface Reflectance (L8SR, June 2016). The differences between LEDAPS and LaSRC algorithms are available on: USGS/b 2016. In any case, it must be highlighted that LEDAPS uses the National Centres for Environmental Prediction (NCEP - http://www.ncep.noaa.gov/) data sources in order to assess the atmospheric composition. LaSRC, instead, uses the MODIS remotely sensed data for the same purpose.

Some Authors believe that applying different atmospheric correction methods (and using different sources to assess the atmospheric composition) can reduce the consistency between TM and OLI remote sensed images (i.e., Zhu, Fu et al. 2016; Schroeder et al. 2006).

Both the used images had been orthorectified using Ground Control Points (GCP) and a Digital Elevation Model (DEM) to correct for relief displacement[7].

---

[5] See: ESPA (Earth Resources Observation and Science/EROS Center Science Processing Architecture) on demand interface (https://espa.cr.usgs.gov/).

[6] LEDAPS applies Moderate Resolution Imaging Spectroradiometer (MODIS) atmospheric correction software to Level-1 data products (see the standard parameters in: https://landsat.usgs.gov/landsat-processing-details). All the environmental variables external to the satellite scene (for instance: water vapor, ozone, aerosol optical thickness, digital elevation, etc.) are used, together with Landsat image and input to the Second Simulation of a Satellite Signal in the Solar Spectrum (6S, see: Vermote et al. 1997) radiative transfer model to generate all the higher-level products.

[7] These image elaboration produces the so called "L1T Data Type" (to deepen: https://landsat.usgs.gov/landsat-processing-details).

5   Image Elaboration

The satellite scenes were subset according to the 19 official HCMC urban and semi-Urban Districts (source: General Statistics Office of Viet Nam – http://gso.gov.vn). An irregular polygon was built in order to contain the 19 urban and semi-urban districts borders (Fig. 5). The reason of the irregular shape of the masking polygon is due to the path of the satellite which, as known, follows a near polar orbit[8].

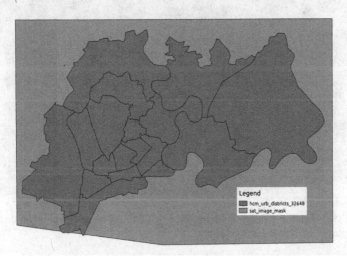

Fig. 5. The 19 urban and semi-urban districts of HCMC. The irregular polygon which contains the urban districts area was used to mask the Landsat images to obtain the study area. The masking polygon is cut on the down – left side because of the slight inclination from a longitudinal line of the near polar orbit followed by the Landsat satellites.

Figure 6 shows HCMC urban district area in the 1988 Landsat 5 scene while Fig. 7 shows the same area in the 2017 Landsat 8 scene.

Both the Landsat images are displayed in false colours composite (NIR band displayed by the red channel, RED band/green channel, GREEN band/blue channel). Looking at the figures, a greater presence of water in the 1988 scene is clear. Furthermore, in the 1988 scene both the main rivers of the area (the Dong Nai and Saigon rivers) have a lot of suspended particles and sediments in their water (revealed by the cyan tone of the water). This could be explained by the different season of the two Landsat scenes. The 1988 image is in fact acquired in late June, which is in the local rainy season (May to October). The 2017 image is instead acquired in mid February, a generally local dry period.

Another clear difference between the two images is connected with the urban area. This last is represented by the light grey structures which stand out from the red vegetated

---

[8] Both Landsat 5 and 8 orbits are inclined Westward of 8.2° from a longitudinal line (see: https://landsat.usgs.gov/).

Fig. 6. The 1988 Landsat 5 image covering the 19 HCMC urban and semi-urban districts. The image is displayed in false colours composite.

Fig. 7. The 2017 Landsat 8 image covering the 19 HCMC urban and semi-urban districts. The image is displayed in false colours composite.

areas. The 2017 scene shows a substantial increase of these structures in the North (all around the airport) and North-East directions.

The two scenes were then classified in an unsupervised manner, using the so called "Hill Climbing" algorithm to form the clusters (Rubin 1967; Bailey 1994). We chose to isolate 10 clusters with 25 iterations. Then we assigned a land cover class to each cluster using:

- the same scene and another Landsat scene acquired 1988 and displayed in Google Earth;
- the same scene and a higher spatial resolution ortophoto acquired in 2016 and displayed in Google Earth.

The obtained 10 land cover classes were then recoded in 8 classes (1988 image) and 7 classes (2017 image). So, the final land cover classes for the two Landsat scene became the following:

- 1988: Residential discontinuous/bare soil; Road/urban; Crop; Grass/bare soil; Water/ swamp; Forest; Bush; Mature crop/forest.
- 2017: Residential discontinuous; Built; Road/urban; Water; Crop; Forest; Grass/ crop.

The land cover classes with double lettering were mixed classes, which include both the land cover types (with a general prevalence of the first type). Looking at the land cover types in the two considered years, it is clear that in 1988 there is a more accurate subdivision of the natural land cover classes (Grass, Forest, Bush, Mature crops, ecc). In the 2017 case there is on the contrary a more accurate subdivision of the built up classes (Residential discontinuous, Built, Road/urban). This is due to the prevalence of the natural land cover classes in the 1988 and of the built up classes in the 2017 (as a result of urbanization in the period).

Figure 8 shows the 1988 Landsat 5 image (classified in 8 land cover classes). Figure 9 shows the 2017 Landsat 8 image (7 land cover classes).

We checked these classifications with an Accuracy Assessment (AA) procedure.

To this aim, we identified 21 random points on the study area. The land cover class of these 21 points was then controlled using as reference:

- 1988: the same scene and another Landsat scene acquired 1988 in Google Earth.
- 2017: a high spatial resolution ortophoto acquired in 2016 in Google Earth.

We built two error matrix (one for each considered year) and then we calculated the following overall accuracies: 1988: 71%; 2017: 86%. As an example, Table 1 shows the error matrix for the 2017 classified image.

Legend

hcm_1988

■ Res disc/bare s
■ Road/urban
□ Crop
■ Water/swamp
■ Forest
■ Bush
□ Mature crop/forest
□ Grass/bare s

Fig. 8. The 1988 Landsat 5 image classified in 8 land cover classes.

Legend

hcm_2017

■ Res dis/bare
■ Built
■ Road/urban
■ Water/swamp
■ Forest
□ Crop
□ Grass/crop

Fig. 9. The 2017 Landsat 8 image classified in 7 land cover classes.

Table 1. The error matrix for the 2017 Landsat 8 image classification. The rows are the reference data (ref) while the columns the classified data (lds). The overall accuracy is calculated by adding all the numbers of the matrix diagonal and dividing the result for the sample size. In this case: $3 + 2 + 3 + 2 + 2 + 3 + 3/21 = 0,857$.

Classes	Res dis/ bare s ref	Built ref	Road/ urban ref	Water/ swamp ref	Forest ref	Crop ref	Grass/ crop ref	Tot rows
Res dis/ bare s lds	3	0	0	0	0	0	0	3
Built lds	0	2	0	0	0	0	0	2
Road/ urban lds	0	0	3	0	0	0	0	3
Water/ swamp lds	0	0	0	2	0	0	0	2
Forest lds	0	0	0	0	2	0	0	2
Crop lds	0	0	0	1	1	3	0	5
Grass/ crop lds	0	1	0	0	0	0	3	4
Tot columns	3	3	3	3	3	3	3	21

Looking at the two classified Landsat images (Figs. 8 and 9), we can make the following observations:

- a greater presence of water (river, swamp and rice crop areas) in the southern parts of the 1988 image with respect of the 2017 image (we could explain this with the different season in which the two images were acquired);
- the historical center of HCMC (just South of the airport) is mainly occupied by the "Res disc/bare s" class in the 1988 while the same area is mainly occupied by the "Built" and "Road/urban" classes in the 2017 (we could explain this with a certain intensification of the local urbanization during the observed period);
- in the areas around and North to the airport and in the North-East side areas is clear a consistent replacement of the "environmental" classes (Forest, Bush, Mature crop and Grass) with the "urbanized" classes (Res disc, Built, road/urban).

6   Change Detection Procedures

To assess the land cover changes during the observed period, we ran a couple of change detection procedures.

We checked the pixel numbers of the land cover classes and we calculated the square km area in each class (in the two considered years). Figures 10 and 11 show the so created histograms. As you can see, the Km^2 in each class are provided below each histogram.

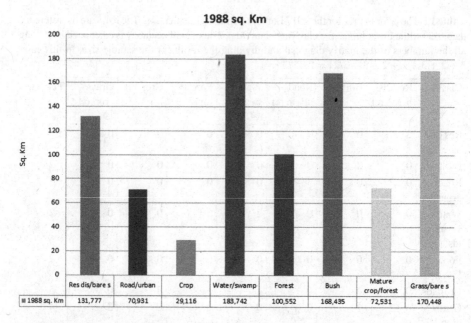

Fig. 10. The 1988 Landsat 5 image classified in 8 land cover classes: the square Km in each land cover class and the histogram created on the basis of its land cover value.

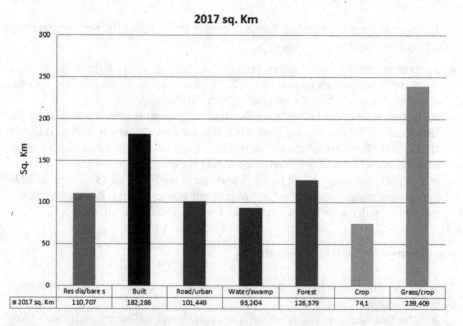

Fig. 11. The 2017 Landsat 8 image classified in 7 land cover classes: the square Km in each land cover class and the histogram created on the basis of its land cover value.

The above written considerations on the basis of the visual analysis of Figs. 8 and 9 are confirmed by the histograms and the numeric consistency of each class:

"Urban" classes. The "Res dis/bare s" class decreased from 131.177 to 110.707 Km^2. The "Road/urban" class increased about 30 Km^2. In 2017 a new urban class appeared: the "Built" one (with 182.286 Km^2).

"Environmental" classes. In 1988 we registered 5 classes connected to vegetation while the same were only 3 in 2017. We cannot say much more because we don't think that these classes are consistent (homogeneous) in the two years. For instance: "Forest" is included in one class in 2017 while the same is spread in two in 1988 ("Forest" and "Mature crop/forest"). A clear difference between the two years is the missing of the "Bush" class in 2017 (in 1988 the same was 168.435 Km^2 wide).

- "Water" class. It is clear the decrease of the "Water" class between the years. As we previously said, this could be explained by the different season of the two Landsat scenes (for this reason in 1988 we added the swamp to the class that in 2017 is mainly constituted by rivers).

In order to verify if there is a connection between urban growth and road network development we considered the current graph of the road network in the study area. At this aim, we isolated in OpenStreetMap environment (OSM) the local "primary road" and "secondary road" tags. Joining these two tags, we created a vector layer covering the same area of the two Landsat scenes. Then we created a 250 meters buffer area around the roads. With this "road buffered" layer we finally masked the 2017 classified Landsat scene. We checked the pixel numbers of the different land cover classes (in the 2017 masked scene) and then we calculated the Km^2 area in each class.

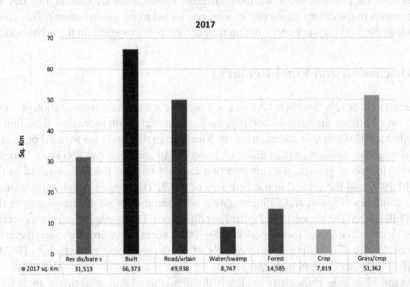

	Res dis/bare s	Built	Road/urban	Water/swamp	Forest	Crop	Grass/crop
2017 sq. Km	31,513	66,373	49,938	8,747	14,585	7,819	51,362

Fig. 12. The 2017 Landsat 8 image classified in 7 land cover classes masked with the road network (primary and secondary roads) buffered layer (250 m around the road lines). The Km^2 in each land cover class and the histogram created on the basis of its land cover value.

Figure 12 shows the histograms of the 2017 classified image that was masked with the road buffered layer.

Comparing the histograms of Figs. 11 and 12, it is clear that the "road buffered" one shows some differences especially in the "urban" classes (Res dis/bare s; Built; Road/urban). Table 2 shows in fact the ratios between each class Km^2 and the total considered Km^2 (both in the entire image case and in the "road buffered" image case).

Table 2. The 2017 land cover classes (sq. Km). The "sq. Km 2017" column shows each class sq Km of the entire 2017 classified image; the "Class/tot 2017" column shows the ratio between each class and the total sq. Km (entire image); the "sq. Km road buf 2017" column shows each class sq Km of the road buffered 2017 classified image; the "Class/tot road buf 2017" columns shows the ratio between each class and the total sq. Km (road buffered entire image).

Classes	sq. Km 2017	Class/tot 2017	sq. Km road buf 2017	Class/tot road buf 2017
Res dis/bare s	110,707	0,12	31,513	0,14
Built	182,286	0,20	66,373	0,29
Road/urban	101,449	0,11	49,938	0,22
Water/swamp	93,204	0,10	8,747	0,04
Forest	126,379	0,14	14,585	0,06
Crop	74,1	0,08	7,819	0,03
Grass/crop	239,409	0,26	51,362	0,22
Total	927,536		230,338	

If we consider the first three classes (the first three rows of the table, the classes connected to the urbanisation), we can notice that there is a certain increment of the ratio values from the entire image to the road buffered. The changes are smaller and they are all decreases in the other classes (the classes connected to the environment). This could mean that the road network construction may have a positive effect on the urbanisation.

7   Discussion and Final Remarks

In the last decades the Southeast Asian countries knew a relevant urbanization process, rising several times the mega-urban regions (see Sect. 2). With more than 8 million of inhabitants, HCMC is now the main city of Vietnam. In this study we focused our attention to its urban and semi-urban districts, covering an area of about 930 km2. In order to assess its recent growth, we compare two Landsat images, the first acquired in the June of 1988 and the second in the February of 2017. The simple visual interpretation of these images (Figs. 6 and 7) highlights a substantial increase of urban area in the North (all around the airport) and North-East directions. Demographic data, concerning each district and collected for the period 1989–2010, seem to confirm the same: thematic maps of density (Fig. 4) put in evidence a sort of 'demographic sprawl' from HCMC historical to its semi-urban districts.

On the other side, difficulties in clearly distinguishing residential urban areas from the bare soils (mainly in the Landsat image of 1988) are one of the main limits of the unsupervised classification procedure. So, in order to quantify urban areas, we identify a mixed class (residential discontinuous and bare soil) and a 'road/urban class', i.e. dense residential housing along main roads. Overall, these classes cover over than 200 Km^2 in the 1988. In the 2017 the situation appears clearer: a more accurate subdivision of three built up classes (residential discontinuous, built and road/urban) provides an estimation of the urban growth, doubling in the last forty years (almost 400 km^2). Road network seems to drive this urbanization growth. For the 2017 Landsat classified image, comparing land cover classes within a road buffered zone (500 meters), we observed how the percentage rate of built up classes is always higher than in entire image (Table 2).

Water management is another main challenges of HCMC. As well know, its climate is strongly influenced by monsoonal regime; the annual average rainfall is about 2,000 mm and, frequently, heavy rainfalls occur in June and September (People's Committee of Ho Chi Minh City 2002). Besides, almost half of HCMC lies less than a meter above sea level: localized urban inundations have intensified by the recent fast urbanization (as put in evidence from the Landsat image of 1988, too). For these reasons in these decades developing the drainage system is a priority: since 1998, large investments has been made by several international administrations (government of Belgium, Japan International Cooperation Agency and the World Bank) to improve the drainage system in HCMC (ADB 2016).

The comparison between the two classified Landsat images (Figs. 7 and 8) put in evidence also a 'built up intensification', mainly in the historical district of HCMC. However, this doesn't mean a comparable growth of population. In fact, in order to

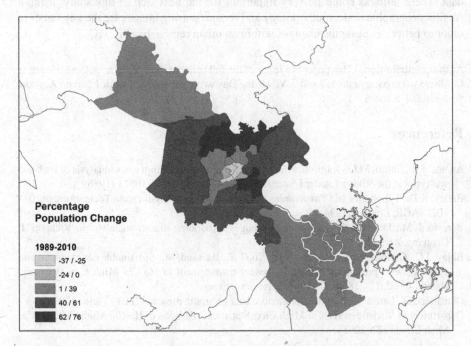

Fig. 13. The thematic map of population growth rate (period 1989–2010) within the HCMC districts (algorithm: manual classification) (sources of data: Department of Statistical Office of HCMC 1977–2001; Statistical office of HCMC 2010).

estimate the percentage population change within the districts in the period 1989–2010, we evaluate the population growth rate (%) as follow:

$$Population\ growth\ rate(\%) = \left(\frac{Pop\,2010 - Pop\,1989}{Pop\,1989} \right) * 100$$

The thematic map of percentage population change (Fig. 13) visualize the heavy decrease in the historical districts (1, 3, and 5), until very high negative values (−37%/ −25%) in a relatively short time (about thirty years). On the other side, in the districts surrounding the center, values of increase are very marked (until +76%). Occurred changes in the functions of districts during this period could be the main reasons explaining this discrepancy between results of satellite image classification and demographic data. If the center is nowadays more similar to the 'core city' (see Sect. 2), the surrounding landscape deeply changes becoming residential districts mainly.

This research would be like a first stage in the monitoring the recent HCMC growth. Likewise to other studies (i.e., Mauro 2016), a methodology merging several different sources (like satellite images, demographic data and participative cartography) helps to better define main transformations occurred during these last decades in the "fast-growth towns", like HCMC. We also highlight limits and potential of unsupervised procedure in order to classify Landsat images: if the good results of accuracy assessment prove its reliability, however this method seems to be very influenced by the quality of the chosen data. These remarks could be very important for the next step of this study: using a smaller geographic scale, methodology and remote sensing images are the key issues in order to better delineate the changes within an urban region, like HCMC.

Author contribution. This paper is a result of the full collaboration of all the authors. However G. Mauro wrote paragraphs 1, 2 and 7, Võ Hoàng Duy wrote paragraph 3, while Favretto A. wrote paragraphs 4, 5 and 6.

References

Adams, J.B., Smith, M.O., Johnson, P.E.: Spectral mixture modelling: a new analysis of rock and soil types at the Viking Lander I Site. J. Geophys. Res. **91**(B10), 10513 (1986)

Bailey, K.D.: Typologies and Taxonomies. An Introduction to Classification Techniques, pp. 07–102. SAGE, London (1994)

Beresford, M.: Doi Moi in review the challenges of building market socialism in Vietnam. J. Contemp. Asia **38**(2), 221–243 (2008)

Bolay, J.C., Cartoux, S., Cunha, A., Ngoc Tu, T.T., Bassand, M.: Sustainable development and urban growth: precarious habitat and water management in Ho Chi Minh City, Vietnam. Habitat Intl. **21**(2), 185–197 (1997). Elsevier Science

Dematteis, G., Lanza, C.: Le città del mondo. Una geografia urbana. UTET, Torino (2011)

Department of Statistic of Ho Chi Minh City: Statistical yearbook of Ho Chi Minh City. Ho Chi Minh City (1977–2001)

Downes, Nigel K., Storch, H., Schmidt, M., Nguyen, T.C.V., Dinh, L.C., Tran, T.N., Hoa, L.T.: Understanding Ho Chi Minh City's urban structures for urban land-use monitoring and risk-adapted land-use planning. In: Katzschner, A., Waibel, M., Schwede, D., Katzschner, L., Schmidt, M., Storch, H. (eds.) Sustainable Ho Chi Minh City: Climate Policies for Emerging Mega Cities, pp. 89–116. Springer, Cham (2016). doi:10.1007/978-3-319-04615-0_6

Drakakis-Smith, D., Dixon, C.: Sustainable urbanization in Vietnam. Geoforum 28(1), 21–38 (1997). Elsevier Science

General Statistics Office (GSO): Statistical Handbook 2011. Vietnam: General Statistics Office of Vietnam (2011). http://www.gso.gov.vn/

General Statistics Office (GSO): Statistical Yearbook of Vietnam 2015. Vietnam: General Statistics Office of Vietnam (2015). http://www.gso.gov.vn/

Gubry, P., Huong, L.T.: Ho Chi Minh City: a future megacity in Vietnam. Vietnam Socio-Econ. Devel. 40, 56–75 (2004)

Gubry, P., Huong, L.T.: Are the 'left behind' really left? Shared advantages in rural-urban migration from Mekong delta to Ho Chi Minh City. Vietnam Socio-Econ. Devel. 44, 54–70 (2005)

Jones, G.W., Douglass, M. (eds.): The Rise of Mega-Urban Regions in Pacific Asia – Urban Dynamics in a Global Era. Singapore University Press, Singapore (2008)

Kontgis, C., Schneider, A., Fox, J., Saksena, S., Spencer, J.H., Castrence, M.: Monitoring peri-urbanization in the greater Ho Chi Minh City metropolitan area. Appl. Geogr. 53, 377–388 (2014)

Mauro, G.: Dinamiche urbane e città post-socialiste: monitoraggio mediante telerilevamento. Casi di studio. Studi Monografici, 1, Associazione Italiana di Cartografia (AIC). Edizioni Universitarie Triestine (EUT), Trieste (2016). http://hdl.handle.net/10077/12841

Mc Gee, T.G., Shaharudin, I.: Reimagining the "Peri-Urban" in the mega-urban regions of southeast Asia. In: Maheshwari, B., Thoradeniya, B., Singh, Vijay P. (eds.) Balanced Urban Development: Options and Strategies for Liveable Cities. WSTL, vol. 72, pp. 499–516. Springer, Cham (2016). doi:10.1007/978-3-319-28112-4_30

McGee, T.G.: The emergence of desakota regions in Asia: expanding a hypothesis. In: Ginsburg, N.J., Koppel, B., Mc Gee, T.G. (eds.) The Extended Metropolis. Settlement transition in Asia, pp. 3–26. University of Hawaii Press, Honolulu (1991)

Nguyen, T.B., Samsura, A., Van der Krabben, E.: Saigon – Ho Chi Minh. Cities 50, 16–27 (2016)

People's Committee of Ho Chi Minh City: Environmental management strategy for Ho Chi Minh City to 2010. Ho Chi Minh City: DOSTE (2002)

Phun Le Vo: Urbanization and water management in Ho Chi Minh City, Vietnam-issues, challenges and perspectives. GeoJournal 70, 75–89 (2007)

Rubin, J.: Optimal classification into groups. An approach for solving the taxonomy problem. J. Theor. Biol. 15, 103–144 (1967)

Saksena, S., Fox, J., Spencer, J., Castrence, M., DiGregorio, M., Epprecht, M.: Classifying and mapping the urban transition in Vietnam. Appl. Geogr. 50, 80–89 (2014)

Schneider, A.: Monitoring land cover change in urban and peri-urban areas using dense time stacks of landsat satellite data and a data mining approach. Remote Sens. Environ. 124, 689–704 (2012)

Schroeder, T.A., Cohen, W.B., Song, C., Canty, M.J., Yang, Z.: Radiometric correction of multi-temporal Landsat data for characterization of early successional forest patterns in western oregon. Remote Sens. Environ. 103, 16–26 (2006)

Simon, D.: Urban environments: issues on the peri-urban fringe. Annu. Rev. Environ. Resour. 33(1), 167–185 (2008)

Son, N.T., Chen, C.F., Chen, C.R., Chang, L.Y., Thanh, B.X.: Urban growth mapping from Landsat data using linear mixture model in Ho Chi Minh City, Vietnam. J. Appl. Remote Sens. **6**, 1–14 (2012)

Son, N.T., Chen, C.F., Chen, C.R., Thanh, B.X., Vuong, T.H.: Assessment of urbanization and urban heat islands in Ho Chi MinhCity, Vietnam using Landsat data. Sustain. Cities Soc. **30**, 150–161 (2017)

Statistical office in Ho Chi Minh City: Population and population density in 2010 by district. HCMC (2010). http://www.pso.hochiminhcity.gov.vn/

Storch, H., Downes, N.K.: A scenario based approach to assess Ho Chi Minh City's urban development strategies against the impact of climate changes. Cities **28**(6), 517–526 (2011)

Thin, N.X., Kopec, J.: Investigation of Land Cover Change and Land Surface Temperature for the Megacity Ho Chi Minh City using Landsat Imagery. In: EnviroInfo 2013: Enviromental Informatics and Renewable Energy. Shaker Verlag, Aachen (2013)

United Nations (UN): World Urbanization Prospects: The 2014 Revision. United Nations, New York (2014)

USGS: Landsat Surface Reflectance-Derived Spectral Indices. Product Guide. Version 3.3, pp. 1–28, December 2016

USGS: Earth Resource Observation and Science (EROS) Center Science Processing Architecture (ESPA) on Demand Interface. Version 3.7, pp. 1–33 (2017)

USGS/b: Provisional Landsat 8 Surface Reflectance Code (LaSRC). Product Guide. Version 3.4, 1–28 December 2016

Van, T.T., Phuong, D.T.K., Phan Van, Y., Xuan Bao, H.D.: Mapping changes of surface topography under urbanization process in Ho Chi Minh City, Vietnam, Using Satellite Imagery. In: Proceedings, First International Electronic Conference on Remote Sensing, pp. 1–7 (2015)

Vermote, E.F., Tanr, D., Deuz, J.L., Herman, M., Morcrette, J.J.: Second simulation of the satellite signal in the solar spectrum, 6S: an overview. IEEE Trans. Geosci. Remote Sens. **35**(3), 675–686 (1997)

Vermote, E., Justice, C., Claverie, M., Franc, B.: Preliminary analysis of the performance of the Landsat 8/OLI land surface reflectance product. Remote Sens. Environ. **185**, 46–56 (2016)

Zhu, Z., Fu, Y., Woodcock, C.E., Olofsson, P., Vogelmann, J.E., Holden, C., Wang, M., Dai, S., Yu, Y.: Including land cover change in analysis of greenness trends using all available Landsat 5, 7, and 8 images: a case study from Guangzhou, China (2000–2014). Remote Sens. Environ. **185**, 243–257 (2016)

Quantifying Sustainable Growth Through a Morphological Approach Comparison to Population Density Measurements

Malgorzata Hanzl[1(✉)] and Lia Maria Dias Bezerra[2]

[1] Institute of Architecture and Town Planning, Lodz Technical University,
Al. Politechniki 6A, 90-924 Lodz, Poland
mhanzl@p.lodz.pl
[2] Faculty of Architecture, Warsaw University of Technology,
Koszykowa 55, 00-659 Warsaw, Poland

Abstract. Sustainable urban planning has to maintain an adequate relationship between demographic dynamics and the development of physical urban structures. The discrepancy between potential urban land capacities and actual population data indicates demographic growth or shrinkage, which needs to be considered as an essential issue of urban strategic planning. In order to maintain proper population densities, one of the key challenges is the establishment of reliable and quick methods to quantify both potential and real densities. The current paper reviews available methods of density calculations with a focus on possibilities to integrate GIS tools. It uses an assessment matrix to evaluate the advantages and disadvantages of each method. A fresh look is given to the usage of urban morphology, which is particularly efficient at the small-scale urban areas and in situations of data scarcity.

Keywords: Urban morphology · Population density · GIS

1 Introduction

Citizens, politicians and urban planners require comprehensive and clear evidence to support efficient planning and policy making [1]. In order to maintain the quality of planning outcomes both at local and regional level, urban planners verify and base their approach upon quantitative analyses and simulation tools. The application of quantitative methods relates to many aspects of the urban structures, but density analyses should be dealt with additional attention as it primarily supports the relation between population growth and physical development.

The necessity to look for new and robust methods is especially urgent when it comes to preparing for healthy urban growth and development. The configuration of urban areas is key to provide responsible urban settlements in the age of scarcity. Therefore, an adequate database for the assessment of plans and programs provide the foundation of a reliable outcome. At the European level, due to the implementation of the INSPIRE Directive [2], data has become slowly but progressively available.

© Springer International Publishing AG 2017
O. Gervasi et al. (Eds.): ICCSA 2017, Part III, LNCS 10406, pp. 327–337, 2017.
DOI: 10.1007/978-3-319-62398-6_23

The growing field of GIS and GIScience application in urban planning is an opportunity to establish a set of available methods and tools that are able to support future development. We review and compare existing methods of estimating density and residential capacity with a focus on the usage of urban morphology analysis. In order to illustrate the methodological calculations, we present case studies of density measurements related to residential typology in settlements neighboring Warsaw and Lodz in central Poland.

2   Density for Future Urban Development

The configuration of urban areas will play an increasing significant role in providing future-proofed human settlements. The culmination of climate change, scarcity of resources, environmental disasters, population growth and urban living brings evermore attention and responsibility to how cities are developed and therefore planned [3, 4]. Contemporary trends of urbanism have given more importance to the concentration of people and of proposing compact cities with higher densities as a headline. However, by paying attention solely to the nominal density, urban form and population growth have been increasing dissociated and need to be revisited and understood in depth. In the past decades, urban land has been consumed in rates without precedent. Roughly, as population doubles, land use triples [5]. In total numbers, such rapid space consumption has been decreasing the overall density in cities while expanding its borders.

In order to be able to provide quality urban settlements urban planners, and administrators need to position themselves ahead of space consumption and migration in order to guarantee public transportation accessibility, affordable housing, high quality open spaces and urban land compactness as an integrated system. When cities expand or concentrate, necessary land for public streets, infrastructure and open spaces must be secured for the quality of urban living.

2.1   Case Study of Polish Urban Planning

The current situation of Polish urban planning raises concerns, as it is still subject to uncontrolled expansion onto cities' outskirts in green areas, forests and agricultural land. Although market-induced suburbanization has been seen around the world since the second half of the 20th century, it has only been present in Poland during the last 25 years. Polish sprawl is reminiscent of the socialist urbanization tradition, based on large housing districts designed without any regard to the land cost or efficient land usage - such practices were part of urban plans then and are still used in current planning [6]. Only recently with the implementation of the 2015 Law on Landscape [7] has there been a requirement to reestablish some relation between population growth and urban area for new developments, although it misses proper regulation on the theme. Although absent in current Polish legislations, efficient methods of measuring density and its capacity constitutes a robust base for urban planning.

2.2   Results of the INSPIRE Directive Implementation in Poland

The potential to implement new innovative methods for density measurement has been strengthen recently due to the gradual implementation of the INSPIRE Directive [2] (2007/2/EC). The directive was introduced in Poland as part of the Law on Infrastructure for Spatial Information of 4th March 2010 and has a strong impact on the way basic data for planning is shared and on methods to conduct planning analyses. This impact should expand in future along with the popularization of GIS workshops and further use of new methods. The timetable of the directive's implementation assumed that reference data - such as cadastral divisions and built structures - would be available by June 2017. The availability of WMS data, which may be effortlessly used as a reference layer, makes it possible to conduct multiple analyses without time-consuming bureaucratic procedures.

3   Density Measurements

Density is a widely used concept and has numerous different applications. The concept of density is broadly used across science. Its origins may be derived from physics, where a unit of volume divides any given mass quantity. A unit of area in urban studies substitutes the unit of volume. Mass quantity can express a number of people, households and building characteristics, which are quantified and attributed to a chosen area [8]. Density may characterized and be applied to the multiple scales, at the level of countries, regions, metropolitan areas, cities, and neighborhoods – even down to a plot or dwelling unit.

However simple in its concept, there is not a strict definition of how density should be measured. Maybe because of the broad usage, but certainly due to the lack of standard, the comparison between areas can be difficult [9, 10], especially among countries. The comparison and even conversion of density measurements can only be made with some assumptions. These can be of mainly two natures: The first has a statistical nature, such as average dwelling size and occupancy rate - and varies according to countries, for instance. And the second, is more methodological, such as the area's plot or building measurement, which can be blurred by mixed uses in a complex development project, for example, or gross floor area measurements sometimes including or exclude balcony overhangs and undercroft parking [11].

Besides the definition or measurement of the object per se, the denominator can also be troublesome. The definition of the boundary area is, according to Berghauser-Pont and Haupt [12], one of the most problematic and important for density outcomes. Within the units of measure, the definition of net and gross area can vary widely, which can include and exclude access roads, for example, in the case of measuring a plot or block. Scale and averages are also able to influence density outcomes - averages can misinterpret otherwise heterogeneous areas and scale gives or takes importance to non-built land.

Physical density in urban studies represents the measurement of individuals, dwellings or other physical structures of the built space. In itself, it doesn't express any judgment, as it is a neutral indicator. Different physical density measurements have been used to express and guide human settlements [13]. They are mainly divided into two: measures of population and dwelling density and those derived from building structures' density.

3.1 Population Density

Population density is expressed as the number of people in a given amount of area. It can be the number of inhabitants of a country, city or neighborhood, the number of people in a household, the number of employees in a business center, the number of dwellings in a planning zone, and so forth. As happens with other density measurements, it is also subject to average and scale issues. For example, when considering the number of inhabitants in a city divided by the total area of the city, certainly this population density is lower than when considering only the amount of built land or the total city area subtracted by its open space areas or water bodies. Population density can be further detailed into net and gross area, but there is no consensus on how to measure it, therefore a clear and precise methodology is needed to validate the measurement.

3.2 Dwelling Density

Dwelling density is the number of dwellings or household units in a given area. It has been used historically in urban planning and can express transformations over a period of time. The number of people living in a household can vary from one person to many, made up by a young family, extended family members or even multi-family households. The variation can be due to an external phenomenon, as high prices of the housing market, or internal such as a growing family, or socio-cultural traditions. If the comparison's time frame considers decades the household composition may undergo significant changes, however, the number of dwellings might remain the same.

3.3 Building Density

Other measurements of physical density have been used to describe and prescribe space besides using population or dwelling, such as floor area ratio, coverage, spaciousness, building height, among others. The relationship of population and building density to urban form has gained interest due to the fast rates of urbanization seen in the past decades. However, when discussing population or dwelling density in a city, it is often reduced to a measure of building typology. Common enough, discussion on population density is likely to influence the perception of building typologies, as it is mistakenly translated to high-rise buildings, with somewhat smaller dwellings and many inhabitants. Without a doubt, building typology is a constituent determinant to density but is not the sole component of density.

The rapid rates of land consumption along with urban population growth have awoken interest and research on space and resource-saving urban settlements. In order to understand how to prescribe these future settlements, more recent mathematical and geometrical analysis research the relationship between built measurements and the urban form, which has been able to be translated into models that are capable of analyzing performance and therefore establishing an methodological future-proofing.

4 Density Analysis Approaches

4.1 A Morphological Approach

Urban fabric analyses utilizing morphological development, including the historical transformation influenced by cultural and civilizational factors, grew popular in recent years after the Modernism movement. The analysis of urban structure units facilitates calculations thanks to generalization levels involved from the outset. The proposed morphological methodology uses the definition of urban region developed by Conzen. As such, the smallest morphological cell understood as the basic planning unit may be distinguished based on its morphological characteristics. The classification basis is divided into three form complexes defined as part of this Conzenian approach [14]:

1. Town plan containing its parcel division;
2. Building forms and typologies;
3. Land use or activities, representing the functional aspect of a unit.

The application of the above classification is commonly used in practical urban planning workshops, especially those that discuss the creation of comprehensive or land use plans. Such Conzenian morphological approach, provides the base on which zoning regulations are applicable in local plans of urban development.

4.2 Residential Capacity

Urban carrying capacity is the maximum amount of urban human activities that can be supported by the urban environment without damaging the environment or the ability to maintain urban life quality [15]. Through thorough analysis of determining factors for urban development, such as environment, resources, infrastructure, a cap development density can be stipulated. Development density is understood as the limit to the population growth or physical development at a given set of parameters and is directly related to their densities. Therefore, the ability of the urban structure to absorb the population or physical growth is the development density limit. However, other authors [16] recommend that planning instruments such as density controls limit capacity. The analysis of the residential capacities allied to the population density as demonstrated previously is able to contribute to the understanding of the development maximum and aid efficient city planning.

5 Population Estimation Methods

Our further considerations focus on population density measurements as an element that relates the development of a city's physical forms to its population increase or decrease. As a factor that should aid in determining the amount of land required for a community settlement, it can contribute to the set of preliminary assumptions for almost any planning document. Simultaneously, this elementary relation is not an explicit requirement in many planning instruments, giving place to speculation and waste of resources, especially the consumption of green fields. The uncontrolled growth of urban areas results in sprawling cities with all its known consequences for communities' budgets and citizens' lives.

Size and distribution analysis of human settlements is fundamental to provide guidance for its future and comprehend the present phenomenon. Various methods have been developed and applied to estimate population. Population studies commonly use census data as its primary source of information; however, it is not applicable to all studies due to its usual decennial characteristic and reporting of all official instead of de facto residents in the area. Population estimation methods are present in a wide variety of literature, in fields such as urban planning, statistics and geography. The chosen method varies according to time, resources, accuracy – ultimately its goal - and to available data. Conventional methods use direct sample surveying of areas at a time, but this can become costly and time demanding.

Many attempts have been made to register and estimate population. Clark [17] made one of the first attempts to find mathematical support for the connection between population and location in the urban geography field. Clark created a simple gravitational population density model that demonstrated how the population distribution is influenced by morphology – as distance to the center of the city and other infrastructures and facilities. From then on, remote sensing have been applied to extract population estimations [18] and its relationship with urban areas, land use, dwelling units, image pixel characteristics (building materials, for example) and other physical or socioeconomic characteristics [19, 20].

Applied GIS techniques and usage of remote sensing data have proved to be efficient, especially with the more recent high-resolution commercial images and automated image processing techniques. Population estimations inherently have become highly accurate, less expensive and less time consuming.

5.1 Building Footprint Approach

The traditional and most common approach to counting densities present in architectural and urban planning and design practice uses the combined data on size of dwellings, building footprint and number of floors or Floor Area Ratio factors in order to obtain an estimate on residential population capacities. Multiplying numbers of inhabitants per dwelling by the number of dwelling units determines the residential capacity of a building. Another approach to the same task is the usage of dwelling densities in order to relate the building footprint and population capacity of a building or housing estate. This method is straightforward, popular and is easy to implement in the GIS practice. On the other hand, it requires precise data on dwelling structure, numbers of flats and inhabitants per household, which often are not available. While it is useful and commonly applicable in small-scale elaborations, it may be time and resource consuming at the whole city scale - especially with incomplete data.

A version of such a method was developed by Smith and Crooks [21] and assumes the usage of address points in order to relate the numbers of dwellings to specific buildings. The possibility to count residential units in buildings enabled their classification into residential types: detached, semi-detached, terraced or multi-family houses.

Another layer of information available was presence of services. The analysis using this combined information on address and building levels has been performed in London in recent years.

5.2 Morphological Typology Approach

The morphological method may be applied at various scales, including a general, systematic approach in the city scale. An urban structure typology provides a consistent and comprehensive framework enabling its descriptions by taking into account the features defined beforehand: parcellation, form of buildings and land use. The method enables follow-up changes, which take place in the urban environment. The resulting dataset permits easy presentation of manifold aspects of the urban environment, through simple selection and highlighting of desired features. Addition of the parameter of 'completeness' of urban structures, determined based on the comparison to predefined pattern considered 'finished' for a given type, open further possibilities to assess the extent of areas requiring intervention.

An example of the application of the morphological method in the scale of an entire town was the Study of Conditions and Directions of Urban Development document elaborated by a team headed by Mirosław Wiśniewski [22] through GIS mapping - ArcView 3.2, described in Hanzl [23]. The study contained the whole city area within its administrative boundary. The area was divided into morphogenetically uniform units, ranging in scale of one to a few dozens land plots. The use of attribute concatenation as classified by the above approach enabled the division into these units. The combination of values from several fields generated a matrix, thereby determining a type of individual record. Additionally, a parameter assessing the urban structure completeness was introduced, which enabled the analysis to optionally calculate its capacity.

The method has then been used and further developed as the basis for teaching students of the Urban Structure Division in the Institute of Architecture and Town Planning at the Lodz University of Technology, headed by Prof. Weronika Wiśniewska after Prof. Jacek Wesołowski, as well as in other research works of the institute [24]. The assessment of urban densities, including population density measurements are one of the main topics of research and teaching curriculum, Fig. 1 represents the aforementioned analysis.

This method assumes a typological classification of residential structures based on its morphogenetic characteristics with special focus on population capacities. The generalization is made of units larger than one single lot, enabling faster results than when estimating values for each individual building. This paper showcases the outcomes of mapping residential typologies structures in the areas neighboring Lodz, Poland, with the objective to assess existing densities and planned development capacities against the backdrop of the demographic dynamics in the region.

A similar method has been implemented as part of the "GIS – Parametric Description of Urban Space" course in the Architecture for the Society of Knowledge master level program in the Faculty of Architecture at the Warsaw University of Technology, tutored by M. Hanzl, Fig. 2 showcases the results of an exercise on density capacity calculations for Góra Kalwaria, Poland. The application of the described method using GIS aided by

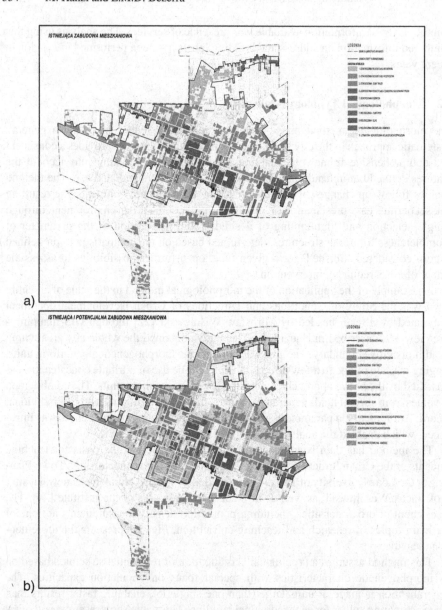

Fig. 1. Urbanism and Sustainability Course, MArch 3rd sem. 2015/16, Student: Aleksandra Kwaśniak, tutor: M. Hanzl, Institute of Architecture and Town Planning, Lodz University of Technology. (1.a) Current residential development. (1.b) Potential residential development.

WMS data available through INSPIRE in Poland proved successful. This first experience shows that classifications done prior to quantification and attributing of typical densities estimations per typology type significantly increases the computation possibilities and easiness of the process. In specific cases, it proved useful in situations of fragmented or scarce data.

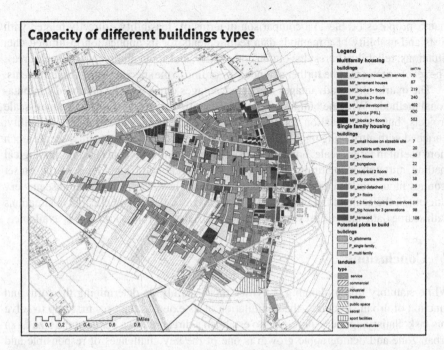

Fig. 2. GIS – Parametric Description of Urban Space Course, MArch 1st sem. 2016/17, Students: Aleksandra Grzybek, Magdalena Koczewska, Magdalena Stepniak, and Sonia Molenda, tutor: M. Hanzl, Faculty of Architecture at the Warsaw University of Technology

6   Discussion

Determining which method to choose in order to satisfy the estimation task depends on the scale of the project and its characteristics case by case. The goal defined in the current paper of relating population growth and physical development capacities requires the implementation of efficient methods in a whole-city scale. Given such amount of data, computational, automatic or semi-automatic methods are useful and can become facilitators. In order to assess the actual values of the shown approaches, an assessment

Table 1. Assessment matrix

Approach	Building footprint	Building footprint & address points	Morphological approach
Feasibility	+	±	±
Data requirements	–	–	+
Reliability	+	+	+
Output information quality	+	+	+
Applicability in large scale	–	+	+

matrix proposes (Table 1) a comparison in terms of: feasibility - directly related with costs and usability of a method; data requirements for its application in limited data situations; reliability of results; output complexity; and applicability in large scale areas. The set of criteria may be further extended according to the specific project requirements.

The matrix shows advantages and disadvantages of each of the proposed computational methods. With the building footprints, counting seems very useful in small-scale projects, but its application for larger scale is dubious due to the data availability. Enriched with attributing people distribution to address points, the method seems much more useful in larger scale, however it still requires buildings' data. The morphological method, through recognition of buildings and parcellation typologies at the outset requires more work on assessment in the beginning, however its application seem very efficient in the scale of the whole town. The latter is especially applicable in situations with scarce data, and in cases where only a WMS data as reference layer is available.

7 Conclusions

While statutory urban planning activities focus mainly on determining the form and function of urban structures, the delimitation of its extent is the very first step to solve this task. Satisfying the requirement to establish a direct relation between the size of an urban zone and demographic growth is one of the key challenges of responsible and sustainable urban development. Too large of an urban zone would encourage urban sprawl accompanied with its negative consequences. Thus, the decision-making and planning activities need more practical and robust methods integrating demographic and physical aspects of urban fabric.

Against the backdrop of density calculations, population densities take a very special place, relating physical structure and demographics dynamics. The discrepancy between potential urban land capacities and actual population data can indicate growth or shrinking processes, which need to be dealt with as an essential issue of urban strategic plans.

This paper reviews the available approaches to density and capacity calculations, with a focus on the integration methods of GIS tools into the measurement process. The advantages and disadvantages of each method have been discussed, however they largely vary depending on the project location, area size, time and other resource availability. Special attention has been paid to the application of analytical tools offered by urban morphology methods. The review proved these methods particularly efficient in the situation of scarce, raw data or when the WMS usage is the only reference available.

Acknowledgements. We are grateful to the students whose work has helped us to apply and investigate the exposed issues.

References

1. Faludi, A., Waterhout, B.: Introducing evidence-based planning. disP Plan. Rev. **165**, 4–13 (2006)
2. INSPIRE Homepage. http://inspire.ec.europa.eu/. Accessed 18 Mar 2016

3. Laconte, P.: Introduction: assessing the assessments. In: Laconte, P., Gossop, C. (eds.) Sustainable Cities. Assessing the Performance and Practice of Urban Environments, pp. 1–14. I.B. Tauris, London (2016)
4. Newman, P., Kenworthy, J.: Sustainability and Cities: Overcoming Automobile Dependence. University of Chicago Press, Chicago (1999)
5. Angel, S.: Planet of Cities. Lincoln Institute of Land Policy, Cambridge (2012)
6. Lorens, P.: Rebuilding the post-socialist cities in the age of Neo-Liberalism – issues and challenges for the planning profession. In: 48th ISOCARP Congress, pp. 1–11 (2012)
7. Polish Parliament: Amending Act for the Strengthening of Landscape Protection. In: Polish Ustawa o zmianie niektórych ustaw w związku ze wzmocnieniem narzędzi ochrony krajobrazu. Dz.U. 2015.744, 24 April 2015
8. Rapoport, A.: Toward a redefinition of density. Environ. Behav. 7(2), 133–158 (1975)
9. Alexander, E.: Density measures: a review and analysis. J. Archit. Planning Res. 10(3), 181–202 (1993)
10. Churchman, A.: Disentangling the concept of density. J. Plan. Lit. 13(4), 389–411 (1999)
11. Bezerra, L.M.D.: Showcasing the use of available open data resources for urban density analysis. In: Słyk, J., Bezerra, L. (eds.) Education for Research, Research for Creativity, Architecture for the Society of Knowledge, vol. 1, pp. 254–259. Wydział Architektury Politechniki Warszawskiej, Warsaw (2016)
12. Berghauser-Pont, M., Haupt, P.: Space Matrix: Space, Density and Urban Form. NAI Publishers, Rotterdam (2010)
13. Cheng, V.: Understanding density and high density. In: Ng, E. (ed.) Designing High-Density Cities for Social and Environmental Sustainability. Routledge, New York (2010)
14. Baker, N.J., Slater, T.R.: Morphological regions in english medieval towns. In: Urban Landscapes International Perspectives. Routledge, London, New York (2000)
15. Oh, K., Jeong, Y., Lee, D., Lee, W.: Determining sustainable development density using the urban carrying capacity assessment system. CASA Working Papers Series 78 (2004)
16. Godschalk, D.R., Parker, F.H.: Carrying capacity: a key to environmental planning. J. Soil Water Conserv. 30, 160–165 (1975)
17. Clark, C.: Urban population densities. J. Roy. Stat. Soc. 114, 490–496 (1951)
18. Langford, M., Unwin, D.J.: Generating and mapping population-density surfaces within a geographical information system. Cartogr. J. 31, 21–25 (1994)
19. Liu, X.: Estimation of the spatial distribution of urban population using high spatial resolution satellite imagery. Ph.D. Thesis, University of California, Santa Barbara (2003)
20. Wu, S., Qiu, X., Wang, L.: Population estimations methods in GIS and remote sensing: a review. GIScience Remote Sens. 42, 80–96 (2005)
21. Smith, A.D., Crooks, A.T.: From buildings to cities: techniques for the multi-scale analysis of urban form and function. CASA Working Papers Series 155 (2010)
22. Lodz City Council: Study of Conditions and Directions of Spatial Development of Lodz, Resolution Nr LXXVII/1793/02 of City Council in Lodz of 03.04.2002; chief designer Wiśniewski, M. (2002)
23. Hanzl, M.: Virtual city models as a tool for urban tissue evaluation. In: 23rd Urban Data Management Symposium Proceedings, Prague (2003)
24. Warsza, R.: Urbanizacja strefy podmiejskiej na przykładzie wybranych gmin łódzkiego obszaru metropolitalnego po roku 1990. Ph.D. Thesis, unpublished, Lodz (2012)

Exploring the Resilience of Urban Systems Using Fuzzy Cognitive Maps

Marta Bottero[1]([⊠]), Giulia Datola[2], and Roberto Monaco[1]

[1] Department of Regional and Urban Studies and Planning,
Politecnico di Torino, Turin, Italy
{marta.bottero,roberto.monaco}@polito.it
[2] Politecnico di Torino, Turin, Italy
giulia.datola@studenti.polito.it

Abstract. In the context of cites, a very innovative approach refers to the theory of urban resilience, which is represented by the ability of an urban system to absorb, adapt and respond to stresses and strains, including issues related to sustainability, governance and economic development. The paper aims at exploring the problems related to urban resilience, with specific attention to the use of Fuzzy Cognitive Maps (FCMs) which constitute a recent approach for representing complex systems and for supporting scenario planning and strategic decision making. Starting from a real case related to the regeneration program of the city of Collegno (Italy), the paper illustrates the application of the FCM method for modeling urban resilience dynamics and for exploring future scenarios of transformation.

Keywords: Decision making-process · Urban regeneration · Dynamic behavior · Scenario analysis · Urban resilience

1 Introduction

When speaking about cities, an emerging approach is related to the theory of the urban resilience [1]. Urban resilience generally refers to the ability to absorb, adapt and respond to changes in an urban system, including different recent urban issues, such as sustainability, governance and economic development. Examples of factors affecting urban resilience can be related to the vulnerability of flooding, the infrastructural development, the presence of architectural and cultural heritage, the existence of social barriers, the demographic change, only to mention some elements. It is imperative for cities to be resilient if they can be considered smart [2]. The proposed research aims at investigating the problems related to urban resilience, with particular reference to urban regeneration processes [3]. In this sense, it has been noted that urban regeneration means not only building-restoration operations, but also programs aiming at eliminating social decline, increasing the quality of life of the inhabitants, supporting the valorization of cultural resources, protecting the environmental system, bringing economic development, and so on. In fact, as mentioned by Roberts [4], urban areas are complex and dynamic systems, reflecting the processes that drive physical, social, environmental, and economic transition and generating themselves important changes.

© Springer International Publishing AG 2017
O. Gervasi et al. (Eds.): ICCSA 2017, Part III, LNCS 10406, pp. 338–353, 2017.
DOI: 10.1007/978-3-319-62398-6_24

Taking into consideration this complexity, it is of particular importance to provide the decision makers with integrated evaluation tools [5] able to consider the multiplicity of objectives and values when dealing with urban regeneration processes and to include the opinions and the needs of the different stakeholders involved. The research will adopt a multi-disciplinary approach to urban resilience based on the theory of evolutionary resilience [6]. This theory is based on the idea that the very nature of the systems may change over time with or without an external disturbance [7, 8]. This theory suggests that a structured way of addressing complexity in urban systems is, instead of seeking to predict changes, to seek to accept and accommodate that unpredictable changes will occur. Under this perspective, resilience is not conceived of as a return to normality, but rather as the ability of socio-ecological systems to change, adapt and transform in response to stresses and strains [9]. This evolutionary understanding of resilience has been articulated using the metaphor of the famous panarchy model of Holling [10]. Under these circumstances, the evaluation of urban transformation scenarios is therefore a complex decision problem where different aspects need to be considered simultaneously. More precisely, under the perspective of evolutionary resilience, urban systems are considered as complex adaptive systems, that are able to create self-organizing patterns through multi-directional feedback processes. It can be stated that it is possible to describe, model and theorize complex adaptive systems behaviors, though not with the ease and precision of ordered systems.

Mention has to be made to the fact that, even if the idea of urban resilience is getting more and more important for the assessment of urban transformation scenarios, the applications of this concept for supporting real world decision making processes are poor and very limited. In this sense, recent debates on the difficulties of incorporating resilience policies into practice reveal that practical and operational implementations of the concept of urban resilience on real case studies are not available.

For this reason, the present paper aims at filling in the existing gap between urban resilience theory and practice, proposing the use of the method of Fuzzy Cognitive Map [11] for assisting Decision Makers and urban planners and designers in the planning and management of resilient urban systems.

2   Methodology

2.1   Definition and Background

The technique of Fuzzy Cognitive Maps (FCMs) represents a natural extension of cognitive maps [12] by embedding to them the use of Fuzzy Logic. FCMs have been introduced by Bart Kosko [11], who suggested their use to those knowledge domains that involve an high degree of uncertainty. He extended Axerlod's work [12], which consisted in the introduction of the cognitive maps in the context of decision making for the representation of social scientific knowledge and decision making processes in the field of social and political systems. Mention has to be made to the fact that the cognitive mapping approach to decision making uses elements from other fields, such as: psycho-logic and graph theory [38].

FCMs are used to represent complex systems, by an aggregate network of concepts and weighted interconnections. For their graphical representation, FCMs are also used to note experts' different knowledge about the behavior of the same system. The technique of FCMs is often employed to reveal the dynamic behavior of the system, describing how the system could evolve in time through causal relationships. For this reason, this approach is considered as a useful tool in the context of scenario planning and decision making, because it can be used for the evaluation of alternatives by applying a complementary analysis.

FCMs are flexible tools that have been applied in different contexts [13], including environmental assessment [14–16], engineering and technological management [17], energy [18]. Mention has to be made to the fact that the present paper represents one of the first applications of FCMs in the domain of urban systems and transformations.

2.2   Properties

FCMs are organized as follows:

- *Concepts*: $C_1, C_2, \ldots, C_n$. These represent the variables that compose the system;
- *State vector*: $A = (a_1, a_2, \ldots, a_n)$, where a_i denotes the initial state and the value of the general concept C_i. The values that are assigned to the concepts are included in the range [0;1];
- *Directed edges*: which symbolize the cause – effect relationship between concepts C_1, C_2 and are visualized as arrows in the graph;
- *Adjacency matrix* $E = \{e_{ij}\}$ where e_{ij} is the weight of the direct edge C_iC_j. The values that are assigned to each relationship are included in the range [−1;1]. The value 0 means that between the general concepts C_i and C_j there is not any causal relationship.

From this list, we can see that FCMs are described by two types of representation:

- A first graphical representation, which includes concepts and directed edges;
- A second mathematical representation, that is made of state vector and adjacency edges.

Figure 1 provides a graphical representation of a FCM.

2.3   Mathematical Methods and Simulation of Dynamic Behavior

As already said, FCMs are used to describe and simulate the dynamic behavior of complex systems. For this operation, it is necessary to refer to the mathematical representation and to the relative mathematical methods of reference, since the simulation is the result of the iteration process between the state vector A and the adjacency matrix E.

The iteration process is performed by the following formula:

$$A_i^{(t+1)} = f(A_i^{(t)} \cdot E) \tag{1}$$

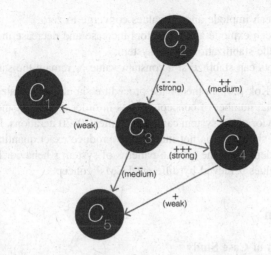

Fig. 1. Graphical representation of a Fuzzy Cognitive Map (Source: Author processing)

where:

- $A_i^{(t+1)}$ is the value of concept C_i at moment $t + 1$;
- $A_i^{(t)}$ is the value of concept C_i at moment t;

The function f is a threshold function [3, 19–21], used to normalize the values assumed by concepts, at each iteration, in the range [−1; 1].

The calculation of a new state vector can be repeated infinitely and four possible paths can emerge (Fig. 2):

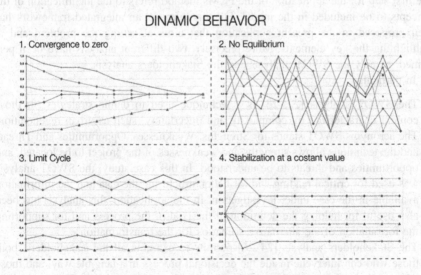

Fig. 2. Dynamic behaviors (Source: Author processing)

1. The concepts can implode and all values converge to zero;
2. The concepts can explode and all factors increase and decrease indefinitely;
3. There is a cyclic stabilization of the system;
4. All the concepts can stabilize at a constant value or remain the same in time.

According to Kok [20], in theory the procedure should be repeated at least $2 \times n$ (where n is the total number of concepts) times in order to identify indirect effects. In practice, the behavior of the system can emerge after 20–30 iterations. It is important to highlight that the simulation is not intended to produce exact quantitative values but rather it aims at identifying the general patterns of system's behavior by means of the analysis of the values achieved by different FCMs' concepts.

3   Application

3.1   Description of Case Study

The case study considered in the present paper is related to the urban regeneration program of the city of Collegno (Northern Italy). The program, promoted by the Municipal Administration, aims at finding answers to the economic and social needs of the city and to give uniformity to a territory afflicted by an unregulated development and by the presence of many decommissioned areas, both industrial and not.

The objectives of the program are related to the qualification of the city as "Collegno Social Town", to the creation of a nice and livable place and to the elimination of physical and environmental barriers.

3.2   Identifying the Concept

The first step for the application of the FCMs method refers to the identification of the concepts to be included in the model. For this purpose, an integrated framework has been proposed in the present application that aims at setting the problem and at highlighting the key elements. More precisely, two different analysis have been performed, namely the SWOT analysis and the Stakeholders analysis.

In particular:

- The SWOT analysis [22, 23] is a technique used to define strategies, in those context characterized by complexity and uncertainty, such as urban regeneration. The acronyms SWOT stands for Strengths, Weaknesses, Opportunities and Threats and the technique allows strengths and weaknesses of the project to be located, and opportunities and threats to be understood. In this case study, the SWOT analysis was used for critical reading and for better structuring the data and the information available in the case under investigation. In the application, this analysis has been also useful for helping the definition of the goal of the process and for supporting the formulation of the alternative scenarios for the transformation.
- The Stakeholders analysis [24–26] permits to examine all the stakeholders, both those who can intervene inside the decisional process in a tangible way, and those who, in their turn, are influenced by the transformation program. This analysis is

fundamental in the context of urban transformations, because it allows to identify who are the participants of the process and which resources and objectives they are able bring into play, showing possible conflicts. Therefore, stakeholders analysis, besides being useful to understand which and how many actors participate to the transformation process, represents the complexity of the decisional process, indicating objectives and criteria for the evaluation of the alternative strategies.

From the two aforementioned analysis it was possible to define the most important drivers of the transformation that can be summarized in Table 1. In particular, SWOT and stakeholders analysis allowed the complexity of the problem to be decomposed and the general aspects that characterize the transformation to be defined, namely environmental, economic, social, regeneration, mobility and services factors. The aspects have been then further investigated in order to obtain a set of measurable attributes for the evaluation of the alternatives. These attributes represent the concepts of the FCMs.

Table 1. Concepts description (Source: Author processing)

Concept	Description
C_1 Public/private spaces	Ratio between public and private surfaces
C_2 Co-working spaces	Surface of the structures for workshop, meeting, training courses
C_3 Co-housing inhabitants	Number of residents in new co-housing buildings
C_4 Permeable surface/territorial surface	Ratio between permeable areas and overall territorial surface of the program
C_5 Urban gardens	Total area used for community and private urban gardens
C_6 Waste production	Amount of waste produced in a year by the activities of the program
C_7 Residential areas	Surface for residential functions
C_8 Retail areas	Surfaces for commercial functions
C_9 Sport and leisure areas	Surfaces for sport and cultural activities
C_{10} Mixité index	Index that describes the functional mix of the area
C_{11} Slow mobility	Surface of the pedestrian tracks and bicycle lanes
C_{12} New public parking	Number of new public parking lots
C_{13} Car sharing/bike sharing	Number of car and bike sharing points
C_{14} Total Economic Value	Estimate of the social benefits delivered by the program
C_{15} Investment cost	Total cost of the program
C_{16} New jobs	Number of new jobs created
C_{17} Regeneration	Regenerated surface
C_{18} Via De Amicis regeneration	Qualitative index showing the level of the regeneration of Via De Amicis
C_{19} Territorial index	Ratio between the maximum buildable volume and the territorial surface

3.3   Alternative Transformation Projects

In this experimentation the integrated approach was applied to for the evaluation of six different alternatives related to the development of the urban regeneration program of Collegno. Table 2 provides a synthesis of the main characteristics of the six alternatives.

Table 2. Six alternative projects for the urban regeneration program (Source: Author processing)

Alternative projects	Description
Cultural District	This strategy is based on the creation of new cultural services for the area, including a new public library and residences for university students
Smart City	The goal of this strategy consists in providing a new identity to the area based on the concept of smart city.
Startup	This project focuses on the creation of innovative business activities in the area.
City and Craft	This strategy is based on the valorization of the small economic activities in the area and on the creation of a new urban park in the Northern part of the area.
Sharing City	The objective of this project is mainly related to the valorization of the public spaces in the area, with special attention to innovative shared solution for living and working.
Green infrastructures	The main intent of this strategy is to improve the livability of the territory, with particular attention to the creation of new green infrastructures, such as pedestrian and bicycle paths.

The six alternatives have been evaluated according to the concepts highlighted in Sect. 3.2. In order to move on to the application of FMCs, the subsequent step consists in translating the performance of each alternative to the corresponding state vector, through a standardization operation. It is necessary to recall that with the support of FCMs it is possible to confer an initial value to each concept, thus describing the initial system conditions.

In this case the performances of each alternative have been translated in the state vector in order to represent and compare their initial conditions. In particular, for the standardization of the performance of the different alternatives, the following formula has been used:

$$a_i = (x_i - x_{min})/(x_{max} - x_{min}) \qquad (2)$$

where x_i is the value of the initial performance of an alternative over a concept, x_{min} and x_{max} being their minimum and maximum value.

It is important to mention that the formula (2) was used for both the criteria that have to be minimized and for those that have to be maximized. This because in the application of the FCMs, the different concepts are interrelated to each other through the causal relations, that can result in increasing or decreasing the influenced concepts.

Following the aforementioned procedure, the state vectors have been calculated and the final values are reported in Table 3.

Table 3. State vectors related to the alternative strategies (Source: Author processing)

	Concept	Cultural district	Smart city	Startup	City and crafts	Sharing city	Green infrastructures
C_1	Public/private space	0,42	0,27	0	1	0,2	0,41
C_2	Co-working spaces	0,37	0,45	1	0,17	0,04	0
C_3	Co-housing inhabitants	0,1	0	0,04	0,11	1	0,37
C_4	Permeable surface/territorial surface	0,94	0	0,59	0,41	0,44	1
C_5	Urban gardens	0,1	0	0,36	1	0,32	0,17
C_6	Waste production	1	0,41	0,19	0,72	0	0,83
C_7	Residential areas	0	0,1	0,02	0,2	1	0
C_8	Retail areas	0,04	0,46	1	0,85	0,21	0
C_9	Sport and leisure areas	0,29	1	0,06	0	1	0,18
C_{10}	Mixitè index	0,59	0,23	1	0	0	0,49
C_{11}	Slow mobility	0,09	0,26	0	0,19	1	0,39
C_{12}	New public parking	0,17	1	0,67	0	0,39	0,18
C_{13}	Car sharing /bike sharing	0,29	0,59	0	0,06	0,71	1
C_{14}	Total Economic Value	0,28	0	0,41	0,97	1	0
C_{15}	Investment cost	0,66	0,54	1	0,79	0	0,67
C_{16}	New jobs	0,24	0,43	0	0,15	1	0,16
C_{17}	Regeneration	0,31	0,13	1	0,67	0	0,31
C_{18}	Via De Amicis Regeneration	0	1	0,5	0,5	1	1
C_{19}	Territorial Index	0,64	0,09	0,26	1	0,69	0

3.4   Quantifying the Relationships

When the different state vectors are defined, is it possible to move to real FCM evaluation through the use of the proposed integrated approach. The first phase concerns the choice of the experts' panel and the interviews. For the purpose of the evaluation, a team of three experts was formed with scientific background in urban design, history of architecture and economic evaluation. It has to be mentioned that the three experts also represent the plurality of actors and visions resulting from stakeholders analysis; as an example, it is possible to notice that the expert in economics has been chosen because through his knowledge and experience he could represent and take into account the interests and objectives of private and public economic actors involved in the transformation.

The evaluation has been conducted according to two subsequent phases:

- A first phase concerning individual interviews to the experts;
- A second phase related to a focus group with the three experts working together.

3.4.1   Individual FCMs

Considering the important contribution of the experts, in order to enhance the success of the experimentation, the definition and elaboration of the procedures to be followed for conducting the interviews are crucial. In the light of these considerations, a specific methodology for the development of the interviews has been conceived according to five subsequent steps that are described as follows:

- Introduction of the FMCs method;
- Description of the context and illustration of the application of the method;
- Drawing of the FCMs;
- Weighting of causal relations;
- Filling in of a feedback questionnaire.

The goal of the individual interviews was to allow the different experts to draw independently their own FCMs, in order that each one identifies and highlights the elapsing relationships among the concepts. In this way each expert could express an individual opinion about the system, putting in evidence how different concepts can influence each other, relying on the specific experience and knowledge about urban regeneration.

As far as the weighting phase is concerned, the procedure proposed by Kok [20] was followed in the present application. In particular, a [−1; 1] scale has been used for the evaluation of the relationships between the concepts of the FCM, where the value −1 means the existence of a strongly negative relationship, the value −0,66 represents a medium negative relationship, the value −0,33 indicates a weakly negative relationship, the value 0 means absence of relationship, the value 0,33 indicates the existence of a weakly positive relationship, the value 0,66 refers to a medium positive relationship and the value of 1 concerns a strongly positive relationship.

As an example, Fig. 3 represents the FCM drawn by the expert in economic evaluation. The map is composed by 19 concepts and the expert identified 29 interrelationships among the concepts. In this map, the most central concept is "C_{14} Total Economic Value", followed by the concepts "C_{17} Urban regeneration" and "C_4 Permeable surface/Territorial surface".

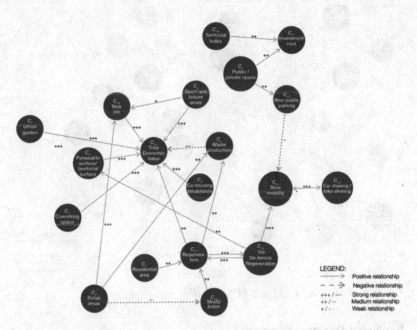

Fig. 3. FCM drawn by economic evaluation expert (Source: Author processing)

3.4.2   Collective FCM

As mentioned before, the second phase of the work consisted in a collective discussion for the generation of a common FCM. For this purpose, a focus group with the three experts was organized. In this case, the experts were asked to work together in order to design the common FCM. For supporting the work of the focus group, the differences among the three individual FCMs have been firstly discussed. This was the case for example of the relationship existing between the concepts "C_{11} Slow mobility" and "C_{12} New public parking", that was defined as strongly negative by the urban design expert and weakly positive by the expert in history of architecture. This difference was discussed in the focus group and the expert in history of architecture argued that in order to incentive the slow mobility, a number of public parking should be created for allowing people to change transport mean from car to public transport. The expert of urban design was convinced by this argumentation and they decided for a weakly positive relationship between the concepts C_{11} and C_{12}. Analogous discussions were carried on in the focus group about the differences existing in the individual FCMs with the aim of finding consensus on the final map that is represented in Fig. 4. As it possible to see, the focus group identified as the most central concept "C_{14} Total Economic Value", followed by the concepts "C_1 Public/private space" and "C_{19} Territorial index".

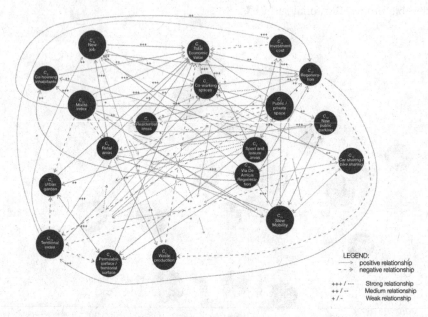

Fig. 4. Collective FCM (Source: Author processing)

3.5 Exploring Dynamic Scenarios

Once performed all the interviews with the experts and weighted the cause-effect relationships, it was possible to move to the next step of the FCMs application that is constituted by the iterative process generating the development of scenarios. The iterative process has been executed following the formula (3):

$$A_i^{(t+1)} = f\left(A_i^{(t)} \cdot E\right) \tag{3}$$

In this specific case of application, the threshold function [17–19] used is represented the following Eq. (4):

$$f(x) = \tanh(x) \tag{4}$$

The choice of this function was suggested by the purpose of the present application [21], that is related to the evaluation of alternative scenarios on the base of their stability and the extent of the long-term effects. In fact, through the use of this formula the different criteria can take any normalized value in the range [−1;1], allowing to represent the degree of increase, reduction or the stability of each concept, with respect to the initial conditions.

To illustrate the results, we will refer only to the collective FCM as it constitutes the integrated vision of the three experts on the decision problem under investigation. Figure 5 represents the output of the change of the state vector. It is important to recall that in the present application the state vector is represented by the configuration of the six alternative transformation projects for the area under examination. The dynamic behaviors have been obtained through the support of Excel software. In fact one of the goal of this work was to simplify the method in order to ease its development. Indeed, using the Excel programme we referred to simple matrix operations, which allowed us to relate the initial state vector and the adiacency matrix.

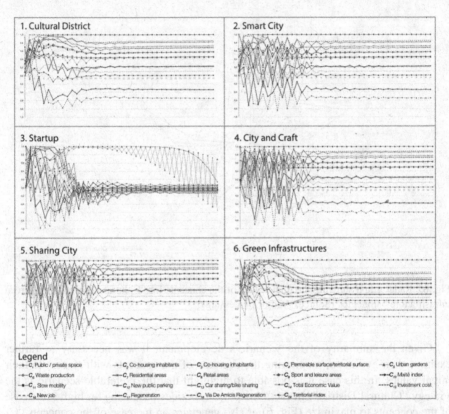

Fig. 5. Scenario simulation of the six alternatives (Source: Author processing)

4 Discussion of the Results

The different equilibriums among the six considered alternatives can be explored making use of different criteria related to:

- Resilience and adaptation, that refer to the capacity of the urban system to change, adapt and transform in response to stresses and strains. In this case, the number of oscillations in each system, their amplitude and frequency have been measured;

- Number of iteration required by the system for reaching the equilibrium;
- Final values of the concepts at the equilibrium considering the alternative systems.

According to the aforementioned criteria, the scenarios that can be considered most stable for number of iterations and amplitude of oscillations are the strategies "Cultural District" and "Green Infrastructures". Both scenarios assume the same number of iterations to achieve a balance and globally the concepts seem to assume almost the same final values [27] (Fig. 6).

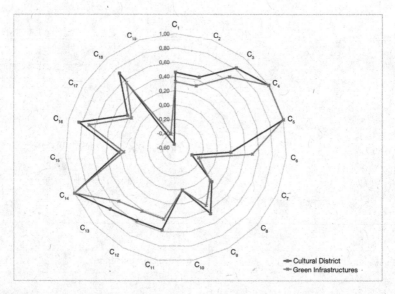

Fig. 6. Radar graph showing the final values of the concepts for "Cultural District" and "Green Infrastructure" strategies (Source: Author processing)

Given the similarity of the scenario's development, it was necessary to further examine their evolution, monitoring the decrease of the concepts with respect to their initial values. In this case it is possible to highlight that the preferable scenario is the strategy "Cultural District". In fact, this project, besides producing an higher increase of the concepts to maximize (Fig. 6), it also generates an increase of the concepts "C_1 Public/private spaces" and "C_{18} Via De Amicis regeneration", compared to the initial conditions, unlike the "Green Infrastructures" strategy's evolution, that produces a decrease of the initial condition, referring to the same concepts.

It is important to underline that this evaluation is not based on the final results considered in a static way, but it is especially grounded on the analysis of the scenario's evolution. Therefore, it is considered as "preferable" the scenario that determines an improvement compared to its initial conditions [28, 30, 32, 37], also keeping in mind the coherence of the development of scenarios with the goals of the urban regeneration program under investigation.

At the end of the analysis of the dynamic behavior obtained from the simulation, it is also crucial to highlight that the result of the FCMs is configured as a semi-quantitative dynamic modeling, i.e. the results are all quantitative, all in numerical form, but their interpretation can only be qualitative [3].

5 Conclusions

The paper illustrated the application of the FCMs for the evaluation of alternative strategies in the context of an urban regeneration program and it represents one of the first application of the FCM approach in the domain of urban and territorial transformations [31, 34]. The method proved to be efficient in addressing the complexity of the decision problem under examination and in investigating semi-qualitative scenarios for modeling urban resilience. However, as a modelling tool, FCMs have not been exploited to their full capacity in urban and territorial planning. Therefore, despite the global coherence of the obtained results, a number of future challenges for a proper development of the method can be found.

To start with, more research should be done for the construction of the adjacent matrix for the FCMs application. In this sense, it can be noticed that the simulation of the dynamic behavior of the scenarios directly depend on the status of the variables included in the state vector and mostly on the identified causal relations [29]. For this reason, it would be interesting to investigate the use of more rigid procedures for developing the interviews to the experts and for evaluating the interconnections among the concepts of the network.

Secondly, different procedures for the normalization of the values of the state vectors and for the calibration of the starting inputs of the model should be examined [33, 35, 36].

Thirdly, it would be necessary to better investigate the semi-quantitative character of the temporal dynamics described by the FCMs model. In particular, it could be interesting to explore how to translate the number of iterations of model into specific temporal units. This could be done by means of the comparison of the results of the model with the effects in the system under investigation over a period that is known.

Finally, sensitivity and robustness analysis could be performed to test the stability of the results when varying the inputs.

Acknowledgements. The alternative projects used for the FCMs application are based on the work performed by the students of the multidisciplinary design studio "Architecture and Urban Economics" (professors Mauro Berta, Marta Bottero, Edoardo Piccoli and Francesca Bagliani) in the Master Program in Architecture Construction City at Politecnico di Torino (Italy).

References

1. Meerow, S., Newell, J.P., Stults, M.: Defining urban resilience: A review. Landsc. Urban Plan. **147**, 38–49 (2016)
2. Desouza, K.C., Flanery, T.H.: Designing, planning, and managing resilient cities: A conceptual framework. Cities **25**, 89–99 (2013)

3. Olazabal, M., Pascual, U.: Use of fuzzy cognitive maps to study urban resilience and transformation. Environ. Innov. Societal Transitions **18**, 18–40 (2015)
4. Roberts, P., Hugh, S.: Urban Regeneration: A Handbook. Sage Publication, London (2000)
5. Bottero, M.: A multi-methodological approach for assessing sustainability of urban projects. Manage. Environ. Qual. Int. J. **26**(1), 138–154 (2015)
6. Colucci, A.: Le città resilienti: approcci e strategie. Università degli studi di Pavia, Pavia (2012)
7. Holling, C.S.: Resilience and stability of ecological systems. Annu. Rev. Ecol. Syst. **4**, 1–23 (1973)
8. Holling, C.S.: Engineering resilience versus ecological resilience. In: Schulze, P. (ed.) Engineering within Ecological Constraints. The National Academies Press, Washington, DC (1996)
9. Folke, C., Carpenter, S. R., Walker, B., Scheffer, M., Chapin, T., Rockström J.: Resilience thinking: integrating resilience, adaptability and transformability. Ecol. Soc. 15(4) (2010). http://www.ecologyandsociety.org/vol15/iss4/art20/
10. Holling, C.S., Gunderson, L.H.: Panarchy: Understanding Transformations in Human and Natural Systems. Island Press, Washington DC (2002)
11. Kosko, B.: Fuzzy cognitive maps. Int. J. Man Mach. Stud. **24**, 65–75 (1986)
12. Axelrod, R.: Structure of Decision: The Cognitive Maps of Political Elites. Princeton University Press, Princeton (1976)
13. Papageorgiou, E.I., Salmeron, J.L.: A review of fuzzy cognitive maps research during the last decade. IEEE Trans. Fuzzy Syst. **21**(1), 69–79 (2013)
14. Özesmi, U., Özesmi, S.: A participatory approach to ecosystem conservation: fuzzy cognitive maps and stakeholder group analysis in Uluabat Lake, Turkey. Environ. Manage. **31**(4), 518–531 (2003)
15. Ozemi, U., Ozemi, S.L.: Ecological models based on people knowledge: A multy – step fuzzy cognitive mapping approach. Ecol. Model. **176**, 43–64 (2004)
16. Misthos, L.S., Messaris, G., Damigos, D., Menegaki, M.: Exploring the perceived intrusion of mining into the landscape using the fuzzy cognitive mapping approach. Ecol. Eng. **101**, 60–74 (2017)
17. Jetter, A.: Fuzzy cognitive maps for engineering and technology management: what works in practice? In: PICMET Proceedings (2006)
18. Jetter, A., Schweinfort, W.: Building scenarios with fuzzy cognitive maps: an exploratory study of solar energy. Futures **43**, 52–66 (2010)
19. Jetter, A.J., Kok, K.: Fuzzy cognitive maps for futures studies – a methodological assessment of concepts and methods. Futures **61**, 45–57 (2014)
20. Kok, K.: The potential of fuzzy cognitive maps for semi-quantitative scenario development, with an example from Brazil. Glob. Environ. Change **19**, 122–133 (2008)
21. Tsadiras, A.K.: Comparing the inference capabilities of binary, trivalent and sigmoid fuzzy cognitive maps. Inf. Sci. **178**, 3880–3894 (2008)
22. Storti, D.: L'analisi SWOT. In: Working paper. Istituto Nazionale di Economia Agraria, Roma (2009)
23. Bottero, M., Lami, I., Lombardi, P.: Analytic network process: la valutazione di scenari di trasformazione urbana e territoriale. Alinea, Firenze (2008)
24. Jones, P.S.: Urban regeneration's poisoned chalice: is there an impasse in (community) participation-based policy? Urban Stud. **40**(3), 581–601 (2003)
25. Dente, B.: Understanding Policy Decisions. Springer, Heidelberg (2014)
26. Yang, J.R.: An investigation of stakeholder analysis in urban development projects: Empirical or rationalistic perspectives. Int. J. Project Manage. **32**, 838–849 (2014)

27. Salmeron, J.L., Vidal, R., Mena, A.: Ranking fuzzy cognitive map based scenarios with TOPSIS. Expert Syst. Appl. **39**, 2443–2450 (2012)
28. Blečić, I., Cecchini, A.: Verso una pianificazione antifragile: Come pensare al futuro senza prevederlo. FrancoAngeli editore, Milano (2016)
29. Gerogiannis, C.V., Maftei, A. V., Papageorgiou, I. E.: Critical success factors on online music streaming services, a case study of applying the fuzzy cognitive maps method. In: Conference paper, pp. 1077–1084 (2016)
30. Davoudi, S., Shaw, K., Haider, L.J., Quinlan, A.E., Peterson, G.D., Wilkinson, C., et al.: Resilience: A bridging concept or a dead end? "Reframing" resilience: Challenges for planning theory and practice interacting traps: Resilience assessment of a pasture management system in Northern Afghanistan Urban resilience: What does it mean in planning practice? Resilience as a useful concept for climate change adaptation? The politics of resilience for planning: A cautionary note. Plann. Theory Pract. **13**(2), 299–333 (2012)
31. Jones, P.S.: Urban regeneration's poisoned chalice: is there an impasse in (community) participation-based policy? Urban Stud. **40**(3), 581–601 (2003)
32. Ahern, J.: From fail-safe to safe-to-fail: Sustainability and resilience in the new urban world. Landscape Urban Plann. **100**, 341–343 (2011)
33. Sharif, A.M., Irani, Z.: Exploring fuzzy cognitive mapping for IS evaluation. Eur. J. Oper. Res. **173**, 1175–1187 (2006)
34. Bottero, M., Mondini, G., Oppio, A.: Decision Support Systems for evaluating urban regeneration. Procedia Soc. Behav. Sci. **223**, 923–928 (2016)
35. Monaco, R., Servente, G.: Introduzione ai modelli matematici nelle scienze territoriali. Celid, Torino (2012)
36. Monaco, R.: A mathematical model for territorial integrated evaluation. In: Brunetta, Smart Evaluation and Integrated Design in Regional Development, Ashgate, Farnham, Surrey (2015)
37. Murgante, B., Borruso, G.: Smart cities in a smart world. In: Rassia, S.T., Pardalos, P.M. (eds.) Future City Architecture for Optimal Living. Springer Optimization and its Applications, vol. 102, pp. 13–35. Springer, Heidelberg (2015)
38. Axelrod, R.: Structure of Decision: The Cognitive Maps of Political Elites. Princeton University Press, Princeton (1976)

Seismic Risk Assessment of Hospitals
in Lima City Using GIS Tools

Sandra Santa-Cruz[1], Juan Palomino[1], Nicola Liguori[1(✉)],
Marco Vona[2], and Rodrigo Tamayo[1]

[1] Pontifical Catholic University of Peru, Lima, Peru
{ssantacruz,jpalominob,nicola.liguori,rtamayol}@pucp.edu.pe
[2] University of Basilicata, Potenza, Italy
marco.vona@unibas.it

Abstract. In this work, seismic risk assessment of hospitals in Lima city is
presented. The aim of this paper is to evaluate the seismic risk of the Lima's health
system at Metropolitan scale. Seismic Risk Analysis has been carried out utilizing
the Comprehensive Approach for Probabilistic Risk Assessment methodology
(CAPRA). Geographic Information System (GIS) tools have been used to model
the risk components: hazard, exposure and vulnerability. A total of 41 hospitals
have been evaluated in order to obtain risk indicators in terms of economic losses.
The results show that after an 8.2 magnitude earthquake with an epicenter in the
coast of Lima, 85% of hospital buildings have more than 10% of structural
damage. Furthermore, the expected annual loss (EAL) is 2% of the replacement
value, which is high and uncompetitive compared with the values of the insurance
sector market. This study seeks to understand and evaluate the hospitals seismic
risk at metropolitan level in order to define measures, priorities and actions for
the future development of Lima's health system.

Keywords: Seismic risk assessment · Economic losses · Public infrastructure ·
Exposure · GIS

1 Introduction

The seismic risk can be assessed following a probabilistic approach, from its components: hazard, vulnerability and exposure [1, 2]. This approach incorporates the uncertainty associated with each component. Several risk assessment tools are available
nowadays to professionals and researchers. In this work, CAPRA methodology was used
to assess the seismic risk of hospitals in Lima. CAPRA is an initiative driven by the
World Bank and it has been used not only for risk assessment but to help the development
of comprehensive disaster management strategies [3–6]. Some examples of the use of
this methodology include the holistic risk assessment of cities or entire countries, development of hybrid loss exceedance curves, tsunami risk assessment, between others [7–
11]. The toolkit of this methodology is CAPRA-GIS, a geographic information system
that allows the integration of the previously developed components, and the subsequently risk calculation in terms of economic losses. Using this software, probabilistic

© Springer International Publishing AG 2017
O. Gervasi et al. (Eds.): ICCSA 2017, Part III, LNCS 10406, pp. 354–367, 2017.
DOI: 10.1007/978-3-319-62398-6_25

metrics like the Expected Scenario Loss (ESL), the Expected Annual Loss (EAL) and the Probable Maximum Loss (PML) are calculated.

2   General Overview of the Methodology

The steps followed to assess the seismic risk in this work are the following:

1. Seismic hazard and site effects assessment. Seismic hazard model was developed by the Geophysical Institute of Peru (IGP), while the local site effects in Lima were studied by the National Institute of Civil Defense (INDECI).
2. Data collection and exposure model generation. Field data collection of hospitals was carried out in order to gather the most important structural characteristics of buildings. Different building types were defined, and corresponding vulnerability functions were assigned to each building (vulnerability functions were defined in the vulnerability module).
3. Vulnerability assessment. The vulnerability of buildings was taken into account using vulnerability functions. This relationship relates the intensity of the hazard and the expected damage of the building. In order to obtain these functions, approximate and simplified methods were used and capacity curves were estimated. In addition, two types of vulnerability modifiers were included in the vulnerability functions: plan and vertical irregularities.
4. Seismic risk assessment. The previously modeled components of risk were integrated in order to obtain the seismic risk in terms of probable economic losses. Three risk indicators were obtained: Expected Scenario Loss (ESL), Expected Annual Loss (EAL) and Probable Maximum Loss (PML)

The exposure model, vulnerability functions and the risk assessment were carried out by the PUCP, while the hazard model was developed by the previously mentioned institutions (IGP and INDECI). Each risk component previously modeled was adjusted

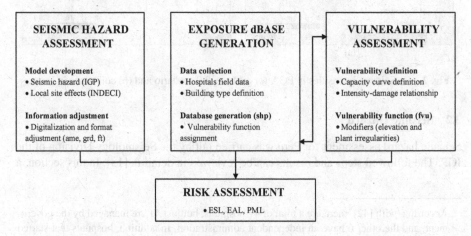

Fig. 1. Methodology flowchart.

to the required format in order to be compatible with CARA-GIS requirements. The flowchart of the methodology is shown in Fig. 1.

3   Seismic Risk Assessment of Hospitals in Lima City

3.1   Study Area

The study area was Lima city, the capital of Peru. It has 2,812 km^2 of extension and around 10 million inhabitants in its metropolitan area [12]. The city has 41 hospitals[1] and more than 200 health facilities. The geographic distribution of hospitals is shown in Fig. 2(a).

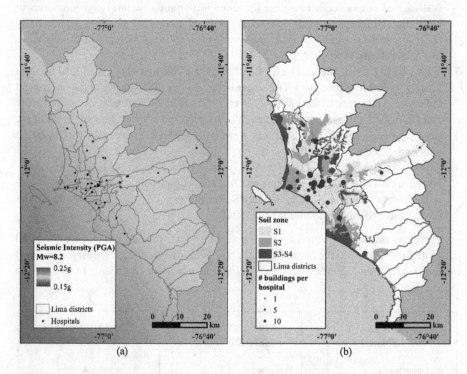

(a)   (b)

Fig. 2.   (a) Seismic intensities in PGA for a Mw = 8.2 scenario and (b) soil zones in Lima.

3.2   Seismic Hazard

Seismic hazard assessment for Peru was carried out by the Seismology Division of the IGP. The followed steps and results can be reviewed in detail in [13]. In this section, a

---

[1] According with [42], there are a total of 47 hospitals, but just 41 are managed by the government, and the other 6 have an independent administration. In addition, hospitals that started operating after the data collection date were not included in this work.

summary and brief description is presented highlighting the file format characteristics and the geographical information. The methodology followed was the Probabilistic Seismic Risk Analysis (PSHA), which takes into account the uncertainty of earthquake events and allows a better representation of their nature. The methodology was proposed by [14, 15] and summarized in four steps by [16].

The seismic hazard was calculated using CRISIS [17] considering the sum of the effects of all the seismic sources and the distance between each source and points of interest to be evaluated[2]. CRISIS has an incorporated functionality to export *.ame files directly from the software, to be used subsequently in CAPRA-GIS. Figure 2(a) shows the seismic intensities in PGA for a Mw = 8.2 scenario, near the coast of Lima. Table 1 shows the GIS characteristics of the hazard model and *.ame file format.

Table 1. Seismic hazard and site effects model characteristics.

Characteristic		Description	
Model		Seismic hazard	Site effects
Software		CRISIS2007 v7.6	SiteEffects v1.0
Format		*.ame	*.grd, *.ft
Coordinate system		Geographic	
Datum		GCS_WGS_1984	
Angular units		Degree	
Grid spacing		0.1°	0.0005°
Extension	Top	−0.038606°	−11.752067°
	Bottom	−18.350928°	−12.490027°
	Left	−81.328230°	−77.187737°
	Right	−68.652279°	−76.666245°

Site effects

In addition to the seismic hazard model, a local site effects grid was created using soil characteristics information of Lima. A microzonation study was carried out by the INDECI [18], and four different homogenous soil zones were defined (Fig. 2(b)). It can be seen that the majority of hospitals are located in non-amplification soil zones. Due to the lack of information about the dynamic soil characteristics, spectral amplification functions were created considering the constant amplification factor used in the Peruvian Seismic Design Code [19].

Using the amplification values for each spectral ordinate it is possible to calculate the spectral acceleration at surface level, multiplying this value by the spectral acceleration at firm ground. In order to include this information inside each soil zone, SiteEffects software was used [20]. This program allows creating a binary file that contains a grid with the soil zone and its corresponding amplification function for each point of the grid inside the study area. With this file included in risk calculation, each event's intensity

---

[2] Seismic sources geometry and their seismicity parameters can be managed in ArcGIS [22], as shapefiles (*.shp) than can be imported in CRISIS.

(contained in the *.ame file) is multiplied by the corresponding spectral amplification factor value before calculating damage in the buildings.

3.3 Exposure Model

An exposure model contains information of infrastructure or population that is exposed to hazards. In order to develop this model it is necessary to identify relevant attributes of exposed assets: location, geometric and structural characteristics, economic value, human occupation level, between others [21]. This information can be obtained from different sources and scale levels, depending on the size and scope of the study. Once the information is gathered, it has to be georeferenced and stored in GIS format. Software like ArcGIS [22] can be used to perform this task.

In this work, due to the lack of information regarding hospitals, a field data collection was performed in order to develop a complete exposure model. With the gathered information and complementary official data, a high resolution exposure model was developed containing information building by building. This allowed the subsequently vulnerability function assignment of each building.

Data Collection Attributes
In order to develop the exposure model it is necessary to define the attributes that have to be part of the model database. Official reports and detailed information previously published regarding Peruvian hospitals were reviewed in order to define relevant attributes to be taken into account [23–27]. In addition, data collection methodologies from other countries and type of assets (such as schools, dwellings, etc.) were included in this review process [28–31]. As a result of this evaluation, five general groups of information were defined (Table 2).

Table 2. Information groups in the exposure model.

	Group	Attributes
I	Building information	Hospital name, building name, building description, use
II	General characteristics	Year of construction, number of storeys, built area
III	Structural system and irregularities	Predominant construction material, structural system, replacement cost, plan and vertical irregularities
IV	Structural and constructive deficiencies	Short column, cracks, excessive deflections
V	Others	Field inspector remarks and comments

Data Collection Form
Digital forms with a database format where developed to help the data collection process. They included all the attributes shown in Table 2. This digital format eliminates the need of the usual digitalization process of physical forms. Mobile devices were used to fill the forms. Similar tools have been used in previous census carried out by the National Institute of Statistics and Informatics of Peru [32].

Data Collection

Field data collection was carried out using mobile devices. The identification of structural information (such as structural system and structural irregularities) was performed following the "FEMA 154-Rapid Visual Screening" guidelines [28]. Mobile devices also allowed georeferencing and photographing the buildings. Mobile applications were used to review and export the collected data. On average, buildings were evaluated in 25 min each. Mobile device environment and utilized applications are shown in Fig. 3.

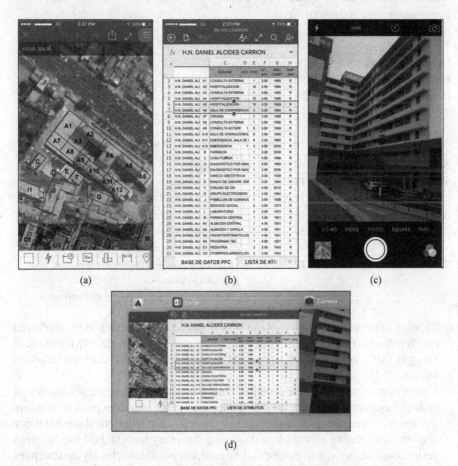

(a)   (b)   (c)

(d)

Fig. 3. Field data collection using mobile devices: (a) georeferencing, (b) data collection form, (c) photographing, (d) multitasking environment

Hospital Building Classes

Using the collected data and available information of hospitals, it was possible to define a set of building classes. Four attributes were considered: type of construction, year of construction, number of storeys and structural irregularities. The generation of vulnerability functions of each building class is described in Sect. 3.4. Then, each building is related to a building class. The subdivision of building classes is shown in Table 3, while the other attributes are shown in Table 4. The attributes description is the following:

Table 3. Building classes subdivision

Type of construction	COD	Year of construction	Number of storeys	Structural irregularity
Reinforced concrete frames	PORT	POST/PRE	B/M/A	IP/IA
Reinforced concrete frames w/walls	DUAL			
Reinforced masonry	MC			
Unreinforced masonry	MH	–	1	IP
Precast building	PREF	–	1	IP
Industrial building	NI	POST/PRE	1	IP

Table 4. Attributes abbreviation and description

Attribute		Abbreviation	Description
Year of Cnst.	<1997	PRE	Designed before 1997 Seismic Design Code
	>1997	POST	Designed after 1997 Seismic Design Code
Number of storeys	Low	B	1–3 storeys (typical: 2)
	Medium	M	4–7 storeys (typical: 5)
	High	A	>8 storeys (typical: 12)
Struct. irregularity	Plan	IP	Reentrant corners, diaphragm openings, non-parallel systems
	Vertical	IA	Soft story, setbacks, vertical discontinuities

- Type of construction: This attribute was organized in six categories: reinforced concrete frames (PORT), reinforced concrete frames with walls (DUAL), reinforced masonry (MC), unreinforced masonry (MH), precast building (PREF) and industrial building (NI).
- Year of construction: The year of construction was used to estimate the seismic design code of the structure. In Peru, the 1997 code [33] was the inflection point from where the structures were design with the necessary lateral stiffness that could prevent major displacements during earthquakes. Assuming that every hospital building has been designed according with its corresponding code, it is possible to classify the structures as pre 1997 code (PRE) and post 1997 code (POST).
- Number of storeys: This attribute was grouped in three categories: 1–3 storeys (B), 4–7 storeys (M) and +8 storeys (A).
- Structural irregularities: Following the FEMA-154 guidelines [28] (ATC, 2002), two structural irregularities were considered: plan (IP) and vertical (IA).

Hospital Economic Value

The building cost was established as the replacement value of modern hospitals in Peru [34] (e.g. hospitals designed according to the current regulations, after the 2007 Pisco earthquake [35]). This cost does not include medical equipment and mechanical systems. The average replacement cost per square meter was set at S/. 2,010³. With this value, it is possible to estimate the total replacement cost of each building, multiplying the total area of the building by the cost per square meter rate. With this rate, the total replacement cost of Lima hospitals is S/. 1,618,489,637.

Exposure Model Generation
Using the collected information of each building (geometry, attributes, building class, economic value), the exposure model was generated using the software ArcGIS v10.2.0 [22]. This software allowed to manage and export the database in a Shapefile format, that is subsequently used in CAPRA-GIS. There are three fields that CAPRA-GIS will use to calculate the seismic risk: VALFIS (total replacement cost), VALHUM (building occupancy) and SE_SISMO (name of the building class related to a vulnerability function). The field VALHUM is not used in this work since it is not focused on human risk. The exposure model characteristics are shown in Table 5. The number of buildings per hospital is shown in Fig. 2(b).

Table 5. Exposure model characteristics

Characteristic	Description	Characteristic	Description
Model	Exposure	Angular units	Degree
Software	ArcGIS v10.2.0	Number of fields	50
Format	Shapefile	Type of fields	Text/Numeric
Coordinate system	Geographic	Number of objects	737
Datum	GCS_WGS_1984	Type of objects	Polygon

3.4 Vulnerability

The structural vulnerability of each typology was expressed using vulnerability functions. It is defined as the relationship between hazard intensity and the Damage Ratio (DMR). This relationship was established using the methodology proposed by [1, 36]. Due to the lack of information, structural parameters of HAZUS [37] regarding building class attributes were used to model the vulnerability functions, except for the unreinforced masonry structures where a Peruvian reference was used [38].

The uncertainty of the vulnerability is taken into account through the definition of the standard deviation, using the equation proposed by the ATC-13 report [39]. Figure 4 shows the vulnerability functions for each structural type and year of construction subtype. A detailed description of vulnerability functions developed for this study is shown in [43].

---

³ Currency conversion: S/. 1.00 ≈ US$ 0.30).

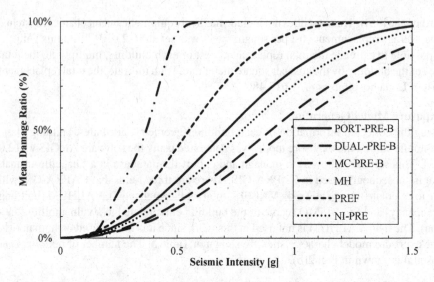

Fig. 4. Vulnerability functions for Pre-code/1-3 storeys building classes.

4 Seismic Risk Results

The seismic risk in this work is expressed in terms of three risk indicators: Expected Scenario Loss (ESL), Expected Annual Loss (AL) and Probable Maximum Loss (PML). In this section, a brief explanation of the calculation of these indicators is shown, as well as the results regarding hospitals of Lima. The software CAPRA-GIS v2.0.0 was utilized to combine the hazard, exposure and vulnerability models, and results were exported to ArcGIS in order to create specific maps. In addition, CAPRA methodology is compatible with the Peruvian standard [40].

Expected Scenario Loss (ESL)
The $ESL_{j,i}$ is the expected scenario loss in the building j due to the occurrence of scenario i; V_j is the vulnerability function of building j, and $Pr_{i,j}(I)$ is the probability that the intensity is I, at location j in a scenario i. This last value depends on the standard deviation of the intensity, explained in Sect. 3.2. The $ESL_{j,i}$ can be calculated with the Eq. (1).

$$ESL_{j,i} = \sum_I V_j(I)Pr_{i,j}(I) \tag{1}$$

From this, it is possible to calculate the Total Expected Scenario Loss ($TESL_i$), shown in Eq. (2). It is defined as the sum of the $ESL_{j,i}$ considering the total number of buildings Nb, for the scenario i. The results of ESL for an Mw = 8.2 seismic scenario in Lima coast are shown in Table 6 and Fig. 5, while Fig. 6 shows the ESL per building class.

Table 6. ESL (Mw = 8.2) and EAL for hospitals in Lima.

	# buildings	%	Built area (m²)	%
TESL = S/. 427,152,404 (26%)				
ESL < 10%	108	15%	78,095	10%
10% < ESL < 30%	488	66%	604,128	75%
30% < ESL < 70%	73	10%	27,141	3%
70% < ESL < 100%	68	9%	95,855	12%
Total EAL = S/. 21,193,294 (2%)				
EAL < 8‰	118	16%	97,353	12%
8‰ < EAL < 20‰	391	53%	486,361	60%
EAL > 20‰	228	31%	221,504	28%

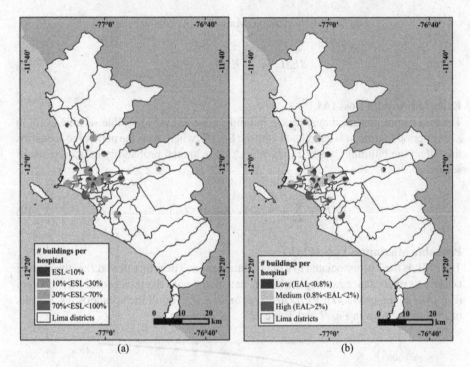

(a)   (b)

Fig. 5. (a) ESL for a Mw = 8.2 scenario in Lima and (b) EAL for hospitals in Lima. Each pie-chart represents one hospital, and the size of the piechart is proportional to the number of buildings.

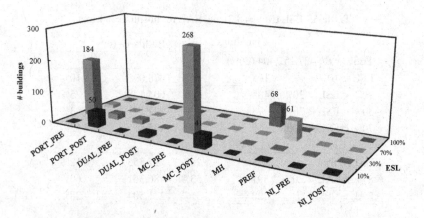

Fig. 6. ESL distribution (Mw = 8.2) per building class.

$$TESL_i = \sum_{j=1}^{Nb} ESL_{j,i} \tag{2}$$

Expected Annual Loss (AL)

The EAL represent the annual loss in building j due to every possible seismic event in a long period of time. It is calculated with the Eq. (3), where Ns is the number of scenarios that affect the building j and $Pr_i(ocurrence)$ is the annual probability of occurrence of scenario i.

$$EAL_j = \sum_{i=1}^{Ns} \left(Pr_i(ocurrence)ESL_{j,i} \right) \tag{3}$$

Probable Maximum Loss (PML)

The PML is the loss associated to a long return period. The return period Tr is the inverse of the loss exceedance rate $v(p)$, which is calculated with the total probability theorem (Eq. (4)), as the product of $Pr_i(ocurrence)$ and $TESL_i$, for all the scenarios Ns. Results of PML are shown in Fig. 7 and Table 7.

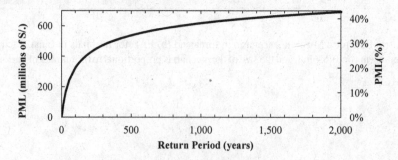

Fig. 7. Probable maximum loss curve

Table 7. PML for fixed return periods

T (years)	PML (%)	PML (S/.)
50	13.9%	S/. 225,275,753
100	19.9%	S/. 322,454,268
200	25.8%	S/. 418,056,280
500	33.1%	S/. 536,376,365
1,000	38.2%	S/. 617,576,042
2,000	42.7%	S/. 691,576,945

$$v(p) = \frac{1}{Tr} = \sum_{i=1}^{Ns} \left(Pr_i(ocurrence) \right) \left(TESL_i \right) \tag{4}$$

5   Discussion and Conclusions

A seismic risk assessment of 41 hospitals in Lima city is presented. The results show that the total loss for the Mw = 8.2 scenario is S/. 427,152,404 and the EAL is S/. 31,853,330. The PML for a seismic event with a return period of 500 years is approximately S/.500 million.

The results show a high loss that is most likely due to the vulnerability of the structures. The most important factor that influences the vulnerability is the years of construction of buildings, which is related to the building code used to design them. In fact, 617 (83%) buildings have been designed with obsolete seismic code (PRE). Consequently, it is clear that buildings designed after the 1997 have an acceptable structural performance. The results show a positive behavior that concern the soil type on which the hospital buildings are. In specific, 550 (75%) building hospitals are built on a firm soil, and have no acceleration amplification effects.

The approach shown in this work is certainly useful not only to evaluate the infrastructures at large scale (as in Lima city), but also for small scale like a singular hospital. In addition, the GIS tools allowed to manage the data with efficiency, with the option to be upgraded and improved in future analyses. Output data certainly can help decision makers to take decision about how manage emergency, retrofitting or rebuilt plans so short, medium or long term intervention measures. Nowadays, some guidelines and example are present in the literature. Reports like FEMA P-420 [41] has published guidelines for incremental seismic rehabilitation. Whit this approach, decision maker, authorities and owners could establish a balance between the budget to invest and the years to reach a retrofitting goal.

This study was focused exclusively on the physical risk, therefore future analysis that include more components (e.g. non-structural and functional vulnerability) could be done. Furthermore, the vulnerability curves were obtained utilizing US database like HAZUS (FEMA, 2011), due to the lack of Peruvian data, so improvement is necessary in this field. Finally, in order to reduce as much as possible the losses and increase the performance of the health system, retrofitting or rebuilding plans have to be developed.

References

1. Ordaz, M., Miranda, E., Reinoso, E., Pérez-Rocha, L.E.: Seismic loss estimation model for Mexico City, Auckland (2000)
2. Cardona, O., et al.: Probabilistic seismic risk assessment for comprehensive risk management: modeling for innovative risk transfer and loss financing mechanisms. In: World Conference on Earthquake Engineering, Beijing (2008)
3. ERN-AL: Comprehensive Approach for Probabilistic Risk Assessment (CAPRA), Mexico, D.F. (2010)
4. Cardona, O.D., Ordaz, M., Reinoso, E., Yamín, L., Barbat, A.: Comprehensive approach for probabilistic risk assessment (CAPRA): International Initiative for disaster risk management effectiveness, Ohrid (2010)
5. Cardona, O.D., Ordaz, M., Reinoso, E., Yamín, L., Barbat, A.: Enfoque integral para la Evaluación Probabilista del Riesgo (CAPRA): Iniciativa Internacional para la Efectividad de la Gestión del Riesgo de Desastre, Granada (2011)
6. Cardona, O.D., Ordaz, M., Reinoso, E., Yamín, L., Barbat, A.: Comprehensive Approach to Probabilistic Risk Assessment: International Initiative for Risk Management Effectiveness - CAPRA, Lisboa (2012)
7. Marulanda, M., Carreño, M., Cardona, O., Ordaz, M., Barbat, A.: Probabilistic earthquake risk assessment using CAPRA: application to the city of Barcelona, Spain. Nat. Hazards 69(1), 59–84 (2013)
8. Carreño, M., Cardona, O.D., Barbat, A., Velásquez, C., Salgado, M.: Holistic seismic risk assessment of port of spain: an integrated evaluation and tool in the framework of CAPRA, Istambul (2014)
9. Velásquez, C., et al.: Hybrid loss exceedance curve (HLEC) for disaster risk assessment. Nat. Hazards 72(2), 455–479 (2014)
10. Mora, M., et al.: Prioritizing interventions to reduce seismic vulnerability in school facilities in Colombia. Earthq. Spectra 31(4), 2535–2552 (2015)
11. Jaimes, M., et al.: A new approach to probabilistic earthquake-induced tsunami risk. Ocean Coast. Manag. 119, 68–75 (2016)
12. INEI: Una mirada a Lima Metropolitana, Lima (2014)
13. Tavera, H., et al.: Seismic hazard analysis in Peru. In: 16 World Conference on Earthquake Engineering, Santiago de Chile (2017)
14. Esteva, L.: Criterios para la construcción de espectros para diseño sísmico, Caracas (1967)
15. Cornell, A.: Engineering seismic risk analysis. Bull. Seismol. Soc. Am. 58(5), 1583–1606 (1968)
16. Reiter, L.: Earthquake Hazard Analysis: Issues and Insights. Columbia University Press (1990)
17. Ordaz, M., Aguilar, A., Arboleda, J.: CRISIS2007 Ver 7.4, México, D.F. (2007)
18. INDECI-PNUD: Estudio SIRAD. Recursos de respuesta inmediata y de recuperación temprana ante la ocurrencia de un sismo y/o tsunami en Lima Metropolitana y Callao, Lima (2011). http://sirad.indeci.gob.pe/static/SIRAD_Publicacion_ES.pdf
19. RNE NTE E.030: Norma Técnica de Edificación E.030 - Diseño Sismorresistente. Mnisterio de Vivienda, Construcción y Saneamiento, Lima (2003)
20. ERN-AL: Site Effects 1.0.0., Evaluación de Riesgos Naturales - America Latina, Mexico, D.F. (2010)
21. Lavell, A.: I. International Agency Concepts and Guidelines for Disaster Risk Management, II. The Transition from Risk Concepts to Risk Indicators, Manizales (2003)
22. ESRI: ArcGIS 10.2 for Desktop, Redlands (2013)

23. Lazares, F., Rios, J.: Metodología para determinación de la vulnerabilidad estructural en instalaciones hospitalarias, Lima (1996)
24. OPS: Diagnóstico de la Vulnerabilidad Sísmica en Hospitales del Perú, Lima (1997)
25. Reque, K.: Diagnóstico preliminar de la vulnerabilidad para establecimientos de salud en el Perú, Lima (2006)
26. INDECI-PNUD: Proyecto SIRAD: Sistema de Información sobre Recursos para Atención de Desastres, Lima (2010)
27. PREDES: Evaluación de vulnerabilidad de infraestructura de salud y educación en Lima y Callao, Lima (2011)
28. ATC: FEMA-154: Rapid visual screening of buildings for potential seismic hazards: A handbook, Washington, D.C. (2002)
29. NSET: Guidelines for seismic vulnerability assessment of hospitals, Nepal (2004)
30. CENAPRED: Guía Básica para la Elaboración de Atlas Estatales y Municipales de Peligros y Riesgos. Evaluación de la vulnerabilidad física y social, México, D.F. (2006)
31. OPS: Índice de Seguridad Hospitalaria: Formularios para evaluación de hospitales seguros. Hospitales seguros frente a desastres, Washington, DC (2008)
32. INEI: Censo de Infraestructura Educativa - CIE 2013, Lima, Perú (2014)
33. RNE NTE E.030: Diseño Sismorresistente, Lima (1997)
34. MINSA: Hospital technical files, Lima (2013)
35. Rios, F., Zavala, C.: Impact of the Pisco-Peru earthquake of August 15th 2007 on health facilities, Beijing (2008)
36. Miranda, E.: Assessment of the seismic vulnerability of existing buildings, Acapulco (1996)
37. FEMA: HAZUS-MH 2.1. Multi-hazard loss estimation methodology: earthquake model. Technical Manual, Washington, D.C. (2011)
38. Tarque, N., Crowley, H., Pinho, R., Varum, H.: Displacement-based fragility curves for seismic assessment of adobe buildings in Cusco, Peru. Earthq. Spectra **28**(2), 759–794 (2012)
39. ATC: Earthquake Damage Evaluation Data for California (Report ATC-13), Redwood City (1985)
40. SBS: Resolución SBS N° 1305–2005. Reglamento para la constitución de la reserva de riesgos catastróficos y de siniestralidad incierta, Lima (2005)
41. FEMA: Engineering guideline for incremental seismic rehabilitation (FEMA P-420 report), Washington, D.C. (2009)
42. Santa-Cruz, S.: Evaluación probabilista del riesgo sísmico de escuelas y hospitales en la ciudad de Lima. Componente 2: Evaluación probabilista del riesgo sísmico de locales escolares, Probabilistic seismic risk assessment of schools and hospitals in the city of Lima, Pontificia Universidad Catolica del Peru, Lima, Internal report (2013)
43. Santa-Cruz, S., Palomino, J., Niño, M.: Development of seismic vulnerability functions for Lima hospitals using simplified methods. In 11th US National Conference on Earthquake Engineering, Los Angeles (2018). (submitted)

Smart City Governance in the Geo-resources Planning Paradigm in the Metropolitan City of Cagliari (Italy)

Ginevra Balletto and Chiara Garau[✉]

DICAAR – Department of Civil and Environmental Engineering
and Architecture, University of Cagliari, Cagliari, Italy
{balletto, cgarau}@unica.it

Abstract. The purpose of this paper is to identify environmental issues related to the geo-resources demand, which arises by the new context of the metropolitan city of Cagliari, in the framework of the existing environmental and place-based policies. This is achieved through the correlation of the main planning tools (the Regional Plan of Extractive Activities [RPEA] for geo-resources planning sector, and the urban masterplan [UMP] for urban planning sector), in order to identify environmental indicators, useful for monitoring and for decision support systems. This comparison defined a new integrated methodological approach between urban, place-based and environmental policies, referring to geo-resources planning, in line with the newest paradigm of smart region and of the panarchy process. This approach allowed to evaluate the delayed impacts of UMPs, and its environmental impacts, resulting from the quarry activities of geo-resources (such as natural aggregates). In fact, quarry activity is the leading effect in UMPs (because the materials of construction are obtained principally by it), and it simultaneously decreases the environmental sustainability, increasing the environmental debt.

Keywords: Smart cities · Smart urban governance · Environmental geo-resources planning · Panarchy · Urban and regional policies · Urban masterplan · Environmental footprint

1 Introduction

The geo-resource planning allows to identify the thresholds of environmental balance between urban needs resulting from planning tools and environmental protection [1, 2]. Specifically, the geo-resources planning is a regional tool (The Regional Plan of Extractive Activities, RPEA (*Piano Regionale Attività Estrattive,* PRAE). It defines regulations and guidelines addressed to professionals and to authorities in the planning, governance and control of mining activities, aimed at achieving specific objectives of sustainable development of the mining sector. The correlation between the building

---

This paper is the result of the joint work of the authors. In particular, paragraphs 3, 4, and 5 have been jointly written by the authors. Ginevra Balletto has written paragraph 2. Chiara Garau has written paragraph 1.

© Springer International Publishing AG 2017
O. Gervasi et al. (Eds.): ICCSA 2017, Part III, LNCS 10406, pp. 368–379, 2017.
DOI: 10.1007/978-3-319-62398-6_26

activity and quarry activity is direct (urban planning gives rise to a material demand) and is cyclically and consequential renewed (as a result of maintenance and urban renewal) [3].

In fact, the interpretation of the dispersed contemporary city with its urban sprawl has made possible to state how the single urban nucleus necessarily needs to trigger reciprocity mechanisms with the neighboring landscape [4]. However, this need expressed in the territory makes the same dispersed city as the one that generates greater demand for materials than the compact historical city [5]. Compared to other Italian realities, the Region of Sardinia has a limited demographic weight and its urban centers have characteristics of polycentric urban development, typical of the urban dispersion phenomenon a low density. In addition, particularly in Sardinia the extraction of natural aggregates (NA) respects the 'principle of proximity' refers to the place of destination and, as a result of modest commercial value attributed to natural aggregates (NA), their commercialization is limited, and more properly attributable to the entire island of Sardinia [6].

According to [7], authors identified the effects in terms of geo-resources (NA) arising from the municipal urban planning, in relation to municipalities of the metropolitan city of Cagliari, selected as case-studies. The metropolitan city of Cagliari (Fig. 1) is

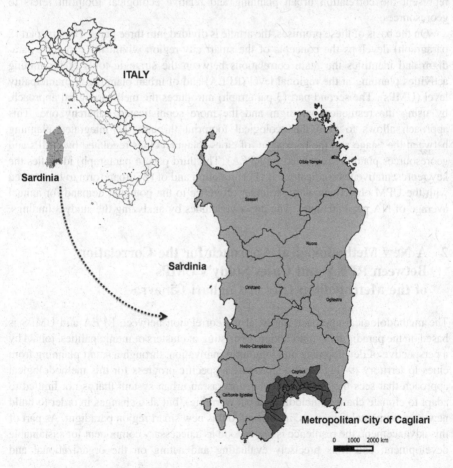

Fig. 1. The metropolitan city of Cagliari (Italy)

established from the Regional law 2/2016 'Reform of the system of local autonomy of Sardinia' (from the Italian *Riordino del sistema delle autonomie locali della Sardegna*).

The Metropolitan city of Cagliari is constituted by seventeen municipalities—with Cagliari as a leader. The other municipalities are Assemini, Capoterra, Decimomannu, Elmas, Maracalagonis, Monserrato, Pula, Quartu Sant'Elena, Quartucciu, Sarroch, Selargius, Sestu, Settimo, Sinnai, Villa San Pietro, and Uta. They include about 431,000 inhabitants, in an area of 1,250 square kilometres (ISTAT, 2015). Different urban planning tools—from those that are strategic to urban master plans or sector plans—continue to be used at various levels [7]. In particular, all seventeen municipalities— such as every Italian municipality from small village to sprawling municipality—have an urban masterplan (UMP) that regulates and protects the urban and territorial processes of transformation, in accordance with the Italian National Law no. 1150 of 1942 and with the Sardinian Regional Law no. 45 of 1989.

The comparative analysis between the Regional Plan of Extractive Activities (RPEA) of Sardinia [8] and the urban masterplans (UMPs) of selected municipalities of metropolitan city of Cagliari makes it possible to identify functional indicators to represent the correlation urban planning and relative ecological footprint refers to georesources.

On the basis of these premises, the article is divided into three parts. The first part (2 paragraph) develops the concepts of the smart city-region within the panarchy paradigm and identifies the main correlations between the strategic tools of for mining activities planning at the regional level (RPEA) and of urban planning at municipality level (UMPs). The second part (3 paragraph) introduces the methodological approach, by using the resilience paradigm and the more sophisticated panarchy one. This approach allows to hold the ecological footprint through the integrated planning between the 'stage and the backstage' of cities (planned cities regulated by UMPs and georesources planning regulated by RPEA). The third part (4 paragraph) identifies the key representativeness indicators of (1) correlation and of (2) urban form to be pursued with the UPM objectives with particular reference to the potential demand for annual average of NA per inhabitant. The paper concludes by analyzing the study's findings.

2 A New Methodological Approach for the Correlation Between RPEA and Cases Study's UMPs of the Metropolitan City of Cagliari Ginevra

The methodological approach aimed at the correlation between RPEA and UMPS is based on the paradigm of smart region, consisting of clusters of municipalities, joined by a perspective of development and long-term innovation, through a smart planning from cities to territory [9–11]. Authors propose a specific progress for this methodological approach that sees the resilient city/territory as an urban system that is not limited to adapt to climate change (including global warming), but also changes in order to build new environmental responses, in relation to this new smart region paradigm. As part of this advancement, the resilience is understood as a necessary component for sustainable development, and it is precisely evaluating and acting on the organizational and management models of urban systems that the smart region is able to express the maximum potential, even in reference to the geo-resources. In other words, if the smart region had identified as a coin, one side was the cities cluster and the other was waste or quarry materials (the geo-resourses field). In fact, the main pillars of smart city paradigm (economy, mobility, environment, people, living and governance) produce interactions beyond geographies-reference of the city boundaries, going to affect the province, the region (when it comes to an island) or even national and international dimension.

The literature defines the term 'panarchy' the specificity of socio-ecological systems that undergoes influences, status and process, by nested interactions that act on different (urban and regional) scales [12, 13]. Specifically, the panarchy with external effects is the ability of a city-territory of change by building social responses, new economic and environmental conditions. These then allow the city- territory to resist in the long run to the stresses of the environment and to those of urban competence. Namely, the nested relationships within virtuous municipalities resulting by multi level actions from neighborhoods to metropolitan city create optimal conditions in order to express the process of panarchy. The opposite (the panarchy with internal effects) is the process having only internal effects without relationships between other urban contexts.

Figure 2 represents at a glance the internal and external panarchy resulting from the correlation between RPEA and UMPs (Fig. 1).

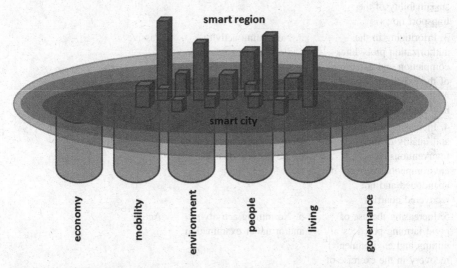

Fig. 2. Smart city and region: internal (urban scale) and external (extra-urban scale) effects. Green represents the positive externalities and the red one negative externalities in the smart region [14] (Color figure online)

From an operational point of view, such correlations between RPEA and UMPs allowed to identify (1) the internal and external effects, after having extrapolated (2) the objectives of the two different planning tools. In turn, the internal and external effects have been divided into active effects (positive for the environment) and passive (negative for the environment) (Table 1).

Table 1. Comparison between RPEA, selected UMPs goals and panarchy with external-internal effects

Goals RPEA	Goals of selected UMPs	Panarchy with external effects of extra-urban scale	Panarchy with internal effects of urban scale
1. Orienting to criteria of sustainability the authorization procedures for issuing permits, in order to open new quarries or mines	1. No mining activity and/or under examination	Active	–
2. Limiting the opening of new mines or quarries for the extraction of materials whose supply is, however, already ensured by mining activities into operation in respect of market constraints, and of sustainability of the transport flows	2. No mining activity and/or under examination	Passive	–
3. Prioritizing in the authorization procedures completion and extension of the existing activity, relative to the opening of new mining activities	3. No mining activity and/or under examination	Passive	–
4. Increasing the number and quality of the interventions of environmental recovery of abandoned and not recovered quarries	4. Quarrying park, recovery and enhancement of the historic quarries	Active	Active
5. Increasing the use of good farming practices of mining and environmental recovery in the exercise of mining	5. No mining activity and/or under examination	Active	–
6. Encouraging the use of environmental certifications of mining activities	6. No mining activity and/or under examination	Passive	
7. Improving the quality level of the design of extractive operations and interventions of	7. No mining activity and/or under examination	Passive	

(*continued*)

Table 1. (*continued*)

Goals RPEA	Goals of selected UMPs	Panarchy with external effects of extra-urban scale	Panarchy with internal effects of urban scale
environmental recovery or redevelopment of abandoned mining areas			
8. Rationalizing the authorization and control procedures of mining activities	8. No mining activity and/or under examination	Passive	
9. Encouraging the reuse of waste from extractive activities and with similar requirements in public works specifications and in EIA of public works (the movements of excavated land and rocks - that follow the environmental recovery of abandoned mining areas - improve the EIA in public work)	9. Operational procedures in tenders	Active	Active
10. Promoting economic development of supply chains in the extractive industry	10. Operational procedures for tenders, redevelopment of historical city centers and private building activity	Active	Active

Interestingly, the effects of panarchy on extra urban scale does not correspond to the objectives stated in the UMPs. In this sense, it is also interesting to note also that 50% of the goals of RPEA (goals 2, 3, 6, 7, 8) does not present a concrete explanation, so as to reduce the much desired environmental sustainability in urban planning.

3 Methodology

The many challenges that urban areas are facing are closely interconnected, not only in the major pillars of the smart cities paradigm (economy, mobility, environment, people, living and governance), but also in terms of spatial terms. Today, the main objective of the EU strategy is to contain the environmental impacts arising from the cities, through integrated planning to contain (or gradually eliminate) the environmental debt [15].

The evaluation of the mining demand for aggregate materials—associated with the demand coming from the implementation of the UMP—is the main prerequisite for identifying policies and urban and regional dynamics and responsible skills [5, 16]. This starting by the most representative indicator of effectiveness: the average potential per capita consumption of natural aggregates [7].

In fact, in order to meet the demand for aggregates of a context, the amount of material consumed in the considered territory in a given period is crucial to know. The activities of mining planning use this information to estimate the aggregate needs of an area.

Among the many approaches, the authors have chosen to adopt the evaluation of aggregate demand in reference to local urban planning tools predictions [16], stating that in Sardinia the consumption is equivalent to the demand for aggregates, because Sardinia can rely solely on own resources due to the modest market value of aggregates. In fact, this island-region cannot import the aggregates required for the building industry, due to the high transport costs.

Usually, local planning tools refer to a time period of 10 years. Therefore, the evaluation of aggregate demand in reference to local urban planning tools is based on the assumption that the UMPs forecasts will be released during this time. In reality, this condition does not always come true, and interventions under the UMPs may be modified or delays and involve much longer timeframes. The assessment of the requirement of inert according to this methodology has been derived from planned volumetries in the single homogeneous urban areas (expressed in square meters), curtailed the already built-up areas, in function of the respective spatial indexes (expressed in cubic meters/square meter).

In the evaluation of aggregate demand, the authors considered the following zoning districts, where we expect the greatest building activity:

- Historic centre zone ('A' zone);
- Residential completion zone ('B' zone);
- Residential expansion zone ('C' zone); and
- Tourism zone ('F' zone)

The quantity of materials required for the realization of the works envisaged by the UMPs are obtained by correcting the volumetries with relative coefficients of utilization. According to [7], authors considered the UMPs of the municipalities of Cagliari, Decimomannu, Maracalagonis, Quartucciu, Quartu Sant'Elena, and Sarroch. The choice of these six municipalities sample compared to the 17 municipalities of the metropolitan city Cagliari arises from the following reasons:

- Cagliari and Quartu Sant'Elena are the most populous municipalities of Sardinia
- Sarroch is influenced by a broader regional scale industrial zone
- Decimomannu, Maracalgonis, and Quartucciu are characterized by an average population increase of about 15.15%

Such synthetic reasons are the main connotation elements having implications for growth - urban renewal of the metropolitan city of Cagliari.

4 Results

In [7], the indicator capable of representing the correlation between UMP and demand for construction materials is the so-called average requirement per year per capita. This allows to confirm the literature that asserts how compact cities consume less material than dispersed and/or ramified ones [17].

After having proceeded to assess in detail for each homogeneous zone the character of even seasonal residentiality (A, B, C, and F), the progress of this work consists in clarifying the new urban expansion and urban redevelopment, for civil works (housing, services, etc.) and for the road.

Table 2 shows how the choices of UMPs are developed in NA, of expansionary or conservative type, because they have generated as a result new construction or maintenance, in the sectors of urban planning - housing and traffic. This has also generated different and substantial percentages on the demand for building materials and, more generally, for the ecological footprint [18].

Table 2. Incidence percentage of NA for urban expansion and redevelopment

	% aggregates for urban expansion	% aggregates for urban redevelopment	% aggregates for urban expansion	% aggregates for urban redevelopment	% aggregates for urban expansion	% aggregates for urban redevelopment
	Cagliari		Decimonannu		Maracalagonis	
A zone	0	100	5.77	94.23	0	100
B zone	65.9	34.1	75.7	24.3	0	100
C zone	97.4	2.4	100	0	100	0
F zone					60.57	39.58
	Quartucciu		Quartu Sant'Elena		Sarroch	
A zone	0	100	10.91	89.09	0	100
B zone	0	100	56.35	43.65	73.26	26.74
C zone	94.14	5.86	62.86	37.14	48.49	51.51
F zone			71.13	28.87	31.02	68.98

In summary, the percentage of NA refers to new construction or maintenance allows to express the containment of the consumption of soil [19], referred to urban and to geo-resources sectors.

In particular, Table 2 shows the percentage of NA for expansion and redevelopment, highlighting different behaviors represented in Fig. 3, through a binary-geographic representation. It allows to distinguish the following phenomena with the following binary attributions:

(1) urban expansion (−1)
(2) conservation-redevelopment (+1)
(3) balance between expansion and conservation-redevelopment (0):

    when the expansion is equal to and less than the 10–12% of redevelopment;
    when the redevelopment is equal to less than 10–12% expansion.

Figure 3 shows how all A zones are subject to urban redevelopment, (having panarchy effects of urban and extra-urban area of active type). The B zones are subject to urban renewal for municipalities of Quartucciu and Quartu St. Elena; for C zones only the Municipality of Maracalagonis, finally for the F zones (when present in the UMPs) no municipality is virtuous.

It is clear, therefore, that, as regards the geo-resources, the municipalities closer to the city of Cagliari are the most virtuous (Fig. 3).

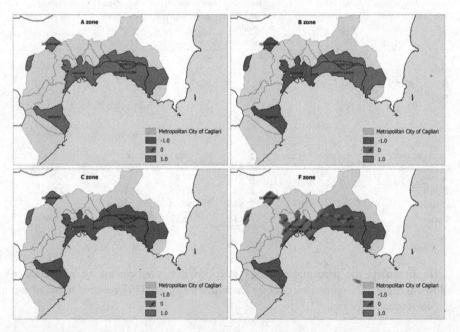

Fig. 3. The four quadrants show the expansion and urban redevelopment in relation to homogeneous areas (A, B, C and F zones) in the 6 municipalities of the metropolitan city of Cagliari

5 Conclusions

The metropolitan city of Cagliari, as cities cluster, is to be understood as a reticular system of urban areas where the risk of urban welding, in generating peripheries negatively affected by its environmental consequences described above.

In particular, large unburned free spaces allow to preserve and strengthen the structure of the urban network and at the same time they contain the ecological footprint resulting from the potential demand of geo-resources (NA).

Within the framework of the urban planning of the metropolitan city [20], the proposition of green spaces and corridors between one center to another, or between clusters of municipalities (Fig. 4) takes on a strategic value, when not welded.

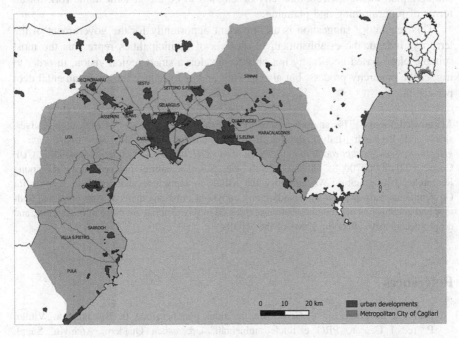

Fig. 4. Agglomerates of municipalities in the Metropolitan city of Cagliari

In fact, green spaces and green corridors can reduce not only the urban dependence of the smaller towns than that prevailing, but also the environmental impacts of the urban own.

So then the urban plan of the metropolitan city (only covered by statute [21]) has a marked significance of integrated urban development, both for direct implications on the geo-resources without underestimating the equally important redevelopment of quarry no longer productive landscapes [22], which as a result of progressive urban expansion have been incorporated into the urban fabric, giving the historical quarry character [23].

This dynamic vision and spatial multi, connected to all pillars offers a more powerful vision region in territorial terms.

In this view, the urban planning of the metropolitan city of Cagliari must necessarily be integrated both in spatial terms (clusters of communes) and in new proposed fields terms, such as geo-resource planning. This latter can no longer be neglected in every urban plan, recognized as a smart tool, where 'urban stage and backstage' [24] are linked by nested interactions for topics and levels.

In this sense the statute of the metropolitan city of Cagliari confirms these principles. It establishes the approval and implementation of the strategic plan for metropolitan city with 'programming guidelines, general, sectoral and transversal development goals in the medium and long term, priorities for intervention, timing and method of implementation, modalities and monitoring tools' [21]. This allows to strategic plan of the metropolitan city of Cagliari to be the general framework for all forms of programming and planning.

This regulatory suggestion is an important opportunity for the government of the territory. Indeed, the establishment of clusters of municipalities represents the most suitable place-based geography not only to develop a smart region vision, in order to trigger the panarchy process, but also to limit and/or to reduce the environmental debt per capita.

Acknowledgments. This study was supported by the MIUR (Ministry of Education, Universities and Research [Italy]) through a project entitled *Governing tHe smart city: a gOvernance-centred approach to SmarT urbanism - GHOST* (Project code:RBSI14FDPF; CUP Code: F22I15000070008), financed with the SIR (Scientific Independence of Young Researchers) programme. We authorize the MIUR to reproduce and distribute reprints for Governmental purposes, notwithstanding any copyright notations thereon. Any opinions, findings and conclusions or recommendations expressed in this material are those of the authors, and do not necessarily reflect the views of the MIUR.

References

1. Dall'Ara, E., Pistocchi, A.: Georisorse, decisioni, pianificazione. In: Biscaglia, A., Vitillo, P. (eds.) Cesena, PRG e tutele ambientali, Urbanistica Quaderni Archivio, Suppl. Urbanistica 117, pp. 97–103 (2002)
2. Del Monte, M., et al.: Geomorphological classification of urban landscapes: the case study of Rome (Italy). J. Maps 12(sup1), 178–189 (2016)
3. Yang, Z., Tanimoto, C. (eds.): Ancient Underground Opening and Preservation. Taylor & Francis Group, London (2016)
4. Bianchetti, C.: Abitare la città contemporanea, Skira, pp. 102–103 (2003)
5. Balletto, G., Mei, G., Garau, C.: Relationship between quarry activity and municipal spatial planning: a possible mediation for the case of Sardinia, Italy. Sustainability 7(12), 16148–16163 (2015)
6. Balletto, G.La: Pianificazione Sostenibile Delle Risorse (Sustainable planning of environmental resources). Franco Angeli, Milano (2005)

7. Garau, C., Balletto, G., Zamperlin, P.: A reflection on smart governance in the new metropolitan city of cagliari. In: The 9th International Conference on Innovation in Urban and Regional Planning, Valentino Castle – Viale Mattioli 39, Turin (14th – 15th September 2016), pp. 135–142 (2016)
8. Regional Plan of Extractive Activities (Piano Regionale Attività Estrattive). https://www.regione.sardegna.it/documenti/1_82_20080627104231.pdf. Accessed 30 Nov 2015
9. Garau, C.: Perspectives on cultural and sustainable rural tourism in a smart region: the case study of marmilla in sardinia (Italy). Sustainability 7(6), 6412–6434 (2015)
10. Priano, F.H., Armas, R.L., Guerra, C.F.: A model for the smart development of island territories. In: International Conference on Digital Government Research, pp. 465–474 (2016)
11. Garau, C.: Smart paths for advanced management of cultural heritage. Reg. Stud. Reg. Sci. 1 (1), 286–293 (2014)
12. Brown, E.D., Williams, B.K.: Resilience and resource management. Environ. Manage. 56 (6), 1416–1427 (2015)
13. Berkes, F., Ross, H.: Panarchy and community resilience: sustainability science and policy implications. Environ. Sci. Policy 61, 185–193 (2016)
14. Murgante, B., Borruso, G.: Smart city or smurfs city. In: Murgante, B., et al. (eds.) ICCSA 2014. LNCS, vol. 8580, pp. 738–749. Springer, Cham (2014). doi:10.1007/978-3-319-09129-7_53
15. Seppelt, R., Cumming, G.S.: Humanity's distance to nature: time for environmental austerity? Landscape Ecol. 31, 1645–1651 (2016)
16. Furcas, C., Balletto, G.: Effects of quarrying activity and the construction sector on environmental sustainability. A brief report on the rapid growth of emerging Central and Eastern European States. Diam. Appl. Tecnol. 70, 74–81 (2012)
17. Fertner, C., Große, J.: Compact and resource efficient cities? Synergies and trade-offs in European cities. Eur. Spat. Res. Policy 23(1), 65–79 (2016)
18. Lu, Y., Chen, B.: Urban ecological footprint prediction based on the Markov chain. J. Clean Prod. (2016). doi:10.1016/j.jclepro.2016.03.034
19. Bimonte, S., Stabile, A.: Land consumption and income in Italy: a case of inverted EKC. Ecol. Econ. 131, 36–43 (2017)
20. Law 56/2014 (known as the Delrio law)
21. Statute of the Metropolitan City of Cagliari can be downloaded at the following link: http://www.provincia.cagliari.it/ProvinciaCa/resources/cms/documents/Statuto_CM.pdf
22. Yang, X.: MaterialScape: the transformation and revitalization of an abandoned limestone quarry into an educational and recreational public park. Muncie, Indiana (2016). https://studylib.net/doc/11007538/materialscape--the-transformation-and-revitalization-of-a...
23. Historic Quarries. http://www.historic-quarries.org/
24. Piccinini, L.C., Chang, T.F.M., Taverna, M.: Confini e stratificazioni nel backstage del mosaico paesistico-culturale. Agribus. Paesaggio Ambiente 13, 114–122 (2010)

Quality of Experience for Personalized Sightseeing Tours: Studies and Proposition for an Evaluation Method

Mayeul Mathias[1]([⊠]), Camille Béguin[5]([⊠]), Juan-Manuel Torres-Moreno[1,2,3]([⊠]),
Didier Josselin[1,2,4]([⊠]), Delphine Picolot[4], Fen Zhou[1,2]([⊠]),
and Marie-Sylvie Poli[2,5]([⊠])

[1] Laboratoire Informatique d'Avignon,
Université d'Avignon et des Pays de Vaucluse, Avignon, France
{mayeal.mathias,juan-manuel.torres,didier.josselin,
fen.zhou}@univ-avignon.fr
[2] FR 3621 Agorantic,
CNRS Université d'Avignon et des Pays de Vaucluse, Avignon, France
[3] Département de Génie Informatique et Génie Logiciel,
École Polytechnique de Montréal, Montréal, QC, Canada
[4] UMR 7300 ESPACE, CNRS,
Université d'Avignon et des Pays de Vaucluse, Avignon, France
[5] Centre Norbert Elias, Université d'Avignon et des Pays de Vaucluse,
Avignon, France
{camille.beguin,marie-sylvie.poli}@univ-avignon.fr

Abstract. According to several studies about touristic practices, we propose an adaptive method to measure the Quality of Experience (QoE) of a personalized sightseeing tour which compares a proposed tour (sequence of points of interest and activities) to a reference tour and gives a correspondence score based on two complementary measures: the cultural interest and the journey rhythm (related to the profile of the tourist group). The method is applied to provide tours for the largest theater festival in Europe, which is held every year in Avignon (France).

1 Introduction

Journey recommendation for tourism is a rising topic of these recent years with important efforts from researchers and engineers covering multiple disciplines such as computer science, psychology and geography ([15] provides an overview of the wide range of methods used in the literature). Today, this problematic has several facets and definitions, therefore different related evaluation methods. When it comes to recommendation software, we identify two key points : the execution time (*i.e.* the time the system needs to generate a tour) and the quality of the proposition (*i.e.* the satisfaction of the tourist about the tour provided). Whereas the execution time is intuitive and easily comparable, measuring the quality of a sightseeing tour proposition is quite difficult and can lead to complex tasks. Indeed, satisfaction relies on personal perceptions that are

© Springer International Publishing AG 2017
O. Gervasi et al. (Eds.): ICCSA 2017, Part III, LNCS 10406, pp. 380–395, 2017.
DOI: 10.1007/978-3-319-62398-6_27

hard to model and simulate. A natural solution is to use real-world experiments by submitting a survey to a group of tourists (such as described in [17]), to generate tours according to tourist preferences and to get their feedback on the proposed journeys. In order to compare multiple tour generators, this method requires a lot of resources, since each proposition will have to be evaluated in the same conditions, either by asking each judge to rate several tours with the same expectations or by growing the panel of judges (to keep a coherent Cohen's kappa [5]). While this is appropriate to assess and then confirm a final product, this is not suitable to compare different recommendation systems or adjust an algorithm according to those criteria.

Ergo we conducted different studies about touristic practice in order to determine the most relevant factors of satisfaction [2,19]. These surveys show that we cannot only consider the importance of items covered by the tour (which is the primary today). Accordingly, we propose an adaptable method to measure the quality of experience of a personalized sightseeing tour which compares a proposed tour to a reference tour and gives a correspondence score. The latest is based on two accordance measures, the first one rates the cultural interest of activities proposed throughout the tour and the second one rates the rhythm of the journey. The method is flexible and can be used to compare a proposed tour to a reference (the primary design goal) but also to measure the difference between two propositions or the similarity between tours of different tourists (useful for profiles generation).

Paper organization

The remaining of this paper is organized as follows. In Sect. 2, we do a literature review of recommendation methods applied to sightseeing tours as well as the notion of satisfaction in the domain of tourism. Section 3 presents a general model of the problem and analyze a study on well known cultural places to determine some key factors of the quality of experience associated to tourism. Then, an evaluation method is proposed in Sect. 4. Section 5 details an application showing its suitability. Lastly, we discuss about the limits and the different application contexts and propose several improvements to complete this work.

2 Literature Review

2.1 Recommendation Systems and Tourism Evaluation Techniques

A lot of researches are focused on the touristic planning, but a vast majority is bounded to a specific case (such as [18] or [10]) and thus is hard to apply in general cases. However, the notion of service that a tour can propose is evolving and some studies (such as [25]) integrate monuments, attractions and also restaurants and hotels.

When it comes to evaluating the quality of service of a cultural institution such as a museum, satisfaction surveys are widely used and have proven their efficiency ([6]). Even though some techniques (such as [17]) give a generic layout to construct these surveys, their realization and analysis require a lot of time and human interventions (to get a representative panel). Consequently, they do not fit the need of rapid evaluation of a recommendation system.

At the time of writing, there is no consensus about the evaluation methods to compare different recommendation systems but recent works (by [16] or [20]) reveal that the personalization is now an important feature of recommendation systems. Current recommenders tackling the personalization problem are mainly focused on two evaluation techniques. The first one is the capacity of a system to reproduce a known tour (such as in [11] or [9]) by comparing the sets of items proposed by the recommender and a reference case (similarly to information retrieval problems). The second method (such as in [13] or [1]) valuates the ability to select a suitable subset of items by rating each of them and by comparing the accumulated scores to those of the overall collection.

However, we notice that an association of both personal dimension (knowledge, perception of the world and self-identity) and commercial products (services and facilities) is necessary in order to offer to the tourist a satisfying experience as denoted by [23]. Thus, the sole use of the interest of cultural monuments proposed by a tour is not enough to evaluate a recommendation system.

In order to retrieve the preferences of a tourist, the concept of "personas" is widely used and allows to create different profiles of visitors, designed by interviewing users and identifying specific needs and expectations [3].

2.2 Geographical and Cultural Points of Interest

A tourist tour is a subtle combination of Points of Interest to reach some freedom space to fill an activity or a leisure. One of the first geographer having worked on such tours in a general point of view is [7]. He designed a 3D space including space and time [8]. More recently, [4] designed what they called "actograms" which are organized sequences of locations separated and labeled by activities. Both models can easily be used for a tour representation as a sequence of locations separated in time, or as a graph of nodes related by oriented, valued and tagged edges (see Definition 1 below) (Fig. 1).

These "actograms" can be drawn by activity recognition techniques, which allow to estimate the sequence of activities of a tourist [14]. Moreover, the significant use of smart-phones leads to facilitate the recognition of some activities as shown by [24] and the use of social networks and the emergence of smart cities ease to retrieve a tourist tour and thus to establish reference cases.

3 Personalized Sightseeing Tour Planning

In this section, we first outline the problem and define a general model to represent any visit tour. Then we present a study about tourism practices and show some key factors for the enjoyment of a touristic journey.

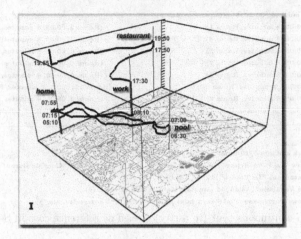

Fig. 1. Space and Time 3D Representation of a day activity (from [8])

3.1 The Personalized Visit Tour Recommendation Problem

The problem of recommending a personalized visit tour can be expressed by Definition 1.

Definition 1. *Among the possible activities (or Points of Interest) within a territory and given the preferences of a tourist, recommending a personalized visit tour is equivalent to proposing a list of activities, each delimited in space and time, that correspond to his preferences while respecting the constraints of both the tourist and the territory.*

This definition encompasses three concepts: activities, preferences and constraints. An activity is anything a tourist can do, such as for example visiting a monument, attending to a theater piece or going to the restaurant. The preferences are the cultural tastes of the tourist (*e.g.* enjoying sporting activities, disliking an art form). Finally the constraints are limitations imposed by the tourist or the territory on the tour or the activities (*e.g.* dates, maximum cost or time per activity, opening hours, start and end locations).

Consequently, a tour can be modeled by an ordered sequence of 4-tuple $\langle a, s, d, l \rangle$ under constraints, where:

- a is the activity proposed to the visitor;
- s the moment the activity starts;
- d the duration of the activity;
- l a function giving at any time $t \in [s; s + d]$ the tourist location.

This sequence cannot contain temporal overlap in activities (which would be tantamount to proposing two activities at the same time) but is not constrained to be continuous (*i.e.* the tour can be a complete schedule or simply a set of things to do during the journey) and possibly be spread on multiple days. Figure 2 shows

```
((Enter the museum, 00:00, 5 minutes, Entrance)
 (Room 1, 00:05, 8 minutes, Room 1)                    (Room 2, 00:05, 8 minutes, Room 2)
 (Room 3, 00:05, 8 minutes, Room 3)                    (Room 4, 00:05, 8 minutes, Room 4)
 (Room 5, 00:05, 8 minutes, Room 5)                    (Room 6, 00:05, 8 minutes, Room 6)
 (Room 7, 00:05, 8 minutes, Room 7)                    (Room 6, 00:05, 8 minutes, Room 6)
 (Room 8, 00:05, 8 minutes, Room 8)                    (Room 9, 00:05, 8 minutes, Room 9)
 (Room 10, 00:05, 8 minutes, Room 10)                  (Room 11, 00:05, 8 minutes, Room 11)
 (Room 8, 00:05, 8 minutes, Room 8)                    (Room 6, 00:05, 8 minutes, Room 6)
 (Room 12, 00:05, 8 minutes, Room 12)           (Exit the museum, 00:05, 1 minute, Exit))
```

(a) Continuous tour (in a museum)

```
((Park car, 09:00, 10 minutes, Car park "Les italiens"),
 (Show "Le Petit Prince", 09:50, 1 hour and 10 minutes, Theatre "Cour de Barouf")
 (Restaurant "Le Potard", 12:00, 1 hour, ),
 ("Le Venaissin", 14:45, 45 minutes, Main square of the city)
 (Show "Andromaque", 16:45, 1 hour and 35 minutes, Theatre "l'Oulle"))
```

(b) Non continuous tour (in a city) – used as reference case in Sect. 5

```
((Calvet Museum, thursday at 09:30, 2 hours, Avignon),
 (Popes' Palace, thrusday at 15:00, 3 hours, Avignon),
 (Monument "La Chartreuse", friday at 14:00, 1 hour, Villeneuve),
 (Monument "Fort Saint-André", friday at 15:00, 35 minutes, Villeneuve))
```

(c) Tour spread on multiple days

Fig. 2. Examples of visit tours

some examples of visit tours, at different geographical scales and with different granularities of information.

This paper neither discuss the definitions or methodologies used to represent or collect the activities proposed by a region nor the preferences and constraints of a tourist. The tour modeling described above is usable no matter how an activity is defined by the recommender (automatic system or not). Each recommendation system studied from previous works (see Sect. 2) generates tours that can be represented by this model. The latest even allows more complex tours such as ones including activities with different start and end locations.

3.2   Study of Touristic Habits

In collaboration with two research laboratories of sociology and geography, we conducted a study divided in two surveys to determine several visitor profiles. The first one [2] was related to the tourist expectations and their tour organization. The second one [19] was focused on a specific event: the Avignon theater festival (a case study in Sect. 5), trying to identify specific profiles.

The first survey [2] was structured around two main fields: the visitor expectations and the way in which (s)he organizes the tour. This survey took place in Avignon from the 8th to the 17th of June 2015 at three different places in the town center involving 276 participants from different countries and age brackets (see Table 1).

The first part of the investigation attempted to determine the tourist expectations before his arrival. They were asked to select the monuments that they

Table 1. Repartitions of respondents

(a) Age distributions

Age	Participants
Less than 25	36
26-35	54
36-49	39
50-60	55
More than 60	78
Without response	14

(b) Native countries

Region	Participants
France	58
North america	40
United Kingdom	31
Germany	29
Netherlands	23
Belgium	18
China and Japan	14
Australia	10
Est Europe	7
Switzerland	6
South America	5
Other	6
Without response	29

planned to visit as well as the types of the most interesting cultural places. Although nearly all of the respondents identified the extremely famous monuments of the city as points of interest, Fig. 3 shows a variety of cultural tastes (note that the dominance of the category" Castles and fortifications" can be explained by the nature of the famous monuments). This implies that even if we use the monument popularity as a decisive factor of interest no matter the visitor profile, his personal preferences have to be taken into account when building longer tours.

The second key point of this survey was to analyze how visitors organize their schedule. The fundamental result is that the rhythm of the journey is an important factor when the tourist is drawing his stay. We also proposed to visitors to identify the pattern the best suited to their habits. Tables 2a and b show that there are various scheduling patterns and, even though we can identify some tendencies depending on the expectations or the accompanying persons[1], we cannot fit a scheduling policy.

The second survey [19] aimed to create specific profiles of visitors of the Avignon theater festival. It highlights similar conclusions and characteristics in the personal cultural choice process. Theater famous pieces or shows were booked in advance, while many others were of interest but not priority. The obtained profiles also show diverse scheduling patterns and open the question of the flexibility of these organization methods according to the tourist profile.

---

[1] Note that no correlation was found between the expectations of a tourist and the persons accompanying him.

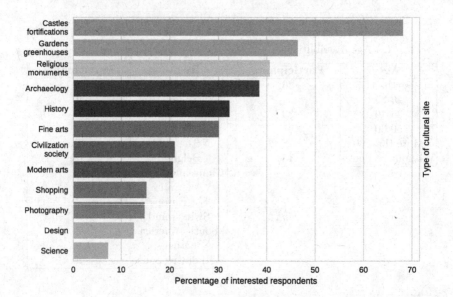

Fig. 3. Interests in cultural places

Table 2. Organization of the stay of the respondents

(a) According to their expectations

Trip organization	Adventure	Entertainment	Discovering a new culture	Change of scene	Rest
Maximize the activities all the days	51.7%	39.4%	39.0%	42.2%	27.3%
Alternate activities and rests during the day	29.3%	42.4%	37.2%	37.2%	56.4%
Alternate intense days and relaxing days during the trip	19.0%	18.2%	23.8%	20.6%	16.3%

(b) According to the accompanying persons

Trip organization	Alone	As a couple	With friends	As a family
Maximize the activities all the days	30.4%	33.1%	46.6%	31.3%
Alternate activities and rests during the day	43.5%	42.9%	29.3%	45.8%
Alternate intense days and relaxing days during the trip	26.1%	24.0%	24.1%	22.9%

4   Evaluating the Quality of Experience

Given the precedent results, we can connect the quality of experience for personalized sightseeing tours to both the interest of the tour and the pace of the journey. In this section, we first detail an evaluation method based on these two criteria and then suggest different computation algorithms to measure each of them.

4.1 General Formulation

In order to evaluate the quality of experience, the final score is divided into two independent accordance measures. The first one estimates the cultural interest of the tour and the second one the rhythm of the journey. The survey suggests that the activities selected by a tourist depend on the interest he has in them, but also on the way they correspond to his scheduling habits. Therefore these two measures rate the attractiveness of a tour by considering complementary points of view and, although the interest and the pace are not strictly independent, measuring them separately is necessary to keep a fast and comprehensive computation method. That is why we propose to use a variation of the F_β score [21], a weighted harmonic mean of both accordance measures. Equation 1 gives a satisfaction score for a tour as modeled by Sect. 3.

$$\text{QoE} = (1 + \beta^2) \times \frac{\text{interest} \times \text{pace}}{(\beta^2 \times \text{interest}) + \text{pace}} \tag{1}$$

Evaluating the quality of experience with this method provides several advantages. First of all, it does not require a human intervention to evaluate each tour, leading to rapidly compute a score for numerous tours. Consequently, it is reproducible: the exact same score will be given for the same input, which makes this method suitable to compare different recommendation systems on a typical scenario or a unique recommender on various use cases. Secondly, it takes into account both the interest and the pace of the visit, the latter cannot be overlooked for journeys of several hours or even days as observed in Sect. 3.2. Moreover, as shown by [22], the β factor can be used to emphasize the interest (if $\beta < 1$) or the pace (if $\beta > 1$) of the evaluated tour or even consider only one of these measures. This allows to adapt the evaluation to the priorities of the visitor and the potential flexibility of its agenda.

4.2 Cultural Preferences

The first accordance measure is focused on the cultural interest and thus only takes into account which activities are proposed by the tour. We describe two ways to estimate this interest, depending on the context and the available information. Firstly by using the F-measure to compare the proposed tour to a reference case, it reflects the ability of a recommender to propose a well defined tour and it is a metric compatible with the evaluation used by [11] or [9] which try to predict the exact tour of a tourist. The second computation method does not require a reference tour but uses a prediction function to compute the interest of each activity, allowing to rate systems that use this approach to compute a tour (such as [13] or [1]).

Comparing the proposition to a reference tour by using the F-score formulates this measure into a simple information retrieval problem. The precision and recall are computed against a reference set of activities. Equations 2a and 2b define the notions of precision and recall for the interest of a personalized sightseeing tour.

$$interest = (1 + \beta^2) \times \frac{precision \times recall}{(\beta^2 \times precision) + recall} \qquad (2)$$

$$precision \quad = \frac{|\{\text{activities in } tour\} \cap \{\text{activities in } reference\}|}{|\{\text{activities in } tour\}|} \qquad (2a)$$

$$recall \quad = \frac{|\{\text{activities in } tour\} \cap \{\text{activities in } reference\}|}{|\{\text{activities in } reference\}|} \qquad (2b)$$

The interest measure (given by Eq. 2) evaluates the proposed tour according to the reference tour (that is not given to the recommendation system). The reference tour can be obtained from the tourist retrospectively or designed by an expert. This method is especially adapted for a trip that will include all interesting activities for a given profile.

Estimating the interest by using a prediction function for each activity can be relevant when the satisfying tours are too diversified and when it is difficult to identify a reference tour. This may be the case for short stays in territories offering a significant number of activities.

We propose here to rely on a deterministic prediction function, giving for each activity a relevance score indicating the adequacy towards the cultural taste of the tourist. Equation 3 expresses the interest of a tour as a ratio of the activities relevance in the proposed tour to the relevance of available activities.

$$interest = \frac{\sum\limits_{a \in A_t} \text{relevance}(a)}{\sum\limits_{a \in A} \text{relevance}(a)} \qquad (3)$$

With:

- *relevance* a prediction function giving for an activity $a \in A$ the relevance in the tour;
- A_t the set of unique activities proposed by the *tour*.

This accordance measure normalizes the interest of a tour between 0 and 1 (as $A_t \subset A$) by considering the activities proposed regardless of their order or the number of times they are included. Using a relevance function allows to evaluate the interest of the tour according to different criteria, such as the presence of the activity in the reference tour (Eq. 4a) or a similarity between the activity and the tourist (Eq. 4b) using vector-space representation as showed by [13] or [16].

We also propose to use the popularity as a relevance factor (Eq. 4c), by ranking the different activities according to their fame. Social networks analysis and natural language processing ([12]) have proven to be effective in such tasks.

$$relevance_1(a) = \begin{cases} 1 & \text{if } a \text{ is in the reference tour,} \\ 0 & \text{otherwise} \end{cases} \tag{4a}$$

$$relevance_3(a) = similarity(a, \text{tourist preferences}) \tag{4b}$$

$$relevance_2(a) = popularity(a) \tag{4c}$$

Another advantage of using a relevance ratio over the classical F-score is that we can evaluate the interest of a tour according to different outlooks. Moreover, with the popularity measure, it is possible to compare a tour according to popular references without having to validate a large number of reference tours.

These two computation methods cover the majority of existing evaluation techniques used by other works (see Sect. 2) and, although the comparison of two tours requires the use of a single method in the interest measure, it allows to focus on the evaluation of the tour pace, which is often neglected by existing recommendation systems.

4.3   Pace Comfort

The second accordance measure is meant to evaluate the pace of the journey. Surveys clearly show that this aspect cannot be overlooked when evaluating a tour and that there exist different types of tourists, with different visit patterns. In this section, we explore a concept widely used in geography to represent the trip of a tourist and we suggest a method to evaluate a tour in respect of a reference case.

A tour can be represented as an actogram describing a relation between time and activities that form it. This representation highlights the use and the time distribution of the activities within a tour which is appropriate to compare pace differences.

The tour modeling defined by Sect. 3 allows different granularities, whether on the duration (a stay of several hours or crossing multiple days) or on the continuity (from an exhaustive schedule to key activities) of the journey. However, an actogram is a continuous sequence of actions and motions. As a consequence, a tour can be represented as either a complete actogram if it is continuous or a partial actogram if not.

To have a single type of actograms without losing or speculating information about the journey, we have to rely only on complete actograms. While it does not require any modification for continuous tours, we propose to transform other tours by adding a null action between two non consecutive activities, starting at the end of the first activity and ending at the begin of the second one.

This measure is meant to evaluate the rhythm of the tour, in other words the variations in the types of activities and not the variations of activities themselves.

Therefore, when it is possible, we substitute each activity by its type, allowing to merge consecutive segments with a same type of activities. In addition to simplify the final actogram, this allows to require simpler reference tours as they do not need to contain a detailed schedule. Again, those reference tours can be obtained by the tourist after his stay (as a test case) or designed by an expert (cf. Sect. 5). Moreover, as shown in the literature review, the construction of actograms is possible thanks to activity recognition and smart-phones usage.

This method produces simple actograms oriented to the tourist occupation over the time. As this operation is performed by the evaluation process after tours generation, the consistency of the two actograms is guaranteed as long as the same rules are applied during merging. Figure 4 shows an actogram representing a stay for a typical profile of visitor in the Avignon theater festival (from [19]).

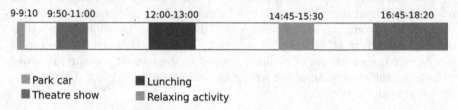

Fig. 4. Actogram of the tour presented in Fig. 2b

The comparison of two actograms can be used to measure their accordance from the pace perspective. When comparing a proposition tour to a reference, we can establish an evaluation of the **pace comfort**, giving the consistency between the proposed and actual schedules.

We propose to compare the complete actogram representations of both tours by applying a penalty cost to each difference between them. Equation 5 estimates the pace of a proposition tour against a reference tour as the opposite of a deviation ratio.

$$pace = 1 - \frac{\sum\limits_{\langle a_r, a_p, \Delta t \rangle \in D} penalty(a_r, a_p) \times \Delta t}{penalty_{max} \times T_{max}} \tag{5}$$

With:

- $D = \langle a_r, a_p, \Delta t \rangle$: the differences between actograms representing the tour and the reference, composed of activities for the reference and the proposition tour and the duration of the difference;
- $penalty$: a matrix giving for each pair of different activities (or types) a penalty cost;
- $penalty_{max}$ the maximum penalty cost;
- T_{max} the duration of both actograms.

The deviation ratio takes into account the differences between both actograms, each characterized by the two conflicting activities (or their type) and a duration. This duration is weighted by a cost given by the penalty matrix, allowing to emphasize or ignore some differences.

In order to determine the differences, we first align the two actograms by prepending or appending a null action to obtain two actograms begining and finishing at the same moments. So, determining the differences amounts to find the moments when both actograms present different activities.

The resulting deviation ratio acts as a normalization process of the penalty of a tour. Indeed, as both actograms have the same duration, $\sum \Delta t \leq T_{max}$ and thus the deviation ratio ranges from 0 and 1. Consequently, the resulting pace measure estimates the accordance of two tours and ranges from 0 to 1.

The method presented to estimate a pace comfort responds to the necessity to quantify the quality of experience in sightseeing tours. Studies show that it is an important aspect of the visit that cannot be overlooked.

5   Case Study

The evaluation method proposed in this paper is mainly intended to compare two recommendation algorithms. We chose to demonstrate its suitability on the Avignon Festival, a theater festival regrouping more than 26 000 performances of 1 381 plays spread over one month (cf. Fig. 5). From the official website[2], we extracted the complete program, consisting of the following information:

- The theater list and location (see Fig. 5);
- The list of plays and shows, with the dates, hours and durations;
- A title, a description and a list of keywords for each show or play.

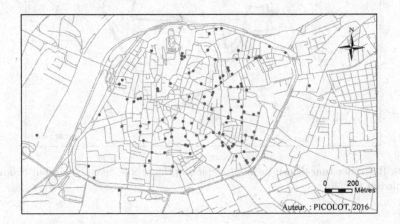

Fig. 5. Location of the theaters in Avignon during the festival.

---

[2] http://www.avignonleoff.com.

In order to observe how the two measures perform, we designed three base-line recommendation systems. The first one does not take into account neither the interest nor the pace but randomly selects activities (while avoiding tempo-ral overlap). The second one is focused on the interest and proposes the most relevance activities. The last one aims at satisfying the pace constraints of the tourist by filling the appropriate time slots with any available activity (randomly selecting an activity when many of them match the time window).

For this use case, the most appropriate way to compute the interest measure is to use a similarity relevance function (see Eq. 4b). We decided to express both the preferences of a tourist as a subset of the 35 keywords given by the different plays. Consequently, we can estimate the interest of a play for the tourist by using the Jaccard distance between its preferences and the keywords of the play.

Works of [19] expose different tourist profiles of this event, giving typical actograms and personas that we used as reference tours and visitor preferences. We performed this case study on the "Family without children" profile for which the actogram is given in Fig. 4. It consists of attending a play in the morning, a lunch followed by a relaxing activity and, in the late afternoon or evening another play.

We simulated tours on the 4th, 16th and 25th of July, generating for each of these days 50 tours (as the methods involve a random selection) and computed the average scores. In addition, we conceived a tour by ourselves (presented in Fig. 2b and shown in Fig. 6), that tries to fit the best to the profile.

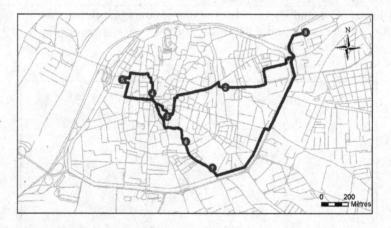

Fig. 6. Reference tour drawn by hand, depicting the profile "Family without children" (detailed in Fig. 2b)

Figure 7 presents the evaluation of the different methods. As expected, the interest measure (Fig. 7a) rewards the "interest focused" system while the pace measure rewards (Fig. 7b) the "pace focused" system. It shows that both mea-sures do what they are designed for, evaluate a tour by a certain point of view, without considering other parameters. The conceived tour obtains a good interest measure without being higher than the interest focused baseline (as many play could satisfy the requirements) but an excellent pace score, due to the fact that no recommendation system was designed to take into account the lunching and activities times. The Fig. 6 illustrates what could be a relevant tour for a family during the Avignon theater festival.

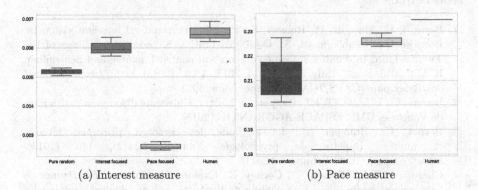

(a) Interest measure   (b) Pace measure

Fig. 7. Interest and pace measures of different recommendation systems

This demonstrates that both accordances measure complement each other, allowing to discriminate good interest-focused recommendation systems but with different scheduling strategies. As the interest measure is inspired by current evaluation metrics, comparing two systems may require to only focus on the pace measure in order to have an idea of their differences in that domain.

6   Discussion and Future Work

Designing a good recommendation system is a complex and difficult task, that requires to take into account the variety of profiles and habits of tourists. With this study, we hope to show some key factors to consider when building such system. In addition we proposed new measures to help to the comparison and tuning of algorithms. These measures are a first draw of a new paradigm for the sightseeing tours evaluation.

Future work should focus on establishing other accordance measures, each evaluating a more specific aspect of the tour. A first idea is to consider the substitutions of two types of activity when comparing tours allowing to grow the set of reference cases depending on the tolerance of a visitor towards the exchange of two activities during its stay. Finally, the implementation and comparison of two recommendation systems applied on the Avignon theater festival is an high priority to demonstrate the interest of this work.

It is to highlight that in the survey about tourism preferences in Avignon [2], we can also observe that 70% of participants declare using Internet before their arrival, most of the time to prepare their tour and identify places of interest (more than 74%). This points out the importance of a new generation of recommendation systems, able to respond to personal preferences and constraints of each visitor, by proposing tours adapted to cultural preferences and touristic habits.

References

1. Berre, D.L., Marquis, P., Roussel, S.: Planning personalised museum visits. In: Borrajo, D., Kambhampati, S., Oddi, A., Fratini, S. (eds.) Proceedings of the Twenty-Third International Conference on Automated Planning and Scheduling, ICAPS 2013, Rome, Italy, June 10–14, 2013. AAAI (2013). http://www.aaai.org/ocs/index.php/ICAPS/ICAPS13/paper/view/6025
2. Béguin, C.: P'ARTCOURT, Rapport de Master. Université d'Avignon et des Pays de Vaucluse, UMR ESPACE-AGORANTIC (2015)
3. Bornet, C., Brangier, É.: La méthode des personas: principes, intérêts et limites. Bulletin de psychologie Numéro **524**(2), 115 (2013). https://doi.org/10.3917/bupsy.524.0115
4. Chardonnel, S., Thévenin, T., Cochey, E.: Explorer les temporalités urbaines de l'agglomération de dijon: Une analyse de l'enquête -ménage-déplacement par les programmes d'activités. 'Espace, Populations, Sociétés (2007)
5. Cohen, J.: A coefficient of agreement for nominal scales. Educ. Psychol. Measur. **20**(1), 37–46 (1960)
6. Daignault, L.: Les musées et leurs publics. Presses de l'Université du Québec (2014)
7. Hägerstrand, T.: What about people in regional. Regional Science Association Papers XXIV (1970)
8. Kraak, M.J.: The space-time cube revisited from a geovisualization perspective. In: Proceedings of the 21st International Cartographic Conference (ICC) 'Cartographic Renaissance', Durban, 10–16 August (1988)
9. Lim, K.H.: Personalized recommendation of travel itineraries based on tourist interests and preferences. In: Cena, F., Desmarais, M., Dicheva, D. (eds.) Late-breaking Results, Posters, Demos, Doctoral Consortium and Workshops Proceedings of the 24th ACM Conference on User Modeling, Adaptation and Personalisation (UMAP 2016), Halifax, Canada, July 13–16, 2016. CEUR Workshop Proceedings, vol. 1618. CEUR-WS.org (2016). http://ceur-ws.org/Vol-1618/DC_6.pdf
10. Liu, Q., Ge, Y., Li, Z., Chen, E., Xiong, H.: Personalized travel package recommendation. In: 2011 IEEE 11th International Conference on Data Mining. Institute of Electrical and Electronics Engineers (IEEE), December 2011. https://doi.org/10.1109/icdm.2011.118
11. Lu, C., Laublet, P., Stankovic, M.: Travel attractions recommendation with knowledge graphs. In: Blomqvist, E., Ciancarini, P., Poggi, F., Vitali, F. (eds.) EKAW 2016. LNCS, vol. 10024, pp. 416–431. Springer, Cham (2016). doi:10.1007/978-3-319-49004-5_27. https://doi.org/10.1007/978-3-319-49004-5_27
12. Mathias, M., Moussa, A., Torres-Moreno, J.M., Zhou, F., Poli, M.S., Josselin, D., El-Bèze, M., Linhares, A.C., Rigat, F.: Optimisation using natural language processing: Personalized tour recommendation for museums. In: Proceedings of the 2014 Federated Conference on Computer Science and Information Systems. Polish Information Processing Society PTI , September 2014. https://doi.org/10.15439/2014f336

13. Mathias, M., Zhou, F., Torres-Moreno, J.M., Josselin, D., Poli, M.S., Linhares, A.C.: Personalized sightseeing tours: a model for visits in art museums. Int. J. Geogr. Inf. Sci. **31**(3), 591–616 (2016). https://doi.org/10.1080/13658816.2016.1233332
14. Minnen, D., Westeyn, T., Starner, T., Ward, J., Lukowicz, P.: Performance metrics and evaluation issues for continuous activity recognition. Perform. Metrics Intell. Syst. **4**, 141–148 (2006)
15. Mishra, H.M., Deshmukh, D.M.V.M.: Travel package recommendation system: a literature review. Int. J. Sci. Res. (IJSR) **5**(3), 1915–1917 (2016). https://doi.org/10.21275/v5i3.nov162170
16. Mittal, R., Sinha, V.: A personalized time-bound activity recommendation system. In: 2017 IEEE 7th Annual Computing and Communication Workshop and Conference (CCWC). Institute of Electrical and Electronics Engineers (IEEE), January 2017. https://doi.org/10.1109/ccwc.2017.7868485
17. Nowacki, M.M.: Evaluating a museum as a tourist product using the servqual method. Museum Manage. Curatorship **20**(3), 235–250 (2005). http://www.sciencedirect.com/science/article/pii/S026047790500021X
18. Olson, R.: Computing the optimal road trip across europe (2015). http://www.randalolson.com/2015/03/10/computing-the-optimal-road-trip-across-europe/
19. Picolot, D.: Recherche et construction de parcours culturels au sein du festival OFF d'Avignon, Master de Géographie. Université d'Avignon et des Pays de Vaucluse, UMR ESPACE-AGORANTIC (2016)
20. Popat, K., Thorat, T., Vidhate, M., Rane, N., Ghuse, N.D.: Personalized and relational approach for travel package recommendation. In: 2015 International Conference on Green Computing and Internet of Things (ICGCIoT). Institute of Electrical and Electronics Engineers (IEEE), October 2015. https://doi.org/10.1109/icgciot.2015.7380596
21. Powers, D.M.: Evaluation: From precision, recall and F-measure to ROC, informedness, markedness and correlation. J. Mach. Learn. Technol. **2**(1), 37–63 (2011)
22. Rijsbergen, C.J.V.: Information Retrieval, 2nd edn. Butterworth-Heinemann, Newton (1979)
23. Räikkönen, J., Honkanen, A.: Does satisfaction with package tours lead to successful vacation experiences? J. Destin. Market. Manage. **2**(2), 108–117 (2013). https://doi.org/10.1016/j.jdmm.2013.03.002
24. Su, X., Tong, H., Ji, P.: Activity recognition with smartphone sensors. Tsinghua Sci. Technol. **19**(3), 235–249 (2014). https://doi.org/10.1109/tst.2014.6838194
25. Wang, K.C., Jao, P.C., Chan, H.C., Chung, C.H.: Group package tour leader's intrinsic risks. Ann. Tour. Res. **37**(1), 154–179 (2010). https://doi.org/10.1016/j.annals.2009.08.004

Workshop on Deep Cities: Intelligence and Interoperability (DEEP CITY 2017)

Towards a Decision Support Tool for Assessing, Managing and Mitigating Seismic Risk of Electric Power Networks

Sonia Giovinazzi[1]([✉]) [iD], Maurizio Pollino[2] [iD], Indranil Kongar[3], Tiziana Rossetto[3] [iD],
Emanuela Caiaffa[2], Antonio Di Pietro[2], Luigi La Porta[2], Vittorio Rosato[2] [iD],
and Alberto Tofani[2]

[1] Sapienza University of Rome, Rome, Italy
sonia.giovinazzi@uniroma1.it
[2] ENEA Laboratory for the Analysis and Protection of Critical Infrastructures (APIC),
Rome, Italy
{maurizio.pollino,emanuela.caiaffa,antonio.dipietro,
luigi.laporta,vittorio.rosato,alberto.tofani}@enea.it
[3] Earthquake and People Interaction Centre (EPICentre),
University College London, London, England
{indranil.kongar.10,t.rossetto}@ucl.ac.uk

Abstract. Recent seismic event worldwide proved how fragile the electric power system can be to seismic events. Decision Support Systems (DSSs) could have a critical role in assessing the seismic risk of electric power networks and in enabling asset managers to test the effectiveness of alternative mitigation strategies and investments on resilience. This paper exemplifies the potentialities of CIPCast, a DSS recently created in the framework of the EU-funded project CIPRNet, to perform such tasks. CIPCast enables to perform risk assessment for Critical Infrastructures (CI) when subjected to different natural hazards, including earthquakes. An ad-hoc customization of CIPCast for the seismic risk analysis and management of electric power networks is featured in this paper. The international literature describes effective and sound efforts towards the creation of software platforms and frameworks for the assessment of seismic risk of electric power networks. None of them, unfortunately, achieved the goal of creating a user-friendly and ready available DDS to be used by asset managers, local authorities and civil protection departments. Towards that and building on the international literature, the paper describes metrics and methods to be integrated within CIPCast for assessing the earthquake-induced physical and functional impacts of the electric power network at component and system level. The paper describes also how CIPCast can inform the service restoration process.

Keywords: Decision Support System (DSS) · Damage Scenario · Seismic risk · Electric power system · Resilience · Decision Making Processes

1 Introduction

Critical Infrastructures (CI) such as electrical grids, gas, water, telecommunication, roads, and railways networks are technological systems the correct functioning of which

© Springer International Publishing AG 2017
O. Gervasi et al. (Eds.): ICCSA 2017, Part III, LNCS 10406, pp. 399–414, 2017.
DOI: 10.1007/978-3-319-62398-6_28

might impact on the life quality of citizens. CI protection is needed to guarantee the physical integrity of CI and the continuity of the services that they deliver. In particular, recent seismic event worldwide proved how fragile the electric power system can be to seismic events and similarly the critical importance of guaranteeing the functionality of the electric power service to support emergency management, recovery operations and the daily life of the affected communities. In the 1994 Northridge earthquake, for example, all of the Los Angeles Department of Water and Power's (LADWP's) 1.5 million power customers lost service, many for a week or more [1]. The 22nd February 2011 Christchurch, New Zealand, earthquake caused an estimated 629 million customer minutes of outages [2] that, in-turn, induced consequences on the functionality of the local telecommunication and waste networks. The impact could have been much worst. In fact, most of the power outages were caused by liquefaction damage to cables while above-ground components, including overhead lines and substations performed well, thanks to a seismic upgrade program that was implemented few years before the earthquake [3].

During the emergency and recovery phases, the local asset managers expressed the need and wish to perform scenario analysis [4] aiming to: compare alternative repair/reconstruction strategies; asses risks to mitigate risks, with a multi-hazard perspective; support the business case for investing into resilience. Decision Support Systems (DSSs) could have a critical role in assessing the seismic risk of electric power networks and in enabling asset managers to test the effectiveness of alternative mitigation strategies and to support business cases for investing into the resilience enhancement of the network.

The international literature describes effective and sound efforts towards the creation of software platforms and frameworks for the assessment of seismic risk of electric power networks. None of them, unfortunately, achieved the goal of creating a user-friendly and ready available DDS to be used by asset managers, local authorities and civil protection departments. Just to provide some examples (an exhaustive literature review is out of the scope of the paper) the American Lifeline Alliance, ALA, defined guidelines and accompanying commentaries [5] to provide a multilevel process by which the performance of electric power system in natural hazards and human threat events could be assessed. The HAZUS platform [6], developed in USA for estimating risks from natural hazards on the built-environment included: (a) fragility curves for different components of electric power networks (i.e. substations, generation plants, and distribution circuits) giving the probability of reaching or exceeding four levels of damage, for a given level of ground motion; (b) a simplified methodology for assessing the residual system performance in term of a probabilistic estimation of power outages; (c) functionality restoration curves for electric substations and distribution circuits and for generation facilities, based on [7]. After that, an attempt to advance the modelling of the post-earthquake restoration processes for electric power networks was made by [8], that proposed discrete event simulation models to estimate geographically-disaggregated, quantitative restoration curves, including an explicit representations of the company's decision variables (e.g. repair crews and material available, etc.).

Finally, in Europe, the EU-funded Syner-G project, developed an integrated methodology and a software tool, referred to as OOFIM Object-Oriented Framework for Infrastructure Modelling and Simulation [9, 10] for the systemic seismic vulnerability and risk assessment of complex systems, including electric power networks. Syner-G compared and selected models for the seismic vulnerability assessment of electric power networks' components [11] and implemented the OOFIM tool on a real case study, namely the seismic probabilistic assessment of the functional performance (in terms of flows, connectivity loss and power loss) of the medium-high transmission network in Sicily region [12]. To achieve the goal of creating a user-friendly and ready available DSS to be used by Electric power network (EPN) asset managers, local authorities and civil protection departments, this paper proposes an ad-hoc customization of a recently created DSS, namely CIPCast, which enables to operationally perform risk prediction on Critical Infrastructures (CI) for different kind of natural hazards, including earthquakes. In particular, building on the available international literature, this paper proposes models and metrics to be integrated within the different functional blocks that constitute CIPCast (Fig. 1) to allow for the seismic risk analysis and management of electric power networks.

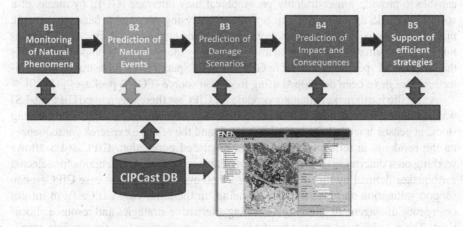

Fig. 1. CIPCast [25]: main functional blocks (Bi), Database and Graphic User Interface (GUI).

2 CIPCast Decision Support System

CI protection is a major issue for Nations, due to its transnational relevance. EU has thus issued directives to Member States in favour of an increased level of protection, recognizing the fact that CI constitute a unique, large system covering all the EU area [13]. In support of these EU directives, the APIC Lab[1] of ENEA has targeted the development and implementation of a DSS specific for CI protection, referred to as CIPCast. CIPCast was conceived and developed in the framework of two different projects, namely the EU-funded project "CIPRNet" (*Critical Infrastructures Preparedness and Resilience Research Network*) and the project "RoMA" (*Resilience enhancement of a Metropolitan Area*), funded by MIUR (the Italian Ministry of Research) as part of the research call "Smart Cities and Communities".

---

[1] Laboratory for the Analysis and Protection of Critical Infrastructures.

Making reference to simulated or real hazard scenarios, CIPCast DSS, can predict *"Damage Scenarios"* in term of punctual damages to the different CI components and *"Impact Scenarios"*, where services outages induced by the physical damage to CI [14] components, are assessed at micro- (local scale) or meso- (regional scale) level. Finally CIPCast can estimate *"Consequences Scenarios"*, starting from Impact Scenarios and via a consequences analysis, in term of estimated consequences on the affected communities (https://www.ciprnet.eu/ads.html).

CIPCast was conceived as a combination of free/open source software environments [15] including Geographic Information System, GIS features, which play a major role in the construction of such a tool. In the last few years, the geo-scientific community has been focusing on the use of GIS technologies and techniques for supporting natural disaster early warning and emergency management tasks. Multi-source data and GIS-integrated analysis can contribute to a better emergency planning, providing fundamental information for immediate response [16, 17]. The developed CIPCast DSS is capable to provide a user-friendly geographical user interface (GUI), by means of a specific WebGIS application, for querying and analysing geographic data and thematic maps, execute processes and simulations, produce and evaluate scenarios, etc. The creation of this information consultation tool, enriched by the geospatial component, implies the adoption of specific and suitable GIS and SDI (Spatial Data Infrastructures) architectures that have been developed using free/open source (FOSS) packages [18–20].

A specific Earthquake Simulator module for CIPCast (hereafter named CIPCast-ES) was developed and customised to assess the earthquake-induced damage to the building stock, at census tract and single building level, and the relative expected consequences on the residents in term of casualties and displaced population. CIPCast-ES allows working on a deterministic base, simulating damage and impact scenarios for selected earthquakes defined by the end-users, or for real events. In the first case CIPCast can support mitigation and preparedness planning; in the latter case CIPCast can inform emergency management allowing for testing alternative strategies and resource allocations. The possibility to account for the seismic microzonation (i.e. the possible amplification of the seismic hazard and therefore of the expected impacts due to soil conditions) was also included within CIPCast-ES, and was used for the case study of Florence Municipality, where a seismic microzonation study, providing the-specific amplification factor AF was provided [21].

3   Methods and Data

Different steps are necessary for estimating earthquake-induced damage, functional impacts and restoration timeframe for distributed infrastructures [22, 23], summarised below as:

1. *Hazard assessment*: generation of ground shaking and ground deformation maps and selection of the most appropriate earthquake hazard parameters to describe them;
2. *Classification of infrastructure components*: inventory and classification of the infrastructure components according to a defined taxonomy, so that the elements

expected to behave similarly, by sustaining similar damages when subjected to an earthquake event, can be grouped together;

3. *Physical damage and functional impact metrics*: selection of appropriate scales for classifying earthquake induced physical damage to each component (e.g. for above-ground components: structural and non-structural damage to the building housing the component and damage to the equipment) and the residual operability of the component that do not necessarily correlate with the level and extent of the physical damage.

4. *Damage assessment*: identification of an appropriate hazard-damage relationship to be used for assigning a damage level/status (metrics in step 3) to each component identified and classified (step 2) as a function of the hazard estimated (as for step 1);

5. *System performance assessment*: estimation of the residual performance of the whole infrastructure accounting for the damages estimated at component level, via serviceability analysis and/or connectivity analysis; possibly adjust for interdependency effects from other systems;

6. *Service restoration assessment*: estimation of the repair and service restoration timeframe at both component and whole system level, based on empirical data/expert judgement and/or resource modelling.

Figure 1 shows the main functional blocks (Bi) of CIPCast [24, 25] and the relevant components i.e. the Database and the Graphic User Interface (GUI). CIPCast block B1 gets external data from many different sources (e.g., seismic data), to establish the current external conditions. CIPCast B2 estimates the expected manifestation strength for predictable events. In B3 CIPCast elaborates a "Damage Scenario", correlating the strength of the expected hazard manifestations with the vulnerability of the different CI elements in the affected areas, in order to estimate the probability that the manifestation could effectively damage (and, in the positive case, to what extent) the CI elements. B4 converts the damages expected for the CI elements into outages of the service. B5 is devoted to inform and support the response, by allowing testing and comparing different strategies for restoring the service by prioritising repairs and deploying physical and human resources.

Table 1. CIPCast functional blocks and proposed steps for building capacity within CIPCast-ES for estimating earthquake-induced risk to electric power networks.

CIPCast functional blocks	CIPCast-ES – Electric power networks
B1	Seismic Hazard representation
B3	Classification of infrastructure
	Damage metrics at component level
	Damage assessment: physical and operational at component level
B4	System performance assessment[a]
B5	Service restoration assessment[a]

[a]*Already built into CIPCast-ES*

Table 1 summarises how the above-mentioned steps for estimating earthquake-induced risk to infrastructures should be customised for electric power networks and for implementation within CIPCast-ES and how they correlate with CIPCast functional blocks Bi (1–5). Steps 5 and 6 namely (Table 1) are already built into CIPCast. Further details are provided in the sub-sections below.

3.1 Seismic Hazard Representation

In order to evaluate the performance of a distributed infrastructure system after an earthquake, it is necessary to know the damage state and functionality at each component simultaneously and hence also the ground motion at each site simultaneously. A brief overview is provided on how to possibly assess and represent seismic hazard within CIP-Cast ES for distributed infrastructures, including: (1) description of the ground shaking in terms of Peak Ground Acceleration (PGA) and Peak Ground Velocity (PGV) at bedrock; (2) representation of amplification due to peculiar soil conditions; (3) estimation of ground deformation (PGD), and Liquefaction Potential Index, (LPI); (4) possible representation of uncertainties. A complete argument on the subject is out of the scope of the paper and can be found, e.g. in [26].

Description of ground shaking in term of PGA and PGV - CIPCast-ES allows the performance of deterministic seismic hazard analysis, for both real events and for end-user defined events. In the first case, and as far as the Italian territory is concerned, CIPCast-ES receives, within 1 min from the occurrence of the earthquake, the GPS coordinates of the earthquake epicentre, the hypocentre depth and the measured Moment Magnitude M_W (Richter scale) from the Italian National Institute of Geophysics and Volcanology, INGV, in Italy (http://cnt.rm.ingv.it/). A shake map is then generated using a suite of ground motion prediction equations (GMPEs). Currently CIPCast-ES implements Sabetta and Pugliese GMPE [27] in terms of PGA and different GMPEs in terms of Macroseismic Intensity I [21]. The seismic performance of above ground components of electric power networks, such as substations, can be assessed against PGA. However buried components such as cables would need to be assessed against Peak ground Velocity (PGV). Further attenuation laws will need to be included within CIPCast-ES to allow for that.

Representation of soil amplifications - After the prediction of the ground shaking either in term of PGA or PGV, possible site amplification due to soil condition would need to be accounted for. CIPCast-ES allows doing so, if a map of amplification factor AF (describing the ratio between the spectral acceleration Sa of the ground motion at the ground surface-and at the bedrock) is provided. Further potentialities will be built within CIPCast-ES to allow for modelling site amplification directly within the selected GMPE itself, or simply by inputting the site class and/or a share wave velocity 0-30-meters depth (Vs30) value for each site in the ground motion field.

Estimation of PGD and LPI - The possibility to estimate PGD, conditional upon the intensity of the estimated ground shaking, should be also included within CIPCast-ES as PGD proved to be an issue for both above ground and buried components of electric power networks. Principal causes of PGD [28] will be estimated in CIPCast-ES as follow: (a) coseismic fault displacement in the near-fault area will be calculated via semi-empirical correlations as a function of the earthquake magnitude (e.g. the ones available from Petersen et al., 2011); (b) landslides triggered by seismic shaking [29] - this capability will be included in CIPCast-ES as discussed in the Conclusion section of this paper); (c) liquefaction, lateral spreading, and seismic settlement will be estimated in term of liquefaction potential index (LPI) that proved to be a good predictor for the damages induced on buried cables [30].

Representation of uncertainties - GMPEs are derived empirically, further to the deterministic part, which calculates the median value of ground motion, GMPEs include random variables representing the variability that occurs within a single event (intra-event) and between separate events (inter-event) [31]. For analysis of spatially distributed systems the requirement for simultaneous ground motions at multiple sites means that the ground motions must be spatially correlated. For the sake of computational efficiency, straightforward approaches for obtaining correlated ground motion fields in CIPCast-ES, will be preferred to complex geostatistical methods [26].

3.2 Classification of Infrastructure Components

The purpose of classifying infrastructure into taxonomy is to group together elements that can be expected to behave similarly following an earthquake. Classification of infrastructure systems require firstly the identification of the different components included in the system and secondly the identification of the typologies/characteristics of the different components.

An electric power network may comprise different components: generation plants, substations and related sub-components, transmission lines (Table 2). Each of these serves a different function in the system. *Generation plants* are responsible for production of electric power; *transmission lines* transport the electricity from one location to another; *substations*, supply the power at load/consumer end. The sub-stations have different components, namely: *transformers* (usually step-down) to change the voltage level to a standard distribution level voltage; *feeders* connect the consumer/load end with the substation (with respect to a distribution system/substation); the terminal substation of each feeder ends with a *switch*. For each of the aforementioned components and sub-components there are different typologies, relating to structural or operational attributes. Transmission lines, for example, can vary based on their position (overhead lines or underground cables), their insulation material or their size. Substations may vary by load capacity or voltage[2]. Table 2 shows the assumed infrastructure taxonomy for this work, their key constituent components and component attributes. The component attributes are the descriptors that could be used to group components into distinct typologies. Components can sometimes be pieces of equipment housed inside a building. In this case the attribute 'seismic design level' refers to whether the building is seismically designed or whether the component is anchored. Sometimes components are made up of a systemic arrangement of smaller sub-components. In this case 'seismic design level' refers to whether or not these sub-components are anchored.

---

[2] Primary Substations (PS) contain High Voltage (HV) to Medium Voltage (MV) transformers; Secondary Substations (SS), Medium Voltage (MV) to Low Voltage (LV) transformers.

Table 2. Example of infrastructure system taxonomy for electric power network.

Components		Attributes	Graph	Damage metric
Generation plants		Capacity, seismic design level	Node	Damage level
Substations		Voltage, seismic design level	Node	Damage level
Transmission lines	Cables	Insulation Material, Cable material, Size	Edge	Repair Rate
	Overhead Lines	Material	Edge	Repair rate

An inventory is an enumeration of the components and facilities in each of the typologies considered by the assumed taxonomy. Preparation of an inventory for infrastructure can be difficult since attributes cannot be identified by simple visual inspection and in many cases the components are not visible (e.g. buried lines). The inventory should therefore be prepared by collecting data from available sources. In the case of infrastructure however usually the only source is the system operator. To protect commercial interests and due to concerns over security, this type of information is not usually available in the public domain to a high level of detail and so depending on the granularity of the modelling exercise, it may be necessary to work in partnership with infrastructure owners [32]. It is quite critical to know the geographical location of each component. Availability of GIS layers of the entire network would be ideal: for instance, within CIPCast development, this has been possible in the framework of "RoMA" project, thanks to the partnership and cooperation of ACEA Distribuzione SpA – Areti, the major electrical distribution operator in Lazio Region (Italy).

3.3 Damage Metrics at Component Level

The damage scales used to model infrastructure damage vary depending on the type of component being assessed. All networked infrastructures can be represented as an arrangement of 'point' components, also known as *nodes* and linear components, also known as *edges*, e.g. for an electric power transmission system represented diagrammatically as a network, the generation plant and substations are nodes and the overhead lines and buried cables are edges (Table 2).

Damage to infrastructure nodes can be described either in terms of physical damage or operational failure. Where components are housed inside buildings, it may be necessary to separately assess the operational state of the equipment and physical damage to the building. For infrastructure components housed in buildings, it is possible for the structure to be significantly damaged yet the component is fully operational as none of the equipment is damaged. Conversely, it is possible for the structure to be sound yet the component does not function because equipment inside has been damaged. The HAZUS methodology [6] considers both generation plants and substations (Table 3) as nodes of the electric power network classifying them in term of power output and voltage respectively and distinguishing, furthermore, whether or not their components are anchored (i.e. designed with special seismic tiedowns or tiebacks) or unanchored (i.e. designed according to normal requirements). Four damage states are defined for generation plants and substations, i.e.: slight/minor damage, moderate damage, extensive damage and complete damage (Table 3). In this application, the damage scale proposed for the building housing sub-stations is the 5 level damage scale defined by the European Macroseismic Scale, EMS-98 [33] already used by CIPCast-ES.

Table 3. Damage state definitions for substations (modified after [6])

Substations sub-components	Damage states			
	Minor[a]	Moderate	Extensive	Complete
Disconnect switches	5%[a]	40%	70%	100%
Switches	5%	40%	70%	100%
Current transformers	–	40%	70%	100%
Transformers	–	–	70%	1000%
Building[b]	D1–D2	D3	D4	D5

[a]*"Failure of 5% of disconnect switches or failure of 5% of circuit breakers or building being in D1–D2 damage state"*; [b]*EMS-98 (Gruntal 1998) damage levels.*

While damage to infrastructure nodes is usually classified qualitatively, damage to infrastructure edges can be assessed quantitatively in term of repair rate. The repair rate, RR, is a deterministic calculation of the number of damages that a cable is expected to experience per unit of length, usually per kilometre. The relationship between repair rate and earthquake hazard commonly follows a power law or a linear relationship although more complex functions do exist. Most repair rate functions have been derived empirically. The typical form of a power law repair rate function is shown in Eq. 1, and a corresponding linear relationship is shown in Eq. 2:

$$RR = a \cdot IM^b \tag{1}$$

$$lnRR = c \cdot ln IM + d \tag{2}$$

where RR is the repair rate, IM is the earthquake hazard parameter and a, b, c, d are coefficients determined using some regression technique [34]. To account for different material properties or soil conditions, the repair rate function may include additional multiplying factors, which vary according to attribute, or a set of functions may be proposed for different conditions.

3.4 Damage Assessment at Component Level

Fragility curves for generation plants and sub-stations. Fragility functions are used to evaluate earthquake-induced damage to generation plants and sub-stations of electric power network. For a given level of ground motion intensity, fragility functions determine the probability that a structure or component will be in, or exceeded, the ith damage state, D_{si}. Fragility functions are often described by a lognormal probability distribution function as in Eq. 3, although it is noted that this distribution may not always be the best fit:

$$P_f\left(D_s \geq D_{s_i}|IM\right) = \Phi\left[\frac{1}{\beta} \cdot \ln\left(\frac{IM}{IM_{mi}}\right)\right] \tag{3}$$

where Pf($\cdot$) indicates the probability of being at or exceeding a particular damage state, D_{si}, for a given seismic intensity level defined by an earthquake intensity measure, IM (e.g. PGA, PGV, PGD etc.), Φ is the standard cumulative probability function, IM_{mi} is the median threshold value of the earthquake intensity measure IM required to cause the ith damage state and β is the total standard deviation. According to Eq. 3, fragility curves can be therefore drawn providing the values of the two parameters, IM_{mi} and β, as a function of IM. Cavalieri et al. [11, 35] provided an exhaustive overview on the main recent works on fragility functions for electric power system components along with the defining IM_{mi} and β parameters for each one of them. Table 4 provides, as an example IM_{mi} and β parameters for substations, as defined by HAZUS [6], making reference to empirical data/expert judgments and using Boolean logic and probabilistic combination of damage functions for jointly accounting for the performance of the constituting sub-components (listed in Table 3).

Table 4. Fragility function parameters for macro-components.

Damage State	Low voltage				Medium voltage				High voltage			
	U		A		U		A		U		A	
Slight /Minor	IM^a	β	IM	β	IM	β	IM	β	IM	β	IM	β
	0.13	0.65	0.15	0.70	0.10	0.60	0.15	0.60	0.09	0.50	0.11	0.50
Moderate	0.26	0.50	0.29	0.55	0.20	0.50	0.25	0.50	0.13	0.40	0.15	0.45
Extensive	0.34	0.40	0.45	0.45	0.30	0.40	0.35	0.40	0.17	0.35	0.20	0.35
Complete	0.74	0.40	0.9	0.45	0.50	0.40	0.70	0.40	0.38	0.35	0.47	0.40

^{a}IM is IMmi as defined in Eq. 3, expressed in PGA[g]
^{b}Low (34.5 kV to 150 kV), Medium (150 kV to 350 kV), High (350 kV and above)

Differently from HAZUS, SYNER-G methodology [11] provides fragility functions for individual sub-components identifying all potential failure modes for the whole substation. As such, it is possible to determine the failure probability of the substation using fault tree analysis, where 'failure' refers to the substation's ability to distribute power rather than a physical damage state. SYNER-G fragility functions have been adapted from the work of Vanzi [36], specifically referring to Italian substations. Kongar et al. [32] reality-checked the reliability of both the aforementioned approaches comparing the damage predicted for substation with the ones observed after the Canterbury earthquake sequence 2010–2011. Both the approaches overestimated the damage and the loss of functionality. The adoption and implementation of either one or the other approach within CIPCast-ES will need to be carefully calibrated as discussed in the conclusions.

Repair rate relationship for buried cables. Kongar et al. [30] produced for the first time evidence-based repair rates for the prediction of damage to buried cables, processing and analysing the damaged caused to them by 2010–2011 Canterbury, New Zealand, earthquake sequence. The analysis showed that the fragility of buried cables is influenced more by liquefaction than by ground shaking, and that lateral spread can cause more damage than settlement alone. Kongar et al. [30] distinguished four different earthquake-induced geotechnical hazard zones (Table 4). Along with the typology of hazard and its intensity, the insulation material was identified as a critical factor influencing cable fragility. In Christchurch three materials were used for the insulation of 11 kV cables, namely: paper-insulated lead covered armoured (PILCA); cross-linked polyethylene (XLPE); and PILCA cables reinforced with high-density polyethylene (PILCA HDPE); plus some further unknown materials (Other). After the Canterbury earthquake sequence repair rates in PILCA cables resulted considerably higher than those observed in XLPE cables [30].

Conversely, Kongar et al. [30] analysis showed no trend between *cable age* and repair rates and a non-significant difference in repair rates for different *conducting materials* (conducting materials used in Christchurch included copper and aluminium). Table 5 shows the repair rate function [30] that will be built into CIPCast-ES: repair rate functions refer to PILCA cables; coefficients are proposed to modify the 'base' PILCA functions for other materials. Therefore to estimate the repair rate for typologies, other than PILCA, one can calculate the repair rate for PILCA cables first and then multiply by the corresponding coefficient in Table 4.

Table 5. Repair rate function for PILCA cables, for different earthquake-induced geotechnical hazard zones, and coefficients for alternative insulation material typologies.

Earthquake-induced geotechnical hazard Zones	Repair rate function	Material dependant coefficient		
	PILCA	XLPE	PILCA HDPE	Other
A - No Liquefaction	_a	0.06	0.38	1.31
B - All Liquefaction	RR = 4.317PGD-0.324	0.26	0.82	1.07
C - Liquefaction with settlement only	RR = 1.23PGD	0.31	0.67	1.48
D - Liquefaction with lateral spreading	RR = 7.951PGD + 0.18	0.14	1.75	0.00

[a]*No reliable relationship*

3.5   System Performance Assessment According to CIPCast-RecSIM

There are two paradigms for measuring system performance: connectivity analysis and serviceability analysis. Connectivity analysis determines whether two points in the system remain connected and as such can be used to determine whether a demand node (customer) remains connected to a source node. Serviceability analysis determines not just whether a customer is connected to a service but also what is the quality of that service. Possible serviceability metrics for electric power networks might include: power supply/demand ratio; voltage reduction. CIP-Cast ES can perform system performance assessment, thanks to a discrete-time event-based Java simulator, referred to as RecSIM [25], already built into built CIPCast B5 module (Fig. 1). By taking into account the predicted critical scenario, CIPCast-RecSIM can perform system performance assessment for a specific area of the electrical grid, both in term of connectivity and serviceability analysis (i.e. can map the evolution of the electric network in term of outages, after the damage and/or loss of functionality of some of the components). *"kilo-minutes of outages (kmin)"* is the reference key performance indicator (KPI) for the serviceability analysis within RECSIM, as this is a metric normally used by electrical operators, committed to provide, in the event of outages, the services back with a prede-fined Quality Level expressed in *kmin*:

$$kmin = \sum_{k=1}^{N} u_k T_k \tag{4}$$

where *kmin* is the sum of the products between the number of minutes of outages times Tk for each kth substation; u_k is the number of electric customers fed by the kth substation considered for the interval time of interest. According to the definition provided for *kmin* in Eq. 3 a short duration blackout in a highly populated area can produce a higher number of kilo-minutes of outages than longer outages in less populated areas. Figure 2 reports an example of serviceability analysis carried out by means of CIPCast-RecSIM module. As a consequence of a simulated earthquake, inducing the failure of some components of the Medium Voltage (MV) power grid, *kmin,* for the census tracks (where costumers of the electric power system are located, represented as polygons) interested by the outages can be visualised in Fig. 2, where different colours (from green to red) represent different ranges of *kmin.*

Fig. 2. CIPCast- RecSIM: example of geographical interface. Different colours (from green to red) represent different ranges of Quality Level expressed *kmin* (Color figure online)

The "Consequences Analysis" module (see B4 in Fig. 1) can produce furthermore a more "societal-oriented" assessment of the impacts [37] by estimating the reduction of wellbeing for different societal sectors (e.g. citizens, economic activities, public services etc.) and the social and economic costs caused by the unavailability (or partial availa-bility) of primary services such as electricity, telecommunications, drinkable water, mobility etc. Further to the models already built into CIPCast-RecSIM for this societal-oriented impact assessment [25] other relationships will be added to assess the expected impacts on businesses of different industry sectors as a function of the outages duration for the electric power service [38].

3.6   CIPCast-RecSIM: Service Restoration Assessment

The purpose of restoration functions is to evaluate the time that it might take for damaged infrastructure components to be repaired based on their damage state and/or the average percentage of repairs that might take place within a specified time period [39]. Such functions may be derived empirically or estimated via resource modelling as a function of the available resources and work rate. CIPCast B5, by means of RecSIM, can evaluate the repair times at component-level and after that re-evaluate the system performance metrics at time-steps after the earthquake accounting for improved system conditions. Towards that CIPCast-RecSIM can simulate the basic functioning mechanisms of a switched and controllable electrical network, while accounting for the procedures usually performed in case of failure and the restoration functions for the different components, the number of emergency crews and power generators available to the electric operator. CIPCast B5 aims at informing CI operators and emergency managers on appropriate intervention, mitigation, and recovery strategies. At the current stage of development, the support actions are mainly related to the optimization of the system recovery sequence, in order to minimize the crisis impact on the continuity, measured in term of *kmin,* as defined in Eq. 3.

4   Conclusions

The paper demonstrated the feasibility and value of developing an ad-hoc DSS for assessing and mitigating the seismic risk to electric power network. The authors are collaboratively working on the steps described in the paper and on testing the reliability of the proposed models on real cases in Europe, including the recent earthquake sequence in Central Italy, where the network data are available thanks to the cooperation of ACEA. The CIPCast-ES will allow end-users to perform the assessment of possible earthquake-induced impacts on the overall system (accounting also for interdependencies) [40] and to estimate the possible consequences on citizens and on environment, starting from both real data (acquired by distributed sensors and monitoring networks), and from the elaboration of simulated scenarios.

As future developments, CIPCast will be further enhanced with additional functionality, primarily the use of Earth Observation data to improve the territorial analysis, particularly considering the landslide risk [29]. Secondly the integration of additional data for environmental monitoring, and finally the capability of collecting crowdsourced data (e.g., real-time road traffic conditions), allowing the citizens to provide useful information to be exploited by the Public Authorities for improving the situational awareness in Metropolitan areas. In turn, the availability of a huge amount of data stored and processed within CIPCast will allow the Authorities to provide to the CP, the CI

Operators and the citizens effective information in real time, therefore improving the decision processes for crisis and emergencies management.

Acknowledgments and Disclaimer. This article was derived from the FP7 project CIPRNet, which has received funding from the European Union's 7th Framework Programme for: research, technological development and demonstration, under grant agreement no. 312450. Thanks to S. Liotta and S. Alessandroni (ACEA-Areti) for their fruitful cooperation to the implementation of the outages propagation model within the CIPCast-RecSIM. The contents of this article do not necessarily reflect the official opinion of the EU. Information and views expressed in the paper are based on personal research experiences, therefore responsibility for that lies entirely with the authors. There are several variables and data uncertainties that might affect and alter the results reported in the paper.

References

1. Schiff, A.J.: Northridge earthquake: lifeline performance and post- earthquake response. (1997)
2. Kwasinski, A., Eidinger, J., Tang, A., Tudo-Bornarel, C.: Performance of electric power systems in the 2010–2011 Christchurch, New Zealand. Earthq. Seq. Earthq. Spectra. **30**, 205–230 (2014)
3. Giovinazzi, S., Wilson, T., Davis, C., Bristow, D., Gallagher, M., Schofield, A., Villemure, M., Eidinger, J., Tang, A.: Lifelines performance and management following the 22 February 2011 Christchurch Earthquake, New Zealand: highlights of resilience. Bull. New Zeal. Soc. Earthq. Eng. **44**, 402–417 (2011)
4. Giovinazzi, S., Wilson, T.M.: Recovery of lifelines following the 22nd February 2011 Christchurch earthquake: successes and issues. In: NZSEE Conference. NZSEE, Christchurch, NZ (2012)
5. A.L.A. - American Lifelines Alliance: Guideline for assessing the performance of Electric Power System in Natural Hazard and Human Threat Events (2005)
6. NIBS: HAZUS MR4 Technical Manual. National institute of Buildilng Sciences, Washington, DC (2004)
7. Rojahn, C.: Earthquake Damage Evaluation Data for California. ATC, Redwood City Calif (1985)
8. Cagnan, Z., Davidson, R.: Post-earthquake restoration modeling of electric power systems. In: Proceedings of the 13th World Conference on Earthquake Engineering (2004)
9. Franchin, P.: A computational framework for systemic seismic risk analysis of civil infrastructural systems. In: Pitilakis, K., Franchin, P., Khazai, B., Wenzel, H. (eds.) SYNER-G: Systemic Seismic Vulnerability and Risk Assessment of Complex Urban, Utility, Lifeline Systems and Critical Facilities. GGEE, vol. 31, pp. 23–56. Springer, Dordrecht (2014). doi: 10.1007/978-94-017-8835-9_2
10. OOFIMS - Object-Oriented Framework for Infrastructure Modelling and Simulation. https://sites.google.com/a/uniroma1.it/oofims/
11. Cavalieri, F., Franchin, P., Buriticá Cortés, J.A.M., Tesfamariam, S.: Models for seismic vulnerability analysis of power networks: comparative assessment. Comput. Civ. Infrastruct. Eng. **29**, 590–607 (2014)

12. Cavalieri, F., Franchin, P., Pinto, P.E.: Application to selected transportation and electric networks in Italy. In: Pitilakis, K., Franchin, P., Khazai, B., Wenzel, H. (eds.) SYNER-G: Systemic Seismic Vulnerability and Risk Assessment of Complex Urban, Utility, Lifeline Systems and Critical Facilities. GGEE, vol. 31, pp. 301–330. Springer, Dordrecht (2014). doi: 10.1007/978-94-017-8835-9_10

13. Council Directive 2008/114/EC, 8 December 2008. http://eur-lex.europa.eu/legal-content/EN/ALL/?uri=celex:32008L0114

14. Tofani, A., Di Pietro, A., Lavalle, P.L., Pollino, M., Rosato, V., Alessandroni, S.: CIPRNet decision support system: modelling electrical distribution grid internal dependencies. J. Polish Saf. Reliab. Assoc. **6**, 133–140 (2015)

15. Pollino, M., Modica, G.: Free web mapping tools to characterise landscape dynamics and to favour e-participation. In: Murgante, B., Misra, S., Carlini, M., Torre, C.M., Nguyen, H.-Q., Taniar, D., Apduhan, B.O., Gervasi, O. (eds.) ICCSA 2013. LNCS, vol. 7973, pp. 566–581. Springer, Heidelberg (2013). doi:10.1007/978-3-642-39646-5_41

16. Pollino, M., Fattoruso, G., Rocca, A.B., Porta, L., Curzio, S.L., Arolchi, A., James, V., Pascale, C.: An open source gis system for earthquake early warning and post-event emergency management. In: Murgante, B., Gervasi, O., Iglesias, A., Taniar, D., Apduhan, B.O. (eds.) ICCSA 2011. LNCS, vol. 6783, pp. 376–391. Springer, Heidelberg (2011). doi: 10.1007/978-3-642-21887-3_30

17. Pollino, M., Fattoruso, G., La Porta, L., Della Rocca, A.B., James, V.: Collaborative open source geospatial tools and maps supporting the response planning to disastrous earthquake events. Futur. Internet. **4**, 451–468 (2012)

18. Steiniger, S., Hunter, A.J.S.: Free and open source GIS software for building a spatial data infrastructure. In: Bocher, E., Neteler, M. (eds.) Geospatial Free and Open Source Software in the 21st Century, pp. 247–261. Springer, Heidelberg (2011)

19. Pollino, M., Caiaffa, E., Carillo, A., Porta, L., Sannino, G.: Wave energy potential in the mediterranean sea: design and development of DSS-WebGIS "Waves Energy". In: Gervasi, O., Murgante, B., Misra, S., Gavrilova, M.L., Rocha, A.M.A.C., Torre, C., Taniar, D., Apduhan, B.O. (eds.) ICCSA 2015. LNCS, vol. 9157, pp. 495–510. Springer, Cham (2015). doi:10.1007/978-3-319-21470-2_36

20. Modica, G., Pollino, M., Lanucara, S., Porta, L., Pellicone, G., Fazio, S., Fichera, C.R.: Land suitability evaluation for agro-forestry: definition of a web-based multi-criteria spatial decision support system (MC-SDSS): preliminary results. In: Gervasi, O., et al. (eds.) ICCSA 2016. LNCS, vol. 9788, pp. 399–413. Springer, Cham (2016). doi: 10.1007/978-3-319-42111-7_31

21. Matassoni, L., Fiaschi, A., Giovinazzi, S., Pollino, M., La Porta, L., Rosato, V.: A geospatial decision support tool for seismic risk management: Florence (Italy) case study. In: Computational Science and Its Applications - ICCSA 2017. LNCS. Springer International Publishing (2017). [Submitted Paper]

22. Kongar, I., Rossetto, T.: A methodological hierarchy for modelling lifelines interdpendencies in risk management. In: SECED Conference: Earthquake Risk and Engineering towards a Resilient World, 9–10 July 2015, Cambridge, UK (2015)

23. Kongar, I., Giovinazzi, S.: Damage to infrastructure: modeling. In: Beer, M., Kougioumtzoglou, I.A., Patelli, E., Au, I.S.-K. (eds.) Encyclopedia of Earthquake Engineering, pp. 1–14. Springer, Heidelberg (2014)

24. Rosato, V., Pietro, A., Porta, L., Pollino, M., Tofani, A., Marti, J.R., Romani, C.: A decision support system for emergency management of critical infrastructures subjected to natural hazards. In: Panayiotou, C.G.G., Ellinas, G., Kyriakides, E., Polycarpou, M.M.M. (eds.) CRITIS 2014. LNCS, vol. 8985, pp. 362–367. Springer, Cham (2016). doi: 10.1007/978-3-319-31664-2_37

25. Di Pietro, A., Lavalle, L., La Porta, L., Pollino, M., Tofani, A., Rosato, V.: Design of DSS for supporting preparedness to and management of anomalous situations in complex scenarios. In: Setola, R., Rosato, V., Kyriakides, E., Rome, E. (eds.) Managing the Complexity of Critical Infrastructures: A Modelling and Simulation Approach, pp. 195–232. Springer International Publishing, Cham (2016)

26. Weatherill, G., Esposito, S., Iervolino, I., Franchin, P., Cavalieri, F.: Framework for seismic hazard analysis of spatially distributed systems. In: Pitilakis, K., Franchin, P., Khazai, B., Wenzel, H. (eds.) SYNER-G: Systemic Seismic Vulnerability and Risk Assessment of Complex Urban, Utility, Lifeline Systems and Critical Facilities. GGEE, vol. 31, pp. 57–88. Springer, Dordrecht (2014). doi:10.1007/978-94-017-8835-9_3

27. Bindi, D., Luzi, L., Pacor, F., Sabetta, F., Massa, M.: Towards a new reference ground motion prediction equation for Italy: update of the Sabetta-Pugliese (1996). Bull. Earthq. Eng. 7, 591–608 (2009)

28. Kramer, S.L.: Geotechnical Earthquake Engineering. Prentice Hall, New York (1996)

29. Borfecchia, F., De Canio, G., De Cecco, L., Giocoli, A., Grauso, S., La Porta, L., Martini, S., Pollino, M., Roselli, I., Zini, A.: Mapping the earthquake-induced landslide hazard around the main oil pipeline network of the Agri Valley (Basilicata, southern Italy) by means of two GIS-based modelling approaches. Nat. Hazards 81, 759–777 (2016)

30. Kongar, I., Giovinazzi, S., Rossetto, T.: Seismic performance of buried electrical cables: evidence-based repair rates and fragility functions. Bull. Earthq. Eng. 15, 1–31 (2016)

31. Douglas, J.: Ground Motion Prediction Equations 1964–2010, Berkeley, CA (2011)

32. Kongar, I., Rossetto, T., Giovinazzi, S.: The effectiveness of existing methodologies for predicting electrical substation damage due to earthquakes in New Zealand. In: Vulnerability, Uncertainty, and Risk, pp. 752–761. American Society of Civil Engineers, Reston, VA (2014)

33. Grünthal, G., Musson, R., Schwarz, J., Stucchi, M.: European Macroseismic Scale 1998 (EMS-98). entre E uropèen de G éodynamique et de Séismolo gie, Luxembourg (1998)

34. (ALA), A.L.A.: Seismic fragility formulation for water systems. Part 1 - Guideline. American Society of Civil Engineers, ASCE (2001)

35. Cavalieri, F., Franchin, P., Pinto, P.E.: Fragility functions of electric power stations. In: Pitilakis, K., Crowley, H., Kaynia, A.M. (eds.) SYNER-G: Typology Definition and Fragility Functions for Physical Elements at Seismic Risk. GGEE, vol. 27, pp. 157–185. Springer, Dordrecht (2014). doi:10.1007/978-94-007-7872-6_6

36. Vanzi, I.: Seismic reliability of electric power networks: methodology and application. Struct. Saf. 18, 311–327 (1996)

37. Petermann, T., Bradke, H., Lüllmann, A., Poetzsch, M., Riehm, U.: What Happens During a Blackout Consequences of a Prolonged and Wide-ranging Power Outage. Books on Demand, Stoughton (2014)

38. Giovinazzi, S., Brown, C., Seville, E., Stevenson, J.R., Hatton, T., Vargo, J.J.: Criticality of infrastructures for organisations. Int. J. Crit. Infrastruct. 12, 331 (2016)

39. Çağnan, Z., Davidson, R.A., Guikema, S.D.: Post-earthquake restoration planning for los angeles electric power. Earthq. Spectra. 22, 589–608 (2006)

40. Tofani, A., Di Pietro, A., Lavalle, L., Pollino, M.R.V.: Supporting decision makers in crisis management involving interdependent critical infrastructures. In: The International Emergency Management Society (TIEMS) 2015. TIEMS, Rome (2015)

An Approach to Provide Shared Architectural Principles for Interoperable Smart Cities

Vatsal Bhatt[1], Arianna Brutti[2], Martin Burns[3], and Angelo Frascella[2(✉)]

[1] United States Green Building Council (USGBC), Washington, DC, USA
vbhatt@usgbc.org
[2] Italian National Agency for New Technologies,
Energy and Sustainable Economic Development (ENEA), Bologna, Italy
{arianna.brutti,angelo.frascella}@enea.it
[3] National Institute of Standards and Technology (NIST), Gaithersburg, USA
martin.burns@nist.gov

Abstract. Smart City projects are moving from trials to complete Smart City realizations. Smart Cities must work as complex ecosystems of interoperable and composable services yet there is currently a proliferation of less than interoperable and portable vertical services. To diminish the barriers among these silos different approaches have been attempted but no single one of them has garnered general acceptance and adoption. The international initiative Internet of Things Enabled Smart City Framework (IES-City) convenes a broad set of stakeholders to build a consensus foundation of architectural principles for interoperable Smart Cities. IES-City evaluates global existing frameworks, tools and applications to distil a common set of Pivotal Points of Interoperability (PPI). PPI have the potential to enable both interoperability and suitable variation and reduce barriers to composable Smart City deployments. The IES-City concept is that such PPI exist in practice and need only be discovered. This paper describes the IES-City methodology.

Keywords: Smart City interoperability · Frameworks · Applications · Architectural principles

1 Introduction

Many cities are pursuing a path for becoming "smart" (by various definitions). Indeed, the city stakeholders have understood that this process provides a clear and strong opportunity, not only for improving the quality of life of the citizen, but also in the direction of economic growth and sustainable deployment.

Such cities are becoming promoters of investment and actions for passing from the phase of trial projects to the realization of "Smart Cities". For example, Korea is investing 50 M€ for making smart the city of Busan [1] and the city of Wien has invested 46 M€ for upgrading homes (21.000 interested people) [2]. More generally, the broad international response to the United States National Institute of Standards and Technology (NIST)'s Global City Teams Challenge (GCTC) [3] provides clear evidence of the great interest on this topic.

© Springer International Publishing AG 2017
O. Gervasi et al. (Eds.): ICCSA 2017, Part III, LNCS 10406, pp. 415–426, 2017.
DOI: 10.1007/978-3-319-62398-6_29

This new kind of city activity raises the level of optimism about the future for deployment of Smart Cities: new and striking smart services could be realized if the different applications and solutions worked as a set of harmonized ecosystems; however, maximum benefits can only be achieved if this growth in deployment is accompanied by increasing interoperability and innovation. From this perspective, it becomes essential to define approaches and methodologies that support automated interaction between (new and pre-existing) systems and support the design and development of replicable and reusable solutions. Interoperability can be defined as "capability of two or more networks, systems, devices, applications, or components to exchange and readily use information, securely, effectively, and with little or no inconvenience to the user" [4]. Interoperable systems share a common meaning for the exchanged information, and this information must elicit agreed-upon types of responses. Clearly, interoperability is a complex property of a set of features and layers: semantic, informational, communications, and organizational.

Moreover, in a system of systems, like a Smart City, the interoperability levels must be implemented both within each system and across the different systems. It is essential for Smart City applications to be composable. That is, once an initial application is provided, it should be possible to build on the application by adding new features and function to the benefit of the city and its citizens. However, in many cases, the complexity of adding features that a supplier did not anticipate and provide can make the cost prohibitive. From a city stakeholder perspective, this can result in vendor lock-in. That is the only team that can expand a deployment in this sense is the one that created it. While this can be efficient in some cases, most often the prospect of vendor lock-in and the non-integrative nature of it can hinder cities from making purchases and, thus, slow market growth. Reducing the barrier to adding a second feature can help increase the viability in the market of the first feature.

As a consequence of this complexity, the path to interoperability needs, on the one hand, a cyclic interaction among research (where new ideas and architectures come up), pilots (where they are tested), standardization (where appropriate for a large scale application) and the availability of a set of tools (e.g. software tools to support adoption, conformance and interoperability tests for assuring interoperability and best practices) with the aim of facilitating the achievement of the a critical mass consensus for adoption [5]. On the contrary, what has emerged to date is the development of several independent and uncoordinated architectural designs. This is positive from the point of view of having a wide range of potential solutions to choose from, but the lack of convergence among them is an obstacle to achieving the critical mass needed for broad adoption.

Starting from these issues, a group of international partners[1] led by NIST began work on the IoT-Enabled Smart City Framework (IES-City pronounced "Yes City") with the objectives of providing a foundation of language/taxonomy and common architectural

---

[1] The other founder partners are Italian National Agency for New Technologies (ENEA), United States Green Building Council (USGBC), American National Standards Institute (ANSI), European Telecommunications Standards Institute (ETSI), Ministry of Science ICT and Future Planning (MSIP), Telecommunications Industry Association (TIA) and FIWARE Foundation, but a lot of international Entities and Industries are taking part to the effort.

principles for supporting the creation of interoperable Smart Cities. The methodology for developing these principles is to distill them by comparing different architectural efforts [6].

This paper presents the activities completed to date in IES-City effort and is structured as follows:

- Section 2 gives a quick overview of the problem and of the state of art;
- Section 3 explains the IES-City approach;
- Section 4 is focused on the results produced up-to-now by IES-City; and
- Section 5 presents conclusions and the next steps.

2 The Problem and Current Solutions

Presently, Smart City projects focus mainly on vertical integration within existing infrastructures (for example, energy, transport, health, etc.), while horizontal interoperability, needed for cities to function as a cohesive ecosystem, is not well-developed [7]. Often this top-down approach lacks an integrated perspective, preferring a problem-oriented (or bottom-up) approach, since this one is more immediate, manageable and requires little or no analysis.

At the same time, many existing Smart City Information and Communications Technologies (ICT) deployments are based on closed, that is inextensible and proprietary systems, instead of open systems, in which may be unique to a particular vendor. This results in non-interoperable, poorly portable solutions, non-extensible within projects in a city and between cities.

As a result, vertical applications are proliferating and becoming disconnected 'silos' (i.e. vertical logical structures, implementing separately various layers of the Smart City applications: sensors, data filtering, etc.) and are not able to interoperate.

This situation diminishes the ability to achieve benefits available at the city scale by aggregation and re-elaboration of data collected by several and heterogeneous sensors, devices and applications. Thus, the urgent problem is how to break down the barriers among silos (see Fig. 1).

While standards and open architectures can be interoperability enablers, broad adoption in the Smart City context is limited by the following:

- Adequate standards are lacking.
- Architectural efforts are not harmonized and there is no apparent convergence among them. So, even when ICT solutions are based on standardized open reference specifications, there remains a risk of insufficient interoperability.
- Harmonization is impeded by a current lack of consensus on both common language/ taxonomy and Smart City architectural principles (the definition of "Smart City" itself is not unique [9]).

- Standardization agencies and consortia, like ISO/IEC JTC1, IEC, IEEE, ITU[2]..., are working to generate the needed standards, but a mechanism for harmonizing or comparing them is lacking.

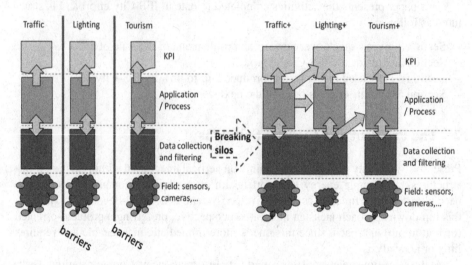

Fig. 1. Breaking down the barriers to creating Smart Cities

Approaches for addressing these critical issues have been attempted by different stakeholders, including:

- *Identification of an optimal implementation policy*: The European project called ESPRESSO, for example, makes recommendations aiming to favor the adoption of a global Smart City Strategy [8]. These recommendations comprise the use of standards, specification of data formats and avoidance of supplier lock-in. This approach fits well with new Smart City projects and can prevent the creation of new silos but it does not give guidance on how to break down barriers between existing silos.
- *Understanding the Smart City standard landscape*: The British Standards Institution (BSI) conducted an analysis of existing Smart City-oriented standards. The result was a report, called "Mapping Smart City Standards [10]", in which the method for identification of the standards and their related gaps plus a summary of the inter-domain Smart City standards, was organized by three levels: technical standards, process standards, and strategic standards. These kinds of analyses are fundamental to facing barriers to interoperability.
- *Definition of reference technological frameworks for Smart City project implementations*: many private and public or non-profit efforts are defining their implementation set of tools for building Smart Cities. An example of open source architecture

[2] International Organization for Standardization (ISO), International Electrotechnical Commission (IEC), Joint Technical Committee (JTC), Institute of Electrical and Electronic Engineers (IEEE), International Telecommunication Union (ITU).

is 'KM4CITY' developed by the University of Florence [11] and there are numerous others.

- *Initiatives putting together many cities around one common architecture*: Various organizations are building cooperative groups of cities around various architectures. For example, the City Protocol Society [12] is developing a network of cities including Amsterdam, Dubai, Barcelona and Montevideo based on its Functional Platform and the Open & Agile Smart Cities (OASC) initiative comprises more than 50 cities using FIWARE based architectures [13]. Another approach being driven by the Global City Team's Challenge, convenes sets of cities and providers as "super clusters" to produce open "blueprints" for sets of Smart City applications [3]. These approaches contribute to our reaching critical mass in the use of interoperable architectures, while not requiring that any one architecture "win the race".
- *Architecture agnostic frameworks for catalyzing Smart City performance*: The U.S. Green Building Council (USGBC) has launched the Leadership in Energy and Environmental Design (LEED) for Cities performance-based certification [14] on the Arc platform, enabling cities worldwide to measure and improve performance and make the outcomes from Smart City sustainability and quality of life applications visible.

The previous approaches are certainly useful, but no single one offers a globally consistent Smart Cities framework i.e., a globally shared set of requirements. Lacking is a higher-level perspective for assessing the relationship between the available approaches and architectures. A larger goal should be to identify and distill a common vocabulary and a set of common architectural principles, and promote consensus around standardized interfaces for interoperability. This is the approach chosen by the IES-City initiative.

3 The IES-City Framework Approach

3.1 The Working Groups

To analyse the Smart City Applications and Framework landscape from different points of view and provide results suitable for different kinds of stakeholders, the IES-City Framework activity has been split into different working groups with different scope and aims:

- Application Framework Working Group: Assimilates and evaluates global frameworks that are facilitating urban decision making process and deployment of Smart City applications. It is compiling an initial list of applications and domains for Smart City applications. The application frameworks being utilized today, are analyzed based on their functional requirements, evaluating cities' readiness while implementing such applications, and critically assessing benefits for the city and its citizens.
- Consensus Pivotal Points of Interoperability (PPI) Working Group: Approaches the problem from the perspective of developers. It is producing distillations of prominent technology suites currently in use in Smart City applications worldwide. Through a

technical investigation methodology, the suites are analyzed against the NIST Cyber-Physical Systems (CPS) Framework [15] Aspects and Concerns to expose potential PPI where a common concern is addressed with a common technical solution.

- Deployed PPI Working Group: Analyzes significant and complex Smart City deployments, using a limited set of case studies, to identify potential PPI that were needed to make such complexity realizable.

3.2 The Starting Point: The CPS Framework

The CPS Framework [15] provides a holistic concern-driven analytical concept for conceptualizing, realizing and assuring cyber-physical systems. Cyber-physical systems are a superset of the Internet of Things (IoT) including all things which have both cyber and physical parts, whether they communicate with other systems or not. The IES-City Framework uses this reference as an analytical tool for reducing complex architectures to what is termed "CPS Framework Normal form" to expose potential PPI. That is, to identify support for Aspects/Concerns and the technical solutions identified by an architecture to help expose the PPI.

The framework (see Fig. 2) has two principle concepts – Aspects/Concerns, and Facets. Facets are modes of thinking applied during a systems engineering process for a cyber-physical system. They group various activities throughout the life cycle of CPS, from idea through creation through decommissioning. Note that a CPS can be a device, a system of devices, or a system of systems.

The three Facets are *conceptualization, realization,* and *assurance.* There are many system engineering processes in use throughout the domains of CPS (i.e. Smart Cities, Smart Grids, Smart Manufacturing, Smart Transportation, etc.). Any given process involves a sequence of activities that typically include use case development, requirements analysis, design and test, and verification. These activities sort cleanly into the

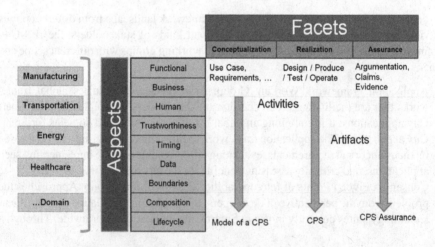

Fig. 2. NIST CPS framework

three Facets that group these activities and produce sets of linked artifacts that comprise a complete data set describing the CPS.

The Aspects group common Concerns that should be considered in any given CPS and drive their realization, through properties or requirements of the CPS that are verified through test and assured by relating those properties and artifacts to consensus methods for judging that the properties have been satisfied. To have the best requirements defining and satisfying the needs of technical development, it is important to evaluate a rich set of Concerns at each activity of conceptualization and at each level of functional decomposition of the CPS. This way, for example, cyber security is considered during business case development, use case development, CPS component decomposition, etc. This avoids the failure to consider important requirements which must later be 'bolted on' to a design when discovered late.

- The Application Framework working group has used the Aspects/Concerns as a means of describing the high-level functional requirements for each application and sub-application reviewed.
- The Consensus PPI working group is using the set of Aspects/Concerns as a means of normalizing approaches to enable a comparative analysis of the disparate technologies being reviewed. Each technology will have its own method of presenting a specification. These methods will have diagrams and detailed documentation that may be highly stylized to the community for which they are being presented. Yet, for example, they may all be using IP addressing to identify nodes in a network. This would correspond to the Functional/Communications/Network concern and 'IP addressing of nodes' would be a property or requirement that addresses the concern related to network layer interoperability.
- The Deployed PPI working group is using the Aspects/Concerns to organize the analysis of several prominent complex Smart City deployments.

3.3 The Innovative Aspect: PPI Concept

Pivotal Points of Interoperability (PPI) introduces the notion that there are design choices made in Smart City technology deployments that are aligned with choices made independently in other Smart City deployments. This consensus provides a defacto standardization and knowledge of these common choices can reduce the complexity of smart City integration and thereby enhance the ability to acquire/sell, deploy, and use Smart City systems. In essence,

- If you standardize everything, you get no innovation;
- If you standardize nothing, you get limited interoperability or impeded integration.

The hypothesis of the IES-City Framework is that not only are there good candidates for PPI, but there may already be existing PPI that are consensus choices – not by agreement but by independent election. For example, the use of IP addresses for the identification of communications end-point addresses is one choice that all implementers of IoT have made. Some other possible PPI might include PKI infrastructure for authentication and confidentiality, the use of APIs and REST or Publish/Subscribe data exchange patterns, domain-specific semantic models, and a universal time reference. Note that these are possible examples and are not intended as recommendations.

By detecting potential PPI, IES-City intends to reduce the barriers to deployment of Smart City applications and thereby help streamline and grow the industry.

Each technology suite that is used to deploy a Smart City application has a set of requirements and documentation that, while essential, can be an obstacle to understanding by external parties who may want to integrate with the technology due to its overwhelming volume and style.

If you consider the left side of Fig. 3, the diagonal arrow, drawn from the lower left to the upper right exemplifies this notion of impenetrable complexity. Without being able to rely on some well-known interfaces, the complexity of adding a new feature, the "distance to interoperability" is large. Yet if there were a set of well-established common features, as illustrated on the right, the 'distance to interoperability' can be reduced.

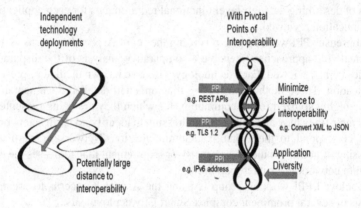

Fig. 3. Benefit of PPI

4   The Current Status

4.1   Application Framework Outcomes

The Application Framework Working Group analyzed the Smart City application space to provide needed tools and methodologies for stakeholders to choose and/or design Smart City applications. Mainly, it focuses on three aspects:

- the breadth of the applications;
- the city's readiness to integrate Smart City applications; and
- the benefits that can be expected from evaluated solutions.

Breadth of Applications. The breadth of a Smart City application, provides a set of coordinates - features, to identify the list of requirements for an application category, to satisfy Smart City needs. A shared list of requirements offers a common base for developing and deploying PPI-focused Smart City applications. In this sense, each identified requirement, mapped on the CPS framework, can provide an opportunity to discover PPIs.

In order to assess the breath of applications, a list of Categories and Sub-categories (classifying the world of the applications for Smart Cities) has been identified starting from literature [16, 17]; then, overlaying it with "Aspects" and "Concerns" defined in the Framework for Cyber-Physical Systems, resulting in a set of requirements for each Sub-category. Based on this categorization, a tool is being developed, where features are used as inputs describing the kind of application to be evaluated. The tool will provide users with requirements needed to be supported by an application.

The tool has different potential users, with different needs. For example:

- Developers: identifying a list of requirements needed to develop an application.
- Urban decision makers: need to choose an application matching city requirements.
- Vendors: evaluating the breadth of applicability of their offerings.

City Readiness. After identifying the breadth of applications and their functional requirements, urban stakeholders should assess the city's readiness from various perspectives, including but not limited to, infrastructure, institutional requirements, policies, finances and stakeholder adaptability. This is somewhat orthogonal to the functional requirements identified in earlier sections.

For example, a chosen application may rely on the existence of an emergency response communications infrastructure and the existing communications between response departments such as police and fire. While many cities may have such formal infrastructures, some may be lacking them.

The readiness dimension provides such indicators analyzed for each application, offering city stakeholders an ability to determine the viability and complexity of acquiring specific applications. Analyzing readiness provides guidance to a city in road-mapping the evolution and deployment of Smart City applications.

Benefits Metrics and Business Case. Urban decision makers need to be equipped with essential frameworks, metrics, and tools to justify benefits of Smart City applications and to establish a viable business-case for practically deploying it in the city with the necessary public resources. Carefully crafted benefits metrics and business-cases are expected to bring win-win situation to all involved stakeholders - benefiting the city government, private sector enterprises and people. However, since priorities for each stakeholder group, for various applications, differ substantially, a wide set of benefits metrics and business-cases have been evaluated from global cities deploying Smart City applications:

- A significant goal for the public sector is growth in economic activity. This includes increased and better jobs in the science, technology, engineering, and mathematics fields, local Gross Domestic Product (GDP) growth, increase in exports and quality of life, decrease in the cost of serving citizens (enabling greater services), sustainability (both environmental and social), and less negative externalities.
- The private sector stands to benefit substantially from increased smart city technologies deployment. New markets and revenue potential become available. Through

innovation, new services are developed and pursued. New capabilities lead to new approaches to performing existing services yielding increased productivity.

- People living in smart communities benefit from improved service delivery and cost savings in areas such as energy and transportation. By empowering citizens through increased information about their lifestyles, greater productivity becomes a reality.

4.2 The Pivotal Points of Interoperability

The Consensus PPI working group defined a methodology for detecting PPI and is using it to evaluate four frameworks, namely oneM2M [18], FIWARE [21], US Department of Transportation's Connected Vehicle Reference Interface Architecture (CVRIA) [19], and OpenIoT [20]. This list may be expanded later.

The methodology is based on the idea of "zone of concerns". A zone of concerns is a concept related to *where sets of technologies may apply*. For example, the communications requirements (concerns) for connecting a sensor to a cellular network are different than those for connecting a cell-phone application to a cloud service provider. For a given technology suite, a determination is made by the proponent of the technology as to whether there is one or more than one "zone of concerns" for their analysis.

At a practical level, the analysis is done with a simple spreadsheet whose rows are the Aspects/Concerns from the CPS Framework. For each zone of concerns, a "tab" of the spreadsheet is created. Then the analyst, based on their own technology specifications, reviews each row for applicability. For example, does my technology address confidentiality? If the answer is yes, the analyst inserts a reference on how it applies and where it is discussed. Finally, if the solution that addresses the concern is an open standard, this standard(s) is identified. At the end of the activity, all the spreadsheets are combined revealing patterns of where technology suites have addressed similar sets of concerns, and, potentially, where the same or similar solutions were chosen.

A key benefit of this approach is the ability to compare not only standards and architectures, but also actual deployments of Smart City applications.

The result will expose candidates for PPI. The strength of consensus will be magnified by the number and reach of the solutions analyzed.

5   Conclusions and Next Steps

Interoperability is fundamental for Smart Cities and standards are a means to that end. An important issue is that if everything were standardized, innovation may be over-constrained. Thus, a trade-off between standardization and innovation must be found. The IES-City initiative takes on this challenge by focusing on the concept of Pivotal Point of Interoperability (PPI) that provides guidance for finding an agreement on standardized interfaces that enable the composition of Smart City systems without locking out innovation.

The IES-City work is still in progress, and PPI are being identified through a comparative analysis of existing architectural efforts and solutions including examples of application integration across cities, standards supporting the modular integration of functions at city scale, best practices, existing tools, and methodologies that enable users to understand and use Smart City capabilities and technologies. Once a consistent list of PPI is available, it will be submitted to the IES-City stakeholders (e.g. cities, ICT developers, Smart City project designers, etc.) to validate and further enrich it. The result will be a White Paper providing common architectural principles (PPI) and a vocabulary for Smart City technologies. Potential users include:

- organizations and consortia developing standards, to give greater coherence to their standardization activities;
- city decision makers, to choose Smart City solutions starting from common and shared principles; and
- application developers, to design and deploy solutions suitable for improving the quality of Smart City services.

References

1. IES-City Framework Library. http://www.iec.ch/whitepaper/smartcities. Accessed 2 May 2017
2. Smart City Wien - Smarter Together. https://smartcity.wien.gv.at/site/en/smarter-together-2/. Accessed 2 May 2017
3. Global City Team's Challenge Super Cluster Activity. https://www.nist.gov/el/cyber-physical-systems/smart-americaglobal-cities. Accessed 2 May 2017
4. Locke, G., Gallagher, P.D.: NIST Special Publication 1108 - NIST Framework and Roadmap for Smart Grid Interoperability Standards, Release 1.0. NIST (2010)
5. De Sabbata, P., et al.: Promoting interoperability through research, standardisation and demonstration. In: Proceedings of 6th Conference of the Italian Chapter of AIS (itAIS 2009), Olbia (2009)
6. IES-City, IoT Enabled Smart City Framework Work Programme. https://pages.nist.gov/smartcitiesarchitecture/. Accessed 2 May 2017
7. IEC, Orchestrating infrastructure for sustainable Smart Cities. White paper (2014). http://www.iec.ch/whitepaper/smartcities. Accessed 13 May 2017
8. ESPRESSO Smart City Strategic Growth Map. http://espresso.espresso-project.eu/wp-content/uploads/2017/02/Espresso-brochure-full.pdf. Accessed 2 May 2017
9. Hollands, R.G.: Will the real Smart City please stand up? In: City: Analysis of Urban Trends, Culture, Theory, Policy, Action, vol. 12, no. 3, pp. 303–320 (2008)
10. BSI Mapping Smart City Standards. https://www.bsigroup.com/LocalFiles/en-GB/smart-cities/resources/BSI-smart-cities-report-Mapping-Smart-City-Standards-UK-EN.pdf. Accessed 2 May 2017
11. Florence University, KM4CITY. http://www.km4city.org/. Accessed 5 Feb 2017
12. Aloisi, J.: Empowering and improving cities through collaboration. In: IES-City Workshop, Gaithersburg MD (2016). https://pages.nist.gov/smartcitiesarchitecture/events/kickoffworkshops/NIST_March24. Accessed 5 Feb 2017
13. FIWARE, More than 50 cities are now part of the Open & Agile Smart Cities (OASC) initiative. https://www.fiware.org/news/more-than-50-cities-are-now-part-of-the-open-agile-smart-cities-oasc-initiative. Accessed 5 Feb 2017
14. USGBC, LEED for Cities Pilot - Performance Score to LEED Certification. http://www.usgbc.org/cityperformance. Accessed 5 Feb 2017
15. NIST, CPS PWG Cyber-Physical Systems Framework Release 1.0, Technical report (2016)

16. NASSCOM, Integrated ICT and Geospatial Technologies - Framework for 100 Smart Cities Mission. Technical report (2014)
17. Correia, L.M.: Smart Cities Applications and Requirements, Net!Works European Technology Platform. White Paper (2010)
18. OneM2M. http://www.onem2m.org/. Accessed 13 May 2017
19. United States Department of Transportation Connected Vehicle Reference Implementation Architecture. https://www.standards.its.dot.gov/DevelopmentActivities/CVReference. Accessed 13 May 2017
20. OpenIoT. http://www.openiot.eu/. Accessed 13 May 2017
21. FIWARE. https://www.fiware.org/. Accessed 13 May 2017

Online Anomaly Detection on Rain Gauge Networks for Robust Alerting Services to Citizens at Risk from Flooding

Grazia Fattoruso[1]([✉]), Annalista Agresta[1], Saverio De Vito[1], Antonio Buonanno[1], Mario Molinara[2], Claudio Marocco[2], Francesco Tortorella[2], and Girolamo Di Francia[1]

[1] DTE/FSN/DIN Lab., ENEA Research Center Portici,
P.leFermi, 1, 80055 Portici, NA, Italy
grazia.fattoruso@enea.it
[2] Electromagnetism, Information Engineering
and Mathematics Department, University of Cassino and Southern Lazio,
Via G. di Biasio, 43, Cassino, Italy

Abstract. The modern cities are addressing their innovation efforts for facing not just the common stresses cities accumulate daily, but also the sudden shocks can occur such as urban floods. Networked gauge stations are instrumental to robust floods alerts though they suffer from error and fault. For capturing the anomalous behavior of networked rain gauges, the use of an online anomaly detection methodology, based on the Support Vector Regression (SVR) technique, has here been investigated and developed. The specific anomaly case of incorrectly zero sensor readings has been efficiently addressed by a centralized architecture and a prior-knowledge free approach based on SVRs that simulate the normality profile of the networked rain gauges, on the basis of the spatial-temporal correlation existing among the observed rainfall data. Real data from the pilot rain gauge network deployed in Calabria (South Italy) have been used for simulating the anomalous sensor readings. As a result, we conclude that SVR-based anomaly detection on networked rain gauges is appropriate, detecting the eventual rain gauge fault effectively during the rainfall event and by passing through increased alert states (green, yellow, orange, red).

Keywords: Anomaly detection · Support vector regression · Urban flooding · Networked rain gauges · Smart city sensor networks

1 Introduction

Over the last years, the modern cities have addressed their innovation efforts towards the smart city paradigm in order to contribute at improving citizens' quality of life. Essentially, they have tried to provide services at citizens for facing not just the common stresses cities accumulate daily, but also the sudden shocks can occur such as earthquakes, floods, fires, terrorism and so on.

Indeed, cities have always faced the natural hazards and demonstrated their resilience in the face of them. Although, currently, natural hazards pose a new challenge at

© Springer International Publishing AG 2017
O. Gervasi et al. (Eds.): ICCSA 2017, Part III, LNCS 10406, pp. 427–442, 2017.
DOI: 10.1007/978-3-319-62398-6_30

the smart cities such as boosting the cities' response to adverse natural events by providing more robust and effective monitoring, forecasting and alerting services to the communities at risk.

Among natural disasters, floods are the most serious regarding the number of people impacted and the deaths caused [1, 2]. An urban flood hazard essentially occurs because the surface runoff caused by heavy and variable rainfall, recently more frequent, cannot be relieved promptly.

Nowadays, flood emergency is faced by the control rooms with a comprehensive and robust set of decision making capabilities based on advanced technologies. In particular, warning and safety management systems are available including multi-models platforms (i.e. rainfall–runoff, flow routing and hydraulic models combined into model cascades), able to build in (near-) real time robust flood forecasting scenarios [3, 4].

Also, such systems receive mainly data in continuous by networked fixed and mobile gauge stations such as water level measurement stations, precipitation stations, and meteorological radar stations [5–7]. These data are essentially related to the water-level fluctuation and the precipitation amount and distribution. Currently, combined with conventional in situ sensing networks, the use of visual sensing based on networked cameras, distributed within the river catchments, is experimented for monitoring and analyzing the flood status and accurately measuring the water level changes in rivers [8].

Thus, in situ sensing networks distributed along the drainage systems and into surrounding areas are linked to control centers by telemetry, providing inputs into alerting procedures as well as forecasting models so that the operators can monitor the situation and give warnings against indicator or trigger rainfall and water levels.

It is evident that the environmental monitoring networks are instrumental to robust forecasting and alerting services to be provided at communities at risk of flooding. Consequently, ensuring networks security becomes a task of primary importance. Indeed, the information received at the control rooms is not always accurate, because the sensing networks are essentially prone to error and fault.

Focusing on the rain gauge networks, the observed rainfall data used for generating alerting scenarios are commonly characterized as a two-dimensional random fields taking into account the time and space variability of the rainfall process in a statistical way. An anomalous behaviour of the networked rain gauges can generate unbefitting estimated rainfall fields, impacting on the reliability of provided services. Thus, the rain gauges network behavior has to be evaluated reliable before using the collected rainfall data.

In order to detect the anomalous behavior of networks in smart city applications, several anomaly detection techniques have been applied. In particular, they are based on a centralized approach [9] (i.e. on the network status information received at the city data centers) rather than on a distributed one [10] (i.e. on sensor measurements clustered and reported to a central node for analysis).

This research work has intended to investigate and develop an on line anomaly detection methodology in rain gauges networks based on Support Vector Regression (SVR) techniques for minimizing the impact of rain gauges fault on urban flood alerting services.

The specific anomaly case of incorrectly zero sensor readings (i.e. rain gauges can record zero rainfall depths while precipitation occur) has been addressed on a pilot rain gauges network, deployed in Calabria (South Italy), according the requirements of the Local Civil Protection Authority.

The developed anomaly detection system detects the eventual rain gauge fault (i.e. incorrectly zero sensor readings) at the operators by passing through increased alert states (green, yellow, orange, red) according to fixed threshold values. A map viewer visualizes eventually faulty rain gauges by a green symbol for normal sensor behavior, orange-yellow symbols for increasing probability of sensor fault and red one for sensor fault.

Assuming the existing rain gauges network as optimal one [4, 7], once the online anomaly detection system has detected the faulty rain gauges, the performance of resulting rain gauge network can be estimated by analyzing estimation accuracy of the rain fields built on the operative gauges [7]. Also, on the basis of the residual performance estimation, an effective gauges repair and service restoration timeframe can be elaborated in order to minimize the effects on the reliability of the provided alerting services.

2 Related Work

The services provided by the smart cities are essentially based on data gathered by wireless sensor networks (WSN) and other elements of the Internet of Things [9].

In situ sensing networks, fixed or mobile, involved in the floods emergency management, essentially consist of water level and rain gauges stations. Over the last decades, these gauge stations have pervasively been deployed in river zones, enhancing the surveillance initially performed by humans as well as providing a continuous monitoring of the hydrological variables.

In order to rapidly deploy these networks, floods managers have often taken advantage of services procured from external providers. Indeed, in many cases, they have outsourced not only the implementation and deployment of the networks, but also the administration thereof. In this regard, although network service providers are contractually obliged to ensure certain levels of security, in practice, the operational rooms cannot always determine the precision and accuracy of the received data [9, 11], especially within the flood warning time. Nevertheless, ensuring observed data quality such as rainfall data is fundamental for proving robust flooding alerts.

Recent literature has proposed the use of anomaly detection algorithms, in order to facing security problems can generally affect the smart city networks. Accordingly the centralized perspective of smart city administration, these algorithms do not require access to the networked sensing nodes nor knowledge of the specific technology used. Rather, they use the only network status information received at the city data centers to determine if the behavior of the networks is reliable.

In this regard, in [9], the authors have compared different anomaly detection algorithms, among the most frequently used in the literature for this purpose [12, 13], and analyzed their behavior, taking into account the minimum quantity of network status information that they require. As a result of their study, one-class Support Vector Machines (SVMs) has resulted the most appropriate technique.

The anomaly detection techniques, more commonly used in applications related to sensing networks, fall into the scope of statistics, clustering and machine learning [12, 13]. Depending on the characteristics of the specific scenario and on the requirements of the application, some algorithms perform better than others.

Just as an example, in [14], the authors have used geostatistics and time series analysis to detect outliers in readings of meteorological sensors. They selected outlier detection based on temporal and spatial real data as the most appropriate technique (with false positive rate around 3%) in a scenario in which there exists a spatio-temporal correlation and a network dense enough.

Other authors, such as in [15], have used anomaly detection techniques based on the distance to the neighbor sensors though they require a high computational work. While classification as well as regression techniques based on SVM have proven to be effective in several contexts related to anomaly detection [9, 16–18].

As regards the regression techniques based on machine learning (SVR), they depends on the kernel parameters and the adequacy of the data sets (in particular of the training set). SVRs use the same features that are central to SVM. In SVMs, datasets are often first transformed to a higher dimensional feature space using a kernel trick. Optimization is then used to find the hyperplane that best separates datasets in this transformed feature space. The vectors that define the hyperplane are referred as support vectors. The process of finding the support vectors can be computational intensive due to the tuning required as well as the quadratic optimization that is involved. The only addition in SVR is a loss function that determines the degree of complexity and generalization provided by the regression [17].

In this work, among the main classes of SVR approaches, we have used ε-SVR one for reconstructing the normality profile of networked rain gauges and capturing the spatial-temporal correlation among them.

The sensitivity of the SVR model is greatly dependent on the value specified for ε, a parameter which determines the number of support vectors and the number of bias support vectors. In addition to ε, values for two other parameters such as a regularization constant (C) and gamma (γ), can also affect the performance of the SVR model, so that they have to selected accurately. Lastly, different types of kernel functions are available in SVM. A Radial Basis Function (RBF) has been used which can learn complex regions.

Once building SVR models for each networked rain gauge, the anomaly detection procedure has been defined evaluating, for each rain gauge, the mismatch between the real rain gauge behavior and the related SVR estimator over fixed time period. The eventual rain gauge fault is detected at the operators by passing through increased alert states (green, yellow, orange, red) according to fixed threshold values.

3   Methodology

The problem of the anomaly detection in WSN investigated within this research work is closely related to the problem of capturing networked rain gauges fault in order to minimize their impacts on flood forecasting and alerting services. Generally, rain gauges fault is detected by the operating center by: (1) missing sensor readings; (2) incorrect sensor readings and (3) anomalous peaks in sensor readings.

Focusing on the anomaly type *incorrect sensor readings,* we have intended to address the specific anomaly case of incorrectly zero sensor readings (i.e. rain gauges can record zero rainfall depths while precipitation occur), according to specific requirements of the pilot operating room.

In this context, the normal behavior of each networked rain gauge station can be defined with respect to the pattern of response of the neighboring gauge stations and past readings thereof, taking into account the spatial-temporal correlation existing among them. Therefore, according to the centralized management of urban floods hazard, previously discussed, the anomaly detection on the networked rain gauges cannot be embedded in some or all the gauges. Rather it has to be performed on the entire network from the data collection point (i.e. control room).

Thus, an anomaly detection methodology has been developed by: (1) selecting a centralized architecture for performing the anomaly detection on the entire network from the data collection point; (2) classifying the anomalies to be detected as spatial-temporal ones; (3) selecting a prior-knowledge free approach based on SVR techniques for building the normality profile of the rain gauges; (4) finally, building the anomaly detection procedure based on the event difference detected by the examined real rain gauge and the related rain estimator over fixed time period.

In the following, an approach for generating SVR models that capture the known spatial-temporal correlation among the rain gauges stations is presented. Then a strategy of using such models for anomaly detection is described

3.1 Anomaly Detection Algorithm

For developing the anomaly detection procedure, the first step has been to generate SVR models for the networked rain gauges.

For this purpose, an ε-SVR has been selected and thus the model parameters evaluated by minimizing the prediction error. Then, in addition to ε, values for the regularization constant (C) and gamma (γ), have been evaluated by a grid search method.

In particular, the SVR model, that reconstructs the normality profile of each networked rain gauge on the basis of the spatial-temporal correlation among the neighboring rain gauges stations, has been defined in Eq. 1:

$$x_j^k(t) = \sum_{m=0}^{k} x_j(t - m) \text{ for each } j = \{1 \dots n\} \tag{1}$$

where n is the number of rain gauges clustered within a same macro-basin (rain gauges cluster).

The reconstructed value will be:

$$\hat{x}_i^k(t) = f_i\left(x_j^k(t)_{j=\{1...n\},j\neq i}\right) i = \{1...n\} \tag{2}$$

where $\hat{x}_i^k(t)$ and $x_i^k(t)$ are the rain intensity values respectively reconstructed and gathered by the gauge location i at the time t, f_i is the regressor function evaluated on the rain intensity values of the other $n-1$ gauge locations over the time interval $[t, t-k]$, with k fixed.

After training the SVR model for each networked rain gauge, by defining:

$$w_i^k(t) = \left\{x_j^k(t)_{j=\{1...n\},j\neq i}\right\} \tag{3}$$

as the measurements·vector gathered by the $n-1$ rain gauges within the same macro basin, we can write the reconstructed value as:

$$\hat{x}_i^k(t) = f_i\left(w_i^k(t)\right) \tag{4}$$

Fixed a rainfall threshold σ_i, we have assumed that $\hat{x}_i^k(t) > \sigma_i$ means rainfall event is predicted.

So if rain gauge j measures a rainfall value $x_i^k(t) = 0$ while the estimator $\hat{x}_i^k(t) > \sigma_i$, the anomaly is detected.

At this point, we have defined the function:

$$pm^{M,k}(t) = \sum_{r=0}^{M-1} \left[\hat{x}_i^k(t-r) > \sigma_j\right] \cdot \left[x_i^k(t-r) > 0\right] \tag{5}$$

and the function $PM^{M,k}(t)$ has been defined on a moving window of M measurements as following:

$$PM^{M,k}(t) = \frac{pm^{M,k}(t)}{pm^{M,k}(t) + \sum_{r=0}^{M-1}\left[\hat{x}_i^k(t-r) > \sigma_j\right] \cdot \left[x_i^k(t-r) = 0\right]\left[\hat{x}_i^k(t-r) > \sigma_j \cdot close\ off\right]} \tag{6}$$

where

- $[\pi]$ is the Iverson bracket i.e. a logical proposition into a number that is 1 if the proposition is satisfied, and 0 otherwise;
- the term $\sum_{r=0}^{M-1} \left[\hat{x}_i^k(t-r) > \sigma_j\right] \cdot \left[x_i^k(t-r) > 0\right]$ calculates the number of events detected both by the real rain gauge that the related SVR estimator;
- the term $\sum_{r=0}^{M-1} \left[\hat{x}_i^k(t-r) > \sigma_j\right] \cdot \left[x_i^k(t-r) > 0\right] +$

$$\sum_{r=0}^{M-1} \left[\hat{x}_i^k(t-r) > \sigma_j\right] \cdot \left[x_i^k(t-r) = 0\right]\left[\hat{x}_i^k(t-r)close\ off\right]$$

calculates the number events detected by SVR estimator but not by the real rain gauge.

The function $PM(t)$ varies within the real interval [0,1]. In particular, $PM(t)$ is near zero (detecting an anomaly) if there is a mismatch between the real rain gauge behaviour and the related SVR estimator, while $PM(t)$ is near 1 if the real rain gauge and the related SVR estimator record rainfall.

For a more robust detection, a precision matching function $PMP(t)$ based on a moving weighted average has been defined as:

$$PMP(t) = (1 - \alpha) \cdot PM(t-1) + \alpha \cdot PM(t) \tag{7}$$

For improving the visualization of the temporal variation of the function $PMP(t)$, the following cumulative temporal function has been defined:

$$DPMP(t) = \begin{cases} DPMP(t-1)+1 & \text{if} \quad PMP(t) - PMP(t-1) < 0 \\ DPMP(t-1) & \text{if} \quad PMP(t) - PMP(t-1) = 0 \\ 0 & \text{if} \quad PMP(t) - PMP(t-1) > 0 \end{cases} \tag{8}$$

Thus, the defined anomaly detection procedure calculates the $DPMP(t)$ over a giventime period, detecting the anomaly - incorrectly zero rain sensor reading by passing through increased alert states (yellow, orange, red), according to fixed threshold values (Fig. 1).

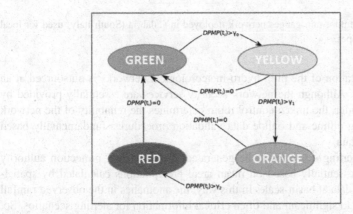

Fig. 1. State diagram that describes the behaviour of defined anomaly detection procedure. (Color figure online)

Three threshold values γ_i are defined for passing by the yellow, to orange and red alert states. At each time t, the function $DPMP(t)$ can assume value 0 and pass into graph to green state when $PMP(t) - PMP(t-1) > 0$ that means real rain gauge behaviour agrees with the related SVR estimator one.

4 Case Study

The proposed anomaly detection methodology aimed at capturing networked sensors fault has been applied to the pilot rain gauges network (Fig. 2) of the Local Civil Protection Authority, deployed in Calabria (South Italy).

Fig. 2. Map of the pilot rain gauges network deployed in Calabria (South Italy) used for local civil protection scopes.

The administration of the pilot hydro-meteorological networks is outsourced at an external provider. Although the network security services are essentially provided by the external provider, the linked control room determines the reliability of the network behavior by using offline and online data validation procedures, fundamentally based on the received data.

As regards alerting scenarios to be generated, the local civil protection authority uses procedures essentially based on mean areal precipitations calculated by spatializing *live* rainfall data at basin-scale. In this way, the anomalies in the observed rainfall data can translate to significant and often critical information for alerting scenarios. So, this makes necessary applying robust anomaly detection procedure.

The used offline and online anomaly detection procedures capture the rain gauges fault by detecting (1) missing sensor readings; (2) incorrect sensor readings; (3) anomalous peaks in sensor readings.

In this research work, the only anomaly of *incorrectly zero sensor readings* (a specific case of incorrect sensor readings anomaly) has been addressed in the pilot rain gauges network, in order to meet the pilot control room' requirements of online detecting and notifying it.

Just as an example, in the following graph (Fig. 3), an anomaly case of incorrectly zero sensor readings is showed, detected in the Nocelle Rain Gauge (Calabria) only after some days, by an offline data validation procedure. It was due to the rain gauge fault.

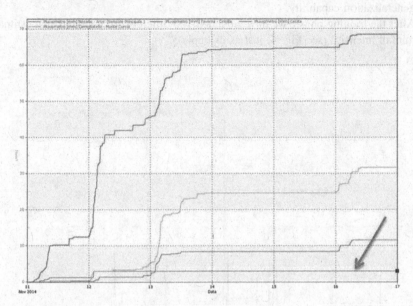

Fig. 3. Offline comparison of observed rainfall data graphs related to the Nocelle rain gauge station (grey line) and some near ones. It is evident that the slope of the grey line (rain intensity data gathered by Nocelle station) becomes flat from day 12th through day 17th against those the other near rain gauges.

Thus, the proposed anomaly detection methodology intended to support the pilot operating room for online alerts of rain gauges fault in order to make more robust the flood alerting scenarios.

4.1   Building SV Regressors

For our research objective, a SVR model has been built for each pilot rain gauge. The rainfall data gathered by these probes have constituted the input to the SVR models.

The pilot network included 100 rain gauges while the experimental dataset covered 1-year rainfall from 01/05/2013 to 31/10/2014 data at 1-min intervals (i.e. 789120 1-min rainfall events).

So, the networked rain gauges have been divided within 14 macro-basins and the rainfall data cumulated over a k-time (i.e. k = 15) period (i.e. 52608 k-length rainfall events).

The period from 01/05/2013 to 30/09/2014 has been used to train the SVR and make a complete tuning while the period from 01/10/2014 and 31/10/2014 to test the gauge fault detection system;

By using the Libsvm package [19], for building SVR models, the RBF linear kernel has been selected after different trials with linear and polynomial kernels. By an heuristic evaluation, the SVRs have been trained setting the parameters k = 15 and ε = 0,01, resulting the best tradeoff between the required measurement accuracy and the generalization capability.

After the training phase, we have obtained 100 different SVR models that estimate the rainfall intensity (see Fig. 4, just as example).

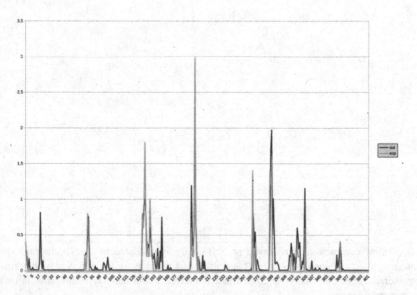

Fig. 4. Comparison between the estimated rainfall intensity (blue line) and observed rainfall intensity (red line) related to the Scilla Villagio del Pino rain gauge (detailed graph). (Color figure online)

4.2 Applying the Anomaly Detection Procedure

According to the developed anomaly detection procedure, the following parameters have been defined for the pilot rain gauge network (Table 1).

Table 1. Anomaly detection procedure parameters' values defined for the pilot rain gauge network

Parameter	Value	Description
σ_j	0.15	Rainfall threshold for detected precipitation events by the SVR estimator
M	10	Length of moving window used for positive matching function
α	0.125	Weight used for calculating $PMP(t_i)$
γ_0	60	Threshold value for passing in the yellow state
γ_1	200	Threshold value for passing in the orange state
γ_2	300	Threshold value for passing in the red state

Running the developed procedure, in operating phase, for each pilot networked rain gauge, the observed rain intensity value is compared with the estimated rain intensity value, calculated over a 15 min.

If a given rain gauge is recording a zero rain event at the time t while the related SVR estimator a non-zero rain event, the evaluation procedure starts in order to establish if a real anomaly has been detected as well as statistic data drifts.

The evaluation procedure examines over a M-long time period the mismatch between the real rain gauge behaviour and the related SVR estimator. If this state continues, the anomaly - incorrectly zero rain sensor reading - is detected and notified to the operators by passing through increased alert states (yellow, orange, red), according to the fixed threshold values $\gamma_0, \gamma_1, \gamma_2$.

By any state, the rain gauge can pass in the normal state (green colour) when its behaviour agrees with the related rain estimator.

On the basis of the developed anomaly detection procedure, an online map viewer (Fig. 5) visualizes the eventually faulty rain gauges by a green symbol for normal sensor behavior, orange - yellow symbols for increasing probably sensor fault and red one for sensor fault.

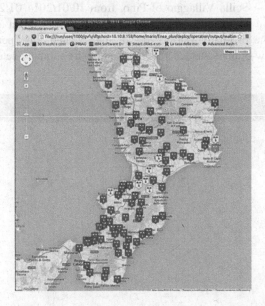

Fig. 5. Map viewer of the online anomaly detection system that notifies the control room operators of eventually faulty rain gauges (Color figure online)

5   Results

The proposed anomaly detection procedure has been tested on data collected from 10/01/2014 to 10/31/2014 by introducing artificial fault in each of the 100 pilot rain gauges.

The anomalous behavior (i.e. rain gauge fault) has been simulated by forcing the zero readings when precipitation occurs, over a fixed time period.

The global performance in terms of Confusion Matrix is reported in Table 2.

Table 2. Confusion matrix

		Predicted condition	
		FAULT	NON FAULT
True condition	FAULT	91	4
	NON FAULT	5	0

In the following, the results are illustrated for two pilot rain gauges – Scilla Villaggio of Pino and Reggio Calabria Rosario, in the case of normal sensor behavior (case 1) and in the case of presence of sensor fault (case 2), using the real rainfall measurements related to October 2014.

Case 1

The graphs in Fig. 6 shows the SVR estimator behaviour and the alert states bar related to the rain gauges – Scilla Villaggio of Pino, from 10/01/2014 01:28 to 10/31/2014 23:58, in absence of anomalous sensor readings. We can notice that any false positive is generated by the estimator during the all investigated time period neither any intermediate (yellow-orange) state alert is returned by the anomaly detection procedure.

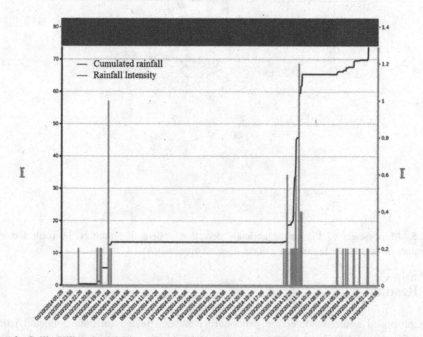

Fig. 6. Scilla Villaggio del Pino. Graph of the estimated rainfall over October 2014 and alert states bar generated by the proposed anomaly detection procedure

Similarly, regarding the Reggio Calabria Rosario station, the estimator behaviour matches the real readings during the all investigated time period.

Case 2

The graphs of the Figs. 7 and 8 show the SVR estimators behaviour and the alert states bar related to the rain gauges – Scilla Villaggio of Pino and Reggio Calabria Rosario, from 10/01/2014 00:16 to 10/06/2014 19:46. Over this period, the rain gauges are forced to zero rainfall readings, simulating an anomalous behaviour.

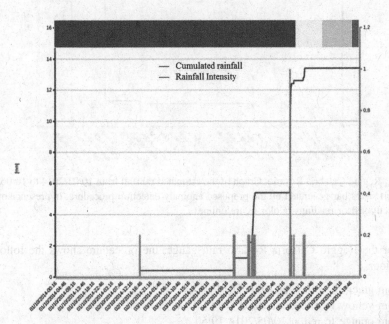

Fig. 7. Scilla Villaggio of Pino. Graph of the estimated rainfall from 10/01/2014 to 10/06/2014 and alert states bar generated by the proposed anomaly detection procedure, in presence of zero incorrectly sensor readings (Color figure online)

We can notice that, while the estimators correctly simulate the rainfall events, the anomaly detection procedure detects the mismatch between the real sensor readings and the estimated ones, passing from the warning states (yellow and orange) to notification sensor fault state (red).

For the Scilla Villaggio of Pino, the procedure shows the following behavior:

– from green to yellow at 10/05/2014 18:44
– from yellow to orange at 10/06/2014 7:59
– from orange to red at 10/06/2014 22:44

It is to be noticed that the duration of rainfall events (not consecutive) is totally 48 min and the total rainfall amount is 17,6 mm. Thus, we can conclude that if the duration of an only rainfall event is 48 min and rainfall depth is at least 17, 6 mm, the developed procedure detects the rain gauge fault during the rainfall event.

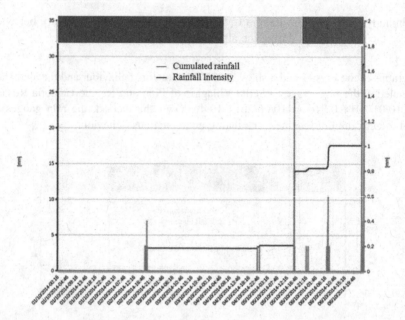

Fig. 8. Reggio Calabria Rosario. Graph of the estimated rainfall from 10/01/2014 to 10/06/2014 and alert states bar generated by the proposed anomaly detection procedure, in presence of zero incorrectly sensor readings (Color figure online)

For the Reggio Calabria Rosario rain gauge, the procedure shows the following behaviour:

- from green to yellow at 10/04/2014 06:44
- from yellow to orange at 10/04/2014 22:14
- from orange to red at 10/05/2014 19:59

Similarly, for the Reggio Calabria Rosario rain gauge, if the duration of an only rainfall event recorded by this station is 50 min and the rainfall depth is at least 12,6 mm, the developed procedure detects online the rain gauge fault, during the rainfall event.

6   Conclusion

Observed rainfall data are instrumental to robust urban flood alerting services though the networked rain gauges suffer from error and fault.

For facing network security issues, anomaly detection techniques are often applied. Some of them perform better than others, depending on the characteristics of the specific scenario and on the requirements of the application.

This research work has intended to investigate the use of computational intelligence techniques in the anomaly detection process applied to networked rain gauges. In fact, the online anomaly detection methodology, here investigates and developed, efficiently addresses the specific anomaly case of incorrectly zero sensor readings, by a centralized architecture and a prior-knowledge free approach based on SVRs that simulate the normality profile of the networked rain gauges, on the basis of the spatial-temporal correlation existing among the observed rainfall data.

Evaluating, for a given rain gauge, the mismatch between the real rain gauge behavior and the related SVR estimator over fixed time period, the eventual rain gauge fault is effectively detected during the rainfall event at the operators by passing through increased alert states (green, yellow, orange, red).

Then, the eventually faulty rain gauges are visualized into an online map viewer using a green symbol for normal sensor behavior, orange-yellow symbols for increasing probability of sensor fault and red one for sensor fault.

We believe that, in the near future, the flood managers will increasingly resort to CI-based approaches in order to provide more effective and robust urban natural risk forecasting and alerting services in a smart city context.

Acknowledgements. This research work has been funded by PON R&C 2007-2013 Smart Cities and Communities and Social Innovation/ABSIDE-AQUASYSTEM Project. The authors thanks the local Protection Civil Authority, Multi-risks Functional Center of Calabria (South Italy) that supported this research.

References

1. Webster, P.J.: Meteorology: Improve weather forecasts for the developing world. Nature **493** (7430), 17–19 (2013)
2. Borga, M., Stoffel, M., Marchi, L., Marra, F., Jakob, M.: Hydrogeomorphic response to extreme rainfall in headwater systems: flash floods and debris flows. J. Hydrol. **518**, 194–205 (2014)
3. Agresta, A., Fattoruso, G., Pollino, M., Pasanisi, F., Tebano, C., Vito, S., Francia, G.: An ontology framework for flooding forecasting. In: Murgante, B., Misra, S., Rocha, Ana Maria A.C., Torre, C., Rocha, J.G., Falcão, M.I., Taniar, D., Apduhan, Bernady O., Gervasi, O. (eds.) ICCSA 2014. LNCS, vol. 8582, pp. 417–428. Springer, Cham (2014). doi:10.1007/978-3-319-09147-1_30
4. Fattoruso, G., Agresta, A., Guarnieri, G., Lanza, B., Buonanno, A., Molinara, M., Marocco, C., De Vito, S., Tortorella, F., Di Francia, G.: Optimal sensors placement for flood forecasting modelling. Procedia Eng. **119**, 927–936 (2015)
5. Marin-Perez, R., García-Pintado, J., Gómez, A.S.: A real-time measurement system for long-life flood monitoring and warning applications. Sensors **12**(4), 4213–4236 (2012)
6. Fattoruso, G., Agresta, A., De Vito, S., Di Francia, G., Pollino, M., Pasanisi, F.: Integration of wireless sensor network and hydrologic/hydraulic ontologies for flooding forecasting. In: Compagnone, D., Baldini, F., Di Natale, C., Betta, G., Siciliano, P. (eds.) Sensors. LNEE, vol. 319, pp. 327–330. Springer, Cham (2015). doi:10.1007/978-3-319-09617-9_57
7. Fattoruso, G., Longobardi, A., Pizzuti, A., Molinara, M., Marocco, C., De Vito, S., Tortorella, F., Di Francia, G.: Evaluation and design of a rain gauge network using a statistical optimization method in a severe hydro-geological hazard prone area. In: Proceedings of International Conference on Applied Mathematics and Computer Science, Rome, Italy, 27–29 January 2017 - AIP Conference Series (2017, In press)

8. Lo, S.W., Wu, J.H., Lin, F.P., Hsu, C.H.: Visual sensing for urban flood monitoring. Sensors **15**(8), 20006–20029 (2015)
9. Garcia-Font, V., Garrigues, C., Rifà-Pous, H.: A comparative study of anomaly detection techniques for smart city wireless sensor networks. Sensors **16**(6), 868 (2016)
10. Rajasegarar, S., Leckie, C., Palaniswami M.: Distributed anomaly detection in wireless sensor networks. In: 10th IEEE Singapore International Conference on Communication Systems (2006)
11. Modares, H., Salleh, R., Moravejosharieh, A.: Overview of security issues in wireless sensor networks. In: 2011 Third International Conference on Computational Intelligence, Modelling and Simulation (CIMSiM), pp. 308–311. IEEE (2011)
12. Chandola, V., Banerjee, A., Kumar, V.: Anomaly detection: A survey. ACM Comput. Surv. (CSUR) **41**(3), 15 (2009)
13. Xie, M., Han, S., Tian, B., Parvin, S.: Anomaly detection in wireless sensor networks: A survey. J. Netw. Comput. Appl. **34**(4), 1302–1325 (2011)
14. Zhang, Y., Hamm, N.A., Meratnia, N., Stein, A., Van De Voort, M., Havinga, P.J.: Statistics-based outlier detection for wireless sensor networks. Int. J. Geogr. Inf. Sci. **26**(8), 1373–1392 (2012)
15. Liu, F., Cheng, X., Chen, D.: Insider attacker detection in wireless sensor networks. In: Proceedings of the International Conference on Computer Communications, Honolulu, HI, USA, pp. 1937–1945, 13–16 August 2007
16. Su, J., Long, Y., Qiu, X., Li, S., Liu, D.: Anomaly detection of single sensors using OCSVM_KNN. In: Wang, Yu., Xiong, H., Argamon, S., Li, X., Li, J. (eds.) BigCom 2015. LNCS, vol. 9196, pp. 217–230. Springer, Cham (2015). doi:10.1007/978-3-319-22047-5_18
17. Kromanis, R., Kripakaran, P.: Support vector regression for anomaly detection from measurement histories. Adv. Eng. Inform. **27**(4), 486–495 (2013)
18. Bernieri, A., Ferrigno, L., Laracca, M., Molinara, M.: Crack shape reconstruction in eddy current testing using machine learning systems for regression. IEEE Trans. Instrum. Meas. **57**(9), 1958–1968 (2008)
19. Chang, C., Lin, C.J.: LIBSVM: A library for support vector machines. ACM Trans. Intell. Syst. Technol. (TIST) **2**(3), 27 (2011)

Computational Intelligence for Smart Air Quality Monitors Calibration

Elena Esposito[✉], Saverio De Vito, Maria Salvato,
Grazia Fattoruso, and Girolamo Di Francia

C.R. Portici, ENEA DTE-FSN-DIN, P. Le Enrico Fermi 1, Portici, 80055 Naples, Italy
elena.esposito@enea.it

Abstract. Machine learning techniques will take an increasingly central role in the distributed sensing realm and specifically in smart cities scenarios. Pervasive air quality monitoring as one of the primary city service requires a significant effort in term of data processing for extracting the needed semantic value. In this paper, after briefly reviewing the emerging relevant literature, we compare several machine learning tools for the purpose of devising intelligent calibration components to be run on board or in cloud computing architectures for pollutant concentration estimation. Two cities field experiments provide the needed on field recorded datasets to validate the approaches. Results are discussed both in terms of performance and computational impact for the specific application.

Keywords: Machine learning · Air quality · Chemical sensor networks · Sensor fusion · Smart cities

1 Introduction

Air quality represents a major concern for citizens worldwide. Decades of medical literature have highlighted the influence of poor air quality on life quality and expectancy [1, 2]. Actually, several pathologies have been correlated with significant concentrations of different pollutants ranging from headache or acute respiratory syndromes depending on short term exposure to severe lungs diseases including asthma, COPD and, ultimately, cancer. As such, monitoring and controlling air quality is considered paramount for public health and, more generally, community economy. Air quality monitoring in cities is regulated by law in most countries. However, in the vast majority of cases, measures methodologies and techniques aims to representing a coarse grained picture of air quality condition in cities both in time and space domain by using sparse and costly, but highly accurate and precise monitoring stations [3]. The informativeness of such data in terms of personal exposure at street level density is rather limited since pollutant concentration and related exposure can vary dramatically in a few meters [4, 5]. The availability of personal exposure data as well as high spatial density information on pollutant concentration can sustain active, healthy and more conscious life styles and choices [6]. For example, one can avoid high polluted streets when planning his path through the city, this may help elderlies and children have to maintain an active lifestyle. Information about a street air quality can influence real estate market helping people to choose their

© Springer International Publishing AG 2017
O. Gervasi et al. (Eds.): ICCSA 2017, Part III, LNCS 10406, pp. 443–454, 2017.
DOI: 10.1007/978-3-319-62398-6_31

home. Ultimately, it may help local administration to implement an informed control of car traffic and design public transport strategies so to positively affect, in a measurable way, the citizen's life. In order to obtain such information, the building of a high density, intelligent measurement mesh is needed and regulatory framework are beginning to suggest the adoption of low cost microsensor based solutions. However, at the current technology state of the art, chemical sensing is affected by multiple issues including lack of specificity, low sensitivity, insufficient stability over time and limited responsiveness [7]. This severely limits their adoption for such safety critical task. Ongoing on the field measurement campaign highlights such limitations that seem to affect even newest commercial developments. On the other hand, the use sensor fusion and machine learning techniques have demonstrated to positively and significantly affect precision and accuracy in real world campaigns [8]. Several approaches have been proposed in the literature impacting on different segments of the semantic extraction chain. These may be integrated in a proposal for the design of future intelligent and pervasive air quality networks featuring a complex network of interacting fixed and mobile air quality nodes supported by sensor fusion and intelligent data analysis components operating along the data processing path in a fog computing architecture. One of the most critical steps of chemical multisensory device data processing is extracting reliable and timely concentration estimations from the chemical sensor array responses stream. In turn concentration estimations may be used to extract synthetic exposure indexes that may be easily communicated to users and general public. Data driven nonlinear multivariate calibration algorithms have been proposed for off-line to high speed, real time concentration estimation in on field operating air quality monitors including Neural Networks, Support Vector Machines, Gaussian Processes, Reservoir Computing and so on. Still, partially due to the lack of publicly available dataset, no comparison data are available. After briefly reviewing the most promising approaches and proposing an integrated architecture, this work will provide a design and performance driven comparison of these computational intelligence methods. We hope that this may prove interesting in guiding the machine learning practitioner in the choosing the most effective solution for the sought application.

2   Related Works

Last few years have seen an increase in testing activities aiming to the adoption of microsensors based air quality monitors for pervasive measurements. At the same time researchers have focused their activities in trying to overcome their limitations. A significant role has been taken by data driven approaches both in terms of single node data analysis and sensor networks data fusion. These efforts have led to development of several strategies for tackling calibration, calibration transfer, drift counteraction and sensor fusion. Calibration methodologies and algorithms aim to find an optimal functional relationship among pollutants concentrations and actual sensor responses. Multivariate calibration as opposed to univariate calibration has shown to partially solve the non-specificity issue reducing cross interferences by subtracting (explicitly or implicitly) the additive response term due to interferent pollutants or environmental conditions like temperature or humidity. This relationship usually takes into account instantaneous sensor responses; however, recent advancements have highlighted the need for harvesting information content of sensor response history. This has proven very effective in reducing sensors slow dynamic issues affecting the system responsiveness to rapid changes of pollutant concentrations that may occur in mobile or street plane monitoring applications. For this reason, we my express the calibration relationship in a more general way:

$$C_p(t) = f(r(t), r(t - T), r(t - 2T), \dots, r(t - nT)), \tag{1}$$

where Cp is the concentration of the p-th pollutant, vector $r(t)$ represents the response of the sensor array at time t, T is the sampling period, n is the length of past response samples observation window and f is the calibration function. Lab based measurements may be used to build a suitable dataset exploring the combinatorial space resulting from the interaction of multiple gases and environmental conditions in a mixture. This dataset may be used to find an optimal $C(t)$ with solutions ranging from physically rooted parametric to data driven non parametric models. The major disadvantage is the significant volume of such space that generates significant requests in term of human and machine time. Conversely, on field calibration methodology resort to sensor responses recorded in the real world scenario along with the response of high accuracy and precision analyzers providing ground truth. Both approaches suffer from representativity issues. Actually, the recorded dataset may be not representative of the actual conditions that the calibrated system will encounter in its operating life negatively affecting the performances [9]. Section 2.1 will briefly review the use of machine learning algorithms for this particular task.

Calibration transfer strategies try to solve sensor properties variability due to intrinsic repeatability limitations of the fabrication process. Due to these, the calibration law will be unique to each air quality monitoring node hence determining an unbearable increase in the total cost of production. In this framework, Direct standardization (DS) applies a signal transformation among different units in order to standardize ad correct the response of a slightly different multisensory unit. DS has been tested for application to concentration estimation problems showing capable to significantly reduce the estimation error while transferring a master calibration to a slave unit suffering baseline shifts [10]. Drift counteraction have been tackled with several approaches ranging from signal correction strategies including simple baseline correction to advanced machine learning strategies as semisupervised learning [11, 12]. None of them provided for a definitive answer to ageing and poisoning issues. Semisupervised learning and Learning in Dynamic Environments frameworks may represent a suitable choice for correcting issues due to the change in stimuli (pollutant concentrations) joint distribution imposed by seasonalities. Martinoli and coauthors proposed a rendez-vous calibration strategy in which one node may exchange its knowledge on actual pollutant concentration with another providing an example of cooperative recalibration in the network [13]. Distributed or mobile chemical multisensory networks offer an interesting research ground. Lilienthal and coauthors have produced a significant amount of insights in the fusion of chemical sensors data recorded by mobile robots in lab based or outdoor environments often resorting to Kriging-like solutions with exogenous inputs [14, 15]. Apart from source identification and localization for olfactive nuisances (see [16]), the reconstruction of a 2D map of the pollutant concentration in the city is the most interesting aspect for air quality monitoring. Recently, on field recorded air quality data by a mobile actor have been fused together by a space time averaging strategy [5]. In that work the authors discuss the actual difficulties of such endeavor in a real world scenario. Finally, as recently shown by Fishbain and Moreno, sensor fusion strategies may be used to significantly reduce the error of poorly calibrated air quality nodes [17].

2.1 Addressing Calibration with Machine Learning Components

Machine learning components provide a solidly grounded framework for obtaining multivariate regression algorithms that may be coded for real time analysis of sensor responses and pollutant concentration estimations both on board and in a cloud based solution.

Starting in 2007, De Vito et al., proposed the use of neural networks for the multivariate calibration of chemical multisensory devices for air quality monitoring applications highlighting the performance boost with respect to univariate solutions, the knowledge arising from sensor-feature selection, the performance impacts of seasonalities and ageing related drift [18]. The same group have proposed dynamic machine learning architectures for reducing slow dynamic issues for emerging mobile applications [8]. M. Gerboles and his group at JRC have confirmed these findings on extensive sets of sensors technologies and pollutants [19]. The use of dynamic SVMs in regression configuration has been analyzed by Vembu et al. [20] reporting slight advantages with respect to simple tapped delay configurations. Gaussian Processes have been introduced with the motivation of obtaining a stochastic extension completing concentration estimations with real time accuracy estimation information [21]. Recently, Reservoir computing has been tested for similar applications in lab based non controlled settings [22]. Their architecture guarantees a redundant solution with simplified design and model selection feature. According to our knowledge, matured during the cooperative efforts of the EuNetAir COST action, the discussed techniques appear as the most promising and best representative of the capabilities of machine learning techniques. Actually shallow neural networks represent an easy to implement non-parametric and iconically "black box" weighted functional model that have been extensively tested along decades. Regression SVMs represents the term of reference for most kernel based machine learning applications resorting to a selection of training instances to actual represents functional dependencies. Gaussian processes, also known as Kriging, represent a statistically grounded lazy learner intrinsically capable of stochastic prediction. Recently introduced Reservoir computing may represent a new horizon of machine learning computing in which redundant randomly connected computing units may find hidden relationships in feature-time space while simple linear architecture at their output stage may be easily trained to exploit them. The next chapters will depict the results of a comprehensive comparison encompassing both performance and design based considerations using two different datasets recorded during extensive on field deployments in real world environments.

3   Experimental Setting

3.1   Datasets Description

Two different types of datasets have been taken into account, the first has been extracted from a pervasive deployment of multisensory devices, with sampling period at 20 s and the second ones extracted from a deployment of multisensory devices located in a polluted area recording hourly averaged responses. Thereby we are able to evaluate the dynamic aspect and to compare the considered methodologies on different timeframes.

In particular, the first dataset involves an open sampling multisensory device, the SnaQ system [23]. It was developed by a partnership led by the Center for Atmospheric Sciences (CAAS) of University of Cambridge (UK) and was equipped with two different NO_2 Electrochemical (EC) sensor units (s. u.), one NO Alphasense EC sensor unit, two different O_3 Alphasense EC sensor units plus T, RH, wind speed and wind direction units. It was deployed in multiple instances within the city Centre of Cambridge as a part of a pervasive deployment. One of them was located on the roof of the Chemical Dept. together with a conventional reference station operated by CAAS. This station relied on certified chemiluminescence and spectrometer based analyzers. The sampling period of the SnaQ system was set at 20 s, while the reference station provides ground truth readings of target gases at 60 s intervals. The conventional station target gases were CO, NO, NO_2, NO_x, O_3, SO_2 and Total Oxidants gases. We considered all raw instantaneous sensors readings and compared the estimations results with the conventional analyzer samples when available (one out of three sensor readings). Baseline and temperature correction by datasheet procedure have been implemented. Eventually, five weeks of continuous measurements have been extracted by the available recordings to build a suitable dataset for our comparison effort. The second dataset (ENEA Pirelli dataset, available on line at [24]) was recorded on the field in a significantly polluted area, at road level, within an Italian city. It contains about one year (recorded from March 2004 to February 2005) of hourly averaged responses from an array of 5 MOX sensors embedded in an Air Quality Multisensor Device. The sensor devices respectively targeted CO, NMHC, NO_x, NO_2, O_3 pollutants plus T, RH and AH. A conventional fixed air pollution monitoring station, operated by regional environmental monitoring agency, provided ground truth readings during the recording campaign. It is worth to note that while the both the devices operated in continuous operation mode, the timeframe of the datasets differs considerably as well as the devices sensors technology. This diversity contributes to the generality of the obtained results.

3.2   Machine Learning Architectures

In this contribution, we consider several popular Machine Learning (ML) methodologies that were compared for their capability to learn accurate nonlinear multivariate calibration functions by data. Furthermore they are screened for their capability to provide a solution to the need of on board/on cloud implementation. The architectures here considered are: Shallow Neural Networks (NN), Support Vector Regressors (SVR), Gaussian Processes Regressors (GPR), Multiple Linear Regressors (MLR) along with their dynamic versions, obtained considering different Tapped Delay Lengths (TDL). Furthermore we provide a comparison with Reservoir Computing (RC) neural architecture, that is inherently dynamic. These methodologies have been selected for their well-known generalization properties and their promising results in chemical multisensory calibration problems. They were compared on the basis of the obtained results and their computational complexity. The first architecture considered, shallow NN, is characterized by multiple layers of information processing nonlinear functional units interacting by means of one way weighted connections. For the computation of prediction mode complexity, we will consider the number of operations needed to perform the sum of the weighted inputs of each neuron and the computation of the neurons activation function. Their computational complexity, supposing to have a single hidden layer and a single output, is $O(nk)$, where k is the number of function invocations for each hidden layer being k the number of hidden neurons in the layer and n is the dimension of input vectors space. SVR are selected for their potential enhanced performance and computational advantages. Their regression function can be computed by means of a small subset of training points called the support vectors. The SVR generalization performance (estimation accuracy) depends on a good setting of hyperparameters the kernel parameters. The problem of optimal parameter selection is further complicated by the fact that SVR model complexity (and hence its generalization performance) depend simultaneously on all the relevant parameters. The prediction complexity of kernel SVR depends on the choice of kernel and it is typically proportional to the number of support vectors. For most kernels, including polynomial and RBF, computation and storage complexity is bound by $O(n_{sv}d)$, where n_{sv} is the number of support vectors and d is the dimension of the input space. GP, a lazy learner probabilistic model, follow a nonparametric approach to regression and offers a stochastic regression function. It's completely characterized by its mean and covariance function or kernel. The computational cost is $O(kn^3)$, where k is the number of function evaluations needed for maximization and n is the number of observations. For large n, estimation of parameters or computing predictions can be very expensive. MLR here used is the standard multiple linear model, that has been trained using the Matlab function *fitlm*, in which we have selected the model containing an intercept and linear terms for each predictor. The computational cost of this algorithm depends on the size of the input matrix, in particular the matrix product $X\beta$, where X is the input features. Finally, RC approach originates from the echo state network paradigm and has been introduced in chemical multisensors field by [22]. This approach is based on a network structure that is characterized by multiple recurrently and randomly interconnected non-linear units, the so called reservoir, that perform a time-expansion of the input sequence. This expanded version of the actual input is fed to a MLR based processing layer that eventually performs the sought prediction. An interesting feature of this algorithm is that the recurrent non-linear dynamic units, more properly their weighted interconnections, are not trained; once randomly wired they will not be affected by a training procedure. On the contrary, the output linear layer is trained in a supervised fashion versus ground truth recordings. The random interconnection process is regulated by two parameters namely *input scaling*, chosen such that the input activity can induce sufficient activity in the reservoir and *spectral radius*, chosen to ensure that the resultant activity of the reservoir, when the inputs occur, is sufficiently diverse for different inputs. The computational complexity is $O(N_x^2)$, where N_x is the dimension of neuron activations function space the storage complexity being bound by the same term.

3.3 Parameters Tuning and Performances Analysis

In the first place, the selected methodologies have been compared looking at their capability to model and generalize sensors response to target gas concentration relationships. The two datasets have been partitioned in training/validation and test sets. The validation set allowed us to select the best performing hyperparameters value set and tapped delay length for each of the above mentioned machine learning methodologies. The test set, instead, has been used to evaluate the purely inductive performance. Different Training set lengths have been used so to analyze the response of the different methodologies in terms of generalization capabilities. Hyperparameters selection has been performed by brute force exploration of model hyperparameters subspaces for all architectures. The performance indicators used are Mean absolute error (MAE) defined as the sample mean of absolute prediction error and its Standard Deviation (STD). For NN, GPR and RC approaches, each training and test procedure has been repeated 30 times averaging performance indicators values, so to reduce the uncertainty in performance indicators computation induced by the random choice of booting parameters, respectively initial weights, results of kernel parameters preliminary selection and random Reservoir units wiring architecture. Best performing architectures for each ML technique, defined by their hyperparameters *tuple*, have been selected to be compared. For NN, the hyperparameters that we have considered are the number of hidden neurons (HNN) and the epochs number (EN). We have chosen HNN in [3, 5, 7, 10, 15, 20] and EN in [100, 200, 300, 400, 500, 600, 900]. The hyperparameters space selected for SVR consists of the Kernel Scale $\gamma \in (2^{-15}, 2^5)$, the Box Constraint $C \in (2^{-5}, 2^{15})$ and the half the width of Epsilon-insensitive band $\varepsilon \in (0.1{:}0.1{:}11)$. The Kernel Function was previously chosen to be the RBF. For GPR methodology, the considered hyperparameters are the initial value for the noise standard deviation of the Gaussian process model (σ) and the Kernel (Covariance) Function $\in$ ('squaredexponential', 'Matern32', 'Matern52'). Finally, for RC computing, we have considered the Spectral Radius $\rho \in (0.1{:}0.1{:}1)$, the Input Scaling IS $\in (0.1{:}0.1{:}9)$ and the Reservoir Units RU $\in$ [10, 20, 30, 50, 100, 150, 200, 250].

4   Results

All tests were performed with different training set lengths (TSL) and different observation windows lengths (TDL); the results are reported in Table 1 for the first dataset, in Table 2 for the second dataset. By looking at the results expressed in Table 1, we can observe that dynamic versions of the machine learning architectures outperform, almost every time, their static version. However, in the second setup, we can observe no consistent performance amelioration (see Table 2). We believe that this is due to the particular sampling methodology that encompasses hourly averaging of sampled data. This procedure averages out any sensor related dynamic information from the dataset. Accordingly, the use of dynamic information in the first setup, may help the calibration function to obtain more accurate and precise estimation particularly when rapid concentration transients are concerned, as suggested in [8]. We can observe that best performances, regardless of the length of the training set, are obtained, for each methodology, at a minimum observation window length of 3 (SVR, GP, MLR) or 4 min (NN). In particular, for SnaQ dataset SVR with training set length equal to 2 weeks and TDL = 3 min has provided the best overall results, i.e. MAE = 1.05 ppb with respect to MAE = 1.10 ppb obtained with NN at its best that was obtained with three weeks long training set. For ENEA Pirelli dataset, the best overall results are provided by GPR (MAE = 0.47 ppm

Table 1. Results obtained by all the selected ML methodologies for first considered dataset at different TDLs and four different training set lengths. No Tapped delay information is reported for the inherently dynamic RC methodology which performs an inner time dimension expansion. For RC, the minimum MAE obtained in the 30x execution procedure is also reported.

ML methodology	Number of samples for TRAIN-VAL-TEST	Tapped delay length				
		20 s	1 min	3 min	4 min	5 min
		MAE in ppb (STD)				
NN	1440-10080-40285	1.62 (0.08)	1.57 (0.13)	1.47 (0.11)	1.54 (0.14)	1.53 (0.14)
	10080-10080-31645	1.26 (0.05)	1.19 (0.06)	1.17 (0.04)	1.17 (0.04)	1.16 (0.04)
	20160-10080-21565	1.39 (0.04)	1.32 (0.03)	1.18 (0.03)	1.17 (0.03)	1.18 (0.02)
	30240-10080-11485	1.38 (0.04)	1.24 (0.03)	1.10 (0.02)	1.10 (0.03)	1.10 (0.03)
GPR	1440-10080-40285	3.34 (0)	2.61 (0.05)	2.25 (0.17)	2.18 (0.20)	2.19 (0.25)
	10080-10080-31645	1.55 (0.02)	1.30 (0.02)	1.20 (0.02)	1.20 (0.02)	1.22 (0.01)
	20160-10080-21565	1.40 (0.01)	1.22 (0.05)	1.10 (0.03)	1.10 (0.03)	1.10 (0.03)
	30240-10080-11485	1.33 (0.01)	1.17 (0.004)	1.06 (0.002)	1.06 (0.003)	1.06 (0.002)
SVR	1440-10080-40285	1.41	1.34	1.26	1.29	1.28
	10080-10080-31645	1.51	1.30	1.25	1.25	1.16
	20160-10080-21565	1.31	1.15	1.05	1.05	1.05
	30240-10080-11485	1.32	1.18	1.10	1.07	1.07
MLR	1440-10080-40285	1.81	1.66	1.63	1.65	1.67
	10080-10080-31645	1.62	1.47	1.40	1.40	1.40
	20160-10080-21565	1.55	1.40	1.30	1.30	1.30
	30240-10080-11485	1.58	1.48	1.39	1.38	1.38
RC	1440-10080-40285	3.02 (0.31)/2.33				
	10080-10080-31645	2.74 (0.95)/1.44				
	20160-10080-21565	1.55 (0.76)/1.16				
	30240-10080-11485	1.25 (0.03)/1.20				

at three weeks training set). Coming to relative performances of the single techniques, we can observe that in SnaQ dataset, best performance for each training set length are provided by SVR architectures 3 out of 4 times. Furthermore considering each (TSL, TDL) setting separately, a similar behavior can be observed with SVR scoring best 12 times out of 20. However performance obtained by NN and GPR are relatively similar. For the second dataset, we observe almost a tie between SVR and GPR scoring best respectively 5 and 7 times out of 12. Regarding RC models, even if outperforming MLR, it seems not able to compete on average with more classic approaches, but it should be consider the significant variance due to the random training of the reservoir connections and the short time that RC networks need to be trained. Finally MLR is always outcompeted by the presented approaches.

Table 2. Results obtained by all the selected ML methodologies for the second considered dataset at different TDLs and four different training set lengths. No Tapped delay information is reported for the inherently dynamic RC methodology which performs an inner time dimension expansion. For RC, the minimum MAE obtained in the 30x execution procedure is also reported.

ML methodology	Number of samples for TRAIN-VAL-TEST	Tapped Delay Length		
		1 h	3 h	5 h
		MAE in ppb (STD)		
NN	24-168-7482	0.90 (0.10)	0.96 (0.43)	1.22 (0.37)
	168-168-7338	0.83 (0.11)	0.86 (0.19)	0.79 (0.14)
	336-168-7170	0.71 (0.10)	0.79 (0.13)	0.69 (0.09)
	504-168-7002	0.61 (0.06)	0.76 (0.12)	0.71 (0.12)
GPR	24-168-7482	0.62 (0)	0.80 (0.02)	0.67 (0.02)
	168-168-7338	0. 95(0)	0.75 (0.09)	0.78 (0.02)
	336-168-7170	0.61 (0.05)	0.50 (0)	0.75 (0)
	504-168-7002	0.55 (0)	0.47 (0)	0.52 (0)
SVR	24-168-7482	0.67	0.92	1.17
	168-168-7338	0.56	0.69	0.53
	336-168-7170	0.50	0.54	0.56
	504-168-7002	0.64	0.53	0.54
MLR	24-168-7482	1.79	–	–
	168-168-7338	1.82	1.97	1.70
	336-168-7170	1.24	1.43	1.36
	504-168-7002	1.09	1.33	1.30
RC	24-168-7482	1.42 (0.28)/0.94		
	168-168-7338	1.37 (0.21)/1.09		
	336-168-7170	1.17 (0.25)/0.88		
	504-168-7002	0.96 (0.14)/0.79		

5   Conclusions and Discussion

In the previous paragraph of this work, we have provided the results of a performance based comparison among the most promising machine learning architectures for the calibration of microsensor based air pollution monitoring systems. In order to choose the right architecture for on board or in-cloud raw sensor data processing, computational aspects should be considered. Actually, by considering a tradeoff between performance and computational and storage complexity, Neural networks emerge as a possible solution. Its compact and efficient knowledge representation may result decisive for its selection. In facts even if outcompeted by SVR solutions in several of the presented settings, its model design time fixed complexity permits a much more rapid execution with respect to SVR solutions that are bound to the number of selected support vectors. In our scenario, the number of selected support vectors of the winning solution never went under 80% of the training set sample dimension, which overcome the slight performance advantage. GPR, at least in its original formulation, is hindered by its lazy learner nature. Like SVRs it can be considered an interesting choice when the size of the training set is limited. RC, instead, provides a redundant time expansion that does not allow for an efficient knowledge representation. On the other hand, its design is simplified by its inherently dynamic structure that allows skipping the observation window optimization task whenever it is needed i.e. when rapid response is concerned like in mobile deployments.

Summarizing, our results shows that nonlinear approaches consistently outperform multivariate linear regression. Furthermore, whenever information on sensors dynamic can be extracted and exploited in the dataset, dynamic machine learning systems outperform static approaches by providing faster responses to rapid concentration changes. The latter are expected to be common in mobile and pervasive deployments where devices may encounter or being exposed temporarily to moving gas plumes. SVR approach seem to steadily but slightly outcompete the other compared architectures including shallow neural networks that however, due to their powerful and efficient knowledge representation, still represent a suitable solution for the desired task.

References

1. Pope, C.A., Ezzati, M., Dockery, D.W.: Fine-particulate air pollution and life expectancy in the United States. N. Engl. J. Med. **360**(4), 376–386 (2009)
2. Setton, E., Marshall, J.D., Brauer, M., Lundquist, K.R., Hystad, P., Keller, P., Cloutier-Fisher, D.: The impact of daily mobility on exposure to traffic-related air pollution and health effect estimates. J. Expo. Sci. Environ. Epidemiol. **21**(1), 42–48 (2011)
3. Ambient air quality and cleaner air for Europe 2008/50/EC Directive. http://eurx.europa.eu/LexUriServ/LexUriServ.do?uri=OJ:L:2008:152:0001:0044:en:PDF
4. Vardoulakis, S., Fisher, B.E.A., Pericleous, K., Gonzalez-Flesca, N.: Modelling air quality in street canyons: a review. Atmos. Environ. **37**(2), 155–182 (2003). Elsevier
5. Van den Bossche, J., Theunis, J., Elen, B., Peters, J., Botteldooren, D., De Baets, B.: Opportunistic mobile air pollution monitoring: a case study with city wardens in Antwerp. Atmos. Environ. **141**, 408–421 (2016). doi:10.1016/j.atmosenv.2016. ISSN 1352-2310

6. de Nazelle, A., Fruin, S., Westerdahl, D., Martinez, D., Ripoll, A., Kubesch, N., Nieuwenhuijsen, M.: A travel mode comparison of commuters' exposures to air pollutants in Barcelona. Atmos. Environ. **59**, 151–159 (2012). doi:10.1016/j.atmosenv.2012.05.013. ISSN 1352-2310

7. Borrego, C., et al.: Assessment of air quality microsensors versus reference methods: the EuNetAir joint exercise. Atmos. Environ. **147**, 246–263 (2016). doi:10.1016/j.atmosenv. 2016.09.050. ISSN 1352-2310

8. Esposito, E., De Vito, S., Salvato, M., Bright, V., Jones, R.L., Popoola, O.: Dynamic neural network architectures for on field stochastic calibration of indicative low cost air quality sensing systems. Sens. Actuators B Chem. **231**, 701–713 (2016). doi:10.1016/j.snb. 2016.03.038. ISSN 0925-4005

9. Castell, N., Dauge, F.R., Schneider, P., Vogt, M., Lerner, U., Fishbain, B., Broday, D., Bartonova, A.: Can commercial low-cost sensor platforms contribute to air quality monitoring and exposure estimates? Environ. Int. **99**, 293–302 (2017). doi:10.1016/j.envint.2016.12.007

10. Fonollosa, J., Fernández, L., Gutiérrez-Gálvez, A., Huerta, R., Marco, S.: Calibration transfer and drift counteraction in chemical sensor arrays using direct standardization. Sens. Actuators B Chem. **236**, 1044–1053 (2016). ISSN 0925-4005

11. Marco, S., Gutierrez-Galvez, A.: Signal and data processing for machine olfaction and chemical sensing: a review. IEEE Sens. J. **12**(11), 3189–3214 (2012)

12. De Vito, S., Fattoruso, G., Pardo, M., Tortorella, F., Di Francia, G.: Semi-supervised learning techniques in artificial olfaction: a novel approach to classification problems and drift counteraction. IEEE Sens. J. **12**(11), 3215–3224 (2012)

13. Arfire, A., Marjovi, A., Martinoli, A.: Model-based rendezvous calibration of mobile sensor networks for monitoring air quality. In: IEEE Sensors 2015, Busan, pp. 1–4 (2015)

14. Lilienthal, A., Duckett, T.: Building gas concentration gridmaps with a mobile robot. Robot. Auton. Syst. **48**(1), 3–16 (2004). doi:10.1016/j.robot.2004.05.002. ISSN 0921-8890

15. Lilienthal, A.J., Reggente, M., Trincavelli, M., Blanco, J.L., Gonzalez, J.: A statistical approach to gas distribution modelling with mobile robots - the Kernel DM+V algorithm. In: 2009 IEEE/RSJ International Conference on Intelligent Robots and Systems, St. Louis, MO, pp. 570–576 (2009)

16. Capelli, L., Sironi, S., Del Rosso, R.: Electronic noses for environmental monitoring applications. Sensors **14**(11), 19979–20007 (2014). Basel, Switzerland. PMC. Web. 20 Mar 2017

17. Fishbain, B., Moreno-Centeno, E.: Self-calibrated wireless distributed environmental sensory networks. Sci. Rep. **6**, Article number: 24382

18. De Vito, S., Piga, M., Martinotto, L., Di Francia, G.: CO, NO_2 and NO_x urban pollution monitoring with on-field calibrated electronic nose by automatic bayesian regularization. Sens. Actuators B Chem. **143**(1), 182–191 (2009). doi:10.1016/j.snb.2009.08.041. ISSN 0925-4005

19. Spinelle, L., Gerboles, M., Villani, M.G., Aleixandre, M., Bonavitacola, F.: Field calibration of a cluster of low-cost commercially available sensors for air quality monitoring. Part B: NO, CO and CO_2. Sens. Actuators B Chem. **238**, 706–715 (2017). doi:10.1016/j.snb. 2016.07.036. ISSN 0925-4005

20. Vembu, S., Vergara, A., Muezzinoglu, M.K., Huerta, R.: On time series features and kernels for machine olfaction. Sens. Actuators B Chem. **174**, 535–546 (2012). doi:10.1016/j.snb. 2012.06.070. ISSN 0925-4005

21. Monroy, J.G., Lilienthal, A., Blanco, J.L., González-Jimenez, J., Trincavelli, M.: Calibration of MOX gas sensors in open sampling systems based on Gaussian processes. In: 2012 IEEE Sensors, Taipei, pp. 1–4 (2012)

22. Fonollosa, J., Sheik, S., Huerta, R., Marco, S.: Reservoir computing compensates slow response of chemosensor arrays exposed to fast varying gas concentrations in continuous monitoring. Sens. Actuators B Chem. **215**, 618–629 (2015). doi:10.1016/j.snb.2015.03.028. ISSN 0925-4005
23. Mead, M.I., et al.: The use of electrochemical sensors for monitoring urban air quality in low-cost, high-density networks. Atmos. Environ. **70**, 186–203 (2013)
24. https://archive.ics.uci.edu/ml/datasets/Air+Quality

Smart Stormwater Management
in Urban Areas by Roofs Greening

Mirka Mobilia(✉) and Antonia Longobardi

University of Salerno, Fisciano, Italy
mmobilia@unisa.it

Abstract. By 2050 the world population will grow to about 9 billion contributing to deep changes in urban areas structure. This would increase the effect of water deficiency and along with projected climate changes the impact of urban floodings, urban heat islands or drought. Smart cities could be key part of the solution contributing to improve the quality life of citizen in urban areas with the adoption of smart, intelligent technologies and infrastructure for energy, water, mobility, buildings, and government. The concept of smart water refers to the ability to provide and manage this primary resource in quantitative and qualitative terms in order to satisfy the future needs of population. The green roof (GR) is a technique belonging to the sectors of smart energy and smart water. It could provide several benefits: sound and thermal insulation of the buildings, mitigation of the urban heat island effects, reduction of air pollution, additionally, GR induces important hydraulic advantages acting as an effective tool for reducing flood risk in urban area with runoff reduction, attenuation and delay of the peak flow. In this paper, the retention capacity of two green roof test beds located in the campus of University of Salerno has been investigated. The analysis has referred to measures of runoff and rainfall conducted in 2017 during the months of February and March. The two roofs substantially differ in the composition of the water storage layer made up of expanded clay in GR1 and of commercial drainage panels in GR2. The retention capacity of the two test beds has been compared. The results confirm that both green roofs, although to a different extent, are effective for the reduction of total runoff volume of rainwater falling on their area.

Keywords: Smart city · Smart water · Green roofs · Retention capacity · Mediterranean climate

1 Introduction

The percentage of people living in urban areas [1] in the world has grown fast from 10% in 1950 to 54% in 2014 and it is expected to further increase by 2050, reaching a peak of 66%. This rapid increase could address in the future, along with the climate change, huge implications on the quality of life of citizens including water deficiency, urban floodings, urban heat islands or drought [2]. Because of a stringent need to react to the changing situations, in the last decades the new concept of smart city has emerged in the scientific literature [3–6]. Several definitions of smart city have been proposed in time [7–9]. The Department for Business, Innovation and Skills [10] defines the smart

© Springer International Publishing AG 2017
O. Gervasi et al. (Eds.): ICCSA 2017, Part III, LNCS 10406, pp. 455–463, 2017.
DOI: 10.1007/978-3-319-62398-6_32

city as process, or as a series of steps to improve the livability and resilience of the citizens to new conditions while The European Commission's [11] defines the smart city as a series of sustainable integrated solutions to make more sustainable urban life. Regardless the different definitions, the smart city is seen as an advanced kind of city overcoming the challenges of urbanization in order to improve the quality of life in cities using smart solutions [12]. The proposed solutions need to be brainy, integrated, cost and resource-efficient and they should positively affect the environmental and financial sustainability and the human health [13]. Smart cities include six categories required to work jointly in order to reach the common purpose of improving the quality of life for the citizens. These categories are smart energy, smart mobility, smart water, smart public services and smart integration. The concept of smart water refers to water and wastewater infrastructures that allow to effectively manage this irreplaceable resource since the growth of population leads to a larger water consumption [14]. The green roof (GR) technique is regarded as a potential adaptive measure belonging to the sectors of smart energy and smart water because it could provide several benefits contributing to the public welfare [15, 16]. This technique creates an attractive roof for the occupants, furthermore it supplies to the building a natural look and reduces the visual impact caused normally by a conventional grey roof and finally it promotes the establishment of animals ecosystems. A green roof could act as a sound insulation barrier reducing the transmission of noise inside the building [17]. GRs also provide a thermal insulation during winters and summers, with a consequent reduction of the energy consumption and of the heating and cooling costs [18]. The green infrastructures give significant contribution to mitigate urban heat island effects. [19]. In addition, the plants of a green roof can behave like a filter for the urban air, trapping particulate matter [20]. Additionally, green roofs induces also important hydraulic advantages acting as an effective tool for reducing flood risk and the frequency of occurrences of this kind of multiple damaging hydrological phenomena in urban area [15] that in the last decades has significantly increased [21]. In particular the hydraulic benefits of a green cover are: runoff reduction [22, 23], attenuation and delay of the peak flow [24, 25]. In order to investigate and quantify the hydrological benefits resulting from an extensive green roof in a Mediterranean area, two green roof test beds (GR1, GR2) have been located in the campus of University of Salerno. The two green roofs have a surface of 2.5 m^2 and the vegetation layer consists of succulents native to the temperate climate. The analysis has focused on the retention capacity of the eco roofs and not on the detention effect (temporal delay) and have referred to measures of runoff and rainfall conducted in 2017 during the months of February and March. The precipitation has been recorded using a tipping bucket type raingauge with a 5-minutes time step while the weight of the tanks storing the runoff from the roofs is daily measured using a high accuracy scale. Because the retention capacity of the benches is strongly influenced by the rainfall event characteristics, the duration, depth and intensity of each storm event having caused the runoff response, has been investigated. The two roofs substantially differ in the composition of the water storage layer because in GR1, it is made up of expanded clay while GR2 one replicated a commercial roof using drainage panel. In this work, the relationship between the retention capacity of the storage systems and the characteristics of the triggering events has been analyzed as well as the comparison of the hydrological performances of the two types of test bed. The results confirm that both green roofs, although to a different extent, are effective for the reduction of total runoff volume of rainwater falling on their area and the efficiency varies with the type of phenomena.

2 The Experimental Site

In January 2007 two green roof test beds were installed at the laboratory of hydraulic, Department of Civil Engineering of University of Salerno (40.770425, 14.789427 altitude of 282 m). Unisa is located in Fisciano, (Southern Italy) and it is featured by a Mediterranean climate with warm or hot, dry summers and mild or cool, wet winters. Average monthly precipitation is about 821 mm/year [26], the drier month is July with 25 mm and the wetter is November with 120 mm while the average annual temperature is 14.8 °C with maximum value of 23.0 °C during August and minimum value of 7.6 °C during January. The two experimental roofs are of extensive type with short-stemmed plants. They differ for the drainage layer setting. They are placed on bench of stainless steel with a surface of 2.5 m2 (1 × 2.5 m) and a double pitch slope of 1%. All over the walls of the bed, three lines of holes at the height of 0, 2.5 and 5 cm from the bottom of the table, have been planned to drain rainwater to the outlet. The holes have a diameter of 1 cm and they are 8 cm away from each other.

From the holes, runoff flows in underlying 8 cm wide open channels set up all around the perimeter of the bench. The open channels are equipped with L-section top lids fixed by metallic clamps and removable for periodic inspection. From the channel the flow is collected into a circular outlet section with a diameter of 10 cm. From this section, a pipe channels runoff into a tank. The tank is manually emptied through a water tap every time the maximum capacity of 50 L is reached. The tank weight is continuously monitored to measure the stored water and quantify the amount of runoff during storm events. The two green roofs include three layers: the vegetation layer made up of succulent plants typical of Mediterranean climate (Mesembryanthemum), 10 cm deep support substrate with peat and zeolite and total porosity of 94%, finally the water storage layer with a depth of 5 cm. A Non-woven filter mat is interposed between the substrate and the storage layer. For one of the test bed (GR1), the drainage layer is made up of expanded clay with diameters from 8 to 20 mm and it ensures a reserve of 32 L/m2. For the second installation (GR2), the drainage layer is made up of a commercial drainage panel MODì filled with expanded clay (Fig. 2). Each panel of 58 × 58 cm is supplied in 13 trays filled with clay acting as water reservoirs and providing, empty, according to the manufacturer's specification, a reserve of 14 L/m2. The site is fully and continuously (5 min resolution) monitored with a meteorological station including a tipping bucket type raingauge for rain with the minimum recordable depth of 0.25 mm rainfall, a thermohygrometer for air humidity and temperature, a pyranometer for solar radiation, 4 soil moisture sensors, 2 for each test bed located upstream and downstream at a distance of 10 cm from the shorted sides. The configuration of the experimental site is shown in Fig. 1.

Fig. 1. Green roofs Experimental site in Salerno

Fig. 2. Drainage layer with clay and commercial panel filled with clay

3   Preliminary Analysis

The monitoring campaign has started on 16th February 2017. Since then 5 rainfall and runoff events have been recorded. These events have been analyzed (Table 1) and the following characteristics have been investigated for each storm: rain peak intensity with duration of 5 min, cumulative rainfall depth, duration. Duration reaches a maximum value of 1080 min and a minimum value of 105 min, rainfall values range between 1.8 mm and 67 mm while maximum intensity ranges from 7.2 to 100.6 mm/h.

Table 1. Recorded rainfall events characteristics

Event		Duration	Cumulative rainfall	Maximum intensity (duration 5 min)
From	To	min	mm	mm/h
18/02/2017 00:00	19/02/2017 00:00	180	5,8	7,2
25/02/2017 00:00	26/02/2017 00:00	535	5,8	9,6
01/03/2017 00:00	02/03/2017 00:00	105	1,8	7,2
06/03/2017 19:00	07/03/2017 09:00	790	67,1	100,6
07/03/2017 14:00	08/03/2017 09:00	1080	30,5	15,2

For each test bed and recorded event, the hydrological performance in term of retention capacity "R" have been derived. The retention capacity is given by:

$$R = 1 - C^* \tag{1}$$

where C* is the coefficient of discharge regarded as the ratio between runoff depth stored in the tank and rainfall depth fallen on the experimental bed (Table 2).

Table 2. Retention capacity of GR1 and GR2.

Event		Retention capacity (%)	
From	To	GR1	GR2
18/02/2017	19/02/2017	50,1	40,2
25/02/2017	26/02/2017	47,8	34,1
01/03/2017	02/03/2017	56,8	56,2
06/03/2017	07/03/2017	62,4	63,0
07/03/2017	08/03/2017	58,5	47,3
Mean (%)		55,1	48,2

The results underline that, overall, the best performances can be achieved by the GR1 installation showing a mean value of R of about 55% against 48.2% of GR2. With regard to the single rainfall events, GR1 returns higher values of the retention capacity than GR2, except during the event between 6th and 7th of March for which GR1 and GR2 are characterized by the same percentage of retention capacity of about 63%. This relevant rainfall event represents the largest peak intensity event among the monitored. The rainfall intensity probably affects the GR performances. The same analysis shows that the larger the duration of the event, the larger the retention capacity of the roofs. During long and low-intensity events, a large amount of rainwater infiltrates into ground because the rainfall intensity is lower than the infiltration capacity of the vegetation support layer (Fig. 3). For the same reasons, comparing the performances to the cumulative rainfall depth (Fig. 4), it can be deduced that the events featured by a substantial volume of rain falling in a long time but with a low intensity, lead to higher percentage of retention as long as the cumulated precipitation is lower or equals the storage capacity of the drainage layer. For GR1 the reserve is 32 L/m^2 while for GR2 it is 14 L/m^2 respectively corresponding to 32 mm and 14 mm of storable rainwater. These values underline how the cumulative rainfall depth exceeds the storage capacity of GR1 only during the event starting on 6th of March and during the events of 6th and 7th of March for GR2. The retention capacity in relation to the intensity (Fig. 5) of the event shows how, apparently, the retention increases with increasing intensity but actually the data are not enough for this statement because the trend of the interpolation line is strongly driven by a single event with high intensity, while all other the events with lower intensity are concentrated in a different region for rainfall intensity. In general, GR2 returns lower performances than GR1 and in addition, GR2 is, compared to GR1, largely affected by the rain variability and its characteristics in fact the percentage of retention for GR2 varies from 34.1% to 63% while for GR1 from 47.8% to 62.4% with a range of variation respectively of 28.9% and 14.7%.

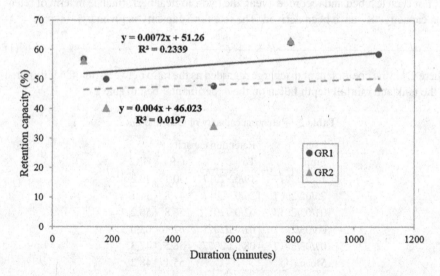

Fig. 3. Retention capacity of two green roofs vs duration of storm events

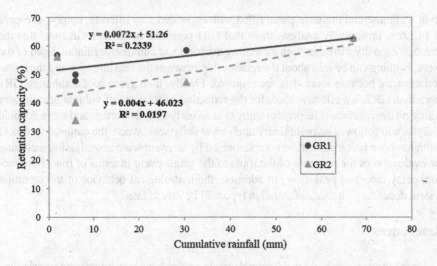

Fig. 4. Retention capacity of two green roofs vs cumulative rainfall depth

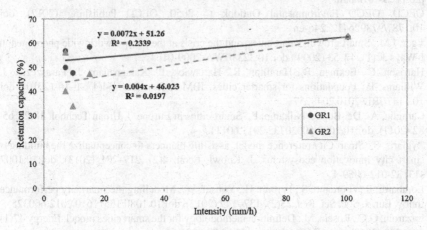

Fig. 5. Retention capacity of two green roofs vs intensity of the storm events

4   Conclusions

Smart cities include several technologies able to face the problems derived by the overcrowding of urban areas among these, green infrastructure are accounted for.

In this work the hydrological performances, in terms of retention capacity, of two extensive green roof test beds, have been investigated in order to quantify the effectiveness of this technique in a Mediterranean area. The two benches are located in the campus of University of Salerno and the monitoring campaign of rainfall and runoff started on February 2017. The two roofs substantially differ in the composition of the water storage layer and consequently in its storage capacity. The drainage layer of GR1 is made up of expanded clay providing a reserve of 32 L/m^2 while the drainage layer of GR2 is made up of a commercial drainage panel filled with expanded clay offering, empty, a reserve of 14 L/m². Preliminary analysis show that GR1 performs better than GR2 and that the retention capacity increases with increasing duration and cumulative rainfall depth of the event. Nothing can be said about the relationship between the rain intensity and the retention capacity because more data are required. Finally, both green roofs, although GR1 more than GR2, are effective tools for the reduction of total runoff volume of rainwater falling on their surface. The present study is at an early stage so further and more detailed analysis will follow. The preliminary analysis at daily scale where the cumulative runoff depth has been recorded, will be complemented by an event scale investigation including the evaluation of the response of the roofs to the single event in terms of runoff production, delay time and peak flow. In addition, the hydrological behavior of the retention system depending on the configuration type will be investigated.

References

1. United Nations. http://www.un.org/en/development/desa/news/population/world-urbanization-prospects-2014.html
2. OECD: OECD Environmental Outlook to 2050. OECD Publishing (2012). doi: 10.1787/9789264122246-en
3. Eger, J.M.: Smart growth, smart cities, and the crisis at the pump a worldwide phenomenon. I-Ways 32(1), 47–53 (2009). doi:10.3233/IWA-2009-0164
4. Harrison, C., Eckman, B., Hamilton, R., Hartswick, P., Kalagnanam, J., Paraszczak, J., Williams, P.: Foundations for smarter cities. IBM J. Res. Dev. 54(4), 1–16 (2010). doi: 10.1147/JRD.2010.2048257
5. Caragliu, A., Del Bo, C., Nijkamp, P.: Smart cities in Europe. J. Urban Technol. 18(2), 65–82 (2011). doi:10.1080/10630732.2011.601117
6. Zygiaris, S.: Smart City reference model: assisting planners to conceptualize the building of smart city innovation ecosystems. J. Knowl. Econ. 4(2), 217–231 (2013). doi:10.1007/s13132-012-0089-4
7. Lombardi, P., Giordano, S., Farouh, H., Yousef, W.: Modelling the smart city performance. Innov. Eur. J. Soc. Sci. Res. 25(2), 137–149 (2012). doi:10.1080/13511610.2012.660325
8. Lazaroiu, G.C., Roscia, M.: Definition methodology for the smart cities model. Energy 47(1), 326–332 (2012). doi:10.1016/j.energy.2012.09.028
9. Marsal-Llacuna, M.L., Colomer-Llinas, J., Melendez-Frigola, J.: Lessons in urban monitoring taken from sustainable and livable cities to better address the Smart Cities initiative. Technol. Forecast. Soc. Change 90, 611–622 (2014)
10. Department for Business, Innovation and Skills: SMART CITIES: Background paper. London, UK (2013)
11. European Commission, Smart Cities and Communities: The European
12. Innovation Partnership on Smart Cities and Communities. http://ec.europa.eu/eip/smartcities/
13. Guan, L.: Smart steps to a battery city. Gov. News 32(2), 24–27 (2012)
14. Ahvenniemi, H., Huovila, A., Pinto-Seppä, I., Airaksinen, M.: What are the differences between sustainable and smart cities? Cities 60, 234–245 (2017). doi:10.1016/j.cities.2016.09.009
15. Waterworld. http://www.waterworld.com/articles/print/volume-29/issue-12/water-utility-management/smart-water-a-key-building-block-of-the-smart-city-of-the-future.html

16. Macháč, J., Louda, J., Dubová, L.: Green and blue infrastructure: an opportunity for smart cities? In: Smart Cities Symposium Prague (SCSP), pp 1–6. IEEE Press (2016). doi:10.1109/SCSP.2016.7501030

17. Meng, T., Hsu, D., Wadzuk, B.: Green stormwater infrastructure use and perception on related smart services: the case of Pennsylvania. World Environmental and Water Resources Congress 2016 (2016)

18. Yang, H.S., Kang, J., Choi, M.S.: Acoustic effects of green roof systems on a low-profiled structure at street level. Build. Environ. **50**, 44–55 (2012). doi:10.1016/j.buildenv.2011.10.004

19. Niachou, A., Papakonstantinou, K., Santamouris, M., Tsangrassoulis, A., Mihalakakou, G.: Analysis of the green roof thermal properties and investigation of its energy performance. Ener. Build. **33**(7), 719–729 (2001). doi:10.1016/S0378-7788(01)00062-7

20. Susca, T., Gaffin, S.R., Dell'Osso, G.R.: Positive effects of vegetation: Urban heat island and green roofs. Environ. Pollut. **159**(8), 2119–2126 (2011). doi:10.1016/j.envpol.2011.03.007

21. Longobardi, A., Nazzareno, D., Mobilia, M.: Historical storminess and hydro-geological hazard temporal evolution in the solofrana river basin—southern Italy. Water **8**(9), 398 (2016). doi:10.3390/w8090398

22. Mobilia, M., Longobardi, A., Sartor, J.: Green roofs hydrological performance under different climate conditions. WSEAS Trans. Environ. Dev. **11**, 264–271 (2015)

23. Mobilia, M., Longobardi, A., Joachim, F.S.: Including a-priori assessment of actual evapotranspiration for green roof daily scale hydrological modelling. Water **9**(2), 72 (2017). doi:10.3390/w9020072

24. Burszta-Adamiak, E.: Analysis of the retention capacity of green roofs. J. Water Land Dev. **16**(1), 3–9 (2012). doi:10.2478/v10025-012-0018-8

25. Trinh, D.H., Chui, T.F.M.: Assessing the hydrologic restoration of an urbanized area via an integrated distributed hydrological model. Hydrol. Earth Syst. Sci. **17**, 4789–4801 (2013). doi:10.5194/hess-17-4789-2013

26. CLIMATE-DATA.ORG. https://it.climate-data.org/location/14223/

Workshop on Econometrics and Multidimensional Evaluation in the Urban Environment (EMEUE 2017)

Genetic Algorithms for Real Estate Market Analysis

Vincenzo Del Giudice[1], Pierfrancesco De Paola[1(✉)], and Fabiana Forte[2]

[1] University of Naples Federico II, Piazzale Vincenzo Tecchio, 80125 Naples, Italy
{vincenzo.delgiudice,pierfrancesco.depaola}@unina.it
[2] University of Campania Luigi Vanvitelli, Via San Lorenzo, 81031 Aversa, Italy
fabiana.forte@unicampania.it

Abstract. This work use Genetic Algorithms (GA) in order to interpret the existing relationship between real estate rental prices and geographic location of housing units for a central urban area of Naples. The choose of algorithm parameters are discussed on the basis of a real estate sample located in Santa Lucia and Chiaia neighborhoods. Main aim of this paper is verify the reliability of GA for real estate appraisals purposes and, at the same time, to show the potentiality but also the limits of GA in this field in terms of analysis of the housing markets.

Keywords: Genetic algorithms · Geoadditive models · Hedonic price models · Housing market · Real estate appraisals

1 Introduction

The real estate sector requests accurate appraisals for property values, this is because various stakeholders pursue several objectives as keep under control real estate values or update their profitability returns [1]. For these reasons, the interpretation of housing market becomes a critical issue together to its evolution and dynamism, and at the same time appropriate techniques in able to analyze adequately the characteristics of real estate market are strongly needed [2].

Land and building are the two main components that are involved in the building production process. They are economic factors that are distinguishable even when the urban and building transformation process are completed. The scarcity of buildings in an urban area is then closely related to the available lands for constructions. This is a technical constraint that mainly depends by the geographical location of lands and by the urban planning policies, the latter are aspects that cannot be overcome by intrinsic factors of real estate market.

Urban land is a limited factor, however it has an unlimited duration over the time. Due to these its features, the urban lands are subject to a specific and intrinsic income. In fact, geographical location shapes the real estate markets and makes them sensitive to economic and social variations. Therefore, if nature of each urban land is unique, however this uniqueness strongly conditions the value and usefulness of the same urban land.

© Springer International Publishing AG 2017
O. Gervasi et al. (Eds.): ICCSA 2017, Part III, LNCS 10406, pp. 467–477, 2017.
DOI: 10.1007/978-3-319-62398-6_33

Said this, any real estate market analysis cannot be treated without a necessary identification of sub-markets, or areas where are homogeneous the mechanisms of price formation and the factors that affect real estate demands and supplies [3–19].

There is no doubt that more accurate is the analysis of real estate market if it's performed for each single submarket. For to identify homogeneous real estate submarkets in an urban area a key parameter is geographical location.

In this paper, Genetic Algorithms were implemented with the aim to identify the effect on real estate rental values deriving by geographical location of housing units. The analysis is carried out through the elaboration of rental prices of housing units located in a central urban area of Naples (Santa Lucia and Chiaia neighborhoods).

2   A Brief Literature History

In the last years, problems concerning real estate market analysis has grown up very fast, as this knowledge is very relevant for real estate predictions, investments, and taxation issues.

The most relevant difficulty in the forecast of real estate prices has always been the subjectivity of judgments to be processed for to obtain reliable real estate values [20]. For this reason, Multiple Regression Analysis (MRA) has been considered for long time as the most flexible technique able to provide reliable predictions and information on real estate values and market analysis. As possible alternative, mostly in economic or financial fields, Artificial Neural Networks (ANNs) have been experimented by researchers for forecasting purposes [21–27].

In literature, however, the comparison between MRA and ANNs often presents controversial aspects and not clearly shows the superiority of one or the other method [28–31].

As alternative to above approaches Genetic Algorithms have been experimented over the time.

GA are stochastic search techniques that may explore wide and complex spaces based on Charles Darwin's evolutionary principle [32–35]. Multi-parameter optimization problems, characterized by objective functions subject to constraints, are the main operating areas suitable for GA. Initialization, Selection, Crossover and Mutation are the four stages in which the search process is developed by GA [36].

The history of GA began with the first computer simulations on evolution, the latter began to spread in the 1950 s. In the 1960 s, Rechenberg [37] introduced the "evolutionary strategy", and the topic was further expanded by Schwefel [38]. Instead, Fogel, Owen and Walsh [39] developed the "evolutionary programming", or a particular technique whose possible solutions were finite state machines. During those years, other experiences were carried on automatic learning and algorithms inspired to evolution and genetic [40].

However, only with Holland [33], and after with Goldberg [32], GA have had a wide spreading in many scientific fields, mainly thank to the improvement of power of computational machines, making possible a constantly wider practical application of those methods.

Holland's original idea, citing Mitchell [41], *"was not to design algorithms to solve specific problems, but rather to formally study the phenomenon of adaptation as it occurs in nature and to develop ways in which the mechanisms of natural adaptation might be imported into computer systems"*.

Holland's GA, as presented in his book [33], is a technique useful to pass from an initial population of chromosomes to a new one, more fit to the environment, using a natural selection mechanism and the genetic operators of crossover, mutation and inversion. Each chromosome is made of a certain number of genes (i.e. bits); each gene is in turn the instance of an allele (i.e. 0 or 1). So, a 7-bits chromosome could present itself like this: 1011010. The selection operator decides which chromosomes can reproduce, so that the best chromosomes (the fitter to the environment) produce a number of offspring larger than the worst chromosomes (the less fit). The crossover operator swaps subsets of two chromosomes, with a procedure similar to that of biological recombination between two haploid organisms (single-chromosome). The mutation operator randomly alters allele's value in some locations of the chromosomes. The inversion operator inverts the order of a contiguous section of the chromosome.

Nowadays the diffusion of GA is so large that a majority of big companies use them to solve a wide range of problems, like scheduling, data fitting, trend spotting and budgeting problems.

3 Genetic Algorithms

GA are adaptive techniques, particularly suitable in the resolution of optimization problems, able to seek - for a complex and prefixed fitness function - its maximum or minimum point.

In this circumstance, other traditional analytical techniques are not usable due to the impossibility to explore the space of possible random solutions.

More generally, GA are adaptive heuristic search techniques based on the ideas of natural selection and genetic evolution. As already mentioned previously, at the basis of GA there are the concepts of simulation processes in natural systems necessary for evolution, the latter initially postulated by Charles Darwin with its theory on survival [41, 42].

Then GA represent, in other terms, a clever utilization of a random search within a preset search space in order to solve a prearranged problem.

GA have been applied in a wide number of ways but their effective representation and selection of fitness function are the key parameters in their applications.

The relevance of GA in the applications is attributable to possibility of use them easily, even though they are, at the same time, reliable and adaptable algorithms able to search better solutions quickly in complex multidimensional problems. In particular, there are three specific conditions that, if verified, suggest the use in operational applications of GA:

- the space of solutions is complex, wide or its knowledge is very poor;
- the knowledge about domain is poor or isn't possible decoding or restricting the space of solutions;

- traditional tools or techniques on mathematical analysis are unavailable.

In analogy with a biological system, it's possible to assume that also the built environment is characterized by a given issue to be solved and it's constituted by subjects of the population that are solvers for the problem to be addressed.

On the individuals of the population, the environment exerts a pressure that is continuously in evolution, pressure identifiable as a specific fitness function able to provide for each person a high accuracy degree about solutions, proposed by the same people, for the problem under investigation.

Derived from biology field, crossover and mutation are main genetic operators considered in study cases. Whereby, referring to the concepts about natural selection, the best individuals of present generation, if coupled together, will produce better subsequent and future generations of new individuals that can provide an entire population of possible solutions for the problem of interest.

In this way, there is a continuous improvement of genetic characteristics and in the number of individuals compared with previous generations. Thus, the better features are crossed and exchanged in the course of future generations. Exploring in detail the most suitable research areas, the optimal solution is identified by best individuals generated in the time.

Generally, can be distinguished five domains where GA are usefully applied, even if these domains don't have clearly defined boundaries [46]:

- Control;
- Design;
- Simulation and identification;
- Planning;
- Classification, modelling and machine learning.

For the latter domain the use of GA is directed to the construction of models able to interpret an underlying phenomenon or for forecasting purposes [12].

4 Case Study

For the implementation of GA the constitution of an initial population (random or derived by heuristics rules) is the first step; after, an evolutionary cycle has to be generated, and in correspondence of each iteration must be produced a new population using genetic operators to the previous population.

GA focuses on the identification of maximum or minimum point for a default fitness function. Therefore, the best solutions must be selected with subsequent iterations and, then, must recombine between them, so a continuous evolution towards the optimal state occurs. In particular, to each individual generated from its previous population is assigned a specific value that depends by quality degree of solution. Subsequently, more suitable individuals are recombined for to produce new generations, until there is convergence to the value attributable to the best individual.

The proposed model focuses on the interpretation of rental prices as the result of a multicriteria choice process.

The criteria of selection may be expressed by the characteristics of housing units, which are fundamental in the mechanism of formation of real estate values. For to determine the marginal price of geographic location, that contributes to define real estate rental prices, the original sample (initial population) has been defined with detection of real estate rental prices that refer to the recent past (last two months) and to housing units with similar building type and located in a central urban area of Naples (n. 64 housing units located in Santa Lucia and Chiaia neighborhoods).

Other non-homogenous real estate characteristics, besides the geographic location, were detected for each real estate sampled and, in particular (see Table 1):

- real estate rental price expressed in euro (*RERP*);
- commercial area expressed in square meters (*AREA*);
- maintenance status (*MAIN*) expressed with a scores scale: 2 if the housing unit is in optimum conditions, 1 if maintenance status is good, 0 otherwise (mediocre status);
- number of floor level of housing unit (*FLOOR*).

Table 1. Statistical description of variables

Variable	Std. Dev.	Median	Mean	Min	Max
RERP	6.000	963,51	1.692	400	6.000
AREA	71,29	100	122,311	30	460
MAIN	0,63	2	1,49	0	2
FLOOR	1,55	2	2,44	0	7

The geographical position (GEO) was expressed assigning a prefixed sequence of characters to each housing unit, so as to classify every housing unit as falling to a defined area among those already identified in a study focused on the city of Naples [4]. The cited study used a Geoadditive Model based on Penalized Spline functions for the housing market segmentation and, specifically, by this work it's possible to subdivide the urban area considered in five subareas with homogeneous values as Fig. 1 shows (A, B, C, D, E). More precisely, mentioned areas were so defined:

- Area A: mean rental price up to € 1.700,00 (sequence: 1,0,0,0,0);
- Area B: mean rental price from € 1.700,00 to € 1.750,00 (sequence: 0,1,0,0,0);
- Area C: mean rental price from € 1.750,00 to € 1.800,00 (sequence: 0,0,1,0,0);
- Area D: mean rental price from € 1.800,00 to € 1.850,00 (sequence: 0,0,0,1,0);
- Area E: mean rental price over € 1.850,00 (sequence: 0,0,0,0,1).

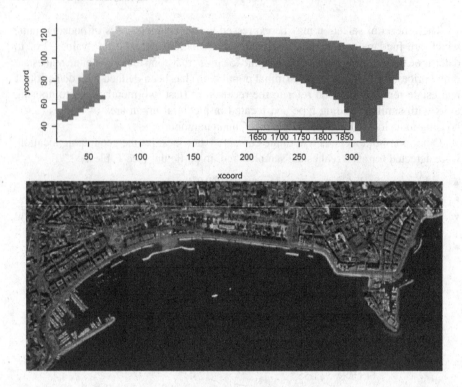

Fig. 1. Spatial distribution of real estate rental values [4].

The fitness function adopted is the Residual Sum of Squares (*RSS*) for to obtain the residuals as difference between observed real estate rental prices and fitted values provided by the model [42]:

$$RSS = \sum_i \varepsilon_i^2 = \sum_i (y_i - \bar{y}_i)^2 = \sum_i (y_i - m_0 - m_i x_i)^2, \; for \; i = 1, 2, \ldots, n. \qquad (1)$$

where y_i are the observed rental prices, $\bar{y}_i$ are the fitted values, x_i is the measure of *i-th* real estate characteristic selected, m_0 and m_i are, respectively, the constant or statistical error and the coefficient of *i-th* real estate characteristic (marginal contribution that the selected variables provide to real estate rental values).

"Genetic Algorithms" tool was used in MatLab software for to process the proposed model.

In MatLab software numerous times iterations were performed, changing in several iterative cycles, one by one, constraints and model key parameters, directing the process to the minimization of the sum of squared residuals. Data processing has allowed to determine genetic code able to generate the optimal solution:

- Population type: Double vector;
- Population size: 64;
- Fitness scaling: Proportional;

- Selection: Stochastic uniform;
- Reproduction: elite count=1; crossover fraction= 0,1;
- Mutation: Constraint dependent;
- Crossover: Heuristic;
- Migration: Both;
- Stopping criteria: Generations=5000;
- Plot function: best fitness; stopping.

Table 2 shows the values of m_i coefficients.

Table 2. Coefficients of geographic locations and real estate characteristics (GA).

GA		
$m_0 = -20,74$		m_{ij}
Characteristics/area		
1	AREA	13,21
2	MAIN	10,67
3	FLOOR	0,90
4	A	47,45
5	B	23,53
6	C	136,69
7	D	-34,47
8	E	-37,30

The vector of coefficients directly allows the estimation of marginal rental prices for the single real estate characteristics. The rental price function is additive as follows:

$$y_i = f(C_j) = C_0 + \sum_{j=1}^{n} C_j = m_0 + \sum_{j=1}^{n} m_{ij} x_{ij} \tag{2}$$

Expected values are calculated with Eq. (2) and, then, also the error between fitted values and observed rental prices. Tables 2 and 3 show model results.

Table 3. Model results compared with MRA

Description	GA	MRA
Max overestimation (%)	25,67%	21,23%
Max underestimation (%)	24,04%	48,52%
Mean error (%)	10,62%	11,50%
No. Cases of overestimation (> 15%)	6	4
No. Cases of underestimation (< −15%)	4	8

Also, model results are compared with those derivable from the application of MRA (with intercept) on the same real estate sample.

Firstly, comparison between GA and MRA highlights that marginal prices, for each single real estate characteristic, are different to each other.

Secondly, although there is a substantial similarity between GA and MRA in result terms, GA show their superiority in order to interpret the real estate rental market (10,62% for GA versus 11,50% for MRA in terms of absolute percentage error, equal to a better prediction in favour of GA in measure of 7,65% about), as also it's detectable from the low value of statistical error ($m_0 = -20,74$).

5   Concluding Remarks

Hedonic models are widespread in urban studies, but for them statistical techniques as Genetic Algorithms, Linear Programming, Semi-parametric or non parametric regressions, Artificial Neural Networks are certainly less commons [3–16, 30, 31, 46–54].

Currently, only few are the works that use Genetic Algorithms for real estate appraisal purposes [43–45]. Genetic Algorithms were used in this case study with the aim to determine the marginal price with which the geographic location takes part to the formation of real estate rental prices. This problem has been addressed using a preliminary segmentation of a central urban area of Naples developed with a Geoadditive Model on the same real estate data. Even if the results obtained by model are excellent (better forecasting results for GA in measure of 7,65% about), Genetic Algorithms not improve, significantly, similar performance obtainable with traditional parametric approaches (see MRA).

The improvement obtainable with Genetic Algorithms is mostly due to use of non-linear functions. In this sense, the computing capabilities of Genetic Algorithms and the modelling ability of other and more complex prediction or fitness functions utilizable for appraisal purposes (in order to better consider the non-linearity of typical real estate phenomena), might certainly provide in future even better results.

References

1. Manganelli, B., Morano, P.: Estimating the market value of the building sites for homogeneous areas. In: Advanced Materials Research. Sustainable Development of Industry and Economy, vols. 869–870, pp. 14–19 (2014)
2. Manganelli, B.: Real Estate Investing. Springer, Cham (2015)
3. Del Giudice, V., De Paola, P.: Undivided real estate shares: appraisal and interactions with capital markets. In: Applied Mechanics and Materials, Trans Tech Pubblications, Vols. 584–586 (2014)
4. Giudice, V., Paola, P.: Spatial analysis of residential real estate rental market with geoadditive models. In: d'Amato, M., Kauko, T. (eds.) Advances in Automated Valuation Modeling. SSDC, vol. 86, pp. 155–162. Springer, Cham (2017). doi:10.1007/978-3-319-49746-4_8
5. Del Giudice, V., De Paola, P., Forte, F.: The appraisal of office towers in bilateral monopoly's market: evidence from application of Newton's physical laws to the directional centre of naples. Int. J. Appl. Eng. Res. 11(18), 9455–9459 (2016). R.I.P
6. Giudice, V., Evangelista, P., Paola, P., Forte, F.: Knowledge management and intellectual capital in the logistics service industry. In: Lehner, F., Fteimi, N. (eds.) KSEM 2016. LNCS, vol. 9983, pp. 376–387. Springer, Cham (2016). doi:10.1007/978-3-319-47650-6_30

7. Giudice, V., Manganelli, B., Paola, P.: Depreciation methods for firm's assets. In: Gervasi, O., Murgante, B., Misra, S., Rocha, A.M.A.C., Torre, C., Taniar, D., Apduhan, Bernady O., Stankova, E., Wang, S. (eds.) ICCSA 2016. LNCS, vol. 9788, pp. 214–227. Springer, Cham (2016). doi:10.1007/978-3-319-42111-7_17

8. Manganelli, B., Paola, P., Giudice, V.: Linear Programming in a Multi-Criteria Model for Real Estate Appraisal. In: Gervasi, O., Murgante, B., Misra, S., Rocha, A.M.A.C., Torre, C., Taniar, D., Apduhan, Bernady O., Stankova, E., Wang, S. (eds.) ICCSA 2016. LNCS, vol. 9786, pp. 182–192. Springer, Cham (2016). doi:10.1007/978-3-319-42085-1_14

9. Giudice, V., Manganelli, B., Paola, P.: Spline Smoothing for Estimating Hedonic Housing Price Models. In: Gervasi, O., Murgante, B., Misra, S., Gavrilova, Marina L., Rocha, A.M.A.C., Torre, C., Taniar, D., Apduhan, Bernady O. (eds.) ICCSA 2015. LNCS, vol. 9157, pp. 210–219. Springer, Cham (2015). doi:10.1007/978-3-319-21470-2_15

10. Del Giudice, V., De Paola, P.: Geoadditive Models for Property Market. Appl. Mech. Mater. Trans. Tech. Pubblications **584–586**, 2505–2509 (2014)

11. Del Giudice, V., De Paola, P.: The effects of noise pollution produced by road traffic of Naples Beltway on residential real estate values. Appl. Mech. Mater. Trans. Tech. Pubblications **587–589**, 2176–2182 (2014)

12. Del Giudice, V., De Paola, P., Manganelli, B., Forte, F.: The monetary valuation of environmental externalities through the analysis of real estate prices. Sustainability **9**(2), 229 (2017). MDPI Switzerland

13. Del Giudice, V., De Paola, P., Cantisani, G.B.: Rough Set Theory for real estate appraisals: an application to Directional District of Naples. Buildings **7**(1), 12 (2017). MDPI Switzerland

14. Del Giudice, V., De Paola, P., Cantisani, G.B.: Valuation of real estate investments through Fuzzy Logic. Buildings **7**(1), 26 (2017). MDPI

15. Del Giudice, V., De Paola, P., Forte, F.: Using genetic algorithms for real estate appraisal. Buildings **7**(2), 31 (2017). MDPI

16. Del Giudice, V., Manganelli, B., De Paola, P.: Hedonic analysis of housing sales prices with semiparametric methods. Int. J. Agric. Environ. Inf. Syst. **8**(2), 65–77 (2017). IGI Global Publishing

17. Morano, P., Tajani, F.: Estimative analysis of a segment of the bare ownership market of residential property. In: Murgante, B., Misra, S., Carlini, M., Torre, C.M., Nguyen, H.-Q., Taniar, D., Apduhan, Bernady O., Gervasi, O. (eds.) ICCSA 2013. LNCS, vol. 7974, pp. 433–443. Springer, Heidelberg (2013). doi:10.1007/978-3-642-39649-6_31

18. Morano, P., Tajani, F.: Bare ownership of residential properties: insights on two segments of the Italian market. Int. J. Hous. Markets Anal. **9**(3), 376–399 (2016)

19. Goodman, A.C., Thibodeau, T.G.: Housing market segmentation. J. Hous. Econ. **7**, 121–143 (1998)

20. Wiltshaw, D.G.: A comment on methodology and valuation. J. Property Res. **12**, 157–161 (1995)

21. Ahn, J.J., Lee, S.J., Oh, K.J., Kim, T.Y.: Intelligent forecasting for financial time series subject to structural changes. Intell. Data Anal. **13**, 151–163 (2009)

22. Chen, W.S., Du, Y.K.: Using neural networks and data mining techniques for the financial distress prediction model. Expert Syst. Appl. **36**, 4075–4086 (2009)

23. Dong, M., Zhou, X.S.: Knowledge discovery in corporate events by neural network rule extraction. Appl. Intell. **29**, 129–137 (2008)

24. Lee, K., Booth, D., Alam, P.: A comparison of supervised and unsupervised neural networks in predicting bankruptcy of Korean firms. Expert Syst. Appl. **29**, 1–16 (2005)

25. Lu, C.J.: Integrating independent component analysis-based denoising scheme with neural network for stock price prediction. Expert Syst. Appl. **37**, 7056–7064 (2010)

26. Oh, K.J., Han, I.: Using change-point detection to support artificial neural networks for interest rates forecasting. Expert Syst. Appl. **19**, 105–115 (2000)
27. Versace, M., Bhatt, R., Hinds, O., Shiffer, M.: Predicting the exchange traded fund DIA with a combination of genetic algorithms and neural networks. Expert Syst. Appl. **27**, 417–425 (2004)
28. Dehghan, S., Sattari, G., Chehreh, C.S., Aliabadi, M.A.: Prediction of uniaxial compressive strength and modulus of elasticity for Travertine samples using regression and artificial neural networks. Min. Sci. Technol. **20**, 41–46 (2010)
29. Hua, C.: Residential construction demand forecasting using economic indicators: a comparative study of artificial neural networks and multiple regression. Constr. Manage. Econ. **14**, 125–134 (1996)
30. Nguyen, N., Cripps, A., Value, P.H.: A comparison of multiple regression analysis and artificial neural networks. J. Real Estate Res. **22**(3), 313–336 (2001)
31. Worzala, E., Lenk, M., Silva, A.: An exploration of neural networks and its application to real estate valuation. J. Real Estate Res. **10**(2), 185–202 (1995)
32. Goldberg, D.E.: Genetic Algorithms in Search, Optimization and Machine Learning. Addison-Wesley, New York (1989)
33. Holland, J.H.: Adaptation in Natural and Artificial Systems: an Introductory Analysis with Applications to Biology, Control and Artificial Intelligence. The MIT Press, Cambridge (1975)
34. Oh, K.J., Kim, T.Y., Min, S.: Using genetic algorithm to support portfolio optimization for index fund management. Expert Syst. Appl. **28**, 371–379 (2005)
35. Koza, J.: Genetic programming. The MIT Press, Cambridge (1993)
36. Wong, F., Tan, C.: Hybrid neural, genetic, and fuzzy systems. In: Deboeck, G.J. (ed.) Trading on the Edge, pp. 243–261. Wiley, New York (1994)
37. Rechenberg, I.: Evolutionsstrategie: Optimierung Technischer Systeme Nach Prinzipien der Biologischen Evolution. FrommannHolzboog, Stuttgart (1973)
38. Schwefel, H.P.: Numerical Optimization of Computer Models. Wiley, Hoboken (1981)
39. Fogel, L.J., Owens, A.J., Walsh, M.J.: Artificial Intelligence Through Simulated Evolution. Wiley, New York (1966)
40. Reed, P., Minsker, B.S., Goldberg, D.E.: Designing a competent simple genetic algorithm for search and optimization. Water Resour. Res. **3612**, 3757–3761 (2000)
41. Mitchell, M.: An Introduction to Genetic Algorithms. MIT Press, Cambridge (1999). Massachusetts London, Fifth printing
42. Nga, T., Skitmoreb, M., Wongc, K.F.: Using genetic algorithms and linear regression analysis for private housing demand forecast. Build. Environ. **43**(6), 1171–1184 (2008)
43. Tajani, F., Morano, P., Locurcio, M., D'Addabbo, N.: Property valuations in times of crisis: artificial neural networks and evolutionary algorithms in comparison. In: Gervasi, O., Murgante, B., Misra, S., Gavrilova, Marina L., Rocha, A.M.A.C., Torre, C., Taniar, D., Apduhan, Bernady O. (eds.) ICCSA 2015. LNCS, vol. 9157, pp. 194–209. Springer, Cham (2015). doi:10.1007/978-3-319-21470-2_14
44. De Mare, G., Lenza, T.L.L., Conte, R.: Economic evaluations using genetic algorithms to determine the territorial impact caused by high speed railways. Int. J. Soc. Educ. Econ. Manage. Eng. **6**(11), 672–680 (2012). World Academy of Science, Engineering and Technology
45. Manganelli, B., Mare, G., Nesticò, A.: Using genetic algorithms in the housing market analysis. In: Gervasi, O., Murgante, B., Misra, S., Gavrilova, Marina L., Rocha, A.M.A.C., Torre, C., Taniar, D., Apduhan, Bernady O. (eds.) ICCSA 2015. LNCS, vol. 9157, pp. 36–45. Springer, Cham (2015). doi:10.1007/978-3-319-21470-2_3

46. Narulaa, S.C., Wellingtonb, J.F., Lewisb, S.A.: Valuating residential real estate using parametric programming. Eur. J. Oper. Res. **217**(1), 120–128 (2012)
47. Kontrimasa, V., Verikasb, A.: The mass appraisal of the real estate by computational intelligence. Appl. Soft Comput. **11**(1), 443–448 (2011)
48. Bourassa, S.C., Cantoni, E., Hoesli, M.: Predicting house prices with spatial dependence: a comparison of alternative methods. J. Real Estate Res. **32**, 139–159 (2010)
49. Brooks, C., Tsolacos, S.: International evidence on the predictability of returns to securitized real estate assets: Econometric models versus neural networks. J. Property Res. **20**, 133–155 (2003)
50. Chica-Olmo, J.: Prediction of housing location price by a multivariate spatial method: cokriging. J. Real Estate Res. **29**, 92–114 (2007)
51. Juan, Y.K., Shin, S.G., Perng, Y.H.: Decision support for housing customization: a hybrid approach using case-based reasoning and genetic algorithm. Expert Syst. Appl. **31**, 83–93 (2006)
52. Peterson, S., Flanagan, A.B.: Neural network hedonic pricing models in mass real estate appraisal. J. Real Estate Res. **31**, 148–164 (2009)
53. Rossini, P.: Artificial neural networks versus multiple regression in the valuation of residential property. Australian Land Econ. Rev. **3**, 1–12 (1997)
54. Wilson, I.D., Paris, S.D., Ware, J.A., Jenkins, D.H.: Residential property price time series forecasting with neural networks. Knowl.-Based Syst. **15**, 335–341 (2002)

Bayesian Neural Network Models
in the Appraisal of Real Estate Properties

Vincenzo Del Giudice[1], Pierfrancesco De Paola[1(✉)],
and Fabiana Forte[2]

[1] University of Naples "Federico II", Piazzale Vincenzo Tecchio,
80125 Naples, Italy
{vincenzo.delgiudice,pierfrancesco.depaola}@unina.it
[2] University of Campania "Luigi Vanvitelli",
Via San Lorenzo, 81031 Aversa, Italy
fabiana.forte@unicampania.it

Abstract. Neural Networks (NNs) had wide interest due to empirical achievements on a wide range of learning issues. NNs are highly expressive models that can learn complex function approximations from input/output, with a particular ability to train them on massive data sets with stochastic optimization. The Bayesian approach to NNs can potentially avoid some of the problems of stochastic optimization. The use of Bayesian learning is well suited to the problem of real estate appraisals, in fact, Bayesian inference techniques are very interesting in order to deal with a small and noisy sample in the field of probabilistic inference carried out with neural model. For this purpose it has here been experimented a NNs model with Bayesian learning. The output distribution has been calculated operating a numerical integration on the weights space with the help of Markov Chain Hybrid Monte Carlo Method.

Keywords: Neural Networks Models · Bayesian approach · Markov Chain Hybrid Monte Carlo Method · Real estate appraisals

1 Introduction

The appraisal of real estate goods carried out with parametric approaches is strongly influenced by dimension and quality of real estate sample available. The minimum dimension of real estate sample necessary to implement statistical inference models is, as known, related to the number of independent variables explaining the real estate characteristics, which mostly influence the real estate prices [1, 10–22].

Furthermore, the market data referring to real estate sales intrinsically reflect the typical distortions of a market which is characterized by low transparency, that is the reason why any real estate sample must be considered as affected by noise [8, 34].

Traditional statistical models, as well as neural ones, used to determine the econometric function of the real estate price, assume that the price distribution (depend variable) is representative of a deterministic function of the real estate characteristics

© Springer International Publishing AG 2017
O. Gervasi et al. (Eds.): ICCSA 2017, Part III, LNCS 10406, pp. 478–489, 2017.
DOI: 10.1007/978-3-319-62398-6_34

considered (independent variables). If considered, the noisiness of statistical sample is generally modelled hypothesizing that the outputs are affected by a Gaussian noise with zero mean and constant variance which does not depend on input variables. Then, interpolating function is chosen using the maximum likelihood criterion which corresponds to the minimization of a square-error function. In this sense, it has been shown that in case of an output noise independent from the input variables, the maximum likelihood criterion provides distorted results because systematically underestimates the variance of noise itself [2, 4, 5].

The possibility of characterizing the interpolating function in probabilistic terms and, thus, of obtaining as output a distribution of the prices instead of a deterministic value, jointly with the capability to model the noise variance of output as function of the input variables using small samples, are the aspects that mainly make us lean in favour of the use of a Bayesian approach for real estate appraisals.

For this purpose it has here been experimented a Neural Network model with Bayesian learning.

In general, Neural Networks (NNs) had wide interest due to empirical achievements on a wide range of learning issues. NNs are highly expressive models that can learn complex function approximations from input/output examples [27], with a particular ability to train them on massive data sets with stochastic optimization [6] and the backpropagation algorithm [38]. These aspects have resulted in successes for NNs on many fields of applied science and economy.

The Bayesian approach to Neural Networks can potentially avoid some of the problems of stochastic optimization [31, 32]. In fact, Bayesian methods consider the uncertainty in parameter estimates and can extend and transform this uncertainty into predictions. Often, Bayesian approaches are more robust to overfitting, since they average over parameter values instead of choosing a single point estimate. Different approaches have been proposed in literature for Bayesian learning of neural networks, based on, e.g., the Laplace approximation [31, 32], Hamiltonian Monte Carlo [35–37], expectation propagation [29], and variational inference [26]. These approaches have not seen widespread adoption due to their lack of scalability for network architecture and data size. An exception is the scalable variational inference approach of Graves [25], but this method seems to perform poorly in practice due to noise from Monte Carlo approximations within the stochastic gradient computations. A different scalable solution based on expectation propagation was proposed by Soudry et al. [39], although its extension to continuous weights is unsatisfying as it does not produce estimates of posterior variance.

2 Bayesian Approach for Neural Network Modelling

Traditional parametric models generally assume that the distribution of data targets t_k (real estate prices) is represented by a deterministic function of the inputs, adding the Gaussian noise characterized by a normal distribution with zero mean and constant standard deviation which does not depend on the input vectors[1]. In such case the input-output functional relation is expressed by the following formula [37]:

$$t_k = h_k(x) + \varepsilon_k \qquad (1)$$

where the distribution of ε_k is given by:

$$\rho(\varepsilon_k) = \frac{1}{(2\pi\sigma^2)^{1/2}} \cdot exp\left(\frac{\varepsilon_k^2}{2\sigma^2}\right) \qquad (2)$$

The choice of the function $h_k(x)$ can occur either with a parametric approach that non parametric. In the first case we primarily need to define the functional form which, in relation to the statistic criteria and to the knowledge of the phenomenon to be studied, better than anyone else nears the data set observations. In the second case, as for example the neural one, the input-output mapping is connected to the realization of pattern learning phase.

In both cases, the need arises to select the optimal status of the so-called free parameters of the model which in the parametric case represent the coefficients which define in an univocal way the interpolating function, whereas in the neural case they refer to the determination of the synaptic weights matrix.

Very often the criterion used to determine the parameters which rule a regression model is the maximum likelihood, which corresponds to the determination of the free parameters set so to minimize a square-error function expressed as the sum of the square differences between model output and corresponding target[2].

By indicating with $\{x^n, t^n\}$ the training data set and assuming that each observation is drawn, independently from the others, from the same distribution, the likelihood L can be written as a product between the conditional probability of the target data conditioned on the input data considered separately[3]

$$L = \prod_n p(t^n | x^n) \qquad (3)$$

---

[1] In the econometric appraisal of real estate prices the stochastic component is representative of the whole effect of the many disturbance factors which cannot be expressed through variables endogenous to the model. Such factors can be explained by: (1) the practical impossibility to assess the regression model with reference to the different samples drawn by the population of known-price sales; (2) the impossibility to quantify the influence of some important market factors (role of broker, contractual power in particular conditions, etc.) or institutional factors, for example, expectations related to fiscal charging, etc.; (3) the impossibility, once acknowledged the influence of a factor, to obtain quantitative information about it; (4) the need to use a number of explicative variables not too high also in relation to low sample size; (5) the chance that real estate sample is influenced by errors in the survey, as well as by random elements in the answers of interviewed (buyers, sellers and brokers).

[2] In real estate valuations each error is representative of the difference between the real estate value obtained from the model and the corresponding price drawn on the market.

[3] In the general case in which one does not hypothesize the independence of the observation, the problem becomes that of determining the conditional density of the target data $p(t \mid x)$ conditioned on the input data.

For computational reason, instead of maximizing the likelihood functional it is better to minimize the negative of its logarithm, so that the error function is given by

$$E = -\ln L = -\sum_n \ln p(t^n|x^n) \qquad (4)$$

The function $h_k(x)$ can be modelled through a neural network where the output $y_k(x, w)$ depends by the input vectors x and synaptic weights w. By using the formulae (1) and (2) the target distribution is given by:

$$p(t_k|x) = \frac{1}{(2\pi\sigma^2)^{1/2}} \cdot exp\left(\frac{\{v_k(x,w) - t_k\}^2}{2\sigma^2}\right) \qquad (5)$$

In the hypothesis of the distribution of independent target variables t_k we can write

$$p(t|x) = \prod_{k=1} p(t_k|x), \qquad (6)$$

hence the error function can be written as follows:

$$E = \frac{1}{2\sigma^2}\sum_{\alpha > 1}^{N}\sum_{k=1}^{C}\left\{y_k(x^n, w) - t^k\right\}^2 + Nc\ln\alpha + \frac{Nc}{2}\ln(2\pi) \qquad (7)$$

The second and the third term as well as the factor $1/\sigma^2$ do not depend on the weights w and can be omitted in order to minimize the error function which thus takes on the know form[4]:

$$E = \frac{1}{2}\sum_{n=1}^{N}\|y(x^n, w) - t^n\|^2 \qquad (8)$$

It has demonstrated that in case of infinitely large data set and highly flexible neural model, that is to say with a number of sufficiently large adaptive weights, the network output is representative of the conditional mean of the target data corresponding to the input vectors [2–5].

The expression of the error or cost function E has been derived in the hypothesis that the target data distribution is Gaussian. In case it is not reasonable to assume such an hypothesis, for instance when the distribution is multimodal, the use of the previ-

---

[4] The sum of quadratic-error function remains valid even if a parametric approach is used, and the interpolating function will have a pre-defined algebraical form and will be expressed as a function of the parameters characterizing the functional form itself. The individuation of the parameters set which make the coat function minimum is, as known, almost always linked to the use of the square minimum algorithm, while in the case of neural network the algorithm mostly used is the back-propagation.

ously described approach can obviously lead to distorted results, very difficult to interpret[5].

Furthermore, very often in the econometric applications, and in particular in the field of real estate valuation, the low transparency of information market together with the stationary market conditions, force the analysts to work with single and small data set.

The sample observations are also affected by noise not always distributed in a uniform way and independent by the input vectors. For example, about the problem of information asymmetry, typical of the housing market, distortions in the market price can very often be driven by single real estate broker's behaviour and, then, with non-uniformity features.

The hypothesis of noise independence from the input vectors is reasonable in market condition with perfect competition, where the correspondence between the usefulness connected with all real estate characteristics and the related market price is strictly ruled by the market. When such market conditions fall, the price reflects, more or less relevantly, strong unbalances from the side of the demand or supply.

For these latter considerations, the Bayesian approach seem to be very interesting in order to deal with a small and noisy sample in the field of probabilistic inference carried out with neural model [28].

A similar approach allows to express the uncertainty in the weights value through a probability distribution $p(w \mid D)$ conditioned on the data set. In this way the neural network is represented no longer by a single vector of the synaptic weights obtained by applying the maximum likelihood criterion, but by a density probability on the weights space. The main consequence is that the output of a similar model will have a probabilistic feature and will be represented by any distribution with regards to which it is possible to calculate the most probable value as well as the confidence interval of each single prevision.

Also, Bayesian approach appears to be particularly interesting in order to determine the real estate market values in harmony with the theoretical-methodological foundations of appraisal theory, these last interested to find the most probable value among all possible values. Nevertheless, the possibility to associate to each prevision (in terms of most probable value) the corresponding confidence interval which stems out in endogenous way from the model, and with reference to generic distribution (i.e. multimodal), represents an important contribution of the model in the field of real estate appraisal.

Besides this, the Bayesian treatment allows to select the regularization coefficients and, thus, the model complexity only using the training set and then without a validation set.

---

[5] All the deductive-axiomatic apparatus of the appraisal theory is based upon the hypothesis that the real estate sample is randomly drawn by a normal population referred to similar real estate sales with known price, and that with increasing of the sample dimension its distribution can be approximated to the normal [9]. Hardly ever these statistical hypothesis are mirrored in practice and this is because [33]: (a) the behaviour of the subjects which deal with the sampling hardly ever follows criteria which are based on random logic; (b) the atypicalness of real estate goods systematically invalidates the normal postulation of the population.

This latter circumstance is particularly important when there is a limited data set, as often occurs in real estate appraisals.

The Bayesian method thus allows to avoid the overfitting problem which is typical of the conventional approach used for the network training and, at least on principle, it does not limit the model complexity [37]. Finally, a similar approach allows the comparison between different models of neural network (i.e. nets with different numbers of hidden neurons, or different types of nets such as M.L.P. or R.B.F., etc.) just by using the training data [2–5].

The issue of determination of the value distribution of outputs can be solved by using the integration on multidimensional space of the synaptic weights. By using the rule of probability marginalization it's possible to express the output distribution for a given vector of input x in the following form:

$$p(t|x, D) = \int p(t|x, w)p(w|D)dw \qquad (9)$$

where $p(w \mid D)$ is the posterior weights distribution on the target data $D \equiv (t^1, ..., t^N)$, that can be expressed starting from a prior distribution $p(w)$ by using the known Bayes theorem[6]:

$$p(w|D) = \frac{p(D|w)p(w)}{p(D)} \qquad (10)$$

where in (10) the denominator of arithmetical ratio is a normalization factor.

Practically the integration over the weights space is analytically untreatable, so that the main approximation methods are two. The first leads to an analytical integration in the restrictive hypothesis that the posterior weights distribution is expressed with a Gaussian distribution centred on the most probable weights vector [31, 32]. On the other hand, the second method operates a numerical integration by using the Monte Carlo technique [35–37] which is otherwise impossible to conduct with the traditional integration technique given the high dimensionality of the problem.

3   The Appraisal of Real Estate with the Markov Chain Hybrid Monte Carlo Method

The application has been made by using a data sample relative to a definite ambit of the Naples real estate market. The sample is made to 65 housing sales. The housing units present the same building typology and are situated in a homogeneous urban area under the profile of the distribution of main public and private services.

For each housing unit, the market price and the amounts of respective real estate characteristics are known as following: the market price (*PRICE*) expressed in €/total square metres; the number of services (*SERV - X1*) of the housing unit; the outer

---

[6] The maximum likelihood approach represent a particular approximation of which we only consider the most probable weights vector which corresponds to the distribution peak.

surface (*OUTSUR - X2*) expressed in square metres; floor level (*FLOOR - X3*) where the housing unit is situated; the state of maintenance and preservation (*MAPR - X4*) expressed with a score scale: 1 = mediocre, 3 = good, 5 = very good; panoramic quality of housing unit (*PAN - X5*) expressed with a score scale: 1 = without panoramic views, 3 = half of views of the housing unit are panoramic, 5 = all views of housing unit are panoramic; the location statement (*LOC - X6*) expressed with a dichotomous measure: 1 = rent free, 0 = not free; the distance from railway station (*STAT - X7*) also expressed with a dichotomous measure: 1 = < 500 m, 0 = > 500 m.

The selection of the most significant real estate characteristics was verified on the basis of a direct knowledge of the market and following a statistical pre-processing connected to the need to determine the intrinsic dimensionality of the data set used [24].

This is done to reduce the effects of correlation among the variables and to obtain a better coverage of the characteristics space. The reduction of dimensionality has to be conducted to enable the identification of the optimal balance between loss of information (as a results of the elimination of a variable) and the need to conserve relevant information contained in the data set [30].

The Bayesian model proposed is of M.L.P. type with a single hidden layer which is made up of thirty units and which has been trained by using just 35 housing sales drawn from the real estate sample. This in order to verify the approach capacity of working with small dimension samples also related to the input vector dimensionality. The remaining part of the sample (30 housing sales) has been used to test the network generalization capacity.

The first stage has been that of choosing a weights prior distribution which in some way should reflect a possible prior knowledge which the analyst may have about the input-output mapping form. Generally the form used is the exponential one of the type[7]:

$$p(w) = \frac{1}{Z_w(\alpha)} exp(-\alpha E_w) \tag{11}$$

where $Z_w(\alpha)$ is a normalization factor, α is called hyperparameter in as much it controls the distribution of other parameters (weights and biases) and is determined during the training phase, while:

$$E_w = \frac{1}{2} \|w\|^2 \tag{12}$$

is a function which favours small values for the network weights in order to encourage the network smooth mapping[8].

---

[7] Different are the possible functions for the prior distribution of weights, see Buntine et al. [7] and Neal [37].

[8] The problem of a very good balance between bias and variance in order to avoid overfitting phenomena by the training data suggests the choice of a function smooth network [2].

In the same way for the distribution $p(D \mid w)$ an exponential form has been chosen so that:

$$p(D|w) = \frac{1}{Z_D(\beta)} exp(-\beta E_D) \tag{13}$$

where $Z_D(\beta)$ is a normalization factor, β is a hyperparameter determined during the training phase which controls the noise variance and E_D is the classical square function derived from the maximum likelihood.

Using Bayes theorem (10) the posterior weights conditioned on the training set is this given by the following relation:

$$p(w|D) = \frac{1}{Z_S} exp(-\beta E_D - \alpha E_w) \tag{14}$$

where Z_S is a normalization factor[9].

The output distribution (9) has been calculated operating a numerical integration on the weights space with the help of *Markov Chain Hybrid Monte Carlo Method* [21, 35, 36]. The basic idea is of selecting random sample of points w_i, in the weights space paying attention to generate such sample so that it may be representative of the distribution $p(w \mid D)$. Then is necessary to make sure that the selected weights vectors are in the region where the $p(w \mid D)$ is reasonably large. This can be done considering the vector sequence, where each following vector depends on the previous, adding a stochastic component so that:

$$w_{new} = w_{old} + \varepsilon \tag{15}$$

where ε is a small random vector chosen, for example, by a spherical Gaussian distribution with a small variance parameter. In order to avoid w_{new} orientating towards the direction where the posterior probability is low, it's possible to use the information about the gradient which can be obtained by using a standard back-propagation algorithm. Such method is known by the name of *Hybrid Monte Carlo* [23]. By using the *Hybrid Monte Carlo Algorithm* it is then possible to generate a sample w_i and in correspondence to each x input vector we can calculate the network prevision $y(x_i, w_i)$, so we can assess the distribution $p(t \mid x, D)$ as the sum of the single $y(x_i, w_i)$. At the same time during the training phase the hyperparameters can be assessed with the *Gibbs sampling* technique[10].

In Table 1 the most probable value, the related confidence interval 95% and the corresponding relative percentage error are given for each real estate pattern of the test

---

[9] It is easy verify that, with α and β fixed, increasing the training set dimension the first is a representative term of the maximum likelihood, whereas the second is a representative term of the prior knowledge that decreases so that larger is the set and better the only term of maximum likelihood approximates the most probable weights distribution. Conversely for small data sets the role of the prior term in the determination of the most probable solution is essential [37].

[10] The elaboration have been carried out with Netlab free software (Aston University, Birmingham).

Table 1. Statistical description of variables

Variable	Std. Dev.	Median	Mean	Min	Max
Price	1,06	3,44	3,40	1,18	6,11
Serv	0,50	1,00	1,45	1,00	2,00
Outsur	11,75	12,00	13,89	0,00	40,00
Floor	1,45	3,00	2,65	0,50	7,00
Mapr	1,46	3,00	2,94	1,00	5,00
Pan	1,28	1,00	1,89	1,00	5,00
Loc	0,49	1,00	0,62	0,00	1,00
Stat	0,50	0,00	0,46	0,00	1,00

set referred to sales not used to assess the model and thus completely unknown to it. The model has show a very good performance in forecast capacity terms with an absolute average error of 6,61%. In particular, the confidence intervals are less wide where the given input density is larger and this is because in the region with a high data density the contribution to the output variance due to the weights uncertainty has a trend which is in inverse relation to the probability density, and thus the variance on the output is mostly due to the noise term [40].

4 Concluding Remarks

The real estate appraisal carried out with the Bayesian approach occurs following a probabilistic model which, as it does not undergo the traditional theoretical hypothesis of the statistical inference (Gaussian noise with zero mean and constant standard deviation which does not depend from the input vectors), allows to characterize the appraisal previsions in terms which correspond to the phenomenical reality of the analyzed real estate market. Furthermore, the possibility to associate to each prevision the corresponding confidence interval endogenously to the model, represents an important appraisal advancement towards the improvement in the reliability of the real estate appraisals (Table 2).

Table 2. Model performance

No.	X1	X2	X3	X4	X5	X6	X7	Price	Lower bound	Most probable value	Upper bound	% Error
1	2	0	2	5	1	1	0	5,00	4,34	4,63	4,95	−7,40
2	2	10	5	3	1	1	1	4,65	4,06	4,37	4,67	−6,10
3	1	0	0,5	1	1	1	1	4,00	3,80	4,14	4,44	3,55
4	2	0	3	5	1	0	1	2,24	2,22	2,42	2,62	8,04
5	2	20	1	3	1	1	1	4,00	4,13	4,40	4,67	10,00
6	1	10	2	5	3	1	1	4,32	3,60	3,86	4,12	−10,63
7	1	10	3	3	1	0	1	3,04	2,57	2,72	2,87	−10,53
8	2	20	5	1	1	1	0	4,61	4,18	4,42	4,68	−4,12

(*continued*)

Table 2. (*continued*)

No.	X1	X2	X3	X4	X5	X6	X7	Price	Lower bound	Most probable value	Upper bound	% Error
9	2	20	1	3	5	1	1	3,14	2,69	2,99	3,29	−4,76
10	1	15	1	1	3	1	1	3,66	3,31	3,61	3,91	−1,34
11	1	30	3	3	3	1	0	4,07	3,86	4,12	4,38	1,20
12	1	0	1	3	3	0	0	2,22	2,16	2,40	2,84	8,11
13	2	25	3	3	1	1	1	6,11	4,99	5,22	5,45	−14,57
14	2	10	2	1	3	0	0	2,42	2,35	2,53	2,72	4,55
15	2	15	2	3	1	0	1	2,36	2,27	2,54	2,81	7,63
16	2	20	4	3	1	0	0	2,89	2,99	2,86	3,14	−1,00
17	2	20	4	1	1	1	1	4,39	3,66	3,93	4,20	−10,47
18	1	0	2	3	1	1	1	5,15	4,16	4,46	4,76	−13,40
19	2	15	4	3	1	1	0	4,23	3,85	4,10	4,35	3,07
20	2	0	0,5	5	1	1	0	2,89	2,35	2,68	2,97	−7,34
21	1	15	4	5	1	1	0	4,34	3,71	3,98	4,25	−8,23
22	2	10	3	1	3	0	0	4,00	3,48	3,72	3,96	−7,00
23	2	20	3	3	5	1	0	3,91	3,74	4,01	4,27	2,43
24	1	20	1	1	1	0	0	1,22	0,88	1,18	1,19	−2,96
25	1	10	4	3	3	1	0	3,20	3,26	3,52	3,78	10,00
26	1	30	2	3	1	1	0	2,13	1,97	2,27	2,57	6,57
27	2	15	5	5	3	1	0	2,67	2,23	2,50	2,74	−6,37
28	2	15	6	1	1	1	0	2,27	2,00	2,40	2,72	5,73
29	1	10	4	3	3	1	0	4,19	3,56	3,82	4,03	−8,83
30	1	12	3	5	1	1	0	3,44	3,37	3,52	3,72	2,33

The analysis has shown an excellent prevision capacity of the model corresponding to a learning set not very numerous (35 housing sales), also considering the dimension of the real estate patterns (dimension equal to 7). This is because the Bayesian learning, for its own nature, does not need a set for the model validation and for the overfitting checking. The confidence intervals have a good appraising coherence showing themselves larger where the input data set density is smaller.

From point of view of the model selection, it should be noted the possibility of using a high number of coefficients regularization to obtain smoother interpolating functions with reduced computational costs compared to the traditional approaches.

Further developments may concern the possibility to obtain, during the model assessment phase, information which indicate the need to introduce further data in order to improve the prevision capability of the model itself (active learning). Besides, very interesting, appears to be the possibility of considering the relative importance of the several input vectors by using different value of the hyperparameters for each input (automatic relevance determination).

References

1. Brotman, B.A.: Linear and non linear appraisals models. Appraisal J. **58**, 249–253 (1990)
2. Bishop, C.M.: Bayesian methods for neural networks, Technical report, Department of Computer Science and Applied Mathematics, Aston University, Birmingham (1995)
3. Bishop, C.M.: Neural Network for Pattern Recognition, 2nd edn. Oxford University Press, New York (1996)
4. Bishop, C.M.: Neural network: a pattern recognition perspective. In: Fiesler, E., Beale, R. (eds.) Handbook of Neural Computation. Oxford University Press, New York (1996)
5. Bishop, C.M., Qazac, C.S., Regression with input-dependent noise: a bayesian treatment. In: Advances in Neural Information Processing Systems, vol. 9. MIT Press (1997)
6. Bottou, L.: Large-scale machine learning with stochastic gradient descent. In: Lechevallier, Y., Saporta, G. (eds.) Proceedings of COMPSTAT 2010, pp. 177–186. Physica-Verlag HD, Heidelberg (2010)
7. Buntine, W.L., Weigend, A.S.: Bayesian back-propagation. Complex Syst. **5**, 603–643 (1991)
8. Child, P.D., Ott, S.H., Riddiough, T.J., Incomplete information, exercise policy and valuation of claims on noisy real assets, Discussion paper, MIT Real Estate Center, Cambridge, USA (1997)
9. Del Giudice, V., De Paola, P.: Undivided real estate shares: appraisal and interactions with capital markets. Appl. Mech. Mater. **584–586**, 2522–2527 (2014). Trans Tech Pubblications
10. Del Giudice, V., De Paola, P.: Spatial analysis of residential real estate rental market. In: d'Amato, M., Kauko, T. (eds.) Advances in Automated Valuation Modeling. SSDC, vol. 86, pp. 9455–9459. Springer, Cham (2017). doi:10.1007/978-3-319-49746-4
11. Del Giudice, V., De Paola, P., Forte, F.: The appraisal of office towers in bilateral monopoly's market: evidence from application of Newton's physical laws to the Directional Centre of Naples. Int. J. Appl. Eng. Res. **11**(18), 9455–9459 (2016). R.I.P
12. Giudice, V., Evangelista, P., Paola, P., Forte, F.: Knowledge Management and Intellectual Capital in the Logistics Service Industry. In: Lehner, F., Fteimi, N. (eds.) KSEM 2016. LNCS, vol. 9983, pp. 1–12. Springer, Cham (2016). doi:10.1007/978-3-319-47650-6_30
13. Giudice, V., Manganelli, B., Paola, P.: Depreciation Methods for Firm's Assets. In: Gervasi, O., et al. (eds.) ICCSA 2016. LNCS, vol. 9788, pp. 214–227. Springer, Cham (2016). doi:10.1007/978-3-319-42111-7_17
14. Manganelli, B., Paola, P., Giudice, V.: Linear programming in a multi-criteria model for real estate appraisal. In: Gervasi, O., et al. (eds.) ICCSA 2016. LNCS, vol. 9786, pp. 182–192. Springer, Cham (2016). doi:10.1007/978-3-319-42085-1_14
15. Giudice, V., Manganelli, B., Paola, P.: Spline smoothing for estimating hedonic housing price models. In: Gervasi, O., Murgante, B., Misra, S., Gavrilova, M.L., Rocha, A.M.A.C., Torre, C., Taniar, D., Apduhan, B.O. (eds.) ICCSA 2015. LNCS, vol. 9157, pp. 210–219. Springer, Cham (2015). doi:10.1007/978-3-319-21470-2_15
16. Del Giudice, V., De Paola, P.: Geoadditive models for property market. Appl. Mech. Mater. **584–586**, 2505–2509 (2014). Trans Tech Pubblications
17. Del Giudice, V., De Paola, P.: The effects of noise pollution produced by road traffic of Naples Beltway on residential real estate values. Appl. Mech. Mater. **587–589**, 2176–2182 (2014). Trans Tech Pubblications
18. Del Giudice, V., De Paola, P., Manganelli, B., Forte, F.: The monetary valuation of environmental externalities through the analysis of real estate prices. Sustainability **9**(2), 229 (2017). MDPI Switzerland

19. Del Giudice, V., De Paola, P., Cantisani, G.B.: Rough set theory for real estate appraisals: an application to directional district of Naples. Buildings **7**(1), 12 (2017). MDPI Switzerland

20. Del Giudice, V., De Paola, P., Cantisani, G.B.: Valuation of real estate investments through fuzzy logic. Buildings **7**(1), 26 (2017). MDPI

21. Del Giudice, V., De Paola, P., Forte, F.: Using genetic algorithms for real estate appraisal. Buildings **7**(2), 31 (2017). MDPI

22. Del Giudice, V., Manganelli, B., De Paola, P.: Hedonic analysis of housing sales prices with semiparametric methods. Int. J. Agri. Environ. Inf. Syst. **8**(2), 65–77 (2017). IGI Global Publishing

23. Duane, S., Kennedy, A.D., Pendeleton, B.J., Roweth, D.: Hybrid Monte Carlo. Phys. Lett. B **195**(2), 216–222 (1987)

24. Fukunaga, K.: Introduction to Statistical Pattern Recognition, 2nd edn. Academic Press, San Diego (1990)

25. Graves, A.: Practical variational inference for neural networks. Adv. Neural. Inf. Process. Syst. **24**, 2348–2356 (2011)

26. Hinton, G., Camp, D.V.: Keeping neural networks simple by minimizing the description length of the weights. In: Proceedings of the Sixth Annual Conference on Computational Learning Theory, pp. 5–13 (1993)

27. Hornik, K., Stinchcombe, M., White, H.: Multilayer feedforward networks are universal approximators. Neural Netw. **2**(5), 359–366 (1989)

28. Jaynes, E.T.: Bayesian methods: general background. In: Justice, H.D. (eds.) Maximum Entropy and Bayesian Methods in Applied Statistics. Cambridge University Press (1986)

29. Jylanki, P., Nummenmaa, A., Vehtari, A.: Expectation propagation for neural networks with sparsity-promoting priors. J. Mach. Learn. Res. **15**(1), 1849–1901 (2014)

30. Jordan, M.L., Bishop, C.M.: Neural networks. In: Tucker, A. (ed.) Handbook of Computer Science. CRC Press (1996)

31. MacKay, D.J.C.: Bayesian interpolation. Neural Comput. **4**(3), 720–736 (1992)

32. MacKay, D.J.C.: The evidence framework applied to classification networks. Neural Comput. **4**(5), 720–736 (1992)

33. Morano, P., Tajani, F.: The break-even analysis applied to urban renewal investments: a model to evaluate the share of social housing financially sustainable for private investors. Habitat Int. **59**, 10–20 (2017)

34. Morano, P., Tajani, F.: Estimative analysis of a segment of the bare ownership market of residential property. In: Murgante, B., Misra, S., Carlini, M., Torre, C.M., Nguyen, H.-Q., Taniar, D., Apduhan, B.O., Gervasi, O. (eds.) ICCSA 2013. LNCS, vol. 7974, pp. 433–443. Springer, Heidelberg (2013). doi:10.1007/978-3-642-39649-6_31

35. Neal, R.M.: Bayesian training of back-propagation networks by the hybrid Monte Carlo method, Technical report, Dept. of Computer Science, University of Toronto, Canada (1993)

36. Neal, R.M.: Probabilistic inference using Markov Chain Monte Carlo method, Technical report, Dept. of Computer Science, University of Toronto, Canada (1993)

37. Neal, R.M.: Bayesian learning for neural network, Ph.D. thesis, University of Toronto, Canada (1994)

38. Rumelhart, D.E., Hintont, G.E., Williams, R.J.: Learning representations by back-propagating errors. Nature **323**(6088), 533–536 (1986)

39. Soudry, D., Hubara, I., Meir, R.: Expectation backpropagation: Parameter-free training of multilayer neural networks with continuous or discrete weights. Adv. Neural. Inf. Process. Syst. **27**, 963–971 (2014)

40. William, C.K.I., Qazac, C., Bishop, C.M., Zhu, H.: On the relationship between bayesian error bars and the input data density. In: Proceedings of 4th International Conference on Artificial Neural Networks, University of Cambridge (1995)

An Assessment Model for the Periodic Reviews of the Market Values of Property Assets

Francesco Tajani[1]([✉]), Klimis Ntalianis[2], and Felicia Di Liddo[3]

[1] Department of Civil Engineering Sciences and Architecture,
Polytechnic University of Bari, Bari, Italy
francescotajani@yahoo.it
[2] Department of Marketing, Technological Educational Institute of Athens, Athens, Greece
kda175@gmail.com
[3] Department of Architecture and Design, Sapienza University of Rome, Rome, Italy
felicia.di@hotmail.it

Abstract. In this paper a mass appraisal methodology for the periodic reviews of the market values of special properties that constitute the asset balance of relevant real estate portfolios has been developed. Using the information published by Italian databases, a study sample of office properties of medium and large size, located in the city of Milan (Italy) and sold in the last decade, has been obtained. After having identified the main characteristics that contribute to the formation of property prices for the study sample considered, a model for the "quick" assessment of similar properties for intended use and explanatory variables of the prices and located in the same territorial context has been defined through the implementation of a genetic algorithm. The methodology developed satisfies the need to perform repetitive valuations, that should be not only contextualized to the spatial characteristics, but also timed to the different stages of evolution of the property cycles.

Keywords: Real Estate Funds · Market value · Mass appraisal · Investment management company · Independent advisor · Genetic algorithm

1 Introduction

The current global economic situation has been characterized by high uncertainties about the future trends. Although the forecasts in the GDP annual changes in the main countries show a positive sign, as a consequence of the widespread growth expectations, there are strong doubts about the size of real improvements. According to the OECD [17], the Brexit should cause −0.5% on the UK growth in 2017 and 2018, and −1.5% in 2019, with cascading effects on the rest of Europe.

In Italy, Greece and Spain, in particular, the uncertainty of the property market is structural. In recent years, social, economic and fiscal factors have produced deep

---

The work must be attributed in equal parts to the authors.

© Springer International Publishing AG 2017
O. Gervasi et al. (Eds.): ICCSA 2017, Part III, LNCS 10406, pp. 490–500, 2017.
DOI: 10.1007/978-3-319-62398-6_35

modifications in the property market, that currently appears as a fragile system characterized by continuous transformations. Despite the efforts of the European Central Bank, the attitude of the banks remains cautious and it is characterized by financial products that favor borrowers with appropriate liquidity and strong guarantees. Moreover, taxes on real estate have reached in a few years unprecedented levels. The formation of anomalous prices, the contraction in sales and the lengthening of the sale time are the main consequences [14].

In this context, the major market difficulties are related to the special properties, i.e. properties that, on the one hand, are characterized by large sizes, on the other hand, incorporate market values which complicate their commercialization, due to the high risk associated with the costs for the purchase, the eventual transformation and the relative management [11].

In recent years, the widespread diffusion of innovative financial instruments, such as the Real Estate Funds, has allowed the activation of a sales market for these types of properties, overcoming the generalized problem of scarcity of public and private resources [12, 19, 21] and ensuring a better management and the possible reactivation of complex properties.

Long time used in other countries as a diversification tool in pension investments [8, 9], in Italy the Real Estate Funds have been also spreading through (i) a favorable tax regime, (ii) the possibility that the promoters can be territorial Entities and/or private subjects, (iii) the establishment of an asset underlying the Real Estate Fund constituted by public and/or private properties.

With Arts. 33 and 33-bis of Decree Law No. 98/2011 new financial vehicles to increase the economic and social value of public properties have been introduced. Art. 33 provides for the creation of an *integrated* system of Real Estate Funds, with the aim of increasing the efficiency of the redevelopment and valorization processes concerning properties owned by the State and by the local Communities. Specifically, by Decree of the Minister of Economy and Finance, the constitution of an Asset Management Company has been provided for the establishment and the management of one or more Real Estate Investment Funds, that pursue strategic objectives, including the reduction of public debt.

Overall, the number of Real Estate Funds authorized by the Bank of Italy has increased from 312 in 2011 to 395 in 2016 [20]. Given that these are medium-long term investments - the minimum expected duration of Real Estate Funds is ten years, whereas the maximum duration can reach up to thirty years - there is the evident need for highly reliable valuations of the market value of the assets in the Real Estate Funds [6]: not surprisingly, the legislation provides for a periodic semi-annual review of the valuations, highlighting the central role of the independent advisor [18].

In this framework, the use of tools for the evaluation of property values is essential for the operators involved in Real Estate Funds (buyers, sellers, institutions, insurance companies, banks, etc.). The continuing uncertainty causes the need to use models which, besides being characterized by a strong theoretical and methodological basis, are able to provide consistently reliable valuations in the short term [4, 7, 10].

2 Aim

In the Measure dated January 19th, 2015, the Bank of Italy [2] emphasizes the peremptoriness that the Management Companies of Real Estate Funds acquire policies, procedures, information tools, techniques and professional resources that constantly ensure a "true and fair representation of the asset value" of the managed Fund. In the cited Measure the need to forecast the "current and future trend of the real estate market for the location of each property" of the investment Fund is highlighted.

Taking into account the extra-ordinary characters of the properties that usually compose the Real Estate Funds (structured offices, shopping malls, hotels, nursing homes, etc.), the absence of a significant market of transactions of similar properties leads to prefer, among the evaluative procedures, the *income approach* through the development of a Discounted Cash Flow Analysis (DCFA). As known, the preliminary determination of the variables that contribute to the definition of the market value to be estimated (cash flows, time horizon, actualization rate, going out cap rate, terminal value, growth rates, etc.) is preparatory for the implementation of a DCFA. In particular, each of the estimated rates inevitably takes into account a share of uncertainties that significantly affects the output of the property valuation, related to the experience and the sensitivity of the evaluator in the appreciation of the different risk components.

With reference to the market value assessments of properties that constitute Real Estate Funds, aimed to periodic reviews of the asset values of the financial tool, in this research a methodology for mass appraisal of special properties has been developed. Starting from the information published by Italian databases, a study sample of 122 office properties characterized by medium and large size, located in the city of Milan (Italy) and sold in the period 2004–2015, has been obtained. For each property, the main technological, locational and economic characteristics that contribute to the formation of property prices have been detected, in order to define, through the use of an hybrid data-driven technique that combines the effectiveness of genetic programming with the advantage of classical numerical regression, a model for the "quick" assessment of similar properties in terms of intended use and explanatory variables of the selling prices and located in the same territorial context.

The model developed could be used for the determination of "comparative" values with the estimates values obtained by the analytical procedure of a DCFA, in order to ensure a further control instrument of the results from the subjects involved, that are *(i)* the independent advisors, which are responsible of producing highly reliable economic judgments about the properties of the Real Estate Funds, *(ii)* the Management Company, in order to monitor in detail the consistency of the values estimated by the independent advisors, *(iii)* the investors in the Real Estate Funds and any institutions involved (banks, Public Administrations, insurance companies, etc.), for which it will be possible to directly and transparently check the evolution over time of the assets market values of the Real Estate Fund and consequently the performance of the own investment.

The paper is structured as follows. In Sect. 3, the database used for the implementation of the methodology developed is described, by specifying the variables considered. In Sect. 4, the method applied for the elaboration of the model is explained, the calculation for the case study is carried out and the results are illustrated. Finally, in Sect. 5 the conclusions of the work are discussed.

3   The Case Study

The case study concerns a sample of 122 office properties characterized by medium and large size, located in the city of Milan (Italy) and sold in the period 2004–2015. The choice of reporting the analysis to the office intended use was influenced by the composition of the borrowed database [16], in which the number of transactions relating to properties of different intended uses from the office one with medium and large size was small for the present research purposes. In the databases published, for each property different information are reported, including the selling price and the year of sale, the intended use, the exact location, the total gross floor surface, the year of construction and the year of the last renovation. In Fig. 1 the localization of each property of the study sample in the city of Milan is represented.

Fig. 1. Localization of the properties of the study sample in the city of Milan

With regard to the timing of the transactions considered, the individuals of the study sample are more or less "spread" within the period of analysis. The highly cyclical trend of the real estate market in the last decades does not allow to consider an uniformity of the economic factors that contribute to the formation of the selling prices in a period of over two years. Therefore, in order to consider the entire sample of 122 detected properties sufficiently consistent for mass appraisal analysis, two "market" variables have been introduced among the characteristics that contribute to the formation of the selling price. These variables are able to take into account in the final model the real estate market trends and to adequately represent the phase of real estate cycle that pertains to the homogeneous zone in which each property is located. These two economic variables are the *average market value* and the *average market rent* published by the Real Estate Observatory (OMISE) of the Italian Revenue Agency [1], and relative to the "structural offices" intended use, to the OMISE Micro-zone in which the property is located and to the year of sale. In particular, the "Micro-zone", defined according to the Presidential Decree No. 138/1998 and ensuing Regulation issued by the Ministry of Finance, for the Italian regulation, is a part of the urban area that must be urbanistically homogeneous and at the same time must constitute a homogeneous real estate market segment. Finally, the inclusion of the two economic variables described allows to borrow the logic of a *static* econometric analysis, applied on the study sample of 122 detected properties, and to simultaneously obtain an adaptable model to the economic evolutions related to different time of evaluation.

3.1 The Variables of the Model

For each property of the selected sample, the main characteristics involved in the explanation of the selling prices (P) have been detected. In particular, the explanatory variables considered are the following:

- *technological* characteristics: the total *surface* (S) of the property, expressed in square meters of gross floor area; the quality of the *maintenance conditions* (A), taken as a qualitative variable and differentiated, through a synthetic evaluation, by the categories "to be restructured", "good" and "excellent". In the model, for this explanatory variable two dummies have been considered, respectively for the state "good" (Ag) and "excellent" (Ae);
- *locational* characteristics: the *distance from the nearest subway* (W), expressed in minutes it takes to walk to it; the *distance from the Central Station* of Milan (T), expressed in minutes it takes to walk to it; the *distance from the nearest highway* (G), expressed in minutes it takes to get there by car; the *distance from the nearest urban park* (V), expressed in minutes it takes to walk to it; the *distance from the Milan Cathedral* (C), expressed in minutes it takes to walk to it; the *number of the accommodation facilities* (H) within 300 m from the property;
- *economic* characteristics: the *average market value* (Q), expressed in euro per square meter of gross floor area, published by the OMISE of the Italian Revenue Agency, relative to the "structural offices" intended use, to the OMISE Micro-zone in which the property is located and to the year of sale; the *average market rent* (L), expressed in euro per square meter of gross floor area and per month, published by the OMISE of the Italian Revenue Agency, relative to the "structural offices" intended use, to the OMISE Micro-zone in which the property is located and to the year of sale.

For the definition of the quality of the *maintenance conditions* (A), the information obtained from the databases consulted about the year of construction and the year of last renovation have been integrated through surveys conducted on site and by web. In particular, the "good" state indicates immediately usable office properties, whereas the "excellent" state refers to properties characterized by high architectural values (*trophy* properties). With reference to the data of the locational characteristics timed to the year of sale of each property, thematic maps published on web sites, reports, street maps, planning documents of the city of Milan have been consulted, in order to "photograph" the real situation to the period of interest.

As regards the main statistics of the values of the variables for the database considered, given the extra-ordinariness of the properties of the database, the mean of the *selling prices* is equal to 28,050,000 €, with values ranging between 1,100,000 € and 175,200,000 €, whereas the mean of the total *surface* is equal to 8,518 m², with minimum and maximum values respectively equal to 950 m² and 35,000 m². In Figs. 2 and 3 two thematic maps are represented, that describe the spatial distribution of the *selling prices* and of the total *surfaces* of the sample study in the city of Milan.

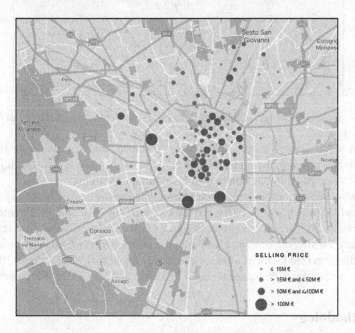

Fig. 2. Spatial distribution of the selling prices of the sample study in the city of Milan

All the properties of the study sample are relatively close to a metro station and a highway: the mean values of the variables *distance from the nearest subway* and *distance from the nearest highway* are respectively equal to seven minutes walking - value range: [1–30] - and eight minutes by car - value range: [1–20]. Higher mean values are instead reported for the *distance from the nearest urban park* - the mean value is equal to eleven minutes walking, and the maximum value arrives at fifty-two minutes walking -, for the *distance from the Central Station* - the mean value is equal to fifteen minutes walking, and the maximum fair arrives at fifty-one minutes walking -, for *the number of the accommodation facilities* within 300 m - the mean value is equal to twenty-one, and the

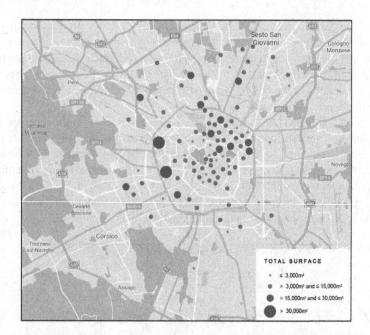

Fig. 3. Spatial distribution of the total surfaces of the sample study in the city of Milan

maximum value arrives at sixty-five. Larger distances are recorded *from the Milan Cathedral*, characterized by a mean value equal to twenty-one minutes walking and a maximum value equal to one hundred and two minutes walking.

The mean values for the dummy variables related to the quality of the *maintenance conditions* (A) show that 57% of the properties of the study sample is characterized by a "good" state, 26% are *trophy* properties and, consequently, 17% requires renovation investments. Finally, the economic variables *average market value* and *average market rent* are characterized by mean values respectively equal to 4,228 €/m^2 and 20.33 €/m^2 for month, with maximum values up to 14,575 €/m^2 and 75.13 €/m^2 for month.

4   Methodology

The econometric methodology implemented for the elaboration of the model to be used for the "quick" assessment of special properties located in the city of Milan is an hybrid data-driven technique, called *Evolutionary Polynomial Regression*. Implemented in the real estate sector in different applications for forecasting purposes [13, 15, 22], the method proposed can be considered as a generalization of the stepwise regression, that is linear with respect to regression parameters, but it is non-linear in the model structures. Equation (1) shows a generic non-linear model structure of the methodology:

$$Y = a_0 + \sum_{i=1}^{n} [a_i \cdot (X_1)^{(i,1)} \cdot \ldots \cdot (X_j)^{(i,j)} \cdot f((X_1)^{(i,j+1)} \cdot \ldots \cdot (X_j)^{(i,2j)})] \tag{1}$$

where n is the number of additive terms, a_i are numerical parameters to be valued, X_i are candidate explanatory variables, (i, l) - with $l = (1,..., 2j)$ - is the exponent of the l-th input within the i-th term in Eq. (1), f is a function selected by the user among a set of possible mathematical expressions. The exponents (i, l) are also selected by the user from a set of candidate values (real numbers).

The iterative investigation of model mathematical structures, implemented by exploring the combinations of exponents to be attributed to each candidate input of Eq. (1), is performed through a population based strategy that employs a genetic algorithm, whose individuals are constituted by the sets of exponents in Eq. (1) and chosen by the user. In particular, the methodology does not require the exogenous definition of the mathematical expression and the number of parameters that fit better the data collected, since it is the iterative process of the genetic algorithm that returns the best solution.

The accuracy of each equation returned is checked through its Coefficient of Determination (COD), defined in Eq. (2):

$$COD = 1 - \frac{N-1}{N} \cdot \frac{\sum_N (y_{estimated} - y_{detected})^2}{\sum_N (y_{detected} - mean(y_{detected}))^2}, \tag{2}$$

where $y_{estimated}$ are the values of the dependent variable estimated by the methodology, $y_{detected}$ are the collected values of the dependent variable, N is the sample size in analysis. The fitting of a model is greater when the COD is close to the unit value.

Therefore, the methodology leads to a range of solutions for the user, among which it is possible to select the most appropriate solution according to the specific needs, the knowledge of the phenomenon in analysis and the type of experimental data used.

4.1   The Model: Application of the Methodology to the Case Study

The methodology is implemented considering the base model structure reported in Eq. (1) with no function f selected and, taking into account the results obtained in several studies [3], the dependent variable is represented by the natural logarithm of the selling price ($Y = ln\,(P)$). Each additive monomial term is assumed to be a combination of the inputs (i.e. the explanatory variables) raised to the proper exponents. Candidate exponents belong to the set $(-2; -1; -0.5; 0; 0.5; 1; 2)$, in order to have a wide range of solutions, among which the best compromise between performance statistics and the empirical reliability of the relationships between candidate inputs and the dependent variable should be defined. The maximum number n of additive terms in final expressions is assumed to be eleven, that is equal to the number of explanatory variables considered.

The analysis carried out has allowed to identify the most appropriate model, characterized by the functional form in Eq. (3), that links the selling prices with all the explanatory variables considered:

$$ln(P) = 14.0925 - 10.185 \cdot \frac{C}{S} - 0.00020569 \cdot H^{0.5} \cdot Q^{0.5} \cdot L^{0.5} + 0.0060682 \cdot T^{0.5} \cdot Ae \cdot Q^{0.5} +$$
$$+ 0.01838 \cdot \frac{W \cdot T^2}{C^2} + 0.049377 \cdot \frac{S^{0.5}}{T^2} + 0.02679 \cdot S^{0.5} - 0.00004398 \cdot S^{0.5} \cdot W \cdot T \cdot Ae + \tag{3}$$
$$+ 1.2183 \cdot 10^{-12} \cdot V^2 \cdot C^{0.5} \cdot H \cdot Ag \cdot Q^2 + 1.0816 \cdot 10^{-10} \cdot G^2 \cdot C \cdot Ag^{0.5} \cdot Q \cdot L^2 +$$
$$- 4.2123 \cdot 10^{-10} \cdot S^2 \cdot W^{0.5}.$$

The performance indicators show a high statistical reliability of the model obtained: the COD is equal to 88.82%; the Root Mean Square Error, that is the square root of the mean of the squared errors between the prices of the original sample and the values estimated through the model, is equal to 2.96%; the Mean Absolute Percentage Error, that is the average percentage error between the detected prices and the values estimated, is equal to 1.98%; the Maximum Absolute Percentage Error, that is the maximum percentage error between the detected prices and the values estimated through the model, is equal to 13.07%.

Therefore, with reference to office properties characterized by medium and large size located in the city of Milan, the assessment of the market values of properties similar to the sample study analyzed may be developed entering into Eq. (4), that is the exponential transformation of Eq. (3), the amount of detected features.

$$P = exp(14.0925 - 10.185 \cdot \frac{C}{S} - 0.00020569 \cdot H^{0.5} \cdot Q^{0.5} \cdot L^{0.5} + 0.0060682 \cdot T^{0.5} \cdot Ae \cdot Q^{0.5} +$$
$$+ 0.01838 \cdot \frac{W \cdot T^2}{C^2} + 0.049377 \cdot \frac{S^{0.5}}{T^2} + 0.02679 \cdot S^{0.5} - 0.00004398 \cdot S^{0.5} \cdot W \cdot T \cdot Ae + \tag{4}$$
$$+ 1.2183 \cdot 10^{-12} \cdot V^2 \cdot C^{0.5} \cdot H \cdot Ag \cdot Q^2 + 1.0816 \cdot 10^{-10} \cdot G^2 \cdot C \cdot Ag^{0.5} \cdot Q \cdot L^2 +$$
$$- 4.2123 \cdot 10^{-10} \cdot S^2 \cdot W^{0.5}).$$

In Fig. 4 the detected prices of the sample analyzed are compared with the prices estimated by the model of Eq. (3). The graphical representation shows the statistical goodness of the results: an almost exact match of the values is widely verified.

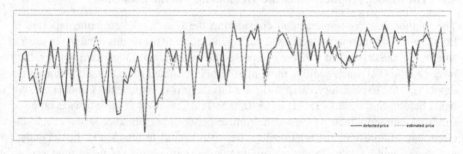

Fig. 4. Comparison between the detected prices (continuous line) and the estimated prices (broken line)

5   Conclusions

The high volatility of the financial market, related to the uncertainties about the real dimension of the non-performing bank loans and to the delicate geo-political international balances, the continuing crisis in the real estate sector, generated by the subprime market and by the banking credit crunch, and the general lack of resources, have led private and public entities to a growing interest in alternative investment forms, such as the Real Estate Funds. By investing primarily in corporate real estate, characterized by large sizes and located in highly attractive locations for potential tenants, these tools allow to ensure, on the one hand, a good profitability at a rather low risk for investors, on the other hand, the reactivation of a market of special properties, that would be alternatively characterized by an absolute stagnation [5].

However, the experiences of recent years have highlighted the main weaknesses of these financial products, related to the frequent lack of expertise able to ensure assessments of the property assets that reflect the actual market trends. For this reason, several regulations have been promulgated (among all, the UNI 11558:2014) aimed at certifying the independent advisor figure, responsible for the periodic assessments of the properties that constitute the asset of the Real Estate Funds.

The methodology developed in this research, tested using the model obtained for the case study of the city of Milan, represents an evaluative support characterized by "quick" implementation for the various subjects involved in the periodic reviews of the asset values of the Real Estate Fund. This method could accompany the classical analytical approaches (DCFA), in order to provide an additional control tool of the results obtained. In particular, the inclusion of the economic variables *average market value* and *average market rent*, regularly published and updated by the Italian Revenue Agency for all the municipal micro-zones of the country, satisfies the need to perform repetitive valuations, that are not only contextualized to the spatial characteristics, but also timed to the different evolution stages of the real estate cycles.

Acknowledgements. The writers would like to thank the Central Observatory of the Real Estate Market and Estimative Services (Italian Revenue Agency), for his availability to provide the necessary real estate data for the analysis carried out and explained in the paper.

References

1. Agenzia delle Entrate. www.agenziaentrate.gov.it
2. Banca d'Italia: Regolamento sulla gestione collettiva del risparmio (2015)
3. Cassel, E., Mendelsohn, R.: The choice of functional forms for hedonic price equations: comment. J. Urban Econ. **18**(2), 135–142 (1985)
4. Del Giudice, V., De Paola, P.: Geoadditive models for property market. Appl. Mech. Mater. **584**, 2505–2509 (2014)
5. Del Giudice, V., De Paola, P.: Undivided real estate shares: appraisal and interactions with capital markets. Appl. Mech. Mater. **584–586**, 2522–2527 (2014)
6. Gregoriou, G.N., Sedzro, K., Zhu, J.: Hedge fund performance appraisal using data envelopment analysis. Eur. J. Oper. Res. **164**(2), 555–571 (2005)
7. Guarini, M.R., Battisti, F.: Benchmarking multi-criteria evaluation methodology's application for the definition of benchmarks in a negotiation-type public-private partnership. A case of study: the integrated action programmes of the Lazio Region. Int. J. Bus. Intell. Data Min. **9**(4), 271–317 (2014)

8. Hebb, T.: Pension funds and urban revitalization. Labor & Worklife Program Harvard Law School (2005)
9. Kallberg, J.G., Liu, C.H., Greig, D.W.: The role of real estate in the portfolio allocation process. Real Estate Econ. **24**(3), 359–377 (1996)
10. Casas, G.L., Scorza, F.: Sustainable planning: a methodological toolkit. In: Gervasi, O., et al. (eds.) ICCSA 2016. LNCS, vol. 9786, pp. 627–635. Springer, Cham (2016). doi: 10.1007/978-3-319-42085-1_53
11. Manganelli, B.: The break-even point of the utilities in the real estate market of bilateral monopoly. Int. J. Appl. Eng. Res. **11**(8), 5395–5399 (2016)
12. Montrone, S., Perchinunno, P., Di Giuro, A., Rotondo, F., Torre, C.M.: Identification of "hot spots" of social and housing difficulty in urban area: scan statistics for housing market and urban planning policies. In: Murgante, B., Borruso, G., Lapucci, A. (eds.) Geocomputation and Urban Planning. SCI, vol. 176, pp. 57–78. Springer, Heidelberg (2009). doi: 10.1007/978-3-540-89930-3_4
13. Morano, P., Tajani, F., Locurcio, M.: Land use, economic welfare and property values: an analysis of the interdependencies of the real estate market with zonal and macro-economic variables in the municipalities of Apulia Region (Italy). Int. J. Agric. Environ. Inf. Syst. **6**(4), 16–39 (2015)
14. Morano, P., Tajani, F.: The break-even analysis applied to urban renewal investments: a model to evaluate the share of social housing financially sustainable for private investors. Habitat Int. **59**, 10–20 (2017)
15. Morano, P., Tajani, F., Locurcio, M.: GIS application and econometric analysis for the verification of the financial feasibility of roof-top wind turbines in the city of Bari (Italy). Renew. Sustain. Energy Rev. **70**, 999–1010 (2017)
16. Nomisma. www.nomisma.it
17. Organization for Economic Co-operation and Development (OECD). www.oecd.org
18. Pattitoni, P., Petracci, B., Spisni, M.: NAV discount in REITs: the role of expert assessors. Appl. Econ. Lett. **20**(2), 194–198 (2013)
19. Rega, C., Bonifazi, A.: Strategic Environmental Assessment and spatial planning in Italy: sustainability, integration and democracy. J. Environ. Planning Manage. **57**(9), 1333–1358 (2014)
20. Scenari Immobiliari: I Fondi Immobiliari in Italia e all'estero (2016)
21. Scorza, F.: Towards self energy-management and sustainable citizens' engagement in local energy efficiency agenda. Int. J. Agric. Environ. Inf. Syst. **7**(1), 44–53 (2016)
22. Tajani, F., Morano, P., Locurcio, M., Torre, C.: Data-driven techniques for mass appraisals. Applications to the residential market of the city of Bari (Italy). Int. J. Bus. Intell. Data Min. **11**(2), 109–129 (2016)

Tentative Reflections on Construction of Assessment Models for Buildings' Sustainability Certification

Maria Fiorella Granata[✉]

Department of Architecture, University of Palermo, Viale delle Scienze - building 14,
90128 Palermo, Italy
maria.granata@unipa.it

Abstract. All over the word several rating systems have been produced to certificate the sustainability level of buildings. Experts agree on considering sustainability a typical field for multicriteria decision analysis, but buildings' rating systems do not comply in a consistent manner this assessment approach. Proposals for using classical and hybrid ranking procedures are aimed to quantify the relative attractiveness of buildings, but do not give information on their absolute attractiveness. While several studies propose suitable application of multicriteria decision making techniques for assessing buildings' sustainability with the purpose of choosing the best solution or obtaining a ranking on a set of alternative solutions, the present work focuses on assessment aimed at buildings' sustainability certification, analyzing the aggregation phase of the assessment procedure. This work is intended to give some tentative reflections on construction of assessment models for buildings' sustainability certification systems in the effective methodological frame of multicriteria decision analysis.

Keywords: Buildings' sustainability · Certification system · Multicriteria decision analysis · Absolute assessment · Aggregation phase

1 Introduction

Since the nineties of the past century the impact of building sector emerged as one of the major factors of pressure on natural environment [1]. From then on all over the word hundreds [2] of rating systems (LEED, BREAM, EcoQuantum, Energy Star, etc.) have been developed to certificate the environmental quality of buildings and a growing number of buildings have been subjected to voluntary certification. Rating systems are the result of government entities or non-government organizations' efforts to measure buildings' sustainability. They are aimed at certify the quality of buildings focusing on different areas of sustainability and are conceived for various types of projects [2]. They generally fall into the classes of total quality assessment systems (e.g. LEED, BREAM), environmental systems based on life cycle analysis (e.g. EcoPro, EcoQuantum, BEES, Equer), energy consumption evaluation systems (e.g. Energy Star, Energy Certification of Building, Nabers Energy) [3] and water consumption evaluation systems (Nabers Water). This work focuses the so called "total quality assessment" of buildings, which integrates the different dimensions of sustainability.

© Springer International Publishing AG 2017
O. Gervasi et al. (Eds.): ICCSA 2017, Part III, LNCS 10406, pp. 501–515, 2017.
DOI: 10.1007/978-3-319-62398-6_36

Scope of buildings' quality certification is providing stakeholders with an inclusive judgment from numerous criteria describing the various assessment dimensions. Overall assessment of buildings' performance plays an important role, since it affects real estate market and construction industry [4–6], but the usefulness of formal evaluation models depends on quality of their intrinsic formal characteristics and their implementation [7, 8].

Several approaches have been applied to assess public and private performances of buildings [9]. Monetary (cost benefit analysis, cost revenue analysis, life-cycle cost analysis) and physical approaches (e.g. CO_2 balance, emergy analysis, energy and water consumption analyses) have been adopted in one-dimensional methods [10]. Nevertheless, since the last sixties it was clear that the assessment of total quality of buildings requires a multi-criteria approach, in order to take into consideration both factors easily quantifiable in monetary or physical terms and factors that cannot be easily quantified, such as the social, cultural, esthetical and perceived ones [10]. Buildings are very complex objects whose description requires the consideration of several features relevant for various actors having multiple conflicting points of view. Therefore, assessing the comprehensive sustainability of buildings fits the typical domain of multi-dimension decision problems.

Multiple-Criteria Decision Analysis (MCDA) offers several approaches to address choosing, sorting and ranking problems of the available alternatives. In MCDA models the aggregation step has the fundamental role to reproduce preferences of decision maker or synthesize a set of scores in a unique meaningful global score. In order to accomplish this task, the used procedure must be appropriate to the special condition of application. The knowledge of conditions implied by the different models of aggregation is essential for choosing approaches consistent with preferences of the decision maker and for a better understanding of assumptions, limitations or advantages deriving from techniques used for the aggregation of criteria in decision-making.

The present work suggests framing the development of rating and scoring tools into multi-criteria decision analysis and focuses the procedural aspects on construction of building's assessment models. It aims at exploring the application of MCDA methods in assessment protocols for buildings' sustainability certification. In particular, some tentative suggestions are given in order to develop rating tools able to give global assessments coherent with decision makers' preferences by a well established formal method.

The next part of this paper is articulated as follows. First, on the ground of literature on buildings' rating systems and assessment (Sect. 2) and of the procedural approach in existing rating protocols (Sect. 3), the aim and content of this work is detailed (Sect. 4). Then some tentative suggestion for effective assessment tools for buildings' sustainability certification (Sect. 5) is given. The paper concludes discussing the previous analysis and outlining future working out (Sect. 6).

2   Literature on Building Rating Systems and Ranking

The wide literature on building's total quality assessment testifies a topical interest on this issue. It can be divided into two main threads concerning the existing rating systems and the assessment of buildings by multicriteria decision methods.

Several studies analyze and compare various rating systems in relation to the set of criteria used [e.g. 5, 6, 10–12], the system of weights adopted [e.g. 2] and characteristics of the tools like cost of certification, influence, availability, applicability to different use of building, accuracy and user-friendliness transparency and communicability of results [2, 11]. Even the studies oriented toward a more complete analysis of the entire elements constituting a rating system [13] do not analyze thoroughly the question of the aggregation of marginal performances in an overall judgment.

Literature on assessment of building quality through multicriteria techniques is as much as wide too. New scholarly assessment procedures have been proposed concerning the energy performance [i.e. 14, 15] or the global environmental performance of buildings [16]. General [17] and particular [18] frameworks for assessing sustainability on urban scale were also proposed.

Scholars agree on the need of defining proper sets of criteria [3, 19, 20] and weights [21, 22] concordantly with regional climate and context conditions, such as local building material and techniques, income level and other social, cultural, economic and environmental factors [4].

Various methods have been applied by scholars to determine rankings of buildings. For instance, Medineckiene et al. [23] used a modified version of Analytic Hierarchic Process (AHP), Drejeris e Kavolynas [24] used the COPRAS technique to assess the comprehensive sustainability of buildings, Nilashi et al. [16] proposed a tool for assessing the performance of green buildings based on fuzzy logic and AHP.

3   Procedural Aspects in Rating Protocols for Buildings' Global Sustainability Certification

Literature is rich in studies analyzing and comparing the most used rating systems, but in the generality results that it is not clear how "preference information" used have been derived and implemented by the assessment procedure. Each rating tool uses its own set of criteria and weights and proposes a system of scores from which the global assessment is drawn. Generally, in available rating systems the aggregation of scores relating the single criteria is made by a summation of all the points awarded to each criterion. All criteria are assumed to be of equal importance (e.g. LEED) or weights are assigned to them (e.g. BREAM). The final outcome is a comprehensive score that is generally divided in a prefixed number of classes corresponding to different total quality levels of buildings. Each class is reached if the total score belongs to the prefixed range of values, but this information is not linked to an immediate and clear significance in terms of building's performance.

4   Aim and Content of This Work

As recalled in Sect. 2, a large literature proposes a variety of buildings' assessment methods developed in the methodological framework of MCDA. They are aimed at giving contribution in improving the quality of assessments related to buildings and in the generality solve ranking or choosing problems on a given set of alternatives according the relative decision maker' preferences. Ranking and choosing problems involve relative evaluations of the alternatives [7].

Ranking and choosing problems fit well assessments required in circumstances like design competitions and allocation of public funds or other incentives, but they do not fit the certification problem of buildings' global sustainability, whose goal is assessing the quality of a building in absolute terms. Certification systems of buildings' environmental total quality award a global score to a building with the ultimate scope of assigning it to a class of quality. In MCDA, the assignment of actions to pre-defined and ordered categories is called "sorting problem".

Buildings scored for certification are considered independently each other and in different times. Furthermore, sorting procedures assign an alternative to a class only on the basis of its comparison to reference actions defining the categories [7]. Sorting problems involve absolute evaluation of alternatives, which is each action is considered independently from the others [7].

Therefore, in rating systems an absolute assessment of alternatives is required. Furthermore, an immediate and clear semantic meaning to the various levels of building quality would be desirable.

The aim of the present work is to identify suitable multicriteria decision methods for scoring or directly sorting buildings according to their level of sustainability. The following points outline the peculiarities of the decision problem here considered:

1. The set of buildings to be assessed is not known a priori.
2. The required outcome of assessment is an overall score (on which the assignment to a class of total quality is based) on each building or the direct assignment of each building to a pre-ordered class of global quality.
3. The performances of a building on criteria can be cardinal data (i.e. a real number) or ordinal data (i.e. linguistic grade or number having the same significant).
4. Preference data may be characterized by different type of uncertainty. External uncertainty concerns the imperfect knowledge of alternatives' consequences (as it is the case of data on future phases of building's life-cycle) while internal uncertainty is related to vagueness information or linguistic information by decision-maker [25]; therefore, probabilistic and fuzzy data may be considered.
5. Compensation among criteria may be accepted or not depending on the sustainability paradigm on which the building certification standard wishes to lay on. Compensation among criteria is allowed when a weak idea of sustainability is accepted, whilst it is not allowed if a strong conception of sustainability is adopted [26, 27].
6. Interaction among criteria may easily occurs dealing with very complex objects like buildings, but a consistent family of criteria [28] can also be defined by careful

analysis of relevant points of view if a certain loss of preference information is tolerated.

7. After global scores have been assigned to some buildings it is required that the ranking of buildings do not undergo rank reversal when other new buildings are assessed through the rating standard.

8. A clear and immediate meaning of the assessment output would be appropriate, considering the important environmental, technical, economic and social roles of building certification.

5 Constructing a Consistent Evaluation Model for Buildings' Total Quality Rating

5.1 Literature References

Choosing a suitable multicriteria decision method in a given decision process is a hard task. Recent literature on this technical issue comprehends a few works concerning multicriteria decision methods addressing general decision problems and sustainability assessment.

In particular, the latter topic is dealt with by De Montis et al. [29] and Rowley et al. [30]. De Montis A. et al. propose a comparative study aimed at clarify the quality of various multicriteria decision methods with respect to the general sustainability issue, while by Rowley H.V. et al. provide an analysis of theoretical implications behind the multicriteria procedures used in quantitative sustainability assessments like life-cycle analysis.

Guitouni and Martel [31] and Roy and Słowiński [32] give guides for choosing suitable methods in general decision problems.

5.2 The Method

In order to identify suitable multicriteria decision methods for assessing buildings in terms of sustainability, the guide by B. Roy and R. Słowiński [32] is adopted in the present work. The proposed hierarchy of fundamental questions leading to right methods concerns: the type of results the method is expected to bring; the requirements on preference scales; the acquisition of preference information; the handling of imperfect knowledge; the acceptance of compensation among criteria; the existence of interaction among criteria; the intelligibility, axiomatic characterization and weaknesses of the considered methods [32].

Following this path in the case here considered the first level of analysis concerns the identification of multicriteria decision methods giving as an outcome a score or a sorting solution. Then, the other questions have to be considered.

Consistency between properties of the original performance scales and properties required by the considered method have to be verified. When selected methods cannot handle original scales of the evaluation criteria, the possibility of transform original scales in a way such that the properties of scales required by the considered method are satisfied have also to be verified.

The need to take into account uncertainties in the definition of performances can be handled by sensitivity and robustness analysis, introducing the probability theory approach and/or the fuzzy theory approach, and using semi and pseudo criteria.

Acceptation of compensation between bad and good performances on some criteria has to be decided on. Methods based on aggregation of criteria into a synthetic criterion assigning a numerical value to each potential action are compensative ones; outranking methods allow a more limited compensation; methods based on the use of "if..., then..." decision rules do not admit any compensation [32].

The opportunity of taking into account interactions among criteria has to be considered, together with the ability of decision method to satisfy the needs of comprehension from stakeholders involved.

"Secondary" questions can also be considered on the adequacy of axiomatic characterization of the selected methods with the considered decision context and the analysis of the impact of weak points in the selected methods which can affect the output of the assessment [32].

5.3 Analysis of Major Aggregation Methods

Generalities. Multicriteria scoring or sorting problems arise when buildings are assessed to certify their sustainability level. As much as the sorting one, the scoring problem can be considered as an aggregation problem [33].

MCDA aims to provide the decision maker indications for decisions in real world situations, on the basis of information provided by the decision maker about his preferences [7]. In MCDA aggregation transforms a multi-dimensional input, which is the performances of an alternative on different points of view, into a synthetic single-dimensional output [7]. Several multicriteria decision procedures are able to address an aggregation problem in choosing, sorting and ranking problems [28] on a set of alternatives. According to Figueira, Greco and Erghott [25] the main aggregation approaches belong to the classes of Multiple Attribute Utility/Value Theory, outranking methods and other "non-classical" approaches, as the decision rule approach [34] and the fuzzy integral approach [35].

Scoring methods. In the outranking approach [36] a preference degree is assigned to the ordered pair of alternatives with respect to each criterion and the global preference degree is obtained by aggregating all the partial preference degrees. Procedures belonging to the outranking approach (ELECTRE [37], PROMETHEE [38]) operate by pair-wise comparison of alternatives and are suitable to ranking problems [7]. They do not give absolute assessments and are not useful in dealing with the scoring problem in consideration where buildings to be assessed are not known a priori.

The MultiAttribute Value/Utility Theory (MAVT/MAUT) [39, 40] assumes that the preferences of decision maker can be expressed by a certain unknown function that aggregates the various points of view taken into account [41]. The distinction between MAVT and MAUT refers respectively to preferences under conditions of certainty or risk [40]. When MAUT/MAVT approach is applied the identification of global assessment function is a difficult task. If the key condition of mutual preferential independence among the considered criteria (that is, the trade-offs between a couple of criteria do not depend on all other criteria) is satisfied the simpler additive form of comprehensive utility function might be assumed [41]. When aggregation of information in an overall assessment of alternatives is based on the construction of a value/utility function, weights have the meaning of trade-offs among the criteria [41] and have to be defined using special procedures aimed at eliciting intercriteria preferences of decision maker [39, 42]. These characteristics make the method very data intensive when a very complex evaluation is attending to, but MAUT approach is also considered a rigorous methodology to incorporate risk and uncertainty preferences into the assessment [43]. Methods belonging to the value-focused approach are compensatory, i.e. allows that an inadequate performance of an action with respect to a given criterion can be balanced by a good performance on another criterion [41].

Since comparisons between buildings are not allowed in the assessment problem in consideration, the preference disaggregation approach [44] seems to be a suitable solution for inferring the wanted decision models. By the "ordinal regression", global preference models are indirectly derived from the analysis of decision maker's overall preference on some reference set of alternatives [45]. The UTA method [44] is the most used method for the additive ordinal regression [45].

In addition to MAUT approach other multicriteria aggregation procedures based on a synthesizing criterion [46] might be used in scoring problems. The Simple Multi-Attribute Rating Theory (SMART) [42], the TOPSIS method [47] and the AHP [48] are among the major operational models, in which imperfect knowledge can be taken into account by probabilistic or fuzzy models [46]. Methods belonging to the value-focused class of aggregation approaches admit only true-criteria.

The Simple Multi-Attribute Rating Technique (SMART) is the weighted linear additive version of MAVT. It is affected by the drawbacks of the weighted arithmetic mean: it assumes that all criteria are measured on the same quantitative measurement scale, that differences between values on different criteria are comparables, and that different performances on criteria can compensate each other [41]. In assessment of building sustainability the natural scales of criteria do not satisfy these requirements. The use of averaging operators on nominal and ordinal information is meaningfulness from the measurement theory point of view [7]. Vinke P. [41] suggests the use of average method when dealing with criteria that represent various aspects of the same global characteristic, when performances on criteria can be expressed in the same unit and are totally compensatory. In multicriteria building assessments, it could be the case of evaluations on single dimension of sustainability, as when quality of buildings is analyzed for energy or water consumptions.

The Technique for Order Preference by Similarity to Ideal Solution (TOPSIS) requires the conversion of the various criteria dimensions into non-dimensional criteria by a normalization of performance values on criteria that make it unusable for the assessment problem in consideration in which the set of alternatives is unknown a priori.

Main advantages of Analytic Hierarchy Process (AHP) lie in its ability of handling both quantitative and qualitative judgments. The original formulation of the AHP requires comparative judgments on criteria and alternatives at each level of the hierarchy and obtains the preference information for the criteria using the eigenvector method [49]. This situation does not apply to building rating procedures where alternatives are not disposable a priori. But, the AHP also permit the rating of alternatives one at a time on the basis of absolute judgments. According the "absolute measurement" way to derive priorities, paired comparisons involve the sole criteria and each alternative is rated adding the corresponding intensity rating under each criterion [49]. Furthermore, the use of the ideal mode in priorities normalization, that is doing normalization through dividing the score of each alternative by the score of the best alternative under each criterion, prevents the unwanted phenomenon of rank reversal [49].

From previous analysis results that disaggregation approaches based on MAUT/ MAVT and AHP used in the "absolute measurement" modality have the requisite for applicability in assessment problems in which a set of alternative is not known a priori and can attribute a global score to each assessed building.

But, when a score is assigned to each certified building it would be appreciable if scores could be interpreted as the degree of quality (sustainability) attained so that the difference between two scores might express the quality differential between the buildings. Nevertheless, when the multicriteria assessment output is expressed by numbers it is not always obvious to interpret these numbers in terms of the level of performance achieved: differences between global scores of two alternatives cannot be interpreted in terms of preference difference [7]. This is an important drawback for application of MAVT/MAUT and AHP methods in scoring of sustainable building, where a correspondence of score and preference differences seems to be essential. Scoring of building having a useful interpretation is admitted by the construction of special value functions that in general do not decompose additively [7]; while the "additive model of preference differences" is subjected to strong axiomatic limitations [7]. These methods are uncommon and not much explored in practical problems.

Analogous considerations can be referred to the fuzzy integral approach. Fuzzy integrals can be used to build models of the preferences of the decision maker and are able to represent the interaction between criteria in a range of variation from synergy to redundancy. The use of interacting criteria avoids the exclusion of a criterion (together with the information it brings [41]) from the decision model owing to its correlation with another one. Fuzzy integrals as well as value-focused models can associate global scores to each alternative, but they cannot be interpreted as values measuring the distances among quality of alternatives [35].

Sorting methods. In consideration of the above, a prudent choice could be tackling the assessment of buildings oriented towards quality certification by a direct assignment to ordered classes of quality. In the case a sorting solution is preferred various methods can provide this type of outcome. In the following part of the present section main features of a few of them based on different approach (ELECTRE TRI, UTADIS, TOMASO and the DRSA methods) are recalled.

ELECTRE TRI (by W. Yu, 1992) assigns alternatives to pre-defined and pre-ordered categories on the basis of an outranking relation built using the concordance-discordance principles [7, 37]. The assignment of a given alternative to a certain category is made on the basis of a comparison of alternatives to the limiting profiles of categories [37]. The assignment method can use an optimistic or a pessimistic procedure. Using the former procedure, an alternative is always assigned to a higher category when than when using the pessimistic approach [7]. The ELECTRE TRI procedure requires the definition of the limiting profile for each category and of the preference parameters (weights, indifference and preference thresholds, veto thresholds). When ELECTRE methods are implemented, the elicitation of preference parameters values is a critical task. In order to overcome the drawback of direct elicitation of preference parameters, some special techniques for ELECTRE TRI have been proposed for complete and partial inference of preference parameters [37]. The simultaneous inference of weights, veto thresholds and category limit (complete inference) requires the solution of a non linear mathematical programming model that is computationally difficult for real-world problems [37].

The UTilités Additives DIScriminantes (UTADIS) technique (by Jacquet-Lagrèze É, 1995] is derived from the UTA method in order to deal with sorting problems [50]. It applies the preference disaggregation approach assuming the existence of an additive value/utility function consistent as possible with the decision maker's global preferences. The decision maker provides his global evaluation on a set of references alternatives classifying them into pre-defined ordered classes. Then a consistent additive utility model is derived by linear programming techniques [50].

The Technique for Ordinal MultiAttribute Sorting and Ordering (TOMASO) method (by Marichal J-L and Roubens M., 2001) is a sorting procedure able to deal with interacting points of view [51]. It comprehends some fundamental steps: first the criteria evaluation are turned into scores; then the aggregation phase is implemented, using the Choquet integral to obtain a global net score associated to each alternative (the fuzzy measure associated to the Choquet integral is assessed from a subset of alternatives that are assigned beforehand to the classes by the decision maker by solving a linear constraint satisfaction problem). Alternatives are assigned to graded classes on the basis of these global scores [51]. The fuzzy measure assessed do not immediately indicates the global importance of criteria nor their level of interaction. But the Shapley importance indexes and interaction indices can be derived from it, thus giving a measure respectively of the overall importance of each point of view and of the extent of positive or negative interaction of criteria [51]. Some advantages of TOMASO method can be recognized. First of all the possibility of a less restrictive definition of criteria, which are not supposed to be independent as in the case of other sorting method (for instance, PROMETHEE TRI and ELECTRE TRI). Independence of criteria can be a quite restrictive condition for building sustainability assessment. Secondly, the decision maker does not have to provide preference information (weights, thresholds) that is obtained from a set of well-known alternatives. Furthermore, the TOMASO method can use purely ordinal data obtained by asking the decision maker some questions on global evaluations concerning the alternatives. Some difficulties inherent in the TOMASO method concern the necessity to turn the original ordinal evaluations of alternatives on criteria in scores and the possibility that the linear program to be solved in order to find the fuzzy measure has no solution [51]. In this case Meyer and Roubens [51] suggest to find the required fuzzy measure by solving a quadratic program.

The Dominance-based Rough Set Approach (DRSA) [52] is the mathematical basis of the decision rule approach to the multiple-criteria decision making. It is based on the original rough sets theory [53], modified by the substitution of the indiscernibility relation by a dominance relation in the rough approximation of decision classes, in order to make it suitable for use in the decision support. DRSA model uses the preference disaggregation logic, according to which the set of decision rules induced from examples can be then applied to potential actions. In the decision rule approach information about decision maker' preferences are expressed in an enough natural manner by decision rules of the type "if ... then" and the output is a set of decision rules which play the role of a model of global preference. The main features of the rule preference approach are synthesized by Greco and Matarazzo [54] as follows. With regard to the input, the decision maker have to give information about his preferences only in terms of exemplary decisions information while parameters of the preference model, such as weights, rates of substitution and thresholds are not required; heterogeneous information (qualitative and quantitative, preference-ordered or not, crisp and fuzzy evaluations and ordinal and cardinal scales of preference, with a hierarchical structure and with missing values) can be processed; furthermore, the inconsistencies should not be removed prior to analysis, since rough set analysis is able to handle inconsistent preferences [54]. With regard to the output information, the preference model induced from the initial information is expressed in the easily interpretable language of decision rules. In addition, the rough set analysis supplies some knowledge about the importance of attributes or criteria and their interaction, the minimum sets of attributes or criteria (reducts) that contain the most relevant knowledge in the exemplary decisions, the set of criteria that are not reducible (core) [54].

Other sorting procedures were proposed in the MCDA framework, as ELECTRE-SORT [55], TOPSIS-SORT [56], PROMETHEE SORT [57]. In some cases various versions of a basic sorting model have been proposed [58]. Giving an exhaustive list and analysis of sorting methods is beyond the purpose of this work, which is solely intended to identify some major potentially suitable approach for multicriteria certification of building sustainability.

A final remark concerns the social value of buildings' sustainability certification. As discussed in the previous dedicated section, building sustainability assessment should involve interests of whole society, represented by several stakeholders having special and conflicting points of view on the decision problem. When an assessment problem is processed in a natural way as a multiple decision makers problem group decision-making methods are required [59]. Most group decision-making methods concerns the choosing and ranking problems [60], but some proposals for group multi-criteria sorting problems can be recognized. Without any pretention of completeness, some methodology to support groups in multicriteria sorting problems are here recalled. They are based on multiple-attribute utility theory [61, 62], dominance-based rough set approach [60], outranking approach [63–65].

6   Conclusions

Certification of buildings' sustainability could be usefully addressed by MCDA models able to reproduce the preferences of decision makers.

Selecting a multicriteria aggregation procedure is a crucial activity from which depends the effectiveness of decision models. The selected model has to be consistent with input preference information and output information needed by the decision makers [7, 32]. Each multicriteria aggregation procedure presupposes theoretical assumptions that must match the real-world decision problem.

In this study, main characteristics of the major aggregation models in MCDA were analyzed in order to single out those potentially suitable for assessments oriented to certification of buildings' sustainability.

From this viewpoint, an important question regards the different types of relating criteria.

Building rating systems communicate important information to various stakeholders of real estate market, such as policy makers, property owners, landlords, tenants, owner-occupiers, designers, developers and building societies, property companies, investors, etc. Each type of stakeholder is interested to different information [1] and an effective comprehensive building assessment should include all the requirements of the various parties involved [4].

When assessing the sustainability of buildings all the fundamental (environmental, social and economic) dimensions have also to be included. Furthermore, dealing with buildings' sustainability requires the inclusion of the whole life-cycle of constructions, from the first designing phase to the constructing, operating, maintaining and removing ones. This is a very difficult task, since the knowledge of future phases of a building life-cycle are uncertain and even technical information on past phases can be imprecise [10].

As a consequence, the multicriteria assessment model should be able to deal with all types of criteria: measurable criteria, enabling the preferential comparison of intervals of the evaluation scale; ordinal criteria, when the evaluation scale is discrete and has only an ordinal meaning; probabilistic criteria, when uncertainty in the buildings' performances can be modeled by probability distributions; and fuzzy criteria, when buildings' performances are intervals of the criterion's evaluation scale [66].

A great variety of criteria must be considered and the assessing procedure should be able to deal in a consistent manner with mixed data. The usual approach adopted in dealing with various types of criteria is the conversion into a single type of values. This approach belong to current practice, however it have some drawbacks. For instance, turning ordinal values into numbers give ranking results depending on which numbers are chosen [33] while the recourse to fuzzy numbers to consider uncertain and imprecise knowledge requires the definition of membership functions that may be affected by certain arbitrariness [67]. The best approach to this question is to avoid transformations of data before their processing [68].

Another important question concerns the true meaning of a given level of sustainability attached to a building by a rating system. As it results from the previous analysis, procedures based on a synthesizing criterion can operate on single alternative associating a global score to each of them, but they however give as output ordinal information reproducing the decision makers' preferences [7]. Global scores on buildings obtained by multicriteria aggregation methods cannot be interpreted in the generality as meaningful measures of absolute differences of quality among buildings, while they are significant as ordinal measures of their sustainability.

In the light of the mentioned drawbacks, scoring buildings through multicriteria aggregation methods do not seem the best way of dealing with assessments for sustainability certification. On the contrary, multicriteria sorting methods can provide a direct assignment of buildings to ordered classes of sustainability in a consistent manner with decision makers' preferences.

A third important question concerns the social role of buildings' global sustainability certification. Considering this role, the possibility to express in a natural language the assessment results would be particularly useful in building certification.

In this perspective, the dominance-based rough set approach seems to be a particularly appropriate model for representing the preferences of decision makers in assessments for total quality certification of buildings. In fact, it is can deal with quantitative and qualitative, crisp and fuzzy information without require any additional information like a grade of membership or a value of possibility; it can determine the relevance of the criteria individually considered and obtain information on their interaction; it can identify the subsets of criteria containing the relevant knowledge of exemplary decisions in order to reduce the complexity of the analysis and make the assessment model clearer for stakeholders.

Finally, the author points out that this paper is not intended as an exhaustive guide for multicriteria assessment of buildings' total quality. It is only aimed to give some tentative reflections on construction of assessment models for buildings' sustainability certification systems in the methodological frame of multicriteria analysis. The broad literature on multicriteria decision making remains the comprehensive reference for those who want to go into MCDA axiomatic features thoroughly. This work is only a first tentative suggestion on this topic. Further researches are required to test the usefulness of models identified for building sustainability certification purposes.

Acknowledgements. Author is grateful to the anonymous referees for their helpful observations.

References

1. Cole, R.J.: Emerging trends in building environmental assessment methods. Build. Res. Inf. **26**(1), 3–16 (1998)
2. Pacific Northwest National Laboratory: Sustainable Building Rating Systems. Summary, operated for the U.S. Department of Energy by Battelle (2006). https://www.gsa.gov
3. Berardi, U.: Sustainability assessment in the construction sector: rating systems and rated buildings. Sustain. Dev. **20**(6), 411–424 (2012)
4. Ding, G.K.C.: Sustainable construction-The role of environmental assessment tools. J. Environ. Manage. **86**, 451–464 (2008)
5. CoreNet Global: International Sustainability Systems Comparison. Prepared for CoreNet Global by Ove Arup & Partners Ltd. (2014) http://www.corenetglobal.org

6. Crawley, D., Aho, I.: Building environmental assessment methods: applications and development trends. Build. Res. Inf. **27**(4/5), 300–308 (1999)
7. Bouyssou, D., Marchant, T., Pirlot, M., Tsoukiàs, A., Vincke, P.: Evaluation and Decision Models with Multiple Criteria. Springer, New York (2006)
8. World Green Building Council: Quality Assurance Guide for Green Building Rating Tools, Version 1.1 (2015). http://www.worldgbc.org
9. Granata, M.F.: Valore e costo dell'architettura sostenibile. Estimo e territorio **5**, 12–23 (2006)
10. Granata, M.F.: Economia eco-sistemica ed efficienza bioarchitettonica della città. FrancoAngeli, Milano (2008)
11. Nguyen, B.K., Altan, H.: Comparative review of five sustainable rating systems. Procedia Eng. **21**, 376–386 (2011)
12. Chandratilake, S.R., Dias, W.P.S.: Sustainability rating systems for buildings: comparisons and correlations. Energy **59**, 22–28 (2013)
13. Wallhagen, M., Glaumann, M., Eriksson, O., Westerberg, U.: Framework for detailed comparison of building environmental assessment tools. Buildings **3**, 39–60 (2013)
14. Loh, E., Crosbie, T., Dawood, N., Dean, J.: A framework and decision support system to increase building life cycle energy performance. J. Inf. Technol. Constr. **15**, 337–353 (2010)
15. Koo, C., Hong, T., Lee, M., Park, H.S.: Development of a new energy efficiency rating system for existing residential buildings. Energy Policy **68**, 218–231 (2014)
16. Nilashi, M., et al.: A knowledge-based expert system for assessing the performance level of green buildings. Knowl.-Based Syst. **86**, 194–209 (2015)
17. Bentivegna, V., Curwell, S., Deakin, M., Lombardi, P., Mitchell, G., Nijkamp, P.: A vision and methodology for integrated sustainable urban development: BEQUEST. Build. Res. Inf. **30**(2), 83–94 (2002)
18. Cilona, T., Granata, M.F.: A choquet integral based assessment model of projects of urban neglected areas: a case of study. In: Murgante, B., Misra, S., Rocha, Ana Maria A.C., Torre, C., Rocha, J.G., Falcão, M.I., Taniar, D., Apduhan, Bernady O., Gervasi, O. (eds.) ICCSA 2014. LNCS, vol. 8581, pp. 90–105. Springer, Cham (2014). doi:10.1007/978-3-319-09150-1_8
19. Ali, H.H., Al Nsairat, S.F.: Developing a green building assessment tool for developing countries – Case of Jordan. Build. Environ. **44**, 1053–1064 (2009)
20. Alyami, S.H., Rezgui, Y., Kwan, A.: Developing sustainable building assessment scheme for Saudi Arabia: Delphi consultation approach. Renew. Sustain. Energy Rev. **27**, 43–54 (2013)
21. Yu, W., Li, B., Yang, X., Wang, Q.: A development of a rating method and weighting system for green store buildings in China. Renewable Energy **73**, 123–129 (2015)
22. Khalil, N., Kamaruzzaman, S.N., Baharum, M.R.: Ranking the indicators of building performance and the users' risk via analytical hierarchy process (AHP): Case of malaysia. Ecol. Ind. **71**, 567–576 (2016)
23. Medineckiene, M., Zavadskas, E.K., Björk, F., Turskis, Z.: Multi-criteria decision-making system for sustainable building assessment/certification. Arch. Civ. Mech. Eng. **15**, 11–18 (2015)
24. Drejeris, R., Kavolynas, A.: Multi-criteria evaluation of building sustainability behavior. Procedia Soc. Behav. Sci. **110**, 502–511 (2014)
25. Figueira, J., Greco, S., Ehrgott, M.: Introduction. In: Figueira, J., Greco, S., Ehrgott, M. (eds.) Multiple Criteria Decision Analysis: State of the Art Surveys, pp. xxi-xxxvi. Springer, New York (2005)
26. Costanza, R., et al.: The value of the world's ecosystem services and natural capital. Nature **387**, 253–260 (1997)

27. De Mare, G., Granata, M.F., Nesticò, A.: Weak and strong compensation for the prioritization of public investments: multidimensional analysis for pools. Sustainability **7**(12), 16022–16038 (2015)
28. Roy, B.: Méthodologie Multicritère d'Aide à la Décision. Economica, Paris (1985)
29. De Montis, A., De Toro, P., Droste-Franke, B., Omann, I., Stagl, S.: Assessing the quality of different MCDA methods. In: Getzner, M., Spash, C., Stagl, S. (eds.) Alternatives for Environmental Valuation, pp. 99–133. Routledge, Abingdon (2004)
30. Rowley, H.V., Peters, G.M., Lundie, S., Moore, S.J.: Aggregating sustainability indicators: Beyond the weighted sum. J. Environ. Manage. **111**, 24–33 (2012)
31. Guitouni, A., Martel, J.-M.: Tentative guidelines to help choosing an appropriate MCDA method. Eur. J. Oper. Res. **109**, 501–521 (1998)
32. Roy, B., Słowiński, R.: Questions guiding the choice of a multicriteria decision aiding method. EURO J. Decis. Process **1**, 69–97 (2013)
33. Grabisch, M.: How to score alternatives when criteria are scored on an ordinal scale. J. Multi-Criteria Decis. Anal. **15**, 31–44 (2008)
34. Greco, S., Matarazzo, B., Slowinski, R.: Decision rule approach. In: Figueira, J., Greco, S., Ehrgott, M. (eds.) Multiple Criteria Decision Analysis: State of the Art Surveys, pp. 507–561. Springer, New York (2005)
35. Grabisch, M.: The application of fuzzy integrals in multicriteria decision making. Eur. J. Oper. Res. **89**, 445–456 (1996)
36. Roy, B.: Classement et choix en presence de points de vue multiples (la méthode ELECTRE). RAIRO **8**, 57–75 (1968)
37. Figueira, J., Mousseau, V., Roy, B.: ELECTRE methods. In: Figueira, J., Greco, S., Ehrgott, M. (eds.) Multiple Criteria Decision Analysis: State of the Art Surveys, pp. 133–162. Springer, New York (2005)
38. Brans, J.P., Mareschal, B.: Promethee methods. In: Figueira, J., Greco, S., Ehrgott, M. (eds.) Multiple Criteria Decision Analysis: State of the Art Surveys, pp. 163–195. Springer, New York (2005)
39. Von Neumann, J., Morgenstern, O.: Theory of Games and Economic Behaviour, 2nd edn. Princeton University Press, Princeton (1947)
40. Keeney, R.L., Raiffa, H.: Decisions with Multiple Objectives Preferences and Value Tradeoffs. Wiley, New York (1976)
41. Vincke, P.: Multicriteria Decision-Aid. Wiley, Chichester (1992)
42. Von Winterfeldt, D., Edwards, W.: Decision Analysis and Behavioral Research. Cambridge University Press, Cambridge (1986)
43. Velasquez, M., Hester, P.T.: An analysis of multi-criteria decision making methods. Int. J. Oper. Res. **10**(2), 56–66 (2013)
44. Jacquet-Lagrèze, È., Siskos, J.: Assessing a set of additive utility functions for multicriteria decision making: The UTA method. Eur. J. Oper. Res. **10**, 151–164 (1982)
45. Angilella, S., Greco, S., Lamantia, F., Matarazzo, B.: Assessing non-additive utility for multicriteria decision aid. Eur. J. Oper. Res. **158**, 734–744 (2004)
46. Roy, B.: Paradigms and challenges. In: Figueira, J., Greco, S., Ehrgott, M. (eds.) Multiple Criteria Decision Analysis: State of the Art Surveys, pp. 3–24. Springer, New York (2005)
47. Hwang, C.-L., Youn, K.: Multiple Attribute Decision Making - Methods and Application: A State of the Art Survey. Springer, New York (1981)
48. Saaty, T.L.: The Analytic Hierarchy Process. McGraw-Hill, New York (1980)

49. Saaty, T.: The analytic hierarchy and analytic network processes for the measurement of intangible criteria and for decision making. In: Figueira, J., Greco, S., Ehrgott, M. (eds.) Multiple Criteria Decision Analysis: State of the Art Surveys, pp. 345–407. Springer, New York (2005)

50. Spronk, J., Steuer, R.E., Zopounidis, C.: Multicriteria decision aid/analysis in finance. In: Figueira, J., Greco, S., Ehrgott, M. (eds.) Multiple Criteria Decision Analysis: State of the Art Surveys, pp. 799–857. Springer, New York (2005)

51. Meyer, P., Roubens, M.: Choice, ranking and sorting in fuzzy multiple criteria decision aid. In: Figueira, J., Greco, S., Ehrgott, M. (eds.) Multiple Criteria Decision Analysis: State of the Art Surveys, pp. 471–506. Springer, New York (2005)

52. Greco, S., Matarazzo, B., Słowiński, R.: Rough sets methodology for sorting problems in presence of multiple attributes and criteria. Eur. J. Oper. Res. **138**(2), 247–259 (2002)

53. Pawlak, Z.: Rough sets. Int. J. Inf. Comput. Sci. **11**, 341–356 (1982)

54. Greco, S., Matarazzo, B.: Decision rule approach. In: Figueira, J., Greco, S., Ehrgott, M. (eds.) Multiple Criteria Decision Analysis: State of the Art Surveys, pp. 507–561. Springer, New York (2005)

55. Ishizaka, A., Nemery, P.: Assigning machines to incomparable maintenance strategies with ELECTRE-SORT. Omega **47**, 45–59 (2014)

56. Sabokbar, H.F., Hosseini, A., Banaitis, A., Banaitiene, N.: A novel sorting method TOPSIS-SORT: An application for Tehran environmental quality evaluation. Ekonomika a management 2(XIX), 87–104 (2016)

57. Araz, C., Ozkarahan, I.: A multicriteria sorting procedure for financial classification problems: The case of business failure risk assessment. In: Gallagher, M., Hogan, J., Maire, F. (eds.) Intelligent Data Engineering And Automated Learning - IDEAL 2005, LNCS, vol. 3578, pp. 563–570. Springer, Berlin-Heidelberg (2005)

58. Zopounidis, C., Doumpos, M.: Multicriteria classification and sorting methods: A literature review. Eur. J. Oper. Res. **138**(2), 229–246 (2002)

59. Munda, G.: Social multi-criteria evaluation (SMCE): methodological foundations and operational consequences. Eur. J. Oper. Res. **158**(3), 662–677 (2004)

60. Chakhar, S., Saad, I.: Dominance-based rough set approach for groups in multicriteria classification problems. Decis. Support Syst. **54**, 372–380 (2012)

61. Greco, S., Kadzinski, M., Mousseau, V., Słowiński, R.: Robust ordinal regression for multiple criteria group decision: UTAGMS-GROUP and UTADISGMS-GROUP. Decis. Support Syst. **52**(3), 549–561 (2012)

62. Dyer, R.F., Forman, E.H.: Group decision support with the AHP. Decis. Support Syst. **8**, 99–124 (1992)

63. Dias, L.C., Clímaco, J.N.: ELECTRE TRI for groups with imprecise information on parameter values. Group Decis. Negot. **9**, 355–377 (2000)

64. Damart, S., Dias, L.C., Mousseau, V.: Supporting groups in sorting decisions: Methodology and use of a multi-criteria aggregation/disaggregation DSS. Decis. Support Syst. **43**, 1464–1475 (2007)

65. Jabeur, K., Martel, J.-M.: An ordinal sorting method for group decision-making. Eur. J. Oper. Res. **180**, 1272–1289 (2007)

66. Jacquet-Lagrèze, È., Siskos, J.: Preference disaggregation: 20 years of MCDA experience. Eur. J. Oper. Res. **130**, 233–245 (2001)

67. Pawlak, Z., Skowron, A.: Rudiments of rough sets. information. Science **177**, 3–27 (2007)

68. Munda, G.: Intensity of preference and related uncertainty in non-compensatory aggregation rules. Theor. Decis. **73**, 649–669 (2012)

Local Communities and Management of Cultural Heritage of the Inner Areas. An Application of Break-Even Analysis

Francesco Calabrò[✉] [ID]

Department of Patrimonio, Architettura, Urbanistica – PAU, Mediterranea University
of Reggio Calabria, Salita Melissari, 89124 Reggio Calabria, Italy
`francesco.calabro@unirc.it`

Abstract. This paper describes an application of Break-Even Analysis (BEA) as an instrument to support public decision-makers in identifying the type of entity to be entrusted with the management of architectural heritage, in the case of absence of public resources for this purpose. The case study is localized in Gerace, a Calabrian small town, in the South of Italy. In particular, in this case, the BEA verifies the economic sustainability of the management of such assets; BEA compares the implications of the entrusting to two different types of entity, private for-profit and private not-for-profit, which have different structures of operating costs. The application of BEA allows us to understand how the expected levels of demand generate sufficient revenue to allow a balanced budget, when the management entity is a private not-for-profit; but they are not sufficient to ensure the profitability needed when the management will be entrusted to a private for profit entity. This implies the need to involve the local community in the management of cultural heritage, through a direct commitment: this role is crucial, for example, in the Inner Areas, when the tourist's flows are insufficient to guarantee the profitability for private for profit subjects. However, if the heritage is a relevant tourist attractor, profits are not directly generated by the management of the asset, but significant impacts are still produced on the local economy. This is the reason because the local community have to guarantee anyway the enjoyment of its heritage.

Keywords: Inner areas · Local communities · Management models · Economic sustainability · Break-Even Analysis

1 Introduction

The sustainability of the management of cultural heritage is today one of the most difficult challenges for the transmission to future generations of the set of knowledge, values, traditions incorporated therein [1, 2].

The condition of progressive contraction of available public resources, far from being one of the known cyclical phases, looks more and more like a structural condition to deal with, even in the future, as highlighted by numerous authors, including: [3, 4].

The long phase of public debt expansion that characterized the period after the Second World War brought the precarious equilibrium conditions for public finances [5, 6]. The economic crisis has a two-way cause-effect relationship with the public finances:

© Springer International Publishing AG 2017
O. Gervasi et al. (Eds.): ICCSA 2017, Part III, LNCS 10406, pp. 516–531, 2017.
DOI: 10.1007/978-3-319-62398-6_37

the level of public debt makes it essential a progressive reduction in government spending; in turn, this leads to a reduction in aggregate demand, with detrimental effects on the entire economy, with a consequent decline in state revenues derived from fees, etc. [7], among others.

These are the reasons that lead to assess as structural the condition of progressive contraction of available public resources, as for the conservation and enhancement of cultural heritage, as is the case for other sectors [8].

This condition leads to the search for innovative solutions to pursue the objectives of conservation and enhancement of heritage, nevertheless [9]: this contribution aims the deepening of the economic estimation and assessment instruments capable of verifying the economic viability and sustainability of innovative solutions for the management of cultural heritage, with particular reference to the architectural and landscape heritage.

The need to ensure the financial viability of the cultural heritage in the process is even more felt in the presence of forms of public-private partnership: subjects of different nature, they have different cost structures, whereas it can be considered invariable the structure of revenues.

In particular, this paper illustrates, through a case study, a technique, Break Even Analysis (BEA), which can help in decision-making, in the phase of intervention planning: it can assist in identifying the most suitable type of management's subject for the examined case and the consequent definition of the management model.

2 The Cultural Heritage Effects on Local Economies

Literature, Italian and foreign, which deals with the effects of cultural heritage in the local economic systems is really vast [10–14], only to mention a few. It is one of the fundamental principles of sustainable development as well as one of the cornerstones of European policies for regional development [15, 16], etc.

Among the various aspects highlighted in the literature, of particular interest for the purpose of this paper it is the turistic fruition of the cultural heritage, which can be considered a particular form of export.

Cultural tourism, in fact, may constitute a prospect of great interest for the most disadvantaged areas: if properly organized, it can generate significant effects on local economies. It is not only interested the system of receptivity but, more generally, the entire production system: the particular type of tourist, in fact, particularly appreciates the specificities of the territories, including the products and culinary preparations [17].

2.1 Local Communities of the Inland Areas for the Enhancement of Cultural Heritage

The less developed regions, such as Calabria, are often characterized by contradictory phenomena, even more accentuated in the Inner Areas: on the one hand a significant budget in cultural heritage, slightly or anything enjoyed; by the other the weakening of the productive system, with the consequent gradual abandonment of agricultural activity and anthropogenic desertification of large areas [18].

There are many factors that determine the short competitiveness of the productive systems of these areas and the difficulties of their products to penetrate markets; among them, we can mention, for example: the lack of sufficient critical mass of product, the high production costs, insufficient efficiency in the public administration, insufficient qualification and characterization of the products, etc.

Even more so in these areas, cultural tourism can be a significant opportunity; for those territories, therefore, it is vital to allow the use of their cultural heritage also to activate tourist flows and, through them, rebuild the economic systems and fight depopulation trend.

In this direction, the local communities have a fundamental role [19]: in a condition of absence of public resources for the management of cultural heritage, the effects that can generate their use are nevertheless evident; in these cases, local communities must become aware that only through their direct engagement is possible to stop the regressive phenomena and trigger development processes based on the enhancement of local resources [20, 21].

3   A Classification of Subjects' Nature, Activities and Costs

As pointed out before, to overcome the known limits of the public entities in the management phase, there are many reminders of the Code of Cultural Heritage and Landscape [22], to the need to involve private entities in the development of cultural heritage, distinguishing between profit and not-for-profit entities [23].

In fact, to the purpose of this Article, the most relevant distinction is related to the nature of the activity, not of the subject: there are, in fact, numerous cases of subject with not-for-profit nature but that carry out economic activities. In such cases does not change the cost structure between a not-for-profit or profit subject, but the tax regime to which they are subject, in addition, of course, the prohibition for not-for-profit organizations to distribute profits [24, 25].

Each of types of the subject identified has different characteristics. In the case of public bodies is known the rigidity in the management phase, due to procedural constraints imposed by current legislation, which is often associated with the difficulties to acquire the necessary skills. The private entities for profit normally are characterized by greater operational efficiency, which, however, must match an adequate return on investment, with the risk to overshadow the public interests, prominent in the case of the management of cultural heritage; furthermore, this type of subjects has a cost structure characterized by high fixed costs for human resources. The not-for-profit organizations arise from determined values shared by the members: usually, these subjects carry out volunteer activities without economic relevance, but also have the opportunity to manage economic activities linked to its objectives. In organizational terms, they are characterized by an intermediate level of efficiency between public entities and private for-profit, due on the one hand by the absence of the procedural constraints typical of public bodies, the other hand by the voluntary nature of participation of members, when it comes without economic returns activities [26].

The involvement of private entities for the purpose of enhancement of cultural heritage focuses attention on the economic dimension of these processes, since it entail the need for such subjects to maintain the financial viability of any business and, in the case for-profit activities, to ensure adequate levels of profit.

The purpose of this paper is precisely to verify the conditions that ensure the economic and financial balance in the enhancement processes in the public-private partnership, in relation to managing entities with different nature, which are associated with different management models: for that aim, therefore, it is particularly important to understand how the cost structure change if change the management models, while we can consider invariable the structure of revenues.

3.1 Nature of Entities and of Activities

Basing on the nature of the activities and of the managing entity, it is possible to hypothesize the following three models (Table 1):

Table 1. Managing models by type of subject

Managing model	Nature of entity and activities
Model P - Profit	Entity profit, activities profit
Model NP - Not-for-profit	Entity not-for-profit, activities not-for-profit
Model M - Mixed	Entity not-for-profit, activities profit

The first model requires no special in-depth: it responds to the classical model of business entities, for which the economic and financial balance occurs only if is guaranteed an adequate level of profit. Given the fixed costs for human resources that characterize it, this model is inapplicable where the visitor flows are not so significant as to generate substantial revenues.

In not-for-profit model, the managing entity, carrying out not-for-profit activities, benefits from the volunteer commitment of the members and other parties at no charge. Them for those activities do not receive any compensation, except possibly an occasional form, in addition to the reimbursement of any costs incurred. Another significant cost item for human resources absent in this model, is the one for management, that is, the organization of production factors [27]. In this way, the fixed cost of human resources is greatly reduced, sometimes transforming this type in variable cost (being occasional performances), significantly reducing the operating costs in the presence of limited flows of users. It is a usable model when a community attaches particular importance to a given asset, the management of which, however, does not generate revenue sufficient to allow coverage of the operating costs of entity for profit or similar entities.

In the mixed model, however, the subject not-for-profit, conducts activities from which it draws significant revenues, such as to be regarded as economic activities in all respects. In this case, it can be equated to a subject for profit in terms of the cost structure, because the involved human resources must be paid as provided in the legislation for those particular tasks. The only differences are that: there is not-for-profit; any surpluses are reinvested in the same activity and can not be distributed among the members; sometimes it goes also considered the cost for the managerial duties, but is not a constant of the model.

It is to highlight that the management model, for the same asset, it can also change over time: it can happen that, in the start-up phase, a subject not-for-profit undertakes the management as volunteer activities. Thereafter, if the demand reaches adequate levels, the same subject can turn the activity in business or act as a start-up for the birth of a subject of entrepreneurial nature.

In any case, the choice of the management model does not depend solely by economic and financial equilibrium: even in the presence of potential adequate profits, is necessary to verify what actually is able to express a territory under the profile of the managing subject. May occur, for example, the absence of subjects of entrepreneurial circles concerned to take over the management of an asset, or can prevail political reasons, which argue in favour of a particular model.

The verification of the economic and financial equilibrium of an asset management, however, allows the decision maker to make informed choices, thereby reducing the possibility of error, and by bringing more transparency in decision-making.

3.2 The Nature of Costs

First, it serves a distinction among the different types of cost that private entities can incur with respect to the enhancement of the architectural heritage, essentially referable to two macro categories [28]: investment costs and management costs.

In fact, the enhancement of heritage requires, first, an initial investment to make usable the asset, and includes the masonry work for its fitness for use, and equipment and furnishings to its usability. In relation to the intrinsic characteristics, the state of preservation and the future use, such investment may be more unbalanced towards the building work or, conversely, to equipment and furnishings.

Initial investment completed, begins the management, which involves a number of costs including: human resources, utilities, maintenance, depreciation and amortization, other goods and services [29]. It is to point out that, among the management costs, the depreciation of equipment and furnishings and the provisions for extraordinary maintenance are particularly significant, for the purposes of assessing the economic sustainability of the projects: this guarantees the replacement of equipment and furniture and the usability of the asset over time, thereby allowing the sustainability of the initiative.

In turn, the operating costs can be divided into two categories, fixed costs and variable costs. As you know, the fixed costs are not related to production volumes, as is the case for the variable costs. Some of the items listed above are characterized by the presence of a fixed component and a variable, such as the utilities or some kinds of human resources.

As seen above, it is precisely the heading Human resources, usually among those with higher incidence, to vary significantly with the several management models: in the case of for-profit activities, in fact, it constitutes one of the major fixed costs of management.

In the case of subjects for profit, the economic-financial balance occurred only in the presence of an adequate level of profit: for this reason, in tests for financial sustainability, this item can also be treated as an operating cost and subtracted from revenue.

4   Profitability and Public-Private Partnership Forms

In relation to the capacity of the asset in question to generate revenue, in theory it can be hypothesized five (six) different conditions of profitability:

Band A. High profitability
Band B. Medium to high profitability
Band C. Average profitability
Band D. Lower-middle profitability
Band E. Low profitability

Then, there is the case of insufficient profitability or nothing (sixth profitability assumptions), which implies the absence of the minimum conditions for any form of public-private partnership and entrusts exclusively to public bodies the responsibility to make available the particular case of asset. This assumption, however, is less and less feasible in reality, due to the progressive decline of available resources in the delivery of public services [30–32].

Each of the first five of profitability conditions it can be associated with five different forms of public-private partnership, with the consequent management models (Fig. 1).

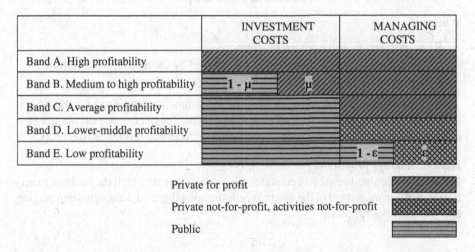

Fig. 1. Distribution of investment and managing costs between public and private entities

Band A. High profitability
This condition occurs when the discounted revenues that can be generated from the use of a certain asset, are greater than the sum of the investment costs necessary to make it accessible and of the operating costs, related to the life cycle of the intervention:

$$\Sigma Ra > \Sigma CI + \Sigma CGa$$

Where:

ΣRa = summation of discounted revenues
ΣCI = summation of the investment costs
ΣCGa = summation of discounted operating costs

In this case, the function of public entity is to govern the way of intervention, to ensure the conservation of the identifying characteristics of the asset, and the modalities of management, to ensure a proper use of the good. During the managing phase, also paid by the public entity is the burden of monitoring in order to ensure the compliance with the contract terms and, more generally, to maintain an adequate usability of the good.

This condition can be found in other types of works of public interest, and it is the basis of project financing; in the reality of cultural heritage is more difficult to find, first because of the high initial investment required for the proper physical recovery of the artefacts, that is, in respect of their identifying characteristics.

Band B. Medium to high profitability
This condition occurs when the discounted revenues that can be generated from the use of certain property, allow full coverage of discounted operating costs, related to the life cycle of the intervention, and the recovery of an aliquot μ of the initial investment:

$$\Sigma Ra > \Sigma \mu CI + \Sigma CGa$$

Where:

ΣRa = summation of discounted revenues
$\Sigma \mu CI$ = aliquot of initial investment costs covered by the discounted revenues
ΣCGa = summation of discounted operating costs

In this case, the public entity, in addition to its functions provided for the case A (which are however applicants in all cases), has the burden of covering the aliquot $(1 - \mu)$ of the investment costs, in order to ensure the intervention economic feasibility.

Band C. Average profitability
For average profitability we can consider the condition under which the revenue generated from the management of the asset exceeds the operating cost, although the managing entity is a private for profit:

$$\Sigma Ra > \Sigma CGa$$

In this case, the asset can be recovered only to the condition that the public entity assume for the entire the initial investment costs. It is this, for example, a case possible if the interventions are carried out by public entities making use of the European funds.

Band D. Lower-middle profitability

For medium to low profitability, we can consider the condition under which the revenue generated from the management of the asset exceed or equalize the operating costs, provided, however, that the managing entity is a private not-for-profit:

$$\Sigma Ra \geq \Sigma CGa$$

Even in this case, the asset can be recovered only on condition that the public partner takes for the entire the initial investment costs: this case is even more frequent (potentially) of the previous in the cases of operations carried out by public entities making use of the European funds.

Band E. Low profitability

For low profitability we mean the condition in which the revenue generated from the management of the asset are able to cover only a rate ε of the operating costs, although the managing entity is a private not-for-profit:

$$\Sigma Ra > \Sigma \varepsilon CGa$$

In this case, the asset can be recovered and made available only on the condition that the public entity assume an aliquot $(1 - \varepsilon)$ of the management costs, over the total of the initial investment costs. Even this may be a recurring case when the interventions are carried out by public entities making use of the European funds.

For the assessment of the economic and financial sustainability of projects, in this case it is of great interest to understand if the rate of costs, covered from the revenue, includes or less the extraordinary maintenance costs and depreciation of equipment and furnishings. In this case, in fact, the public contribution may be limited, for example, to few kind of costs, so for example for utilities and cleaning, but would safeguard the maintenance over time of the usability of the good and functional services.

5   The Economic and Financial Sustainability of Projects of Enhancement

Of particular interest appears, for the purpose of enhancement of the architectural heritage, the verification of profitability band in which they fall; this allows the identification of the most suitable type of managing entity, for which it is verified the economic and financial sustainability. It happens often, especially in Italian regions Convergence objective, that the public authorities are in receipt of EU funding for the physical recovery of buildings and their furnishings and equipment, but then are not able to ensure the management directly and have to resort to the indirect management [33]. Often, the assets remain unavailable because there are not conditions of adequate profitability for entrepreneurial entities. It must to verify, so, if the asset fall in the C Band (Investment by public, managing by private for profit), in the D Band (Investment by public, managing by private not-for-profit) or, even in the E Band (Investment by public, managing by private not-for-profit with public contribution to the managing).

In these cases, the verification of the economic and financial sustainability of enhancement projects in public-private partnership is done taking into account the operating costs and revenues [34]. This analysis allows to verify the relationship between the revenues generated from the use of the asset and the costs incurred by the managing subject: the overall balance obviously depends not only on the cost structure but also by the level of revenues. The revenues will be considered virtually independent of the management model, while, as we have seen, the cost structure is heavily dependent by it [35].

It is clear that the revenues that can be generated by the projects are a function of the demand, in turn dependent on a number of factors, some independent of the asset or the project [36, 37], such as, for example:

- The catchment area of potential users (an asset placed in a big city or in a town with strong tourist presence, for example, has a higher potential of one located in a small town or in town not frequented by tourists);
- The intended use of the asset and related functions that are localized within it;
- The presence of assets and/or similar functions in the vicinity;
- The inherent attractiveness of the asset in question;
- The effectiveness of the communication and marketing strategies and the availability of resources for such activities.

5.1 The Break-Even Analysis

The break-even analysis (BEA) is a decision support tool used for different purposes in the field of validation, in economic terms, of the various types of investment projects [38].

In the present case, the use of break-even analysis allows to identify the management model most appropriate to the level of estimated presences. In other words, considering the different cost structures of the alternative management models, the BEA allows to identify for which level of demand they reach the minimum condition of equilibrium, giving the possibility to see which model is applicable to the estimated level of demand in the specific case. In terms of costs, the subjects for profit have a structure of fixed costs, mainly due to the costs for human resources, other than the entities not-for-profit, when they perform not-for-profit activities, while is very similar in the case of for-profit activities.

6   The Case Study: The Cultural Park of the "Geracese" History and Memory

The case study in which it was tested the approach described above concerns the realization of the "Cultural Park of "Geracese" History and Memory" in the centre of Gerace, a small town in Calabria, in southern Italy, of early-medieval origins [39].

The project includes a series of actions aimed at achieving full usability of three religious buildings in public ownership, through the completion of their recovery and their reuse; the three assets will destined to the localization of cultural functions that make perceptible the main features of the geracese cultural heritage: the religious traditions, the settlement layering, and the medieval culture.

Specifically, there is the localization: in the St. Martino's church, a museum dedicated to the ancient history of the diocese of Gerace; in the St. Maria del Mastro's church, a documentation centre on the historical layering of the city centre; in the St. Caterina's church, a medieval study centre and documentation.

For all three actions are planned interventions of physical recovery of artifacts and upgrading work with the mounting of exhibition areas and the provision of equipment and furnishings required. The planned investment is € 1,500,000.00, fully covered by the POR Calabria 2007–2013 funds.

Pictures. St. Caterina's church, St. Maria del Mastro's church, St. Martino's church

Currently about 13,000 visitors throughout the year visit Gerace: it is, in Calabria, a major destination for cultural tourism, attracted by the rich historical and architectural heritage still present and in fairly good condition. One of the main shortcomings is the lack of services for full enjoyment and understanding of the heritage; through the planned intervention, you want to work on this very weakness, thus reinforcing the attractiveness of the village and its ability to generate economic flows.

On the basis of currently detectable tourists in Gerace and assuming an increase of 25%, can be generated by marketing actions planned to support the project, it is conceivable for the Park an annual flow of visitors, in the fully operational year (the third) of about 16,000 units.

The question asked is: given the assumed functions and the flow of visitors estimated, in which profitability condition is the intervention in question. It is conceivable to place in foster care the management to privates or it must to be managed by a public body? In the first case, what type of subject must be, for profit or not-for-profit?

6.1 The Application of Break-Even Analysis

The trial was held simulating the cash flows associated with two different management models: one of type P (for profit) and one of type NP (not-for-profit), identifying for both, through successive iterations, the breakeven point between costs and revenues.

The starting point was an estimate of the revenues, hypothesized the same for both models, and linked to the type of services provided, which consist of:

– Entrance to the Park
– Guided tours
– Supply of audio guides
– Sale informational material such as monographs etc.
– Sale gadgets

The whole of services provided and products sold produces annual revenues estimated at € 160,000.00 [40].

In terms of costs, the managing entity, of whatever nature, will have to bear:

– Fixed costs for human resources
– Other fixed costs (provisions for extraordinary maintenance, depreciation, etc.)
– Variable costs (gadgets and editorial material purchase, consumables etc.).

6.2 The Costs of the Managing Entity in the Model P – for Profit

To ensure the delivery of services foreseen by the project it is required a series of figures, between which at least one person that ensures the simultaneous opening of each of the three poles in which is articulated the park, for a total of three units, over to at least one guide and the director. The whole of human resources employed involves an annual fixed cost of € 134,600.00.

Other fixed costs (provisions for extraordinary maintenance, depreciation etc.) amount to € 21,200, while the variable costs (gadgets and editorial material purchase, consumables etc.) amount to 2.80 €/visitor.

In the presence of this cost structure, the break even point is obtained in the presence of 21,640 visitors a year (Tables 2 and 3), far above the estimated flow.

Table 2. Estimate of managing costs for the break-even point of the Model P – for Profit

Service	Variable unit cost for visitor	Visitors	Costs
Fixed costs for human resources			134.600 €
Other fixed costs			21.200 €
Variable costs	2,80 €/visitor	21.640	60.600 €
Total of costs			216.400 €

Table 3. Estimate of revenues for the break-even point of the Model P – for Profit

Service	Percentage of users on the total number of visitors	Quantities sold	Unit price	Revenues
Entrance to the park	100%	21.640	4,50 €	97.380 €
Guided tours	30%	6.492	4,00 €	25.968 €
Supply of audio guides	20%	4.328	5,00 €	21.640 €
Sale informational material	30%	6.492	6,00 €	38.952 €
Sale gadgets	50%	10.820	3,00 €	32.460 €
Total of revenues				216.400 €

6.3 The Costs of the Managing Entity in the Model NP – Not-for-Profit

The eventual not-for-profit entity may limit the use of employees through the voluntary commitment of the members that could provide some services for free, such as the one to allow the opening of the poles, especially in periods with lower turnout; in the summer months, however, the volume of activity could require the temporary employment of personnel.

Some costs for human resources, in addition, may also be attributed to variable costs, such as the one of the guides, because are occasional services directly related to the influx of visitors. Furthermore, it would not be necessary the compensation of the general activity of management: under these conditions, the annual fixed costs for human resources would amount to € 55,300.00. Other fixed costs (provisions for extraordinary maintenance, depreciation etc.) amount again to € 21,200, while the variable costs (guides, gadgets and editorial material purchase, consumables etc.) amount to € 4.80/visitor.

In presence of this costs structure, the break-even point is obtained at 14,715 visitors a year, enough below the estimated flow (Tables 4 and 5).

Table 4. Estimate of managing costs for the break-even point of the Model NP – Not-for-Profit

Service	Variable unit cost for visitor	Visitors	Costs
Fixed costs for human resources			55.300 €
Other fixed costs			21.200 €
Variable costs	4,80 €/visitor	14.715	70.630 €
Total of costs			147.130 €

Table 5. Estimate of revenues for the break-even point of the Model NP – Not-for-Profit

Service	Percentage of users on the total number of visitors	Quantities sold	Unit price	Revenues
Entrance to the park	100%	14.715	4,50 €	66.215 €
Guided tours	30%	4.415	4,00 €	17.650 €
Supply of audio guides	20%	2.943	5,00 €	14.715 €
Sale informational material	30%	4.415	6,00 €	26.480 €
Sale gadgets	50%	7.358	3,00 €	22.070 €
Total of revenues				147.130 €

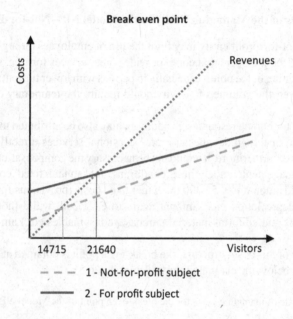

7　Conclusions

The use of break-even analysis in the illustrated case study has allowed us to verify that the managing of the particular cultural asset in question is referable to the profitability hypothesis "D" - medium-low. The managing can be entrusted to a private entity, type not-for-profit, on condition that the members contribute voluntarily and freely in the activities, while there are no conditions for business profit.

It is now a case very recurrent, especially in smaller towns and in the presence of limited flows of visitors, since public resources to ensure the management of the assets is increasingly constrained, insufficient to ensure the provision of such services.

If local communities recognize the fundamental role that cultural heritage can play in the economic development of their territory, they must to take upon oneself the burden of the managing of this heritage, through the direct commitment, voluntary and free. Only to these conditions can be guaranteed the usability of the assets, when the visitor flows are not sufficient to ensure at least an average level of profitability.

It is necessary to point out, however, that in this case the break-even analysis made it possible to verify that the financial and economic sustainability of the intervention is fully guaranteed, since the revenues allow the full coverage of the operating costs, including the extraordinary maintenance and depreciation, at no additional cost to the public sector.

Involvement of no profit entities, however, it is relevant not only about the economic sustainability of the project, but also for the empowerment of the local communities and the re-appropriation of their identity, indispensable to trigger virtuous processes of local development.

The research in this field will continue, applying the methodology to other cases study, verifying, in particular, the variations in the distribution of costs in different situations. Another aspect that deserves attention, always in terms of costs structure, it is as varies the incidence of human resources if the subject for profit recourse to new forms of contractualization provided by the innovations in the field [41, 42].

It is necessary to point out, however, that it is a field that has many risks in terms of social sustainability: we need to clearly distinguish what is a voluntary commitment, for free, from what is work. The enhancement of cultural resources must to be for the territories an opportunity for development and not an additional ground of job insecurity or worse, the incentive of forms of illegal labour.

Acknowledgements. This study has been supported by the project of the *Mediterranea* University of Reggio Calabria: Marine Energy Lab - PON03PE00012_1 - P.O.N. RICERCA E COMPETITIVITA' 2007-2013 Avviso n. 713/Ric. del 29/10/2010 - Titolo III - "Nuovi distretti e laboratori".

References

1. Fusco Girard, L., Cerreta, M., De Toro, P., Forte, F.: The Human Sustainable City: Values. Approaches and Evaluative Tools. Routledge, London (2007). pp. 65–93
2. Drury, P., McPherson, A.: Conservation principles: policies and guidance for the sustainable management of the historic environment (2008)
3. Gualerzi, D.: The Coming of Age of Information Technologies and the Path of Transformational Growth: A Long Run Perspective on the 2000s Recession. Routledge (2009). pp. 20–22
4. Hagemann H., Seiter. S.: Growth, productivity, and employment: consequences of the new information and communication technologies in Germany and the US. In: Growth, Distribution, and Effective Demand: Alternatives to Economic Orthodoxy: Essays in Honor of Edward J. Nell, p. 98. M. E. Sharpe Inc., New York (2004)
5. Dornbusch, R., Reynoso, A.: Financial factors in economic development. Am. Econ. Rev. **79**(2), 204–209 (1989)
6. Lopes, A., Giannola, A.: Politiche di intervento, sviluppo economico del mezzogiorno e debito pubblico. Il Mulino, Bologna (1992)

7. Sutherland, A.: Fiscal crises and aggregate demand: can high public debt reverse the effects of fiscal policy? J. Public Econ. **65**(2), 147–162 (1997)
8. Bodo, C., Bodo, S.: Country Profile: Italy, in Compendium of cultural policies and trends in Europe, edited by Council of Europe, Ericarts, Bruxelles: Council of Europe (2011). http://www.culturalpolicies.net/web/profiles-download.php
9. Donolo, C.: Dalle politiche pubbliche alle pratiche sociali nella produzione di beni pubblici? Osservazioni su una nuova generazione di policies. Stato e mercato **25**(1), 33–66 (2005)
10. Fusco Girard, L., Nijkamp, P. (eds.): Cultural Tourism and Sustainable Local Development. Ashgate Publishing, Ltd. (2009)
11. Santagata, W.: Cultural districts, property rights and sustainable economic growth. Int. J. Urban Reg. Res. **26**(1), 9–23 (2002)
12. Scott, A.J.: The cultural economy of cities. Int. J. Urban Reg. Res. **21**(2), 323–339 (1997)
13. Rizzo, I., Throsby D.: Cultural heritage: economic analysis and public policy. In: Handbook of the Economics of Art and Culture, vol. 1, pp. 983–1016 (2006)
14. Mazzanti, M.: Cultural heritage as multi-dimensional, multi-value and multi-attribute economic good: toward a new framework for economic analysis and valuation. J. Soc. Econ. **31**(5), 529–558 (2002)
15. Camagni, R., Capello, R., Nijkamp, P.: Towards sustainable city policy: an economy-environment technology nexus. Ecol. Econ. **24**(1), 103–118 (1998)
16. Crevoisier, O.: The innovative milieus approach: toward a territorialized understanding of the economy? Econ. Geogr. **80**(4), 367–379 (2004)
17. Long, L.M. (ed.): Culinary Tourism. University Press of Kentucky, Lexington (2004)
18. Mollica E.: Le aree interne della Calabria, Soveria Mannelli (CZ), Rubbettino (1996)
19. Boccella, N., Cassalia, G., Salerno, I.: Community led practices and cultural planning: methodological approaches and practices for sustainable urban development. In: Advanced Engineering Forum, vol. 11, pp. 125–130. Trans Tech Publications, Switzerland (2014). doi: 10.4028/www.scientific.net/AEF.11.125
20. Della Spina, L., Ventura, C., Viglianisi, A.: Enhancement and governance of the local tourist destinations in integrated perspective. Procedia Soc. Behav. Sci. **223**, 327–334 (2016). doi: 10.1016/j.sbspro.2016.05.379
21. Hampton, M.P.: Heritage, local communities and economic development. Ann. Tour. Res. **32**(3), 735–759 (2005)
22. Decreto Legislativo 22 gennaio 2004, n. 42, Codice dei beni culturali e del paesaggio
23. Bilancia, P. (ed.): La valorizzazione dei beni culturali. Modelli giuridici di gestione integrata, vol. 642. FrancoAngeli (2006)
24. Propersi, A.: Il sistema di rendicontazione negli enti non profit. Dal bilancio d'esercizio al bilancio di missione. Vita e pensiero (2004)
25. Francesconi, A.: Comunicare il valore dell'azienda non profit. Wolters Kluwer Italia (2007)
26. Giuffrida, S., Napoli, G., Trovato, M.R.: Industrial areas and the city. Equalization and compensation in a value-oriented allocation pattern. In: Gervasi, O., et al. (eds.) ICCSA 2016. LNCS, vol. 9789, pp. 79–94. Springer, Cham (2016). doi:10.1007/978-3-319-42089-9_6
27. Fazzi, L., Giorgetti, G.: Il bilancio sociale per le organizzazioni non profit. Teoria e pratica. Guerini e Associati (2005)
28. Pelfrey, S.: Cost categories, behavior patterns, and break-even analysis. J. Nurs. Adm. **20**(12), 10–14 (1990)
29. Baraldi, S., Cifalinò, A., Sacco, P.: I sistemi di programmazione e controllo. Giappicheddi, Torino (I), pp. 15–29 (2011)
30. Aas, C., Ladkin, A., Fletcher, J.: Stakeholder collaboration and heritage management. Ann. Tour. Res. **32**(1), 28–48 (2005)

31. Franch, M.: Le frontiere manageriali per la valorizzazione della cultura e dell'arte. Cultura, arte e management: frontiere e connessioni, pp. 95–107 (2010)
32. Nesticò, A., Macchiaroli, M., Pipolo, O.: Costs and benefits in the recovery of historic buildings: the application of an economic model. Sustainability 7(11), 14661–14676 (2015). doi:10.3390/su71114661. MDPI AG, Basel
33. Bencardino, M., Nesticò, A.: Demographic changes and real estate values. A quantitative model for analyzing the urban-rural linkages. Sustainability 9(4), 536 (2017). doi:10.3390/su9040536
34. Kaplan, R.S., Atkinson, A.A., Morris, D.J.: Advanced Management Accounting, vol. 3. Prentice Hall, Upper Saddle River (1998)
35. Kong, E.: The development of strategic management in the non-profit context: Intellectual capital in social service non-profit organizations. Int. J. Manag. Rev. 10(3), 281–299 (2008)
36. Tajani, F., Morano, P.: Evaluation of vacant and redundant public properties and risk control: a model for the definition of the optimal mix of eligible functions. J. Prop. Invest. Financ. 35, 75–100 (2017). doi:10.1108/JPIF-06-2016-0038
37. Cochrane, J., Tapper, R.: Tourism's contribution to World Heritage Site management. In: Managing World Heritage Sites, pp. 97–109 (2006)
38. Morano, P., Tajani, F.: The break-even analysis applied to urban renewal investments: a model to evaluate the share of social housing financially sustainable for private investors. Habitat Int. 59, 10–20 (2017). doi:10.1016/j.habitatint.2016.11.004
39. Campanella, R.: Un progetto di territorio per il turismo sostenibile. LaborEst 10, 17–22 (2015)
40. Tramontana C.: The management of cultural heritage: the importance of not-for-profit subjects, In: Advanced Engineering Forum, vol. 11, pp. 542–548. Trans Tech Publications, Switzerland (2014). doi:10.4028/www.scientific.net/AEF.11.542
41. Della Spina, L., Scrivo, R., Ventura, C., Viglianisi, A.: Urban renewal: negotiation procedures and evaluation models. In: Gervasi, O., et al. (eds.) ICCSA 2015. LNCS, vol. 9157, pp. 88–103. Springer, Cham (2015)
42. Della Spina, L., Ventura, C., Viglianisi, A.: A multicriteria assessment model for selecting strategic projects in urban areas. In: Gervasi, O., et al. (eds.) ICCSA 2016. LNCS, vol. 9788, pp. 414–427. Springer, Cham (2016)

Choice Experiments:
An Application for the Corona Verde
Landscape in Turin (Italy)

Marta Bottero[1](✉), Giada Cozza[2], Roberto Fontana[3],
and Roberto Monaco[1]

[1] Department of Regional and Urban Studies and Planning,
Politecnico di Torino, Turin, Italy
{marta.bottero,roberto.monaco}@polito.it
[2] Politecnico di Torino, Turin, Italy
giada.cozza@studenti.polito.it
[3] Department of Mathematical Sciences, Politecnico di Torino, Turin, Italy
roberto.fontana@polito.it

Abstract. How to evaluate a landscape in constant evolution and transformation? What does it constitute and determine the economic value of landscape? The present paper aims at investigating the role of evaluation tools for the assessment of the characteristics of a landscape. In line with the definition provided by the European Landscape Convention, the research deserves specific attention to the analysis of the landscape from the point of view of the values perceived by people. In particular, the paper focuses on the Choice Experiments technique that allows individual preferences and choices to be studied about several alternative scenarios. Starting from a real case concerning the Corona Verde landscape in the metropolitan area of Turin (Italy), the contribution investigates the role of Choice Experiments for supporting decision processes concerning landscape management and protection.

Keywords: Landscape economic value · Questionnaires · SAS · Total economic value · Econometric models

1 Introduction

Today, landscape covers an important role, not only in the ecological and environmental management, but also as ecological resource and as component of individuals' welfare [1]. In the land-use planning, there is a growing need for evaluation, which allows the identification of every components of landscape to be developed, considering not only spatial and environmental factors [2], but also social and cultural elements [3]. This permits to pass from a purely ecological approach toward a human approach, in which the benefits for present and future generations can be valued, both in monetary and not-monetary terms [4].

In this sense, it is important to consider evaluation approaches able to appraise all the characteristics of a landscape without excluding the perception that the population has of it, as established in the definition of landscape that the European Landscape

© Springer International Publishing AG 2017
O. Gervasi et al. (Eds.): ICCSA 2017, Part III, LNCS 10406, pp. 532–546, 2017.
DOI: 10.1007/978-3-319-62398-6_38

Convention provides. According to this approach, landscape is seen in its entirety, through the identification of the full range of objective and subjective components. The objective components concern the biophysical structure of landscape as extension, morphology and presence of urban orders; the subjective components are correlated to the observer: everyone observes the landscape and perceives different characteristics of it, independently of his/her preferences and experiences [1].

It has been noted that in order to evaluate environmental and landscape systems, it is necessary to attribute a value to all the benefits that can be delivered; therefore, it is highly important to define which advantages a landscape is able to produce and how they can be valued [5, 6]. The search of the values, which characterize the identity of a territory, is an inevitable demand in the evaluation of this kind of good [7].

In the light of the aforementioned considerations, the paper aims at investigating the role of Choice Experiments (CE) method in the decision problems related to protection, management and development of environmental and landscape goods [8]. More precisely, the objective of the study refers to an estimation of the economic value of a specific landscape, through the calculation of the Total Economic Value (TEV). It has been generally agreed that the TEV approach is suitable for dealing with the economic valuation of environmental and landscape goods and it is composed by use values, which come from the utility perceived by consumers through the enjoyment of the good, and non-use value, described by the existence value, tied to the will to preserve the good and the desire to enjoy by future generations. Following this definition, the preferences of the individuals who benefit the good become decisive and the CE method has been chosen for its capacity of considering the value that residents and tourists attach to landscape goods.

This paper is divided into 4 sections: after the introduction, the second section focuses on the Choice Experiments method; the third section describes the application of Choice Experiments to a real case study concerning the Corona Verde landscape in Turin (Italy); the last section discusses the results of the research and proposes ideas for the future.

2   Choice Experiments Methodology

Choice Experiments (CE) refers to a statistical methodology using preferences expressed to investigate consumers' attitude in front of several versions of a product or service [9]. Generally speaking, CE methodology aims at disaggregating the good to examine components from which the individuals obtain benefits; the disaggregation allows to investigate the trade-off existing among different attributes and the trade-off represents the marginal willingness to pay, when an attribute is the cost [10]. The method seems to be particularly useful in the context of the evaluation of public goods, as landscape; in fact, this method is able to reveal preferences and to measure shadow prices in the context of multi-attribute goods [11]. The development of a CE includes the following steps:

- Definition of a set of attributes, that describe landscape; each attribute is declined according to different levels where one of the attributes is usually the price.
- Combination of these levels and attributes to build hypothetical scenarios, composed at least by 2 alternatives [12] that are subsequently introduced to interviews.

All the possible combinations compose the full factorial design, that usually involves a very high number of alternatives; to obviate to the problem, it possible to apply other methods, such as the orthogonal design, that is able to reduce the complexity, ensuring at the same time the right evaluation of the main effects [13].

- Questionnaire for asking people to state their preferences about these alternative scenarios; every scenario is described in terms of its attributes and levels.
- Econometric analysis of individual responses by means of multinomial logit models, where the probability of choice of one alternative depends on attributes and socioeconomic variables.

Table 1 summarizes the steps describing CE technique.

Table 1. CE method's steps

Steps	Description
1	To find attributes that best describe the good under examination and to decline them in different levels
2	To combine attribute and levels between them to create hypothetical scenarios for interviews
3	To design questionnaire with hypothetical scenarios
4	To implement the econometric analysis and to calculate the TEV of the good

CE method has been widely used for the estimation of environmental goods [14, 15], while few applications exist dealing with assessment of the value of landscape and cultural heritage [1, 16, 17].

3 Case Study

3.1 Corona Verde Landscape

In this study, the Choice Experiments method has been applied to Corona Verde Landscape in Piedmont (Fig. 1). Since 1997 Savoy Residences, which form the "crown of delight", have been included in the UNESCO World Heritage List (World Heritage List Id., N. 823). The global significance of this good is also given by the integration of the system with the context: the Corona Verde Project, a strategic project at the regional level that promotes the creation of green infrastructures to integrate the "crown of delight" of Savoy Residences with the idea of a green belt. The idea of the project is to create a wide green belt around the city to contain urban development and to protect large green areas surrounding the cities, formed by metropolitan parks, rivers and natural areas [18].

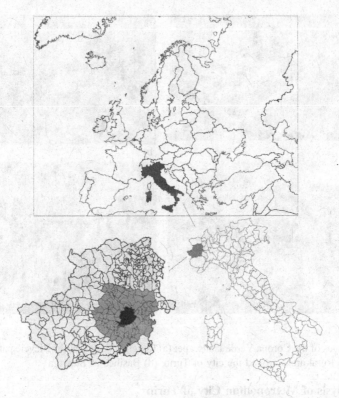

Fig. 1. The territory of the Corona Verde project (Color figure online)

The Corona Verde Project aims to highlight the values, opportunities and potentialities of the green metropolitan area, proposing redevelopments, which are able to reconstruct the image and the identity of this territory. One of the main objectives of the project is related to the valorization of the regional and provincial ecological network, with enhancement of the naturalistic and river areas, including the protection of rural and peri-urban ones [19]. The program aims to create a system of green areas connected among them and with the Royal Residences, with the purpose of ensuring usability to residents and tourists. The strategy of Corona Verde Project has different objectives, including the enhancement of the existing system of protected areas and those in project; the valorization of cultural sites, particularly for the Royal Residences system; the promotion of a project for the Metropolitan City of Turin, in order to supplement the areas constructed with green areas; the preservation of agricultural areas and their activities; the creation of new conservation projects and ecological reconstruction for degraded and abandoned areas; the enhancement of rural, urban and suburban buildings, revitalizing their potentialities; the redevelopment of rivers and water resources, including historical irrigation networks; the construction of cultural conditions with the aim of creating a requalitifation of this area to be extended and durable (Fig. 2).

Fig. 2. Images of the Corona Verde landscape: (a) Reggia di Venaria, (b) Bicycle path along the Po river, (c) Rural areas around the city of Turin, (d) Basilica of Superga

3.2 Analysis of Metropolitan City of Turin

According to the CE technique, basin analysis is a crucial point to explain the social and cultural context in which the good under examination is placed. Regarding the present application, the territory considered is the area of the Metropolitan City of Turin, which is one of the main actors of the transformation promoted by the Corona Verde program.

Firstly, the population of the 316 municipalities belonging to this area has been analyzed using the data provided by Italian National Statistical Institute. The data show a slow decline of the population, after a peak reached in 2013; moreover, the analysis puts in evidence that the population mostly belong to the age range from 45 to 59, followed by age range from 30 to 44. It is interesting to highlight that the Italian National Statistical Institute predicts that the oldest part of the population will continue to grow in the coming years, until it will reach about the 30% of the population in 2043, while the portion of the population that includes young people will have a strong decline over the next years.

Subsequently, tourism sphere has been analyzed; as far as tourism in lakes and hills of the Province of Turin is concerned, the data show that there is an increase in arrivals and presences starting from 2013: this data may be significant in identifying best places where Municipal Authorities can make hypothesis for tourism growth. Undoubtedly, the Royal Residences are very well-established attractions in Piedmont landscape: in 2013, the Reggia of Venaria hosted more than the 30% of the total number of tourists in the Crown of Delight, as to become part of the ten most visited Italian sites.

Playing a leading role in the local economy, tourism is the driving force behind the areas' morphological changes: in fact, the growth of cultural tourism influences political choices destined to the countryside, which in turn have an impact on residents of sites that are subject of transformation, which, consequently, change their attitude towards the territory, recognizing and protecting as attractive poles sites so far unknown [20, 21].

3.3   Experimental Design and Questionnaire

As mentioned in Sect. 2, Choice Experiments technique requires the determination of attributes that identify the characteristics of the good under consideration, as well as a mosaic of history, human activities, variety of settlements and natural beauty [22]. In the case study under investigation, six attributes have been identified with the help of an experts' panel with from Politecnico di Torino who worked in the design of the Corona Verde program. Each attribute has been further divided into three levels.

The following attributes have been defined (See Table 2):

Table 2. Attributes and levels

Attributes	Levels
Signs of vegetation	1: meadows 2: orchards and vineyards 3: forests
Agritourism landscape	1: urbanized areas (low) 2: historic settlements and limited recreational activities (medium) 3: historic settlements and traditional agriculture (high)
Outside activities	1: water activities (boating, kayak, etc.) 2: relax (resting and pic-nic areas) 3: cycling, hiking, horse riding
Cultural and architectural heritage	1: places of religious interest 2: villas, palaces and castles 3: Royal Residences
Accessibility ways	1: bycicle path 2: private transport (car) 3: public transport
Cost_Residents	0 € 150 € 250 €
Cost_Tourists	0 € 40 € 60 €

(1) Signs of vegetation, that considers how people perceive and store a territory, depending on the presence of signs; in this case, the signs considered are forests, orchards and vineyards or meadows;

(2) Agritourism landscape, that deals with the promotion of multifunctionality of local activities through the reuse of the heritage of historical farmhouses and the creation of innovative agritourism services; this attribute considers different possibilities for the use of rural landscapes;

(3) Outside activities, meant as leisure or sports engaged in the outdoors, but also relaxing activities, with resting and picnic areas;

(4) Cultural and architectural heritage, defined as a fundamental characteristic that describes the landscape taken in consideration; in this case, the Royal Residences of "crown of delight", but also villas, palaces and castles and places of religious interest are considered;

(5) Accessibility ways, meant as chance to easily reach a place that belongs to Corona Verde, whether by public or private transport or bicycle path;

(6) Cost, that is the most probable amount of money for an *una tantum* tax that residents would be willing to pay in order to support investments to improve this area or an entry ticket that tourists would be willing to pay for visiting the sites.

The levels of attribute "cost" were defined by a questionnaire administered to a limited sample of residents and tourists. Moreover, in this case study the pre-test was also used to translate qualitative attributes using an ordinal scale, in order to determine a base level for each attribute for the development of the CE evaluation. The pre-test was, therefore, the exploratory investigation to evaluate *ex ante* the subjects' preferences, i.e. in the period preceding the issuance of the survey. It was preparatory to the actual questionnaire, because it concerned a research conducted on a small sample of the population, to get initial reactions and to investigate the degree of understanding of descriptive attributes. It was useful in the evaluation of the dimension of each level to discover the attitudes of people and to measure the willingness to pay. To evaluate this aspect, people had to answer an open-ended question, with a different formulation for tourists and residents, so as to present a payment constraint that simulates real contexts to be accepted and plausible.

Table 2 presents attributes and levels, according to the ordinal scale, as a pre-test's results.

Attributes and levels have been combined by a partial factorial design to create hypothetical alternatives to be submitted to respondents for the evaluation. The creation of scenarios has been made with the support of the SAS® statistical software, following the steps for drawing up a generic choice design, intended as a situation in which we obtain information about the preferences of respondents on the characteristics of the good under consideration. As mentioned before, the software processed multiple choice-set designs, including orthogonal designs; these designs permits to overcome the problem of presenting a high number of scenarios. The orthogonality of the design ensures the evaluation of the main effects and avoids the respondents' preferences depend on biased construction of alternatives of the questionnaire. Two different choice-set designs and, consequently, two questionnaires were prepared in the present application: a preparatory questionnaire, made of 18 alternatives that was useful for exploring the decision context and a final questionnaire, made of 36 alternatives that was employed for the elaboration of the CE method.

With reference to the final questionnaire, using the SAS® software the 36 alternatives were grouped to form 12 choice-sets of 3 alternatives each. During the questionnaire, respondents were asked to make a choice among the 3 alternatives of each choice-set according to their preferences about the landscapes under examination.

Figure 3 provides an example of the Choice Experiments question.

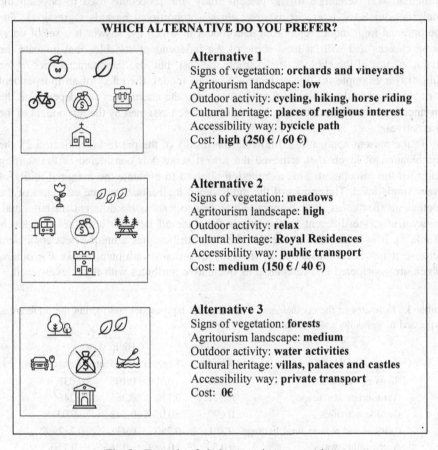

WHICH ALTERNATIVE DO YOU PREFER?

Alternative 1
Signs of vegetation: **orchards and vineyards**
Agritourism landscape: **low**
Outdoor activity: **cycling, hiking, horse riding**
Cultural heritage: **places of religious interest**
Accessibility way: **bycicle path**
Cost: **high (250 € / 60 €)**

Alternative 2
Signs of vegetation: **meadows**
Agritourism landscape: **high**
Outdoor activity: **relax**
Cultural heritage: **Royal Residences**
Accessibility way: **public transport**
Cost: **medium (150 € / 40 €)**

Alternative 3
Signs of vegetation: **forests**
Agritourism landscape: **medium**
Outdoor activity: **water activities**
Cultural heritage: **villas, palaces and castles**
Accessibility way: **private transport**
Cost: **0€**

Fig. 3. Example of choice experiments question

3.4 Econometric Model

A total of 140 respondents (divided into tourists and residents in the area of Corona Verde Landscape) were surveyed in the month of November 2016 using an on-line questionnaire that was submitted through the social networks, like Facebook and others. The answers were analyzed by means of the SAS® software, in order to estimate the relevance of each attribute and their relative levels: the statistical model assumes that for each individual n, a level of utility is associated with each alternative j; the alternative j will be chosen if and only if the utility, in the nucleus of choices, is higher than the one of the other alternatives; this utility can depend on attributes of the object or on socio-economic characteristics of individuals [23]. Kuhfeld [24] suggested important steps about model planning and analysis and proposed the use of the multinomial logit model, in which the probability to select an alternative is considered as dependent by attributes and by socio-economic variables [23]. This model was implemented by McFadden [25] and is based on Quandt's stochastic utility theory. In particular, with reference to the present study, the procedure used to develop the analysis with SAS® software is *proc phreg* (proportional hazards regression). The multinomial logit model refers to a data model in which the answer is a set of unordered choices and with at least some of the independent variables that indicate the characteristics of the choices (for example the cost) but also the characteristics of the subject (for example the age or income); in this model, the effect of an independent variable is tied to the choice of the subject among the alternatives and depends on the distance between the variable's values that have been assigned by the respondent to the alternatives.

In the present application, following the results of the pre-test (see Sect. 3.2), the combination of levels that achieved the lowest score was considered as the starting point for the calculation. This assumption allowed to evaluate the marginal utility of every single level. The results of the multinomial logit model are the estimates of the coefficients (ß) that are used to appraise how respondents assess different attributes and, consequently, the different levels: this is the trade-off between attributes and levels (Table 3). It is important to note that the cost attribute has a unique beta coefficient because it has been considered as the only quantitative attribute, unlike the others, which are considered and calculated as qualitative attributes with three levels each.

Table 3. Estimates of the coefficients of multinomial logit model considering the preferences expressed by residents and tourists.

	Medium		High	
	Residents	Tourists	Residents	Tourists
Signs of vegetation	0,180	−0,309	0,105	0,037
Agritourism landscape	0,221	0,158	0,365	0,246
Outside activities	0,090	−0,054	0,242	−0,057
Cultural and architectural heritage	0,391	0,280	0,411	0,212
Accessibility ways	−0,309	−0,089	−0,165	−0,156
Cost_ Residents	−0,005			
Cost_Tourists	−0,014			

The calculation of beta coefficients was done separately for questionnaires addressed to residents and questionnaires addressed to tourists; also the socio-economic characteristics have been investigated because they influence the respondents. As we see in Table 3, the coefficient of cost has a negative sign. This is consistent with economic theory and logic because, if the cost of the option increases the expression of preference for the option decreases. An important reflection arises from comparing the choices undertaken by tourists and those carried out by the residents: the willingness to pay of residents is greater than that of the tourists and the two resulting estimates of the beta coefficients related to the cost attribute are equal to −0,005 for residents and to −0,142 for tourists.

Moreover from the results of Table 3 it is interesting to notice that the outdoor activities attribute for tourists has always a negative sign. This means that respondents tend to prefer water activities (that correspond to the lowest score level according to the results of the pre-test) and to neglect other levels of the attribute, such as relax activities or cycling, hiking and horse riding. Also the attribute "accessibility ways" has a negative sign both for tourists and for residents: in this case respondents prefer bicycle accessibility to the landscapes under examination and they dislike other systems such as private car or public transport.

3.5   Willingness to Pay and Relations Between Decisions and Socio-Economic Context

After having estimated the coefficients from respondents' answers, it was possible to proceed with the assessment of willingness to pay, related to each level of each attribute. It is important to highlight that when one of the two attributes is a monetary value, the trade-off is a measure of its marginal value.

Equation (1) represents the formula to calculate the marginal WTP (Willingness To Pay)

$$WTP_{ik} = -\frac{\beta_{ik}^{(k)}}{\beta_{mon}}, k = 1, \ldots, 5 \tag{1}$$

where $\beta_{ik}^{(k)}$ refers to beta coefficients previously estimated, which show the effect that each attribute has on the probability of choice of the alternative, and β_{mon} indicates the coefficient referred to the monetary attribute, which is expected to be negative and significant, showing the fact that respondents shun expensive alternatives [1].

Table 4 shows the estimates of the WTP for the case under investigation.

Table 4.   Estimation of the willingness to pay of residents and tourists.

	Medium		High	
	Residents	Tourists	Residents	Tourists
Signs of vegetation	37,60 €	−2,15 €	20,85 €	2,60 €
Agritourism landscape	43,70 €	11,10 €	72,35 €	17,35 €
Outside activities	17,85 €	−3,80 €	48,00 €	−4,05 €
Cultural and architectural heritage	77,50 €	19,70 €	81,55 €	15,00 €
Accessibility ways	−61,30 €	−6,30 €	−31,75 €	−11,00 €

Attributes that indicate the preferences of residents and tourists and, thus, guide their choices regarding the alternatives in the questionnaire are the same: the greatest preference is identified with the presence of a cultural heritage and architectural assets within a landscape; secondly, great importance is also attached to the degree of naturalness and maintenance of a landscape, identified through the "agritourism landscape" attribute. However, in contrast with respect to the results of the pre-test, there are also negative WTP values, indicating that the corresponding attributes affect in a negative way respondents' choices; in this case, attributes with negative WTPs are "outside activities" and "accessibility ways".

The economic evaluation of a good needs a set of analytical tools, useful to deepen characteristics of the context in which it operates and to highlight the problems. These tools are used, therefore, to put in evidence the variables that can be crucial in the evaluation of future scenarios, giving useful information to define the guidelines to be pursued.

Among the variables in question, an essential role is covered by factors that refer to the considered population, its demographic characteristics, its social composition, the activities in which it is engaged, levels of education, income; this type of variable has particular importance since it shows the relationship that exists between the landscape under study and its recipients, namely the social subjects that benefit from it. Considering both residents and visitors, it has to be noted that any intervention, especially in the context of environmental public goods, is intended to transform the conditions of social and economic life of a population and it influences the quality of life of the inhabitants. Therefore, socioeconomic variables are very important and their importance grows in all interventions, which deeply and permanently change landscape and territorial conditions.

Estimating a model based on people's opinion, that includes socio-economic variables, is useful for assessing how much the introduction of these variables may change the previously calculated WTPs and, therefore, for analysing how respondents' way of life affects their choice. For this reason, in the questionnaire, questions that refer to the socio-economic sphere of interviewees have been included, namely level of education, profession and monthly income. These data have been analyzed in the multinomial regression model.

The data concerning educational level and profession have been divided into two new levels, in such a way that the sample of 140 respondents has been separated into two groups of 70 answers to make statistical analysis more balanced. Mention has to be made to the fact that income has been excluded for the analysis because most part of the respondents preferred not to answer to this specific question.

Tables 5 and 6 present the results of the analysis of the relationship between "profession/preference" and "education/preference". Table 5 shows that the willingness to pay from category "with income" turns out to be greater than the category "no income" with an average of around 21 €, compared to 15 €. The results of Table 5 are in line to the outcome previously described (Table 3) where the attributes that mostly affect and influence respondents' choices are those related to cultural heritage and to the agritourism landscape. Table 6 shows that the willingness to pay of category "primary education" is greater, with an average of about 21 €, compared to the category "higher education", with an average of about 16 €. Also in this case, the results are consistent with the findings of Table 3.

Table 5. Relation between respondents' profession and their choices.

	Medium		High	
	With inc.	No inc.	With inc	No inc.
Signs of vegetation	9,00 €	16,00 €	3,00 €	19,00 €
Agritourism landscape	47,00 €	22,00 €	65,00 €	45,60 €
Outside activities	0,40 €	1,70 €	44,30 €	−8,75 €
Cultural and architectural heritage	61,00 €	58,00 €	40,00 €	62,00 €
Accessibility ways	−39,00 €	−27,00 €	−19,00 €	−36,00 €

Table 6. Relation between respondents' education and their choices.

	Medium		High	
	Primary	Higher	Primary	Higher
Signs of vegetation	22,00 €	3,00 €	26,00 €	−4,35 €
Agritourism landscape	23,00 €	50,00 €	37,00 €	81,00 €
Outside activities	17,40 €	−16,60 €	32,00 €	−0,50 €
Cultural and architectural heritage	65,00 €	59,00 €	56,00 €	58,00 €
Accessibility ways	−44,00 €	−23,00 €	−18,00 €	−44,00 €

3.6 Landscapes Estimation

As previously mentioned, the coefficients resulting from the CE evaluation reveal the role of the different variables in influencing the final choice. In this sense, the estimation coefficients of Table 3 can be used to evaluate the degree that the interviews do trade-off among the attributes. In particular, from the parameters of the model it is possible to calculate the WTP or consumer surplus for specific landscape scenarios in the Corona Verde area.

Equation (2) represents the formula [1] for the calculation of the consumer surplus.

$$WTP_{i1,\dots i5} = -\frac{\beta_{i1}^{(1)} + \dots + \beta_{i5}^{(5)}}{\beta_{mon}} \tag{2}$$

where WTP indicates the willingness to pay for a single person, in relation to a certain landscape, calculated as the sum of the beta coefficients of levels, divided by the beta coefficient of the cost. The WTP is then extended to the catchment area: in the case of residents, the WTP was multiplied by the number of family units in the catchment area related to the landscape under examination, while in the case of tourists the WTP was multiplied by the number of tourist arrivals registered in the municipalities of reference. The sum of the overall consumer surplus of both residents and tourists provide the Total Economic Value (TEV) of the good under examination.

The evaluation has been developed for a number of specific landscapes of the Corona Verde program, including the Historic Palace of Stupinigi, the green infrastructural bypass, the Natural Reserve of Orco and Malone Confluence, the hill of Rivoli and the hill on the side of the Po river; each one of the considered landscapes encloses a combination of attributes, which perfectly described it. Landscapes have been identified as much different as possible, so that each level of each attribute can be represented and the complexity of the case study of the Corona Verde area can be fully investigated.

As an example, we can consider the landscape of the Historic Palace of Stupinigi. In this case the landscape is characterized by the presence of forest, historic settlements and traditional agriculture, relaxing activities, Royal Residences and bicycle accessibility. Using the coefficients of Table 3 and the formula (2) it was possible to estimate the individual WTP both for residents and for tourists as follows:

$$WTP_{Res} = -\frac{0,105 + 0,365 + 0,09 + 0,411 - 0}{-0,005} = 194,2 \, \text{€} \tag{3}$$

$$WTP_{Tou} = -\frac{0,037 + 0,24 - 0,054 + 0,213 - 0}{-0,014} = 31,6 \, \text{€} \tag{4}$$

These values have been then extended to the overall population of reference, which is composed by 20.544 family units of residents and 49.304 tourists arrivals, leading to a Total Economic Value for the landscape of the Historic Palace of Stupinigi of around 5,5 millions of Euro.

4 Discussion and Conclusion

In recent years, human activities have imposed major changes landscapes around the world. In fact, the landscapes are constantly changing because they are the expression of the dynamic interaction between natural and cultural forces. These rapid changes lead to the need of preserving, managing and developing landscapes based on a balanced relationship between social needs, economic activity and environmental system.

In this context, Choice Experiments evaluation technique can enrich the decision-making processes that affect the landscape, thanks primarily to its flexibility and the ability to take into account the multidimensional nature of the landscapes and to provide detailed information. The technique makes it possible the definition of landscape as a function of its properties or characteristics and this aspect could become an important reference for planners and Decision Makers in rural and urban design of landscape. Therefore, CE constitutes an approach that is well suited for the description of a territory: the larger the size of the territory, the higher will be the number of features that describe it.

In this work, this technique has been applied on Corona Verde landscape, in order to estimate its monetary value; although the scenery is not classified as a market good, this does not means that the intangible benefits that the population draws from its use are not measurable by a monetary value.

The application of this evaluation methodology is today considered innovative regarding the analysis of economic individual preferences within the framework of public and mixed goods, as it allows to estimate use and non-use values and it permits to appraise the importance that people attribute to different characteristics that underline such a choice. Furthermore, the structuring of the elicitation format using repeated choices, although it may increase the complexity for interviewees, it is considered more flexible and allows to obtain more information to create a complete database. The answers obtained from the questionnaires can be linked with socio-economic data provided by the respondents, such as age, education level, occupation and income. The focal point of Choice Experiments technique is the opportunity to present the good in an unbundled way, that is, through in a multi-attribute and multi-dimensional way, which takes into account not only the aspects merely quantitative, but also qualitative characteristics, that can arise from individual perceptions of residents and tourists. In this sense, one of the most important strengths of the method consists in the fact that it goes from a biocentric vision to an anthropocentric one, that can express indicators of the quality of human life [26, 27]. The fact that the technique is based on an anthropocentric approach is of particular interest in the emphasis placed on socio-economic variables, which therefore become an indicator of how a territory is developed and how the choices of citizens and tourists are crucial in addressing, in turn, the choices of the DMs in the context of the definition of actions and strategies for the valorization and management of environmental and landscape system [28].

In conclusion, the landscape constitutes a multidisciplinary subject, hugging many different sectors, but all representable through the identification of attributes, able to describe all facets of an area, with the possibility of being assessed with the methodology here described. Final results suggest that rating methods for the detection of stated preferences play a very important role in the management and maintenance of the landscape, as they give information about how people perceive a territory, and consequently its conservation and development; it seems to be a method suitable for supporting in an appropriate way decision processes concerning landscape preservation and planning, especially considering the emphasis about the preferences of users, who are intended as the main source of information to achieve the goal of landscape evaluation.

References

1. Tagliafierro, C., Longo, A., Eetvelde, V., et al.: Landscape economic valuation by integrating landscape ecology into landscape economics. Environ. Sci. Policy **32**, 26–36 (2013)
2. Gobattoni, F., Lauro, G., Leone, A., Monaco, R., Pelorosso, R.: A procedure for the mathematical analysis of landscape evolution and scenarios assessment. Landsc. Urban Plan. **103**, 289–302 (2011)
3. Cassatella, C., Peano, A.: Landscape Indicators: Assessing and Monitoring Landscape Quality. Spinger, Berlin (2011)
4. Potschin, M.B., Haines-Young, R.H.: Landscape and sustainability. Landsc. Urban Plan. J. **75**(3–4), 155–161 (2006)
5. Tempesta, T., Thiene, M.: Percezione e valore del paesaggio. Franco Angeli, Milano (2006)
6. Bottero, M.: Assessing the economic aspects of landscape. In: Cassatella, C., Peano, A. (eds.) Landscape Indicators: Assessing and Monitoring Landscape Quality, pp. 167–192. Springer, Berlin (2011)
7. Stellin, G., Rosato, P.: La valutazione economica dei beni ambientali: Metodologia e casi studio. CittàStudi Edizioni, Torino (1998)

8. Rolfe, J., Bennett, J., Louviere, J.: Choice modelling and its potential application to tropical rainforest preservation. Ecol. Econ. **35**, 289–302 (2000)
9. Lancaster, K.J.: A new approach to consumer theory. J. Polit. Econ. **2**, 132–157 (1966)
10. Bennett, J.W.: Some Fundamentals of Environmental Choice Modelling. Research Report n. 11, University of New South Wales (1999)
11. Bottero, M., Ferretti, V., Mondini, G.: Constructing multi-attribute value functions for sustainability assessment of urban projects. In: Murgante, B., et al. (eds.) ICCSA 2014. LNCS, vol. 8581, pp. 51–64. Springer, Cham (2014). doi:10.1007/978-3-319-09150-1_5
12. Hanley, N., Mourato, A.: Choice Modelling Approaches: A Superior Alternative for Environmental Valuation? EAERE Conference, Oslo (1999)
13. Fontana, R.: Fractional factorial design for model based evaluation of customer preferences. Commun. Stat. Theory Methods **43**(4), 693–703 (2014)
14. Boxall, P., Adamowicz, V., Swaitt, J., Wilson, M., Louvriere, J.: A comparison of state methods for environmental valuation. Ecol. Econ. **18**(3), 243–253 (1994)
15. Adamowicz, V., Hanley, N., Wright, R.E.: Using choice experiments to value the environment. Environ. Resour. Econ. **11**, 413–428 (1998)
16. Alpìzar, F., Vega, D.C.: Choice experiments in environmental impact assessment: the toro 3 hydroelectric project and the recreo verde tourist center in costa rica. Impact Assess. Project Apprais. **4**, 252–262 (2011)
17. Oppio, A., Bottero, M., Ferretti, V.: Designing adaptive reuse strategies for cultural heritage with choice experiments. In: Stanghellini, S., Morano, P., Bottero, M., Oppio, A. (eds.) Appraisal: From Theory to Practice. GET, pp. 303–315. Springer, Cham (2017). doi:10.1007/978-3-319-49676-4_23
18. Cassatella, C.: The 'Corona Verde' Strategic Plan: an integrated vision for pro-tecting and enhancing the natural and cultural heritage. Urban Res. Pract. **6**(2), 219–228 (2013)
19. Polito, DITER – Dipartimento Interateneo Territorio: Progetto Corona Verde. Technical report (2007)
20. Burns, P.M., Novelli, M.: Tourism and Politics: Global Frameworks and Local Realities. Elsevier, Amsterdam (2007)
21. Strielkowski, W., Riganti, P., Wang, J.: Tourism, cultural heritage and eservices: using focus groups to assess consumer preferences. Tourismos **7**(1), 21–59 (2012)
22. Tosco, C.: I beni culturali: Storia, Tutela e valorizzazione. Il Mulino, Bologna (2014)
23. Mazzanti, M., Montini, A.: Valutazione economica multi-attributo mediante esperimenti di scelta. Aspetti metodologici e strumenti di analisi econometria. Siep - XIII Conference (2001)
24. Kuhfeld, W.F.: Marketing Research Methods in SAS. SAS Institute Inc., Cary (2010)
25. McFadden, D.L.: Conditional Logit analysis of qualitative choice behaviour. In: Zarembka, P. (ed.) Frontiers in Econometrics, pp. 105–142. Academic Press, New York (1974)
26. Martijn van der Heide, C., Heijman, W.J.M.: The Economic Value of Landscapes. Routledge, Oxon (2013)
27. Mondini, G.: Il progetto di sostenibilità. In: Bottero, M., Mondini, G. (eds.) Valutazione e sostenibilità: Piani, programmi, progetti, pp. 23–57. Celid, Torino (2009)
28. Giuffrida, S., Ventura, V., Trovato, M.R., Napoli, G.: Axiology of the historical city and the cap rate. Valori e Valutazioni **18**, 41–56 (2017)

Public and Private Interests in Urban Regeneration Programs: The Case Study of Trieste Historic Centre

Mauro Crescenzo[1](✉) (iD), Marta Bottero[2], and Luigi Buzzacchi[2]

[1] Architect, Trieste, Italy
mauro.crescenzo@gmail.com
[2] Department of Regional and Urban Studies and Planning,
Politecnico di Torino, Turin, Italy
{marta.bottero,luigi.buzzacchi}@polito.it

Abstract. This paper focuses on the evaluation of the economic aspects related to urban transformations, with particular attention to the relationships among the different interests involved. Starting from the application of the Discounted Cash-Flow Analysis, the study investigates public and private perspectives in the development of the regeneration of the historic center of the city of Trieste (Italy). Different scenarios are considered and evaluated from the point of view of the public and private convenience considering the Internal Rate of Return and the Net Present Value indicators. The final results are also verified by means of specific sensitivity analyses that allow the validity of the proposed model to be tested.

Keywords: Discounted Cash-Flow analysis · Internal rate of return · Feasibility analysis · Sensitivity analysis · Urban economics

1 Introduction and Overview

This paper focuses on the economic evaluation of urban regeneration processes [1] concerning historic centres. Despite these long-term view evaluations are quite consolidated [2, 3] and have been used for assessing several urban development operations (e.g. Hamburg [4], Barcelona, Malmö, Berlin, Amsterdam [5]), limited studies investigates their application related to the regeneration of historic centres [6], which are characterized by high complexity of values and needs.

This paper is part of a wider research work[1] which aims at examining the case study of Trieste historic centre by suggesting a sustainable planning approach (i.e. an integrated Multicriteria Analysis framework) that considers the broad spectrum of problems, aspects and Stakeholders involved within the decision process. For the present article, in particular, the sensitive economic point of view has been screened and further developed, examining - in order to promote awareness and to aid the framing of possible solutions - an innovative Public fund proposal for its contribution to boosting

---

[1] Master thesis [8] developed by Mauro Crescenzo and Sara De Matteis with the supervision of professors Marta Bottero, Mauro Berta and Valentina Ferretti at Politecnico di Torino.

© Springer International Publishing AG 2017
O. Gervasi et al. (Eds.): ICCSA 2017, Part III, LNCS 10406, pp. 547–561, 2017.
DOI: 10.1007/978-3-319-62398-6_39

the overall process [7]. Economic purposes, among others, are related to great urban development projects operations [9] (e.g. Bilbao and Copenhagen, in addition to others already mentioned) as they offer opportunities for investors for which economic aspects are crucial [5]. From Private investors' perspective, profits on investments usually ensure the success the operation [10]; however, common benefits can also be obtained [11]. Cities (i.e. urban communities) are in fact lived and shared by many - either Private or Public - individuals: the increase of value (i.e. indirect economic and social benefits) resulting from the operation can be thus shared - maximizing the benefits [10] - with the whole community. The proposal investigated in this paper is thus framed considering both individual (i.e. Private) and community (i.e. Public) economic aspects of the intervention, thanks to the development of various Discounted Cash-Flow Analyses, in a shared economy perspective where both actors involve resources for achieving common goals and benefits. Public effort is in fact usually considered the starting driver of successful urban renewal experiences [10].

After the introduction and the presentation of the case study, the paper is organized as follows: Sect. 2 presents the Discounted Cash-Flow analysis methodological background; Sect. 3 illustrates the application to the historic centre of Trieste, clarifying the subsequent steps of the evaluation model; Sect. 4 illustrates the results and discusses the main findings of the research, Sect. 5 summarizes the main conclusions that can be drawn from the work and contribute to future perspectives and the study of economic aspect and the urban regeneration of historic centres.

1.1 The Historic Centre of Trieste

Trieste is an ancient city with Roman origins located in Northern Italy. The city experienced a very complex development process during the years that deeply marked its urban environment and particularly its historic centre, which is named Cittavecchia. A large depopulation in late 1700 and the following repopulation with the poorest classes of the society [12] led to widespread sanitary problems [13], collapses and a significant abandonment that caused in 1900 the partial completion of several demolition plans and the walling-up of the area that lasted until the early'90. In 1986, the increasing awareness on the problem and the first recovery plans led to the opportunity to start an extensive renovation of Cittavecchia with Communitarian fund obtained for the Urban II Programme in 1998. Moreover, various buildings and archeological areas were recovered and discovered [14] during the intervention, which successfully accomplished various objectives but left incomplete other portions of the area. After several years, this situation increased the fragmentation of the urban fabric and the identity issues that can be perceived today. Archeological areas and public spaces clearly symbolize this condition: despite their great potential they do not properly connect the various interventions and the city itself to the historic centre.

For the evaluation of a proper regeneration proposal it is important to consider the impact on the citizens of the complex development that Trieste faced during the years. The deep scars on the urban tissue due to the extensive abandonment, the poor sanitary conditions and the historic centre confinement for many years, contributed to the existing issues as Cittavecchia were excluded from the city and citizens were deprived of these spaces. Also today it can be in fact perceived a certain type of confinement as Private investors are not motivated to recover their abandoned buildings despite the great potential of the area [15]. Therefore, in order to envisage a successful regeneration for the historic centre it is increasingly required to consider the importance of commitment and the feeling of trust between citizens and local Institutions. In fact it has been noted that trust facilitates the relation between actors, reducing negative outcomes and risks of the operation [16]. Investments can be encouraged and economic development reached if citizens and Stakeholders are motivated to comprehend the potential of the area - sharing then resources [17], goals and aspirations - thanks to long-term solution proposals and inclusive decision-making processes. In this sense, the present paper aims at investigating a particular Public-Private Partnership (PPP) proposal that recalls the Allen and Meyer definition of Organizational Commitment [18]: a psychological state that binds the individual to the organization. If citizens in fact take part to the development acting loyally and responsibly towards the Institutions, as it happens in the relation between the individuals and the organization in which they are employed, a better successful regeneration process can be achieved. The economic literature on PPP also emphasizes the effect on incentives and risk transfer of bundling building and operation into a single contract, with different assumptions on the contractual framework and the quality of the information held by the government [19].

2 Methodological Background

The feasibility analysis applied in the research work and further developed for this paper aims at answering the question "will it work?" for a specific project proposal. The method identifies in fact the full range of costs and incomes of a project, allowing investor to understand if minimum objectives of the intervention will be achievable. According to the scientific literature [20, 21] feasibility analysis is iterative and continuous and it involves the following eight steps: (1) assessing the physical and legal aspects of the site; (2) estimating demand for the space; (3) analyzing competitive space; (4) estimating costs of acquisition, construction or rehabilitation; (5) estimating the cost and availability of borrowed funds; (6) estimating absorption rates; (7) developing cash flow schedules; (8) evaluating the estimated cash flow in terms of acceptability of the expected outcome. A very important part of the overall feasibility study is related to the financial analysis which normally can be addressed through the Discounted Cash-Flow Analysis (DCFA). Particularly, this technique is used to derive economic and financial performance criteria for investment projects [22] in the form of synthetic and easy to interpret indicators that allows the Decision Maker to understand if the project should be accepted or rejected. Net Present Value (NPV) and Internal Rate of Return (IRR) are thus the most used project performance criteria.

Let X be a project with real benefits B_{Xt} and real costs C_{Xt}, in t = 0,1,..., T years from now and r the discount rate. NPV of the project is defined as in Eq. (1):

$$NPV = \sum_{t=0}^{T} \frac{B_t - C_t}{(1+r)^t} \qquad (1)$$

It has been noticed that: (i) If NPV = 0 the discounted benefits are equal to the discounted costs and then we should be indifferent in the decision whether to accept or reject the project; (ii) If NPV > 0 the discounted benefits are larger than the discounted costs and then we should accept the project; (iii) If NPV < 0 the discounted benefits are smaller than the discounted costs and then we should reject the project.

With reference to the Internal Rate of Return (IRR) of the investment, the value can be derived finding the rate of return so that the project breaks even, in order to find the IRR which makes the present value zero as represented in the Eq. (2):

$$\sum_{t=0}^{T} \frac{B_t - C_t}{(1+r)^t} = 0 \Rightarrow r = IRR \tag{2}$$

It is then possible to affirm that a project is admissible if IRR > r (i.e. rate of return exceeds opportunity cost).

3 Application

3.1 The Urban Regeneration Scenarios

The urban regeneration envisaged for Trieste aims, as defined by Roberts [23], at solving the existing problems and achieving lasting improvements on economic, physical, social and environmental conditions with an integrated vision. In particular, three scenarios - that are analyzed from the economic point of view in the present application - have been proposed in the main research work with different functional mixes (Table 1) and design solutions (Fig. 1) for public, private, unused and underused spaces, considering reusing and preservation principles in order to obtain a solution more economic and respectful of the existing heritage.

3.2 Public and Private Perspectives of the Operation

Public sector is increasingly supporting economic regeneration processes with integrated approaches and partnerships in order to ensure a better value to the invested capital [23]. Recent urban development initiatives propose various solutions for Public and Private funding and their relationship - e.g. PPPs (London), Public-owned companies (Hamburg, Barcelona and Copenhagen), mixed approaches (Berlin), more traditional Public-Private cooperation (Amsterdam and Malmö) [5] and private-led operations (Brussels) [9]; however, new coalitions can be forged for the redevelopment of historic centres [11] where large part of the buildings already exists.

In this paper, an innovative approach has been thus proposed and investigated, in relation to a Public contribution that is useful to increase the desirability of the Private investors, to encourage the beginning of the operation and to involve the existing owners within the process. The Discounted Cash-Flow Analysis described in the previous paragraph has been thus applied to identify the convenience of both Private and Public investors. In particular, in this study an innovative public incentive, which

Table 1. Envisaged scenarios for the regeneration of Trieste historic centre

Scenario	Description
Working setting	The proximity to the Institutional buildings and the presence of various existing work realities in the area suggest the solutions proposed in this scenario: large part of the buildings and public spaces are designed to host a large Neighborhood Market, traditional and innovative new work activities and their related services
Touristic environment	The existing historic traces, the cultural identity and other attractions of the area are enhanced and systematized in this scenario with a new Tourist Office, various museums (e.g. an Archaeological one in Piazza Cavana) and various paths between the archaeological areas
Residential location	This scenario aims at creating a more livable environment by converting largest part of the spaces to residential buildings and services. It is in fact enhanced the cooperative use of spaces with a proposed Neighbourhood Community Center in Piazza Cavana, urban gardens and outdoor leisure areas

covers the 60% of the Private construction costs and that will be entirely returned to the Public only if profits will be obtained by the Private investors, has been assumed. In this perspective Public and Private investors are bounded by an economic and psychological agreement, which recalls the Organizational Commitment vision previously introduced, and activate the private interest as various cases - e.g. Hamburg [4], Berlin, Barcelona, London and finally Amsterdam [5] - suggest. Public sector thus coordinates and invests on the operation as it is interested in potential positive effects on the whole area and on the local community [24], while Private investors are encouraged to begin the renovation thanks to the significant profits that can be achieved thanks to the Public contribution. Both sectors share then economic and other indirect advantages that result from the success of the operation as, for example, the revitalization of public spaces and the returns on the Real Estate Market. Moreover, it is important to consider that any goals can be achieved with a detailed contract that is proposed and agreed at the start of the operation [19] (e.g. in Hamburg Public sector tied Private investments to strict criteria previously defined [4]). Other fund opportunities are not considered in the following analyses because of their different nature (as for the non-repayable Public, European and Private grants).

3.3 Development of the Discounted Cash-Flow Analysis

The economic evaluation of Private and Public Conveniences has been developed with the DCFA method that is useful to rationalize and quantify both the advantages and disadvantages of the proposals.

The analyses are based on parametric data that derive from a Property Market Analysis and on detailed hypothesis considering the solutions proposed by each scenario and the specific time frame. The two analyses that have been developed from the Public investor perspective and from the Private one for each scenario have been also

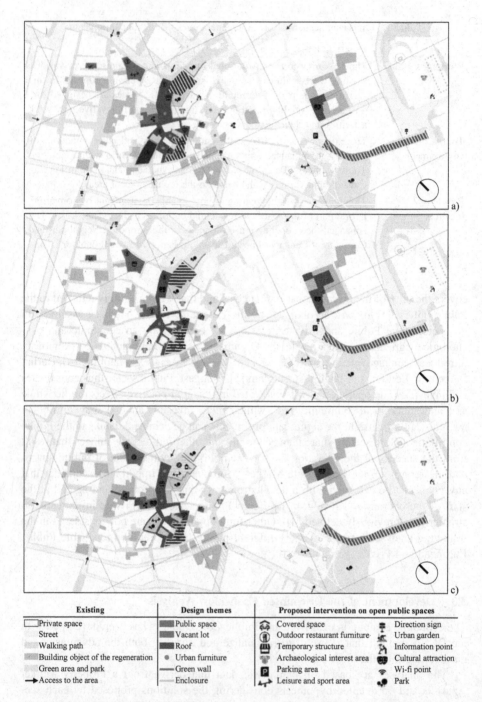

Existing	Design themes	Proposed intervention on open public spaces	
Private space	Public space	Covered space	Direction sign
Street	Vacant lot	Outdoor restaurant furniture	Urban garden
Walking path	Roof	Temporary structure	Information point
Building object of the regeneration	Urban furniture	Archaeological interest area	Cultural attraction
Green area and park	Green wall	Parking area	Wi-fi point
Access to the area	Enclosure	Leisure and sport area	Park

Fig. 1. Proposed interventions [8] for the envisaged scenarios: (a) *Working setting*, (b) *Touristic environment*, (c) *Residential location*

interconnected in order to properly consider the Public fund provided at the beginning of the operation and the following Private returning contribution.

Time Frame of the Evaluation. In order to apply the Discounted Cash-Flow Analysis model, it is necessary to identify the duration of the evaluation [25] that corresponds to the time frame considered for the estimation of the investment feasibility. Due to the size of the operation, the analyses proposed for this paper are based on a periodization of both costs and benefits over a time frame of 30 years that include all the phases of the operation, from the properties acquisitions to the revenues resulting from the completion of the intervention (Table 2).

Table 2. Duration of the phases of the evaluation

Component	Start (year)	Duration (years)	Method
Acquisitions	1	4	Percentage
Construction	1	Private: 5	Percentage
		Public: 6	
60% Fund	1	5	Percentage
Private returning contribution	2	On the sales: 1	Sales plan
		On the rents: 3	Rents plan
Management costs	3	29 + Residual value (+)	Percentage
Sales	2	5	Sales plan
Rents	2	29 + Residual value (+)	Rents plan

Estimation of Costs. Various costs that differ from design and functional proposals have been quantified and distributed over the time frame, including the construction and management costs, the technical and general expenses and the financial charges.

Construction costs result from the interplay of various factors related to the envisaged projects [26] and have been estimated with a parametric approach, considering the good or bad state of conservation of the buildings. Moreover, with specific costs manuals [27], a time scheduling of a single building has been developed (Fig. 2) in order to quantify the percentage weight of the renewal operations over the years. The distribution of the works resulting from this analysis can be described as follows: 35.4% for the first year and 64.6% for the second one.

Annual values that have been used for the distribution over the time frame are shown in Table 3: due to the dimensions of the area and the high number of buildings involved time scheduling values have been refined considering an asynchronous beginning of the renewal operations (assumed to be of 20% on the first year, 30% on the second and third one and 20% on the fourth one).

Furthermore, other aspects have been considered for the Private perspectives, as the costs related to the capital invested for the operation and the taxes, considering constant values and real rates. In particular, the interest expenses and the loan interest have been included in the calculations and they have been assumed equal to 3% (considering TUS as 0.05% and SPREAD as 2.95%) and to1%, respectively. With reference to the taxes,

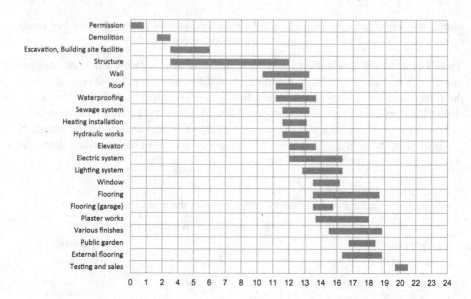

Fig. 2. Time scheduling of a case study building (months on the horizontal axis)

Table 3. Annual distribution of the construction costs

Distribution	1st year	2nd year	3rd year	4th year	5th year
20%	7.1%	12.9%			
30%		10.6%	19.4%		
30%			10.6%	19.4%	
20%				7.1%	12.9%
TOTAL:	7.1%	23.5%	30.0%	26.5%	12.9%

they are represented by IRES (an income tax that deducts the previous losses from the taxable income) and IRAP (a regional tax on productive activities that considers as a taxable income the difference between the profits and the 70% of the costs). Subsequently, for both the cash-flows of Public and Private investments, a limited risk premium has been applied, i.e. a discount rate of 5%.

Estimation of Profits. Expected profits for each proposed destination are quantified with different approaches: selling prices and annual rents have been defined, thanks to parametric prices resulting from a Real Estate Market Analysis and considering also the case that some of the actual owners can maintain the property of their buildings.

The distribution over the time frame of the profits, which is different for the sales and the rents, is based on sales and renting plans that have been envisaged for this research in order to further develop the method and to obtain a more precise result. In particular, the *Sales Plan* proposed for the present application is based upon percentages of 10% of the sales for the first year, 20% for the second one, 35% for the third one, 25% for the fourth one and 10% for the fifth one. The obtained annual profits are then distributed over a time frame of 29 years with a proposed *Rents Plan* that is based on the following cumulated percentages: 10% of successful rents during the first year, 20% of successful ones during the second year, 40% during the third one, 70% during the fourth one and 100% during the fifth one.

Relationship Between Public and Private Investments. As previously mentioned, in the evaluation model it has been assumed that the Public actor provides the 60% of the Private construction costs, contribution that will be returned by the Private investors only if profits are obtained.

The distribution on the time frame of the starting contribution is contextual to the construction operations, while the Private investors return the contribution contextually with the sales or rents. As it is shown in Table 4, the Public and Private involvements are different in each proposed alternative; in particular the Public direct costs are higher for the touristic scenario due to the expenses required for the construction of the proposed museums and for the enhancement of the archaeological areas. The highest Private investment is related to the working alternative and the lowest to the residential one.

Table 4. Public and Private investments required for the start of the intervention

Investment		Working setting	Touristic environment	Residential location
Public	Direct costs	4,476,204 €	11,766,312 €	6,730,041 €
	Contribution to private costs	6,558,142 €	5,770,645 €	5,749,008 €
Private direct costs		4,372,094 €	3,847,097 €	3,832,672 €
Public involvement		72%	82%	77%

4   Results

4.1   Evaluation of the Economic Convenience

The resulting Net Present Value (NPV) and the Internal Rate of Return (IRR) - which are useful to assess the economic convenience of the operation according to the DFCA methodology - have been calculated for the three envisaged scenarios both for Public and for Private investors (Table 5). As an example, Table 6 in Appendix A provides the DCFA table for the evaluation of the *touristic environment* scenario under the Private perspective. As it can be noted from Table 5, the minimum acceptable IRR value of 10% is always achieved and the highest and lowest resulting IRR values are both related to the *working setting* proposal, while the touristic scenario presents the highest IRR among the Public perspective. Furthermore, it is relevant to mention that the analysis performed for this paper does not consider the non-monetary benefits of a Public investment, which can in particular influence the touristic scenario as it proposes a more profitable solution for the public spaces and the archaeological areas of Cittavecchia.

Table 5. Public and private internal rate of return for each scenario

	Working setting	Touristic environment	Residential location
Public IRR	13.1%	14.6%	14.2%
Private IRR	21.2%	20.3%	15.8%

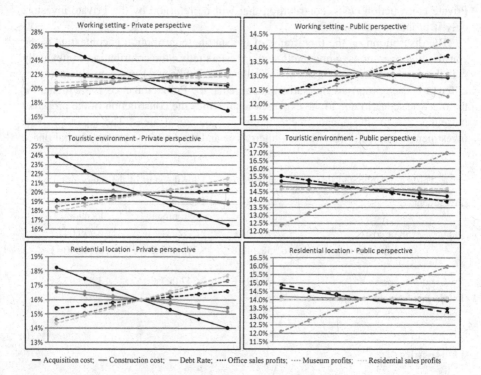

— Acquisition cost;   — Construction cost;   — Debt Rate;   ···· Office sales profits;   ···· Museum profits;   ···· Residential sales profits

Fig. 3. Sensitivity Analyses of Private and Public perspectives for each scenario. A suggestion for the touristic scenario: the proposed archaeological museum [8].

4.2 Sensitivity Analysis

As other experiences proved, results may vary according to different elements: in fact, although many are not completed yet, some operations better succeed (e.g. Barcelona and Berlin) than others (e.g. Amsterdam) [5] in achieving developers' expectations, attracting Private investments and thus increasing common benefits.

For this reason, in order to better investigate the results of the analysis, Sensitivity Analysis is normally applied to test the robustness of the results of the DFCA model taking different scenarios into account: key variables of the evaluation, most uncertain areas of the project and variation of the expected results are thus identified for implementing ad-hoc monitoring. Sensitivity analysis is concerned with a "what if" kind of question to see if the final answer is stable when the inputs are changed. In the present application NPV and IRR have been recalculated by modifying ($\pm5\%$, $\pm10\%$, $\pm15\%$) the value of crucial cost and benefit entries (acquisition costs, construction costs, debt rate, office sales profits, museum profits and residential sales profits). The results are summarized in scatter plots where the x axis represents the percentage variation of the input while the y axis represents the percentage variation of the performance criteria (Fig. 3). The critical variables - represented by the highest angular coefficient - are acquisition costs for all the Private perspectives and museum profits, together with debt rate in working scenario, for the Public ones. More importantly, IRR values are higher than the minimum threshold in every scenario.

5 Discussion of the Results and Conclusions

From the economic point of view, it is important to consider the increasing relevance of the shared economy [28], where both Public and Private investors share resources and goals in order to obtain a more sustainable result. The development of the city and of urban regeneration processes are more and more based on inclusive decision making procedures with a greater balance between feelings of loyalty and responsibility where citizens and Institutions invest and share advantages. It is then increasingly important to accelerate the process motivating the Private investors and enhancing the feeling of trust in local Institution and their comprehension of the regeneration process potential. The DCFA developed for this paper offer a successful interpretation of the complexity that is related to such decision problems, as it is able to interpret and translate the psychological agreement in the economic process, easing the adaptation of the evaluation method to the complex existing dynamics, exploring and proposing innovative perspectives. In particular it is possible to notice that through an operation based on the proposal of a starting public fund that corresponds to the 60% of the Private construction costs subsequently returned with the Private profits, successful economic and non-economic goals can be reached for both Public and Private Investors. The Public profit is in fact obtained for every scenario and can be further enhanced if also non-monetary aspects are considered; at the same time Private actors are moved to invest and take advantages of the profits and of the increase of value resulting on their properties.

Considering the degree of detail that have been developed and the results obtained by the DCFA and the Sensitivity Analyses performed for this paper, it is possible to state that the best overall economic performance is obtained by the *touristic environment* scenario, thanks to the high IRR values resulting from the evaluation, the low influence of the variation on the results and the positive influence of non-monetary benefits that - despite the fact they have not been evaluated for the present paper - could in particular influence this scenario. The proposed application of the method and the obtained results are very useful in decision-making processes similar to the case study of Trieste as they permit to investigate and identify complex economic proposals considering the various economic perspectives of the actors involved. The intention of this paper is in fact to offer a new perspective for the study of urban regeneration processes, thanks to a reasoning that can be further developed to better frame the existing complexity and the potential of each alternative. In particular, the mechanism of Public Private Partnership proposed in the present application seems to be very suitable for addressing the complex and interconnected objectives of urban regeneration policies. In fact, in the model the Public subject acts as a lending institution, granting capital to Private investors at a low interest rate and the loan is then reimbursed by private actors, with an increase of urban quality in the area under investigation and positive effects on local community.

With reference to the future perspectives of the present study, it would be of scientific interest to better develop the Discounted Cash-Flow analyses by means of specific risk analysis in order to include uncertainty in the evaluation model [29]. Further research could explore the application of Cost Benefit Analysis on this case study, focusing more on the integration of a shared economy perspective, considering non-monetary benefits and aspects and verifying their influence on the results [30–33]. Finally, for a better validation of the present application results, the method could be experimented in other contexts, promoting innovative Private investments, the research of non-refundable funds and deepening the weight assessment process.

Fig. 4. A suggestion for the touristic scenario: the proposed archaeological museum [8].

A Appendix

See the Table 6.

Table 6. Discounted cash-flow analysis of the *touristic environment* scenario from the private perspective (P.con. = Private contribution).

Type	State	Cost (€/m²)	Quantity	UI Total €	P.con €	Year 1	Year 2	Year 3	Year 4	Year 5	Year 6	Year 7	Year 8...	Year 30...
Acquisition Costs	-	1,100	2,096 m²	2,515,200	-	251,520	503,040	1,006,080	754,560	0	0	0	0	0
Acquisition Benefits	-	500	4,984 m²	1,993,400		199,340	398,680	797,360	598,020	0	0	0	0	0
Construction costs Residential Highprice	Bad	890	1,596 m²	1,420,440	568,176	41,398	134,334	170,653	149,754	72,237				
Residential Mediumpr.	Good	880	527 m²		143,308	10,434	13,859	27,552	42,502	18,037				
Residential Lowprice	Bad	880	287 m²		91,840	6,692	21,714	27,552	24,206	11,676				
Residential Lowprice	Bad	400	161 m²	64,400	25,760	1,877	6,090	7,728	6,790	3,275				
Shop	Good	410	743 m²	326,920	130,768	9,528	30,918	39,230	34,466	16,626				
Association	Good	410	1,028 m²	421,480	168,592	12,283	39,860	50,578	44,436	21,434				
Hotel Highprice	Bad	70,000	45 n	3,181,500	1,272,600	92,724	300,882	381,780	335,418	161,796				
Hotel Lowprice	Good	47,200	38 n	1,896,462	723,585	12,649	170,841	316,675	190,451	91,988				
Atelier Lowprice	Bad	620	620 m²	154,800	200,880	14,636	47,494	47,694	52,646	25,540				
Exhibition	Bad	900	172 m²	502,200	61,920	4,512	14,640	18,576	16,320	7,872				
Office Highprice	Good	770	1,496 m²	1,151,920	460,768	33,572	108,940	138,230	121,444	58,581				
TOTAL PUBLIC CONTRIBUTION					5,770,645	420,460	1,364,359	1,731,194	1,520,964	733,669				
Management costs Expenses Technical	5	c.costr. %		480,887		96,177	96,177	96,177	96,177	96,177				
Expenses General	3	c.costr. %		192,335		38,471	38,471	38,471	38,471	38,471				
Expenses Ferales	2	c.costr. %		199,397		27,997	27,997	27,997	27,997	27,997				
Association Lowprice	20	Riel.net %		3,220	2			805	1,610	2,415	3,220	3,220	3,220	3,220
Shop	30		161 m²	3,220				7,710	15,420	23,130	30,840	30,840	30,840	30,840
Hotel Highprice	100		1,028 m²	151,500				37,875	75,750	113,625	151,500	151,500	151,500	151,500
Hotel Lowprice	30		1,515 m²	174,960				43,740	87,480	131,220	174,960	174,960	174,960	174,960
Atelier Lowprice	20		2,187 m²	16,200				4,050	8,100	12,150	16,200	16,200	16,200	16,200
Exhibition	30		810 m²	5,160				1,290	2,580	3,870	5,160	5,160	5,160	5,160
Office	30		172 m²	44,800				11,200	22,440	33,660	44,800	44,800	44,800	44,800
			1,496 m²	426,760				106,690	213,380	320,070	426,760	426,760	426,760	426,760
Total costs for the management				7,602,286		694,472	1,575,258	2,429,545	2,144,562	971,829	2,114,562	758,100		
TOTAL PRIVATE COSTS								319,200	1,326,675	1,546,125	2,114,562			
Benefits Residential Highprice	To sell	2,500	1,596 m²	3,990,000		39,900	39,900	52,064	216,391	252,185	758,100			
Residential Lowprice	To sell	2,000	814 m²	650,800		6,508	676	1,352	2,705	4,733	6,762	6,762	6,762	6,762
Shop	To rent	1,800	161 m²	6,762			557	2,853	5,858	14,530	30,776			
Association	To rent	2,200	743 m²	49,334		4,937	9,869	19,738	29,341	34,541	49,334	49,334	49,334	49,334
Hotel Highprice	To rent	2,500	1,515 m²	1,260,494		126,049	252,099	504,198	882,346	1,260,494	1,260,494	1,260,494	1,260,494	1,260,494
Hotel Lowprice	To rent	2,500	2,187 m²	733,397		73,340	146,679	293,359	513,378	733,397	733,397	733,397	733,397	733,397
Atelier Lowprice	To rent	1,500	810 m²	38,880		3,888	7,776	15,552	27,216	38,880	38,880	38,880	38,880	38,880
Exhibition	To rent	2,500	172 m²	18,576		1,858	3,715	7,430	13,003	18,576	18,576	18,576	18,576	18,576
Office	To sell	2,100	1,496 m²	215,424		21,542	43,085	86,170	150,797	215,424	215,424	215,424	215,424	215,424
Returning contribution on the sales					1,777,056	17,771	142,165	590,871	689,680	689,682	837,641	882,693	882,693	2,322,877
TOTAL BENEFITS (sales + rents + acquisitions)				16,505,693	3,883,850	199,340	677,732	1,636,059	3,082,095	3,438,143	3,211,405	2,322,877	2,322,877	2,322,877
ECONOMIC CASH-FLOW - Exposition				3,242,501		-495,132	-1,003,566	-1,112,195	-6,415	1,564,311	1,013,424	1,896,117	1,896,117	1,896,117
FINANCIAL CHARGES - Exposition						-495,132	-1,498,698	-2,610,894	-2,610,894	-1,457,488	106,823	1,120,246	2,133,670	43,848,237
Interest expense (annual)						-14,854			-78,327	-78,519	-43,725			
Loan interest (annual)											1,068		11,202	419,523
FINANCIAL CASH-FLOW (ante taxes)						-495,132	-1,018,420	-1,15,156	-84,442	1,087,300	1,535,586	1,014,492	1,024,626	2,315,638
FINANCIAL CASH-FLOW (post taxes)	27.50%					-495,132	-1,498,698	-2,610,894	-2,617,309	-1,457,488	1,087,300	1,014,492	1,024,626	2,315,638
IRIS	3.90%										-29,376	-113,594	-281,772	-636,800
IRAP								-61,655	-107,557		1,377,616	-78,942	-78,942	-78,942
BTP (30 years)	5%					-495,132	-1,018,420	-1,157,156	-146,397	973,744		656,565	663,912	1,599,896
FINANCIAL CASH-FLOW (post taxes)						0.95	-923,737	0.82	-69,717	0.78	0.75	0.71	0.68	0.23
Ante taxes NPV				19,463,075		-471,555		-999,595	-120,441	847,228	1,134,685	720,980	693,507	535,786
Ante taxes IRR (minimum 10%)				25.60%										
Post taxes NPV				25,923,462		-471,555	-923,737	-999,595	-120,441	762,954	1,027,998	466,608	449,362	370,180
Post taxes IRR (minimum 10%)				20.3%										

References

1. Walker, A.: Project Management in Construction. Blackwell Publishing, Oxford (2002)
2. Schubert, D.: Three contrasting approaches to urban development and waterfront transformations in Hamburg: "String of Pearls", Hafencity and IBA (International Building Exhibition). In: ISOCARP Review 10, International Society of City and Regional Planners, pp. 124–137 (2014)
3. SGS Economics and Planning, Best practice urban renewal, Input into Bays Precinct forum, Sydney (2014)
4. Schleffer, N.: Capitalisation, case study: cities tackling climate change: the case of the International Building Exhibition (IBA) Hamburg. URBACT II capitalisation, Nantes (2015)
5. AURIF, Large scale urban development projects in Europe, Institut D'Amenagement et D'Urbanisms de la Region D'Ile-de-France, Paris (2007)
6. Ribeiro, F.L.: Urban regeneration economics: the case of Lisbon's old downtown. Int. J. Strateg. Property Manage. **12**(3), 203–213 (2008)
7. Buzzacchi, L., Scellato, G., Ughetto, E.: The investment strategies of publicly sponsored venture capital funds. J. Bank. Finance **37**, 707–716 (2013). Elsevier
8. Crescenzo, M., De Matteis, S.: Ri-centro: valutazione di scenari di riqualificazione urbana per il centro storico di Trieste attraverso l'Analisi Multicriteri. MS thesis, Politecnico di Torino (2016)
9. Salet, W.: Framing strategic urban projects. In: Gualini, E., Salet, W. (eds.) Framing Strategic Urban Projects. Routledge, London, p. 14 (2007)
10. SGS Economics and Planning, Urbecon. vol. 2, pp. 2–3 (2015)
11. Urban Redevelopment Authority, Cities in Transformation: Lee Kuan Yew World City Prize. Tien Wah Press, Singapore (2012)
12. Tamaro, A.: Storia di Trieste. vol. 1–2, Edizioni Stock, Roma (1964)
13. Maggi, P., Merlatti, R., Petrucci, G.: a cura di, Sotto Trieste. Percorsi nella città tra storia e archeologia. Tipografia Villaggio del Fanciullo Opicina, Trieste (2009)
14. Morselli, C.: a cura di, Trieste antica. Lo scavo di Crosada. Editreg, Trieste (2007)
15. Ratcliffe, J., Stubbs, M.: Urban Planning and Real Estate Development. UCL Press Limited, London, p. 266 (1996)
16. Grotenbreg, S., Klijn, E.H., Boons, F., van Buuren, A.: The influence of trust on innovative outcomes in Public-Private Partnerships. In: 18th Annual Conference of the International Research Society for Public Management (IRSPM), Carleton University, Ottawa, 9–11 April 2014
17. McQuaid, R.W.: Partnerships and Urban Economic Development. Social Science Working Paper no. 13, Department of Social Sciences, Napier University, Edinburgh (1994)
18. Allen, N.J., Meyer, J.P.: The measurement and antecedents of affective, continuance and normative commitment to the organization. J. Occup. Organ. Psychol. **63**, 1–18 (1990). The British Psychlogical Society
19. Hart, O.: Incomplete contracts and public ownership: remarks, and an application to public-private partnerships. Econ. J. **113**, C69–C76 (2003)
20. Oprea, A.: The importance of investment feasibility analysis. J. Property Investment Finance **28**, 58–61 (2010)
21. Manganelli, B.: Real Estate Investing. Springer, Berlin (2015)
22. French, N., Gabrielli, L.: The uncertainty of valuation. J. Property Investment Finance **22**, 484–500 (2004)
23. Roberts, P.: The evolution, definition and purpose of urban regeneration. In: Roberts, P., Sykes, H. (eds.) Urban Regeneration: A Handbook, pp. 17–85. Sage, London (2000)

24. Guy, S., Hanneberry, J. (eds.): Development and Developers: Perspectives on Property, p. 74. Blackwell Science Ltd, Oxford (2002)
25. Roscelli, R., (ed.) Manuale di Estimo. Valutazioni Economiche ed esercizio della professione. De Agostini - UTET università, Novara (2014)
26. Isaac, D., O'Leary, J., Daley, M.: Property Development: Appraisal and Finance, 2nd edn. Palgrave Macmillan, Basingstoke (2010)
27. Collegio degli Ingegneri e Architetti di Milano, Prezzi e Tipologie Edilizie 2014. Dei Tipografia del Genio Civile (2014)
28. URBACT II Programme, New Urban Economies: How can cities can foster economic development and develop 'new urban economies'. URBACT II capitalisation, Nantes (2015)
29. Tajani, F., Morano, P.: Evaluation of vacant and redundant public properties and risk control: a model for the definition of the optimal mix of eligible functions. J. Property Investment Finance 35(1), 75–100 (2017)
30. Tyler, P., Warnock, C., Provins, A., Lanz, B.: Valuing the benefits of urban regeneration. Urban Stud. 50(1), 169–190 (2013)
31. Bottero, M.: A multi-methodological approach for assessing sustainability of urban projects. Manage. Environ. Qual. Int. J. 26(1), 138–154 (2015)
32. Gabrielli, L., Giuffrida, S., Trovato, M.R.: Functions and perspectives of public real estate in the urban policies: the sustainable development plan of syracuse. In: Gervasi, O., et al. (eds.) ICCSA 2016. LNCS, vol. 9789, pp. 13–28. Springer, Cham (2016). doi:10.1007/978-3-319-42089-9_2
33. Napoli, G., Giuffrida, S., Trovato, M.R.: Fair planning and affordability housing in urban policy. The case of syracuse (Italy). In: Gervasi, O., et al. (eds.) ICCSA 2016. LNCS, vol. 9789, pp. 46–62. Springer, Cham (2016). doi:10.1007/978-3-319-42089-9_4

An Integrated Approach for the Assessment of Urban Transformation Proposals in Historic and Consolidated Tissues

Maria Rosaria Guarini[1], Anthea Chiovitti[2], Fabrizio Battisti[1], and Pierluigi Morano[3(✉)]

[1] Faculty of Architecture, Department of Architecture and Design (DIAP), Sapienza University of Rome, Via Flaminia 359, 00196 Rome, RM, Italy
{mariarosaria.guarini, fabrizio.battisti}@uniroma1.it
[2] Doctoral School in Architecture and Construction (DRACO), Faculty of Architecture, Department of Architecture and Design (DIAP), Sapienza University of Rome, Via A. Gramsci 53, 00197 Rome, RM, Italy
anthea.chiovitti@uniroma1.it
[3] Department of Civil Engineering Sciences and Architecture, Polytechnic University of Bari, Via Orabona 4, 70125 Bari, BA, Italy
p.morano@poliba.it

Abstract. The definition of a refurbishment intervention, in every step of the building process, brings to a complex decision problem; in a diachronic dimension of time, iterative and interactive must be put in relation a large variety of aspects with interrelations, concerning components, stakeholders and procedures that must be considered. The identification of the possible solutions depends on the construction of the evaluation procedures; shared goals with the stakeholders must be defined, on the basis of which can be assessed alternative intervention scenarios and make choices with regard to the matter under consideration. Thereby, in the present work a mixed method model in which are integrated Multi-Criteria Decision Analysis, Strategic Planning Tools and Participation Techniques has been proposed to be applied to refurbishment intervention in historical fabrics.

Keywords: Appraisal · Multi-Criteria decision analysis · Strategic planning tools · Participation techniques

1 Introduction and Aims of the Work

The definition of an urban transformation intervention brings to a complex decision problem involving a large variety of simultaneous and conflicting aspects that could be contemporary considered only by use of appropriate evaluation techniques.

The contribution is the result of the joint work of the four authors; it must be attributed in equal parts to the four authors.

O. Gervasi et al. (Eds.): ICCSA 2017, Part III, LNCS 10406, pp. 562–574, 2017.
DOI: 10.1007/978-3-319-62398-6_40

In the field of urban transformations, when regarding historical fabrics in particular, principal aims of the evaluation are: (i) to lead the definition of hypothesis of intervention; (ii) to support the choice of the hypothesis that better give answer to the aims assumed in relation to specific aspects of complexity.

The goal of the transformation, is usually related to the integration of the intervention in an urban context that – at least in Italy – is almost always signified by stratification and over-layering of tissues and functions [1, 2]. Once established the goal, the achievement of this could be evaluated by the definition of a methodology structured by an integrated approach, mixed method type, that utilize simultaneously different clusters of assessment techniques [20].

Among multiple decision support tools, that can be utilized in the context of urban transformation processes, it must be point out:

- Multi-criteria decision analysis (MCDA), developed and applied since the Sixties' of XX century in different scientific contexts, succeed to support decision processes related to urban transformation [3, 4] and to find the best compromise solution for the mitigation of the previous aims [5, 6];
- Strategic Planning Tools (SPT), developed since the Sixties' of XX century in business management [7, 8], can be applied in urban and territorial planning to choose instruments, abilities and necessary actions to reach system's goals in medium and long period perspectives. SPT are useful in contexts characterized by multi-level activities and multi-actor processes [9, 19];
- Participation Techniques (PT), finalized to include the stakeholders' point of view in the evaluation process, the latters belonging to different categories and directly or indirectly involved in decisional process.

MCDA methods can be implemented in concert with other techniques or evaluation tools to support the choice process including, among different variables, also verbal and qualitative judges [10].

According to the European recommendations, the identification of different solution of the problem is to be correlated to the definition of shared aims with stakeholders. Alternative scenarios of intervention, referring to the analysed problem, can be evaluated on the base of the defined aims [11] by the integration of MCDA and PT. Integration of MCDA and PT with SPT can be useful to support the solution of decision problems in urban transformation allowing to motivate in greater detail the quantity and the typology of variables to be considered depending on the goal of the evaluation.

Therefore, the aim of the present work is to define an evaluation model, according to a specific set of objectives, able to support decision processes related to urban transformation in historic and consolidated tissues.

Considering the indications of some European Community documents (European Commission EC, 2006, Community Directive 2014/24/UE) regarding the actions of development and urban regeneration, transposed in Italy in the Legislative Decree n. 50/2016, the proposed procedure must consider financial, socio-economic, environmental, landscape, procedural and technical aspects that generally characterize urban intervention of transformation. In the context of historic and consolidated tissues have to be taken into account how these aspects can be applied referring to some typical characters observed in Italy and elsewhere in these urban areas: (i) the presence of building plans strongly characterized from the typo-morphological, structural and distributive point of view; (ii) stratified structure of tissues, founded on layers that overlay structures, materials and heterogeneous forms; (iii) spaces, private and public buildings, characterized by a poor adaptability and often (iv) connected to spaces with high socio-identity values.

Further in the text will be described: the evaluation tools utilized in the construction and in the definition of the evaluation methodology proposed (Sect. 2); the structure of evaluation model (Sect. 3); the implementation of the methodology proposed for the case study of the new building for Chamber of Deputies in the historical center of Rome (Sect. 4); the conclusions (Sect. 5).

2 Choice of the Evaluation Tools

In the construction of evaluation procedure methods tools and techniques must be chosen on the base of problems to be solved and referring to the phase of the process in which evaluation is conducted. The choice of the MCDA method in accordance to the full aggregation approach or to the outranking approach can be made considering the set of endogenous ad external variables typifying different decisional contexts [12].

Among MCDA tools that develop analysis by a full aggregation approach, the Analytic Hierarchy Process (AHP) is one of the techniques that allow to point out the best option by a pair-wise comparison based on a rational scale, structured in hierarchical levels [13]. In this way, is it possible to easily and intuitively solve the problem of the choice of the best performing proposal of urban transformation, breaking up the complex problem into sub-problems technically solvable. Ones defined the specific objectives (Os), the criteria (Cn), the sub-criteria (SCn) and the indicators, by appropriate analysis and by PT, the AHP phases can be synthesized in: (a) the recognition of alternatives Ii (concept-design and/or design); (b) the construction of Matrix of Coefficients (MC) gathering the performances that various alternatives record according to SCn of evaluation; (c) the calculation of local priorities (Pij) of Cn and SCn according to the Goal, by the construction of bi-dimensional matrix of pairwise comparison through the assignment of weights Wj to Cn and SCn; (d) the calculation of global priorities (Pi) (and ranking) by the construction of bi-dimensional matrix of pairwise comparison through the aggregation of the performances recorded in the Matrix of Coefficients with local priorities (Pij).

Among SPT, the Strengths, Weaknesses, Opportunities, and Threats (SWOT) analysis can be utilized to identify the before mentioned factors referring to an intervention that has to be realized in a certain system or settling context. SWOT analysis can be implemented in a static way, directly translating information gathered from analysis into actionable choices, or in a relational or dynamic way [14], considering SWOT elements as input data to be used in following steps by the integration of SWOT analysis with other techniques. In the methodology proposed, SWOT analysis is used in a dynamic way, integrated with PT (Stakeholder Analysis), for the definition of a vector of weights Wj to be attributed to each Cn and SCn, adopted for the implementation of AHP. SWOT factors are defined thanks to the consultation of experts (focus group) and they are expressed referring to urban, legislative, procedural, socio-economic elements in the analysed context.

According to the modalities of stakeholder participation in different phases of evaluation, the choice of PT has to be made taking into account: (i) levels of comprehension (even for non-expert subjects) of contents and of procedures used for gathering and elaboration of judges; (ii) time of implementation and (iii) level of conflict in stated judges [4]. Among PT the Focus Group (FG) is characterized by a medium level of comprehension, a short time for implementation but a high level in risk of conflict; the Stakeholders Analysis (SA) is characterized by a high level of comprehension, a very short time for the implementation and a short level in risk of conflict. In the methodology proposed, these techniques are integrated in AHP because they are used, respectively, to define the necessary elements for the construction of Matrix of Coefficients and for the calculation of local priorities.

3 Framework of the Evaluation Model in Accordance with the Mixed Method Approach

As mentioned before, the methodology proposed is based on the joint use of AHP, SWOT Analysis, FG and SA for the choice of the best solution of intervention in order to better answer to the goal and to the general Objectives (Og) – architectural and urban quality of transformation (QA), technical and functional quality (QT), economical and financial aspects (EF) – and it is structured in accordance with an integrated approach made of a number of consecutive phases (Fig. 1): (i) definition of the elements of evaluation: Criteria (Cn), Sub-criteria (SCn), Indicators (In), Coefficients (Kji) (Phase 1); (ii) weighing of Cn and SCn (Phase 2); (iii) ranking of alternatives Ii and identification of the best compromise solution (Phase 3).

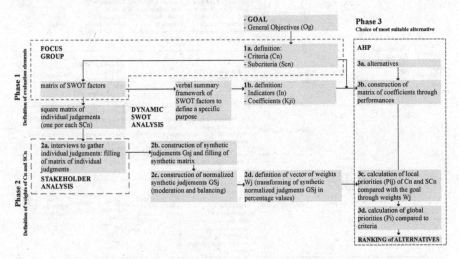

Fig. 1. Framework of methodology proposed

Referring to the specific context where evaluation procedure is applied, evaluation elements must be firstly defined (Phase 1):

(1a) a set of Criteria Cn and Sub-criteria SCn, identified through a FG (consultation of experts) in which experts for each Og define a suitable number of significant elements for the transformations to represent a coherent and equal corpus to measure the best level for achievement of the objectives [15–17].

(1b) a set of Indicators In and Coefficients Kji through the application of a dynamic SWOT analysis, structuring:

   (i) Matrix of SWOT factors: through a FG, for each SCn is defined a point of Strength, Weakness, Opportunity and Threat considered most significant. The result obtained is synthesized in a Matrix of SWOT factors. Defining the SWOT factors it must be taken into account both de facto state and the evolution perspectives, referred to the context where intervention is located, considering currently what effects the alternatives of intervention could generate;

Evaluation Elements				Matrix of SWOT factors			
Goal	General Objiectives	Criteria	Sub-Criteria	Internal Factors		External Factors	
				Strengths	Weaknesses	Opportunites	Threats
The urban void solution by the inclusion of new functions	Economic and finalncial aspects (EF)	Spending control (art. 95, art 96, art 97 D.lgs n. 50/2016; PRG art. 36, comma 1 NT, D.lgs n. 152/2006 s.m.i)	Cost reduction	Rational use of financial resources	Expensive process because of their function "Edifici e Complessi speciali" (cfr. art. 36 delle NTA, comma 1), comprehensive of open space directly connected with public spaces (piazza, gardens, streets) having high urban, morphological, symbolic and functional relevance	Functional, distributive and technical solution allowing a cost reducing	Abnormally low tenders
			Cost sustainability connected with energy saving	Rational use of financial resources implying the research of a balance between resources conservation and socio-economic development	Expensive initial investments bacause of adoption of sustainable and innovative technical solutions	Technical and functional solutions allowing management of cost reducing paying attention to energy saving and pollution control	Abnormally low tenders
			Maintenance costs por year	Rational and effective use of financial resources		Technical and functional solutions allowing management of cost reducing in ordinary and extraordinary maintainace	Abnormally low tenders
		Economic Convinience (Censimento Industria e Servizi 2001 ISTAT; art. 95, art 96, art 97 D.lgs n. 50/2016)	Environmental costs	Cost reducing referred to greehouse gas and other polluting substances emissions	Absence of activities planning on urban context in specific economic sectors	Environmental impact reducing generated from new design functions in the area of historical city centre	Low prediction of environmental impacts in long period
			Costs Benefits ratio	Economic and social regeneration for consolidated city according to design strategies based on economic convenience evaluations (best locationing for economic activities, supplay and demand, geomarketing, highest and best use, contingent values)	Difficolt monetary quantification of intangible aspects	Quantification of collective advantage regarding expected results	Unsuitability of estimation of interest rate

Fig. 2. (continued)

Evaluation Elements				Matrix of SWOT factors			
				Internal Factors		External Factors	
Goal	General Objiectives	Criteria	Sub-Criteria	*Strengths*	*Weaknesses*	*Opportunites*	*Threats*
The urban void solution by the inclusion of new functions	Architectural and Urban quality (QA)	Urban fabric filling in relashionship with the historical development process (PRG art. 20, co. 2, art. 22 comma 1 NTA, G2 Guida per la qualità degli interventi: Capo III)	Alignement of the new building to the urban fabrics before demolition (IGM 1873)	Organic design of urban spaces and riconfiguration of urban routes geometry broken by demolitions	Planimetric and distributive limits to design proposal	Urban void solution by valorization and refurbishments of morphological connections	Limits to design research for innovative solution finding
			Presence of inner courts (covered or uncovered) following the tradition of the historical urban fabric	Conservation of traditional characters of historical urban tissues (T1)	Planimetric, distributive and typo-morphological limits to design proposal	Valorization of urban courtyards as distribution element of several building units in order to guarantee a good permeability with outer spaces	Limits to design research for innovative solution finding
		Organic relashionship between buildings and urban spaces (PRG art. 20, co. 2, art. 22 comma 1 NTA, G2 Guida per la qualità degli interventi: Capo III)	Connection between design spaces, urban spaces and parliamentary functions close to the design area	Organic design of the urban spaces paying attention to volumetric and formal relation between the new buildings and the typical system of open spaces of historical tissues, giving attention to the hierarchies rooling all the technical, functional, symbolic, monumental components of historical centres	Planimetric and distributive limits to design proposal at the urban and architectural scale	Valorization of the urban spaces constituting the context sorrounding the Palazzo di Montecitorio as a main urban landmark	Lack of the design solution in answering to the historical and development processes of the urban tissues
			Mixed use providing by concentration of commercial functions on Matrix route in order to restore its functional and morphological continuity	Regeneration of consolidated and historical tissues (T1) according to morphological strategies	Planimetric, distributive and typo-morphological limits to design proposal	Valorization of the relationship between inner and outer spaces by the refurbishment of the morphological connections	Functional marginalisation of non commercial areas
			Easy access to non parliamentary functions on matrix route (Via di Campo Marzio)	Regeneration of consolidated and historical tissues (T1) according to morphological strategies	Distributive limits to design proposal	Directioning of entry flows to the design funcions	Functional marginalisation of non commercial areas
	Technical and functional quality (QT)	Flexibility and integrability of inner and outer spaces from functional and distributive point of view (UNI 8290 - UNI 10838, Best Practice: Scotish Parliament, Building User Brief)	Minimizing of unmovable structures to reduce the impact on the dinamic and alternative use of spaces	Dynamic and flexible spaces	Landlocked and tiny area of intervention compared with the functional needs	Appropriateness to changes in functional and managerial organisation of spaces in short, medium and long period in relation to the new dynamic and flexible character of contemporary job	Not-appropriateness of the building to the functional needs in short, medium and long period
			Minimizing of tecnical and structural elements to reduce the impact on the dynamic and alternative use of spaces	Maximization in use of inner spaces	Distributive and design limits	Modularity and standardization of technical and structural elements	Compliance of technical solution with costs limits

Fig. 2. Evaluations elements (Part 1) and Matrix of SWOT factors (Part 2)

(ii) Square Matrix of individual judgements: SWOT factors identified are entered as heading, in line (i_S, i_W, i_O, i_M) and in row (j_S, j_W, j_O, j_M), to draw up, for each SCn, a serie of Square Matrix of individual judgements that will be filled in phase 2 of the methodology proposed.

(iii) Verbal summary framework of SWOT factors: a specific purpose to each SCn indicator (In), qualitative and quantitative, and to its qualitative coefficients (Kji) (values between 0 and 1) are defined.

The definition of weight vector Wj of Criteria Cn and Subcriteria SCn (phase 2) is made by:

(2a) carrying out individual interviews (Stakeholder Analysis); during the interviews are asked stakeholders to express a set of individual judgments Gji performing, for each matrix of individual judgments relating to SCn, the pairwise comparison between the ith row element with the jth element column.

(2b) development of synthetic judgments GSJ and synthetic matrices filling; all n x n of synthetic judgments GSj for each SWOT factor is calculated on the average of the individual judgments Gji expressed by stakeholders;

I	II	III	IV	V	VI
Goal	General Objectives	Criteria	Sub-Criteria	Purposes	Indicators
				(Synthesis of SWOT elements)	
The urban void solution by the inclusion of new functions	Architectural and Urban quality (QA)	Urban fabric filling in relashionship with the historical development process	Alignement of the new building to the urban fabrics before demolition (Rilievo IGM 1873)	Architectural and urban quality improvement through the integration between the new intervention and the historical development processes and through the valorization of morphological connections	Total Partial Absent
			Presence of inner courts (covered or uncovered) following the tradition of the historical urban fabric	Architectural and urban quality improvement through regeneration of tissues; prioritization of design proposals according to the most integrated in the context paying attention to volumetric relation between built areas and empty spaces in the historic centre	Present Absent
		Organic relashionship between buildings and urban spaces	Connection between design spaces, urban spaces and parliamentary functions close to the design area	Architectural and urban quality improvement through regeneration of public spaces; prioritization of design proposals according to the most integrated in the context paying attention to the connection between new building and urban spaces	Very high High Medium Low Very low
			Mixed use providing by concentration of commercial functions on Matrix route in order to restore its functional and morphological continuity	Architectural and urban quality improvement through regeneration of public spaces; prioritization of design proposals according to the most suitable to maintain a dynamic socio-economic context	Total Partial Absent
			Easy access to non parliamentary functions on matrix route (Via di Campo Marzio)	Architectural and urban quality improvement through regeneration of public spaces; prioritization of design proposals according to the most integrated in the context paying attention to the concentration of commercial functions on matrix route	Total Partial Absent
	Technical and functional quality (QT)	Flexibility and integrability of inner and outer spaces from functional and distributive point of view	Minimizing of unmovable structures to reduce the impact on the dinamic and alternative use of spaces	Preference of design proposals characterized by open functional and distributive solutions able to answer to flexibility of functions in short, medium and long period according to contemporary dynamism of work's conditions.	Very high High Medium Low Very low
			Minimizing of tecnical and structural elements to reduce the impact on the dynamic and alternative use of spaces	Preference of design proposals that allow high use of space in relation to model of use and to the structural and technical integrability	Total Partial Absent
	Economic and finalncial aspects (EF)	Spending Control	Cost reduction	Spending control referred to realization costs	% on base amount established for call for tenders
			Cost sustainability connected with energy saving	Spending control referred to management costs. Preference of design proposals characterized by functional, distributive, technical solution allowing to reduce cost of using, energy saving and pollution reduction	€/year
			Maintenance costs por year	Spending control referred to maintenance plans for spaces, structures and technical elements. Preference of design proposals characterized by functional, distributive, technical solution allowing to reduce cost of ordinary and extraordinary maintenance	€/year
		Economic Convinience	Environmental costs	Environmental impact reducing and greenhuse gas or other polluting gas emission reducing	€
			Costs Benefits ratio	Economic convenience referred to economic and social regeneration of consolidated and historic city according to strategies able to generate benefits. Accuracy of analysis is based on studi level of detail and on the choice of suitable interest rate	NPVe (€)

Fig. 3. Qualitative and quantitative indicators

(2c) construction of normalized judgments GNj: the set of synthetic judgments GSj built for each factor within the synthetic matrices is transformed into a normalized judgment GNj through operations of:

   (i) Moderation: (i1) the arithmetic sum of synthetic line judgments GSj leads to define Line Vectors; (i2) the sum (which does not take into account whether it is positive or negative) of synthetic judgments GSj leads to define Column Vectors; (i3) a moderation algorithm built starting from the Column Vectors, for the definition of an array of values called Moderator [14]; (i4) definition of moderate Line Vectors through the multiplication of Line Vectors by the Moderator in each Synthesis Matrix.

   (ii) Balancing: construction of a weighted sum of the Line Vectors moderated in each Synthesis Matrix that determines the normalized judgement GNj.

(2d) Normalized Judgments GNj allow to define the Weights Vector Wj of Cn and SCn to be used in the AHP, transforming each Normalized Judgment GNj in terms of proportionality on the base of 100, compared to the sum of the Normalized Judgments GNj (Wj = 100*GSj /0*GSj).

The ranking of the alternatives (phase 3) is obtained by introducing in the hierarchical structure of the AHP, the elements of the evaluation and the weight vector Wj by using of specific software that will produce local (Pij) and global (Pi) priorities of the alternatives, using mathematical algorithms that lead to solve the problem of the consistency of the matrix during pairwise comparisons with the eigenvalues (MEV) method. Further in the text it will illustrate the operational application of the methodology proposed for the case of the new services building for the Chamber of Deputies in Rome (Sect. 4), integrally for phases 1 and 2, partially for phase 3.

Indicators (In)	Coefficients (Kji)
Qualitative	Range of values between 0 – 1
Very high – Total – Present	1
High	0,75
Medium – Partial	0,5
Low	0,25
Very low – Absent	0
Quantitative	
€/tar	Scale of coefficient to be built according to
€	the amount established for call for tenders and according to quantitative aspects referred
NPVe (€) (Net present value)	to managment plans

Fig. 4. Evaluation coefficients

4 Implementation of the Proposed Methodology for the Case Study of the New Services Building for the Chamber of Deputies in Rome

The case study concerns the construction of a new services building for the Chamber of Deputies in Rome remained unsolved from the design competition of 1967, on a not built area close to Montecitorio building, in the historic centre of the city. The transformation proposal is to choose the most suitable intervention solution among various design hypothesis, to solve a break of the historic tissue and to insert new offices and services nearby the Italian Parliament building. In order to identify the characters, that the intervention of a new services building for the Chamber of Deputies in the tissue of the historic centre of Rome should have, were taken into account:

- the needs of the Chamber of Deputies in term of spaces and governmental functions;
- the quantity and quality of functions included in governmental buildings built in recent decades in Italy and in the World;
- the state of planning about what the General Regulatory Plan of Rome requires for the Old City (NTA 2008, PRG Roma, art. 24, co. 1 - historical fabrics;)
- the historical, morphological, functional, distributive characters of the area surrounding Montecitorio building;
- the study of national and international Best Practice in the field of quality and functionality of spaces in the design of government buildings;
- regulatory requirements in the latest updates in the field of public works contracts (Legislative Decree n.50/2016) regarding the economic and financial sustainability, the environmental performances and the energy savings.

According to the goal of the case study the urban void solution by the inclusion of new functions and to the general objectives (Og) and following the aforementioned procedure (cit. Paragraph 3), in Phase 1 activating a Focus Group (consultation: the parliamentary technicians (1), designers and researchers (10)) it succeeded in: (1a) definition of the elements of the evaluation made of 5 Cn, and 12 SCn (Fig. 2 part 1); (1b) construction of the Matrix of SWOT factors (Fig. 2 part 2), setting up the arrays of individual judgments and the verbal summary framework of SWOT factors (assigning a specific purpose to each SCn). On the base of the verbal summary framework qualitative and quantitative indicators (In) (Fig. 3) and qualitative coefficients (Kji) (-values between 0 and 1) (Fig. 4) have been defined. Coefficients (Kji) referred to the economic and financial convenience aspects have not been defined because they need further analysis referred to the technical-economic and procedural characters that were not performed at this phase.

In order to define the Vector of Weights Wj of the Cn and SCn (Phase 2) it proceeded:

(2a) to interview (SA) a sample of parliamentary technicians (3) and a sample of designers and researchers (10) to fill the arrays of individual judgments based on judgments Gji formulated from each of the selected subjects following the procedure described in paragraph 3;

(2b) to calculate for each SCn the average of individual judgment Gji obtaining the synthetic judgments GSji which are reported in the Summary Matrix (Fig. 5a);

a. Synthesis Matrix / **b. Moderation and balancing operations**

		S – Organic design of urban spaces and riconfiguration of urban routes geometry broken by demolitions	W – Planimetric and distributive limits to design proposal	O – Urban void solution by valorization and refurbishments of morphological connections	T – Limits to design research for innovative solution finding	LINE VECTOR (LV_nSc_n)	BREAK-VALUESa (BVa_nSc_n)	BREAK-VALUESp (BVp_nSc_n)	MODERATOR (MSc_{nn})	MODERATE VECTOR (Vm_nSc_n)
S	Organic design of urban spaces and riconfiguration of urban routes geometry broken by demolitions		1	1	2	4	3	50,0	0,5	2,00
W	Planimetric and distributive limits to design proposal	0		0	0	0	5	83,3	0,8	0,00
O	Urban void solution by valorization and refurbishments of morphological connections	2	2		1	5	1	16,7	0,2	0,83
T	Limits to design research for innovative solution finding	1	2	0		3	3	50,0	0,5	1,50

b. Moderation and balancing operations

COLUMN VECTOR (VC_nSc_n)	3	5	1	3	
BREAK-VALUES (BVa_nSc_n)*	3	5	1	3	
ΔVc_nSc_n	5				
BREAK-VALUES (BVa_nSc_n)	1	2	3	4	5
ATTRIBUTION of $BVa_n Sc_n$ to $VC_n Sc_n$	1	2	3	4	5

NORMALIZED JUDGEMENT GNj	1,08

Fig. 5. Synthesis matrix, (a); Construction of normalized judgements GNj, application for SCn1, (b)

(2c) to carry out operations of moderation and balancing of synthetic judgments GSji in order to obtain the construction of normalized judgment GNji; (Fig. 5b);

(2d) to define the vector of weights Wj of Cn and SCn by the translation of normalized judgments GNji in percentage values (Fig. 6).

Cn of *Urban fabric filling* in relationship with the historical development process (30%) and of *Organic relation between buildings and urban spaces* (29%) related to general objective of the architectural and urban quality of transformation (QA) obtained a bigger weight. Cn referred to the general objective of the technical and functional quality (QT) and of the economic and financial aspects (EF) obtained a progressively smaller weight.

General Objectives	Criteria	Sub-Criteria	Wheight subcriteria V%	Wheight criteria V%
Architectural and Urban quality (QA)	Urban fabric filling in relashionship with the historical development process	Alignement of the new building to the urban fabrics before demolition (Rilievo IGM 1873)	17	30
		Presence of inner courts (covered or uncovered) following the tradition of the historical urban fabric	13	
	Organic relashionship between buildings and urban spaces	Connection between design spaces, urban spaces and parliamentary functions close to the design area	6	29
		Mixed use providing by concentration of commercial functions on Matrix route in order to restore its functional and morphological continuity	8	
		Easy access to non parliamentary functions on matrix route (Via di Campo Marzio)	15	
Technical and functional quality (QT)	Flexibility and integrability of inner and outer spaces from functional and distributive point of view	Minimizing of unmovable structures to reduce the impact on the dinamic and alternative use of spaces	4	24
		Minimizing of tecnical and structural elements to reduce the impact on the dynamic and alternative use of spaces	20	
Economic and financial aspects (EF)	Spending Control	Cost reduction	2	8
		Cost sustainability connected with energy saving	5	
		Maintenance costs por year	2	
	Economic Convinience	Environmental costs	5	9
		Costs Benefits ratio	4	

Fig. 6. Definition of vector of weights Wj of Cn and SCn

Five preliminary design drawn up specifically for the present application have been evaluated to obtain the ranking of alternatives. Economic and financial aspects were not analysed at this stage of research, so the implementation of the methodology was partial developing the ranking of alternatives on the base of solely qualitative criteria. The use of *transparent choice* software allowed to calculate the local priority Pji and global priority Pi taking into account the vector of the weights Wj determined in phase 2 and to obtain the ranking of the alternatives (Fig. 7).

Alternatives	Global priorities Pi	Local priorities Pji											
		Architectural and Urban quality (QA)								Technical and functional quality (QT)			
		Urban fabric filling in reationship with the historical development process	Alignement of the new building to the urban fabrics before demolitions	Presence of inner courts (covered or uncovered)	Organic relation between buildings and urban spaces	Connection between design spaces, urban spaces and parliamentary functions	Mixed use provided by concentration of commercial function on Matrix route	Easy access to non parliamentary functions on matrix route		Flexibility and integrability of inner and outer spaces	Minimizing of unmovable structures to reduce impact on the dynamic and alternative use	Minimizing of technical and structural elements to reduce impact on the dynamic and alternative use
Project 3	0,8748	0,8748	0,5785	0,4303	0,1481	0,2963	0,0232	0,0508	0,2223	0,0508	0,0102	0,0004	0,0020
Project 4	0,7431	0,7431	0,4468	0,4303	0,0165	0,2963	0,0232	0,0508	0,2223	0,0508	0,0102	0,0004	0,0020
Project 6	0,7082	0,7082	0,5926	0,4444	0,1481	0,1156	0,0203	0,0508	0,0445	0,0508	0,0102	0,0004	0,0020
Project 2	0,3960	0,3960	0,1025	0,0861	0,0165	0,2935	0,0203	0,0508	0,2223	0,0508	0,0102	0,0004	0,0020
Project 5	0,3751	0,3751	0,1000	0,0836	0,0165	0,2751	0,0020	0,0508	0,2223	0,0508	0,0102	0,0004	0,0020
Project 1	0,1616	0,1616	0,1025	0,0861	0,0165	0,0591	0,0044	0,0102	0,0445	0,0102	0,0020	0,0002	0,0004

Fig. 7. Ranking of alternatives

5 Conclusions

The proposed procedure allowed to define a methodology for evaluating alternatives in complex urban and/or multi-layered contexts like those of historic fabrics, through the construction of a framework of structural elements of the evaluation model and the definition of their relative weight [18]. The total implementation of the first and second phase of the procedure and partial implementation of third phase where weight of the elements of the evaluation of Cn and SCn and ranking of project alternatives were defined, was possible thanks to integrated assessment techniques, consultation of experts, inclusion of stakeholders point of view. The defined set of Cn and SCn is suitable to be used to formulate design guidelines and possibly to integrate the functional and distributive program to support a competition call for design proposals.

The proposed methodology is useful and effective in different contexts. Its organization in phases lends to successive improvement levels able to answer to heterogeneous ambit of complexity. Despite the moderation and balancing operations (step 2c) on synthetic judgments GSj used to define the weight of Cn and SCn, the inconsistency in the expression of individual judgments may cause small changes in percentage points in weighing Cn and SCn. This limitation could be overcome with the development of methods of consistency-check and the development of software and specially designed tools.

References

1. Nesticò, A., Macchiaroli, M., Pipolo, O.: Costs and benefits in the recovery of historic buildings: the application of an economic model. Sustainability 7(11), 14661–14676 (2015)
2. Guarini, M.R., Battisti, F., Buccarini, C.: Rome: requalification program for the street markets in public-private partnership. A further proposal for the Flaminio. Adv. Mater. Res. **838–841**, 2928–2933 (2014)
3. European Commission: Evaluation methods for the european union's external assistance. Evaluation tool, vol. 4 (2006). http://ec.europa.eu/europeaid/sites/devco/files/evaluation-methods-guidance-vol4_en.pdf. Accessed 11 May 2017
4. Guarini, M.R., Battisti, F.: Benchmarking multi-criteria evaluation methodology's application for the definition of benchmarks in a negotiation-type public-private partnership. A case of study: the integrated action programmes of the lazio region. Int. J. Bus. Intell. Data Min. **9** (4), 271–317 (2014)
5. Figueira, J., Greco, S., Ehrgott, M. (eds.): Multiple Criteria Decision Analysis State of the Art Surveys. Kluwer Academic Publishers, Dordrecht (2005)
6. Ishizaka, A., Nemery, P.: Multi-Criteria Decision Analysis, Methods and Software. Wiley, Chichester (2013)
7. Mintzberg, H.: Tracking Strategies: Toward a General Theory. Oxford University Press on Demand, New York (2007)
8. Terrados, J., Almonacid, G., Hontoria, L.: Regional energy planning through SWOT analysis and strategic planning tools. Impact on renewables development. Renew. Sustain. Energy Rev. **11**, 1275–1287 (2007)

9. Kreukels, A., Salet, W., Thornley, A. (eds.): Metropolitan Governance and Spatial Planning: Comparative Case Studies of European City-Regions. Spon Press, Taylor & Francis Group, London and New York (2003)
10. Roy, B., Bouyssou, D.: Aide multicritére à la décision: Méthodes et case. Economica Paris (1995)
11. Manganelli, B., Morano, P., Tajani, F.: Risk assessment in estimating the capitalization rate. WSEAS Trans. Bus. Econ. **11**, 199–208 (2014)
12. Guitoni, A., Martel, J., Vincke, P.: A framework to choose a discrete multicriterion aggregation procedure (1999). http://citeseerx.ist.psu.edu/viewdoc/download?doi=10.1.1.57.6226&rep=rep1&type=pdf. Accessed 11 May 2017
13. Saaty, T.: The Analytic Hierarchy Process. McGraw-Hill, New York (1980)
14. Bezzi, C.: La SWOT dinamica o relazionale. http://www.chersi.it/listing/master2008/4_mod_valutazione/bezzi/SWOT%20dinamica%20o%20relazionale%20(Web%20-%20agosto%202006).pdf
15. Morano, P., Locurcio, M., Tajani, F., Guarini, M.R.: Fuzzy logic and coherence control in multi-criteria evaluation of urban redevelopment projects. Int. J. Bus. Intell. Data Min. **10**(1), 73–93 (2015)
16. Bencardino, M., Nesticò, A.: Demographic changes and real estate values. A quantitative model for analyzing the urban-rural linkages. Sustainability **9**, 536 (2017)
17. Della Spina, L., Ventura, C., Viglianisi, A.: A multicriteria assessment model for selecting strategic projects in urban areas. In: Gervasi, O., Murgante, B., Misra, S., Rocha, A.M.A.C., Torre, C., Taniar, D., Apduhan, Bernady O., Stankova, E., Wang, S. (eds.) ICCSA 2016. LNCS, vol. 9788, pp. 414–427. Springer, Cham (2016). doi:10.1007/978-3-319-42111-7_32
18. Tajani, F., Morano, P.: Evaluation of vacant and redundant public properties and risk control: A model for the definition of the optimal mix of eligible functions. J. Property Investment Finance **35**(1), 75–100 (2017)
19. Torre, C.M., Balena, P., Ceppi, C.: The devaluation of property due to the perception of health risk in polluted industrial cities. Int. J. Bus. Intell. Data Min. **9**(1), 74–90 (2014)
20. Atherton, E., French, N., Gabrielli, L.: Decision theory and real estate development: a note on uncertainty. J. Eur. Real Estate Res. **1**(2), 162–182 (2008)

The Information Value for Territorial and Economic Sustainability in the Enhancement of the Water Management Process

Salvatore Giuffrida[1(✉)], Maria Rosa Trovato[1], and Marcella Falzone[2]

[1] Department of Civil Engineering and Architecture, University of Catania, Catania, Italy
{sgiuffrida,mrtrovato}@dica.unict.it
[2] FALCAM Limited Co, Rome, Italy
falcam@tin.it

Abstract. The Integrated Water Service (IWS) makes use of technological infrastructures that are part of the more general process of the natural water cycle, significantly changing its eco-systemic structure. The management of the aqueducts is a strategic link in the sustainability chain; its mission is to contain the catabolic effects of dialectic between social system and environment, caused by inadequacies in the design, construction and maintenance of capillary networks in large part obsolete. Starting from some analyses of the criticalities of the infrastructure management, the contribution focuses on information as production factor, whose implementation may help resolve major problems, especially in the planning of interventions to improve efficiency of the underground pipelines network. With reference to the ATO of Caltanissetta, we estimate the positive economic impact that the implementation of ICT-based technologies have on the extension of the territory covered by the IWS, given the quality target.

Keywords: ICT · Water service performances assessment · Environmental value · Social value · Customer satisfaction

1 Introduction

The Integrated Water Service (IWS) is a special "production process" aimed at supplying water according to a standard (and hopefully increasing) performance level at an affordable price for the end users.

Water is a highly inelastic and not fungible good; it is one of the main issue of social and political consensus; IWS's quality and tariffs are the benchmark and the target of the water policies [1]. IWS, implemented in Italy by Law n. 36/1994, is nowadays ruled by the Decree n. 152/2006 concerning the set of public utilities including water collection, supply and distribution of water for civil use, sewage and wastewater treatment, which must be managed according to the principles of efficiency, effectiveness and economy, under the responsibility of the Manager within the provincial "ATO" (the local authority water board) according to the Area Plan (AP).

In Sicily L. R. 02/2013 abolished the Area Authority (AATO) and initiated a reorganization of the integrated water management into existing ATO. To date, the thirty

© Springer International Publishing AG 2017
O. Gervasi et al. (Eds.): ICCSA 2017, Part III, LNCS 10406, pp. 575–590, 2017.
DOI: 10.1007/978-3-319-62398-6_41

years AP, have all been adopted and approved in 2002, but no one is revised. One of the main criticalities affecting the IWS management in Sicily, is the poor support information structure; this has important repercussions on the adequacy and effectiveness of decision-making at all levels, at all stages and in respect of all the players.

The strategic performances of IWS, sustainability of the sources and methods of supply, control and maintenance, reduction of losses, tariffs, quality of service and transparency of the process, are all closely linked to ICT. Information is getting the most important input in the "value chain" [2] of business in Services Economy, and many studies are now focusing on the incorporation of "Business analytics" – an emerging technology including big data analytics facilitating decision-making – and Enterprise Information Systems [3, 4].

With reference to the ATO of Caltanissetta, the contribution indicates the information technologies and some diagnostic tools supporting the waste reduction and increasing the extension of the service by improving the network performances.

2   Materials: The Value Chain of the Integrated Water System

2.1   General Frame

The requirements of the IWS, relevant to science valuations, are: technical efficiency, and management; quantitative and qualitative effectiveness; economy. The AP is the basic knowledge platform for planning activities; it indicates the current status of infrastructure (works and equipment), the overall production capacity, the criticalities and untapped potential, under which the ATO determines the quantitative and qualitative objectives of the services to be performed, and optimizes the combination of investments and the tariffs (with the normalized Method) related to the way of concession of the service.

The AP establishes the criteria for determining the different tariffs (real, average, standard and applicable). From the point of view of the allocation of the economic

Table 1. Investments, fees and annual costs in the Sicilian ATO (COVIRI, 2006)

| | Investments | | | | Fees | | | | | | Annual costs (€/m³) | | | | |
	Total investments (millions €)	Rate nvestments (millions €)	Incidence per capita thousands €	Annual incidence per capita (thousands €)	Depuration	Dreinage	Acqueuct	Fixed fee	Total per family	Total per capita	Depuration	Dreinage	Acqueuct	Fixed fee	Total annual cost
Palermo	1261	1050	1,05	35,08	59	21	127	13	220	73	0,28	0,1	0,5	11,6	12,6
Catania	1193	1.022	1,15	38,2	60	20	75	9	165	55	0,31	0,11	0,4	9,2	10,0
Messina	814	692	1,26	41,98	55	19	98	23	194	65	0,28	0,1	0,5	22,8	28,7
Siracusa	486	416	1,24	41,37	69	19	55	9	153	51	0,36	0,1	0,3	9,2	9,9
Ragusa	378	333	1,30	43,17	54	8	163	0	225	75	0,28	0,04	0,9	0,0	1,2
Agrigento	502	354	1,14	37,91	37	37	163	0	237	79	0,33	0,06	0,9	0,0	1,2
Trapani	590	482	1,44	47,95	55	19	154	6	232	77	0,28	0,1	0,8	6,1	8,3
Caltanissetta	319	251	1,17	39,02	60	20	203	3	287	96	0,31	0,11	1,1	3,1	4,7
Enna	290	226	1,64	54,53	55	19	219	10	303	101	0,29	0,1	1,1	10,2	11,8

resources, the analysis of the investments in the Sicilian ATO shows clear gaps in the correspondence between overall size and per capita costs, with evident tariff unfairness (Table 1) [5].

With regard to the overall assessment of efficiency, effectiveness and economy of the IWS, the official surveys [6] indicate the mismatch between the amount of transfers and the effects on the infrastructure and management systems, especially in the weak areas of the country, with consequent high indices of "water distrust tap" and levels of "dispensing irregularities" [7, 8].

Even in matters of efficiency, there are more waste in the weak areas of the country recording a 45% average rate of loss $[1 - (Vol_{collected} - Vol_{billed})/Vol_{collected}]$, slightly above the national average (40%); they are both *real* and *apparent* losses, measuring defects that give rise to forms of distribution inequities [9] (the volumes delivered are not billed).

With regard to the performance monitoring and waste control, the "knowledge factor" is relevant precisely because the supervisor has adopted a system of performance indicators and reporting, designed to monitor and evaluate the interaction between investments and performances: in fact, public transfers as well as contributions and support warranty, allocated at the level of national and regional programming, are bound to monitoring the quality of services, especially with regard to the minimum essential levels and the environmental performances.

For water finance, despite the intention of the Law 36/1994, concerning the deregulation of the ISW, in Italy the financial instruments – for the upgrading and maintenance of infrastructure – mostly involve public funds coming from the CIPE and European and Regional sources [10]. The main are:

- the Program Agreements, implementing the Program of Institutional Arrangements;
- the Objective Law 443/01, which allocates to "Water Schemes" € 4.6 billion for the South, for emergency drinking water, irrigation and industrial uses;
- Regional Operational Program, in Sicily: measures 1.2 - Infrastructure, 1.04a - Water Supply and 1.04b - Sewerage and Sanitation;
- the Project Financing;
- the loans for investment in water works.

The Data analysis [5] indicates that public funding accounts for 41% in the South and Islands, 12% in the Centre and 28% in the North, and that the total of the investments hardly covers 22% of the amount planned. Again, information has a decisive influence on the reconfiguration of investment items, especially today, due to the progressive dematerialization of the performances and the decisive impulse of ICT [11]. The information capital intervenes:

- as *input*:
  - in the *organization*: 1. in a diachronic sense information improves the representation of the causal chains and the formation of prediction scenarios; in a synchronic sense, information allows corporate to optimize internal and external relationships by reducing *gaps and overlaps* of skills, activities, responsibilities.

- in the *qualification of personnel*, improving the "horizontal" dialogue and cooperation within the *operational core*, and the "vertical" relationships with management and the *techno-structure* [12] in terms of awareness about the outcomes;
- in the *structure of the company internal communication*, making it more equitable, flexible and efficient in allocating roles, power and merits;

- as *output*:
  - in the *customer loyalty* improving the customer satisfaction;
  - in the *enhancement of the service* as complex of socio-environmental performances and opportunity for improving the communication between "infrastructural and industrial equipment, urban areas and natural environment" [13, 14].

Some of the main concerns expressed in the ground of protection and enhancement of the water system by the address documents, relate the issue of losses, due to:

- the definite gap between price and value of water;
- the incomparability of this price and the amount of investment in physical and informational improvement of the water networks.

The main criticalities of the water supply network characterized by a high losses rate are:

- the waste of the resources:
  - as an economic good having a prevailing *utility* value (value = price);
  - as an economic good having a prevailing *opportunity* value (value = *full cost recovery* + contributions from external funding sources): in this case the total cost overcomes the price (*price cap*);
  - as itself, having a prevailing *identity*-value;
  - as an ecological-environmental good, having a prevailing eco-systemic value: the waste of water partly frustrates the investments and the irreversible modification of the hydrogeological and geo-morphological layout of land;
  - as a "political good" [15], having a prevailing *social* value: the unfair distribution (low performances, high tariffs) reduces the cohesion of the community

- the reduction of the aqueduct performance in terms of flow rates and pressures and of the consequent periodic inefficiencies;
- the lack of cost control for the destructive losses detection in underground pipelines;
- the interference of this activities with the urban road network;
- the low willingness to pay for increasing the supply cost due to:
  - the progressive decrease of the water availability;
  - the need to extend the infrastructure and improve its performance;
  - the exponential increase in the costs of sustainability due to the higher pressure on the physical and eco-systemic components involved.

2.2 Action and Knowledge in the Value-Chain of IWS

The diagram of Fig. 1 represents the interactions and interconnection between the IWS management and the territorial-environmental social system.

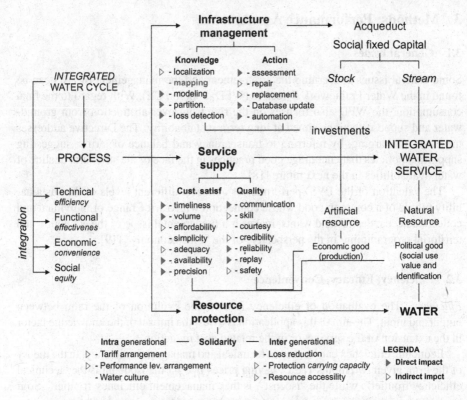

Fig. 1. General scheme of sustainability in the water supply value chain

The water network is part of the social overhead capital, whose "stock-value" depends on the ability to provide "streams" stable, continuous, lasting and increasing. The ecological-environmental and social value of the investments necessary to maintain this *productive* and *adaptive* capacity [16, 17] depends on the ability of the entire system (1) to reduce the pressure on the sources, (2) to simplify the organizational structure of the company. In the management of the water system, *knowledge* and *action* complement each other:

- *knowledge* includes the description system focused on location, mapping, modeling, district metering, monitoring and losses detection;
- *action* includes: (1) assessment, supporting the organization of the activities, the investment and funding allocation, the balance of ordinary (repair) and extraordinary (replace) maintenance; (2) implementation of decisions and programs.

Assessment, in particular, includes the measure of economic efficiency performances (total costs, provided volume, extent of the water network managed per employee, residents served per employee, energy consumed) and effectiveness (water availability, time for repairs, time for new connections, unitary energy consumed, employees) [11].

3   Methods: Performance Assessment

3.1   General Issues

Some general issues concerning the arrangement and the management of IWS can be found in the Water Framework Directive (WFD; 2000/60 CE). With regard to the final consumption, the WFD also focuses on the risk from over-abstraction from ground-water and supposes actions aimed at long term sustainability. The Directive addresses the issue of charging, by referring to transparency and balance of tariffs, suggesting supporting policies that encourage good practices in the face of the structural decline of water availabilities in the next future [18].

The valuation of the IWS' performances connects different levels of the sustaina-bility profile of a common good whose connection with a wide range of individual and collective needs, desires and wants, makes it a fundamental issue of the economic and territorial programming in the perspective of the "blue economy" [19].

3.2   Efficiency, Efficacy, Convenience

Efficiency. The evaluation of efficiency inherits the evolution of the ratio between output and input. The aim of this application is to test the impact of the knowledge factor in the extension of the service, or in the related cost reduction.

Economic efficiency can be seen as technical and managerial efficiency. In the theory of the firm, given two inputs x_1 e x_2, having prices p_1 e p_2, the isoquant is the "technical efficiency frontier", while the "isocost", is the "management efficiency frontier". So it is possible: to maximize the production function $q = f(x_1, x_2)$ constrained to the produc-tion cost $c = x_1 p_1 + x_2 p_2$; minimize the cost at a given level of production (Fig. 2, left).

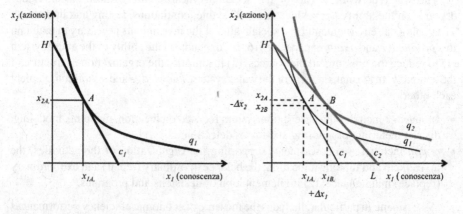

Fig. 2. Sx: trade off and maximization of the production function. Dx: increase of production as effect of the decrease of the "knowledge input" price.

Point A on the left graph of Fig. 2 represents one combination of the two inputs with a low information content, assuming efficient and effective the level of water delivery, and given the prices of the two factors. The point of tangency of q_1 and c_1 represents the equilibrium between technical and management efficiency. Each different combination between the two factors at the same cost would correspond to a lower service level, and each different combination of the two factors, such as to produce the same level of service would result in a higher cost. The Marginal Rate of Technical Substitution of the two factors ($MRTS_{2,1}$) is the ratio between the prices of the two factors.

Efficacy. Therefore, the efficient combination of the two factors needs to be verified from the point of view of effectiveness, here exemplified by the minimum allowable level supply (150 l/inhab/d). The increase in the information factor reduces the costs of knowledge and changes the ratio between the prices of the two factors as represented by the isocost c_2 (Fig. 2 right). Therefore, if total cost doesn't change, the isocost rotates counter clockwise around the point H so that:

- the product increases up to q_2, slightly reducing x_2 and increasing x_1;
- or (Fig. 3 left), keeping q constant, (destroying) action and wasted water replacement definitely decrease to the benefit of targeted and essential interventions. In this case isocost, once in HL, rotates again counter clockwise around point L, until it become tangent to q_1, (Fig. 3 left), and defining the new efficient combination of the two inputs x_{1C}, x_{2C}.

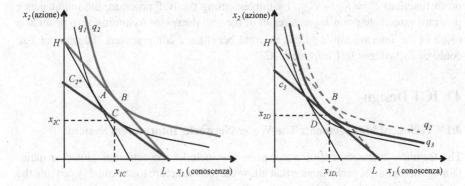

Fig. 3. Sx: Decrease of action input at constant q. Dx: minimum allowable q and new combination of the two inputs.

If production is between of q_1 e q_2, since minimum allowable level supply, q_3, is greater than the current one, q_1, the best inputs combination can be defined by rotating the isocost in c_3 position (Fig. 3 right), in order to find out the actual best level of investment in the knowledge input.

Convenience. In the ground of the management of the water supply it is possible to determine the best extension of the water network maintenance programme by maximizing the difference Revenue-Costs related to the implementation of ICT.

Revenues are the costs of repairs avoided and the value of the recovered water; the cost of ICT factor grows because of the diseconomies of scale related to the widening of mapping and database (Fig. 4).

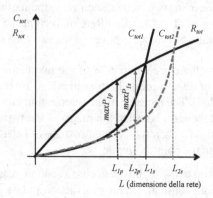

Fig. 4. Comparison between the best extensions from private and public perspective

The best extension of the repaired water network from the perspective of the entrepreneur without ICT program implementation is L_{1p}, determined by maximizing the profit function: $P_1 = R_{tot} - C_{tot1}$; by implementing the ICT program, the maintenance program extends to point L_{2p} as a result of the cost decrease. Assuming zero profit as a result of the internalization of the external benefit not compensated, the optimal size could be L_{1s} without ICT e L_{2s} with ICT.

4   ICT Design

4.1   Technical Management: The Water Networks Information System

The technical management of water networks includes the activities aimed at maintaining the technical performance that allow the infrastructure to sustainably provide the predetermined service levels at the most advantageous rate of return of the inputs. According to a wider notion of input, including the arrangement of natural resources, this definition also supports the public point of view, which is directed to the issue of water management in an eco-socio-systemic perspective [20, 21]: the political-administrative system oversees the balance between prices for users, and environmental costs; the company is supposed to implement the organization factor for which the information is both input and output.

The Water Networks Information System (WNIS), operating on a GIS platform [22], equips the water network with a decision-making platform supporting the management in the perspective of increasing the technical, economic and administrative efficiency, and in the perspective of effectiveness combining service delivery and resource protection, according to the original spirit of the law 36/1994. The WNIS includes:

- the *database of the historical data*, including the features of the existing system;

- the *surveys' database*, integrating historical data with the data used for defining the parameters to be assessed, and therefore with information about the performances;
- a *works' database* that updates historical data about the works of maintenance and/or replacement performed in the course of the management with specific reference to the cost data of the works.

The system is designed to contain the leaks from pipelines by applying the method of partition of the water network (Ministerial Decree n. 99/1997) after the pre-localization. As a result of the repairs of the identified losses, it is possible to quantify the water saving and define the basic level of consumption for each district [23]. Even the partition of the water network is optimized by a mathematical model of the network, which allows the management to simulate the operation in the most varied operating conditions, and to prevent future disruptions. The indicated method enables the control, over time, of the level of loss and the distinction between areas with different priorities of intervention.

4.2 Development of a GIS for the Management of Water Networks

The "complete" case history for the development of a GIS includes: the design of the database; its graphic-alphanumeric population; the collection-integration of data from different subjects and in different formats; the components of the pattern that integrate the paper documents, .DXF and .SHP files [24–26].

The data acquisition process is based on a project GIS (MySQL database) that integrates in a unitary structure the graphic and alphanumeric databases produced by the current Management Authority on the basis of acquisition and digitization of detailed mappings. The GIS implemented for the purpose of technical management consists of features such as Unified Model Language, which defines: the Use Case diagram; the Class and Object diagrams; the Behavior (State and Activity) diagrams; the Sequence diagram; the Collaboration diagram; the Implementation (Component and Deployment) diagrams.

4.3 The Case Study

Some verifications on the positive impacts that the above-mentioned ICT system implementation can generate in terms of overall performance of the SII, were carried out with reference to the ATO 6 – Caltanissetta. Within its administrative boundaries three distinct morphological systems, marked by the watershed of the Salso river can be recognized: the Basin of "Vallone", the Salso Valley, the Basin of Gela river. The ATO comprises 22 municipalities, the total population is 272,402 inhabitants on a 2,128 square kilometers area with a population density of 128 inhabitants per square kilometer.

The main criticalities of the IWS are related to the high level of total losses of the networks that require works for maintenance [27] and expansion of the infrastructure [28], and the improvement of the knowledge support system as the key to success of the new management [29]. For this reason an additional amount of investment has been assigned for programming the new functions in the first ten years, especially to optimize the service: losses containing; supply increasing; sewer functionality improving;

scrubbers empowering etc. The investigation and design finding, and a planning study were included in the one item "knowledge project", for which it is estimated a cost value of € 1,032,913, to be committed in early Plan.

For the management of the IWS in the Province of Caltanissetta six municipal management bodies and five public management entities: the EAS (Sicilian Acqueducts Entity), ASI (Industrial Development Areas) of Gela and Caltanissetta, AGIP and the Reclamation Consortium n. 4 – Caltanissetta.

Regarding the service coverage, the ATO of Caltanissetta includes the towns of medium size: the classes comprising the largest number of municipalities, including the municipalities of less than 5,000 inhabitants (11 of 22) and between 5,000 and 10,000 inhabitants (5 of 22); the class between 10,000 and 50,000 inhabitants has four municipalities, while the large centres with a population exceeding 50,000 inhabitants are two, Caltanissetta and Gela. The overall percentage of the population served is 93.74%, equal to 255,359 units.

The average value of the losses in distribution, real or apparent, is around 41% of the volume injected into the network. There are no known losses in adduction. The average value of per capita consumption is approximately 135 l/inhab/day

Water resources in the territory of the province are small. From wells and municipal sources they are picked up about 2.6 million m^3/year. There are four sources that provide an average volume of about 0.43 million m^3.

The resources currently used in the ATO also come from other sources not directly managed by the municipalities: from the Agip desalter, located in the municipality of Gela, the EAS has withdrawn and injected into the network 6,88 Mm^3. The aqueducts managed by EAS in 2000 have provided the ATO a volume of 12.3 million m^3/year.

With regard to infrastructure, the ATO has distribution networks of drinking water of 1,004 km: only 4% was made before 1950, 22% between 1950 and 1970, 10% between 1970 and 1980, 3% between 1980 and 1990 and finally 18% after 1990. For the remaining 43% no information is available; 32% has been declared to have a good or excellent functionality, 33% sufficient, the remaining 7% bad, poor or insufficient. No description is available for 28%. The development per capita of the distribution network is 3.7 m/inhab.

5 Applications, Results and Discussions

The hypothesis of recombining the input concerns the "operational planning" which, on the basis of the *"Class and Object diagrams, Behavior diagrams* and *Sequence diagrams"* has supposed network mapping scenarios in 60, 90, 120 and 180 days, according to the expected duration for the single task of mapping, which depends on the productivity of labour and the extent and quality of the equipment. The estimated time period should be accompanied by a realistic allocation of costs in relation to the current business resources [30].

The prefigured intervention scenario envisages that the management board wants to calculate the optimal duration of mapping differently combining workers and equipment. Assuming that a two workers-team has an average productivity of 1.5 km of pipeline per day, Table 2 displays the costs calculation and their variation in relation to four different time schedule.

Table 2. Mapping cost calculation in different rapidity hypotheses

Days	60	120	180	240
Number of teams	16	8	4	2
Working days	60	120	180	240
Wage for each 2-workers-team per day	400 €	400 €	400 €	400 €
GPS tool	64.000 €	32.000 €	16.000 €	8.000 €
Ferrofon tool	64.000 €	32.000 €	16.000 €	8.000 €
Transportation	32.000 €	16.000 €	8.000 €	4.000 €
Cost for mapping according to the four hypotheses	3 544.000 €	6 464.000 €	9 328.000 €	12 212.000 €

In the absence of economies or diseconomies of scale, and in case of network homogeneity, the cost of mapping has a linear increase with respect to the size of the mapped network drive. In addition, it is assumed that operators do not face initial difficulties as well as they don't take advantage from the experience gained. Still, the networks in the different municipalities, heterogeneous from the typological and dimensional points of view, their different degree of complexity and the rate of losses, only in some cases allow the management to combine some operations, while in other cases this is contraindicated because it is unnecessarily expensive and not consistent with the programmed *knowledge-system*.

By established international practice, the loss detection is avoided by the managing bodies of water services because, although apparently convenient – due to the short period for the resource recovery – it is difficult to take into account the structural and operating conditions of the network. Therefore men and equipment, most of the times, are employed in areas of the network where, from the point of view of dispersions, do not exhibit levels such as to justify any punctual intervention. The accurate localization of the water losses is then carried out downstream of a project monitoring and control of the level of the dispersions, which takes into account the partition of the network into districts, and then an order of intervention priorities.

The case examined concerns three Municipalities belonging the ATO of Caltanissetta, Marianopoli, Resuttano, Villalba; the following features have been taken into account: the distribution networks of the three municipalities have never been interested by technically advanced maintenance programs; the extent of each network is small enough (<15,000 m) to avoid a division into districts (at least in the first phase); loss percentages are greater than 60%.

The network is 39 km long, and has a flow rate of 21.81 l/s. The area includes 6,842 inhabitants with a theoretical allocation of 275 l/inhab/d. The network showed total losses of 10.53 l/s (1.05 physiological, 4.74 apparent, 4.74 occult), 48% of the total volume. The actual allocation is 142.38 l/inhab/d, lower than the minimum allocation of 150 l/inhab/d as supposed. The estimated unit costs is 150 €/m.

The loss detection carried out with the aid of the correlator and the geophone, makes it possible to recover the volume of water dispersed above the physiological level of loss, within 20 working days. A detailed mapping of the networks would allow the teams to increase their productivity up to 3,000 meters/day/team of pipelines detected, and to complete the operation in 13 working days instead of 20. We analyse two cost scenarios.

1. *Traditional losses detection.* The systematic detection is completed within one month; once the target level of service is reached, revenues (water savings) are accounted. The equilibrium between costs and revenues (saved water) occurs in the third month, when the company gets a revenue of 1,600 €, and the end of the year a total revenue of € 112,000.

2. *Digital mapping losses detection.* The concentration of localization, mapping, systematic detection and repair tasks make it possible to complete the work in half a month and to recover the water making; the trend of revenues-costs function is constant up to half of the first month being null revenues. After two months there is an income of 2,500 € that compensates the costs for the information factor and a gain of around 125,000 € at the end of the year.

In the second scenario, by the end of the year € 13,000 of savings are forecasted: € 6,000 from the least amount of water dispersed, and € 7,000 corresponding to the destructive loss detection works avoided. In the same period, without interventions, the cost in terms of water dispersed and not sold would be around € 147,000.

The heterogeneity of networks ATO suggests starting the process of maintenance and enhancement of the entire network from the simplest networks serving the smaller municipalities in order to compensate the higher initial costs and to take advantage of the staff's increasing experience. This way part of the diseconomies of scale corresponding to the networks of the largest municipalities would be amortized.

The intervention program allows us to compare the costs of the integrated maintenance system (Table 3), and the corresponding revenues determining, with reference to the length of the ATO network, that part (and therefore the municipalities) where it is more advantageous to implement the process. This advantage depends on the difference between revenues and costs.

Figure 5 shows that the program should include 90% of the ATO network (Fig. 5) excluding the municipalities of Campofranco, Mazzarino, and Milena Montedoro. Of

Table 3. Intervention priority and board of investment costs in ICT and losses

	Network lenght	Progr Network lenght	Losses	Total losses per year		Daily cost	Mapping costs	Cumulated mapping costs	Mapping costs	Cumulated Mapping Cost
				Annual	Cumulated					
Marianopoli/EAS	11	11	60%	61497	61497	680	€ 12.716	€ 12.716	€ 15.796	€ 61.497
Resuttano/EAS	15	26	60%	83860	145357	800	€ 13.500	€ 26.216	€ 33.496	€ 145.357
Villalba	13	39	60%	72679	218036	520	€ 8.788	€ 35.004	€ 45.924	€ 218.036
Bompensiere/EAS	6	45	45%	25158	243194	560	€ 4.704	€ 39.708	€ 52.308	€ 243.194
Butera	6	51	45%	25158	268352	560	€ 4.704	€ 44.412	€ 58.692	€ 268.352
Acquaviva/EAS	7	58	40%	24226	292578	600	€ 5.850	€ 50.262	€ 66.362	€ 292.578
Delia/EAS	16	74	40%	59634	352212	640	€ 16.384	€ 66.646	€ 87.226	€ 352.212
Mussomeli	25	99	40%	93178	445389	680	€ 28.900	€ 95.546	€ 123.126	€ 445.389
Riesi	53	152	45%	223906	669295	760	€ 77.110	€ 172.656	€ 215.188	€ 669.295
Santacaterina V./EAS	39	191	45%	164785	834080	880	€ 76.085	€ 248.740	€ 302.276	€ 834.080
Sommatino/EAS	27	218	37%	91705	925785	960	€ 61.286	€ 310.027	€ 371.011	€ 925.785
San Cataldo/EAS	65	283	45%	272545	1198330	1080	€ 189.540	€ 499.567	€ 578.751	€ 1.198.330
Caltanissetta/EAS	230	513	33%	707218	1905548	1200	€ 828.000	€ 1.327.567	€ 1.471.151	€ 1.905.548
Gela/EAS	250	763	45%	1048249	2953797	1320	€ 1.089.000	€ 2.416.567	€ 2.630.151	€ 2.953.797
Niscemi	82	845	45%	343826	3297622	1480	€ 449.032	€ 2.865.599	€ 3.102.143	€ 3.297.622
Vallelunga/EAS	19	864	33%	58422	3356045	1600	€ 121.600	€ 2.987.199	€ 3.229.063	€ 3.356.045
Sutera/EAS	25	889	45%	104825	3460870	1720	€ 184.900	€ 3.172.099	€ 3.420.963	€ 3.460.870
Serradifalco/EAS	29	918	33%	89479	3550348	1840	€ 246.302	€ 3.418.401	€ 3.675.413	€ 3.550.348
Campofranco/EAS	9	927	25%	21198	3571546	1960	€ 87.396	€ 3.505.798	€ 3.765.358	€ 3.571.546
Mazzarino	40	967	25%	93178	3664724	2080	€ 432.640	€ 3.938.438	€ 4.209.198	€ 3.664.724
Milena/EAS	32	999	25%	74542	3739266	2200	€ 387.200	€ 4.325.638	€ 4.605.358	€ 3.739.266
Montedoro/EAS	5	1004	25%	11647	3750913	2320	€ 67.280	€ 4.392.918	€ 4.674.038	€ 3.750.913

course, according to the theory of the firm, i.e. maximizing the difference revenues-costs, the optimal size of the network to be retrained would be reduced to only 300 km.

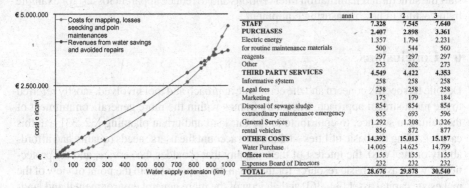

anni	1	2	3
STAFF	**7.328**	**7.545**	**7.640**
PURCHASES	**2.407**	**2.898**	**3.361**
Electric energy	1.357	1.794	2.231
for routine maintenance materials	500	544	560
reagents	297	297	297
Other	253	262	273
THIRD PARTY SERVICES	**4.549**	**4.422**	**4.353**
Informative system	258	258	258
Legal fees	258	258	258
Marketing	175	179	184
Disposal of sewage sludge	854	854	854
extraordinary maintenance emergency	855	693	596
General Services	1.292	1.308	1.326
rental vehicles	856	872	877
OTHER COSTS	**14.392**	**15.013**	**15.187**
Water Purchase	14.005	14.625	14.799
Offices rent	155	155	155
Expenses Board of Directors	232	232	232
TOTAL	**28.676**	**29.878**	**30.540**

Fig. 5. Left: optimal production scale of the program implementation. Right: ATO balance sheet: costs for aggregate items (3 years).

The perspective of economic-financial and environmental sustainability imposes to combine the logic of the market with measures aimed to articulate and differentiate tariffs, in order to support investment in the implementation of the ICT factor and start the improvement of water infrastructure system.

Some other aspects of economic evaluation may suggest a further study. In the ATO balance sheet (Fig. 5 right) it is possible to observe the impact of each of the different items on the total cost of the IWS. On this basis it was possible to develop a hypothesis of the ICT investment cash flow. Qualified literature [31] provides the definition of performance indicators proposed by the International Water Association (IWA): the Current Annual Real Losses (CARL), the Unavoidable Average Real Losses (UARL) and the Infrastructure Leakage Index (ILI); they provide the target performance levels to be achieved with the drastic reduction of losses due to the implementation of the WNIS.

In particular, it established the optimum level ILI (2.76) is possible to calculate the volume of water to be recovered which provides the expected revenue for each year of operation. The graph in Fig. 6 (right) shows that starting from the end of the second year

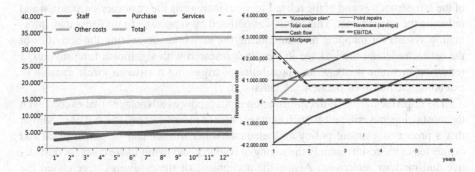

Fig. 6. Left: balance sheet of the ATO (3 years). Right: Cash Flow of the "knowledge plan"

of operation the revenues corresponding to the recovered water, cover the costs of the second phase of the "knowledge project" with a positive cash flow that can be used to start the structural rehabilitation interventions and to reduce apparent losses, for example by investing in new measuring equipment.

6 Conclusions

Despite its specific concern and the economic approach and tool involved, mostly referred to the main-stream approach, this study frames within the more general commitment of the valuation science, to contribute to the fair land and urban planning [32, 33] – in this case regarding the basic utilities – taking into account the users' needs (quality and affordability of the IWS), the interest of the company that provides the service, and the protection of water as the basic resource for the urban development from the point of view of the real estate capital asset [34–36], and an icon of the more general environmental and landscape capital asset [30].

The reduction and control of water losses require significant investments in information input as to the technological level of the fixed capital and the specialization of the staff. In the reform of Integrated Water System, the ATO made it possible to concentrate in a single Management Authority the responsibility for the results of operations, increasing the decision-making power needed to implement innovative programs to achieve the minimum targets of IWS, in total respect of the prescriptions about the protection of the resource and of the hydrogeological system.

The placement of the reservoirs, the development of the linear main pipeline and the arrangement of the reticular aqueducts, can take advantage of the increased efficiency of the service, and of the savings that can be allocated to the investment necessary to prepare a capillary and durable infrastructure.

Even considering these strategic objectives, should be considered that the perceived quality of IWS does not always corresponds to the quality of the infrastructure. This may be due to resource wastage and inefficiencies in maintenance unaccounted in the tariffs. This is the case of Caltanissetta, where no tariff increase was recorded despite the high rate of wiles of the pipeline and the consequent high costs for maintenance works, often ineffective because of the lack of appropriate technology, knowledge and skills.

The implementation of high level ICTs, is part of the process of dematerialization of the infrastructures and of the related services increasing the customer satisfaction and reducing the investments. This result was outlined by supposing to implement an information system for mapping and monitoring the networks, organizing the activities of the teams, reducing the leakage in the pipes research with significant time savings, a reduction in water wastage, and possibility of triggering a virtuous circle capable of extending the radius of the network enhanced.

The implementation of the information input produces advantages that exceed even the most stringent verification, such as the economic-monetary one [35], but on condition that a proper investment policy and adequate water finance can be put in place and connected to the result, namely the saving of resource and to minimize costs for destructive and random detections. Again, the accounting of these savings depends on the perspective of integrating technological information, economic and financial evaluation [23], and socio-environmental communication.

Acknowledgements. S. Giuffrida and M. R. Trovato edited parr. 1–3, 5 and 6; M. Falzone edited parr. 4 and 5.

References

1. Guffanti, L.: La gestione del servizio idrico integrato. In: Guffanti, L., Morelli, M. (eds.) La riforma dei servizi idrici in Italia, pp. 103–137. Egea, Milano (1997)
2. Porter, M.E.: Competitive Advantage. Free Press (1985). ISBN 0-684-84146-0
3. Sun, Z., Strang, K.D., Firmin, S.: Business analytics-based enterprise information systems. J. Comput. Inf. Syst. (2016). doi:10.1080/08874417.2016
4. Trovato, M.R., Giuffrida, S.: A DSS to assess and manage the urban performances in the regeneration plan: the case study of Pachino. In: Murgante, B., et al. (eds.) ICCSA 2014. LNCS, vol. 8581, pp. 224–239. Springer, Cham (2014). doi:10.1007/978-3-319-09150-1_17
5. Comitato per la Vigilanza sull'uso delle Risorse Idriche: Relazione annuale al Parlamento sullo stato dei servizi idrici Anno 2005. Ministero dell'Ambiente, Roma (2006)
6. Comitato per la Vigilanza sull'uso Risorse Idriche: Relazione annuale al Parlamento sullo stato dei servizi idrici Anno 2004. Ministero dell'Ambiente Roma (2005)
7. Comitato per la Vigilanza sull'uso delle Risorse Idriche: Rapporto sullo stato dei servizi idrici (PDF). Ministero dell'Ambiente Roma (2009)
8. Autorità per l'Energia Elettrica e il Gas: Consultazione pubblica per l'adozione di provvedimenti tariffari in materia di servizi idrici, Milano (2012)
9. Abbott, M.B., Vojinovic, Z.: Towards a hydroinformatics praxis in the service of social justice. J. Hydroinformatics **16**, 516–530 (2013). doi:10.2166/hydro.2013.198
10. Brosio, G.: Economia e finanza pubblica. Carocci, Roma (2002)
11. Ancarani, A.: Valutazione delle prestazioni nei servizi. ESI, Napoli (2003)
12. Rebora, G.: Manuale di organizzazione aziendale. Carocci, Roma (2001)
13. Giuffrida, S., Napoli, G., Trovato, M.R.: Industrial areas and the city. Equalization and compensation in a value-oriented allocation pattern. In: Gervasi, O., et al. (eds.) ICCSA 2016. LNCS, vol. 9789, pp. 79–94. Springer, Cham (2016). doi:10.1007/978-3-319-42089-9_6
14. Della Spina, L., Ventura, C., Viglianisi, A.: A multicriteria assessment model for selecting strategic projects in urban areas. In: Gervasi, O., et al. (eds.) ICCSA 2016. LNCS, vol. 9788, pp. 414–427. Springer, Cham (2016). doi:10.1007/978-3-319-42111-7_32
15. Rizzo, F.: Il valore dei valori. FrancoAngeli, Milano (2005)
16. Pires Rosa, M.: Towards an adaptive approach in planning and management process. In: Meire, P., Coenen, M., Lombardo, C., Robba, M., Sacile, R. (eds.) Integrated Water Management. NATO Science Series, vol. 80, pp. 23–32. Springer, Dordrecht (2008). doi:10.1007/978-1-4020-6552-1_3
17. Mallawaarachchi, T., Walker, P.A., Young, M.D., Smyth, R.E., Lynch, H.S., Dudgeon, G.: GIS-based integrated modelling systems for natural resource management. Agric. Syst. **50**(2), 169–189 (1996)
18. Borja, A., Franco, J., Valencia, V., Bald, J., Muxika, I., Belzunce, M.J., Solaun, O.: Implementation of the European water framework directive from the Basque country (northern Spain): a methodological approach. Mar. Pollut. Bull. **48**, 209–218 (2004)
19. Gunter, P.: The Blue Economy: 10 years, 100 Innovation, 100 Million Jobs. Report to the Club of Rome, Paradigm Publications, Taos (NM) (2010)

20. Mitchell, B.: Integrated water resource management, institutional arrangements, and land-use planning. Environ. Plan. A **37**, 1335–1352 (2005)
21. Nguyen, G.T., de Kok, J.L., Titus, M.J.: A new approach to testing an integrated water systems model using qualitative scenarios. Environ. Model Softw. **22**(11), 1557–1571 (2007)
22. Maidment, D.R.: Arc Hydro. GIS for water resource, ESRI (2002)
23. Cammarata, F.: Progetto di massima per il controllo e la localizzazione delle dispersioni idriche nelle reti di distribuzione a servizio del centro storico della città di Caltanissetta. FALCAM, Caltanissetta (2001)
24. Bhave, P.R.: Analysis of flow in water distribution networks. In: Dunlop, E.J. (ed.) WADI Users Manual. Local Government Computer Services Board, Dublin (1991)
25. Booch, G., Jacobson, I., Rumbaugh, J.: The Unified Software Development Process. Addison-Wesley Longman Publishing Inc., Boston (1999)
26. Saleh, H.A., Allaert, G., De Sutter, R., Kellens, K., De Mayer, P., Vanneuville, W.: Intelligent decision support system based geo-information technology and spatial planning for sustainable water management. In: Feyen, J., et al. (eds.) Water and Urban Development Paradigm, pp. 283–285. Taylor & Francis Group, London (2009)
27. Rossman, L.A., Boulos, P.F.: Numerical methods for modelling water quality in distribution systems: a comparison. J. Water Res. Plan. Manag. **122**(2), 137–146 (1996). http://dx.doi.org/10.1061/(ASCE)0733-9496(1996)122:2(137)
28. Alegre, H. (ed.): Performance Indicators for WSS. Alliace House, London (2006)
29. Rossman, L.A.: EPANET 2. Users manual, Water Supply and Water Resources Division National Risk Management Research Laboratory (2000)
30. Naselli, F., Trovato, M.R., Castello, G.: An evaluation model for the actions in supporting of the environmental and landscaping rehabilitation of the Pasquasia's Site Mining (EN). In: Murgante, B., et al. (eds.) ICCSA 2014. LNCS, vol. 8581, pp. 26–41. Springer, Cham (2014). doi:10.1007/978-3-319-09150-1_3
31. Viorel, G. (ed.): Water loss management 2015. In: Conference Proceedings. ARA Publishing, Bucharest (2015)
32. Napoli, G.: Financial sustainability and morphogenesis of urban transformation project. In: Gervasi, O., Murgante, B., Misra, S., Gavrilova, M.L., Rocha, A.M.A.C., Torre, C., Taniar, D., Apduhan, B.O. (eds.) ICCSA 2015. LNCS, vol. 9157, pp. 178–193. Springer, Cham (2015). doi:10.1007/978-3-319-21470-2_13
33. Napoli, G., Giuffrida, S., Trovato, M.R.: Fair planning and affordability housing in urban policy. The case of Syracuse (Italy). In: Gervasi, O., et al. (eds.) ICCSA 2016. LNCS, vol. 9789, pp. 46–62. Springer, Cham (2016). doi:10.1007/978-3-319-42089-9_4
34. Gabrielli, L., Giuffrida, S., Trovato, M.R.: From surface to core: a multi-layer approach for the real estate market analysis of a central area in Catania. In: Gervasi, O., Murgante, B., Misra, S., Gavrilova, M.L., Rocha, A.M.A.C., Torre, C., Taniar, D., Apduhan, B.O. (eds.) ICCSA 2015. LNCS, vol. 9157, pp. 284–300. Springer, Cham (2015). doi:10.1007/978-3-319-21470-2_20
35. Gabrielli, L., Giuffrida, S., Trovato, M.R.: Functions and perspectives of public real estate in the urban policies: the sustainable development plan of Syracuse. In: Gervasi, O., et al. (eds.) ICCSA 2016. LNCS, vol. 9789, pp. 13–28. Springer, Cham (2016). doi:10.1007/978-3-319-42089-9_2
36. Gabrielli, L., Giuffrida, S., Trovato, M.R.: Gaps and overlaps of urban housing sub-market: hard clustering and fuzzy clustering approaches. In: Stanghellini, S., Morano, P., Bottero, M., Oppio, A. (eds.) Appraisal: From Theory to Practice. GET, pp. 203–219. Springer, Cham (2017). doi:10.1007/978-3-319-49676-4_15

From the Object to Land. Architectural Design and Economic Valuation in the Multiple Dimensions of the Industrial Estates

Salvatore Giuffrida[(✉)] and Maria Rosa Trovato

Department of Civil Engineering and Architecture, Catania, Italy
{sgiuffrida,mrtrovato}@dica.unict.it

Abstract. This contribution deals with some economic issues of the enhancement of Tifeo power station in Augusta, facing the Ionian Sicilian coast. The assessment was conducted to verify the economic balance and landscape sustainability of some of the most significant schemes submitted by nine teams entering a design competition organized by the Architecture Department of the University of Palermo. The assessment of the nine schemes focuses on the main issues of the territorial and real estate features involved in the regeneration process and connected with the large and polluted area surrounding the Petrochemical Industrial District of Syracuse. The analysis consists of two approaches: a Discounted Cash Flow Analysis and a Multi Attribute Value Theory pattern.

Keywords: Industrial estate · Land pollution · Sustainable development · DCFA · MAVT · Value substance · Matter, Energy and Information

1 Introduction

This paper will outline some of the hermeneutical trajectories of the regeneration process of ENEL Tifeo Power Station in Augusta. In the perspective of the redevelopment of this area ENEL launched an ideas Contest, hosted by the Department of Architecture of the University of Palermo [1].

The evaluation process of the project proposals, which have been submitted by nine groups of participants, began from the definition of the "salient and resistant" elements, which can be assumed as the starting points of a communication/interlocutory process that can be woven between the company, the local authorities, the scientific community and social community.

The ENEL Tifeo Power Station is strongly characterised with regard to: its location within one of the largest and polluted areas in Italy; the high landscape value of the overall geographic context; its design that has been drawn up by one of the greatest Italian architects of the twentieth century, Giuseppe Samonà. In the perspective of an assessment process, and according to the value substance proposed by F. Rizzo [2], these issues can be interpreted within the general frame of the dialectic order/disorder in the ground of *matter* (pollution), *energy* (renewable *vs.* fossil), *information* (artificial/natural assets).

© Springer International Publishing AG 2017
O. Gervasi et al. (Eds.): ICCSA 2017, Part III, LNCS 10406, pp. 591–606, 2017.
DOI: 10.1007/978-3-319-62398-6_42

This value substance can be considered the maximum and the best degree of abstraction and *reductio ad unum* of the various meanings which the designers detected and proposed in the attempt of complement their personal "gesture" and the needs of a landscape definitely and permanently contaminated.

The regeneration program of the Tifeo Power Station is part of the more general and gradual process of divestment of the whole petrochemical district of Augusta. This settlement, initially welcomed with enthusiasm due the connected expectations of employment and widespread wealth, over time caused a deep and permanent wound in one of the most significant and uncontaminated areas of the Ionian Sea, symbolizing the failure of the industrial decentralization policy and the incompatibility of a development pattern not based on local resources.

The Enel Tifeo ideas contest highlighted several issues, having global (development pattern, sustainability, energy sources conversion) and local (decontamination, reuse and enhancement) relevance, and involving a wide range of values, from monetary up to incommensurable [3], which the "design gesture" aims at complementing.

According to the conceptual pattern of the dissipative structures (Prigogine, 1981), the possibility of creating order out of disorder, on the one hand typically fits the design approach, on the other hand highlights some of the typical appraisal's weaknesses, not as much about its means, but rather about its ends, its directions, the claim of neutrality, its stubborn reference to prices and not to values.

The evaluation methods and techniques today available are extensive and able to meet the complexity of the projects and of the matters they face; both appraisal and assessment integrate many types of values according to the agents more or less strongly involved, or, which by means of the project try to interpret the destiny of a place [4–6]. In this sense, the contribution integrates two evaluation areas:

- the first one integrates the Discounted Cash Flow Analysis within the Residual Value, in order to compare the different design proposals from the monetary point of view;
- the second one performs a Multi-Attribute Value Theory (MAVT) pattern assuming as criteria the objectives highlighted by the designers, and framing them within the approach proposed by F. Rizzo, that interprets economy as a "tras-in-form-a(c)tion process" whose input and output are "*Matter, Energy* and *Information*" in different quantities and shapes [7].

2   Materials. the Tifeo Power Station and the Petrochemical Estate of Augusta

Due to its architectural value, the ENEL Tifeo Power Station can be assumed as the starting point and as the sample of the whole process of divestment, remediation, redevelopment and reuse of one of the Petrochemical district of Augusta.

The vast industrial estate occupies a coastal area of 2,700 hectares along a water front of 26 km and includes the municipalities of Augusta, Priolo Gargallo, Melilli and the northern part of the municipality of Syracuse.

Due to the irreversible transformation of the landscape layout of this large and, once, valuable area, the impact caused by the pollution of all environmental components, included the human one, cannot be in any way compensated; the consequence is the definite reduction of the communicative connection between the economic, the political, the administrative and the environmental-sanitary sub-systems [8].

On the background of the general divestment and redevelopment process the acceptance this landscaping contamination persist; it is the physical track of an impossible hybridization of two strangers development patterns, conflicting to the point of the dramatic and final double loss: of landscape value and of the initial employment, due to the progressive reduction of the industrial activities [9].

The industrial complex is the result of a suffered negotiation process that took place at the very beginning of the aftermath of World War II, some intellectuals, political teams and representatives of civil society, and aimed at addressing the issue of the serious economic, social and human condition of Sicily, whose state of infrastructures, productive and economic backwardness had worsened due to heavy damage dealt by the conflict.

Don Luigi Sturzo [10] himself – trusting in the positive effect of the industrial asset in the perspective of the partial emancipation from poverty, and of human development – sided with the "Industrialists" that prevailed over the "Agriculturalists".

In 1944 the High Commissioner for Sicily obtained from the Central Government an Industrial Credit section at the Bank of Sicily, parallel to those of Mining and Land Credit.

An impressive stream of funding (that began with one billion L. over the 25 for the entire country) started and supported the construction of the industrial district. In 1949, near Augusta, the first refinery Rasiom was built employing the first 650 workers. Once triggered, the process continued creating an integrated industrial and infrastructural district comprising an internal railway, some crude oil extraction areas located in Hyblean Plateau and, not least, in 1958 the Tifeo Power Station over a 15 hectares area, with a first funding of 17 billion L.

With the potential of 210 megawatts which can be produced by the three oil-fired power groups from the Rasiom, the Tifeo Power Station covered the energy needs of the entire island, playing a symbolic role according to its mythological name, evoking winds and storms, but also of the wealth coming from the energy potential of the sulphur deposits and oil fields in Sicily [11]. Until the early '80 s the Petrochemical district reached the current extension, employing in twenty years (1950–70) 20,000 jobs, which today they have reduced in 4,500.

The design of the Tifeo Power Station is extraordinarily innovative (Fig. 1) as its refined complexity, harmonic volumetric articulation, and chromatic solution, suggesting the functional distribution and the tasks of the different parts, making the architectural complex an artefact with a great emotional impact.

The project combines cutting-edge engineering standards and formal organization, anticipating many of successive milestones of the history of Architecture.

In 1961 the project won the prize "ARCHINSI 1961" for the best architectural work carried out in Sicily.

The complex functional structure that arranges the performances of the "thermal machinery" is reflected in the partition of the façades as well as in the volumetric composition. The building consists of one engine room, three boiler-towers, the offices

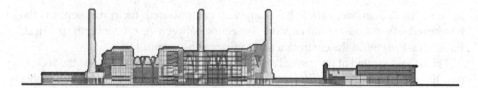

Fig. 1. The Enel TIFEO power station in Augusta

block, the transformers workshop, the auxiliary plant and workers' dwells (nowadays demolished).

The block for the turboalternators is strongly characterised by the rhythm of the forked ribs coming out from the pillars at the first floor entirely in exposed concrete, giving rise to a formal unity resulting by the perfect integration of structural and figurative order.

The inner space articulation is refined as well, sometimes enveloping two and three floors according to the functions of the different areas, suddenly compressing/expanding the space with great effect solutions.

The northern boiler-towers and the three chimney stacks serving the correspondent sections of the engine room have a completely different structure: there are three vertical bodies which are deconstructed in a seemingly disorganized alternation of solids and voids; the three bodies are carved out by loggias and enriched by cantilevers, windows and dividing walls in asbestos-cement panels, which are connected with gangway and pipes.

Due to its dramatic expressiveness and, more in general, to the information content (i.e. the consistency of its formal organization) that can be recognized in it, the Tifeo Power Station can be identified as the symbolic the starting point of the conversion process involving the entire district, hopefully able to coordinate the several issues related to this landscape (dis-)unit and to identify priorities and hierarchies [12].

The conversion of the Tifeo Power Station can be considered as the epitome of a progressive acceptance and resolution of the contradictions that turned a former incomparably beautiful area in a pollution stock [13, 14].

The study on the ENEL Tifeo Power Station area in Augusta proposes issues that can be observed in other areas of the national territory, especially in southern Italy and islands, as the national interest sites in Sicily (Milazzo, Gela and Biancavilla), Sardinia (Porto Torres, Sulcis Iglesiente Guspinese, Maddalena), Puglia (Taranto, Brindisi, Bari and Manfredonia), Basilicata (Tito and Val Basento), Calabria (Crotone Cassano Cerchiaria), Campania (Eastern Naples sites, Vesuvian Coastal Area, Domizio Flegreo Coast, Bagnoli, Sarno River Basin, Plain), and many other industrial estates not included into that list.

Many studies aim at supporting reclamation and reuse projects based on joint public and private actions, such as the ones affecting the Val d'Agri areas in the Province of Potenza (Basilicata region) where ENI and Enterprise Oil exploited two large oil deposits located in the Southern Appenine mountains [15], the Federico II coal-fired power station of ENEL in Cerano, in the Province of Brindisi (Puglia region) and the iron and steel complex of Ilva of Taranto [12].

The valuation science contributes by proposing interpretative patters selecting the appropriate values (the axiological and ethical contents) and valuation patterns able to manage and compare these values.

3 Methods and Procedures

The proposed evaluation process is applied to nine design proposals compared both in terms of economic profitability, and from the point of view of the qualitative value according to the theoretical model of F. Rizzo [2, 16], so in terms of natural (or thermodynamic), bio-genealogical (ecological and economic) and historical-cultural surpluses [9].

3.1 DCFA Analysis

The economic analysis concerns the real estate asset involved in the investment process and not the related business activities whose return is part of the real estate market value of the investments [17–20]. The "Residual Value" is the most effective appraisal tool to support a transformation process [21, 22], as it connects the value of the current asset to the value of the asset once transformed in something different. This evaluation is only apparently simple, because it involve some fundamental od economic theory concerning the production function as proposed by the classic economic theory.

In particular, the value of a real estate asset can be calculated by subtracting from the final value (at the end of the transformation process) the total production costs and the entrepreneurial normal profit considering the rates of the different asset involved in the process (interest on debts, opportunity cost of equity, land and real estate capital, cost of human capital) [23].

This economic-financial approach involves the "residual" component of the process, typically attributable to the economic rent and in its various forms, from the *location rent* to the "information rent".

The general scheme of the transformation value can be represented as follows:

$$S = \frac{V^* - v - k(1 + \bar{r})^m (1 + r')^n}{(1 + \bar{r})^m (1 + r')^n}$$

where: S is the value of the complex in the present state, taking into account the transformation potential, V^* is the final value, v is the present value of the site at current prices, k is the processing cost including the profit for the building entrepreneur, $\bar{r}$ is the well-known weighted average capital cost (*WACC*), r' is the entrepreneurial profit rate for risk, m is the duration of the loan in the short term (the business cycle), and n is the length of the more general transformation process [24].

The process reproduces the scheme of a DCFA from the point of view of the private and public subject:

- the private revenues include:
  - the real estate value of all the buildings as transformed;

- the capitalized value of the energy produced;
- the avoided costs (divestment of plant).
- the public revenues include:
  - the real estate value of the building that is destined to the research centre RET;
  - ordinary concession fees;
  - extraordinary concession fees.
- the private costs include:
  - the implementation costs;
  - cost of soil suitability;
  - the opportunity costs of land and existing buildings;
  - extraordinary concession fees;
  - overheads and tax component;
  - ordinary grant charges for the destinations that will create income.
- the costs for the public subject are the same except for ordinary grant charges.

The evaluation results of the first option are assumed as the benchmark to compare and appraise the eight remaining.

3.2   Multi-attribute Value Theory - MAVT

The Multiple Criteria Decision Aid (MCDA) is part of operational research and deals with structured assessments supporting multi-criteria decision-making problems under uncertainty and not. The approaches proposed within the MCDA can be considered as analytical techniques to explain subjective decisions; they include the approaches that allow us to attribute value judgements by means of the utility function or the value function [25, 26].

The Multi-Attribute Value Theory (MAVT) and Multi Attribute Utility Theory (MAUT) are two MCDA additive approaches, characterised by a similar mathematical representation but different assumptions; the first one can be considered a simplified form of the second that is a more robust and complicated approach, able to take into account also the uncertainty due to the propensity to risk of the decision maker (DM).

MAVT [27–29] can be used to deal with problems involving a discrete and finite set of optional alternatives, which may be evaluated also on the basis of conflicting objectives. MAVT allows us to structure and analyse decision problems by means of attribute trees (also called value trees) and to identify the relative importance of the criteria. In an attribute tree the main objective is declined in hierarchically lower-level objectives (criteria) and in measurable attributes, at the lowest level, the leaf of criteria).

An alternative that is the subject of the decision process is evaluated by means of the functions of value that reflect its performance on each attribute. MAVT is based on the assumption that the DM is rational, prefers the best rather then worst performance values, has a good knowledge about the subject of the decision and is consistent in terms of judgments. In this regard a proper implementation of MAVT supposes the independence of the DM's preferences [28, 29].

Under this assumption a comprehensive evaluation on the alternative can be performed by using the standard additive aggregation rule:

$$V(x) = \sum_{1=1}^{n} w_i v_i(x)$$

where n is the number of attributes, w_i is the weight of the attribute i and $v_i(x)$ is the value function for the single attribute that reflects the performance of the alternative x with respect to the attribute i.

The sum of the weights is normalized to one. The value function $v_i(x)$ ranges from 0, the worst, to 1, the best possible value, namely the performance of the alternative for a given attribute that meets at best the goal.

The weights indicate the relative importance of an attribute from its worst level to the best and by comparison with all other attributes [28–30].

Attributes can be of different nature both quantitative and qualitative.

The MAVT associates a real number $V(x)$ to each alternative x thus generating an order of preference on alternatives consistent with the value judgments, which should be expressed by the DM and should be used to build the value functions.

The MAVT approach can be performed through the following steps [25]:

1. defining and structuring the fundamental objectives and attributes;
2. identifying optional alternatives;
3. evaluating the scores for each alternative and for each criterion;
4. modelling the preferences and the trade-offs;
5. generating the ranking of alternatives.

There are different techniques in the literature for the determination of the weights, which can be grouped into two major categories, namely the numerical estimate of the weights and the weights of indifference [29, 31]; to the first category belong: rankings, direct rating, ratio estimation and swing weights; to the second category belong the trade-off method.

The main strengths of MAVT are [32]:

- a clear structure of the decision process articulated in objectives, criteria and alternative options to solve the problem;
- the possibility to deal with quantitative as well as qualitative dimensions;
- a better understanding of the problem by encouraging the DM and/or decision analyst to represent his preference with a value function; thus MAVT reduces the information amount in order to improve its comprehensibility;
- the improvement of communication for reasoning and negotiations by clarifying the strengths and weaknesses of the alternatives and by making explicit the intermediate and final results;
- the possibility to incorporate the perspective of different stakeholder groups within the structure of the criteria tree, to develop alternative options/solutions for the problem and to draw the value function.

The main weakness MAVT are:

- the full compensability of the criteria that are reduced and expressed in the same unit within the value functions; this implies that a bad performance on a criterion (for example a high environmental impact) can be compensated by a good performance on another (for example a high income); this feature makes MAVT an adequate instrument to operationalize the concept of weak sustainability, but not the idea of strong sustainability.
- the difficulty to meet the mutual independence of the preference conditions that in many cases is simply ignored when applying the additive form of MAVT.

4   Applications

The nine design proposals presented at the ideas contest banned by ENEL and hosted by the Department of Architecture of University of Palermo (Fig. 2) suppose redevelopment interventions different in; typology (more or less transformative); intervention scale (local, namely near to area of Power Station or territorial, i.e. concerning the whole landscape context including Augusta and Syracuse); functions; groups of stakeholders; territorial and infrastructural systems being involved.

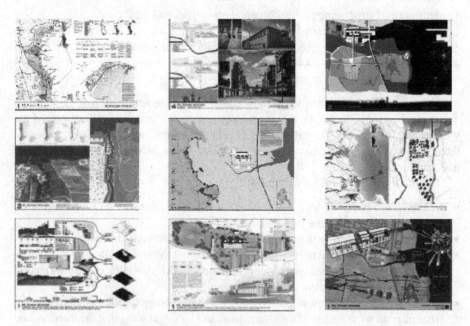

Fig. 2. ENEL Tifeo Power Station projects of the design teams

The projects presented by the nine groups are [1]:

1. *From architecture to the territory. The Tifeo Power Station as an opportunity* (team 1: Cannatà M. and Fernandes F.);

2. *Re_power Station* (team 2: Carpenzano);
3. *The project of a marine biology research centre in Augusta* (team 3: Ferrari M. and Tinazzi C.);
4. *Eh₂ocampo* (team 4: Franciosini);
5. *The recovery of ENEL Tifeo Power Station: a technology centre for the third industrial revolution* (team 5: Messina);
6. *Re_Power Station* (team 6: Moccia);
7. *Re_Power Station* (team 7: Piscopo C. and Scala P.);
8. *Re_Power Station*. "RCEA" Research Center for the Environmental Energy (team 8: Rossi Prodi);
9. *Re_Power Station* (team 9: Trisciuglio).

The invariants of these proposals are represented by physical elements in terms of buildings, technological and territorial infrastructures existing in the area, such as: the building of the turboalternators, the offices block, the three towers, the transformer building, the auxiliary plant with its towers, the canteen, the substations, the cooling tanks, the water intake system, the railway and the Cantreva river.

The general conversion process of the Tifeo area suggests many topical issues at a global (sustainability, energy conversion) and local (decontamination, reuse and exploitation) level, which involve the layer of values in all its joints.

Table 1. Value-MAVT tree for the Enel TIFEO power station

Objective	Sub- objective	Ref.	Specific sub -objective
Redevelopment of Tifeo Power Station	Natural or thermodynamic surplus	A	Air
		B	Water- Catchment basins-Sea
		C	Soil
		D	Land use
		E	Flora and fauna
		F	Biodiversity
	Bioloeical and ecological surplus	G	Human health
		H	Intergenerational ethics
		I	Eco-systemic resilience
		L	Industrial ecolosv
		M	Landscape ecology
		N	Social ecology
	Historical and cultural surplus	O	Archaeological and industrial
		P	Technical-engineering
		Q	Historical and architectural
		R	Archaeological and historical
		S	Territorial management
		T	Historical and cultural identity

Due to the complexity of the proposals and the issues which they deal with, the valuation approach needs to integrate the various axiological layers and coordinate different procedures to capture and systematise functional, symbolic, monetary, extra-monetary, environmental, social, perceptual, structural and stakeholders features [33, 34].

The quantitative and monetary valuation of the investments, i.e. the Discounted Cash Flow Analysis, has considered the real estate and energy components, ignoring the business one that would require a business plan.

This structure of the attributes has been defined by considering the general objective of redevelopment. According to the estimate economic approach that has been considered and MAVT, this general goal has been broken down a sub-objectives (Table 1),

	1	2	3	4	5
A	Polluting substances	Concentration of contaminants	Weather and climatic condition		
B	Surface water pollution	Groundwater pollution	Marine and coastal pollution	Transitional waters pollution	
C	Pollution from heavy metals and metalloids	Organic micro-pollutants			
D	Replacement of agricultural use	Replacement of natural area	Replacement of bathing areas	Replacement of technological networks	
E	Reduction of the fauna because of pollution	Reduction of the flora because of pollution			
F	Reduction of natural ecological mix				
G	Areas exposed to substances hazardous to human health	Cancerous diseases	Mutagenic effects	Accident risk for the population	Accident risk to workers
H	Depletion of water resources	Depletion of marine resources	Depletion of soil resources	Depletion of the landscape	
I	Adaptation of the community	Flora adaptation	Fauna adaptation	Systemic reproduction of the territory and landscape	Access to jobs in the industrial sector
L	Mix of production activities	Degree of conversion of activities	Policies	Financing in the field of industrial conversion	
M	Mix in the sub-units of landscape	Overlapping of landscape units	Degree of influence of the landscape units		
N	Representative capacity of local communities	Representative capacity of local administrators	Process management		
O	Importance of the site from a historical and cultural point of view for the community	Synergies System	Fundings for archaeological and industrial adaptation to a new function		
P	Technical and engineering know-how	Capacity of reclamation	Capacity of adaptation to a new function	Capacity to management of adaptation to a new function	Cost of adaptation to a new function
Q	Notoriety of designer	Quality of the project	Project positioning in the national context	Project positioning in the international context	
R	Compatibility with the archaeological system	Flexibility in adapting to new function			
S	Mix of companies operating in the territory	Synergies between sectors	Public and / or private funds to support the transformation of the territory	Effectiveness of the management model	
T	Perception of the community	Participation in the cultural and historical identity			

Fig. 3. The leaves of the criteria

i.e. were regarded as sub-objectives those of the natural thermodynamic surplus, the surplus bio-ecological and historical and cultural surplus. These sub-objectives in turn were declined in additional sub-objectives or attributes (Fig. 3).

5 Results and Discussions

5.1 Economic and Financial Feasibility: The Residual Value

The analysis on the economic and financial feasibility highlighted the interventions that best respond to the economic profitability criterion in relation to general requirements for the redevelopment of area. The results of the evaluation are summarized in Table 2 comparing the alternatives in terms of monetary normalized values, once assumed option 1 as benchmark. Only the alternative records positive margin.

Table 2. DCFA of the nine planning proposals

	PROGETTI															
	2		3		4		5		6		7		8		9	
RICAVI	priv	pubbl	priv	pubbl	priv	pubbl	priv	pubbl	priv	pubbl	priv	pubbl	priv	pubbl	priv	pubbl
valore immobiliare	8,990	0,000	0,599	0,603	1,498	0,302	6,293	0,603	2,997	0,201	2,997	0,201	2,997	0,201	4,845	0,201
valore attrezzatura portuale	5,292	0,000	0,000	0,000	0,000	0,000	0,000	0,000	13,230	0,000	2,646	0,000	2,646	0,000	0,000	0,000
produzione energia da biogas	0,000	0,000	0,000	0,000	15,833	0,000	0,000	0,000	0,000	0,000	0,000	0,000	0,000	0,000	0,000	0,000
produzione energia da fotovoltaico	0,000	0,000	0,000	0,000	0,388	0,000	2,589	0,000	0,000	0,000	0,000	0,000	3,884	0,000	0,000	0,000
costi evitati (demolizioni)	2,191	0,000	2,191	0,000	2,191	0,000	1,753	0,000	2,191	0,000	2,191	0,000	1,972	0,000	2,191	0,000
oneri concessori ordinari	0,000	2,315	0,000	0,000	0,000	0,000	0,000	1,543	0,000	2,315	0,000	0,772	0,000	0,772	0,000	0,039
COSTI																
opere architettoniche	34,475	0,000	11,492	1,283	5,746	6,417	24,133	1,750	11,492	0,992	11,492	0,583	12,641	0,642	12,641	0,583
spazi aperti	2,866	6,688	1,791	4,180	0,896	2,090	2,687	6,270	2,150	5,016	1,791	4,180	2,150	5,016	1,971	4,598
opere a verde	0,095	0,291	0,059	0,182	0,148	0,545	0,030	0,091	0,059	0,182	0,059	0,182	0,071	0,218	0,059	0,182
infrastrutture viarie e portuali	5,069	7,946	1,690	1,324	0,189	1,059	1,183	1,854	2,534	0,000	1,690	2,649	1,352	2,119	0,456	2,649
impianto biogas	0,000	0,000	0,000	0,000	0,855	0,000	0,000	0,000	0,000	0,000	0,000	0,000	0,000	0,000	0,000	0,000
impianti fotovoltaici	0,000	0,000	0,000	0,000	0,173	0,000	1,153	0,000	0,000	0,000	0,000	0,000	1,557	0,000	0,000	0,000
idoneizzazione suolo	0,121	0,500	0,121	0,500	0,181	0,750	0,145	0,800	0,121	0,000	0,121	0,500	0,121	0,500	0,121	0,500
costi opportunità suoli e fabbricati	4,373	0,909	4,373	0,909	1,182	1,000	4,810	1,000	4,373	0,000	4,373	0,909	4,373	0,909	4,373	0,909
spese generali	0,000	0,000	0,000	0,000	0,000	0,000	0,000	0,000	0,000	0,000	0,000	0,000	0,000	0,000	0,000	0,000
iva	0,000	0,000	0,000	0,000	0,000	0,000	0,000	0,000	0,000	0,000	0,000	0,000	0,000	0,000	0,000	0,000
oneri concessori ordinari	2,315	0,000	0,000	0,000	0,000	0,000	0,000	0,000	0,000	0,000	0,000	0,000	0,000	0,000	0,000	0,000

	2		3		4		5		6		7		8		9	
RICAVI	priv	pubbl	priv	pubbl	priv	pubbl	priv	pubbl	priv	pubbl	priv	pubbl	priv	pubbl	priv	pubbl
valore immobiliare																
valore attrezzatura portuale																
produzione energia da biogas																
produzione energia da fotovoltaico																
costi evitati (demolizioni)																
oneri concessori ordinari																
COSTI																
opere architettoniche																
spazi aperti																
opere a verde																
infrastrutture viarie e portuali																
impianto biogas																
impianti fotovoltaici																
idoneizzazione suolo																
costi opportunità suoli e fabbricati																
spese generali																
iva																
RICAVI																
COSTI																
MARGINE																

5.2 Qualitative Assessment: The MAVT

The nine possible design scenarios have been assessed considering for each of them, three basis scenarios: the state of fact, the future with the project and without the project.

So in total, the project alternatives that will be evaluated are 27.

The value functions were built based on the preferences which have been declared by a group of experts considering from the best performance in terms of objectives to the worst.

The system of weights has been defined by an expert group that declared the weights ranking in ascending order the objectives. In the proposed valuation framework, three basic configurations of weights were set according to the weight given by expert group to the three considered macro-areas of value (Table 3) [35]. Once defined the value functions and the weight system, the evaluation of the alternatives has been performed for the three investigated reference conditions for each alternative.

Table 3. The basic weight system of the axiological grid

Weights	w1	w2	w3
1. natural or thermodynamic	0,33	0,40	0,40
2. bio-ecological	0,33	0,30	0,20
3. historical and cultural	0,33	0,30	0,40

In particular, for the level of the sub-objectives it has been defined an axiological grid on the basis of a system of weights.

This system of weights has allowed to grasp the different gradations of value, in terms of Surplus, as mentioned. The weight system introduced at this level, can support the choice of decision-makers between some configurations which are sometimes conflicting.

The prevalence of a component in the configuration of value, between the three possible, means to reduce or limit the other, and then persuade a planning process with different levels of sustainability in economic, environmental and social terms (Table 3). The evaluation on all the 27 alternatives, three basic (Table 4) for each optional alternative, allows to identify the one which registered the highest level of performance for the overall objectives considered for the redevelopment of the area, which is the best among the all alternatives.

Table 4. Option 1: assessment for the three basic conditions and the different weight systems

	w1	w2	w3
Current state	0,24	0,25	0,24
Future with project	0,53	0,52	**0,53**
Future without project	0,32	0,30	0,33
Max Value Alternative		**0,53**	

The ranking of the alternatives shows the project that best meets the goal of the redevelopment for the area.

The best project is the redevelopment of the ENEL Tifeo Power Station that has been design by team 1, in configuration of the "future with project" (green area surrounded by red, Fig. 4).

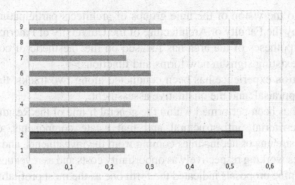

Fig. 4. Option 1: comparison between the three basic scenarios and the different weigh systems (Color figure online)

The evaluation of the best alternative, has been identified according to the weight system w_2, which is characterised by the prevalence of the natural-thermodynamic component, compared to the biological-ecological and historical-cultural ones.

The qualitative assessment results highlights the main overall objective of the redevelopment process, to assume the Tifeo area as a dissipative structure able to create a new order (neg-entropy) and a new direction (information) from the current (landscape) disorder and pollution.

The team project 1 proposal is quite conservative, involves a smaller area, focuses on decontamination, reuse and valorisation issues, proposes new functions such as: *research*, supposing to create the Centre for Advanced Studies on renewable energy of the Sicily Region; *innovation*, supposing a Renewable Energy Technology Centre for conversion of the original function of the Power Station; *environment*, supposing a central waste disposal for the production of biogas, the installation of photovoltaic panels, and of a constructed wetland plant; *information*, supposing to establish a study centre for historical, cultural and industrial archaeology with the creation of a museum in the structure of Power Station.

6 Conclusions

The conversion process of the ENEL Tifeo Power Station of Augusta, is the starting point of a possible new hybridization of the whole petrochemical complex. The entire geographical area, now definitively compromised from the environmental point of view, is a markedly industrial landscape dis-unity, dotted by the erratic presence of recognisable echo-systems, archaeological sites like Megara Hyblea dating from 728 BC, Thapsos dating from the fourteenth century BC., and Stentinello dating from fifth millennium BC, important buildings, like the airship hangar in Augusta (1917–20), physical evidences of traditional architectural culture having noticeable anthropologic value, prospective views of the geographical unit of the Gulf of Augusta and of the massive infrastructures of its commercial harbour.

According to the vision of the nine groups of architects participating to the ideas contest hosted by the Faculty of Architecture of the University of Palermo, the conversion process hypotheses of the area has focused on the "aesthetic of contamination", integrating the existing signs in new forms and functions.

This evaluation experience has been conducted along two tracks, the quantitative and monetary appraisal, and the qualitative assessment.

The former has been performed within the general frame of the Residual Value, and concerns the territorial, infrastructural and real estate components, capturing and discounting the streams of net incomes coming from the investments, and the initial and final stock values working respectively as opportunity costs and as revenues [36–38]. The appraisal of the nine proposals indicated the forth one as the most profitable alternative.

A more general approach, the qualitative one, involving several ecological, environmental and human issues, suggests a plurality of linkages and insights due to the progressive increase of the environmental concerns both from people and from institutions, involving some fundamental achievement of economic theory, in particular, the new paradigm proposed by F, Rizzo aimed at measuring the surplus of value due to each transformation process.

Moving in this direction the qualitative assessment [39–41] performed by using the Multi Attribute Value Theory, framed the contents of the three surpluses within a decision structure able to represent and interpret the aims of the designers groups in terms of natural, bio-genealogical and cultural surpluses, according to some of the main addresses of theoretical non-linear thermodynamics and semantics information theory, i.e. two heuristic areas that allow us to interpret, in the dialectic order/disorder, the various forms of the ethics and aesthetic on (de-)contamination.

According to the ranking of the alternatives, assessed in the three configurations (current state, future with and without project), the proposal n. 1 has been considered the best one. Its "environmental, ecological and human profile" [42] reflects a general feeling valuing preservation of natural eco-systems, the modification of energy production/consumption pattern, the local cultural and anthropological resources, the reduction of soil waste and pollution, as defined by weighting the criteria by an expert group.

Acknowledgements.   S. Giuffrida edited paragraphs 1, 3.1 and 5.1; M.R. Trovato edited paragraphs 2, 3.2, 4, 5.2 and 6.

References

1. Palazzotto, E. (ed.): Re-Power Station. Edizioni Caracol, Palermo (2016)
2. Rizzo, F.: Valore e valutazioni. La scienza dell'economia o l'economia della scienza. FrancoAngeli, Milano (1999)
3. Calabrò, F., Della Spina, L.: The public-private partnerships in buildings regeneration: a model appraisal of the benefits and for land value capture. In: 5nd International Engineering Conference 2014 (KKU-IENC 2014). Advanced Materials Research, Trans Tech Publications, Switzerland, vol. 931–932, pp. 555–559 (2014)
4. Herwijnen, M.V.: Spatial Decision Support for Environmental Management. Vrije Universiteit, Amsterdam (1999)

5. Imperatori, G.: Il project financing. Una tecnica, una cultura, una politica, Il Sole-24Ore, Milano (1995)
6. Trovato, M.R., Giuffrida, S.: The choice problem of the urban performances to support the Pachino's redevelopment plan. Int. J. Bus. Intell. Data Min. Int. J. 9(4), 330–355 (2014). doi: 10.1504/IJBIM.2014.068458
7. Rizzo, F.: Dalla rivoluzione keynesiana alla nuova economia. Dis-equilibrio, tras-informazione e co-efficiente di capitalizzazione, FrancoAngeli, Milano (2002)
8. Luhmann, N.: Sistemi sociali. Fondamenti di una teoria generale. Il Mulino, Bologna (1990)
9. Martinico, F.; Il Territorio dell'industria. Nuove strategie di pianificazione delle aree industriali in Europa. Gangemi, Roma (2001)
10. Caruso, A.: Il piano Marshall e l'economia siciliana, 1947–1952. Università di Catania (2011). http://archivia.unict.it/bitstream/10761/328/4/4.%20LA%20SICILIA%20E%20IL%20PIAN O%20MARSHALL.pdf
11. Sciortino, L., Zaffora, F.: Re_Power Station. In: International Workshop: Re-use and Recover of Augusta Power Station Designed by Giuseppe Samonà into Museum of Electricity. Dipartimento di Architettura dell'Università di Palermo (2014)
12. Torre, C.M., Balena, P., Ceppi, C.: The devaluation of property due to the perception of health risk in polluted industrial cities. Int. J. Bus. Intell. Data Min. 9(1), 74–90 (2014). doi:10.1504/IJBIDM.2014.062885
13. Tietenberg, T.: Economia dell'ambiente. McGraw Hill, Milano (2006)
14. Turner, P.K., Pearce, D.W., Bateman, I.: Economia Ambientale, Il Mulino, Bologna (1994)
15. Casas, G.L., Scorza, F.: Discrete spatial assessment of multi-parameter phenomena in low density region: the val d'agri case. In: Gervasi, O., Murgante, B., Misra, S., Gavrilova, Marina L., Rocha, A.M.A.C., Torre, C., Taniar, D., Apduhan, Bernady O. (eds.) ICCSA 2015. LNCS, vol. 9157, pp. 813–824. Springer, Cham (2015). doi:10.1007/978-3-319-21470-2_59
16. Rizzo, F.: Economia del patrimonio architettonico-ambientale. FrancoAngeli, Milano (1987)
17. Camagni, R.: Perequazione urbanistica "estesa", rendita e finanziarizzazione immobiliare: un conflitto con l'equità e la qualità territoriale. Scienze Regionali 13(2), 29–44 (2014)
18. Chiodelli, F., Moroni, S.: Zoning-integrative and zoning-alternative transferable development rights: Compensation, equity, efficiency. Land Use Policy 52, 422–429 (2016)
19. Salasco, M., Guzzini, E.: Strumenti per la valutazione degli investimenti industriali. Analisi Economico-finanziaria. McGraw Hill, Milano (2009)
20. Napoli, G.: Financial sustainability and morphogenesis of urban transformation project. In: Gervasi, O., Murgante, B., Misra, S., Gavrilova, Marina L., Rocha, A.M.A.C., Torre, C., Taniar, D., Apduhan, Bernady O. (eds.) ICCSA 2015. LNCS, vol. 9157, pp. 178–193. Springer, Cham (2015). doi:10.1007/978-3-319-21470-2_13
21. Micelli, E.: Development rights markets to manage urban plans in Italy. Urban Stud. 39(1), 141–154 (2002)
22. Stanghellini, S. (ed.): Il negoziato pubblico-privato nei progetti urbani. DEI, Roma (2012)
23. Giuffrida, S., Gagliano, F.: Sketching smart and fair cities WebGIS and spread sheets in a code. In: Murgante, B., Misra, S., Rocha, Ana Maria A.C., Torre, C., Rocha, J.G., Falcão, M.I., Taniar, D., Apduhan, Bernady O., Gervasi, O. (eds.) ICCSA 2014. LNCS, vol. 8581, pp. 284–299. Springer, Cham (2014). doi:10.1007/978-3-319-09150-1_21
24. Giuffrida, S., Napoli, G., Trovato, M.R.: Industrial areas and the city. Equalization and compensation in a value-oriented allocation pattern. In: Gervasi, O., Murgante, B., Misra, S., Rocha, Ana Maria A.C.Maria A.C., Torre, Carmelo M.M., Taniar, D., Apduhan, Bernady O.O., Stankova, E., Wang, S. (eds.) ICCSA 2016. LNCS, vol. 9789, pp. 79–94. Springer, Cham (2016). doi:10.1007/978-3-319-42089-9_6
25. Keeney, R.: Common mistakes in making value trade-offs. Oper. Res. 50, 935–945 (2002)

26. Roy, B., Mousseau, V.: A theoretical framework for analysing the notion of relative importance of criteria. J. Multi. Crit. Decis. Anal. **5**, 145–159 (1996)

27. Beinat, E.: Value Functions for Environmental Management. Kluwer Academic Publishers, Dordrecht (1997)

28. Keeney, R., Raiffa, H.: Decisions with multiple objectives: preferences and value trade-offs. Wiley, New York (1976)

29. Von Winterfeldt, D.W., Edwards, W.: Decision Analysis and Behavioral Research. Cambridge University Press, Cambridge (1986)

30. Poyhonen, M., Hamalainen, R.P.: On the convergence of multi-attribute weighting methods. Eur. J. Oper. Res. **129**, 569–585 (2001)

31. Ferretti, V., Bottero, M., Mondini, G.: Decision making and cultural heritage: an application of the Multi-Attribute Value Theory for the reuse of historical buildings. J. Cult. Heritage **15**(6), 644–655 (2014)

32. Bouyssou, D., Marchant, T., Pirlot, M., Tsoukias, A., Pincke, P.: Evaluation and decision models with multiple criteria, pp. 151–153. Springer Science and Business Media Inc., New York (2006)

33. Alterman, R.: Can the "unearned increment" in land values be harnessed to supply affordable housing? In: Financing Affordable Housing and Infrastructure in Cities: Towards Innovative Land and Property Taxation, UN Habitat, Varsaw, pp. 17–18 (2010)

34. Trovato, M.R., Giuffrida, S.: A DSS to assess and manage the urban performances in the regeneration plan: the case study of pachino. In: Murgante, B., Misra, S., Rocha, Ana Maria A.C., Torre, C., Rocha, J.G., Falcão, M.I., Taniar, D., Apduhan, Bernady O., Gervasi, O. (eds.) ICCSA 2014. LNCS, vol. 8581, pp. 224–239. Springer, Cham (2014). doi: 10.1007/978-3-319-09150-1_17

35. Greco, S., Ehrgott, M., Figueira, J.: Multiple Criteria Decision Analysis: State of the Art Surveys. Springer, New York (2005)

36. Woodbury, S.: Transfer of development rights: a new tool for planner. J. Am. Plan. Assoc. **41**(1), 3–14 (1973)

37. Camagni, R.: Il finanziamento della città pubblica: la cattura dei plusvalori fondiari e il modello perequativo.: In Curti, F. (ed.) Urbanistica e fiscalità locale, Maggioli, Ravenna, pp. 321–342 (1999)

38. Henger, R., Bizer, K.: Tradable planning permits for land-use control in Germany. Land Use Policy **27**, 843–852 (2010)

39. Choo, E.U., Bertram, S., Wedley, W.: Interpretation of criteria weights in multicriteria decision making. Comput. Ind. Eng. **37**, 527–541 (1999)

40. Belton, V., Stewart, T.J.: Multiple Criteria Decision Analysis: An Integrated Approach. Kluwer Academic Press, Boston (2002)

41. Montibeller, G., Yoshizaki, H.: A framework for locating logistic facilities with multi-criteria decision analysis. In: Takahashi, Ricardo H.C., Deb, K., Wanner, Elizabeth F., Greco, S. (eds.) EMO 2011. LNCS, vol. 6576, pp. 505–519. Springer, Heidelberg (2011). doi: 10.1007/978-3-642-19893-9_35

42. Naselli, F., Trovato, M.R., Castello, G.: An evaluation model for the actions in supporting of the environmental and landscaping rehabilitation of the pasquasia's site mining (EN). In: Murgante, B., et al. (eds.) ICCSA 2014. LNCS, vol. 8581, pp. 26–41. Springer, Cham (2014). doi:10.1007/978-3-319-09150-1_3

Conflicting Values in Designing Adaptive Reuse for Cultural Heritage. A Case Study of Social Multicriteria Evaluation

Alessandra Oppio[1(✉)] and Marta Bottero[2]

[1] Department of Architecture and Urban Studies,
Politecnico di Milano, Milan, Italy
alessandra.oppio@polimi.it
[2] Interuniversity Department of Regional and Urban Studies and Planning,
Politecnico di Torino, Turin, Italy

Abstract. Over the past two decades the Council of Europe has addressed cultural heritage preservation policies to the use of heritage as cultural capital. Given this definition, the conservation of cultural capital is crucial, for its intrinsic value and as an investment for cultural, social and economic development. Thus, principles and areas of actions have been defined with the aim of underlying the importance of cultural values for territorial identity. Especially for cultural heritage with a potential for tourism, the decisions about valorization interventions are not always consensual, given the coexistence of different instances from local inhabitants and tourists. Selecting among the potential uses the one that could ensure the preservation of physical characters as well as intangible values, fueling economic development, is still a challenging policy and design issue. In this context, this paper proposes the use of a multi-methodological approach based on Choice Experiments and Social Multicriteria Evaluation to support the adaptive reuse on real case study. The NAIADE approach has allowed the decision maker to consider both socio-economic and technical dimensions within the same evaluation framework.

Keywords: Cultural heritage conservation · Stakeholders analysis · NAIADE · Valle d'aosta castles · Adaptive reuse

1 Introduction

Decisions problems about cultural heritage enhancement and conservation are generally complex and ill-structured, given their multidimensional nature and the large set of values they represent. Since the late 90 s, the European Council has encouraged a wider understanding of heritage and its relationship to communities and society. There are several documents, conferences and consultations that prove this long and intense debate. Cultural heritage is considered as a crucial resource for the integration of the different dimensions of development (i.e. cultural, ecological, economic, social and political). Furthermore, it contributes to the protection of cultural diversity and sense of place in the face of growing globalization and to develop dialogue, democratic debate and openness between cultures [1].

© Springer International Publishing AG 2017
O. Gervasi et al. (Eds.): ICCSA 2017, Part III, LNCS 10406, pp. 607–623, 2017.
DOI: 10.1007/978-3-319-62398-6_43

According to this premise, the decisions about what and how to conserve for representing us and our past to future generations should be based not only on a deep knowledge of the cultural heritages and their potential, but also on the recognition of the meanings and uses that society attaches to them. As a consequence, over the past two decades, the theoretical and methodological advancements in the field of cultural heritage evaluation have pointed out some crucial issues: (1) the monetary value of cultural heritage is a crucial instance for cultural policy as markets concerning heritage are not able to reflect the value users and society attach to the cultural goods [2]; (2) the allocation of public resources requires legitimation, transparency and efficiency; (3) the achievement of a balance among goal and instrumental values is still a challenging decision problem, especially for touristic sites; (4) the use of stated preference techniques for estimating the extent of collective willingness to pay for intangibles benefits; (5) the relevance of including several categories of stakeholders into the evaluation processes, starting from the modeling phase of the decision problem [3].

Moreover, the conceptual concurrence among sustainable development paradigm and cultural heritage policies [4] has led relevant changes by introducing innovative preservation practices. The idea of adaptive reuse of cultural heritage [5, 6] into accessible and usable places, by respecting tangible and intangible values, seems to be an increasingly promising strategy for achieving a balance among different instances such as: the preservation of existing buildings involving minimal changes consistent to new uses' requirements; the retention of the symbolic values of historical buildings; the achievement of sustainability principles; the community engagement; the enhancement territorial development processes. The adaptive reuse approach requires to respect the building's heritage significance and add a contemporary layer that provides value for the future [7–9]. Thus, the choice about the highest and best adaptive reuse intervention should be supported by adaptive analytical tools, able to consider subsequent feedbacks both from technical and social side during the evaluation processes. For this purpose, Social Multicriteria Evaluation (SMCE) [10–13] seems to be the most adequate theoretical framework for supporting public policies in multi-values and complex decision contexts, where several and often conflictual are the interests at stake, but all legitimate. The paper proposes an application of the SMCE for defining the most consensual adaptive reuse of a castle located in Val d'Aosta (Northern Italy).

More in deep, after the introduction the rest of the paper is divided into 3 main sections: the second section illustrates the methodological background use for solving the decision problem, focusing more on the use of Social Multicriteria Evaluation and on the NAIADE approach; the third describes the application of abovementioned methodology on a real world case; the last one discusses the results and proposes future research lines.

2 Methodological Background

For addressing the complexity of the decision problem in exam, an integrated evaluation framework has been implemented in the present study. In particular, the

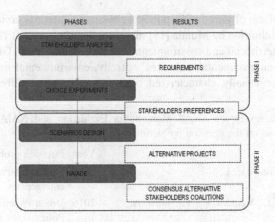

Fig. 1. The integrated evaluation framework

framework is structured according to a multi-methodological approach that has been organized in two main phases (Fig. 1):

(1) The first phase, which is based on the application of the Choice Experiment technique [14–16] aims at designing a set of alternative projects for the reuse of the castles;

(2) The second phase, which is based on the development of the Social Multi-Criteria Evaluation [10], is finalized at selecting the best performing alternative paying particular attention to the social actors involved in the decision problem.

With particular reference to the first phase of the proposed framework, an expert panel was organized in order to better define the decision problem. The expert panel also allowed to formulate the relevant attributes to be considered in the evaluation model and to set the proper levels for the related attributes. The attributes and levels thus defined were used for structuring the experimental design for the application of the CE method [17]. As a result of this evaluation, a set of information has been provided able to structure the generation of alternative reuse projects. These alternatives will be presented in detail in Sect. 3.2 of the present paper.

The present paper focuses on the illustration of the second phase of the afore-mentioned integrated method, which is related to the application of the SMCE. In particular, the NAIADE (Novel Approach to Imprecise Assessment and Decision Environments) has been considered in the research for performing a technical evaluation of the given set of alternatives and for carrying out a social analysis that allows a consensus alternative to be found and final recommendations to be formulated.

2.1 NAIADE

NAIADE (Novel Approach to Imprecise Assessment and Decision Environments) is based on the Social Multicriteria Evaluation approach that was developed by Munda [18, 10] as a useful framework for the application of social choice to complex political problems with the aim of introducing political constrains, interests groups and collusion effects. Since its definition by Munda [18] many applications exist of NAIADE, namely in the context of territorial and environmental conflict management. Given the growing awareness about environmental resources' scarcity, environmental management decision problems are usually characterized by conflicts between different groups and

Table 1. Literature review on Social Multicriteria Evaluation and NAIADE from Scopus database with a focus on the decision problem.

[-]	Authors	Year	Decision problem	NAIADE
[19]	Scuderi, A., Sturiale, L.	2016	Phytosanitary emergencies	V
[20]	Della Spina, L., Ventura, C., Viglianisi, A.	2016	Urban Planning Policy	
[21]	Walter, M., Latorre, T.S., Munda, G., Larrea, C.	2016	Mining extraction development	V
[22]	Torre, C.M., Morano, P., Taiani, F.	2015	Urban Planning Policy	
[23]	Kolinjivadi, V., Gamboa, G., Adamowski, J., Kosoy, N.	2015	Water management	V
[24]	Etxano, I., Garmendia, E., Pascual, U., Hoyos, D., Díez, M.Á., Cadiñanos, J.A., Lozano, P.J.	2015	Protected areas management	
[25]	Gomes, L.F.A.M., De Mattos Fernandes, J.E., De Mello, J.C.C.B.S.	2014	Aircraft selection	V
[26]	Nicolini, E., Pinto, M.R.	2013	Urban Planning	V
[27]	Cerreta, M., Rosa, F., Palma, M., Inglese, P., Poli, G.	2013	Water management	
[28]	De Mello, J.C.C.B.S., Fernandes, J.E.M., Gomes, L.F.A.M.	2012	Aircraft selection	V
[29]	Garmendia, E., Gamboa, G.	2012	Natural resource management	V
[30]	Monterroso, I., Binimelis, R., Rodrìguez-Labajos, B.	2011	Ecosystem management	V
[31]	Oikonomou, V., Dimitrakopoulos, P.G., Troumbis, A.Y.	2011	Protected areas management	V
[32]	Cerreta, M., De Toro, P.	2010	Strategic Environmental Assessment	
[33]	Naidu, S., Sawhney, R., Dhingra, R., Knickerbocker, C.	2010	Nanotechnology development	V
[34]	Browne, D., O'Regan, B., Moles, R.	2010	Energy policy	V
[35]	Garmendia, E., Gamboa, G., Franco, J., Garmendia, J.M., Liria, P., Olazabal, M.	2010	Integrated Coastal Zone Management	V
[36]	Turón, A., Aguarón, J., Escobar, M.T., Gallardo, C., Moreno-Jiménez, J.M., Salazar, J.L.	2010	Public policy	

(continued)

Table 1. (*continued*)

[-]	Authors	Year	Decision problem	NAIADE
[37]	Montrone, S., Perchinunno, P., Di Giuro, A., Rotondo, F., Torre, C.M.	2009	Urban Planning	
[38]	Siciliano, G.	2009	Farming system management	V
[39]	Shmelev, S.E., Rodriguez-Labajos, B.	2009	Sustainability assessment	V
[40]	Zabala, A.	2009	Transport Policy	V
[41]	Munda, G.	2009	Sustainability Policy	
[42]	Ramirez, A., Hagedoorn, S., Kramers, L., Wildenborg, T., Hendriks, C.	2009	Environmental management	V
[43]	Buchholz, T., Rametsteiner, E., Volk, T.A., Luzadis, V.A.	2009	Energy system design	V
[44]	Munda, G., Russi, D.	2008	Rural renewable-energy policy	V
[45]	Kain, J.-H., Söderberg, H.	2008	Knowledge management	V
[46]	Benetto, E., Dujet, C., Rousseaux, P.	2008	Life Cycle Assessment	V
[47]	Tangari, L., Ottomanelli, M., Sassanelli, D.	2008	Transport Policy	V
[48]	Dinca, C., Badea, A., Rousseaux, P., Apostol, T.	2007	Energy policy	V
[49]	Gamboa, G., Munda, G.	2007	Energy policy	V
[50]	Gamboa, G.	2006	Environmental management	V
[51]	Munda, G.	2006	Sustainability management	V
[52]	Wenzel, V.	2005	Water management	V
[53]	Brand, C., Mattarelli, M., Moon, D., Wolfler, C.R.	2002	Transport Policy	V

competing values and interests they hold. Despite cultural heritage represent a resource often subjected to conflictual uses, the overview of NAIADE literature show that it has been still used in this decision domain (See Table 1).

The method implies two types of evaluations:

- a technical evaluation, that is based on the score values assigned to the criteria of each alternative and is performed using an impact matrix (alternatives vs criteria).

In this case the ultimate output given by NAIADE is the alternatives ranking according to set of criteria preferences;

- a social evaluation that analyses conflicts among the different interest groups and, through an equity matrix, which provides a linguistic evaluation of alternatives by each group, studies the possible formation of coalitions among different stakeholders.

The methodology follows these steps: (i) construction of the impact matrix; (ii) pairwise comparison by means of preference relationships. Indifference and preference thresholds have to be defined for this task; (iii) criteria aggregation procedure. NAIADE uses the number of criteria in favor of each alternative instead of another and the intensity of preference; (iv) obtaining the ranking of alternative; (v) performing the coalition formation analysis; (vi) looking for the compromise choice.

The aforementioned steps will be described in detail in the remaining part of the present paper with reference to the application of the NAIADE approach to the case study of the Valle d'Aosta Castles.

3   Case Study

3.1   The Val D'Aosta Castles Between Tourism and Local Communities

In this study the multi-methodological evaluation has been applied to a group of three castles owned and managed by the Regional government in Valle d'Aosta. Consistently to the idea of bringing cultural heritage back to local communities, the Regional Government has enhanced a cultural policy based on the notion of "Restitution" policy [54, 55]. Given the growing reduction of financial resources, the reuse of the abandoned castles becomes an opportunity for fostering economic development whilst improving the quality of life of inhabitants. Among the 13 castles owned by the Region Valle d'Aosta, the study focuses on the Chateau Vallaise (Arnad), the Sant-Germain (Montjovet) and the Ussel castle (Châtillon). With respect to the analysis of intrinsic and positional features of the three castles under evaluation, their potential and alternative adaptive reuses have been defined.

Unless for the landscape quality, that is very high for all the three cases, the castles under evaluation show very different features in terms of state of preservation and age of construction, connections to the transport system, current use and seasonal openings, as well as of surroundings uses. This high variability calls for a specific conservation strategy based on their peculiar characteristics according to general adaptive reuse criteria, aimed at avoiding decay and abandonment of cultural heritage through the enhancement of economic and social resources whilst preserving the architectural object from an historical and cultural point of view. In addition, the assumption of an adaptive conservation approach addresses the choice of reversible and compatible functions that could play a key role for reinforcing local identity, traditions and practices.

In order to support the design of adaptive reuse alternatives, the main categories of stakeholders with different levels of interest/power regarding the castles have been considered and a requirement analysis has been developed with reference to a framework that takes together human based, technical-functional, business-corporate, regulatory-policy aspects (See Table 2).

3.2   Generation of the Alternatives

As stated by Munda and Gamboa [13], one of the main features of the Social Multi-criteria Evaluation framework is that alternatives are constructed considering information from several sources, for instance, the participatory process, technical interviews, and so on.

In the present application the alternative scenarios correspond to different adaptive reuse hypotheses that were elaborated making use of the preferences of tourists and residents as resulting from the application of the CE method (Fig. 2). More precisely, according to the CE findings the most preferred attributes were selected as fundamental elements to be considered in the design of the reuse project for the castles [17].

With reference to the Arnad castle, the alternative scenarios considered for the reuse will be illustrated in the remaining part of the present section.

3.2.1   Scenario 1: Craft University

This scenario is mainly devoted to residents and it foresees the reuse of the spaces of the Arnad Castle as Crafts University. The idea is to offer study courses about the techniques of production of the local products and the regional eno-gastronomic culture. The most representative spaces of the castle, as the rooms containing the precious cycle of paintings, are designed as spaces for lectures, public meetings, and conferences. The area that revolves around the patio is used instead as a space for the display and sale of local products (food stands) while the eastern part of the castle will be dedicated laboratories and spaces aimed at food preparation.

3.2.2   Scenario 2: Food Commerce Activities

The second scenario is mainly targeted to residents and it aims to valorize the Valle d'Aosta culinary excellence by promoting a strong interaction between the castle and the productive and concerned social context of the region. The castle is conceived as a showcase for the local products and the enogastronomic culture of Valle d'Aosta.

The part of the castle interested by the presence of the pictorial cycle is designed as a flexible space, with rest rooms or lecture and conference halls. The patio is an open-air hall for tasting and selling activities. The east wing of the building hosts cook labs recipes and taste education labs or classrooms for food courses. This solution guarantees a good level of conservation of the castle's ancient structure in its most artistically valuable parts and a discrete level of multifunctionality in the most damaged areas, which present more possibilities of intervention.

3.2.3   Scenario 3: Museum and Temporary Exhibitions

This scenario takes into account the expectations of interviewed tourists, who have expressed the desire to preserve as much as possible the original structure of the castle. The rooms that revolve around the patio are designed as temporary exhibition spaces. The high flexibility of these spaces allows diversified uses (events, stands of local products, festivals, etc.). The eastern area of the castle includes didactic laboratories and a small library with attached storage space, always accessible to the public. In the rooms containing the painting cycle, a permanent museum will be created: this exhibition could be centred on the story of the castle and to the Region history and customs.

Table 2. Actors and requirements for adaptive reuse. The requirements have been divided into 4 classes according to Gershenson and Stauffer [56].

Actors/requirements	Human-based end-user			Technical functional							Business corporate			Regulatory Policy
	Availability	Involvement	Attractiveness	Flexibility	Continuity with the architecture	Continuity with the surroundings	Complementarity in time	Complementarity in space	Conservation	Usability	Low investment	Economic feasibility	Complementarity in profitability	Safety regulations
Soprintendenza valle D'aosta region	X	X	X	X	X	X	X	X	X	X	X	X	X	X
Tourists	X		X							X				
Municipalities	X	X	X	X	X	X	X	X		X	X	X	X	
Tourism facilities	X		X				X		X	X				
Local producers	X	X	X	X		X	X	X		X				
Festival organizers	X	X	X			X	X	X		X				
Cultural associations	X	X	X			X		X	X	X				
Inhabitants	X	X	X	X		X	X	X		X				

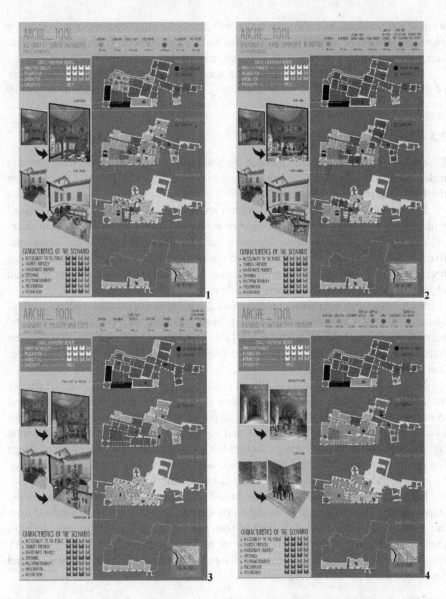

Fig. 2. Alternatives reuse project for the Arnal Castle (1: Craft University; 2: Food commerce activities; 3: Museum and temporary exhibitions, 4: Interactive museum)

3.2.4   Scenario 4: Interactive Museum

This scenario is thought on the needs of a specific target of tourists such as schools, young and families. Internal and external spaces of the castle will address a teaching function through the application of digital tools and educational activities in which the visitors are protagonists. In such context, they will be able to assess traditional practices like producing foods or small objects with local techniques. For this purpose the west wing of the building, including the patio, will house the interactive museum, while the east wing will be occupied by a dining area and a shop of local products. On the other hand, the top floor is managed as a space for laboratory activities or lectures.

This type of scenario allows reaching a good level of preservation, since the spaces of intervention can be set up without affecting permanently the structure of the castle.

3.3   Technical Evaluation

Before applying the NAIADE approach the Stakeholder Analysis has been deepened in order to explicit values and preferences and to define the set of criteria for comparing the four adaptive reuse scenarios.

In a social multicriteria domain, criteria are not given but they should be defined with respect to the role and the position of the stakeholder against the scenario under evaluation. Thus, a collaborative approach has been assumed and the key representatives of the Municipality of Arnad, where the castles under evaluation is located, has been involved in some brainstorming sessions for discussing and identifying the main objectives associated to the conservation decisions.

With help of a questionnaire, followed by a collective brainstorming, a set of quantitative and qualitative criteria have been defined that represent the experts' translation of stakeholders' expectations [13]. The Table 3 describes the stakeholders directly involved in the process of criteria definition, their position against the castles and their needs.

More in deep, the quantitative criteria are defined as follows: possibility of reusing the castle for a different function according to changes of environmental and social systems over time (*Flexibility*); presence of public spaces (*Public spaces*); events for inhabitants (Events); new installations and equipment required by the new function (*Invasivity*). The qualitative criteria include the following elements: the return of image for the municipality of Arnad (*Promotion*); accessibility to the castle (*Accessibility*); investment value (*Cost*); population's needs met by the scenario (*Target*).

Each of the 4 scenarios has been evaluated according to this set of 8 criteria, as the Impact matrix shows (see Table 4) and a first technical ranking has been obtained from the application of the NAIADE method (see Fig. 3). As it possible to see, the most preferred alternative from a technical point of view is the Museum and temporary exhibition (3), followed by the Crafts university (1), the Interactive museum (4) and finally the Food commerce activites (2).

3.4   Social Evaluation

According to the NAIADE approach a second matrix has to be defined and it is represented by the Social Impact Matrix, which is shaped upon the evaluation expressed by each stakeholder by the use of a questionnaire (See Table 5). Differently from the Impact Matrix, that is a technical translation independent from stakeholders' preferences, by the Social or Equity Matrix social actors are allowed to evaluate each alternative using linguistic variables, that are variables whose values are words or

Table 3. Actors, needs and criteria

Actors	Scale of action	Position regarding the castel	Criteria	Needs and expectations
Soprintendenza	Local - Regional	Flexibility of spaces and functions	Flexibility	*possibility of reusing the castle for different functions in the future, according to the changes of the economic and social system over time
		Invasivity control to guarantee cultural heritage adaptive reuse	Invasivity	*reducing the number and dimension of the new installations
			Tradition	* strenghtening local traditions
Arnad Public administration	Local	Public spaces and promotion in order to give back the castle to citiziens	Public Spaces	*improving presence of places always open to the public
			Attraction of new Inhabitants	*increasing the number of new inhabitants and related services
Tourism & Trading Sector	National - International	Events availability, for both tourists and residents	Events	*increasing the possibility to organise events for the town
		Consideration about the Accessibility	Accessibility	*control the amount of people who can access the structure
Experts	National	Consideration about the Targets	Targets	*enlarging the population categories the project refers to
		Consideration about the Costs	Cost	improving investment and economic return
Industry Sector	Local	Promotion of events	Promotion	*reinforcing the return of image for the town of Arnad and strengthening of the castle system
		Flexibility in the duration of the work	Timing	*minimizing the period of realization
Inhabitants	Local	Events	Small scale events	*achievement of population needs rather than of tourists needs
		Consideration of new job opportunities	Social sustainability	*creation of career opportunities and new job positions

Table 4. Impact matrix

Alternatives/Criteria	1	2	3	4
Flexibility	1115	956	1449	1294
Promotion	Very Good	Very Good	More or Less Good	Good
Accessibility	Moderate	Very Good	Good	Very Good
Public spaces	571	571	536	156
Cost	More or Less Good	Moderate	More or Less Bad	Moderate
Events	319	319	910	762
Invasivity	250	661	0	323
Target	More or Less Good	Good	Very Good	Moderate

sentences. Generally speaking, linguistic variables are very useful for characterizing phenomena which are too complex or too-ill defined to be suitable for a description in quantitative terms and they are natural representation of cognitive observations [12]. Fuzzy set theory [57] provides a framework for developing approximate calculus of linguistic variables. In fact, it has been generally agreed that representing observation by means of linguistic variables requires a less complicated transformation with respect to a numerical transformation, thus ensuring less distortion in the evaluation procedure. In the case under investigation, following the NAIADE methodology [12], a multi-level scale has been used for the evaluation of the alternatives, where 11 linguistic judgments were considered: perfect, very good, good, more or less good, moderate, more or less bad, bad, very bad, extremely bad.

Fig. 3. Technical ranking.

Starting from the social matrix, distributional issues can be taken into consideration. In particular, for each pair of interest groups i and j, by using a distance function d_{ij} as conflict indicator, a similarity matrix $s_{ij} = 1/(1+d_{ij})$ can be constructed for all possible pairs of groups, so that a clustering procedure is meaningful. By applying this procedure to the social impact matrix, a coalition dendrogram can be obtained (Fig. 4).

The graph helps visualizing the actors' goals proximity, as in the case of the first coalition: Tourism & Trade sector (G3) and Local Community (G5), whose credibility is very high (0.8051). G3 interests are also shared the municipality of Arnad (G2) and the Soprintendenza (G1), whose preferences focus on the same alternatives (credibility index: 0.79). On the other hand, the Industry sector (G6) and the Experts (G) show a medium high degree of credibility but a major distance. They both target the same objective: improve local economy and costs by preferring the scenario 1 and 2.

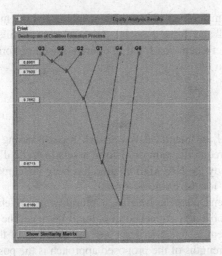

Fig. 4. Dendrogram of coalitions (G1: Soprintendenza, G2 Municipality of Arnad, G3: Tourism & Trade sector, G4: Experts, G5: Local Community, G6: Industries)

Table 5. Social impact matrix.

Actors/Alternatives	1	2	3	4
Soprintendenza	Good	Moderate	Very Good	More or Less Good
Arnad Public Administration	More or Less Bad	Good	Very Good	Very Good
Tourism & Trading Sector	Moderate	More or Less Good	Very Good	Good
Experts	Very Good	Moderate	Moderate	Good
Inhabitants	Moderate	Moderate	Very Good	Good
Industry Sector	Good	Good	More or Less Bad	More or Less Bad

4   Results and Discussion

In the light of the results of the NAIADE application it is possible to state that from a technical point of view (Table 3), the best performing solution is scenario 3, followed by scenarios 1 and 4 and finally by scenario 2. From the point of view of the social conflict analysis (Table 5), it seems that scenarios 1 is the alternative that generates maximum conflict as it is not well appreciated from the coalition of actors G3 (Tourism & Trade sector), G5 (Local community) and G2 (Arnad Public Administration) that has an high level of credibility (0.79). Moreover, it is also possible to notice that scenario 2 is not appreciated from the most part of social actors while scenarios 3 and 4 are ranked in a medium-high position from many considered stakeholders.

In synthesis, it seems correct to state that scenario 3 is the most defensible project both form a technical and from a social point of view, while the other scenarios maximize social conflict (scenarios 1 and 2) or are not well performing from a technical point of view (scenario 4).

5   Conclusions

The research proposed an integrated framework for supporting the decision making process related to the requalification of historic assets in Valle d'Aosta Region (Italy). In particular, in the study the NAIADE method has been developed for the selection of the best re-use project for the castle of Arnad.

In a decisional arena characterized by a plurality of stakeholders with different legitimate values and objectives attached to cultural heritage, the method proved to be able to consider different technical criteria and the opinions of the involved actors.

One of the main strengths of the proposed approach is the possibility of structuring the evaluation not as 'one-shot activity', rather as a social learning process where DM and stakeholders learn about the problems while they are solving them. Moreover, the method allows a common knowledge for DM, local communities and tourists to be created, thus ensuring the strengthening of the social capital.

Despite the strengths of the approach and the coherence of the obtained results, a number of future perspectives for the present study can be envisaged.

To start with, it would be interesting to explore the definition of an interaction protocol for defining actors' values and for filling in the social impact matrix in a more rigorous way.

Secondly, from the point of view of the exploitation of the results, future work could be done for exploring alternative methods, such as the use Threshold model proposed by Gamboa and Munda [13] for the aggregation of criterion scores of alternatives.

Thirdly, more research could be done in the examination of technical and social rankings proposed by the NAIADE method; in particular, it would be interesting to explore a more formal interaction among the two rankings that at the moment are compared and interpreted only from a qualitative point of view.

Finally, future research could consider the development of specific sensitivity on the technical ranking and on the credibility degrees of the coalitions in order to verify the model and the obtained results and to formulate more robust recommendations for the DM.

References

1. Council of Europe: Framework Convention on the Value of Cultural Heritage for Society (2005). www.coe.int
2. Mazzanti, M.: Cultural heritage as multi-dimensional, multi-value and multi-attribute economic good: toward a new framework for economic analysis and valuation. J. Socio-Econ. **31**, 529–558 (2002)

3. Bottero, M.: A multi-methodological approach for assessing sustainability of urban projects. Manage. Environ. Qual. Int. J. **26**(1), 138–154 (2015)
4. Throsby, D.: Economics and Culture. Cambridge University Press, Cambridge (2001)
5. Plevoets, B., Van Cleempoel, K.: Adaptive reuse as a strategy towards conservation of cultural heritage: a literature review. WIT Trans. Built Environ. **118**, 155–164 (2011)
6. Elsorady, D.: The economic value of heritage properties in Alexandria, Egypt. J. Cult. Heritage **15**, 511–521 (2014)
7. Latham, D.: Creative re-use of buildings, vol. II. Donhead Publishing, London (2000)
8. Department of Environment and Heritage (DEH): Adaptive Reuse, Commonwealth of Australia, Canberra (2004). https://www.environment.gov.au. Accessed Mar 2015
9. Bullen, P.A., Love, P.E.D.: Adaptive reuse of heritage buildings. Struct. Surv. **29**(5), 411–421 (2011)
10. Munda, G.: Social multi-criteria evaluation (SMCE): methodological foundations and operational consequences. Eur. J. Oper. Res. **158**(3), 662–677 (2004)
11. Munda, G.: Social Multi-Criteria Evaluation for a Sustainable Economy. Springer, Berlin (2008)
12. Munda, G.: A conflict analysis approach for illuminating distributional issues in sustainability policy. Eur. J. Oper. Res. **194**(2009), 307–322 (2009)
13. Gamboa, G., Munda, G.: The problem of windfarm location: a social multi-criteria evaluation framework. Energ. Policy **35**, 1564–1583 (2007)
14. Lancaster, K.J.: A new approach to consumer theory. J. Polit. Econ. **2**, 132–157 (1966)
15. Adamowicz, W., Boxall, P., Williams, M., et al.: Stated preference approaches for measuring passive use values. Choice experiments and contingent valuation. Am. J. Agr. Econ. **80**, 64–75 (1998)
16. Hanley, N., MacMillan, D., Wright, R.E., et al.: Contingent valuation versus choice experiments: estimating the benefits of environmentally sensitive areas in Scotland. J. Agric. Econ. **49**(1), 1–15 (1998)
17. Oppio, A., Bottero, M., Ferretti, V.: Designing adaptive reuse strategies for cultural heritage with choice experiments. In: Stanghellini, S., Morano, P., Bottero, M., Oppio, A. (eds.) Appraisal: From Theory to Practice. GET, pp. 303–315. Springer, Cham (2017). doi:10.1007/978-3-319-49676-4_23
18. Munda, G.: Multicriteria Evaluation in a Fuzzy Environment. Theory and Applications in Ecological Economics. Physica-Verlag, Heidelberg (1995)
19. Scuderi, A., Sturiale, L.: Multi-criteria evaluation model to face phytosanitary emergencies: the case of citrus fruits farming in Italy. Agric. Econ. – Czech **62**, 205–214 (2016)
20. Della Spina, L., Ventura, C., Viglianisi, A.: A multicriteria assessment model for selecting strategic projects in urban areas. In: Gervasi, O., et al. (eds.) ICCSA 2016. LNCS, vol. 9788, pp. 414–427. Springer, Cham (2016). doi:10.1007/978-3-319-42111-7_32
21. Walter, M., Latorre, T.S., Munda, G., Larrea, C.: A social multi-criteria evaluation approach to assess extractive and non-extractive scenarios in Ecuador: Intag case study. Land Use Policy **57**, 444–458 (2016)
22. Torre, C.M., Morano, P., Taiani, F.: Social balance and economic effectiveness in historic centers rehabilitation. In: Gervasi, O., et al. (eds.) ICCSA 2015. LNCS, vol. 9157, pp. 317–329. Springer, Cham (2015). doi:10.1007/978-3-319-21470-2_22
23. Kolinjivadi, V., Gamboa, G., Adamowski, J., Kosoy, N.: Capabilities as justice: analysing the acceptability of payments for ecosystem services (PES) through 'social multi-criteria evaluation'. Ecol. Econ. **118**, 99–113 (2015)
24. Etxano, I., Garmendia, E., Pascual, U., Hoyos, D., Díez, M.Á., Cadiñanos, J.A., Lozano, P. J.: A participatory integrated assessment approach for Natura 2000 network sites. Environ. Plann. C Gov. Policy **33**(5), 1207–1232 (2015)

25. Gomes, L.F.A.M., De Mattos Fernandes, J.E., De Mello, J.C.C.B.S.: A fuzzy stochastic approach to the multicriteria selection of an aircraft for regional chartering. J. Adv. Transp. **48**(3), 223–237 (2014)
26. Nicolini, E., Pinto, M.R.: Document strategic vision of a Euro-Mediterranean port city: a case study of palermo. Sustainability **5**(9), 3941–3959 (2013)
27. Cerreta, M., Rosa, F., Palma, M., Inglese, P., Poli, G.: A spatial multicriteria assessment decision support system (SMCA-DSS) for east naples: towards a water opportunity map. In: Murgante, B., et al. (eds.) ICCSA 2013. LNCS, vol. 7974, pp. 572–586. Springer, Heidelberg (2013). doi:10.1007/978-3-642-39649-6_41
28. De Mello, J.C.C.B.S., Fernandes, J.E.M., Gomes, L.F.A.M.: Multicriteria selection of an aircraft with NAIADE. In: Proceedings of the 1st International Conference on Operations Research and Enterprise Systems, pp. 427–431 (2012)
29. Garmendia, E., Gamboa, G.: Weighting social preferences in participatory multi-criteria evaluations: a case study on sustainable natural resource management. Ecol. Econ. **84**, 110–120 (2012)
30. Monterroso, I., Binimelis, R., Rodrìguez-Labajos, B.: New methods for the analysis of invasion processes: multi-criteria evaluation of the invasion of Hydrilla verticillata in Guatemala. J. Environ. Manage. **92**(3), 494–507 (2011)
31. Oikonomou, V., Dimitrakopoulos, P.G., Troumbis, A.Y.: Incorporating ecosystem function concept in environmental planning and decision making by means of multi-criteria evaluation: the case-study of Kalloni, Lesbos, Greece. Environ. Manage. **47**(1), 77–92 (2011)
32. Cerreta, M., De Toro, P.: Integrated spatial assessment for a creative decision-making process: a combined methodological approach to strategic environmental assessment. Int. J. Sustain. Dev. **13**(1–2), 17–30 (2010)
33. Naidu, S., Sawhney, R., Dhingra, R., Knickerbocker, C.: Nanomanufacturing under lean and green principles. In: IIE Annual Conference and Expo Proceedings (2010)
34. Browne, D., O'Regan, B., Moles, R.: Use of multi-criteria decision analysis to explore alternative domestic energy and electricity policy scenarios in an Irish city-region. Energy **35**(2), 518–528 (2010)
35. Garmendia, E., Gamboa, G., Franco, J., Garmendia, J.M., Liria, P., Olazabal, M.: Social multi-criteria evaluation as a decision support tool for integrated coastal zone management. Ocean Coast. Manag. **53**(7), 385–403 (2010)
36. Turón, A., Aguarón, J., Escobar, M.T., Gallardo, C., Moreno-Jiménez, J.M., Salazar, J.L.: PRIOR-WK&E: social software for policy making in the knowledge society. In: Communications in Computer and Information Science, 111 CCIS (PART 1), pp. 139–149 (2010)
37. Montrone, S., Perchinunno, P., Di Giuro, A., Rotondo, F., Torre, C.M.: Identification of "hot spots" of social and housing difficulty in urban areas: scan statistics for housing market and urban planning policies. Stud. in Comput. Intell. **176**, 57–78 (2009)
38. Siciliano, G.: Social multicriteria evaluation of farming practices in the presence of soil degradation. a case study in Southern Tuscany, Italy. Environ. Dev. Sustain. **11**(6), 1107–1133 (2009)
39. Shmelev, S.E., Rodriguez-Labajos, B.: Dynamic multidimensional assessment of sustainability at the macro level: the case of Austria. Ecol. Econ. **68**(10), 2560–2573 (2009)
40. Zabala, A.: Walking the green carpet to work. Int. J. Sustain. Dev. **12**(1), 78–94 (2009)
41. Munda, G.: A conflict analysis approach for illuminating distributional issues in sustainability policy. Eur. J. Oper. Res. **194**(1), 307–322 (2009)
42. Ramirez, A., Hagedoorn, S., Kramers, L., Wildenborg, T., Hendriks, C.: Screening CO_2 storage options in the Netherlands. Energy Procedia **1**(1), 2801–2808 (2009)

43. Buchholz, T., Rametsteiner, E., Volk, T.A., Luzadis, V.A.: Multi criteria analysis for bioenergy systems assessments. Energy Policy 37(2), 484–495 (2009)
44. Munda, G., Russi, D.: Social multicriteria evaluation of conflict over rural electrification and solar energy in Spain. Environ. Plann. C Gov. Policy 26(4), 712–727 (2008)
45. Kain, J.-H., Söderberg, H.: Management of complex knowledge in planning for sustainable development: the use of multi-criteria decision aids. Environ. Impact Assess. Rev. 28(1), 7–21 (2008)
46. Benetto, E., Dujet, C., Rousseaux, P.: Integrating fuzzy multicriteria analysis and uncertainty evaluation in life cycle assessment. Environ. Model Softw. 23(12), 1462–1467 (2008)
47. Tangari, L., Ottomanelli, M., Sassanelli, D.: Multicriteria fuzzy methodology for feasibility study of transport projects case study of southeastern trans-european transport axes. Transp. Res. Rec. 2048, 26–34 (2008)
48. Dinca, C., Badea, A., Rousseaux, P., Apostol, T.: A multi-criteria approach to evaluate the natural gas energy systems. Energy Policy 35, 5754–5765 (2007)
49. Gamboa, G., Munda, G.: The problem of windfarm location: a social multi-criteria evaluation framework. Energy Policy 35(3), 1564–1583 (2007)
50. Gamboa, G.: Social multi-criteria evaluation of different development scenarios of the Aysén region. Chile. Ecol. Econ. 59(1), 157–170 (2006)
51. Munda, G.: A NAIADE based approach for sustainability benchmarking. Int. J. Environ. Technol. Manage. 6(1–2), 65–78 (2006)
52. Wenzel, V.: Philosophy and formalization of integrated assessment for decision support applied to water management project GLOWA-Elbe. In: The 9th World Multi-Conference on Systemics, Cybernetics and Informatics, Proceedings, vol. 3, pp. 57–62 (2005)
53. Brand, C., Mattarelli, M., Moon, D., Wolfler, C.R.: STEEDS: a strategic transport-energy-environment decision support. Eur. J. Oper. Res. 139(2), 416–435 (2002)
54. Oppio, A., Bottero, M., Ferretti, V.: Multicriteria spatial analysis for competitive cultural heritage in fringe areas: the case of valle d'aosta castles, advanced engineering forum, new metropolitan perspective. Integr. Approach Urban Sustain. Dev. 11, 579–584 (2014)
55. Oppio, A., Bottero, M., Ferretti, V., Fratesi, U., Ponzini, D., Pracchi, V.: Giving space to multicriteria analysis for complex cultural heritage systems: the case of the castles in Valle D'Aosta Region, Italy. J. Cult. Heritage 16(6), 779–789 (2015)
56. Gershenson, J.K., Stauffer, L.A.: A Taxonomy For Design Requirements From Corporate Customers, Research in Engineering Design. J. Res. Eng. Des. 11(2), 103–115 (1999)
57. Zadeh, L.A.: The concept of a linguistic variable and its application to approximate reasoning. Inf. Sci. 8(3), 199–249 (1975)

Rethinking Feasibility Analysis for Urban Development: A Multidimensional Decision Support Tool

Alberto Colorni[1(✉)], Valentina Ferretti[2], Alessandro Luè[1],
Alessandra Oppio[3], Valerio Paruscio[1], and Luca Tomasini[1]

[1] POLIEDRA – Politecnico di Milano, via G. Colombo, 40, Milan, Italy
{alberto.colorni,alessandro.lue,valerio.paruscio,
luca.tomasini}@polimi.it
[2] LSE – London School of Economics and Political Science,
Houghton Street, London WC2A 2AE, UK
V.Ferretti@lse.ac.uk
[3] DASTU – Politecnico di Milano, via Bonardi, 3, 20133 Milan, Italy
alessandra.oppio@polimi.it

Abstract. Large-scale urban development projects featured over the past thirty years have shown some critical issues related to the implementation phase. Consequently, the current practice seems oriented toward minimal and wide-spread interventions meant as urban catalyst. This planning practice might solve the problem of limited reliability of large developments' feasibility studies, but it rises an evaluation demand related to the selection of coali-tion of projects within a multidimensional and multi-stakeholders deci-sion-making context. This study aims to propose a framework for the generation of coalitions of elementary actions in the context of urban regeneration processes and for their evaluation using a Multi Criteria Decision Analysis approach. The proposed evaluation framework supports decision makers in exploring dif-ferent combinations of actions in the context of urban interventions taking into account synergies, i.e. positive or negative effects on the overall per-formance of an alternative linked to the joint realization of specific pairs of actions. The proposed evaluation framework has been tested on a pilot case study dealing with urban regeneration processes in the city of Milan (Italy).

Keywords: Feasibility analysis · Urban acupuncture · Urban catalyst · Synergy · Multi knapsack approach

1 Introduction

The concept of urban acupuncture refers to small-scale interventions that can be developed in a short time and have a "healing" effect on the surroundings or on the whole city.

On one side, this new idea of planning might solve the problem of large developments' feasibility evaluation, but on the other side it rises an evaluation demand

© Springer International Publishing AG 2017
O. Gervasi et al. (Eds.): ICCSA 2017, Part III, LNCS 10406, pp. 624–638, 2017.
DOI: 10.1007/978-3-319-62398-6_44

related to both the selection and feasibility analysis of coalition of actions within a multidimensional and multi-stakeholders decision context. This study aims to propose a framework for the generation of feasible coalitions of actions in the context of urban regeneration processes and for their evaluation using a Multi Criteria Decision Aiding (MCDA) approach. Given the decomposition of the concept of feasibility into three main criteria (environmental, economic and social), the proposed evaluation framework supports decision makers in exploring different combinations of actions in the context of urban interventions meant as catalysts. Two pillars underpin the proposed framework. The first pillar concerns the modeling and evaluation of synergies and temporal priorities among different combinations of projects. The second pillar concerns the inclusion of stakeholders' preferences and values in the evaluation process of the different combinations of projects. A first test of the evaluation framework on a pilot case study of urban regeneration in the city of Milan (Italy) is proposed. This paper will contribute to the debate on how to innovatively design policies and programs by exploring the use of MCDA and Operational Research in the field of urban development projects. More precisely, after the introduction, Sect. 2 focuses on the notion of urban acupuncture; Sect. 3 proposes an overview of the literature dealing with the design of alternative options for public policy making; Sect. 4 focuses on the methodological approach aimed to define and evaluate synergic coalitions of elementary urban development interventions; Sect. 5 shows the results of the first test of the evaluation model and, finally, Sect. 6 discusses the results and future research perspectives.

2   Feasibility Analysis Under the Urban Catalyst Paradigm

At the end of a long period of urban renewal processes focused on the development of large brownfields, many European cities are facing two interrelated issues [1]. The first deals with the difficulty to fulfill the urban developments undertaken in the last decade, due to the real estate market crisis and the consequent reduction of demand, as well as the inability of local governments to select a set of sustainable interventions.

The second relates to the presence of disused spaces spread across the cities in addition to new constructions still unsold, that represents an opportunity for local governments to define reuse strategies and test innovative planning practices [2]. Abandoned areas and buildings, besides reflecting the demographic, social and economic decline, highlight other signs of change, such as i) the geography of this phenomenon – nuclear and diffused – and dispersed in the tissue; ii) their relationship to a recent historical memory [3] iii) the advanced state of decay with problems of public safety due to the presence of irregular settlements. Thus, the abandoned spaces consisting of punctual and discontinued areas, disused buildings, interrupted interventions scattered in the city can overcome their residual condition when they become part of a system. Under this perspective, the notion of urban acupuncture can be considered as one of the possible lines of action. Urban acupuncture has been firstly introduced by Manuel de Sola Morales [4] with respect to urban planning practice. According to the idea of a city as a living organism, where change in one part generates change in another, local actions placed in specific areas are able to address the overall cities development [5–7]. Large development projects, with their high investments, laborious bureaucratic-administrative processes and not always consensual results, are going to be replaced by widespread and small interventions, meant as urban catalysts [8], capable of activating synergies with existing projects and trigger economic and social development processes.

The extensive literature on the subject of urban catalysts [9, 10] mainly addresses issues related to the scale and form of urban development, disregarding the instance of how to (i) define a system of catalytic pro-jects/interventions; (ii) evaluate how much they meet different objectives; (iii) explore their feasibility with a multidimensional perspective.

The transition from a traditional concept of feasibility focused on an utilitarian vision to a broader notion which encompasses intangible aspects and uncertainty due to chains of effects that are not always predictable, requires to overcome the limitations of sectorial approaches and to introduce valuation approaches co-extensive to planning, programming and design processes [11].

What deserves to be explored and represents a major challenge in the context of decision aiding models and practices is the modeling phase, when objectives are identified and alternative strategies and actions are defined [12]. Moreover, the definition of elementary projects and actions' coalitions requires to pay particular attention to the generation of alternatives [13] which are not given but should be defined starting from a cognitive map of criticalities and potentials of urban contexts, in addition to expectations and values expressed by institutions and inhabitants [14].

3 Literature Review

Creating quality alternatives plays a crucial role in many decision-making contexts, from those without an obviously complete set of alternatives to those without a set of desirable alternatives. One of the fields where the design of alternatives can have the most significant impact in terms of consequences on the local communities, quality of life and sustainability, to name a few, is that of public policy making. Yet, research on the potential usefulness of creating alternatives and how to effectively create alternatives for policy design is scarce [15].

Policy design is one of the eight major steps in the policy cycle, together with is-sue identification, defining policy objectives, policy testing, policy finalisation, policy implementation, policy monitoring and evaluation, policy readjustment and innovation [16]. Being part of the policy cycle, policy design has been explored within the body of literature concerned with policy making but by few fields [15]. The following paragraphs summarise the contribution of these fields.

Policy making has been mainly studied in policy analysis [17], with a large body of literature devoted to retrospective (ex post) analysis of policies (e.g. [18]).

Economists have been also concerned with policy making, focusing much of their research on rational theories of public decision making and formal methods for the ex-ante and ex-post evaluation of public policies (e.g. [19]).

Operational Research and Decision Analysis too have developed methods which aim at supporting different phases of the policy cycle, such as problem structuring methods (e.g. [20]), system dynamics (e.g. [21]), and Urban Operational Research (e.g. [22]), to name the most relevant ones. However, most emphasis in this stream has been on evaluation of alternatives, with limited consideration to support policy design [15].

Most decision problems discussed in the literature consider the set of alternatives on which they apply as "given", although we know that in practice such a set frequently needs to be constructed. There is little in the literature addressing this problem [23], despite the awareness of it (e.g. [24]). Few notable exceptions are summarised below.

Keller and Ho [25] characterize five approaches for the creation of alternatives. Three approaches use attributes, states of nature, or both to generate alternatives, while the remaining approaches refer to general creativity techniques such as brain-storming (e.g. [26]). Another approach to designing alternatives is the value focused thinking one [27] which focuses on the values that should be guiding the decision situation, thus removing the anchor on narrowly defined alternatives and making the search for new alternatives a creative and productive exercise.

Zwicky [28] proposed the use of the morphological box to identify a set of complex alternatives or comprehensive strategies, by decomposing a system into its functional subsystems, creating elements of an alternative that achieve the function of each subsystem, and creating an alternative by combining an element for each subsystem. Similarly, Howard [29] proposed the strategy table to decompose a strategy decision into a set of strategy areas and create possible alternatives for each. These last two procedures systematically identify a comprehensive set of feasible alternatives, even though many of the combinations may be unappealing [30].

Other interesting techniques to support alternatives' design for policy making and territorial planning are Spatial Multicriteria Analysis (e.g. [31]) and Choice Experiments (e.g. [32]), as discussed in Ferretti [33].

Once the set of alternatives has been designed, several decision analysis techniques are available to compare and evaluate such a set (e.g. [23]) Within the context of urban and territorial planning, promising approaches able to take into account coalitions of decision elements are the NAIADE (e.g. [34]) and the Choquet Integral [35]. However, they consider coalitions of actors and criteria, respectively. The present study, by proposing the use of an operational research approach based on the knapsack model to take into account coalitions of alternatives, has thus an innovative value.

4 The Methodological Proposal

Creating quality alternatives plays a crucial role in many decision-making contexts, from those without an obviously complete set of alternatives to those without a set of desirable alternatives. One of the fields where the design of alternatives can have the most significant impact in terms of consequences on the local communities, quality of life and sustainability, to name a few, is that of public policy making. Yet, research on the potential usefulness of creating alternatives and how to effectively create alternatives for policy.

4.1   Actions and Plans

As previously described, the present work considers an approach to urban planning called acupuncture, which means defining a large number of specific actions to be implemented in a certain urban area. The aim of the optimization is to find the best set of actions that maximizes benefits and minimizes costs, given some constraints to be respected. Each set of actions is defined as a plan. A group of "good" plans is the outcome of the optimization model and input of the MCDA.

4.2   Attributes and Criteria

A set number of attributes characterizes each action. Attributes have to be maximized (benefit-like attributes) or minimized (cost-like attributes).

Some attributes (e.g. the social benefits) are qualitative attributes. The transformation to numeric values (for quantitative analysis) has to be done involving experts. The attributes are the main inputs of the optimization algorithm: their definition plays thus a crucial role in determining the results.

Criteria are used to compare and evaluate potential alternative plans.

4.3   Constraints

The alternatives that will be generated might have to respect some constraints. For some attributes, alternatives might simply need to respect a given constraint value instead of targeting optimal values. Two typical examples refer to "costs" and "time", which in some cases have not to be minimized but rather to be kept lower than a certain value, i.e. the available budget and the maximum available time.

4.4   Relations Between Actions

Synergies between Actions

The framework considers the synergies between pairs of actions. A synergy happens when the joint development of two actions leads to a better performance (positive synergy) or to a weaker performance (negative synergy) (e.g. jointly developing a road and a cycle path can lead to a positive synergy from the point of view of the costs).

Synergies between actions (all the feasible pairs) are evaluated with the help of experts using ad hoc questionnaires.

Precedence between Actions

Precedence relations between actions are also considered in the model. Two kinds of precedence relations are included: a temporal precedence and a conditional precedence. Each pair of actions can have a temporal and/or a conditional precedence relation.

The temporal precedence implies that, for example, if two actions A and B are selected to form an alternative plan, B can be developed only after A has been completed.

The conditional precedence means that action B can be included in an alternative only if action A is present as well.

4.5 Solution of the Problem in 2 Steps

The problem is solved in two steps. Initially, a set of "good" alternative plans is generated through an operational research method, based on the Knapsack model (step 1). These alternative plans are then evaluated, ranked and selected through Multi Criteria Decision Aiding methods (step 2).

Step 1: Alternatives' Generation

The solution to the problem would be a plan (a set of actions) that maximizes the benefit-like attributes, minimize the cost-like attributes and respects all the constraints.

In general, multi-objective problems don't have a unique optimal solution, but rather a multi-dimensional Pareto frontier, which is the set of a large number of optimal solutions. This set of solutions can be difficult to show and to explain to the stake-holders involved in the evaluation step.

In order to limit the number of alternatives to be generated and to thus simplify the evaluation step, the optimizations are performed selecting two attributes at a time: each optimization process uses an attribute as a constraint and a second attribute as an objective function. This approach is known as the Knapsack algorithm [36, 37].

Within such a formalization, given an ordered pair of actions, a single solution can be found, i.e. the set of actions that respects the constraint and maximizes the objective function. That means that in a problem with n attributes, $n*(n-1)$ solutions can be found.

This Knapsack approach requires a low computational effort and can thus be applied to problems characterized by a large set of actions. The drawback is that this algorithm finds only a "near-best" solution.

Benchmark with the full calculation approach

The full calculation approach would allow to investigate all the combinations of actions (plans) and so to find the optimal solution. This approach would allow to find the ranking of all the possible solutions instead of the "near-best" one only. The drawback is a high computational effort which limits the operability of the approach when actions are more than 20. In this application, the full calculation approach is used to produce a benchmark for the alternatives found by the Knapsack algorithm and test its ability to find the best solutions.

Step 2: Evaluation

To compare the options (plans) identified in the previous Section, we used multi-attribute value theory (MAVT) [38, 39]. MAVT allows to rank the options by assigning to each one a global value based on its scores with respect to a selected set of criteria. The preferences of the decision-makers are expressed with criteria weights, which are scaling factors between the criteria, and value functions, which represent the level of satisfaction about the criteria scores.

The evaluation step is performed by considering all the available criteria, while the generation step considers only 2 attributes at a time.

5 Case study

The evaluation framework has been tested on a pilot case study of urban regeneration in the city of Milan (Italy). The area of Bovisa, located in the north west part of the city, has been selected among the areas currently under development since a recent competition has encouraged the definition of several requalification proposals, that can be considered as systems of elementary actions. Given the limited availability of economic resources', it is crucial to select a set of actions able to foster development over time. The proposal used to test the evaluation framework is the most consistent with the notion of urban catalyst, as it is aimed at the definition of coalitions of elementary actions selected with respect to their mutual synergies.

5.1 The renewal process of the Bovisa area, Milan, Italy

Bovisa is a strategic area, both from the size point of view, as it covers approximately 87 hectares, and from the accessibility point of view, thanks to the presence of two regional and inter-regional railway stations (FNM Bovisa and Villapizzone). Bovisa is located along the axis that connects the Expo area with the new district of Garibaldi and Porta Nuova (see Fig. 1).

The site is a kind of enclave within the city, with several signs of its former industrial use. Thus, its environmental remediation and redevelopment is part of the larger development strategy of the entire city.

In particular, Bovisa is characterized by the presence of the late nineteenth century urban structure made by small and medium-sized industrial and crafts buildings together with several residential buildings. Starting from the late '70s many industrial buildings have been abandoned or turned into smaller and fragmented workspaces with a progressive expansion of residential use.

The replacement process over the years has been carried out without an overall redesign of the districts. Actually, small industrial activities still coexist with multi-store residential buildings from the early Twenties. Over the last decades a key role has been played by the Politecnico di Milano and the Mario Negri research centre with their support related activities. Figure 2 shows that, with the exception of these two large-scale functions, there is a shortage of quality services to the people, as well as of green areas.

The "drop" shaped Bovisa area, limited by the railway, represents a gap between the surrounding residential districts because of the lack of accesses, links and cycle-pedestrian lines. Even though Bovisa is one of the most easily accessible areas by the regional rail network, the two existing railway stations should be connected to the urban public transport system.

The territorial system under analysis thus represents an integrated and multifunctional urban area, able to create synergies among the strategic functions related to

Fig. 1. The area of Bovisa and the surrounding recent and on-going urban developments. Source: Verso le Nuove Municipalità un atlante, Comune di Milano, Politecnico di Milano DAStU, 2013 (Comune di Milano, Politecnico di Milano DAStU (2013), Verso le Nuove Municipalità un atlante)

university and research and the residential blocks. Particular attention has been paid to the timeline of the development process and its feasibility. Different functional scenarios have been defined by combining flexibility and adaptive reuse (Fig. 3). The basic idea of this proposal is that it is possible to manage urban transformations through the development of spatial elements, whose uses can change over time according to a principle of rotation.

5.2 Results

The set of actions proposed for the Bovisa case study are listed in the following tables. The actions are 18 and are grouped according to 3 main themes:

(A) Infrastructures
(B) Built environment
(C) Green space

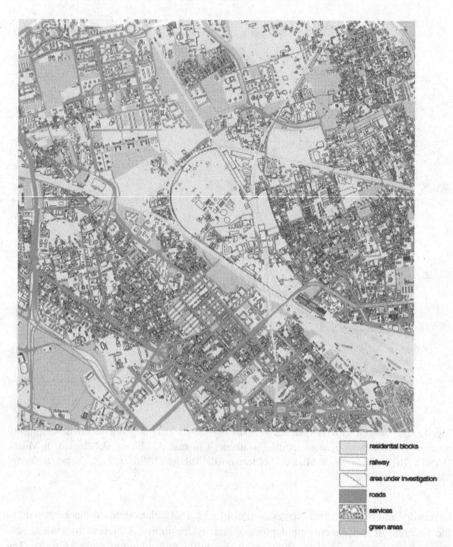

The legend reads:

- residential blocks
- railway
- area under investigation
- roads
- services
- green areas

Fig. 2. Main functions of the Bovisa area. Source: Carta tecnica comunale, 2006

Four attributes (n = 4) are defined for the generation of alternatives: Economic feasibility (eco), Technical feasibility (tec), Social-Environmental feasibility (soc-env) and Costs (cost).

As described above, in order to limit the number of alternatives generated and to facilitate the evaluation step, the optimizations are performed selecting two attributes at a time: each optimization process uses an attribute as a constraint and a second attribute as an objective function. Given an ordered pair, a single solution exists, i.e. the set of actions that respects the constraint and maximizes the objective function.

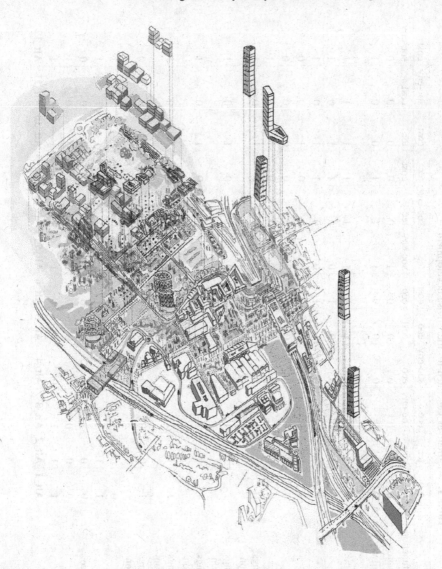

Fig. 3. The proposal for the development of Bovisa selected to test the evaluation framework. Bovisa Call for Ideas, Politecnico of Milano, 2016, Proposal: "Bovisa Connection. Tassel-li urbani per scenari resilienti", Team leader: Andrea Arcidiacono. View of the renewal project by Jacopo Ascari.

Thus, ($n*(n - 1) = 12$) alternatives ($Alt\_1, \ldots, Alt\_12$) have been generated for the Bovisa case study through the proposed approach (Table 1). The actions contributing to the creation of optimal alternatives taking into account a pair of attributes at a time (one as a constraint and one as an objective function) are highlighted in green.

The generated alternatives are composed of a minimum number of 4 actions (Alt_4) to a maximum of 13 actions (Alt_6, Alt_10, Alt_12).

Table 1. Alternatives generated for the Bovisa development

			Constrain	eco	tec	eco	soc-env	eco	cost	tec	soc-env	tec	cost	soc-env	cost
			Objective function	tec	eco	soc-env	eco	cost	eco	soc-env	tec	cost	tec	cost	soc-env
A-Infrastructures	A2	Railway station		0	0	0	0	0	0	1	0	0	0	0	0
	A3	Existing railway station dev		0	0	0	0	0	0	1	1	1	0	0	1
	A4	Bicycle path		1	1	1	0	1	1	1	1	1	1	1	1
	A5	Road		1	0	0	0	0	1	0	0	1	1	0	1
	A6.1	Parking_a		1	1	1	0	1	1	0	0	1	1	0	1
	A6.2	Parking_b		1	0	0	0	0	1	0	0	0	1	0	0
	A6.3	Parking_c		0	0	0	0	0	0	0	0	0	0	0	0
	A7	Viaduct		0	0	1	0	1	1	1	0	0	1	1	1
B-Built environment	B4.1	Old buildings rehabilitation		0	0	1	0	1	1	0	0	0	0	0	1
	B4.2	Old buildings rehabilitation		1	1	1	0	1	1	0	1	0	0	0	1
	B4.3	Old buildings rehabilitation		1	1	1	0	1	1	0	0	0	0	0	1
	B4.4	Old buildings rehabilitation		1	1	1	0	1	1	0	0	0	1	0	1
	B4.5	Old buildings rehabilitation		1	0	0	0	0	1	0	0	0	1	0	0
C-Green	C1	Green_a		0	0	1	0	1	1	1	0	1	0	1	1
	C2	Green_b		1	1	1	0	1	1	1	1	1	1	1	1
	C3	Public space		0	0	1	0	1	0	0	0	0	0	0	0
	C4	Park		0	0	0	0	0	0	1	0	1	1	0	1
	C5	Green_c		1	1	1	0	1	1	1	1	1	1	1	1
Generated alternative				Alt_1	Alt_2	Alt_3	Alt_4	Alt_5	Alt_6	Alt_7	Alt_8	Alt_9	Alt_10	Alt_11	Alt_12

The results of the generation step are inputs for the evaluation step. Synergies (expressed by experts, as significant interplays between pairs of actions in relation to individual attributes) contribute to increase/decrease the performance of the actions in relation to the attributes. In the generation step, when the algorithm considers elementary actions, it also considers pairs of actions and their positive/negative synergies, increasing/decreasing their performances. For the evaluation step the criteria are the same as the attributes selected for the generation step.

The evaluation is performed as follows: the performance of an alternative is calculated as the sum of the attributes of the actions that compose each alternative, taking in account existing synergies. The values of the criteria are then transformed through value functions. These functions assign the value 1 to the best performance of an action, if the attribute is a benefit-like one, or to the worst performance of an action, if the attribute is a cost-like one. The four value functions (i.e. one for each attribute) are then aggregated using the relative weights to obtain an overall score for each single alternative. For this pilot case study, weights are considered homogeneous across the attributes for providing a neutral scenario. The sensitivity analysis on weights should be introduced according to the stakeholders' involvement in order to explore the effects of their preferences on ranking.

The final result of the evaluation is a ranking of the 12 alternatives, as shown in Fig. 4.

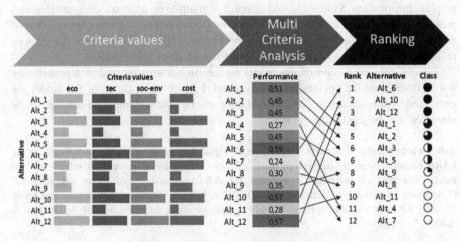

Fig. 4. Ranking of the 12 alternatives

A crucial aspect of the above described procedure consists in the elicitation of both value functions and weights. For the Bovisa case study this elicitation was performed by interviewing experts.

6 Discussion and Conclusions

The results of the first practical test of the evaluation framework seem to support the generation and the ranking of coalitions of elementary actions whose synergies have been evaluated with respect to a set of both qualitative and quantitative criteria. The decision about which coalitions of actions should be developed in order to maximize benefits, given limited economic resources, is supported by an evaluation pro-cess based on value judgments. Despite the approximations due to the limited involvement of real stakeholders and to the limited availability of data on the actions, the notions of urban acupuncture and urban catalyst have been modeled and the complexity given by the coexistence of several interventions to be combined has been reduced by the use of the multi knapsack approach.

This approximation reflects the usual characteristics of urban development projects, i.e. limited time availability, presence of multiple and conflicting interests, need for tools able to support decision makers' understanding and development of arguments for the decision. Further developments of the model refer to: (i) implementation of a dynamic sensitivity analysis, to investigate the robustness of the results, (ii) refinement of actions' performances evaluation, (iii) deeper investigation of synergies (among functions, stakeholders, resources, thematic issues) and value functions. Synergies, in particular, require to be mapped and to be monitored over time as they are considered key drivers for successful urban development. To this end, the introduction of Geographic Information Systems could support a multilayer analysis of synergies and provide a sound basis for evaluation over time (for example in the implementation of monitoring systems and/or as a tool for performance evaluation of both the choices related to different time horizons and the deviations from predictions).

Finally, the application of the model on the Bovisa area represents a preliminary test to investigate the operability of the model. Further applications of the model are envisaged by the authors in decision-making contexts where elementary actions can be identified and be jointly developed.

Acknowledgements. The authors of the paper would like to thank all the participants in the FARB research projects "Innovating the feasibility concept for contemporary urban developments. The role of integrated assessment for defining coalitions of urban interventions" (Politecnico of Milano, Research Funds 2015) (i.e. Grazia Concilio, Anna Moro and Paola Savoldi) for their valuable comments and suggestions about the definition of the evaluation model.

References

1. UN HABITAT: The State of European Cities, Cities, leading the way to a better future (2016). ec.eropa.eu
2. Savoldi, P., Gaeta, L., Micelli, E.: La pianificazione urbanistica tra governo e mercato. In: Angrilli, M. (a cura di), L'urbanistica che cambia, rischi e valori, pp. 184–193. FrancoAngeli, Milano (2012)
3. Augè, M.: Rovine e macerie: Il senso del tempo. Bollati Boringhieri, Torino (2004)

4. De Solà-Morales, M.: The strategy of urban acupuncture. In: Structure Fabric and Topography Conference, Nanjing University (2004)
5. De Solà Morales, M.: Urbanitat Capillar, Lunwerg, Barcelona (2009)
6. Casagrande, M.: Third Generation Eco-City, Taiwan Architect (2007)
7. Lerner, J.: Urban Agupuncture. Island Press, Washington (2014)
8. Attoe, W., Logan, D.: American Urban Architecture: Catalysts in the Design of Cities. University of California Press, Berkeley (1989)
9. Sideroff, D.A.: Neighborhood revitalization through catalyst projects: capacity building and urban design in the West Philadelphia Landscape Project and the Bronx River Project, DSpace@MIT: Massachusetts Institute of Technology Open Educational Resources (OER) (2003), download 2015. http://www.temoa.info/node/258679
10. Landry, C.: Urban agupuncture. Plan. Theory Pract. 6(1), 117–128 (2005)
11. Patassini, D.: Esperienze di valutazione urbana. FrancoAngeli, Milano (2006)
12. Sharifi, M.A., Rodriguez, E.: Design and development of a planning support system for policy formulation in water resource rehabilitation. J. Hydroinf. 4(3), 157–175 (2002)
13. Tsoukias, A.: Aiding to decide and evaluation: chalenges for the future. Valori e Valutazioni 13, 33–36 (2014)
14. Crosta, P.L.: Pratiche. Il territorio 'è l'uso che se ne fa'. FrancoAngeli, Milano (2010)
15. Ferretti, V., Pluchinotta, I., Tsoukiàs, A.: Supporting decisions in Public Policy making processes: generation of alternatives and innovation. Eur. J. Oper. Res. (under review)
16. Lasswell, H.D.: The Decision Process: Seven Categories of Functional Analysis. University of Maryland Press, College Park (1956)
17. Moran, M., Rein, M., Goodin, G.E.: The Oxford handbook of public policy. Oxford University Press, Oxford (2006)
18. Considine, M.: Thinking outside the box? Applying design theory to public policy. Polit. Policy 40(4), 704–724 (2012)
19. Dollery, B., Worthington, A.: The evaluation of public policy: normative economic theories of government failure. J. Interdisc. Econ. 7(1), 27–39 (1996)
20. Rosenhead, J.: Past, present and future of problem structuring methods. J. Oper. Res. Soc. 57(7), 759–765 (2006)
21. Sterman, J.D.: System dynamics modeling: Tools for learning in a complex world. Calif. Manag. Rev. 43(4), 8–25 (2001)
22. Larson, R.C., Odoni, A.R.: Urban Operations Research. Prentice-Hall, Englewood Cliffs (1981)
23. Belton, V., Stewart, T.J.: Muliple Criteria Decision Analysis: An Integrated Approach. Kluwer Academic, Dordrecht (2002)
24. Newstead, S.E., Thompson, V.A., Handley, S.J.: Generating alternatives: A key component in human reasoning? Mem. Cogn. 30, 129–137 (2002)
25. Keller, L.R., Ho, J.L.: Decision problem structuring: generating options. IEEE Trans. Syst. Man Cybern. 18, 715–728 (1988)
26. Ackoff, R.L.: The Art of Problem Solving. Wiley, New York (1978)
27. Keeney, R.L.: Value-Focused Thinking: A Path to Creative Decision making. Harvard University Press, Cambridge (1992)
28. Zwicky, F.: The morphological approach to discovery, invention, re-search and construction. In: Zwicky, F., Wilson, A.G. (eds.) New Methods of Thought and Procedure: Contributions to the Symposium on Methodologies, pp. 273–297. Springer, Berlin (1967)
29. Howard, R.A.: Decision analysis: practice and promise. Manage. Sci. 34(6), 679–695 (1988)
30. Siebert, J., Keeney, R.L.: Creating more and better alternatives for decisions using objectives. Oper. Res. 63(5), 1144–1158 (2015)

31. Geneletti, D., Ferretti, V.: Multicriteria analysis for sustainability assessment: concepts and case studies. In: Morrison-Saunders, A., Pope, J., Bond, A. (eds.) Handbook of Sustainability Assessment, pp. 235–264. Edgar Elgar Publishing, Cheltenham (2015)

32. Oppio, A., Bottero, M., Ferretti, V., Fratesi, U., Ponzini, D., Pracchi, V.: Giving space to multicriteria analysis for complex cultural heritage systems: The case of the castles in Valle D'Aosta Region, Italy. J. Cult. Herit. **16**(6), 779–789 (2015)

33. Ferretti, V.: From stakeholders analysis to cognitive mapping and Multi-Attribute Value Theory: An integrated approach for policy support. Eur. J. Oper. Res. **253**(2), 524–541 (2016)

34. Munda, G.: A conflict analysis approach for illuminating distributional issues in sustainability policy. Eur. J. Oper. Res. **194**(1), 307–322 (2009)

35. Choquet, G.: Theory of capacities. Ann. l'Institute Fourier **5**, 131–295 (1953)

36. Feuerman, M., Harvey, W.: A mathematical programming model for test construction and scoring. Manage. Sci. **19**(8), 961–966 (1973)

37. Zhong, T., Young, R.: Multiple choice knapsack problem: example of planning choice in transportation. Eval. Program Plan. **33**, 128–137 (2010)

38. Keeney, R.L., Raiffa, H.: Decisions with Multiple Objectives. Wiley, New York (1976)

39. De Toro, P., Iodice, S.: Evaluation in Urban Planning: a multi-criteria approach for the choice of alternative. Operational Plans in Cava De' Tirreni. AESTIMUM **69**, 93–112 (2016)

Experimenting CIE and CBA in Urban Restoration

Carmelo Maria Torre[✉], Pierluigi Morano, and Francesco Tajani

Dipartimento DICAR Politecnico di Bari, via Orabona 4 Bari, Bari, Italy
carmelomaria.torre@poliba.it

Abstract. The Community impact evaluation (CIE) is a multi-actor methodology of evaluation: its goal is to identify the convenience of actions/projects, as part of urban policies, according to the Social preferable expressed by different members of the community affected by the policy itself. It traces a methodological approach for the preparation of a social report distributed in the plan's policies. His first methodological application was developed as Planning Balance Sheet in the early sixties, in order to give an answer to the need to overcome the Cost-benefit analysis limit constituted by the failure to evaluate the distributive effects of interventions. Lichfield [1] distinguishes between different social categories those involved in an active way (promoters) or passive (users) in the implementation of an intervention, in different ways. These different modes of involvement are defined by the nature of the different advantages of which each group can enjoy and disadvantages that each group can undergo. They play an active role of the producers, who participate in the implementation of the intervention. instead play a "passive" users, who do not participate in the production process. A first way to determine the distribution effects is therefore to build many budgets disaggregated as there are groups affected by the policy of recovery. If the benefits and costs identified for each social group were all liquidated the procedure would be to build a series of indicators of economic convenience. (Net Present Value and Internal Return Rate) estimated budget for the costs benefits of all the groups involved [2].

To widen the scope you can start by analyzing the advantages and disadvantages not monetizable affecting every social group. The paper illustrates the result of a social supported simulation of future hypothesis of reuse of a monumental site, by the application of a matrix modelled CIE approach.

Keywords: CIE · Cost-benefit · Arrow theorem

1 Introduction

The Community impact evaluation (CIE) is a multi-actor methodology of evaluation: its goal is to identify the convenience of actions/projects, as part of urban policies, according to the Social preferable expressed by different members of the community affected by the policy itself [1]. It traces a methodological approach for the preparation of a social report distributed in the plan's policies.

© Springer International Publishing AG 2017
O. Gervasi et al. (Eds.): ICCSA 2017, Part III, LNCS 10406, pp. 639–650, 2017.
DOI: 10.1007/978-3-319-62398-6_45

His first methodological application was developed in the early sixties by Nathaniel Lichfield, in order to give an answer to the need to overcome the Cost-benefit analysis limit constituted by the failure to evaluate the distributive effects of interventions [2, 3].

Lichfield distinguishes between different social categories those involved in an active way (promoters) or passive (users) in the implementation of an intervention, in different ways. These different modes of involvement are defined by the nature of the different advantages of which each group can enjoy and disadvantages that each group can undergo [4–6]. Producers play an active role, who participate in the implementation of the intervention Instead users play "passive", as who do not participate in the production process [7–9].

The promoters will tend to hinder the implementation of the intervention or to favor it according to whether it is contrary or in accordance with the objectives that are conducted through the activities that lead the producers themselves. Users, in turn, will tend to hinder the realization of plan or the hypothesis according to favor it that it provides a reduction or an increase in supply relative to demand for goods or services, or to the question of "other values" expressed by consumers themselves [10–12]. The paper shows a method for assessing the social profitability of each stakeholder involved in a development or regeneration project, by the support of a Case Study.

In the first part, after general data about the case of study, a synthesis of the Social Planning Balance process will be shown, in the second part a multilevel normalized system of preferences is developed, in the third part, finally, the discussion of result will introduce the final remarks.

2   Facts and Materials

2.1   Case of Study: Assessing Social Impacts of Possible Reuse of Historical Buildings

The case study is represented by a group of buildings and connected inside the Monumental Complex of the Bourbonic Royal Palace of Portici (Fig. 1). The Royal Palace is integrated with a further palace named Mascabruno. The both buildings are inside a wide park, used for equestrian activities and stables. The property has undergone some transformations and has been affected by numerous changes of intended use. The ownership of the fabrics is multiple, and the property is divided between private and public institutions, as the City Council of Portici, the County of Naples and the University of Naples.

Some restoration of all the buildings owned by the County, with the exclusion of Riding area works were carried out 20 years ago. The Horses Stable (named "Cavallerizza") in the Park, as the whole complex of fabrics of the Royal Palace, are characterized by a relevant social value. An experimental multi-actor decision making process was simulated about a social new use for the fabrics of "Cavallerizza". In this experiment the potential restoration and reuse of the Riding School of "Cavallerizza" was framed in a broader project of reuse that encompass the entire Palace of Portici [13].

As regards the Riding School, are to be proposed two possibilities for reuse.

Fig. 1. The monumental area of Portici

First hypothesis: health center. The first hypothesis of reuse for the Royal Palace responds to the provisions of the Health Agreement between the City of Portici and Health Agency, which has among its objectives the transformation of the network of health services in the area [4].

The supply of non-routine health equipment is increasing, particularly to provide a nursing home assistance for the elderly and disabled, an aids information center for people with disabilities and a point of listening to youth problems and prevention of drug addiction. The fabric is under management of an association agreement with the City Health Agency, whose regime of activity is independently from the rest of the complex, having recovered. In this hypothesis it is expected in particular the location of a rehabilitation gym, with annexes services and bar, with restoration, connection, via the grand staircase, between the riding school and the Lower Park. The Province will grant busy in the use of this property in its municipality and Health Agency. They in turn will receive revenue from the management of the Horsing School, used as a rehabilitation gym.

Planned interventions are: the functional adaptation of a Palace named Mascabruno, hosting the facilities of the Faculty of Agriculture, to be used as residence for elderly and chronic disabled people, and further audit – point for drug addicts; the building is the most artistic and architectural relevant part, will host the clinic for the handicapped and administrative offices. The Horsewoman will be used as a rehabilitation gym.

These interventions translate the use of fabrics into the following changes:

(a) placement of commercial activities
(b) partial regeneration of the lower woods
(c) use for recreational purposes of the area surrounding the lower forest
(d) re-use of derelict structures currently
(e) creation of spaces for social and cultural aggregation
(f) physical redevelopment

The pursued objectives by realizing the idea of health care are:

– the recovery of the connection between the group of fabrics and the park
– a better use of the forest;
– the increase of attention and protection to weak social groups.
– the improvement of employment, thanks to the presence of new accommodation and health activities.

Second hypothesis: gallery. The second option is to use the Palace as the Art Gallery of the Province, the municipal library and conference room. The idea stems from the Pinacoteca, expressed by the Province, to allocate the prestigious collection of paintings owned by him in a place of architectonic historical value. It is planned to locate the Pinacoteca in large Palazzo Mascabruno environments, i.e. the former stables of the Royal Palace.

Due to the large size, the complex of fabrics has a public library designed to turn a part of the buildings currently used improperly as an elementary school. The two most valuable objects from an artistic and architectural point of view, which straddle the Street University, may instead house the library and all administrative offices.

Finally the Eques Riding, the restoration object, becomes a conference room, the management of which may be entrusted to private promoters, subject to the availability of space for the Province. At the same time, taking advantage of the opening of the hall itself towards the lower Park, it may constitute a place suited to the organization of meetings or events.

The envisaged interventions are: the recovery of the connection between the complex and the lower park, to improve its use; the functional adaptation of the use of complex Gallery, Municipal Library and conference room.

They cause the following transformations:

1. creation of open spaces to the public
2. setting up of business
3. regeneration of a part of the lower woods
4. use for recreational purposes area adjacent to the lower woods
5. reconfiguration of the near pier for accessibility
6. reuse of abandoned structures
7. creation of spaces for socializing and cultural gathering

The objectives pursued with this assumptions of reuse are:

– better use of available resources, thanks to the versatility of the intended use
– increasing the flow of tourists and visitors;
– the protection of the architectural and environmental values;
– improving the aesthetic quality, and cultural enjoyment of the property;
– promote the image;
– increase in employment levels

2.2   CIE as Complex Way for Social Assessment

The Community Impact Evaluation then analyzes the distribution of social preferable expressing it with a series of indicators quali-quantitative, of diverse nature, through which they are identified different explicate hypothesis usefulness of intervention, and different prices, express or implied, which are paid by different social groups.

Each indicator identifies the utility expressed as the degree of satisfaction of a goal that may be of interest to one or more social groups.

In this context, among the other issues, objectives of public and private entities can clearly converge or diverge, interact positively or negatively [14–16].

In a framework of fragmentation of the subjects involved becomes therefore essential to be able to describe, through these categories design alternatives to be evaluated, in order to determine which aspects of the transformation induced by the project interfere positively or negatively with the objectives of each sector/group and, therefore, ultimately with the preferences of each sector/group [17, 18].

The process is then carried out through a set of phases. The first, namely the "institutional analysis" [19, 20] is descriptive (Fig. 2):

(a) a description of the quantitative and qualitative changes induced by the different hypotheses project/plan, according to a suitable choice of parameters;
(b) identification of social groups, or "sectors" that are affected by the impacts of the plan or the project itself;
(c) identification of sector objectives which affect each social group;
(d) identification of sector goals that the plan favors or contrasts.

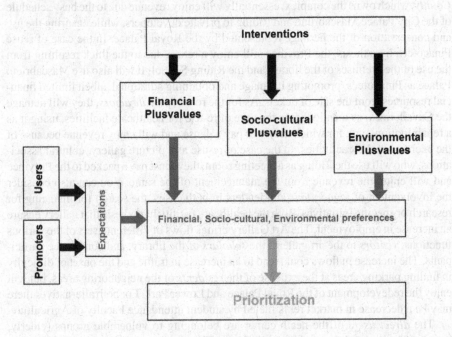

Fig. 2. The logical framework

3 Identifying Stakeholders

As well as the variables referring to the areas of transformation are the descriptive elements of the modification induced by the project, the sector goals are the elements on the basis of which it articulates the preference of each social group [21, 22].

They are therefore the sector goals of a social group which identify the parameters by which to measure the preference of the group itself. For example, if the group is considered one of the residents, the indicators that can express the preferability according to their point of view are those linked to the objective of increased environmental quality, such as the increase of green areas, the increase services, areas subject to conservation and protection and the increase in the value of the social, cultural, financial, etc. they possess.

Some project actions will cause modifications of the physical space and the socio-environmental context, which will change the structure of green areas, the provision of services, will increase or decrease the chances of protection, creating favorable or unfavorable impacts to residents [23, 24]. If the social group considered is that of local entrepreneurs, the objectives that may affect their preference are those of the revaluation of the market, the profitability of economic activities generated by the intervention.

As for the *City Council* (local government), the re-use hypothesis for the establishment of a health center does not have an economic return, as they will be dealt with the costs of the dense structure of the Province, the management and maintenance. It will, however, significant social impacts. As for the possibility of reuse Pinacoteca, the impact on the municipality will still essentially expressed by thick and social returns costs. The *County*, which owns the complex, essentially will enjoy revenue due to the busy schedule of the City Palace Mascabruno and Riding to private developers, while ensuring the use and conservation of the heritage represented by the Royal Palace. In the case of reuse Pinacoteca hypothesis, the Province still enjoy a return due to the thick resulting from the use of the premises of the library and the Riding School; It will also use Mascabruno Palace as Pinacoteca, promoting its image and obtaining additional, albeit limited financial resources from the sale of tickets. As for the role of *private actors*, they will manage the Cavallerizza, as mentioned, in the case of re-use for healthcare facilities, using it as a rehabilitation gym, for which they will pay a dense and will enjoy revenue because of the exercise of their activities. In the case of re-use as a picture gallery, cultural associations, who will use the Riding as a meeting room, they must pay a packed to the Province and will enjoy the revenue from the management of the same. You can also consider the involvement of *foundations* and lenders in both cases, the search for financing for research or specific initiatives. Both the healthcare facility hypothesis that gallery ensure an increase in employment. The Art Gallery brings flows of different users of the various functions: *visitors* to the art gallery, the *scholars* of the library, and conference participants. The increase in flows could lead to an increase in traffic and the onset of difficulty in finding parking areas at the expense of the *residents* of the neighboring areas, but will enjoy the redevelopment of the Royal Palace and Lower Park. For both alternatives there may be a decrease in market rents fueled by student attendance Faculty of Agriculture.

The *direct users* of the heath center are belonging to vulnerable groups (elderly, young offenders and drug addicts, disabled). The *direct users* of the Gallery are: its visitors; Scholars who use the library, the users from the meeting room, which can benefit from an easily reachable by public transport (metro, bus, seaside walk).

4   Assessing Social Impacts of Projects

At this point the impact is determined deductively starting from the intersection of transformations and objectives. Any modification of the physical and social space may favor or oppose the pursuit of a number of objectives. The favorable character or contrast of each transformation can be expressed

- through quantitative indicators, which represent the quantitative indicator that measure the degree of performance relative to a given objective, and the quantitative indicator that measures the transformation made by the project according to a given aspect;
- through qualitative indicators, expressing the relationship between transformations and objectives through scores, ordinal scales or verbal judgments.

All the relationships between indicators are resumed in a coaxial matrix, described as follows.

Transformation-goals matrix. It is the intersecting matrix between Transformations. and Goals of the sectors/groups/stakeholders, described through the impact that each transformation determines on pursuing goals of each stakeholder (Fig. 3). It is expressed the level of satisfaction or objective foreclosure through an intensive impact dependent entity assumed by the variable in the project and the importance of objective impacted by the processing sector. Even the value of each component of the Transformation Goal matrix is standardized in the interval [0–1]. The second one is evaluative type and is constructed from the following evaluation coaxial matrices:

Transformation-projects matrix. Matrix crossover between design alternatives and physical, social, environmental induced by the same alternatives. The intersection is expressed through qualiquantitative variables describing the size and the characteristics of the changes induced by the project. Different projects can determine the same types of processing, entity or different quality, or, in theory, also of the same magnitude.

The interaction Transformation-Project relates a group of transformation with a provided project. Given the Vector of overall transformation V_T: $(T_1 ..... T_n)$ each project produce a set of possible changes represented by a vector V_C: $(T_1 ..... T_j)$ where $(T_1 ..... T_j)$ is a sub-set of $(T_1 ..... T_n)$. The value of each component of V_T and V_C is standardized in a interval [0–1].

Stakehokders-Goals matrix. Matrix representing crossover between social groups and objectives of the sectors/groups/individuals involved. The intersection expresses an intensity of quali-quantitative preference which represents the importance of each objective for different sectors/groups/entities involved. These objectives have a different weight for different groups.

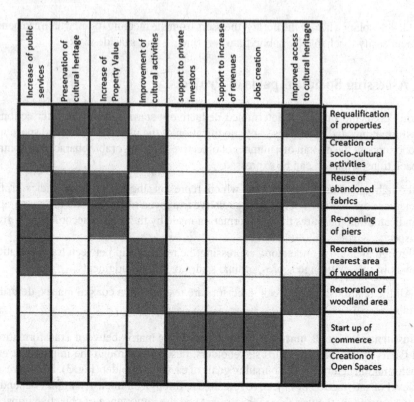

Fig. 3. Interaction between goals of interest for groups and possible transformations provided by projects.

The interaction Stakeholder-Project relates a group of transformation with a provided project. Given the Vector of overall Goals V_G: $(G_1 ..... G_m)$ each Stakehoders is identified with its set of goals represented by a vector V_S: $(S_1 ..... S_i)$ where $(S_1 ..... S_i)$ is a subset of $(G_1 ..... G_m)$. The value of each component of V_G and V_S is standardized in the interval [0-1].

This stage of the procedure is almost similar to that in an environmental impact assessment leads to break the project down into individual actions and the environmental context in components and individual elements on which the impacts are then evaluated.

The final evaluation is carried out through the determination of a synthetic index that represents the average intensity of the impacts on each group generated by each transformation induced by each intervention provided in each design reuse hypothesis. The table gives us the distribution and the average intensity of the impact on each person/group/sector (Fig. 4).

The **final intersection of social preference by stakeholders with project's actions,** syntetizes the preference about all the intersections in which where the intersection of transformations induced by each project, the project objectives and that express the preference of each sector/group/subject directly replaces the intersection between the intensities of the preferences expressed by each sector/group/person for each project.

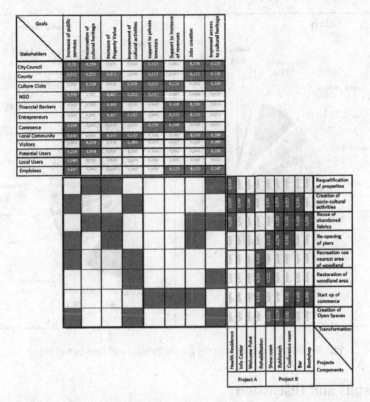

Fig. 4. Coaxial Matrixes where the interaction between goals of interest for stakehoders and possible transformations connect projects to groups according the filter function of qualitative matrix transformation-goals.

The analysis could lead through further processing to a synthesis index, which expresses the preferability of each of the two projects for different groups by determining an average intensity. Due to the unevenness of the impacts it is difficult to build a quantitative comparison of the impact intensity of each group, especially because these intensities are based as well as on different nature of impacts, including impacts on variables in number from group to group.

The breakdown of each average intensity of impact for each group and for each project can be a way to highlight the articulation of preferability. Considering, however, the community benefits from both projects, the simultaneous implementation of both would provide 100% of the benefits and costs (Fig. 5). At this point, placing the sum of the intensities of the impacts of both projects equal to 100, and broken down by medium intensity refers to each group, you can make the comparisons illustrated in the following chart:

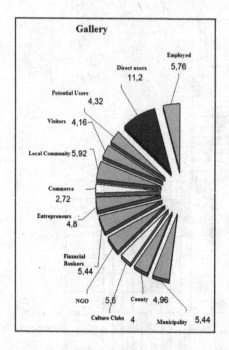
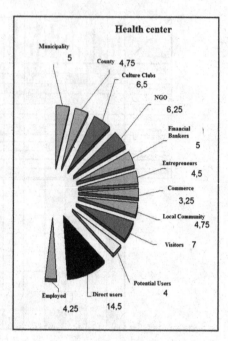

Fig. 5. Distribution of benefits for the project and between groups.

5   Results and Discussion

By comparing the normalized distribution you will notice that there is a strong impact intensity difference between Project A (Health Center) and Project B (Gallery) for the following groups:

(a) visitors (project A: 7%; project B 4.16%);
(b) associations (project A: 6.5%; project B 4%);
(c) direct users (project A: 14.5%; project B 11.2%);
(d) traders (Project A: 3.25%; 2.72% Project B).

Finally, in absolute terms, about the normalized distribution of the impacts should be noted that in general the total benefit of the impacts of the project A exceeds the total benefit of the impacts of the project B. The above differences represent the highest degree of discrimination between groups in preference of a project relative to each other. The final intensity of preferability in essence depends on,

(a) by the number of impacts that affect each social group,
(b) the importance aspect involved by each impact.

This implies that while other groups will have an attitude of equidistance between the two options, visitors, associations, direct and Traders users tend to "shift the decision" in favor of the project that creates for them the most positive impacts. Since the project A preferable to B project for all the highlighted groups, it is more likely to be put in place following a consultation phase involving actors considered in the evaluation.

Acknowledgements. Authors wish to acknowledge the support provided by colleagues of the MITO Lab of the Polytechnic of Bari. Furthermore, even if the paper is the result of a common reasoning, the various parts have been written with this sequence: the introduction (and conclusions) have been written by Pierluigi Morano. The second and the Third Paragraph is due to the effort of Francesco Tajani and the fourth paragraph is due to the effert of Carmelo M. Torre.

References

1. Lichfield, N.: Community Impact Evaluation. UCL Press, London (1995)
2. Sen, A.: The impossibility of a paretian liberal. J. Polit. Econ. **78**(1), 152–157 (1970)
3. Tirole, J.: Collusion and the theory of organizations. In: Laffont, J.J. (ed.) Advances in Economic Theory: Sixth World Congress 2. Cambridge University Press, Cambridge (1992)
4. Arrow, K.J.: Social Choice and Individual Values. Wiley, New York (1973)
5. Munda, G.: Social multi-criteria evaluation: methodological foundations and operational consequences. Eur. J. Oper. Res. **158**(3), 662–677 (2004)
6. Khakee, A.: Evaluation and planning: inseparable concepts. Town Plann. Rev. **64**, 359–374 (1998)
7. Lichfield, N.: Integrating planning and environmental impact assessment. In: Lichfield, N., Barbanente, A., Borri, D., Khakee, A., Prat, A. (eds.) Evaluation in Planning: Facing the Challenge of complexity, pp. 151–176. Kluwer, Dordrecht (1998)
8. Hahn, B.M., Kofalk, S., De Kok, J., Berlekamp, J., Evers, M.: Elbe DSS: a planning support system for strategic river basin planning. In: Geertman, S., Stillwell, J. (eds.) Planning Support Systems Best Practice and New Methods The GeoJournal Library 6, pp. 113–136. Springer, Berlin (2009)
9. Vidal, A.C., Keating, W.D.: Community development: current issues and emerging challenges. Journal of Urban Affairs **26**(2), 125–137 (2004). To Open Restoration to Community
10. Porter, M.E., Kramer, M.R.: The big idea: creating shared value. Harvard Bus. Rev. **89**(1), 2 (2011)
11. Torre, C.M.: Socio-economic dimension in managing the renewal of ancient historic centers. In: Rotondo, F., Selicato, F., Marin, V., Galdeano, J.L. (eds.) Cultural Territorial Systems, pp. 97–106. Springer, Heidelberg (2016)
12. Campagna, M., De Montis, A., Deplano, G.: PSS design: a general framework perspective. Int. J. Environ. Technol. Manage. **6**(1–2), 163–179 (2005)
13. Gaudioso, F.: Ipotesi di Restauro della Cavallerizza di Portici. M.Sc thesis, University Frederic II Library, Naples (2002)
14. Mossetto, G.: Aesetics and Economics. Kluwer, Boston (1993)
15. Greffe, X.: La valeur économique du patrimoine. La demande et l'offre de monuments. Antropos, Paris (1991)
16. Torre, C.M., Attardi, R., Sannicandro, V.: Integrating financial analysis and decision theory for the evaluation of alternative reuse scenarios of historical buildings. In: Gervasi, O., Murgante, B., Misra, S., Rocha, Ana Maria A.C.Maria A.C., Torre, Carmelo M.M., Taniar, D., Apduhan, Bernady O.O., Stankova, E., Wang, S. (eds.) ICCSA 2016. LNCS, vol. 9789, pp. 177–190. Springer, Cham (2016). doi:10.1007/978-3-319-42089-9_13

17. Morano, P., Locurcio, M., Tajani, F., Guarini, M.R.: Urban redevelopment: a multi-criteria valuation model optimized through the fuzzy logic. In: Murgante, B., Misra, S., Rocha, Ana Maria A.C., Torre, C., Rocha, J.G., Falcão, M.I., Taniar, D., Apduhan, Bernady O., Gervasi, O. (eds.) ICCSA 2014. LNCS, vol. 8581, pp. 161–175. Springer, Cham (2014). doi: 10.1007/978-3-319-09150-1_13

18. Bezdek, J.C.: Pattern recognition with fuzzy objective function algorithms. Plenum, New York (1981)

19. North, D.: Institutions, Institutional Changes and Economic Performance. Cambridge University Press, Cambridge (1993)

20. Hogdson, G.M.: What are institutions? J. Econ. Issues 15(1), 1–25 (2006)

21. Pearce, D.W., Mourato, S.: The Economic of Cultural Heritage. Report CSERGE, University College, London (1998)

22. Hercowitz, M.: The Lanzarote Society and Tourism's Metabolism. Universidad Autonoma de Barcelona (2001)

23. Skinner, H.: In search of the genius loci: The essence of a place brand. Mark. Rev. 11(3), 281–292 (2011)

24. Smith, N., Williams, P.: Gentrification of the City. Routledge (2013)

25. Wates, N.: The Community Planning Handbook: How people can shape their cities, towns & villages in any part of the world. Routledge, New York (2014)

Workshop on Emotion Recognition (EMORE 2917)

A Web-Based System
for Emotion Vector Extraction

Valentina Franzoni[1,2], Giulio Biondi[1(⊠)], and Alfredo Milani[1,3]

[1] Department of Mathematics and Computer Science,
University of Perugia, Perugia, Italy
giulio.biondi@studenti.unipg.it, milani@unipg.it
[2] Department of Computer, Control, and Management Engineering,
Sapienza University of Rome, Rome, Italy
franzoni@dis.uniromal.it
[3] Department of Computer Science, Hong Kong Baptist University,
Kowloon Tong, Hong Kong

Abstract. The ability of assessing the affective information content is of increasing interest in applications of computer science, e.g. in human machine interfaces, recommender systems, social robots. In this project, the architecture of a semantic system of emotions is designed and implemented, to quantify the emotional content of short sentences by evaluating and aggregating the semantic proximity of each term in the sentence from the basic emotions defined in a psychological model of emotions (e.g. Ekman, Plutchick, Lovheim). Our model is parametric with respect to the semantic proximity measures, focusing on web-based proximity measures, where data needed to evaluate the proximity can be retrieved from search engines on the Web. To test the performances of the model, a software system has been developed to both collect the statistical data and perform the emotion analysis. The system automatizes the phases of sentence preprocessing, search engine query, results parsing, semantic proximity calculation and the final phase of ranking of emotions.

Keywords: Web document retrieval · Semantic similarity measures · Emotion recognition · Affective data · Affective computing

1 Introduction

Affective computing is a research area of growing interest, in particular the ability of assessing the emotional content can help to improve the effectiveness of applications in a vast amount of scenarios, e.g. analysis of trends and information diffusion in social networks [1–3], recommender systems [4], image recognition [5], semantic context generation [6], social robots and, more generally, in human machine interfaces. Currently, a widely investigated related topic is sentiment analysis, which aim is to produce semantic annotations focusing on classifying the stance (i.e. the sentiment) towards an object, according to its positive, negative or neutral polarity. On the other hand, emotion recognition works at a deeper level, since it is aimed at quantifying the emotional load, with respect to various emotions, conveyed by multimedia objects [7].

© Springer International Publishing AG 2017
O. Gervasi et al. (Eds.): ICCSA 2017, Part III, LNCS 10406, pp. 653–668, 2017.
DOI: 10.1007/978-3-319-62398-6_46

Priming studies carried out by psychologists led to the development of models of emotions, e.g. Ekman, Plutchik and Lovheim [4]. Such models encompass and reduce the wide range of complex human emotions to sets of basic emotions which prove general for all the human beings. Emotion models induce a numerical representation of a multimedia object, consisting in a vector of emotions which quantifies, for each emotion in a model, the associated emotional load with respect to the object. The object can therefore be represented with a Vector Space Model of emotions, i.e. a Vector Emotion Model.

Part of the definition of a framework performing semantic analysis is also the choice of a proper knowledge source. Web-based similarity measures [8–10] evaluate the similarity of terms from the number of occurrences and co-occurrences of terms in a corpus, i.e. the documents indexed by a search engine. Such corpora are constantly updated in the Web, reflecting the natural evolution of knowledge, thus constituting a good basis for real-time applications [11]. Other approaches to similarity [12] are based on ontologies [13]; although ontologies can be very accurate and usually represents meaningful semantic relationships [14, 15], they have a number of drawbacks, since they are manually annotated by experts, often far from completion and reflect the static specialized knowledge of experts, less frequently updated [16].

In this paper, in the second section web-based proximity measures will be explained, in the third and four section models and scales for evaluating emotions will be exposed respectively. In the fifth section, our semantic model of emotion vectors is proposed, with all the phases of implementation and execution. In the sixth section, experimental results are discussed before the conclusions.

2   Web-Based Proximity Measures

Web-based proximity measures [8–10] are used to evaluate the proximity of two terms using Search Engines (SE); the only requirement for a search engine SE to be used for our purpose is to provide the number of hits for a given keyword. The needed data is then easy to obtain by querying the SE; the corpus of indexed documents represents the collective knowledge of the community behind the corpus, and constantly evolves over time in a distributed collaborative way [17]. The number of results obtained is thus time-dependent, resembling the natural process of knowledge evolution. The proposed approach allows the use of any search engine (e.g. Bing, Google, Yahoo) and any semantic proximity measure (e.g. PMI, NGD, Average Confidence, PMING) [18–20], where distances can be transformed into proximities by simple operations of complement and normalization.

Average Confidence (AC) is a symmetric measure, derived from the well known *Confidence* [21] used in rule mining for measuring trust in a rule $X \rightarrow Y$. *Average Confidence* is obtained by mediating the confidences in the rules $w_1 \rightarrow w_2$ and $w_2 \rightarrow w_1$, which describe the logical association between two terms w_1 and w_2.

$$\text{ConfAvg}(w1, w2) = \frac{1}{2}\left(\frac{f(w_1 \wedge w_2)}{f(w_1)} + \frac{f(w_2 \wedge w_1)}{f(w_2)}\right) \tag{1}$$

Pointwise Mutual Information (PMI) [22–24] is a point-to-point measure of association used in statistics and information theory. In this case the *Pointwise Mutual information* between two particular words w_1 and w_2, which appear in webpages indexed by a search engine, is defined as:

$$PMI(w_1, w_2) = \log_2 \frac{P(w_1, w_2)}{P(w_1), P(w_2)} \qquad (2)$$

Normalized Google Distance (NGD) [25, 26] has been introduced as a measure of semantic relation, based on the assumption that two terms w_1 and w_2 describe similar concept if they occur together in a large number of Web documents. The number of documents in which a term appears, i.e. the term frequency, is usually returned by a query to search engine S, and it is used in NGD to define a distance between terms semantically related:

$$NGD(w_1, w_2) = \frac{\max(\log f(w_1), \log f(w_2)) - \log f(w_1, w_2)}{logM - \min(\log f(w_1), \log f(w_2))} \qquad (3)$$

$f(w_1)$, $f(w_2)$ and $f(w_1, w_2)$ are the cardinalities of results returned by S for the query on w_1, w_2, $w_1 \land w_2$ respectively, and M is the number of pages indexed by S.

PMING Distance (PMING) [10, 18] is a weighted convex linear combination consisting of NGD and PMI locally normalized. The weight ρ depends on NGD and PMI differentials. Given two terms w_1 and w_2 in a set of terms or context W, with $f(w_1) \geq f(w_2)$, the PMING distance is a function in *[0,1]* defined as follows:

$$PMING(w_1, w_2) = \rho \left(\log_2 \frac{f(w_1, w_2)M}{F(w_1)f(w_2)\mu_1} \right) + (1 - \rho) \left(\frac{\log f(w_1) - \log f(w_1, w_2)}{(logM - \log f(w_2))\mu_2} \right)$$

$$(4)$$

where μ_1 and μ_2 are constant values depending on the context W, defined as $\mu_1 = max\ PMI(w_1, w_2)$ and $\mu_2 = max\ NGD(w_1, w_2)$, with $(w_1, w_2) \in W$.

In [10, 18] it is shown that PMING outperforms NGD and PMI for clustering and classification of concepts. *Average Confidence* provides the best results for shortest semantic path finding in Wikipedia [21], because the original asymmetric relation *confidence* better reflects the *explanatory relationships*, with respect to other web-based similarity measures.

3 Models of Emotion

In this work three main models of emotions have been considered: the Ekman model, the Plutchik model and the Lovheim model [4]. Other models have been also considered, but without a ground truth they are not suitable for a direct comparison. These models have been developed by psychologists to model the basic emotion that humans feel. The general idea in all these approaches is that all the emotions can be considered as a combination of a set of basic emotions.

The basic emotions of the models implemented are:

$$E_{Ekman.} = [anger, disgust, fear, joy, sadness, surprise] \qquad (5)$$

$$E_{Plutchik} = [anger, anticipation, disgust, fear, joy, sadness, surprise, trust] \qquad (6)$$

$$E_{Lovheim} = [anger, disgust, distress, fear, interest, joy, shame, surprise] \qquad (7)$$

Ekman's model has been developed in the framework of research on facial expressions, which were correctly identified by humans as conveying the basic emotions later included in the model. The Plutchik model, developed within Robert Plutchik's psychological evolutionary theory, is often graphically represented using the *wheel of emotions* or *cone of emotions*, respectively a 2d and 3d graph showing connections between emotions. The more recent model proposed by Lovheim, instead, was developed to establish a relationship between neurotransmitters levels and emotions felt by humans, and can be represented using a cube.

The idea of having emotional dimensions, allow to describe every emotion by a sort of vector of basic emotions. The psychological models do not address issues such as which is the best approach to measure emotions, either quantitative or qualitative, and which scales of values allow operations among those vectors, i.e. emotional processing and algebra.

4 Scales for Statistic Measurement of Behavior

Different statistic measurement scales [27] exist for studying human behaviors. The most common ones are the *Thurstone* and *Guttman* scales, that have main disadvantages for human behavioral evaluation, and *Likert* and *semantic differential* scales, which instead are among the most used for behavioral measurement and for diagnostic tests by human evaluation. In the following paragraph, a brief description of these scales will be given. In general, scales for measuring the behaviors are by rule built of sets of items to which a human is asked to give a feedback, which can be positive or negative. The underlying hypothesis of this approach is that through this feedback it should be possible to measure human behavior with respect to an event or topic along a continuum of goodness/badness of each evaluation point of the scale. A deeper discussion of what is a behavior, and if measuring it makes sense, are not within the scopes of this work, and can be studied in specialized books in the psychology area.

If in some scales of intervals, e.g. temperature scales, is easy to say that a constant unit exists, and that a *zero* arbitrarily chosen can be established, in the empirical system of behavioral models this is not trivial. Also, it is not trivial to proof that the unit does not change during the continuum. It is although possible to perform tests on the distributions of the features, with the aim of elaborating and interpreting results. If in the system it is possible to identify an element of null intensity (i.e. a "zero"), then the system will have all the properties of a numeric system, and transformation rules can be used, including proximity/distance among items.

4.1   Thurstone Scale

Thurstone [28] suggested to measure psychophysical variables with the method of comparative judgements: the probability of a behavioral event (e.g. a crime) can be judged to be more important than another basing on its probability, which becomes a ranking measure. A *Thurstone scale* approximates interval measurements in a straightforward manner, with the assumption that statistical distributions of probability points over a scale are Gaussian. This is debatable sometimes, because this model is non-conformant to the structure of usual behaviors, which distribution can be mono-tone: the relation between the *stimulus* (i.e. the event which generates a behavioral reaction, in this case an emotion) and the *behavior* itself should be linearly growing/decreasing, when a positive/negative *feedback* increases/decreases the good-ness of the object by the point of view of the human evaluator.

4.2   Guttman Scale

The main goal of the *Guttman scale* [29] is to build a scale composed by selected items, where each item is sequential (i.e. if a positive feedback is given to an item, then it means that the positiveness is inherited by all the precedent items in the same set). For example, speaking about age, if a subject says that she is "more than 20 years old", then this sentence constitutes a perfect Guttman scale, because the subject saying "I am more than 20 years old" will positively reply to all the questions about the ages that are smaller than "20". The Guttman scale is part of a family of deterministic scales that includes, among the others, also the *difficulty scale*. The main advantage of the Guttman scale is that it is possible to reproduce the scale starting from the information given by the evaluator. The main problems of the scale are the *numericity* of its construction and the fact that it does not guarantee that the scale is *unidimensional*, therefore sometimes the model is not conformant to real data.

4.3   Likert Scale

Among the three exposed previously, the only measurement scale that has the features needed by psychological test is the Likert scale [30], created in 1932, and still com-monly used. Likert scales are built on a set of feedback sentences where the subject is invited to tell how much she agrees on a statement. Sometimes, scales with 6 positions (where 6 means completely agree, 0 means don't agree at all) or even positions are used, to avoid that the subject stays on a neutral position. The final position will be the summation of the tracks of all the users' evaluations for each item. Ideal evaluations are moderately positive or negative, where an obvious discrimination is not stated. This is the main scale used in recommender systems, however caution is needed when sum-marizing a single value with a Linkert scale.

4.4 Semantic Differential

The Semantic Differential approach [31] uses a set of bipolar scales anchored on each pole through a descriptive adjective on the side of the semantic continuum. It is possible for semantic differential to make comparisons among different objects. Users will evaluate items putting a sign on the position in the scale that can best represent the item, seen as a separation point between the two parts of the scale that it will divide. The final evaluation will be done on the item basing on a differential evaluation on several feedbacks.

Hybrid methods can use a combination of different scales in order to evaluate a set of items/features.

5 Semantic Model of Emotion Vectors

The aim of the project is to develop a model which allows to quantify the emotional content of short sentences, such as news titles. The semantic proximity between each relevant word in a sentence and each emotion in an emotion model is evaluated using web-based similarity measures, which are calculated starting from the number of occurrences and co-occurrences of terms in documents of a corpus.

More formally, let $E_M = \{e_1, \ldots, e_n\}$ emotion model and $\eta_p(w, E_M) = \big(\eta_p(w, e_1), \ldots, \eta_p(w, e_n)\big)$ the Vector Space Model for term w, emotion model E_M and proximity measure p, where each component $\eta_p(w, e_i)$ of the vector represents the proximity between term w and emotion e_i. Then, for sentence:

$$s, \eta_p(s, E_M) = \big(\eta_p(s, e_1), \ldots, \eta_p(s, e_n)\big) \tag{8}$$

will be the vector containing the overall emotional content depending on the whole sentence. Each component $\eta_p(s, e_i)$ is calculated considering the single $\eta_p(w, e_i)$ values. Formally,

$$\eta_p(s, e_i) = AGGR\big(\eta_p(w_1, e_i), \ldots, \eta_p(w_k, e_i)\big) \tag{9}$$

where AGGR can be a parametrical aggregation function [32].

The aggregation functions (9) which have been considered are $AGGR = \{Max, Average\}$. In the first case, the Max aggregation, the components of the sentence emotional vector are obtained by choosing the maximal value for each emotion in the words composing the phrase i.e., it tends to amplify all the emotions. On the other hand, using the second aggregation function points out the average emotional content of the phrase. It is worth noticing that, since the aggregation takes place independently component by component, the resulting emotions vector of the sentence is, in general, different from any constituent term w_i.

5.1   Implementation

The semantic model architecture has been designed on the basis of the key concepts of flexibility, parametrizations and reuse.

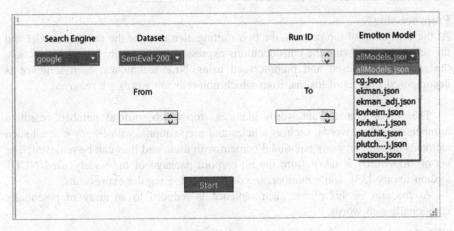

Fig. 1. The program interface. A drop-down menu shows the parametric emotion models, including Ekman, Plutchik and Lovheim.

As shown in the program launcher interface in Fig. 1, the user can provide the values for each of the following parameters:

- *Search engine*: connectors to Google and Bing search interface have been implemented.
- *Dataset*: the user can select the data set on which to perform the analysis; pre-processing may be needed to standardize the data set to the program requirements.
- *Run ID*: a user defined it parameter used as a label for a particular run. Different runs can obtain different result since the search engine statistics varies over time.
- *Emotion model*: the emotion model to be used.
- *From* and *To*: the ids of the first and last sentence to analyze. The analysis can be performed on part of the data set, allowing to distribute the workload among different machines.

The software allows users to specify by a special entry on a configuration file on which proximity measures to perform the analysis among those described above. The Semantic Model is currently implemented in the Python programming language, new proximity measure can be integrated in the code.

The data collection and data analysis phases are supported by completely separated processes; this means that, on one hand, it is possible to gather data from the web and store it to be analyzed later and, on the other hand, analysis can be subsequently performed offline using various proximity metrics without performing web engine searches.

5.2   Data Collection

During the data collection phase, statistics regarding occurrences and co-occurrences of terms are collected from a search engine S. The semantic model can currently gather knowledge from the English localized versions of Google, Bing and Yahoo, while it can be easily extended to query other sources of information.

Preprocessing
At the beginning of the process, the two starting elements are the emotion model and the sentence. Following the considerations expressed in the beginning of this section, the sentence is parsed and preprocessed using NLP techniques; each sentence is decomposed in a set of tokens, from which non-relevant words are removed.

The set of non-relevant words includes stop-words, ordinal numbers, cardinal numbers and short words, such as articles and prepositions, with *length < 3*; all such elements do not carry any emotional content with them and thus can be removed. The set of stop-words is taken from the all-corpora package of the widely used NLTK Python library [33], while numbers are detected using regular expressions.

At the end of this phase, each sentence is reduced to an array of potentially emotionally rich words.

Web Search and results scraping
The set of n words $\{w_1,...,w_n\}$ resulting from the sentence preprocessing step is then used to submit n queries to the search engine where $q_i = w_i$, $i\in[1,n]$.

For each one of the m basic emotions in the given model M, say $E_M = \{e_1,...,e_m\}$, another m queries $q_j = e_j$, $j\in[1,m]$, are submitted and $2*m*n$ queries, each containing a word-emotion pair, are generated where $i\in[1,n]$, $j\in[1,m]$, $q_{ij} = w_i \wedge e_j$ and $q_{ji} = e_j \wedge w_i$. The queries are automatically submitted to the selected search engine and the number of document is scraped from the SERP depending on the page representation used by each particular engine.

Note that from a logical point of view and according to the search engine specifications, the two queries $w_i \wedge e_j$ and $e_j \wedge w_i$ should return identical numbers, i.e. the order among terms should not affect the engine results. The real behavior of search engines is quite different from the specification and give rise to the need of testing both orders for obtaining more reliable values. Moreover, two additional problems may arise during the search phase: banning and results neutrality.

Reproducing a human behavior is fundamental in order to avoid being banned.

A web-driver called Selenium [34] has been used in the script to perform automated browser control. The use of Selenium allows to mimic the behavior of a human user, i.e. opening the search page, typing the query letter by letter in the search box, loading the results page, reading back the content in a search-engine specific way and closing the browser window.

In addition, random delays are introduced between subsequent searches, since humans do not complete queries at the same, constant speed.

Bots that perform automated searches are rapidly banned by Search Engines on a IP address basis; automated queries could be used in a harmful way, to put unnecessary workload on servers, or for Search Engine Optimization (SEO) purposes, to artificially elevate the importance of less famous web-pages. Different types of *banning* can be issued by the search engines, which can return an abnormally low number of hits for a query or no result at all. Despite the adopted precautions, the software can be banned by the search engine; the script is able to detect bans and waits random intervals before trying to perform the query again.

Search engines display customized results to different users basing on various criteria. Users that login with their profile, for example, will receive results that are more consistent with their navigation history and interests. Locations plays also a role in the search phase: users connecting from different places will receive different results, and intermediate caches in the path followed by the data stream could also be relevant.

To minimize this effect, and guarantee *search neutrality*, the data collection phase should be performed by computers connected through the same network, with no cached data and empty browser profiles; this result is easily achieved using Selenium which, by default, opens a new, totally blank profile each time a new browser window is opened.

After all the data for a sentence has been successfully collected, the results are saved in three JSON files, containing respectively occurrences for the emotion keywords, for the sentence words and for pairs, both emotion-word and word-emotion. The number of queries to be performed is function of the emotion model and the sentence: let n number of words in the sentence after preprocessing and m the number of emotions in the emotion model, the number n_q of queries is $n_q = n+m + 2*n*m$. This leads to a rapid increase of the time needed for the analysis, which depends on the size of the data set and the structure of the single elements in the data set.

Calculations have been made to determine the number of machines needed to perform the collection phase in the desired restricted timeframe, which had been set to one day and a half. This is fundamental, since results in a search engine tend to change over time, and data collected in too long periods may prove inconsistent; some keywords can show a peak of occurrences following a particular event in the real world.

5.3   Data Analysis and Emotion Ranking

In the second phase, web-based similarity measures values are calculated for each word in a sentence and each emotion in a model, and the results are stored in a dictionary. The implemented set of measures included Confidence, PMI, NGD, and PMING (see functions (1), (2), (3), (4) in Sect. 2).

The first three measures can be calculated in parallel in one loop, while PMING, in this implementation, requires the maximum value of NGD and PMI at the sentence level. Therefore, a second loop is necessary in order to calculate PMING.

When the single values for each emotion-word pair have been calculated, the set of words in the sentence are aggregated [32] using the AVERAGE and MAX functions (see function (9) in Sect. 5), thus inducing a natural sentence-level emotion ranking. At the end of the analysis, the script saves the results; for each sentence, the dictionary is dumped in a JSON file. The script also outputs some human-readable CSV files, containing aggregate emotion data at a word level and at sentence-level.

6 Experiments and Results

6.1 Data Set

For the preliminary experiments, the SemEval-2007 data set [35] was chosen. SemEval-2007 is built by Istituto per la ricerca scientifica e tecnologica Trento, Italy, and includes 250 news titles and documents from the Web. The choice was made according to two main criteria:

- *Generality*: being SemEval-2007 a general news title dataset, several contexts, with possibly different involved emotions are touched.
- *Ground truth availability*: SemEval-2007 provides human evaluations of the emotional content of sentences; such figures can be used as a benchmark to assess the performance of the SEMO model.
  The data is provided on a Likert scale; each emotion was evaluated by humans in the [0–100] range, with 0 meaning total absence of the emotion and 100 maximum presence. The set of emotions is the one of the Ekman model.

Any other data set of objects which can be represented by emotion vectors can be analyzed.

6.2 Evaluation Criteria

The annotation performed by humans provided with the data set, and the emotion rankings induced by the annotations, constitute a ground truth against which to compare the results of the Semantic Model. Three correlation coefficients have been calculated, in order to assess the performances of the model:

- *Spearman ρ*, is a measure of rank correlation returning a value in the interval *[0,1]*, where the higher the value, the better the performance of the results. Spearman ρ assesses how well the relationship between variables can be described using a monotonic function. It measures the *difference per rank*.
- *Kendall τ*, measures the ordinal association A τ test is a non-parametric hypothesis test for statistical dependence based on the τ coefficient. the Kendall correlation between two variables will be high when observations have a similar rank, i.e. with similar relative positions (or identical for a correlation of 1,) between the two variables, and low when observations have a dissimilar rank (i.e. totally different, for a correlation of −1) between the two variables. The Kendall τ correlation is not affected by the difference of values between the ranks are but only by the *relative rank positions of the observation*.

Both Kendall's τ and Spearman's ρ can be formulated as special cases of the more general *Pearson r*.

- *Pearson r*, measuring the *co-variance of a set of variables*, calculated two by two, divided by the product of their standard deviations. Pearson *r* returns a value ranging in *[0,1]*, where 1 corresponds to highest performance, i.e. identical covariance. Since set having a similar co-variance are similar in Pearson r, it can be straight forwardly applied as evaluation measure to the vector space.
- *Main sentence emotion*, these criteria evaluates if the model is able to determine the main emotion in a sentence with respect to the SemEval-2007 ground truth. The *main emotion* is simply defined as the emotion with the highest rank in the sentence emotion vector.

6.3   Word-Level Experiments

A preliminary evaluation has been performed at a word level, considering the emotional load a term carries for each emotion. The proximity between each term and each emotion is expressed by a normalized value in the [0,1] range. No ground truth is available to compare results, but previous experiments in the context extraction [36, 37] and set distance evaluation [5] fields show that the results can be accepted as sufficiently representative of the knowledge of the Web. The aggregation of results, on Average and Max, will allow to compensate against poor conditions of single words, which measurement may not properly fit the intuitive evaluation of the reader. Results at this level can be evaluated on a classification or clustering base, using accuracy, recall and F1 with respect the data set ground truth.

6.4   Sentence-Level Experiments

In this experiment level, the emotion vector for each sentence is built using the selected proximity measure and search engine, then according to the evaluation criteria, the Spearman, Kendall and Pearson coefficients are calculated for each sentence and compared to the ground truth. The ground truth is also used to compare the main sentence sentiment determined by SEMO in the given setting with respect to the main sentiment provided in the data set.

In Table 1, the resulting emotion vectors for some sentences in the dataset are shown: in each row, it is shown the vector space for the sentence, see Table 2 for decoding the sentence id. In Table 2, the correlation between our results and the ground truth is shown for the same sample from the data set, where for each sentence the ranking correlation values are shown using Kendall τ, Spearman ρ, and Pearson r.

Table 1. Example of the emotion vector spaces for average confidence

ID	Anger	Disgust	Fear	Joy	Sadness	Surprise
22	0.163	0.023	0.370	0.187	0.034	0.224
109	0.093	0.029	0.292	0.302	0.063	0.220
140	0.139	0.031	0.290	0.326	0.034	0.181
154	0.164	0.044	0.365	0.198	0.060	0.169
176	0.175	0.039	0.240	0.293	0.048	0.204
220	0.154	0.032	0.340	0.263	0.042	0.169

Table 2. Correlation values for the emotion vector space Average Confidence

ID	Sentence text	Pearson	Spearman	Kendall
22	*Kidnapped AP photographer freed in Gaza*	0.793	0.886	0.733
109	*The sweet tune of an anniversary*	0.554	0.655	0.577
140	*German Chief Forges Accord on Financing Health Care*	0.643	0.676	0.602
154	*An Old Letter Casts Doubts on Iran's Goal for Uranium*	0.560	0.759	0.596
176	*In God's Name: Religion-Based Tax Breaks: Housing to Paychecks to Books*	0.615	0.621	0.548
220	*Kentucky wants to ban alcohol inhalers*	0.491	0.759	0.596

It is possible to give a graphical visualization of the emotional load of a sentence using the data produced by the semantic model. In Fig. 2, a radar graph shows the per-word emotional load of sentence n.22 of the SemEval-2007 dataset, i.e. the news title: *"Kidnapped AP photographer freed in Gaza"*. In the radar, each color corresponds to a term obtained after preprocessing.

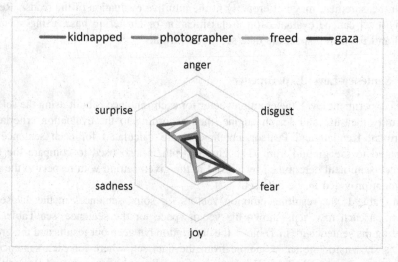

Fig. 2. Visualization of title n.22 using a Radar Graph for $E = E_{Ekman}$. and $\eta = AvgConf$

Figure 3 reports the aggregated results of Average Confidence, PMI and PMING showing the ability of the semantic model of determining the main emotion in the sentence with respect to the ground truth provided by SemEval-2007 [35] data set. Despite of the limited scope of the preliminary experiments, which are still ongoing, it is worth noticing that PMING similarity confirms the improvement of performance over its pure PMI component.

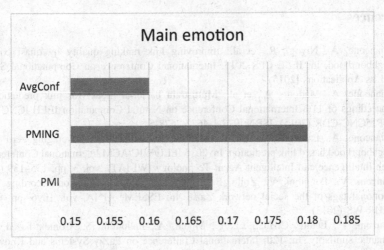

Fig. 3. Percentage of correct guesses for the first emotion

7 Conclusions

In this work, we have proposed a Semantic Model for ranking emotions in sentences using web-based semantic proximity measures and presented a system which implements it using various emotion models and proximity measures. The emotional content of a sentence is evaluated by aggregating the data corresponding to each of its constituent terms; each term is associated to an emotion vector, where each component contains the calculated proximity measure value between the term and an emotion in the chosen emotion model. The emotion models supported by SEMO implementation include Ekman, Plutchik and Lovheim [4] and the proximity measures *NGD, Average Confidence, PMI, PMING* [8, 9, 10]. Preliminary experiments on Ekman's model with PMI, Average Confidence, and PMING show that the approach provides promising results both on word-level and sentence-level, evaluated with respect to Spearman's, Kendall's, and Pearson's coefficients and a general ability of determining the main emotion of the sentence. Future experiments will be done to systematically assess the performance of the approach in the complete SemEval-2007 database, and for other emotion models and search engines.

Acknowledgements. Authors thank Mr. Ka Ho Tam, MSc and Dr. Yuanxi Li, PhD of the Hong Kong Baptist University, for the useful support and revision of the first version before submission.

References

1. Chiancone, A., Niyogi, R., et al.: Improving link ranking quality by quasi common neighbourhood. In: IEEE CPS 2015, International Conference on Computational Science and Its Applications (2015)
2. Chiancone, A., Madotto, A., et al.: Multistrain bacterial model for link prediction. In: Proceedings of 11th International Conference on Natural Computation IEEE ICNC 2015. CFP15CNC-CDR (2015). ISBN: 978-1-4673-7678-5
3. Chiancone, A., Franzoni, V., Li, Y., Markov, K., Milani, A.: Leveraging zero tail in neighbourhood based link prediction. In: 2015 IEEE/WIC/ACM International Conference on Web Intelligence and Intelligent Agent Technology (WI-IAT), vol. 3, pp. 135–139 (2015)
4. Franzoni, V., Poggioni, V., Zollo, F.: Automated book classification according to the emotional tags of the social network Zazie. In: ESSEM, AI*IA, vol. 1096, pp. 83–94. CEUR-WS (2013)
5. Franzoni, V., Leung, C.H.C., Li, Y., Milani, A., Pallottelli, S.: Context-based image semantic similarity. In: 12th International Conference on Fuzzy Systems and Knowledge Discovery (FSKD), Zhangjiajie, pp. 1280–1284 (2015)
6. Franzoni, V., Milani, A.: Context extraction by multi-path traces in semantic networks, In: CEUR-WS, Proceedings of RR 2015 Doctoral Consortium, Berlin (2015)
7. Deng, J.J., Leung, C.H.C., Milani, A., Chen, L.: Emotional states associated with music: classification, prediction of changes, and consideration in recommendation. ACM Trans. Interact. Intell. Syst. 5, 4 (2015)
8. Leung, C.H.C., Li, Y., Milani, A., Franzoni, V.: Collective evolutionary concept distance based query expansion for effective web document retrieval. In: Murgante, B., Misra, S., Carlini, M., Torre, C.M., Nguyen, H.-Q., Taniar, D., Apduhan, B.O., Gervasi, O. (eds.) ICCSA 2013. LNCS, vol. 7974, pp. 657–672. Springer, Heidelberg (2013). doi:10.1007/978-3-642-39649-6_47
9. Matsuo, Y., Sakaki, T., Uchiyama, K., Ishizuka, M.: Graph-based word clustering using a web search engine. University of Tokio (2006)
10. Franzoni, V., Milani, A.: A semantic comparison of clustering algorithms for the evaluation of web-based similarity measures. In: Gervasi, O., et al. (eds.) ICCSA 2016. LNCS, vol. 9790, pp. 438–452. Springer, Cham (2016). doi:10.1007/978-3-319-42092-9_34
11. Wu, L., Hua, X.S., Yu, N., Ma, W.Y., Li, S.: Flickr Distance. Microsoft Research Asia, Beijing (2008)
12. Budanitsky, A., Hirst, G.: Semantic distance in wordnet: an experimental, application-oriented evaluation of five measures. In: Proceedings of Workshop on WordNet and Other Lexical Resources, Pittsburgh, PA, USA, p. 641. North American Chapter of the Association for Computational Linguistics (2001)
13. Miller, G.A., Beckwith, R., Fellbaum, C., Gross, D., Miller, K.: Introduction to wordnet: an on-line lexical database (1993)
14. Tasso, S., Pallottelli, S., Ferroni, M., Bastianini, R., Laganà, A.: Taxonomy management in a federation of distributed repositories: a chemistry use case. In: Murgante, B., Gervasi, O., Misra, S., Nedjah, N., Rocha, A.M.C., Taniar, D., Apduhan, B.O. (eds.) ICCSA 2012. LNCS, vol. 7333, pp. 358–370. Springer, Heidelberg (2012). doi:10.1007/978-3-642-31125-3_28
15. Tasso, S., Pallottelli, S., Bastianini, R., Lagana, A.: federation of distributed and collaborative repositories and its application on science learning objects. In: Murgante, B., Gervasi, O., Iglesias, A., Taniar, D., Apduhan, B.O. (eds.) ICCSA 2011. LNCS, vol. 6784, pp. 466–478. Springer, Heidelberg (2011). doi:10.1007/978-3-642-21931-3_36

16. Newman, M.E.J.: Fast Algorithm for Detecting Community Structure in Networks. University of Michigan, Ann Arbor (2003)

17. Pallottelli, S., Tasso, S., Pannacci, N., Costantini, A., Lago, N.F.: Distributed and collaborative learning objects repositories on grid networks. In: Taniar, D., Gervasi, O., Murgante, B., Pardede, E., Apduhan, B.O. (eds.) ICCSA 2010. LNCS, vol. 6019, pp. 29–40. Springer, Heidelberg (2010). doi:10.1007/978-3-642-12189-0_3

18. Franzoni, V., Milani, A.: PMING distance: a collaborative semantic proximity measure. In: WI–IAT, vol. 2, pp. 442–449. IEEE/WIC/ACM (2012)

19. Franzoni, V., Milani, A.: Heuristic semantic walk. In: Murgante, B., Misra, S., Carlini, M., Torre, C.M., Nguyen, H.-Q., Taniar, D., Apduhan, B.O., Gervasi, O. (eds.) ICCSA 2013. LNCS, vol. 7974, pp. 643–656. Springer, Heidelberg (2013). doi:10.1007/978-3-642-39649-6_46

20. Franzoni, V., Milani, A., Pallottelli, S.: Multi-path traces in semantic graphs for latent knowledge elicitation. In: Proceedings of 11th International Conference on Natural Computation, IEEE ICNC (2015). ISBN: 978-1-4673-7678-5

21. Franzoni, V., Milani, A.: Heuristic semantic walk for concept chaining in collaborative networks. Int. J. Web Inf. Syst. **10**(1), 85–103 (2014)

22. Church, K.W., Hanks, P.: Word association norms, mutual information and lexicography. In: ACL, p. 27 (1989)

23. Turney P.: Mining the web for synonyms: PMI versus LSA on TEOFL. In: Proceedings of ECML (2001)

24. Lin, J.: Divergence measures based on the Shannon entropy. IEEE Trans. Inf. Theor. **37**(1), 145–151 (1991)

25. Cilibrasi, R., Vitanyi, P.: The Google Similarity Distance. ArXiv.org (2004)

26. Joyce, J.M.: Kullback-leibler divergence. In: Lovric, M. (ed.) International Encyclopedia of Statistical Science. Springer (2011)

27. Manning, D., Schutze, H.: Foundations of Statistical Natural Language Processing. The MIT Press, London (2002)

28. Thurstone, L.: Attitudes can be measured. Am. J. Sociol. **33**, 529–554 (1928)

29. Stouffer, S.A., Guttman, L., et al.: Measurement and prediction. In: Studies in Social Psychology in World War II, vol. 4. Princeton University Press (1950)

30. Bartholomeu, D., Silva, M., Montiel, J.: Improving the likert scale of the children's social skills test by means of rasch model. Psychology **7**, 820–828 (2016)

31. Osgood, C.E., Suci, G., Tannenbaum, P.: The Measurement of Meaning. University of Illinois Press, Urbana (1957)

32. Franzoni, V., Leung, Clement H.C., Li, Y., Mengoni, P., Milani, A.: Set similarity measures for images based on collective knowledge. In: Gervasi, O., Murgante, B., Misra, S., Gavrilova, M.L., Rocha, A.M.A.C., Torre, C., Taniar, D., Apduhan, B.O. (eds.) ICCSA 2015. LNCS, vol. 9155, pp. 408–417. Springer, Cham (2015). doi:10.1007/978-3-319-21404-7_30

33. Bird, S., Loper, E., Klein, E.: Natural Language Processing with Python. O'Reilly Media Inc., Sebastopol (2009)

34. http://www.seleniumhq.org/projects/webdriver

35. Strapparava, C., Mihalcea, R.: SemEval-2007 task 14: affective text. In: Proceedings of the 4th International Workshop on Semantic Evaluations (SemEval 2007), pp. 70–74. Association for Computational Linguistics, Stroudsburg, PA, USA (2007)

36. Franzoni, V., Milani, A.: Semantic context extraction from collaborative networks. In: IEEE International Conference on Computer Supported Cooperative Work in Design, CSCWD 2015. IEEE Press (2015)
37. Franzoni, V., Milani, A.: A pheromone-like model for semantic context extraction from collaborative networks. In: 2015 IEEE/WIC/ACM International Conference on Web Intelligence and Intelligent Agent Technology (WI-IAT), Singapore, pp. 540–547. IEEE Press (2015)

Ontology-Based Sentiment Analysis
of Kazakh Sentences

Banu Yergesh[1(✉)], Gulmira Bekmanova[1], Altynbek Sharipbay[1],
and Manas Yergesh[2]

[1] L.N.Gumilyov Eurasian National University, Astana, Kazakhstan
b.yergesh@gmail.com, gulmira-r@yandex.kz,
sharalt@mail.ru
[2] Kazakh University of Technology and Business, Astana, Kazakhstan
shymkent90@mail.ru

Abstract. Sentiment analysis one of the important and interesting task in natural languages. A number of resources and tools have been developed for sentiment analysis of English, Turkish, Russian and other languages. Unfortunately, there was no data and tools available for sentiment analysis in Kazakh. The Dictionary of Kazakh sentiment words has been created during the study. In this work we described the rule-based method using dictionary for sentiment analysis of texts in the Kazakh language, based on the morphological rules and ontological model. Ontological model for rule extraction that determines sentiment was built. Our rule based method achieves 83% accuracy for simple sentences.

Keywords: Sentiment analysis · Kazakh language · Classification · Production rules · Rule-based method · Morphological rules · Ontology

1 Introduction

Sentiment analysis or opinion mining in natural languages is one of the fastest growing technologies of natural language processing. Sentiment analysis, also called opinion mining, is the field of study that analyzes people's opinions, sentiments, evaluations, appraisals, attitudes, and emotions towards entities such as products, services, organizations, individuals, issues, events, topics, and their attributes [1]. Sentiment analysis is considered as a major topic for companies, enterprises who might be interested in identifying opportunities within a new market. Emotions and opinions play a significant role in people's everyday life and their decision-making process. The sentiment analysis tools have been widely accepted in the commercial and social fields. It can be noticed that the number of blogs, reviews, forums, web pages of social networks are growing by the day in worldwide network. Therefore, manual processing such a big amount of data becomes impossible, thus different linguistic and machine learning methods are used [1–11]. Sentiment analysis had been applied on various levels, starting from the whole text level, then going towards the sentence and/or phrase and aspect levels.

© Springer International Publishing AG 2017
O. Gervasi et al. (Eds.): ICCSA 2017, Part III, LNCS 10406, pp. 669–677, 2017.
DOI: 10.1007/978-3-319-62398-6_47

For English a lot of resources and systems have been developed for sentiment analysis of texts by now [1, 2]. A number of researches are conducting on sentiment analysis for Russian [3, 5], Turkish [8–10], Spanish [11], Arabic [12, 13] and other languages. For Spanish [11] proposed an approach to the subjectivity detection on Twitter micro texts that explores the uses of the structured information of the social network framework. For Arabic proposed a semantic approach to discover user attitudes and business insights from Arabic social media by building an Arabic Sentiment Ontology that contains groups of words that express different sentiments in different dialects [13].

The sentiment analysis of texts written in Kazakh language has been studied little. Here some works on sentiment analysis for dual languages, Kazakh and Russian [14, 15]. In [14] described modern approaches of solving the task of sentiment analysis of the news articles in Kazakh and Russian languages by using deep recurrent neural networks. Thereby, research shows that good results can be achieved even without knowing linguistic features of particular language. And here also proposed a deep neural network model that uses bilingual word embedding to effectively solve sentiment classification problem for a given pair of languages. They apply this approach to two corpora of two different language pairs: English-Russian and Russian-Kazakh. It is shown here how to train a classifier in one language and predict in another. This approach achieves 73% accuracy for English and 74% accuracy for Russian. For Kazakh sentiment analysis, propose a baseline method, that achieves 60% accuracy; and a method to learn bilingual embedding from a large unlabeled corpus using a bilingual word pairs [15].

Computers are beginning to acquire the ability to recognize emotions. In 1995 Rosalind W. Picard [16] reported about key issues in "affective computing", computing that relates to, arises from, or influences emotions. Since then, a lot of research has been carried out. Many studies are related to the emotion recognition from texts. [17] suggest an approach for emotion recognition using web-based similarity. Here also proposed emotion ranking model, based on semantic proximity measures, e.g. Confidence, PMI, PMING.

Today, there are a lot of mobile devices, such as smart phones, tablets, cameras and PC around the world. Also, a lot of applications for audio, video posting, chats are implementing day by day. Accordingly, text, audio and video information are increasing. Because of this, the task of extracting emotion from text, image, audio and video information becomes an important task.

The emotion is extracting not only from texts, but also from audio and video content [18, 19], from images [20]. Such applications can be used in as social media marketing, brand positioning, election and financial prediction.

This work can be considered as an introduction and an attempt to apply the linguistic approach for sentiment analysis of the texts written in the Kazakh language. For that reason, this paper describes the rule-based methods used in sentiment analysis and approaches used to determine the sentiment of Kazakhs sentences by formalizing the morphological rules.

2 The Main Methods Use in Sentiment Analysis

According to the work described in [1] the automatic analysis of a sentiment of texts in the natural language carried out by applying the methods such as machine learning methods and lexicon-based methods (Fig. 1).

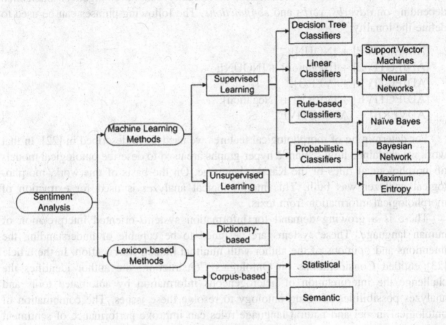

Fig. 1. Sentiment analysis methods

The sentiment analyses of tonality based on machine learning methods are "trained" on a collection of pre-marked texts. These methods include a support vector machine (SVM), logistic regression, naive Bayes classifier, maximum entropy, k nearest neighbor (k-NN) and other methods.

Lexicon-based methods usually use morphological analysis, specifically designed sentiment dictionaries of words and phrases as well as set of linguistic rules and corpora [21].

3 Determining the Sentiment of Phrases in Kazakh Language

Determination of sentiment of sentences in Kazakh language is based on a classification of texts by two features: positive (1) and negative (0). For this purpose, a dictionary of sentiment words was developed which participates in determining the tonality of the text. In Kazakh language the tonality of a phrase is given by parts of speech as an adjective, verb and adverb. After that, morphological rules of parts of speech are formalized that are involved in determining the tonality of the sentence:

words and/or phrases are extracted from the sentence, which contains evaluative words. The overall sentiment of the text is evaluated according to the sentence/phrase tonality.

Adjectives mainly determine the semantic orientation (tonality) of the text, and the noun plays a role of an aspect (object) of discussion. From the extracted phrases we can determine the tonality of the whole text. The tonality of evaluative words might depend on the context and subject area. Also, the tonality can be changed or intensified depending on *adverbs*, *verbs* and *conjunctions*. The following phrases can be used to define the tonality:

[ADJECTIVE] + [NOUN];
[ADJECTIVE] + [Negation] + [NOUN];
[ADJECTIVE] + [VERB];
[ADJECTIVE] + [VERV] + [Negation];
[ADVERB] + [ADJECTIVE].

For determining of morphological features we used work described in [22]. In that work we explained how semantic hyper-graphs are used to describe ontological models of morphological rules of the Kazakh language. On the basis of this work, morphological analyzer was built. This morphological analyzer is used for extraction of morphological information from texts.

There is a growing demand for information systems-oriented interpretation of human language. These systems are designed to be capable of understanding the intentions and opinions of the author with minimal human intervention. In the article [23] entitled Considerations on Ontologies Construction, the author identifies the challenge the interpretation of heterogeneous information by automated tools and analyzes possibilities of using ontology to resolve these issues. The combination of ontological model and natural language rules can improve performance of sentiment analysis.

Ontology is a powerful and widely used tool to model relationships between objects belonging to various subject fields. In the context of computer and information sciences, an ontology defines a set of representational primitives with which to model a domain of knowledge or discourse. The representational primitives are typically classes (or sets), attributes (or properties), and relationships (or relations among class members). The definitions of the representational primitives include information about their meaning and constraints on their logically consistent application.

This formalism determines ontology O as triple (V, R, K), where V is a set of classes of a given subject field, R is a set of relationships between these classes, and K is a set of attributes in the domain [24].

In Fig. 2 presented part of ontology model for determining the sentiment of phrases in the Kazakh. For example, if we have some collocation, it can consist of adjective and noun (verb). The ontology formalism - O (*adjective, has_polarity, adjective with positive (negative) orientation*); O (*collocation, has_polarity, sentiment*).

Ontology has allowed us to present in a model form of phrase with sentiment for further use of OWL in RDF schema. In addition, construction of semantic queries in SPARQL language based on the rule presented in Part 4.

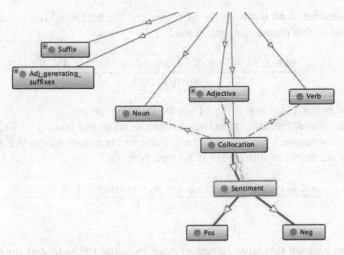

Fig. 2. Ontology for determine the sentiment of the collocation

4   Rules Used to Define the Sentiment

Here we formalized rules for defining the phrases sentiment in the Kazakh language. They described using production rules. For that, we introduce the following meta notations (Table 1).

Table 1. Meta notations

Notation	Definition
W	Set of words of language
L	Set of sentences of language
A	Set of adjectives
N	Set of noun words
V	Set of verbs
V^{-1}	Set of verbs with negative form
D	Set of superlative and comparative adverbs
sent	Predicate of sentiment
¬	Operation of negation words emes/zhok (not/no)
·	Operation of concatenation
$\zeta,\ldots,\xi$	Any string of words, including empty

The production rules for determining the sentiment of an adjective and noun phrases are given below in the sequential form $\frac{A}{B}$, where A - antecedent, B - consequent. In [25] we described some rules. Here we want to represent more rules for determining the sentiment of phrases.

1. If the extracted word is a negative adjective, and the next word is a noun, then the sentiment of this phrase is negative too.

$$\frac{\omega \in L, \omega = \zeta \cdot \alpha \cdot \beta \cdot \xi, \alpha \in A, sent(a) = 0, \beta \in N}{sent(\omega) = 0}$$

here and below ζ, ξ - any string of words, including empty.
Example, nashar (negative adjective) kalam (noun) (a bad pencil) $\rightarrow$ NEG

2. If there is a negation word "emes" (not) between the negative adjective and noun, then the sentiment of this phrase is become positive.

$$\frac{\omega \in L, \omega = \zeta \cdot \alpha \cdot \beta \cdot \gamma \cdot \xi, \alpha \in A, sent(a) = 0, \beta = \neg, \gamma \in N}{sent(\omega) = 1}$$

Results
Example, zhaman (negative adjective) emes (negation) kino (noun) (movie is not bad) $\rightarrow$ POS
The production rules for defining the sentiment of an adjective and verb phrases are following:

3. If an adjective follows by a verb phrase, then the word coming after the verb should be checked. If the adjective is negative and there is a negation word (emes/zhok (not)) after verb, then the sentiment of this phrase is positive.

$$\frac{\omega \in L, \omega = \zeta \cdot \alpha \cdot \beta \cdot \gamma \cdot \xi, \alpha \in A, sent(a) = 0, \beta \in V, \gamma = \neg}{sent(\omega) = 1}$$

Example, damsiz (negative adjective) bolgan (verb) emes/zhok (negation) (was not tasteless) $\rightarrow$ POS.

4. If an adjective follows by a verb phrase, then the word coming after the verb should be checked. If the adjective is positive and there is a negation word (emes/zhok (not)) after verb, then the sentiment of this phrase is negative.

$$\frac{\omega \in L, \omega = \zeta \cdot \alpha \cdot \beta \cdot \gamma \cdot \xi, \alpha \in A, sent(a) = 1, \beta \in V, \gamma = \neg}{sent(\omega) = 0}$$

Example, damdi (positive adjective) bolgan (verb) zhok (negation) (it was not tasty) $\rightarrow$ NEG.

5. If the superlative or comparative adverbs comes before adjective with negative sentiment, then the sentiment of this phrase is negative.

$$\frac{\omega \in L, \omega = \zeta \cdot \alpha \cdot \beta \cdot \xi, \alpha \in D, \beta \in A, sent(\beta) = 0}{sent(\omega) = 0}$$

For example, tym (adverb) ashy (negative adjective) (too spicy) $\rightarrow$ NEG.

5 Results

Also implemented system based on described rules for Kazakh language. Here the fragment of implemented program is given (Fig. 3).

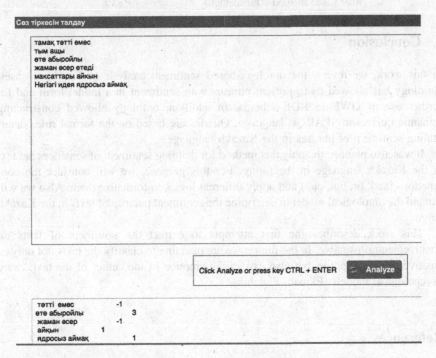

Fig. 3. Program fragment. Example for collocations [adjective] + [verb], [adjective] + [noun], [adverb] + [adjective]

Explanation for Fig. 3.: Тамақ тәтті емес (the meal is not tasty), тым ащы (too spicy), өте абыройлы (highly respected), жаман әсер етеді (bad influences), мақсаттары айқын (have clear objectives), негізгі идея ядросыз аймақ (main idea is a place without nuclear).

In addition, the sentiment might also depend on the conjunctions between words or sentences

– if there are connecting conjunctions, the sentiment does not change;
– if between words or sentences comes dividing or adversative conjunctions, then semantic orientation of sentence changes to opposite. For example, bul kampit tatti, birak katty eken (this candy is tasty, but hard).

Here we compare the methods implemented for the Kazakh language (Table 2). Here we can notice that our method gives good results.

Table 2. Results

Method	Accuracy
Long-Short Term Memory (LSTM) [14]	86.3%
Deep learning model for bilingual sentiment [15]	60%
Rule based method (Our method)	83%

6 Conclusion

In this work, we review the ontology-based sentiment analysis of Kazakh phrases. Ontology has allowed us to present phrases with sentiment in a model form and for further use of OWL in RDF schema. In addition, ontology allowed constructing semantic queries in SPARQL language. Queries are based on the formal rules determining sentiment of phrases in the Kazakh language.

It was also planned to apply this method for defining sentiment of sentences ant text in the Kazakh language in the future. For this purpose, we will consider the conjunctions (and, or, but, etc.) and apply different logics to formalize them. Also we will expand the ontological model to determine the sentiment polarity of texts in the Kazakh language.

This work describes the first attempts to extract the sentiment of texts on positive/neutral/negative. In the future, we are planning to classify the texts not only as positive/neutral/negative, but also extract the emotion of the author of the text, using psychological models (Ekman, Plutchik).

References

1. Liu, B.: Sentiment Analysis and Opinion Mining. Morgan & Claypool Publishers, San Rafael (2012)
2. Pang, B., Lee, L.: Opinion mining and sentiment analysis. In: Foundations and Trends® in Information Retrieval. Now Publishers (2008)
3. Loukachevitch, N.V., Chetviorkin, I.I.: Evaluating sentiment analysis systems in Russian. Artif. Intell. Decis. Mak. **1**, 25–33 (2014). (in Russian)
4. Chetviorkin, I., Braslavskiy, P., Loukachevich, N.: Sentiment analysis track at ROMIP 2011. In: Proceedings of International Conference Dialog-2012, vol. 2, pp. 1–14 (2012)
5. Chetvirokin, I., Loukachevitch, N.: Sentiment analysis track at ROMIP 2012. In: Proceedings of International Conference Dialog-2013, vol. 2, pp. 40–50 (2013)
6. Chetviorkin, I., Loukachevitch, N.: Extraction of Russian sentiment lexicon for product meta-domain. In: Proceedings of COLING 2012, pp. 593–610 (2012)
7. Steinberger, J., Lenkova, P., Ebrahim, M., Ehrmann, M., Hurriyetogly, A., Kabadjov, M., Steinberger, R., Tanev, H., Zavarella, V., Vazquez, S.: Creating sentiment dictionaries via triangulation. In: Proceedings of the 2nd Workshop on Computational Approaches to Subjectivity and Sentiment Analysis, ACL-HLT, pp. 28–36 (2011)
8. Akba, F., Uçan, A., Sezer, EA., Sever, H.: Assessment of feature selection metrics for sentiment analyses: Turkish movie reviews. In: Proceedings of the 8th European Conference on Data Mining, pp. 180–184 (2014)

9. Yıldırım, E., Çetin, F., Eryiğit, G., Temel, T.: The impact of NLP on Turkish sentiment analysis. In: Proceedings of the TURKLANG 2014 International Conference on Turkic Language Processing, Istanbul (2014)

10. Eryiğit, G., Çetin, F., Yanık, M., Temel, T., Çiçekli, I.: TURKSENT: a sentiment annotation tool for social media. In: Proceedings of the 7th Linguistic Annotation Workshop & Interoperability with Discourse, ACL 2013, Sofia, Bulgaria (2013)

11. Sixto, J., Almeida, A., López-de-Ipiña, D.: An approach to subjectivity detection on Twitter using the structured information. In: Nguyen, N.-T., Manolopoulos, Y., Iliadis, L., Trawiński, B. (eds.) ICCCI 2016. LNCS, vol. 9875, pp. 121–130. Springer, Cham (2016). doi:10.1007/978-3-319-45243-2_11

12. Mohammad, S., Salameh, M., Kiritchenko, S.: Sentiment lexicons for Arabic social media. In: Proceedings of the 10th Edition of the Language Resources and Evaluation Conference, Portorož, Slovenia (2016)

13. Tartir, S., Abdul-Nabi, I.: Semantic sentiment analysis in Arabic social media. J. King Saud Univ. Comput. Inf. Sci. 29(2), 229–233 (2016)

14. Sakenovich, N.S., Zharmagambetov, A.S.: On one approach of solving sentiment analysis task for Kazakh and Russian languages using deep learning. In: Nguyen, N.-T., Manolopoulos, Y., Iliadis, L., Trawiński, B. (eds.) ICCCI 2016. LNCS, vol. 9876, pp. 537–545. Springer, Cham (2016). doi:10.1007/978-3-319-45246-3_51

15. Abdullin, Y.B., Ivanov, V.V.: Deep learning model for bilingual sentiment classification of short texts. Sci. Tech. J. Inf. Technol. Mech. Optics 17(1), 129–136 (2017)

16. Picard, R.W.: Affective computing. MIT Media Laboratory Perceptual Computing Section Technical Report No. 321. Media Lab. Massachusetts Institute of Technology, Cambridge Univ. (1995)

17. Biondi, G., Franzoni, V., Li, Y., Milani, A.: Web-based similarity for emotion recognition in web objects. In: Proceedings - 9th IEEE/ACM International Conference on Utility and Cloud Computing, UCC 2016, pp. 327–332 (2016)

18. Poria, S., Chaturvedi, I., Cambria, E., Hussain, A.: Convolutional MKL based multimodal emotion recognition and sentiment analysis. In: Proceedings - IEEE International Conference on Data Mining, ICDM, art. no. 7837868, pp. 439–448 (2017)

19. Arunnehru, J., Kalaiselvi Geetha, M.: Automatic human emotion recognition in surveillance video. In: Dey, N., Santhi, V. (eds.) Intelligent Techniques in Signal Processing for Multimedia Security. SCI, vol. 660, pp. 321–342. Springer, Cham (2017). doi:10.1007/978-3-319-44790-2_15

20. Jiang, R., Ho, A.T.S., Cheheb, I., Al-Maadeed, N., Al-Maadeed, S., Bouridane, A.: Emotion recognition from scrambled facial images via many graph embedding. Pattern Recogn. 67, 245–251 (2017)

21. Taboada, M., Brooke, J., Tofiloski, M., Voll, K., Stede, M.: Lexicon-based methods for sentiment analysis. Comput. Linguist. 37(2), 267–307 (2011)

22. Yergesh, B., Mukanova, A., Sharipbay, A., Bekmanova, G., Razakhova, B.: Semantic hyper-graph based representation of nouns in the Kazakh language. Computacion y Sistemas 18(3), 627–635 (2014)

23. Cicortas, A., Iordan, V., Fortis, A.: Considerations on construction ontologies. J. Ann. Comput. Sci. Ser. 1, 79–88 (2009)

24. Gruber, T.R.: Toward principles for the design of ontologies used for knowledge sharing. Int. J. Hum Comput Stud. 43(5–6), 907–928 (1995)

25. Yergesh, B., Sharipbay, A., Bekmanova, G., Lipnitskii, S.: Sentiment analysis of Kazakh phrases based on morphological rules. J. Kyrgyz State Tech. Univ. Named After I. Razzakov. Theor. Appl. Sci. Tech. J. 2(38), 39–42 (2016)

Automatic Detection of a Driver's Complex Mental States

Zhiyi Ma[1]([⊠]), Marwa Mahmoud[2], Peter Robinson[2], Eduardo Dias[3],
and Lee Skrypchuk[3]

[1] Department of Engineering, University of Cambridge, Cambridge, UK
zm273@cam.ac.uk
[2] Computer Laboratory, University of Cambridge, Cambridge, UK
[3] Jaguar Land Rover, Coventry, UK

Abstract. Automatic classification of drivers' mental states is an important yet relatively unexplored topic. In this paper, we define a taxonomy of a set of complex mental states that are relevant to driving, namely: *Happy, Bothered, Concentrated* and *Confused*. We present our video segmentation and annotation methodology of a spontaneous dataset of natural driving videos from 10 different drivers. We also present our real-time annotation tool used for labelling the dataset via an emotion perception experiment and discuss the challenges faced in obtaining the ground truth labels. Finally, we present a methodology for automatic classification of drivers' mental states. We compare SVM models trained on our dataset with an existing nearest neighbour model pre-trained on posed dataset, using facial Action Units as input features. We demonstrate that our temporal SVM approach yields better results. The dataset's extracted features and validated emotion labels, together with the annotation tool, will be made available to the research community.

1 Introduction

Complex mental states occur often in real-world driving, and drivers' mental states can have an impact on their driving behaviours, such as speed, acceleration and traffic violations [26]. Therefore, it would be desirable to identify drivers' complex mental states automatically. This can also be very useful for car manufacturers, such as to make cars smarter.

Although there have been many studies looking at stress level [12,16], drowsiness [13,19], and basic emotions [23] of a driver, there is not much work on detection of complex mental states, which were actually found to occur more often in real life [27]. Also, speech recognition [14], physiological signals [16,22] and grip strength [23] have been investigated in classifying drivers' mental states. However, analysing emotions from drivers' facial expressions are not fully explored, partially due to the challenge of lighting conditions during driving and the relatively subtle expressions exhibited while driving.

In this paper, we present our work on automatic detection of drivers' complex mental states based on facial analysis and real-world driving videos. We looked

© Springer International Publishing AG 2017
O. Gervasi et al. (Eds.): ICCSA 2017, Part III, LNCS 10406, pp. 678–691, 2017.
DOI: 10.1007/978-3-319-62398-6_48

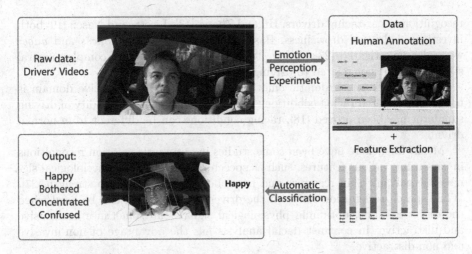

Fig. 1. An overview of our work: The mental states were labeled per frame by human annotators. The features (facial Action Units) were extracted by OpenFace [2]. The long video segments were then processed to small clips and subsampling was used to balance the dataset. Two models were evaluated: per video nearest neighbour model based on an existing classifier and per frame SVM classification.

into four complex mental states that appear frequently in driving scenarios, and performed our automatic classification on natural data. Figure 1 gives an overview of our emotion labeling and classification approach.

The main contributions of our work can be summarised as follows:

1. We present a spontaneous dataset collected in a natural driving scenario and define a set of four categories of complex mental states that are relevant to driving: *Happy, Bothered, Concentrated*, and *Confused*. We obtained our ground truth labels through emotion perception experiment. The features and validated labels[1], together with the annotation tool[2], will be be publicly available to the research community.
2. Using the dataset, we present a methodology for automatic complex mental states classification based on extracting per frame facial Action Units (AU) and using Support Vector Machine (SVM).
3. We compare the SVM models with a nearest neighbour automatic complex mental states classifier pre-trained on posed data [1], and demonstrate that the temporal SVM model achieves significantly better classification results.

1.1 Related Work

Lots of studies have explored automatic emotion recognition, such as [4,5,30]. However, most of these studies were based on the basic emotions [7]. In automotive domain specifically, Katsis et al. [16] studied the automatic stress level

---

[1] Please email marwa.mahmoud@cl.cam.ac.uk for the link and password.
[2] https://github.com/mzy0369/VideoAnnotator.

recognition in car-racing drivers. Hu and Zhang [13], Lisetti and Nasoz [19] both investigated drivers' drowsiness. Basic emotions such as *happiness* and *anger* were also investigated [23]. A few studies have explored more complex mental states [1,9] but not related to driving.

Lots of work on automatic emotion classification in automotive domain is based on simulated racing conditions [12,15,16]. Although the validity of driving simulator has been proved [18], racing conditions can be different from normal driving.

Meanwhile, there have been some studies in automatic emotion recognitions in cars using various features, such as speech recognition [14], physiological signals like galvanic skin response and heart beat [16,22], and grip strength [23]. While speech recognition relies on the driver to talk, which can be hard when the driver is alone, obtaining physiological signals can sometimes be invasive and distractive. In contrast, facial analysis has the advantage of non-invasive and non-distractive.

2   Relevant Mental States

There have been two most common models on constructing computational models of emotions: categorical and dimensional model [11]. Categorical model divides affective states into discrete emotion categories, assuming that there exists such emotions that are hard-wired in our brain. Dimensional model conceptualises emotions as points in a continuous space on the chosen dimensions. So far both theories have shown their merits and demerits [11]. We adopted the categorical approach in our work as it is more intuitive to non-expert labellers.

We chose our taxonomy based on the work of Baron-Cohen et al. [28]. This work contained an exhaustive list of 24 complex mental states groups, with 412 emotion concepts associated. Based on an initial investigation of the videos, eight complex mental states from this list were chosen, i.e. *angry, bothered, disgusted, excited, happy, interested, thinking* and *unsure*, which are believed to be relevant in a driving scenario.

Because the facial expressions of the drivers were mostly subtle, we combined similar groups to form four big categories of complex mental states. *Excited, happy* and *interested* were combined to *Happy*, while *angry, disgusted* and *bothered* to *Bothered*. Hence we defined our taxonomy to constitute of four categories, namely *Happy, Bothered, Concentrated* and *Confused* (see Fig. 2 for some sample frames).

3   Dataset

This section describes five stages of data collection: collecting driving videos, designing annotation tool, conducting emotion perception experiment, validating the collected labels and preparing data for classification.

3.1   Video Collection

The original dataset is composed of 30 video segments of 10 participants driving in a natural environment. The lengths of segments vary from 8 to 20 min. All segments were recorded using a frontal webcam placed on the dashboard in front of the driver, with a frame rate of 30 fps.

Among the 10 drivers, five were driving alone following the instructions on a sat-nav, while the rest were following the instructions given by a co-pilot (passenger). This setup was meant to get varied amount of mental states expressed.

(a) *Happy*   (b) *Bothered*   (c) *Confused*   (d) *Concentrated*

Fig. 2. Samples from videos for each emotion category: *Happy, Bothered, Confused, Concentrated*. The emotion concepts included in each category are: *Happy: Comfortable, Happy*; *Bothered: Frustrated, Nervous, Bothered*; *Confused: Unsure, Confused*; *Concentrated: Thinking, Concentrated*.

3.2   Annotation Tool

In order to collect emotion labels, we developed an annotation tool for real-time annotation. Unlike some available open-source tools such as FEELTRACE [6] and ANNEMO [25], our tool has three features that makes it suitable for our labelling task: (1) It is a stand-alone offline tool. Since the original videos were confidential, this was important for our task. (2) It supports real-time annotation. Given the length of the segments, it was impossible to describe a segment with only one emotion label. (3) As a real-time annotation tool, the interface should be as easy as possible to use, i.e. fewer states with straightforward layout to be chosen from, in order to reduce the reaction time and avoid the need to rewind the video.

We used two annotation modes to further simplify the task of real-time labelling. In every mode, two categories are labelled. To explain each category to non-expert annotators, we explained the meaning of each mental state with their associated emotion concepts [28]. Figure 2 shows sample frames from our videos for each emotion category, accompanied by the emotion concepts included in each category.

In each annotation mode, a continuous scale of 5 levels for each mental state was used, with the higher level indicating a higher intensity. Since the emotional expressions can be subtle in the driver's face, the lower levels encourages annotators to capture a weak mental state appearance. An *Other* option representing level 0 is also included to avoid a forced choice. Figure 3 shows a snapshot.

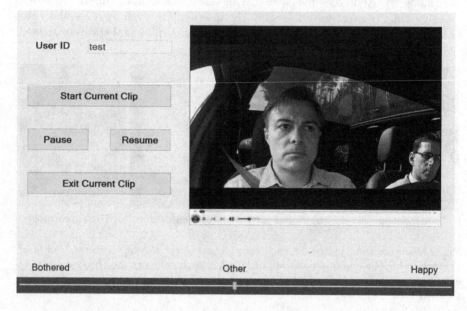

Fig. 3. A snapshot of the video annotation tool interface

Labels are logged by the annotation tool in real-time, and converted to per-frame annotation according the frame rate of the video. The tool is open-source and will be available to the research community.

3.3   Emotion Perception Experiment

Annotators were recruited to our laboratory to label the videos via an emotion perception experiment. All audio in the original video segments were muted to exclude verbal cues.

A total number of 24 segments from 10 drivers were annotated by 48 annotators. Each segment was fully annotated by 6 annotators, half in annotation mode A and half in mode B. Each annotator was rewarded with a £10 Amazon Voucher after finishing annotating three randomly pre-selected segments. To eliminate learning effect, the segments for each annotator were chosen from three different drivers, and the annotation mode was alternate (i.e. ABA or BAB).

3.4   Inter-Rater Agreement Analysis

To evaluate the reliability of the collected labels, we used Krippendorff's Alpha to measure multiple annotators' agreement [17]. It was calculated per video segment for both original continuous scale labels and categorical labels of each mental state category (i.e. converting to binary labels for each mental state without considering the intensity). All level 0's were treated as empty labels in continuous scale labels since it is systematically different from intensity values.

Figure 4 shows Alpha values distributions. For continuous scale labels in annotation mode A, a quarter of the segments have moderate agreement (alpha value 0.4~0.6) while 12.5% have substantial agreement (alpha value 0.6~0.8). Only 21% have fair agreement (0.2~0.4) in mode B (not shown in Fig. 4). Considering each mental state category, *Happy* has the best agreement, indicating it being the most reliably labelled category. The fairly smaller number of segments with moderate agreement from other categories explains the relatively low agreement for mode B annotations.

It can be a challenge to achieve good agreement in collecting large naturalistic datasets [20], especially with mostly non-expert annotators. To deal with this challenge, we adopted a short clip approach in data preparation, which is discussed in Sect. 4.2.

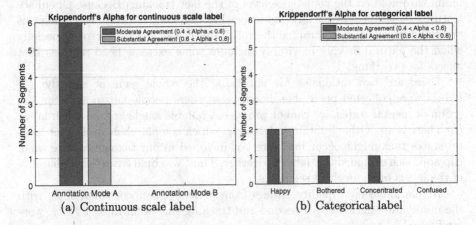

Fig. 4. Krippendorff's Alpha distribution for: (a) continuous scale label of the two annotation modes; (b) categorical label of the each mental state category.

4   Methodology

This section describes the main stages of our automatic mental state estimation approach: feature extraction, data pre-processing (including filtering and balancing), and automatic classification of mental states.

4.1 Feature Extraction

Input features, i.e. facial Action Units (AU) [8] intensities, are extracted by OpenFace [2] from the segments. A continuous scale from 0 to 5 indicating the intensities of 14 AUs are returned respectively per frame. OpenFace is based on the state-of-art AU recognition framework [3,29] with slight modifications tailored for natural video dataset [2]. It outperformed similar softwares DL [10], BA and BG [29] in most AUs on the public dataset SEMAINE [21] and BP4D [31], achieving an average F1-score of 0.48 [2]. Therefore, it is reliable and well-suited to our work.

4.2 Data Pre-processing

Data Filtering. To avoid different annotator's bias when annotating in the continuous scale, categorical labels were used throughout classification.

We adopted a perfect agreement small clip approach to deal with the long segments and low agreement in this experiment. We defined "Perfect agreement" as all three annotators agreeing on the mental state category of the same frame. There are two variables in choosing the small clips: (1) A minimum length of continuous perfect agreement on one of the four mental state categories. This ensures a stable and reliable perceived existence of the mental states. (2) A minimum threshold on the confidence level of the face tracking. Because OpenFace feature extraction depends on reliable facial Action Unit tracking, specifying this threshold is crucial to guarantee the reliability of the feature vector, especially when the natural driving inevitably includes some extreme head motions that affects face tracking.

There are two rationales for not using the whole segment directly: (1) Labels were collected per frame. For frames where people fail to agree on the group of mental states, we cannot produce a reliable single ground truth label. (2) There is an "Other" option in labelling, which is a placeholder of other mental states that might occur but were not included in our taxonomy. The small clip approach excluded this label altogether. Thus, we could ensure the reliability of the labels of those short segments.

To guarantee data quality, frames from perfect agreement small clips, with the minimum length set to 1 second and tracking successful rate of 100%, were used for SVM training.

Data Balancing. One challenge in our work was to balance the dataset. Table 1 shows the total number of frames available for each mental state category. Clearly not many were obtained for *Confused*. The videos show that the associated head pose change and hand-over-face occlusion causes face tracking to fail from time to time. Therefore, the 100% tracking successful rate requirement was waived on *Confused* clips, but only frames that were successfully tracked were used for classification.

We then used random subsampling to balance the number of frames from each mental state category. For each driver, the number of frames from the

Table 1. The number of frames of each mental state from different drivers before subsampling. Numbers in bold represent the baseline adopted for each driver (or sum up for a group of drivers). Subsampling guaranteed having a balanced dataset for the subsequent automatic classification steps.

Driver	Mental states categories			
	Happy	Bothered	Concentrated	Confused
1	702	2086	9937	**100**
2	**90**	384	9292	101
3	**130**	0	1361	469
4	9655	2520	17647	**432**
5	3500	3365	7745	**1616**
6	39	781	997	**456**
7	0	1186	2416	**119**
10	6308	0	1452	**18**
8	6179	2462	8893	**2261**
9	9758	3737	15603	**866**
Total	36361	16521	75343	6438
Subsampled total	6088	6088	6088	6088

mental state that has the minimum number of frames was set as a baseline, and frames were subsampled from the other mental states of this driver to its baseline. When this baseline was 0, we combined a driver's data with another driver into a new fold. Specifically, drivers 6, 7, 10 and drivers 2,3 were combined to be two "drivers", resulting in a total of 7 "drivers", all containing frames from mutually different faces (see Table 1). Subsampling guaranteed having a balanced dataset for the subsequent automatic classification steps.

4.3   Automatic Classification of Mental States

We trained Support Vector Machine (SVM) models with our spontaneous dataset to automatically classify the labelled mental states. A per frame approach was adopted, to match the collected label format.

We first trained two binary classifiers according to the two annotation modes, and then performed a four-class classification. Two approaches for each type of classifiers were used: (1) SVM per frame approach, where the 14 AU intensities were directly used as the feature vector for each frame. (2) Temporal per frame approach, where the context of the video is taken into consideration, and the AU intensities from the previous frame was appended to the current frame to form a 28-dimension feature vector. We experimented with linear and radial basis function (RBF) kernels SVM approaches. To optimise the parameters, we used a leave-one-driver-out cross-validation, with gamma and C varied in the range [0.01, 0.1, 1, 10, 100].

Pre-trained Nearest Neighbour Classification. For comparison purposes, using our spontaneous dataset, we evaluated a nearest neighbour (NN) approach based on a complex mental states classifier [1], pre-trained on posed data [24]. We chose this system as it is based on the same set of complex mental states we use in our experiments. In this approach, a single feature vector is obtained per video, by dividing the AUs and speed of AUs uniformly into different bins. And the three emotion categories whose overall feature vector is the closest to the video's are returned as the classification results.

We used perfect agreement small clips with fixed length of five seconds and 80% successful rate, since previous studies showed that two seconds is the minimum time for human to reliably detect a mental state [9]. There are a total of 18 emotions available in the classifier. We discarded those that are not relevant to our taxonomy, and grouped the rest to match ours according the emotion grouping discussed in Sect. 2. Details are shown in Table 2. An extra emotion called "average" was used in this classifier to normalise the feature vectors. We kept this emotion but did not assign it to any mental states. Overall a total of 10 emotions were used.

Table 2. Emotions grouping for per video NN classifier

Mental state category	Emotions
Happy	Excited, Happy, Interested
Bothered	Angry, Disappointed, Disgusted, Frustrated
Concentrated	Neutral
Confused	Worried
Discarded Emotions	Afraid, Ashamed, Bored, Hurt, Joking, Pround, Sad, Sneaky, Surprised

5   Experimental Results

This section presents the classification results of our experiments. We use F1-score to report the performance of each system.

5.1   Per Frame Approaches Using SVM

In all of these experiments, we used a user-independent 7 fold cross validation method. The normalised confusion matrices for binary and four-class classifiers are shown in Fig. 5. Table 3 tabulates the F1-score for each mental state and overall for each classifier. The statistical significances were calculated using F1-score for each mental state with a one-tail t-test, which indicates the statistically significant improvements from random choice F1-score (0.5 and 0.25 for binary and four-class, respectively).

All SVM training methods achieved F1-scores significantly higher than chance except for *Concentrated-Confused* SVM per frame classifier. In general,

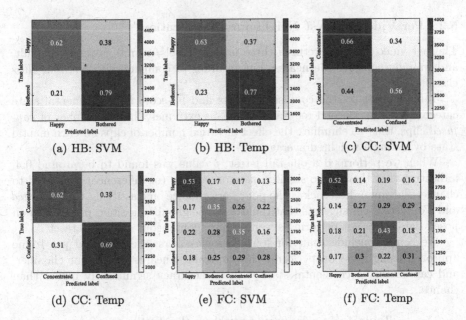

Fig. 5. Normalised confusion matrices for per frame approaches. "HB" stands for "*Happy-Bothered* binary classifier", "CC" for "*Concentrated-Confused* binary classifier", and "FC" for "Four-Class classifier". "SVM" means "SVM per frame approach", and "Temp" is short for "temporal per frame approach".

Table 3. The F1-scores of binary and four-class SVM classifiers

Classifier	F1-score					Chance F1-score
	Overall	Happy	Bothered	Concentrated	Confused	
HB SVM*	0.70	0.67	0.73	-	-	0.50
HB Temp*	0.70	0.68	0.72	-	-	
CC SVM	0.61	-	-	0.63	0.59`	
CC Temp*	0.66	-	-	0.64	0.67	
FC SVM*	0.37	0.50	0.34	0.34	0.31	0.25
FC Temp*	0.38	0.51	0.28	0.41	0.32	

* Indicates a statistically significant difference of $p < 0.05$ compared with chance F1-score

Happy-Bothered classifiers perform better than their counterparts *Concentrated-Confused* classifiers, which agrees with the inter-rater agreement results that showed that *Happy* and *Bothered* are more reliably detected by human annotators. Moreover, the SVM temporal approach had the best performance.

Overall, we can see that our per frame approaches using SVM managed to classify the four mental states categories. The four-class classifiers achieved significantly better results than chance. Concurrent states might have affected the classification results. This will be discussed in Sect. 6.

5.2 Per Video Nearest Neighbour Classification

The per video classifier returns three nearest labels/mental states by default, and we only consider the nearest one in order to compare with our four-class classifiers.

Table 4 tabulates the confusion matrix and F1-score for each mental state category. The five-second requirement means extremely limited number of *confused* clips, thus we eliminate the effect of varied number of clips for each mental state by taking a weighted average.

When we performed a one-tail t-test, p value was found to be around 0.4, indicating that there is no significant improvement (or difference) compared to chance. The main drawback is the poor performance on classifying *Concentrated* and *Confused*. This suggests that the nearest neighoubr classifier, pre-trained on posed data, does not perform as well on our spontaneous driving dataset.

We could conclude that, for four-class classifiers, the temporal per frame approach using SVM outperforms the pre-trained nearest neighbour classifier, and can classify each mental state with an accuracy significantly higher than chance.

Table 4. Per video nearest neighbour classification, $p < 0.4$

		Predicted label				F1-score	Chance F1-score
		Happy	Bothered	Concentrated	Confused		
True label	Happy	111	34	9	3	0.51	0.24
	Bothered	20	40	3	10	0.27	0.11
	Concentrated	146	145	104	11	0.40	0.63
	Confused	5	5	3	0	0	0.02
Overall	-	-	-	-	-	0.40	0.46

6 Discussion and Challenges

One big challenge in mental states classification is the existence of concurrent states. From the four-class confusion matrix in Fig. 5, we can see that *Bothered* and *Confused* are generally confused with each other, while *Happy* and *Concentrated* are less confused and usually well-identified. This explains the relatively low accuracy of the former two compared with the latter.

Another challenge is the unbalanced dataset. As Table 1 shows, *Confused* has the least amount of data, which might have affected the results despite the efforts to balance the dataset using subsampling. However, this is common because we do not expect *Confused* to happen too often in a natural driving scenario.

One last aspect is the driving setup. As described half of the drivers were instructed by a co-pilot (passenger) while the rest were alone following a sat-nav. It was observed that drivers tend to be more expressive when they are accompanied. This might have increased the frequency of all the happiness label.

7   Conclusion

We presented the taxonomy of four categories of mental states that are believed to be related to the driving context. We have used a spontaneous dataset of drivers' videos, and evaluated two models of automatic mental states detection. Comparing our approach with a per video pre-trained classifier, our temporal per frame SVM classifier performs significantly better. We presented our real-time annotation tool and discussed the challenges of obtaining validated ground truth labels. We also discussed the challenges of having an unbalanced dataset, which is expected for this type of natural dataset. The dataset features and labels will be publicly available to the research community.

For future work, we would like to use different models such as Hidden Markov Models (HMM). It may also be worth using a multi-modal approach integrating speech and body with the facial features. Finally, more context-related data is needed. Not having enough data, especially for *Confused*, affected the classification results.

Acknowledgment. The work presented in this paper was funded and supported by Jaguar Land Rover, Coventry, UK.

References

1. Adams, A., Robinson, P.: Automated recognition of complex categorical emotions from facial expressions and head motions. In: 2015 International Conference on Affective Computing and Intelligent Interaction (ACII), pp. 355–361. IEEE (2015)
2. Baltru, T., Robinson, P., Morency, L.P., et al.: Openface: an open source facial behavior analysis toolkit. In: 2016 IEEE Winter Conference on Applications of Computer Vision (WACV), pp. 1–10. IEEE (2016)
3. Baltrušaitis, T., Mahmoud, M., Robinson, P.: Cross-dataset learning and person-specific normalisation for automatic action unit detection. In: 2015 11th IEEE International Conference and Workshops on Automatic Face and Gesture Recognition (FG), vol. 6, pp. 1–6. IEEE (2015)
4. Bartlett, M.S., Littlewort, G., Frank, M., Lainscsek, C., Fasel, I., Movellan, J.: Recognizing facial expression: machine learning and application to spontaneous behavior. In: 2005 IEEE Computer Society Conference on Computer Vision and Pattern Recognition (CVPR 2005), vol. 2, pp. 568–573. IEEE (2005)
5. Cohn, J.F., De la Torre, F.: Automated face analysis for affective. In: The Oxford Handbook of Affective Computing, p. 131 (2014)
6. Cowie, R., Douglas-Cowie, E., Savvidou, S., McMahon, E., Sawey, M., Schröder, M.: 'FEELTRACE': An instrument for recording perceived emotion in real time. In: ISCA Tutorial and Research Workshop (ITRW) on Speech and Emotion (2000)
7. Ekman, P.: An argument for basic emotions. Cogn. Emot. **6**(3–4), 169–200 (1992)
8. Ekman, P., Rosenberg, E.L.: What the Face Reveals: Basic and Applied Studies of Spontaneous Expression Using the Facial Action Coding System (FACS). Oxford University Press, New York (1997)
9. El Kaliouby, R., Robinson, P.: Real-time inference of complex mental states from facial expressions and head gestures. In: Kisačanin, B., Pavlović, V., Huang, T.S. (eds.) Real-time Vision for Human-computer Interaction, pp. 181–200. Springer, Heidelberg (2005)

10. Gudi, A., Tasli, H.E., den Uyl, T.M., Maroulis, A.: Deep learning based FACS action unit occurrence and intensity estimation. In: 2015 11th IEEE International Conference and Workshops on Automatic Face and Gesture Recognition (FG), vol. 6, pp. 1–5. IEEE (2015)

11. Gunes, H., Schuller, B.: Categorical and dimensional affect analysis in continuous input: Current trends and future directions. Image Vis. Comput. **31**(2), 120–136 (2013)

12. van den Haak, P., van Lon, R., van der Meer, J., Rothkrantz, L.: Stress assessment of car-drivers using EEG-analysis. In: Proceedings of the 11th International Conference on Computer Systems and Technologies and Workshop for PhD Students in Computing on International Conference on Computer Systems and Technologies, pp. 473–477. ACM (2010)

13. Hu, S., Zheng, G.: Driver drowsiness detection with eyelid related parameters by support vector machine. Expert Syst. Appl. **36**(4), 7651–7658 (2009)

14. Jones, C.M., Jonsson, I.M.: Automatic recognition of affective cues in the speech of car drivers to allow appropriate responses. In: Proceedings of the 17th Australia Conference on Computer-Human Interaction: Citizens Online: Considerations for Today and the Future. Computer-Human Interaction Special Interest Group (CHISIG) of Australia, pp. 1–10 (2005)

15. Katsis, C., Goletsis, Y., Rigas, G., Fotiadis, D.: A wearable system for the affective monitoring of car racing drivers during simulated conditions. Transp. Res. Part C: Emerg. Technol. **19**(3), 541–551 (2011)

16. Katsis, C.D., Katertsidis, N., Ganiatsas, G., Fotiadis, D.I.: Toward emotion recognition in car-racing drivers: A biosignal processing approach. IEEE Trans. Syst. Man Cybern. Part A: Syst. Hum. **38**(3), 502–512 (2008)

17. Krippendorff, K.: Agreement and information in the reliability of coding. Commun. Methods Measures **5**(2), 93–112 (2011)

18. Lee, H.C., Cameron, D., Lee, A.H.: Assessing the driving performance of older adult drivers: on-road versus simulated driving. Accid. Anal. Prev. **35**(5), 797–803 (2003)

19. Lisetti, C.L., Nasoz, F.: Affective intelligent car interfaces with emotion recognition. In: Proceedings of 11th International Conference on Human Computer Interaction, Las Vegas. Citeseer (2005)

20. Mahmoud, M., Baltrušaitis, T., Robinson, P., Riek, L.D.: 3D corpus of spontaneous complex mental states. In: D'Mello, S., Graesser, A., Schuller, B., Martin, J.-C. (eds.) ACII 2011. LNCS, vol. 6974, pp. 205–214. Springer, Heidelberg (2011). doi:10.1007/978-3-642-24600-5_24

21. McKeown, G., Valstar, M.F., Cowie, R., Pantic, M.: The semaine corpus of emotionally coloured character interactions. In: 2010 IEEE International Conference on Multimedia and Expo (ICME), pp. 1079–1084. IEEE (2010)

22. Nasoz, F., Ozyer, O., Lisetti, C.L., Finkelstein, N.: Multimodal affective driver interfaces for future cars. In: Proceedings of the Tenth ACM International Conference on Multimedia, pp. 319–322. ACM (2002)

23. Oehl, M., Siebert, F.W., Tews, T.-K., Höger, R., Pfister, H.-R.: Improving human-machine interaction–a non invasive approach to detect emotions in car drivers. In: Jacko, J.A. (ed.) HCI 2011. LNCS, vol. 6763, pp. 577–585. Springer, Heidelberg (2011). doi:10.1007/978-3-642-21616-9_65

24. O?Reilly, H., Pigat, D., Fridenson, S., Berggren, S., Tal, S., Golan, O., Bölte, S., Baron-Cohen, S., Lundqvist, D.: The EU-emotion stimulus set A validation study. Behav. Res. Methods **48**(2), 1–10 (2015)

25. Ringeval, F., Sonderegger, A., Sauer, J., Lalanne, D.: Introducing the RECOLA multimodal corpus of remote collaborative and affective interactions. In: 2013 10th IEEE International Conference and Workshops on Automatic Face and Gesture Recognition (FG), pp. 1–8. IEEE (2013)

26. Roidl, E., Frehse, B., Höger, R.: Emotional states of drivers and the impact on speed, acceleration and traffic violations? a simulator study. Accid. Anal. Prev. **70**, 282–292 (2014)

27. Rozin, P., Cohen, A.B.: High frequency of facial expressions corresponding to confusion, concentration, and worry in an analysis of naturally occurring facial expressions of americans. Emotion **3**(1), 68 (2003)

28. Baron-Cohen, S., Ofer Golan, S.W.: A new taxonomy of human emotions (2004)

29. Valstar, M.F., Almaev, T., Girard, J.M., McKeown, G., Mehu, M., Yin, L., Pantic, M., Cohn, J.F.: FERA 2015-second facial expression recognition and analysis challenge. In: 2015 11th IEEE International Conference and Workshops on Automatic Face and Gesture Recognition (FG), vol. 6, pp. 1–8. IEEE (2015)

30. Whitehill, J., Bartlett, M., Movellan, J.: Automatic facial expression recognition for intelligent tutoring systems. In: 2008 IEEE Computer Society Conference on Computer Vision and Pattern Recognition Workshops, CVPRW 2008, pp. 1–6. IEEE (2008)

31. Zhang, X., Yin, L., Cohn, J.F., Canavan, S., Reale, M., Horowitz, A., Liu, P., Girard, J.M.: BP4D-spontaneous: a high-resolution spontaneous 3D dynamic facial expression database. Image Vis. Comput. **32**(10), 692–706 (2014)

EmEx, a Tool for Automated Emotive Face Recognition Using Convolutional Neural Networks

Matteo Riganelli[1], Valentina Franzoni[2(✉)], Osvaldo Gervasi[1], and Sergio Tasso[1]

[1] Department of Mathematics and Computer Science,
University of Perugia, Perugia, Italy
matteoriganelli@gmail.com,
{osvaldo.gervasi,sergio.tasso}@unipg.it
[2] Department of Computer, Control, and Management Engineering,
Sapienza University of Rome, Rome, Italy
franzoni@dis.uniroma1.it

Abstract. The work described in this paper represents the study and the attempt to make a contribution to one of the most stimulating and promising sectors in the field of emotion recognition, which is health care management. Multidisciplinary studies in artificial intelligence, augmented reality and psychology stressed out the importance of emotions in communication and awareness. The intent is to recognize human emotions, processing images streamed in real-time from a mobile device. The adopted techniques involve the use of open source libraries of visual recognition and machine learning approaches based on convolutional neural networks (CNN).

Keywords: Image recognition · Emotion recognition · Face detection · Machine learning · CNN

1 Introduction

The study aims to support people with health disorders that can reduce communication skills (e.g. muscle wasting, stroke, autism, or, more simply, pain) to automatically detect basic emotions, in order to generate a real-time feedback or to be fed in more complex systems. In this way, a user who can not recognize emotions herself (e.g. for a visual or cognitive impairment) can be assisted with augmented emotional stimuli; on the other hand, a user who has difficulties in expressing emotions (e.g. speaking impairment or difficulty) can be monitored to infer expressions of suffering, to intervene accordingly. The proposed system is called *EmEx* (Emotion Extraction), and exploits the high precision of CNN processing, precisely designed to process images. A special classification of emotions is then set up, divided into basic emotions: anger, sadness, disgust, happiness, neutral. A graphic user interface allows to create a set of emotion events in relation to the above-mentioned model, i.e. a personalized training set;

© Springer International Publishing AG 2017
O. Gervasi et al. (Eds.): ICCSA 2017, Part III, LNCS 10406, pp. 692–704, 2017.
DOI: 10.1007/978-3-319-62398-6_49

the neural network will be created appropriately. Finally, another part of the ad hoc software makes use of the convolutional neural model to detect the type of emotion in a video stream, where the same user who trained the network appears. The particularity of EmEx is, in fact, to be user-centered: the user trains the network on her/his own face expressions, the software supports a personalized emotional feedback for each particular user. Personal traits, such as scars or flaws, or individual variations in emotion feeling and expression, will not avoid the training and recognition, but instead help it.

Through an in-deep study of the elements that characterize the problem, the system is made able to overcome those barriers that have so far imposed such a problem. The proposed system has also robustness and scalability properties, verified in previous works. On the other hand, the main technical difficulty can concern the ambient light setting, which needs a proper setup:

- **Robustness:** The algorithm must be able to operate even in the presence of low quality data (low resolution, bad light conditions, etc.);
- **Scalability:** The user position in front of the camera should not be conditioned by the fact that it has a fixed distance, in order to avoid constraining the person under recognition.
- **Luminosity:** An important problem is precisely that of the variation of light. In computer vision ([2]), the variation of the lens involves an alteration of the information. No complete control of the detected information is achieved, the system will be able to withstand variations in brightness without compromising the original information.

The proposed solution has been implemented in C++ language and has methods available in OpenCV graphics libraries, hence it is compatible with all operating systems. The use of these graphics libraries is due to their high reliability and constant support from an increasingly growing community of developers and users. Moreover, these libraries are widely used in many research projects and prototypes based on an open source approach. The open source approach greatly facilitated our work, thanks to the high number of examples available that simplified many developing phases, the accurate and extensive documentation, and the opportunities of sharing and improving our work with the community of developers.

2   Related Work

Deep Learning and Image Classification

The recent scientific focus on Deep Learning towards the end of the XX century has contributed to the rebirth of a major interest in neural networks. The true impact of Deep Learning began in the context of speech recognition around year 2010, when two Microsoft Research employees, Lil Deng and Geoenix Hinton, realized that using large amounts of data for training a deep neural network resulted in lowering error rates far below the state of the art [28]. New discoveries in the field of hardware have certainly contributed to the rise of interest in Deep Learning. In particular, the ever-powerful GPUs seem to be able to perform the countless mathematical calculations of matrices and vectors in Deep Learning [17–19]. Actual GPUs allow to reduce workout times from the weeks to a day.

Recently, deep learning has been used for several researches aiming at classification of images and learning, trying to solve the limitations of machine learning, which reside in overfitting and domain dependence, with image adaptation, kernel randomization [20] and transfer learning [29].

Commitment has been dedicated by researchers to exploit domain dependence as a feature, where personalized classification can be easily done on a particular user or entity, especially for smart-home systems [43] and microblog sentiment tagging [45].

Alternative approaches consider evolutionary algorithms [31], random walks on semantic networks of images [35] and max-product neural networks [34].

Convolutional Neural Networks are among the most used methods for affective image classification [30] thanks to their flexibility for transfer learning, and easy availability online [42].

Health Management

For computerized health care management, multidisciplinary studies in Artificial Intelligence, Augmented Reality and Robotics stressed out the importance of computer science for automatizing real-life tasks for assistive and learning objects, such as detecting words from labial movements (i.e. automated lip detection) [37], Virtual reality for prosthetic training [33] or neural tele-rehabilitation of patients with stroke [11], vocal interfaces for robotics applications [38].

As an application of complex networks, it is possible to predict bacteria diffusion patterns [44], as well as epidemiology data [32], having a viral spread. To be mentioned, high advances are happening on medical image recognition and multi-stage feature selection for classification of cancer data [40], and of text corpora for medical or patient feedback in social networks [21].

One of the most promising advances of recent years for health care management is the opportunity to have light-implementation Mobile Apps, that can be easily developed to be used in a friendly manner [9], in order to assist and support disabled users for communication and learning tasks. Such applications can be run directly on personal smartphones or wearables devices, for health monitoring and prognosis [14] as well as for interactive support for people with disabilities or conditions that can influence communication and learning, such as autism spectrum disorders [13]. Using cloud services or networks in the Internet of Things (IoT), it is possible both to connect such devices to high capability servers, both to collect data in a distributed collaborative perspective [26], in order to feed big knowledge bases and increase the capability of the single object, i.e. of its owner, as member of a large interactive collective dynamic knowledge (i.e. Big Data) network.

Affective Computing and Emotion Recognition

Multidisciplinary approaches recently stressed out the importance of recognizing and extracting affective and mental states, in particular emotions, for communication, understanding, and supporting humans in any task with automated detectors and artificial assistants having machine emotional intelligence [6]. In real-life problems, individuals transform overwhelming amounts of heterogeneous data in a manageable and personalized subset of classified items. The process of recognition of moods and sentiments is largely complex, but recent research underlines that basic emotional states such as happiness, sadness, anger, disgust, or neutral state [46] can be recognized based on physiological clues such as heart rate, skin conductance and face expression, differently from sentiment, moods and affect, which are more complex states and can be better managed with a multidimensional approach [22,47]. Since Rosalind Picard defined the challenges for Affective Computing in 2003 [7], numerous advances have been done in the task of emotion recognition, such as defining collective influence of emotions expressed online [15], stating that emotional expressiveness is the crucial fuel that sustains communities; studying cultural aspects of emotions in art [23] and its variations; create emotionally engaging experiences in games [41], where affective changes are crucial to conscious experience of the world around us. Some of the more ethical and important challenges defined by Rosalind Picard, however, still remain open. For example, many of the modalities for emotion recognition (e.g. blood chemistry, brain activity, neurotransmitters) are not easily available, commercial tools are limited [25], data sets for training are not general [24] and people's emotion is so idiosyncratic and variable, that there is a little hope of accurately recognizing individual's emotional states from available data [7].

This paper aims to provide a solution to overcome such difficulties.

3   The Proposed Method: EmEx

The proposed method takes some insights from literature about lip reading [10,12,39], and the GUI-based EmEx software, ad hoc created, will recognize the emotion of the user whose face is in the camera streaming [3]. For the purpose of our work, we need to establish a subdivision of classes (see Fig. 1) as a representation of the Ekman basic emotions [22], which will be our multi-classification features [5] (Table 1).

Then the information represented by the visual expression captured by a special camera will be processed, in order to return a given output. The system will then process the information that can then be returned to output to the user with a real-time feedback as in Fig. 1A, or be further processed by the system, real as in Fig. 1B.

Table 1. Identified classes to represent emotions.

Class	Emotion	Img
0	anger	
1	sad	
2	happines	
3	disgust	
4	fear	
5	neut	

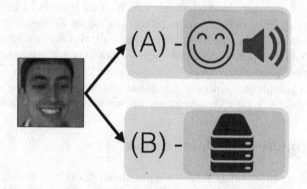

Fig. 1. Simple output scheme: the output can be a real-time feedback (graphic, sound, elements in the interface) or a file to be further processed by an external system.

3.1 Make Data

Creating the data set represents a crucial phase [27], as we are able to train a neural network with a set of images in relation to the above table of emotions. This training phase will enable the user to train a personal network with the appropriate parameters for her case, and our algorithm will automatically recognize emotions of the same user during the actual use of the software, i.e. in the frame acquisition phase. A personalized automation software automatically detects the position of the person's face ([8, 12, 36]) in the camera, and recognizes the emotions, basing on the training set. The software interface is designed to be usable [9], to intuitively guide the user into the various facial expressions in the training phase, in order to form the data set of images and files needed to train the neural network. Besides the automated training, the software interface also permits the user to provide additional frames (e.g. photos) and tag them with an emotion to improve the neural network and its recognition capabilities. On the other hand, a usable list of frames of the training is always accessible by the user, to manually remove in an easy way the eventual noisy frames.

3.2 Make CNN

In order to have a direct approach to the world of conundrum neural networks, the proposed approach focuses on the use of an open source framework. Open source is in fact a powerful method to guarantee security and privacy, where it is possible for each version to check what exactly the code does, and to fix eventual bugs in a collective effort. For our proposal, the choice is on the *Caffe* framework [42], available online. The reason for this choice is the good online documentation and the ease of use of the framework, together with its validated efficiency.

In order to create our user-centered personal data set of emotions, we proceed to set up the files for the proper neural convection training, in accordance with the CNN-based theory. Network layers are thus set up to extract the specific information of the image data, accurately setting the parameters to have an effective recognition. Figure 2 shows the layers of the proposed neural network for emotion recognition [16] CNN, where training data are labeled with emotions, and the results of the layer computation is evaluated in terms of accuracy and loss.

The neural network consists of a number of layers connected to each other. The main level is for the appropriately converted data set and the corresponding tags. The second layer met is the convoluted layer: being directly linked to the data set, in this layer the convolution operations are performed on the images, extracting specific information about each frame in each class. Subsequently, a layer pooling is used to spatially reduce the volume of previously created data in width and height. Such a reduction also leads to reduce the parameters magnitude, and therefore the computational time needed for the network to be computed. For scaling, a maximum and average calculation function of a variable set is used: in our tests we used a max function. After the reduction step, the network continues again with convolutional layers. This time, however, on a more accurate and reduced processing of the data to further improve the refinement of the data. Subsequently, after the layer pooling is applied further, a layer of inner product (innerProduct) groups all the information obtained up to this point. This grouping step has the useful effect to express such information in a single numeric value, that can be processed again in subsequent phases.

After the group layer, the system is able to return a vector representation of neurons (from n to 1). This suggests that, from here onwards, it will no longer be possible to apply unambiguous layers.

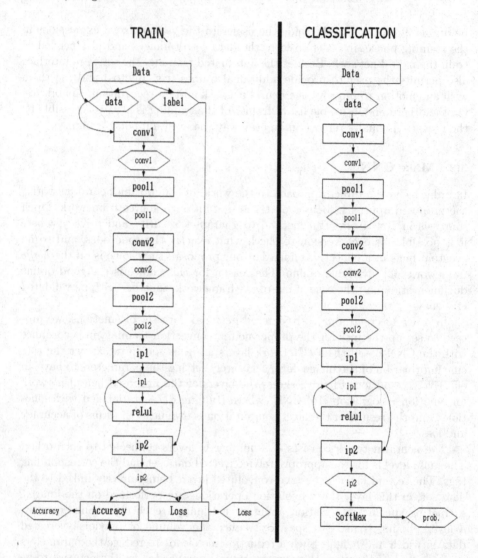

Fig. 2. Representative diagram of CNN network to classify emotions - Train + Classification

Another layer of innerProduct is then applied: it is useful to put these layers in succession, because the last one will have an output parameter that will equal the number of classes needed for the classification. The K final values will be therefore the object of a probability function that will allow the final classification.

It is noticeable that in the TRAIN phase, the network ends with an Accuracy layer for network accuracy calculation, and with a Loss layer for the calculation of the error function needed for a correct and useful training phase. In the

CLASSIFICATION phase, instead, we use the same file but having a SoftMax layer as the final layer: the main purpose of the SoftMax layer is the classification of new images (test set), not present in the data set. This type of layer calculates the likelihood of the most appropriate class in the grading phase, and therefore represents the final solution.

In order to reach the final solution, we created the network, set the parameters of each layer and prepared the various files needed for Caffe to start the train phase with the appropriate command. Each user will be able to setup a personalized network, in an easy and intuitive way, guided by the interface of the EmEx software.

It is also necessary to create a network specially for the classification phase. This will be identical in the layer type to the network used for training but will have as input an image captured by an unknown camera and as output a layer capable of establishing a property for the most appropriate class corresponding to the detected image. The network in question is visible in the picture 2.

3.3   Classification

You can go to the classification step by creating the network template. Here too, software has been designed to process the image by using the Opencv libraries, automatically pulling out the face position, after which frames are captured and their rescue will be controlled by Caffe who will classify them each in the corresponding class of membership, returning the output value. To have a safer result, a check of occurrences is made, that is, the consecutive frames belonging to the same class are counted, and if they exceed a predetermined threshold value then it is likely that the expression will be expressed by the network. In this way you can eliminate some false positives and you can improve the accuracy of the network. Classification is carried out in the so-called 'top-5 accuracy' method. This means that the grading probabilities are reported for each class in descending order, from the most probable to the least probable. In this way it will also be possible to establish a classification of multiple emotions, that is represented by the visual expression of multiple expressions. The software and therefore the neural convection network are able to detect even if the user is expressing both sadness and seriousness at the same time, given the chances of the neural network for each dataset class.

In order to obtain a more reliable final classification, a check of occurrences is carried out, in according with [1,4]. This gives you two benefits. Observing how many times consecutively an emotion can detect noise by eliminating frame sequences below a predetermined threshold. In this way it can be assumed that the emotions that occur a small number of times do not really belong to the emotion expressed by the person. With this step you get two benefits. The first is to significantly reduce the length of the carrier containing the data. Also by observing how many times an emotion occurs, it is possible to detect noise by eliminating emotion sequences below a predetermined threshold. In the practical case this threshold was found empirically. In some cases, this threshold is too low, but it is preferred to leave some rare misconception rather than risking to eliminate a sequence of correct emotions.

4 Discussion of Result

In the present paper we described EmEx, a system designed to identify emotion from face expressions acquired through a webcam. The system is based on Convolutional Neural Networks. The presented results are based on a sample neural network trained on the author Matteo Riganelli. To run tests, we used a personal computer equipped with an Intel core i5-3210M CPU, 2,50 GHz, 4,00 GB of RAM and a Webcam 640×480 px, 30 fps.

By using a specific training phase for each user, the recognition of emotions become more effective. It is advisable to create the data set and the subsequent training phase for each user according to a personalized approach, although this method can also be used without training phase, and introducing a complex and complete data set of samples per each class. A significant advantage in using this system is also the fact that it allows a variable distance of the user from the webcam.

The first step consists in creating an image data set, in the appropriate input format, depicting the training-set and the validation-sets useful to Caffe for the training phase, that, thanks to the personalized layers, allows to calculate the accuracy of the model at certain intervals.

To facilitate the usage of the system by the final user, the ability to interrupt the training phase in advance is provided, so that an expert user who wants to improve some parameters without waiting the completion of the computational phase, is enabled to do it. The template created in such a way will be used for a webcam rating. Finally, the classification program serves the system to classify emotions expressed by the user, based on the previously prepared training data.

Final tests allow to identify the emotion with a given probability, depending on appropriate classes for the face acquired by the webcam, as shown in Fig. 3.

In the two figures, we can see that the expression of happiness can be recognized easily (Fig. 3) while a small uncertainty is present for the trained data for the second classification (Fig. 4). This is due to the fact that it is easy for the system to recognize a smile. A more accurate training for the other emotions can enhance the results.

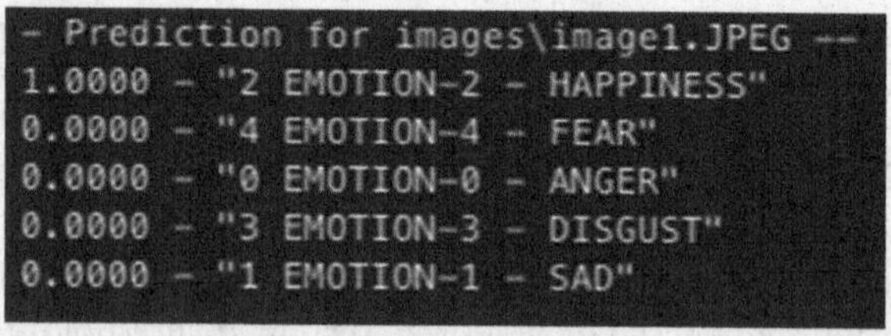

```
-- Prediction for images\image1.JPEG --
1.0000 - "2 EMOTION-2 - HAPPINESS"
0.0000 - "4 EMOTION-4 - FEAR"
0.0000 - "0 EMOTION-0 - ANGER"
0.0000 - "3 EMOTION-3 - DISGUST"
0.0000 - "1 EMOTION-1 - SAD"
```

Fig. 3. Face image classification - 1.

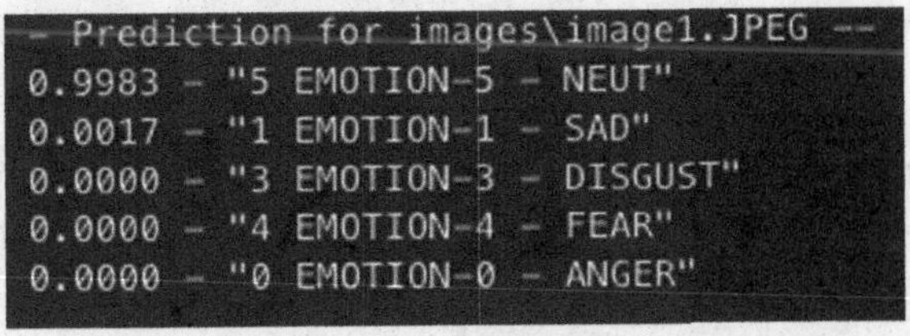

```
-- Prediction for images\image1.JPEG --
0.9983 - "5 EMOTION-5 - NEUT"
0.0017 - "1 EMOTION-1 - SAD"
0.0000 - "3 EMOTION-3 - DISGUST"
0.0000 - "4 EMOTION-4 - FEAR"
0.0000 - "0 EMOTION-0 - ANGER"
```

Fig. 4. Face image classification - 2.

Table 2. Results

Class	Emotion	Img
0	Anger	5/5
1	Sad	5/5
2	Happiness	5/5
3	Disgust	2/5
4	Fear	5/5
5	Neut	3/5

Table 2 shows the number of correct classifications for each type of emotion, carried out in a consecutive image acquisition. In this case 5 consecutive acquisitions for the smile images have been carried out. Small defects are found only for very similar representations as visual expressions.

A better match can be obtained with more examples for the training data set. Future works include a revision of the structure of the neural convolutional network to better fit special applications for different user types.

5   Conclusions

This work is focused on creating a method of recognizing emotions visually. Such a system can be useful to the user with difficulties in expressing or recognizing emotions e.g., users with autism spectrum disorders, sick users in pain, people assisting users to be monitored for health conditions.

This effort has been made possible thanks to recent developments in neural networks, more specifically CNN convolutional neural networks, able to process images accurately.

The use of a simple webcam has led to good results, but a higher resolution camera may improve accuracy, both in training and grading. The experiment demonstrates that this operation can be done with simple tools, good results can be achieved with inexpensive hardware. The proposed classification can be accurate, though having pictures of very similar emotions, visually speaking: this feature is considered an advantage for the proposed user-centered application.

The main disadvantage of the proposed approach is the same of all machine learning techniques, which require in general a complex training phase.

References

1. Mahalanobis, P.C.: On the generalised distance in statistics. Proc. Natl. Inst. Sci. India **2**(1), 49–55 (1936)
2. Cootes, T.F., Taylor, C.J., Cooper, D.H., Graham, J.: Active shape models-their training and application. Comput. Vis. Image Underst. **61**(1), 38–59 (1995). ISSN: 1077-3142
3. Stiefelhagen, R., Yang, J., Waibel, A.: A model-based gaze tracking system. Int. J. Artif. Intell. Tools **6**(2), 193–209 (1997)
4. Levenshtein, V.I.: Binary Codes Capable of Correcting Deletions, Insertions and Reversals, vol. 10, p. 707. Soviet Physics Doklady (1966)
5. Pigeon, S., Vandendorpe, L.: The M2VTS multimodal face database (Release 1.00). In: Bigün, J., Chollet, G., Borgefors, G. (eds.) AVBPA 1997. LNCS, vol. 1206, pp. 403–409. Springer, Heidelberg (1997). doi:10.1007/BFb0016021
6. Picard, R.W., Vyzas, E., Healey, J.: Toward machine emotional intelligence: analysis of affective physiological state. IEEE Trans. Pattern Anal. Mach. Intell. **23**(10), 1175–1191 (2001)
7. Picard, R.W.: Affective computing: challenges. Int. J. Hum. Comput. Stud. **59**(1–2), 55–64 (2003)
8. Eveno, N., Caplier, A., Coulon, P.Y.: Accurate and quasi-automatic lip tracking. IEEE Trans. Circuits Syst. Video Technol. **14**(5), 706–715 (2004). ISSN: 1051-8215
9. Franzoni, V., Gervasi, O.: Guidelines for web usability and accessibility on the Nintendo Wii. In: Gavrilova, M.L., Tan, C.J.K. (eds.) Transactions on Computational Science VI. LNCS, vol. 5730, pp. 19–40. Springer, Heidelberg (2009). doi:10.1007/978-3-642-10649-1_2
10. Lombardi, L., ur Rehman Butt, W., Grecuccio, M.: Lip tracking towards an automatic lip reading approach. JMPT **5**, 1–11 (2014)
11. Gervasi, O., Magni, R., Zampolini, M.: Nu!RehaVR: Virtual reality in neuro tele-rehabilitation of patients with traumatic brain injury and stroke. Virtual Reality **14**(2), 131–141 (2010)
12. Saeed, U., Dugelay, J.-L.: Combining edge detection and region segmentation for lip contour extraction. In: Proceedings of the 6th Conference on Articulated Motion and Deformable Objects, AMDO 2010, Andratx, Mallorca, Spain, 7–9 July 2010. Also published in LNCS, vol. 6169 (2010)
13. Hayes, G.R., Hirano, S., Marcu, G., Monibi, M., Nguyen, D.H., Yeganyan, M.: Interactive visual supports for children with autism. Pers. Ubiquit. Comput. **14**(7), 663–680 (2010)
14. Pantelopoulos, A., Bourbakis, N.G.: A survey on wearable sensor-based systems for health monitoring and prognosis. IEEE Trans. Syst. Man Cybern. Part C Appl. Rev. **40**(1), 1–12 (2010). Art. no. 5306098
15. Chmiel, A., Sienkiewicz, J., Thelwall, M., Paltoglou, G., Buckley, K., Kappas, A., Hołyst, J.A.: Collective emotions online and their influence on community life. PLoS ONE **6**(7) (2011). Art. no. e22207
16. Krizhevsky, A., Sutskever, I., Hinton, G.: ImageNet classification with deep convolutional neural networks. In: Advance in Neural Information Processing System, vol. 25, pp. 1106–1114 (2012)
17. Gervasi, O., Russo, D., Vella, F.: The AES implantation based on OpenCL for multi/many core architecture. In: 2010 International Conference on Computational Science and Its Applications, Fukuoka, ICCSA 2010, pp. 129–134. IEEE Computer Society, Washington, DC (2010). doi:10.1109/ICCSA.2010.44

18. Vella, F., Neri, I., Gervasi, O., Tasso, S.: A simulation framework for scheduling performance evaluation on CPU-GPU heterogeneous system. In: Murgante, B., Gervasi, O., Misra, S., Nedjah, N., Rocha, A.M.A.C., Taniar, D., Apduhan, B.O. (eds.) ICCSA 2012. LNCS, vol. 7336, pp. 457–469. Springer, Heidelberg (2012). doi:10.1007/978-3-642-31128-4_34

19. Mariotti, M., Gervasi, O., Vella, F., Cuzzocrea, A., Costantini, A.: Strategies and systems towards grids and clouds integration: a DBMS-based solution. Future Gener. Comput. Syst. (2017). doi:10.1016/j.future.2017.02.047

20. Neumann, M., Patricia, N., Garnett, R., Kersting, K.: Efficient graph kernels by randomization. In: Flach, P.A., Bie, T., Cristianini, N. (eds.) ECML PKDD 2012. LNCS, vol. 7523, pp. 378–393. Springer, Heidelberg (2012). doi:10.1007/978-3-642-33460-3_30

21. Cheng, V.C., Leung, C.H.C., Liu, J., Milani, A.: Probabilistic aspect mining model for drug reviews. IEEE Trans. Knowl. Data Eng. **26**(8), 2002–2013 (2014). Art. no. 6678354

22. Franzoni, V., Poggioni, V., Zollo, F.: Automated classification of book blurbs according to the emotional tags of the social network Zazie. In: CEUR Workshop Proceedings, vol. 1096, pp. 83–94 (2013)

23. Bertola, F., Patti, V.: Emotional responses to artworks in online collections. In: CEUR Workshop Proceedings, vol. 997 (2013)

24. Saif, H., Fernandez, M., He, Y., Alani, H.: Evaluation datasets for Twitter sentiment analysis a survey and a new dataset, the STS-Gold. In: CEUR Workshop Proceedings, vol. 1096, pp. 9–21 (2013)

25. Cieliebak, M., Dürr, O., Uzdilli, F.: Potential and limitations of commercial sentiment detection tools. In: CEUR Workshop Proceedings, vol. 1096, pp. 47–58 (2013)

26. Tasso, S., Pallottelli, S., Rui, M., Laganá, A.: Learning objects efficient handling in a federation of science distributed repositories. In: Murgante, B., et al. (eds.) ICCSA 2014. LNCS, vol. 8579, pp. 615–626. Springer, Cham (2014). doi:10.1007/978-3-319-09144-0_42

27. Karayev, S., Trentacoste, M.: Recognizing Image Style. University of California Barkley Adobe, Helen Han (2014)

28. LeCun, Y., Bengio, Y., Hinton, G.: Deep learning. Nature **521**(7553), 436–444 (2015). doi:10.1038/nature14539. Nature Publishing Group, a division of Macmillan Publishers Limited. All Rights Reserved. ISBN: 0028-0836

29. Patel, V.M., Gopalan, R., Li, R., Chellappa, R.: Visual domain adaptation: a survey of recent advances. IEEE Signal Process. Mag. **32**(3), 53–69 (2015). Art. no. 7078994

30. Peng, K.-C., Chen, T., Sadovnik, A., Gallagher, A.: A mixed bag of emotions: model, predict, and transfer emotion distributions. In: Proceedings of the IEEE Computer Society Conference on Computer Vision and Pattern Recognition, 07–12 June 2015, pp. 860–868 (2015). Art. no. 7298687

31. Baioletti, M., Milani, A., Santucci, V.: Linear ordering optimization with a combinatorial differential evolution. In: 2015 IEEE Proceedings of the International Conference on Systems, Man, and Cybernetics, SMC 2015, pp. 2135–2140 (2016). Art. no. 7379505

32. Voirin, N., Payet, C., Barrat, A., Cattuto, C., Khanafer, N., Régis, C., Kim, B.-A., Comte, B., Casalegno, J.-S., Lina, B., Vanhems, P.: Combining high-resolution contact data with virological data to investigate influenza transmission in a tertiary care hospital. Infect. Control Hosp. Epidemiol. **36**(3), 254–260 (2015)

33. Phelan, I., Arden, M., Garcia, C., Roast, C. Exploring virtual reality and prosthetic training. In: 2015 IEEE Virtual Reality Conference, VR 2015 - Proceedings, pp. 353–354 (2015). Art. no. 7223441

34. Costarelli, D., Vinti, G.: Max-product neural network and quasi-interpolation operators activated by sigmoidal functions. J. Approx. Theory **209**, 1–22 (2016)

35. Franzoni, V., Milani, A., Pallottelli, S., Leung, C.H.C., Li, Y. Context-based image semantic similarity. In: 2015 Proceedings of the 12th International Conference on Fuzzy Systems and Knowledge Discovery, FSKD 2015, pp. 1280–1284 (2016). Art. no. 7382127

36. Lewis, T.W., Powers, D.M.W.: Lip contour detection techniques based on front view of face. J. Glob. Res. Comput. Sci. **2**(5), 43–46 (2011). ISSN: 2229-371X

37. Gervasi, O., Magni, R., Ferri, M.: A method for predicting words by interpreting labial movements. In: Gervasi, O., et al. (eds.) ICCSA 2016. LNCS, vol. 9787, pp. 450–464. Springer, Cham (2016). doi:10.1007/978-3-319-42108-7_34

38. Bastianelli, E., Nardi, D., Aiello, L.C., Giacomelli, F., Manes, N.: Speaky for robots: the development of vocal interfaces for robotic applications. Appl. Intell. **44**(1), 43–66 (2016)

39. Biondi, G., Franzoni, V., Li, Y., Milani, A.: Web-based similarity for emotion recognition in web objects. In: Proceedings of the 9th International Conference on Utility and Cloud Computing, UCC 2016, Shanghai, China, 6–9 December 2016, pp. 327–332 (2016)

40. Alkuhlani, A., Nassef, M., Farag, I.: Multistage feature selection approach for high-dimensional cancer data. Soft Comput., 1–12 (2016)

41. Canossa, A., Badler, J., El-Nasr, M.S., Anderson, E.: Eliciting emotions in design of games - a theory driven approach. In: CEUR Workshop Proceedings, vol. 1680, pp. 34–40 (2016)

42. Caffe Framework - Github. https://github.com/BVLC/caffe

43. Lou, Y., Wu, W., Vatavu, R.-D., Tsai, W.T.: Personalized gesture interactions for cyber-physical smart-home environments. Sci. China Inf. Sci. **60**(7), 072104 (2017)

44. Franzoni, V., Chiancone, A., Milani, A.: A multistrain bacterial diffusion model for link prediction. Int. J. Pattern Recognit. Artif. Intell. **31**(11) (2017). World Scientific. doi:10.1142/S0218001417590248

45. Cui, W., Du, Y., Shen, Z., Zhou, Y., Li, J.: Personalized microblog recommendation using sentimental features. In: 2017 IEEE International Conference on Big Data and Smart Computing, BigComp 2017, pp. 455–456 (2017). Art. no. 7881756

46. Angelov, P., Gu, X., Iglesias, J.A., Ledezema, A., et al.: Cybernetics of the mind, learning individual's perceptions autonomously. IEEE Syst. Man Cybern. **3**(1), 8–21 (2017)

47. Franzoni, V., Milani, A., Vallverdu, J.: Emotional affordances in human-machine interactive planning and negotiation. In: Proceedings of WI 2017, Workshop on Affective Computing and Emotion Recognition (ACER) (2017)

"Humble" Politicians and Their Multimodal Communication

Francesca D'Errico[✉] and Isabella Poggi

Roma Tre University, Rome, Italy
{francesca.derrico,isabella.poggi}@uniroma3.it

Abstract. The present study deals with the representation and automatic detection of the multimodal communication of humble politicians. Studies in the psychology of political communication have stressed the role of dominance in the self-presentation of politicians, while implicitly excluding the very hypothesis that a political leader can be o can present himself as humble. This work presents two studies on humility and humble politicians. First a survey study has investigated how laypeople define humility, trying to extract the defining features of this notion, such as non-superiority, empathy, equality and others. Then a qualitative analysis has investigated, in the multimodal communication of four humble leaders, which postures, prosodic features, gaze and face expressions specifically convey the semantic features of humility previously hypothesized, and what emotions, detected through Ekman's Action Units, are displayed by those leaders and how they are linked to the features of humility.

Keywords: Humility · Multimodal communication · Emotion expression

1 Introduction

"Pride is concerned with who is right. Humility is concerned with what is right."
Ezra Taft Benson

The concept of humility, so widely promoted in religious literature, has rarely been approached and coherently described in scientific research, in favour of opposite notion like "dominance" as a common expression of one's own power [1].

While Tangney [2] defines the psychological notion of humility as a state/disposition to "forget the self", on the other hand the common sense makes reference to a highest level of self-awareness, in which the humble person is highly aware of her strengths and limits.

In the psychology of organization humble leadership presupposes (1) acknowledgement of personal faults, mistakes and limits, (2) openness to new even contradictory ideas, (3) the tendency to give voice and merits to "employees" [3].

Studies in eastern cultures [3, 4] stress how this may have positive effects on employees, like "voice behaviors (proactive and constructive suggestions)", when they have a positive evaluation of the leader.

This work aims at defining the notion of "humble leadership" in the political field and at describing what characterizes the multimodal communication of "humble"

© Springer International Publishing AG 2017
O. Gervasi et al. (Eds.): ICCSA 2017, Part III, LNCS 10406, pp. 705–717, 2017.
DOI: 10.1007/978-3-319-62398-6_50

political leaders. In order to this goal, first a survey has been conducted to explore the common-sense view of "humility" and of "humble leader", and the assessment of humble political leaders, then a qualitative analysis of the "humble" leaders' communication was carried out, finding out the characterizing features of humble leadership in their discourse and their body communication.

2   Humility. Towards a Socio-Cognitive Definition

To explore the notions of humility and of humble leader, two approaches can be applied. On the one hand, a conceptual analysis can be drawn, in a top-down fashion, from a general model of social relations between humans; on the other hand, the common-sense definition of these notions can be investigated through empirical research, trying to discover how people in real life classify others as humble, and why they do so. This latter approach was first taken in our research, in order to finally come up with an empirically grounded conceptual definition of humility and humble leaders.

To find out how people define humility and how they describe "humble leaders", a survey was conducted on 52 participants (22 Males, 30 Females, mean age 24.1). The 30 questions, phrased on the basis of a previous focus group, asked participants to describe a hypothetically humble behaviour, of both themselves and others; to provide a definition of humility; to name possible humble political leaders; and to find a video on Youtube witnessing their humble communicative behaviour.

Here we only overview the participants' definition of humility, their choice of political leaders as representative of humble communication, with their respective youtube video, and we finally focus on their multimodal analysis.

According to our participants, humility is characterized by the following features:
First, it is

1. a stance (that is, a way of being and behaving with others: STANCE), and it entails:
2. acknowledgement of one's own limits and flaws, and of the consequent possibility of making errors (LIMITS AWARENESS) Such stance towards life and oneself is then (in participants' words),
3. realistic (REALISM) and it causes one
4. to feel equal to others (EQUALITY).
5. not to feel superior to them, not to ostentate or display any superiority, and if actually having some power over others, not to take advantage of it (NON-SUPERIORITY) As a consequence, the behavior of the humble person entails
6. not only feeling but also showing of being on the same level as others, as well as treating them as equal to oneself (FAMILIARITY), and
7. being empathic to them (EMPATHY) which implies CARE and ATTENTION to the other, and hence gives an impression of
8. ALTRUISM, of being oriented to people more than to objects. Humility also entails
9. not crediting any relevance to any external tinsel or symbolic ornament like status symbols or status tout court (ESSENTIALITY), which results in features of
10. INFORMALITY

11. SINCERITY, not caring anything but the real substantive value of people, which again warrants for the impression of REALISM.

Such definition of humility from a cognitive perspective shows how the main goal of a humble person is to be *"like others"*, not more and not less, thus for pursuing this goal s-he does not show nor make appeal to his/her own power, superiority in terms of status, knowledge, merits, contributions, virtues and capabilities. From a communicative point of view s/he considers important "not to put her/himself first" but rather attributes a positive value to a more large dimension of belonging (i.e.others, group, organizations, party) and focuses on the problem rather than on the person who did something. Such horizontal perspective of the humble person, focused on others and on the group, leads to emphasize elements of *similarity*, *familiarity* and *informality*.

3   Multimodal Communication of Humble Leaders

Besides the definition of humility, a further aim of our work was to find out its characterizing elements in the multimodal communication of humble politicians. To search them in real cases, we chose four politicians among those most frequently pointed at by our participants: two Italian leaders from the past, Enrico Berlinguer and Aldo Moro, and two from present or recent leaders, José Mujica and Barack Obama. For each of them we selected a video from a real TV program: three interviews for the former three, and the "farewell speech" of Obama after his second presidential term; then each video was subject to a qualitative analysis of the Leader's multimodal communication.

3.1   Method

Our goal in analysing humble communication was to find out if and how the features of humility mentioned by our participants are expressed by the multimodal communication of humble politicians, and in particular of the four leaders considered as most representative of humble leadership.

Therefore we analyzed the fragments of their communication in terms of the annotation scheme of Table 1. In the scheme, the timeline of the behaviors taken into exam is represented vertically: at each second the behavior or trait under analysis is analyzed through three rows. For each group of three rows, the first one contains a description of the analyzed signal in terms of the parameters and values of Table 2. In the second row we write the literal meaning we attribute to that signal, and possibly, preceded by an arrow, its indirect meaning, since, according to the principles adopted in previous analysis [5, 6], each signal may have, beyond its literal meaning, a further meaning to be inferred by the Addressee.

Table 1. Annotation scheme of politician's humility

	1 Min	2 Verbal	3 Voice	4 Body	5 Head	6 Gaze	7 Mouth	8 Nose	9 Gesture	10 Clothing
		MUJIC JOSE'S INTERVIEW https://www.youtube.com/watch?v=4GX6a2WEA1Q&t=18s								
Signals	2.30	*"No es una apologia de la pobreza Es una apologia de la sobriedad"* = It is not an apology of poverty but one of sobriety	*Low and slow rhythm*	*Trunk swaying forward*	*Head down towards Interlocutor*	*He stares at Interlocutor fixedly from down upward* + *raised and frowning eyebrows (AU 1, 4, 15)*		*Nose wrinkle*		*Simple shirt*
Meaning		I use short and simple sentences → I care simple essential values		I care you → I am worried for you	I am not dominant	I address you from a down position → I do not put myself in a up position, + I am really concerned about you		I am angry and worried → I ask for attention		I am dressed just like you
Humility Features		ESSENTIALITY		FAMILIARITY	NON-SUPERIORITY	NON-SUPERIORITY + EMPATHY				INFORMALITY

In the third row we write the feature that forms the core of the meaning conveyed: a mental ingredient that may or may not be included within the "humility" features listed above. The signals are distinguished according to their productive modality, that is, the body organs by which they are produced, represented in the columns [7]. So, while column 1 specifies the time in the video and the Sender of the signal under analysis, the subsequent columns contain the modalities taken into account: Verbal (Col.2), Voice (3), Body (4), Head (5) Gaze (6), Mouth (7), Nose (8), Gesture (9), and Clothing (10).

Within each modality, Table 1. distinguishes some specific parameters: e.g., for the body (col.4) we take trunk position and body movement into account, for head (5), movement and direction, and so on (see Table 2.). This is because sometimes a body organ, or even some aspect of its behaviour or traits (like position, direction, movement), may by itself convey a single piece of meaning that when combined with other behaviours or aspects or behaviour makes up a complex message; and even, sometimes the meaning conveyed by one part or aspect of the signal relevantly combines with an aspect of another. For example (see Table 1.), in the multimodal communication by Uruguay president José Alberto Mujica a global meaning resulting in the features of CARE, WORRY FOR OTHERS is conveyed, at time 2.30, by body movement (Mujica *moves his trunk forward and backward, swaying*), head position (*head canting*) and head movement (he *turns toward Interlocutor*), and gaze direction (he *stares at Interlocutor fixedly from down upward*).

Table 2. Description of parameters

Modality	Parameter	
Voice	Voice	High, medium, low
Body	Trunk position	Erected, close, distancing,
	Body movement	Forward, backward
	Movement	Default, nod, shake, canting, toss
Head	Direction	To interlocutor, forward, backward, leftward, rightward
	Direction	Oblique, gazing down, gazing upward, downward, upward,
Gaze	Eyebrows	BROW LOWERED AU4, BROW RAISE AU2, INNER BROW RAISE AU1, LID TIGHTEN AU23
	Eyelids	Default, raising, frown, asymmetrical, AU43
Mouth	Lips	Default, half open, closed, LIP CORNER DEPRESSOR AU15, LIP SUCK AU28, LIPS PRESS AU24, LIP STRETCH AU20, UPPER LIP RAISE AU5, SMILE AU12,
	Lip corners	Default, upward, downward, retracted, MOUTH STRETCH AU27, SMILE AU12, DIMPLER AU14, CHIN RAISED AU17, SMIRK
Nose	Nose	Nose wrinkle, cheek raise - AU 9, 6
Clothing		Simple, formal, informal, sophisticated

Beside analyzing body and head movements, all along the fragment from the Leader's face we also detected his facial expressions by means of I-MOTION. It is an automatic detection system based on Affectiva's Affdex technology to gain emotional reactions via facial expressions.

I-Motion is based on a facial expression algorithm that automatically identifies 6 Basic Emotions, Valence, Excitement, 15 Facial Expressions, 33 Facial Landmarks, Interocular Distance, and Head Pose (www.imotion.com) The 23 Action Units – and the six basic emotions - based on Ekman's studies ([8] Ekman et al.) were automatically detected, each ranging from 0 to 100, where 0 is total absence and 100 full presence of that emotion. Three additional parameters were also automatically detected by i-motions, attention (head orientation toward screen), valence of emotions (positive, vs. negative, AU 4, 9, 10) and engagement (maximum intensity of all actions).

The fragment was analyzed separately by two independent judges; after analysis, critical passages were discussed until reached agreement.

3.2   The Humble Leader: A Multimodal Analysis

Our data from the Italian survey reveal that almost 17% of our participants state they cannot choose a politician when talking of humility because they think this is self-contradictory. 17 participants (39%) indicated foreign politicians: Obama (11f., 25%), Mujica (3f., 7%) and three others (Harold V, the Norwegian King; the French leader Melenchon, and Martin Luther King); 34% of participants chose Italian politicians from the past like Aldo Moro (7%), Enrico Berlinguer (7%), Marco Pannella (5%), Napolitano, Pertini, and Veltroni; only 27% named current Italian politicians chosen from Beppe Grillo's anti-establishment movement "Five Stars Movement"; Virginia Raggi, Di Battista, Di Maio, 21% in to-tal), former prime ministers and presidents Enrico Letta, Sergio Mattarella, Giorgio Napolitano. In order to perform the multimodal analysis of verbal and bodily signals the most frequent have been chosen: Obama and Mujica as current leaders, and Berlinguer and Moro as past time politicians. The qualitative analysis of the fragments presented allows us to describe political leaders' humble communication in detail.

3.3   Enrico Berlinguer

Among the Italian politicians of the past mentioned by participants as humble leaders, we analysed Enrico Berlinguer, secretary of the Italian Communist Party from 1972 to 1984; he is remembered for having raised the moral question regarding the way of power management on the part of the Italian political parties. Berlinguer is a very popular politician, he was respected by opponents and loved by his party militants, so much so that at his funeral in Rome, more than one million people were present (Fig. 1).

In an interview on April 23th, 1983, Berlinguer says at minute 3.18:
I cannot define "Berlinguerian", because I deny that there is such a category as the "Berlinguer-ians"
(*Non posso definire i berlingueriani, perché nego che esiste una categoria di berlingueriani*)

Fig. 1. Berlinguer

With a *low tone of voice* and a *very slow speech rate*, Berlinguer diminishes the fact that there might exist a category with his name; an element of humble communication in this case is the verbal act of *underestimating* and *belittling* one's own merits, by attributing them to a larger category (the entire party, the community) [9]; in this fragment Berlinguer displays a facial expression of slight embarrassment (eyes slightly averted from the Interlocutor) and modesty (coyness AU6,7,12,25, 26, *small smile, head slightly turned down*: [10]).

At minute 4.48 Berlinguer says:
(Esiste un'evoluzione perché le situazioni cambiano e la politica di partito si adegua. L'importante è che tutti i cambiamenti siano adeguati alla situazione e che siano condotti in modo tale che tutti comprendano la necessità e l'opportunità).

(There is an evolution because situations change and the party's politics adapts to them. The important thing is for all changes to be appropriate to the situation and conducted in such a way that everyone understands the need and the opportunity of doing so).

The multimodal analysis of the fragment shows how Berlinguer quietly explains how a party's policy addresses change in such a way as to let everyone understand the need thereof, while emphasizing the word "*tutti*" (all) by opening his arms wide to point how important in his message is to achieve an *ecumenical level of attention*.

In this fragment too (Fig. 2) Berlinguer displays an almost sad, but *serious* gaze (AU 9 + 1 + 4; nose wrinkle, inner brown raised), *staring out into space,* a cue to cognitive effort and attention to the words he is choosing. This conveys a meaning of ATTENTION and CARE to the Interlocutor (he searches the right words because the other person is important for him).

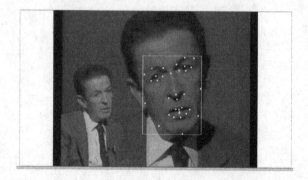

Fig. 2. Berlinguer

Later, Berlinguer *moves forward towards the Interviewer*, and starting from a position of *head canting*, he makes *nods* to approve and integrate the journalist's perspective [11]; he *looks at him straight in his eyes*, conveying that he is "going toward" the interlocutor and trying to get to a common point, a sign of conciliation and mediation of viewpoints (Fig. 3).

Fig. 3. a, b. Berlinguer

3.4 Aldo Moro

Aldo Moro was a politician, an academic and Italian jurist during the sixties until 1978 when he was kidnapped and killed by terrorists of "Red Brigades"; he was five times Prime Minister and chairman of the Christian Democrats, and he was very popular also because he promoted a conciliatory policy towards the Italian Communist Party.

At minute 4.07. Moro says:
"Non mi pento di aver trovato naturale un incontro con tutti i parlamentari."
(I do not regret to have found a natural accordance with all parliament member).

The multimodal analysis evidences Moro's *flat pitch* and *very slow rhythm*, both conveying on the one hand the need to be understood and the other the need to choose the right words to use, given the importance of the other's point of view; the ATTENTION to the other is marked by the cognitive effort and seriousness expressed by the facial expression of sadness/concern (*knitted brows, eyes slightly tighten, lip corner depressed,*

AU 1, 4, 6, 15) and by the *gaze downward, raised* to the Interlocutor only in case of emphasis. At the same time, Moro's *hands bent before chin*, and *swaying toward the interlocutor*, express a state of concentration and sometimes the resolution of an internal reasoning finally communicated externally (Fig. 4).

Fig. 4. Moro

3.5   José Alberto Mujica

The first fragment is from President of Uruguay, José Alberto Mujica, who with his life style demonstrated a humble way to be president. He lives on a small farm in Rincón del Cerro, the suburbs of Montevideo, and also during his tenure he refused to live in the presidential palace. In reference to the small amount of salary he kept for himself (about 800 EUR), which made him deserve the nickname "the poorest President in the world", Mujica said in an interview to the Colombian newspaper El Tiempo that this amount of money was sufficient to him, given that many farmers in his country live on less than this.

In 2015, Josè Mujica recorded an interview For "Human", a collection of stories to answer the film director Yann Arthus-Bertrand's question on "what means to be human".

At minute 2.30 he says
"This is not an apology of poverty but one of sobriety"
(*questa non è un'apologia della povertà ma della sobrietà*)

The multimodal analysis of this fragment, performed by means of the annotation scheme (Table 1), describes Mujica, dressed with a *simple shirt* (col.10) – a signal of INFORMALITY – leaning forward as to communicate a desire to get closer, to create FAMIL-IARITY with the interlocutor (col. 4); his head (col.5) is lowered and directed straight to the camera but, like gaze direction, from down upward, thus positioning him in a down-up position, conveys the meaning that he does not judge or command over the potential listener (NON- SUPERIORITY). His gaze (col.6), by *raised and frowning eyebrows* (AU 1, 4, 15) expresses worry, hence concern about the interlocutor's future (EMPATHY), while *nose wrinkles* (col. 8) and AU7, lid tightener, AU23, lip tightener – the Action Units of anger [7] communicate the importance of the subject by raising attention (Fig. 5).

Fig. 5. Mujica

At 2.39 Mujica says:

Inventamos una montaña de consumo superfluo.... Y lo que estamos comprando es el tiempo de la vida! Porqué quando yo compro algo, o tu, no lo compra con plata, lo compra con el tiempo de vida que use para otener ese plata Pero con esta diferencia: la unica cosa che no se puede comprar es la vida"

(We invent a mountain of unnecessary consumption. ...What we're buying is the time of life! When we buy something, you do not buy it with money, but with the life time it takes to earn that money. With one difference: the only thing you cannot buy is life").

In this fragment Mujica's speech has a *simple phrase structure*, he suggests and gives advice with a *slow rhythm* and a *low intensity of voice*, whispering phrases as if talking to a family member, thus expressing FAMILIARITY. But he emphasizes *"la vida"* (life) with *louder voice* and also *looking directly toward the interlocutor* while *lowering his head* and with a facial expression of anger (*frown, raised eyebrows, nose wrinkles*), which is also another way to display EMPATHY for the possible negative consequences of not being sober (Fig. 6).

Fig. 6. Mujica

3.6 Barack Obama

The most quoted politician in our survey as "humble" politician was Barack Obama, and the speech most frequently chosen by participant was the "farewell speech" issued on January 10th, 2017.

(https://www.youtube.com/watch?v=XcCrH6rWG-0&t=95s). Obama is cited as humble mostly for the moment in which, while thanking his wife, he is blatantly *moved*: in so doing he complies with two rules of humble communication. The first is "do not show your own power, merits, or successes", but rather attribute them to another person through *thanksgiving*. The second is linked to the idea that to express one's emotions, but also to be seen while trying to retain emotional expression describe a politician in all his humanness. Here Obama expresses emotions as if he were in his family and, therefore, he does not hold back his tears (Fig. 7).

At 3:39 Obama names his wife: "*Michelle Obama, southern girl* (…)", he *looks down at her, stops talking*, trying to hold back the emotion and then *swallows up tears*, he *shakes his head* and *bites his lips*.

Then he goes on (3:51): "*over the past 25 years you have been not only my wife or the mother of my children have been my best friend*" and again *presses his lips* to create the *one hand dimpler* (dimpler + lip corner depressor AU15 + lip press AU24 and lip suck AU28), he tries to speak again but *lowers his head* and *raises his eyes bright*.

Fig. 7. Obama

3.7 Humble Leaders and Emotion Detection Through I-Motion

The videos analyzed with a multimodal approach [7] were later analyzed frame by frame through Action Unit detection in order to describe what are the emotions leaking during humble communication. Table 3 shows how the humble politicians have an average engagement (31.6), a high level of attention (direction towards the other person) but a negative emotional valence (−15.8). In particular, among the negative emotions *anger* prevails (10.2), which in this context we can interpret rather as "serious, strict and attentive" and *sadness* (6.1), appearing in our analysis mainly with the meaning of worried, and *disgust* (8.2) as restrained concern (Table 4). Actually, from the multimodal analysis, in addition to the features discovered in our survey, new elements such as SERIOUSNESS emerge, as well as CONCERN for the discussed issues, in particular in Mujica and Moro; so the most common emotions across these four videos are WORRY and SERIOUSNESS/ATTENTION. Such expressions are coherent with the EMPATHIC stance typical of the humble leader. Politicians express these negative emotions to stress how important the issues they are talking about are for their social group or for the human kind in general. On the contrary, positive emotions such as joy and surprise are very low. Upcoming analysis will compare these data with others taken from "non-humble" leaders.

Table 3. Engagement, valence and attention

	Engagement	Valence	Attention
MORO	44,64	−24,75	86,75
BERLINGUER	24,00	−10,05	71,55
MUJICA	42,09	−21,17	95,09
OBAMA	15,97	−7,25	25,15
Mean	31,68	−15,81	69,63

Table 4. Humble leaders' emotions

	Anger	Sadness	Disgust	Joy	Surprise	Fear	Contempt
MORO	18,55	7,29	19,19	0,74	0,42	0,05	1,97
BERLINGUER	0,45	0,08	2,96	0,65	2,38	0,73	6,53
MUJICA	18,71	15,63	5,54	0,86	0,49	0,08	2,10
OBAMA	3,40	1,43	5,42	0,85	2,79	0,12	0,30
Mean	10,28	6,11	8,28	0,78	1,52	0,24	2,73

4   Conclusion

The study presented was aimed, as a first step, at identifying the semantic elments of humility, and investigating its multimodal communication in the political domain. As resulting from our survey, humility entails acknowledgement of one's own limits and flaws, a feeling of equality, and a goal of not showing superior to others, to the point of hiding one's own advantages or merits. In political communication, the humble politician expresses his/her thoughts by treating the interlocutor in a familiar and empathic way. From multimodal analysis it emerges how politicians tend to be empathic by expressing their sadness or anger (as detected from Action Units such as AU7), and this results in an expression of seriousness and worry about the topic at hand. From the automatic detection of emotions, humble politicians seem to express negative emotions more than positive ones. Future analysis will deepen the role played by emotions by comparing humble politicians with dominant ones. A possible difference stands out from our multimodal analysis across time: humility in past politicians was expressed in a more *institutional* manner, speaking more in the name of the party; actual politicians instead tend to express humility in a more familiar way, since the relation between politician and potential voter is more strict. In our observation Obama speaks as a husband, a father, a son and a nephew, and gets moved publicly while thanking his wife: this points out how a more intense and less restrained expression of emotions can be considered as a form of familiarity and confidentiality. To this purpose, future analyses will take into consideration also the intensity dimension of emotion, while also more systematically studying the verbal/rhetorical level.

References

1. Poggi, I., D'Errico, F.: Dominance signals in debates. In: Salah, A.A., Gevers, T., Sebe, N., Vinciarelli, A. (eds.) HBU 2010. LNCS, pp. 163–174. Springer, Heidelberg (2010). doi: 10.1007/978-3-642-14715-9_16
2. Tangney, J.P.: Humility. In: Snyder, C.R., Lopez, S.J. (eds.) Handbook Of Positive Psychology, pp. 411–419. Oxford University Press, New York (2002)
3. Liu, C.: Does humble leadership behavior promote employees' voice behavior?—A dual mediating model. Open J. Bus. Manage. 4(04), 731 (2016)
4. Li, J., Liang, Q.Z., Zhang, Z.Z.: The effect of humble leader behavior, leader expertise, and organizational identification on employee turnover intention. J. Appl. Bus. Res. (JABR) 32(4), 1145–1156 (2016)
5. D'Errico, F., Poggi, I.: Acidity. The hidden face of conflictual and stressful situations. Cogn. Comput. 6(4), 661–676 (2014)
6. Poggi, I., D'Errico, F.: Multimodal acid communication of a politician. In: ESSEM@ AI* IA, pp. 59–70 (2013)
7. Poggi, I.: Mind, Hands, Face and Body: A Goal And Belief View of Multimodal Communication, pp. 1–432. Weidler, Berlin (2007)
8. Ekman, P., Friesen, W.V., Hager, J.C.: Facs manual. A Human Face (2002)
9. Keltner, D., Cordaro, D.T.: Understanding multimodal emotional expressions: Recent advances in basic emotion theory (2015). Emotion Researcher http://emotionresearcher.com/understanding-multimodalemotional-expressions-recent-advances-in-basic-emotion-theory
10. D'Errico, F.: With different words: The arguments that can empower an e-minority. Comput. Hum. Behav. 61, 205–212 (2016)
11. Poggi, I., D'Errico, F., Vincze, L.: Agreement and its multimodal communication in debates: A qualitative analysis. Cogn. Comput. 3(3), 466–479 (2011)

A Deep Learning Semantic Approach to Emotion Recognition Using the IBM Watson Bluemix Alchemy Language

Giulio Biondi[1], Valentina Franzoni[2(✉)], and Valentina Poggioni[1]

[1] Department of Mathematics and Computer Science, University of Perugia,
Via Vanvitelli 1, Perugia, Italy
giulio.biondi@studenti.unipg.it, valentina.poggioni@unipg.it
[2] Department of Computer, Control and Management Engineering,
Sapienza University of Rome, Via Ariosto, 25, Rome, Italy
franzoni@dis.uniroma1.it

Abstract. Sentiment analysis and emotion recognition are emerging research fields of research that aim to build intelligent systems able to recognize and interpret human emotions. Due to the applicability of these systems to almost all kinds of markets, also the interest of companies and industries is grown in an exponential way in the last years and a lot of frameworks for programming these systems are introduced. IBM Watson is one of the most famous and used: it offers, among others, a lot of services for Natural Language Processing. In spite of broad-scale multi-language services, most of functions are not available in a lot of "secondary" languages (like Italian). The main objective of this work is to demonstrate the feasibility of a translation-based approach to emotion recognition in texts written in "secondary" languages. We present a prototypical system using IBM Watson to extract emotions from Italian text by means of Bluemix Alchemy Language. Some preliminary results are shown and discussed in order to stress pro and cons of the approach.

Keywords: Affective computing · Emotion recognition · Sentiment analysis · SEMO · Semantics · Deep learning · Machine learning · Artificial intelligence · Computer science · IBM · Watson · Alchemy language · Language translation

1 Introduction

In recent years, Affective Computing become a trending topic in Artificial Intelligence focusing, among others, on detection and extraction of affective information from different sources e.g., images, music, brain scans, text. Particularly studied is the analysis of text, written either in structured/semi-structured form or in natural language [27–30,33]. Using Natural Language Processing (NLP) techniques, automated agents can gain the ability to process and analyze text at different levels of abstraction, exploiting the speed and computational power of modern systems.

© Springer International Publishing AG 2017
O. Gervasi et al. (Eds.): ICCSA 2017, Part III, LNCS 10406, pp. 718–729, 2017.
DOI: 10.1007/978-3-319-62398-6_51

Among various branches of Affective Computing, it is possible to identify, Sentiment Analysis (SA) and Emotion Recognition (ER):

- Sentiment Analysis studies the polarity of a text, which can be positive, negative or neutral.
- Emotion Recognition extracts and recognizes the emotional content, according to models of emotions accepted as State of the Art, e.g. the Ekman, Plutchik, and Lovheim models.

Several other models are present in literature and others will come, because the hype initiated at the end of last century didn't still finish its effect on the scientific research [31]. Furthermore, the technical advent of new and affordable tools to measure aspects linked to emotional reactions lead to an interdisciplinary worldwide interest to Affective Computing and Emotion Recognition, so that both private and public research groups are studying emotions in different points of view. For our point of view focusing on textual information, different approaches can be followed to analyze text e.g., knowledge-based, statistical or hybrid approaches. Nowadays, companies already invest a lot of resources to fructify information on the sentiment expressed towards a target, e.g. political subjects, brands, a product with its associated reviews; the efficiency of a marketing campaign depends largely on the ability to detect ongoing trends and to foresee future customers' needs.

1.1 Affective computing for marketing applications

Recommender Systems (RS) can use affective computing to implement and augment knowledge about the sentiment/opinion towards a product or a brand, helping sellers to automatically tailor their recommendations to users with a user-centered approach for a better personalization. Along with commercial applications, researchers are applying Affective Computing also to spam detection [23], and to build human-computer interaction systems based on natural language, both spoken [5,32] and written [13,14,18–21,26].

Another application of Emotion Recognition (ER) that is already on the market, is used to detect in real time the interest, involvement and emotions of a customer through video-based techniques. A simple classification of visual features captured with a camera, recognized and tracked while a user is looking, hearing or trying a product, gives sellers immediate feedback about their products and the connected customers' feelings.

1.2 Novel Applications

Novels applications include to use knowledge of emotions as prosthesis knowledge for tutoring, or auto-evaluation of teachers and leaders, who can analyze their facial or written or spoken expressions in order to be aware of emotions and manage them as possible, with the aim of improving their social skills and avoid human misunderstanding of tone. For example the SEMO model of Semantic Emotion Recognition [1,13] allow to detect emotions from text and thus to eventually correct it before sending it via email or posting on social networks [22].

1.3   A Translation-Based Approach

In this work, a translation-based approach to emotion recognition in texts written in "secondary" languages is presented, and the feasibility of such approach is discussed. For this purpose, we present a prototypical system using IBM Watson to extract emotions from Italian text by means of Bluemix Alchemy Language. Some preliminary results are shown and discussed in order to stress pros and cons of the approach. In the first section of this paper an overview of the software tools and platforms that perform our approach is presented. A detailed breakdown of the IBM Alchemy Language API is given, describing each function related to a complete process of emotion recognition and extraction. The second section shows an example of usage of the Sentiment and Emotion APIs, in conjunction with the Language translator module, used here to translate terms from Italian to English. A final discussion concludes the paper.

2   Platform and Tools

2.1   IBM Watson

IBM Watson is an AI system capable of answering questions posed in natural language. Developed within the *DEEPQA* IBM project, it improves the capability of artificial intelligences in understanding questions posed in natural language, providing relevant answers. Watson was firstly shown in public in 2011, when it competed against two human champions in the TV quiz *Jeopardy!*. The stress was put on the ability of the AI to understand questions and provide exact answers with speed comparable to humans: Watson, in fact, won the first prize in the game.

IBM engineers then focused on using Watson as a clinical decision support system, in partnership with the Memorial Sloan-Kettering Cancer Center, New York. The goal was to enable medical personnel to supply the system with a patient's clinical situation, including symptoms and risk factors, and get a list of personalized recommendations, ranked by a confidence index. Tests shown that for particular applications (e.g. lung cancer diagnosis) Watson could dramatically improve the time needed for diagnosis and give relevant suggestions. More generally, the key feature of Watson in the medical field is the ability to process the huge amount of knowledge produced in medical literature on a daily basis, at a speed impossible for humans. Diagnoses can then be performed taking into account the whole literature, possibly leading to improved results, which will then be analyzed and used by human personnel.

After the initial presentation of Watson to the public, a variety of Artificial Intelligence applications have been introduced in the service, using machine learning techniques for rapid exploration of an enormous source of linked data [6,7,15]. Knowledge in several fields was enhanced, ranging from NLP to personality insights for annotating user profiles basing on the content of their messages, emails and tweets. In a future Internet-of-Things (IoT) vision, General Motors is planning to use Watson to improve location-aware services in their cars, and the Imperial College in London is focusing on crime prediction using Watson for pattern analysis. We are showing here how Watson can be used also for emotion recognition, in a simple application on text data [8,17].

2.2   IBM Bluemix

IBM Watson tools are available on Bluemix, the IBM cloud computing PaaS (Platform-as-a-Service). Bluemix serves both as an infrastructure, offering the possibility to rent computing power, network appliances and storage space, and as a software platform, with runtime applications developed in different languages and technologies. Bluemix offers access to various services too; a list of all the available services can be found on the Bluemix website (an IBM account is needed).

2.3   Watson Developer Cloud

IBM *Watson Developer Cloud* offers services for helping users to build cognitive applications; it is the access point for developers to the Watson API, and the basis for the service of Affective Computing. A plethora of services are available on the platform, covering five main areas:

1. Language, recognizing 97 spoken languages;
2. Speech, with NLP functions;
3. Vision, with image recognition;
4. Data Insights for data analysis;
5. Embodied Cognition, including sentiment analysis and alchemy language on linked data.

It is possible to combine functions and libraries belonging to different areas, in order to build complex multimedia applications.

2.4   AlchemyLanguage

AlchemyLanguage is a set of services to build complex applications for textual NLP, with a high level of abstraction used in several applications of emotion recognition (i.e. see [16]. This service is part of the Language area in the Watson Developer Cloud. AlchemyLanguage is composed of two main modules:

1. *AlchemyLanguage functions*: a set of text analysis functions to extract semantic information from input text terms;
2. *AlchemyData*: a database indexing about 300 thousand news and blog articles everyday, in English. Users can create custom NLP queries that will can performed directly on the cloud database, without the need of heavy calculation on local client machines. Results will include the indexed articles, matching the query constraints and enriched with NLP information.

2.5   Sentiment Analysis and Emotion Recognition

Entity Recognition. The *Entities* function extracts entities from text. The user inputs a text, HTML document or URL pointing to a web page, and Watson returns a list of entities, using complex statistical algorithms and NLP technology in the form of a combination of multilingual support, linked data, context-sensitive entity disambiguation, comprehensive type support and quotations extraction. The API supports custom models that can be trained using Watson Developer Studio. Results can include additional content, e.g.:

- linked data (active by default);
- entity-level sentiment;
- emotions associated to detected entities.

Supported languages for the function are: English, French, German, Italian, Portuguese, Russian, Spanish, and Swedish.

Sentiment on Document. The *Sentiment* function analyses the overall sentiment in a given text. The user inputs some text content, HTML documents or URL pointing to the information to analyze, and the system returns the associated sentiment, in the form of a triple:

1. a flag *Mixed*, with *1* meaning that the sentiment is not polarized (i.e. both positive and negative), and *0* meaning that the sentiment is polarized;
2. a weight in the $[-1; 1]$ range representing the sentiment, with *0* meaning Neutral;
3. a polarity value among: *positive, negative* or *neutral*.

Supported languages are: English, French, Italian, German, Portuguese, Russian, and Spanish.

Sentiment on Specific Targets. The *Targeted Sentiment* function works like the precious, but at a different level of abstraction, associating a sentiment to user-specified targets, e.g. a product or a brand. Furthermore, other items can be analyzed as part of other calls, e.g. quotations, entities (*Entities* call), and keywords (*Keywords* call). Thanks to the strong NLP abilities of Watson, target options include also relational and directional functions (*Relations* call). Supported languages for these functions are: Arabic, English, French, German, Italian, Portuguese, Russian, and Spanish.

3   Experimental Use Case: Assigning Emotional Tags to Book Blurbs in Italian Language

In a previous work, the authors of this work tested if it is possible to classify books using emotional by means of classifying terms extracted not from the whole book, but from its presentation blurb (usually in the fourth page of the edition). Experiments has been carried on books written or translated in Italian language, and the final emotions has been compared to the emotional tags given by users of the social network Zazie. Zazie is an Italian product giving to users a place where to review the books they read, assigning them reviews and emotional tags to discover, from collective information, new books to choose, based on their capacity to raise emotions (e.g. happy, sad) or to be read while in particular moods (e.g. relaxed on the coach, distracted on the beach). In [12,14] the authors tested the possibility of automatic classification of books associating to the words of blurbs to emotional tags extracted from WordNet Affect, which is part of the WordNet ontology. In this work, we implement a simple experimentation of what the IBM Alchemy API can do for the same task, using a simple example from the Zazie data set. In [9,11] the Wikipedia semantic network is navigated by using a trace based approach [25] similar to ACO algorithms [2–4,24] and several web-based proximity measures [10], it is worth investigating in future work if the same techniques and proximity measures can be used in the framework of emotion classification.

3.1 Experiment Design

As shown in the previous section, Alchemy APIs provide the user with methods to assign a sentiment/emotion tag. While sentiment can be extracted in a number of languages, including Italian, emotions can be instead recognized only in English. A translation from Italian to English will be therefore exploited using the *Language Translator* module as a preliminary action, then the result will be used with the *Emotion Analysis* module. As an example, we will carry out the Italian text of the blurb from the book *Il turno di notte lo fanno le stelle* by the author Erri De Luca:

> Matthew ha un cuore nuovo. Un cuore di donna. Ed è con una donna, sua compagna di malattia e guarigione in ospedale, che andrà a riprendersi la vita in cima a una montagna, scalandola. Uno straordinario raccontosceneggiatura, dove ogni battito del cuore ha un suono mai udito prima.

3.2 NLP Preprocessing Phase

The *Relations* function extracts triplets (Subject, Action, Object) expressing relations. It is one of the most advanced and interesting tools available in the AlchemyLanguage API, and well demonstrates the power of Watson Data Mining AI in the field of NLP. The user inputs some text content, HTML documents or URLs pointing to the information to analyze, and the system returns a list of sentences along with their elements, performing the following steps, for which we provide a description including a tag "charged" if they are due to an additional payment in the IBM system:

1. *Sentence Parsing*: parses sentences into subject, action, object and location.
2. *Keyword extraction* (charged): extracts keywords information
3. *Entity extraction* (charged): extracts entities information.
4. *Sentiment Analysis* (charged): calculates sentiment at a relational level for subjects, objects and locations, and directional level for actions.
5. *Verb Normalization*: lemmatizes verbs, identifies the tense and detects an eventual negation.

By default, linked data content links are included in the response; users can optionally hide them.

Supported languages are English and Spanish. Italian is not supported, thus our application will require a preliminary translation.

3.3   Results on the Sentiment Analysis Task

In this section a Sentiment tag is assigned to the blurb, among *positive*, *negative* and *neutral*.

The following script queries the *Sentiment Analysis* API and prints the result, in the form of a JSON document, on screen.

Algorithm 1. Sentiment Analysis example code

```
1  import json
2  from watson_developer_cloud import AlchemyLanguageV1
3
4  alchemy_language = AlchemyLanguageV1(api_key=API_KEY)
5  text="Matthew ha un cuore nuovo. Un cuore di donna. Ed
       \'e con una donna, sua compagna di malattia e
       guarigione in ospedale, che andr\'a a riprendersi
       la vita in cima a una montagna, scalandola. Uno
       straordinario racconto-sceneggiatura, dove ogni
       battito del cuore ha un suono mai udito prima."
6  result = alchemy_language.sentiment(text=text,
       language=italian)
7  print(json.dumps(result, indent=2))
```

The following JSON-style document shows the result of the call.

```
1    {
2        "docSentiment":{
3            "mixed" : "0",
4            "score" : "0.467522",
5            "type" : "positive"
6        },
7        "usage": "By accessing AlchemyAPI or using information
8        generated by AlchemyAPI, you are agreeing to be bound by the
9        AlchemyAPI Terms of Use:
10       http://www.alchemyapi.com/company/terms.html",
11       "status": "OK",
12       "totalTransactions": "1"
13   }
```

Listing 1: JSON example

Results include some control information which is common to each API call, i.e.:

- *usage* field, containing a link to the terms of usage of AlchemyAPI;
- *status* field, indicating whether the request was successful or not;
- *totalTransactions* field, indicating how many API calls were necessary to get all the required information. May be higher than one, for example in combined calls.

The sentiment information is embedded in the *docSentiment* object, which is composed of three elements:

- A "Mixed" flag, with 1 meaning that the sentiment is both positive and negative, and 0 meaning that the sentiment is polarized
- A weight in the $[-1; 1]$ range representing the sentiment strength, with 0 meaning *Neutral*
- A Sentiment tag that can be Positive, Negative or Neutral.

In our case, the API reported a Positive polarity for the text, with a score of 0.467522 and no mixed sentiment.

Note: the *mixed* attribute is not included in the result when its value is 0. We decided to include it for clarity purposes.

3.4   Translation and Emotion Analysis

In this section we will show the second step of our example, translating the blurb to the English language and calculating emotional scores.

The following script first queries the *Language Translator* service, prints the result on screen and uses it as input to the *Emotion Analysis* API.

Algorithm 2. Translator and Emotion Analysis example code

```
1   import json
2   from watson_developer_cloud import LanguageTranslatorV2 as
        LanguageTranslator , AlchemyLanguageV1
3   language_translator = LanguageTranslator(
4       username='LT_userName',
5       password='LT_password')
6   alchemy_language = AlchemyLanguageV1(api_key=API_key)
7   text=XXX
8   translation = json.dumps(language_translator.translate(text=text,
        source='it', target='en'), indent=2, ensure_ascii=False)
9   print(translation)
10  result = json.dumps(alchemy_language.emotion(text=translation),
        indent=2)
11  print(result)
```

The translation performed by the Language Translator service:

> Matthew has a new heart. A woman's heart. And it's with a woman, her roommate disease and healing in the hospital, which will recover their lives at the top of a mountain, scalandola. One amazing racconto-sceneggiatura, where each pulse of the heart has a sound never heard before.

The JSON-style document in listing 2 shows the result of the call for Emotion Analysis. The emotion information is embedded in the *docEmotions* object, which contains five emotion-score pairs, as described in Chap. 2, section *Emotion Analysis*. In our case, the API reports *joy* as the prevalent emotion in the text, followed in turn by *fear*.

4   Results Discussion and Conclusion

In this work an overview of the *AlchemyLanguage* API was given and an example use case on the Zazie data set was shown. The main goal of this work was to check if IBM Watson Developer Cloud Services can be used for research purposes in the area of Emotion Recognition and Sentiment Analysis, both as ways to discover new information and ease processes and as benchmarks to compare against laboratory results. The answer is positive, although with some caveats:

```
1   {
2     "docEmotions":
3     {
4       "fear": "0.213389",
5       "joy": "0.301097",
6       "sadness": "0.142693",
7       "anger": "0.200515",
8       "disgust": "0.206219"
9     }
10    "totalTransactions": "1",
11    "language": "english",
12    "usage": "By accessing AlchemyAPI or using information generated
13      by AlchemyAPI, you are agreeing to be bound by the AlchemyAPI
14      Terms of Use:
15      http://www.alchemyapi.com/company/terms.html",
16    "status": "OK"
17  }
```

Listing 2: Emotion analysis results example

– First, even if IBM allows to launch the computation on their dedicated cloud platform, it could prove expensive in terms of time: there is a free daily/- monthly quota for AlchemyLanguage, depending on the different methods for

Language Translator; other services, which we only mentioned, have their own subscription plans. Those amounts are enough for small testing, but working on Big Data may require planning to optimize time: it was calculated that to perform *Sentiment Analysis* on all the blurbs included in the Zazie dataset without incurring in any charge approximately 10 days are needed, with the same time required for *Emotion Analysis*.

- Building and using custom models for specific needs requires a consistent effort in terms of money. The free *one time* quota is 250.000 characters.
- The quality of translation still needs to be improved. In the previously shown example, the system was not able to translate some words, which were left in the original language. This could lead to less precise results, especially in the case when the words

Nevertheless, IBM *AlchemyLanguage*, even in the limited *free* version, represents a good and easy way to access tools at the state of art of Natural Language Processing. It would be interesting to analyze all the services on Watson Developer Cloud and their applications, to test not only text-related but Image Recognition and Speech Recognition ones, to perform Affective Computing and Emotion Recognition from images and audio directly on the IBM cloud.

References

1. Anusha, V., Sandhya, B.: A learning based emotion classifier with semantic text processing. In: El-Alfy, E.-S.M., Thampi, S.M., Takagi, H., Piramuthu, S., Hanne, T. (eds.) Advances in Intelligent Informatics. AISC, vol. 320, pp. 371–382. Springer, Cham (2015). doi:10.1007/978-3-319-11218-3_34
2. Baioletti, M., Milani, A., Poggioni, V., Rossi, F.: An ACO approach to planning. In: Cotta, C., Cowling, P. (eds.) EvoCOP 2009. LNCS, vol. 5482, pp. 73–84. Springer, Heidelberg (2009). doi:10.1007/978-3-642-01009-5_7
3. Baioletti, M., Milani, A., Poggioni, V., Rossi, F.: Ant search strategies for planning optimization. In: ICAPS 2009 Proceedings of the 19th International Conference on Automated Planning and Scheduling, pp. 334–337 (2009)
4. Baioletti, M., Milani, A., Poggioni, V., Rossi, F.: Optimal planning with ACO. In: Serra, R., Cucchiara, R. (eds.) AI*IA 2009. LNCS, vol. 5883, pp. 212–221. Springer, Heidelberg (2009). doi:10.1007/978-3-642-10291-2_22
5. Bhaskar, J., Sruthi, K., Nedungadi, P.: Hybrid approach for emotion classification of audio conversation based on text and speech mining. Procedia Comput. Sci. **46**, 635–643 (2015)
6. Chiancone, A., Franzoni, V., Milani, A.: A multistrain bacterial diffusion model for link prediction. Int. J. Pattern Recogn. Artif. Intell. **31**(11), 157–172 (2017). World Scientific
7. Chiancone, A., Milani, A., Poggioni, V., Pallottelli, S., Madotto, A., Franzoni, V.: A multistrain bacterial model for link prediction. In: Proceedings of the International Conference on Natural Computation, pp. 1075–1079. IEEE Press (2016). doi:10.1109/ICNC.2015.7378141
8. Ferrucci, D.A.: Introduction to this is watson. IBM J. Res. Dev. **56**(34), 1 (2012)

9. Franzoni, V., Mencacci, M., Mengoni, P., Milani, A.: Semantic heuristic search in collaborative networks: measures and contexts. In: Proceedings 2014 IEEE/WIC/ACM International Joint Conference on Web Intelligence and Intelligent Agent Technology, WI/IAT 2014, vol. 1, pp. 187–217. IEEE Press (2014). doi:10.1109/WI-IAT.2014.27

10. Franzoni, V., Milani, A.: Pming distance: a collaborative semantic proximity measure. In: Proceedings of the IEEE/WIC/ACM International Conference on Intelligent Agent Technology, IAT 2012, vol. 2, pp. 442–449. IEEE Press (2012). doi:10.1109/WI-IAT.2012.226

11. Franzoni, V., Milani, A.: A pheromone-like model for semantic context extraction from collaborative networks. In: Proceedings IEEE/WIC/ACM International Joint Conference on Web Intelligence and Intelligent Agent Technology, WI-IAT 2015, 2016-January, pp. 540–547, IEEE Press (2016)

12. Franzoni, V., Poggioni, V., Zollo, F.: Can we infer book classification by blurbs. CEUR Workshop Proceedings, vol. 1127, pp. 16–19. CEUR WS (2014)

13. Franzoni, V., Biondi, G., Milani, A., Li, Y.: Web-based semantic similarity for emotion recognition in web objects. CoRR abs/1612.05734 (2016)

14. Franzoni, V., Poggioni, V., Zollo, F.: Automated classification of book blurbs according to the emotional tags of the social network zazie. In: 1st International Workshop on Emotion and Sentiment in Social and Expressive Media, ESSEM 2013, CEUR Workshop Proceedings, pp. 83–94. CEUR WS (2013)

15. Gentili, E., Milani, A., Poggioni, V.: Data summarization model for user action log files. In: Murgante, B., Gervasi, O., Misra, S., Nedjah, N., Rocha, A.M.A.C., Taniar, D., Apduhan, B.O. (eds.) ICCSA 2012. LNCS, vol. 7335, pp. 539–549. Springer, Heidelberg (2012). doi:10.1007/978-3-642-31137-6_41

16. Gupta, R.K., Yang, Y.: Crystalnest at semeval-2017 task 4: Using sarcasm detection for enhancing sentiment classification and quantification. In: SemEval: 11th International Workshop on Semantic Evaluation, Aug 3–4, 2017, Vancouver, Canada (to appear)

17. High, R.: The Era of Cognitive Systems: An Inside Look at IBM Watson and How it Works. IBM Corporation, Redbooks, Armonk (2012)

18. Houjeij, A., Hamieh, L., Mehdi, N., Hajj, H.: A novel approach for emotion classification based on fusion of text and speech. In: 2012 19th International Conference on Telecommunications (ICT), pp. 1–6, April 2012

19. Huang, S.l., Chen, Y.S.: Developing document classifiers for recognizing article readers' affects. In: Proceedings of the 2012 International Conference on Information Management (2012)

20. Liberati, C., Camillo, F.: Subjective business polarization: Sentiment analysis meets predictive modeling. In: Catania, B., et al. (eds.) New Trends in Databases and Information Systems. AISC, vol. 241. Springer, Cham (2014)

21. Lupan, D., Bobocescu-Kesikis, S., Dascalu, M., Trausan-Matu, S., Dessus, P.: Predicting readers' emotional states induced by news articles through latent semantic analysis. In: SMART 2013 International Conference on Social Media in Academia: Research and Teaching, pp. 79–84. Citeseer (2013)

22. Mancini, L., Milani, A., Poggioni, V., Chiancone, A.: Self regulating mechanisms for network immunization. AI Commun. 29(2), 301–317 (2016)

23. Markines, B., Cattuto, C., Menczer, F.: Social spam detection. In: Proceedings of the 5th International Workshop on Adversarial Information Retrieval on the Web AIRWeb 2009, p. 41 (2009)

24. Milani, A., Poggioni, V.: Planning in reactive environments. Comput. Intell. 23(4), 439–463 (2007)

25. Pallottelli, S., Franzoni, V., Milani, A.: Multi-path traces in semantic graphs for latent knowledge elicitation. In: Proceedings of International Conference on Natural Computation 2016-January, pp. 281–288. IEEE Press (2016). doi:10.1109/ICNC.2015.7378004
26. Ren, F., Quan, C.: Linguistic-based emotion analysis and recognition for measuring consumer satisfaction: an application of affective computing. Inf. Technol. Manage. **13**(4), 321–332 (2012)
27. Shelke, N.: Approaches of emotion detection from text. Int. J. Comput. Sci. Inf. Technol. Res. **2**(2), 123–128 (2014)
28. Shivhare, S.N., Garg, S., Mishra, A.: Emotionfinder: detecting emotion from blogs and textual documents. In: 2015 International Conference on Computing, Communication & Automation (ICCCA), pp. 52–57. IEEE (2015)
29. Shivhare, S.N., Saritha, S.K.: Emotion detection from text documents. Int. J. Data Min. Knowl. Manage. Process **4**(6), 51 (2014)
30. Taboada, M., Brooke, J., Tofiloski, M., Voll, K., Stede, M.: Lexicon-based methods for sentiment analysis. Comput. Linguist. **37**(2), 267–307 (2011)
31. Vallverdú, J., Trovato, G.: Emotional affordances for humanrobot interaction. Adapt. Behav. **24**(5), 320–334 (2016)
32. Vanzo, A., Croce, D., Castellucci, G., Basili, R., Nardi, D.: Spoken language understanding for service robotics in Italian. In: Adorni, G., Cagnoni, S., Gori, M., Maratea, M. (eds.) AI*IA 2016. LNCS, vol. 10037, pp. 477–489. Springer, Cham (2016). doi:10.1007/978-3-319-49130-1_35
33. Wang, H., Xu, H., Liu, L., Song, W., Du, C.: An unsupervised microblog emotion dictionary construction method and its application on sentiment analysis. J. Inf. Comput. Sci. **12**, 2729–2739 (2015)

Community Branding (Co-Bra): A Collaborative Decision Making Process for Urban Regeneration

Maria Cerreta[1(✉)] and Gaia Daldanise[1,2]

[1] Department of Architecture (DiARC), Federico II University of Naples,
Via Toledo 402, 80134 Naples, Italy
{cerreta,gaia.daldanise}@unina.it
[2] National Research Council of Italy (CNR), Institute of Research on Innovation
and Services for Development (IRISS), Via Guglielmo Sanfelice 8, 80134 Naples, Italy
g.daldanise@iriss.cnr.it

Abstract. The paper introduces a methodology for a learning and negotiation process that supports urban regeneration, combining management models and multi-criteria/multi-group evaluation methods. The purpose concerns the urban regeneration issue in an interdisciplinary complex decisional context where Place Branding, Community Planning, Community Impact Evaluation, and Place Marketing interplay in a decision-making process named "Community Branding (Co-Bra)". The processing of data and information elaborated by PROMETHEE (Preference Ranking Organisation METHod for Enrichment Evaluations) is crucial for providing the decision-maker with a ranking of alternatives based on preference degrees. Starting from the analysis carried out for Matera ECoC 2019, the case study of Pisticci (MT), the third-largest town in Basilicata (Italy), tested the methodological approach. The choice of a multidimensional approach, focused on the recognition of social, economic and cultural resources, provides strategies of enhancement of cultural heritage and community network by a "community hub", called "PLUS – Pisticci Laboratorio Urbano Sostenibile" (Pisticci Sustainable Urban Lab).

Keywords: Community identity · Hybrid evaluation · Place branding · Community impact evaluation · PROMETHEE

1 Introduction

In the planning and evaluation cycle, the evaluation may be understood as a decision-making process predicated upon the integration of approaches, methods, and models [1]. A suitable analysis of the problem at hand is essential for correctly addressing it. Doing so requires the identification of the available alternatives and of their consequences, the evaluation of alternatives and the selection of the most appropriate one, and the implementation of the latter [2]. Even so, evaluation is often understood and practised differently [3]: as a means to instrumentally legitimate actions, as a tool for interaction, as a modality to build tactics, as a coding tool, as a conceptual approach or as a process.

© Springer International Publishing AG 2017
O. Gervasi et al. (Eds.): ICCSA 2017, Part III, LNCS 10406, pp. 730–746, 2017.
DOI: 10.1007/978-3-319-62398-6_52

"Learning from comparison" is at the same time the goal and the result of the evaluation process, which may transfer a process in different contexts [5, 6]. Ultimately, evaluation seeks to estimate the significance of the change by analysing threats and opportunities [4]. With regard to the management of change of cultural values and to the promotion of the heritage as "urban strategic management", three key elements emerge in the implementation phase:

- Resources: the costs of preserving and transforming the heritage with the aim of achieving sustainable financing strategies;
- Rules: to reduce conflicts between public and private actors, and to incentivise collaborative strategies;
- Project: the concept that inspires the plan.

The issue of resources includes new channels of financing (public-private, national, international, local), as well as the third sector (foundations, NGOs, associations, cooperatives). The abundance of the latter in some contexts illustrates the vitality and the autonomy of local communities [1]. The issue of rules pertains to both the institutions (that should guarantee sustainable objectives), and to NGOs, which often engage in initiatives aimed at social integration.

Evaluation is interpreted here as a conceptual approach and as a learning process that supports planning. Adopting this interpretation requires interdisciplinary work on regeneration processes, such as research in the fields of Place Branding, Community Planning, and Place Marketing. Starting from *genius loci* definition [5], Place Branding [6–11] is the process that leads to the discovery, creation, development, and implementation of ideas and actions with the aim of (re)building the identity, the distinctive features, and the "sense of place" of a territory. Doing so requires investments in:

- infrastructure and buildings (the *hardware*, or the physical transformation of a territory);
- events and stories (the *software*, or the knowledge, skills and transfer capacity);
- cooperatives of organisational restructuring (the *orgware*, or the ability of actors to organise among themselves);
- symbols and symbolic actions (the *virtualware*, or the communication and transmission of a message [12].

If on the other hand, evaluation is view as a process of knowledge and planning, place branding emerges as a form of culture for the governance of the local supply, in that it introduces a system of principles, rules, and procedures that innovate the governance way of the territory and its society.

The second field, Community Planning [13–15], is a continuous, long-term process of planning, production, and revision of a commonplace. It has no pre-established duration, and the contribution of people and communities becomes a legal obligation [16]. Within community planning, we may distinguish between service-focused and people-focused approaches [17]. The two approaches, however, are complementary and therefore are both essential [18] for the cultural productivity of a territory [19, 20]. The community is both an actor and the end user of such a process. In a similar vein, the growth of the cultural sector implements both its supply and its demand. This highlights the necessity of developing an efficient management of the demand: place marketing [21–26]. Place marketing [23, 27–31] can be defined as a process that aims at enhancing a market-oriented strategy for a place to communicate its own identity. In this perspective, place marketing is interpreted as a production culture for the management of local demand, in that its core goal is the ability to relate different resources, each originating in different scholarly fields, with the surrounding contexts.

In line with this theoretical discussion, the research question focuses on a yet open question concerning policies and strategies for transcalar interventions. How can we build regeneration projects that synergically integrate the cultural, environmental, social, and economic aspects, particularly regarding the governance and management of a territory and the formation of active communities, and that combine innovation with place-based identity?

The paper attempts responding to this research question through the following structure: the first part (Sect. 2) defines the multi-method evaluation systems for place/community identity and cultural values; the second one (Sect. 3) explains the methodological approach of Community Branding (Co-Bra) and the case study results; the third (Sect. 4) shows discussion and conclusions about the whole process.

2   Evaluation for Cultural Values and Community Identity: Hybrid Evaluation Systems

Regarding the evaluation of place identity and image, three main approaches [32] of empirical measurement of place brand can help us to understand these dynamics:

- first, using qualitative methods oriented to end user [33, 34];
- secondly, with quantitative methods like standardised questionnaires on different brand dimensions and attributes [35];
- thirdly, with mixed methods like network analyses [36], multidimensional scaling [37], the laddering technique [38, 39], the brand concept map method [40, 41] or balanced scorecard as a monitoring tool for performances [42].

Furthermore, key measurement models of cultural heritage and perceived image [43] are included in Country Brand Index [44], Nation Brand Index of Anholt GfK Roper or City Brand Index [45] and in CHEI, a measurement scale of the Cultural Heritage Image [43]. Cultural heritage, place identity and collaborative processes [46–51] are complex systems in which any representation [52] is not completely able to reflect and capture all the issues of a problem in a single perspective [53–55]. Especially if we consider cultural values and community identity, the main evaluation approaches that take into account this complexity, in a systemic view, are multi-criteria methods [56]. Multicriteria evaluation (MCE), also known as Multi-Criteria Decision Analysis [57, 58], is a process of simplifying complex decision-making tasks [59] involving a great number of stakeholders, several possible outcomes and many, also intangible, criteria by which to evaluate the outcomes [60].

Among these, multi-actor and multi-group are methods highly discussed [57, 61–64], in particular for the issue of weights attribution. In these methods usually, weights are a "bottleneck" for the decision process, as shown, for example, in ELECTRE methods [62, 65] or in the NAIADE method [66]. However, this solution to the problem is not often adequate for a "social" multi-criteria evaluation [52], where weights of different criteria imply weights to different groups in the community. The main consequence is that weights become importance coefficients and not as a trade-off. In the aggregation stage, this approach implies that conventions used should be non-compensatory mathematical algorithms [67, 68].

The management of a multi-actor policy process involves several layers of decisions and requires a dialogue process among many stakeholders, formal and informal, local and not [52]. For this reason, the multi-criteria process can be participative and transparent, including stakeholders [69] in a social process, from participative multi-criteria evaluation (PMCE) or stakeholders multi-criteria decision aid (SMCDA) to social multi-criteria evaluation (SMCE).

If all relevant actors are involved in the decision process, the support for decision-making process is much higher. Among several methods that include stakeholders from the beginning, Multi-Actor Multi-Criteria Analysis (MAMCA) allows to show explicitly the objectives of the stakeholders and supports the decision maker providing a comparison of different strategic alternatives [70]. The construction of MAMCA criteria is different from the Group Decision Support Systems (GDSS). This method gives preferences set for every actor showing alternatives with most potentials [70].

From this literature framework, the research methodology aims to activate, in the experimental stage, a Deliberative Multi-Criteria Evaluation (DMCE) [60, 71–73] as a process aiming to address multiple decision makers into a Multi-Criteria Assessment (MCA). Combining Multi-Criteria Analysis with a deliberative procedure – the Citizens' Jury – this technique allows effective interaction from multiple decision-makers for deliberating and structuring main issues of the decision-making process. DMCE combines the facilitation properties of Citizens' Jury with analytical and integrated features of the Multi-Criteria Analysis by giving the jury the responsibility of finding an agreement about the weightings on decision criteria.

The target is providing an equitable framework of stakeholder preferences and priorities and impacts, outcomes of different options that are crucial in the decision-making process. In this method, it is used a no-conventional sensitivity analysis, because the analyst is not performing the calculations alone in a laboratory, but in a situation of real-time interaction with the decision makers. The main consequence is a continuous update of decisive parameters (for example, some criteria or options could be included, dropped, or simplified, and/or the weights could change) and the analyses could be iterated until the deliberation goes on.

3   Community Branding (Co-Bra) for Cultural Creative Networks: The Case of Pisticci (Italy)

In order to apply a DMCE framework for redefining territories, communities and their economies, this research relies on a circular methodological approach that combines the Community Impact Evaluation [74] with a set of evaluation and management tools for linking and enhancing local resources: Community Branding (Co-Bra) approach (Fig. 1). By Co-Bra, we mean a strategic, "glocal" process that combines:

- Place Branding for the governance of the local supply;
- Place Marketing for the management of the local demand;
- Community Planning and Community Evaluation to identify opportunities from local cultural production.

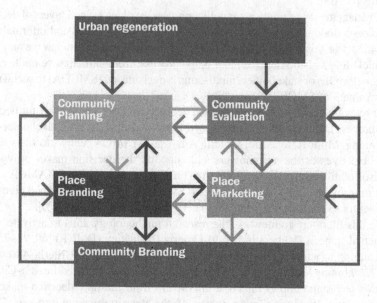

Fig. 1. Community branding (Co-Bra) approach

This approach emerges from the analysis carried out for Matera-Basilicata ECoC 2019 [75], which highlighted the necessity, for the Basilicata region, in the South of Italy, of an open network of cultural activities and creative communities. Its main focus lies on the valorization of the resources and of the relations between traditional and innovative identities within the network.

The proposed approach pushed the research towards further inquiries, which became an integral part of the adopted methodology:

- Which cultural values and how evaluate, "extract" them from the territory?
- Is there an open network that includes cultural activities within local context?
- Which are actors involved?
- What are the available monitoring and intervention tools?

To answer these questions, we have embarked on an exploratory research in Pisticci, the third-largest town in Basilicata (Italy) (Fig. 2). The rich potential of its tangible heritage is particularly visible in a few research projects that aimed at identifying the potential of the territory. This research was carried out in cooperation with Department of Architecture of the Federico II University of Naples and the City Council of Pisticci for the analysis of the strengths of the territory.

Fig. 2. Pisticci municipality

On the other hand, the variety of intangible (cultural and human) resources emerges from cultural and creative initiatives (such as "Imbianchini di Bellezza" - Painters of Beauty, "P-stories", "Lucania Film Festival", "Teatro lab"- Theater Lab, among others). These initiatives arose from local community and associations interaction, which make Pisticci an ideal case for an experiment on Co-Bra approach.

The project is structured along the 12 steps [76] of the Community Impact Evaluation. These were, however, sequenced and adapted to the 5 steps of the Place Branding process [77]. Following the Co-Bra approach, and with the goal of building an efficient/operative link among the three different disciplines, this project borrows the tools and approaches from both the evaluation and from the management repertoires [78–80]. These contribute, through the lived experiences of the community, to the identification and evaluation of the projects and of the actions in the field [94–96].

In the first step, and based on the case-study approach [81], we prepared the data extraction and identified the priorities of the territory. After the analysis of different projects and interventions, we defined the goals of the community branding for the regeneration of the territory.

Starting from desk research, our proposal was structured, in cooperation with local actors, in its vision, mission, and objectives:

- Vision: Networking Pisticci. A "virtual" network of landscapes, resources, and communities balancing tradition and innovation;
- Mission: Valorization of local peculiarities;
- Objectives: Favouring an efficient management of the human and territorial resources; Identifying the actions necessary to preserve the Historical Urban Landscape [82]; Developing community actions to valorize the identity of the latter; Programming meetings to establish an international dialogue about the risks and potentials of the territory.

The following steps drew, on the one hand, on consolidated multi-criteria and multi-group tools for the Deliberative Multi-Criteria Evaluation of alternative choices. On the other hand, we selected some key tools of Place Branding and Place Marketing. From Place Branding, we chose "urban storytelling" and "stakeholder satisfaction" for their aptness at monitoring how communities perceive their cultural heritage. These two tools were used during the second step (the analysis of the current place brand), in order to identify, evaluate, and "extract" the local cultural values from the territory. During this experimental phase, we used the "walk-about" explorative/digital method (a performance-based media storytelling of the group "Urban experience"). "Walking about" emerged as the most natural way to address issues connected to the territory and to its architecture and landscape. This activity helped to define paths and common spaces, as an "embryonic" city, where the most important relations with the territory unfold [83].

This led to a new implementation of the "walk-about" method, called "Luoghi di zonzo" ("Places of wandering") – promoted by "P-Stories" project – where the community was asked about its visions for the future development of Pisticci. With the aid of digital tools, participants were stimulated to enhance their sight and listening senses. This enabled us to collect information and ideas for future projects for the sustainable development of Pisticci, that were based on its history and its alternative vocations.

The collection of the community's stories and of the local vocations emerging from the "walk-about" were useful to structure survey form for questionnaires (both on paper and online), which in turn led to a more detailed understanding of how the community perceives the local traditions and the local innovation initiatives.

This analysis allowed not only a richer description of the territory, but also the identification of the community's priorities, the definition of its experience variables, and, in a second moment, the identification of the community's perceptions through these variables. The multiple-choice survey form was written with the SurveyMonkey software [8] and structured along the indications of the Delphi method [84, 85]. The data, relative to 110 individuals, each of which was classified according to his/her activity and district, was analysed and ordered on a Likert scale. These approaches helped to delineate the community's understanding of Pisticci's identity as "bianco bellezza" (white beauty) and related perceived image – a place of participatory hospitality – and designed image: a place of experience.

Step 3 (co-project and co-evaluation) aimed at identifying the relevant actors and their interests and needs, reconstructing local supply and the related demand. For doing so, it borrowed from the typical tools of community planning and place marketing. The main tools were selected to facilitate interaction among stakeholders and to obtain concrete results, in term of actions and services planned for the community.

The project is based on a physical and digital platform, a "community hub" [86], called "PLUS – Pisticci Laboratorio Urbano Sostenibile" (Pisticci Sustainable Urban Lab). Each of the three main themes (governance, activities, and economic sustainability) had a dedicated co-design round table.

With the goal of aligning the future changes of the territory with the basis of the community's needs, two approaches were used in roundtables: the "World cafè" method for the community planning and the "Canvas business model" for the place marketing. The former [87] was used to facilitate the interaction between the round tables, on the belief that the contribution of the participants is increased if based on action and on informal and free dialogue. The World cafè method revolves around the idea of "incremental and circular discussion", where the debate grows in substance and quality thanks to a regular rotation of the participants. The second is BMC - Business Model Canvas [88], which was aimed at evaluating the strategic choices of creative industries. This model utilises the visual language to develop innovative business models, mirroring the way enterprises create value. The BMC revolutionised the way business models are represented since it presents an enterprise's inner working in a simplified and therefore more accessible manner: this creates a communication advantage. The "Value proposition" of the BMC was utilised to facilitate teamwork, thanks to large posters that allowed participants to discuss the elements of the project by drawing, writing post-it notes, and writing directly on them. This enabled the project to adapt to the organisational logic of the community and favoured the understanding, the discussion and the analysis of the activities, without penalising creative inputs and sharing. As result, the Value Proposition allowed identifying the needs of the different groups and the actions and services of different sectors of the community that may increase advantages and decrease the disadvantages of PLUS.

This working mode defined the community brand identity of the PLUS project and put in place an interaction among values, starting from a network of urban sustainable organisations and from the possible local experiences among them to be planned.

Step 3 includes the co-evaluation of alternative vocations defined as following:

– V 0: assessment of the current situation;
– V 1: hospitality and resilient community;
– V 2: the sacred and the profane;
– V 3: agricultural tradition;
– V 4: density of artisan and creative activities;
– V 5: landscape and biodiversity

Thanks to the cooperation among the participants, it was possible to identify the concrete measures necessary for the construction of the local experiences. The measures were structured according to alternative vocations that have emerged, across four experience variables: recovery of tangible and intangible heritage; digital platform; services for inhabitants and temporary citizens; urban contract. The latter variable seeks to define the models of shared governance by explicitly identifying the "urban contract" among the involved actors [89] (Fig. 3).

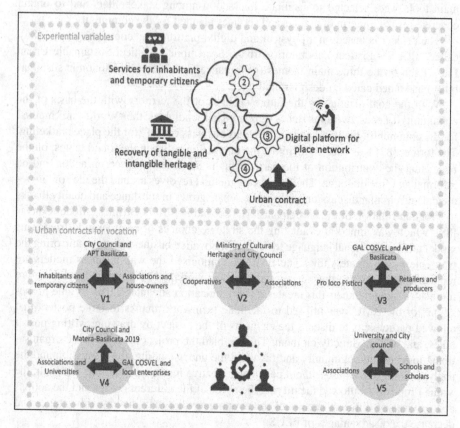

Fig. 3. PLUS project experiential variables and alternative vocations

The likely impact of the measure of each vocation was estimated according to economic, social, and cultural (E, S, C) criteria. These were done with respect to the following macro-criteria: "Hardware", "Software", "Orgware", and "Virtualware". These macro-criteria relate to the types of investments that should be made for place branding strategies. The forecast of their impacts derives from the experience variables, which in turn derives from this approach.

Once the measures, the macro criteria (Hardware, Software, Orgware, Virtualware), as well as the E, S, C (economic, social, and cultural) criteria have been outlined, the sectoral objectives for the evaluation of the relevant sector were defined. The direct and indirect (D, I) impacts were classified according to the relevant experience variables. On the basis of the possible impacts, we built a matrix (on the basis of two main frameworks: the European framework on culture and democracy [90]; and the AUDIS indicators for urban regeneration [91]) to evaluate the different vocations according to 34 economic, social, and cultural indicators.

On this basis, each vocation was assessed according to the criteria and to the macro-criteria, thus defining the following impact categories and relative indicators: Hardware Economic (HE); Hardware Social (HS); Hardware Cultural (HC); Software Economic (SE); Software Social (SS); Software Cultural (SC); Orgware Economic (OE); Orgware Social (OS); Orgware Cultural (OC); Virtualware Economic (VE); Virtualware Social (VS); Virtualware Cultural (VC). The alternative vocations were assessed with a qualitative evaluation scale (9 point scale), chosen through the aggregation procedure based on the PROMETHEE (Preference Ranking Organisation METHod for Enrichment Evaluations) multi-criteria method in which an outranking procedure is applied as the basis of evaluation [92].

The PROMETHEE method is based on the computation of preference degrees which rank all the alternatives and form the best to the worst one. Every preference degree is a score (between 0 and 1) which highlights how an alternative is preferred, from the decision maker's point of view. Three preference flows are computed to consolidate the results of the pairwise comparisons of the alternatives [93]: Phi+ (f+): the positive (or leaving) flow; Phi- (f-): the negative (or entering) flow; Phi (f): the net flow. PROME-THEE II Complete Ranking is based on the net flow Phi, in which the top half of the scale (in green) corresponds to positive scores and the bottom half (in red) to negative scores (Fig. 4). In this study, we used also the PROMETHEE Diamond as a 2-dimensional representation that shows both PROMETHEE I partial and II complete rankings. In the PROMETHEE Diamond, each alternative is represented as a point in the (Phi+, Phi-) plane angled 45 °. The vertical dimension (green-red axis) gives the Phi net flow and a cone is drawn for each alternative. When a cone is overlapping another one it

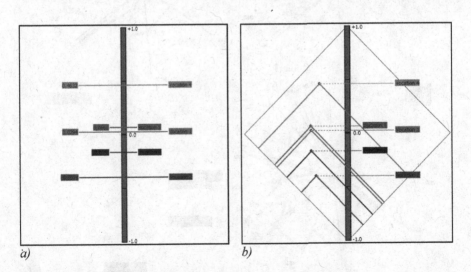

a)   b)

Fig. 4. Evaluation of vocations/alternatives (a) PROMETHEE II Complete Ranking (b) PROMETHEE Diamond (Color figure online)

means that the alternative is preferred to the other one in the PROMETHEE I Partial Ranking. Intersecting cones correspond to incomparable alternatives.

The analysis of the data suggests that Vocation 4 (density of artisan and creative activities) may be the most appropriate one for activating urban regeneration processes in Pisticci, in that it could insert new types of economy and local development (Fig. 5). Following the analysis of the data provided in the previous steps, and the analysis of the measures connected to Vocation 4, the project proceeded to the implementation of the

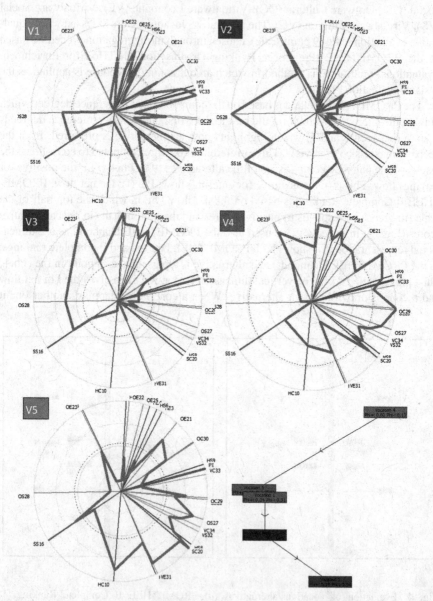

Fig. 5. Evaluation of vocations/alternatives: sensitivity analysis and PROMETHEE Network

PLUS brand (step 4) with the goal of activating different inputs, each founded on experience variables. The sectoral preferences were synthesised through a costs-opportunities analysis and a stakeholders map for emerging coalitions and conflicts.

4   Discussion and Conclusions

The main objective of the evaluation process, i.e. "learning from comparing", was integrated for allowing the evaluator to be not only an "external expert", but rather a facilitator figure within a community-based project. His/her experience on the field becomes itself an evaluation tool, while at the same time helping the negotiation between the different stakeholders. It might be useful to highlight the importance of "learning from perceptions and experiences". If on the one hand, it is true that comparison enables the construction of transferable models, it is also true, on the other, that familiarity with the actual perceptions of a community allows researchers and practitioners to construct more locally-embedded models, since the concrete proposals are the direct expression of the territories. For this reason, it seems necessary to couple quantitative data with qualitative information (in particular, on the perceptions of the local actors), since this increases participants' understanding of the process and the self-organization of the community towards sustainable development [94].

The strength of the whole process should be precisely that of achieving a plan of economically, socially, and culturally feasible interventions. Their feasibility draws on the fact that these interventions are not merely shared with the community, but are produced based on its perceptions and desires. This should happen by seeking to build experiences, as occasions where social ties and alliances are possible among people with diverging interests. Its weakness concerns the long duration of such large and articulated processes, in which a continuous, attentive engagement is required to build trust towards, and awareness of a "community brand" that evolves along the physical transformations of territories and people. The main difficulty lies in communicating that investing time and money in immaterial activities (such as the measures involving place branding and community planning) is a valuable contribution to the material transformation of the built environment in the long period.

However, enacting the five steps of the process (Fig. 6) shows that "learning from perception and from experiences" ensures a continuous evaluation and, at the same time, a continuous action on the territory, thanks to the feedbacks and the trust of the participants, as well as to the strengthening of the groups' organizational abilities.

Thanks to a very productive teamwork, it was possible to plan and implement the contents and the tools of every following phase. In this sense, the process appeared to be a chain of experiences that follow one another, and that becomes real by keeping in mind the three elements of "urban strategic management": resources, rules, project.

In conclusion, networking and territorial re-branding potentials are large in small towns, due to the spontaneity and authenticity of their communities, as well as their lower social and territorial complexity. As a network of creative, micro, district-based communities, with its peculiar landscape and its peasant and artisan tradition, Pisticci may be an ideal testing ground for Co-Bra. The ultimate goal should be the construction

	Phases	Approaches	Tools	Results
Step 1	1. Territorial priorities	Data collection Yin method	Desk analysis	Vision, mission and objectives
Step 2	2. Alternative vocations	Performing, Media, Storytelling	Walk about "I luoghi di zonzo"	Reports with vocations
	3. Territory through vocations	Delphi method	Paper and on line surveys	110 responses
	4. Territorial preferences	Stakeholders satisfaction	Data processing	Filtered data / Urban district
	5. Experiential variables	Stakeholders satisfaction	Data processing	Filtered data / Stakeholders
	6. Community perceptions	Multi-group analysis	Data processing	Perceptions priorities
Step 3	7. Community needs	Canvas World café	Co-design round tables	Needs and actions matrix
	8. Impacts previsions	Multi-criteria analysis	Impacts analysis	Impacts matrix
	9. Impacts evaluation for sectors	Multi-criteria analysis	Sectors analysis	Impacts matrix for sectors
	10. Vocations evaluation	Multi-criteria analysis	Indicators analysis	Indicators matrix
Step 4	11. Synthesis of sectors preferences	Costs / Opportunities Stakeholders map	Results analysis	Coalition and conflicts
Step 5	12. Evaluation report	Results monitoring	Check feasibility	PLUS agenda and mind map
	Evaluation	Management		

Fig. 6. Community branding (Co-Bra) process: steps and results

of opportunities through new forms of development and society that balance tradition and innovation. This potentially could build a place network model for the whole Basilicata region in the wake of Matera 2019: from Pisticci community brand to Lucania (the old name of Basilicata) territorial brand [42].

Acknowledgements. This study has been supported by CNR IRISS of Naples, Department of Architecture (DiARC) of Federico II University of Naples, but also by local organisations and administrations in Basilicata region. In particular, authors are very grateful to "Imbianchini di bellezza", PLUS association, P-stories, Open story lab, "Legambiente circolo Pisticci", Lucania Film Festival, Allelammie, Teatro Lab, AVIS, University of Basilicata, Pisticci Municipality and Basilicata region.

References

1. Trochim, W.M.K., Donnelly, J.P.: The Research Methods Knowledge Base. Mason, Ohio (2006)
2. Cerreta, M., De Toro, P.: Strategic environmental assessment of port plans in italy: experiences, approaches tools. Sustainability 4(12), 2888–2921 (2012)
3. Forss, K., Rebien, C.C., Carlsson, J.: Process use of evaluations: types of use that precede lessons learned and feedback. Evaluation 8(1), 29–45 (2002)
4. Cerreta, M., Salzano, I.: Progetti di conservazione integrata del patrimonio culturale: la valutazione come "processo di apprendimento". In: 7th Congresso Associazione Italiana di Valutazione La rete e l'arcipelago: viaggio tra le pratiche della valutazione italiana, pp. 2–26. AISRe, Milano (2004)

5. Norberg-Schulz, C.: Genius Loci: Towards a Phenomenology of Architecture. Rizzoli, New York (1980)
6. Kavaratzis, M., Ashworth, G.J.: City branding: an effective assertion of identity or a transitory marketing trick? Tijdschr. voor Econ. en Soc. Geogr. **96**(5), 506–514 (2005)
7. Anholt, S.: Competitive identity: The new brand management for nations, cities and regions. J. Brand Manag. **14**(6), 474–475 (2007)
8. Baker, B.: Destination Branding for Small Cities: The Essentials for Successful Place Branding. Creative Leap Books, Portland (2007)
9. Klingmann, A.: Brandscapes: Architecture in the Experience Economy. Mit Press, Cambridge (2007)
10. Skinner, H.: In search of the genius loci: the essence of a place brand. Mark. Rev. **11**(3), 281–292 (2011)
11. Dinnie, K.: City Branding: Theory and Cases. Palgrave Macmillan, Basingstoke (2011)
12. Govers, R., Go, F.: Place Branding–Glocal, Physical and Virtual Identities Constructed, Imagined or Experienced. Palgrave Macmillan, New York (2009)
13. Forester, J.: Beyond dialogue to transformative learning: how deliberative rituals encourage political judgment in community planning processes. Eval. Theor. Practice Urban-Rural Interplay Plan. **37**, 81–103 (1997)
14. Sadan, E., Churchman, A.: Process-focused and product-focused community planning: two variations of empowering professional practice. Comm. Dev. J. **32**(1), 3–16 (1997)
15. Wates, N.: The Community Planning Handbook: How People Can Shape Their Cities, Towns & Villages in Any Part of the World. Earthscan, Abingdon (2000)
16. Community places. http://www.communityplanningtoolkit.org/
17. Sadan, E., Churchman, A.: Global sustainability and community empowerment. Int. Assoc. People Envir. Stud. **14**, 184–192 (1996)
18. Briscoe, C.: Community work in a social service department. Soc. Work Today **7**(2), 47 (1976)
19. D'Auria, A.: Turismo culturale e sviluppo locale: un modello basato sull'uso creativo delle ICTs. L'Acropoli Anno XII (5) (2011)
20. Napolitano, P.: http://www.digicult.it/it/news/the-socio-economic-impact-of-the-cultural-heritage-on-the-communities/
21. Paddison, R.: City marketing, image reconstruction and urban regeneration. Urban Stud. **30**(2), 339–349 (1993)
22. Caroli, M.G.: Il marketing territoriale. FrancoAngeli, Milano (1999)
23. Van den Berg, L., Klaassen, L.H., Van der Meer, J.: Strategische City-Marketing. Schoonhoven Academic Service, Schoonhoven (1990)
24. Braun, E.: City Marketing: Towards an Integrated Approach. ERIM, Rotterdam (2008)
25. Cercola, R., Bonetti, E., Simoni, M.: Marketing e strategie territoriali. EGEA S.p.A, Milano (2009)
26. Napolitano, M., Marino, V.: Cultural heritage e Made in Italy. Casi ed esperienze di marketing internazionale. Editoriale Scientifica, Napoli (2016)
27. Van den Berg, L., Braun, E.: Urban competitiveness, marketing and the need for organising capacity. Urban Stud. **36**(5), 987 (1999)
28. Ashworth, G.J., Graham, B.: Senses of Place, Senses of Time. Routledge, Abingdon (2005)
29. Ashworth, G.J., Voogd, H.: Selling the City: Marketing Approaches in Public Sector Urban Planning. Belhaven Press, London (1990)
30. Gold, J.R., Ward, S.V.: Place Promotion: The Use of Publicity and Marketing to Sell Towns and Regions. Wiley, New York (1994)
31. Ward, S.V.: Selling Places: The Marketing and Promotion of Towns and Cities, 1850–2000. Routledge, London (1998)

32. Kavaratzis, M., Warnaby, G., Ashworth, G.J.: Rethinking Place Branding. Springer, Cham (2015)

33. Calder, B.J.: Focus groups and the nature of qualitative marketing research. J. Mark. Res. 14(3), 353–364 (1977)

34. Supphellen, M.: Understanding core brand equity: guidelines for in-depth elicitation of brand associations. Int. J. Mark. Res. 42(3), 319 (2000)

35. Aaker, J.L.: Dimensions of brand personality. J. Mark. Res. 34(3), 347–356 (1997)

36. Henderson, G.R., Iacobucci, D., Calder, B.J.: Using network analysis to understand brands. In: NA-Advances Consumer Research, vol. 29 (2002)

37. Carroll, J.D., Green, P.E.: Psychometric methods in marketing research: part II, multidimensional scaling. J. Mark. Res. 34(2), 193–204 (1997)

38. Grunert, K.G., Grunert, S.C.: Measuring subjective meaning structures by the laddering method: theoretical considerations and methodological problems. Int. J. Res. Mark. 12(3), 209–225 (1995)

39. Gutman, J.: A means-end chain model based on consumer categorization processes. J. Mark. 46(2), 60–72 (1982)

40. John, D.R., Loken, B., Kim, K., Monga, A.B.: Brand concept maps: a methodology for identifying brand association networks. J. Mark. Res. 43(4), 549–563 (2006)

41. Schnittka, O., Sattler, H., Zenker, S.: Advanced brand concept maps: a new approach for evaluating the favorability of brand association networks. Int. J. Res. Mark. 29(3), 265–274 (2012)

42. Donner, M.I.M.: Understanding place brands as collective and territorial development processes. Wageningen University Press (2016)

43. Mainolfi, G., De Nisco, A., Marino, V., Napolitano, M.R.: Immagine Paese e cultural heritage. Proposta e validazione di una scala di misura formativa della cultural heritage image (CHEI). In: XII Convegno Annuale Società Italiana Marketing, Università degli Studi di Torino (2015)

44. Future Brand. http://www.futurebrand.com/uploads/CBI-14_15-LR.pdf

45. Anholt, S.: The Anholt-GMI city brands index how the world sees the world's cities. Place Brand. 2(1), 18–31 (2006)

46. Forester, J.: Beyond dialogue to transformative learning: how deliberative rituals encourage political judgment in community planning processes. In: Esquith, S.L. (ed.) Political dialogue: Theories and practices. Poznan Studies. In the Philosophy of the Sciences and the Humanities, vol. 46, pp. 295–333. Rodopi (1996)

47. Ostrom, E.: Governing the Commons. Cambridge University Press, New York (2015)

48. Healey, P.: Collaborative planning in perspective. Plan. Theor. 2(2), 101–123 (2003)

49. Clemente, M., Arcidiacono, C., Giovene di Girasole, E., Procentese, F.: Trans-disciplinary approach to maritime-urban regeneration in the case study 'Friends of Molo San Vincenzo', port of Naples, Italy. In: Citta 8th Annual Conference on Planning Research Aesop tg / Public Spaces & Urban Cultures Meeting Generative Places, Smart Approaches, Happy People, pp. 701–718 (2015)

50. De Vita, E., Trillo, C., Oppido, S.: Urban regeneration and civic economics: a community-led approach in Boston and Naples. J. Comp. Cult. Stud. Archit. 9, 28–40 (2016)

51. de Vita, E., Ragozino, S.: Natural commercial centers: regeneration opportunities and urban challenges. Adv. Eng. Forum 11, 392–401 (2014)

52. Munda, G.: Social multi-criteria evaluation: methodological foundations and operational consequences. Eur. J. Oper. Res. 158(3), 662–677 (2004)

53. Funtowicz, S.O., Alier, J.M., Munda, G., Ravetz, J.R.: Information tools for environmental policy under conditions of complexity. Office for official publications of the European communities (1999)

54. O'Connor, M., Faucheux, S., Froger, G., Funtowicz, S.O., Munda, G.: Emergent Complexity and Procedural Rationality: Post-Normal Science for Sustainability. Getting Down to Earth: Practical Applications Of Ecological Economics, pp. 223–248. Island Press, Washington (1996)
55. Rosen, R.: Complexity as a system property. Int. J. Gen Syst 3(4), 227–232 (1977)
56. Ishizaka, A., Nemery, P.: Multi-Criteria Decision Analysis: Methods and Software. Wiley, Chichester (2013)
57. Bana e Costa, C.A.: An additive value function technique with a fuzzy outranking relation for dealing with poor inter-criteria preference information. In: Bana e Costa, C.A. (ed.) Readings in Multiple Criteria Decision Aid. LNCS, pp. 351–382. Springer, Heidelberg (1990)
58. Munda, G.: Multicriteria Evaluation in a Fuzzy Environment. Theory and Applications in Ecological Economics. Contributions to Economics Series. Physical Verlag, Heidelberg (1995)
59. Cerreta, M., Panaro, S., Poli, G.: A knowledge-based approach for the implementation of a SDSS in the partenio regional park (Italy). In: Gervasi, O., et al. (eds.) ICCSA 2016. LNCS, vol. 9789, pp. 111–124. Springer, Cham (2016). doi:10.1007/978-3-319-42089-9_8
60. Proctor, W., Drechsler, M.: Deliberative multicriteria evaluation. Environ. Plan. C Gov. Policy 24(2), 169–190 (2006)
61. Munda, G.: Multiple criteria decision aid: Some epistemological considerations. J. Multi Criteria Decis. Anal. 2(1), 41–55 (1993)
62. Roy, B.: Méthodologie multicritère d'aide à la décision. Economica, Paris (1985)
63. Nijkamp, P., Rietveld, P., Voogd, H.: Multicriteria Evaluation in Physical Planning. Contributions to Economic Analysis. Elsevier, Amsterdam (2013)
64. Vansnick, J.C.: On the problem of weights in multiple criteria decision making (the noncompensatory approach). Eur. J. Oper. Res. 24(2), 288–294 (1986)
65. Roy, B.: Multicriteria Methodology for Decision Aiding. Springer Science & Business Media, New York (2013)
66. Munda, G.: A NAIADE based approach for sustainability benchmarking. Int. J. Environ. Technol. Manag. 6(1–2), 65–78 (2005)
67. Bouyssou, D.: Building criteria: a prerequisite for MCDA. In: Bana e Costa, C.A. (ed.) Readings in Multiple Criteria Decision Aid. LNCS, pp. 58–80. Springer, Heidelberg (1990). doi:10.1007/978-3-642-75935-2_4
68. Roberts, F.S.: Measurement Theory with Applications to Decision Making, Utility and the Social Sciences. Addison-Wesley, London (1979)
69. Banville, C., Landry, M., Martel, J., Boulaire, C.: A stakeholder approach to MCDA. Syst. Res. Behav. Sci. 15(1), 15–32 (1998)
70. Macharis, C., Bernardini, A.: Reviewing the use of multi-criteria decision analysis for the evaluation of transport projects: time for a multi-actor approach. Transp. Policy 37, 177–186 (2015)
71. Kenter, J.O., Reed, M.S., Fazey, I.: The deliberative value formation model. Ecosyst. Serv. 21, 194–207 (2016)
72. Betsch, C.: Chronic preferences for intuition and deliberation in decision making: lessons learned about intuition from an individual differences approach. In: Intuition Judgment and Decision Making, pp. 231–248 (2008)
73. McCrum, G., Blackstock, K., Matthews, K., Rivington, M., Miller, D., Buchan, K.: Adapting to climate change in land management: the role of deliberative workshops in enhancing social learning. Environ. Policy Gov. 19(6), 413–426 (2009)
74. Lichfield, N.: Community Impact Evaluation. University College Press, London (1996)

75. Daldanise, G.: Place (based) branding e rigenerazione urbana. Work. Pap. Riv. online, Urban@it 1 (2016)
76. Fusco Girard, L., Nijkamp, P.: Le valutazioni per lo sviluppo sostenibile della città e del territorio. FrancoAngeli (1997)
77. Place Brand Observer. http://placebrandobserver.com/wp-content/uploads/TPBO-Quick-Guide-Place-Branding-Process.pdf
78. Daldanise, G.: Innovative strategies of urban heritage management for sustainable local development. Procedia Soc. Behav. Sci. **223**, 101–107 (2016)
79. Cannavacciuolo, L., Iandoli, L., Ponsiglione, C., Zollo, G.: Learning by failure vs. learning by habits: entrepreneurial learning micro-strategies as determinants of the emergence of co-located entrepreneurial networks. Int. J. Entrep. Behav. Res. **23**(3), 524–546 (2017)
80. Errichiello, L., Marasco, A.: La strategia della supply chain nei servizi. Econ. E Dirit. del Terziario 3 (2007)
81. Yin, R.K.: Case Study Research: Design and Methods, 5th edn. Sage, London (2013)
82. UNESCO Recommendation on the Historic Urban Landscape. http://whc.unesco.org/en/activities/638
83. Careri, F.: Walkscapes. Camminare Come Pratica Estetica. Einaudi, Milano (2006)
84. Bolognini, M.: Democrazia elettronica: metodo Delphi e politiche pubbliche. Carocci, Roma (2001)
85. Pacinelli, A.: Metodi per la ricerca sociale partecipata. FrancoAngeli, Milano (2008)
86. Calvaresi, C.: https://www.che-fare.com/community-hub-due-o-tre-cose-che-so-di-loro/
87. World Café Community. http://www.theworldcafe.com/
88. Osterwalder, A.: The business model ontology: a proposition in a design science approach. Ph.D. thesis, Universite de Lausanne Ecole des hautes etudes commerciales (2004)
89. Perulli, P.: The Urban Contract: Community, Governance and Capitalism. Routledge, Abingdon (2016)
90. Council of Europe: Indicator Framework on Culture and Democracy – Policy maker's guidebook, Technical report (2016)
91. AUDIS: Linee guida per la rigenerazione urbana, Technical report (2014)
92. Brans, J.P., Mareschal, B.: The PROMETHEE methods for MCDM; the PROMCALC, GAIA and BANKADVISER software. In: Bana e Costa, C.A. (ed.) Readings in Multiple Criteria Decision Aid. LNCS, pp. 216–252. Springer, Heidelberg (1990). doi:10.1007/978-3-642-75935-2_10
93. Mareschal, B.: Visual PROMETHEE 1.4 Manual [PDF]. VPSolutions, Technical report (2013)
94. Cerreta, M., Inglese, P., Manzi, M.L.: A multi-methodological decision-making process for cultural landscapes evaluation: the green lucania project. Soc. Behav. Sci. **216**, 578–590 (2016)
95. Montrone, S., Perchinunno, P., Di Giuro, A., Rotondo, F., Torre, C.M.: Identification of "hot spots" of social and housing difficulty in urban areas: scan statistics for housing market and urban planning policies. In: Murgante, B., Borruso, G., Lapucci, A. (eds.) Geocomputation and Urban Planning, pp. 57–78. Springer, Heidelberg (2009)
96. Montrone, S., Perchinunno, P., Torre, C.M.: Analysis of positional aspects in the variation of real estate values in an Italian Southern metropolitan area. In: Taniar, D., Gervasi, O., Murgante, B., Pardede, E., Apduhan, B.O. (eds.) ICCSA 2010. LNCS, vol. 6016, pp. 17–31. Springer, Heidelberg (2010). doi:10.1007/978-3-642-12156-2_2

Deliberative Spatial Multi-Criteria Evaluation (DSM-CE): Forming Shared Cultural Values

Maria Cerreta[✉] and Simona Panaro

Department of Architecture (DiARC),
Federico II University of Naples, Via Toledo 402, 80134 Naples, Italy
{maria.cerreta, simona.panaro}@unina.it

Abstract. The paper introduces a methodological approach for a Deliberative Spatial Multi-Criteria Evaluation (DSM-CE) able to support cultural enhancement, combining deliberative multi-criteria evaluation methods and Geographic Information System (GIS). The purpose concerns the cultural regeneration issue in an interdisciplinary complex decisional context where an interactive decision-making process among the different stakeholders is oriented to the identification of shared cultural values. The decision-making process has been elaborated for the historic centre of Naples (Italy), in order to activate a culture-led regeneration process and to recognise in the culture the ability to influence site-specific planning actions.

Keywords: Cultural values · Culture-led regeneration · Deliberative multi-criteria analysis · Spatial decision support system

1 Introduction

The starting of urban regeneration processes that enhance local resources through sustainable strategies is an open research theme. The economic crisis and the lack of public funding require, indeed, to rethink the chances and forms of action, especially in the historic centres. The attention of local governments towards the development of cultural processes is justified by the need to reposition the city in the global market and simultaneously create an environment suitable to new forms of technology-based economy, creativity, human capital, and ability to innovate (Mercer 2006; Schneider 2010; Ward 2015). Cultural activities are interpreted as an engine for job growth because they are able to build an enabling environment, in which the multi-dimensional forms of creativity (including the sectors of business and technology) can take root and thrive (Florida 2002).

Creativity is considered a means to stimulate economic activity and improve the image of the city, through the specificity and authenticity of places (Zukin 2010) and, for these reasons, is linked to the development of the experience economy (Pine and Gilmore 1999; Poulsson and Kale 2004), and the various forms of cultural tourism. Indeed, thanks to the development of more flexible and innovative strategies, the tourist experience is more difficult to imitate and, therefore, more competitive (Alvarez 2010). The ability of a destination to compete depends not only on its organisational skills but also on its ability to transform the cultural heritage into highly symbolic activities (OECD 2009).

© Springer International Publishing AG 2017
O. Gervasi et al. (Eds.): ICCSA 2017, Part III, LNCS 10406, pp. 747–763, 2017.
DOI: 10.1007/978-3-319-62398-6_53

The focus has, therefore, shifted to the intangible cultural aspects and lifestyle, making even sites without significant architectural and historical heritage potentially competitive (Richards and Wilson 2007).

It follows that, in the past two decades, the concept of tourism has also changed a lot, thanks to technological innovation developments, including tourists forms of involvement in the daily lifestyles. This step is a very delicate point because the clear risk is that an exclusively competitive approach of the experience economy distorts urban lifestyles through their commodification and staging of everyday experiences, without a true meaning (Richards 2011). In a global context, the roots, before the transfer of knowledge and skills, become a key issue for the survival of the cultural identity of places.

On the other hand, the most relevant potential is inherent in relations systems and their spaces, where it is possible to undergo authentic and participative experiences. Indeed, while the traditional economic values were redistributed, in contemporary approaches (civil economy, circular economy, sharing economy) values can be generated within the cooperative and collaborative processes, fielding different forces and productivity (Zamagni and Zamagni 2008). If the city becomes, therefore, a cultural productivity system, the connections that can be put in place will have a much larger identity values system and the presence of hubs, hybrid spaces and areas of contamination in the territory can spark new opportunities since the networking of the context vital resources.

In the processes of transformation and cultural development of the cities, not only "culture" and "creativity" become indispensable, but also the communities and identifying the community-driven processes (Zamagni and Sacco 2006; Ferilli et al. 2012, 2017), viz., the ways to activate the change through interaction with those communities that guide the transformation.

Transformation and management models of value production processes force us to rethink, at the same time, both the private dimension and the public one, considering the mutual innovation opportunity derived from the exchange and interaction of expertise and shared experiences.

Cooperation becomes the main factor of development and hubs are configured as "learning organisation" (Zamagni and Zamagni 2008), in which the creation and sharing of knowledge are the comparative advantage factors, able to leverage the motivations, extrinsic and intrinsic, of all the actors who contribute to their construction. The harmonious coexistence of cooperative and competitive relations among the same actors (public, private and social) facilitates operating the model of "learning organisation", increasing the level of cultural, creative and social productivity.

The activation of a network of urban and regional hubs, complementary and synergistic, allowing pursuit of the economic model of cooperative competition, able to replace the outdated model of positional competition, recognising the potential value of inter-subjectivity (Zamagni and Sacco 2006; Sacco and Crociata 2013).

The methodological study regards the historic centre of the city of Naples, UNESCO site since 1995, and aims at the finding its perceived and shared values by the city's promoters, in order to enhance the local (material and immaterial) heritage as a network. The paper attempts responding to the above issues through the following structure: the first part (Sect. 2) identifies shared values and the difference between "social" and "cultural" ones; the second one (Sect. 3) explains the methodological approach of a Deliberative Spatial Multi-Criteria Evaluation and the case study results; the third (Sect. 4) shows discussion and conclusions about the whole process.

2 Shared Social Values vs Shared Cultural Values: A Value-Focus Perspective

The research "Culture, Cities and Identity in Europe" (Arfaoui and Heid 2016), developed in collaboration with Culture Action Europe and the Agenda 21 for Culture - UCLG, identifies culture as a tool for economic growth, to reconvert cities, to enable integration and inclusion processes, as a pillar of identity for Europe. Many European cities have already recognised the role and importance of culture and creative industries in local development.

Culture is integrated into urban agendas and local development strategies, including such sectors as innovation, branding, tourism and social inclusion. At the same time, culture is considered as both highlighting the participation in a variety of experiences and cultural practices that the capacity of the cultural services of contributing to economic development, including both creative/cultural work in itself, that the arising or related occupations, often also defined as the cultural and creative industry. Culture, as an integrated and driving component, can make a difference in the processes of urban regeneration: renewing the image of the city and its neighbourhoods, fostering pride and a sense of belonging in residents, attracting investment and tourism, improving the quality of life and social cohesion, enabling new job opportunities in the cultural and creative sectors, etc. As a result, the strategies and cultural initiatives are facing an increasingly wide range of policy objectives, becoming more and more a possible success factor in the urban regeneration processes. In this context, culture is seen as the main catalyst of urban regeneration processes, and for this reason, they are defined as *culture-led regeneration* processes (Fig. 1). This model permits explanation of the relationships between the processes of regeneration and the production of social and human capital, to recognise in the culture the ability to influence specific planning actions, and identify and evaluate the impacts of the processes activated, with particular reference to the human and social dimensions.

The synergistic effect of culture-led regeneration depends, therefore, on how the process is able to create a shared and inclusive social representation, in which the various local communities can learn to expand their ability to interact, creating and sharing information and ideas to cooperate and compete together.

Thus, it expands the audience of subjects potentially interested in collaborating in the construction of an urban renewal strategy that will make the citizens, non-profit institutions, small and medium-sized enterprises, artisans and training bodies, true promoters and protagonists of change. The tourism economy related to cultural heritage and urban renewal processes should be reconsidered in this perspective (Šebová et al. 2014).

The relationship between cultural production and cultural tourism is considered unbalanced, since the latter is mainly defined as the ability to maintain the cities within those attraction mechanisms and enhancement of talent, as part of a tourist offer that can lead to degenerative mechanisms (Sacco et al. 2015).

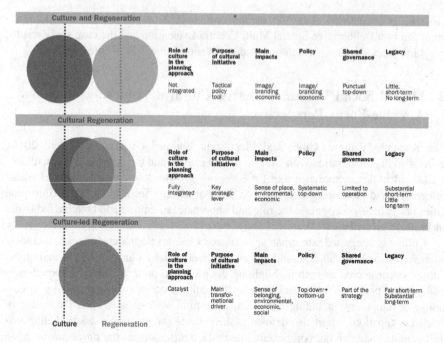

Fig. 1. Culture and regeneration interplay

In this context, we need to encourage the development of cultural capital in the territory, by networking, in a bottom-up approach, the existing projects and ensuring that the different actors have a chance to meet and share their knowledge.

The cultural capital is recognised as a real resource capable of producing value, for which sharing, cooperation and development of new projects related to the economy of culture should be promoted.

It follows that the territorial branding accepts new challenges (Zenker et al. 2010) and the same tourist economy can become more attentive to the possibility of offering authentic experiences and to developing strategies for inclusive urban renewal, avoiding the removal of residents from the centers of interest, and improving well-being and quality of city services.

Cultural productivity and the active involvement of the community in the production process are an integral part of regeneration strategies that cities activated with a "culture-led" approach to local development, to be built on their specific profiles, using culture to differentiate the supply compared to other cities and to increase their competitiveness.

The formation and implementation of collective place brands involve the participation of multiple stakeholders groups (such as public organisations, NGOs, enterprises, investors, residents, and tourists) (Beckman and Zenker 2012), actively engaged in the branding co-creation process, giving their own place brand meaning (Kavaratzis 2012). These branding strategies are aimed at an economic, social and cultural place development, and involve public-private interaction and collaborative processes among various local actors. The collective place branding can become, therefore, an instrument of territorial development co-creation, able to trigger cross-sector synergies. It is not just about marketing, but is also considered a collective territorial governance and development project, which sets in motion different processes, depending on various contextual variables, revealing different local dynamics and taking into account three main issues: territorial embeddedness, i.e. place identity, with the anchorage and dynamics of local actors within their territory; local governance and cooperation as driving processes; development policies and public interventions, that set the conditions.

Conventional economic approaches to evaluation, including the welfare economic theory and the evaluation of non-market benefits of the cultural heritage, tend to approach value as unidimensional. Value to society is considered through aggregation of individual valuations, with the assumption that these valuations reflect underlying preferences and values (Klamer 2003). However, such an approach may not capture collective meanings and significance ascribed to cultural resources, missing relevant shared dimensions of value.

In the above perspective, deliberative and participatory approaches to evaluation are increasingly advocated as a way to include the multidimensionality of value within decision-making, considering notions of communal values and collective intentionality. Recent frameworks for evaluation (TEEB 2010; UK NEA 2014) include "shared", "social" or "shared social" values as value categories in order to better manage conflicts over natural resources, assess the social impacts of policy and develop effective management strategies. The same categories can be useful for the management and evaluation of cultural resources.

The concept of shared value has often been used to refer to values that are shared by groups or communities or to refer to cultural values more generally or as synonymous with public values (Sagoff 1986), a result of deliberative and social processes. Indeed, shared values may also refer to values held in common by groups in particular contexts (Kenter et al. 2015).

Whereas the concept of social value refers to the values of a particular community or the cultural values and norms of society, but can also be used to refer to the public interest, values for public goods, altruistic values, values related to welfare or well-being, the willingness-to-pay (WTP) of a group, or values derived through a social process. At the same time, the concept of shared social value refers to subsets or combinations of the various value concepts described above, in relation to deliberative decision-making, characterized by complexity and post-normality (Funtowicz and Ravetz 1993).

Shared social values can be considered as the outcome of processes of effective social interaction, open dialogue and social learning, linked to shared meanings, and depend on the creation activated among cultural groups, as a result of a social learning process (Stagl 2004). These methods underline that values related to complex goods are not pre-formed, and need to be constructed through a transformative process of deliberation and learning (Christie et al. 2012; Kenter et al. 2011). According to Kenter et al. (2015), overcoming the limitations of neoclassical economic valuation in assessing shared, social and shared social values, deliberative and interpretive approaches for their elicitation incorporate notions of common and cultural importance through social and collaborative processes.

3 Deliberative Spatial Multi-Criteria Evaluation for the Naples Historic Center (Italy)

The research aims at developing a methodology for tracing the potentials of the historical centre of the city of Naples. It was, thus, elaborated an interpretational model of the context, which analyses the value in use, value of non-use and the intrinsic values (Fusco Girard and Nijkamp 1997), in order to identify the shared ones (Porter and Kramer 2011), the ongoing dynamics and the actions that could enable a culture-led regeneration (Vickery 2007; UNESCO 2009).

Therefore, once defined the potentials of the historic city centre, the research intends to suggest a strategy for the enhancement of its cultural heritage as a network. More specifically, the study has been led within the "Social Network of Historical District Entity - SNECS" research project, University of Naples Federico II, Department of Architecture (DiARC).

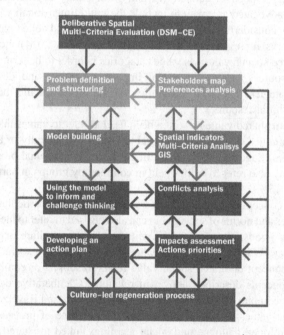

Fig. 2. The methodological approach

The research focuses on improving the stakeholders involvement into the new enhancing policies of Naples' historical centre, with the wider goal of structuring a functional methodology for inclusive decision-making processes. This methodology falls within four stages, of which the first two have already been tested (Fig. 2):

- *Problem definition and structuring.* It includes the institutional analysis aimed at the identification of relevant stakeholders for the studied issue, the practical investigation carried out through semi-structured and in-depth interviews, the processing of the interviews and the preferences to clarify the terms of the decisional problem (i.e. the criteria and the network of potential actors, places and actions with the related levels of relevance).

- *Model building.* It includes the selection of indicators pertinent to the decisional problem, the elaboration of spatial indexes through GIS data processing, the recognition of suitable areas within Naples historical centre by the use of the WLC method, the definition of synergetic actions through the analysis of conflicts and coalitions carried out with the support of the NAIADE method.

- *Using the model to inform and challenge thinking.* It consists in consulting the local actors for checking the strategic actions, their localisation in order to understand their risks and potential consequences, and for implementing them.

- *Developing an action plan.* It regards the assessment of the impacts, the definition of a scale of preferences for the actions and their planning during the time.

In the methodology have been set two different consulting stages of the local actors, the first one (phase 1) to structure the decisional problem, the second one (phase 3) to check and implement the decisional process. This work is still in progress, and, below, will be shown the results of stages 1 and 2.

3.1   Problem Definition and Structuring

In the first phase of the methodological approach, through the institutional analysis (Lapassade 2006), a heterogeneous group of stakeholders has been selected. Apart from people with institutional roles related to the protection/knowledge/promotion of cultural heritage, the research also addressed to operators offering an alternative form of visiting the historical centre or private citizens that host visitors and tourists in their private properties, thanks to web platforms (such as Airbnb). The stakeholders' map was drawn up by considering the following categories:

- Promoters of cultural heritage;
- Operators of the creative, leisure and tourism industry;
- Experts of the SNECS research project.

The operators in the tourism/leisure industry have been interviewed through semi-structured interviews, while experts and advisers through in-depth interviews.

The processing of soft data was led through a semantic analysis (Perea and Rosa 2002; Lepore and Stone 2007), which allowed to disclose the relevant issues and the preferences of the interviewees, useful, in addition, to trace the guidelines and identify the criteria for the study of the context.

The overall of the operators interviewed affirm the need to give visitors the opportunity to discover places outside the traditional routes. There is as a mater of fact, a widespread rediscovery of the historical cultural heritage of the city, due to the rise of tourists' number in recent years. However, the touristic promotion of the city is still limited to the traditional sights. On the contrary, the citizenship is showing more and more interested in broadening their knowledge of the local heritage to less known sights and innovative forms of cultural promotion (e.g. night museum visits; speleological visits to the lower ground of Castel Nuovo, a kayak tour along the city's seashore; a tour through the Underground stations). Nevertheless, these events are not regularly arranged or widely sponsored, apart from the month of May dedicated to the cultural heritage promotion by the local Institutions, "Maggio dei Monumenti". In fact, during this month a great deal of the local cultural events are officially scheduled, and it becomes possible to visit places normally not open to the public.

Among the operators, in particular, the hosts of Airbnb platform interviewed are already promoting the city in alternative ways, since they recommend to their guest visiting places and events they would attend, very often away from the most touristic sites. Their answer to the question "Find a motto to promote your city?" has been, indeed, "Experience Naples like me that was born and raised here".

The Experts, as well, suggest to give more relevance to the cultural activities and events focused on strengthen the identity and sense of belonging to the city, and to develop new modes of interaction with the huge cultural and archaeological heritage of the city by the use of IT systems for communicating knowledge and the specificities of the context. However, tangible proposals in this field are only made by specialists who are currently working on an enhancing plan of city's heritage in the Art Underground Stations, by testing and developing new modes of representation (e.g. video mapping).

Another key point regard public transports and mobility (pedestrian routes or underground lines, and their intermodal integration). On the one hand, some railways and metro lines are seen as good transport links to most popular hotspots for the city life, on the other hand, mobility services on roads, including bus services, are considered inadequate. Many interviewees mention indeed their difficulties to reach some areas of the city centre, characterized by a high concentration of the cultural heritage, by public transports as a reason for their alienation from the city's cultural life; on the contrary the opening of new underground stations in the historic centre has determined new bustling zones in town.

In particular, in the city of Naples for the extension of the underground Line 1, also called "Metropolitana dell'Arte, Architettura e Archeologia" (the Art, Architecture and Archaeology Underground), the stations have been placed close to the areas of the highest cultural interest within the historic city centre. However, there is much to be done for the intermodal integration of all modes of transports and the improvement of transport links to the city centre, especially for some districts.

Through the identification of same keywords and their relative returning in the interviews have been, thus, recognized the main topics and the guidelines for describing the local context in its characteristic features, in particular: the local services' system (namely cultural and touristic services, public services, commercial services, recreational and restaurant services); the local public transports, the innovation and research; the safety standards. These criteria are, thus, according to interviewees, the key points for designing actions of urban regeneration intended to enhance the city's (material and immaterial) cultural heritage.

3.2   Model Building

In the building of the methodological model was given prominence to a set of indicators capable of describing the criteria in details. They are mostly based on institutional sources, apart from the safety parameter, which was elaborated on a mapping of local crime realised by a local newspaper. The mapping is a VGI, Volunteered Geographic Information (Goodchild 2012); they are maps voluntarily created by the users and are freely available online, for this reason, are often used despite needing a quality assurance checking. This group of indicators, selected on each criterion, is shown in Table 1.

Table 1. Criteria and indicators

Criteria	Indicators	Measure unit	Territorial coverage	Year	Source
Tourist services	Number of employees in the hospitality industry	Number	Cadastral sections	2011	ISTAT
Cultural services	Number of creative, artistic and entertainment activities	Number	Cadastral sections	2011	ISTAT
	Number of libraries, archives and other cultural activities	Number	Cadastral sections	2011	ISTAT
	Number of cultural sites	Number	Points	2015	Comune di Napoli
Leisure Services	Number of recreational and amusement activities	Number	Cadastral sections	2011	ISTAT
Commercial activities	Number of stores and commercial activities	Number	Cadastral sections	2011	ISTAT
Catering services	Number of restaurants and catering services	Number	Cadastral sections	2011	ISTAT
	Number of cafè, bars, pubs	Number	Cadastral sections	2011	ISTAT
Public transport	Number of underground station	Number	Points	2017	Comune di Napoli
Public service	Number of post office	Number	Cadastral sections	2011	ISTAT
	Number of public office and police stations	Number	Cadastral sections	2011	ISTAT
	Number of schools and educational services	Number	Cadastral sections	2011	ISTAT
	Number of hospitals and health services	Number	Cadastral sections	2011	ISTAT
Innovation	Number research and development activity	Number	Cadastral sections	2011	ISTAT
Safety standards	Number of criminal acts	Number	Points	2015	napolitoday.it

The indicators, thus selected, have been later worked out in order to identify for each criterion a single or more indexes that would provide an overall picture of the city's historic centre. By comparing the historic centre's data with those of the entire city of Naples, it was possible to elaborate the indexes for assessing the vitality level of the historic centre in comparison with the other city's areas.

Reporting the data in the GIS system allowed, lastly, their spatial simplification, which itself enabled to better understand the current phenomena and support, in the further stages, the decisional process on where to locate future actions. Through data processing, normalization and reclassification the following indexes have been created:

– ID01, the density of public services, which shows the number of public services within a specific cadastral section, compared with the number of public services in the city;
– ID02, the density of catering services, which shows the number of catering services within a specific cadastral section, compared with the number of the catering services in the city;
– ID03, the local specialization for the hospitality industry, which shows the number of employees in hotel industry within a specific cadastral section compared with the number of employees in the same field in the entire city area;
– ID04, the density of creative and leisure activities, which shows the number of creative and leisure activities within the specific cadastral sections, compared with the number of creative and leisure activities in all the city;
– ID05, index of accessibility to services for each cadastral section. It regards the total number services offered in the cadastral section according to the distance of the area to the closest underground station;
– ID06, the density of cultural sites, which shows the number of cultural sites and the activity of public sites using the Kernel density spatial analysis;
– ID07, the density of criminal acts, which shows the number of murders, muggings, prostitutes using the Kernel density spatial analysis.
– ID08, the density of stores and commercial activities, which shows the number of stores and commercial activities within the specific cadastral sections, compared with the number of stores and commercial activities in the city.

The spatial indexes allow understanding the distribution of the services, the activities and the cultural sites, as well as the level of security. The density maps achieved let describe the geography and the intensity of relations concentrating around some specific areas, which are already attractive places for the historical city centre (city sights). The information processed in the previous steps has been arranged according to a matrix of assessment built in the following categories: groups, goals, actions, spatial indexes. At this point, from the interviewees' preferences have been obtained the weights of the spatial indexes so as to develop a preference map of the historic centre, making use of the WLC multi-criteria method (Weighted Linear Combination) integrated with the GIS system.

The multi-criteria analysis tools integrated with the GIS software allowed to develop an evaluation map, which relates geographic data to value judgements (Malczewski 2006; Montrone et al. 2010; Bonifazi et al. 2016), showing the areas of potentiality (green) and the critical areas (red) (Fig. 3). Through the assigning of weight, the preferences of the interviewees have been related to the resources of the historical city centre.

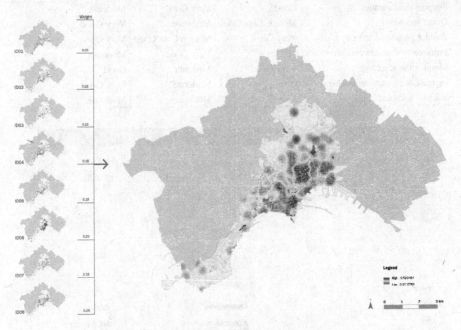

Fig. 3. The evaluation map (Color figure online)

This evaluation map allows to summarize the studied issues and offers a supporting tool for the subsequent consultation of the relevant stakeholders in the next stages. In order to support the consultation, it was also carried out the analysis of the conflicts and coalitions among the stakeholders by using the NAIADE method (Novel Approach to Imprecise Assessment and Decision Environments, Munda 1995).

NAIADE, through the equity matrix and a sequence of mathematical reductions, enables to build the dendrogram of coalitions showing possible alliance formation among social groups (Table 2; Fig. 4).

In such manner, were found a series of synergistic actions easily shared by the stakeholders. At this stage, it was elaborated a sample of the strategic map that locates the synergistic actions, acquired with the NAIADE method, according to the preference areas found with the WLC analysis.

Table 2. The equity matrix

Alternatives	Stakeholders		
Strategic actions	Promoters	Operators	Experts
Start an info-point	Very Good	Moderate	Good
Improve transports and mobility	Good	Very Good	Good
Increase services	Moderate	Good	Moderate
Improve security	Moderate	Good	Moderate
Support communities	Good	Very Good	Moderate
Direct tourism	More o Less Good	Moderate	Very Good
Build a picture of the city	Very Good	More o Less Good	Very Good
Promote new routes and itineraries	Moderate	Very Good	Moderate
Monitor the results	Very Good	Moderate	Good
Increase the use of technology	Good	Moderate	Very Good
Start up a cultural hub	Very Good	Moderate	Moderate

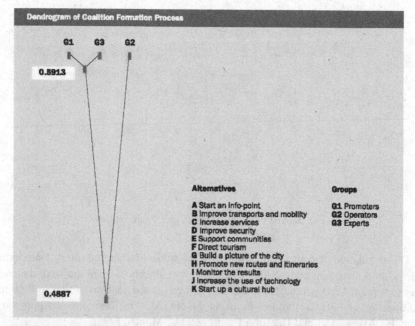

Fig. 4. The dendrogram of coalitions and the actions ranking

This strategic map considers the potentialities and the critical points of local resources and contributes thus to explicate stakeholders' preferences concerning the resources of the historical centre, providing a proposal capable of limiting potential conflicts, combining objective and subjective analysis (Fig. 5).

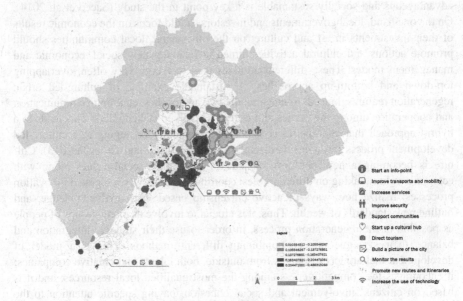

Fig. 5. The strategic map

These two methodological phases have allowed understanding the goals of every group of actors, taking into account the potential conflicts and the opportunities related to the localization of the resources, formerly analysed in the previous stages.

In the following stages, these issues will be properly discussed and examined with the stakeholders, furtherly extending the decisional process and defining a site-specific action plan.

4   Conclusions and Discussion

The experimental methodology elaborated in the Naples historic center intends to start a fruitful dialogue among stakeholders interested in a culture-led regeneration of the city. The purpose of the research is, thus, to construct an inclusive decisional process, whose key steps are to outline a framework of knowledge suitable to the different stakeholder's objectives and to identify shared strategic actions.

Stakeholders' preferences have, therefore, led the analysis of the existing local resources, and the shared actions for the enhancement of the historic centre have been correlated to them. In such manner, an interpretative model of the ongoing potentials was built in support of the following stage of consultation and openness of the decision-making process.

A growing and widespread awareness, which stems from practice and experience, suggests how the culture-led renovation fosters the establishment of new social and creative places. However, unless they are properly included into the economic and social trends of the place, they could even worsen social exclusion and alienation (Zukin 2010). Therefore, finding the conditions for culture to be economically advantageous and socially sustainable is a key point in the study (Sacco et al. 2014). On the one hand, local governments and investors should focus on the economic results of their investments in art and culture; on the other hand, local communities should promote actions and cultural activities aimed at realizing new social, economic and management modes. These different attitudes tend to merge very often, overlapping top-down and bottom-up approaches. A sustainable example of culture-led urban regeneration requires, indeed, to integrate the two approaches, enabling communication and cooperation among the parties and different involved stakeholders. This leads to a hybrid approach that attempts to consider the complexity belonging to a culture-led development process through interdisciplinary tools (Sacco and Crociata 2013). Culture is becoming a new platform, capable of generating social values along with economic values, taking on different roles: coordinate organically integrated innovation processes; realize new ways of active citizenship based on shared knowledge; and outline new standards of wealth. Thus, it is crucial to involve as many groups of people as possible in the regeneration process, in order to use their strategic integration and balance their systemic effects, combining different methods. This is a model of development that attracts resources from outside, both talents and creative companies; it encourages the competitiveness among the most qualified local resources; and it is based on citizens' involvement and social cohesion, paying specific attention to the promotion of actions that foster the community's capability-building and social enterprises (Sacco et al. 2012, 2014; Sassano et al. 2016; Cannavacciuolo et al. 2017). A culture-led regeneration process needs social and economic conditions to let culture trigger the change.

The inclusive regeneration processes and the integrated enhancement of Naples historical city should steadily encourage those activities and areas of interest where culture, creativity and economy cooperate for the development of the local community in productive ways. According to the UN-Habitat (2004), in order to feed creativity, cities should have a generous and inclusive culture, an attitude of openness and integration. It has been defined with the word "moxie" the ability to face adversities with courage. The word denotes feelings such as bravery, strength, energy and curiosity for all that is different and new. It becomes a strong drive for change that can trigger innovating processes.

Acknowledgements. This study has been supported by "Social Network of Historical District Entity - SNECS" research project, University of Naples Federico II, Department of Architecture (DiARC), Project code: PON03PE_00163_1 - MIUR 3972 del 20/11/2014.

References

Mercer, C.: Cultural planning for urban development and creative cities (2006). http://www.burgosciudad21.org/adftp/Shanghai_cultural_planning_paper.pdf

Schneider, B.: Cities and Regions: their cultural responsibility for Europe and how they can fulfil it. A manual, A soul for Europe. TOGETHER project, European Parliament (2010). http://www.asoulforeurope.eu/sites/www.asoulforeurope.eu/files/media_pdf/Manual%20Cities%20%26%20Regions.pdf

Ward, J.: Report on the role of intercultural dialogue, cultural diversity and education in promoting EU fundamental values. European Parliament – Committee on Culture and Education (2015). http://www.europarl.europa.eu/sides/getDoc.do?pubRef=-//EP//TEXT+REPORT+A8-2015-0373+0+DOC+XML+V0//EN

Florida, R.: The Rise of the Creative Class: And How It's Transforming Work, Leisure, Community and Everyday Life. Basic Books, New York (2002)

Zukin, S.: Naked City: The Death and Life of Authentic Urban Places. Oxford University Press, Oxford (2010)

Pine, J., Gilmore, J. (eds.): The Experience Economy. Harvard Business School Press, Boston (1999)

Poulsson, S.H.G., Kale, S.H.: The experience economy and commercial experiences. Mark. Rev. **4**, 267–277 (2004)

Alvarez, M.D.: Creative cities and cultural spaces: New perspectives for city tourism. Int. J. Cult. Tourism Hospitality Res. **4**, 171–175 (2010)

OECD: The impact of culture on tourism. OECD, Paris (2009)

Richards, G., Wilson, J. (eds.): Tourism, Creativity and Development. Routledge, London (2007)

Richards, G.: Creativity and tourism: The state of the art. Ann. Tourism Res. **38**(4), 1225–1253 (2011)

Zamagni, S., Zamagni, V. (eds.): La cooperazione. Il Mulino, Bologna (2008)

Zamagni, S., Sacco, P.L. (eds.): Teoria economica e relazioni interpersonali. Il Mulino, Bologna (2006)

Ferilli, G., Sacco, P.L., Blessi, G.T.: Cities as creative hubs: From instrumental to functional values of culture-led local development. In: Girard, L.F., Nijkamp, P. (eds.) Sustainable City and Creativity: Promoting Creative Urban Initiatives, pp. 110–124. Ashgate, London (2012)

Ferilli, G., Sacco, P.L., Tavano, B.G., Forbici, S.: Power to the people: When culture works as a social catalyst in urban regeneration processes (and when it does not). Eur. Plan. Stud. **25**(2), 1–18 (2017)

Sacco, P.L., Crociata, A.: Conceptual regulatory framework for design and evaluation of complex, participative cultural planning strategies. Int. J. Urban Reg. Res. **37**(5), 1688–1706 (2013)

Arfaoui, M., Heid, K.: Culture, Cities and Identity in Europe, European Economic and Social Committee, Brussel (2016). http://www.eesc.europa.eu

Šebová, M., Džupka, P., Hudec, O., Urbančíková, N.: Promoting and financing cultural tourism in Europe through European capitals of culture: A case study of Košice, European capital of culture 2013. Economic Interferences XVI(36) (2014)

Sacco, P., Ferilli, G., Blessi, G.T. (eds.): Cultura e sviluppo locale. Verso il distretto culturale evoluto. Il Mulino, Bologna (2015)

Zenker, S., Knubben, E., Beckmann, S.C.: Your city, my city, their city, our city: Different perceptions of a place brand by diverse target groups. In: 6th International Conference Thought Leaders in Brand Management, Lugano, Switzerland, 18–20 April 2010

Beckman, B., Zenker, S.: Place branding: A multiple stakeholder perspective. In: 41st European Marketing Academy Conference, Lisbon, Portugal, 22–25 May 2012

Kavaratzis, M.: From "necessary evil" to necessity: stakeholders' involvement in place branding. J. Place Manage. Dev. 5(1), 7–19 (2012)

Klamer, A.: A pragmatic view on values in economics. J. Econ. Methodol. 10, 191–212 (2003)

TEEB: The economics of ecosystems and biodiversity: The ecological and economic foundations. Earthscan, London (2010)

UK National Ecosystem Assessment: UK National Ecosystem Assessment Follow-on. Phase: Synthesis Report. UNEP-WCMC, Cambridge (2014)

Sagoff, M.: Values and preferences. Ethics 96, 301–316 (1986)

Kenter, J.O., O'Brien, L., Hockley, N., Ravenscroft, N., Fazey, I., Irvine, K.N., Reed, M.S., Christie, M., Brady, E., Bryce, R., Church, A., Cooper, N., Davies, A., Evely, A., Everard, M., Fish, R., Fisher, J.A., Jobstvogt, N., Molloy, C., Orchard-Webb, J., Ranger, S., Ryan, M., Watson, V., Williams, S.: What are shared and social values of ecosystems? Ecol. Econ. 111, 86–99 (2015)

Funtowicz, S.O., Ravetz, J.R.: Science for the post-normal age. Futures 25, 739–755 (1993)

Stagl, S.: Valuation for sustainable development: The role of multicriteria evaluation. Vierteljahrsh Wirtsch Forsch 73, 53–62 (2004)

Christie, M., Fazey, I., Cooper, R., Hyde, T., Kenter, J.O.: An evaluation of monetary and non-monetary techniques for assessing the importance of biodiversity and ecosystem services to people in countries with developing economies. Ecol. Econ. 83, 69–80 (2012)

Kenter, J.O., Hyde, T., Christie, M., Fazey, I.: The importance of deliberation in valuing ecosystem services in developing countries: Evidence from the Solomon Islands. Glob. Environ. Change 21, 505–521 (2011)

Fusco Girard, L., Nijkamp, P.: Le valutazioni per lo sviluppo sostenibile della città e del territorio. Angeli, Milano (1997)

Vickery, J.: The Emergence of Culture-led Regeneration: A Policy Concept and its Discontents. Warwick, Centre for Cultural Policy Studies (2007). http://wrap.warwick.ac.uk/36991/1/WRAP_Vickery_ccps.paper9.pdf

UNESCO: Measuring the Economic Contribution of Cultural Industries (2009). http://www.uis.unesco.org/culture/Documents/FCS-handbook-1-economic-contribution-culture-enweb.pdf

Lapassade, G.: Groupes, organisations, institutions. Anthropos, Paris (2006)

Perea, M., Rosa, E.: The effects of associative and semantic priming in the lexical decision task. Psychol. Res. 66, 180–194 (2002)

Lepore, E., Stone, M.: Logic and semantic analysis: Philosophy of logic. In: A volume in Handbook of the Philosophy of Science, pp. 173–204 (2007)

Goodchild, M.F., Li, L.: Assuring the quality of volunteered geographic information. Spatial Stat. 1, 110–120 (2012)

Malczewski, J.: GIS-based multicriteria decision analysis: A survey of the literature. Int. J. Geogr. Inf. Sci. 20(7), 703–726 (2006)

Montrone, S., Perchinunno, P., Torre, C.M.: Analysis of positional aspects in the variation of real estate values in an Italian southern metropolitan area. In: Taniar, D., Gervasi, O., Murgante, B., Pardede, E., Apduhan, Bernady O. (eds.) ICCSA 2010. LNCS, vol. 6016, pp. 17–31. Springer, Heidelberg (2010). doi:10.1007/978-3-642-12156-2_2

Bonifazi, A., Sannicandro, V., Attardi, R., Cugno, G., Torre, C.M.: Countryside vs city: A user-centered approach to open spatial indicators of urban sprawl. In: Gervasi, O., Murgante, B., Misra, S., Rocha, A.M.A.C., Torre, C.M., Taniar, D., Apduhan, B.O., Stankova, E., Wang, S. (eds.) ICCSA 2016. LNCS, vol. 9789, pp. 161–176. Springer, Cham (2016). doi:10.1007/978-3-319-42089-9_12

Munda, G.: Multicriteria Evaluation in a Fuzzy Environment: Theory and Applications in Ecological Economics. Physica-Verlag, Heidelberg (1995)

Sacco, P.L., Ferilli, G., Tavano, B.G.: Understanding culture-led local development: A critique of alternative theoretical explanations. Urban Stud. **51**(13), 2806–2821 (2014)

Sacco, P.L., Ferilli, G., Blessi, G.T.: Culture 3.0: A new perspective for the EU active citizenship and social and economic cohesion policy. In: The Cultural Component of Citizenship: An Inventory of Challenge. European House for Culture. Access to the Culture Platform, pp. 195–213 (2012)

Sassano, G., Graziadei, A., Amato, F., Murgante, B.: Involving citizens in the reuse and regeneration of urban peripheral spaces. In: Nunes Silva, C., Local, B.J. (eds.) Government and Urban Governance in Europe, pp. 193–206. Springer, Heidelberg (2016)

Cannavacciuolo, L., Iandoli, L., Ponsiglione, C., Zollo, G.: Learning by failure vs learning by habits: entrepreneurial learning micro-strategies as determinants of the emergence of co-located entrepreneurial networks. Int. J. Entrep. Behav. Res. **23**(3), 524–546 (2017)

UN-Habitat: State of the World's Cities Report 2004/2005. Globalization and Urban Culture. United Nations Human Settlements Programme, Earthscan, London (2004)

Author Index

Printed in the United States
By Bookmasters